Leading Issues in
Economic Development

Leading Issues in Economic Development

SEVENTH EDITION

GERALD M. MEIER
Stanford University

JAMES E. RAUCH
University of California, San Diego

New York   Oxford
OXFORD UNIVERSITY PRESS
2000

Oxford University Press

Oxford   New York
Athens   Auckland   Bangkok   Bogota   Bombay   Buenos Aires
Calcutta   Cape Town   Dar es Salaam   Delhi   Florence   Hong Kong
Istanbul   Karachi   Kuala Lumpur   Madras   Madrid   Melbourne
Mexico City   Nairobi   Paris   Singapore   Taipei   Tokyo   Toronto

and associated companies in
Berlin   Ibadan

Library of Congress Cataloging-in-Publication Data

Leading issues in economic development / [edited by] Gerald M. Meier, James E.
Rauch.– 7th ed.
        p. cm.
    Includes bibliographical references and index.
    ISBN 0-19-511589-9 (paper)
    1. Economic development. I. Meier, Gerald M. II. Rauch, James E.

  HD82.L3273 2000
  338.9—dc21

                                                    99-059308

 Printing (last digit) 10 9 8 7 6 5 4 3 2
Printed in the United States of America
on acid-free paper

To the next generation of development economists.
                                                        –G.M.M.

To my mother and to the memory of my father.
                                                        –J.E.R.

CONTENTS

EXHIBITS

PREFACE

The economics of development is one of the most exciting subjects in social science. Why, two centuries after the Industrial Revolution, are poverty and its attendant ills so prevalent in most of the world? And what can be done about it? Nobel Prize–winning economist Robert Lucas wrote of the questions addressed by development economics, "Once one starts to think about them, it is hard to think about anything else" ["On the Mechanics of Economic Development," *Journal of Monetary Economics* 22 (July 1988), p. 5].

Development economics is also a very frustrating subject. Unlike most areas within economics, there exists no consensus on what the student should know. Two scholars can with equal justification write two completely different textbooks.

The aim of this book is to convey as much of the excitement of development economics and as little of the frustration as possible. To this end we have avoided writing the ordinary type of textbook, instead culling the most insightful readings from the diffuse field of development and bringing them into conceptual order. By using this distinctive approach we allow for a variety of perspectives while keeping in sight the most important overarching themes. The section "Using This Book" (p. xix) describes our strategy of combining excerpted readings ("Selections") with our own "Overviews," "Notes," "Comments," and "Exhibits."

After being responsible for the previous six editions of *Leading Issues in Economic Development* over the past 35 years, Professor Meier has now selected Professor Rauch to upgrade and modernize this seventh edition and to perpetuate subsequent editions. This edition is mainly Professor Rauch's effort. It reflects his desire to strengthen the analytical and quantitative dimensions of development economics and to illuminate contemporary—and future—problems of development policymaking. In all, it provides fresh and serious attention to the interplay between development experience, changing views of economists, and policy.

While this seventh edition maintains the format of previous editions, the inclusion of a new author has brought many changes relative to the sixth edition:

- New chapters on income distribution and on development and the environment have been added while other chapters have been consolidated.
- Most of the Selections and Notes are new.
- The representation in the Selections of articles from leading professional journals has increased.
- The Selections make greater use of statistical analysis, and an Appendix, "How to Read a Regression Table," has been added to ensure that these Selections are easily accessible to all readers.

We wish to express our appreciation to the authors and publishers who have granted permission to use excerpts from publications for which copyrights exist. Specific acknowledgment is given with each Selection. Some parts of the original versions of the excerpted materials have been omitted out of consideration for relevance and to avoid repetition. In some instances, tables and diagrams have been renumbered and the footnotes have been deleted or renumbered.

We would like to thank a number of extremely busy people who generously took time out to provide advice or to comment on portions of the manuscript: Richard Carson, Graham Elliott, Peter Evans, and Dani Rodrik. We would also like to acknowledge the valuable research assistance of Neville Francis, Timothy Kane, Paula Lindsay, and Donald McCubbin. James Rauch wishes to thank his wife, Doris

Bittar, for making room in her life for this book during its final months of preparation. Kenneth MacLeod has been a very helpful and patient editor. Finally, we are grateful to the entire profession of social scientists whose writings on development provide the foundation for this volume.

USING THIS BOOK

Instructors and students can use this book more like a main text or more like a supplementary reader. To facilitate the latter approach the contents have been designed to allow individual freedom of choice in deciding what chapters and Selections to read and in what sequence. If the former approach is taken, the organizational and thematic guidance of the chapter Overviews can be followed and the chapters can be read in numerical order.

The chapters include the following materials:

Overviews: These are introductory essays that show how the subsequent chapter materials fit together and elucidate one or more overarching themes. They sometimes contain ideas that are not explicitly presented by the other chapter materials.

Selections: These are the core of the book. They present a broad sample of the major contributions by scholars and practitioners on the central issues in economic development. Each Selection has been edited for the sake of brevity and to highlight the points of greatest relevance for the chapter in which it appears.

Notes: These serve two purposes. One is to expound important ideas that are extant in the literature but are not presented as clearly or simply as we would like. The other is to present more original material that complements the Selections.

Comments: Like the Notes, these serve two purposes. One is to clarify or expand upon the immediately preceding Selection. The other is to suggest additional readings on the subject of the immediately preceding Selection.

Exhibits: These are tables and charts that provide empirical illustrations and data on topics under discussion.

Starting with Selection III.1, some Selections include regression tables. Readers without econometric training are urged to refer to the Appendix to get the most insight from these Selections.

Introduction

Overview

The subject of this book is the economics of less developed countries, sometimes called "developing countries." Yet we must admit from the start that there is no universally accepted definition of "less developed country" (LDC). Roughly speaking, the definition in use by the writers whose work is excerpted in this book is the countries of Latin America, North Africa and the Middle East, sub-Saharan Africa, and Asia minus Japan and the countries that were formerly members of the Soviet Union: in short, what used to be called the Third World. When the border that separated East and West Germany became obsolete, so did the boundaries that separated the classification "Second World" from the classifications "First World" and "Third World." Yet the countries of Eastern Europe and the former Soviet Union, no matter how poor, are currently labeled "transition" countries rather than "less developed" countries, and are the subject of "transition economics" rather than "development economics." Moreover, a number of formerly Third World countries such as Israel, Singapore, and Taiwan would appear to have graduated to "more developed" or "industrialized" status.

Given this current state of flux regarding country classifications, it seems more important than ever to be careful about how to measure a country's level of "development." The Note that begins the first section below starts with the measure by which countries are ordered in Exhibit I.A.1 (and in many other Exhibits in this book): per capita GNP in U.S. dollars. As described in the Note, because of evidence that the purchasing power of U.S. dollars is greater in poor than in rich countries, per capita GNP in U.S. dollars is increasingly being replaced by the second measure in Exhibit I.A.1, per capita GNP in "international dollars." Exhibit I.A.2 shows that this "correction" of exchange-rate converted per capita income tends to be greater, the poorer the country relative to the United States. Selection I.A.1 by Jagdish Bhagwati and the following Comment attempt to explain why services are so much cheaper relative to commodities in poor countries than in rich countries, cheaper services being the chief reason the purchasing power of the dollar is greater in poor countries. Exhibit I.A.1 also contains an indicator of poverty that is used to supplement (or replace) per capita income as a measure of development. The development of an internationally comparable poverty line is discussed in the selection by the World Bank, I.A.2. The last two columns of Exhibit I.A.1, life expectancy and adult illiteracy, are used as inputs to the Human Development Index (HDI), the last measure of development discussed in Note I.A.1. Exhibit I.A.3 shows exactly how the HDI is computed, Exhibit I.A.4 shows that countries can have very similar per capita incomes yet quite different HDI values, and Exhibit I.A.5 ranks countries from highest to lowest HDI values. The HDI owes much to the work of Amartya Sen, which is the subject of the Comment following Exhibit I.A.5.

The first section concludes with Exhibit I.A.6, which shows two important systematic differences between low- and high-income countries that are not included in any of the measures of development discussed in the Note. First, population growth is higher in low-income countries. The (unweighted) average annual growth rate of population for the low-income economies in Exhibit I.A.6 was 2.6 percent in the period 1980–90 and 2.3 percent in the period 1990–95, compared with 1.0 percent and 0.8 percent respectively, for the high-income economies. The cause of more rapid population growth in low-income countries is easily traced to an incomplete "demographic transition" from high birth rates and death rates to low birth rates and death rates. The (unweighted) average birth rates for the low- and high-income economies in 1995 were 38 births per thousand persons and 13 births per thousand persons, respectively. (All figures reported in this paragraph and the next not computed from Exhibit I.A.6 were computed from the 1997 *World Development Indicators* CD-ROM.) The (unweighted) average death rates for the low- and high-income economies in 1995 were 13 deaths per thousand persons and 8 deaths per thousand persons, respectively. Thus population growth is more rapid in low-income countries because death rates have dropped to near the level of high-income countries but birth rates have not. A key factor in bringing down death rates in low-income countries was control of major infectious diseases. This control was fostered by international aid agencies and its success did not require high incomes in the recipient countries. One consequence of the much higher birth rates in low-income countries is that their populations tend to be much younger than in high-income countries. The (unweighted) average share of the population less than 15 years old was 43 percent in the low-income economies in 1995 compared with 21 percent in the high-income economies.

The second important systematic difference between low- and high-income countries shown in Exhibit I.A.6 is the much higher proportion of the labor force engaged in agriculture in the former. The (unweighted) average share of the labor force engaged in agriculture in the low-income economies was 68 percent in 1990 compared with 7 percent in the high-income economies. Reasons for this enormous difference include the tendency of poor households to spend a much higher fraction of their income on food than rich households and the tendency of poor countries to export cash crops in exchange for manufactures. (The historical origins of the latter tendency and its contemporary persistence are described in chapters II and IV, respectively.) It is also the case that productivity in agriculture relative to industry is much smaller in the typical low-income country than in the typical high-income country. The unweighted averages of the values of agricultural and industrial output per worker in 1990 were respectively $727 and $3,414 in the low-income economies and $21,819 and $43,657 in the high-income economies. Average measured industrial productivity was thus 4.7 times higher than agricultural productivity in the low-income economies but only 2.0 times higher in the high-income economies. The reasons poor countries have had such exceptional difficulty in raising agricultural productivity are explored in Chapter VII.

The next section begins with Exhibit I.B.1, an overview of progress and shortcomings of less developed countries as a whole during the period 1960–93. The first selection, by the World Bank, reviews the per capita income growth, low inequality, and reduction in poverty achieved by the "high-performing East Asian economies" (HPAEs): Hong Kong, Indonesia, Japan, the Republic of Korea, Malaysia, Singapore, Taiwan, and Thailand. (Though not a less developed country, Japan is included because it clearly served as a model for the other countries.) Until 1997 these countries, especially the "Four Tigers" (Hong Kong, Korea, Singapore, and Taiwan), set the standards of performance that less developed countries in the rest of the world have struggled to live up to. Yet the question of exactly what policies followed by the HPAEs should be imitated by other countries to achieve comparable performance remains a subject of fierce debate, to which the World Bank in this selection made a very influential contribution.

The dramatic reversal of East Asian economic performance in 1997–98 may eventually prove to have as much influence on economic policies in the rest of the world as did their decades of success, though again the lessons to be extracted will be subject to contentious debate. Exhibit I.B.2 shows a dramatic (projected) fall in GDP growth in 1998 for all the HPAEs (plus the Philippines) except Taiwan. The following selection by the World Bank is an early attempt to understand the causes of the crisis. The selection absolves long-term "structural" problems of blame and focuses on short-term mistakes in macroeconomic management and financial panic. A key statistic is a more than $100 billion reversal between 1996 and 1997 of net private capital flows to Indonesia, the Republic of Korea, Malaysia, the Philippines, and Thailand. This statistic has ensured that one of the major policy debates emerging from the crisis will be the desirability of open capital accounts, given the presence of poorly regulated financial sectors in most less developed countries. If the HPAEs fail to recover quickly, instead experiencing a "lost decade" of economic growth as did Latin America in the 1980s, the advocates of "good luck" rather than "good policy" as the major cause of superior economic performance will have received considerable ammunition (see Selection III.6 by Easterly et al.).

A common theme of the selections describing recent economic performance in China, Latin America, and India is that perceived failures of development, both in absolute terms and relative to the Four Tigers, have led to dramatic policy reforms. These reforms generally reduced state involvement in the economy, and the Note following these selections cautions the reader against jumping to conclusions about the proper role of the state in economic development, especially in light of the longer historical record that is the subject of Chapter II. The last selection of this section describes the dismal economic performance of sub-Saharan Africa and notes that, although the need for policy reform was at least as great there as in

Latin America, for example, governments have typically been much less forthcoming in providing it. In discussing the underlying causes of government failure in sub-Saharan Africa the selection anticipates a number of the selections in Chapter IX.

The section that concludes this introductory chapter concerns development economics as a discipline. Note I.C.1 discusses the evolution of the discipline from the late 1940s to the 1980s, and Comment I.C.1 examines its "classical" antecedents. Comment I.C.2 addresses the question of how development economics is different from the rest of economics. This question has perhaps become more urgent with the rise of "new" or "endogenous" growth theory in the late 1980s and early 1990s, which is described in Note I.C.2. Endogenous growth theory has changed the relationship of development economics to the neoclassical mainstream, both by bringing ideas from development economics into the mainstream and by allowing the mainstream to analyze economic growth in less developed countries more effectively. As will be evident to readers of this book, however, development economics is much broader than growth theory, old or new.

I.A. MEASURING DEVELOPMENT

Note I.A.1. The Evolution of Measures of Development

The traditional measure of development is per capita income measured in U.S. dollars. This is the measure by which countries are ranked by the World Bank in Exhibit I.A.1. Countries with GNP per capita in 1995 less than U.S. $765 are labeled "low-income economies," countries with GNP per capita in 1995 greater than U.S. $9,385 are labeled "high-income economies," and all countries in between are labeled "middle-income economies." It is tempting to then call the low- and middle-income economies "less developed countries" and the high-income economies "more developed countries."

(Sometimes GDP per capita is used instead of GNP per capita. Gross domestic product is defined as the total final outputs of goods and services produced within a country's territory by residents and nonresidents. Gross national product equals GDP plus factor incomes accruing to residents from abroad, less the income earned in the domestic economy accruing to nonresidents. GNP per capita is the correct measure of income per head, but GDP per capita is often easier to estimate.)

Per capita income is an average over all the residents of a country, and as such can obscure important regional differences. For example, according to an estimate for 1975, per capita income in the southeast region of Brazil was double that in the northeast region even after correcting for differences in cost of living (World Bank 1991, p. 41). This problem extends to all attempts to measure development at the national level. This practice has persisted nevertheless because many countries lack reliable regional-level data and because most crucial policy decisions are made at the national level.

In the 1970s various attempts were initiated to correct, supplement, or replace per capita income in U.S. dollars as a measure of development. These attempts were motivated by three major problems with this measure:

1. As is obvious to anyone who has spent U.S. dollars in poor countries, their purchasing power is much greater there than in rich countries. GNP per capita in U.S. dollars therefore gives an exaggerated estimate of the differences in average standards of living between poor and rich countries.
2. Per capita GNP is a "one dollar, one vote" average. Even if the majority of the population is very poor, a rich minority can raise per capita GNP to a relatively high level.
3. Per capita GNP does not directly measure well-being. Populations in countries with similar per capita GNPs may differ widely in average levels of health, for example.

To understand the first problem it is helpful to start by showing why we might expect the purchasing power of a dollar to be *equal* across countries. Consider the dollar cost of purchasing commodity i in the United States versus country j. Suppose the price of commodity i in the United States equals P_i^{US}, measured in U.S. dollars, the price of commodity i in country j equals P_i^j, measured in the currency of country j, and the exchange rate equals e, measured in U.S. dollars per unit of currency of country j. Then the dollar cost of purchasing commodity i is the same in the United States and in country j if

$$P_i^{US} = eP_i^j \qquad (1)$$

Equation (1) is known as the *law of one price*. Why should we expect this "law" to hold? Suppose it does not. If $P_i^{US} > eP_i^j$, then one could buy commodity i in country j, resell it in the United States, and make a guaranteed profit. This process, known as *international commodity arbitrage,* will bid up the price of commodity i in country j and bid down the price of commodity i in the United States until equation (1) holds. International commodity arbitrage also rules out $P_i^{US} < eP_i^j$.

Implicit in the preceding argument is the assumption that international trade is perfectly free: there are no transport costs and no tariffs or other trade barriers. Since this assumption does not hold in the real world, dollar prices may in fact differ across countries. In particular, most services have extremely high transportation costs. If haircuts are cheaper in country j than in the United States, it is impossible for an arbitrageur to buy haircuts in country j and resell them in the United States, and extremely expensive for a consumer to fly from the United States to country j to get a cheap haircut. Housing and local transportation are similar to haircuts in this regard, though many business services such as accounting can be cheaply transported electronically. If the dollar prices of services are much lower in poor countries, while the dollar prices of goods are kept close across countries by international commodity arbitrage, than the overall cost of a standardized basket of goods and services will be lower in poor countries.

Selection I.A.1 by Bhagwati gives two explanations for why nontraded services should be cheaper in poor countries. Both explanations essentially boil down to the following: wages are lower in poor countries, labor is a major input to production of services, and technology for producing services does not differ dramatically across countries, so that lower wages translate into lower costs of production.

In the 1970s the International Comparison Project (ICP) under the direction of Kravis, Heston, and Summers (1982) collected price data in 34 countries. As expected, the prices of services relative to goods tended to rise with per capita income, as shown in Figure 1 and Table 1 in Selection I.A.1. Using a rather involved procedure described fully in their book, Kravis, Heston, and Summers went on to estimate per capita GDP for all 34 countries measured in "international dollars" whose purchasing power is, in theory, the same everywhere. In Exhibit I.A.2 the ratio of per capita GDP measured in international dollars to per capita GDP measured in U.S. dollars, labeled the "exchange-rate-deviation index," is plotted against per capita GDP in international dollars (measured relative to the United States). There is a strong tendency for the exchange-rate-deviation index to rise as "real per capita GDP" falls. In other words, the poorer the country, the more its per capita GDP measured by exchange-rate conversion of local currency into U.S. dollars tends to underestimate the average purchasing power of its citizens relative to U.S. citizens.

In Exhibit I.A.1 the World Bank has extended the work of the ICP to produce estimates of 1995 per capita GNP (not GDP) in international dollars for nearly all the countries in the Exhibit. Including only countries with both U.S. dollar and international dollar figures, the (unweighted) averages of U.S. dollar per capita GNP for the low- and high-income countries are $365 and $22,275, respectively, while the (unweighted) averages of international dollar per capita GNP for the low- and high-income countries are $1,372 and $27,251, respectively. The U.S. dollar figures thus give the impression that the typical high-income country is 61 times as rich as the typical low-income country, while the international dollar figures reduce that ratio to 20.

Measuring per capita GNP in international dollars does not change the fact that it is an average over the entire population and thus does not address the second problem with using per capita GNP as a measure of development described above. If we think a major goal of development is reduction of poverty, we might want to supplement (if not replace) per capita GNP with a measure of the extent of poverty. Attempts to develop an internationally comparable "poverty line" and measure the extent of poverty across countries are described in the selection by the World Bank below. In Exhibit I.A.1 the World Bank uses one international dollar a day as its poverty line, and reports estimates of the percentage of each country's population living below that line. It is clear that averages do indeed conceal a great deal. For example, the 1995 per capita GNPs measured in international dollars for Brazil and Tunisia are $5,400 and $5,000, respectively, but 28.7 percent of the Brazilian population was living on less than one international dollar a day compared with only 3.9 percent of the Tunisian population.

Just as one can find in Exhibit I.A.1 countries that have similar average incomes but differ greatly in the extent of poverty, so one can find countries with similar average incomes that differ greatly in life expectancy and literacy. The 1995 per capita GNPs measured in international dollars for Egypt and Sri Lanka are $3,820 and $3,250, respectively, yet Egyptian life expectancy at birth was only 63 years and 49 percent of Egyptian adults were illiterate compared with Sri Lankan life expectancy of 72 years and adult illiteracy of 10 percent. This kind of observation motivated some in the 1970s to advocate discarding income-based measures of development altogether in favor of direct measurement of the extent to which the "basic needs" of the population were being met. A major effort in this direction was development of the Physical Quality of Life Index or PQLI (Morris 1979). This index was based on a country's life expectancy, infant mortality rate, and literacy rate. The successor to the PQLI is the Human Development Index (HDI) devised by the United Nations Development Program. As shown in Exhibit I.A.3, the HDI uses life expectancy as its only indicator of health rather than including the infant mortality rate as does the PQLI. The HDI also adds school enrollment rates to the literacy rate to form a weighted index of educational attainment that is averaged into the overall index. The most important difference between the HDI and the PQLI, however, is that the HDI gives a one-third weight to an index based on per capita GDP measured in international dollars, although the index heavily discounts income above a certain threshold to account for diminishing marginal utility (another dollar of income is valued much less by someone earning $100,000 annually than by someone earning $1000). The HDI is thus intended to be a more comprehensive measure of development than either the PQLI or per capita income.

Despite the inclusion of per capita GDP in the construction of the Human Development Index, Exhibit I.A.4 shows that countries with similar per capita incomes can still differ substantially in their HDI scores. Exhibit I.A.5 ranks 175 countries from highest to lowest 1994 HDI values, and shows the differences between their rankings by per capita GDP measured in international dollars and their HDI rankings. Many of the biggest positive differences (countries ranked much higher by HDI than by per capita income) are for socialist or formerly socialist countries, and many of the biggest negative differences (countries ranked much higher by per capita income than by HDI) are for countries that are major oil exporters. The former observation can be partly explained by the more equal distribution of income in these countries. If one takes $1,000 annually from someone earning $100,000 and gives it to someone earning $1,000, the health of the first person is unlikely to suffer while the health of the second person may improve significantly. However, it is likely that the more important reason the socialist and formerly socialist countries have high HDI values relative to their per capita incomes is that their governments both made provision of educational and health services a very high priority and commanded the share of national resources needed to deliver these services. The latter observation that major oil exporters have low HDI values relative to their per capita incomes can be partly explained by the fact that a major mineral discovery or sharp increase in the price of a mineral (such as the quadrupling of the price of oil that occurred during 1973–74) can make a country wealthy almost literally overnight, while it takes time for that higher income to generate greater health and educational attainment. One should, however, not let individual cases exaggerate the differences in ranking between per capita GDP in international dollars and the Human Development Index: the correlation coefficient between the two rankings is 0.958.

References

Kravis, Irving B., Alan Heston, and Robert Summers. 1982. *World Product and Income: International Comparisons of Real Gross Product* (Baltimore: Johns Hopkins).

Morris, Morris David. 1979. *Measuring the Condition of the World's Poor: The Physical Quality of Life Index* (New York: Pergamon Press).

World Bank. 1991. *World Development Report 1991* (New York: Oxford University Press).

Exhibit I.A.1. Basic Indicators

	Population (millions) mid-1995	Surface area (thousands of sq. km)	GNP per capita[a] Dollars 1995	GNP per capita[a] Avg. ann. growth (%) 1985–95	PPP estimates of GNP per capita[b] US = 100, 1987	PPP estimates of GNP per capita[b] US = 100, 1995	PPP estimates of GNP per capita[b] Current int'l $ 1995	Poverty % of people living on less than $1 a day (PPP) 1981–95	Life expectancy at birth (years) 1995	Adult illiteracy (%) 1995
Low-income economies	3,179.9 t	40,606 t	430 w	3.8 w					63 w	34 w
Excluding China and India	1,050.3 t	27,758 t	290 w	−1.4 w					56 w	46 w
1 Mozambique	16.2	802	80	3.6	2.5	3.0	810c	..	47	60
2 Ethiopia	56.4	1,097	100	−0.3	2.0	1.7	450	33.8	49	65
3 Tanzania[d]	29.6	945	120	1.0	2.6	2.4	640	16.4	51	32
4 Burundi	6.3	28	160	−1.3	3.2	2.3	630c	..	49	65
5 Malawi	9.8	118	170	−0.7	3.1	2.8	750	..	43	44
6 Chad	6.4	1,284	180	0.6	2.5	2.6	700c	..	48	52
7 Rwanda	6.4	26	180	−5.4	3.8	2.0	540	45.7	46	40
8 Sierra Leone	4.2	72	180	−3.6	3.2	2.2	580	..	40	..
9 Nepal	21.5	141	200	2.4	4.0	4.3	1,170c	53.1	55	73
10 Niger	9.0	1,267	220	..	3.6	2.8	750c	61.5	47	86
11 Burkina Faso	10.4	274	230	−0.2	3.3	2.9	780c	..	49	81
12 Madagascar	13.7	587	230	−2.2	3.1	2.4	640	72.3	52	..
13 Bangladesh	119.8	144	240	2.1	4.8	5.1	1,380	..	58	62
14 Uganda	19.2	236	240	2.7	4.7	5.5	1,470c	50.0	42	38
15 Vietnam	73.5	332	240	..	..	..	..	..	68	6
16 Guinea-Bissau	1.1	36	250	2.0	2.8	2.9	790c	87.0	38	45
17 Haiti	7.2	28	250	−5.2	5.8	3.4	910c	..	57	55
18 Mali	9.8	1,240	250	0.8	2.3	2.0	550	..	50	69
19 Nigeria	111.3	924	260	1.2	4.4	4.5	1,220	28.9	53	43
20 Yemen, Rep.	15.3	528	260	..	..	..	..	..	53	..
21 Cambodia	10.0	181	270	..	..	..	..	..	53	35
22 Kenya	26.7	580	280	0.1	5.7	5.1	1,380	50.2	58	22
23 Mongolia	2.5	1,567	310	−3.8	10.6	7.2	1,950	..	65	..
24 Togo	4.1	57	310	−2.7	5.5	4.2	1,130c	..	56	48
25 Gambia, The	1.1	11	320	..	4.5	3.5	930c	..	46	61
26 Central African Republic	3.3	623	340	−2.4	5.0	4.0	1,070c	..	48	40
27 India	929.4	3,288	340	3.2c	4.4	5.2	1,400	52.5	62	48
28 Lao PDR	4.9	237	350	2.7	..	..	..	..	52	43
29 Benin	5.5	113	370	−0.3	6.9	6.5	1,760	..	50	63
30 Nicaragua	4.4	130	380	−5.4	11.8	7.4	2,000c	43.8	68	34
31 Ghana	17.1	239	390	1.4	7.4	7.4	1,990c	..	59	..
32 Zambia	9.0	753	400	−0.8	4.2	3.5	930	84.6	46	22

33 Angola	10.8	1,247	410	−6.1	8.9	4.9	1,310	..	47	..
34 Georgia[f]	5.4	70	440	−17.0	28.1	5.5	1,470	..	73	..
35 Pakistan	129.9	796	460	1.2	8.4	8.3	2,230	11.6	60	62
36 Mauritania	2.3	1,026	460	0.5	6.0	5.7	1,540[c]	31.4	51	..
37 Azerbaijan[f]	7.5	87	480	−16.3	21.8	5.4	1,460		70	..
38 Zimbabwe	11.0	391	540	−0.6	8.6	7.5	2,030	41.0	57	15
39 Guinea	6.6	246	550	1.4	..	..	..	26.3	44	..
40 Honduras	5.9	112	600	0.1	7.9	7.0	1,900	46.5	67	27
41 Senegal	8.5	197	600	..	7.3	6.6	1,780	54.0	50	67
42 China	1,200.2	9,561	620	8.3	6.3	10.8	2,920	29.4	69	19
43 Cameroon	13.3	475	650	−6.6	15.1	7.8	2,110	..	57	37
44 Côte d'Ivoire	14.0	322	660	..	8.2	5.9	1,580	17.7	55	60
45 Albania	3.3	29	670	..	..	..	..	..	73	..
46 Congo	2.6	342	680	−3.2	11.5	7.6	2,050	..	51	25
47 Kyrgyz Republic[f]	4.5	199	700	−6.9	13.6	6.7	1,800	18.9	68	..
48 Sri Lanka	18.1	66	700	2.6	10.6	12.1	3,250	4.0	72	10
49 Armenia[f]	3.8	30	730	−15.1	25.4	8.4	2,260	..	71	..
Middle-income economies	1,590.9 t	60,838 t	2,390 w	−0.7 w			..		68 w	18 w
Lower-middle-income	1,152.6 t	40,323 t	1,670 w	−1.3 w			..		67 w	
50 Lesotho	2.0	30	770	1.2	6.1	6.6	1,780[c]	50.4	61	29
51 Egypt, Arab Rep.	57.8	1,001	790	1.1	14.3	14.2	3,820	7.6	63	49
52 Bolivia	7.4	1,099	800	1.8	9.1	9.4	2,540	7.1	60	17
53 Macedonia, FYR	2.1	26	860	..	..	..	..	..	73	..
54 Moldova[f]	4.3	34	920	..	..	..	..	6.8	69	..
55 Uzbekistan[f]	22.8	447	970	−3.9	12.6	8.8	2,370	..	70	..
56 Indonesia	193.3	1,905	980	6.0	9.8	14.1	3,800	14.5	64	16
57 Philippines	68.6	300	1,050	1.5	10.3	10.6	2,850	27.5	66	5
58 Morocco	26.6	447	1,110	0.9	13.2	12.4	3,340	1.1	65	56
59 Syrian Arab Republic	14.1	185	1,120	0.9	18.5	19.7	5,320	..	68	..
60 Papua New Guinea	4.3	463	1,160	2.3	8.5	9.0	2,420[c]	2.6	57	28
61 Bulgaria	8.4	111	1,330	−2.6	23.4	16.6	4,480	..	71	..
62 Kazakstan[f]	16.6	2,717	1,330	−8.6	24.2	11.2	3,010	53.3	69	..
63 Guatemala	10.6	109	1,340	0.3	13.2	12.4	3,340	30.4	66	44
64 Ecuador	11.5	284	1,390	0.8	15.8	15.6	4,220	19.9	69	10
65 Dominican Republic	7.8	49	1,460	2.1	13.7	14.3	3,870	17.7	71	18
66 Romania	22.7	238	1,480	−3.8	22.2	16.2	4,360	4.7	70	..
67 Jamaica	2.5	11	1,510	3.6	11.3	13.1	3,540	2.5	74	15
68 Jordan	4.2	89	1,510	−4.5	23.8	15.1	4,060[c]	1.6	70	13
69 Algeria	28.0	2,382	1,600	−2.4	26.5	19.6	5,300	..	70	38
70 El Salvador	5.6	21	1,610	2.8	8.2	9.7	2,610	..	67	29
71 Ukraine[f]	51.6	604	1,630	−9.2	20.7	8.9	2,400	..	69	..
72 Paraguay	4.8	407	1,690	1.2	13.3	13.5	3,650	..	68	8
73 Tunisia	9.0	164	1,820	1.9	18.3	18.5	5,000	3.9	69	33

Exhibit I.A.1. Continued

	Population (millions) mid-1995	Surface area (thousands of sq. km)	GNP per capita[a] Dollars 1995	GNP per capita[a] Avg. ann. growth (%) 1985–95	PPP estimates of GNP per capita[b] US = 100 1987	PPP estimates of GNP per capita[b] US = 100 1995	PPP estimates of GNP per capita[b] Current int'l $ 1995	Poverty % of people living on less than $1 a day (PPP) 1981–95	Life expectancy at birth (years) 1995	Adult illiteracy (%) 1995
74 Lithuania[f]	3.7	65	1,900	–11.7	25.2	15.3	4,120	2.1	69	..
75 Colombia	36.8	1,139	1,910	2.6	20.7	22.7	6,130	7.4	70	9
76 Namibia	1.5	824	2,000	2.9	15.8	15.4	4,150[c]	..	59	..
77 Belarus[f]	10.3	208	2,070	–5.2	26.3	15.6	4,220	..	70	..
78 Russian Federation[f]	148.2	17,075	2,240	–5.1	30.9	16.6	4,480	1.1	65	..
79 Latvia[f]	2.5	65	2,270	–6.6	24.5	12.5	3,370	..	69	..
80 Peru	23.8	1,285	2,310	–1.6	17.9	14.0	3,770	49.4	66	11
81 Costa Rica	3.4	51	2,610	2.8	19.8	21.7	5,850	18.9	77	5
82 Lebanon	4.0	10	2,660	..	..	..	..	..	68	8
83 Thailand	58.2	513	2,740	8.4	16.2	28.0	7,540	0.1	69	6
84 Panama	2.6	76	2,750	–0.4	26.1	22.2	5,980	25.6	73	9
85 Turkey	61.1	779	2,780	2.2	20.4	20.7	5,580	..	67	18
86 Poland	38.6	313	2,790	1.2	21.5	20.0	5,400	6.8	70	..
87 Estonia[f]	1.5	45	2,860	–4.3	25.5	15.6	4,220	6.0	70	..
88 Slovak Republic	5.4	49	2,950	–2.8	17.6	13.4	3,610	12.8	72	..
89 Botswana	1.5	582	3,020	6.1	15.3	20.7	5,580	34.7	68	30
90 Venezuela	21.7	912	3,020	0.5	33.0	29.3	7,900	11.8	71	9
Upper-middle-income	438.3 t	20,514 t	4,260 w	0.2 w	22.4	18.6	5,030[c]	23.7	69 w	14 w
91 South Africa	41.5	1,221	3,160	–1.1	..	..	..	..	64	18
92 Croatia	4.8	57	3,250	..	..	..	..	..	74	..
93 Mexico	91.8	1,958	3,320	0.1	27.8	23.7	6,400	14.9	72	10
94 Mauritius	1.1	2	3,380	5.4	39.0	49.0	13,210	..	71	17
95 Gabon	1.1	268	3,490	–8.2	..	..	..	..	55	37
96 Brazil	159.2	8,512	3,640	–0.8	24.2	20.0	5,400	28.7	67	17
97 Trinidad and Tobago	1.3	5	3,770	–1.7	38.1	31.9	8,610[c]	..	72	2
98 Czech Republic	10.3	79	3,870	–1.8	44.9	36.2	9,770	3.1	73	..
99 Malaysia	20.1	330	3,890	5.7	22.9	33.4	9,020	5.6	71	17
100 Hungary	10.2	93	4,120	–1.0	28.9	23.8	6,410	0.7	70	..
101 Chile	14.2	757	4,160	6.1	24.6	35.3	9,520	15.0	72	5
102 Oman	2.2	212	4,820	0.3	33.2	30.2	8.14[c]	..	70	..
103 Uruguay	3.2	177	5,170	3.1	23.6	24.6	6,630	..	73	3
104 Saudi Arabia	19.0	2,150	7,040	–1.9	43.0	..	..	..	70	37
105 Argentina	34.7	2,767	8,030	1.8	31.6	30.8	8,310	..	73	4

Economy	Population (millions)	Area (thousands sq km)	GNP per capita (dollars)	GNP per capita avg. annual growth (%)	PPP	PPP	PPP (international dollars)	Life expectancy	Adult illiteracy (%)
106 Slovenia	2.0	20	8,200	..	..	..	..	74	..
107 Greece	10.5	132	8,210	1.3	44.2	43.4	11,710	78	..
Low- and middle-income	4,770.8 t	101,444 t	1,090 w	0.4 w				65 w	30 w
Sub-Saharan Africa	583.3 t	24,271 t	490 w	-1.1 w				52 w	43 w
East Asia and Pacific	1,706.4 t	16,249 t	800 w	7.2 w				68 w	17 w
South Asia	1,243.0 t	5,133 t	350 w	2.9 w				61 w	51 w
Europe and Central Asia	487.6 t	24,355 t	2,220 w	-3.5 w				68 w	..
Middle East and N. Africa	272.4 t	11,021 t	1,780 w	-0.3 w				66 w	39 w
Latin America and Caribbean	477.9 t	20,414 t	3,320 w	0.3 w				69 w	13 w
High-income economies	902.2 t	32,039 t	24,930 w	1.9 w				77 w	..
108 Korea, Rep.	44.9	99	9,700	7.7	27.3	42.4	11,450	72	h
109 Portugal	9.9	92	9,740	3.6	41.6	47.0	12,670	75	..
110 Spain	39.2	505	13,580	2.6	50.5	53.8	14,520	77	..
111 New Zealand	3.6	271	14,340	0.8	63.3	60.6	16,360	76	h
112 Ireland	3.6	70	14,710	5.2	44.2	58.1	15,680	77	h
113 †Israel	5.5	21	15,920	2.5	56.3	61.1	16,490	77	..
114 †Kuwait	1.7	18	17,390	1.1	86.3	88.2	23,790[c]	76	21
115 †United Arab Emirates	2.5	84	17,400	-2.8	84.4	61.1	16,470	75	21
116 United Kingdom	58.5	245	18,700	1.4	72.0	71.4	19,260	77	h
117 Australia	18.1	7,713	18,720	1.4	70.1	70.2	18,940	77	h
118 Italy	57.2	301	19,020	1.8	72.5	73.7	19,870	78	h
119 Canada	29.6	9,976	19,380	0.4	84.6	78.3	21,130	78	h
120 Finland	5.1	338	20,580	-0.2	72.9	65.8	17,760	76	h
121 †Hong Kong	6.2	1	22,990[g]	4.8	70.7	85.1	22,950[g]	79	8
122 Sweden	8.8	450	23,750	-0.1	77.7	68.7	18,540	79	h
123 Netherlands	15.5	37	24,000	1.9	70.5	73.9	19,950	78	h
124 Belgium	10.1	31	24,710	2.2	76.3	80.3	21,660	77	h
125 France	58.1	552	24,990	1.5	77.6	78.0	21,030	78	h
126 †Singapore	3.0	1	26,730	6.2	56.1	84.4	22,770[c]	76	9
127 Austria	8.1	84	26,890	1.9	75.0	78.8	21,250	77	h
128 United States	263.1	9,364	26,980	1.3	100.0	100.0	26,980	76	h
129 Germany	81.9	357	27,510	..	..	74.4	20,070	76	h
130 Denmark	5.2	43	29,890	1.5	78.7	78.7	21,230	75	h
131 Norway	4.4	324	31,250	1.7	78.6	81.3	21,940	78	h
132 Japan	125.2	378	39,640	2.9	75.3	82.0	22,110	80	h
133 Switzerland	7.0	41	40,630	0.2	105.4	95.9	25,860	78	h
World	5,673.0 t	133,483 t	4,880 w	0.8 w				67 w	..

†Economies classified by the United Nations or otherwise regarded by their authorities as developing. aAtlas method. bPurchasing power parity. cThe estimate is based on regression; others are extrapolated from the latest International Comparison Programme benchmark estimates. dIn all tables, GDP and GNP cover mainland Tanzania. eGDP growth rates were revised after the statistics for this publication were finalized. fEstimates for economies of the former Soviet Union are preliminary; their classification will be kept under review. gData refer to GDP. hAccording to UNESCO, illiteracy is less than 5 percent.

t = total   w = weighted average

Source: World Bank, World Development Report 1997 (New York: Oxford University Press, 1997), pp. 220–221.

Exhibit I.A.2. Exchange-Rate-Deviation Index in Relation to Real GDP per Capita, Thirty-four Countries, 1975

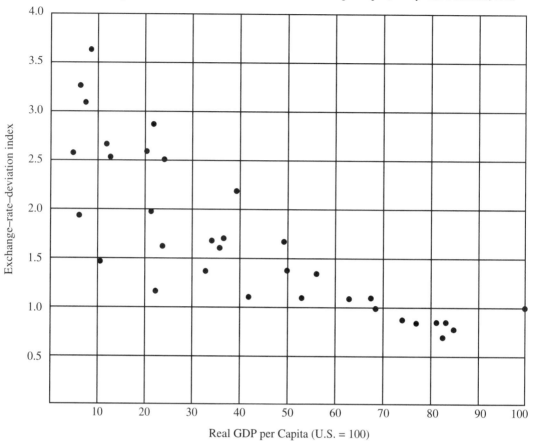

Source: Kravis, Irving B., Alan Heston, and Robert Summers, *World Product and Income: International Comparisons of Real Gross Product* (Baltimore: Johns Hopkins, 1982), p. 11.

Selection I.A.1. Why Are Services Cheaper in the Poor Countries?*

I. The Empirical Phenomenon

In their important work on international comparisons of national incomes and of comparative price structure, Kravis, Heston and Summers (1982, p. 8) have noted that "services are much cheaper in the relative price structure of a typical poor country than in that of a rich country."

This phenomenon has been documented now fairly systematically by the data, gathered under their guiding hand, of the United Nations International Comparison (ICP) which covers 34 countries. Table 1 reproduced from their work (1982), and Fig. 1 based on rows 3 and 11–13, indeed show this tendency for the relationship between relative service prices and real per capita GDP in this Kravis–Heston–Summers 34-country 6-group sample. The tendency is strongly evident except for the intermediate groups III and IV.

II. The Kravis–Heston–Summers Explanation: International Productivity Differences

An explanation of this phenomenon was provided by Kravis–Heston–Summers as follows:

As a first approximation it may be assumed for purposes of explaining the model that the prices of traded goods, mainly commodities, are the same in different countries. With similar prices for traded goods in all countries, wages in the industries producing traded goods will differ from country to country according to differences in productivity–a standard conclusion of Ricardian trade theory. In each country the wage level established in the traded goods industries will determine wages in the industries producing nontraded goods, mainly services. Because international productivity differences are smaller for such industries, the low wages established in poor countries in the low-productivity traded goods industries will apply also to the not-so-low productivity service and other nontraded goods industries. The consequences will be low prices in low-income countries for services and other nontraded goods (1982, p. 21).

This is an interesting explanation and indeed is to be found also in Balassa (1964) and Samuelson (1964) and, as Kravis has pointed out to me, in a splendid early analysis in Harrod (1933, chap. IV). Kravis et al. explore it further and insightfully. But it does raise, within the parameters of its own approach, the question whether we cannot formalise

it in general equilibrium, also extending the formalisation beyond the excessively limiting Ricardian framework of a single factor, labour, so that we get closer to a more realistic and meaningful formulation.

This can indeed be done, drawing on two elements of general-equilibrium analysis as practised by international trade theorists: (i) the use of the Lerner diagrammatic technique relating goods to factor prices, as used to advantage in analysing technical change in the 2-good case by Findlay and Grubert (1959) and the pattern of comparative advantage and the Heckscher–Ohlin theorem in the many-good case by Bhagwati (1972) and Deardorff (1979); and (ii) the notion that we can go beyond the single-factor Ricardian theory by taking multifactor production functions with Hicks-neutral productivity differences internationally, this generalisation having been proposed in Bhagwati (1964).[1]

Then, to formalise the Kravis–Heston–Summers argument in a general equilibrium, 2-factor model, take Fig. 2. X and Y are two "traded" commodities; S is the non-traded service. Suffixes R and P refer to the Rich and Poor countries respectively. Assume the standard restrictions on constant-returns-to-scale production functions in each activity. Putting a wage-rental price line, ω, tangent to the corresponding isoquants then defines, as shown by Lerner, the corresponding goods price vector. Evidently, $\bar{X}_R$ will exchange for $\bar{Y}_R$ and each, in turn, for $\bar{S}_R$, in the Rich country.[2]

The Kravis–Heston–Summers argument assumes that in the Poor country, if the same traded-goods prices prevail due to free trade and productivity is indeed lower by λ in the traded sector, $\lambda\bar{X}_P$, exchanges for $\lambda\bar{Y}_P$ yielding, of course, the same $X{:}Y$ price ratio. But the service sector is equally productive as in the Rich country. Hence, $\lambda\bar{X}_P$ exchanges for $\lambda\bar{Y}_P$ but for $\bar{S}_P$. Hence, trade will link the Rich and the Poor countries but lead to $\bar{S}_R = \lambda\bar{S}_P$ ($\lambda > 1$), yielding therefore the observed

---

[1]Thus, if I and II are countries, and X and Y are two activities using factors K and L, let

$$X^{\mathrm{I}} = \phi^{\mathrm{I}}(K_x, L_x) \text{ and } X^{\mathrm{II}} = \lambda\phi^{\mathrm{I}}(K_x, L_x).$$

If $\lambda > 1$, country II has Ricardian-style neutral productivity advantage in producing good X. The Ricardian theory of comparative advantage is then reformulated in Bhagwati (1964) in terms of comparative λ differences across trading countries.

[2]Evidently, since they are tangent to the same factor price line, $P_x\bar{X}_R = P_y\bar{Y}_R = P_s\bar{S}_R (= \omega OQ$ worth of wages). Therefore $p_x/p_y = \bar{Y}_R/\bar{X}_R$, etc.

*From Jagdish N. Bhagwati, "Why Are Services Cheaper in Poor Countries?" *Economic Journal* 94 (June 1984): 279–285. Reprinted by permission.

Table 1. Nominal and Real per Capita Absorption of GDP in the Form of Services and Commodities, and Price Indexes, by Real per Capita GDP Group, 1975

			Income group			
	I	II	III	IV	V	VI
1. Number of countries	8	6	6	4	9	1
Real GDP per capita (U.S. = 100)						
2. Range	0–14.9	15–29.9	30–44.9	45–59.9	60–89.9	90 and over
3. Mean	9.01	23.1	37.3	52.4	76.0	100.0
Per capita expenditures converted at exchange rate						
4. GDP (U.S. = 100)	3.7	12.1	24.2	38.7	82.3	100.0
5. Commodities (U.S. = 100)	5.0	15.2	31.1	50.6	92.7	100.0
6. Services (U.S. = 100)	2.0	8.1	15.5	23.4	69.1	100.0
7. Share of services	22.2	28.4	27.4	25.6	36.8	43.9
Per capita quantity indexes (based on PPP-conversion of expenditures)						
8. Commodities (U.S. = 100)	8.8	23.4	37.5	53.8	77.4	100.0
9. Services (U.S. = 100)	9.4	22.7	37.0	49.2	73.0	100.0
10. Share of services	33.8	31.7	31.8	30.3	31.2	32.3
Price indexes (U.S. = 100)						
11. GDP	40.6	51.7	64.7	73.5	107.5	100.0
12. Commodities	57.2	65.9	83.1	94.0	119.0	100.0
13. Services	20.7	34.1	41.2	46.3	94.6	100.0
14. 13/12	0.36	0.52	0.49	0.49	0.79	1.00

Line 2 $\dfrac{\text{(expenditure in domestic currency/population)} \div \text{purchasing power parity}}{\text{GDP in U.S./U.S. population}} \times 100$.

Line 3 Simple average of values within each income class.

Line 4 $\dfrac{\text{(expenditures in domestic currency/population)} \div \text{exchange rate}}{\text{GDP in U.S./U.S. population}} \times 100$.

Lines 6, 7, 9, 10, and 13 include public consumption as well as household expenditures.
Lines 11–13 purchasing power parity ÷ exchange rate × 100.
Source: Kravis–Heston–Summers (1982).

phenomenon that the relative price of the service sector is lower in the Poor country.

This theoretical, general-equilibrium[3] formulation of the Kravis–Heston–Summers argument is based on a more satisfactory notion of "productivity" advantage than simply labour productivity and is fully rigorous. But it does also imply at least two other unrealistic consequences: that the wage-rental ratio, ω, is equal across countries and that

[3]A conventional demand side can be readily added to the model to close it. Evidently, the configuration of demand and factor endowments must be such that, within each country, the wage-rental ratio is the same, as in the argument formalised via Fig. 1. With presumably the relative endowment of labour higher in the poor countries, this implies that the argument permits demand there to be skewed more in favour of services. Line 10 in Table 1, and private conversation with Kravis, suggest however that the share of services in total expenditure is not differentially greater in the poor countries. Demand differences have been discussed also by Samuelson (1964) in the context of the purchasing power parity doctrine.

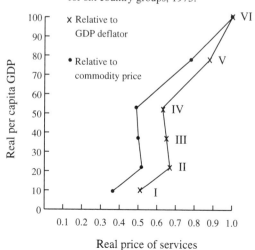

Figure 1. Relative price of services and per capita GDP for six country groups, 1975.

Figure 2

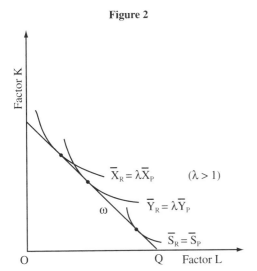

$$\overline{X}_R = \lambda \overline{X}_P \quad (\lambda > 1)$$

$$\overline{Y}_R = \lambda \overline{Y}_P$$

$$\overline{S}_R = \overline{S}_P$$

K/L ratios are also equal across countries within each activity. One *could* weaken some of these implications by, for example, parametrically shifting the $\overline{X}$ and $\overline{Y}$ isoquants for the Poor country to the right, to allow for the observed fact that Poor countries seem to have lower K/L ratios in each activity than Rich countries. But that would be surely an *ad hoc* procedure.

Besides, it is not evident to me at all that the non-traded sectors do have "productivity" parity in the proper theoretical sense (as against simply looking at labour productivity differences) whereas the traded sectors are technologically inferior, in the Poor countries relative to the Rich countries. It is arguable that technology diffuses fairly substantially through sale of technology, direct investment, etc. in the traded sectors and that this implies that the λ parameter in Fig. 2 is not important. On the other hand, services today are not by any means technically stagnant and hence there is probably a not insignificant λ in the services sector in favour of the Rich countries.

Can we therefore build an explanation of the observed phenomenon of real price of services being lower in Poor countries *without* resorting to a particular specification of comparative-productivity ranking between countries in their traded (commodity) and non-traded (services) sectors, while *also* explaining the *labour*-productivity rankings? I believe it is indeed possible to do so, as shown immediately below. In fact, I propose to develop an explanation which, while altogether ignoring differential ("true") productivity differences across sectors between countries, manages to "explain" simultaneously a number of related empirical observations in Kravis, Heston, and Summers (1982)

as also the fact that groups III and IV in Table 1 do not conform to the central phenomenon being discussed in this paper.

III. An Alternative Explanation

Consider then the same basic model as in Fig. 1. But now assume, as in Fig. 3, that the Rich and Poor countries have identical production functions in each sector: "productivity" differences are thus assumed to be non-existent. Let ω_R be the wage–rental ratio obtaining in the Rich country, implying that $\bar{X}_R$ exchanges for $\bar{Y}_R$ for $\bar{S}_R$.

If, however, the Poor country were to have this wage–rental ratio, its overall endowment ratio $(\bar{K}/\bar{L})_P$ for all employment would have to be spanned by OA and OC, with AOC (not drawn) constituting the McKenzie–Chipman diversification cone. But if, as in Fig. 3, $(\bar{K}/\bar{L})_P$ lies outside this diversification cone, ω_R is not feasible and the Poor country, being so abundantly endowed with labour, would have to have a *lower* wage–rental ratio such as ω_P. The consequence is that production of X is no longer possible at the goods price ratio $\bar{X}_R = \bar{Y}_R$ given from the Rich country, whereas $\bar{Y}_P$ will now exchange, *not* for $\bar{S}_P$ but for $\bar{S}_P$, the choice of K/L ratios being OE and OD respectively in the Poor country. The new diversification cone defined by EOD, of course, spans $(\bar{K}/\bar{L})_P$. This immediately means that the relative price of services is cheaper in the Poor country, since $\bar{S}_P > \bar{S}_P$.

But, aside from yielding the central phenomenon to be explained, my construct also shows that one may find that labour productivity in services relative to labour productivity in commodities is higher in consequence in the Poor country. For, at

Figure 3

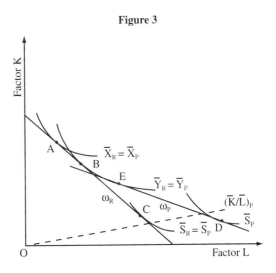

ω_P relative to ω_R, these are *two* effects lowering K/L ratio in commodities (and hence lowering the labour productivity in them) whereas there is only *one* effect lowering it in services. The two effects in commodities are: (i) the elimination of X, the most K-intensive good, from production; and (ii) the substitution effect from B to E in Y-production. The one effect in services is simply the corresponding substitution effect from C to D. . . .

It is, in fact, remarkable that this is precisely what Kravis, Heston, and Summers (1982) report:

Kuznets' own work relating first to 1950 and later to 1960 and the independent work of Chenery and Syrquin (1975) summarizing the period 1950–70 show clearly that the productivity of the service sector relative to the commodity sector tends to be inversely related to the income level of the country. This finding is confirmed when sectoral productivity indexes, circa 1975 are regressed against real per capita GDP for the 20 ICP Phase III countries for which data for such indices were available. In the following regression, productivity in the service industries (SP) relative to productivity in the commodity industries (CP) of each country is taken as the dependent variable and the ICP estimate of 1975 real per capita GDP (r) is the independent variable (standard errors are shown in parenthesis):

$$\ln(SP/CP) = 7.3988 - 0.3100 \ln r \quad \bar{R}^2 = 0.618$$
$$(0.4349) \quad (0.0550) \quad \text{S.E.E.} = 0.198$$
$$\text{n} = 20$$

The coefficient of r is negative and highly significant. The higher the country's per capita income, the lower its service sector productivity relative to its commodity sector productivity.

My explanation also implies that, as $\bar{K}/\bar{L}$ endowment ratio rises, and therefore GDP per capita increases, the wage–rental ratio would tend to rise and hence for K/L ratios in each sector to rise. I.e., in Fig. 3, the (K/L) ratio at OE in the Poor country is exceeded by those at OB and OA in the Rich country; also, that at OD is exceeded by that at OC. This again is observed statistically by Kravis, Heston, and Summers (see Table 2).

Finally, it is clear that these effects, both the central phenomenon of the relative service decline with GDP per capita and the associated comparative labour productivity observations between sectors and within sectors across countries, depend in my construct on the fact that, for the pair of countries being compared, their comparative factor endowments are sufficiently apart so as not to permit them to be at the same wage–rental ratio and hence to be in the same diversification cone. If therefore two countries or groups of countries are close together, in GDP per capita, we would expect that

Table 2. Capital/Labour Ratios*

Income group	Commodities	Services
I	4.39	2.48
II	9.24	5.16
III	5.64	6.21
IV	6.91	6.32
V	16.27	9.44
VI	21.94	10.96

*$1000 worth of capital per man-year.

the several correlative phenomena explained in this paper would also be correspondingly weak.

And this seems more or less to be so. Thus, if we examine Table 2, it is evident that the capital/labour ratios in the two "sectors" (commodities and services) are not substantially changed between country groups II–IV. This would suggest that these lie more or less within the same diversification cone and hence we would not expect to observe substantial change in the relative price of services within the range of per capita GDP variation defined by these groups. It is therefore somewhat remarkable that, as Table 1 and Fig. 1 show, the relative price of services is indeed fairly constant over groups II–IV! My explanation, therefore, seems yet additionally compelling.[4]

[4]Kravis has kindly drawn my attention to Kravis and Lipsey (1983) where a "factor proportions" explanation, consonant with that advanced in this paper, is stated.

References

Balassa, B. (1964). "The purchasing-power parity doctrine: a reappraisal." *Journal of Political Economy,* vol. 72 (December), pp. 584–96.

Bhagwati, J. N. (1964). "The pure theory of international trade: a survey." Economic Journal, vol. 74 (March), pp. 1–84.

——— (1972). "The Heckscher–Ohlin theorem in the multi-commodity case." *Journal of Political Economy,* vol. 80 (September/October), pp. 1052–5.

Chenery, H. and Syrquin, M. (1975). *Patterns of Development 1950–1970,* London: Oxford University Press.

Deardorff, A. (1979). "Weak links in the chain of comparative advantage." *Journal of International Economics,* vol. 9 (May), pp. 197–209.

Findlay, R. and Grubert, H. (1959). "Factor intensities, technological progress and the terms of trade." *Oxford Economic Papers,* vol. 11 (March), pp. 111–21.

Harrod, R. F. (1933). *International Economics.* Cambridge Economic Handbooks. London: Nisbet & Cambridge University Press.

Kravis, I., Heston, A., and Summers, R. (1982). "The share of services in economic growth" (mimeograph). In *Global Econometrics: Essays in Honor of Lawrence R. Klein* (ed. F. G. Adams and Bert Hickman). Cambridge: MIT Press.

Kravis, I. and Lipsey, R. (1983). "Toward an explanation of national price levels." Princeton Studies in International Finance, No. 52.

Samuelson, P. A. (1964). "Theoretical notes on trade problems." *The Review of Economics and Statistics,* vol. 46 (May), pp. 145–54.

Comment I.A.1. The Productivity and Factor Proportions Explanations Again

The preceding selection by Bhagwati uses graphical tools from international trade theory to present two explanations of why services are cheaper relative to commodities in poor than in rich countries, the first based on differences between productivity in rich and poor countries and the second based on differences between factor proportions in rich and poor countries. The intuition behind the productivity difference explanation is given in the quotation at the beginning of the selection. No comparable intuition is given for the factor proportions explanation, however, so we provide the following. Suppose the fact that poor countries have less physical capital per worker than rich countries leads to a higher cost of capital relative to labor in poor countries than in rich countries. Suppose further that commodities use more capital relative to labor in production than do services, as Table 2 of the selection indicates. One then expects commodities to be produced more expensively relative to services in poor than in rich countries. If prices reflect costs of production, then services will be cheaper relative to commodities in poor than in rich countries.

Selection I.A.2. Burden of Poverty*

The burden of poverty is spread unevenly—among the regions of the developing world, among countries within those regions, and among localities within those countries. Nearly half of the world's poor live in South Asia, a region that accounts for roughly 30 percent of the world's population. Sub-Saharan Africa accounts for a smaller, but still highly disproportionate, share of global poverty. Within regions and countries, the poor are often concentrated in certain places: in rural areas with high population densities, such as the Gangetic Plain of India and the island of Java, Indonesia, or in resource-poor areas such as the Andean highlands and the Sahel. Often the problems of poverty, population, and the environment are intertwined: earlier patterns of development and the pressure of rapidly expanding populations mean that many of the poor live in areas of acute environmental degradation.

The weight of poverty falls most heavily on certain groups. Women in general are disadvantaged. In poor households they often shoulder more of the workload than men, are less educated, and have less access to remunerative activities. Children, too, suffer disproportionately, and the future quality of their lives is compromised by inadequate nutrition, health care, and education. This is especially true for girls: their primary enrollment rates are less than 50 percent in many African countries. The incidence of poverty is often high among ethnic groups and minorities such as the indigenous peoples in Bolivia, Ecuador, Guatemala, Mexico, and Peru and the scheduled castes in India.

In many but not all cases, low incomes go hand in hand with other forms of deprivation. In Mexico, for example, life expectancy for the poorest 10 percent of the population is twenty years less than for the richest 10 percent. In Côte d'Ivoire the primary enrollment rate of the poorest fifth is half that of the richest. National and regional averages, often bad enough in themselves, mask appallingly low life expectancy and educational attainment among the poorest members of society. . . .

Poverty is not the same as inequality. The distinction needs to be stressed. Whereas poverty is concerned with the absolute standard of living of a part of society—the poor—inequality refers to relative living standards across the whole society. At maximum inequality one person has everything and, clearly, poverty is high. But minimum inequality (where all are equal) is possible with zero poverty (where no one is poor) as well as with maximum poverty (where all are poor).

This report defines poverty as the inability to attain a minimal standard of living. To make this definition useful, three questions must be answered. How do we measure a standard of living? What do we mean by a minimal standard of living? And, having thus identified the poor, how do we express the overall severity of poverty in a single measure or index?

The Poverty Line

All the measures are judged in relation to some norm. For example, we deem life expectancies in some countries to be low in relation to those attained by other countries at a given date. The choice of the norm is particularly important in the case of the consumption-based measures of poverty.

A consumption-based poverty line can be thought of as comprising two elements: the expenditure necessary to buy a minimum standard of nutrition and other basic necessities and a further amount that varies from country to country, reflecting the cost of participating in the everyday life of society. The first part is relatively straightforward. The cost of minimum adequate caloric intakes and other necessities can be calculated by looking at the prices of the foods that make up the diets of the poor. The second part is far more subjective; in some countries indoor plumbing is a luxury, but in others it is a "necessity."

The perception of poverty has evolved historically and varies tremendously from culture to culture. Criteria for distinguishing poor from nonpoor tend to reflect specific national priorities and normative concepts of welfare and rights. In general, as countries become wealthier, their perception of the acceptable minimum level of consumption—the poverty line—changes. . . .

Rather than settle for a single number, this chapter employs two: $275 and $370 per person a year. (The amounts are in constant 1985 PPP prices.) This range was chosen to span the poverty lines estimated in recent studies for a number of countries with low average incomes—Bangladesh, the Arab Republic of Egypt, India, Indonesia, Kenya, Morocco, and Tanzania. The lower limit of the range coincides with a poverty line commonly used for India.

*From World Bank, *World Development Report 1990* (New York: Oxford University Press, 1990), pp. 2, 26–29. Reprinted by permission.

How Much Poverty Is There?

Once the poor have been distinguished from the nonpoor, the simplest way to measure poverty is to express the number of poor as a proportion of the population. This *headcount index* is a useful measure, although it is often criticized because it ignores the extent to which the poor fall below the poverty line. The income shortfall, or *poverty gap,* avoids this drawback. It measures the transfer that would bring the income of every poor person exactly up to the poverty line, thereby eliminating poverty. . . .

The use of the upper poverty line—$370— gives an estimate of 1,115 million people in the developing countries in poverty in 1985. That is roughly one-third of the total population of the developing world. Of these, 630 million—18 percent of the total population of the developing world— were extremely poor: their annual consumption was less than $275, the lower poverty line. Despite these massive numbers, the aggregate poverty gap—the transfer needed to lift everybody above the poverty line—was only 3 percent of the developing countries' consumption. The transfer needed to lift everybody out of extreme poverty was, of course, even smaller—just 1 percent of the developing countries' consumption. Mortality for children under 5 averaged 121 per thousand for all developing countries, aggregate life expectancy was 62 years, and the overall net primary school enrollment rate was 83 percent. These figures hide considerable variation within and among countries. Table 1 sets out a detailed regional breakdown of these estimates. . . .

Nearly half of the developing world's poor, and nearly half of those in extreme poverty, live in South Asia. Sub-Saharan Africa has about one-third as many poor, although in relation to the region's overall population, its poverty is roughly as high. Table 1 also shows that both South Asia and Sub-Saharan Africa have low scores on several other social indicators; in Sub-Saharan Africa, in particular, life expectancy and primary school enrollment rates are alarmingly low, and under 5 mortality rates are alarmingly high. The Middle Eastern and North African countries have the next highest poverty, according to all the indicators. They are followed by Latin America and the Caribbean and by East Asia. China's overall performance is impressive, although the size of its population means that a relatively low headcount index still translates into large numbers of poor.

Although developing countries had made substantial progress in reducing poverty over the past

Table 1. How Much Poverty Is There in the Developing Countries? The Situation in 1985

	Extremely Poor			Poor (including extremely poor)			Social Indicators		
	Headcount			Headcount			Under 5 Mortality (per thousand)	Life Expectancy (years)	Net Primary Enrollment Rate (percent)
Region	Number (millions)	Index (percent)	Poverty Gap	Number (millions)	Index (percent)	Poverty Gap			
Sub-Saharan Africa	120	30	4	180	47	11	196	50	56
East Asia	120	9	0.4	280	20	1	96	67	96
China	80	8	1	210	20	3	58	69	93
South Asia	300	29	3	520	51	10	172	56	74
India	250	33	4	420	55	12	199	57	81
Eastern Europe	3	4	0.2	6	8	0.5	23	71	90
Middle East and North Africa	40	21	1	60	31	2	148	61	75
Latin America and the Caribbean	50	12	1	70	19	1	75	66	92
All developing countries	633	18	1	1,116	33	3	121	62	83

Note: The poverty line in 1985 PPP dollars is $275 per capita a year for the extremely poor and $370 per capita a year for the poor.

The headcount index is defined as the percentage of the population below the poverty line.

The poverty gap is defined as the aggregate income shortfall of the poor as a percentage of aggregate consumption.

three decades, there was only a slight improvement in the aggregate incidence of poverty in the latter half of the 1980s. The number in poverty, therefore, increased at close to the rate of population growth (a compound annual rate of about 1.5 percent). The key challenge is to resume the more rapid rate of poverty reduction of earlier years. This will require higher economic growth rates during the rest of the 1990s and improved patterns of growth that benefit the poor.

Exhibit I.A.3. The Human Development Index

The HDI is based on three indicators: longevity, as measured by life expectancy at birth; educational attainment, as measured by a combination of adult literacy (two-thirds weight) and combined primary, secondary and tertiary enrolment ratios (one-third weight); and standard of living, as measured by real GDP per capita (PPP$).

For the construction of the index, fixed minimum and maximum values have been established for each of these indicators:

- Life expectancy at birth: 25 years and 85 years
- Adult literacy: 0% and 100%
- Combined gross enrolment ratio: 0% and 100%
- Real GDP per capita (PPP$): $100 and $40,000 (PPP$).

For any component of the HDI, individual indices can be computed according to the general formula:

$$\text{Index} = \frac{\text{Actual } x_i \text{ value} - \text{minimum } x_i \text{ value}}{\text{Maximum } x_i \text{ value} - \text{minimum } x_i \text{ value}}$$

If, for example, the life expectancy at birth in a country is 65 years, then the index of life expectancy for this country would be

$$\frac{65 - 25}{85 - 25} = \frac{40}{60} = 0.667.$$

The construction of the income index is a little more complex. The world average income of $5,835 (PPP$) in 1994 is taken as the threshold level ($y*$), and any income above this level is discounted using the following formulation based on Atkinson's formula for the utility of income:

$$W(y) = y* \text{ for } 0 < y < y*$$

$$= y* + 2[(y - y*)^{1/2}] \text{ for } y* \leq y \leq 2y*$$

$$= y* + 2(y*^{1/2}) + 3[(y - 2y*)^{1/3}] \text{ for } 2y* \leq y \leq 3y*$$

$$y = y* + 2(y*^{1/2}) + 3[(y - 2y*)^{1/3}] + n\{[1 - (n-1)y*]\}^{1/n}$$

$$\text{for } (n-1)y* \leq y \leq ny*.$$

To calculate the discounted value of the maximum income of $40,000 (PPP$), the following form of Atkinson's formula is used:

$$W(y) = y* + 2(y*^{1/2}) + 3(y*^{1/3}) + 4(y*^{1/4}) + 5(y*^{1/5})$$

$$+ 6(y*^{1/6}) + 7(y*^{1/7}) + 8[(40,000 - 7y*)^{1/8}].$$

This is because $40,000 (PPP$) is between $7y*$ and $8y*$. With the above formulation, the discounted value of the maximum income of $40,000 (PPP$) is $6,154 (PPP$).

The construction of the HDI is illustrated with two examples—Greece and Gabon, an industrial and a developing country.

Country	Life expectancy (years)	Adult literacy rate (%)	Combined enrolment ratio (%)	Real GDP per capita (PPP$)
Greece	77.8	96.7	82	11,265
Gabon	54.1	62.6	60	3,641

Life expectancy index

$$\text{Greece} = \frac{77.8 - 25}{85 - 25} = \frac{52.8}{60} = 0.880$$

$$\text{Gabon} = \frac{54.1 - 25}{85 - 25} = \frac{29.1}{60} = 0.485$$

Adult literacy index

$$\text{Greece} = \frac{96.7 - 0}{100 - 0} = \frac{96.7}{100} = 0.967$$

$$\text{Gabon} = \frac{62.6 - 0}{100 - 0} = \frac{62.6}{100} = 0.626$$

Combined primary, secondary and tertiary enrolment ratio index

$$\text{Greece} = \frac{82 - 0}{100 - 0} = 0.820$$

$$\text{Gabon} = \frac{60 - 0}{100 - 0} = 0.600$$

Educational attainment index

$$\text{Greece} = [2(0.967) + 1(0.820)] \div 3 = 0.918$$

$$\text{Gabon} = [2(0.625) + 1(0.600)] \div 3 = 0.617$$

Adjusted real GDP per capita (PPP$) index

Greece's real GDP per capita at $11,265 (PPP$) is above the threshold level, but less than twice the threshold. Thus the adjusted real GDP per capita for Greece would be $5,982 (PPP$) because $5,982 = [5,835 + 2(11,265 - 5,835)^{1/2}]$.

Gabon's real GDP per capita at $3,641 (PPP$) is less than the threshold level, so it needs no adjustment.

Thus the adjusted real GDP per capita (PPP$) indices for Greece and Gabon would be:

$$\text{Greece} = \frac{5,982 - 100}{6,154 - 100} = \frac{5,882}{6,054} = 0.972$$

$$\text{Gabon} = \frac{3,641 - 100}{6,154 - 100} = \frac{3,541}{6,054} = 0.584$$

Human development index

The HDI is a simple average of the life expectancy index, educational attainment index and adjusted real GDP per capita (PPP$) index, and so is derived by dividing the sum of these three indices by 3.

Country	Life expectancy index	Educational attainment index	Adjusted real GDP per capita (PPP$) index	HDI
Greece	0.880	0.918	0.972	0.923
Gabon	0.485	0.617	0.584	0.562

Source: United Nations Development Program, *Human Development Report 1997* (New York: Oxford University Press, 1997), p. 122.

Exhibit I.A.4. Similar Income, Different Human Development, 1993

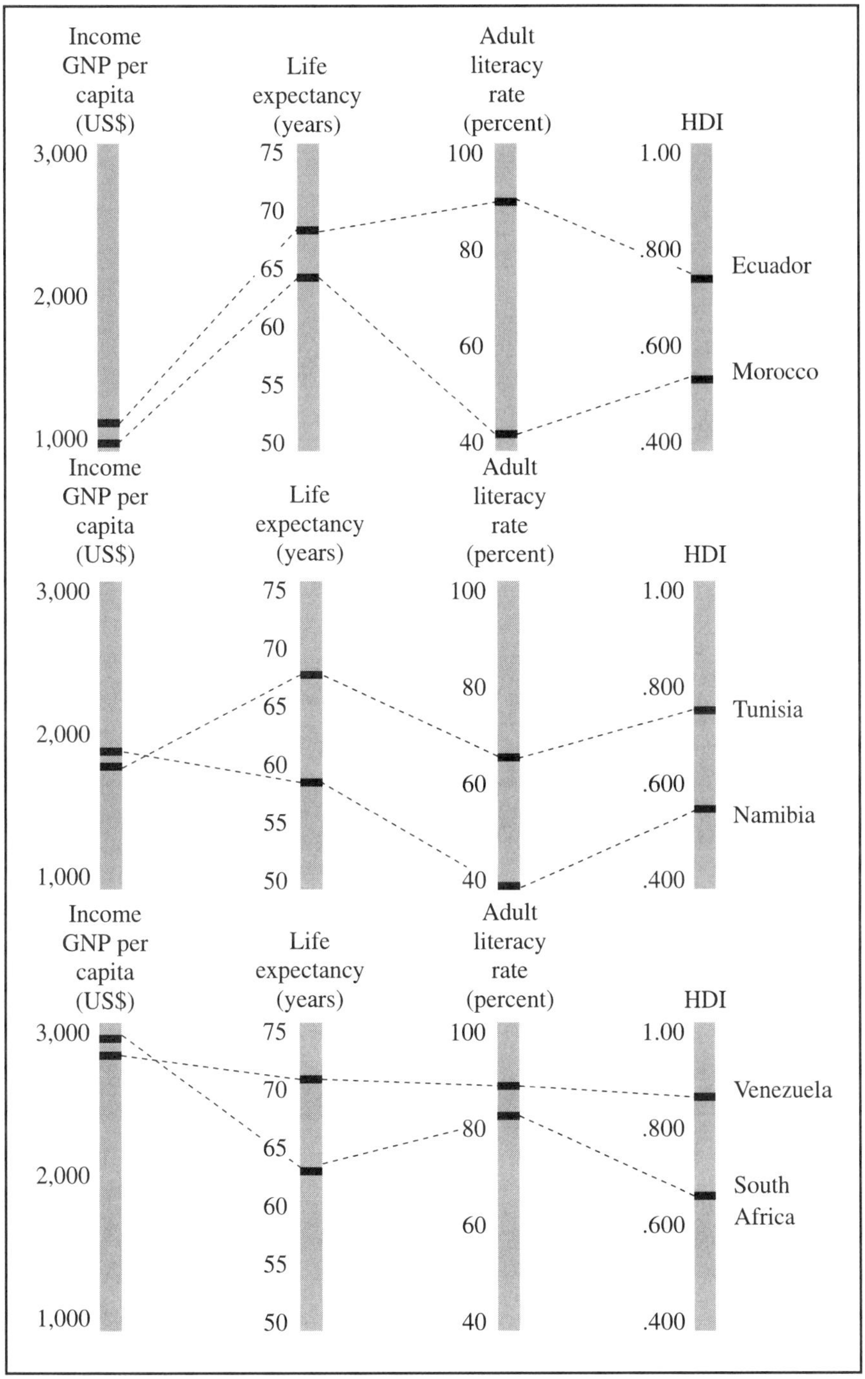

Income GNP per capita (US$)

Life expectancy (years)

Adult literacy rate (percent)

HDI

3,000
2,000
1,000

75
70
65
60
55
50

100
80
60
40

1.00
.800
.600
.400

Ecuador

Morocco

Income GNP per capita (US$)

Life expectancy (years)

Adult literacy rate (percent)

HDI

3,000
2,000
1,000

75
70
65
60
55
50

100
80
60
40

1.00
.800
.600
.400

Tunisia

Namibia

Income GNP per capita (US$)

Life expectancy (years)

Adult literacy rate (percent)

HDI

3,000
2,000
1,000

75
70
65
60
55
50

100
80
60
40

1.00
.800
.600
.400

Venezuela

South Africa

Source: United Nations Development Program, *Human Development Report 1996* (New York: Oxford University Press, 1996), p. 30.

Exhibit I.A.5. Human Development Index Rankings

HDI rank	Life expectancy at birth (years) 1994	Adult literacy rate (%) 1994	Combined first-, second- and third-level gross enrolment ratio (%) 1994	Real GDP per capita (PPP$) 1994	Adjusted real GDP per capita (PPP$) 1994	Life expectancy index	Education index	GDP index	Human development index (HDI) value 1994	Real GDP per capita (PPP$) rank minus HDI rank[a]
High human development										
1 Canada	74.6	97.0	80	17,052	6,040	0.83	0.91	0.98	0.907	—
2 France	79.0	99.0	100[b]	21,459	6,073	0.90	0.99	0.99	0.960	7
3 Norway	78.7	99.0	89	20,510	6,071	0.89	0.96	0.99	0.946	13
4 USA	77.5	99.0	92	21,346	6,073	0.88	0.97	0.99	0.943	6
5 Iceland	76.2	99.0	96	26,397	6,101	0.85	0.98	0.99	0.942	-1
6 Netherlands	79.1	99.0	83	20,566	6,071	0.90	0.94	0.99	0.942	9
7 Japan	77.3	99.0	91	19,238	6,067	0.87	0.96	0.99	0.940	13
8 Finland	79.8	99.0	78	21,581	6,074	0.91	0.92	0.99	0.940	0
9 New Zealand	76.3	99.0	97	17,417	6,041	0.85	0.98	0.98	0.940	15
10 Sweden	76.4	99.0	94	16,851	6,039	0.86	0.97	0.98	0.937	15
11 Spain	78.3	99.0	82	18,540	6,064	0.89	0.93	0.99	0.936	11
12 Austria	77.6	97.1[c]	90	14,324	6,029	0.88	0.95	0.98	0.934	19
13 Belgium	76.6	99.0	87	20,667	6,072	0.86	0.95	0.99	0.932	1
14 Australia	76.8	99.0	86	20,985	6,072	0.86	0.92	0.99	0.932	-1
15 United Kingdom	78.1	99.0	79	19,285	6,068	0.89	0.95	0.99	0.931	4
16 Switzerland	76.7	99.0	86	18,620	6,065	0.86	0.95	0.99	0.931	5
17 Ireland	78.1	99.0	76	24,967	6,098	0.88	0.91	0.99	0.930	-12
18 Denmark	76.3	99.0	88	16,061	6,037	0.85	0.95	0.98	0.929	8
19 Germany	75.2	99.0	89	21,341	6,073	0.84	0.96	0.99	0.927	-8
20 Greece	76.3	99.0	81	19,675[d]	6,069	0.86	0.93	0.99	0.924	-3
21 Italy	77.8	96.7[c]	82	11,265	5,982	0.88	0.92	0.97	0.923	15
22 Hong Kong	77.8	98.1[c]	73	19,363	6,068	0.88	0.90	0.99	0.921	-4
23 Israel	79.0	92.3	72	22,310	6,075	0.90	0.86	0.99	0.914	-17
24 Cyprus	77.5	95.0	75	16,023	6,037	0.87	0.88	0.98	0.913	3
25 Barbados	77.1	94.0	75	13,071[e,f]	6,021	0.87	0.88	0.98	0.907	8
26 Singapore	75.9	97.3	76	11,051	5,979	0.85	0.90	0.97	0.907	11
27 Luxembourg	77.1	91.0	72	20,987	6,072	0.87	0.85	0.99	0.900	-15
	75.9	99.0	58	34,155	6,130	0.85	0.85	1.00	0.899	-26

28	Bahamas	72.9	98.1	75	15,875	6,036	0.80	0.90	0.98	0.894	0
29	Antigua and Barbuda	74.0	96.0	76	8,977[e]	5,947	0.82	0.89	0.97	0.892	16
30	Chile	75.1	95.0	72	9,129	5,950	0.83	0.87	0.97	0.891	13
31	Portugal	74.6	89.6[c]	81	12,326	6,014	0.83	0.87	0.98	0.890	3
32	Korea, Rep. of	71.5	97.9	82	10,656	5,974	0.77	0.93	0.97	0.890	5
33	Costa Rica	76.6	94.7	68	5,919	5,853	0.86	0.86	0.95	0.889	27
34	Malta	76.4	86.0[g]	76	13,009[e,f]	6,021	0.86	0.83	0.98	0.887	−1
35	Slovenia	73.1	96.0	74	10,404[e]	5,970	0.80	0.89	0.97	0.886	3
36	Argentina	72.4	96.0	77	8,937	5,946	0.79	0.90	0.97	0.884	10
37	Uruguay	72.6	97.1	75	6,752	5,895	0.79	0.90	0.96	0.883	15
38	Brunei Darussalam	74.9	87.9	70	30,447[e,f]	6,125	0.83	0.82	1.00	0.882	−36
39	Czech Rep.	72.2	99.0	70	9,201	5,951	0.79	0.89	0.97	0.882	3
40	Trinidad and Tobago	72.9	97.9	67	9,124	5,949	0.80	0.88	0.97	0.880	4
41	Dominica	72.0	94.0	77	6,118[e]	5,868	0.78	0.88	0.95	0.873	16
42	Slovakia	70.8	99.0	72	6,389	5,882	0.76	0.90	0.96	0.873	12
43	Bahrain	72.0	84.4	85	15,321	6,034	0.78	0.85	0.98	0.870	−14
44	United Arab Emirates	74.2	78.6	82	16,000[h]	6,036	0.82	0.80	0.98	0.866	−17
45	Panama	73.2	90.5	70	6,104	5,868	0.80	0.84	0.95	0.864	14
46	Fiji	71.8	91.3	79	5,763	5,763	0.78	0.87	0.94	0.863	16
47	Venezuela	72.1	91.0	68	8,120	5,930	0.79	0.83	0.96	0.861	1
48	Hungary	68.8	99.0	67	6,437	5,884	0.73	0.88	0.96	0.857	5
49	Saint Kitts and Nevis	69.0[g]	90.0[g]	78	9,436	5,955	0.73	0.86	0.97	0.853	−9
50	Mexico	72.0	89.2	66	7,384	5,913	0.78	0.81	0.96	0.853	0
51	Colombia	70.1	91.1	70	6,107	5,868	0.75	0.84	0.95	0.848	7
52	Seychelles	72.0[g]	88.0[g]	61	7,891[e]	5,925	0.78	0.79	0.96	0.845	−3
53	Kuwait	75.2	77.8	57	21,875	6,074	0.84	0.71	0.99	0.844	−47
54	Grenada	72.0[g]	98.0[g]	78	5,137[e]	5,137	0.78	0.91	0.83	0.843	17
55	Qatar	70.9	78.9	73	18,403	6,063	0.76	0.77	0.99	0.840	−33
56	Saint Lucia	71.0[g]	82.0[g]	74	6,182[e]	5,872	0.77	0.79	0.95	0.838	−1
57	Saint Vincent	72.0[g]	82.0[g]	78	5,650[e]	5,650	0.78	0.81	0.92	0.836	6
58	Poland	71.2	99.0	79	5,002	5,002	0.77	0.92	0.81	0.834	14
59	Thailand	69.5	93.5	53	7,104	5,906	0.74	0.80	0.96	0.833	−8
60	Malaysia	71.2	83.0	62	8,865	5,945	0.77	0.76	0.97	0.832	−13
61	Mauritius	70.7	82.4	61	13,172	6,022	0.76	0.75	0.98	0.831	−30
62	Belarus	69.2	97.9	80	4,713	4,713	0.74	0.92	0.76	0.806	13
63	Belize	74.0	70.0[g]	68	5,590	5,590	0.82	0.69	0.91	0.806	1
64	Libyan Arab Jamahiriya	63.8	75.0	91	6,125[e]	5,869	0.65	0.80	0.95	0.801	−8
	Medium human development	67.1	82.6	64	3,352	3,352	0.70	0.76	0.54	0.667	—
65	Lebanon	69.0	92.0	75	4,863[e,f]	4,863	0.73	0.86	0.79	0.794	8
66	Suriname	70.7	92.7	71	4,711	4,711	0.76	0.85	0.76	0.792	10
67	Russian Federation	65.7	98.7	78	4,828	4,828	0.68	0.92	0.78	0.792	7

Exhibit I.A.5. Continued

HDI rank	Life expectancy at birth (years) 1994	Adult literacy rate (%) 1994	Combined first-, second- and third-level gross enrolment ratio (%) 1994	Real GDP per capita (PPP$) 1994	Adjusted real GDP per capita (PPP$) 1994	Life expectancy index	Education index	GDP index	Human development index (HDI) value 1994	Real GDP per capita (PPP$) rank minus HDI rank[a]
68 Brazil	66.4	82.7	72	5,362	5,362	0.69	0.79	0.87	0.783	0
69 Bulgaria	71.1	93.0	66	4,533	4,533	0.77	0.84	0.73	0.780	9
70 Iran, Islamic Rep. of	68.2	68.6c	68	5,766	5,766	0.72	0.68	0.94	0.780	−9
71 Estonia	69.2	99.0	72	4,294	4,294	0.74	0.90	0.69	0.776	8
72 Ecuador	69.3	89.6	72	4,626	4,626	0.74	0.84	0.75	0.775	5
73 Saudi Arabia	70.3	61.8	56	9,338	5,953	0.76	0.60	0.97	0.774	−32
74 Turkey	68.2	81.6	63	5,193	5,193	0.72	0.75	0.84	0.772	−4
75 Korea, Dem. People's Rep. of	71.4	95.0	75	3,965c,f	3,965	0.77	0.88	0.64	0.765	10
76 Lithuania	70.1	98.4g	70	4,011	4,011	0.75	0.89	0.65	0.762	8
77 Croatia	71.3	97.0	67	3,960d	3,960	0.77	0.87	0.64	0.760	10
78 Syrian Arab Rep.	67.8	69.8	64	5,397	5,397	0.71	0.68	0.87	0.755	−12
79 Romania	69.5	96.9g	62	4,037	4,037	0.74	0.85	0.65	0.748	3
80 Macedonia, FYR	71.7	94.0	60	3,965f	3,965	0.78	0.83	0.64	0.748	5
81 Tunisia	68.4	65.2	67	5,319	5,319	0.72	0.66	0.86	0.748	−12
82 Algeria	67.8	59.4	66	5,442	5,442	0.71	0.62	0.88	0.737	−17
83 Jamaica	73.9	84.4	65	3,816	3,816	0.82	0.78	0.61	0.736	7
84 Jordan	68.5	85.5	66	4,187	4,187	0.73	0.79	0.68	0.730	−3
85 Turkmenistan	64.7	97.7g	90	3,469e	3,469	0.66	0.95	0.56	0.723	12
86 Cuba	75.6	95.4	63	3,000e	3,000	0.84	0.85	0.48	0.723	17
87 Dominican Rep.	70.0	81.5	68	3,933	3,933	0.75	0.77	0.63	0.718	1
88 Oman	70.0	35.0	60	10,078	5,965	0.75	0.43	0.97	0.718	−49
89 Peru	67.4	88.3	81	3,645	3,645	0.71	0.86	0.59	0.717	5
90 South Africa	63.7	81.4	81	4,291	4,291	0.64	0.81	0.69	0.716	−10
91 Sri Lanka	72.2	90.1	66	3,277	3,277	0.79	0.82	0.52	0.711	9
92 Latvia	67.9	99.0	67	3,332	3,332	0.71	0.88	0.53	0.711	6
93 Kazakstan	67.5	97.5	73	3,284	3,284	0.71	0.89	0.53	0.709	6
94 Paraguay	68.8	91.9	62	3,531	3,531	0.73	0.82	0.57	0.706	2
95 Ukraine	68.4	98.8c	76	2,718	2,718	0.72	0.91	0.43	0.689	14

96	Samoa (Western)	68.1	98.0[g]	74	2,726[e]	2,726	0.72	0.90	0.43	0.684	12
97	Botswana	52.3	68.7	71	5,367	5,367	0.45	0.69	0.87	0.673	-30
98	Philippines	67.0	94.4	78	2,681	2,681	0.70	0.89	0.43	0.672	12
99	Indonesia	63.5	83.2	62	3,740	3,740	0.64	0.76	0.60	0.668	-7
100	Uzbekistan	67.5	97.2[g]	73	2,438	2,438	0.71	0.89	0.39	0.662	14
101	Mongolia	64.4	82.2	52	3,766	3,766	0.66	0.72	0.61	0.661	-10
102	Albania	70.5	85.0	59	2,788[c,f]	2,788	0.76	0.76	0.44	0.655	4
103	Armenia	70.8	98.8	78	1,737	1,737	0.76	0.92	0.27	0.651	24
104	Guyana	63.2	97.9	67	2,729	2,729	0.64	0.88	0.43	0.649	3
105	Georgia	73.1	94.9	69	1,585	1,585	0.80	0.86	0.25	0.637	31
106	Azerbaijan	71.0	96.3	72	1,670	1,670	0.77	0.88	0.26	0.636	25
107	Kyrgyzstan	67.8	97.0[g]	73	1,930	1,930	0.71	0.89	0.30	0.635	18
108	China	68.9	80.9	58	2,604	2,604	0.73	0.73	0.41	0.626	3
109	Egypt	64.3	50.5	69	3,846	3,846	0.66	0.57	0.62	0.614	-20
110	Moldova, Rep. of	67.7	98.9[c]	67	1,576[d]	1,576	0.71	0.88	0.24	0.612	28
111	Maldives	62.8	93.0	71	2,200	2,200	0.63	0.86	0.35	0.611	7
112	El Salvador	69.3	70.9	55	2,417	2,417	0.74	0.66	0.38	0.592	3
113	Bolivia	60.1	82.5	66	2,598	2,598	0.59	0.77	0.41	0.589	-1
114	Swaziland	58.3	75.2	72	2,821	2,821	0.55	0.74	0.45	0.582	-10
115	Tajikistan	66.8	96.7[g]	69	1,117	1,117	0.70	0.87	0.17	0.580	35
116	Honduras	68.4	72.0	60	2,050	2,050	0.72	0.68	0.32	0.575	7
117	Guatemala	65.6	55.7	46	3,208	3,208	0.68	0.52	0.51	0.572	-16
118	Namibia	55.9	40.0	84	4,027	4,027	0.52	0.55	0.65	0.570	-35
119	Morocco	65.3	42.1	46	3,681	3,681	0.67	0.43	0.59	0.566	-26
120	Gabon	54.1	62.6	60	3,641[e]	3,641	0.49	0.62	0.58	0.562	-25
121	Viet Nam	66.0	93.0	55	1,208[e,f]	1,208	0.68	0.80	0.18	0.557	26
122	Solomon Islands	70.8	62.0	47	2,118	2,118	0.76	0.57	0.33	0.556	0
123	Cape Verde	65.3	69.9	64	1,862	1,862	0.67	0.68	0.29	0.547	3
124	Vanuatu	65.9	64.0[g]	52	2,276	2,276	0.68	0.60	0.36	0.547	-7
125	São Tomé and Principe	67.0[i]	67.0[i]	57	1,704[c,f]	1,704	0.70	0.64	0.26	0.534	3
126	Iraq	57.0	56.8	53	3,159[c,f]	3,159	0.53	0.56	0.51	0.531	-24
127	Nicaragua	67.3	65.3	62	1,580[c,f]	1,580	0.70	0.64	0.24	0.530	10
128	Papua New Guinea	56.4	71.2	38	2,821	2,821	0.52	0.60	0.45	0.525	-24
129	Zimbabwe	49.0	84.7	68	2,196	2,196	0.40	0.79	0.35	0.513	-10
130	Congo	51.3	73.9	56	2,410	2,410	0.44	0.68	0.38	0.500	-14
	Low human development	56.1	49.9	47	1,308	1,308	0.52	0.49	0.20	0.403	—
131	Myanmar	58.4	82.7	48	1,051	1,051	0.56	0.71	0.16	0.475	25
132	Ghana	56.6	63.4	44	1,960	1,960	0.53	0.57	0.31	0.468	-8
133	Cameroon	55.1	62.1	46	2,120	2,120	0.50	0.57	0.33	0.468	-12
134	Kenya	53.6	77.0	55	1,404	1,404	0.48	0.70	0.22	0.463	5
135	Equatorial Guinea	48.6	77.8	64	1,673[c,f]	1,673	0.39	0.73	0.26	0.462	-5

Exhibit I.A.5. Continued

HDI rank	Life expectancy at birth (years) 1994	Adult literacy rate (%) 1994	Combined first-, second- and third-level gross enrolment ratio (%) 1994	Real GDP per capita (PPP$) 1994	Adjusted real GDP per capita (PPP$) 1994	Life expectancy index	Education index	GDP index	Human development index (HDI) value 1994	Real GDP per capita (PPP$) rank minus HDI rank[a]
136 Lao People's Dem. Rep.	51.7	55.8	50	2,484^e	2,484	0.45	0.54	0.39	0.459	-23
137 Lesotho	57.9	70.5	56	1,109	1,109	0.55	0.66	0.17	0.457	14
138 India	61.3	51.2	56	1,348	1,348	0.60	0.53	0.21	0.446	5
139 Pakistan	62.3	37.1	38	2,154	2,154	0.62	0.37	0.34	0.445	-19
140 Comoros	56.1	56.7	39	1,366	1,366	0.52	0.51	0.21	0.412	1
141 Nigeria	51.0	55.6	50	1,351	1,351	0.43	0.54	0.21	0.393	1
142 Zaire	52.2	76.4	38	429^e	429	0.45	0.64	0.05	0.381	31
143 Zambia	42.6	76.6	48	962	962	0.29	0.67	0.14	0.369	15
144 Bangladesh	56.4	37.3	39	1,331	1,331	0.52	0.38	0.20	0.368	0
145 Côte d'Ivoire	52.1	39.4	39	1,668	1,668	0.45	0.39	0.26	0.368	-13
146 Benin	54.2	35.5	35	1,696	1,696	0.49	0.35	0.26	0.368	-17
147 Togo	50.6	50.4	50	1,109	1,109	0.43	0.50	0.17	0.365	4
148 Yemen	56.2	41.1	52	805^{e,f}	805	0.52	0.45	0.12	0.361	14
149 Tanzania, U. Rep. of	50.3	66.8	34	656	656	0.42	0.56	0.09	0.357	21
150 Mauritania	52.1	36.9	36	1,593	1,593	0.45	0.37	0.25	0.355	-15
151 Central African Rep.	48.3	57.2	37	1,130	1,130	0.39	0.50	0.17	0.355	-2
152 Madagascar	57.2	45.8^j	33	694	694	0.54	0.42	0.10	0.350	16
153 Cambodia	52.4	35.0^g	58	1,084^{e,f}	1,084	0.46	0.43	0.16	0.348	1
154 Nepal	55.3	27.0	55	1,137	1,137	0.51	0.36	0.17	0.347	-6
155 Bhutan	51.5	41.1	31	1,289	1,289	0.44	0.38	0.20	0.338	-10
156 Haiti	54.4	44.1	29	896	896	0.49	0.39	0.13	0.338	5
157 Angola	47.2	42.5	31	1,600	1,600	0.37	0.39	0.25	0.335	-24
158 Sudan	51.0	44.8	31	1,084^{e,f}	1,084	0.43	0.40	0.16	0.333	-4
159 Uganda	40.2	61.1	34	1,370	1,370	0.25	0.52	0.21	0.328	-19
160 Senegal	49.9	32.1	31	1,596	1,596	0.41	0.32	0.25	0.326	-26
161 Malawi	41.1	55.8	67	694	694	0.27	0.60	0.10	0.320	7
162 Djibouti	48.8	45.0	20	1,270^{e,f}	1,270	0.40	0.37	0.19	0.319	-16
163 Guinea-Bissau	43.2	53.9	29	793	793	0.30	0.46	0.11	0.291	1

164	Chad	47.0	47.0	25	700	700	0.37	0.40	0.10	0.288	2
165	Gambia	45.6	37.2	34	939[e]	939	0.34	0.36	0.14	0.281	-5
166	Mozambique	46.0	39.5	25	986	986	0.35	0.35	0.15	0.281	-9
167	Guinea	45.1	34.8	24	1,103[e]	1,103	0.34	0.31	0.17	0.271	-14
168	Eritrea	50.1	25.0	24	960[e,f]	960	0.42	0.25	0.14	0.269	-9
169	Burundi	43.5	34.6	31	698	698	0.31	0.33	0.10	0.247	-2
170	Ethiopia	48.2	34.5	18	427	427	0.39	0.29	0.05	0.244	4
171	Mali	46.6	29.3	17	543	543	0.36	0.25	0.07	0.229	1
172	Burkina Faso	46.4	18.7	20	796	796	0.36	0.19	0.11	0.221	-9
173	Niger	47.1	13.1	15	787	787	0.37	0.14	0.11	0.206	-8
174	Rwanda	22.6[k]	59.2	37	352	352	0.00	0.52	0.04	0.187	1
175	Sierra Leone	33.6	30.3	28	643	643	0.14	0.30	0.09	0.176	-4
	All developing countries	61.8	69.7	56	2,904	2,904	0.61	0.65	0.46	0.576	—
	Least developed countries	50.4	48.1	36	965	965	0.42	0.44	0.14	0.336	—
	Sub-Saharan Africa	50.0	55.9	42	1,377	1,377	0.42	0.51	0.21	0.380	—
	Industrial countries	74.1	98.5	83	15,986	6,037	0.82	0.93	0.98	0.911	—
	World	63.2	77.1	60	5,798	5,798	0.64	0.71	0.94	0.764	—

Source: United Nations Development Program, *Human Development Report 1997* (New York: Oxford University Press, 1997), pp. 146–148. Complete reference information for the notes that follow can be found in the source publication.

Note: Figures in italics are Human Development Report Office estimates. Countries with the same HDI value are ranked on the basis of the fourth decimal place, not shown here.

[a]A positive figure indicates that the HDI rank is better than the real GDP per capita rank (PPP$), a negative the opposite; [b]Capped at 100; [c]UNESCO 1995b. Data refer to 1995; [d]UNECE estimate based on data from the 1993 European Comparison Programme; [e]Preliminary update of the Penn World Tables using an expanded set of international comparisons, as described in Summers and Heston 1991; [f]Extrapolations are provisional; [g]UNICEF 1997; [h]Estimate based on World Bank calculations using GDP-GNP ratio from UNDP 1996d; [i]World Bank 1995c; [j]Human Development Report Office estimate based on national sources; [k]1990–95 data from UN 1996b.

Column 1: calculated on the basis of data from UN 1996b; *column 2:* UNESCO 1996b; *column 3:* UNESCO 1996a; *column 4:* unless otherwise noted, calculated on the basis of estimates from World Bank 1997a.

Comment I.A.2. Capabilities and Entitlements

In delimiting the nature of poverty, Amartya Sen has stated that

poverty is not just a matter of being relatively poorer than others in the society, but of not having some basic opportunities of material well-being—the failure to have certain minimum "capabilities." The criteria of minimum capabilities are "absolute" not in the sense that they must not vary from society to society, or over time, but people's deprivations are judged absolutely, and not simply in comparison with the deprivations of others in that society. If a person is seen as poor because he is unable to satisfy his hunger, then that diagnosis of poverty cannot be altered merely by the fact that others too may also be hungry (so that this person may not be, relatively speaking, any worse off than most others). . . . A person's advantage is judged in this approach by his capabilities, viz., what he can or cannot do, can or cannot be. The relevant capabilities are of many different kinds (e.g., being free from starvation, from hunger, from undernourishment; participating in communal life; being adequately sheltered; being free to travel to see friends; and so on). The ranking of "capability vectors" can be used to rank people's advantages vis à vis others. But in the context of poverty analysis, it is a question of setting certain absolute standards of minimum material capabilities relevant for that society. Anyone failing to reach that absolute level would then be classified as poor, no matter what his relative position is vis a vis others. Poverty, in this view, is not ultimately a matter of incomes at all; it is one of a failure to achieve certain minimum capabilities. The distinction is important since the conversion of real incomes into actual capabilities varies with social circumstances and personal features.[1]

Sen has also maintained that the most important thematic deficiency of traditional development economics is its concentration on national product, aggregate income, and total supply of particular goods rather than on the "entitlements" of people and the "capabilities" that these entitlements generate. Entitlement refers to the set of alternative commodity bundles that a person can command in a society using the totality of rights and opportunities that he or she has.

For an elaboration of entitlements and capabilities, see Amartya K. Sen, "Development: Which Way Now?" *Economic Journal* (December 1983), *Poverty and Famines: An Essay on Entitlement and Deprivation* (1981), *Choice, Welfare and Measurement* (1982), "Poor, Relatively Speaking," *Oxford Economic Papers* (July 1983), and *Commodities and Capabilities* (1985).

The case for a "capabilities-orientated" rather than a "goods-orientated" social welfare function is also argued by K. Griffin and J. Knight, "Human Development: The Case for Renewed Emphasis," *Journal of Development Planning* (1989).

---

[1]Amartya Sen, "A Sociological Approach to the Measurement of Poverty: A Reply to Professor Peter Townsend," *Oxford Economic Papers* (December 1985): 669–70.

Exhibit I.A.6. Population and Labor Force

	Population						Labor force									
	Total (millions)		Avg. annual growth rate (%)		Aged 15–64 (millions)		Total[a] (millions)		Avg. annual growth rate(%)		Female (%)		Agriculture (%)		Industry (%)	
	1980	1995	1980–90	1990–95	1980	1995	1980	1995	1980–90	1990–95	1980	1995	1980	1990	1980	1990
Low-income economies	2,378 t	3,180 t	2.0 w	1.7 w	1,351 t	1,934 t	1,156 t	1,575 t	2.2 w	1.7 w	40 w	41 w	73 w	69 w	13 w	15 w
Excluding China and India	709 t	1,050 t	2.7 w	2.4 w	371 t	563 t	317 t	467 t	2.6 w	2.5 w	40 w	41 w	72 w	67 w	10 w	12 w
1 Mozambique	12	16	1.6	2.6	6	9	7	8	1.2	2.4	49	48	84	83	7	8
2 Ethiopia	38	56	3.1	1.9	19	28	17	25	2.9	2.3	42	41	86	80	2	2
3 Tanzania	19	30	3.2	3.0	9	15	10	15	3.2	2.9	50	49	86	84	4	5
4 Burundi	4	6	2.8	2.6	2	3	2	3	2.6	2.7	50	49	93	92	2	3
5 Malawi	6	10	3.3	2.7	3	5	3	5	3.0	2.5	51	49	88	95	5	5
6 Chad	4	6	2.4	2.5	2	3	2	3	2.1	2.5	43	44	88	81	3	4
7 Rwanda	5	6	3.0	-1.7	3	4	3	4	3.2	2.0	49	49	93	92	3	3
8 Sierra Leone	3	4	2.1	1.0	2	2	1	2	1.8	2.0	36	36	70	67	14	15
9 Nepal	15	21	2.6	2.5	8	12	7	10	2.4	2.4	39	40	95	95	1	0
10 Niger	6	9	3.3	3.3	3	4	3	4	3.0	2.9	45	44	93	91	3	4
11 Burkina Faso	7	10	2.6	2.8	4	5	4	5	2.0	2.1	48	47	92	92	3	2
12 Madagascar	9	14	2.9	3.1	5	7	4	6	2.5	3.1	45	45	85	84	6	7
13 Bangladesh	87	120	2.4	1.6	44	64	41	60	2.8	2.1	42	42	74	64	9	16
14 Uganda	13	19	2.4	3.2	6	9	7	9	2.2	2.7	48	48	89	93	4	5
15 Vietnam	54	73	2.1	2.1	28	43	26	37	2.7	1.9	48	49	73	72	13	14
16 Guinea-Bissau	1	1	1.8	2.1	0	1	0	1	1.3	1.8	40	40	86	85	2	2
17 Haiti	5	7	1.9	2.0	3	4	3	3	1.3	1.7	45	43	71	68	8	9
18 Mali	7	10	2.5	2.9	3	5	3	5	2.3	2.7	47	46	93	93	2	2
19 Nigeria	71	111	3.0	2.9	38	58	30	44	2.6	2.8	36	36	55	43	8	7
20 Yemen, Rep.	9	15	3.3	5.0	4	8	2	5	3.7	4.9	33	29	70	58	13	16
21 Cambodia	6	10	2.9	2.8	3	5	3	5	2.8	2.5	56	53	76	74	7	8
22 Kenya	17	27	3.4	2.7	8	14	8	13	3.6	2.7	46	46	83	80	6	7
23 Mongolia	2	2	2.9	2.1	1	1	1	1	3.1	2.9	46	46	40	32	21	22
24 Togo	3	4	3.0	3.0	1	2	1	2	2.6	2.8	39	40	69	66	10	10
25 Gambia, The	1	1	3.6	3.7	0	1	0	1	3.4	3.2	45	45	84	82	7	8
26 Central African Republic	2	3	2.4	2.2	..	2	1	2	1.7	1.8	48	47	85	80	3	3
27 India	687	929	2.1	1.8	394	562	300	398	1.9	2.0	34	32	70	64	13	16
28 Lao PDR	3	5	2.7	3.0	2	3	2	2	2.3	2.7	45	47	80	78	6	6
29 Benin	3	5	3.1	2.9	2	3	2	2	2.7	2.5	47	48	67	62	7	8
30 Nicaragua	3	4	2.9	3.1	1	2	1	2	2.9	4.0	28	36	39	28	24	26
31 Ghana	11	17	3.3	2.8	6	9	5	8	3.1	2.7	51	51	61	60	13	13
32 Zambia	6	9	3.0	2.9	3	5	2	4	3.1	2.8	45	45	76	75	8	9
33 Angola	7	11	2.7	3.1	4	5	3	5	2.1	2.8	47	46	76	75	8	8

Exhibit I.A.6. Continued

	Population				Aged 15–64 (millions)		Labor force									
	Total (millions)		Avg. annual growth rate (%)				Total[a] (millions)		Avg. annual growth rate(%)		Female (%)		Agriculture (%)		Industry (%)	
	1980	1995	1980–90	1990–95	1980	1995	1980	1995	1980–90	1990–95	1980	1995	1980	1990	1980	1990
34 Georgia	5	5	0.7	−0.2	3	4	3	3	0.4	−0.1	49	46	32	26	27	31
35 Pakistan	83	130	3.1	2.9	44	70	29	46	2.9	3.3	23	26	62	56	15	20
36 Mauritania	2	2	2.6	2.5	1	1	1	1	2.0	2.7	45	44	72	55	7	10
37 Azerbaijan	6	8	1.5	1.0	4	5	3	5	1.0	1.7	47	44	35	31	28	29
38 Zimbabwe	7	11	3.3	2.4	3	6	3	5	3.6	2.2	44	44	74	69	12	8
39 Guinea	4	7	2.5	2.7	2	3	3	3	2.1	2.4	47	47	91	87	1	2
40 Honduras	4	6	3.3	3.0	2	3	1	2	3.6	3.8	25	30	56	40	14	19
41 Senegal	6	8	2.9	2.7	3	4	3	4	2.6	2.7	42	42	81	76	6	7
42 China	981	1,200	1.5	1.1	586	811	539	709	2.2	1.1	43	45	76	74	14	15
43 Cameroon	9	13	2.8	2.9	5	7	4	5	2.4	3.1	37	38	73	70	8	9
44 Côte d'Ivoire	8	14	3.8	3.1	4	7	3	5	3.1	2.3	32	33	65	60	8	10
45 Albania	3	3	2.1	−0.1	2	2	1	2	2.6	0.8	39	41	57	55	23	23
46 Congo	2	3	3.1	2.9	1	1	1	1	3.1	2.6	43	43	58	48	13	14
47 Kyrgyz Republic	4	5	1.9	0.5	2	3	2	2	1.6	1.2	48	47	34	32	29	26
48 Sri Lanka	15	18	1.4	1.3	9	12	5	8	2.3	2.0	27	35	52	49	18	21
49 Armenia	3	4	1.4	1.2	2	2	2	2	1.6	1.1	48	48	21	17	43	41
Middle-income economies	1,236 t	1,591 t	1.8 w	1.4 w	717 t	981 t	513 t	688 t	2.1 w	1.8 w	36 w	38 w	38 w	32 w	28 w	27 w
Lower-middle-income	905 t	1,153 t	1.7 w	1.4 w	527 t	712 t	387 t	507 t	1.8 w	1.7 w	38 w	40 w	41 w	36 w	27 w	27 w
50 Lesotho	1	2	2.7	2.1	1	1	1	1	2.3	2.3	38	37	41	41	33	28
51 Egypt, Arab Rep.	41	58	2.5	2.0	23	34	14	21	2.5	2.7	26	29	61	43	17	23
52 Bolivia	5	7	2.0	2.4	3	4	2	3	2.6	2.6	33	37	53	47	18	18
53 Macedonia, FYR	2	2	0.7	0.9	1	1	1	1	1.2	1.3	36	41	34	22	31	41
54 Moldova	4	4	0.9	−0.1	3	3	2	2	0.2	0.2	50	49	43	33	26	30
55 Uzbekistan	16	23	2.5	2.1	9	13	6	9	2.2	2.8	48	46	38	34	25	25
56 Indonesia	148	193	1.8	1.6	83	120	59	89	2.9	2.5	35	40	59	57	12	14
57 Philippines	48	69	2.4	2.2	27	40	19	28	2.7	2.7	35	37	52	45	15	15
58 Morocco	19	27	2.2	2.0	10	16	7	10	2.6	2.6	34	35	56	45	20	25
59 Syrian Arab Republic	9	14	3.3	3.0	4	7	2	4	3.0	3.5	23	26	39	34	28	24
60 Papua New Guinea	3	4	2.2	2.3	2	2	2	2	2.1	2.3	42	42	83	79	6	7
61 Bulgaria	9	8	−0.2	−0.7	6	6	5	4	−0.4	−0.6	45	48	20	14	45	50
62 Kazakstan	15	17	1.2	−0.2	9	10	7	8	1.1	0.5	48	47	24	22	32	31
63 Guatemala	7	11	2.8	2.9	4	6	2	4	2.9	3.5	22	26	54	52	19	17
64 Eucador	8	11	2.5	2.2	4	7	3	4	3.5	3.2	20	26	40	33	20	19
65 Dominican Republic	6	8	2.2	1.9	3	5	2	3	3.1	2.6	25	29	32	25	24	29
66 Romania	22	23	0.4	−0.4	14	15	11	11	−0.2	0.1	46	44	35	24	41	47
67 Jamaica	2	3	1.2	1.0	1	2	1	1	2.1	1.8	46	46	31	24	16	23

68 Jordan	2	4	3.7	5.7	1	2	1	1	4.9	5.3	15	21	24	21	32	32
69 Algeria	19	28	2.9	2.2	9	16	5	9	3.7	4.1	21	24	36	26	27	31
70 El Salvador	5	6	1.0	2.2	2	3	2	2	1.7	3.4	27	34	43	36	19	21
71 Ukraine	50	52	0.4	-0.1	33	34	26	26	-0.1	-0.2	50	49	25	20	39	40
72 Paraguay	3	5	3.0	2.7	2	3	1	2	2.9	2.9	27	29	45	39	20	23
73 Tunisia	6	9	2.5	1.9	3	5	2	3	2.7	3.0	29	30	39	28	30	32
74 Lithuania	3	4	0.9	0.0	2	2	2	2	0.7	-0.2	50	48	28	18	38	40
75 Colombia	28	37	1.9	1.8	16	23	9	16	3.9	2.7	26	37	39	25	20	22
76 Namibia	1	2	2.7	2.7	1	1	0	1	2.3	2.5	40	41	56	49	15	15
77 Belarus	10	10	0.6	0.2	6	7	5	5	0.5	0.2	50	49	26	20	38	40
78 Russian Federation	139	148	0.6	0.0	95	99	76	77	0.2	0.0	49	49	16	14	44	42
79 Latvia	3	3	0.5	-1.2	2	2	1	1	0.2	-1.1	51	50	16	16	42	40
80 Peru	17	24	2.2	2.0	9	14	5	9	3.1	3.1	24	29	40	36	18	18
81 Costa Rica	2	3	2.8	2.3	1	2	1	1	3.8	2.5	21	30	35	26	23	27
82 Lebanon	3	4	2.5	1.9	2	2	1	1	3.5	2.9	23	28	13	5	26	22
83 Thailand	47	58	1.7	0.9	26	39	24	34	2.6	1.3	47	46	71	64	10	14
84 Panama	2	3	2.1	1.7	1	2	1	1	3.1	2.4	30	34	29	26	19	16
85 Turkey	44	61	2.3	1.7	25	38	19	28	2.9	2.1	35	35	60	53	16	18
86 Poland	36	39	0.7	0.3	19	26	19	19	0.1	0.6	45	46	30	27	38	36
87 Estonia	1	1	0.6	-1.1	1	1	1	1	0.4	-0.8	51	49	15	14	43	41
88 Slovak Republic	5	5	0.6	0.3	3	4	2	3	0.9	0.7	45	48	14	12	36	32
89 Botswana	1	1	3.5	2.5	0	1	0	0	3.4	2.5	50	46	64	46	10	20
90 Venezuela	15	22	2.6	2.3	8	13	5	8	3.5	3.0	27	33	15	12	28	28
Upper-middle-income	331 t	438 t	2.0 w	1.7 w	191 t	269 t	126 t	182 t	2.7 w	2.0 w	29 w	34 w	31 w	21 w	29 w	27 w
91 South Africa	29	41	2.4	2.2	16	24	11	16	2.7	2.4	35	37	17	14	35	32
92 Croatia	5	5	0.4	0.0	3	3	2	2	0.3	0.1	40	43	24	15	32	32
93 Mexico	67	92	2.3	1.9	35	54	22	36	3.5	2.8	27	31	37	28	29	24
94 Mauritius	1	1	0.9	1.3	0	1	0	0	2.3	1.8	26	32	27	17	28	43
95 Gabon	1	1	3.0	2.8	0	1	0	1	2.1	1.9	45	44	76	61	14	19
96 Brazil	121	159	2.0	1.5	71	101	48	71	3.2	1.6	28	35	37	23	24	23
97 Trinidad and Tobago	1	1	1.3	0.8	1	1	0	1	1.2	1.8	32	36	11	11	39	31
98 Czech Republic	10	10	0.1	-0.1	6	7	5	6	0.2	0.4	47	47	13	11	56	45
99 Malaysia	14	20	2.6	2.4	8	12	5	8	2.8	2.7	34	37	41	27	19	23
100 Hungary	11	10	-0.3	-0.3	7	7	5	5	-0.8	0.1	43	44	18	15	43	38
101 Chile	11	14	1.7	1.5	7	9	5	6	2.7	2.1	26	32	21	19	25	25
102 Oman	1	2	3.9	6.0	1	1	0	1	3.4	5.1	7	14	50	48	22	26
103 Uruguay	3	3	0.6	0.6	2	2	1	1	1.6	1.0	31	40	17	14	28	27
104 Saudi Arabia	9	19	5.2	3.7	5	10	3	6	6.5	3.2	8	13	45	20	16	20
105 Argentina	28	35	1.5	1.3	17	21	11	14	1.3	2.0	28	31	13	1	34	32
106 Slovenia	2	2	0.5	-0.1	1	1	1	1	0.3	0.1	46	46	58	5	42	44
107 Greece	10	10	0.5	0.6	6	7	4	4	1.2	0.9	28	36	31	23	29	28
Low- and middle-income	3,614 t	4,771 t	2.0 w	1.6 w	2,069 t	2,916 t	1,669 t	2,263 t	2.2 w	1.7 w	38 w	40 w	63 w	58 w	17 w	18 w
Sub-Saharan Africa	381 t	583 t	3.0 w	2.6 w	196 t	305 t	173 t	257 t	2.7 w	2.6 w	42 w	42 w	72 w	68 w	9 w	9 w

Exhibit I.A.6. Continued

	Population						Labor force									
	Total (millions)		Avg. annual growth rate (%)		Aged 15–64 (millions)		Total[a] (millions)		Avg. annual growth rate(%)		Female (%)		Agriculture (%)		Industry (%)	
	1980	1995	1980–90	1990–95	1980	1995	1980	1995	1980–90	1990–95	1980	1995	1980	1990	1980	1990
East Asia and Pacific	1,360 t	1,706 t	1.6 w	1.3 w	796 t	1,119 t	704 t	951 t	2.3 w	1.3 w	43 w	45 w	73 w	70 w	14 w	15 w
South Asia	903 t	1,243 t	2.2 w	1.9 w	508 t	732 t	389 t	532 t	2.1 w	2.1 w	34 w	33 w	70 w	64 w	13 w	16 w
Europe and Central Asia	437 t	488 t	0.9 w	0.3 w	277 t	317 t	219 t	238 t	0.6 w	0.5 w	46 w	46 w	27 w	23 w	37 w	36 w
Latin America and Caribbean	358 t	478 t	2.0 w	1.7 w	201 t	293 t	130 t	197 t	3.0 w	2.3 w	27 w	33 w	34 w	25 w	25 w	24 w
High-income economies	816 t	902 t	0.7 w	0.7 w	522 t	605 t	368 t	432 t	1.2 w	0.9 w	39 w	42 w	9 w	5 w	35 w	31 w
108 Korea, Rep.	38	45	1.2	0.9	24	32	16	22	2.3	1.9	39	40	37	18	27	35
109 Portugal	10	10	0.1	0.1	6	7	5	5	0.4	0.5	39	43	26	18	36	34
110 Spain	37	39	0.4	0.2	23	27	14	17	1.3	1.0	28	36	19	12	37	33
111 New Zealand	3	4	0.8	1.4	2	2	1	2	2.0	1.5	34	44	11	10	33	25
112 Ireland	3	4	0.3	0.5	2	2	1	1	0.4	1.7	28	33	19	14	34	29
113 †Israel	4	6	1.8	3.5	2	3	1	2	2.3	3.5	34	40	6	4	31	29
114 †Kuwait	1	2	4.4	–4.9	1	1	0	1	5.8	–1.6	13	27	2	1	32	25
115 †United Arab Emirates	1	2	5.7	5.8	1	1	1	1	5.1	3.9	5	13	4	7	37	24
116 United Kingdom	56	59	0.2	0.3	36	38	27	29	0.6	0.3	39	43	3	2	38	29
117 Australia	15	18	1.5	1.1	10	12	7	9	2.3	1.4	37	43	6	5	32	26
118 Italy	56	57	0.1	0.2	36	39	23	25	0.8	0.4	33	38	13	9	38	32
119 Canada	25	30	1.2	1.3	17	20	12	15	1.9	1.0	40	45	7	3	33	25
120 Finland	5	5	0.4	0.5	3	3	2	3	0.6	0.1	46	48	12	8	35	31
121 †Hong Kong	5	6	1.2	1.6	3	4	2	3	1.6	1.3	34	37	1	..	50	37
122 Sweden	8	9	0.3	0.6	5	6	4	5	1.0	0.3	44	48	..	5	..	26
123 Netherlands	14	15	0.6	0.7	9	11	6	7	2.0	0.6	31	40	6	3	31	28
124 Belgium	10	10	0.1	0.4	6	7	4	4	0.2	0.5	34	40	3	3	35	29
125 France	54	58	0.5	0.5	34	38	24	26	0.4	0.8	40	44	8	5	35	36
126 †Singapore	2	3	1.7	2.0	2	2	1	1	2.3	1.7	35	38	2	0	44	37
127 Austria	8	8	0.2	0.8	5	5	3	4	0.5	0.5	40	41	10	8	41	28
128 United States	228	263	0.9	1.0	151	172	110	133	1.4	1.1	42	46	3	3	31	38
129 Germany	78	82	0.1	0.6	52	56	37	40	0.6	0.3	40	42	7	4	45	38
130 Denmark	5	5	0.0	0.3	3	4	3	3	0.7	0.1	44	46	7	6	31	28
131 Norway	4	4	0.4	0.5	3	3	2	2	0.9	0.7	40	46	8	6	29	25
132 Japan	117	125	0.6	0.3	79	87	57	66	1.1	0.6	38	41	11	7	35	34
133 Switzerland	6	7	0.6	1.0	4	5	3	4	1.5	0.8	37	40	6	6	39	35
World	4,429 t	5,673 t	1.7 w	1.5 w	2,590 t	3,521 t	2,037 t	2,695 t	2.0 w	1.6 w	38 w	40 w	53 w	49 w	20 w	20 w

[a] Participation rates from ILO are applied to population estimates to derive labor force estimates. t = Total w = weighted average

Source: World Bank, *World Development Report 1997* (New York: Oxford University Press, 1997), pp. 220–221.

I.B. ECONOMIC PERFORMANCE OF LESS DEVELOPED COUNTRIES: THE RECENT PAST

Exhibit I.B.1. Balance Sheet of Human Development—Developing Countries

Progress	Deprivation
Health	
• In 1960–93 average life expectancy increased by more than a third. Life expectancy is now more than 70 years in 30 countries.	• Around 17 million people die each year from curable infectious and parasitic diseases such as diarrhoea, malaria, and tuberculosis.
• Over the past three decades the population with access to safe water almost doubled—from 36% to nearly 70%.	• Of the world's 18 million HIV-infected people, more than 90% live in developing countries.
Education	
• Between 1960 and 1991 net enrolment at the primary level increased by nearly two-thirds—from 48% to 77%.	• Millions of children are still out of school—130 million at the primary level and 275 million at the secondary level.
Food and Nutrition	
• Despite rapid population growth, food production per capita increased by about 20% in the past decade.	• Nearly 800 million people do not get enough food, and about 500 million people are chronically malnourished.
Income and Poverty	
• During 1960–93 real per capita income in the developing world increased by an average 3.5% a year.	• Almost a third of the population—1.3 billion people— lives in poverty.
Women	
• During the past two decades the combined primary and secondary enrolment ratio for girls increased from 38% to 78%.	• At 384 per 100,000 live births, maternal mortality is still nearly 12 times as high as in OECD countries.
• During the past two decades fertility rates declined by more than a third.	• Women hold only 10% of parliamentary seats.
Children	
• Between 1960 and 1993 the infant mortality rate fell by more than half—from 150 per thousand live births to 70.	• More than a third of children are malnourished.
• The extension of basic immunization over the past two decades has saved the lives of about three million children a year.	• The under-five mortality rate, at 97 per thousand live births, is still nearly six times as high as in industrial countries.
Environment	
• Developing countries' contribution to global emissions is still less than a fourth that of industrial countries, though their population is four times the industrial world's.	• About 200 million people are severely affected by desertification.
	• Every year some 20 million hectares of tropical forests are grossly degraded or completely cleared.
Politics and Conflicts	
• Between two-thirds and three-quarters of the people in developing countries live under relatively pluralistic and democratic regimes.	• At the end of 1994 there were more than 11 million refugees in the developing world.

Source: United Nations Development Program, *Human Development Report 1996* (New York: Oxford University Press, 1996), p. 20.

Selection I.B.1. The East Asian Miracle*

East Asia has a remarkable record of high and sustained economic growth. From 1965 to 1990 the twenty-three economies of East Asia grew faster than all other regions (see figure 1). Most of this achievement is attributable to seemingly miraculous growth in just eight economies: Japan; the "Four Tigers," Hong Kong, the Republic of Korea, Singapore, and Taiwan, China; and the three newly industrializing economies (NIEs) of Southeast Asia, Indonesia, Malaysia, and Thailand. Moreover, these eight economies have been unusually successful at sharing the fruits of growth. Compared with other developing economies, they have had lower and declining levels of inequality. Rapid growth and improving equity are the defining characteristics of the East Asian miracle and the eight high-performing East Asian economies (HPAEs) that are the subject of our study[1] . . .

The HPAEs' low and declining levels of inequality are also a remarkable exception to historical experience and contemporary evidence in other regions. The positive association between growth and improving equity in the HPAEs, and the contrast with other economies, is illustrated in figure 2. Forty economies are ranked by the ratio of the income share of the richest fifth of the population to the income share of the poorest fifth and per capita real GDP growth during 1965–90. The northwest corner of the figure identifies economies with high growth (GDP per capita greater than 4.0 percent) and low relative inequality (ratio of the income share of the top quintile to that of the bottom quintile less than 10). All of the high growth, low inequality economies are in East Asia. Seven are HPAEs; only Malaysia, which has an index of inequality above 15, is excluded, while China enters. For the eight HPAEs, rapid growth and declining inequality have been shared virtues.

As the result of rapid shared growth, human welfare has improved dramatically. In the HPAEs, the proportion of people living in poverty dropped sharply—for example, from 58 percent in 1972 to

17 percent in 1982 in Indonesia, and from 37 percent in 1973 to less than 15 percent in Malaysia in 1987. Absolute poverty also declined in other developing economies since the early 1970s, but much less steeply, from 54 to 43 percent in India and from 50 to 21 percent in Brazil. A host of other social and economic indicators, from education to appliance ownership, have also improved rapidly in the HPAEs, and now are at levels that sometimes surpass those in industrial economies.

Understanding East Asia's Success

What caused East Asia's success? Superior accumulation accounted for most of the growth in the HPAEs. Private domestic investment, combined with rapidly growing human capital, were the principal engines of growth. High levels of domestic financial savings sustained the HPAEs' high investment levels. Agriculture, while declining in relative importance, nonetheless experienced rapid growth. Manufactured exports grew extremely rapidly, facilitating the absorption of foreign technology. Population growth rates declined more rapidly in the HPAEs than in other parts of the developing world, leading to more rapid growth in per capita consumption and larger surpluses for reinvestment. In addition, and partly because of these factors, the HPAEs may have been better at allocating resources to high-return activities. Finally, the HPAEs have had unusually high productivity growth; change in total factor productivity, a key measure of productivity, is higher in the HPAEs than in most other developing economies.

While some of the HPAEs benefited from a head start in terms of the education and public administration systems, most of their growth resulted from getting the policy basics right. Macroeconomic management was unusually good, providing the stable environment essential for private investment. Policies to increase the integrity of the banking system, and to make it more accessible to nontraditional savers, increased the levels of financial savings. Education policies that focused on primary and secondary schooling generated rapid increases in labor force skills. Agricultural policies stressed productivity change and did not tax the rural economy excessively. Governments either actively encouraged family planning or, at the minimum, did not restrict family planning choices. Finally, all the HPAEs kept price distortions within

*From World Bank, "The East Asian Miracle," *The East Asian Miracle: Economic Growth and Public Policy: Summary* (Washington, D.C.: The World Bank, 1993), pp. 1–12. Reprinted by permission.

[1]Recently China, particularly southern China, has recorded remarkably high growth rates using policies that in some ways resemble the HPAEs. This very significant development is beyond the scope of our study, mainly because China's ownership structure, methods of corporate and civil governance, and reliance on markets are so different from the HPAEs, and in such rapid flux, that cross-economy comparison is problematic.

Figure 1. Average Growth of GNP per Capita, 1965–90

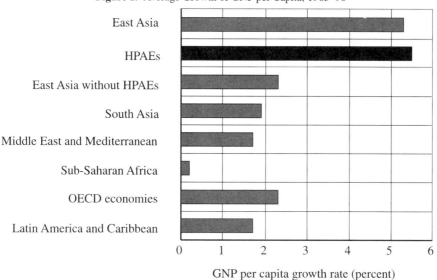

GNP per capita growth rate (percent)

reasonable bounds and were open to foreign ideas and technology, policies that, along with other fundamentals, facilitated efficient allocation and helped to set the stage for high productivity growth.

But these fundamental policies do not tell the entire story. In each of these economies the government also intervened to foster development, often systematically and through multiple channels. Policy interventions took many forms: targeted and subsidized credit to selected industries, low deposit rates and ceilings on borrowing rates to increase profits and retained earnings, protection of domestic import substitutes, subsidies to declining industries, the establishment and financial support of government banks, public investments in applied research, firm- and industry-specific export targets, development of export marketing institutions, and wide sharing of information between public and private sectors.

At least some of these interventions violate the dictum of establishing for the private sector a level playing field, a neutral incentives regime. Yet these strategies of selective promotion were closely associated with high rates of accumulation, generally efficient allocation and, in the fastest-growing economies, high rates of productivity growth. Were some selective interventions, in fact, good for growth?

In addressing this question we face a central methodological problem. Since we chose the HPAEs for their unusually rapid growth, we know

before we begin analysis that their interventions did not inhibit growth. But it is very hard to establish statistical links between growth and a specific intervention, and even more difficult to establish causality. Because we cannot know what would have happened in the absence of a specific policy, we cannot prove conclusively whether interventions increased growth rates. Moreover, because the HPAEs differed from less successful economies both in their closer adherence to policy fundamentals and in the manner in which they implemented interventions, separating the relative impact of fundamentals and interventions is virtually impossible. Thus, in attempting to distinguish interventions that contributed to growth from those that were either growth neutral or harmful to growth we cannot offer a rigorous counterfactual scenario. Instead, we have had to rely on analytical and empirical tools to produce what Keynes would have called an "essay in persuasion."

Our judgment is that in a few economies, mainly in Northeast Asia, government interventions appear in some instances to have resulted in higher and more equal growth than otherwise would have occurred. However, the prerequisites for success were so rigorous that policymakers seeking to follow similar paths in other East Asian economies met with failure. Thus, the problem is not only to try to understand which policies contributed to growth with equity, but also to understand the institutional and economic circumstances which made them viable.

Figure 2. Income Inequality and Growth of GDP, 1965–89

GDP growth per capita (percent)

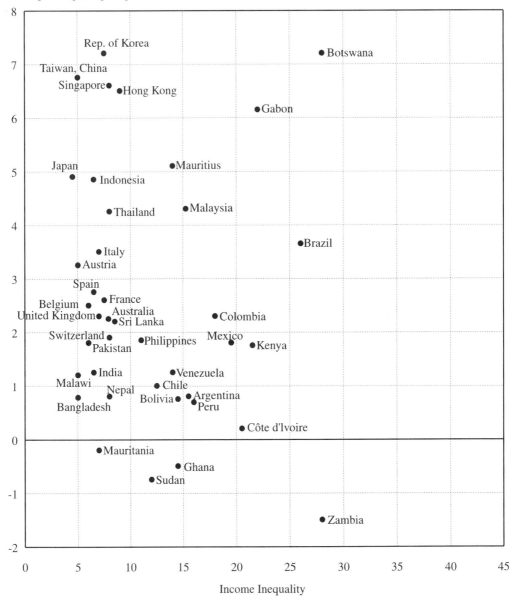

Note: Income inequality is measured by the ratio of the income shares of the richest 20 percent and the poorest 20 percent of the population.

Circumstances, Public Policy, and Growth

Geography and culture clearly have been important factors in East Asia's rapid growth. Ready access to common sea lanes and relative geographical proximity are the most obvious shared characteristics of the successful Asian economies. Intraregional economic relationships date back many centuries to China's relations with tribute states—the kingdoms that became Cambodia, Japan, Korea, Laos, Myanmar, and Viet Nam. To the south, Muslim traders sailed from India to Java, trading at points in between, for hundreds of years before the arrival of European ships. These traditional ties, reinforced in the nineteenth and twentieth centuries by surges of emigration, have fostered elements of a common trading culture, including two lingua francas, Bahasa and Hokein

Chinese, that continue to be felt in the region today.

In our own century, cheap ocean transport and shared historical experiences further knit together a far-flung, culturally disparate region. Throughout Southeast Asia, ethnic Chinese with links to Hong Kong and Taiwan, China, and drawing on a common cultural heritage have been more and more active in intraregional trade and investment. Such links and geographical proximity probably facilitated attempts to emulate Japan's success: Korea borrowed Japanese techniques for building large trading companies and directing the structure of industry; Malaysia focused first on developing heavy industry and more recently on building business-government relationships; and Singapore used Japanese experience in penetrating foreign markets and shifting industry to knowledge-intensive branches. More broadly, Japan's example undoubtedly inspired policymakers throughout East Asia.

Finally, geographical proximity facilitated capital flows, particularly in the last decade, as Northeast Asian manufacturers of labor-intensive exports moved their factories south to take advantage of lower wages. Successive waves of investment, first from Japan and later from Hong Kong, Korea, Singapore, and Taiwan, China, have washed over Indonesia, Malaysia, and Thailand. The appreciation of the Japanese yen and U.S. restrictions on Japanese imports created rare opportunities for other East Asian producers to enter international markets. Producers of garments, shoes, television sets, automobiles and other products, first in Korea and Taiwan, China, and later in Southeast Asia, took advantage of these episodes to establish lucrative market positions. These capital flows were mostly encouraged by generally liberal treatment of foreign investment; where investment has been restricted, informal credit and information networks have helped investors to move capital relatively freely.

If geography, history, and culture were an adequate explanation for the HPAEs' success, other economies would have little to learn from East Asia's success stories. Fortunately, evidence suggests that this is not the case. Many HPAEs passed through periods of macroeconomic instability and low growth before making policy changes that launched them on a high-growth trajectory. Moreover, economies that are part of the same matrix of geography, culture, and history as the HPAEs but continue to follow different economic policies—the Democratic People's Republic of Korea and the Philippines are two widely divergent examples—have yet to share in the East Asian miracle. These facts suggest that policies rather than circumstances have been decisive.

Policy Explanations for Rapid Growth

Among the variety of policy explanations, two broad views have emerged. Adherents of the neoclassical view have stressed East Asia's success in getting the basics right. Its proponents argue that the successful Asian economies have been better than others at providing a stable macroeconomic environment and a reliable legal framework to promote domestic and international competition. They also stress that the orientation of the HPAEs toward international trade and the absence of price controls and other distortionary policies have led to low relative price distortions. Investments in people, education, and health are legitimate roles for government in the neoclassical framework, and its adherents stress the importance of human capital in the HPAEs' success.

Adherents of the revisionist view have successfully shown that East Asia does not wholly conform to the neoclassical model. Industrial policy and interventions in financial markets, common in East Asia, are not easily reconciled with the neoclassical framework. Some policies in some economies are much more in accord with models of state-led development. Moreover, while the neoclassical model would explain growth with a standard set of relatively constant policies, the policy mixes used by East Asian economies were diverse and flexible. Revisionists argue that East Asian governments "led the market" in critical ways. In contrast to the neo-classical view, which acknowledges relatively few cases of market failure, revisionists contend that markets consistently fail to guide investment to industries that would generate the highest growth for the overall economy. In East Asia, the revisionists argue, governments remedied this by deliberately "getting the prices wrong," using incentives and subsidies to boost industries that would not otherwise have thrived.

While the revisionist school has provided valuable insights into the history, role, and extent of East Asian interventions, demonstrating convincingly the scope of government actions to promote industrial development in Japan, Korea, Singapore, and Taiwan, China, its proponents have not established that interventions, per se, accelerated growth. Moreover, some important government interventions in East Asia, such as Korea's promotion of heavy and chemical industries, have had little apparent impact on industrial structure. In other instances, such as Singapore's effort to squeeze out labor-intensive industries by boosting wages and Malaysia's heavy industry push, policies have clearly backfired. Thus neither view fully accounts for East Asia's phenomenal growth. . . .

A Functional Approach to Understanding Growth

To accommodate this shifting diversity of policies, we have developed a framework which links rapid growth to the attainment of three functions. In this view, each of the HPAEs maintained macroeconomic stability and accomplished three functions of growth: accumulation, efficient allocation, and rapid technological catching up. They did this with shifting combinations of policies, ranging from market-oriented to state-led, both across economies and over time.

Figure 3 gives a schematic view of the functional approach to understanding East Asia's success. We classify policy choices (first column) into two broad groups, fundamentals and selective interventions. Among the most important fundamental policies are macroeconomic stability, high investments in human capital, stable and secure financial systems, limited price distortions, and openness to foreign technology. Selective interventions include

mild financial repression (keeping interest rates positive, but low), directed credit, selective industrial promotion, and export-push trade policies. Using this framework, we have tried to understand how government policies, both fundamental and interventionist, may have contributed to accumulation, more efficient allocation, or productivity growth.

To be successful, an intervention must address one or more market failures; for if such failures do not exist, markets by definition will perform the allocation function more efficiently than any intervention. Coordination problems, such as lack of information or lack of risk markets, are a frequent cause of market failure and are particularly common in the early stages of development. Some of East Asia's most successful interventions can be seen as government-initiated responses to these coordination problems—responses which emphasize cooperative behavior among private firms and clear performance-based standards of success.

Competitive discipline (second column of figure 3) is crucial to efficient investment. Most economies employ only market-based competition. We argue that some HPAEs have gone a step further by creating contests that combine competition with the benefits of cooperation, among firms and between government and the private sector. Such contests range from very simple nonmarket

Figure 3. A Functional Approach to Growth

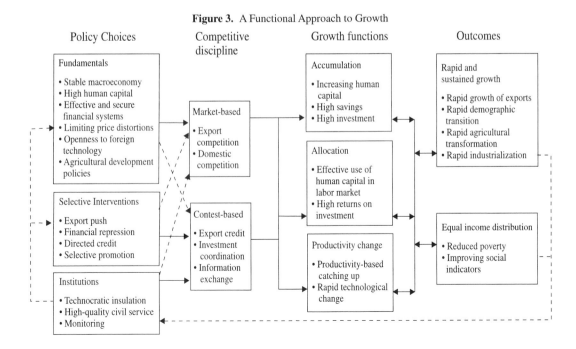

allocation rules such as access to rationed credit for exporters, to very complex coordination of private investment in the government-business deliberation councils of Japan and Korea. The key feature of each contest, however, is that the government distributes rewards—for example, access to credit or foreign exchange—based on performance, which the government and competing firms monitor. To succeed, selective interventions must be disciplined by competition, via either markets or contests.

Economic contests, like all others, require competent and impartial referees—that is, strong institutions. Thus, a high-quality civil service with the capacity to monitor performance, and which is insulated from political interference, is an essential element of contest-based competition. Of course, a high-quality civil service also augments a government's ability to design and implement non-contest-based policies.

Our framework is only an effort to order and interpret information. No HPAE government set out to achieve the functions of growth. Rather they used multiple, shifting policy instruments in pursuit of more immediate economic objectives. Pragmatic flexibility—the capacity and willingness to change policies—is as much a hallmark of the HPAEs as any single policy instrument.

Exhibit I.B.2. East Asian GDP Growth, 1996–1998

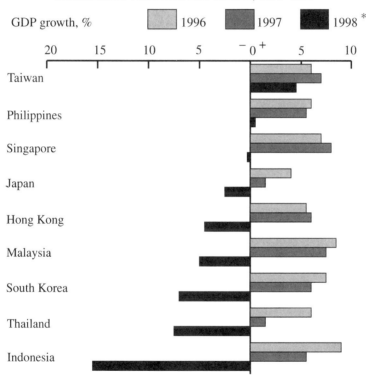

* Forecast

Source: "Survey: Taiwan." *The Economist* 349 (November 7, 1998): p. 4.

Selection I.B.2. East Asian Crisis: An Overview*

Why Did East Asia Falter?

... Several structural problems were well known and analyzed prior to the collapse of the Thai baht in July 1997. Did these structural problems finally produce the exhaustion of the East Asian model, much as import substitution in Latin America became fully exhausted during the crisis decade of the 1980s? Or, was the crisis in East Asia the result of short-term macroeconomic mistakes and financial panic, a type of macro-financial accident?

Rapid growth, urbanization, and industrialization were spawning new and difficult development problems prior to the crisis. These were building in three dimensions. First, rapid growth, in the absence of sophisticated financial and capital markets and with a large government presence, left the corporate and financial sectors unusually reliant on financing long-term investment with short-term debt capital (this will be discussed below). Second, economic growth was undermining the traditional protection mechanisms for the unemployed, the sick, and the elderly. East Asia relied on high personal savings and family ties to provide security for its elderly. It came to rely on growth itself to provide an ever more buoyant labor market. The forces of growth, with their demands for an increasingly mobile labor force, migration, and wider scope for personal consumption, were putting strains on traditional ways of solving social problems. In the transition countries of China and Vietnam, the old commune and state enterprise system of welfare was under analogous strains with the spread of markets. In the wealthiest countries, lifetime employment guarantees in the corporate sector were proving increasingly out of tune with the modern economy's needs for rapid change and flexibility. Third, a weakness of a different kind resulted from the exploitation of national resources, particularly forests. Southeast Asian growth was fueled, in part, by over-logging, intensive exploitation of fisheries, and wasteful agricultural practices. Although national income accounts are difficult to adjust for environmental damage, some estimates are that Malaysia's growth in gross domestic product (GDP) would have been approximately 20 percent less if adequate allowance had been made for resource depletion.

*From World Bank, "East Asian Crisis: An Overview," *East Asia: The Road to Recovery* (Washington, D.C.: World Bank, 1998), pp. 3–15. Reprinted by permission.

Nonetheless, there is not much evidence that these long-term development problems alone were enough to drag down growth, much less precipitate a sudden reversal of fortune. Productivity growth was generally within the normal range for developing countries. In that sense the "miracle" was no miracle at all. Rapid growth relative to other countries was achieved by dint of sacrifice reflected in East Asia's famously high savings rates, hard work as reflected in the dramatic increases in labor force participation rates, and investments in education as reflected in the skill level of the workforce. Productivity, per se, is less important than increases in per capita income, whatever the source, and East Asia simply out-performed other regions of the world by this more meaningful measure.

Even if declining returns to investment eventually were to set in, the question is when and whether they would be sufficient to precipitate sharp slowdown or crisis. ... any growth slowdown associated with diminishing returns is likely to be well into the 21st century, not the mid-1990s. The main sources of the crisis will have to be found elsewhere.

Emergence of Structural Vulnerability

Three forces interacted to leave some countries in the region—notably Thailand, Korea, and Indonesia—vulnerable to external shocks: a burgeoning availability of private capital, especially short-term capital, that was in search of higher returns; macroeconomic policies that permitted capital inflows to fuel a credit boom; and newly liberalized, but insufficiently regulated financial markets that were growing rapidly. The scenario played out as follows: The push from global capital markets, often without due diligence and beyond prudent limits, interacted with poorly regulated domestic financial systems to fuel a domestic credit expansion. This manifested itself as an asset price bubble, particularly in Thailand, and added to the excessive debt of already over-leveraged firms, which exposed the region to the shocks of changing investor expectations.

Ready Availability of Capital

Globalization of financial markets has been occurring at a dizzying pace. From 1990 to 1997, the volume of private capital flows to developing countries rose more than fivefold—from US$42 billion in 1990 to US$256 billion in 1997. While world trade grew by about 5 percent annually, private capital flows grew by nearly 30 percent annually. The most mobile forms of flows, commercial bank debt and portfolio investments, set the pace (see figure 1).

Propelling this expansion was an aggressive search for ever higher returns to capital. "Emerging markets" were booming, and offered greater profitability than investments in developed countries. Banks and financial institutions, often trapped in slow-growing but highly competitive home markets, scanned the globe for investment opportunities.

The very success of East Asia made it an ideal location and the combination of rapid growth, low debt ratios, and a history of sound macroeconomic management attracted capital like a magnet.

From Inflows to Credit Boom: Macroeconomic and Exchange Rate Policy

. . . Most of the Association of Southeast Asian Nations (ASEAN) countries adopted a nominal anchor policy by pegging loosely to the U.S. dollar in the run-up to the crisis, switching from real exchange rate targeting in the earlier period. Informal pegs to the U.S. dollar encouraged capital inflows due to large interest rate differentials. Predictable nominal rates encouraged unhedged external borrowing. A wedge was driven between the actual and equilibrium real exchange rates due

to a loss of competitiveness and declining corporate profitability on the one hand, and a real appreciation on the other. Exceptions were Singapore and Hong Kong (China) where labor markets were flexible and productivity gains were high. Thus, the link to the U.S. dollar in Hong Kong (China) or the strong currency policy in Singapore did not result in a real exchange rate misalignment. To further complicate matters, the yen depreciated against the U.S. dollar throughout much of 1996, so the pegged currencies lost competitiveness against the important yen market. But, the most important effect was the incentives the policy gave to borrow abroad. Exchange rate policies played a particularly large role in motivating capital flows. By reducing the perceptions of exchange rate risks, incentives to hedge external borrowing were suppressed and, moreover, the relatively narrow exchange rate movements created a bias toward short-term borrowing.

Between 1994 and 1997, the net private capital inflows as a share of the rapidly expanding GDP increased throughout the East Asia 5. The exception was Thailand where, by 1994, the net private capital inflows had already reached 14.5 percent of GDP (see figure 2).

. . . These inflows fueled the domestic credit boom throughout most of the region. In the East Asia 5, broad money (M2) expanded at a near 20 percent annual rate in 1996 and 1997. This was nearly twice the rate of China, Taiwan (China), Hong Kong (China), and Singapore—countries that would later fare better in the storm of specula-

Figure 1. Private flows to developing countries have skyrocketed

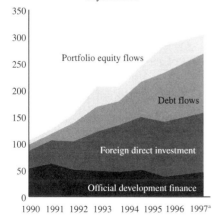

ªPreliminary.

Source: World Bank Debt Reporting System.

Figure 2. Private flows become increasingly important to East Asia

Net private capital flows to East Asia, 1994–96

Source: World Bank Global Development Finance, 1998.

tive attacks. The credit boom, in turn, led to an increase in assets prices, creating the appearance of high returns. Property values in Bangkok, Seoul, and Jakarta rose at double digit rates through 1996. Rising asset prices provided greater collateral to banks, and led to greater lending. At the same time, middle- and upper-class owners of these assets, feeling more well-heeled, consumed more freely. Rising aggregate demand encouraged yet more foreign borrowing.

Weak Financial Systems Led to Poor Investments and Excessive Risks

As capital inflows increased, the quality of intermediation became increasingly important. Invested in high-return activities to creditworthy borrowers, these capital inflows had the potential to spur East Asian growth. However, incremental additions to investments appear to have yielded a lower return. As indicated in figure 3, the incremental capital-output ratio in Thailand and Korea, after some fluctuations in previous decades, rose every year after 1988.

East Asian countries receiving foreign capital primarily through the domestic banking system or through direct corporate borrowing became more vulnerable than countries relying predominantly on foreign direct investment. This was especially true in Thailand. Private decisions resulted in an excessive buildup of risky forms of leverage on the balance sheets of financial institutions and non-financial corporations, in particular of short-term foreign currency debt in excess of foreign currency resources available on short notice. In several East Asian countries in the late 1980s, short-term debt relative to overall external liabilities began rising sharply.

Capital inflows and the credit boom increased vulnerability in two dimensions. On the one hand, the ratio of short-term debt to foreign reserves, a rough measure of a country's ability to meet its current obligations from its own liquid resources, rose sharply from 1994 to 1997, except for Indonesia, where it remained at high levels. In the three most-affected countries—Korea, Indonesia, Thailand—short-term debt-to-reserves ratios had risen to well over 150 percent by June 1997. Malaysia and the Philippines were not as badly exposed, with ratios at less than 100 percent. Credit growth was evident in the high ratio of broad money to reserves, and the two were correlated, as seen in figure 4. A broader measure of vulnerability, the ratio of M2 money to reserves, indicates the potential for a "run" on the foreign exchange reserves of a

Figure 3. Korea and Thailand require ever greater investment to achieve the same level of output growth

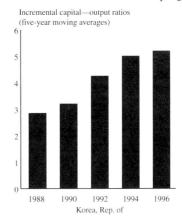

Incremental capital—output ratios
(five-year moving averages)

Korea, Rep. of

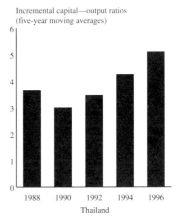

Incremental capital—output ratios
(five-year moving averages)

Thailand

Source: World Bank Global Development Finance 1998.

country with a fixed exchange rate by its own residents when there is a loss of confidence in the local currency. Countries with exchange controls and less open capital accounts are less vulnerable than this measure would otherwise indicate because of the difficulty in shifting funds out of the country.

Patterns of indebtedness varied across countries. In Thailand, finance companies and banks, availing themselves of extremely low-interest, yen-denominated loans, borrowed through government sanctioned channels to invest in real estate. Financial institutions' net foreign liabilities rose from 6 percent of domestic deposit liabilities in 1990 to one-third by 1996 (Global Economic Prospects (GEP), 1998). Korean banks also increased their exposure to foreign borrowing. In Indonesia, however, corporations became the primary borrowers from foreign sources, with much of it coming from "off-shore."

Figure 4. Vulnerability indicators
(*Selected countries, June 1997*)

Broad money-to-reserves ratios, in percent

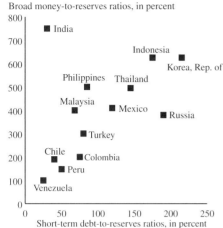

Short-term debt-to-reserves ratios, in percent

Source: BIS, IMF, and GEP, 1998.

Three microeconomic factors accentuated the incentives to borrow abroad. First, the implicit insurance—for example, the fixed exchange rate—provided to financial institutions motivated excessive risk-taking, including large foreign exchange risks, that were passed on to the rest of the domestic economy. Second, high domestic funding costs and market segmentation added to the incentives to borrow abroad. In Thailand during the period 1991–96, domestic financial intermediation costs accounted for 28 percent of the nominal baht interest cost. The domestic cost of funds was significantly higher than the costs of borrowing "offshore," even after taking into account exchange rate risks, which only added further incentive to borrow foreign funds. Since this access to foreign markets was only available to the largest and best credit corporations, these firms and banks enjoyed a market advantage, and undoubtedly used their access to political leaders to protect their position, making it more difficult for regulators to limit "off-shore" borrowing to prudent levels. Third, the creation of "off-shore" financial markets in which local corporations could, because of regulatory and tax advantages, obtain lower-cost finance than in domestic markets. This situation was the most severe in Thailand.

The inflows also fed into a system of corporate finance that heightened risks from abrupt changes in interest or foreign exchange rates. The corporate sector had grown rapidly during the previous decades in a context of under-developed bond markets and over-reliance on bank financing. The debt-equity ratio of Korean corporates, for exam-

ple, was over 317 percent by the end of 1996, twice the U.S. ratio, and four times the Taiwanese ratio. The top 30 Korean chaebols had even higher leverage, on average more than 400 percent in 1996. Correspondingly, interest burdens are very high in East Asian countries. In Korea, for example, the interest-expenses-to-sales ratio of all manufacturing corporations in 1995 was about 6 percent, compared to 2 percent for Taiwan (China) and 1 percent for Japan. This would present a painful dilemma to macroeconomic policy makers when the crisis hit: they could use interest rate adjustments to maintain exchange rate stability but only at the cost of imperiling their highly leveraged corporate sectors and creating a domestic liquidity crunch.

In retrospect, it is also clear that the regulations necessary to manage the integration of global external finance had not kept pace with capital inflows. Inconsistent reforms and inappropriate sequencing of liberalization added to the buildups of vulnerabilities. For example, licensing and supervision regulation of merchant banks in Korea permitted groups of companies to own both banks and the same groups of firms to whom they were lending. In Indonesia, the number of banks expanded very rapidly and the supervisory authorities spent too little time screening the integrity of owners and managers to keep out applicants with poor prospects or fraudulent ventures. In Thailand, the scope of finance companies' activities greatly increased in the 1990s without a commensurate improvement in their supervision. In several East Asian countries, the capital account was liberalized for inward and outward flows for foreign investors; domestic investors, however, did not always have the opportunity to invest abroad and thus, could not diversify their risks. Finally, throughout the region, regulations requiring prudential management of currency risks, credit evaluation, and public financial reporting were wholly inadequate.

The time bomb was loaded. Rising global liquidity fed huge amounts of capital into a poorly regulated institutional setting with limited transparency, and related party lending, often with negligible due diligence from foreign lenders. Implicit and explicit government guarantees on the exchange rate and selected investments fed into a domestic credit boom that macroeconomic policy failed to manage. East Asian countries had taken risks that left them exposed to shocks in several ways:

• Widening current account deficits, financed with short-term debt, exposed the economies to sudden reversals in capital inflows.

- Weaknesses in the under-regulated financial sector had allowed expansion of lending into risky investments of inflated values, often with currency and maturity mismatches, which exposed entities to exchange rate risks.
- Corporations, often with insider relationships with banks and having little incentive to use capital efficiently, became even more highly leveraged when presented with additional funding options from abroad, which exposed them to relatively small interest rate shocks.

This created a potentially explosive situation that only required detonation.

Trigger

Macroeconomic imbalances and financial sector weaknesses were most pronounced in the case of Thailand: the current account deficit, which reached very high levels of 8 percent of GDP, was financed by short-term inflows. The heavy inflows and credit boom channeled substantial investment into real property, creating an asset price bubble. The private sector had borrowed huge amounts from abroad and, taking advantage of the promise of a pegged exchange rate, did not hedge against foreign currency risks. Thai borrowers, many of which were under-regulated finance companies, invested in the booming property market. In the mid-1990s, an investor could borrow in yen at near zero interest rates and invest in Bangkok skyscrapers, whose expected annual return was 20 percent.

In 1996, export growth hit a wall. After growing 20 percent in 1995, exports actually contracted by 1 percent in 1996. Although all East Asian exports had slowed in conjunction with diminished world demand, Thailand was the worst hit. The impact was the result of three elements: the loss of wage competitiveness associated with appreciation; the demand for its products, particularly electronics, slumped badly in world markets; and because growth in its markets, notably Japan, slowed sharply. At the same time, prices of real assets stopped growing. Vacancy rates increased in 1996 as the supply of office space began to outpace demand. The finance companies began to experience serious difficulties in early 1997. The government response to furnish them with liquidity, only added to the supply of funds in the market ready to attack the peg.

Equity investors were the first to withdraw. The stock market peaked for the year in February, and fell by more than 30 percent by year's end. As the yield curve tilted against Thai borrowers, short-

Figure 5. The East Asia flu became contagious

Index of values of East Asian currencies (July 2, 1997 = 100)
East Asian 5

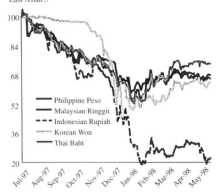

- Philippine Peso
- Malaysian Ringgit
- Indonesian Rupiah
- Korean Won
- Thai Baht

Index of values of East Asian currencies (July 2, 1997 = 100)
East Asian 5

- Singapore Dollar
- Taiwan Dollar
- Japanese Yen

Source: Bloomberg.

term borrowing became increasingly common. Perceptions began to take hold in the market that asset prices were getting too high and the exchange rate was misaligned. In early 1997, total private capital flows started to taper off. In the first half of 1997, bond issues and syndicated loans fell by 30 percent relative to the same period in the previous year. Confidence took a further hit when Somprasong Land defaulted on a Eurobond issue.

When the baht came under attack in February 1997, the government intervened heavily to support the peg. The central bank issued some US$23 billion in forward foreign exchange contracts at a time when reserves were hovering around US$25 billion. As investors' perceptions continued to sour, the finance companies came under pressure, and the government had to pump a large volume of liquidity to support them. Even more baht were chasing fewer dollars. Soon capital began to seek safe haven, and reserves fell. Finally, on July 2, 1997, the government yielded to the market forces and abandoned the peg. The crisis that was to rock East Asia and reverberate throughout world financial markets had begun.

Contagion

The Thai devaluation triggered a withdrawal of capital from the region as a financial panic progressively set in. Developments in Thailand caused investors to look more critically at weaknesses they had previously ignored. In the process, they discovered new information that amplified their concerns, especially about the health of the financial system and the magnitude of short-term debt. Market doubts were compounded by the lack of transparency about the financial and corporate sectors, and thus, about the magnitude of contingent liabilities. Once investors lost confidence that reserves would cover short-term debt, both foreign and domestic investors scrambled to get out. Markets became much less forgiving. The lack of a mechanism for orderly workouts of corporate and bank debt undoubtedly contributed to the full-scale financial panic that swept Thailand, Korea, and Indonesia, and to a lesser extent Malaysia.

Contagion produced simultaneous declines in asset prices and spurred capital outflows. Within the space of six months, capital outflows from the region erased the inflows of the first semester, and turned the net flow to a negative US$12 billion. As shown in table 1, in the space of a year net capital flows reversed by more than US$100 billion.

. . . Trade links between countries meant that declines in demand of imports in one country led to decline in exports in other countries. . . .

Intra-regional exports among East Asian countries accounted for almost 40 percent of total exports in 1996, up from 32 percent in 1990. If Japan

is included, the figure rises to 50 percent. These high levels of intra-regional trade reflect a process of specialization and outsourcing of activities from the more advanced, to the lower income countries in the region. About three-fourths of the intra-regional trade is in raw materials, intermediate inputs, and capital equipment which accounts for more than 50 percent of the total East Asian imports of these products. Such trade complementarity probably increased the speed and directness of the contagion. . . .

From Currency and Financial Crisis to Economic and Social Crisis

As the Thai crisis spread throughout Southeast Asia, and then to Korea, the currency crisis became a financial crisis, which became, in turn, an economic and social crisis. These have had sweeping domestic political ramifications in Korea and Thailand, where transitions were managed relatively free of disruption. Indonesia experienced an even more profound political crisis.

The outflow of capital in 1997 required huge swings in current account balances. New surpluses were achieved primarily through import compression and reductions in income, rather than through exports. . . . While exports experienced some increase, their performance has not been sufficient to make the current account adjustments without steep economic contraction. Private investment-savings balances have undergone adjustment, and deflated demand.

Monetary and fiscal policy was tightened as countries struggled to cope with the financial panic that had induced a run on their currencies. Rising interest rates were intended to increase the price of domestic assets and make them more attractive to holders of foreign currency funds. But, this raised difficult tradeoffs. High rates compounded the problems of the debt-laden corporate sector. Interest costs rose at exactly the time their profits were falling with the advancing recession, and many could not service their debts. Non-performing loans on the balance sheets of the banks increased, forcing them to call in loans in a struggle to maintain cash flow. . . .

Unemployment has risen as the economies have contracted. In virtually every country in the region, unemployment is at a 20-year high. In some countries, the unemployed have suffered in relative silence; in others, the contraction has led to social protests.

Table 1. Private Capital Flows Reverse . . . with a Vengeance

Net private capital flows in five East Asian economies (US$ billion)	1996	1997
Private flows (net)	97.1	−11.9
Non-debt flows	18.7	2.1
Foreign direct investment	6.3	6.4
Portfolio equity investment	12.4	−4.3
Debt flows	78.4	−14.0
Banks	55.7	−26.9
Non-banks	22.7	12.9

Source: IIF, Capital Flows to Emerging Market Economies.

Selection I.B.3. Completing China's Move to the Market*

China's economic reform process officially began with the Communist Party Plenum of December 1978. From the outset, China's reforms differed markedly from those of eastern Europe and the Common-wealth of Independent States. China was exhausted from 20 years of dealing with Mao's messianic visions, but it was in no sense ready for revolution. There was nothing comparable to eastern Europe's desire to be like western Europe, the sooner the better. China faced no economic crisis that required immediate and fundamental change, only dissatisfaction with the pace of existing growth, a dissatisfaction fueled in part by increasing awareness of the far better economic performances of China's immediate neighbors. The Communist Party held all of the important reins of power both in 1978 and 15 years later. Where Deng Xiaoping differed from his predecessors was in the strength of his desire to turn China into a wealthy and powerful state and his lack of interest in Maoist ideas of a new kind of society where such things as material incentives would play little or no role. But Deng and his associates had no economic reform blueprint.

In this context, a gradual approach to economic reform was inevitable. Mao Zedong was the believer in "big bangs." Mao's successors were willing to try almost anything if it worked. They also had a sense that some sectors, notably agriculture and foreign trade, were more in need of reform than others, such as industry. Mao's bias against foreign technology and foreign products had severely hurt China's modernization, and per capita grain output in 1978 was the same as it was in the mid-1950s. These latter views led to a sequencing of the economic reforms, first agriculture and foreign trade, and only later industry. At no time during the early years of reform did the senior leadership of China think that they were aiming toward a full market system.

It was as much by luck as by design, therefore, that China stumbled on a strategy that has proved remarkably successful in moving the economy from a Soviet-style command system to what by the early 1990s was an economy governed in large part by market forces, however distorted some of those market forces may have been. That the eco-nomic reforms initiated in December 1978 and continuing thereafter have been successful cannot be seriously doubted. The data in Tables 1 and 2 tell the basic story. China's gross domestic product grew by over 8 percent a year for 14 years, or roughly 7 percent per capita. The 8.8 percent GDP growth rate figure may overstate the real rate by a small amount (mainly because small-scale industries sometimes only report output figures in current prices which may not always be deflated by the statistical authorities), but there is no question that growth has been rapid. This rate is roughly double the GDP growth rate of the previous two decades, 1957–1978.[1] The foreign trade story is even more impressive. In the 1970s, China's exports grew by a modest 3.4 percent a year if one takes away the impact of OPEC-generated increases in the price of petroleum and related across-the-board inflation. This real growth rate rose to 14.1 percent a year during the first decade of reform and 70 percent of these exports were manufactures (petroleum and mining products by 1988 accounted for under 8 percent of exports, as contrasted to 25 percent in 1980).

China's impressive export performance was partly due to the reforms, but it also reflects the fact that China began its reform period from a more advantageous position than did the reformers of eastern Europe, the C.I.S., and Vietnam. The breakup of the Council for Mutual Economic Assistance (CMEA) forced these latter countries to abandon many of their markets with each other and reorient their trade to the west. China went through a similar process in the early 1960s and it was very disruptive to the economy, but by 1978 China had long since completed this adjustment. China also had no foreign debt to pay off in 1978, unlike the situation in China in 1960 or eastern Europe after 1989. China's other big advantage in 1978 was that it began the reform period with no overt inflation and not much repressed inflationary pressure. Reform did not have to begin with a stabilization program. . . .

[1]The Chinese net material product indexes for the pre-1978 years are based mainly on 1950s price calculations that give much too heavy a weight to the fast-growing industrial sector and hence exaggerate real NMP growth. Following methods similar to those used in Table 1, I recalculated Chinese NMP for the 1952–1978 period using 1978 prices as the base. This recalculation produced NMP growth rates of 4.8 percent for 1952–1978 or 4.2 percent per year for 1957–1978 (Perkins, 1981).

*From Dwight Perkins, "Completing China's Move to the Market," *Journal of Economic Perspectives* 8 (Spring 1994): 23–34. Reprinted by permission.

Table 1. China's GDP and Its Components

	1978	1984	1988	1990	1992
GDP	669.4	1,097.0	1,625.9	1,769.5	2,162.9
(billion 1990 yuan)					
–per capita (1990 yuan)	695	1051	1464	1548	1846
–per capita (index)	100.0	151.2	210.6	225.3	266.6

	Growth rates (in % per year)			
	1984/1978	1988/1984	1992/1988	1992/1978
Agriculture	7.3	3.1	4.3	5.2
Industry	8.9	14.2	10.4	10.8
Services	10.1	13.5	5.8	9.8
GDP	8.6	10.3	7.5	8.8

Note: The Chinese GDP figures were calculated by applying the indexes in "comparable prices" for 1978, 1984, 1988, and 1992 to the current price estimates of the three components of GDP in 1990. This produces rough constant price GDP figures for these years and an index that differs slightly from the official Chinese GDP index for this period.

Sources: State Statistical Bureau, 1992, p. 6; State Statistical Bureau, 1991, pp. 33, 79; and "Statistical Communique of the State Statistical Bureau of the PRC on the 1992 National Economic and Social Development," February 18, 1993, *Beijing Review,* March 8–14, 1993, vol. 36, no. 10, pp. 31–40; and State Statistical Bureau, 1993, pp. 19, 21.

Table 2. Growth Rate of China's Foreign Trade (in percent per year)

	Nominal		Real	
	Exports	Imports	Exports	Imports
1972/1952	7.4	4.8	—	—
1978/1972	19.0	25.0	3.4	13.0
1988/1978	17.2	17.6	14.1	10.2
1992/1978	16.7	15.4	—	—

Sources: Same as in Table 1 plus, for the real rates, China Foreign Trade Yearbook compiling committee, 1984, p. IV-5; and China Foreign Trade Yearbook Compiling Committee, 1990, p. 303. Appropriate price deflators were not available for the post-1988 period.

Rural Reform

The two principal components of China's rural reforms were the gradual freeing up of the markets for agricultural commodities and the decollectivization of Chinese rural society.

The market for secondary crops and household products was freed up almost immediately after the December 1978 party plenum. Free markets, or rural trade fairs as they were called, had existed before 1978 but were tightly controlled when they were allowed to function at all. However, the state retained a near monopoly of the trade in major crops such as grain, until 1985, and state contracts for the purchase of grain and other key agricultural commodities were made voluntary, although the word "voluntary" as used in China often retains elements of coercion. By the latter half of the 1980s around 60 percent of agricultural commodities were bought and sold on competitive markets, as compared to only 8 percent in 1978 (Lu and Timmer, 1992). By 1990 this share had risen to about 80 percent; markets supplied 89 percent of all aquatic products, 80 percent of fruits, 76 percent of vegetables, 68 percent of meat and eggs, and about half of all grain (*China Daily,* December 17, 1992). . . .

Decollectivization happened more or less spontaneously. What began as experiments to help the poorest areas in certain provinces spread quickly to other regions. Only when lower level party officials would try to halt or reverse the process did the center move in with orders to let happen what was happening. By the end of 1983, the system of people's communes and the production teams of 20–30 families that had operated as a collective unit had ceased to exist in most of the country.[2]

[2]Discussion of this process from a village viewpoint is in the essays by a variety of people who spent time in Chinese villages in the early 1980s (Parish, 1985; Zweig, 1989).

Household agriculture was the norm and the state soon determined that household contracts for the use of the land would last for 15 years.

The response of agriculture to decollectivization and the freeing up of rural markets was immediate and dramatic. The basic picture can be seen in the data in Table 3. Production of all crops including grain grew at an unprecedented rate; from 1978 to 1984, the growth rate for agricultural value-added was five times what it had been over the previous two decades. Farm income and consumption grew even more rapidly, although the data are less reliable than those for output. Improving terms of trade for agriculture, plus non-agricultural sources of income, account for most of the difference between output versus consumption or income growth.

These growth statistics also indicate that the agricultural output spurt was a one-shot affair largely exhausted by the end of 1984, when most crop production returned to its long-term growth rate, in part because farmers preferred to invest their resources in rural industry (Huang, 1993). Reforms also could not alter the fact that China is attempting to feed 1.1 billion people on less than a tenth of a hectare per capita, and crop yields in the best-endowed provinces are already comparable to those in such advanced agricultural systems as Japan, South Korea or Taiwan. Politically, however, the 1978–1984 spurt gave enormous credibility to market-oriented reforms and to the individuals who designed those reforms. The political lesson for future reformers from China's experience is obvious but often forgotten—try to begin the reform process with a clear winner. . . .

Foreign Trade and Investment

In China's Soviet-style foreign trade system, all trade was handled by government corporations that had a monopoly over all purchases and sales in particular sectors. All foreign exchange was turned over to the Bank of China, the foreign exchange bank. There was an "air lock" between all producing enterprises and world markets so that prices on world markets had no influence on the domestic price structure. Foreign firms often did not even know to which industrial enterprise the equipment they were selling was going or from which enterprise the items they were purchasing were coming. In addition to this, throughout the Cultural Revolution period (1966–1976) there was active political hostility toward foreign trade in general and foreign technology in particular. Foreign investment did not exist.

After Mao Zedong's death in 1976, policies began to change. The first move was to encourage domestic enterprises to buy inputs from abroad rather then to discourage such purchases. Enterprises responded with such alacrity that China by 1978 found itself with a growing trade deficit, despite increasing prices for China's petroleum exports. Imports in nominal dollar terms rose 51 percent in 1978 and by 44 percent in 1979. Clearly, new and increasing sources of foreign exchange had to be discovered.

In 1979, reforms were introduced to facilitate exports of manufactures and (for the first time) to allow for foreign investment (Lardy, 1992). In essence, these efforts involved the breakup of the monopoly on foreign trade held by the state corporations, and transferring this authority to regional

Table 3. Agricultural Growth Rate (in percent per year)

	1978/1957	1984/1978	1988/1984	1992/1988
(1) Agricultural value added	1.4[a]	7.3	3.1	4.3
(2) Gross value of crop output	2.9	6.8	1.0	3.7
(3) Grain output	2.1	5.0	–0.8	2.9
(4) Farm household net income per capita (real)	—	15.0[b]	2.3	7.6

[a]The 1957–1978 figure is the growth rate of agriculture's share of net material product.

[b]The changeover from a production team to a household based accounting system makes it difficult to compare net income figures before and after this changeover. Hence the 1978–1984 figure is particularly unreliable.

—Indicates data not available to the author.

Sources: Rows (1)–(3) were derived from data in "Communique of the State Statistical Bureau of the PRC on the 1992 National Social and Economic Development, pp. 31–40; State Statistical Bureau, 1989, pp. 742–743; State Statistical Bureau, 1991, pp. 243, 294–295.

The raw data for row (4) are from the same sources. The percentage increases in net income were derived from per capita data in current prices divided by the rural retail price index.

Table 4. Foreign Direct Investment in China (in billions of U.S. dollars per year)

	1979–1982	1983–1985	1986–1988	1989–1990	1991	1992
Contracted direct foreign investment	1.50	3.44	3.95	6.10	11.98	58.12
Direct foreign investment actually used	0.29	1.19	2.46	3.44	4.37	11.01

Sources: "Official predicts $10 billion more in investment," *China Daily,* April 26, 1993, Business Supplement, p. 1; "Foreign funds hit record $25 billion," *China Daily,* June 2, 1993, p. 2; State Statistical Bureau, *Zhonguo tongji nianjian,* 1991, p. 629; State Statistical Bureau, *Zhonguo tongji nianjian,* 1992, p. 641; and State Statistical Bureau, *Zhongguo tongji nianjian,* 1993, p. 647.

corporations (but not to producing enterprises for the most part). Special economic zones (export processing zones) were set up to free foreign investors and other exporters from red tape. Various export subsidies were introduced and China's currency was devalued from 1.7 yuan to the U.S. dollar in 1981 to 2.9 yuan to the dollar in 1985 to 4.8 yuan to the dollar in 1990. This 182 percent rise was much more than the 87 percent increase in Chinese retail prices or the 40 percent rise in the ratio of Chinese to U.S. retail prices.

Foreign trade responded to these incentives in dramatic fashion, as indicated by the data in Table 2. The response of foreign direct investment was equally dramatic, as the data in Table 4 indicate. A Soviet-style economy geared to producing low quality goods for a captive domestic market was suddenly competing head-to-head with its East Asian neighbors, the most dynamic exporters of manufactured goods in the world. What accounts for this extraordinary change?

. . . One cannot prove the point systematically, but connections with Hong Kong probably account for much of China's success. In 1979, 22.6 percent of Chinese exports went to Hong Kong and 79 percent of those exports stayed in Hong Kong. By 1987, despite the increasing knowledge of foreign markets on the Chinese mainland, Hong Kong's share of all exports rose to 31.1 percent (of a much larger total than in 1979) and 62 percent of these exports to Hong Kong were reexported. Among manufactures, Hong Kong's share was much higher, ranging from 46 percent for textile fabric to 62 percent for clothing and 87 percent for machinery (Sung, 1991). By 1992 Hong Kong's share in total Chinese exports (including re-exports) had risen further to 44 percent (General Administration of Customs, 1993). In the 1990s, a similar process seems to be happening through Taiwan. In effect, the formidable marketing talents of Hong Kong and Taiwan are being grafted onto the manufacturing capacity of the mainland.

References

China Foreign Trade Yearbook compiling committee, *Zhongguo duiwai jingji maoi nianjian 1984.* Beijing: China Foreign and Economic Trade Publishers, 1984.

"Communique of the State Statistical Bureau of the PRC on the 1992 National Social and Economic Development Plan," *Beijing Review,* March 8–14, 1993, 36:10, 31–40.

General Administration of Customs, *China's Customs Statistics,* Series No. 40, No. 1, 1993.

Huang, Yiping, "Government Intervention and Agricultural Performance in China," unpublished doctoral dissertation, Australian National University, 1993.

Lardy, Nicholas, *Foreign Trade and Economic Reform in China, 1978–1990.* Cambridge: Cambridge University Press, 1992.

Lu, Mai, and Peter C. Timmer, "Developing the Chinese Rural Economy: Experience of the 1980s and Prospects of the Future," HIID Development Discussion Paper No. 428.AFP, September 1992.

Parish, William L., ed., *Chinese Rural Development: The Great Transformation.* Armonk: M. E. Sharpe, 1985.

Perkins, Dwight H., "An American View of the Chinese Economy. In Jingji yanjiu compilation group, *Guowai jingji xuezhe lun zhongguo ji fazhanzhong guojia jingji.* Beijing: China Finance and Economic Publishers, 1981, 4–5.

"Rural Market Needs Further Strengthening," *China Daily,* December 17, 1992, p. 4.

State Statistical Bureau, *Zhongguo tongji nianjian,* 1989.

State Statistical Bureau, *Zhongguo tongji nianjian,* 1991.

State Statistical Bureau, *Zhongguo tongji nianjian,* 1992.

State Statistical Bureau, *Zhongguo tongji nianjian,* 1993.

Sung, Yun-Wing, *The China-Hong Kong Connection: The Key to China's Open Door Policy.* Cambridge: Cambridge University Press, 1991, 106–7.

Zweig, David, *Agrarian Radicalism in China, 1968–1981.* Cambridge: Harvard University Press, 1989.

Selection I.B.4. Latin American Economic Development: 1950–1980*

In the thirty years between 1950 and 1980, Latin America experienced rapid growth. During this period, output expanded at an annual rate of 5.5% with per capita increases averaging 2.7% a year. Table 1 provides country details. The star is clearly Brazil, whose share in regional product increased from less than a quarter to more than a third. At the other extreme are two groups: the Southern Cone (Argentina, Chile and Uruguay), whose mid-century leading position in the region was eroded by below average performance; and a group of smaller countries, including several in Central America. On average, Latin America's record, viewed from an immediate post-World War II perspective, is impressive. It far exceeded the target of the Alliance for Progress implemented in 1961, which called for an annual rate of 2% per capita. It also compared very favourably with European per capita income growth in the aftermath of the Industrial Revolution, which was 1.3% from 1850 to 1900 and 1.4% between 1900 and 1950. Long-term US economic growth has been at 1.8%.

Yet two factors combine to make the 1950–80 Latin American growth performance seem less positive. One is its dramatic reversal in the 1980s, a period in which GDP per capita fell by 8.3%. By 1989, with the exception of Brazil, Chile, Colombia and the Dominican Republic, per capita GDP had fallen below its 1980 level. At the extreme, Venezuela, Nicaragua and El Salvador show levels below those attained in 1960. The 1980s have truly been a lost decade and thus one tends to underestimate the earlier achievement.

The second circumstance diminishing the accomplishment from 1950 to 1980 has been the surging performance of the Asian countries. Led by the four newly industrialising countries of South Korea, Hong Kong, Singapore and Taiwan, but extending to many others, Asia has vaulted ahead in the 1980s at an average per capita income growth rate in excess of 5%. This contrast is now widely interpreted as proving the errors of the import substitution strategy favoured by Latin America throughout most of the post-war period. Two of the pillars of that strategy were emphasis upon industrialisation through governmental intervention and barriers to trade. . . .

*From Eliana Cardoso and Albert Fishlow, "Latin American Development: 1950–1980," *Journal of Latin American Studies* 24 (1992): 197–202, 212–217. Reprinted by permission.

Sources of Growth

During the 1950s, most Latin American countries moved toward an import substitution strategy. They chose this path because it seemed to fit their circumstances. After the Great Depression of the 1930s, the disruption of the Second World War, and the boom and bust created by the Korean War, the international economy did not seem to be a propitious engine of growth. Nor did the United States place economic development and Latin America high on its agenda; the Marshall Plan instead gave priority to Europe and the Cold War.

Latin American economic thought and practice emerged against this historical backdrop, influenced but not determined by a group of economists working at the Economic Commission for Latin America in Santiago under the leadership of Raul Prebisch. These contributions amended the orthodox view of economic growth through comparative advantage and capital accumulation in three ways: the specification of macroeconomic adjustment, the identification of microeconomic distortions and, following from the above, a strong role for government intervention.

Attention to the foreign exchange constraint rather than to savings as the determinant of growth in peripheral countries was the principal macroeconomic novelty. In a world where the terms of trade moved against traditional primary export products, domestic production would have to substitute for non-essential imports, leaving foreign exchange for the needed inputs. Moreover, while technical progress in agriculture would leave labour unemployed, dynamic industry could absorb the growing population with increasing productivity and incomes. Domestic production required protection against imports and a deliberate bias against exports of resources required by industry. In the microeconomic sphere, emphasis was placed on imperfections and discontinuities, both of which impeded effective operation of price signals. Whether in agriculture—where land concentration was notorious—or in industry—where new privileges provided shelter from market forces—the competitive model was flawed.

These macro- and microeconomic conditions militated in favour of a strong state presence. Regulation and direction were needed. Development was a consequence of policy, not a natural evolutionary process. Conscious and comprehensive planning was desirable, and the Economic Com-

Table 1. Per Capita Gross Domestic Product (GDP) and Growth Rates of Latin America Countries[a]
(per cent and dollars of 1975)

	Share in total population (%)	Share in regional GDP (%)		GDP per capita, dollars of 1975		Growth rate of GDP per capita (% per year)	
	1980	1950	1980	1950	1980	1950–80	1981–89[d]
Brazil	35.6	22.2	34.2	637	2,152	4.2	0.0
Mexico	20.2	18.5	23.1	1,055	2,547	3.0	–1.0
Argentina	8.0	21.2	11.8	1,877	3,209	1.8	–2.6
Colombia	7.5	7.2	6.3	949	1,882	2.3	1.5
Venezuela	4.3	7.2	7.1	1,811	3,310 (3,647)[e]	1.5 (2.4)[e]	–2.8
Peru	5.1	4.9	3.9	953	1,746	2.1	–2.7
Chile	3.2	5.7	3.4	1,416	2,372	1.8	1.1
Uruguay	0.8	3.1	1.2	2,184	3,269	1.4	–0.8
Ecuador	2.3	1.4	1.6	638	1,556	3.1	–0.1
Guatemala	2.0	1.6	1.2	842	1,422	1.8	–2.0
Dominican Rep.	1.7	1.1	1.1	719	1,564	2.6	0.2
Bolivia	1.6	1.4	0.8	762	1,114	1.3	–2.9
El Salvador	1.3	0.8	0.5	612	899	1.3	–1.9
Paraguay	0.9	0.8	0.7	885	1,753	2.4	0.0
Costa Rica	0.6	0.5	0.6	819	2,170	3.3	–0.7
Panama	0.5	0.5	0.5	928	2,157	2.9	–1.9
Nicaragua	0.7	0.5	0.4	683	1,324	2.3	–3.7
Honduras	1.0	0.6	0.4	680	1,031	1.4	–1.3
Haiti	1.6	0.8	0.2	353[c]	439	0.7	–2.1
Latin America[b]						2.7 (3.0)[e]	–0.8

[a]Countries ordered by average share in regional GDP between 1950 and 1985; [b]Latin America except Cuba; [c]1960; [d]preliminary; [e]Venezuelan data adjusted for changes in the terms of trade.

Note: The growth rate of Venezuela's per capita GDP between 1950 and 1980 is 1.9 per cent per year in IMF: IFS. For Chile and Honduras, the average growth rate per capita per year from Summers and Heston is 0.004 higher than in IMF: IFS, and for Nicaragua it is almost 0.01 larger. The average for Latin America is practically unaffected by the growth rates of Honduras and Nicaragua due to their small share in the population of the region.

Sources: Robert Summers and Alan Heston, "Improved International Comparisons of Real Products and Its Composition: 1950–1980," *Review of Income and Wealth,* June 1984; and ECLAC, *Preliminary Overview of the Latin American Economy* (Santiago, 1989).

mission for Latin America pioneered the application of input–output models in the region.

Import substitution was a disequilibrium development strategy. It confronted three limitations that had an increasing impact on economic performance towards the end of the 1950s. One was the deterioration in the balance of trade, the second was sectoral imbalance, and the third was deterioration of the public sector accounts.

Protection led to overvalued exchange rates, which acted as a tax on exports. The consequence was an eventual reduction in export supply. Yet industrialisation required increased inputs of capital goods and intermediate imports. As trade deficits increased, foreign investment became a critical requirement, not only for its modern technology but also for its provision of foreign exchange. This was an ironic and unanticipated consequence of a strategy which derived its strong political appeal from its emphasis upon national productive capability.

In sectoral terms, import substitution policies exaggerated industrial growth at the expense of agriculture, with three consequences. First, food prices were kept artificially low, benefiting urban incomes at the expense of rural incomes. Second, relatively capital-intensive manufactures absorbed only a diminishing fraction of the increment in the labour force, swelling the service sector and placing pressure on government to serve as an employer of last resort. Third, physical targets dominated cost-effectiveness calculations, as if the higher shadow price of foreign exchange could justify any project.

The third disequilibrium was fiscal. As the initial real resources taxed away from primary exports began to diminish, subsidies to industrial investment had to come from explicit taxes. At the same time, government responsibilities had increased, placing new pressures upon the budget from the expenditure side. Monetisation of the deficit was an irresistible lure, and one with a nine-teenth-century precedent in Latin America. Inflation and the need for stabilisation began to loom as a problem in several countries towards the end of the 1950s.

These disequilibria were temporarily averted by the Alliance for Progress. New inflows of official capital simultaneously eased the pressure on the external accounts and public sector deficits, while PL 480 imports increased supplies of food. Governments also attempted to correct some of the policy excesses by more realistic exchange rates and greater promotion of exports. These efforts, however were not enough. By the mid-1960s the Alliance was faltering, the victim of changing policy perceptions in the United States and Latin America alike. Reforms were not easy, nor were resources unlimited. More orthodox policies became the order of the day, frequently under military tutelage, setting the state for a new phase of economic expansion.

When the limits of the import substitution strategy were recognised in the 1960s, important modifications to commercial policy were introduced. Tariffs were frequently reduced, especially in the highest categories, while crawling-peg exchange-rate systems accommodated high domestic rates of inflation and averted the overvaluation (earlier so predominant). Explicit concern for inducing non-traditional exports produced special export subsidy programmes in many countries during the period after 1965. In the context of a more buoyant international market such reinforcements produced positive results, and export growth and diversification in the region increased.

At the same time, larger private capital inflows provided an option for several countries of the region. From the end of the 1960s and reinforced by the oil surpluses after 1973, the Eurodollar market was in pursuit of new players and found many of them in the region. Governments could finance both more imports and also larger public sector deficits.

Domestic policies tended to retreat somewhat from regulation. Although prices were given greater scope to direct resources, the commitment to industrialisation remained, safeguarding an intrusive role for the public sector even under the orthodox policies pursued by military governments. The Brazilian "miracle" of the late 1960s and 1970s was a clear descendant of import substitution, not to be confused with an outward orientation. The large domestic market still dominated production decisions.

This period of adaptation and relatively success-ful adjustment of the earlier model (growth rates showed general region-wide improvement) was brought to an abrupt end by the international disequilibrium ushered in by the oil price rise in 1973. The post-oil shock experience in the region was substantially conditioned by mounting indebtedness and a deterioration of domestic policy in a more difficult external environment. This period saw the rise of international monetarism as a means of reducing inflation in the Southern Cone countries, but at the expense of a substantial increase in external liabilities. It saw growing indebtedness of oil producers based upon the new greater value of oil in the ground. Finally, it saw Brazil labour under its progressively larger debt service payments and domestic pressures to sustain its exhilarating pace of industrial expansion. For the region as a whole, output growth slowed in the 1970s, but remained at satisfactory levels.

The precariousness of the Latin American economies only became fully apparent when a new oil price rise, an abrupt increase in real interest rates, and an OECD recession coincided in the early 1980s. Countries of the region had badly chosen their adjustment style after 1973. It was not simply that they blindly followed the original import substitution bias of the 1950s, as Maddison has argued. Rather it was their especially asymmetric opening to the world economy, featuring vast financial flows with much more limited trade penetration. Moreover, new fiscal distortions reduced the room for manoeuvre. To make growth continue in the late 1970s, government deficits were incurred that could no longer be so easily financed. Stop–go macroeconomic responses could be found in a much larger number of countries during this period, but they were only a prelude to the stop–stop policies that ultimately became necessary in the 1980s. . . .

Poverty and Income Distribution

Perhaps the biggest limitation of Latin American development in the postwar period has been its modest social achievements in the process of economic growth. Growth is essential for achieving social goals. But growth is not enough. Economic growth and industrialisation in Latin America blended with mass poverty, social tensions, regional imbalances, widespread political instability and acute injustice.

Altimir has developed a widely used definition of poverty for ten Latin American countries in the 1970s on the basis of available household surveys and population censuses. His poverty lines (annual household consumption per capita ranging from 150 to 250 dollars of 1970) are country-specific, based on the cost of a nutritionally adequate diet multiplied by two. According to Altimir's estimate, in 1970, 40% of Latin American households were poor and had an average purchasing power from 40 to 55% below the poverty line. Only in Argentina was the income gap as low as 25%. The extent of poverty was higher in rural than in urban areas in all Latin American countries. Even in Argentina, Chile and Uruguay, the most heavily urbanised countries in the region, the extent of rural poverty was not less than 20% of rural households. In Mexico, the three bottom deciles of the income distribution were entirely rural. In Brazil, 70% of the lowest four deciles in the mid-1970s were rural households. The poorest are usually landless labourers who purchase all or a large part of their food. In the urban areas the poorest are self-employed (rather than wage earners), workers in construction (the most likely entry point for immigrants), and those employed in public make-work programmes such as those in Chile.

In 1970 the extent of destitution (risk of severe nutritional deficiency) varied quite substantially from 1% of the population in Argentina to 45% in Honduras. About one-fifth of all households in Latin America had incomes that were insufficient to pay for an adequate diet. Musgrove's study of nutrition in ten Latin American cities in 1966–69 confirmed the high levels of destitution poverty, ranging from 18% in Caracas to 56% in Quito. Table 2 shows different estimates of the percentage of population living in poverty in 1970 for twelve Latin American countries.

The basic survey data from which the indices of poverty are drawn present many problems. These surveys undercount the disproportionately poor groups, and those who participate in surveys under-report their incomes (as shown by comparisons with independent sources of data). One therefore has more confidence in the measurement of trends than in figures for any one year. Molina published an update of Altimir's work, based on the assumption that poverty lines grew at one-quarter the rate of average income in any country. Despite considerable growth in the 1970s, the consequences are disappointing. Table 3 shows only a slight drop in the percentage of the population living in poverty in most countries in 1981 compared to 1970, with substantial progress in Brazil and Mexico. Because of their weight in the regional total, the incidence of poverty in Latin America dropped from 39% to 35%. Nonetheless, the number of poor increased.

Table 2. Latin America, 1970: Percentage of Population Living in Poverty

	Kakwani	Altimir		
		A Destitution	B Poverty	C Relative poverty
Brazil	17.3	25	49	54
Mexico	4.2	12	34	48
Argentina		1	8	28
Venezuela	4.6	10	25	38
Colombia	13.1	18	45	48
Peru	25.3	25	50	48
Chile	0.9	6	17	39
Uruguay	6.1	4[a]	10[a]	25[a]
Costa Rica	1.5	6	24	36
Honduras	27.5	45	65	58
Ecuador	21.5			
El Salvador	20.8			

Notes: Kakwani's poverty line is 150 dollars of 1970; Altimir's poverty lines for 1970: the national averages of the line of destitution, A, vary between 87 dollars for Honduras and 151 dollars for Argentina. The national averages of the line of absolute poverty, B, vary between 162 dollars for Honduras and 296 dollars for Argentina. Relative poverty, C, is defined as less than half the average per capita income of all households.

[a]urban poverty.

Sources: M. Kakwani, *Income Inequality and Poverty: Methods of Estimation and Policy Implications* (New York, 1980); Oscar Altimir, *The Extent of Poverty in Latin America,* World Bank Staff Working Paper No. 522 (Washington, D.C., 1982).

Table 3. Incidence of Poverty in Latin America, 1970–81

	1970		1981	
	Head count[a]	Poverty gap[b]	Head count[a]	Poverty gap[b]
Argentina	8.0	0.5	8.0	0.5
Brazil	49.0	8.2	43.0	4.2
Chile	17.0	1.9	16.0	1.6
Colombia	45.0	7.7	43.0	5.3
Costa Rica	24.0	3.6	22.0	2.7
Honduras	65.0	23.1	64.0	21.8
Mexico	34.0	3.9	29.0	2.6
Panama	39.0	6.8	37.0	5.7
Peru	50.0	13.4	49.0	12.8
Venezuela	25.0	2.8	24.0	3.6
All 10	39.0	5.3	35.0	3.6

[a]Percent of population below the poverty line.

[b]Shortfall of the average income of the poor from the poverty line as a proportion of GDP.

Source: Sergio Molina, "Poverty: Description and Analysis of Policies for Overcoming It," CEP AL *Review,* no. 18, Dec. 1982.

Although the number of poor increased, they undoubtedly saw some improvement in their standard of living between 1950 and 1980 as health and schooling improved. Growth of the urban population brought expanded opportunities. Life expectancy in Latin America increased from 55 years in 1960 to 63.7 years in 1980, and infant mortality declined from 107 per thousand to 69 per thousand. Access to literacy rose. The data in Table 4 show a strong positive correlation between incomes per head and life expectancy. There is no correlation between incomes per head and infant mortality rates.

Aggregate figures, however, may overstate reality. Merrick, for instance, asserts the existence of a dual population structure in Brazil. He shows a modern demographic elite passing through the mortality transition and into controlled natality at a pace similar to late-industrialising societies. This southeast-urban sector coexists with the northeast-rural sector, where high fertility and mortality rates correspond to the level of traditional underdeveloped societies.

Relative shares of income also count. They are relevant not only to issues of equity, but also to the assessment of policies to overcome absolute poverty. Average income per capita in most Latin American countries exceeds that in the majority of African and Asian countries, yet extreme poverty exists as a result of unequal income distribution. In the Latin American context it is impossible to look at poverty without considering redistribution as a potential solution.

Table 5 presents the share of the richest quintile as a multiple of the poorest quintile, as well as Gini indices for thirteen Latin American countries. The levels of inequality depicted by these indices are striking, as they exceed those found in most other parts of the developing world. There is little indication that the situation has improved much after

Table 4. Economic and Social Indicators, Latin America,[a] 1980

	GDP per head[b] (index)	Urban population (% of total)	Infant mortality (per thousand)	Life expectancy (years)	Population per physician (1981)	Literacy ratio (1978)
Y > $2,000 in 1980						
Venezuela	100.0	83	41.7	67.4	1,000	82
Uruguay	98.8	84	39.7	70.9	500	94
Argentina	96.9	82	45.2	70.4	540[g]	93
Mexico	76.9	67	56.0	65.2	1,210	82[h]
Chile	71.7	81	43.2	67.1	1,930	89[i]
Costa Rica	65.6	43	27.5	72.2	1,440	90[h]
Panama	65.2	54	21.7	70.4	1,010	82
Brazil	65.0	68	83.3	63.1	1,300	76
Y > $1,000 in 1980						
Colombia	56.9	64	56.4	62.9	1,710[g]	81[h]
Paraguay	53.0	39	46.8	64.6	1,750	84
Peru	52.7	65	87.7	57.7	1,440	80
Dominican Rep.	47.3	51	68.3	61.4	1,400	67
Ecuador	47.0	45	81.6	61.2	760[g]	77
Guatemala	43.0	39	65.9	58.5	8,610[g]	46[j]
Nicaragua	40.0	53	90.5	56.4	2,230	90
Bolivia	33.7	44	131.3	50.2	2,000	63[k]
Honduras	31.1	36	88.5	58.2	3,100	60
Y < $1,000 in 1980						
El Salvador	27.2	41	77.9	63.0	2,550	62
Haiti	13.3	28	114.6	53.2	9,200	23[h]

Y = Income per head.

[a]Latin America except Cuba, countries ordered by size of GDP per capita in 1980; [b]indices of GDP per capita in 1980, Venezuela = 100. Venezuela GDP per capita not corrected for changes in the terms of trade = 3,310 dollars of 1975; [g]1980; [h]1980; [i]1970; [j]1975; [k]1976.

Sources: Summers and Heston, *Improved International Comparisons;* World Bank, *World Tables;* IMF, *International Financial Statistics,* PRE-ALC, and ECLAC.

Table 5. Income Shares and Gini Indices,* 14 Latin American countries, c. 1970

	Income share of bottom 20% (percent)		Income share of top 20% as multiple of bottom 20%			Gini index	
	a	b	a	b	c	a	c
Brazil	3.0	2.0	21	33	15	.574	
Mexico	3.7	2.9	15	20	16	.524	.567
Argentina	6.9	4.4	7	11	7	.437	.425
Venezuela	2.7	3.0	24	18	18	.622	.531
Colombia	3.5		17		15	.557	.520
Peru		1.9		32	26		.591
Chile	4.8		12		14	.506	.503
Ecuador	3.5		16		24	.526	.625
Dominican Rep.	4.3		13			.493	
El Salvador	3.2		18		11	.539	.532
Costa Rica	5.0	3.3	11	17	9	.416	.466
Panama	3.0		20		24	.557	.558
Uruguay					13		.449
Honduras					21		.612
For comparison: OECD average	5.5		9			.380	

*The Gini index is a measure of income inequality which varies from 0 (complete equality) to 1 (complete inequality).

Sources: ªManek Kakwani, *Income Inequality and Poverty: Methods of Estimation and Policy Implications* (New York, 1980); ᵇWorld Bank, *World Development Report 1988* (New York, 1988); ᶜJacques Lecaillon et al., *Income Distribution and Economic Development: An Analytical Survey* (Geneva, 1984).

1970. Moreover, there is reason to believe that the 1980s have witnessed an increased share of income going to capital and a reduced share to labour, thereby leading to further deterioration. While efforts to eradicate absolute poverty appear feasible in resource cost (although difficult to implement), relative inequality may prove much more stubborn. From the standpoint of politics, extreme relative inequality may create enough discontent to hamper effective economic policy.

Selection I.B.5. The Launching of the Reforms*

The Latin American reforms of the 1980s and early 1990s are impressive. Most countries opened up their economies to international competition, implemented major stabilization programs, and privatized a large number of state-owned firms. Toward mid-1993, analysts and the international financial media were hailing the market-oriented reforms as a success and proclaiming that some Latin American countries were on the way to becoming a new generation of "tigers." Foreign investors rapidly moved into the region, and consultants and academics scrambled to analyze the Chilean, Mexican, and Argentine experiences in order to learn firsthand how these countries, which only a few years ago seemed hopeless, had become highly attractive for international business. Also, policymakers and politicians in Eastern Europe turned to Latin America for lessons on how to move toward a market-oriented economic system.

By 1992, the reforms were beginning to bear fruit, as more and more countries began to recover and to experience higher rates of growth (see table 1). Also, macroeconomic equilibrium had been achieved in most countries, exports were expanding, and productivity had grown substantially. Additionally, starting in 1991 private foreign capital entered the region at a pace that surprised even the most optimistic observers.

In spite of this progress, a decade after the crisis a number of problems persisted. Physical infrastructure had deteriorated severely, and in many countries the extent of poverty had increased. Despite spectacular progress, inflation continued to be high, refusing, even in some of the best cases, to drop back to single digits. Moreover, in some countries, the economic reforms were not accompanied by the modernization of political institutions. This created tensions, and in some cases political unrest, including serious crises in Brazil, Guatemala, Haiti, Peru, and Venezuela. Additionally, in many countries—Mexico and Argentina, in particular—large capital inflows financed large and growing current account deficits and generated sizable pressures toward appreciation of the real exchange rate, and increased the vulnerability of the external sector. The uprising of the Zapatistas in Chiapas, Mexico, in early 1994 reminded analysts, in a brutal

way, that Latin America's modernization process was far from over. By early 1994, Latin America still faced tremendous challenges, including maintaining prudent macroeconomic policy, effectively managing capital infows, alleviating poverty, reducing inequality, significantly increasing domestic savings, and creating solid economic, social, and political institutional foundations for long-term growth and development.

Even though it is difficult to date exactly the beginning of the reforms in each country, it is possible to argue that they only acquired full and generalized force in the late 1980s and early 1990s, after attempts to use traditional structuralist-inspired policies to solve the crisis had failed. At the time the reforms were initiated, different countries in the region experienced very different initial conditions. Some faced rapid inflation and highly distorted incentive systems; others faced relatively mild inflation and moderate distortions. The economic role of the state, including the importance of state-owned enterprises, also varied, as did the historical experiences with growth. While Brazil and Mexico, for example, grew rapidly between 1960 and 1975, growth performance in the Southern Cone—Argentina, Chile, and Uruguay—was dismal during the same period.

Although the intensity and scope of the reforms differed across countries, it is possible to classify them into four broad groups according to the approximate time of initiation of the reforms: early reformers, second-wave reformers, third-wave reformers, and nonreformers (table 1). Generally speaking, early reformers moved more rapidly in the transformation, having made progress in many areas. Chile represents a case on its own, having initiated the reforms in 1975, almost a decade before anyone else. The Chilean reforms are advanced and have touched almost every aspect of economic life. Mexico initiated the reforms in 1985 and moved broadly and deeply, building new institutions that have helped create the bases of a new economic system. The social development in Chiapas in early 1994 and the assassination of presidential candidate Luis Donaldo Colosio, however, introduced some doubts on the exact direction in which the Mexican reforms will move in the years to come. The second- and third-wave reformers started the transformation process in the late 1980s and early 1990s, and vary in the intensity and scope of reforms. Some countries, such as Argentina, rapidly and simultaneously dealt with

---

*From Sebastian Edwards, "The Launching of the Reforms," *Crisis and Reform in Latin America: From Despair to Hope* (New York: Oxford University Press, 1995), pp. 6–9. Reprinted by permission.

Table 1. Selected Macroeconomic Indicators in Latin America and the Caribbean, 1982–92

Country	Growth in per capita GDP as a percentage of constant prices				Annual inflation rate (percentage)[a]		
	Average 1982–86	Average 1987–92	1991	1992	1982–86	Average 1987–92	Average 1992
Early reformers							
Bolivia	−5.0	0.7	1.7	1.3	776.5	15.8	12.1
Chile	−2.0	5.2	4.3	8.7	21.2	19.1	15.4
Mexico	−2.6	1.0	1.7	0.5	73.2	48.4	15.5
Average	−3.2	2.3	2.5	3.5	290.3	27.8	14.3
Weighted average	−2.6	1.4	1.9	1.3	79.1	45.1	15.4
Second-wave reformers							
Costa Rica	−1.0	2.0	−0.1	4.9	29.4	20.6	21.8
Jamaica	−1.2	2.3	0.0	1.3	17.1	28.9	68.1
Trinidad and Tobago	−0.6	−2.0	1.7	−0.9	11.1	8.5	6.5
Uruguay	−3.0	2.7	2.2	6.8	53.0	80.5	68.5
Average	−1.5	1.3	0.9	3.0	27.6	34.6	41.2
Weighted average	−1.8	1.5	1.2	4.0	33.5	43.9	45.6
Third-wave reformers							
Argentina	−0.9	0.6	7.6	7.5	316.5	446.7	24.9
Brazil	1.3	−1.3	−0.3	−2.5	157.9	850.8	1,157.0
Colombia	0.8	2.0	1.2	1.1	20.6	27.3	27.0
El Salvador	−1.2	1.0	1.5	2.5	17.9	18.5	11.2
Guatemala	−4.0	0.8	0.3	1.6	12.0	19.2	10.0
Guyana	−4.3	−0.2	5.6	6.8	16.7	57.4	14.2
Honduras	−2.1	0.7	0.1	1.3	5.9	13.3	8.8
Nicaragua	−3.4	−4.9	−3.5	−2.4	123.1	2,151.3	20.3
Panama	0.5	−1.1	7.2	5.5	1.8	0.9	1.8
Paraguay	−3.1	1.0	−0.3	−1.0	19.2	24.5	15.1
Peru	−1.7	−4.9	1.2	−4.8	102.7	733.1	73.5
Venezuela	−2.3	1.6	7.8	5.1	10.2	40.2	31.4
Average	−1.7	−0.4	2.4	1.7	67.0	363.0	116.8
Weighted average	0.3	−0.6	2.0	0.3	159.5	623.8	695.7
Nonreformers							
Dominican Republic	−1.0	0.4	−2.6	5.7	16.7	35.7	4.5
Ecuador	−0.7	0.0	2.1	1.5	29.0	51.9	54.6
Haiti	−2.2	−4.1	−4.8	−6.7	7.6	8.2	25.2
Average	−1.3	−1.3	−1.8	0.2	17.7	31.9	28.0
Weighted average	−1.0	−0.4	−0.3	1.9	22.2	41.1	34.2
Latin America and the Caribbean							
Average	−1.8	0.2	1.6	2.0	83.6	212.4	72.2
Weighted average	−0.7	0.1	1.9	0.8	129.2	421.7	459.3

Note: GDP, gross domestic product.

[a] Average growth in consumer price index for the period; compound growth rates.

Source: Data base of the World Bank, International Economics Department, supplemented by staff estimates.

many sectors, while others moved timidly and selectively on structural reforms or were reluctant until mid-1994 to enact credible and sustainable macroeconomic stabilization programs (Brazil).

Table 1 also contains data on macroeconomic indicators for twenty-four countries for 1982–92. Four features stand out. First, in almost every country the years immediately following the debt crisis (1982–86) resulted in severe declines in GDP per capita. Second, starting in 1987, GDP per capita began to recover in many countries. Growth was stronger among advanced reformers than among countries that delayed the adjustment process. With a few exceptions, most countries experienced respectable to strong growth in 1992. Third, after accelerating in the second half of the 1980s, inflation declined substantially throughout the region. Once again, advanced reformers, as a group, made the greatest progress in this area.

Selection I.B.6. Indian Economic Reforms: Background, Rationale, Achievements, and Future Prospects*

1. Achievements and Failures Since Independence

First, the extent of poverty, that is, the proportion of the population with monthly per capita private consumption expenditure below a very modest poverty line[1] has indeed gone down, from over half the population in the mid fifties to about a third in the late eighties, and further to less than a fifth in 1993–94 according to official estimates. Most of the reduction occurred in the eighties during which period GDP grew over 5% per year as compared to around 3.5% per year in the previous three decades. Unfortunately, this spurt in growth was achieved by fiscal expansion financed by domestic credit and external borrowing. As such, the reduction in poverty arising from a more rapid *but* debt-led growth, without structural reforms, meant its future sustainability was doubtful.

Second, in contrast to the targets for income growth of 5.5%–7.5% per year in the various five year plans since the second, national income grew only at an average rate of less than 4% per year in the *forty year* period (1950–51 to 1990–91). Except for the fifth, and the fiscally profligate sixth and seventh plans (1975–1990), when national income grew by 5.5% per year, in all four previous plans the rate of growth did not exceed 4%.

Third, self-sufficiency, at very modest levels of consumption, has been achieved in a number of commodities including, notably, foodgrains.

Fourth, life expectancy at birth increased from about 32 years around 1950 to about 55 years around 1990, and the rate of infant mortality fell from over 175 per 1000 live births in 1950 to under 100 in 1990. Literacy rate rose from 17% in 1950–51 to 52% in 1990–91. These achievements are modest in comparison to the achievements of other developing countries in South Asia (e.g. Sri Lanka) and elsewhere.

Fifth, industrial production, as measured by the general index, rose twelve-fold between 1950 and 1992. Although the share of manufacturing industry in GDP rose modestly from about a sixth to a fifth between 1950–51 and 1990–91, its share in gainful employment changed much more slowly, with agriculture continuing to be dominant, still accounting for over two-thirds of the labour force in the late eighties as compared to about three-fourths in the early fifties.

Sixth, the share of gross domestic capital formation in GDP almost doubled from 14.7% in 1950–51 to 23.6% in 1990–91. However, there was no commensurate increase in the rate of growth of GDP because of the capital-intensive character of the investment.

Seventh, the public sector became dominant, with the share of the public sector (administration and enterprises) in GDP exceeding 25%, and in the economy's capital stock about 45%, at the end of the eighties. All major banks and insurance companies were nationalized in 1969 and these accounted for over 90% of the financial sector's assets in the early nineties. While the public sector banks have succeeded in mobilizing savings and in extending banking to rural areas and directed credit to "priority" sectors, the subsidies and defaults have become so large that the policy of subsidized and directed credit has become unsustainable and the net worth of the banking sector has been eroded.

Eighth, until the 1991 reform measures, government control over production, investment, technology and locational choice, prices and foreign trade had become so extensive that there was no possibility of exercising the discretion vested in the layers of bureaucracy by the system of controls in a rational manner. A chaotic system of incentives and opportunities of rent seeking were created.

Ninth, the development strategy that emphasized import-substituting industrialization, and the foreign trade and exchange control regime that sustained it, reduced the role of the external sector in development. India's share in world exports fell from its level above 2% at independence to about 0.5% in 1990. The share of foreign trade (exports plus imports) in GDP at market prices was virtually unchanged, increasing from 12% in 1950–51 to 14% in 1990–91.

The concern that the poor might not be sharing in whatever growth that was occurring emerged early on and led to the appointment, in 1960, of the Mahalanobis Committee on Distribution of Income and Levels of Living. Even more significant, in 1962 the Perspective Planning Discussion of the Planning Commission prepared a study for provid-

---

*From T. N. Srinivasan, "Indian Economic Reforms: Background, Rationale, Achievements, and Future Prospects," Yale University (September 1996), pp. 10–16. Reprinted by permission.

[1]Poverty lines of Rs. 15 per capita for rural areas and Rs. 20 per capita for urban areas at 1960–61 prices were set by an expert committee of the Planning Commission in the early sixties.

ing the basic needs of the entire Indian population in fifteen years (Srinivasan and Bardhan, 1974, Chapter 1). It anticipated the basic needs approach to development that was later propounded by international agencies. Unfortunately, these laudable efforts did not lead to any rethinking of the development strategy. . . .

2. Rao-Manmohan Singh Reforms: Origins and Rationale

Bhagwati (1992) has succinctly summarized the factors that explain Indian economic failure. As he put it,

I would divide them into three major groups: extensive bureaucratic controls over production, investment and trade; inward-looking trade and foreign investment policies; and a substantial public sector, going well beyond the conventional confines of public utilities and infrastructure.

The former two adversely affected the private sector's efficiency. The last, with the inefficient functioning of public sector enterprises, impaired additionally the public sector enterprises' contribution to the economy. Together, the three sets of policy decisions broadly set strict limits to what India could get out of its investment. [p. 48]

. . . The systemic failures identified by Bhagwati and others were well known even prior to the initiation of the Rao-Manmohan Singh reforms. Indeed during the final years of Mrs. Gandhi's prime-ministership and that of Rajiv Gandhi hesitant and limited reforms had been initiated. These in effect removed egregious distortions here and there but left the basic control system intact. It is arguable whether a coherent and systemic reform would have come about but for the acute crisis faced by the Indian economy in early 1991. This crisis was brought about by several factors. First, of course, was the unsustainable fiscal profligacy of the eighties financed in part by external borrowing at hard commercial terms: total expenditure of the centre, states and union territories rose to around 33% of GDP by 1990–91 from an average of around 20% in the seventies. Revenues accounted for only 21% of GDP in 1990–91, thus creating a large (12%) fiscal deficit. Second, the Gulf War of 1990 raised the cost of imported crude oil, substantially reduced exports to the gulf area, eliminated inward remittances from emigrant Indian workers in West Asia and besides resulted in expenditures on bringing them home. Third, with an unstable coalition government at the centre, political uncertainties adversely affected the confidence of external creditors, including in particular non-resident Indians (NRI). The rate of inflation rose to double digits. The outflow of NRI deposits and the lengthening

(shortening) of the lag between exports (imports) and corresponding foreign exchange receipts (payments) in anticipation of a devaluation resulted in a steep fall in foreign exchange reserves to the equivalent of the cost of just two weeks of imports.

The government then in power attempted to tackle the severe crisis through a series of draconian measures. As Ministry of Finance (1992, p. 10) put it, "By June 1991, the balance of payments crisis had become overwhelmingly a crisis of confidence in the Government's ability to manage the balance of payments. The loss of confidence had itself undermined the Government's capability to deal with the crisis by closing off all recourse to external credit. A default on payments, for the first time in our history, had become a serious possibility in June 1991."

The Rao government that came to power on June 26, 1991, although it took immediate policy measures to avoid defaulting on external debt, recognized the long-term problems with India's economic management that underpinned the development strategy of the previous decades. In July 1991, the government announced a series of far reaching reforms. These included an initial devaluation of the rupee and subsequent market determination of its exchange rate, abolition of import licensing with the important exceptions that the restrictions on imports of manufactured consumer goods and on foreign trade in agriculture remained in place, convertibility (with some notable exceptions) of the rupee on the *current account;* reduction in the number of tariff lines as well as tariff rates; reduction in excise duties on a number of commodities; some limited reforms of direct taxes; abolition of industrial licensing except for investment in a few industries for locational reasons or for environmental considerations, relaxation of restrictions on large industrial houses under the Monopolies and Restrictive Trade Practices (MRTP) Act; easing of entry requirements (including equity participation) for direct foreign investment; and allowing private investment in some industries hitherto reserved for public sector investment. A National Renewal Fund for assisting workers currently employed in enterprises that would have to be scaled down or closed altogether was established. Reform of the financial sector included simplification of the interest rate structure with the elimination of interest rate floors on large loans, replacement of fixed term deposit rates by an interest rate ceiling, reductions in government preemption of loanable funds and monetization, and improving the capital position of the banks.

These reforms are *systemic* and conceived as a package of coordinated action in several areas.

They go beyond liberalizing the more irksome controls at the margin and are based on the realization that the benefits from reforming one sector could be limited if other related sectors are not also reformed.

3. Achievements of Reforms

Any meaningful evaluation of any policy reform is possible only by comparing the economy after the reforms are completed and have had their full and intended effect, with a counterfactual state that the economy would have been in, given the same economic environment exogenous to policy, had there been no reforms. Such an evaluation requires specifying a model of the economy with its parameters immune to Lucas-critique, an almost impossible task! A comparison of the performance of the economy prior to and after reforms is simplistic and will confound the reform effects with effects of exogenous shocks. Indian reform process has been in place for only five years and is as yet incomplete. As such, while it is too soon to see the medium to longer term beneficial effects of reforms, recent economic performance will surely reflect in part the inevitable and unavoidable short-term costs. Over-interpreting recent trends is thus a danger. With these caveats let me proceed.

Ministry of Finance (1996a, 1996b) provides ample evidence that achievements thus far of economic reforms have been remarkable. The reforms have "led to a revival of strong economic growth, rapid expansion of productive employment, a reduction of poverty and a marked decline in inflation" (Ministry of Finance, 1996b, p. 1). Further "the growth achieved in the post-crisis period was a noteworthy achievement by international standards and was more sustainable than the growth in the immediate pre-crisis period." In brief,

- growth of GDP at factor cost, which had fallen to a mere 0.8% in 1992–93 accelerated significantly to 6.3% in 1994–95 and is provisionally placed at 7% in 1995–96. *This is the first time that a growth rate of this magnitude was not due to exceptional agricultural growth.*
- industrial growth, after attaining 9.3% in 1994–95, accelerated to 12.4% during April 95–February 1996. What is even more remarkable, production of capital goods, which had been heavily protected in the pre-liberalization era, and had fallen for three years in a row after liberalization, grew by 24.9% in 1994–95 and by 20.4% during April–February 1996.
- wholesale price inflation, which exceeded 10%

in 1993–94 and 1994–95 has slowed to 4.4% in 1995–96
- growth in the value of exports in US dollar terms has ranged between 18.4% and 20.9% in the three years 1993–96
- current account deficit as a proportion of GDP has remained below 2% as compared to 3.2% in the crisis year of 1990–91
- foreign currency assets, which had fallen to less than a billion dollars at the height of the crisis, rose to $20.8 billion at the end of 1994–95 and have since declined to $17 billion at the end of 1995–96
- gross domestic savings as a proportion of GDP, after falling to little over 21% in 1992–93 and 1993–94 from a level of 23.6% in 1990–91 has recovered to 24.4% in 1994–95. However gross domestic capital formation at 25.2% of GDP in 1994–95 is yet to surpass the level of 27.0% in 1990–91.

Ministry of Finance (1996a) points to the clear beneficial effects of reforms on living standards and social indicators:

Following an initial deterioration resulting from the 1991 crisis, the setbacks to real agricultural wages, mortality rates and the growth of employment, were soon reversed. After declining by 6.2 per cent in the crisis year of 1991–92 the growth of real wages of unskilled agricultural labour has averaged 5.1 per cent per annum in the next three years. Provisional estimates by the Planning Commission indicate that in 1993–94 the incidence of poverty had declined to below 19 per cent of India's total population. After the crisis-induced low of 1991–92, annual economy-wide employment growth is estimated to have averaged 6.3 million jobs per year over 1992–93 to 1994–95, with 7.2 million additional employment in 1994–95. This has to be viewed against estimates of annual employment increase of 4.8 million in the 1980s.

These achievements are impressive.

References

Bhagwati, Jagdish (1992), *India's Economy: The Shackled Giant,* Oxford: Clarendon Press.

Ministry of Finance, Government of India (1992), *Economic Survey 1991–92,* New Delhi: Government of India Press.

——— (1996a), *Economic Survey 1995–96,* New Delhi: Government of India Press.

——— (1996b), *Economic Survey 1995–96: An Update,* New Delhi: Government of India Press.

Srinivasan, T. N. and P. K. Bardhan (1974), *Poverty and Income Distribution in India,* Calcutta: Statistical Publishing Society.

Note I.B.1. The Triumph of Laissez-Faire?

The selections above on China, Latin America (by Edwards), and India all describe how "reforms" that reduced state involvement in the economy have led to accelerated economic growth and better performance in achieving other important goals such as alleviating poverty or reducing inflation. It may appear that the long debate over whether the state or the market should guide development has been decided in favor of the latter. The purpose of this Note is not to contribute to this debate but simply to forestall a rush to judgment by the reader.

First, we should point out that while the direction of reform is clear, the ultimate goal is not. Should the goal be a "minimal" state, whose only economic role is to enforce private contracts? Should the goal be a state that, while relying on the private sector as the "engine of growth," redistributes income from the rich to the poor and is a major provider of education, health care, and physical infrastructure such as roads and sewers? Or should the state "lead the market," as described in the foregoing selection on East Asia? Recall that this selection grudgingly concludes that "in a few economies, mainly in Northeast Asia, government interventions appear in some instances to have resulted in higher and more equal growth than otherwise would have occurred."

Second, while reduction of state involvement has appeared to benefit development in the recent past, the longer historical record is less clear. In Selection II.1, Lloyd Reynolds identifies "turning points" when countries began "intensive growth," that is, growth of output in excess of growth in population, leading to rising average standards of living. Reynolds dates the turning point in China to 1949, when the Communist Party came to power, and dates the turning point in India to 1947, when the country gained independence. Thus intensive growth in China and India began with the inception of exactly the high levels of state intervention whose partial reversal is described in the selections above! Reynolds notes a general tendency toward increased prominence of government in the years following 1945, marked by an increase in the public expenditure share of GNP from perhaps 5 percent before 1940 to around 15 percent by 1980. During this period, "Countries which had reached the turning point before 1940 continued to grow, usually at an accelerated rate." Of course the coincidence of an increased state role in the economy and more rapid economic growth does not imply that the former caused the latter, and indeed Exhibit III.1 shows that, looking across countries, rapid growth is associated with neither a high nor a low average share of government expenditure in GDP during the period 1960–89. Nevertheless, none of this evidence is favorable to the view that reducing state involvement in the economy is the key to successful development.

Selection I.B.7. Explaining Africa's Development Experiences*

The Record

Official estimates show that, on average, incomes in sub-Saharan Africa (SSA) are today no higher than 20 years ago and are well down over the last decade. There have also been comparatively large and persistent balance of payments and inflation problems, very low levels of saving and investment, and a declining productivity of investment. Table 1 summarizes some of the evidence and compares the African record with that of other low-income countries.

The economic comparisons are clearly to the disadvantage of SSA. The comparatively poor record on export volumes, and the failure to diversify out of primary product exports, is arguably the most serious of these. The social indicators are better, showing improving mortality rates and school enrollments but even here, other low-income countries mostly made more progress, and the dietary comparison is particularly adverse. Progress with the enlargement of secondary school enrollments was a notable exception to these unfavorable comparisons. There are, however, concerns that in some SSA countries the quality of schooling has deteriorated and there is evidence of declining enrollment rates in recent years. . . .

There are, of course, large differences in the resource endowments, structures, performances and problems of African economies. There are major differences between the situations of oil-importing and exporting countries. The Franc Zone arrangements place most Francophone African countries in a special category. Countries in the Sahelian zone and the Horn of Africa have a special vulnerability to uncertain rainfall.

Figure 1 illustrates the wide spread of experiences by reference to the growth of per capita income in 1965–1990. Over that period substantial increases are shown for a number of countries, while in a slightly larger number, average incomes are today lower than they were a quarter of a century ago. The record is not uniformly bad. Yet strong performers like Botswana and Mauritius are distinguished more by their special circumstances than by their potential as role-models. The more recent record has been worse and most of the countries listed in Figure 1 were unable to prevent declines in per capita incomes during the 1980s.

*From Overseas Development Institute, *Explaining Africa's Development Experiences,* Briefing Paper, June 1992. Reprinted by permission.

Some of the worst performers, such as Sudan and Mozambique, are not included in the Figure; nor is it weighted by population. (Nigeria's stagnation and Zaire's decline far outweigh the growth of the smaller countries.) Yet there are many common characteristics and substantial similarities in experience; this paper is concerned with what the economies of SSA have in common rather than with the differences. . . .

Economic Policies

The poor quality of past economic policies is often blamed for SSA's unhappy experience, particularly policy biases which contributed to the poor export and balance-of-payments record. There was a tendency until the early 1980s to maintain fixed and over-valued exchange rates, with a two-fifths average real appreciation during the 1970s. Overvaluation reduced the profitability of exporting and this disincentive was compounded by other policy biases. A substantial proportion of export receipts was often with-held from producers as a result of export taxes (overt or covert) and the inflated costs of state monopoly marketing agencies. Exceptionally high levels of industrial protection also acted as a tax on exporters, by raising the cost of local inputs and biasing relative prices in favour of import substitution. Inadequate supporting services and a crumbling infrastructure often made things worse.

Implicit in the above was another common feature of the 1960s and 1970s: relative neglect of agriculture. To the pro-urban bias of import substitution, particularly in manufacturing, and the taxation of cash crops can be added, in some cases, price controls on foodstuffs, depressing the prices paid to farmers; underresourced inefficient research and extension services; and underinvestment in rural infrastructure.

"Financial repression" was another common feature: interest rates controlled at well below market levels; lending decisions based on political and other non-financial criteria; a variety of devices for capturing a disproportionate share of domestic credit to finance the deficits of the public sector. Such "repression" is blamed for holding back the development of financial systems, frustrating the credit requirements of private businesses, and contributing to low-productivity investment.

The large need of the public sector for bank credit reflected two further weaknesses: deteriorat-

Table 1. Comparative Indicators of Economic Performance

		SSA	Low-Income SSA	All-Low Income Countries
Economic Growth, 1980–89 (percent p.a.)				
Income (GNP) per capita		−1.2	−1.1	+0.7
Private consumption per capita		−2.2	−0.5	−0.5
Export volumes		−0.7	−1.8	+0.8
Prices (inflation rate)		+19.6	+30.2	+14.8
Structural Indicators				
Gross domestic savings as percent GDP	1965	14	—	18
	1989	13		26
Gross domestic investment as percent GDP	1965	14	—	19
	1989	15		28
Primary products as percent total exports	1965	92	—	76
	1989	89		48
Energy consumption per capita*	1965	72	—	125
	1989	73		330
Social Indicators (percent change 1965–89)				
Crude death rate		−32	−30	−39
Infant mortality rate		−32	−30	−37
Calorie supply per capita		−1	0	+13
Primary school enrollment		+55	+58	+60
Secondary school enrollment		+314	+292	+207

Note: * = kgs of oil equivalent.

Source: World Bank, various.

Figure 1. Change in per capita GNP, 1965–90 (percent per annum).

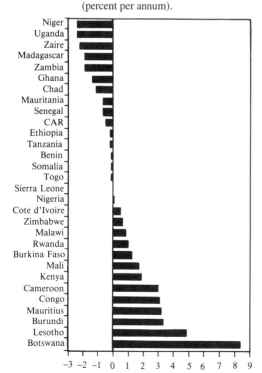

ing fiscal balances and unprofitable public enterprises. The evidence indicates that governments were increasingly unable to meet even their recurrent expenditures from tax revenues, contributing to the deteriorating savings position, and to inflationary and balance-of-payments pressures. The number of public enterprises was greatly expanded and, while some of them performed well, they were the exceptions. The inefficiency of some—in the delivery of agricultural services, export marketing, banking, manufacturing, and retailing— further contributed to the poor economic record under examination.

Another common weakness was a preference in the 1960s and 1970s for the use of controls and discretionary powers rather than policy interventions which operate through market incentives. Controls over imports and prices, a multitude of licensing requirements, and other restrictions on economic life often had the effect of tying-up high-level manpower, created large opportunities for corruption, and spawned parallel (black) markets.

The economic role of the state was in these ways often expanded well beyond its capacity to perform efficiently. It seems likely that this over-expansion contributed to the serious decline in the productivity of investment which also occurred. It may also have undermined the state as an instrument for economic change, by widening the gap between the expectations created and the ability of governments to satisfy these expectations, alienating the people. Some of the chosen forms of intervention themselves hastened the decline of the state, by creating parallel markets, shrinking the tax base, and eroding those aspects of economic life within the control of the state.

Some governments failed notoriously to provide basic security for their peoples. Wars—civil and international—, political instability, and breakdowns of the rule of law have brought suffering to a multitude of Africans—displacing many, forcing others to retreat into the subsistence economy or to operate in the twilight zone of the parallel economy, contributing to the creation of burdensome armies.

The Effects of Personal Rule

Some of the policy weaknesses identified above were also in evidence in various Asian and Latin American countries. One of the features which has placed SSA into a special category, however, was the slowness of its governments to respond to the deteriorating economic results produced by these weaknesses. In many cases deficient policies were sustained for many years so the question arises, why was the policy response so slow? Why were policies harmful to the economy allowed to remain for so long even though governments' popularity, even legitimacy, was undermined by the resulting economic decline? Why were so many of the subsequent policy changes initiated from outside and why has progress with these reforms been slow? In the search for answers to these questions, political, historical, and cultural forces appear to be at least as important as the economic factors described above.

For many political scientists "personal rule" models of African political systems are particularly persuasive. They see the position of modern African rulers and their governments as maintained by patron-client relationships, largely based on familial and ethnic loyalties. Followers are rewarded with preferential access to loans, import licenses, contracts, and jobs. Institutional rules and constitutional checks are swept aside in the struggle to maintain power. The distinction between the public and private domains becomes blurred.

Governments which conform to this model are unlikely to care much about broad-based, long-term economic development. Indeed they are seen as destructive of it, with the pursuit of personal aggrandizement and short-term political advantage leading to economic irrationality. As rule becomes more personalized and power more concentrated, so policies are apt to become less predictable, more arbitrary. Manipulating the distribution of wealth becomes more important than its creation.

Despite its explanatory value, there are particularly large dangers of over-generalizing here and of appearing to denigrate all African governments. Nonetheless, the personal rule model appears able to predict and explain a number of the policy weaknesses described earlier:

- The proliferation of generally over-manned public enterprises and, more generally, the over-expansion of the state relative to the private sector to maximize opportunities for patronage.
- The preference for direct controls and discretionary actions over interventions that work impersonally through the market, for similar motives.
- Inward-looking import-substitution policies, to provide further opportunities for rewarding important urban groups; and the neglect of (politically unimportant) peasant farmers.
- Financial repression and politicized credit allocation mechanisms, in order to have cheap credit to offer to supporters.
- The persistence of anti-development policies long after their ill-effects have become apparent, because their primary function was to provide a system of rewards and maintain the ruler in power, rather than to promote development per se.

History and Social Structure

It is evident that personal rule and clientelist-based politics occur in many parts of the world but they do appear to have been particularly pervasive in Africa. If this is so, the question becomes why the region has offered such fertile soil for the growth of this style of politics. A full exploration of Africa's development experience thus requires reference to social structures, values, and historical experiences unique to SSA. . . .

Initial Conditions and Structural Weaknesses

Whatever the validity of these wider political and cultural factors, they do not alone explain Africa's development experience. Further explanations are provided by reference to other conditions at the time of independence, and to chronic weaknesses in the structures of its economies, in respect of which the average African economy was at a serious disadvantage relative to other developing countries at the beginning of the 1960s.

- Populations were largely illiterate and there were acute shortages of educated and trained personnel. Thus, in 1960 the proportion of people enrolled in tertiary education relative to the population aged 20–24 was less than half of one percent in 16 of the 18 SSA countries for which estimates are available, compared to 2 percent for all low-income countries taken together and 4 percent for middle-income countries. This has had serious and long-lived consequences for attempts at modernization, and for SSA's capacity to absorb and adapt modern technologies. Modern approaches to the determinants of economic growth place real importance upon such human and technological capacities.
- As another aspect of under-developed human resources, the relative absence of an indigenous entrepreneurial class equipped to employ modern know-how to the development of substantial productive firms.
- The heavy dependence on primary product exports induced by the colonial approach to development; the consequentially under-developed condition, and distorted nature, of the infrastructure of transport and communications, oriented towards trade with Europe rather than internal development.
- The tiny size of the domestic market for industrial goods (which today for a typical SSA country is about 1/300 that of an average-size industrial country), operating as a major constraint upon industrialization (a constraint greatly aggravated by import-substitution strategies based on the home market).
- Market mechanisms operated poorly, due to the poverty of the economies, their small size, weak communications and infrastructure, low literacy, and scarcities of modern skills. These conditions created extensive dualism and much monopoly outside of traditional agriculture and marketing.

These initial conditions can, in turn, be seen as resulting in inflexible economic structures and a low economy-wide capability of adapting to changing needs. Combined with a predominantly primary production base, these conditions interacted with personal rule to reduce economic responsiveness. This helps explain the static composition of exports, and could be why the response of African economies to structural adjustment programmes has been sluggish by comparison with other developing economies.

In respect of most of the initial conditions just surveyed, the SSA situation was worse (often much worse) than was typical of countries in Asia and Latin America at a comparable stage, helping to answer the question, why Africa? With hindsight, absolutely and comparatively poor development performance could have been predicted, although that was not how it was seen at the time. It is therefore inappropriate to describe the SSA experience as one of "failure." Sustained rapid development would have been extraordinary.

I.C. THE DISCIPLINE OF DEVELOPMENT ECONOMICS

Note I.C.1. Evolution of Development Economics

Modern development economics arose in the late 1940s as an economic counterpart to the political independence of the emerging countries of Asia, Africa, and the Caribbean. Its influence spread rapidly to Latin America and other low-income areas. Regions that had been considered in the eighteenth century as "rude and barbarous," in the nineteenth century as "backward," and in the prewar period as "underdeveloped" now became the "less developed countries" or the "poor countries"—and the "emergent countries" and "developing economies."

But how was the development to be achieved? Although political independence can be legislated, economic independence cannot. An understanding of the forces of development was necessary, and the design of appropriate policies to support these forces was essential. To accomplish this, the creative participation of economists was needed.

The new development economics had some relation to the old growth economics of classical economists (Smith, Malthus, Ricardo)—a concern with the heavy variables of capital, population, and the objective of what Adam Smith termed the "progress of opulence" in the progressive state.[1]

But the new development economists went beyond their classical and neoclassical predecessors to consider the kinds of policies that an active state and the international community could adopt to accelerate a country's rate of development. And the new development economics, with its concern for economic theory and policy analysis, became more analytic than the prewar phase of colonial economics, which had been characterized by narrow institutional studies and economic anthropology.

The term "economic development" constituted a persuasive definition: an increase in real income per head as a desirable objective. During the 1950s and early 1960s, development policies emphasized the maximization of growth of GNP through capital accumulation and industrialization based on import substitution. In view of a distrust of markets and a belief in the pervasiveness of market failure, governments also turned to central planning. There was general optimism with respect to what could be accomplished by emphasizing planned investment in new physical capital, utilizing reserves of surplus labor, adopting import-substitution industrialization policies, embracing central planning of change, and relying on foreign aid. But there was pessimism regarding the external conditions of development—the international environment within which the national development process would have to progress—and the export of primary products: low price elasticities of demand, low income elasticities of demand, fluctuations in export revenue, deteriorating terms of trade—all these pessimistic views regarding primary-product exports reinforced the inward-looking import-substitution policies.[2]

Policy makers were adopting these policies not simply because of advice from economists, but also because of ideology and political economy.[3] Chapter IX considers from the perspective of political economy the more general problem of why governments of developing countries do what they do—either in accordance with or contrary to professional economic advice. Nonetheless, much of the thinking in the new development economics could be appealed to in support of these policies. A "big push"[4] or "critical minimum effort"[5] was believed necessary to break out of a "low level equilibrium trap."[6] An increase in the proportion of national income invested above 10 percent was advocated for a "take-off," with industry as the leading sector.[7] "Balanced growth"—the synchronized application of capital to a wide range of industries—was advocated by Nurkse:

> A frontal attack—a wave of capital investments in a number of different industries—can economically succeed while any substantial application of capital by an individual entrepreneur in any particular industry may be blocked or discouraged by the limitations of the preexisting market. . . . [T]hrough the application of capital over a wide range of activities, the general level of economic activity is raised

and the size of the market enlarged. . . . [Balanced growth] is a means of getting out of the rut, a means of stepping up the rate of growth when the external forces of advance through trade expansion and foreign capital are sluggish or inoperative.[8]

Hirschman, however, advocated unbalanced growth in order to maximize induced decision making and to take advantage of forward and backward linkages in the production process.[9] Unlike the neoclassical economists, who assumed a smoothly working market-price system, some of the early development economists adopted a more structuralist approach to development problems. Structuralist analysis attempted to identify specific rigidities, lags, shortages and surpluses, low elasticities of supply and demand, and other characteristics of the structure of developing countries that affect economic adjustments to development policy. The structuralist view also was pessimistic about the responsiveness of agents to price signals and incentives. Instead of neoclassical flexibility and substitutability, the structuralist view emphasized low elasticities of supply and market imperfections that limit the mobility of factors and the responsiveness of agents. Myrdal, Prebisch, and Singer were especially prominent in reinforcing the pessimistic view with respect to exports of primary products.[10]

During the late 1960s and early 1970s came a second phase of development economics, which focused more directly on poverty and inequality. It was argued that growth in GNP is not a sufficient condition for the removal of poverty: income was not trickling down to the lowest income groups, and the number of people living in absolute poverty was increasing in many countries. The very meaning of development was questioned, and instead of worshiping at the altar of GNP, many economists added other dimensions to the objectives of development. The World Bank emphasized redistribution with growth.[11] The International Labor Organization (ILO) concentrated on basic human needs.[12] Much of the development literature turned from an emphasis on industrial development to one on rural development. Impressed by studies of human capital formation,[13] economists also shifted their attention from physical capital to human resources. And the concern with appropriate technology broadened the problem of what could or should be borrowed from the more developed countries.[14]

The most substantial change in the content of development economics came during the 1970s and 1980s—decades marked by the resurgence of neoclassical economics.[15] There was increasing criticism of policy-induced distortions and the nonmarket failures associated with the implementation of public policies. This led to a critique of comprehensive and detailed administrative controls. With the renewed attention to the application of neoclassical economics, price distortions were to be removed: "'Getting prices right' is not the end of economic development. But 'getting prices wrong' frequently is."[16] It had long since become evident that economic rationality characterizes agents in the less developed countries as well as in the more developed.[17] Beyond the removal of price distortions, neoclassical economics advocated getting all policies right. Markets, prices, and incentives became central. Inward-looking strategies of development were to give way to liberalization of the foreign-trade regime and export promotion. Inflation was to submit to stabilization programs. State-owned enterprises were to be privatized. A poor country was now considered poor because of inappropriate policies, and good economics—that is, neoclassical economics—was good for the developing country.

In the 1950s, the pioneers in development had asked why underdeveloped countries were underdeveloped, and they formulated grand theories and general strategies. In contrast, the focus in the 1970s and 1980s became increasingly directed to the heterogeneity of the developing countries and to an explanation of differential rates of country performance. Analysis moved from highly aggregated growth models to disaggregated micro models. More emphasis was placed on applied research that was country-specific, based on empirical data, and on the application of neoclassical principles to policy issues. In an increasing number of countries, these changes in development thought produced an improvement in agricultural policies, a liberalization of the foreign-trade regime, and a professionalism in project appraisal.[18]

In contrast to the position of the early development economists, who eschewed the universal use of neoclassical economics and thought the "special case" irrelevant for development policy, many economists now emphasize the universality of neoclassical economics and dismiss the claim that development economics is a special subdiscipline in its own right. Hirschman, for instance, has written provocatively about the rise and decline of development economics.[19] So, too, does Kreuger state:

> Once it is recognized that individuals respond to incentives, and that "market failure" is the result of inappropriate incentives rather than of nonresponsiveness, the separateness of development economics as a field largely disappears. Instead, it becomes an applied field, in which the tools and insights of labor economics, agricultural economics, international economics, public finance and other fields are addressed to the special questions and policy issues that arise in the context of development.[20]

Many other students of development, however, believe that an obituary of development economics is not in order. Thus Sen argues that there is still much relevance in the broad policy themes that traditional development economics has emphasized: (1) industrialization, (2) rapid capital accumulation, (3) mobilization of underemployed manpower, and (4) planning and an economically active state.[21] And Lewis recognizes that "the overlap between Development Economics and the Economics of the Developed is bound to be great, but there are also differences that are rather large, which is why each also has some tools of its own."[22]

Perhaps the issue of the relevance of neoclassical economics to developing countries can be best resolved by concluding that the task of development economists is made difficult not because they must start afresh with a completely new set of tools or because they confront problems that are wholly different from those in advanced countries, but because they must acquire a sense of the different assumptions that are most incisive for analyzing a problem within the context of a poor country. In particular, this calls for special care in identifying different institutional relations, in assessing the different quantitative importance of some variables, and in allowing some elements that are usually taken as givens—such as population, "state of the arts," institutions, and supply of entrepreneurship—to become endogenous variables in development analysis.

Notes

1. For more detailed reference to early growth economists, see G.M. Meier and R.E. Baldwin, *Economic Development: Theory, History, Policy* (1957); G.M. Meier, *Emerging from Poverty* (1984), chap. 5; William J. Baumol, *Economic Dynamics* (1959); Irma Adelman, *Theories of Economic Growth and Development* (1961); and Lionel Robbins, *Theory of Economic Development in the History of Economic Thought* (1968).

2. See Jagdish Bhagwati, "Development Economics: What Have We Learned?," *Asian Development Review* 2, no. 1 (1984): 24–29.

3. See, for example, Albert O. Hirschman, "Political Economy of Import Substituting Industrialization," *Quarterly Journal of Economics* (February 1968).

4. P.N. Rosenstein-Roden, "Problems of Industrialization of Eastern and Southeastern Europe," *Economic Journal* (June–September 1943).

5. Harvey Leibenstein, *Economic Backwardness and Economic Growth* (1957), chap. 8.

6. Richard R. Nelson, "A Theory of the Low-Level Equilibrium Trap in Underdeveloped Economies," *American Economic Review* (December 1956): 894–908.

7. W. W. Rostow, *The Stages of Economic Growth* (1960).

8. Ragnar Nurkse, *Problems of Capital Formation in Underdeveloped Countries* (1953), pp. 13–15.

9. Albert O. Hirschman, *The Strategy of Economic Development* (1958).

10. Gunnar Myrdal, *Economic Theory and Underdeveloped Regions* (1957); Raúl Prebisch, "The Economic Development of Latin America and Its Principal Problems," *Economic Bulletin for Latin America* 7 (1950); Hans Singer, "Gains and Losses from Trade and Investment in Underdeveloped Countries," *American Economic Review* (May 1950).

11. World Bank, *Redistribution with Growth* (1974).

12. International Labor Organization, *The Basic Needs Approach to Development* (1977).

13. T.W. Schultz, "Investment in Human Capital," *American Economic Review* (March 1961): 1–17.

14. Frances Stewart, *Technology and Underdevelopment* (1977).

15. I.M.D. Little, *Economic Development* (1982), chap. 9.

16. C. Peter Timmer, "Choice of Techniques in Rice Milling in Java," *Bulletin of Indonesian Economic Studies* (July 1973).

17. The usual postulates of rationality and the principles of maximization or minimization have quite general applicability. For illustrative evidence, see P. T. Bauer and B. S. Yamey, *The Economics of Under-Developed Countries* (1957), pp. 91–101; W. J. Barber, "Economic Rationality and Behavior Patterns in an Underdeveloped Area: A Case Study of African Economic Behavior in the Rhodesias," *Economic Development and Cultural Change* (April 1960): 237–51; and W. O. Jones, "Economic Man in Africa," *Food Research Institute Studies* (May 1960): 107–34.

18. Gerald M. Meier, "On Getting Policies Right," in *Pioneers in Development*, 2d ser., ed. Gerald M. Meier (1987), pp. 3–11.

19. Albert O. Hirschman, "Rise and Decline of Development Economics," in *Essays in Trespassing* (1981).

20. Anne O. Krueger, "Aid in the Development Process," *World Bank Research Observer* (January 1986): 62–63.

21. Amartya K. Sen, "Development Which Way Now?" *Economic Journal* (December 1983).

22. W. Arthur Lewis, "The State of Development Theory," *American Economic Review* (March 1984): 2.

Comment I.C.1. Classical Growth Theory

Prior to the neoclassical marginalist revolution in the 1870s, classical economists had been very much interested in economic growth—Adam Smith's "progressive state." According to Smith, the level of output per head, together with the growth of output, "must in every nation be regulated by two different circumstances: first by the skill, dexterity, and judgement with which its labor is generally applied; and, secondly, by the proportion between the number of those who are employed in useful labor, and that of those who are not so employed."

The major sources of growth are (1) growth in the labor force and stock of capital, (2) improvements in the efficiency with which capital is applied to labor through greater division of labor and technological progress, and (3) foreign trade that widens the market and reinforces the other two sources of growth.

Once begun, the growth process becomes self-reinforcing in the progressive state. As long as the growth in wealth favors profits, there are savings and additional capital accumulation, and hence further growth. And with capital accumulation, the demand for labor rises, and a growing labor force is absorbed in productive employment.

Smith also attributed overwhelming importance to the division of labor, in the broad sense of technical progress. The division of labor entails improved efficiency of labor, and increasing specialization leads to rising per capita income. By extending the division of labor, improvements in production reduce the amount of input per unit of output. According to Smith, however,

> the division of labor is limited by the extent of the market. . . . When the market is very small, no person can have any encouragement to dedicate himself entirely to one employment, or want of power to exchange all that surplus part of the produce for his own labor, which is over and above his own consumption, or such parts of the produce of other men's labor as he has occasion for.

The division of labor increases wealth, which, in turn, widens the market, enabling the division of labor to be carried further forward.

If capital accumulation, division of labor, and foreign trade are sources of a nation's economic growth, then—according to Smith—growth can be promoted through the extension of market institutions and the activity of competition.

Some of Smith's insights retain much relevance. To Smith and the modern economists, growth is the outcome of a logical process. Both search for some laws and generalizations. Modern economists emphasize, as did Smith, capital accumulation as a driving force in the growth process. So, too, do they concentrate on increasing productivity. They also point to the possibilities for development based on foreign trade. And at the forefront of development discussions, economists seek to find a proper division between reliance on the market-price system and dependence on governmental actions.

Among the classical economists, the development views of Thomas Malthus, David Ricardo, and John Stuart Mill are also significant.

From the 1870s to the 1930s, the theory of value and resource allocation dominated economic thought. Economic analysis turned its attention to the conditions that would make possible various optima rather than the conditions that would allow an economy to achieve ever-changing optima of ever-increasing range. Not the movement of aggregate output in the entire economy, but the movement of particular lines of production toward an equilibrium position became the neoclassicist's concern. To tighten up the economy and avoid inefficiency was the neoclassicist's objective. Rigorous analysis of individual markets and of price formation was the neoclassicist's hallmark. In *The Theory of Economic Growth* (1955), W. Arthur Lewis could therefore say that "no comprehensive treatise on the subject has been published for about a century. The last great book covering this wide range was John Stuart Mill's *Principles of Political Economy,* published in 1848."

For studies of the classical economists' views on economic growth, see Lionel Robbins, *The Theory of Economic Development in the History of Economic Thought* (1968); William J. Baumol, *Economic Dynamics* (1959); Irma Adelman, *Theories of Economic Growth and Development* (1961); G. M. Meier and R. E. Baldwin, *Economic Development: Theory, History, Policy* (1957); G. M. Meier, *Emerging from Poverty* (1984), chap. 5.; G. M. Meier, ed., *From Classical Economics to Development Economics* (1994).

Comment I.C.2. Development Economics as a Special Subject

In the years following World War II, the subject of development economics was formulated in its own right. Investigating issues that went beyond the earlier growth economics of classical economists (Smith, Malthus, Ricardo), a "new development economics" began to be formulated by a number of economists. For the outstanding contributions made in the formative period of the 1950s, see Gerald M. Meier and Dudley Seers, eds., *Pioneers in Development* (1984). Also, H. W. Arndt, *Economic Development: The History of an Idea* (1989).

Several retrospective papers have considered the evolution of development thought over the past four decades. Most useful in tracing the changing views of development economists are Albert Hirschman, "The Rise and Decline of Development Economists," in *Essays in Trespassing* (1981); Ian Livingstone, "The Development of Development Economics," *O.D.I. Review,* no. 2 (1981); Amartya Sen, "Development: Which Way Now?" *Economic Journal* (December 1983); Jagdish Bhagwati, "Development Economics: What Have We Learned?" *Asian Development Review* 2 (1984); W. Arthur Lewis, "The State of Development Theory," *American Economic Review* (March 1984); and "The Methodological Foundations of Development Economics" [special issue], *World Development* (February 1986).

Although development economists now rely much more on standard neoclassical principles that apply to rich and poor countries alike, the subject of development economics still has sufficient distinctive characteristics to distinguish it as a special subdiscipline in economics. This distinction is recognized in two recent surveys of the subject. Nicholas Stern's "Survey of Development," *Economic Journal* (September 1989) is addressed to "economists and students of economics who do know the tools of their trade but not necessarily how they have been applied to and fashioned for the analysis of the economics of developing countries." Bliss also argues that general economic principles are precisely too general to give us insights into applications for less developed economies. Alone, the parts of economic theory and method that apply more or less universally tell us less than we need in particular application. To give them life they have to be enlarged and translated. When this is done a specialty is created. Development economics consists in part of the refinement of general economics to deal with questions which arise in the context of development, and partly of certain special ideas which have proved useful in studying developing countries.[1]

[1]Christopher Bliss, *Handbook of Development Economics* (1989), p. 1188.

Note I.C.2. New Endogenous Growth Theory

At various times in the history of thought, economists have stressed increasing returns as an endogenous explanation for economic growth. Adam Smith did so in emphasizing that growth in productivity was due to the division of labor, which depends upon the extent of the market. Alfred Marshall also emphasized that the role of "nature" in production may be subject to diminishing returns, but the role of "man" is subject to increasing returns. And again, in an earlier period, J. M. Clark also observed that "knowledge is the only instrument of production that is not subject to diminishing returns."[1] Allyn Young also related economic progress to increasing returns that were external to the firm as a result of the progressive division and specialization among industries and the use of roundabout methods of production.[2]

Nobel laureate Kenneth Arrow gave a dynamic interpretation to increasing returns by emphasizing "Learning by Doing."[3] This was an early attempt to render technological progress endogenous in growth models by making the productivity of a given firm an increasing function of cumulative aggregate investment for the industry. (Note that Arrow emphasized cumulative investment, not cumulative output.)

Most recently, new endogenous growth models have gone beyond Robert Solow's neoclassical growth model that exhibited diminishing returns to capital and labor separately and constant returns to both inputs jointly, and that left technological progress as a residual.[4] The new growth theory examines production functions that show increasing returns because of specialization and investment in "knowledge" capital. Technological progress and human capital formation are endogenized within general equilibrium models of growth. New knowledge is generated by investment in the research sector. The technological progress residual is accounted for by endogenous human capital formation. With knowledge being treated as a public good, spill-over benefits to other firms may then allow aggregate investment in knowledge to exhibit increasing returns to scale. This in turn allows investment in knowledge capital to persist indefinitely and to sustain long-run growth in per capita income. A policy implication is that governments can promote growth by providing incentives to agents in the knowledge-producing, human capital–intensive sectors. Developing countries can also be aided by the international transfer of technology. See Paul M. Romer, "Increasing Returns and Long-run Growth," *Journal of Political Economy* (October 1986), and "Endogenous Technological Change," *Journal of Political Economy* (October 1990); and Robert Lucas, Jr., "On the Mechanics of Economic Development," *Journal of Monetary Economics* (July 1988).

For less developed countries, the implication of the new growth theory is to place more emphasis on human capital—even more than on physical capital, and to emphasize the benefit from the exchange of ideas that comes with an open economy integrated into the world economy. A discussion of the implications of new growth theory for the ability of government policies to affect long-run growth in LDCs is contained in the Overview to Chapter III.

It is also suggested by some empirical studies that the new endogenous growth models conform better to the evidence on diversity in growth rates among countries over the past three or four decades then does the neoclassical growth model. See Isaac Ehrlich, "The Problem of Development: Introduction," *Journal of Political Economy* (October 1990): S2–S3, S7; and Jati K. Sengupta, "Growth in NICs in Asia: Some Tests of New Growth Theory," *Journal of Development Studies* (January 1993): 342–57.

In contrast to the critics of the Solow model, another study of cross-country variation in income explains much of the variation in terms of an augmented neoclassical production-function model that includes accumulation of human capital as well as physical capital, but maintains the Solow assumption of decreasing returns to scale in capital. Even when denying the new growth theory's emphasis on externalities to capital accumulation, the augmented Solow model can explain most of the international variation in income per capita by differences in saving, education, and population growth. See N. Gregory Mankiw, David Romer, and David

N. Weil, "A Contribution to the Empirics of Economic Growth," *Quarterly Journal of Economics* (May 1992): 407–37. We are still left, however, with the challenge to understand the determinants of saving, population growth, and worldwide technological change that remain as exogenous variables in neoclassical growth models.

For an evaluation of different models of growth, see the symposium "New Growth Theory," *Journal of Economic Perspectives* (Winter 1994): 3–72.

Notes

1. J. Maurice Clark, *Studies in the Economics of Overhead Costs* (1923), p. 120.

2. Allyn A. Young, "Increasing Returns and Economic Progress," *Economic Journal* (December 1928): 527–42.

3. Kenneth Arrow, "The Economic Implications of Learning by Doing," *Review of Economic Studies* (June 1962): 155–73.

4. Robert M. Solow, "A Contribution to the Theory of Economic Growth," *Quarterly Journal of Economics* (February 1956): 65–94.

CHAPTER II

Historical Perspective

Overview: The Division of the World

In order to analyze the problems of contemporary poor countries it is essential to understand how they became "less developed" than today's rich countries and how they have attempted to catch up. The main focus of this chapter is on the division of the world into agricultural and industrialized countries, with the latter located until recently entirely outside the tropics.

The first selection, by Lloyd Reynolds, examines economic growth of large countries (1980 population at least 10 million) in Asia, Latin America, North Africa and the Middle East, and sub-Saharan Africa during the period 1850–1980. Reynolds begins by noting that prior to this period many countries in these regions had for a century or more been experiencing what he calls "extensive growth," meaning growth in output that is absorbed by growth in population, leaving per capita income unchanged. He argues that developments during the period of extensive growth provided "important conditioning factors" such as nation-building for later growth in per capita income. When this "intensive growth" began in many countries during the "world economic boom" from 1850–1914, it was invariably led by exports of primary products to Europe and North America. This was by no means inevitable, since many countries in Western (but not Central) Europe responded to the industrial revolution that began in Britain in the late eighteenth century through imitation rather than trade. The question of why imitation did not take hold in the countries studied by Reynolds leads us to the second selection, by W. Arthur Lewis.

Lewis states his argument with an elegance and economy that cannot be improved:

> In a closed economy, the size of the industrial sector is a function of agricultural productivity. Agriculture has to be capable of producing the surplus food and raw materials consumed in the industrial sector, and it is the affluent state of the farmers that enables them to be a market for industrial products. If the domestic market is too small, it is still possible to support an industrial sector by exporting manufactures and importing food and raw materials. But it is hard to begin industrialization by exporting manufactures. Usually one begins by selling in a familiar and protected home market and moves on to exporting only after one has learnt to make one's costs competitive.

> The distinguishing feature of the industrial revolution at the end of the eighteenth century is that it began in the country with the highest agricultural productivity—Great Britain—which therefore already had a large industrial sector. The industrial revolution did not create an industrial sector where none had been before. It transformed an industrial sector that already existed by introducing new ways of making the same old things. The revolution spread rapidly in other countries that were also revolutionizing their agriculture, especially in Western Europe and North America. But countries of low agricultural productivity, such as Central and Southern Europe, or Latin America, or China had rather small industrial sectors, and there it made rather slow progress.

The assumption that "it is hard to begin industrialization by exporting manufactures" is crucial to Lewis's argument. We examine this assumption in detail in Note II.1. The assumption of a closed economy is also made in the next two selections, respectively by Kiminori Matsuyama and by Kevin Murphy, Andrei Shleifer, and Robert Vishny, which can be seen as formalizing and extending different aspects of Lewis's argument.

Matsuyama's model makes it clear that an income elasticity of demand for agricultural output (food) that is less than 1 (a well-established empirical regularity known as Engel's Law) is necessary for Lewis's argument to work. Otherwise, an increase in agricultural productivity would, by increasing income, cause a more than proportionate increase in demand for agricultural output that would require a greater share of the labor force to be employed in agriculture, shrinking rather than expanding the industrial sector. This assumption is only implicit in Lewis's argument—the "surplus food" that agriculture has to be capable of producing is a surplus over an assumed subsistence requirement that causes people with low incomes to spend a high proportion of their incomes on food.

Matsuyama also extends Lewis's argument by claiming that manufacturing is the locus of economic growth because only there does productivity increase through learning-by-doing take place. Higher agricultural productivity thus increases not only the level but also the rate of growth of income, because it leads to employment of a larger share of the labor force in manufacturing and thus more rapid learning-by-doing. Two important assumptions are that learning-by-doing is not subject to diminishing returns (there is no tendency to run out of things to learn), and that no individual manufacturing firm has an incentive to increase employment and output to learn more, because each firm is small relative to the industry as a whole and benefits from learning-by-doing in the entire industry. The learning-by-doing model of productivity increase will be discussed in more detail in Note IV. A.1.

It is important to note what happens in Matsuyama's model when the assumption of a closed economy is removed. Now any shortage of agricultural output relative to domestic demand can be met by imports in exchange for exports of manufactures. High agricultural productivity is no longer needed to free up labor for manufacturing and generate demand for manufacturing output. On the contrary, high agricultural productivity allows farmers to attract workers out of the manufacturing sector and thus *lowers* the rate of income growth. The "curse" of abundant arable land and mineral resources will be a major theme covered in Chapter IV.

The model of Murphy, Shleifer, and Vishny makes clear the importance of increasing returns to scale in the "new ways of making the same old things." Because of larger fixed costs, factory production cannot yield lower unit cost than handicraft production unless the volume of output is sufficiently large. With a closed economy, achieving a large volume of output depends on domestic demand. Murphy, Shleifer, and Vishny argue further that domestic demand is not only a function of average income (and thus average agricultural productivity), but also of the distribution of income. A small group of wealthy plantation owners might generate a demand for sterling silver cooking utensils too small to justify investment in a factory to make them, but the same income spread over a middle class of owner-cultivators may generate a volume of demand for flatware sufficient to support factory production. Thus both high agricultural productivity and a relatively equal distribution of agricultural income promote the introduction of modern manufacturing techniques in place of traditional handicrafts.

Returning to the selection by Lewis, he addresses how the tropical countries fared once they settled into the pattern of development through exports of primary products. He begins by noting that this development attracted immigration of about 50 million people from China and India to work on plantations, in mines, or in construction projects. He argues that the prices of tropical primary products could therefore not rise above the level that supported a Chinese or Indian standard of living, so that export production was not a way out of the trap of low tropical food productivity. This argument assumes that the land needed to grow tropical cash crops was abundant, so that tropical farmers could not get rich from the rent on their land. This assumption does not hold for mineral-bearing lands, but the rents on these lands went to foreign investors. In contrast, the prices of primary product exports such as wool and frozen meat from the temperate countries of recent settlement, Canada, Argentina, Chile, Australia, New Zealand, and South Africa, had to sustain a European standard of living. Lewis's model of relative wage and price determination in the temperate and tropical worlds is presented in detail in Note II.2.

The period of favorable conditions for export-led growth came to an end with World War I, which initiated what Reynolds calls "the longest depression" from 1914–45. Only a handful of countries in Reynolds's sample began intensive growth in this period marked by two world wars and the Great Depression. Following World War II was the period Reynolds calls "the greatest boom," which ended in 1973. Both the initiation of intensive growth in countries including China and India and its continuation in many other countries in Reynolds's sample was now led by industrial production for the home market rather than exports of primary products. Governments played a key role in this change and indeed tended to expand their influence in every sphere of economic life. This part of the Reynolds selection is very wide ranging and provides an excellent background for issues that will be treated in much greater detail in the remaining chapters of this book.

As indicated in section I.B, the role of government has been scaled back in many less developed countries since 1983 when Reynolds wrote his article. Comment II.1 addresses one aspect of this retreat, the privatization of state-owned enterprises.

The delay in the onset of intensive growth in what we now call less developed countries relative to Western Europe, combined with slower intensive growth in many of these countries, led to a huge divergence in per capita incomes between the leading countries and all others. This divergence is documented in the final selection by Lant Pritchett. He estimates that the ratio of per capita income of the 17 richest countries to all others increased from 2.4 in 1870 to 4.6 in 1990.

Selection II.1. The Spread of Economic Growth to the Third World: 1850–1980*

First, I deal only with growth in the simplest sense of capacity to produce. This is not meant to minimize the importance of how the product is distributed. But that is another large subject to include which would have stretched my study entirely too thin.

Second, I have excluded all countries with a 1980 population of less than 10 million people, which excludes about eighty countries at one stroke. Again, this does not mean that small countries are uninteresting, or that they do not differ in significant ways from larger countries. I can plead only the need to spare effort.

The countries included, forty-one in number, are as follows:

Latin America:	Argentina, Brazil, Chile, Colombia, Cuba, Mexico, Peru, Venezuela.
North Africa and Middle East:	Algeria, Egypt, Iran, Iraq, Morocco, Sudan, Turkey.
Africa (sub-Saharan):	Ethiopia, Ghana, Ivory Coast, Kenya, Mozambique, Nigeria, Tanzania, Uganda, Zimbabwe, Zaire, Zambia.
Asia:	Afghanistan, Bangladesh, Burma, China, Indonesia, India, South Korea, Malaysia, Nepal, Pakistan, Philippines, Japan, Sri Lanka, Taiwan, Thailand.

. . . An increase in capacity to produce may be "absorbed" either in population growth, or in a rise of per capita income, or both. A situation in which increased capacity is fully absorbed by population, with no uptrend in per capita income, I define as *extensive growth*. This does not imply that the increase in capacity precedes a "choice" as to how it shall be absorbed. Rather, there is a (largely) exogenous growth of population, which stimulates a growth of productive capacity, initially through cultivation of additional land, often followed by intensification of cultivation methods.

A situation in which capacity to produce is rising appreciably faster than population, so that there is a sustained rise in per capita income, I define as *intensive growth*. . . . The time at which extensive growth turns into intensive growth, a change which is not inevitable and in some countries has not yet occurred, I call the *turning point*. . . .

II. The Era of Extensive Growth

A. Economic Organization

The era in which population and output are growing at about the same rate is a long one. It typically lasts for a century or more, and in some countries has been documented over several centuries.[1] . . .

It is better to say that the economy is dominated at this stage by *household production*. Each family produces not only most of its own food, but most of its housing and clothing, plus a wide range of services—education, healing, recreational activity, religious observance. We commonly observe that at this stage 80 to 90 percent of the population live in rural areas—isolated farms, or small villages close to farmland. This was true in Europe in 1700. The 80 percent ratio is still true in China today. This is sometimes wrongly regarded as indicating the size of the "agricultural sector." All it really means is that most economic activity is family activity. A careful record of time use by rural family members will reveal that agricultural activities take perhaps 50 to 60 percent of the total, the remainder going to "industrial" and service activities.

A corollary is that the apparent shrinkage of the agricultural sector and the expansion of other sectors as economic growth proceeds is partly fictitious. In part, it represents a transfer of household activities to specialized commercial producers whose activities are more readily detected and measured. But people always have clothes and they always have housing, no matter how these goods are produced.

So household production is central during the period of extensive growth. But this is not inconsistent with a substantial amount of marketed out-

---

*From Lloyd G. Reynolds, "The Spread of Economic Growth to the Third World," *Journal of Economic Literature* 21 (September 1983): 941–975. Reprinted by permission.

[1]Some scholars suggest that, for countries now considered developed, the era of extensive growth lasted from about 1500 to 1800 (cf. Maddison, 1982, p. 6).

put, a widespread development of markets, and trade and transport over long distances. Nor is it inconsistent with substantial changes in commodities, techniques, market organization, and trade routes over the course of time. What some might view as a "primitive" economy is, in fact, quite complex, sophisticated, and responsive to change.

As regards West European countries, this view would be readily accepted. It is well known that these economies become increasingly diversified, commercialized, and linked by trade relations during the sixteenth and seventeenth centuries, well before the industrial era. There was substantial development of towns and town markets, extensive development of manufacturing by handicraft methods, substantial interchange of goods between town and country, creeping technical progress in agriculture, internal trade along rivers and canals, overseas trade around the shores of the Mediterranean and the Baltic and North Seas.

There is a tendency, however, to assume that similar statements cannot be made about third-world countries, that their pre-turning point economies were more primitive, static, agriculture-oriented than their European counterparts. As evidence to the contrary, consider first the case of China, as documented by Albert Feuerwerker (1969), Dwight Perkins (1975), Alexander Eckstein (1977), and others. The period before 1949 can be considered one of extensive growth, which had been going on more or less continuously since establishment of the Ming dynasty in 1368. Over the years 1368–1949, the population of the country increased about eight times. Crop acreage increased about four times, while yields per acre doubled. What did the economy look like in these earlier centuries?

Agriculture was central, but far from all-important. Feuerwerker estimates that agricultural output was about two-thirds of national output in the 1880s. This is close to Eckstein's estimate of 65 percent for 1933, suggesting the absence of significant structural change before 1940. Rural *population,* of course, was substantially higher—perhaps 80 percent of the total, as indeed it is today. But the rural population was doing many things other than growing foodstuffs.

"Industry," which at this stage meant handicrafts, produced perhaps 7–8 percent of national output. This work was done overwhelmingly in individual farm households. But there was also co-operative activity by a number of households in rice milling, wheat milling, salt and pottery production; and there were some larger workshops in urban areas. Trading activities constituted another

7–8 percent, and transport perhaps 5 percent of national output. Government in the late nineteenth century was raising in taxes about 7 1/2 percent of national output, a figure not out of line with tax ratios in European countries during the nineteenth century.

Trade was carried on in a stable hierarchy of markets, ranging from local to international in scope. Perhaps three-quarters of total trade went on in some 70,000 basic local markets, in which peasants and handicraftsmen exchanged their surplus produce. This local trade absorbed perhaps 20 percent of total farm output, and this proportion seems not to have changed much over the centuries. Trade was thoroughly monetized and commercialized but restricted in geographic scope.

Longer-distance trade was restricted by transport costs, and involved only objects of sufficient value to warrant the cost. Trade moved mainly along waterways, notably the vast Yangtze network, and by vessels ranging from tiny sampans to large freighters. In North China, less well-supplied with waterways, most goods had to move by carts, which was slow and expensive. It is estimated that only 5–7 percent of national output went into interprovincial trade, and perhaps 1–2 percent into foreign trade. Even by 1900 the trade network had changed only a little at the seacost fringes, and scarcely at all within the country.

The government apparatus which presided over this economic activity was a meritocracy populated by the small educated elite. Perhaps because of the sheer size of the country, provincial and local governments were relatively more important than in smaller countries. Regular (or irregular) tribute was paid to the Emperor, but the Emperor was far away. Even in the 1890s, scholars estimate that only 40 percent of tax revenues went to the central government. Government did little to promote economic growth, but it was adequate for maintenance of the economy at a relatively constant level of per capita output.

A more surprising illustration comes from West Africa. One might visualize the economic organization of this region in pre-colonial times as unusually primitive and culture-bound. But evidence assembled by A. G. Hopkins (1973) suggests that the reality was rather different.

While rural villages predominated, there was also considerable urbanization. For example, Ibadan in the mid nineteenth century had a population of 70,000 and city walls with a circumference of 24 miles. There was much mobility of population, associated mainly with shifting pasturage of livestock and with trading activities. While production occurred mainly within the household there was an active market for non-family labor, though for the most part this was a slave rather than a hired-labor market. (Slaves were preferred because the cost of acquiring and maintaining them was less than the cost of hiring wage labor.)

Agriculture was the basic economic activity, with cereals predominating in the savanna and root crops, which yield more calories per acre, predominating in the forest. The early food crops had come mainly from Asia by way of the Middle East. After the beginnings of European contact many new crops were introduced, especially from South America. Successful innovations included corn, cassava, groundnuts, tobacco, and cocoa. The crops which survived and spread did so for the good reason that the value of output exceeded the cost of production. This responsiveness to change refutes the idea of a static "traditional" economy.

As regards industry, Hopkins (1973, p. 48) notes that "pre-colonial Africa had a range of manufacturing industries which closely resembled that of pre-industrial societies in other parts of the world . . . based on clothing, metal working, ceramics, construction, and food processing." Kano was a major textile center, a kind of Manchester of West Africa. Leather goods were prominent in cattle-raising areas. Pottery production was widely diffused throughout the region. While most of these handicraft activities were smallscale and carried on within family units, they were often regulated by guild rules which any European would have recognized as familiar.

The extensive development of trade and markets should be emphasized, as an offset to stereotypes of purely subsistence production. Local trade was carried on in regular town markets, to which people walked from a radius of ten miles or so, bringing in foodstuffs and carrying back craft products. Nearby towns arranged to rotate their market days to avoid overlapping. Perhaps more surprising, there was a highly organized network of long-distance trade routes, extending as far as from the Lake Chad area to Dakar, and from Kano to the Mediterranean coast. Long-distance trade usually moved in caravans, which individual traders could join for part or all of their journey, and which provided protection from bandits as well as other external economies. There were recognized trade centers along these routes for the assembly, break-up, or re-export of shipments. There was an elaborate system of local agents and commission men, banking and credit facilities, even a code of commercial morality. All in all, there was no lack of economic motivation and business ability. . . .

B. Population and Food Supply

During the era of extensive growth, population is increasing by definition; and this increase begins very early. Durand estimates that population was growing at a low rate almost everywhere in the world from at least 1750 onward (Population Problems, 1967, pp. 136–59). (A possible exception is tropical Africa, for which estimates before 1900 are dubious.) Growth rates were low by modern standards. In Europe, the average growth rate was about 0.7 percent per year from 1800–1850 and 0.8 percent from 1850–1900. Kuznets' estimate for the less developed countries places their average population growth at 0.35 percent from 1800–1850 and 0.56 percent from 1850–1900 (Richard A. Easterlin, 1980, pp. 471–516).

The great killers are famine, war, and plague. Once these are somewhat under control, population tends to grow through a modest excess of births over deaths. At this stage of development, the fertility rate is mainly the result of uncontrolled reproduction. People are not sure that they will be able to have as many surviving children as they would prefer to have. In Easterlin's terminology, the desired number of children, C_d, is greater than the natural fertility rate, C_n; so the former is dominant, and there is no incentive to population control (Tilly, ed. 1978, pp. 57–134).

To speak of a "natural fertility rate" does not imply that this is a universal constant for all countries. Even the uncontrolled birth rate is influenced by such things as: (1) the percentage of women who marry; (2) average age at marriage, which varies presently from around 30 in Ireland to 25 in the United States to 20 in tropical Africa; (3) the rate at which fecundity declines with age; (4) the average interval between births, which is influenced by social factors such as breastfeeding customs and taboos on intercourse during breast feeding, and so may vary from less than two years to more than three years; (5) the probability of husband or wife dying before the end of the childbearing period. Because of these factors, uncontrolled birth rates range from about 35 to 55 per thousand.

The mortality rate is somewhat influenced by economic factors. Famine, traditionally an important cause of death, has been gradually eliminated by reductions in the cost of transporting food within and among countries. More recently, improvements in nutrition, sanitation, and literacy have reduced child mortality from diarrhea and other diseases. To a large extent, however, the determinants of mortality are exogenous, related to the progress of medical science; and this progress is somewhat discontinuous. Techniques developed during the two world wars to reduce mortality among soldiers later proved applicable to civilian populations. Thus after a gradual sag of mortality rates up to 1914, we see a marked drop after 1920 and another marked drop after 1945.

Even during the period of extensive growth one often observes a slight acceleration in the population growth rate. This seems to be due to a (largely exogeneous) secular decline in mortality. Fertility rates fluctuate somewhat with good or bad harvests; but they do not show any marked secular trend during the period of extensive growth.

We have defined extensive growth as a situation in which population growth is matched by growth of national output and in particular of food supply. When we see population growing, how do we know that this second condition is met? The data for some of the larger third-world countries such as Brazil, India, China, and Indonesia have been worked over with considerable care. These studies suggest that food output per capita was either stationary or rising very slowly in the pre-modern period. Usually, however, we have to resort to negative reasoning. *If* population growth had been accompanied by marked deterioration of living standards, one would expect this to have been reported by informed observers. While reports of short-term hardship arising from drought and other natural disasters are common in the literature, reports of a secular decline in living standards are rare. In general, growing populations manage to feed themselves at a near-stationary level.

How is this feat accomplished? Least interesting, though very important historically, is simply extension of the cultivated area. As of 1900, most countries in our sample still had substantial reserves of unused land, which shrank only gradually in succeeding decades. The spreading out of population over a larger area, with at least a proportionate increase in agricultural output, is familiar from experience in "areas of new settlement," such as North America, South America and Australia, and presents no analytical problems.

More interesting is intensification of cultivation, which tends to accompany acreage expansion and becomes dominant when the frontier finally closes. Using length of the fallow period as an intensity indicator, one can lay out a spectrum of cultivation systems, ranging from "slash-and-burn" through bush fallow to short fallow, annual cropping with no fallow period, and multicropping. Ester Boserup (1965 and 1981) has argued persuasively that movement along this spectrum is a normal response to exogenous population growth. The pop-

ulation increase which requires larger food supplies also tends to produce them by bringing about a shift toward more intensive land use. She uses cross-section analysis across countries to test the relation between population density and the cultivation system, with good results.

More intensive cultivation systems, of course, require larger factor inputs per unit of land. Labor inputs present no problem. More mouths to feed are accompanied by more hands to cultivate, reaching a high point in Chinese or Javanese rice-growing, which resembles gardening more than farming. When the soil is no longer allowed to recuperate through fallow periods, larger fertilizer inputs also become necessary—at this stage, mainly organic rather than chemical fertilizer. Multicropping, and even annual cropping in areas of deficient rainfall, typically requires large investments of labor time in drainage and irrigation facilities.

In this way it is possible to raise crop yields *per acre* in the most intensive cultivation systems several times over yields in less intensive systems. Yield *per farm worker* will tend to fall, but perhaps not very much. Shigeru Ishikawa (1981) has made cross-country studies of rice cultivation in which yield per hectare on the vertical axis is charted against available hectares per farm worker on the horizontal axis. The results conform quite closely to a rectangular hyperbola, sometimes called an "Ishikawa curve." Data for the same country, such as Japan or Taiwan, in successive time periods show a similar pattern. A country moves upward to the left along the Ishikawa curve as land availability decreases.

A further possibility is changes in the agricultural product mix. Potatoes and other root crops yield substantially more calories per acre than do most grain crops, and thus a reallocation of land among crops can substantially raise caloric availability. Another way in which densely populated countries adjust is through de-emphasis of livestock production. Boserup finds a strong inverse relation between population density and pasture area/cultivated area and livestock/person ratios. Large animals are a very inefficient way of converting acreage into calories, though pigs and chickens are somewhat more efficient. Densely populated areas tend to get a high proportion of their animal protein from fish.

Several of these possibilities can be illustrated from the experience of China, which has been analyzed by Dwight Perkins (1969). As we noted earlier, over the period 1349–1949 China's population increased about eight times, its cultivated acreage only about four times. But yields per acre roughly doubled, indicating that this "traditional economy" was not immune to technical change. Perkins notes several kinds of change:

i. Some improvement of seeds, partly developed and diffused within China, partly imported from abroad.
ii. Introduction of new crops from America after 1600. Corn and potatoes were especially important, partly because they could be grown in areas not hospitable to other crops. As the frontier gradually closed and the man/land ratio rose after 1850, farmers adjusted to this partly by shifting to crops (including cash crops such as cotton and raw silk) which yielded more food or income per acre and at the same time required more labor for their cultivation.
iii. A gradual extension of double cropping, accompanied by irrigation projects to provide the necessary control of water supply. By 1900 irrigation had been extended to almost all the feasible acreage. Population growth in a sense *produced* more double-cropping by providing more labor both for seasonal peaks of cultivation and for water-control projects.
iv. An increase of inputs, notably fertilizer inputs. More people produced more nightsoill. So did more pigs, whose numbers apparently kept up with population growth. Perkins suggests that without this side-benefit, pork production would have been unprofitable.

This is not meant to suggest that adaptation of agriculture to population growth was entirely painless. But the possibilities of adaptation, even in pre-modern times, were apparently greater than one might have anticipated.

C. The Non-Agricultural Sectors

Industrial output grows along with population and agricultural output; and there is a gradual shift in the locus of manufacturing activity from the household to specialized workshops and cottage industry. Since clothing is a major consumer good, textiles tend to take the lead in this process. The "putting-out system," in which a merchant supplies materials to home spinners and weavers and then collects and markets their product, is familiar to readers of European economic history; but it was by no means confined to that continent. Quite similar systems existed in China, India, and many other third-world countries. In addition to textiles, one typically finds an array of other handicraft industries supplying household necessities.

Handicraft production in turn gives way eventually to factory production, with textiles and raw materials processing in the lead. Handicraft products are often forced to compete first with imported factory goods, and later on with the output of domestic factories. Whether factory production appears during the period of extensive growth depends on the era we are discussing. In the substantial number of countries which reached the turning point before 1900, factories were almost absent at the turning point, and did not become important for five or six decades thereafter. This is why, for these countries, it is wrong to take the onset of industrialization as marking the beginning of intensive growth. But when we come to the years 1900–1950, by which time modern industrial techniques were increasingly well known throughout the world, we find considerable industrial development in countries such as Egypt, Turkey, India, and China which were still in the extensive growth phase. And since 1950 efforts to initiate intensive growth have been strongly identified with forced-draft industrial development.

Even during the extensive growth period the economy has trade relations with other countries, typically exchanging primary products for manufactured consumer goods. The volume of trade grows along with the size of the economy, but it may not grow any faster. A marked rise in the export/GNP ratio occurs only after the turning point—indeed, we rely heavily on this ratio in dating the turning point.

Governmental systems varied widely among the three continents we are discussing. In Latin America, the first half-century of independence was a period of nation-building. While Brazil's transition to independence was relatively peaceful, in most other countries there was a prolonged period of civil wars among rival factions of the élite. Not until around 1850, and in some countries not until around 1880, did stable governments emerge. These were oligarchies, with a change of regime meaning replacement of one élite group by another; but there was enough continuity and domestic order to permit expansion of private economic activity. In Asia, most of the countries in our sample were colonies, though China, Thailand, and the Ottoman Empire remained independent. . . .

In Africa, while there were a few substantial kingdoms, political units were generally small and fragmented along tribal lines. The "countries" which emerged with the partition of Africa among the European powers in the late nineteenth century were synthetic creations lacking any natural legitimacy in the eyes of the population; and the fragility of these creations may be partly responsible for relatively poor African performance since independence.

Nineteenth-century governments, whether indigenous or colonial, collected only a small percentage of national income, mainly from head taxes, land taxes, and trade taxes. Expenditures were mainly for the Army, the civil service, and consumption of the ruling group, with little remaining for economic or social purposes. But there was some building of roads, railroads, ports and warehouses for trade and military purposes. Interestingly enough, some colonial governments were more active on this front than were most independent countries. . . .

D. The Question of Preconditions

To what extent can developments during the period of extensive growth be regarded as a preparation for, or a pre-requisite for, the turning-point to intensive growth?

. . . Important conditioning factors during the period of extensive growth include: (1) nation-building, which in many countries is a recent and precarious process, still going on with varying degrees of success; (2) small technical changes which add up to what we might call "the importance of the unconspicuous"; (3) changes in crops, water control systems, and cultivation methods which enable food output to at least keep up with population, and which lay a foundation for eventually leaping ahead of population; (4) gradual reduction of transport costs and extension of long-distance trade; (5) growth of manufacturing production outside the household, or even within the household through the "putting-out system."

These factors are perhaps especially important for countries which have *recently* embarked on intensive growth, and which had a long prior exposure to the world economy. For example, India in 1947 had a tradition of national unity and democratic government, a well-staffed civil service, a substantial educational system, much physical infrastructure, a long tradition of handicraft manufacturing, and the beginnings of factory industry, notably in textiles. Some of these things could be said also of China, Pakistan, Egypt, Turkey, and other recent developers. They were taking off, not from a situation of stagnation, but from an economy already visibly in motion. . . .

III. The Turning Point

The striking fact which emerges from Table 1 is that about two-thirds of the countries which have

Table 1. A Turning-point Chronology

1840	Chile	1900	Cuba
1850	Brazil	1910	Korea
1850	Malaysia	1920	Morocco
1850	Thailand	1925	Venezuela
1860	Argentina	1925	Zambia
1870	Burma	1947	India
1876	Mexico	1947	Pakistan
1880	Algeria	1949	China
1880	Japan	1950	Iran
1880	Peru	1950	Iraq
1880	Sri Lanka	1950	Turkey
1885	Colombia	1952	Egypt
1895	Taiwan	1965	Indonesia
1895	Chana	—	Afghanistan
1895	Ivory Coast	—	Bangladesh
1895	Nigeria	—	Ethiopia
1895	Kenya	—	Mozambique
1900	Uganda	—	Nepal
1900	Zimbabwe	—	Sudan
1900	Tanzania	—	Zaire
1900	Philippines		

thus far achieved a turning point (22 out of 34) had done so by around 1900. The years 1900–1945 are a "hollow period," during which only four countries appear on the list. After 1945 the procession speeds up again, with eight countries reaching the turning point soon thereafter. We shall argue that this chronology stems from three major epochs in the world economy, which will be reviewed briefly.

(1) *World economic boom, 1850–1914.* It is clear in retrospect that this era was unusually favorable to world-wide diffusion of economic growth. Output in the early developing countries of Europe and North America was rising rapidly, and with it their demand for imports of primary products. Kuznets (1966) estimates the median growth rate of output in these countries from 1860–1914 at about 3 percent per year, which meant median growth of about 2 percent a year in per capita terms.

Rapid economic growth in Europe and North America opened up the possibility of enlarged trade with other continents. But this possibility could scarcely have been realized without an improvement and cheapening of transport. This involved replacement of sailing ships by steam-driven steel ships, which reduced ocean freight rates by 1913 to about 30 percent of their 1870 level; a world-wide railroad boom, which peaked in the years 1870–1914, and which produced even more spectacular reductions in overland transport costs; and building of a worldwide telegraph network linking would-be sellers and buyers. Completion of the Suez Canal in 1869 was a particularly important development for Asian countries trading with Europe.

Available estimates of growth in the volume of international trade have been analyzed by Kuznets (1967). They show the sum of exports and imports growing at an average rate of 50.3 percent per decade from 1850–1880, and 39.5 percent per decade from 1881–1913. The ratio of world trade to world output was thus rising quite rapidly. Kuznets estimates that this ratio had reached 33 percent by 1913.

Trade was of course dominated by the countries of Europe and North America, which accounted for about three-quarters of combined exports and imports. Latin America, Africa, and Asia accounted for about 20 percent of trade in 1876–1880 and 22 percent in 1913, not far from their proportion in recent decades. The implication is that third-world countries were keeping up with the general pace of world trade. This is confirmed by the investigations of Lewis (1969), who finds that the volume of tropical exports grew at 3.6 percent per year from 1883–1913. Agricultural exports grew a bit slower than this, but mineral exports grew faster. Indeed, during this period total exports from the tropical countries grew at almost exactly the same rate as industrial production in the advanced countries. While terms of trade between primary products and manufactures show short-term fluctuations, Lewis (1970) concludes that there was no appreciable trend over the period as a whole.

The third-world countries which embarked on intensive growth during this period fall into three groups: (a) all of the Latin American countries in our sample with the exception of Venezuela. The turning point dates in most cases mark the beginning of political stability after the prolonged civil wars which followed independence. Growth was invariably export-led, the nature of the exports varying from case to case. Argentina and Chile were able to grow and export wool, wheat, meat, and other temperate-zone products. Brazil relied on tropical products, initially sugar with coffee becoming dominant from the 1840s onward. Coffee also dominated the early export trade of Colombia. Minerals were important in Chile—at first nitrates, later copper. Minerals dominated Mexico's nineteenth-century exports, though agricultural products, cattle, and timber grew gradually in importance. Peru also had a combination of agricultural and mineral exports. Cuba was a sugar island. But everywhere exports, directed mainly toward European and North American markets, were the key to economic expansion.

(b) Four of the Asian countries which were drawn into the world export boom lie in an arc from Ceylon through Burma and Malaya to Thailand. Their turning points can be dated generally from the 1850s, though Ceylon had large and growing coffee exports from the 1830s onward. In Burma and Thailand a rising flow of rice exports came mainly from peasant producers expanding into uncultivated land, a pattern to be repeated later in West Africa. In Malaya the early export product was tin, produced mainly by relatively small entrepreneurs of Chinese origin, but by 1900 rubber had emerged as a second major product. Ceylon's exports came initially from large foreign-owned plantations—coffee plantations from 1830–1970, tea plantations after the coffee trees had been ruined by plant disease. Toward the end of the century, however, smallholder production of coconuts, rubber, and other crops became increasingly important, and by 1913 the export list was quite diversified.

Next there is the case of Japan, which did not appear unusual at the time, and which seems exceptional in retrospect only because of that country's ability to sustain and accelerate its growth rate over the subsequent century. This case is so well documented that details would be superfluous. But it is worth noting that Japan, like the other countries listed, showed a consistently strong export performance. Exports plus imports were about 10 percent of GNP in the 1870s, but had risen to 30 percent by 1910–1913. Over the years 1881–1914, Japanese exports grew about twice as rapidly as world exports. Up to 1900 this is mainly the story of raw silk, after 1900 mainly the story of cotton textiles.

To round out the Asian experience, Taiwan was ceded to Japan after China's defeat in the Sino-Japanese war of 1894–1895; and Japan set out energetically to turn the island into a rice bowl for the home country. The Philippines passed under American control after Spain's defeat in the Spanish-American War of 1898. There followed a period of rapid export-led growth, dominated by sugar and aided by a preferential trade agreement with the United States.

(c) Toward the end of the century several areas of Africa were drawn into the intensive growth process. Algeria in North Africa; Nigeria, Ghana, and Ivory Coast in West Africa; Kenya, Uganda, and Tanganyika in East Africa; and Southern Rhodesia (Zimbabwe) in Central Africa. To speak of these as "countries" is to speak of colonial creations. Europeans drew the boundaries, established unified administration over numerous tribal areas, and created an impression of nationhood which, while it took on some substance over the years, was never as strong as in the ancient kingdoms of Asia.

Most of the Asian and Latin American countries mentioned participated in the pre-1914 boom for periods of forty to sixty years. The new African colonies were latecomers, who participated for a generation or less. They nevertheless got in on the tail-end of the boom. Their exports rose sharply up to 1914; and this gave them an initial momentum which they never entirely lost. Wheat, fruits, and wine from Algeria; palm products, cocoa, coffee, and timber from West Africa; cereals from Kenya, cotton from Uganda, sisal and coffee from Tanganyika; cereals, gold, and other minerals from Southern Rhodesia—all flowed into international trade in growing volume. Exports from Ghana, Nigeria, Ivory Coast, and Uganda came almost entirely from African smallholders, who brought additional land under cultivation in the pattern observed earlier in Southeast Asia. In Algeria, Kenya, and Southern Rhodesia, on the other hand, substantial white settlements created dualistic economies in which most of the exports came from European-owned farms.

(2) *The Longest Depression, 1914–1945.* This phrase, borrowed from Lewis (1978a), is adequately descriptive. It was a bleak period for the world economy, marked by two world wars, the Great Depression, and a marked slowdown in the growth of world production and trade. The growth rate of industrial production in the "developed" countries fell from 3.6 percent in 1883–1913 to 2.7 percent in 1913–1929 and 1.3 percent in 1929–1938. This is significant in view of Lewis' finding that the growth rate of primary exports from tropical countries is closely related to growth of industrial production in the advanced economies. And in fact the growth rate of tropical exports fell from 3.7 percent per year in 1883–1913 to 3.2 percent in 1913–1929 and 1.9 percent in 1929–1937. This decline in export volume was accompanied by a mild sagging of primary products' terms of trade against manufactures even before 1929, and a sharp drop after 1929. The import capacity of third-world countries was sharply reduced.

Under these depressed conditions, countries which had been growing quite rapidly before 1914 now grew more slowly. It is significant, too, that only four additional countries reached the turning

point during this period, and these cases can be attributed to special circumstances. Korea was formally taken over by Japan in 1910 and, as in the earlier case of Taiwan, Japan set about to develop the country as an auxiliary to the Japanese economy. A French protectorate was established in Morocco in 1912 as part of a deal among the European powers, and effective control over most of the territory had been gained by 1920. Here, as earlier in Algeria, French settlers in effect implanted a new "modern" economy on top of the indigenous economy, initiating a growth process whose benefits went disproportionately to the Europeans.

In Venezuela, which had remained a stagnant backwater dominated by military dictators and an agricultural oligarchy, the discovery of oil in the early twenties set off a rapid transformation of both the economy and the political structure. Venezuela was the first great oil exporter and remains a key member of OPEC, which it took the initiative in founding in the 1960s. In Zambia (then Northern Rhodesia), rich copper deposits began to be exploited by foreign-owned companies in the late twenties. While these properties have now passed from foreign to national ownership, copper remains a dominant factor in the economy.

(3) *The Greatest Boom, 1945–1973.* The evolution of the world economy during this period is still fresh in mind and can be reviewed very briefly. The years 1945–1973 saw an unprecedented boom in world production and trade, a "second golden age" with growth rates well above those of the "first golden age" of 1870–1914. The average annual growth rate of GNP in the OECD countries from 1950–1973 was 4.9 percent, compared with an 1870–1913 average of 2.5 percent and a 1913–1950 figure of 1.9 percent. These high output rates, plus reduction of trade barriers, plus continued reduction of transport costs (supertankers, container ships, jet aircraft, great expansion of road mileage and truck transport) produced an even faster growth in the volume of inter-national trade. Angus Maddison (1982) shows the export volume of the OECD countries rising at 8.6 percent per year from 1950–1973. Thus export/GNP ratios rose substantially.

Exports from third-world countries, while still growing rapidly by historical standards, grew somewhat less rapidly than developed country exports, so that their percentage of world exports fell from 25.3 percent to 17.7 percent. There was some diversification of the export mix. Manufactured goods formed only 7.6 percent of third-world exports in 1955, but by 1970 this had risen to 16.7

percent (and the percentage was to double again by 1980). Meanwhile exports of foodstuffs had fallen from 36.7 percent to 26.5 percent of the total, reflecting not only demand constraints but also increasing domestic food consumption associated with population growth and rising per capita incomes. The great grain-surplus areas are now the United States, Canada, Australia, and Europe. Thus the old distinction between "developed" exporters of manufacturers and "less developed" exporters of primary products has become increasingly blurred. The terms of trade between primary products and manufactures show no marked trend over the period 1945–1973. . . . Eight additional countries reached the turning point in the 1950–1980 period; and this includes the two Asian giants, China and India, plus Pakistan and Indonesia. In both China and undivided India one could make a case for a slight rise in per capita income from 1900–1940. But the increase, if present at all, is so slight that in our judgment the turning point for India and Pakistan should be dated from independence in 1947, and for China from the revolution of 1949.

Four additional countries—Egypt, Turkey, Iraq and Iran—lie in an arc across the Middle East. There is some ambiguity about the correct dating for these countries. They experienced some political and economic modernization from the 1920s onward. But the 1929 depression and the 1939 war followed so soon afterwards that they had scarcely made a significant beginning before 1945. It seems most reasonable, then, to locate their turning points in the postwar period.

The case of Indonesia is also complex and somewhat ambiguous. Exports from Indonesia rose from 1880–1930 at a quite respectable rate. But to an unusual degree these exports came from foreign-owned mines and plantations, and a large share of the proceeds remained in foreign hands. Particularly in densely-populated Java, the benefits to the local population seem to have been meagre. As a matter of judgment, then, we prefer to locate Indonesia's turning point after the achievement of independence. Even then, GNP per capita did not begin to rise perceptibly until the overthrow of President Sukarno and installation of the present regime in the mid-sixties.

(4) *Some Laggards.* We note finally that seven countries in our sample remain in the phase of extensive growth and show no sign of a sustained rise in per capita income. These countries are Afghanistan, Nepal, Bangladesh, Ethiopia, Sudan, Mozambique, and Zaire. There does not seem to

be any single reason for their failure to achieve intensive growth. This failure results rather from varying combinations of geographic remoteness (Afghanistan, Nepal, most of Ethiopia, Zaire, and Sudan), absence of transport facilities and other infrastructure (all seven countries except Bangladesh), internal political turmoil (absent only in Nepal and post-1970 Sudan), colonial authorities who fled the country with no real preparation for independence (Mozambique, Zaire), primitive governments (Afghanistan, Ethiopia, Nepal), and massive misgovernment (Zaire). . . .

IV. Intensive Growth: Then and Now

. . . In the long era before 1940 the early developing countries followed a broadly similar growth pattern, which we shall try to characterize. The years after 1945 brought substantial changes in the political and economic setting. Countries which had reached the turning point before 1940 continued to grow, usually at an accelerated rate, but with significant changes in the growth pattern. Further, countries reaching the turning point after 1945 set off on a somewhat different course from the outset.

A. Intensive Growth Before 1940.

(1) *Population and food supply.* Nineteenth-century population growth rates were low, typically below one percent. Kuznets estimates the average rate of population increase in third-world countries at only about 0.6 percent per year from 1850–1900 (Easterlin, ed., 1980, pp. 471–516). There was some acceleration after 1920, however, due mainly to a reduction of mortality rates associated with medical progress, Kuznets' estimate of average third-world population growth in the twenties is 1.3 percent.

Growing population and rising per capita income imply growing demand for food, at a rate which can be estimated from income elasticities of demand. Closed-economy growth models typically suggest that, unless food output rises at the minimum required rate, the internal terms of trade will turn in favor of agriculture. Rising food prices will put upward pressure on money wage rates, and this will choke off industrial growth in Ricardian fashion. In actual open economies, however, the situation is different. A country with flourishing exports of oil, minerals, timber, rubber, cotton, or whatever can trade these products for food, thus relaxing the domestic food supply constraint.

Pre-1940 experience in this respect is mixed.

Many countries, perhaps most, did manage to keep food output rising in line with the moderate growth of demand. This was done mainly by extending the cultivated area. Crop yields usually did not change significantly, though extension of irrigation and multiple-cropping raised yields in Egypt and China, while improved seeds and other technical changes did so in Japan, Taiwan, and Korea.

What is rather surprising is how many countries fell into the habit of trading non-food exports for food imports, allowing not only the absolute volume of imports but the imported percentage of domestic consumption to rise over time. Notable examples were Chile, Peru, Mexico, Venezuela, Sri Lanka, Burma, Malaysia, Egypt, Iraq, and Iran. This could in some cases be regarded as a sensible exploitation of comparative advantage. But the main explanation seems to be government inattention to agriculture. Where government did have an active agricultural policy, as in Japan and its colonies, good results were achieved despite serious land constraints.

(2) *Manufacturing*. The development of manufacturing after the turning point follows a standard pattern, as regards both organization of production and type of product. As agricultural production becomes more labor-absorbing and more profitable, and as manufactures can be purchased from outside on more favorable terms, the rural family sheds some of its goods-producing functions and passes them over to specialized producers. Indeed, not only goods production but production of many services—education, healing, religion, dispute settlement—tends to move outside the family, which becomes more strictly a producer of *agricultural* goods rather than a multi-purpose producer of everything.

The manufacturing activities displaced from the household are taken over in the first instance by individual artisans and small-scale "rural industries." In almost every country this was the dominant form of manufacturing organization throughout the period we are considering. Opening of the economy to trade, of course, means that these local industries are early forced to compete with factory-made imports. But even in India, often cited as the classic case, and also in Southeast Asia and elsewhere, the extent of "handicraft destruction" has often been exaggerated. It was most pronounced in textiles, and especially in spinning, where the factory's technical superiority is very large. It was notably less in other goods, particularly heavy or bulky goods where transport costs provide some natural protection. Costs of inland transport also meant that

import competition was most severe in port cities, less so in the interior. The typical outcome was that handicraft production continued to grow, but at a rate below that of domestic consumption, so that the imported *share* of total supply rose.

As imports penetrate and reveal the market, this leads in time to initiation of local factory production. But time is required. The prospective market must be large enough to absorb the output of at least one plant of minimum efficient size. And even then, capital and entrepreneurship does not appear automatically. There is typically a lag, often of forty or fifty years, between the beginning of intensive growth and the appearance of large factories with power-driven equipment. Even in the Latin American countries, with relatively high per capita income and independent governments able to levy tariffs, factory industry was still very limited as of 1900. By 1940 it was more substantial; and an initial manufacturing base had been established also in India, China, Taiwan, Korea, and the Philippines. In most of the African countries, however, as well as in Sri Lanka, Burma, Malaysia, and Thailand, factory industry was virtually absent. For the third world as a whole, handicraft production must still have provided more than half of manufacturing output, and much more than half of manufacturing employment.

As regards type of product, textiles are normally the leading sector, because clothing is a basic need and the potential market is large. Further, the capacity to produce cotton and other fibers is widely distributed throughout the world, so that domestic raw materials are usually available. In addition to an assured domestic demand—often demonstrated initially by large cloth imports—the emergence of textiles is facilitated by relatively small minimum efficient scale of plant, a well-known technology, ready availability of used as well as new textile machinery, and limited requirements of skilled labor.

Other early industries are concerned mainly with agricultural processing for home use or for export—rice mills, flour mills, sawmills, palm oil extraction, and so on. These are followed by light consumer goods industries such as shoes, clothing, beverages, leather goods, ceramics, furniture, and household utensils, as well as building materials and simple agricultural implements. As the market continues to grow, additional industries appear in a sequence charted by Walther Hoffman (1958) and Hollis Chenery (1960, 1979). "Middle industries" such as chemicals and petroleum products appear, followed eventually by "late" or heavy-goods industries, dominated by metals, machinery, and transport equipment.

As of 1940 most third-world countries had proceeded only a short distance through this sequence. Most were at the stage of raw material processing, with at most a small development of textiles. Even the dozen or so more industrialized countries were producing mainly finished consumer goods, with capital goods and intermediates forming only a small percentage of manufacturing output.

(3) *The foreign sector.* Little need be added to what was said about exports in earlier sections. Typically, exports rose considerably faster than population or national output. During the 1850–1914 era, countries which had reached the turning point had population growth rates somewhat below 1 percent, GNP growth rates of perhaps 2 to 3 percent, but export growth of 3 to 4 percent, and occasionally even higher. From 1914–1945, output and export growth rates were lower; and there were also large short-term fluctuations associated with war and depression.

The largest import items were usually foodstuffs and cotton cloth, with other consumer goods making up most of the balance. Except for railroad equipment and other infrastructure requirements, capital goods imports were usually small, though by 1920–1940 industrial development in some Latin American countries was far enough along to require substantial machinery imports.

Private capital (mainly British and French up to 1914, with the United States prominent after 1920) flowed to these countries through several channels. The British were the main railroad builders all over the world, providing not only finance but physical equipment and engineering and construction skills, often followed by ownership and management of the completed lines. There was substantial direct investment in mineral exploitation and plantation agriculture. There was also private portfolio investment, particularly in Latin American government securities. Little foreign capital went into manufacturing, which was largely indigenous as regards both financing and entrepreneurship. When we say "indigenous," of course, we must recall the prominence of ethnic Chinese entrepreneurs throughout Southeast Asia. There were also foreign-owned manufacturing firms—Japanese and British textile mills in China, American firms in Cuba and the Philippines, British firms in India and other colonial areas. But these were rarely dominant. The textile and steel pioneers in India were Indians, not British.

(4) *The public sector.* The years before 1940 were an era of small government. Colonial administrations typically raised perhaps 5 percent of GNP through readily collectible trade and excise taxes, and spent the proceeds on a limited array of public services—roads, urban streets and sewerage, a small development of primary education and health facilities, a police force. But independent governments in Latin America and elsewhere were scarcely more enterprising. It is doubtful that the public goods/GNP percentage was higher in these countries than in the colonies. It is doubtful also that there was an uptrend in this percentage before 1914, with perhaps a slight uptrend from 1914–1940.

Government was more active as regards capital formation, particularly railroad building. Colonial administrators typically floated loans for this purpose in the home market, committing the colony to meet interest and principal repayments from tax revenue. Latin American governments also took the initiative in financing railroad building in one way or another—issuing government bonds, guaranteeing private bond issues, occasionally giving land concessions to the railroad companies. . . .

B. The Post-1945 Environment and Some Consequences

The years around 1945 mark a watershed in several respects:

i. About half the countries in our sample were decolonized and became independent countries.

ii. There was a marked change of political climate in most parts of the world, with much more emphasis on the economic functions of government. Economic growth was no longer something that happened or failed to happen, but something to be planned and promoted.

iii. The pace of scientific and technical progress quickened, especially in the fields of medicine and agriculture, accompanied by improved channels for diffusion of technical progress.

iv. There was a marked increase in the flow of capital from richer to poorer countries. In the first instance this was mainly "official" capital flowing through government-to-government channels; but private long-term investment and commercial bank lending grew in relative importance over the course of time.

v. Finally, there was the unprecedented growth of output and trade in the "developed" countries, which did more than any other single factor to generate rapid growth in the third world.

This changed environment, as suggested earlier, had two kinds of consequence: countries which were growing before 1940 tended to grow faster, but along somewhat different lines; and, in countries which reached the turning point only after 1945, intensive growth showed a somewhat different pattern than that followed by early developers. The growth of Pakistan from 1950–1980 looks more like Brazil from 1950–1980 than like Brazil from 1850–1900. These points can best be explained through a sector-by-sector review.

(1) *Population and food supply.* There was substantial technical progress before and during World War II in anti-insect chemicals, antibiotics, and other branches of medical science. After 1945 these new techniques were disseminated rapidly by the World Health Organization and national aid agencies, at low or zero cost to the recipient countries. The result was a striking decline in mortality rates, even in the poorest countries, and a corresponding rise in rates of natural increase. The Kuznets estimates for all third-world countries cited earlier show the average rate of natural increase rising from 1.3 percent in 1920–1930 to 2.0 percent in 1950–1955 and 2.6 percent in 1970–1975. The average crude death rate fell from 31 per thousand in 1937 to 16 per thousand in 1970–1975.

It is worth noting that a number of third-world countries already show signs of retracing the demographic pattern observed earlier in the "developed" countries, in which the birth rate follows the death rate downward with a considerable lag. Indeed, twenty-four of our forty countries show a significant drop in the crude birth rate between 1960 and 1980. Drops of 10 points or more have occurred in

Brazil (43–30) Colombia (46–30)

Chile (37–22) Peru (47–36)

Venezuela (46–35) Cuba (32–18)

South Korea (43–24) Taiwan (40–21)

Philippines (46–34) Indonesia (46–35)

Thailand (44–30) Malaysia (45–31)

Turkey (43–32)

Declines of 8 points have occurred in Mexico and India. China's energetic population control program is said to have achieved substantial success. Even if these declines continue, however, the eventual steady state population numbers projected by demographers are startlingly large.

Higher population growth rates since 1945 mean that required rates of food output growth are now considerably higher. At the same time reserves of uncultivated land are smaller, and in China and South Asia are virtually zero. Governments have become more active in agriculture, but this activity has often taken unfavorable forms. The post-1950 tendency to regard industrialization as the key to growth has led in many countries to trade and exchange policies which turned the internal terms of trade sharply against agriculture. A desire to ensure cheap food for industrial workers and other city people has often led to farm price controls which discouraged production. Experiments with socialized agriculture, a tenure form not favorable to high productivity, have disorganized production in some countries.

The most encouraging postwar development has been rapid technical progress in rice, wheat, corn, and a number of other crops. Countries which have moved energetically to incorporate these developments in their agricultural systems have been able to achieve remarkable yield increases within a few years. It is probably fair to say also that, in most countries, government policies were more favorable to agriculture in the seventies than in the fifties. The glitter of rapid industrialization is somewhat tarnished, the importance of agricultural output is more widely appreciated, and the requirements for agricultural progress are better understood.

Country performance since 1950 has been variable. Countries which have done outstandingly well, with increases of 30 to 60 percent in *per capita* food output between the early fifties and 1980, are Brazil, Mexico, Malaysia, Taiwan, Thailand, Sri Lanka, and Venezuela. India and China have achieved a slight gain in per capita output despite population pressure and land scarcity. Of the remaining 32 countries in our sample, 17 show a modest increase in per capita output over the period, the median increase being about 15 percent. But the other 15 countries have been falling behind, showing a median *decrease* of 15 percent in food output per capita. It is not surprising that there is a marked relation between agricultural performance and overall economic performance. Of the twelve countries which rank lowest in terms of 1950–1980 GNP growth rate, ten also show a decline in food output per capita. Eight of these countries are in Africa, the others being Afghanistan and Nepal.

(2) *The public sector.* Economic growth before 1940 was largely private enterprise growth, though

government's infrastructure contribution was usually substantial. But since 1945, private enterprise in most third-world countries has been in retreat. Public ownership, government regulation, economic planning, and the welfare state are in vogue. This world-wide tendency has been reinforced in some countries by nationalist sentiment. Where many of the private enterprisers are foreigners (and in Southeast Asia, even Chinese long resident in the country are "foreigners," as are Indians in East Africa), while the indigenous population controls the government, transferring economic activities from foreign to indigenous control is naturally interpreted as requiring transfer to government control.

This increased prominence of government takes several forms:

i. A marked rise in the public consumption share of GNP. We suggested earlier that before 1940 this share may have averaged 5 percent. By 1980 the median for countries in our sample was 15 percent, and a half-dozen countries were already in the 20–25 percent range. There are several reasons for this uptrend. Partly because of international demonstration effects, there has been insistent public demand for expansion of education, health facilities, housing and urban amenities, and other public services; and independent governments are under stronger pressure to respond to these demands than were the colonial administrators. Some countries have chosen the popular course of subsidizing urban food consumption and, more recently, consumption of petroleum products. There has been a tendency toward over-staffing and over-payment of government employees, again understandable on political grounds. And some countries have continued to enlarge their military establishments, which often control the government.

ii. A marked increase in public ownership of economic activities, extending beyond infrastructure to mining, manufacturing, finance, and trade. The reasons, in addition to ideological and nationalistic considerations, include the vogue of industrialization in the fifties and sixties, and the urge to launch large new enterprises in a situation where government seemed best able to mobilize the necessary investment funds. Rapid, government-propelled industrialization was preferred to the slower pace which would have resulted from relying on private initiative and finance.

iii. A marked increase in government investment expenditure. GDCF/GNP ratios have risen substantially, and in most countries of our sample now exceed 20 percent. Government is typically responsible for half or more of national capital formation, and its capital expenditures often rival current expenditures in size. Accelerated economic growth has increased the need for investment in roads, electric power, and other infrastructure facilities; and in addition government is typically the main source of finance for manufacturing investment.

iv. A tendency toward increasingly complex regulation of private economic activity. In addition to foreign trade and exchange controls, one finds licensing systems for new private enterprises, price controls for farm products, government marketing systems for these products, urban price controls sometimes accompanied by rationing, interest rate and wage rate regulations, and much else besides. In the best cases, this reflects an effort at coherent economic planning. But in many cases it comes closer to random interventionism, which can scarcely promote growth. In some countries, too, the structure of public administration is incapable of enforcing the complex controls, and private initiative reasserts itself through smuggling, black marketing, and other evasions of control.

(3) *Manufacturing.* All of the late developing countries except Indonesia and Pakistan already had by 1950 a modest base of factory industry developed during the period of extensive growth. India and China, in particular, had sizeable textile industries dating from the nineteenth century, as well as the beginnings of light consumer goods and engineering industries. Several of the early developers, too, had a substantial industrial base by 1950, including Argentina, Brazil, Chile, Mexico, Egypt, and the Philippines. In many other countries, however, and particularly in Africa, handicrafts greatly predominated, and factory industry was starting almost from zero.

One would have expected the high growth rate of per capita income after 1950 to stimulate industrial growth. It is well documented that, as per capita income rises, both the broader "industrial" share and the narrower manufacturing share of GNP increase steadily. Both import substitution and growth of domestic consumption contribute to this result. Chenery's (1960) analysis yields "growth elasticities" with respect to per capita income of 1.31 for consumer goods output, 1.50 for intermediate goods, and 2.16 for capital goods. Import substitution accounts for most of the relative increase in output of investment goods and intermediate goods. For consumer goods, on the other hand, growth of final demand is the dominant factor.

Manufacturing output did in fact grow rapidly in most countries, substantially raising its share of GNP. In 1950, the median manufacturing share in the countries of our sample was a bit below 10 percent. By 1980 the median had risen to 16 percent and twelve countries were in the 20–30 percent range, that is, approaching the structure characteristic of "developed countries." This group includes the major Latin American countries plus Egypt, Turkey, Sri Lanka, Philippines, Taiwan, South Korea, and China. In addition, India, Pakistan, and Thailand were only slightly below the 20 percent level. The data also show the expected shift toward heavier types of industry. In most of the growing economies of Asia and Latin America, though not in Africa, import substitution in consumer goods is now substantially complete—indeed, a half-dozen countries have substantial *exports* of consumer goods. Except in China and Brazil, import substitution in intermediates and capital goods is less far along, many countries still importing one-third to two-thirds of their requirements.

During the fifties and sixties manufacturing was the fair-haired child of most third-world governments. In addition to mobilizing capital for manufacturing investment and building supporting infrastructure, governments promoted industrialization by familiar techniques—high rates of effective protection, often accompanied by quantitative import restrictions; foreign exchange licensing and an overvalued exchange rate; preferential treatment in imports of materials and machinery; preferential access to capital through government lending institutions; a variety of tax holidays and tax rates for new industries; and pegging of interest rates at low, even negative, levels. These policies often involved substantial resource costs in terms of ill-conceived projects, implicit taxation of agriculture which discouraged farm production, and discrimination against exports. As this became evident, some countries moved from the early sixties onward toward a more outward-looking policy stance, involving trade and exchange policies which were more nearly neutral as between exports and import-substituting activities, plus higher interest rates and more realistic and flexible exchange rates. Notable examples are Brazil, Colombia, Taiwan, South Korea, Pakistan, and (recently) Sri Lanka. The growing efficiency of manufacturing industries in these countries, and their increasing success in export markets, can be traced partly to this policy shift.

The question of how far post-1950 manufacturing growth was a "normal" response to growth of domestic markets, and how far it was accelerated by government promotional efforts, would need to be examined country by country. Overall, my impression is that the effect of market expansion may have been underestimated in the literature, while the effect of promotional policies may have been overstated, especially in view of the fact that these policies had negative as well as positive effects.

An important aspect of post-1950 manufacturing expansion is the marked increase in the public-sector share of assets and output. Before 1940, third-world manufacturing industries were almost entirely in private hands. Since 1950, in most countries, government has not only been the main source of industrial finance through government investment banks, commercial banks, and direct budget allocations, but has gone beyond this to ownership and management of manufacturing establishments. The public-sector share of manufacturing is often 20 to 25 percent, and sometimes reaches 75 to 80 percent. The reasons vary from country to country: a long-standing statist tradition, as in Turkey and other remnants of the Ottoman Empire; socialist ideology of the British Labor Party type, as in India; a desire to transfer industry from foreign to national ownership, which tended to be interpreted as public ownership, as in Egypt or Burma; and a perhaps natural tendency for government investment banks to acquire majority equity ownership and thus responsibility for management, as in Mexico or Brazil.

In most countries, however, the private manufacturing sector, even when discriminated against by public policy, has enough vitality to remain important; and in perhaps half of our countries it is predominant. Multinational investment is important in a few of the most industrialized countries. But in general local entrepreneurship predominates, with capital being accumulated in classical fashion by reinvestment of earnings.

In most countries the structure of manufacturing remains quite dualistic. There is a strong persistence of small-scale industry, in the face of policies which usually discriminate against it; and even a marked persistence of handicraft activity in the countryside. There are still many countries in which handicraft and small-scale industries provide more than half of manufacturing employment, though a considerably smaller share of manufacturing output and capital stock. This very gradual replacement of the old by the new is not unlike what was happening a century ago.

(4) *The foreign sector.* Exports continue to be an

important part of the growth story. In most countries of our sample exports form 20 percent or more of GNP. In most countries, too, the export GNP ratio was stable or rising from 1950–1980. Exceptions include India, Egypt, Turkey, and several African countries with poor overall performance.

The primary export pessimism voiced by Prebisch and others in the fifties has turned out to be unwarranted. Primary products as a whole have done well. The export elasticities with respect to industrial output in the "developed" countries which Lewis calculated for 1883–1965 seem still to hold good. The behavior of terms of trade is always debateable, depending somewhat on the choice of series and of a base year. But there is no clear evidence that the terms of trade between primary products and manufactures have moved appreciably against primary products since 1945.

Growth of primary exports has been accompanied in many countries by a healthy diversification of exports, reducing the risks associated with any one crop. Notable examples are Thailand, Malaysia, Ivory Coast, Brazil, and Colombia. Further, a growing number of countries have been able to diversify into manufactured exports, sometimes termed "export substitution." This requires prior development of an industrial base. But it also requires the shift described earlier to outward-looking trade policies, and can be aided further by correct pricing of capital, labor, and foreign exchange. Some countries made this transition successfully during the sixties, but many have not yet done so. As a result, about half of third-world exports of manufactures come from a Far Eastern "gang of four" (Taiwan, South Korea, Hong Kong, Singapore), while another quarter comes from a Latin America "gang of four" (Brazil, Argentina, Mexico, Colombia).

Before 1940 export proceeds were used mainly to finance consumption. Since 1950 they have been used increasingly to finance investment. Except for food, consumer goods are a small and declining percentage of imports in most countries. Capital goods, fuels, and intermediates dominate the import list.

Comparing international capital flows from 1950–1980 with, say, 1850–1914, we note two main differences. First, recent capital transfers have been larger not only in absolute amount but relative to GNP and capital formation in the recipient countries; and second, long-term capital now flows mainly from governments to governments rather than through private channels. This institutional fact of life may be partly responsible for the relative expansion of the public sector in most third-world countries since 1950.

A country-by-country analysis would no doubt reveal that the productivity of foreign capital has varied widely from case to case, depending on the country's "absorptive capacity," which may reflect mainly the economic competence of government. In well-managed economies, foreign borrowing has no doubt been helpful in raising capital formation rates well above the pre-1940 level. But poorly-governed countries which lack the internal requisites for growth have (rightfully) had difficulty in borrowing; and where grant money has been poured into these countries, the returns have often been close to zero.

(5) *GDP growth rates.* For almost all countries in our sample there are official estimates of GDP and its components from about 1950 onward. But this is not as great an advantage as may appear. First, the quality of the data is highly variable and, if a rating scale could be constructed, many countries would probably deserve a C or D. Second, the estimates have several sources of upward bias. Two biases emphasized by Kuznets (1972) are: (1) that the ratio of industrial to agricultural prices is substantially higher in the LDCs than in developed countries, leading to overweighting of the fast-growing industrial sector; (2) that the estimated growth of service outputs is partly spurious, since it contains the "regrettable necessities" arising from urbanization, industrialization, and (in some countries) militarization. One suspects also that faster-growing activities such as large-scale manufacturing and infrastructure are overweighted simply because they are more visible and easier to measure than is household production in the countryside.

Taking the data at face value, they show a median growth rate of real GDP for the countries in our sample of 4.9 percent over the period 1950–1980. Because of relatively high population growth rates, the median rate of increase in real GDP per capita was only 2.3 percent. This is clearly below the median for the OECD countries over the same period. In this sense, the first-world/third-world gap has increased.

Perhaps more significant, however, is the marked variation of growth rates *among* third-world countries. At the top of the league are South Korea, Taiwan, Brazil, Thailand, and Malaysia with 1960–1980 growth rates of real per capita income above 4 percent. These countries have been gaining on the OECD countries, while at the same time pulling farther ahead of other third-world economies. At the bottom of the league are Ghana,

Nepal, Sudan, Uganda, and Zaire, whose per capita income growth since 1950 has been zero or negative. This growing disparity of income levels makes it less and less meaningful to speak of all third-world economies as a group.

C. Concluding Comment

We shall not try to summarize what is already a very condensed argument. But several points seem worth making:

(1) Yes, things are different now. Intensive growth before 1940 was leisurely and intermittent, invariably export led, with moderate population growth, food output growing mainly through acreage expansion rather than technical progress, factory industry absent in most countries and only modestly developed in others, a low capital formation rate, and a small public sector. Since 1950, in both early and recent developers, population has grown considerably faster, per capita income in most countries has also grown faster, there are cases of non-export led growth, increases in agricultural output have relied increasingly on technical progress as land reserves shrink, factories have proliferated and in many countries now dominate the manufacturing sector, capital formation rates have doubled or more, and government's economic role has greatly expanded.

(2) At the same time there are strong elements of continuity with the pre-1940 period. Among these we may note: continuing pressure of growing population and food demand on agricultural output; continuing importance of exports, and the tendency for a high growth rate to be associated with export success; importance of infrastructure development, which has always been the responsibility of government; a broadly unchanged sequence of manufacturing development, as regards both form of organization and type of product; and the importance of international linkages through trade, capital flows, and technological transfer.

References

Boserup, Ester. *The conditions of agricultural growth. The economics of agrarian change under population pressure.* London: Allen and Unwin; Chicago: Aldine Pub. Co., 1965.

———. *Population and technological change: A study of long term trends.* Chicago: U. of Chicago Press, 1981.

Chenery, Hollis. "Patterns of Industrial Growth," *Amer. Econ. Rev.,* Sept. 1960, *50,* pp. 624–54.

———. *Structural change and development policy.* Oxford: pub. for the World Bank by Oxford U. Press, 1979.

Durand, J. Dana. *Historical estimates of world population: An evaluation.* Philadelphia: Population Studies Center, U. of Pennsylvania, 1974.

Easterlin, Richard A., ed. *Population and economic change in developing countries: A conference report.* Universities-National Bureau Committee for economic research; No. 30. Chicago: U. of Chicago Press, 1980.

Hoffman, Walther. *The growth of industrial economies.* Manchester: U. of Manchester Press, 1958.

Ishikawa, Shigeru. *Essays on technology, employment and institutions in economic development: Comparative Asian experience.* Tokyo: Kinokuniya Bookstore Co., 1981.

Kuznets, Simon. *Modern economic growth: Total output and production structure.* New Haven: Yale U. Press, 1966.

———. "Quantitative Aspects of the Economic Growth of Nations: X. Level and Structure of Foreign Trade: Long-term Trends," *Econ. Develop. Cult. Change,* Jan 1967, *15*(2, Part II), pp. 1–140.

———. "Problems in Comparing Recent Growth Rates for Developed and Less Developed Countries." *Econ. Develop. Cult. Change,* Jan. 1972, 20, pp. 185–209.

Lewis, W. Arthur. *Aspects of tropical trade, 1883–1965.* Stockholm: Almqvist & Wiksell, 1969.

———. *Tropical development, 1880–1913: Studies in economic progress.* London: Allen & Unwin, 1970.

———. *Growth and fluctuations, 1870–1913.* London and Boston: Allen & Unwin, 1978a.

Maddison, Angus. *Phases of capitalist development.* Oxford: Oxford U. Press, 1982.

Tilly, Charles, ed. *Historical studies of changing fertility.* Princeton: Princeton U. Press, 1978.

Hopkins, A. G. *An economic history of West Africa.* NY: Columbia U. Press, 1973.

Eckstein, Alexander. *China's economic revolution.* London and NY: Cambridge U. Press, 1977.

Feuerwerker, Albert. *The Chinese economy, ca 1870–1911.* Ann Arbor: Michigan papers in Chinese Studies, no. 5. U of Michigan, Centre for Chinese Studies, 1969.

Perkins, Dwight M. *Agricultural development in China, 1368–1968.* Chicago: Aldine Press, 1969.

———, ed. *China's modern economy in historical perspective,* Stanford: Stanford U. Press, 1975.

Comment II.1. State-owned Enterprises and Privatization

For a variety of reasons—not only economic, but also historical, ideological, and sociopolitical—governments of LDCs have often relied on public enterprise to try to achieve their development goals. In many LDCs, state-owned enterprises (SOEs) account for 10 to 40 percent of GDP. The major economic reasons for establishing state-owned enterprises have been to mobilize savings, create employment, provide public goods, and invest in large-scale capital-intensive projects that are natural monopolies or are subject to economies of scale or are especially risky for private investors.

There has, however, been growing concern about the performance of SOEs. One reason is that SOEs make large and growing claims on the budget and may resort to external debt for financing. In a number of countries, the public-enterprise deficit has been identified as a proximate cause of excessive credit creation, leading to monetary expansion, price inflation, and, ultimately, balance-of-payments pressures. SOEs also often undertake policies of controlling prices of public services, food grains, and other basic wage goods, which often prevent the public enterprises from covering their costs, with corresponding fiscal and monetary repercussions. For an elaboration of these macroeconomic aspects of SOEs, see Robert H. Floyd et al., *Public Enterprise in Mixed Economies: Some Macroeconomic Aspects* (1984).

At the micro level, there is also much concern about efficiency in production, profitable investment decisions, and nondistorting pricing policies. Various ways of improving SOE efficiency are now being emphasized—from the provision of systems for monitoring and evaluating performance to the sale of state-owned enterprises and promotion of privatization programs. On problems of management and control, see World Bank, *World Development Report, 1983* (1983), chap. 8.

Other instructive references are Deepak Lal, "Public Enterprises," in *Policies for Industrial Progress in Developing Countries,* ed. John Cody, Helen Hughes, and David Wall (1980); Leroy P. Jones, *Public Enterprise in Less Developed Countries* (1982); Tony Killick, "Role of the Public Sector in the Industrialization of African Developing Countries," *Industry and Development* (1985); Malcolm Gillis, "Role of State Enterprises in Economic Development," *Social Research* (Summer 1980); George Yarrow, "Privatization in Theory and Practice," *Economic Policy* (April 1984); and Gabriel Roth, *Private Provision of Public Services in Developing Countries* (1987).

In recent years, there have been numerous cases of privatizing state-owned enterprises—in terms of either ownership or management—in an effort to improve their efficiency and reduce their financial burden on the government's budget. For an appraisal of these cases, see Steve H. Hanks, ed., *Privatization and Development* (1987); Paul Cook and Colin Kirkpatrick, eds., *Privatization in LDCs* (1988); John Vickers and George Yarrow, *Privatization: An Economic Analysis* (1988); William Glade, ed., *Privatization of Public Enterprises in Latin America* (1991); Mary Shirley and John Nellis, *Public Enterprise Reform: Lessons of Experience* (1991); Sunita Kikeri et al., *Privatization: The Lessons of Experience* (1992); Leroy Jones et al., *Selling Public Enterprises: A Cost–Benefit Methodology* (1990); and Paul H. Boeker, ed., *Latin America's Turnaround: Privatization, Foreign Investment and Growth* (1993).

The study by Vickers and Yarrow (1988) is especially instructive in demonstrating how ownership of a firm will have significant effects on its behavior and performance, since changes in property rights will alter the structure of incentives faced by decision makers in the firm.

Selection II.2. The Division of the World and the Factoral Terms of Trade*

The Division of the World

How did the world come to be divided into industrial countries and agricultural countries? Did this result from geographical resources, economic forces, military forces, some international conspiracy, or what?

In talking about industrialization, we are talking about very recent times. England has seen many industrial revolutions since the thirteenth century, but the one that changed the world began at the end of the eighteenth century. It crossed rapidly to North America and to Western Europe, but even as late as 1850 it had not matured all that much. In 1850 Britain was the only country in the world where the agricultural population had fallen below 50 percent of the labor force. Today some 30 Third World countries already have agricultural populations equal to less than 50 percent of the labor force—17 in Latin America, 8 in Asia not including Japan, and 5 in Africa not counting South Africa. Thus, except for Britain, even the oldest of the industrial countries were in only the early stages of structural transformation in 1850.

At the end of the eighteenth century, trade between what are now the industrial countries and what is now the Third World was based on geography rather than on structure; indeed India was the leading exporter of fine cotton fabrics. The trade was also trivially small in volume. It consisted of sugar, a few spices, precious metals, and luxury goods. It was then cloaked in much romance, and had caused much bloodshed, but it simply did not amount to much.

In the course of the first half of the nineteenth century industrialization changed the composition of the trade, since Britain captured world trade in iron and in cotton fabrics; but the volume of trade with the Third World continued to be small. Even as late as 1883, the first year for which we have a calculation, total imports into the United States and Western Europe from Asia, Africa, and tropical Latin America came only to about a dollar per head of the population of the exporting countries.[1]

There are two reasons for this low volume of trade. One is that the leading industrial countries—Britain, the United States, France, and Germany—were, taken together, virtually self-sufficient. The raw materials of the industrial revolution were coal, iron ore, cotton, and wool, and the foodstuff was wheat. Between them, these core countries had all they needed except for wool. Although many writers have stated that the industrial revolution depended on the raw materials of the Third World, this is quite untrue. Not until what is sometimes called the second industrial revolution, at the end of the nineteenth century (Schumpeter's Third Kondratiev upswing based on electricity, the motor car and so on), did a big demand for rubber, copper, oil, bauxite, and such materials occur. The Third World's contribution to the industrial revolution of the first half of the nineteenth century was negligible.

The second reason why trade was so small is that the expansion of world trade, which created the international economic order that we are considering, is necessarily an offshoot of the transport revolutions. In this case, the railway was the major element. Before the railway the external trade of Africa or Asia or Latin America was virtually though not completely confined to the seacoasts and rivers; the railway altered this. Although the industrial countries were building railways from 1830 on, the railway did not reach the Third World until the 1860s. The principal reason for this was that, in most countries, railways were financed by borrowing in London—even the North American railways were financed in London—and the Third World did not begin to borrow substantially in London until after 1860. The other revolution in transport was the decline in ocean freights, which followed the substitution of iron for wooden hulls and of steam for sails. Freights began to fall after the middle of the century, but their spectacular downturn came after 1870, when they fell by two-thirds over thirty years.

For all these reasons, the phenomenon we are exploring—the entry of the tropical countries significantly into world trade—really belongs only to the last quarter of the nineteenth century. It is then that tropical trade began to grow significantly—at about four percent a year in volume. And it is then that the international order that we know today established itself.

Now it is not obvious why the tropics reacted to the industrial revolution by becoming exporters of agricultural products.

*From W. Arthur Lewis, "The Division of the World and The Factoral Terms of Trade," *The Evolution of the International Economic Order* (Princeton, NJ: Princeton University Press, 1978), pp. 4–20. Reprinted by permission.

[1]For the sources of this and other statistics used here, and generally for more detailed historical analysis, the reader may consult my book, *Growth and Fluctuations 1870–1913*, Allen and Unwin, London 1978.

As the industrial revolution developed in the leading countries in the first half of the nineteenth century it challenged the rest of the world in two ways. One challenge was to imitate it. The other challenge was to trade. As we have just seen, the trade opportunity was small and was delayed until late in the nineteenth century. But the challenge to imitate and have one's own industrial revolution was immediate. In North America and in Western Europe, a number of countries reacted immediately. Most countries, however, did not, even in Central Europe. This was the point at which the world began to divide into industrial and non-industrial countries.

Why did it happen this way? The example of industrialization would have been easy to follow. The industrial revolution started with the introduction of new technologies in making textiles, mining coal, smelting pig iron, and using steam. The new ideas were ingenious but simple and easy to apply. The capital requirement was remarkably small, except for the cost of building railways, which could be had on loan. There were no great economies of scale, so the skills required for managing a factory or workshop were well within the competence and experience of what we now call the Third World. The technology was available to any country that wanted it, despite feeble British efforts to restrict the export of machinery (which ceased after 1850), and Englishmen and Frenchmen were willing to travel to the ends of the earth to set up and operate the new mills.

Example was reinforced by what we now call "backwash." A number of Third World countries were exporting manufactures in 1800, notably India. Cheap British exports of textiles and of iron destroyed such trade, and provided these countries an incentive to adopt the new British techniques. India built its first modern textile mill in 1853, and by the end of the century was not only self-sufficient in the cheaper cottons, but had also driven British yarn out of many Far Eastern markets. Why then did not the whole world immediately adopt the techniques of the industrial revolution?

The favorite answer to this question is political, but it will not wash. It is true that imperial powers were hostile to industrialization in their colonies. The British tried to stop the cotton industry in India by taxing it. They failed because the Indian cotton industry had the protection of lower wages and of lower transportation costs. But they did succeed in holding off iron and steel production in India till as late as 1912. The hostility of imperial powers to industrialization in their colonies and in the "open door" countries is beyond dispute. But the world

was not all colonial in the middle of the nineteenth century. When the coffee industry began to expand rapidly in Brazil around 1850, there was no external political force from Europe or North America that made Brazil develop as a coffee exporter instead of as an industrial nation. Brazil, Argentina, and all the rest of Latin America were free to industrialize, but did not. India, Ceylon, Java, and the Philippines were colonies, but in 1850 there were still no signs of industrialization in Thailand or Japan or China, Indo-China or the rest of the Indonesian archipelago. The partition of Africa did not come until 1880, when the industrial revolution was already a hundred years old. We cannot escape the fact that Eastern and Southern Europe were just as backward in industrializing as South Asia or Latin America. Political independence alone is an insufficient basis for industrialization.

We must therefore turn to economic explanations. The most important of these, and the most neglected, is the dependence of an industrial revolution on a prior or simultaneous agricultural revolution. This argument was already familiar to eighteenth-century economists, including Sir James Steuart and Adam Smith.

In a closed economy, the size of the industrial sector is a function of agricultural productivity. Agriculture has to be capable of producing the surplus food and raw materials consumed in the industrial sector, and it is the affluent state of the farmers that enables them to be a market for industrial products. If the domestic market is too small, it is still possible to support an industrial sector by exporting manufactures and importing food and raw materials. But it is hard to begin industrialization by exporting manufactures. Usually one begins by selling in a familiar and protected home market and moves on to exporting only after one has learnt to make one's costs competitive.

The distinguishing feature of the industrial revolution at the end of the eighteenth century is that it began in the country with the highest agricultural productivity—Great Britain—which therefore already had a large industrial sector. The industrial revolution did not create an industrial sector where none had been before. It transformed an industrial sector that already existed by introducing new ways of making the same old things. The revolution spread rapidly in other countries that were also revolutionizing their agriculture, especially in Western Europe and North America. But countries of low agricultural productivity, such as Central and Southern Europe, or Latin America, or China had rather small industrial sectors, and there it made rather slow progress.

If the smallness of the market was one constraint on industrialization, because of low agricultural productivity, the absence of an investment climate was another. Western Europe had been creating a capitalist environment for at least a century; thus a whole new set of people, ideas and institutions was established that did not exist in Asia or Africa, or even for the most part in Latin America, despite the closer cultural heritage. Power in these countries—as also in Central and Southern Europe—was still concentrated in the hands of landed classes, who benefited from cheap imports and saw no reason to support the emergence of a new industrial class. There was no industrial entrepreneurship. Of course the agricultural countries were just as capable of sprouting an industrial complex of skills, institutions, and ideas, but this would take time. In the meantime it was relatively easy for them to respond to the other opportunity the industrial revolution now opened up, namely to export agricultural products, especially as transport costs came down. There was no lack of traders to travel through the countryside collecting small parcels of produce from thousands of small farmers, or of landowners, domestic or foreign, ready to man plantations with imported Indian or Chinese labor.

And so the world divided: countries that industrialized and exported manufactures, and the other countries that exported agricultural products. The speed of this adjustment, especially in the second half of the nineteenth century, created an illusion. It came to be an article of faith in Western Europe that the tropical countries had a comparative advantage in agriculture. In fact, as Indian textile production soon began to show, between the tropical and temperate countries, the differences in food production per head were much greater than in modern industrial production per head.

Now we come to another problem. I stated earlier that the industrial revolution presented two alternative challenges—an opportunity to industrialize by example and an opportunity to trade. But an opportunity to trade is also an opportunity to industrialize. For trade increases the national income, and therefore increases the domestic market for manufactures. Import substitution becomes possible, and industrialization can start off from there. This for example is what happened to Australia, whose development did not begin until the gold rush of the 1850s, and was then based on exporting primary products. Nevertheless by 1913 the proportion of Australia's labor force in agriculture had fallen to 25 percent, and Australia was producing more manufactures per head than France or Germany. Why did this not happen to all the other agricultural countries?

The absence of industrialization in these countries was not due to any failure of international trade to expand. The volume of trade of the tropical countries increased at a rate of about 4 percent per annum over the thirty years before the first world war. So if trade was the engine of growth of the tropics, and industry the engine of growth of the industrial countries, we can say that the tropical engine was beating as fast as the industrial engine. The relative failure of India tends to overshadow developments elsewhere, but countries such as Ceylon, Thailand, Burma, Brazil, Colombia, Ghana, or Uganda were transformed during these thirty years before the First World War. They built themselves roads, schools, water supplies, and other essential infrastructure. But they did not become industrial nations.

There are several reasons for this, of which the most important is their terms of trade. Thus, we must spend a little time analyzing what determined the terms of trade.

The Factoral Terms of Trade

The development of the agricultural countries in the second half of the nineteenth century was promoted by two vast streams of international migration. About fifty million people left Europe for the temperate settlements, of whom about thirteen million went to what we now call the new countries of temperate settlement: Canada, Argentina, Chile, Australia, New Zealand, and South Africa. About the same number—fifty million people—left India and China to work mainly as indentured laborers in the tropics on plantations, in mines, or in construction projects. The availability of these two streams set the terms of trade for tropical and temperate agricultural commodities, respectively. For temperate commodities the market forces set prices that could attract European migrants, while for tropical commodities they set prices that would sustain indentured Indians. These were very different levels.

A central cause of this difference was the difference in agricultural productivity between Europe and the tropics. In Britain, which was the biggest single source of European migration, the yield of wheat by 1900 was 1,600 lbs. per acre, as against the tropical yield of 700 lbs. of grain per acre. The European also had better equipment and cultivated more acres per man, so the yield per man must have been six or seven times larger than in tropical regions. Also, in the country to which most of the

European migrants went (the United States), the yield differential was even higher, not because of productivity per acre, which was lower than in Europe, but because of greater mechanization. The new temperate settlements could attract and hold European immigrants, in competition with the United States, only by offering income levels higher than prevailed in Northwest Europe. Since Northwest Europe needed first their wool, and then after 1890 their frozen meat, and ultimately after 1900 their wheat, it had to pay for those commodities prices that would yield a higher-than-European standard of living.

In the tropical situation, on the other hand, any prices for tea or rubber or peanuts that would offer a standard of living in excess of the 700 lb. of grain per acre level were an improvement. Farmers would consider devoting idle land or time to producing such crops; as their experience grew, they would even, at somewhat higher prices, reduce their own subsistence production of food in order to specialize in commercial crops. But regardless of how the small farmer reacted, there was an unlimited supply of Indians and Chinese willing to travel anywhere to work on plantations for a shilling a day. This stream of migrants from Asia was as large as the stream from Europe and set the level of tropical prices. In the 1880s the wage of a plantation laborer was one shilling a day, but the wage of an unskilled construction worker in Australia was nine shillings a day. If tea had been a temperate instead of a tropical crop, its price would have been perhaps four times as high as it was. And if wool had been a tropical instead of a temperate crop, it could have been had for perhaps one-fourth of the ruling price.

This analysis clearly turns on the long-run infinite elasticity of the supply of labor to any one activity at prices determined by farm productivity in Europe and Asia, respectively. This is applied to a Ricardian-type comparative cost model with two countries and three goods. The fact that one of these goods, food, is produced by both countries determines the factoral terms of trade, in terms of food. As usual one can elaborate by increasing the number of goods or countries, but the essence remains if food production is common to all.

One important conclusion is that the tropical countries cannot escape from these unfavorable terms of trade by increasing productivity in the commodities they export, since this will simply reduce the prices of such commodities. Indeed we have seen this quite clearly in the two commodities in which productivity has risen most, sugar and rubber. The factoral terms of trade can be im-

proved only by raising tropical productivity in the common commodity, domestic foodstuffs.

There are interesting borderline cases where the two groups of countries compete. Cotton is an example. In the nineteenth century, the United States was the principal supplier of cotton, but the crop could also grow all over the tropics. The United States maintained its hold on the market despite eager British efforts to promote cotton growing in the British colonies. The U.S. yields per acre were about three times as high as the Indian or African yields, but this alone would not have been enough to discourage tropical production. The United States could not have competed with tropical cotton had southern blacks been free to migrate to the North and to work there at white Northern incomes. It was racial discrimination in the United States that kept the price of cotton so low; or, to turn this around, given the racial discrimination, American blacks earned so little because of the large amount of cotton that would have flowed out of Asia and Africa and Latin America at a higher cotton price.

Cotton was one of a set of commodities where low agricultural productivity excluded tropical competition. The tropics could compete in any commodity where the difference in wages exceeded the difference in productivity. This ruled out not only cotton and tobacco, which fell to the ex-slaves in North America, but also maize, beef, and timber, for which there were buoyant markets, and ground was lost steadily in sugar as beet productivity increased. This left a rather narrow range of agricultural exports and contributed to the overspecialization of each tropical country in one or sometimes two export crops. Low productivity in food set the factoral terms of trade, while relative productivity in other agriculture determined which crops were in and which were out.

Minerals fall into this competing set. Labor could be had very cheaply in the tropical countries, so high productivity yielded high rents. These rents accrued to investors to whom governments had given mining concessions for next to nothing, and the proceeds flowed overseas as dividends. Mineral-bearing lands were not infinitely elastic, but the labor force was. With the arrival of colonial independence over the last two decades, the struggle of the newly independent nations to recapture for the domestic revenues the true value of the minerals in the ground, whether by differential taxation, by differential wages for miners, or by expropriation, has been one of the more bitter aspects of the international confrontation.

Given this difference in the factoral terms of

trade, the opportunity that international trade presented to the new temperate settlements was very different from the opportunity presented to the tropics. Trade offered the temperate settlements high income per head, from which would immediately ensue a large demand for manufactures, opportunities for import substitution, and rapid urbanization. Domestic saving per head would be large. Money would be available to spend on schools, at all levels, and soon these countries would have a substantial managerial and administrative elite. These new temperate countries would thus create their own power centers, with money, education, and managerial capacity, independent of and somewhat hostile to the imperial power. Thus, Australia, New Zealand, and Canada ceased to be colonies in any political sense long before they acquired formal rights of sovereignty, and had already set up barriers to imports from Britain. The factoral terms available to them offered them the opportunity for full development in every sense of the word.

The factoral terms available to the tropics, on the other hand, offered the opportunity to stay poor—at any rate until such time as the labor reservoirs of India and China might be exhausted. A farmer in Nigeria might tend his peanuts with as much diligence and skill as a farmer in Australia tended his sheep, but the return would be very dif-

ferent. The just price, to use the medieval term, would have rewarded equal competence with equal earnings. But the market price gave the Nigerian for his peanuts a 700-lbs.-of-grain-per-acre level of living, and the Australian for his wool a 1600-lbs.-per-acre level of living, not because of differences in competence, nor because of marginal utilities or productivities in peanuts or wool, but because these were the respective amounts of food that their cousins could produce on the family farms. This is the fundamental sense in which the leaders of the less developed world denounce the current international economic order as unjust, namely that the factoral terms of trade are based on the market forces of opportunity cost and not on the just principle of equal pay for equal work. And of course nobody understood this mechanism better than the working classes in the temperate settlements themselves, and in the United States. The working classes were always adamant against Indian or Chinese immigration into their countries because they realized that, if unchecked, it would drive wages down close to Indian and Chinese levels.[2]

---

[2]I have borrowed passages from my paper "The Diffusion of Development" in Thomas Wilson, Editor, *The Market and the State*, Oxford University Press, Oxford 1976.

Note II.1. Why Not Export First?

In the selection by W. Arthur Lewis, Lewis states that "it is hard to begin industrialization by exporting manufactures. Usually one begins by selling in a familiar and protected home market." In this Note the word we want to accent is *familiar*. It is one thing to export a homogeneous product like sugar. If a trader sees that the price differential between the home and foreign market is sufficient to cover the customs and transportation costs, he ships the product. Prices convey all the relevant information. It is another thing to export a differentiated product like garments or shoes. A trader cannot act on the price differential between domestic and foreign shoes because they bundle together different characteristics. Your shoes may be a poor fit (so to speak) for foreign consumers and thus sell (if they sell at all) for a price well below your expectations. Learning about foreign markets is an expensive process, and a continuous one, because styles and specifications are always changing.

This point is best illustrated by Japan, the only country *not* populated by Western Europeans to industrialize successfully during the "world economic boom" period 1850–1914. In Selection II.1 Reynolds notes that Japan began intensive growth as a raw silk exporter, but that by 1900 its exports were dominated by cotton textiles. Japan solved the problem of breaking into foreign markets by developing the general trading companies known as the *sogo shosha*. These trading companies were unique, among both developed and less developed countries, in both their size and their scope until imitations began in Korea and Turkey in the 1970s and 1980s, respectively. In their book on the sogo shosha, Yoshino and Lifson write of their operation in the late nineteenth and early twentieth centuries (1986, p. 23):

> Particularly important . . . was the role the sogo shosha played in providing export opportunities for the myriad small Japanese firms in cottage industries, which, like their counterparts in developing countries today, faced many problems in trying to break into the world market. The sogo shosha fed them market information, helped them design products, extended credit, and, most important, developed foreign outlets for their products.

An alternative to expensive cultivation of foreign markets is to establish export-oriented manufacturing through foreign direct investment (FDI). Writing about industrialization of the British West Indies, Lewis (1950) advised, "since it is difficult and expensive to break into a foreign market by building up new distribution outlets, this is most likely to succeed if the islands concentrate on inviting manufacturers who are already well established in foreign markets." Since Lewis wrote these words there has indeed been substantial export-oriented manufacturing FDI in less developed countries, and in fact many smaller LDCs could be said to have begun industrialization in this manner. Typically such FDI begins with assembly of components imported from the source country (Gereffi 1994). More integrated manufacturing in the host country comes later, if at all.

Could such an industrialization strategy have worked in the tropics in the 1850–1914 period? There is reason for doubt. First, the wage differential between the host and source countries was much smaller than it is now, and transportation costs were much larger, so FDI in export-oriented assembly operations may not have been profitable. Second, investments in agro-processing, mining, and infrastructure (especially railroads) associated with primary-product exports may have seemed like such good bets that few foreigners willing to risk their capital in far-off countries could have been persuaded to try export-oriented manufacturing instead. We conclude that, at least during the late nineteenth and early twentieth centuries, it is reasonable to take the size of the domestic market to be a key variable determining the ability of countries to industrialize.

References

Gereffi, Gary. 1994. "The International Economy and Economic Development." In Neil J. Smelser and Richard Swedberg (eds.), *The Handbook of Economic Sociology* (Princeton, N.J.: Princeton University Press and Russell Sage Foundation), pp. 206–33.

Lewis, W. Arthur. 1950. "The Industrialization of the British West Indies." *Caribbean Economic Review* (May).

Yoshino, M. Y., and Thomas B. Lifson. 1986. *The Invisible Link: Japan's* Sogo Shosha *and the Organization of Trade*. (Cambridge, Mass.: MIT Press).

Note II.2. The Lewis Model of the World Economy

In *Aspects of Tropical Trade, 1883–1965,* W. Arthur Lewis (1969) presents in much more detail the model of determination of the factoral and commodity terms of trade sketched in the preceding selection. He gives a series of numerical examples to illustrate his results. Here we adopt more general notation that allows us to present his results more compactly.

We begin with a table showing fixed outputs per labor hour (labor productivities) in manufactures, food, and cash crops:

Table 1. Output per Labor Hour

	Cash Crops	Food	Manufactures
Region 1	q_C^1	q_F^1	
Region 2		q_F^2	q_M^2

Region 1 represents either the tropical countries of Africa, Asia, and Latin America or the temperate countries of recent settlement such as Australia and Canada. Region 2 represents the industrialized "core" consisting of Western Europe and the United States. For the time being we ignore the possibility that region 1 could produce manufactures or that region 2 could grow cash crops (or produce synthetic substitutes for them).

It is assumed that all three goods are freely traded, that labor is perfectly mobile within regions but immobile across them, and that food is always produced in both regions. This last assumption is especially crucial, because it means that productivity in food determines the opportunity cost of labor in both regions. In other words, labor can be had for production of cash crops within region 1 or manufactures within region 2 only by paying wages sufficient to attract workers out of food production. This requirement, combined with competition, determines the prices of cash crops and manufactures in terms of food.

More formally, if labor is paid its marginal value product in all sectors (equal to its average value product in this model), perfect intraregional mobility of labor implies:

$$p_C q_C^1 = q_F^1 = w^1 \quad \text{or} \quad p_C = \frac{q_F^1}{q_C^1} \tag{1}$$

and

$$p_M q_M^2 = q_F^2 = w^2 \quad \text{or} \quad p_M = \frac{q_F^2}{q_M^2} \tag{2}$$

where p denotes price and w denotes wage. It follows immediately that the factoral terms of trade, the rate at which region 1 labor hours implicitly exchange for region 2 labor hours, are given by

$$\frac{w^1}{w^2} = \frac{q_F^1}{q_F^2} \tag{3}$$

and that the commodity terms of trade, the rate at which cash crops exchange for manufactures, are given by

$$\frac{p_C}{p_M} = \frac{q_F^1/q_C^1}{q_F^2/q_M^2} \tag{4}$$

We see that a region can only improve its factoral or commodity terms of trade by increasing its productivity in food. Productivity increases in a region's specialty only serve to drive down its price. Lewis (1969) documents the sharp decreases in the prices of rubber and sugar that took place from 1880–84 to 1960–64. He claims these were the only two tropical crops that showed dramatic productivity increases during this period. Letting region 1 represent the tropics, equation (4) shows that increases in cash crop productivity must drive down the price of tropical cash crops relative to manufactures. By the same token, if a cash crop is grown with unchanged productivity in a region with higher food productivity, its price must be proportionately higher. Suppose that food productivity in the temperate countries of recent settlement were four times higher than in the tropics. If region 1 now represents these temperate countries, the numerators of both equation (3) and equation (4) must be increased by a factor of 4. This explains Lewis's statement in the preceding selection, "If tea had been a temperate instead of a tropical crop its price would have been perhaps four times as high as it was. And if wool had been a tropical instead of a temperate crop it could have been had for perhaps one-fourth of the ruling price."

Above all, the standard of living within a region is primarily determined by its food productivity. From equations (1) and (2) we see that, for example, if the tropics (represented by region 1) were to double its productivity in food, its wage would double not only in terms of food but in terms of manufactures as well, whereas if the tropics were to double its productivity in cash crops, its wage would double only in terms of cash crops. This explains Lewis's statement in the preceding selection that "the market price gave the Nigerian for his peanuts a 700-lbs-of-grain-per-acre level of living, and the Australian for his wool a 1600-lbs-per-acre level of living, not because of differences in competence, nor because of marginal utilities or productivities in peanuts or wool, but because these were the respective amounts of food that their cousins could produce on the family farms."

A puzzling feature of this analysis is that demand plays no role in the determination of prices. Suppose, for example, that consumer preferences in the industrialized world were to change so that demand for tea or wool increased at given prices and incomes. With tea or wool output unchanged, its price would increase, increasing the marginal value product of labor in tea or wool production and attracting labor out of food production. This leads to an expansion of tea or wool output, which as we have seen must continue until the price of tea or wool is driven down to its original level (given by equation (1)) *provided the wage in food production is unchanged.* Would it not be the case, however, that the marginal product of labor in food production would increase as pressure on scarce food-producing land is reduced? The answer suggested by the preceding selection is that the labor supply of China and India is too large for the increased demand for labor in tea production to significantly reduce the labor-land ratios there, but could we say the same of the labor supply of Britain, the source of immigrants to Australia? A more credible answer, we believe, is to simply extend to food-producing land the assumption of abundance that Lewis makes for land suitable for cash crop production. Land cannot become less scarce if it is not scarce to begin with, so any tendency for the opportunity cost of immigrant labor to rise would be checked by region 1 residents leaving their food-producing land to work in cash crop production. The assumption of an unlimited supply of food-producing land can also be applied to region 2 if we think of it as including the United States.

We now allow for the possibilities that region 1 could produce manufactures and that region 2 could grow cash crops, or produce synthetic substitutes for them. We modify Table 1 appropriately:

Table 2. Output per Labor Hour

	Cash Crops	Food	Manufactures
Region 1	q_C^1	q_F^1	q_M^1
Region 2	q_C^2	q_F^2	q_M^2

Under what conditions does the pattern of trade above still apply? Consumers in region 1 must find imported manufactures cheaper than domestically produced output, and consumers in region 2 must find imported cash crops cheaper than domestically produced output. These conditions are given by, respectively,

$$p_M^2 = \frac{q_F^2}{q_M^2} < \frac{q_F^1}{q_M^1} = p_M^1 \tag{5}$$

and

$$p_C^1 = \frac{q_F^1}{q_C^1} < \frac{q_F^2}{q_C^2} = p_C^2 \tag{6}$$

where we have now superscripted the prices of cash crops and manufactures to indicate which region is producing them. Under these conditions region 1 does not produce manufactures and region 2 does not produce cash crops, just as in the model with which we started. We see that, as expected, these conditions are more likely to hold, the higher is the productivity of region 2 in manufactures relative to region 1 and the higher is the productivity of region 1 in cash crops relative to region 2. In contrast, an increase in a region's food productivity raises its cost of labor and thus makes it less likely that region will continue to export its specialty. For example, an increase in region 2 food productivity makes it less likely that condition (5) will hold. Lewis (1969) therefore notes that "a relative rise in food productivity in the temperate world forces the tropical countries to industrialize."

Reference

Lewis, W. Arthur. 1969. *Aspects of Tropical Trade, 1883–1965* (Stockholm: Almqvist and Wicksell).

Selection II.3. Agricultural Productivity, Comparative Advantage, and Economic Growth*

For many years, economists have discussed the role of agricultural productivity in economic development. Generations of development economists have stressed improving agricultural productivity as an essential part of successful development strategy. For example, Nurkse (1953, p. 52) argued that "[e]veryone knows that the spectacular industrial revolution would not have been possible without the agricultural revolution that preceded it," and Rostow (1960, p. 8) stated that "revolutionary changes in agricultural productivity are an essential condition for successful take-off." A casual reading of recent development textbooks suggests that this view seems to have achieved almost the status of an axiom in development economies.[1]

According to this conventional view, which is based in part on the experiences of the Industrial Revolution in Britain, there are *positive* links between agricultural productivity and industrialization. First, rising productivity in food production makes it possible to feed the growing population in the industrial sector. With more food being produced with less labor, it releases labor for manufacturing employment. Second, high incomes generated in agriculture provide domestic demand for industrial products. Third, it increases the supply of domestic savings required to finance industrialization.

However, a comparative look at some regional experiences of industrialization tells a different story. For example, why were Belgium and Switzerland the first to become leading industrial countries in continental Europe, while the Netherlands lagged behind and did not take off until the last decades of the nineteenth century? Or why did industrialization of the United States during the antebellum period, mainly in the cotton textile industry, occur in New England, not in the South? Economic historians who studied these experiences found their answer in the Law of Comparative Advantage, which implies a *negative* link between agricultural productivity and industrialization; see Mokyr's

(1976) comparative study of industrialization in Belgium and the Netherlands, and Field (1978) and Wright (1979) for industrialization in New England and the South. According to this view, the manufacturing sector has to compete with the agriculture sector for labor. Low productivity in agriculture implies the abundant supply of "cheap labor" which the manufacturing sector can rely on.

The key to understanding these two conflicting views can be found in the difference in their assumptions concerning the openness of economies. Note that the logic behind the conventional wisdom crucially rests on the implicit assumption that the economy is an effectively closed system. This assumption, which may be appropriate for Britain during the half-century of the Seven Year War, the War of American Independence, the French Revolution, and the Napoleonic Wars, should not be taken for granted for many developing countries.[2] In an open trading system, where prices are mainly determined by the conditions in the world markets, a rich endowment of arable land (and natural resources) could be a mixed blessing. High productivity and output in the agricultural sector may, without offsetting changes in relative prices, squeeze out the manufacturing sector. Economies which lack arable land and thus have the initial comparative (but not necessarily absolute) advantage in manufacturing, on the other hand, may successfully industrialize by relying heavily on foreign trade through importing agricultural products and raw materials and exporting manufacturing products, as recent experiences in the newly industrialized economies in East Asia suggest.[3]

In an attempt to highlight the point made above, this paper presents a two-sector model of endogenous growth. The model is essentially of the Ricardo–Viner–Jones variety, with one mobile factor (called labor) combined with diminishing returns technologies. There are two additional features. First, preferences are non-homothetic and the in-

*From Kiminori Matsuyama, "Agricultural Productivity, Comparative Advantage, and Economic Growth," *Journal of Economic Theory* 58 (December 1992): 317–322. Reprinted by permission.

[1]My samples include Gillis et al., 1983, Hayami and Ruttan 1985, Herrick and Kindleberger 1983, Timmer 1988, and Todaro 1989. Timmer claims that this view "has not been challenged (p. 277)."

[2]The effect of continuous wars on the British Industrial Revolution remains in dispute. In particular, the extent to which trade in food was disrupted has been questioned, given the closer integration of the Irish and British economies during the period; see Thomas 1985.

[3]Although my main concern here is output growth, I found the empirical findings reported in Rauch 1989 highly suggestive. He found that per capita consumption growth will be slower in countries with relatively large endowments of land per capita.

come elasticity of demand for the agricultural good is less than unitary. Second, manufacturing productivity rises over time because of learning-by-doing. For the closed economy case, an exogenous increase in agricultural productivity shifts labor to manufacturing and thereby accelerates economic growth. The model therefore provides a formalization of the conventional wisdom, which asserts that agricultural revolution is a precondition for industrial revolution. For the open economy case, however, there exists a negative link between agricultural productivity and economic growth. An economy with less productive agriculture allocates more labor to manufacturing and will grow faster. For a sufficiently small discount rate, it will achieve a higher welfare level than the rest of the world. The productive agricultural sector, on the other hand, squeezes out the manufacturing sector and the economy will de-industrialize over time, and, in some cases, achieve a lower welfare level. The model is also used to illustrate the Dutch disease phenomena.

Once stated, the contrast between the results in the closed and open economies is quite intuitive, but has often escaped the attention that it deserves. It suggests that the openness of economies should be an important factor to be kept in mind when planning development strategies and predicting growth performances. At the turn of the century, those schooled in the conventional wisdom might have predicted that Argentina, with her fertile and vast pampas land, would grow faster than Japan, with her mountainous land and limited natural resources. To them, what happened to these two economies during the last 90 years may be puzzling. Or, to many, it provides prima-facie evidence that cultural or political factors are important determinants of economic development.[4] The result for the open economy case arguably offers an economic explanation for this "puzzle." . . .

The economy consists of two sectors: manufacturing and agriculture. Both sectors employ labor. Abstracting from the issue of population growth, the size of the population is constant and equal to L. The total labor supply is also constant and nor-

malized to one. . . . Technologies in the two sectors are given by

$$X_t^M = M_t F(n_t),$$

$$F(0) = 0, F' > 0, F'' < 0, \tag{1}$$

$$X_t = AG(1 - n_t),$$

$$G(0) = 0, G' > 0, G'' < 0, \tag{2}$$

where n_t is the fraction of labor employed in manufacturing as of time t (time is continuous). Both sectors operate under diminishing returns. Agricultural productivity, A, which may reflect the level of technology, land endowment, and climate, among other things, is constant over time and treated as an exogenous parameter. On the other hand, productivity in the manufacturing sector, M_t, which represents knowledge capital as of time t, is predetermined, but endogenous. Knowledge accumulates as a by-product of manufacturing experience, as follows[5]:

$$\dot{M}_t = \delta X_t^M, \quad \delta > 0. \tag{3}$$

These learning-by-doing effects are purely external to the individual firms that generate them. With complete spillovers, each manufacturing firm treats M_t as given when making production and employment decisions. Thus, competition between the two sctors for labor leads to the equilibrium condition in the labor market,

$$AG'(1 - n_t) = p_t M_t F'(n_t), \tag{4}$$

where p_t is the relative price of the manufacturing good.

All consumers in this economy share identical preferences given by

$$W = \int_0^\infty [\beta \log(c_t^A - \gamma) + \log(c_t^M)] \, e^{-\rho t} \, dt,$$

$$\beta, \gamma, \rho > 0, \tag{5}$$

where c_t^A and c_t^M denote consumption of the agriculture good (food for simplicity) and the manufacturing good, as of time t. The parameter γ represents the subsistence level of food consumption and satisfies

$$AG(1) > \gamma L > 0. \tag{6}$$

The first inequality states that the economy's agricultural sector is productive enough to provide the subsistence level of food to all consumers. With a positive γ, preferences are non-homothetic and the

---

[4]For example, one political scientist argues that liberal theory, by which he means economies as commonly taught in North American universities, "tends to neglect the political framework, . . . , yet the process of economic development cannot be divorced from political factors." He then asks "How else can one explain the remarkable economic achievements of resource-poor Japan and the troubles of resource-rich Argentina? (Gilpin (1987) p. 269)"

[5]For simplicity, it is assumed that knowledge capital never depreciates. Introducing a depreciation generates possibility of a growth trap in this model.

income elasticity of demand for food is less than unitary. The low income clasticity is introduced partly because of its central role in the logic behind the conventional view and partly because of the empirically indisputable Engel's law; see Crafts (1985). It is also assumed that all consumers have enough income to purchase more than γ units of food. Then, from (5), demand for the two goods by a consumer satisfies $c_t^A = \gamma + \beta p_t c_t^M$. Aggregation over all consumers yields

$$C_t^A = \gamma L + \beta p_t C_t^M, \tag{7}$$

where the upper case letters denote aggregate consumption.

To proceed further, let us assume that the economy is a closed system. This requires that $C_t^M = X_t^M = M_t F(n_t)$ and $C_t^A = X_t^A = AG(1 - n_t)$. Combining them with Eqs. (4) and (7) yields

$$\phi(n_t) = \frac{\gamma L}{A}, \tag{8}$$

where $\phi(n) \equiv G(1 - n) - \beta G'(1 - n)F(n)/F'(n)$, which satisfies $\phi(0) = G(1), \phi(1) < 0$, and $\phi' < 0$. From (6), (8) has a unique solution in $(0,1)$. Since the right-hand side is decreasing in A, this solution can be written as

$$n_t = v(A), \quad \text{with} \quad v'(A) > 0.$$

Thus, the employment share of manufacturing is constant over time and positively related to A. From (3), output in manufacturing grows at a constant rate, $\delta F(v(A))$, also positively related to A. Aggregate food consumption and production stay constant at the level given by

$$C^A = X^A = AG(1 - v(A))$$

$$= \frac{\gamma L + A\beta G'(1 - v(A)) F(v(A))}{F'(v(A))},$$

which is also increasing in A. Under the closed economy assumption, the model predicts that an increase in agricultural productivity releases labor to manufacturing and immediately increases its output and accelerates its growth. It also causes a permanent increase in the level of food production. Therefore, the utility of the representative consumer, who consumes C^A/L and C_t^M/L, unambiguously increases with agricultural productivity. These results can thus be considered as a formalization of the conventional wisdom, which asserts that agricultural revolution is a precondition for industrial revolution and supports the development strategy that emphasizes the Green Revolution. Although the underlying mechanism is very simple, this is, to my best knowledge, the first attempt to model a positive link between agricultural productivity and the growth *rate* of the economy. . . . Engel's law plays a crucial role here. If γ is zero, the solution to (8) is independent of A, and thus agricultural productivity has no effect on growth. If γ is negative, and so food is a luxury good, then a rise in agricultural productivity slows down the economy.

References

N. F. R. Crafts. Income clasticities of demand and the release of labor by agriculture during the British industrial revolution: A further appraisal, *J. Europ. Econ. Hist.* 9 (1980), 153–168; reprinted in J. Mokyr (Ed.), "The Economics of the Industrial Revolution," Rowman & Allanheld, Totawa, NJ, 1985.

A. J. Field, Sectoral shifts in Antebellum Massachusetts: A reconsideration, *Exploration Econ. Hist,* 15 (1978), 146–171.

M. Gillis. D. Perkins, M. Roemer, and D. Snodgrass, "Economics of Development," Norton, New York, 1983.

R. Gilpin, "The Political Economy of International Relations," Princeton Univ. Press, Princeton, NJ, 1987.

Y. Hayami and V. W. Ruttan, "Agricultural Development: An International Development," rev. expanded edition, Johns Hopkins Univ. Press, Baltimore, MD, 1985.

B. Herrick and C. Kindleberger, "Economic Development," 4th ed., McGraw-Hill, New York, 1983.

J. Mokyr, "Industrialization in the Low Countries, 1795–1850," Yale Univ. Press, New Haven, CT., 1976.

R. Nurkse, "Problems of Capital Formation in Underdeveloped Countries," Oxford Univ. Press, New York, 1953.

J. E. Rauch, "The Question of International Convergence of Per Capita Consumption," UCSD Working paper, August 1989.

W. W. Rostow, "The Stages of Economic Growth: A Non-Communist Manifesto," Cambridge Univ. Press, Cambridge, UK, 1960.

B. Thomas, Food supply in the United Kingdom during the Industrial Revolution, *Agr. Hist.* 56 (1982), 328–342; reprinted in J. Mokyr (Ed.), "The Economics of the Industrial Revolution," Rowman & Allanheld, Totawa, NJ, 1985.

C. P. Timmer, The agricultural transformation, *in* "Handbook of Development Economics" Vol. I (H. Chenery and T. N. Srinivasan, Eds.), North-Holland, Amsterdam, 1988.

M. P. Todaro, "Economic Development in the Third World," 4th ed., Longman, New York, 1989.

G. Wright, Cheap labor and Southern textiles before 1880, *J. Econ. Hist.* 39 (1979), 655–680.

Comment II.2. Income Elasticity of Demand for Food in the Matsuyama Model

Readers who enjoy mathematical economic models may find Matsuyama's model simpler and more convincing than the summary presented in the Overview for this chapter. For these readers we add a few details to the demonstration that the preferences given by equation (5) yield an income elasticity of demand for agricultural output (food) less than 1.

To maximize the integral given in equation (5), at every point in time the consumer must set the ratio of the marginal utility from consumption of manufactures to the marginal utility from consumption of food equal to the price ratio p_t, yielding $(c_t^A - \gamma)/\beta c_t^M = p_t$. This aggregates to equation (7). Moreover, consumers cannot save in Matsuyama's model, so at every point in time they consume their entire aggregate income, which we denote by Y_t: $C_t^A + p_t C_t^M = Y_t$. Combining this last equation with equation (7) and eliminating C_t^M gives us aggregate consumption of food as a function of aggregate income: $C_t^A = (\beta Y_t + \gamma L)/(1 + \beta)$. Finally, income elasticity $(dC_t^A/dY_t)(Y_t/C_t^A) = \beta Y_t/(\beta Y_t + \gamma L)$, which is less than 1 as long as γ is positive.

Selection II.4. Income Distribution, Market Size, and Industrialization*

We present a model of industrialization caused by an increase in agricultural productivity or by an export boom, that raises incomes and therefore demand for domestic manufactures. As domestic markets become larger, increasing returns production technologies that could not break even in smaller markets come into profitable use and industry expands. The key role of productive agriculture or exports for generating domestic demand for manufactures has been emphasized in earlier work of Rosenstein-Rodan [1943], Nurkse [1953], Lewis [1953, 1954], Ranis and Fei [1961], and especially Fleming [1955]. Empirically, Ohkawa and Rosovsky [1960] document the great increases in agricultural productivity in turn of the century Japan, and Johnston and Mellor [1961] note the importance of the demand from farmers for growth of industry during that period. Similarly, Thorbecke [1979] and Ranis [1979] present evidence for the dramatic progress of agriculture in postwar Taiwan, and Ranis in particular stresses the role of demand by farmers at the initial stages of Taiwan's industrialization. Lewis [1953] makes increases in farm productivity and in cash crop exports a cornerstone of his proposed development strategy for the Gold Coast, on the theory that increased rural purchasing power would foster industrialization.

The vibrancy of domestic agriculture or exports is not, however, always sufficient to bring about any industrialization. In some cases, although farm or export income is generated, it does not go to potential customers of domestic industry, and the relevant markets remain as narrow as ever. For industrial markets to expand, the composition of demand must concentrate buying power in the hands of consumers of manufactures. Large population, homogeneous tastes, and concentrated population all help to create large markets for manufactures.[1] But also of great importance to industrialization is the distribution of income, since the middle class are the natural consumers of manufactured goods. As has been pointed out by Baldwin [1956] and North [1959], extreme concentration of wealth in the hands of the very rich will manifest itself in the demand for handmade and imported luxuries rather than for domestic manufactures, even when farm or export income grows. The necessity of a middle class as the source of the buying power for domestic manufactures is the central message of our paper.

The effects of income distribution on the extent of industrialization seem to be important in a number of historical episodes. For example, in the first half of the nineteenth century, the United States greatly surpassed England in the range of consumer products it manufactured using mass production techniques. In contrast to high quality handmade creations of the English artisans, American producers offered standardized mass-produced utilitarian items such as rifles, cutlery or balloon-frame houses (which an English architect called bare, bald white cubes). This difference in production techniques seems to be accounted for by the difference in the composition of demand [Rosenberg, 1972]. Whereas in England manufactures were demanded by the quality-conscious upper class, that could not have possibly generated a large market, the American demand came from a large number of relatively well-off farmers. The large demand from this land-rich middle class enabled American manufactures to profitably sustain mass production.

This difference in the composition of demand and of techniques of production in the two countries have been described in the catalog for the 1851 London Crystal Palace exhibition (cited in Rosenberg [1972] p. 50):

The absence in the United States of those vast accumulations of wealth which favor the expenditure of large sums on articles of mere luxury, and the general distribution of the means of procuring the more substantial conveniences of life, impart to the productions of American industry a character distinct from that of many other countries. The expenditure of months or years of labour upon a single article, not to increase its intrinsic value, but solely to augment its cost and its estimation as the object of *virtu,* is not common in the United States. On the contrary, both manual and mechanical labour are applied with direct reference to increasing the number or the quantity of articles suited for the wants of a whole people, and adapted to promote the enjoyment of that moderate competency that prevails upon them.

In the model presented below, the U. S. experience can be understood in terms of distribution of returns from farming and the demand by farmers for industrial goods.

Perhaps the best example of a country in which

*From Kevin M. Murphy, Andrei Shleifer, and Robert W. Vishny. "Income Distribution, Market Size, and Industrialization," *Quarterly Journal of Economics* 104 (August 1989): 537–545. Reprinted by permission.

[1]Chenery, Robinson, and Syrquin [1987] report that industrialization usually begins at a much lower level of income in high-population countries.

the distribution of rewards from a boom in a leading sector has led first to the failure and then to the success of industrialization is Colombia in the second half of the nineteenth century. In the 1850s and 1860s Colombia experienced a large boom in tobacco exports, which, however, failed to lead to widespread economic development. From about 1880 to 1915, Colombia went through a boom in coffee exports, the effect of which on industrialization has been much more widely pronounced. Harbison [1970] explains the difference between the two episodes by the fact that, technologically, tobacco had to be grown on large plantations and hence the income from the boom went to a very small number of plantation owners who spent it on luxury imports, whereas coffee was grown on small family enterprises with the result that income accrued to a large number of people who then demanded domestic manufactures. Harbison's [1970] analysis of Colombia illustrates precisely the point developed in our work:

The lion's share of increased prosperity generated by coffee production was enjoyed by the large poor rural *mestizo campesino* class, not the small group of rich white urban landlords. These peasants, in turn, certainly did not buy for themselves and their children foreign travel and foreign education or other luxury imports. . . . Since such items could not be produced in Colombia, the use of tobacco-generated incomes to purchase these luxury imports had resulted in a long-term depression and decline in Colombian artisan manufacture without compensating growth in another domestic sector. But coffee generated incomes in the hands of Antioqueno farmers who spend precisely on those necessities. . . . The rapid expansion of coffee production redistributed income toward that segment of the population most likely to spend the incremental income on items characterized by high potential for generating domestic incomes—i.e. on domestic goods whose large-scale production could utilize modern low-cost technology—and not on imports.

Colombia's experience with the two leading sector booms thus shows exactly how income distribution affects the consequences of such booms.

The central economic assumption underlying our interpretation of these examples is the relevance of local demand composition, as opposed to the world markets, for the choice of techniques. If world trade is costless and free of barriers, this assumption is untenable. In practice, however, transport costs, difficulties of penetrating foreign markets, and especially protectionism make the sizes of local markets relevant for a wide range of goods in many countries. In this paper we first focus on the case of a closed economy with agriculture serving as the source of high-powered demand for

manufactures, and then let this role be played also by mineral or cash crop exports. . . . [In our model] each consumer spends all of his income on food until he gets z units of it. If he has income left over, he spends all of it on manufactures. He expands the menu of manufactures he buys in order of marginal utility per unit price. Richer consumers end up with a superset of manufactures bought by poorer consumers. . . .

Each [manufactured] good q is assumed to be produced in a separate sector that is small relative to the economy. Two technologies are assumed to be available for producing each good q. First, $\alpha >$ 1 units of labor can be applied to produce one unit of output of any good q using the constant returns to scale (CRS), or "backstop," technology. In addition, good q can be produced with a fixed investment of C units of labor and a variable labor requirement of one per unit of output. The idea of two alternative technologies has been used by Shleifer [1986] and Shleifer and Vishny [1988] to illustrate the importance of market size in promoting the switch to IRS technology. Here, since the size of the market for q is equal to the number of consumers whose menu includes q (customer base), income distribution will determine the profitability of producing q with increasing returns.

Industrialization in this paper is taken to be substitution of increasing returns technologies for constant returns technologies in production of some goods. It seems very plausible to associate increasing returns with events that are commonly linked to industrialization, such as mass production, escape from the farm, concentration of labor in the same location, etc. . . .

In the equilibrium we propose, all sectors producing goods 0 through Q for some Q industrialize. The entering monopolists displace the fringe in these sectors, but do not cut prices. The price of each manufacturing good is therefore αw, regardless of whether it is produced in an industrialized or a backstop sector. . . .

When all sectors $(0,Q)$ industrialize, and prices in all of them are kept at αw, the sector Q for whose monopolist it is marginally profitable to enter is one where variable profits just cover the fixed cost. Denote by N^* the sales of that sector, equal to the minimum efficient scale. For this sector, the break-even condition is

$$(\alpha w - w) N^* = Cw, \qquad (1)$$

or

$$N^* = \frac{C}{(\alpha - 1)}. \qquad (2)$$

Since the range of goods consumed declines with income, consumers of Q are the N^* richest people in the economy.

References

Baldwin, Robert E., "Patterns of Development in Newly Settled Regions," *The Manchester School,* XXIV (1956), 161–79.

Chenery, Hollis B., Sherman Robinson, and Moshe Syrquin. *Industrialization and Growth: A Comparative Study* (New York: Oxford University Press, 1987).

Fleming, J. Marcus, "External Economies and the Doctrine of Balanced Growth," *Economic Journal,* LXV (1955), 241–56.

Harbison, Ralph W., "Colombia," in *Tropical Development 1880–1913,* W. A. Lewis, ed. (Evanston: Northwestern University Press, 1970), pp. 64–99.

Johnston, Bruce F., and John W. Mellor, "The Role of Agriculture in Economic Development," *American Economic Review,* LI (1961), 566–93.

Lewis, W. Arthur, *Report on the Industrialization of the Gold Coast* (Accra: Government Printing Office of the Gold Coast, 1953).

———, "Economic Development with Unlimited Supplies of Labor," *The Manchester School,* XXII (1954), 139–91.

North, Douglass C., "Agriculture in Regional Economic Growth," *Journal of Farm Economics,* LI (1959), 943–51.

Nurkse, Ragnar, *Problems of Capital Formation in Underdeveloped Countries* (Oxford: Basil Blackwell, 1953).

Ohkawa, Kazushi, and Henry Rosovsky, "The Role of Agriculture in Modern Japanese Economic Development," *Economic Development and Cultural Change,* IX part 2 (1960), 43–68.

Ranis, Gustav, "Industrial Development," in *Economic Growth and Structural Change in Taiwan,* Walter Galenson, ed. (Ithaca and London: Cornell University Press, 1979).

Ranis, G., and J. C. H. Fei, "A Theory of Economic Development," *American Economic Review,* LI (1961), 533–65.

Rosenberg, Nathan, *Technology and the American Economic Growth* (New York: M. E. Sharpe, 1972).

Rosenstein-Rodan, Paul N., "Problems of Industrialization of Eastern and South-eastern Europe," *Economic Journal,* LIII (1943), 202–11.

Shleifer, Andrei, "Implementation Cycles," *Journal of Political Economy,* XCIV (1986), 1163–90.

———, and Vishny, Robert W. "The Efficiency of Investment in the Presence of Aggregate Demand Spillovers," *Journal of Political Economy,* XCVI (1988), 1221–31.

Thorbecke, Eric, "Agricultural Development," in *Economic Growth and Structural Change in Taiwan,* Walter Galenson, ed. (Ithaca and London: Cornell University Press, 1979).

Comment II.3. *Minimum Market Size in the Murphy–Shleifer–Vishny Model*

Here we link equation (2) to the discussion of the Murphy–Shleifer–Vishny model in the Overview. The fixed cost C of introducing factory production of a given manufacture must be spread out over a sufficient number of units to make the average cost of factory production at least as low as that of handicraft production. Average cost of factory production equals $(C/N + 1)w$, where N is the number of units produced and w is the wage rate, and αw is the average cost of handicraft production. Solving the equation $(C/N + 1)w = \alpha w$ for N yields equation (2). As we would expect, the minimum number of units N^* depends positively on the fixed cost C and negatively on α, the number of labor hours needed to produce one unit of output using handicraft methods. Given the consumer preferences assumed by Murphy, Shleifer, and Vishny, N^* is also the minimum number of consumers above the level of income such that they demand one unit of the manufacture in question, that is, the minimum market size for successful introduction of factory techniques for this manufacture.

Selection II.5. Divergence, Big Time*

Divergence in relative productivity levels and living standards is the dominant feature of modern economic history. In the last century, incomes in the "less developed" (or euphemistically, the "developing") countries have fallen far behind those in the "developed" countries, both proportionately and absolutely. I estimate that from 1870 to 1990 the ratio of per capita incomes between the richest and the poorest countries increased by roughly a factor of five and that the difference in income between the richest country and all others has increased by an order of magnitude.[1] This divergence is the result of the very different patterns in the long-run economic performance of two sets of countries.

One set of countries—call them the "developed" or the "advanced capitalist" (Maddison, 1995) or the "high income OECD" (World Bank, 1995)—is easily, if awkwardly, identified as European countries and their offshoots plus Japan. Since 1870, the long-run growth rates of these countries have been rapid (by previous historical standards), their growth rates have been remarkably similar, and the poorer members of the group grew sufficiently faster to produce considerable convergence in absolute income levels. The other set of countries, called the "developing" or "less developed" or "nonindustrialized," can be easily, if still awkwardly, defined only as "the other set of countries," as they have nothing else in common. The growth rates of this set of countries have been, on average, slower than the richer countries, producing divergence in relative incomes. But amongst this set of countries there have been strikingly different patterns of growth: both across countries, with some converging rapidly on the leaders while others stagnate; and over time, with a mixed record of take-offs, stalls and nose dives. . . .

Calculating a Lower Bound for Per Capita GDP

There is no historical data for many of the less developed economies, and what data does exist has enormous problems with comparability and reliability. One alternative to searching for historical data is simply to place a reasonable lower bound on what GDP per capita could have been in 1870 in any country. Using this lower bound and estimates of recent incomes, one can draw reliable conclusions about the historical growth rates and divergence in cross-national distribution of income levels.

There is little doubt life was nasty, brutish and short in many countries in 1870. But even deprivation has its limit, and some per capita incomes must imply standards of living that are unsustainably and implausibly low. After making conservative use of a wide variety of different methods and approaches, I conclude that \$250 (expressed in 1985 purchasing power equivalents) is the lowest GDP per capita could have been in 1870. This figure can be defended on three grounds: first, no one has ever observed consistently lower living standards at any time or place in history; second, this level is well below extreme poverty lines actually set in impoverished countries and is inconsistent with plausible levels of nutritional intake; and third, at a lower standard of living the population would be too unhealthy to expand.

Before delving into these comparisons and calculations, it is important to stress that using the purchasing power adjustments for exchange rates has an especially important effect in poor countries. While tradable goods will have generally the same prices across countries because of arbitrage, nontradable goods are typically much cheaper in poorer countries because of their lower income levels. If one applies market exchange rates to convert incomes in these economies to U.S. dollars, one is typically far understating the "true" income level, because nontradable goods can be bought much more cheaply than market exchange rates will imply. There have been several large projects, especially the UN International Comparisons Project and the Penn World Tables, that through the collection of data on the prices of comparable baskets of goods in all countries attempt to express different countries' GDP in terms of a currency that represents an equivalent purchasing power over a basket of goods. Since this adjustment is so large and of such quantitative significance, I will denote figures that have been adjusted in this way by $P\$$. By my own rough estimates, a country with a per capita GDP level of \$70 in U.S. dollars, measured in market exchange rates, will have a per capita GDP of $P\$250$.

The first criteria for a reasonable lower bound

*From Lant Pritchett, "Divergence, Big Time," *Journal of Economic Perspectives* 11 (Summer 1997): 3–4, 6–12. Reprinted by permission.

[1]To put it another way, the standard deviation of (natural log) GDP per capita across all countries has increased between 60 percent and 100 percent since 1870, in spite of the convergence amongst the richest.

on GDP per capita is that it be a lower bound on measured GDP per capita, either of the poorest countries in the recent past or of any country in the distant past. The lowest five-year average level of per capita GDP reported for any country in the Penn World Tables (Mark 5) is P$275 for Ethiopia in 1961–65; the next lowest is P$278 for Uganda in 1978–82. The countries with the lowest level of GDP per capita ever observed, even for a single year, are P$260 for Tanzania in 1961, P$299 for Burundi in 1965 and P$220 for Uganda in 1981 (in the middle of a civil war). Maddison (1991) gives estimates of GDP per capita of some less developed countries as early as 1820: P$531 for India, P$523 for China and P$614 for Indonesia. His earliest estimates for Africa begin in 1913: P$508 for Egypt and P$648 for Ghana. Maddison also offers increasingly speculative estimates for western European countries going back much further in time; for example, he estimates that per capita GDPs in the Netherlands and the United Kingdom in 1700 were P$1515 and P$992, respectively, and ventures to guess that the average per capita GNP in western Europe was P$400 in 1400. Kuznets's (1971) guess of the trough of the average per capita GDP of European countries in 900 is around P$400.[2] On this score, P$250 is a pretty safe bet.

A complementary set of calculations to justify a lower bound are based on "subsistence" income. While "subsistence" as a concept is out of favor, and rightfully so for many purposes, it is sufficiently robust for the task at hand. There are three related calculations: poverty lines, average caloric intakes and the cost of subsistence. Ravallion, Datt and van de Walle (1991) argue that the lowest defensible poverty line based on achieving minimally adequate consumption expenditures is P$252 per person per year. If we assume that personal consumption expenditures are 75 percent of GDP (the average for countries with GDP per capita less than P$400) and that mean income is 1.3 times the median, then even to achieve median income at the lowest possible poverty line requires a per capita income of $437.[3]

As an alternative way of considering subsistence GDP per capita, begin with the finding that estimated average intake per person per day consistent with working productively is between 2,000 to 2,400 calories.[4] Now, consider two calculations. The first is that, based on a cross-sectional regression using data on incomes from the Penn World Tables and average caloric intake data from the FAO, the predicted caloric consumption at P$250 is around 1,600.[5] The five lowest levels of caloric availability ever recorded in the FAO data for various countries—1,610 calories/person during a famine in Somalia in 1975; 1,550 calories/person during a famine in Ethiopia in 1985; 1,443 calories/person in Chad in 1984; 1,586 calories/person in China in 1961 during the famines and disruption associated with the Cultural Revolution; and 1,584 calories/person in Mozambique in 1987—reveal that nearly all of the episodes of average daily caloric consumption below 1,600 are associated with nasty episodes of natural and/or man-made catastrophe. A second use of caloric requirements is to calculate the subsistence income as the cost of meeting caloric requirements. Bairoch (1993) reports the results of the physiological minimum food intake at $291 (at market exchange rates) in 1985 prices. These calculations based on subsistence intake of food again suggest P$250 is a safe lower bound.

That life expectancy is lower and infant mortality higher in poorer countries is well documented, and this relation can also help establish a lower bound on income (Pritchett and Summers, 1996). According to demographers, an under-five infant

---

[2]More specifically, Kuznets estimated that the level was about $160, if measured in 1985 U.S. dollars. However, remember from the earlier discussion that a conversion at market exchange rates—which is what Kuznets was using—is far less than an estimate based on purchasing power parity exchange rates. If we use a multiple of 2.5, which is a conservative estimate of the difference between the two, Kuznets's estimate in purchasing power equivalent terms would be equal to a per capita GDP of $400 in 1985 U.S. dollars, converted at the purchasing power equivalent rate.

[3]High poverty rates, meaning that many people live below these poverty lines, are not inconsistent with thinking of these

poverty lines as not far above our lower bound, because many individuals can be in poverty, but not very far below the line. For instance, in South Asia in 1990, where 33 percent of the population was living in "extreme absolute poverty," only about 10 percent of the population would be living at less than $172 (my estimates from extrapolations of cumulative distributions reported in Chen, Datt and Ravallion, 1993).

[4]The two figures are based on different assumptions about the weight of adult men and women, the mean temperature and the demographic structure. The low figure is about as low as one can go because it is based on a very young population, 39 percent under 15 (the young need fewer calories), a physically small population (men's average weight of only 110 pounds and women of 88), and a temperature of 25°C (FAO, 1957). The baseline figure, although based on demographic structure, usually works out to be closer to 2,400 (FAO, 1974).

[5]The regression is a simple log-log of caloric intake and income in 1960 (the log-log is for simplicity even though this might not be the best predictor of the level). The regression is

ln (average caloric intake) = 6.37 + .183*ln (GDP per capita),

(59.3)(12.56).

with t-statistics in parentheses, N = 113, and R-squared = .554.

Figure 1. Simulation of Divergence of Per Capita GDP, 1870–1985 (showing only selected countries)

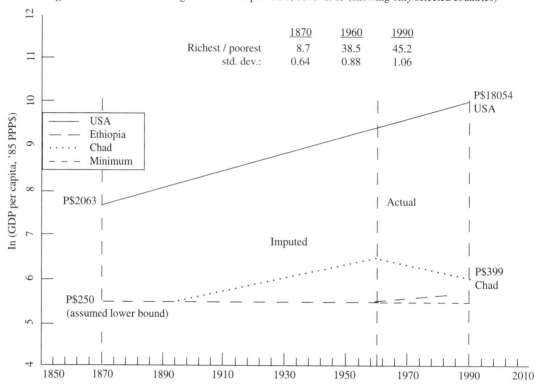

mortality rate of less than 600 per 1000 is necessary for a stable population (Hill, 1995). Using a regression based on Maddison's (1991) historical per capita income estimates and infant mortality data from historical sources for 22 countries, I predict that infant mortality in 1870 for a country with income of P250$ would have been 765 per 1000.[6] Although the rate of natural increase of population back in 1870 is subject to great uncertainty, it is typically estimated to be between .25 and 1 percent annually in that period, which is again inconsistent with income levels as low as P250$.[7]

[6]The regression is estimated with country fixed effects:

$$\ln (IMR) = -.59 \ln (GDP \text{ per capita}) - .013*Trend$$
$$(23.7) \qquad\qquad\qquad (32.4)$$

$$- .002*Trend*(1 \text{ if} > 1960)$$
$$(14.23)$$

N = 1994 and t-statistics are in parentheses. The prediction used the average country constant of 9.91.

[7]Livi-Basci (1992) reports estimates of population growth in Africa between 1850 and 1900 to be .87 percent, and .93 percent between 1900 and 1950, while growth for Asia is estimated to be .27 1850 to 1900, and .61 1900 to 1950. Clark (1977) estimates the population growth rates between 1850 and 1900 to be .43 percent in Africa and India and lower, .33 percent, in China.

Divergence, Big Time

If you accept: (a) the current estimates of relative incomes across nations; (b) the estimates of the historical growth rates of the now-rich nations; and (c) that even in the poorest economies incomes were not below P250$ at any point—then you cannot escape the conclusion that the last 150 years have seen divergence, big time. The logic is straightforward and is well illustrated by Figure 1. If there had been no divergence, then we could extrapolate backward from present income of the poorer countries to past income assuming they grew at least as fast as the United States. However, this would imply that many poor countries must have had incomes below P100$ in 1870. Since this cannot be true, there must have been divergence. Or equivalently, per capita income in the United States, the world's richest industrial country, grew about four-fold from 1870 to 1960. Thus, any country whose income was not fourfold higher in 1960 than it was in 1870 grew more slowly than the United States. Since 42 of the 125 countries in the Penn World Tables with data for 1960 have levels of per capita incomes below $1,000 (that is, less than four times $250), there must have been substantial divergence between the top and bot-

Table 1. Estimates of the Divergence of Per Capita Incomes Since 1870

	1870	1960	1990
USA (P$)	2063	9895	18054
Poorest (P$)	250	257	399
	(assumption)	(Ethiopia)	(Chad)
Ratio of GDP per capita of richest to poorest country	8.7	38.5	45.2
Average of seventeen "advanced capitalist" countries from Maddison (1995)	1757	6689	14845
Average LDCs from PWT5.6 for 1960, 1990 (imputed for 1870)	740	1579	3296
Average "advanced capitalist" to average of all other countries	2.4	4.2	4.5
Standard deviation of natural log of per capita incomes	.51	.88	1.06
Standard deviation of per capita incomes	P$459	P$2,112	P$3,988
Average absolute income deficit from the leader	P$1286	P$7650	P$12,662

Notes: The estimates in the columns for 1870 are based on backcasting GDP per capita for each country using the methods described in the text assuming a minimum of P$250. If instead of that method, incomes in 1870 are backcast with truncation at P$250, the 1870 standard deviation is .64 (as reported in Figure 1).

tom. The figure of P$250 is not meant to be precise or literal and the conclusion of massive divergence is robust to any plausible assumption about a lower bound.

Consider some illustrative calculations of the divergence in per capita incomes in Table 1. I scale incomes back from 1960 such that the poorest country in 1960 just reaches the lower bound by 1870, the leader in 1960 (the United States) reaches its actual 1870 value, and all relative rankings between the poorest country and the United States are preserved.[8] The first row shows the actual path of the U.S. economy. The second row gives the level of the poorest economy in 1870, which is P$250 by assumption, and then the poorest economies in 1960 and 1990 taken from the Penn

World Tables. By division, the third row then shows that the ratio of the top to the bottom income countries has increased from 8.7 in 1870 to 38 by 1960 and to 45 by 1990. If instead one takes the 17 richest countries and applies the same procedure, their average per capita income is shown in the fourth row. The average for all less developed economies appearing in the Penn World Tables for 1960 and 1990 is given in the fifth row; the figure for 1870 is calculated by the "backcasting" imputation process for historical incomes described above. By division, the sixth row shows that the ratio of income of the richest to all other countries has almost doubled from 2.4 in 1870 to 4.6 by 1990.

The magnitude of the change in the absolute gaps in per capita incomes between rich and poor is staggering. From 1870 to 1990, the average absolute gap in incomes of all countries from the leader had grown by an order of magnitude, from $1,286 to $12,662, as shown in the last row of Table 1.

[8]The growth rate of the poorest country was imposed to reach P$250 at exactly 1870, and the rate of the United States was used for the growth at the top. Then each country's growth rate was assumed to be a weighted average of those two rates, where the weights depended on the scaled distance from the bottom country in the beginning period of the imputation, 1960. This technique "smushes" the distribution back into the smaller range between the top and bottom while maintaining all cross country rankings. The formula for estimating the log of GDP per capita (GDPPC) in the ith country in 1870 was

$$GDPPC_i^{1870} = GDPPC_i^{1960} * (1/w_i)$$

where the scaling weight w_i was

$$w_i = \frac{(1 - \alpha_i) * \min(GDPPC^{1960})}{P\$250 \; + \alpha_i * GDPPC_{USA}^{1960}/GDPPC_{USA}^{1870}}$$

and where α_i is defined by

$$\alpha_i = \frac{(GDPPC_i^{1960} - \min(GDPPC^{1960}))}{(GDPPC_{USA}^{1960} - \min(GDPPC^{1960}))}.$$

References

Bairoch, Paul, *Economics and World History: Myths and Paradoxes.* Chicago: University of Chicago Press, 1993.

Chen, Shaohua, Gaurav Datt, and Martin Ravallion, "Is Poverty Increasing in the Developing World?" World Bank Policy Research Working Paper No. 1146, June 1993.

Clark, Colin, *Population Growth and Land Use.* London: Macmillan, 1977.

FAO, *Calorie Requirements: Report of the Second Committee on Calorie Requirements.* Rome: FAO, 1957.

FAO, *Handbook on Human Nutritional Requirements.* Rome: Food and Agriculture Organization and World Health Organization, 1974.

Hill, Kenneth, "The Decline of Childhood Mortality." In Simon, Julian, ed., *The State of Humanity.* Oxford: Blackwell, 1995, pp. 37–50.

Kuznets, Simon, *Economic Growth of Nations: Total Output and Production Structure.* Cambridge, Mass.: Belknap Press, 1971.

Livi-Basci, Massimo, *A Concise History of World Population.* Cambridge, Mass: Blackwell, 1992.

Maddison, Angus, *Dynamic Forces in Capitalistic Development: A Long-Run Comparative View.* New York: Oxford University Press, 1991.

Maddison, Angus, *Monitoring the World Economy, 1820–1992.* Paris: Development Centre of the Organisation for Economic Co-operation Development, 1995.

Pritchett, Lant, and Lawence H. Summers, "Wealthier is Healthier," *Journal of Human Resources,* 1996, 31:4, 841–68.

Ravallion, Martin, Gaurav Datt, and Dominique van de Walle, "Quantifying Absolute Poverty in the Developing World," *Review of Income and Wealth,* 1991, 37:4, 345–61.

World Bank, *World Development Report: Workers in an Integrating Economy.* Washington, D.C.: Oxford University Press for the World Bank, 1995.

CHAPTER III

Savings and Investment

Overview: Savings—The Engine of Growth?

Few doubt that investment in physical and human capital, financed primarily by domestic savings, is crucial to the process of economic development. Educational attainment is included in the Human Development Index discussed in Chapter I, making accumulation of human capital partially synonymous with development according to this measure. Achievement of high per capita incomes without accumulation of modern infrastructure, plant, and equipment seems a virtual impossibility, absent the kind of enormous mineral wealth that places a few oil-exporting countries among the high-income ranks. We are therefore not surprised to see the strong cross-country associations between rapid per capita income growth and high rates of fixed investment and school enrollment in Exhibit III.1. The importance of domestic savings follows from the well-known strong cross-country correlation between the savings and investment shares of GDP (Feldstein and Horioka 1980).

Whether or not savings and investment play a *leading* role in development, serving as "the engine of growth," has on the other hand been a source of controversy since the early days of development economics. The controversy centered on the role of saving to finance investment in physical capital. W. Arthur Lewis (1954, p. 155) wrote, "The central problem in the theory of economic development is to understand the process by which a community which was previously saving and investing 4 or 5 per cent of its national income or less, converts itself into an economy where voluntary saving is running at about 12 to 15 per cent of national income or more." Albert Hirschman (1958) took the opposite position, arguing that if opportunities for profitable projects were there, the requisite investable funds would be forthcoming. Saving could not create such opportunities, and would be wasted in their absence. For example, in an article entitled "The Vice of Thrift," the *Economist* (1998, p. 85) states, "it has become clear that the surge in investment in East Asia in the 1990s was a sign of weakness, not strength. Much of the money was wasted on speculative property deals or unprofitable industrial projects."

Outside of development economics, the received wisdom from growth theory was for many years that savings could not be the engine of growth because of diminishing returns to investment in physical capital. As the stock of physical capital per head increased, the rate of return on investment inevitably fell so low that the incentive for further saving was eliminated. An exceptionally thrifty population could only postpone the inevitable until a higher stock of capital per head was reached. Thus in the long run the propensity to save could only affect the level of per capita income, not its growth rate. The engine of growth was taken to be improvement in technology, which was considered to be exogenous to the saving process. The impotence of savings extended to government policy. Policy could affect the rate of growth of per capita income only if it could affect the rate of technological progress. This was frustrating, given the kind of robust cross-country associations between government policies and per capita income growth that are displayed in Exhibit III.1.

(As an aside, we should note that the economic indicators often called "policies" in the cross-country growth literature are at best only indicators of government policies. For example, governments commonly legislate import quotas and tariffs and export subsidies, but they do not target the share of exports in GDP.)

The advent of "endogenous growth theory," described in section I.C, changed the message of growth theory regarding savings and policies. The accumulation of physical and human capital through saving was argued to be associated with an accumulation of knowledge that staved off diminishing returns. Without diminishing returns savings could propel growth indefinitely, and policies that changed the rate of saving could change the rate of growth.

The debate over diminishing versus constant or increasing returns, and over exogenous versus endogenous growth theory, is of questionable relevance for development economics. One can argue that the level of capital per head in less developed countries is so low that diminishing returns do not apply, even if they are relevant for more developed countries. As Easterly, Kremer, Pritchett, and Summers state (1993, p. 479), "if countries are far from their steady states, models in which country characteristics determine income look similar to those in which country characteristics determine growth rates." Nevertheless, the development of endogenous growth theory gave a powerful new intellectual foundation to the position within development economics that savings is the engine of growth, and that growth rates can be changed by policies that affect the incentive to save. The AK model, attributable to Rebelo (1991), proved an especially useful vehicle for demonstrating how policies such as those listed in Exhibit III.1 could have the effects on growth found in the data. Easterly, King, Levine, and Rebelo (1991) show how policies affect growth in the AK model either by changing the incentive to save or changing the efficiency of saving as measured by the extent to which the marginal private product of capital reflects its marginal social product. Note III.1, based loosely on pages 12–21 of their paper, shows how a simplified version of the AK model yields the results that growth is positively affected by the propensity to save, negatively affected by government income taxation to finance consumption, and ambiguously affected by government income taxation to finance investment in infrastructure.

Recent evidence has favored Hirschman's view that investment and saving tend to follow rather than lead growth. In Selection III.1, Magnus Blomström, Robert Lipsey, and Mario Zejan find that growth in per capita GDP helps to forecast the share of investment in GDP (growth "Granger-causes" investment) but investment does not help to forecast growth. Similar findings for savings, using both country- and individual-level data, are reported by Carroll and Weil (1994). These findings can be interpreted as evidence that growth creates opportunities that induce saving and investment, but unfortunately they do not tell us what causes growth in the first place.

A similar long-running controversy in development economics concerns the financial system: does its development lead or follow growth? One might think that if savings and investment follow growth, so must financial development. In Selection III.3, however, Ronald McKinnon claims that "the quality, if not the quantity, of investment improves significantly when interest rates are positive and financial intermediation is robust." It could be that growth is induced when improved financial intermediation allows savings to be channeled to the most profitable projects, even if an increase in the number of projects holding quality constant cannot have the same effect.

The selection by U Tun Wai describes the functioning of unorganized or traditional money markets in a situation of financial underdevelopment. In the next selection McKinnon makes the case against financial repression, where a policy of maintaining low interest rates discourages people from putting their savings in the banking system and creates an excess demand for bank credit, which the government then helps to allocate. The following Comment notes that financial liberalization also has its dangers, especially when it leads to large inflows of short-term foreign investment. Hugh Patrick addresses the question of "demand-following" versus "supply-leading" finance in a historical context in Selection III.4. Finally, the selection by Ross Levine presents cross-country evidence that financial depth in 1960, measured by the ratio of liquid liabilities of the financial system to GDP, predicts per capita GDP growth over the next 30 years.

Recall that one of the attractions of new growth theory, and of the AK model in particular, was its ability to generate results consistent with the apparently robust correlation between government policies and growth in per capita income. In the final selection of this chapter (Selection III.6), William Easterly, Michael Kremer, Lant Pritchett, and Lawrence Summers find that indicators of country fiscal, trade, and other policies such as those shown in Exhibit III.1 are very persistent across the decades of the 1960s, 1970s, and 1980s, but that country growth in GDP per worker is not. Assuming that a policy that is good for growth in one decade is also good for growth in the next, this is a puzzle for new (endogenous) growth theory: countries that maintain the same policies from one decade to the next should maintain the same growth rates. Easterly and colleagues also find that "shocks" to per capita income such as changes in the prices of a country's exports relative to imports (its terms of trade) have large effects on growth even over the decade-long periods they examine. The net effect of their work is to call into question whether policies can really affect long-run growth after all, and to ask whether much of the difference in growth across countries is actually due to luck in receiving favorable versus unfavorable shocks. The Comment following their selection suggests that Easterly and co-workers may have somewhat overstated the case for the importance of shocks relative to policies.

One can argue that the problem Selection III.6 poses for the application of new growth theory to the study of development runs deeper. A basic analytical tool for both new and old growth theory is a theoretical construct called the "aggregate production function" (see Note III.1), which translates total labor hours and the total value of physical (and perhaps human) capital into total output. This construct is not useful unless the efficiency with which total inputs generate total output is stable or changes in a predictable way. In fact, the growth of this efficiency (known as total factor productivity growth) has not been persistent across decades: see Figure 3 in Selection III.6. Put differently, persistent rates of growth of the total labor force and total capital stock (through investment) have not translated into a persistent rate of growth of GDP. In the next chapter we return to a more disaggregated view of the economies of less developed countries.

References

Carroll, Christopher D., and David N. Weil. 1994. "Saving and growth: A reinterpretation." *Carnegie-Rochester Series on Public Policy* 40 (June): 133–192.

Easterly, William, Robert King, Ross Levine, and Sergio Rebelo. 1991. "How Do National Policies Affect Long-Run Growth? A Research Agenda." World Bank Working Paper No. 794 (October).

Easterly, William, Michael Kremer, Lant Pritchett, and Lawrence Summers. 1993. "Good Policy or Good Luck? Country Growth Performance and Temporary Shocks." *Journal of Monetary Economics* 32 (December): 459–483.

The Economist. 1998. "The Vice of Thrift." *The Economist* 346 (March 21): 85–86.

Feldstein, Martin S., and Charles Horioka. 1980. "Domestic Saving and International Capital Flows." *Economic Journal* 90 (June): 314–329.

Hirschman, Albert O. 1958. *The Strategy of Economic Development* (New Haven, Conn.: Yale University Press).

Lewis, W. Arthur. 1954. "Economic Development with Unlimited Supplies of Labour." *The Manchester School* 22: 139–191.

Rebelo, Sergio, 1991. "Long Run Policy Analysis and Long Run Growth." *Journal of Political Economy* 99: 500–521.

Exhibit III.1. Economic and Social Indicators in Fast and Slow Growth Economies (Cross-country averages, 1960–1989)

	Fast-growers	Slow-growers
Share of investment in GDP	0.27	0.17
Secondary school enrolment rates	0.27	0.07
Primary school enrolment rates	0.90	0.52
Government expenditures/GDP	0.14	0.13
Government consumption/GDP	0.08	0.12
Inflation rate	8.42	16.51
Standard deviation of inflation	8.75	19.38
Black market exchange rate premium	4.65	75.03
Standard deviation of black market premium	6.53	105.69
Share of exports in GDP	0.44	0.29

Mean per capita growth rate = 1.92 per cent; fast growers are countries whose per capita growth rate is greater than or equal to the mean plus one standard deviation. The cutoff growth rate was 4 per cent and the number of fast growers is 12. Slow growers are countries with per capita growth rates that are lower than or equal to the mean minus one standard deviation. The cutoff growth rate for slow growers was –0.2 per cent and the number of slow growers is 15.

Source: Easterly, William, Robert King, Ross Levine, and Sergio Rebelo. "Policy, Technology Adoption, and Growth." In Luigi L. Pasinetti and Robert M. Solow, eds., *Economic Growth and the Structure of Long-Term Development* (New York: St. Martin's, 1994), p. 76.

Note III.1. The AK Model

To begin, we express output per capita y as a function of an aggregate of physical and human capital per head k:

$$y = f(k) \tag{1}$$

Note that all economic activity has been aggregated into one sector that produces GDP or income. Unlike the models of Chapter II, no distinction is made between agriculture and industry. Next, we choose a very special functional form for the aggregate production function:

$$f(k) = Ak \tag{2}$$

where A is a constant that does not vary across time or countries. It follows that the marginal product of capital per head is constant rather than diminishing.

There are two time periods in the model: the present (period 1) and the future (period 2). Using equations (1) and (2), we can compute the rate of growth of per capita income g:

$$g = \frac{(y_2 - y_1)}{y_1} = \frac{(Ak_2 - Ak_1)}{Ak_1} = \frac{(k_2 - k_1)}{k_1} \tag{3}$$

where subscript denotes time period. We define investment $i \equiv k_2 - k_1$, the change in capital per head. Investment is assumed to be financed entirely by domestic savings per head s, so that $i = s$: there is no use of foreign savings by borrowing abroad (nor is domestic savings used to finance foreign investment). Substituting into equation (3) yields

$$g = \frac{s}{k_1} \tag{4}$$

Growth in income per capita is determined by savings in proportion to the initial stock of capital.

Since k_1 is inherited from the past and therefore fixed, we can close the model by determining the value of s. We assume that the choice of s is made by a consumer who represents all consumers in the sense that all consumers are assumed to have the same preferences and same income. The representative consumer has income y given by equation (1) and preferences given by

$$U(c_1, c_2) = \ln(c_1) + \frac{\ln(c_2)}{(1 + \rho)} \tag{5}$$

where c denotes consumption per head (i.e., consumption of the representative consumer), ln is the natural logarithm function, and ρ is a parameter called the "discount rate." The natural logarithm function yields diminishing marginal utility of consumption, discussed in connection with the Human Development Index in Chapter I, Section I.A. The discount rate is greater, the more the consumer values present relative to future consumption, that is, the more impatient the consumer is. Thus a lower discount rate is associated with a greater propensity to save.

Savings are given by the excess of present income over present consumption:

$$s = y_1 - c_1 = Ak_1 - c_1 \tag{6}$$

where we have used equations (1) and (2). We assume the capital stock is not consumable, and since there is no borrowing from abroad consumption cannot exceed income and $s \geq 0$. We will choose parameters so that this constraint on savings is never binding, however, and hence will ignore it in what follows. Since the capital stock is not consumable, and the consumer has no later period to save for, he or she will consume exactly his or her income in the future:

$$c_2 = y_2 = Ak_2 = A(k_1 + i) = A(k_1 + s) \tag{7}$$

where we have used equations (1) and (2). Substituting equations (6) and (7) into equation (5) yields the following expression for utility:

$$U = \ln(Ak_1 - s) + \frac{\ln(A(k_1 + s))}{(1 + \rho)} \tag{8}$$

We assume that the consumer chooses s so as to maximize utility. Using the fact that $d \ln x/dx = 1/x$ and rearranging, we obtain the first-order condition $Ak_1 - s = (1 + \rho)(k_1 + s)$, which we can solve for s to get

$$s = \frac{[A - (1 + \rho)]k_1}{2 + \rho} \tag{9}$$

We see that savings are increasing in A, the marginal product the consumer receives on the capital he or she invests, and decreasing in ρ, so that greater impatience yields lower propensity to save, as expected. This solution is valid (the constraint $s \geq 0$ is not violated) provided $A \geq 1 + \rho$.

Finally, substitution of equation (9) into equation (4) yields equilibrium growth in income per capita:

$$g = \frac{A - (1 + \rho)}{2 + \rho} \tag{10}$$

Two points should be made about this result. First, a thriftier (lower ρ) population will generate more rapid growth. Second, the rate of growth is independent of the initial level of capital per head: there is no tendency for richer countries to grow slower or faster than poor ones. This prediction is supported by cross-country data. However, when policies such as those in Exhibit III.1 are controlled for, it is found that poor countries grow faster than rich ones, a result commonly termed "conditional convergence." Barro and Sala-i-Martin (1995, chap. 12) provide a good review of the evidence.

With savings as the engine of growth, we expect policies that reduce the incentive to save to lower the growth rate. Consider for example income taxation at rate τ to finance government consumption expenditure. In the real world government consumption expenditure might take a form such as food subsidies, but here it is simply a lump-sum grant t to the representative consumer. Although the government budget constraint ensures that $t = \tau y$, the representative consumer treats t as exogenous because it equals total tax receipts divided by the total population and is thus only negligibly affected by his or her own income. Individual savings affect the consumer's after-tax future income but not the size of his or her future government grant, hence the incentive to save is reduced by the fact that the consumer keeps only $1 - \tau$ of the return on his or her investment.

Because the representative consumer's present income and present government grant are both exogenous, equation (6) is unchanged:

$$s = (1 - \tau)y_1 + t_1 - c_1 = (1 - \tau)y_1 + \tau y_1 - c_1 = y_1 - c_1 = Ak_1 - c_1 \tag{6'}$$

In equation (7), on the other hand, the representative consumer's future after-tax income is determined by his or her savings, while the future government grant is still exogenous:

$$c_2 = y_2 = (1 - \tau)y_2 + t_2 = (1 - \tau)Ak_2 + t_2 = (1 - \tau)A(k_1 + i) + t_2 = (1 - \tau)A(k_1 + s) + t_2 \tag{7'}$$

Substituting equations (6') and (7') into equation (5) yields a new expression for utility:

$$U = \ln(Ak_1 - s) + \frac{\ln((1 - \tau)A(k_1 + s) + t_2)}{(1 + \rho)} \tag{8'}$$

We obtain the new first-order condition $(1 - \tau)A(Ak_1 - s) = (1 + \rho)[(1 - \tau)A(k_1 + s) + t_2]$. Substituting for t_2 using the government budget constraint, we can solve for s to get

$$s = \frac{[(1 - \tau)\,A - (1 + \rho)]k_1}{2 + \rho - \tau} \tag{9'}$$

Note that this solution is valid (the constraint $s \geq 0$ is not violated) provided $(1 - \tau)A \geq 1 + \rho$. Finally, substitution of equation (9′) into equation (4) yields the new equilibrium growth in income per capita:

$$g = \frac{[(1 - \tau)A - (1 + \rho)]}{2 + \rho - \tau} \tag{10'}$$

As expected, growth is lower, the higher is the income tax rate:

$$\frac{dg}{d\tau} = \frac{-(1 + \rho)(1 + A)}{(2 + \rho - \tau)^2} \tag{11'}$$

This result is consistent with the evidence in Exhibit III.1 that countries with high ratios of government consumption (such as expenditure on food subsidies) to GDP grow slower than countries where this ratio is low, provided that this higher expenditure is financed by higher taxes that reduce the incentive to save. Exhibit III.1 also shows that fast- and slow-growing countries do not differ in their ratios of *total* government expenditure to GDP. We can understand this finding in terms of the AK model if we think of income tax revenue as financing government investment in infrastructure that is complementary to private capital as well as financing government consumption. A high tax rate then reduces the incentive to save directly, but can increase the incentive to save indirectly by financing accumulation of a larger stock of government-owned capital that increases the return to investment in privately owned capital. Thus a low share of government expenditure in GDP might correspond to inadequate infrastructure, while a high share might correspond to excessive taxation, leading on average to no difference between the government expenditure share of slow- and fast-growing countries. Readers who would like to see this result demonstrated in a formal model should see Easterly, King, Levine, and Rebelo (1991, p. 21).

References

Barro, Robert J., and Xavier Sala-i-Martin. 1995. *Economic Growth* (New York: McGraw-Hill).

Easterly, William, Robert King, Ross Levine, and Sergio Rebelo. 1991. "How Do National Policies Affect Long-run Growth? A Research Agenda." World Bank Working Paper No. 794 (October).

Selection III.1. Is Fixed Investment the Key to Economic Growth?*

The strong relationship between fixed capital formation shares of GDP and growth rates since World War II has led many writers, such as De Long and Summers [1991, 1992], to conclude that the rate of capital formation or of capital formation in the form of equipment, determines the rate of a country's economic growth.[1] Yet, the strong association between fixed investment or equipment investment and growth, particularly over spans of fifteen to twenty years, does not prove causality. The effects may very well run from growth to capital formation, so that rapid growth leads to high rates of capital formation. An earlier study by Lipsey and Kravis [1987] found that for five-year periods within the longer spans, the rate of growth was more closely related to capital formation rates in succeeding periods than to contemporary or preceding rates. That result suggested that the observed long-term relationships were due more to the effect of growth on capital formation than to the effect of capital formation on growth.

In this paper we address that issue by again examining changes in capital formation and growth over successive five-year periods, but with more formal methods of studying the direction of causation. Our aim is to determine directions of influence and their timing between capital formation ratios and rates of growth. . . .

A first test of the timing issue is provided in the first part of Table 1, which shows simple regressions of five-year growth rates in per capita GDP on preceding, current, and succeeding period fixed capital formation rates (ratios of fixed capital formation to GDP).[2] The coefficients, t-statistics, and $\bar{R}^2$'s increase as one moves from the preceding period to the current one and then from there to the succeeding period. From this timing relationship we are led to suspect that the case for effects run-

*From Magnus Blomström, Robert E. Lipsey, and Mario Zejan. "Is Fixed Investment the Key to Economic Growth?" *Quarterly Journal of Economics* 111 (February 1996): 269–273. Reprinted by permission.

[1]See Levine and Renelt [1992] for a survey of the literature.

[2]We chose five-year periods, partly to dilute cyclical influences, partly to maximize the number of countries included and to use most of the years of the ICP benchmark surveys (the basis for the Summers and Heston estimates), for which the data should be most reliable. However, there is no theoretical basis for this interval, and it might be worthwhile to experiment with others also. Much shorter intervals might, however, give results reflecting business cycle developments rather than the longer term influences that are important for development.

A list of the 101 countries included in the study is provided in Blomström, Lipsey, and Zejan [1994].

ning from growth rates to subsequent capital formation is stronger than that for the effects running from capital formation to subsequent growth.

One risk in using pooled time series and cross-section data, is that the cross-sectional differences among countries reflect permanent characteristics of the countries that encourage or discourage both fixed investment and economic growth. Examples of such characteristics might be the efficiency of government, the degree of corruption, the level of violence, or the attitude of governments and populations toward individual achievement or enterprise. Any such relationship could give a false impression that high fixed capital formation resulted in high growth, or vice versa. To eliminate any such bias, we include country dummies. The effect is to remove cross-sectional differences among countries, leaving only time-series variations to be explained. The main result persists when intercountry differences are eliminated: growth seems to precede capital formation (see the second part of Table 1).

A more formal way of examining the direction of causality is to apply tests in the Granger-Sims causality framework [Granger 1969; Sims 1972]. We first estimate the following equations:

(i) $RGDPC_t = f(RGDPC_{t-1}, RGDPC_{t-2})$

(ii) $RGDPC_t = f(RGDPC_{t-1}, RGDPC_{t-2}, INV_{t-1})$,

where $RGDPC$ is growth in real income per capita, INV is the ratio of fixed capital formation to GDP, and t is the period (see Table 1). We interpret investment to be Granger-causing growth when a prediction of growth on the basis of its past history can be improved by further taking into account the previous period's investment.

Estimating (i) and (ii) gives the following results (t-values are in parentheses):

$$RGDPC_t = 0.661 + 0.227\ RGDPC_{t-1}$$
$$(7.0) \quad (3.7)$$

$$+\ 0.142\ RGDPC_{t-2}$$
$$(2.1)$$

$$\bar{R}^2 = 0.06 \quad n = 303$$

$$RGDPC_t = 0.660 + 0.228\ RGDPC_{t-1}$$
$$(6.7) \quad (3.5)$$

$$+\ 0.142\ RGDPC_{t-2} - 0.002\ INV_{t-1}$$
$$(1.9) \qquad\qquad (0.02)$$

$$\bar{R}^2 = 0.06 \quad n = 303$$

Table 1. Regressions of Growth in Real GDP per Capita on Fixed Capital Formation Ratios without and with Country Dummies

	Fixed capital formation/GDP		
	Preceding period	Current period	Following period
Country dummies excluded			
Coefficient	0.30	0.60	0.80
t-statistic	(3.42)	(5.71)	(8.94)
$\bar{R}^2$	0.03	0.07	0.16
No. of obs.	404	404	404
Country dummies included			
Coefficient	−1.00	−0.01	1.65
t-statistic	(3.95)	(0.04)	(6.78)
$\bar{R}^2$	0.16	0.12	0.23
No. of obs.	404	404	404

Real GDP per capita growth, 1965–1970, 1970–1975, 1975–1980, and 1980–1985 (ratio of end year over initial year).

Ratio of fixed capital formation to GDP, measured in current purchasing power parities, averaged over five-years periods (1960–1965, 1965–1970, 1970–1975, 1975–1980, 1980–1985, and 1983–1988).

Source: Summers and Heston (1991).

Thus, we cannot reject the null hypothesis that capital formation in the preceding period has no explanatory power with respect to growth in the current period, given the past history of growth in that country. The past history of growth is a poor predictor of current growth, but lagged investment does not improve the prediction.

We can then reverse the question to ask whether past growth has an effect on current capital formation rates, given the history of capital formation rates. The results are as follows (t-values are in parentheses):

$$INV_t = 2.48 + 0.948\ INV_{t-1} - 0.075\ INV_{t-2}$$
$$\quad\ (4.6)\ \ (15.3)\qquad\qquad (1.27)$$

$$\bar{R}^2 = 0.79 \quad n = 303$$

$$INV_t = -7.35 + 0.828\ INV_{t-1} - 0.012\ INV_{t-2}$$
$$\quad\ (4.9)\ \ (13.7)\qquad\qquad (0.21)$$

$$+ 9.49\ RGDPC_{t-1}$$
$$(6.9)$$

$$\bar{R}^2 = 0.82 \quad n = 303.$$

The significant t-statistic on $RGDPC_{t-1}$ suggests that past growth has a significant effect on current capital formation even after past capital formation is taken into account. Even though the past history of capital formation rates predicts current rates well, past growth rates improve the prediction. . . .

In sum, informal and formal tests using only fixed investment ratios as independent variables give evidence that economic growth precedes capital formation, but no evidence that capital formation precedes growth. Thus, the causality seems to run in only one direction, from economic growth to capital formation.

References

Blomström, Magnus, Robert E. Lipsey, and Mario Zejan, "Is Fixed Investment the Key to Economic Growth?" NBER Working Paper No. 4436, 1993.

Blomström, Magnus, Robert E. Lipsey, and Mario Zejan, "What Explains the Growth of Developing Countries?" in William Baumol, Richard Nelson, and Edward Wolff, eds., *International Convergence of Productivity* (London: Oxford University Press, 1994), pp. 243–59.

De Long, J. Bradford, and Lawrence Summers, "Equipment Investment and Economic Growth," *Quarterly Journal of Economics,* CVI (1991), 445–502.

De Long, J. Bradford, and Lawrence Summers, "Equipment Investment and Economic Growth: How Strong Is the Nexus?" *Brookings Papers on Economic Activity* (1992), 157–211.

Granger, C. W. J., "Investigating Causal Relations by Econometric Models and Cross-Spectral Methods," *Econometrica,* XXXVII (1969), 424–38.

Levine, Ross, and David Renelt, "A Sensitivity Analysis of Cross-Country Growth Regressions," *American Economic Review,* LXXXII (1992), 942–63.

Lipsey, Robert, and Irving Kravis, *Saving and Economic*

Growth: Is the United States Really Falling Behind? (New York: The Conference Board, 1987).

Sims, Christopher A., "Money, Income and Causality," *American Economic Review,* LXII (1972), 540–52.

Summers, Robert, and Alan Heston, "The Penn World Table (Mark 5): An Extended Set of International Comparisons, 1950–1988," *Quarterly Journal of Economics,* CVI (1991), 327–68.

Selection III.2. Interest Rates in the Organized Money Markets of Underdeveloped Countries, and Interest Rates Outside the Organized Money Markets of Underdeveloped Countries*

The size of an organized money market in any country may be indicated by either or both of the following ratios, although neither measurement is perfect: the ratio of deposit money to money supply and the ratio of the banking system's claims (mostly loans, advances, and bills discounted) on the private sector to national income. . . .

The ratio of deposit money to money supply actually measures banking development of the money market. However, to the extent that the development of commercial banking is synonymous with the development of the money market this ratio may be used as an indicator of the growth of a money market. In most underdeveloped countries, there are hardly any lending agencies of importance other than commercial banks. There are no discount houses or acceptance houses, and savings institutions (including life insurance companies) are in the early stages of development. . . .

Both ratios might be expected to be low in an underdeveloped country and high in a developed one. The ratio of deposit money to money supply should be higher in a more developed country because, with economic development, there is also development of the banking system. . . .

The structure of interest rates in the organized money markets of underdeveloped countries is usually more or less the same as in the developed ones. The short-term rate of interest is generally much below the long-term rate, as indicated by the spread between the government treasury bill rate and the government bond yield; the rate at which bills of exchange are discounted is also lower than the rate at which loans and advances are granted.

The lowest market rates are usually the call loan rates between commercial banks. The next lowest are those paid by commercial banks on short-term deposits, followed by the government treasury bill rate. Then come the rates at which commercial banks discount commercial paper, varying according to the type of security and the date of maturity. In most countries, especially in Asia, the govern-

ment bond yield comes next, followed by the lending rates of commercial banks. . . .

In general, the level of interest rates in underdeveloped countries, even in organized money markets, is higher than in the more developed countries. The more notable difference between the two groups of countries, however, is that the range of interest rates is generally much wider in underdeveloped countries. The volume of loans granted at relatively low rates in an underdeveloped country is not very important, as only limited amounts of financial assets are available to serve as collateral for lending at low rates. It is usually the foreign business firms with longer experience and larger capital which are able to borrow at the lower rates. Most of the indigenous firms have to pay the higher rates; this is especially true where foreign banks occupy an important position in the banking system. . . .

In spite of the small direct dependence of commercial banks on the central banks for funds, the latter are able to influence market rates by changes in the bank rate because of their economic, and at times their legal, position in the domestic money market, with wide powers for selective credit control, open market operations, and moral pressures.

The general expectation is that the long-term trend of interest rates in underdeveloped countries, at least in the organized markets, should be downward. Generally speaking, in these countries the banking systems and with them the money markets are likely to develop at a faster rate than the other sectors of the economy. The long-term supply of loanable funds therefore tends to increase more rapidly than the long-term demand. Where, for one reason or another, the growth of banking has been restricted or the banking system subjected by law to many restrictions, including controls on interest rates and of the purposes for which loans may be granted (as in a number of countries in Latin America), the long-term trend of interest rates may, however, not be downward. . . .

In [the above] examination . . . of the interest rate structure and the lending practices of organized money markets in underdeveloped countries, . . . it was shown that these differed much less than might have been expected from those prevailing in most developed countries. In underdeveloped countries, however, unorganized money markets

*From U Tun Wai, "Interest Rates in the Organized Money Markets of Underdeveloped Countries," *International Monetary Fund Staff Papers*, Vol. 5, No. 2 (August 1956). pp. 249–50, 252–53, 255, 258, 276–78: "Interest Rates Outside the Organized Money Markets of Underdeveloped Countries," ibid., Vol. 6. No. 1 (November 1957), pp. 80–83, 107–9, 119–25. Reprinted by permission.

also play a very important role, and any study of credit conditions in these countries that is to be adequate must be extended to cover the unorganized as well as the organized markets. Efforts have often been made to repair the deficiencies of the unorganized markets by government action designed to stimulate the development of cooperative credit or to provide credit through agricultural banks, etc.; it is convenient to include these government-sponsored institutions in a study of unorganized money markets in general.

Interest rates in the unorganized money markets of underdeveloped countries are generally very high in relation both to those in the organized money markets and to what is needed for rapid economic development. These high interest rates are caused by a disproportionately large demand for loanable funds coupled with a generally inelastic and limited supply of funds. The large demand stems from the special social and economic factors prevalent in the rural areas of underdeveloped countries. The low level of income leaves little surplus for saving and for the accumulation of capital for self-financing of agricultural and handicraft production. The uncertainty of the weather, which affects crop yields and incomes, causes an additional need for outside funds in bad years. A significant portion of the demand for loanable funds in rural areas is for financing consumption at levels much higher than are warranted by the low income of the peasant. . . .

The supply of loanable funds in the unorganized money markets is very limited and inelastic because the major source is the money-lender, and only very small quantities are supplied by indigenous bankers and organized institutions, such as cooperative credit societies and land mortgage banks. The moneylender in most cases is also a merchant or a landlord and therefore is willing to lend only at rates comparable with what he could earn by employing his capital in alternative uses which are often highly profitable. The lenders in the unorganized money markets do not have the facilities for mobilizing liquid funds available to commercial banks in organized markets and therefore the supply of funds is rather inflexible. Since the unorganized money markets are generally not closely connected with the organized money markets, there is little possibility of increasing the supply of loanable funds beyond the savings of the lending sector of the unorganized money markets. The limited supply of loanable funds indeed reflects the general shortage of capital in underdeveloped countries.

The disadvantages of the high rates of interest in the unorganized money markets are well known and include such important effects as "deadweight" agricultural indebtedness, alienation of land from agriculturalists to money-lenders and the agrarian unrest that is thus engendered, and a general slowing down of economic development. . . .

The organized money markets in underdeveloped countries are less fully integrated than the money markets in developed countries. The unorganized money markets in underdeveloped countries are even more imperfect, and indeed it is questionable whether the existing arrangements should be referred to as "markets." They are much less homogeneous than the organized markets and are generally scattered over the rural sector. There is very little contact between the lenders and borrowers in different localities. The usual textbook conditions for a perfect market are completely nonexistent: lenders and borrowers do not know the rates at which loans are being transacted in other parts of the country; the relationship between borrower and lender is not only that of a debtor and creditor but is also an integral part of a much wider socioeconomic pattern of village life and rural conditions.

In unorganized money markets, moreover, loans are often contracted and paid for not in money but in commodities; and the size of the average loan is very much smaller than in the organized money markets. Both borrowers and lenders in the two markets are often of quite different types. In the organized money markets, the borrowers are mainly traders (wholesale and retail) operating in the large cities and, to a less extent, manufacturers. Agriculturalists rarely account for a significant portion of demand except in those underdeveloped countries where export agriculture has been developed through plantations or estates. In the unorganized money markets, the borrowers are small agriculturalists, cottage industry workers, and some retail shopkeepers. The lenders in the organized money markets consist almost exclusively of commercial banks. In the unorganized markets, the suppliers of credit consist of a few financial institutions, such as cooperatives, private and government-sponsored agricultural banks, indigenous bankers, professional moneylenders, large traders, landlords, shopkeepers, relatives, and friends. Proper records of loans granted or repaid are usually not kept, and uniform accounting procedures are not adopted by the different lenders. Loans are granted more on a personal basis than in the organized money markets, and most of the loans granted by the moneylenders and by other noninstitutional sources are unsecured beyond the verbal promise of the borrower to repay.

The unorganized money market may be divided into three major parts: (1) a part in which the supply is dominated by indigenous bankers, cooperatives, and other institutions, and the demand by rural traders and medium-sized landlords; (2) a part in which the demand originates mainly from small agriculturalists with good credit ratings, who are able to obtain a large portion of their funds from respectable moneylenders, traders, and landlords at high but reasonable rates of interest, that is, rates that are high in relation to those prevailing in the organized money market but not exorbitant by the standards of the unorganized money market; (3) a part in which the demand originates from borrowers who are not good credit risks, who do not have suitable collateral, and who in consequence are driven to shady marginal lenders who charge exorbitant rates of interest. . . .

Many explanations have been offered for the high interest rates that generally prevail in unorganized money markets. One theory is that interest rates are high there because they are determined by custom and have always been high. This might be called the theory of the customary rate of interest. . . .

The theory of customary rates is not satisfactory, however, because it does not explain how or why the custom of high rates developed. The true explanation has to be found in the economic and social conditions of underdeveloped countries, which cause the demand for loanable funds to be large in relation to the available supply. Some writers tend to explain the high rates of interest in terms of demand factors while others emphasize supply. . . .

The difference in the levels of interest rates between the organized and unorganized money markets stems partly from the basic differences between the sources of supply of funds in the two markets. In an organized money market, facilities for the expansion of credit are open to the commercial banks, which have the use of funds belonging to depositors. These banks are therefore able to charge relatively low rates of interest and yet make satisfactory profits for the shareholders. On the other hand, moneylenders in an unorganized money market have little influence on the supply of funds at their disposal and, furthermore, their supply price tends to be influenced by the alternative uses to which their funds can be put.

A number of institutional factors are also responsible for high rates of interest in unorganized money markets. The size of the loan is usually small and thus the fixed handling charges are relatively high. Defaults also tend to be larger in unorganized money markets. These higher defaults are due not so much to a lower standard of morality and willingness to repay debts as to the fluctuations in prices and incomes derived from agricultural products, which reduce the ability of the agriculturalists to repay debts at inopportune times. . . .

The list of causes of high interest rates could be extended to include other social and economic factors in underdeveloped countries—even to fairly remote factors, such as the system of land tenure which prevents land from being used as collateral. A general statement, however, is that interest rates in the unorganized money markets of underdeveloped countries are high because the economy is underdeveloped and the money market unorganized. . . .

Any program to bring down interest rates in unorganized money markets must be comprehensive and should be guided by the principle that interest rates can be lowered only by reducing the demand for loanable funds as well as by increasing the supply. . . .

A reduction in borrowing for productive purposes may not be desirable, especially as the amount of self-financing which can take its place is negligible. Such borrowing can be reduced in the long run only through an increase in savings from higher agricultural output and income. It is not sufficient that the ability of the farmer to save be increased. The willingness to save must also be created. The problem of cheap agricultural credit is inseparable from the whole problem of agricultural development, including such measures as increasing the use of fertilizers and proper seeds; making available adequate marketing facilities, including proper grading, transportation, and storage of crops; and providing an efficient agricultural extension service. . . .

Even if it is true that the cure for high rates of interest is to be found more on the demand side than on the supply side, the supply of credit should also be increased. Supply should be increased in such a way that legitimate credit needs are met at cheaper rates without encouraging borrowing for consumption. This can be achieved by increasing the supply of institutional credit while at the same time taking steps to discourage borrowing from noninstitutional lenders. In this connection, it could be argued that legislation regarding moneylenders which has had the effect of drying up noninstitutional credit may be a blessing in disguise—although in a manner different from that intended by legislators.

Increasing the supply of institutional credit is a difficult problem, but the efforts of governments have had a fair degree of success. One problem is that of getting the commercial banks to lend more to agriculture. . . .

One way of inducing the organized financial institutions to lend more to agriculture is by making agriculturalists more creditworthy and generally reducing the risks of lending by lessening the impact of some of the natural calamities (floods, plant and animal diseases); improving the human factor, i.e., reducing carelessness and increasing honesty; reducing the uncertainties of the market through crop insurance, stabilized agricultural prices, etc. The lenders might also take certain steps, such as spreading loans between different types of borrower and region and supervising the use of loans for productive purposes.

Selection III.3. Financial Liberalization in Retrospect: Interest Rate Policies in LDCs*

When governments tax and otherwise distort their domestic capital market, the economy is said to be financially "repressed."[1] Usury restrictions on interest rates, heavy reserve requirements on bank deposits, and compulsory credit allocations interact with ongoing price inflation to reduce the attractiveness of holding claims on the domestic banking system. In such a repressed financial system, real deposit rates of interest on monetary assets are often negative, and are difficult to predict when inflation is high and unstable. Thus, the demand for money—broadly defined to include saving and term deposits as well as checking accounts and currency—falls as a proportion of GNP.

But these monetary assets naturally dominate the financial portfolios of small savers in less developed countries. Thus Edward Shaw and I hypothesized that repressing the monetary system fragments the domestic capital market with highly adverse consequences for the quality and quantity of real capital accumulation:

1. The flow of loanable funds through the organized banking system is reduced, forcing potential investors to rely more on self-finance:
2. Interest rates on the truncated flow of bank lending vary arbitrarily from one class of favored or disfavored borrower to another;
3. The process of self-finance within enterprises and households is itself impaired. If the real yield on deposits—as well as coin and currency—is negative, firms cannot easily accumulate liquid assets in preparation for making discrete investments. Socially costly inflation hedges look more attractive as a means of internal finance.
4. Significant financial deepening outside of the repressed banking system becomes impossible when firms are dangerously illiquid and/or inflation is high and unstable. Robust open markets in stocks and bonds, or intermediation by trust and insurance companies, require monetary stability.

*From Ronald I. McKinnon, *Financial Liberalization in Retrospect: Interest Rate Policies in LDCs,* Center for Economic Policy Research Publication No. 74, Stanford University (July 1986), pp. 1–3, 5–9, processed. Reprinted by permission.

[1]Terminology introduced by Edward Shaw (1973) and McKinnon (1973). Further discussion of optimal financial management in a repressed economy is found in McKinnon and Mathieson (1981). A more general review of the literature on financial repression and liberalization can be found in Fry (1982).

Remedying financial repression is implicit in its definition. We suggested keeping positive and more uniformly high real rates of interest within comparable categories of bank deposits and loans by eliminating undue reserve requirements, interest ceilings, and mandated credit allocations on the one hand, while stabilizing the price level through appropriate macroeconomic measures on the other. Then, savers and investors would better "see" the true scarcity price of capital, and thus reduce the great dispersion in the profitability of investing in different sectors of the economy.

These strictures for liberalizing the financial system seem now like mere truisms to most economists—although not to politicians. Today, both the World Bank and the International Monetary Fund stress the importance of stabilizing the domestic price level, and increasing the flow of generally available loanable funds at close to market-clearing interest rates. From the perspective of the 1980s, those countries with substantially positive real interest rates and high real financial growth—such as Japan, Taiwan, and Singapore—are regarded as leading success stories.

In the 1980s, this new emphasis on the advantages of financial liberalization is quite remarkable. Well into the 1970s, many development economists had still favored the generation of "forced" saving through inflation—or through shifts in the internal distribution of income by such means as turning the internal terms of trade against agriculture in order to transfer an economic "surplus" to the industrial sector. Credit subsidies, at below market rates of interest, were once widely promoted as a means of stimulating socially desirable investments. Unless so manipulated or repressed, the financial sector was not viewed as a leading force in the development process.

Outside of the centrally planned economies, however, there is now widespread agreement that flows of saving and investment should be voluntary, and significantly decentralized in an open capital market at close to "equilibrium" interest rates. . . .

What lessons have been learned about financial repression in steady states—say over a decade or more? Countries that have sustained higher real rates of interest have generally had robust real financial growth leading to higher real economic growth. Some data on private holdings of "broad" money throw light on these issues. Table 1 pre-

Table 1. Bank Loanable Funds in Typical Semi-industrial LDCs (ratio of M2 to GNP)

Country	1960	1965	1970	1975	1980	Mean 1960–80
Latin America						
Argentina	0.245	0.209	0.267	0.168	0.234	0.225
Brazil	0.148	0.156	0.205	0.164	0.175	0.170
Chile	0.123	0.130	0.183	0.099	0.208	0.149
Colombia	0.191	0.204	0.235	—	0.222	0.210
Mean ratio of M2 to GNP for four Latin American countries						0.184
Asia and the Middle East						
India	0.283	0.262	0.264	0.295	0.382	0.297
Philippines	0.186	0.214	0.236	0.186	0.219	0.208
Sri Lanka	0.284	0.330	0.275	0.255	0.317	0.291
Turkey	0.202	0.223	0.237	0.222	0.136	0.204
Mean ratio of M2 to GNP for four Asian countries						0.247

Source: International Monetary Fund, *International Financial Statistics* (various issues).

sents ratios of the broad money supply (M2) to gross national product (GNP).[2] One noticeable characteristic is that even the slower-growing Asian countries (shown in the lower panel) tend to be more financially developed than typical Latin American countries (shown in the upper panel). However, both groups of slowly or erratically growing economies have fairly low ratios of M2 to GNP, averaging about 0.22.

In contrast, Table 2 shows financial development in the really rapid-growth economies—West Germany, Japan, South Korea, Taiwan, and Singapore. A high and rising M2/GNP ratio indicates a large real flow of loanable funds. Because capital markets in these economies were dominated by banks, ratios of M2 to GNP encompass the main domestic flow of loanable funds in the system. By 1980 Japan, Taiwan, and Singapore had M2/GNP ratios of 0.75 or more. Only South Korea had a much lower ratio of M2 to GNP (0.34), and had to make up for this shortage of domestic loanable funds by borrowing heavily abroad. The other countries shown in Table 2 are now net international creditors.

Although a higher rate of financial growth is positively correlated with successful real growth, Patrick's problem [Selection III.4] remains unresolved: what is the cause and what is the effect? Is finance a leading sector in economic development,

or does it simply follow growth in real output which is generated elsewhere? Perhaps individuals whose incomes grow quickly want financial assets simply as a kind of consumer good (i.e., an incidental outcome of the growth process). To disentangle these issues, Table 3 presents some data from a recent study on interest-rate policies in developing countries (IMF 1983). Pure data availability and membership of the IMF were the criteria on which countries were selected.

For any one country over time, the real interest rate can vary a great deal, even from positive to negative or vice versa. For the period from 1971 to 1980, the IMF calculated an average real interest rate for each country on a fairly common asset, usually a thirty-day deposit. Countries were then classified according to whether their average real interest rate was positive, mildly negative, or highly negative. Because most of these countries have fragmented interest-rate structures, a representative interest rate is not easy to select. Nevertheless the IMF managed to devise the three-way classification in Table 3.

Using this same sample of countries from the IMF study, real financial growth (which is not the same as measured personal saving) is shown to be positively correlated with real GDP growth in Figure 1. The left-hand panel of Figure 2 shows that those countries that maintain positive real rates of interest have higher growth in real financial assets, as might be expected. Most importantly, the right-hand panel of Figure 2 shows a significant positive correlation between real rates of interest and real growth in GDP. . . .

[2]These ratios are taken from IMF, *International Financial Statistics,* various issues. The IMF defines M2 as money plus quasi-money plus deposits outside commercial banks. M2 is a stock tabulated as of 30 June for each calendar year, whereas GNP is the flow of output for that year.

Table 2. Bank Loanable Funds in Rapidly Growing Economies (ratio of M2 to GNP)

Country	1955	1960	1965	1970	1975	1980
Germany[a]	0.331	0.294	0.448	0.583	0.727	0.913
Japan	0.554[b]	0.737[b]	0.701[b]	0.863	1.026	1.390
South Korea	0.069	0.114	0.102	0.325	0.323	0.337
Taiwan	0.115	0.166	0.331	0.462	0.588	0.750
Singapore	—	—	0.542[b]	0.701	0.668	0.826

[a]As well as deposits and currency, the German series includes bank bonds sold directly to the public.

[b]The bias is downward because deposit information on specialised credit institutions was not collected.

Source: International Monetary Fund, *International Financial Statistics* (various issues).

Table 3. Selected Developing Countries Grouped According to Interest-Rate Policies: Growth of Real Financial Assets and Real GDP, 1971–80 (compound growth rates, percent per annum)

	Financial Assets[a]	GDP
1. Countries with Positive Real Interest Rates		
Malaysia	13.8	8.0
South Korea	11.1	8.6
Sri Lanka	10.1	4.7
Nepal	9.6	2.0
Singapore	7.6	9.1
Philippines	5.6	6.2
2. Countries with Moderately Negative Real Interest Rates		
Pakistan[b]	9.9	5.4
Thailand	8.5	6.9
Morocco	8.2	5.5
Colombia	5.5	5.8
Greece	5.4	4.7
South Africa	4.3	3.7
Kenya	3.6	5.7
Burma	3.5	4.3
Portugal	.8	4.7
Zambia	−1.1	0.8
3. Countries with Severely Negative Real Interest Rates		
Peru	3.2	3.4
Turkey	2.2	5.1
Jamaica	−1.9	−0.7
Zaire	−6.8	0.1
Ghana	−7.6	−0.1

[a]Measured as the sum of monetary and quasi-monetary deposits with the banking sector, corrected for changes in the consumer price index.

[b]The period covered is 1974–80.

Source: International Monetary Fund, *Interest Rate Policies in Developing Countries.* Occasional Paper, no. 22, October 1983.

Figure 1. Selected developing countries: growth of real GDP and real financial assets, 1971–80.

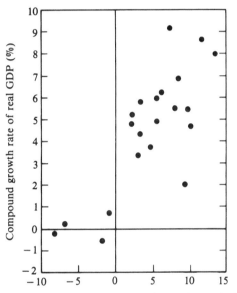

Compound growth rate of real financial assets[a] (%)

[a]As defined in Table 3. *Source:* International Monetary Fund, *Interest Rate Policies in Developing Countries,* Occasional Paper, no. 22, October 1983.

With this kind of regression analysis, care must be taken in deciding which variables are exogenous and which endogenous. Positive correlations between growth in financial assets and growth in GDP do not show which way the causality operates. However, for the purposes of portfolio choice by individual investors, a case can be made for treating the real rate of interest as exogenous. Governments frequently intervene to set ceilings on nominal rates of interest on bank deposits, and at the same time they determine the aggregate rate of price inflation; the real rate of interest, therefore, is very much determined by public policy. Thus the

Figure 2. Selected developing countries grouped according to interest-rate policies: growth of real financial assets and real GDP, 1971–80.

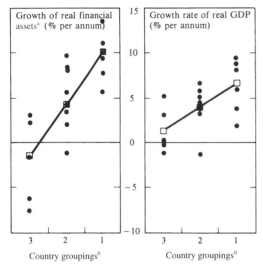

[a]As defined in Table 3

[b]See Table 3 for specifications of these groupings.

Source: International Monetary Fund, *Interest Rate Policies in Developing Countries,* Occasional Paper, no. 22, October 1983.

In an inflationary economy, real rates of interest on financial assets are usually negative. Because of inflation, however, the private sector is forced to abstain from current consumption. Individuals must keep adding to their nominal money balances in order to prevent their real balances from declining. But this inflation "tax" extracted by the government is classified in the GNP accounts as if it were private saving. However, real personal financial assets are not accumulating, and the flow of loanable funds to the private sector may be quite low—even though the flow of private "saving," as measured in the GNP accounts, might be quite high. Typically, therefore, systematic relationships cannot be derived from cross-sectional data between the flow of personal saving and real rates of interest, or between personal saving and inflation. From cross-country comparisons of "long-run" experiences over a decade or more, however, the positive correlation between real interest rates and real growth seems unambiguous.

Apparently the quality, if not the quantity, of investment improves significantly when interest rates are positive and financial intermediation is robust.

References

Fry, Maxwell J. (1982). "Models of Financially Repressed Developing Economies." *World Development* 10 (September).

McKinnon, Ronald I. (1973). *Money and Capital in Economic Development.*

McKinnon, Ronald I., and Donald Mathieson (1981). "How to Manage a Repressed Economy." *Princeton Essays in International Finance,* no. 145.

Shaw, Edward S. (1973). *Financial Deepening in Economic Development.*

presumption is that nonrepressive financial policies, resulting in significantly positive real rates of interest, contribute to higher economic growth.

Any positive link between real rates of interest and personal saving, as measured in the GDP accounts, is much less apparent. The results of cross-country statistical studies linking inflation rates to aggregate saving have been quite ambiguous. This ambiguity is puzzling: shouldn't saving be discouraged as inflation erodes the real values of financial assets?

Comment III.1. Financial Liberalization

The policy implications of models of financial repression are that economic growth can be increased by removing interest rate ceilings and bringing the deposit rate of interest up to the free-market equilibrium rate, by eliminating selective or quantitative credit programs, and by ensuring that financial markets operate competitively with freedom of entry.

A number of developing countries have undertaken such policies of financial liberalization along with their stabilization programs. According to the McKinnon analysis of financial repression, economic liberalization and monetary stabilization are complementary concepts. When inflation is high and uncertain, the full deregulation (liberalization) of markets in goods, financial capital, or labor services cannot work well. In determining how to bring domestic inflation under control in a liberalizing economy, the government must attempt to keep interest rates, exchange rates, and wage rates properly aligned during the process of disinflation.

This policy has proved difficult in a number of countries. The general case favoring financial liberalization has been called into question by a series of bank panics and bankruptcies in the Southern Cone of Latin America. See Carlos Diaz-Alejandro, "Good Bye Financial Repression, Hello Financial Crash," *Journal of Development Economics* (September–October 1985), and Vittorio Corbo and Jaime de Melo, eds., "Liberalization with Stabilization in the Southern Cone of Latin America" [special issue], *World Development* (August 1985).

From these country cases, it is clear that macroeconomic stabilization policies must precede deregulation of banks and other financial institutions. The developing country must also avoid overborrowing from abroad when a liberalization program appears to be successful. See Ronald I. McKinnon, "Monetary Stabilization in LDCs and the International Capital Market," Stanford Center for Research in Economic Growth (June 1986, mimeographed), and *The Order of Economic Liberalization* (1991); World Bank, *World Development Report 1989* (1989), chap. 9. The risk of overborrowing has been made especially clear by the East Asian Crisis of 1997–1998 (see Section I.B).

Contrary to the models of financial repression, however, the empirical evidence is ambiguous regarding whether a rise in real deposit rates has a positive effect on saving ratios. Higher interest rates increase the benefits of saving but at the same time reduce the need for saving. The existence of informal curb markets in developing countries may also limit the influence of interest rates on saving.

A number of empirical studies conclude that the net response of savings to interest rates is small. See Rudiger Dornbusch and Alejandro Reynoso, "Financial Factors in Economic Development," in *Policymaking in the Open Economy,* ed., Dornbusch (1993), chap. 4; papers by Paul Collier and Colin Mayer, and Maxwell J. Fry in *Oxford Review of Economic Policy* 5 (1989); and Alberto Giovannini, "Saving and the Real Interest Rate in LDCs," *Journal of Development Economics* 18 (1985).

Even though the increase in savings and hence the quantity of investment may be small, there have been substantial gains in the quality of investment in countries that have undertaken financial liberalization. This result conforms to the better allocation of investment through the market instead of by government direction. Financial liberalization tends to be most effective in raising economic growth through higher productivity of investment.

For other discussions of how to pursue financial liberalization and price stability, see Ronald I. McKinnon and Donald J. Mathieson, *How to Manage a Repressed Economy,* Princeton Essays in International Finance, no. 145 (December 1981); Basant Kapur, "Alternative Stabilization Policies for Less Developed Countries," *Journal of Political Economy* (August 1976); S. Van Wijnbergen, "Interest Rate Management in LDCs," *Journal of Monetary Economics* (September 1983); and L. Taylor, *Structuralist Macroeconomics* (1983).

Selection III.4. Financial Development and Economic Growth in Underdeveloped Countries*

Typical statements indicate that the financial system somehow accommodates—or, to the extent that it malfunctions, it restricts—growth of real per capita output. For example,

It seems to be the case that where enterprise leads finance follows. The same impulses within an economy which set enterprise on foot make owners of wealth venturesome, and when a strong impulse to invest is fettered by lack of finance, devices are invented to release it . . . and habits and institutions are developed.[1]

Such an approach places emphasis on the demand side for financial services; as the economy grows it generates additional and new demands for these services, which bring about a supply response in the growth of the financial system. In this view, the lack of financial institutions in underdeveloped countries is simply an indication of the lack of demand for their services.

We may term as "demand-following" the phenomenon in which the creation of modern financial institutions, their financial assets and liabilities, and related financial services is in response to the demand for these services by investors and savers in the real economy. In this case, the evolutionary development of the financial system is a continuing consequence of the pervasive, sweeping process of economic development. The emerging financial system is shaped both by changes in objective opportunities—the economic environment, the institutional framework—and by changes in subjective responses—individual motivations, attitudes, tastes, preferences.

The nature of the demand for financial services depends upon the growth of real output and upon the commercialization and monetization of agriculture and other traditional subsistence sectors. The more rapid the growth rate of real national income, the greater will be the demand by enterprises for external funds (the saving of others) and therefore financial intermediation, since under most circumstances firms will be less able to finance expansion from internally generated depreciation allowances and retained profits. (The pro-

portion of external funds in the total source of enterprise funds will rise.) For the same reason, with a given aggregate growth rate, the greater the variance in the growth rates among different sectors or industries, the greater will be the need for financial intermediation to transfer savings to fast-growing industries from slow-growing industries and from individuals. The financial system can thus support and sustain the leading sectors in the process of growth.

The demand-following supply response of the growing financial system is presumed to come about more or less automatically. It is assumed that the supply of entrepreneurship in the financial sector is highly elastic relative to the growing opportunities for profit from provision of financial services, so that the number and diversity of types of financial institutions expand sufficiently; and a favorable legal, institutional, and economic environment exists. The government's attitudes, economic goals, and economic policies, as well as the size and rate of increase of the government debt, are of course important influences in any economy on the nature of the economic environment. As a consequence of real economic growth, financial markets develop, widen, and become more perfect, thus increasing the opportunities for acquiring liquidity and for reducing risk, which in turn feeds back as a stimulant to real growth.[2]

The demand-following approach implies that finance is essentially passive and permissive in the growth process. Late eighteenth and early nineteenth century England may be cited as a historical example. In fact, the increased supply of financial services in response to demand may not be at all automatic, flexible, or inexpensive in underdeveloped countries. Examples include the restrictive banking legislation in early nineteenth century France, religious barriers against loans and interest charges, and Gerschenkron's analysis of the abortive upswing of Italian industrial development in the 1880s "mainly, it is believed, because the modern investment bank had not yet been established in Italy."[3] In underdeveloped countries today, similar obstacles, together with imperfections

*From Hugh T. Patrick, "Financial Development and Economic Growth in Underdeveloped Countries," *Economic Development and Cultural Change,* Vol. 14, No. 2 (January 1966), pp. 174–77. Reprinted by permission.

[1]Joan Robinson, "The Generalization of the General Theory," in *The Rate of Interest and Other Essays* (London, 1952), pp. 86–87.

[2]Cf. W. Arthur Lewis. *The Theory of Economic Growth* (London, 1955), pp. 267–86.

[3]Alexander Gerschenkron, *Economic Backwardness in Historical Perspective—A Book of Essays* (Cambridge, 1962) p. 363. See also Chapter 4.

in the operation of the market mechanism, may dictate an inadequate demand-following response by the financial system. The lack of financial services, thus, in one way or another restricts or inhibits effective growth patterns and processes.

Less emphasis has been given in academic discussions (if not in policy actions) to what may be termed the "supply-leading" phenomenon: the creation of financial institutions and the supply of their financial assets, liabilities, and related financial services in advance of demand for them, especially the demand of entrepreneurs in the modern, growth-inducing sectors. "Supply-leading" has two functions: to transfer resources from traditional (non-growth) sectors to modern sectors, and to promote and stimulate an entrepreneurial response in these modern sectors. Financial intermediation which transfers resources from traditional sectors, whether by collecting wealth and saving from those sectors in exchange for its deposits and other financial liabilities, or by credit creation and forced saving, is akin to the Schumpeterian concept of innovation financing.

New access to such supply-leading funds may in itself have substantial, favorable expectational and psychological effects on entrepreneurs. It opens new horizons as to possible alternatives, enabling the entrepreneur to "think big." This may be the most significant effect of all, particularly in countries where entrepreneurship is a major constraint on development. Moreover, as has been emphasized by Rondo Cameron,[4] the top management of financial institutions may also serve as entrepreneurs in industrial enterprises. They assist in the establishment of firms in new industries or in the merger of firms (the advantages of economies of scale may be more than offset by the establishment of restrictive cartels or monopolies, however), not only by underwriting a substantial portion of the capital, but more importantly by assuming the entrepreneurial initiative.

By its very nature, a supply-leading financial system initially may not be able to operate profitably by lending to the nascent modern sectors.[5] There are, however, several ways in which new financial institutions can be made viable. First, they may be government institutions, using government capital and perhaps receiving direct government subsidies. This is exemplified not only by Russian

experience in the latter half of the nineteenth century, but by many underdeveloped countries today. Second, private financial institutions may receive direct or indirect government subsidies, usually the latter. Indirect subsidies can be provided in numerous ways. Commercial banks may have the right to issue banknotes under favorable collateral conditions; this technique was more important in the eighteenth and nineteenth centuries (national banking in Japan in the 1870s; wildcat banking in the United States) than it is likely to be in present underdeveloped countries, where this right is reserved for the central bank or treasury. Nonetheless, modern equivalent exist. They include allowing private financial institutions to create deposit money with low (theoretically, even negative) reserve requirements and central bank rediscount of commercial bank loans at interest rates effectively below those on the loans. Third, new, modern financial institutions may initially lend a large proportion of their funds to traditional (agricultural and commercial) sectors profitably, gradually shifting their loan portfolio to modern industries as these begin to emerge. This more closely resembles the demand-following phenomenon; whether such a financial institution is supply-leading depends mainly on its attitude in searching out and encouraging new ventures of a modern nature.

It cannot be said that supply-leading finance is a necessary condition or precondition for inaugurating self-sustained economic development. Rather, it presents an opportunity to induce real growth by financial means. It thus is likely to play a more significant role at the beginning of the growth process than later. Gerschenkron implies that the more backward the economy relative to others in the same time period (and the greater the forced-draft nature of the economic development effort), the greater the emphasis which is placed on what I here term supply-leading finance.[6] At the same time, it should be recognized that the supply-leading approach to development of a country's financial system also has its dangers, and they should not be underestimated. The use of resources, especially entrepreneurial talents and managerial skills, and the costs of explicit or implicit subsidies in supply-leading development must produce sufficient benefits in the form of stimulating real economic development for this approach to be justified.

In actual practice, there is likely to be an interaction of supply-leading and demand-following

---

[4]Rondo Cameron, "The Bank as Entrepreneur." *Explorations in Entrepreneurial History,* Series 2, Vol. 1, No. 1 (Fall 1963), pp. 50–55.

[5]Except in the extreme case where inherent profit opportunities are very high, and supply-leading stimulates a major entrepreneurial effort.

[6]Gerschenkron, *Economic Backwardness in Historical Perspective.*

phenomena. Nevertheless, the following sequence may be postulated. Before sustained modern industrial growth gets underway, supply-leading may be able to induce real innovation-type investment. As the process of real growth occurs, the supply-leading impetus gradually becomes less important, and the demand-following financial response becomes dominant. This sequential process is also likely to occur within and among specific industries or sectors. One industry may initially be encouraged financially on a supply-leading basis and as it develops have its financing shift to demand-following, while another industry remains in the supply-leading phase. This would be related to the timing of the sequential development of industries, particularly in cases where the timing is determined more by governmental policy than by private demand forces. . . .

Selection III.5. Financial Development and Economic Growth: Views and Agenda*

A Parable

Consider Fred, who has just developed a design for a new truck that extracts rocks from a quarry better than existing trucks. His idea for manufacturing trucks requires an intricate assembly line with specialized labor and capital. Highly specialized production processes would be difficult without a medium of exchange. He would find it prohibitively costly to pay his workers and suppliers using barter exchange. Financial instruments and markets that *facilitate transactions* will allow and promote specialization and thereby permit him to organize his truck assembly line. Moreover, the increased specialization induced by easier transactions may foster learning-by-doing and innovation by the workers specializing on their individual tasks.

Production requires capital. Even if Fred had the savings, he would not wish to put all of his savings in one risky investment. Also, he wants ready access to savings for unplanned events; he is reluctant to tie up his savings in the truck project, which will not yield profits, if it does yield profits, for a long time. His distaste for risk and desire for liquidity create incentives for him to (a) diversify the family's investments and (b) not commit too much of his savings to an illiquid project, like producing a new truck. In fact, if Fred must invest disproportionately in his illiquid truck project, he may forgo his plan. Without a mechanism for managing risk, the project may die. Thus, *liquidity, risk pooling, and diversification* will help him start his innovative project.

Moreover, Fred will require outside funding if he has insufficient savings to initiate his truck project. There are problems, however, in mobilizing savings for Fred's truck company. First, it is very costly and time consuming to collect savings from individual savers. Fred does not have the time, connections, and information to collect savings from everyone in his town and neighboring communities even though his idea is sound. Banks and investment banks, however, can mobilize savings more cheaply than Fred due to economies of scale, economies of scope, and experience. Thus, Fred may seek the help of a financial intermediary to *mobilize savings* for his new truck plant.

*From Ross Levine, "Financial Development and Economic Growth: Views and Agenda," *Journal of Economic Literature* 35 (June 1997): 701–709. Reprinted by permission.

Two additional problems ("frictions") may keep savings from flowing to Fred's project. To fund the truck plant, the financial intermediaries—and savers in financial intermediaries—require information about the truck design, Fred's ability to implement the design, and whether there is a sufficient demand for better quarry trucks. This information is difficult to obtain and analyze. Thus, the financial system must be able to acquire *reliable information* about Fred's idea before funding the truck plant. Furthermore, if potential investors feel that Fred may steal the funds, or run the plant poorly, or misrepresent profits, they will not provide funding. To finance Fred's idea, outside creditors must have confidence that Fred will run the truck plant well. Thus, for Fred to receive funding, the financial system must monitor *managers and exert corporate control*.

While this parable does not contain all aspects of the discussion of financial functions, it provides one cohesive story of how the five financial functions may interact to promote economic development. . . .

The Level of Financial Development and Growth: Cross-Country Studies

Consider first the relationship between economic growth and aggregate measures of how well the financial system functions. The seminal work in this area is by Goldsmith (1969). He uses the value of financial intermediary assets divided by GNP to gauge financial development under the assumption that the size of the financial system is positively correlated with the provision and quality of financial services. Using data on 35 countries from 1860 to 1963 (when available) Goldsmith (1969, p. 48) finds:

(1) a rough parallelism can be observed between economic and financial development if periods of several decades are considered; [and]
(2) there are even indications in the few countries for which the data are available that periods of more rapid economic growth have been accompanied, though not without exception, by an above-average rate of financial development.

Goldsmith's work, however, has several weaknesses: (a) the investigation involves limited observations on only 35 countries; (b) it does not systematically control for other factors influencing economic growth (Levine and David Renelt 1992); (c) it does not examine whether financial development is associated with productivity growth and capital accumulation; (d) the size of financial intermediaries may not accurately measure the functioning of the financial system; and (e) the close association between the size of the financial system and economic growth does not identify the direction of causality.[1]

Recently, researchers have taken steps to address some of these weaknesses. For example, King and Levine (1993a, 1993b, 1993c) study 80 countries over the period 1960–1989, systematically control for other factors affecting long-run growth, examine the capital accumulation and productivity growth channels, construct additional measures of the level of financial development, and analyze whether the level of financial development predicts long-run economic growth, capital accumulation, and productivity growth. (Also, see Gelb 1989; Gertler and Rose 1994; Roubini and Sala-i-Martin 1992; Easterly 1993; and the overview by Pagano 1993.) They use four measures of "the level of financial development" to more precisely measure the functioning of the financial system than Goldsmith's size measure. Table 1 summarizes the values of these measures relative to real per capita GDP (RGDP) in 1985. The first measure, DEPTH, measures the size of financial intermediaries and equals liquid liabilities of the financial system (currency plus demand and interest-bearing liabilities of banks and nonbank financial intermediaries) divided by GDP. As shown, citizens of the richest countries—the top 25 percent on the basis of income per capita—held about two-thirds of a year's income in liquid assets in formal financial intermediaries, while citizens of the poorest countries—the bottom 25 percent— held only a quarter of a year's income in liquid assets. There is a strong correlation between real per capita GDP and DEPTH. The second measure of financial development, BANK, measures the degree to which the central bank versus commercial banks are allocating credit. BANK equals the ratio of bank credit divided by bank credit plus central bank domestic assets. The intuition underlying this measure is that banks are more likely to provide the five financial functions than central banks.

There are two notable weaknesses with this measure, however. Banks are not the only financial intermediaries providing valuable financial functions and banks may simply lend to the government or public enterprises. BANK is greater than 90 percent in the richest quartile of countries. In contrast, commercial banks and central banks allocate about the same amount of credit in the poorest quartile of countries. The third and fourth measures partially address concerns about the allocation of credit. The third measures, PRIVATE, equals the ratio of credit allocated to private enterprises to total domestic credit (excluding credit to banks). The fourth measure, PRIVY, equals credit to private enterprises divided by GDP. The assumption underlying these measures is that financial systems that allocate more credit to private firms are more engaged in researching firms, exerting corporate control, providing risk management services, mobilizing savings, and facilitating transactions than financial systems that simply funnel credit to the government or state owned enterprises. As depicted in Table 1, there is a positive, statistically significant correlation between real per capita GDP and the extent to which loans are directed to the private sector.

King and Levine (1993b, 1993c) then assess the strength of the empirical relationship between each of these four indicators of the level of financial development averaged over the 1960–1989 period, F, and three growth indicators also averaged over the 1960–1989 period, G. The three growth indicators are as follows: (1) the average rate of real per capita GDP growth, (2) the average rate of growth in the capital stock per person, and (3) total productivity growth, which is a "Solow residual" defined as real per capita GDP growth minus (0.3) times the growth rate of the capital stock per person. In other words, if $F(i)$ represents the value of the ith indicator of financial development (DEPTH, BANK, PRIVY, PRIVATE) averaged over the period 1960–1989, $G(j)$ represents the value of the jth growth indicator (per capita GDP growth, per capita capital stock growth, or productivity growth) averaged over the period 1960–1989, and X represents a matrix of conditioning information to control for other factors associated with economic growth (e.g., income per capita, education, political stability, indicators of exchange rate, trade, fiscal, and monetary policy), then the following 12 regressions are run on a cross-section of 77 countries:

$$G(j) = \alpha + \beta F(i) + \gamma X + \varepsilon \qquad (1)$$

There is a strong positive relationship between

---

[1]Goldsmith (1969) recognized these weaknesses, e.g., "there is no possibility, however, of establishing with confidence the direction of the causal mechanisms, i.e., of deciding whether financial factors were responsible for the acceleration of economic development or whether financial development reflected economic growth whose mainsprings must be sought elsewhere" (p. 48).

Table 1. Financial Development and Real Per Capita GDP in 1985

Indictors	Very rich	Rich	Poor	Very poor	Correlation with Real per Capita GDP in 1985	(P-value)
DEPTH	0.67	0.51	0.39	0.26	0.51	(0.0001)
BANK	0.91	0.73	0.57	0.52	0.58	(0.0001)
PRIVATE	0.71	0.58	0.47	0.37	0.51	(0.0001)
PRIVY	0.53	0.31	0.20	0.13	0.70	(0.0001)
RGDP85	13053	2376	754	241		
Observations	29	29	29	29		

Source: King and Levine (1993a)

Very rich: Real GDP per Capita > 4998
Rich: Real GDP per Capita > 1161 and < 4998
Poor: Real GDP per Capita > 391 and < 1161
Very poor: Real GDP per Capita < 391

DEPTH =   Liquid liabilities to GDP
BANK =   Deposit money bank domestic credit divided by deposit money bank + central bank domestic credit
PRIVATE =   Claims on the non-financial private sector to domestic credit
PRIVY =   Gross claims on private sector to GDP
RGDP85 =   Real per capita GDP in 1985 (in constant 1987 dollars)

each of the four financial development indicators, $F(i)$, and the three growth indicators $G(j)$, long-run real per capita growth rates, capital accumulation, and productivity growth. Table 2 summarizes the results on the 12 β's. Not only are *all* the financial development coefficients statistically significant, the sizes of the coefficients imply an economically important relationship. Ignoring causality, the coefficient of 0.024 on DEPTH implies that a country that increased DEPTH from the mean of the slowest growing quartile of countries (0.2) to the mean of the fastest growing quartile of countries (0.6) would have increased its per capita growth rate by almost one percent per year. This is large. The difference between the slowest growing 25 percent of countries and the fastest growing quartile of countries is about five percent per annum over this 30 year period. Thus, the rise in DEPTH alone eliminates 20 percent of this growth difference.

Finally, to examine whether finance simply follows growth, King and Levine (1993b) study whether the value of financial depth in 1960 predicts the rate of economic growth, capital accumulation, and productivity improvements over the next 30 years. Table 3 summarizes some of the results. In the three regressions reported in Table 3, the dependent variable is, respectively, real per capita GDP growth, real per capita capital stock growth, and productivity growth averaged over the period 1960–1989. The financial indicator in each of these regressions is the value of DEPTH in 1960. The regressions indicate that financial depth in 1960 is significantly correlated with each of the

growth indicators averaged over the period 1960–1989.[2] These results, plus those from more sophisticated time series studies, suggest that the initial level of financial development is a good predictor of subsequent rates of economic growth, physical capital accumulation, and economic efficiency improvements over the next 30 years even after controlling for income, education, political stability, and measures of monetary, trade, and fiscal policy.[3]

[2] There is an insufficient number of observations on BANK, PRIVATE, and PRIVY in 1960 to extend the analysis in Table 3 to these variables. Thus, King and Levine (1993b) use pooled, cross section, time series data. For each country, data permitting, they use data averaged over the 1960s, 1970s, and 1980s; thus, there are potentially three observations per country. They then relate the value of growth averaged over the 1960s with the value of, for example, BANK in 1960 and so on for the other two decades. They restrict the coefficients to be the same across decades. They find that the initial level of financial development is a good predictor of subsequent rates of economic growth, capital accumulation, and economic efficiency improvements over the next ten years after controlling for many other factors associated with long-run growth.

[3] These broad cross-country results hold even when using instrumental variables—primarily indicators of the legal treatment of creditors taken from LaPorta et al. 1996—to extract the exogenous component of financial development (Levine 1997). Furthermore, though disagreement exists (Woo Jung 1986 and Philip Arestis and Panicos Demetriades 1995), many time-series investigations find that financial sector development Granger-causes economic performance (Paul Wachtel Rousseau 1995). These results are particularly strong when using measures of the value-added provided by the financial system instead of measures of the size of the financial system (Klaus Neusser and Maurice Kugler 1996).

Table 2. Growth and Contemporaneous Financial Indicators, 1960–1989

Dependent Variable	DEPTH	BANK	PRIVATE	PRIVY
Real Per Capita GDP Growth	0.024***	0.032***	0.034***	0.032
	[0.007]	[0.005]	[0.002]	[0.002]
R^2	0.5	0.5	0.52	0.52
Real Per Capita Capital Stock Growth	0.022***	0.022**	0.020**	0.025***
	[0.001]	[0.012]	[0.011]	[0.001]
R^2	0.65	0.62	0.62	0.64
Productivity Growth	0.018**	0.026**	0.027***	0.025***
	[0.026]	[0.010]	[0.003]	[0.006]
R^2	0.42	0.43	0.45	0.44

Source: King and Levine (1993b)

*significant at the 0.10 level, **significant at the 0.05 level, ***significant at the 0.01 level.
[p-values in brackets]
Observations = 77

DEPTH =   Liquid liabilities to GDP
BANK =   Deposit bank domestic credit divided by deposit money bank + central bank domestic credit
PRIVATE =   Claims on the non-financial private sector to total claims
PRIVY =   Gross claims on private sector to GDP
Productivity Growth = Real Per Capita GDP Growth – (0.3) * Real Per Capita Capital Stock Growth

Other explanatory variables included in each of the 12 regressions: log of initial income, log of initial secondary school enrollment rate, ratio of government consumption expenditures to GDP, inflation rate, and ratio of exports plus imports to GDP.

Table 3. Growth and Initial Financial Depth, 1960–1989

	Per Capita GDP Growth, 1960–1989	Per Capita Capital Growth, 1960–1989	Per Capita Productivity Growth, 1960–1989
Constant	0.035***	0.002	0.034***
	[0.001]	[0.682]	[0.001]
Log (Real GDP per Person in	−0.016***	−0.004*	−0.015***
1960)	[0.001]	[0.068]	[0.001]
Log (Secondary school enrollment	0.013***	0.007***	0.011***
in 1960)	[0.001]	[0.001]	[0.001]
Government consumption/GDP	0.07*	0.049*	0.056*
in 1960	[0.051]	[0.064]	[0.076]
Inflation in 1960	0.037	0.02	0.029
	[0.239]	[0.238]	[0.292]
(Imports plus Exports)/GDP	−0.003	−0.001	−0.003
in 1960	[0.604]	[0.767]	[0.603]
	0.028***	0.019***	0.022***
DEPTH (liquid liabilities) in 1960	[0.001]	[0.001]	[0.001]
R^2	0.61	0.63	0.58

Source: King and Levine (1993b)

*significant at the 0.10 level, ** significant at the 0.05 level, *** significant at the 0.01 level.
[p-values in brackets]
Observations = 57

The relationship between the initial level of financial development and growth is large. For example, the estimated coefficients suggest that if in 1960 Bolivia had increased its financial depth from 10 percent of GDP to the mean value for developing countries in 1960 (23 percent), then Bolivia would have grown about 0.4 percent faster per annum, so that by 1990 real per capita GDP would have been about 13 percent larger than it was.[4] Thus, finance does not merely follow economic activity. The strong link between the level of finan-

[4]These examples do not consider causal issues or how to increase financial development.

cial development and the rate of long-run economic growth does not simply reflect contemporaneous shocks that affect both financial development and economic performance. There is a statistically significant and economically large empirical relationship between the initial level of financial development and future rates of long-run growth, capital accumulation, and productivity improvements. Furthermore, insufficient financial development has sometimes created a "poverty trap" and thus become a severe obstacle to growth even when a country has established other conditions (macroeconomic stability, openness to trade, educational attainment, etc.) for sustained economic development (Berthelemy and Varoudakis 1996).

Some recent work has extended our knowledge about the causal relationships between financial development and economic growth. For example, Rajan and Zingales (1996) assume that financial markets in the United States are relatively frictionless. This benchmark country then defines each industry's efficient demand for external finance (investment minus internal cash flow). They then examine industries across a large sample of countries and test whether the industries that are more dependent on external finance (in the United States) grow relatively faster in countries that begin the sample period with better developed financial systems. They find that industries that rely heavily on external funding grow comparatively faster in countries with well-developed intermediaries (as measured by PRIVY) and stock markets (as measured by stock market capitalization) than they do in countries that start with relatively weak financial systems. Similarly, using firm-level data from 30 countries, Demirgüç-Kunt and Maksimovic (1996) argue that firms with access to more developed stock markets grow at faster rates than they could have grown without this access. Furthermore, when individual states of the United States relaxed intrastate branching restrictions, this boosted bank lending quality and accelerated real per capita growth rates even after controlling for other growth determinants (Jayaratne and Strahan 1996). Thus, using firm- and industrial-level data for a broad cross-section of countries and data on individual states of the United States, recent research presents evidence consistent with the view that the level of financial development materially affects the rate and structure of economic development.

Not surprisingly, these empirical studies do not unambiguously resolve the issue of causality. Financial development may predict growth simply because financial systems develop in anticipation of future economic growth. Furthermore, differences in political systems, legal traditions (LaPorta et al. 1996), or institutions (Engerman and Sokoloff 1996; North 1981) may be driving both financial development and economic growth rates. Nevertheless, the body of evidence would tend to push many skeptics toward the view that the finance-growth link is a first-order relationship and that difference in financial development can alter economic growth rates over ample time horizons.

References

Berthelemy, Jean-Claude and Varoudakis, Aristomene. "Economic Growth, Convergence Clubs, and the Role of Financial Development," *Oxford Econ. Pap.,* Apr. 1996, *48*(2), pp. 300–28.

Demirgüç-Kunt, Asli and Maksimovic, Vojislav. "Financial Constraints, Uses of Funds, and Firm Growth: An International Comparison." World Bank mimeo, 1996.

Easterly, William. "How much Do Distortions Affect Growth?" *J. Monet. Econ.,* Nov. 1993, *32*(4), p. 187–212.

Engerman, Stanley L. and Sokoloff, Kenneth L. "Factor Endowments, Institutions, and Differential Paths of Growth Among New World Economies: A View from Economic Historians of the United States," in *How Latin America fell behind.* Ed.: Stephen Haber. Stanford, CA: Stanford U. Press, 1996, pp. 260–304.

Gelb, Alan H. "Financial Policies, Growth, and Efficiency." World Bank PPR Working Paper No. 202, June 1989.

Gertler, Mark and Rose, Andrew. "Finance, Public Policy and Growth," in Gerard Caprio, Jr., Izak Atiljas, and James A. Hanson. *Financial Reform.* New York: Cambridge Univ. Press, 1994, pp. 13–45.

Goldsmith, Raymond, W. *Financial structure and development.* New Haven, CT: Yale U. Press, 1969.

Jayaratne, Jith and Strahan, Philip E. "The Finance-Growth Nexus: Evidence from Bank Branch Deregulation" *Quart. J. Econ.,* Aug. 1996, *111*(3), pp. 639–70.

King, Robert G. and Levine, Ross. "Financial Intermediation and Economic Development," in *Financial intermediation in the construction of Europe.* Eds.: Colin Mayer and Xavier Vives. London: Centre for Economic Policy Research, 1993a, pp. 156–89.

———. "Finance and Growth: Schumpeter Might Be Right," *Quart. J. Econ.,* Aug. 1993b, *108*(3), pp. 717–37.

———. "Finance, Entrepreneurship, and Growth: Theory and Evidence," *J. Monet. Econ.,* Dec. 1993c, *32*(3), pp. 513–42.

Laporta, Rafael et al. "Law and Finance." National Bureau of Economic Research Working Paper No. 5661. July 1996.

Levine, Ross and Renelt, David. "A Sensitivity Analysis of Cross-Country Growth Regressions," *Amer. Econ. Rev.,* Sept. 1992, *82*(4), pp. 942–63.

North, Douglass C. *Structure and change in economic history.* New York: Norton, 1981.

Pagano, Marco. "Financial Markets and Growth: An Overview," *Europ. Econ. Rev.,* Apr. 1993, 37(2–3), pp. 613–22.

Rajan, Raghuram G. and Zingales, Luigi. "Financial Dependence and Growth." U. of Chicago mimeo, May 1996.

Roubini, Nouriel and Sala-i-Martin, Xavier. "Financial Repression and Economic Growth." *J. Devel. Econ.,* July 1992, 39(1), pp. 5–30.

Selection III.6. Good Policy or Good Luck? Country Growth Performance and Temporary Shocks*

Much of the new growth literature stresses country characteristics as the dominant determinant of growth performance. A vast empirical literature tests the effects of country characteristics on growth. This paper presents a fact suggesting the emphasis on country characteristics is misguided: growth rates are highly unstable over time, while country characteristics are highly persistent. The correlation across decades of countries' growth rates of income per capita is around 0.1 to 0.3, while most country characteristics display cross-decade correlations of 0.6 to 0.9. Correlations of growth across periods as long as two decades—period lengths comparable to those used in the cross-section empirical literature—are similarly low. With a few famous exceptions, the same countries do not do well period after period; countries are "success stories" one period and disappointments the next. . . .

Table 1 presents correlations of the least-squares growth rate of GDP per worker between 1960–69, 1970–79, and 1980–88.[1] The R^2 obtained by regressing the current growth rate on the previous decade's growth was less than 10 percent. Little of the variation of growth rates is explained by past growth.[2] This low persistence result is robust over the choice of country sample, time period, and sectoral performance measure.

Fig. 1 displays the scatterplot of the growth rates for 115 countries over two periods, 1960–73

and 1974–88. The dotted lines show the averages in each period. A large portion of the sample is contained in the off-diagonal quadrants: above average in 1960–73 and below average in 1974–88, or vice versa. The rank correlation is 0.21 in the figure.

The boxes in the corners represent the deciles of the period growth rates. The northeast box represents countries with growth in the top deciles in both periods. The southwest box shows the countries persistently in the bottom decile. The northeast box (persistent success) contains Botswana and the famous Asian Gang of Four (Hong Kong is actually just short of being the top decile in the first period). The East Asian success story is well-known, while Botswana has benefited from extensive diamond mines and from a democratic government that has avoided some of its neighbors' economic mistakes. The widespread perception of strong country effects in growth is strongly influenced by the Gang of Four; without them and Botswana, the already low correlation of growth rates between periods is cut in half. In contrast, persistence is not raised much by deleting a small number of outliers.

Persistence is also low for several subsamples of countries. The second, third, and fourth rows of table 1 show the correlations for nonoil countries, the OECD countries, and the nonoil developing countries. The only exception is a high correlation between the 60s and 70s in the small sample of OECD countries, but this reverts to zero between the 70s and 80s. . . .

The most straightforward explanation of the low persistence of growth rates would be that the country characteristics usually thought to determine growth are themselves not persistent. This section shows this explanation to be untenable: country characteristics are persistent. Fig. 2 shows persistence of country characteristics between the 60s and 70s and between the 70s and 80s for a sample of 45 countries for which data is available for all variables and time periods. The variables chosen are those that appear in the classic growth regression of Barro (1991), as well as several others common in the literature. All of the country characteristics display far higher persistence than growth rates. Many other country characteristics, like culture and geography, must be even more persistent.

However, some aggregate index of policy vari-

*From William Easterly, Michael Kremer, Lant Pritchett, and Lawrence Summers. "Good Policy or Good Luck? Country Growth Performance and Temporary Shocks," *Journal of Monetary Economics* 32 (December 1993): 459–480. Reprinted by permission.

[1]The data on real GDP per worker is taken from the Penn World Tables Mark 5 of Summers and Heston (1991). We obtained similar results using World Bank data on growth rates of output per worker valued at constant local prices. Results are also similar with GDP per capita; we used GDP per worker since it is a better measure of productivity change. The use of the least-squares growth rate reduces the sensitivity to endpoints; conventional compound growth rates are even less persistent. We have *a priori* excluded high-income oil exporters, i.e., Kuwait and Saudi Arabia, because their growth depends entirely on variations in oil production. Including Kuwait would raise persistence (to about 0.35) because it has strikingly negative growth in all periods.

[2]Others who have previously noted this include De Long and Summers (1991). Levine and Renelt (1991), and Fischer (1987). Quah (1993) has recently presented a similar finding, notably the instability of growth across periods in Markov transition matrices.

Table 1. Simple and Rank Correlations of Growth Rates Across Periods

Sample	Sample size	60s with 70s correlation coefficient		70s with 80s correlation coefficient	
		Simple	Rank	Simple	Rank
All countries	100	0.212	0.233	0.313	0.157
All nonoil	89	0.153	0.227	0.301	0.187
OECD	22	0.729	0.701	0.069	0.086
Developing countries, nonoil	67	0.099	0.150	0.332	0.251

Figure 1. Per worker growth rates per year, 1960–73 and 1974–88.

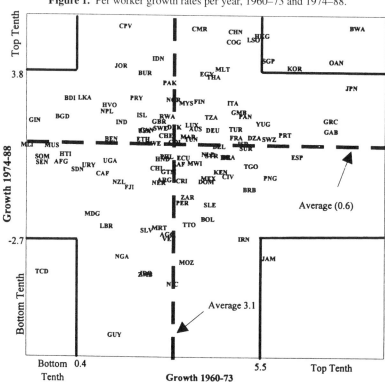

Note: Growth rates are least-squares growth per worker for each country for periods shown. The three-letter World Bank codes for country names, which are also used in Summers and Heston (1991) and Barro and Wolf (1989), are used for each point.

ables could still have low persistence.[3] To construct such an index, we use the variables shown in fig. 2 with a pooled time-series cross-section regression on 10-year averages. Table 2 shows regressions using the Barro (1991) variables with the exception of his *PPI60DEV* (deviation of the relative price of investment from the sample mean),

which is not available in individual decades for a sufficient sample. (Our government consumption variable does not exclude spending on defense and education as Barro's did, due to lack of decade data on the latter.) We allow the intercepts to vary across decades. We also perform a second regression with a broader set of country characteristics. The fitted values from this regression (denoted Barro Index and Augmented Barro Index, respectively) are also far more persistent than growth rates, as shown in fig. 2.

Rates of factor accumulation are much more

[3]Since the persistence of a linear combination of variables depends on the positive or negative covariance among them, it is possible for an aggregate index of country policies to show lower persistence than any of its components.

Table 2. Pooled Cross-Section Time Series Regressions of Long-term Growth on Policy Variables with Decade Averages[a,b] Dependent variable: Growth rate of GDP per worker

Independent Variables	Barro Regression	Augmented Barro Regression
GDP per worker	–0.013	–0.012
(initial)	(–2.62)	(–2.93)
Primary enrollment	0.019	0.013
(initial, lagged 10 years)	(2.16)	(1.63)
Secondary enrollment	0.026	0.0097
(initial, lagged 10 years)	(2.12)	(0.86)
Assassinations per	–0.013	–0.013
million (avg)	(–1.19)	(1.40)
Revolutions and coups	–0.0029	0.004
(avg)	(–0.52)	(0.90)
Share of government	–0.0089	0.035
consumption in GDP (avg)	(–0.29)	(1.18)
Log black market		–0.038
premium (avg)		(–3.74)
Inflation (avg)		0.0042
		(0.92)
Share of trade in		–0.0059
GDP (initial)		(1.18)
Ratio M2/GDP		0.025
(initial)		(3.88)
Summary statistics		
Observations	135	135
R^2	0.43	0.58

[a]Absolute values of t-statistics calculated with MacKinnon–White (1985) heteroskedasticity-consistent standard errors in parentheses. Dependent variable is the least-squares growth rate of Summers–Heston (1991) output per worker.

[b]Pooled regression has separate decade constant terms, not reported.

persistent than growth rates. To compute an index of factor accumulation, we regressed aggregate growth (not per capita) on investment and labor force growth, using a sample of 115 countries which have data for all three decades. Fig. 3 shows that investment, labor force growth, and the fitted value of growth predicted by the two are much more persistent than growth. The residuals from this regression can be interpreted, under certain assumptions, as the deviations of total factor productivity (TFP) growth for each country from the global mean.[4] As shown in the graph, TFP growth rates are even less persistent than growth rates.

[4]The coefficients of the regression were as follows (*t*-statistics in parentheses): constant term –0.004 (–0.81), on invest-

Shocks and Policies

This section argues that shocks, especially shocks to the terms of trade, are an important determinant of variations in growth rates over 10-year periods, and that they can help account for low persistence.

Below we test how much of the variation in growth rates between countries can be statistically explained in terms of differences in policies, and how much is due to differences in shock variables, such as the terms of trade, external transfers, the change in the number of war-related casualties per capita on national territory, and the presence of a debt crisis. We show that much of the variance in growth rates, even over periods as long as a decade, can be directly explained by shocks.[5] Moreover, shocks indirectly influence growth by changing policy variables. Thus the low persistence of shocks, particularly external shocks, helps explain the low persistence of growth rates.

Table 3 shows the simple correlations of three shock variables with growth rates.[6] The variables are (1) the growth in dollar export prices times the initial share of exports in GDP minus the growth in import prices times the initial share of imports in GDP (terms of trade change), (2) the change in war casualties per capita on national territory, and (3) a dummy measuring countries likely to have a debt crisis in the 1980s.[7] Growth is strongly correlated with terms of trade improvements and high exter-

ment share 0.073 (4.1), on labor force growth 0.65 (4.92), on a dummy for the 60s 0.030 (9.0), on a dummy for the 70s 0.019 (4.99). R-squared was 0.23 and there were 345 observations (decade averages for 60s, 70s, and 80s for 115 countries). As is well-known, the regression can be interpreted as a cross-country estimate of a production function under the rather heroic assumptions of constant capital-output ratios across countries, exogenous capital and labor growth, and constant parameters across countries of the (Cobb–Douglas) production function. The coefficient on labor growth is the estimate of the labor share, which is a reasonable 0.65. However, the implied estimate of the capital-output ratio [(1 – 0.65)/0.073 = 4.87] seems too high.

[5]The finding that shocks play an important role in growth at long horizons is reminiscent of the importance attributed to technology shocks in the real business cycle literature [e.g., Long and Plosser (1983)].

[6]Our thinking about proper definitions of shock variables benefited from the related work of McCarthy and Dhareshwar (1991).

[7]This is a dummy variable measuring whether the debt to GDP ratio was above 50 percent in 1980 in low- and middle-income countries. We do not have comparable statistics for rich countries, but in any case no rich country experienced an external debt crisis. Data on terms of trade, exports, imports, external debt, and GDP are from the World Bank's internal database; data on war casualties are from Sivard (1991).

Figure 2. Persistence coefficients of country characteristics.

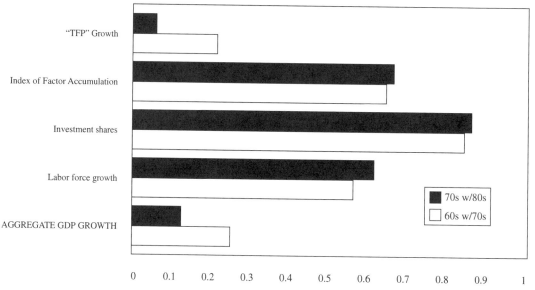

Note: Persistence coefficients are the cross-decade correlations of the variables indicated for the sample of 45 countries for which data are available on all variables.

Figure 3. Persistence of factor accumulation across 115 countries.

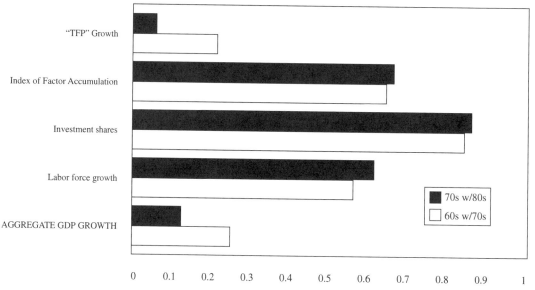

Note: Persistence coefficient is cross-decade correlation of variable shown. Index of factor accumulation is the fitted value from a regression of growth on investment shares and labor force growth. 'TFP' growth is the residual in this regression.

nal debt in the 80s, and with war in the 70s (and weakly with war in the 80s).

When shock variables are added to a regression with a small set of significant country characteristics, they have substantial explanatory power com-

pared to policy variables (table 4). We add the three variables from the previous paragraph and, for completeness, the per annum increase in official transfers. The partial R^2 of the policy variables (enrollments, black market premium, M2/GDP) in

Table 3. Simple Correlations of Growth and Shocks[a]

Correlation of Growth with	1970s	1980s
Terms of trade change	0.10	0.45***
Change in war casualties	−0.31***	−0.12*
Dummy for high external debt, 1980		−0.19**

[a]Asterisks indicate significance levels: *10%, **5%, ***1%.

Table 4. Growth Regressions with Shock Variables[a] Dependent variable: Per annum growth rate of GDP per worker

Independent variables	1970s		1980s	
GDP per worker (initial)	−0.0023	−0.0047	−0.021	−0.016
	(0.349)	(0.74)	(2.06)	(1.74)
Primary enrollment (initial,	0.00019	0.00033	0.00003	0.00002
lagged 10 years)	(1.27)	(1.97)	(0.180)	(0.123)
Secondary enrollment (initial,	−0.00039	−0.00033	0.00053	0.0003
lagged 10 years)	(2.10)	(1.83)	(2.09)	(1.38)
Black market premium	−0.041	−0.032	−0.017	−0.009
(avg, log)	(2.51)	(2.11)	(1.51)	(0.64)
Ratio M2/GDP (initial)	0.016	0.026	0.030	0.023
	(0.980)	(1.92)	(2.29)	(2.03)
Shock variables				
Per annum terms of trade gain		0.0042		0.0085
as share of GDP		(2.36)		(2.24)
Per annum transfers increase as		0.015		−0.014
share of GDP		(1.43)		(1.69)
War-related casualties per		−1.40		−0.78
capita (avg)		1.83		(0.69)
Heavily indebted (initial)				−0.07
				0.82
Summary statistics				
Observations	80	80	80	80
R^2	0.265	0.369	0.257	0.371

[a]*T*-statistics, in parentheses, computed using MacKinnon–White (1985) heteroskedasticity-consistent standard errors.

the 1970s was 0.26 and of the shocks 0.14, while in the 1980s the partial R^2 of the policy variables was 0.10 versus 0.15 for shock variables.[8]

The terms of trade effect is large and strongly significant in both periods. In the 1980s a favorable terms of trade shock of 1 percentage point of GDP per annum raises the growth rate by 0.85 percentage point per annum. Recall that GDP is measured in constant prices, so there is no direct effect of a terms of trade shock on growth. This increase

[8]The partial R^2 of x for y after partialling out z is the R^2 of the regression of the components of y and x orthogonal to z. This is not the incremental R^2 and the components do not sum to the total R^2. Both partial R^2s exclude the initial level of GDP.

in growth is far larger than it would be created simply through the effect of the increased income on savings. Even if all the shock passed into saving, and the rate of return to capital were (optimistically) 20 percent, growth would only increase by 0.2 percentage points.

Persistence and Growth Theory

. . . This section examines the interpretation of low persistence under two types of growth models. In the first type of model, long-run growth depends on country characteristics. For example, in the AK model of Rebelo (1991), growth depends on tax rates. In closed economy versions of Romer (1990) or Aghion and Howitt (1992), technological change, and therefore economic growth, depend on a country's patent system and market size. In simple versions of these models, low persistence of growth rates implies that random shocks are important in determining the long-run path of output. In the second type of model, which includes both the neoclassical model with exogenous technological change and some models of technological diffusion, growth is a world-wide process, and country characteristics determine the relative level of income. In these models, low persistence is consistent with shocks of any size, and shocks may play only a minor role in determining the long-run path of output, despite being an important determinant of variance in decade-long growth rates.

Models in Which Country Characteristics Determine Long-run Growth

In a simple model in which country characteristics determine growth, the persistence coefficient can be interpreted as reflecting the magnitude of variance in underlying growth rates across countries relative to the variance of random shocks. . . . In this simple model, low persistence implies that luck is important relative to policies in determining the long-run path of output. This model in which country characteristics determine long-run growth thus leaves much of growth unexplained. . . .

Models in Which Worldwide Technological Progress Determines Long-run Growth

Under a different type of model, worldwide technological progress determines long-run growth, and country characteristics determine steady state relative levels of income. This category includes not only the neoclassical model [Solow (1956)], but also some models of technological diffusion. . . . If there is a wide dispersion of distances between countries' initial incomes and their steady states, then transitional dynamics will dominate the effect of the random error term. The countries furthest below their steady state will grow the fastest. Relative growth rates will initially be highly persistent. However, as all countries approach their steady state levels of income, persistence will fall because transitional dynamics will become less important relative to the random error term. Asymptotically countries will converge to an ergodic distribution around the steady state, in which persistence will be negative since coun-

tries which receive a positive random shock one period will tend to fall back towards the steady state the next period.[9]

. . . Just as these models predict high persistence following a large shock to the income of a group of countries, such as a war, they predict high persistence following a large shock to the policies of a country, such as a major policy reform. As mentioned earlier, a group of East Asian countries and Botswana had consistently high growth. It seems plausible that many of them adopted policies at the beginning of the period that led to steady state levels of income far above their initial income levels. On the other hand, few countries were consistent bad performers. This may indicate that countries with high levels of income do not often change to policies that give them a low level of steady state income.

. . . One difficulty with this type of model is that it does not explain why we observe countries outside the ergodic distribution around the steady state. Barro and Sala-i-Martin (1992) have suggested countries may be outside this distribution due to large, infrequent shocks, such as wars, depressions, or industrial revolutions. Such shocks could plausibly affect only a subset of countries, thus creating a wide distribution of ratios of actual to steady state relative income.

[9]We consider the impact of shocks to income, but shocks to policy would have similar consequences, since these alter the steady state level of income and transitional dynamics are determined by the difference between initial and the steady state level of income.

References

Aghion, P. and P. Howitt, 1992, A model of growth through creative destruction, Econometrica 60, 323–351.

Barro, R. J., 1991, Economic growth in a cross section of countries, Quarterly Journal of Economics 106, 407–443.

Barro, R. J. and X. Sala-I-Martin, 1992, Convergence, Journal of Political Economy 100, 223–251.

Barro, R. J. and H. C. Wolf, 1989, Data appendix for economic growth in a cross section of countries, Mimeo. (Harvard University and MIT, Cambridge, MA).

De Long, J. B. and L. H. Summers, 1991, Equipment, investment, relative prices, and economic growth, Quarterly Journal of Economics CVI, 445–502.

Fischer, S., 1987, Economic growth and economic policy, in: V. Corbo, M. Goldstein, and M. Khan, eds., Growth-oriented adjustment programs (IMF and World Bank, Washington, DC) 151–178.

Levine, R. and D. Renelt, 1991, Cross-country studies of growth and policy: Some methodological conceptual, and statistical problems, PRE working paper 608 (World Bank, Washington, DC).

Long, J. and C. Plosser, 1983, Real business cycles, Journal of Political Economy 91, 39–69.

MacKinnon, J. G. and H. White, 1985, Some heteroskedasticity-consistent covariance matrix estimators with improved finite sample properties, Journal of Econometrics 29, 305–325.

McCarthy, F. D. and A. Dhareshwar, 1991, Economic shocks and the global environment, Mimeo. (World Bank, Washington, DC).

Quah, D., 1993, Empirical cross-section dynamics in economic growth, European Economic Review 37, 426–434.

Rebelo, S., 1991, Long run policy analysis and long run growth, Journal of Political Economy 99, 500–521.

Sivard, R. L., 1991, World military and social expenditure (WMSE Publications, Leesburg, VA).

Romer, P., 1990, Endogenous technological change, Journal of Political Economy 98, S71–S102.

Solow, R., 1956, A contribution to the theory of economic growth, Quarterly Journal of Economics 70, 65–94.

Summers, R. and A. Heston, 1991, The Penn world table (Mark 5): An expanded set of international comparisons 1950–88, Quarterly Journal of Economics CVI, 327–368.

Comment III.2. Policies Versus Shocks: A Closer Look

The main thrust of the selection by Easterly and colleagues is to cast doubt on the importance of country characteristics or policies as determinants of growth in country income per worker and to elevate the importance given to "shocks" as determinants of growth even over periods as long as a decade. In this Comment we argue that they overstate their case in favor of "good luck" and against "good policy" by counting as luck a variable that is heavily influenced by policy, and by ignoring the possibility that the extent to which bad luck is translated into poor economic performance is itself dependent on country characteristics or policies.

In 1982 the "debt crisis" broke over many less developed countries, leading to a "lost decade" of economic growth in Latin America and elsewhere. Easterly et al. conceive of the debt crisis as an exogenous shock to these countries, yet the "shock variable" they use to indicate which countries were likely to have a debt crisis is a dummy measuring whether the debt/GDP ratio was above 50 percent in 1980 in low- and middle-income economies. Clearly the debt/GDP ratio did not get to be that high independent of government policies. In fact, in many cases the governments themselves were the biggest debtors.

Another shock variable used by Easterly et al. is the change in a country's terms of trade. This is driven by developments in international markets and can more reasonably be thought of as exogenous to government policies. However, the extent to which a deterioration in a country's terms of trade negatively affects its growth in per capita income may still be influenced by government policies or country characteristics. In a paper entitled "Where Did All the Growth Go? External Shocks, Social Conflict, and Growth Collapses" (National Bureau of Economic Research Working Paper No. 6350, January 1998), Dani Rodrik has argued (p. 2) that "the effect of shocks on growth is larger the greater the latent social conflict in an economy and the weaker its institutions of conflict management." The idea is that the impact of a negative terms of trade shock on growth is magnified by fighting over who should bear the costs of adjustment, and that more resources are devoted to this fight when the political mechanisms for resolving distributional conflict are less well established.

As is clear from Figure 1 in Selection III.6, the years 1974–88 were a period of "growth collapse" for many countries: average per worker growth was 0.6 percent per year compared with 3.1 percent for 1960–1973. Rodrik finds in Table 4 of his paper that, in the absence of indicators of latent social conflict or strength of institutions of conflict management, the difference in growth between these two periods (he actually uses 1975–89 versus 1960–75) is negatively associated with volatility in a country's terms of trade (not the same as the change in the terms of trade used by Easterly et al.). He then adds an index of the quality of government institutions, based on numerical evaluations produced by a country rating service, and an index of ethnolinguistic fractionalization. The latter is an indicator of latent social conflict and the former is an indicator of the strength of institutions of conflict management. Quality of government institutions is found to have a positive effect on the growth differential and ethnolinguistic fractionalization is found to have a negative effect, while the negative association of terms of trade volatility with the growth differential disappears. Rodrik obtains the same result when an index of democracy is used instead of an index of the quality of government institutions.

CHAPTER IV

International Trade and Technology Transfer

Overview

The division of the world described in Chapter II established a pattern of international trade in which poor, mainly tropical countries exported primary products to rich temperate countries in exchange for manufactures. Exhibit IV.A.1 shows the extent to which this pattern has continued in the present. We see that on average primary products account for more than half of the value of merchandise exports for every group of countries except the high-income group. Moreover, countries whose exports are dominated by primary products also tend to have their exports concentrated in a small number of commodities (the correlation between the primary product export share and the index of export concentration in Exhibit IV.A.1 is 0.69).

Selection IV.A.1 by Jeffrey Sachs and Andrew Warner presents evidence that countries with a larger value of primary product exports relative to GDP in 1970 grew more slowly in the following two decades. Their results hold, but less strongly, for countries with a larger share of primary product exports in total exports in 1970. Given the high primary product export shares shown in Exhibit IV.A.1, these results are still very relevant for most contemporary LDCs. There are indeed very few current examples of rapidly growing countries with exports dominated by natural resource-based products, and even these few have special characteristics that make it hard to generalize from their experience. Botswana has vast diamond reserves for a population of roughly 1 million. The ability of Chile to export temperate produce during the northern hemisphere off-season has little relevance for tropical countries.

In the period following World War II virtually every LDC government capable of implementing a coherent economic policy attempted to encourage industrialization by protecting domestic manufacturing from import competition. Among their motivations were the perception that exports of primary products were a dead end and some form of the infant-industry argument presented in Note IV.A.1. As a result, in the next selection, IV.A.2, Gustav Ranis looks at what follows the first phase of import-substituting industrialization to find differences in trade policies and economic performance across countries. He argues that countries that were able to complete the process of substitution for imports of labor-intensive, low-technology goods such as consumer nondurables faced a choice between two ways of continuing rapid growth of manufacturing production. They could remove protection for consumer nondurables producers in the hope that the infants had grown up and could expand into foreign markets, or they could extend protection to more capital-intensive, high-technology goods such as consumer durables. South Korea and Taiwan took the first path and the more advanced countries of Latin America took the second. Ranis suggests that, in part, the first path was forced on South Korea and Taiwan by lack of natural resources needed to generate exports sufficient to finance the imports of intermediate and capital goods still needed during the next phase of import substitution. Ranis's argument is supported by the finding of Sachs and Warner in the preceding selection that natural resource abundance is associated with less openness to international trade. Auty (1994) argues that China and India took the same path as Latin America despite poor resource endowments because they were "market-rich": their huge populations made their domestic markets large enough to allow economies of scale to be achieved even in the capital-intensive industries protected in the second phase of import substitution.

By the 1970s, South Korea, Taiwan, and Latin American countries such as Brazil and Mexico appeared to have wound up in the same place, with diversified industrial structures and substantial exports of labor-intensive manufactured goods. Ranis claims, however, that as a result of the different paths taken, both light and heavy industry in Korea and Taiwan were internationally competitive whereas Latin American industry suffered from high costs, requiring subsidies to push out manufactured exports and continued tariff and quota protection for the domestic market. As we saw in section I.B, Latin America (and India) ultimately felt compelled to undertake substantial liberalization in the 1980s and 1990s. The delay in liberalization relative to East Asia has been blamed for Latin America's relatively high income inequality and for the severity of the 1982 debt crisis and the lost decade of growth that followed (and for the prolonged slow growth of India).

Ranis argues that the introduction of more capital-intensive and technologically sophisticated industry in South Korea and Taiwan was much more of a market process in East Asia than in Latin America. Selection IV.A.3 by Alan Deardorff and Comment IV.A.1 show how such a market process might work. Accumulation of physical and human capital drives down the costs of renting capital equipment and employing skilled labor relative to the cost of employing unskilled labor, thereby reducing the cost of producing goods that make intensive use of physical and human capital relative to goods that make intensive use of unskilled labor. When this accumulation proceeds far enough, domestic production of the former goods can be profitable even at international prices.

In the selection by Bela Balassa, IV.A.4, the consequences of overriding market signals are alleged to be particularly severe in the second stage of import-substituting industrialization. Essentially this is due to the much larger minimum efficient scale in capital-intensive than in labor-intensive industries. For intermediate goods such as petrochemicals and steel, efficient plant size is large. For consumer durables such as automobiles and refrigerators, the network of upstream suppliers of components needs to be large, and downstream assemblers are more efficient if they can dedicate separate plants to separate models. Domestic markets in most LDCs were too small to support the efficient levels of plant size and horizontal and vertical specialization for industries protected in the second stage of import substitution, making international cost competitiveness and the consequent ability to export imperative.

The next selection, by Jagdish Bhagwati and Anne Krueger, describes how the use of quantitative restrictions on imports rather than tariffs made protection of domestic industry from foreign competition even more costly. In Selection IV.A.6 by the World Bank, the first recommendation for reform of trade policy is to replace quantitative restrictions with tariffs. The subsequent Comment notes that liberalization of foreign trade is often part of a reform package that includes macroeconomic stabilization, decontrol of domestic financial markets, and liberalization of capital flows from abroad, and addresses the order in which these reforms should be undertaken.

In Selection IV.A.7, Dani Rodrik disputes the claim that the move of South Korea and Taiwan into capital-intensive industry was primarily a market process, and argues that a reduction in the relative cost of skilled labor is at best a precondition rather than sufficient for LDCs to advance beyond production of consumer nondurables. He asserts that exactly the characteristics of capital-intensive industry emphasized in the selection by Balassa—the need for large plants and large networks of component suppliers—induce a need for coordination of investments among upstream and downstream firms. The Korean and Taiwanese governments intervened to facilitate this coordination, while reliance on the market may have led to a coordination failure where (for example) potential automobile assemblers did not build plants because of inadequate supply of parts and potential suppliers of parts did not build plants because of inadequate demand by assemblers.

Rodrik assumes that domestic assemblers cannot import foreign components and domestic component suppliers cannot export to foreign assemblers, thereby avoiding coordination failure. The possibility that supplier networks could be located abroad also weakens Balassa's case against establishment of production of consumer durables for the domestic market only. The Note that concludes section IV.A evaluates whether the assumption that intermediate goods are nontraded is appropriate and points out that an industrialization strategy that relies heavily on backward and forward linkages may create growth-reducing bottlenecks.

In section IV.A trade is viewed as an arms-length form of exchange. Trade may also be associated with more direct and personal contact such as repeated movement of engineers and other skilled personnel between developed country buyers and LDC suppliers. In the first Note of section IV.B we argue that this contact is a major source of transfer of technology and managerial know-how, and discuss the organization of this contact through international production networks or "global commodity chains." In Selection IV.B.1 Howard Pack describes how Korea and Taiwan moved beyond technology transfer from foreign buyers to more systematic means of acquiring foreign technology, including encouragement of large firms to obtain technology licenses (Korea) and establishment of central technology diffusion institutions (Taiwan).

Foreign direct investment is also an important form of contact between more and less developed countries. In Selection IV.B.2. Ann Harrison reports her findings that in Morocco and Venezuela firms with foreign equity participation exhibit much higher levels of productivity, but that there appeared to be no technology spillovers to domestically owned firms. On the other hand, she found that in Mexico location near multinational exporters increased the likelihood that domestically owned firms would export, possibly indicating spillovers of knowledge regarding foreign markets.

Note IV.B.2 draws on material from both sections to describe three views of the effect of international trade on the economic growth of less developed countries. It can be seen as a link backward to the concerns with the rate of aggregate growth and the "engine of growth" that were so prominent in Chapter III.

Reference

Auty, Richard M. 1994. "Industrial Policy Reform in Six Large Newly Industrializing Countries: The Resource Curse Thesis." *World Development* 22 (January): 11–26.

IV.A. TRADE

Exhibit IV.A.1. Share of Primary Products in Merchandise Exports and Index of Export Concentration

	Primary Product Export Share (%)*	Export Concentration**
Low-income Economies		
Mozambique	88.0	0.384
Ethiopia	94.6	0.623
Tanzania	85.7	0.264
Burundi	82.5	0.565
Malawi	94.8	0.696
Chad	85.1	
Rwanda	98.5	0.564
Sierra Leone	59.8	0.586
Nepal	1.2	0.525
Niger	97.8	
Burkina Faso	89.2	0.600
Madagascar	83.5	0.332
Bangladesh	22.4	0.284
Uganda	99.1	0.818
Vietnam	86.4	0.241
Guinea-Bissau	87.4	
Haiti	39.2	0.201
Mali	98.4	
Nigeria	99.5	0.901
Yemen, Rep.	95.6	
Kenya	70.7	0.310
Togo	89.2	0.384
Gambia, The	99.3	
Central African Republic	73.8	
India	22.1	0.141
Lao PDR	69.2	
Benin	92.1	
Nicaragua	79.1	0.283
Ghana	99.1	0.359
Zambia	84.1	
Angola	99.9	0.912
Pakistan	16.9	0.239
Mauritania	99.5	0.612
Zimbabwe	62.6	0.311
Honduras	90.8	0.378
Senegal	77.5	0.300
China	15.6	0.074
Cameroon	92.1	0.375
Cote d'Ivoire	94.8	0.405
Congo	97.9	0.810
Sri Lanka	25.5	0.218
Average	76.6	0.442
Middle-income economies		
Lower-middle-income		
Egypt, Arab Rep.	59.5	0.265
Bolivia	81.2	0.225
Indonesia	49.4	0.162
Philippines	20.4	0.321
Morocco	48.5	0.167
Syrian Arab Republic	64.4	0.655
Papua New Guinea	88.9	0.408
Guatemala	71.9	0.223
Ecuador	92.2	0.366
Dominican Republic	20.9	0.166
Romania	23.6	
Jamaica	31.0	0.493
Jordan	51.3	0.270
Algeria	96.4	0.555
El Salvador	55.1	0.305
Paraguay	86.0	0.321
Tunisia	20.6	0.207

Exhibit IV.A.1. Continued

	Primary Product Export Share (%)*	Export Concentration**
Colombia	61.1	0.238
Peru	85.2	0.254
Costa Rica	66.3	0.294
Lebanon	39.5	0.169
Thailand	26.0	0.087
Panama	79.7	0.402
Turkey	25.7	0.113
Poland	28.5	
Venezuela	85.6	0.524
Average	56.1	0.300
Upper-middle-income		
South Africa	30.4	0.266
Mexico	22.2	0.129
Mauritius	29.5	0.317
Gabon	98.9	0.852
Brazil	45.1	0.087
Trinidad and Tobago	55.3	0.343
Czech Republic	15.7	
Malaysia	24.0	0.165
Hungary	32.2	
Chile	85.1	0.280
Oman	85.3	0.747
Uruguay	61.0	0.176
Saudi Arabia	92.9	0.728
Argentina	66.1	0.136
Greece	50.0	0.120
Average	52.9	0.334
High-income economies		
Korea, Rep.	6.6	0.125
Portugal	16.6	0.104
Spain	21.0	0.140
New Zealand	69.8	0.152
Ireland	21.5	0.166
Israel	8.5	0.268
Kuwait	95.3	0.932
United Arab Emirates	53.8	0.683
United Kingdom	17.3	0.065
Australia	66.9	0.211
Italy	9.9	0.055
Canada	32.6	0.139
Finland	15.6	0.202
Hong Kong	4.6	0.153
Sweden	14.2	0.111
Netherlands	33.4	0.063
Belgium	17.7	0.112
France	20.4	0.063
Singapore	13.9	0.195
Austria	11.6	0.062
United States	19.1	0.073
Germany	9.7	0.084
Denmark	31.8	0.086
Norway	65.8	0.367
Japan	2.8	0.129
Switzerland	6.5	0.105
Average	26.4	0.186

*Data are for 1995 or latest available year. Primary products are the sum of all food items (SITC 0 + 1 + 22 + 4), agricultural raw materials (SITC 2 less (22 + 27 + 28)), fuels (SITC 3), and ores and metals (SITC 27 + 28 + 68). SITC = Standard International Trade Classification.

**Data are for 1994. Concentration is measured by the Hirschman-Herfindahl index normalized to range from 0 (minimum concentration) to 1 (maximum concentration). See p. 205 of Source for exact formula.

Source: United Nations Conference on Trade and Development. *Handbook of International Trade and Development Statistics 1995* (New York: United Nations), 1997.

Selection IV.A.1. Natural Resource Abundance and Economic Growth*

I. Introduction

One of the surprising features of economic life is that resource-poor economies often vastly outperform resource-rich economies in economic growth. The basic pattern is evident in a sample of 95 developing countries in Figure 1, where we graph each country's annual growth rate between 1970–90 in relation to the country's natural resource-based exports in 1970, measured as a percent of GDP. Resource-based exports are defined as agriculture, minerals, and fuels. On average, countries which started the period with a high value of resource-based exports to GDP tended to experience slower growth during the following twenty years. . . .

II. A Summary of the Theory

In Matsuyama's model there are two sectors, agriculture and manufacturing. Manufacturing is characterized by learning-by-doing that is external to individual firms, that is, the rate of human capital accumulation in the economy is proportional to total sectoral production, not to the production of an individual firm. Hence the social return to manufacturing employment exceeds the private return. Any force which pushes the economy away from manufacturing and towards agriculture will lower the growth rate by reducing the learning-induced growth of manufacturing. Matsuyama shows that trade liberalization in a land-intensive economy could actually slow economic growth by inducing the economy to shift resources away from manufacturing and towards agriculture.

In Matsuyama's model, the adverse effects of agricultural production arise because the agricultural sector directly employs the factors of production that otherwise would be in manufacturing. Such a framework may be useful for studying labor-intensive production of natural resources, such as in agriculture, but is less relevant for a natural resource sector like oil production, which uses very little labor, and therefore does not directly draw employment from manufacturing. However, it is not difficult to extend Matsuyama's same point in a setting that is more appropriate for natural resource intensive economies, using the framework of the Dutch disease models. . . .

In our version of the Dutch disease model, the economy has three sectors: a tradeable natural resource sector, a tradeable (non-resource) manufacturing sector, and a non-traded sector. Capital and labor are used in the manufacturing and non-traded sectors, but not in the natural resource sector. The greater the natural resource endowment, the higher is the demand for non-tradeable goods, and consequently, the smaller is the allocation of labor and capital to the manufacturing sector. Therefore, when natural resources are abundant, tradeables production is concentrated in natural resources rather than manufacturing, and capital and labor that otherwise might be employed in manufacturing are pulled into the non-traded goods sector. As a corollary, when an economy experiences a resource boom (either a terms-of-trade improvement, or a resource discovery), the manufacturing sector tends to shrink and the non-traded goods sector tends to expand.

The shrinkage of the manufacturing sector is dubbed the "disease," though there is nothing harmful about the decline in manufacturing if neoclassical, competitive conditions prevail in the economy. The Dutch Disease can be a real disease, however—and a source of chronic slow growth—if there is something special about the sources of growth in manufacturing, such as the "backward and forward linkages" stressed by Hirschman and others, if such linkages constitute production externalities, or the learning-by-doing stressed by Matsuyama. If manufacturing is characterized by externalities in production, then the shrinkage of the manufacturing sector caused by resource abundance can lead to a socially inefficient decline in growth.[1] The economy loses the benefits of the external economies or increasing returns to scale in manufacturing. . . .

III. Evidence on Natural Resource Abundance and Growth 1970–1989

In this section we show the evidence of an inverse association between natural resource abun-

*From Jeffrey D. Sachs and Andrew M. Warner, "Natural Resource Abundance and Economic Growth," Harvard Institute for International Development (November 1997), pp. 1–25. Reprinted by permission.

[1]Various authors have subscribed to the maintained assumption that manufacturing has larger positive externalities than other forms of economic activity. The empirical support for this is based on the observations that countries with more diversified exports seem to do better, and that growth tends to be positively correlated with growth in manufacturing production and manufacturing exports, rather on micro-level evidence. Therefore it remains somewhat speculative.

Figure 1. Growth and Natural Resource Intensity

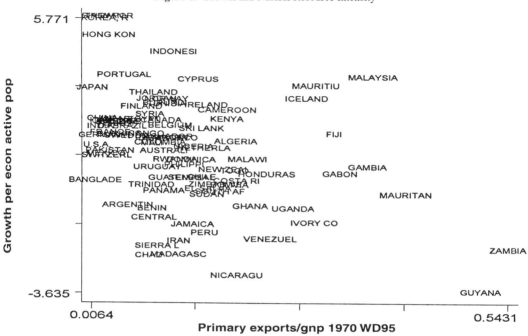

dance and growth during the period 1970–1990.
. . .

We start in Table 1 with a series of regressions that are designed mainly to demonstrate that the inverse association obtains after controlling for a number of other regressors. In the first regression, we regress growth in GDP (divided by the economically active population between 1970 and 1990, denoted GEA7090) on the log of initial GDP (per economically active population, denoted LGDPEA70) and the share of primary exports in GDP in 1970 (SXP). A higher share of primary exports in 1970 is associated with lower growth in the next two decades, with an estimated coefficient of –9.43 and a t-statistic of –4.75. To gauge the size of this coefficient, note that SXP is measured as a share of GDP, with a cross-country mean in 1970 of 0.16 and a standard deviation of 0.16. Regression 1.1 implies that a unit standard deviation increase in the share of primary exports in 1970 would be associated with a reduction in annual growth of 1.51 percentage points (–1.51 = –9.43*0.16). . . .

It is possible that this negative association between natural resource intensity and growth is spurious, reflecting an association between resource wealth and something else that affects growth. Some common arguments are that resource-rich countries are more likely to adopt im-port-substituting, state-led development strategies, are less likely to accumulate capital at home because they can live off natural resource rents, are more prone to rent-seeking and to develop large inefficient bureaucracies, or are less likely to develop market supporting legal institutions. In addition, a long-standing view in the development literature is that countries that specialize in natural resource exports are more likely to suffer from unpredictable and disruptive shocks in global commodity prices.

Therefore, the remaining regressions in Table 1 are designed to show that the resource intensity variable remains significant after controlling for variables that measure a number of these ideas. In regression 1.2 we add a variable for outward orientation, SOPEN, that measures the fraction of years between 1965 and 1989 that the country was integrated with the global economy. A country is said to be integrated if it maintained reasonably low tariffs and quotas, and did not have an excessively high black market exchange rate premium, was not socialist, and avoided extreme state-control of its export sector [see Sachs and Warner, 1995 for more details on the formal criteria]. A country that was open every year between 1965 and 1989 received a value SOPEN = 1. A country that was always closed during these years received a value SOPEN = 0.

Table 1. Partial Associations Between Growth (1970–90) and Natural Resource Intensity (1971)

Dependent Variable: GEA7090					
	(1.1)	(1.2)	(1.3)	(1.4)	(1.5)
LGDPEA70	–0.11	–0.96	–1.34	–1.76	–1.79
	(0.55)	(–5.16)	(–7.77)	(–8.56)	(–8.82)
SXP	–9.43	–6.96	–7.29	–10.57	–10.26
	(–4.75)	(–4.55)	(–5.57)	(–7.01)	(–6.89)
SOPEN	—	3.06	2.42	1.33	1.34
		(8.05)	(7.06)	(3.35)	(3.44)
INV7089	—	—	1.25	1.02	0.81
			(5.63)	(3.45)	(2.63)
RL	—	—	—	0.36	0.40
				(3.54)	(3.94)
DTT7090	—	—	—	—	0.09
					(1.85)
Adjusted R^2	0.20	0.55	0.67	0.72	0.73
Sample size	87	87	87	71	71
Standard error	1.62	1.22	1.04	0.93	0.92

The numbers in parentheses are *t*-statistics. The variable SXP is the measure of primary resource intensity. These regressions are designed to show that the inverse association between growth and natural resource intensity is robust to the inclusion of a number of other variables and to the exclusion of outlying observations. The regressions exclude four countries (Chad, Gabon, Guyana, and Malaysia) that were deemed to be outliers according to a procedure suggested by Belsley, Kuh and Welsch 1980, which considers both the leverage and the residuals in deciding whether an observation is an outlier. If these four countries were not excluded, the estimated coefficients on SXP would range from –6.0 to –8.5, with *t*-ratios always exceeding 4 in absolute value.

We have also tried other policy-related variables in these regressions such as the fiscal deficit or the average inflation rate. We found that these variables were not significant when SOPEN was in the regression, so we have dropped them in favor of SOPEN. However, we cannot exclude the possibility that there are other unobserved or mismeasured policy variables that are correlated with SOPEN. The SOPEN variable may therefore be picking up some of the effects of these variables in addition to openness. Nevertheless, although the data do not allow us to distinguish sharply between openness and other correlated policies, the regression results do show that the package of policies captured by SOPEN were strongly and positively associated with growth during the 1970–1989 period.[2] In addition, the natural resource variable remains significant after controlling for this variable.

The other variables considered in Table 1 are designed to control for capital accumulation, institutional quality, and global commodity price shocks. The variables considered are: INV7089, the investment to GDP ratio averaged over the period 1970–1989; RL, the rule of law variable used in Knack and Keefer [1995] and Barro [1996]; and DTT7090, average annual growth of the ratio of export to import prices between 1971 and 1990.

The regressions in Table 1 show that the share of primary exports in GDP remains significant after controlling for these variables. Although the regressions in Table 1 are exploratory, and thus we are somewhat hesitant to stress a structural interpretation, we do think the results are informative about the following general points. First, whatever the exact nature of the adverse effect of natural resource abundance on economic growth, the evidence suggests that it is not simply a proxy for institutional quality or import-substituting industrialization policy, to the extent that these are measured by RL and SOPEN. It also seems that the adverse effect is not operating mainly by lowering investment rates, since the negative correlation is maintained even after controlling for investment

[2]For the vast majority of the developing world, the basic policy choice whether to follow an inward-looking or outward-looking development strategy was decided before 1970 and was maintained until the late 1980's. So we see little evidence that reverse causality from growth to the SOPEN variable is an important econometric issue with these regressions. We present our argument in further detail in Sachs and Warner 1995.

Table 2. Associations Between Growth and Resource Intensity Using Alternative Measures of Resource Intensity

Dependent Variable: GEA7089

	(2.1)	(2.2)	(2.3)	(2.4)
SXP	−8.28	—	—	—
	(−6.67)			
SNR	—	−6.45	—	—
		(−3.95)		
PXI70	—	—	−2.50	—
			(−3.89)	
LAND	—	—	—	−0.39
				(−3.78)
Adjusted R^2	0.73	0.63	0.63	0.64
Sample size	74	74	73	74
Standard error	0.97	1.12	1.14	1.12

The numbers in parentheses are *t*-statistics. The natural resource intensity variables are first, the SXP variable used in Table 1, which measures natural resource exports divided by GDP in 1970; second, SNR (mineral production divided by GNP in 1970); third, PXI70 (natural resource exports divided by total exports in 1970), and LAND (the log of arable land area divided by population). The other explanatory variables in the regressions are LGDPEA70, SOPEN, RL, DTT7090 and LINV7089.

rates.[3] Further, since SXP remains significant after controlling for long-run changes in the external terms-of-trade, resource intensity is not simply a proxy for adverse trends in global export prices of resource intensive economies.[4] The effect also remains significant after we control for regional dummy variables. Finally, it is interesting to note that even within the small set of fast growing Asian tigers there is an adverse effect of natural resource abundance, since resource-poor Singapore, Hong Kong, and Korea have grown faster than resource-rich Malaysia and Thailand. . . .

We also checked robustness by trying alternative measures of natural resource abundance. In Table 2 we report the estimated natural resource coefficients from four regressions, each of which varies only the measure of natural resource intensity. Regression 2.1 is a version of regression 1.5, using other full-sample instead of excluding the outliers. Regression 2.2 replaces SXP with SNR, which measures the share of mineral production in GDP in 1971. This is constructed using country-specific production data from the U.S. Bureau of Mines for the top twenty-three minerals in 1971. These production figures were then valued at U.S. import prices and divided by the U.S. dollar value of GDP to obtain SNR. Regression 2.2 shows that mineral production in 1971 is also negatively associated with subsequent growth. Our third measure of resource intensity is PX170, the share of primary exports in total exports in 1970 (rather than the share of primary exports in GDP, which is SXP). Our fourth measure is the log of land area per person in 1971. Regressions 2.3 and 2.4 show that both are also negatively associated with subsequent growth.[5]

The reason we prefer the SXP variable to these alternatives involves both theory and measurement issues. In the Dutch disease model we present in

[3]We are sympathetic to the criticism that investment may be endogenous and thus either should not be included in this specification, or should be estimated with instrumental variables. However, we include it nevertheless to make the point that the SXP effect is significant even after controlling for investment. Our conclusions about SXP and SOPEN would obtain if we dropped investment from the regressions.

[4]We have also controlled for additional variables that are not reported in table I. First, other measures of the quality of government institutions, such as the bureaucratic quality indicator from Political Risk Services, tend to be collinear with the rule of law variable. So the regression evidence does allow us to distinguish between various measures of institutional quality. Second, we have tried a variable which measures the standard deviation of the terms of trade rather than just the change, but it was not significant. Third, we tried an income inequality measure in an earlier draft of this paper, but it was not significant, and tended to severely reduce the sample. Fourth, an oil economy dummy was not significant.

[5]We also experimented with preliminary data developed at the World Bank, that attempts to measure the productive wealth of the world's economies, and to allocate that wealth among human capital, physical capital, and natural resources. We used the proportion of natural resource wealth in total productive wealth as a measure of resource abundance. As with the other measures, a high proportion of resource wealth is associated with slower economic growth, holding constant other relevant variables.

the working paper version of this paper, what matters is the share of the economy's labor force employed in non-tradeables production rather than tradeable manufactures. This share depends on the level of demand for non-tradeables which, in turn, depends on the wealth effect from natural resources. The size of this wealth effect is better captured by the share of resource exports in total GDP rather than just exports (hence the preference for SXP over PX170).

Political economy arguments call for measurement of the actual or potential economic rents associated with natural resources. It appears impossible to base this on cross-country data on proven reserves of minerals. Reserve data exists for major natural resources such as crude oil and natural gas, but not for the others, and this is important if one wants to include developing countries in the sample. In our view, SXP has better coverage of primary production than SNR, which measures only minerals and fuel production. In addition, from looking at the Bureau of Mines' data for 1971, on which SNR is based, it is clear that mineral production for some of the poorer countries was simply not recorded, or contains obvious guesses. Therefore we think that SXP simply has fewer gross measurement errors than SNR and prefer it largely on that basis. Finally, we prefer SXP to land area per person because land is not a very precise measure of primary production, though land abundance does tend to be correlated with our measures of natural resource abundance. . . .

Another way to approach the evidence is to try to identify cases of high-growth, resource-abundant economies, which would be counter-examples to our general proposition. Are there developing economies that are in the top quartile of resource abundance (measured by SXP, for example) and that have sustained high levels of growth? We find only two cases of developing countries (defined as 1971 income <$5,000 per capita on a PPP basis) that were in the top quartile on SXP, and had sustained per capita growth of greater than or equal to 2.0 percent per annum for the period 1970–89. These countries are Malaysia and Mauritius. The fact that there are only two such cases is, of course, striking, since the top quartile of SXP includes 23 developing countries. Both Malaysia and Mauritius were quite open to trade, at least in the sense of having zero-tariff Export Processing Zones to stimulate labor-intensive manufacturing exports. Both have had their growth sustained by the very rapid development of such exports. Thus, even in these cases, it is manufacturing exports rather than resource-led

growth that accounts for the sustained high levels of economic growth.[6] . . .

IV. Pathways Connecting Resource-Intensity and Growth

We find evidence that natural resource abundance may affect growth indirectly through the extent of trade openness. First, we postulate, and find supporting evidence, for a U-shaped relation between openness (measured as SOPEN, on the y-axis) and resource intensity (measured as SXP, on the x-axis). Our reasoning is as follows. Resource abundance squeezes the manufacturing sector, as in the Dutch Disease. In almost all countries, the squeeze of manufactures provokes some protectionist response that aims to promote industrialization despite the Dutch Disease effects. For the most highly resource-endowed economies, however, such as the oil-rich states of the Middle East, the natural resource base is so vast that there is no strong pressure to develop an extensive industrial sector (other than in oil-based sectors such as petrochemicals and refining). Thus, for the most extreme resource-based cases, openness to trade (SOPEN) would tend to be high. The overall effect would therefore be a U-shaped relationship between SXP and SOPEN.

There is statistical support for this idea in regression 3.4 (Table 3), where we find a negative estimated coefficient on the level of SXP and a positive coefficient on SXP^2. The dependent variable SOPEN, is a fraction that ranges between 1 (if a country was open for the whole period 1965–1989) and 0 (if a country was never open). The estimated trough of the "U" is when the share of primary exports in GDP equals 0.29. For countries below that value—which is almost all countries in the sample—higher primary exports tend to promote economic closure (that is, a low value of SOPEN). Above that threshold, higher SXP tends to promote openness. Two interesting examples on the positive part of the "U" are Malaysia and Saudi Arabia. These countries are extremely resource rich, and have also had a long tradition of open trade.

---

[6]Botswana is sometimes also included as an example of a natural resource abundant economy that grew rapidly. Data from the Ministry of Finance in Botswana (reported in Modise [1996]) indicate that in 1970, when we measure SXP, diamond exports were only about 5 percent of GDP. What happened was that several diamond mines began producing in the next 15 years. One possible interpretation of Botswana's growth is that they have had a 20-year natural resource boom, driven not by a rise in world diamond prices, but rather by diamond discoveries and consequent production increases.

Table 3. Associations Between Natural Resource Abundance and Other Explanatory Variables

Dependent Variables:

	National Saving % GDP, 70–89 (NS7089) (3.1)	Investment Ratio % GDP, 70–89 (LINV7089) (3.2)	Human Capital Accumulation Change, 70–90 (DTYR7090) (3.3)	Share of Years Open 65–89 (SOPEN) (3.4)	Relative Price of Investment Goods 70–89 (LPIP70) (3.5)
LGDPEA70	6.38 (7.69)	—	0.05 (0.45)	—	–0.16 (–2.71)
SXP	0.19 (0.03)	0.40 (1.19)	–0.95 (–1.05)	–1.89 (–2.51)	0.08 (0.26)
SXP^2	—	—	—	3.24 (3.20)	—
SOPEN	—	0.14 (1.19)	—	—	–0.40 (–3.24)
RL	—	0.06 (2.22)	—	—	—
LPIP70	—	–0.82 (–7.53)	—	—	—
LAND	—	—	—	–0.09 (–3.64)	—
Adjusted R^2	0.36	0.67	–0.01	0.21	0.31
Sample size	104	80	90	104	102
Standard error	7.64	0.31	0.89	0.40	0.43

The numbers in parentheses are t-statistics.

Since the vast majority of our countries have SXP values on the negatively sloped part of the "U" relation, we evaluate the effect of SXP growth via SOPEN at the mean of SXP (0.16), along the negatively sloped part of the U-shaped relation. Starting from the mean of SXP, our estimates imply that a unit-standard deviation increase in SXP from its mean (that is, from 0.16 to 0.32) reduces SOPEN by 0.06. Taken at face value, since SOPEN measures the fraction of years between 1965 and 1989 that a country is rated as open, this estimate implies that a country with a value of SXP one standard deviation above the mean would have been open for about 1.4 years less on average than a country with the mean value of SXP.

We also look at the cross country relationship between natural resource abundance and four other variables: savings rates, investment rates, rates of human capital accumulation and the relative price of investment goods. First, regarding savings rates, we do not find strong evidence that resource abundant economies have higher savings rates. Simple bi-variate data plots show that only three resource abundant economies, Gabon, Kuwait, and Saudi Arabia, had unusually high average savings rates (over the period 1970–1989). But if we exclude these three countries there is no clear cross-country relation. Moreover, even with the three high-savings countries included in the sample, a regression of average saving rates on the level of GDP and SXP does not yield a significant coefficient on SXP (see regression 3.1 in Table 3, which also controls for initial GDP). Therefore, although it is possible that a more elaborate study would change this conclusion, the simple evidence does not support a positive association between resource abundance and average savings.

We reach similar conclusions when we examine the data on investment and human capital association. As we show in regression 3.2 in Table 3, average investment rates are not significantly associated with natural resource abundance. There is some evidence of a positive relation between investment (this is sensitive to whether investment is entered as a ratio or in logs) and openness and the rule of law variable, and some evidence of a negative relation with the relative price of investment goods, but after controlling for these variables, no significant effect of natural resource intensity. We also find little direct evidence that more resource intensive countries have had significantly lower rates of human capital accumulation, as shown in regression 3.3. We have tried excluding outliers (Bahrain, Korea, and Kuwait) from the human capital regression, and estimating stock-adjustment equations where the change in the human capital stock is regressed on the initial level of human capital, SXP and initial income, but still find no statistical relation between SXP and human capital accumulation.

References

Barro, R. "Determinants of Economic Growth: A Cross-Country Empirical Study," Paper prepared for the Lionel Robbins Lectures, London School of Economics, January 1996.

Belsley, D. A., Kuh, E. and R. E. Welsch. *Regression Diagnostics.* New York: John Wiley and Sons, 1980.

Knack, Stephen and Philip Keefer. "Institutions and Economic Performance: Cross-country Tests using Alternative Institutional Measures." *Economics and Politics,* VII, 1995, pp. 207–227.

Modise, D. Modise, "Managing Mineral Revenues in Botswana," paper presented to the UNCTAD group of experts on development policy for Resource-based economies, Geneva, 1996.

Sachs, J. D. and A. M. Warner. "Economic Reform and the Process of Global Integration," *Brookings Papers on Economic Activity,* 1995:1, pp.1–118.

Note IV.A.1. Import-substituting Industrialization and the Infant-Industry Argument

The vast majority of countries that have become major exporters of manufactures initially protected their manufacturing sectors against foreign competition. Examples range from British protection against the cotton textiles of India in the eighteenth century through Taiwanese protection in the 1950s and early 1960s. The policy of government intervention to encourage domestic industrial production to replace imports has become known as *import-substituting industrialization,* or ISI. An important motivation for this policy is the *infant-industry argument.*

The infant-industry argument is deceptively simple. It states that industries in which a country has a long-run comparative advantage may be stifled by foreign competition if they are not protected from imports during an initial period in which firms learn to get their costs down. This sounds reasonable, but one may ask: if these firms are going to become internationally competitive, why do they not borrow to cover their losses during the learning period and repay the loans out of future profits, like any business start-up? Evidently a more sophisticated version of the infant-industry argument is required, one that explains why firms acting on their own will not achieve the socially optimal outcome, and how government policy can generate better results. Put differently, the existence of a "market failure" must be established, and it must be shown that the government can at least partially correct this failure.

There are many such versions of the infant-industry argument. The one presented here is based on Bardhan (1971). Consider a manufacturing industry in which firms are trying to adapt foreign production technology to the particular economic and social environment of their country. This is a trial-and-error process: the more any firm produces, the more it learns about what works and what does not, and the more efficient it becomes. This process is known as "learning-by-doing" and was a key feature of the Matsuyama model in Chapter II. An alternative way to describe a firm experiencing learning-by-doing is to say it is engaged in "joint production": it simultaneously produces commodities and knowledge. This kind of knowledge, however, cannot be patented. While the commodities can be sold, the knowledge easily leaks out to competing firms through many channels such as interfirm movement of personnel or the "watching and talking" that occurs in an industrial district. Here is the market failure: firms do not have to pay for the knowledge produced by their competitors, so each firm has an incentive to "free-ride" on the production of the industry as a whole.

Government can correct this market failure by granting each firm in the industry a subsidy per unit output, thereby compensating the firm for the value of the knowledge it generates for other firms as a by-product of its production process. Note that this policy is not identical to a policy of protecting domestic firms from foreign competition. Tariff or quota protection raises the price of imports and thereby raises the price domestic firms can charge for their output, which is equivalent to the effect of a production subsidy, but it also raises prices for domestic consumers. Nevertheless, the infant-industry argument is frequently used to justify taxes or quantitative restrictions on imports. One reason for this is ease of administration relative to production subsidies. All governments maintain customs services that collect trade taxes and enforce quotas and other regulations. LDC governments have especially limited administrative capacity, and it is easier to use an existing agency to implement protective tariffs or quotas than to create a new agency to administer production subsidies.

Finally, it is important to remember that the infant-industry argument supports a *temporary* policy to aid import-competing manufacturing. Once the learning process is complete, government help is no longer justified. One of the rebuttals made to the infant-industry argument is that an industry powerful enough to get government help when an infant will surely be powerful enough to retain that help when it is an adult. This is another reason a production subsidy is preferable to import protection: the former is a drain on the government budget while the latter adds to government revenues, so the government has a greater incentive to end subsidies when they are no longer needed.

Reference

Bardhan, Pranab K. 1971. "On Optimum Subsidy to a Learning Industry: An Aspect of the Theory of Infant Industry Protection." *International Economic Review* 12: 54–70.

Selection IV.A.2. Typology in Development Theory: Retrospective and Prospects*

A Brief Demonstration of the Comparative Historical Analysis Approach

Consider the development record of three countries representing three distinct types: Kenya, as the relatively land surplus, natural resources rich, human resources deficient, "African type"; Mexico, as the moderately labor surplus, relatively natural resources and human resources rich, "Latin American type"; and Taiwan, as the heavy labor surplus, relatively natural resources poor, human resources rich, "East Asian type." I could devote much more space to spelling out these dimensions of the differences in the initial conditions, the precise degree of labor surplus measured by man-land ratios, the human-capital endowment measured by literacy or educational attainment rates, the natural resources endowment measured by the relative availability of exportable minerals or cash crops (see Table 1). Other dimensions—such as size, with Taiwan and Kenya fairly small, and Mexico somewhat intermediate—could be added as well, leading to a large potential number of typological cells. But this is not my purpose here. Instead, I want to demonstrate the approach at a rather elementary level in application to these three representatives of country types.

The beginning of the transition growth effort is set rather arbitrarily at the point when the system moves from its "colonial" pattern, during which it exports mainly primary products in return for the import of consumer nondurables, deployed to attract workers to the export enclave, and capital goods, deployed to permit the expansion of the export enclave. The next subphase almost invariably is an effort at primary import-substitution, once the newly independent country is able to get control of its foreign exchange earnings, supplemented by foreign capital. The beginning of the transition period has thus been placed around 1960 for Kenya, shortly before independence; in 1930 for Mexico, given that independence was much earlier and that the Great Depression gave a tremendous impetus to import substitution; and around 1952 for Taiwan after both retrocession from Japan and political separation from the mainland. According to Table 1, Kenya can be characterized as small in size, intermediate in labor surplus, poor in human capital, and poor in natural resources. The Latin American type, Mexico, may be viewed as intermediate in size, low in labor surplus, low in human capital, and rich in natural resources. The East Asian type, Taiwan, is small in size, heavy in labor surplus, rich in human capital, and poor in natural resources. . . .

Notice in Figure 1 (row 1) that during the colonial or pretransition era in the three countries under observation, the agricultural sector A is exporting traditional raw materials or mineral products X_A to the foreign country F and is importing producer goods M_P for the expansion of the enclave, along with manufactured consumer nondurables M_{CN} consumed, in addition to the food domestically produced D_F by the domestic households H. Export earnings may, of course, be supplemented by "private" foreign capital—Japanese foreign capital in Taiwan, U.S. foreign capital in Mexico, and British foreign capital in Kenya. The policy setting to sustain this modus operandi of the economy during the preindependence or colonial period in all three country cases includes an industrial policy specifying the role of domestic industry within the colonial system, with minimal infant-industry protection outside those narrow bounds and most colonial investments focused on overheads and services to facilitate the raw material or cash crop export.

There also are major differences in the colonial heritage of the three countries during this pretransition phase: the commodity content of the traditional export X_A was related to what the colonial power is basically interested in procuring. For example, in Kenya and Mexico agricultural research and such infrastructural investments as ports and railways by colonial and early postcolonial governments supported exports of traditional cash crops. In contrast, Japan was almost entirely interested in food production, and Taiwan's exports of rice and sugar were certainly instrumental in focusing attention on the provision of small-scale rural infrastructural investments, such as roads, irrigation, and electricity, and on such organizational innovations as land reform, as early as 1905, and the creation of farmers' associations. This helped prevent the development of a dualistic agriculture and an undue separation between agriculture and nonagriculture. It also set the stage for a dynamic rural economy.

*From Gustav Ranis, "Typology in Development Theory: Retrospective and Prospects," in Moshe Syrquin, Lance Taylor, and Larry E. Westphal, eds., *Economic Structure and Performance* (Orlando: Academic Press, 1984) pp. 29–37. Reprinted by permission.

Table 1. Initial Conditions[a]

	Size[b]	Labor surplus[c]	Human capital resources[d]	Mineral, fuel, and other natural resources
Kenya	8,017 (1960)	3.9 (1960)	20 (1962)	Moderate (no coal or oil but good in cash crops).
Mexico	16,589 (1930)	0.7 (1930)	30 (1930)	Rich (zinc, lead, copper, silver, iron ore, mercury, sulphur/oil reserves among largest in world).
Taiwan	7,981 (1950)	9.2 (1950)	50 (1950)	Poor (good coal, some natural gas, little oil).

[a]*Sources:* U.N. Demographic Yearbook (size), FAO Production Yearbook (arable land), UNESCO Statistical Yearbook (literacy), U.S. AID Data book (mineral and fuel resources).
[b]Population, in thousands.
[c]Man-arable land ratio, in hectares.
[d]Literacy rate (%).

The initial transition subphase (row 2 in Figure 1), almost universally adopted in contemporary LDCs, is primary import substitution (PIS).

The progress of PIS can be observed in the ratio of the value of M_{CN} to the value of total merchandise imports M over time, as D_{CN} gradually replaces M_{CN} (see Table 2). This ratio had already reached a low level plateau for Mexico by 1950, indicating that the inevitable termination of this subphase with the exhaustion of domestic markets had already been reached. Taiwan was nearing the completion of this subphase in the early 1960s, after about a decade. Kenya seems to be nearing the point of completing it at this stage. To protect and support the new infant industrial class, public policy effected the gradual displacement of the previously imported nondurable consumer goods M_{CN} by the domestically produced variety D_{CN} in all three cases. X_A continues to fuel the process, with the foreign exchange earnings now, however, used to import the producers' goods M_P needed for the construction of the nondurable-consumer-goods industries in the newly important nonagricultural sector (NA). This description corresponds rather closely to what Chenery (1979, p. 29) calls the early phase of the transition "characterized by the emphasis on primary exports, easy import substitution, and the availability of external aid on soft terms."

Once the initial subphase of transition has run out of steam, developing countries have a rather momentous political decision about the second subphase. The alternatives for the second subphase are illustrated by the divergence between Mexico and Taiwan in row 3 of Figure 1. (It is more instructive to concentrate in what follows on the comparison between Mexico and Taiwan—because of Kenya's much later start and less favor-

able initial conditions, especially its more limited industrial entrepreneurial capacity.) One possible strategy, adopted by Mexico and certainly representing the majority LDC case, is to shift to a secondary-import-substitution growth path. The (minority) Taiwan case stands in some contrast in that the primary-export-substitution subphase basically consists of exporting to international markets the same nondurable consumer goods (X_{CN}) previously supplied only to the domestic market; while any consumer durables required for final consumption are likely to be mainly imported (M_{CD}).

The third transition subphase (row 4 of Figure 1) follows more or less naturally from the choice of the second subphase. It is fair to say that the objective of all developing countries is ultimately to produce for the domestic market and to export a wide and increasingly sophisticated range of industrial products. In Taiwan this is likely to represent a natural sequel to the primary-export-substitution pattern in that, once the labor surplus has been exhausted, there is a natural tendency to shift toward the more capital-intensive and technology-intensive product mixes for the domestic market and, given its relatively small size, to export such commodities simultaneously, or at least soon. Thus the extent of simultaneity of the secondary-import-substitution/secondary-export-substitution (SIS/SES) growth subphase is very much a function of the size of the domestic market. Note that systems poor in natural resources, like Taiwan, will ultimately be food importers (row 4).

The SIS/EP (export promotion) growth path in Mexico, on the other hand (row 4), indicates the aforementioned desire to export industrial manufactured goods even if the labor-intensive industrial export phase has been "skipped." It is accomplished by superimposing industrial exports on the

Figure 1. Comparative subphases of development: (1) colonial or pretransition; (2) initial transition; (3) second transition subphase; (4) third transition subphase. A, agricultural sector; D_{CD}, domestically produced consumer durables; D_{CN}, domestically produced consumer nondurables; D_F, domestically produced food; EP, export promotion; F, foreign country; H, households; M_{CD}, imports of consumer durables; M_{CN}, imports of consumer nondurables; M_F, imports of foodstuffs; M_p, imports of producer goods; NA, nonagricultural sector; PES, primary export substitution; PIS, primary import substitution; SES, secondary export substitution; SIS, secondary import substitution.

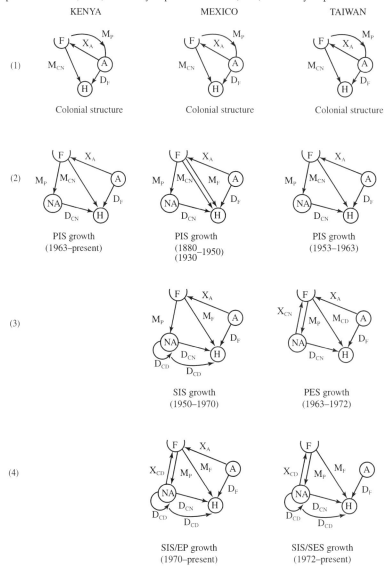

KENYA   MEXICO   TAIWAN

continued secondary import substitution structure of sub-phase 2—which can be accomplished only through the direct or indirect subsidization of such exports. At a high level of aggregation of industrial exports, it is difficult to distinguish SIS/EP growth from SIS/SES growth. When manufacturing exports are decomposed further, however, it is found that 20% of Mexico's were consumer nondurables in 1970, compared with 41% of Taiwan's (Fei, Ranis, Kuo, 1979). To be emphasized, moreover, is that the Mexican development path continues to be clearly much less export oriented overall and gives evidence of a much lower proportion of manufactured exports than does Taiwan's, even if the focus is on changes over time rather than on absolute levels—thus reducing the impact of differences in country size.

In summary, traditional exports, recently aug-

Table 2. Primary Import Substitution $(M_{CN}/M)^a$

	1950	1962	1970	1977
Kenya	—	16.4	14.3	6.9
Mexico	5.8	4.3	5.7	4.6
Taiwan	17.2 (53)^b	8.1 (60)^b	5.8	2.9

^{a}Consumer nondurable industries = 61 leather, etc.; 64 paper, paper board, etc.; 65 textiles; 84 clothing; 851 foot-wear; 892 printed matter. Source: U.N. Yearbook of International Trade Statistics.

^{b}Computation not completely comparable to others due to lack of Standard Industrial Classification data. Numbers in parentheses indicate the year to which the data refers.

mented by oil and always by foreign capital, could continue to fuel the industrialization effort in Mexico, including the export of fairly sophisticated capital and consumer durables. In Taiwan the burden of financing continued industrialization was, in contrast, gradually shifted to exports of nondurable consumer goods during the crucial PES phase, thus getting industry to help increasingly in paying the way—in the foreign exchange allocation sense—for its continued expansion. . . .

I am entitled, in fact enjoined, to ask why there is such a deviation in pattern between the East Asian and Latin American types—or as Chenery might put it, why there is such a deviation of the "minority" East Asian type from the "majority" Latin American pattern approaching "average" regression performance. Partly, of course, the Latin American representative, Mexico, is substantially larger in size than the East Asian representative, Taiwan. And, as has already been indicated, it has a much lower level of labor surplus and a much better natural resource endowment. Consequently, even if policies had been identical in the two cases, a less pronounced and probably shorter primary export substitution phase could be anticipated in Mexico, given its generally higher levels of income and lower levels of labor surplus. Its relatively stronger natural resource endowment, even before petroleum became important, can be expected to yield a relatively stronger exchange rate and, by way of the "Dutch disease," be less favorable for potential labor-intensive manufacturing exports typical of the PES subphase.

In addition to these endowment-driven phenomena is the package of policy interventions that further curbed any underlying tendency to move toward more diversified production and exports by way of the PES subphase. This set of policies or strategies is based, in part, on economic forces but also deeply grounded in political economy. In other words, natural resource bonanzas and abundant capital inflows render the exchange rate strong and

exert a politico-psychological effect, making it not only feasible for the system to continue to afford heavy protectionism and the relatively inefficient growth path chosen but also politically difficult to deviate from that path. It is increasingly well understood that a shift from PIS to PES must overcome the resistance of (1) industrialists, reluctant to shift from certain and large unit-profit rates on a larger volume in export markets; and (2) the civil service, threatened with a reduction of its influence or power as controls are reduced. The shift also flies in the face of much of organized labor's tendency, especially in the Latin American case, to keep its eye on wage rates rather than the wage bill and the income of working families.

Thus, a country like Mexico, given the relative abundance of its natural resources and easy access to foreign capital, could afford to pay for the prolongation of import substitution and attempt to skip the primary export substitution subphase. It also found this politically much easier to do. Until recently Mexico thought it could afford the relatively costly choice of an SIS/EP growth path in the belief that its natural resources were plentiful enough, foreign capitalists responsive enough, and the employment-distribution outcomes tolerable enough. Unfortunately there now is considerable doubt at least about the second of these assumptions.

The East Asian cases, including the representative, Taiwan, on the other hand, did not have the same options from the outset. The agricultural sector could be viewed as a temporary, if important, source of fuel. But the system's long-run comparative advantage had to be sought else-where: first in its human resources, and then, increasingly, through the contribution of routinized science and technology as during the epoch of modern growth. The secular shortage of natural resources, in particular, and the unwillingness of foreign capital to support continued import substitution in a relatively small domestic market forced an early change in policy toward the use of human resources and away from land-based resources. Once a more market-oriented growth pattern had been established, it began to have its own modus operandi: one of flexibility, responsiveness to changing endowment conditions, and a changing international environment.

References

Chenery, H. B. (1979). *Structural Change and Development Policy*. New York: Oxford University Press.

Fei, J. C. H., G. Ranis, and S. Kuo (1979). *Growth with Equity: The Taiwan Case*. London: Oxford University Press.

Food and Agriculture Organization (1952, 1961). *Production Yearbook*. Rome: Food and Agriculture Organization.

United Nations (1949–1950, 1980). *Demographic Yearbook*. New York: United Nations.

United Nations (1951, 1962, 1970, 1980). *Yearbook of International Trade Statistics*. New York: United Nations.

UNESCO (United Nations Educational, Scientific and Cultural Organization) (1963). *Statistical Yearbook*. Paris: United Nations.

US AID (United States Agency for International Development) (1974, 1975). *Economic Data Book*. Washington, D.C.: Department of State, AID, Division of Statistics and Reports.

Selection IV.A.3. An Exposition and Exploration of Krueger's Trade Model*

Krueger (1977) proposed a variant of the H–O model that is a hybrid of it with the specific-factors model.[1] Her model includes an agricultural sector that employs labour and land plus a manufacturing sector that employs labour and capital.[2] Capital and land are immobile between sectors, but capital is mobile within the manufacturing sector, which is modelled as capable of producing any of a large number of manufactured goods. These can be traded internationally, with a large number of countries among which factor prices are assumed to be unequal. The agricultural good—call it food—is also traded internationally.

Technologies in both agriculture and manufacturing are identical internationally and display constant returns to scale. Goods and factors are priced competitively, so that goods prices, together if necessary with factor endowments, determine factor prices in each country. Factor endowments are assumed to differ enough among countries to prevent factor price equalization even in the manufacturing sector. Thus world prices are such that, without interference, no country could produce more than a subset of the manufactured goods.

Countries at different levels of development may, depending also on their endowments of land, produce and perhaps export more or less capital-intensive manufactured goods. Also, unless they have very extreme factor endowments, they will import a variety of manufactured goods, some more capital intensive, and some less, than what they produce themselves. Finally, with exports of food also possible, a country with much land might import *all* manufactured goods, even when it produces only one of them.

All this can be seen in figure 1. The figure combines Lerner–Pearce unit-value-isoquants for de-

termining specialization within the manufacturing sector with the beaker-shaped diagram of the specific-factors literature. Together the two panels determine specialization and factor prices for a country with given factor endowments and facing given (free trade) prices of all goods.

To see how it is done, consider first the top panel, which is similar to figures in Deardorff (1979). Given world prices of three manufactured goods, p_1, p_2, and p_3, unit-value isoquants are drawn as M_1, M_2, and M_3 and are then connected by common tangents to form their convex hull.[3] This hull acts as a unit-value isoquant for manufacturing as a whole. Its slope indicates the ratio of the wage, w, to the rental on capital, r_K, that is implied by the marginal products of these factors in manufacturing. Along straight segments of the hull two goods[4] are produced in the sector, and marginal products of both factors are invariant with respect to small changes in the sector's employment of capital and labour.[5] Along curved portions of the hull, on the other hand, only one manufactured good is produced and marginal products of factors decline as their employment increases.

Given the capital stock $\bar{K}$, therefore, one can infer the behaviour of the manufacturing-sector wage as the level of employment in that sector, L_M, is varied. Moving to the right along the horizontal line at $\bar{K}$ in the top panel, one passes into and out of regions of specialization and non-specialization. For levels of manufacturing employment below L^0, for example, the sectoral capital-labour ratio is above the minimum $\underline{k}_3$ needed for specialization in M_3. In this region the manufacturing wage, which is the value of labour's marginal product in manufacturing, V_L^M, is also its value marginal product in producing only M_3. As L_M rises in this region, the capital-labour ratio in M_3 falls, and so must the manufacturing wage. This is shown by the curve w_M in the lower panel.

When L_M rises above L^0, the manufacturing sec-

*From Alan V. Deardorff, "An Exposition and Exploration of Krueger's Trade Model," *Canadian Journal of Economics* 17 (November 1984): 733–740. Reprinted by permission.

[1]The simple H—O model and the specific-factors model are both special cases of a generalized Heckscher–Ohlin model, in which there are arbitrary numbers of goods, factors, and countries. The generalized model retains some but not all of the properties of the simple model. See Deardorff (1979, 1982) and Ethier (1983). The Krueger model, too, is a special case of the generalized H—O model.

[2]The names "land" and "capital" are to indicate that these factors are not mobile between the agricultural and manufacturing sectors and need not otherwise have the properties of actual land and capital. The factor "land," in particular, could be thought of as representing a variety of factors that are specific to agriculture, including agricultural capital.

[3]The diagram can easily accommodate more than three goods, but three can make the points in this paper.

[4]I assume that world prices permit production of no more than two manufactured goods in any freely trading country. With only three manufactured goods in the sector, this is necessary in order to permit factor prices to differ internationally. With a larger number of goods that would not be necessary. The reader may think of figure 1 as including many additional undrawn isoquants, tangent to the hull along the straight segments.

[5]This of course is the familiar phenomenon of the factor-price equalization theorem of Samuelson (1949).

Figure 1

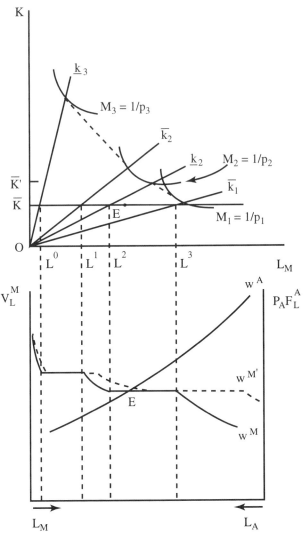

tor begins production of M_2 as well as M_3. Factor prices become fixed, since the capital-labour ratio in the sector can now fall without changing the ratios $\underline{k}_3$ and $\bar{k}_2$ employed in each of the two industries. Thus the manufacturing wage in the lower panel becomes flat throughout this region of non-specialization—that is, between L^0 and L^1. Proceeding further to the right, the sector alternates between specialization and non-specialization, and the w_M curve below alternates downward sloping and horizontal segments.

Once constructed in this way, the w_M curve can be combined with another curve representing the agricultural wage, w_A, to determine the equilibrium allocation of labour between the sectors. This

is the usual beaker-shaped diagram of the specific-factors model. The horizontal dimension of the beaker is the labour endowment, $\bar{L}$. Agricultural employment, L_A, is measured leftwards from the right-hand wall of the beaker. The agricultural wage must equal the value of the marginal product of labour in agriculture, $P_A F_L^A$. Given the endowment of land, $\bar{T}$, which is specific to that sector, and given also the world price of the agricultural good, P_A, that marginal product is a decreasing function of agricultural employment, as drawn.

Labour-market equilibrium with free mobility of labour between sectors requires the same wage in both. Thus equilibrium is at E, where the w_M and w_A curves intersect. The pattern of specialization

Figure 2

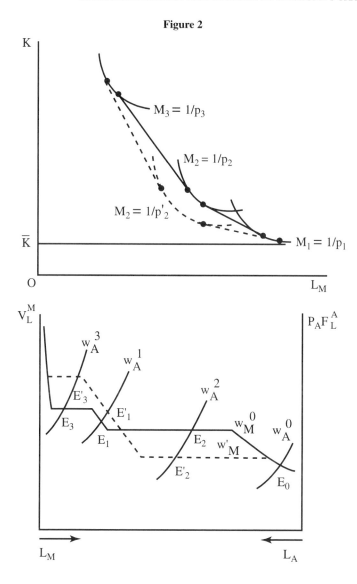

can be inferred from the segment of the w_M curve in which this intersection appears, and other behaviour in the manufacturing sector can be found in the upper panel.[6] As drawn, for example, the equilibrium entails production of both M_1 and M_2, using capital-labour ratios $\bar{k}_1$ and $\underline{k}_2$ in their production.

The diagram lends itself readily to comparative-static analysis and yields conclusions about effects of growth on trade that were a subject of Krueger's paper. For example, an increase in the capital stock

to $\bar{K}'$ shifts the w_M curve proportionately rightward, to $w_M{}'$. As drawn, this causes manufacturing to specialize completely in M_2. However, it is also clear that, for other initial equilibria, some capital accumulation can occur without changing the pattern of specialization, the wage, and total manufacturing employment. Note the contrast to the simpler specific factors model where accumulation of either specific factor necessarily raises the wage.

Comparison of economies with different endowments of land can also be done, although I leave the diagram to the reader. An increase in land shifts the w_A curve upward and causes an unambiguous decline in manufacturing employment, together with Rybczynski-like effects on separate

<hr>

[6]The point E in the upper panel could be used as the upper-right corner of an Edgeworth Box, showing allocation of capital and labour between industries M_1 and M_2.

manufacturing outputs in regions of nonspecialization.[7] One can easily derive Krueger's interesting conclusion that a country with little capital may none the less produce quite capital-intensive manufactured goods if it is also well endowed with land. . . .

Consider now the effects of price increases due to tariffs. These can occur for any good, but I focus primarily on that manufactured good, M_2, of intermediate capital intensity. A rise in p_2 captures all the qualitative effects of any manufactured-good price increase, including what one would find in a model with a larger number of goods. I also briefly note the effects of an increase in the price of the agricultural good.

A rise in the price of M_2 shifts the unit-value isoquant for M_2 radially inward, as shown in figure 2. The common tangents with the other two isoquants also adjust, rotating to maintain their tangencies. This alters all the capital-labour ratios at which these tangencies occur and thus changes the boundaries of all regions of specialization. The central region, for specialization in M_2, expands, while those for both M_1 and M_3 contract.

Factor prices are also altered by the price change in much of the diagram. Within regions of non-specialization these are most easily inferred from marginal products in M_1 and M_3, since their prices have not changed. In the lower region where M_1 and M_2 are produced, the capital-labour ratio in M_1 must fall. Thus, at world prices the wage falls and the rental on capital rises. Just the opposite

happens in the upper non-specialization region, since k rises in M_3. Finally, in the central region, where only M_2 is produced, all marginal products in terms of M_2 remain constant for given capital-labour ratios. Since the domestic price of M_2 has risen, however, both w and r_K rise in terms of world prices by the amount of the price increase.

These partial equilibrium effects on the wage are shown in the lower panel of figure 2 as altering the shape of the w_M curve from $w_M{}^0$ to $w_M{}'$. The horizontal portions of the curve shift vertically— one up, one down—while the downward sloping centre portion shifts up vertically by the amount of the price increase.

References

Deardorff, A. V. (1979) "Weak links in the chain of comparative advantage." *Journal of International Economics* 9, 197–209.

——— (1982) "The general validity of the Heckscher–Ohlin Theorem." *American Economic Review* 72, 683–94.

Ethier, W. J. (1983) "Higher dimensional trade theory." Chap. 3 of R.W. Jones and P.B. Kenen, eds, *Handbook of International Economics,* vol. 1 (Amsterdam: North-Holland).

Krueger, A. O. (1977) "Growth, distortions, and patterns of trade among many countries." *Princeton Studies in International Finance,* No. 40 (Princeton, NJ Princeton University).

Rybczynski, T. M. (1955) "Factor endowments and relative commodity prices." *Economica* 22, 336–41.

Samuelson, P. A. (1949) "International factor-price equalization once again." *The Economic Journal* (June), 181–97.

[7]For example, as manufacturing employment falls in the region between L^2 and L^3, output of M_2 rises and output of M_1 falls, much as in Rybczynski (1955).

Comment IV.A.1. Moving Up the Ladder and Changes in Relative Costs of Factors of Production

Let us think of "capital" in the preceding selection as an aggregate of physical and human capital, as we did in Note III.1 on the AK model. Figure 1 can then be used to show how a country that is accumulating physical and human capital will "move up the ladder" from less to more capital- and skill-intensive goods (goods with higher value-added per worker) without the aid of government policy. The key is Deardorff's result that the w_M curve shifts right as the capital stock increases. Consider a country with a capital stock that is sufficiently small, and consequently a w_M curve that lies sufficiently far to the left, that the intersection of this curve with the w_A curve occurs on its rightmost downward-sloping portion associated with complete specialization of the manufacturing sector in production of M_1, the most labor-intensive good. Now allow this country to accumulate capital. The w_M curve shifts right, causing its intersection with the w_A curve to move up, corresponding to a higher wage and lower rental on capital. With the cost of capital falling relative to the cost of labor, eventually firms can introduce production of the more capital-intensive good M_2 and break even at its international price: the first kink in the w_M curve is reached. As capital continues to accumulate, its increased supply shifts the mix of manufacturing production toward M_2 and away from M_1 rather than driving down the rental rate. When the second kink in the w_M curve is reached, the manufacturing sector is completely specialized in production of M_2. Further accumulation of capital again causes the wage to rise and the rental on capital to fall, and the country gradually moves up to the next step on the ladder.

Protection can of course accelerate the introduction of more capital-intensive production. With a tariff on imports of M_2, firms can introduce its production when the economy has accumulated less capital: as shown in Figure 2, the first kink in the w_M curve occurs further to the right.

Note that Krueger's model, as set forth by Deardorff, assumes constant returns to scale in production of all goods. In contrast, the selections in this section by Balassa and Rodrik emphasize that increasing returns to scale are a very important feature of capital-intensive production. This is one reason why moving up the ladder to more capital- and skill-intensive goods may not be as smooth as Krueger's model suggests it can be.

Selection IV.A.4. The Process of Industrial Development and Alternative Development Strategies*

Early Stages of Industrial Development

The Generation of a Surplus in the Primary Sector

Industrial development generally begins in response to domestic demand generated in the primary sector, which also provides investible funds for manufacturing industries. Demand for industrial products and investible savings represent possible uses of the surplus generated in agriculture (understood in a larger sense to include crops, livestock, fisheries, and forestry) or in mining as primary output comes to exceed subsistence needs. More often than not, the surplus generated in the primary sector is associated with export expansion. The effects of primary exports on industrial development, in turn, depend to a considerable extent on input-output relationships and on the disposition of incomes generated in the export sector.

Infrastructure in the form of ports, railways, and roads often represents important inputs for primary exports, and their availability may contribute to the development of industrial activities. In turn, the disposition of incomes generated in the export sector is affected by ownership conditions. In the case of foreign ownership, a substantial part of the surplus may be repatriated, although taxing the earnings of foreign capital does add to domestic incomes. There are leakages in the form of investing and spending abroad and consuming imported luxuries in the case of domestic ownership, too, in a system of plantation-type agriculture and large-scale mining. And, as Douglas North noted, plantation owners have little incentive to finance human investment in the form of general education.

By contrast, in cases where family-sized farms predominate, demand is generated for the necessities and the conveniences of life, as well as for education. This demand contributes to the development of domestic industry, which enjoys "natural" protection from imports in the form of transportation costs. It further contributes to the accumulation of human capital, which finds uses in manufacturing industries.

The process of industrial development may be accelerated if natural protection is complemented

by tariff or quota protection. This last point leads me to the next step in the industrialization process: the first, or "easy," stage of import substitution.

The First Stage of Import Substitution

With the exception of Britain at the time of the Industrial Revolution and Hong Kong more recently, all present-day industrial and developing countries protected their incipient manufacturing industries producing for domestic markets. There were differences, however, as regards the rate and the form of protection. While the industrial countries of today relied on relatively low tariffs, a number of present-day developing countries applied high tariffs or quantitative restrictions that limited, or even excluded, competition from imports.

At the same time, high protection discriminates against exports, through the explicit or implicit taxation of export activities. Explicit taxation may take the form of export taxes, while implicit taxation occurs as a result of the effects of protection on the exchange rate. The higher the rate of protection, the lower will be the exchange rate necessary to ensure equilibrium in the balance of payments, and the lower will be the amount of domestic currency exporters receive per unit of foreign exchange earned.

The adverse effects of high protection are exemplified by the case of Ghana, where import prohibitions encouraged inefficient, high-cost production in manufacturing industries; taxes on the main export crop, cocoa, discouraged its production; and other crops were adversely affected by the unfavorable exchange rate. Ghana's neighbor, the Ivory Coast, by contrast, followed a policy encouraging the development of both primary and manufacturing activities. As a result, it increased its share of cocoa exports, developed new primary exports, and expanded manufacturing industries.

Differences in the policies applied may largely explain why, between 1960 and 1978, per capita incomes fell from $430 to $390 in Ghana in terms of 1978 prices, compared with an increase from $540 to $840 in the Ivory Coast. This has occurred notwithstanding the facts that the two countries have similar natural-resource endowments and, at the time of independence, Ghana had the advantage of a higher educational level and an indigenous civil service.

Indeed, there is no need for high protection at

*From Bela Balassa, "The Process of Industrial Development and Alternative Development Strategies," Princeton University International Finance Section, Essays in International Finance No. 141 (December 1980): 4–12, 18–22, 24. Reprinted by permission.

the first stage of import substitution, entailing the replacement by domestic production of imports of nondurable consumer goods such as clothing, shoes, and household goods, and of their inputs, such as textile fabrics, leather, and wood. These commodities suit the conditions existing in developing countries when they begin the industrialization process: they are intensive in unskilled labor; the efficient scale of output is relatively low, and costs do not rise substantially at lower output levels; production does not involve the use of sophisticated technology; and a network of suppliers of parts, components, and accessories is not required for efficient operation.

The relative advantages of developing countries in these commodities explain the frequent references made to the "easy" stage of import substitution. At the same time, to the extent that the domestic production of these commodities generates external economies in the form of labor training, the development of entrepreneurship, and the spread of technology, there is an argument for moderate infant-industry protection or promotion.

Inward-oriented Industrial Development Strategies

In the course of first-stage import substitution, domestic production will rise more rapidly than domestic consumption, since it not only provides for increases in consumption but also replaces imports. Once the process of import substitution has been completed, however, the growth rate of output will decline to that of consumption.

Maintaining high industrial growth rates, then, necessitates either moving to second-stage import substitution or turning to the exportation of manufactured goods. This choice represents alternative industrial development strategies that may be followed after the completion of the first stage of import substitution. I first consider second-stage import substitution, representing the application of an inward-looking industrial development strategy, and subsequently examine an outward-oriented strategy that does not discriminate against exports, with favorable effects on the exporting of manufactured goods.

The Choice of Second-Stage Import Substitution

In the postwar period, second-stage import substitution was undertaken in several Latin-American countries, in some South Asian countries, particularly India, and in the Central and Eastern European socialist countries. In Latin America, the choice of this strategy reflected the ideas of Raul Prebisch, in whose view adverse foreign-market conditions for primary exports and the lack of competitiveness in manufactured exports would not permit developing countries to attain high rates of economic growth by relying on export production. Rather, Prebisch suggested that these countries should expand manufacturing industries oriented toward domestic markets. This purpose was to be served by industrial protection, which was said to bring additional benefits through improvements in the terms of trade.

Similar ideas were expressed by Gunnar Myrdal. Myrdal influenced the policies followed by India; they were also affected by the example of the Soviet Union, which chose an autarkical pattern of industrial development. And the European socialist countries faithfully imitated the Soviet example, attempting to reproduce it in the framework of much smaller domestic markets that also lacked the natural-resource base of the Soviet Union.

Second-stage import substitution involves the replacement of imports of intermediate goods and producer and consumer durables by domestic production. These commodities have rather different characteristics from those replaced at the first stage.

Intermediate goods such as petrochemicals and steel tend to be highly capital-intensive. They are also subject to important economies of scale: efficient plant size is large compared with the domestic needs of most developing countries, and costs rise rapidly at lower output levels. Moreover, the margin of processing is relatively small, and organizational and technical inefficiencies may contribute to high costs.

Producer durables, such as machinery, and consumer durables, such as automobiles and refrigerators, are also subject to economies of scale. But in these industries economies of scale relate not so much to plant size as to horizontal and vertical specialization, entailing reductions in product variety and the manufacture of parts, components, and accessories on an efficient scale in separate plants.

Reducing product variety will permit longer production runs that lower production costs through improvements in manufacturing efficiency along the "learning curve," savings in expenses incurred in moving from one operation to another, and the use of special-purpose machinery. Horizontal specialization is, however, limited by the smallness of domestic markets in the developing countries.

Similar conclusions apply to vertical specialization, which leads to cost reductions through the subdivision of the production process among plants of efficient size. General Motors, for example, has ten thousand subcontractors, each producing a part or component. This extended division of the production process has permitted General Motors to produce at a substantially lower cost than its U.S. competitors. A number of years ago, Martin Shubik reached the conclusion that without antitrust legislation only General Motors would survive in the United States, and he predicted the disappearance of several small American car producers. Some producers have in fact disappeared since, and without federal support Chrysler would have met a similar fate.

At the same time, the production of parts, components, and accessories has to be done with precision for consumer durables, and especially for machinery. This, in turn, requires the availability of skilled and technical labor and, to a greater or lesser extent, the application of sophisticated technology.

Given the relative scarcity of physical and human capital in developing countries that have completed the first stage of import substitution, they are at a disadvantage in the manufacture of highly physical-capital-intensive intermediate goods and skill-intensive producer and consumer durables. By limiting the scope for the exploitation of economies of scale, the relatively small size of their national markets contributes to high domestic costs in these countries. At the same time, net foreign-exchange savings tend to be small because of the need to import materials and machinery.

The domestic resource cost (DRC) ratio relates the domestic resource cost of production, in terms of the labor, capital, and natural resources utilized, to net foreign-exchange savings (in the case of import substitution) or net foreign-exchange earnings (in the case of exports). In the absence of serious distortions in factor markets, the DRC ratio will be low for exported commodities. It is also relatively low for consumer nondurables and their inputs, in the production of which developing countries have a comparative advantage. For the reasons already noted, however, DRC ratios tend to be high in the manufacture of intermediate goods and producer and consumer durables. The establishment of these industries to serve narrow domestic markets is therefore predicated on high protection, and the rates of protection may need to be raised as countries "travel up the staircase" represented by DRC ratios. This will occur as goods produced at earlier stages come to saturate domestic markets and

countries embark on the production of commodities that less and less conform to their comparative advantage. High protection, in turn, discriminates against manufactured and primary exports and against primary activities in general.

Characteristics of Inward-oriented Development Strategies

In the postwar period, several capitalist countries in Latin America and South Asia and the socialist countries of Central and Eastern Europe adopted inward-oriented industrial development strategies, entailing second-stage import substitution. Capitalist countries generally utilized a mixture of tariffs and import controls to protect their industries, while socialist countries relied on import prohibitions and industry-level planning. Notwithstanding these differences, the principal characteristics of the industrial development strategies adopted in the two groups of countries show considerable similarities.

To begin with, while the infant-industry argument calls for temporary protection until industries become internationally competitive, in both groups of countries protection was regarded as permanent. Also, in all the countries concerned, there was a tendency toward what a Latin-American economist aptly described as "import substitution at any cost."

Furthermore, in all the countries concerned, there were considerable variations in rates of explicit and implicit protection across industrial activities. This was the case, first of all, as continued import substitution involved undertaking activities with increasingly high domestic costs per unit of foreign exchange saved. In capitalist countries, the generally uncritical acceptance of demands for protection contributed to this result; in the absence of price comparisons, the protective effects of quantitative restrictions could not even be established. In socialist countries, the stated objective was to limit imports to commodities that could not be produced domestically or were not available in sufficient quantities, and no attempt was made to examine the implicit protection that pursuit of this objective entailed.

In both groups of countries, the neglect of intra-industry relationships further increased the dispersion of protection rates on value added in processing, or effective protection, with adverse effects on economic efficiency. In Argentina, high tariffs imposed on caustic soda at the request of a would-be producer made formerly thriving soap exports unprofitable. In Hungary, the high cost of domestic steel, whose production was based largely on imported iron ore and coking coals, raised costs for steel-using industries. Large investments in the steel industry, in turn, delayed the substitution of aluminum for steel, although Hungary had considerable bauxite reserves.

Countries applying inward-oriented industrial development strategies were further characterized by the prevalence of sellers' markets. In capitalist countries, the smallness of national markets limited the possibilities for domestic competition in industries established at the second stage of import substitution, while import competition was virtually excluded by high protection. In socialist countries, the system of central planning did not permit competition among domestic firms or from imports, so that buyers had neither a choice among domestic producers nor access to imported commodities.

The existence of sellers' markets provides little inducement to cater to users' needs. In the case of industrial users, it led to backward integration as producers undertook the manufacture of parts, components, and accessories themselves in order to minimize supply difficulties. This outcome, observed in capitalist as well as socialist countries, led to higher costs, since economies of scale were foregone.

Also, in sellers' markets, firms had little incentive to improve productivity. In capitalist countries, monopolies and oligopolies assumed importance; the oligopolists often aimed at the maintenance of market shares while refraining from actions that would invoke retaliation. In socialist countries, the existence of assured outlets and the managers' emphasis on short-term objectives discouraged technological change.

The managers' emphasis on short-term objectives in socialist countries had to do with uncertainty as to the planners' future intentions. In capitalist countries, fluctuations in real exchange rates (nominal exchange rates, adjusted for changes in inflation rates at home and abroad) created uncertainty for business decisions. These fluctuations, resulting from intermittent devaluations in the face of rapid domestic inflation, aggravated the existing bias against exports, because the domestic-currency equivalent of export earnings varied with the devaluations, the timing of which was uncertain.

In countries engaging in second-stage import substitution, distortions were further apparent in the valuation of time. In capitalist countries, negative real interest rates adversely affected domestic savings, encouraged self-investment—including inventory accumulation—at low returns, and pro-

vided inducements to transfer funds abroad. Negative interest rates also necessitated credit rationing, which generally favored import-substituting investments, whether the rationing was done by the banks or the government. In the first case, the lower risk of investments in production for domestic than for export markets gave rise to such a result; in the second case, the preference given to import-substituting investments reflected government priorities. Finally, in socialist countries, ideological considerations led to the exclusion of interest rates as a charge for capital and an element in the evaluation of investment projects.

There was also a tendency to underprice public utilities in countries following an inward-oriented strategy, either because of low interest charges in these capital-intensive activities or as a result of a conscious decision. The underpricing of utilities particularly benefited energy-intensive industries and promoted the use of capital.

In general, in moving to the second stage of import substitution, countries applying inward-oriented development strategies deemphasized the role of prices. In socialist countries, resources were in large part allocated centrally in physical terms; in capitalist countries, output and input prices were distorted, and reliance was placed on nonprice measures—import restrictions and credit allocation.

Effects on Exports and on Economic Growth

The discrimination in favor of import substitution and against exports did not permit the development of manufactured exports in countries engaging in second-stage import substitution behind high protection. There were also adverse developments in primary exports, because low prices for producers and consumers reduced the exportable surplus by discouraging production and encouraging consumption. In fact, instead of improving the external terms of trade, import protection turned the internal terms of trade against primary activities and led to a decline in export market shares in the countries in question. Decreases in market shares were especially pronounced in cereals, meat, oilseeds, and nonferrous metals, benefiting developed countries, particularly the United States, Canada, and Australia.

The volume of Argentina's principal primary exports, chiefly beef and wheat, remained, on average, unchanged between 1934–38 and 1964–66, while world exports of these commodities doubled. In the same period, Chile's share of world copper exports, which accounted for three-fifths of the country's export earnings, fell from 28 per cent to 22 per cent.

Similar developments occurred in socialist countries, where the allocation of investment favored industry at the expense of agriculture. In Hungary, exports of several agricultural commodities, such as goose liver, fodder seeds, and beans, declined in absolute terms, and slow increases in production made it necessary to import cereals and meat, which earlier were major export products.

The slowdown in the growth of primary exports and the lack of growth of manufactured exports did not provide the foreign exchange necessary for rapid economic growth in countries pursuing inward-oriented industrial development strategies. The situation was aggravated by the increased need for foreign materials, machinery, and technological know-how, which reduced net import savings. As a result, economic growth was increasingly constrained by the scarcity of foreign exchange, and intermittent foreign-exchange crises occurred when attempts were made to expand the economy at rates exceeding that permitted by the growth of export earnings.

The savings constraint became increasingly binding as high-cost, capital-intensive production at the second stage of import substitution raised capital-output ratios, requiring ever-increasing savings ratios to maintain rates of economic growth. At the same time, the loss of income because of the high cost of protection reduced the volume of savings and, in capitalist countries, negative interest rates contributed to the outflow of funds.

In several developing countries, the cost of protection is estimated to have reached 6 to 7 per cent of GNP. There is further evidence that the rate of growth of total factor productivity was lower in countries engaging in second-stage import substitution than in the industrial countries. Rather than reduce the economic distance between the industrial and the developing countries, then, infant-industry protection may have caused this lag to increase over time. . . .

The Choice of a Development Strategy: Lessons and Prospects

Inward- vs. Outward-oriented Development Strategies

The evidence is quite conclusive: countries applying outward-oriented development strategies performed better in terms of exports, economic growth, and employment than countries with continued inward orientation, which encountered increasing economic difficulties. At the same time, policy reforms aimed at greater outward orientation brought considerable improvement to the economic performance of countries that had earlier applied inward-oriented policies.

It has been suggested, however, that import substitution was a necessary precondition for the development of manufactured exports in present-day developing countries. In attempting to provide an answer to this question, a distinction needs to be made between first-stage and second-stage import substitution.

I have noted that, except in Britain and Hong Kong, the exportation of nondurable consumer goods and their inputs was preceded by an import-substitution phase. At the same time, there were differences among the countries concerned as regards the length of this phase and the level of protection applied. First-stage import substitution was of relatively short duration in the present-day industrial countries and in the three Far Eastern developing countries that subsequently adopted an outward-oriented strategy; it was longer in most other developing countries, and these countries also generally had higher levels of protection.

Nor did all nondurable consumer goods and their inputs go through an import-substitution phase before the Far Eastern countries began to export them. Synthetic textiles in Korea, plastic shoes in Taiwan, and fashion clothing in Singapore all began to be produced largely for export markets. Plywood and wigs, which were Korea's leading exports in the late sixties and early seventies, did not go through an import-substitution phase either.

Wigs provide a particularly interesting example, because they reflect the responses of entrepreneurs to incentives. Korea originally exported human hair to the industrial countries, especially the United States. Recognizing that human hair was made into wigs by a labor-intensive process, entrepreneurs began to exploit what appeared to be a profitable opportunity to export wigs, given the favorable treatment of exports in Korea and the limitations imposed by the United States on wigs originating from Hong Kong. The supply of human hair soon proved to be insufficient, however, and firms turned to exporting wigs made of synthetic hair. Wigs made with synthetic hair were for a time Korea's second-largest single export commodity, after plywood.

The example indicates that entrepreneurs will export the commodities that correspond to the country's comparative advantage if the system of incentives does not discriminate against exports. It also points to the need to leave the choice of exports to private initiative. It is highly unlikely that government planners would have chosen wigs as a potential major export or that they would have effected a switch from human to synthetic hair in making them. Even if a product group such as toys were identified by government planners, the choice of which toys to produce would have to be made by the entrepreneur, who has to take the risks and reap the rewards of his actions. At the same time, providing similar incentives to all export commodities other than those facing market limitations abroad and avoiding a bias against exports will ensure that private profitability corresponds to social profitability. This was, by and large, the case in countries pursuing an outward strategy.

These considerations may explain why Singapore and Taiwan did not need a planning or targeting system for exports. Export targets were in effect in Korea, but the fulfillment of these targets was not a precondition of the application of the free-trade regime to exports or of the provision of export incentives. While successful exporters were said to enjoy advantageous treatment in tax cases and export targets may have exerted pressure on some firms, these factors merely served to enhance the effects of export incentives without introducing discrimination among export products. At any rate, most firms continually exceeded their targets. A case in point is the increase in Korean exports by two-thirds between the second quarter of 1975 and the second quarter of 1976, exceeding the targets by a very large margin.

The reliance on private initiative in countries that adopted an outward-oriented development strategy can be explained by the need of exporters for flexibility to respond to changing world market conditions. Furthermore, government cannot take responsibility for successes and failures in exporting that will affect the profitability of firms. For these reasons Hungary, among socialist countries, gave firms the freedom to determine the product composition of their exports after the 1968 economic reform and especially after 1977.

In the Latin-American countries that reformed their incentive systems in the period preceding the 1973 oil crisis, the expansion of manufactured exports was not based on export targets either. The question remains, however, whether the development of exports in these countries was helped by the fact that they had undertaken second-stage import substitution.

This question can be answered in the negative as far as nondurable consumer goods and their inputs are concerned. Had appropriate incentives been provided, these commodities could have been exported as soon as first-stage import substitution was completed, as was the case in the Far Eastern countries. In fact, to the extent that the products in question had to use some domestic inputs produced at higher than world market costs, exporters were at a disadvantage in foreign markets. It can also be assumed that the inability to exploit fully economies of scale and the lack of sufficient specialization in the production of parts, components, and accessories in the confines of the protected domestic markets retarded the development of exports of intermediate products and producer and consumer durables.

More generally, as a Hungarian economist has pointed out, there is the danger that second-stage import substitution will lead to the establishment of an industrial structure that is "prematurely old," in the sense that it is based on small-scale production with inadequate specialization and outdated machinery. Should this be the case, any subsequent move toward outward orientation will encounter difficulties. Such difficulties were apparent in the case of Hungary and may also explain why, although exports grew rapidly from a low base, their share in manufacturing output remained small in the Latin-American countries that moved toward outward orientation from the second stage of import substitution.

In contrast, in the period following the oil crisis the Far Eastern countries increasingly upgraded their exports of nondurable consumer goods and began exporting machinery, electronics, and transport equipment. For several of these products, including shipbuilding in Korea, photographic equipment in Singapore, and other electronic products in Taiwan, exporting was not preceded by an import-substitution phase. There are even examples, such as color television sets in Korea, where the entire production was destined for foreign markets.

Intermediate goods, machinery, and automobiles require special attention, given the importance of economies of scale on the plant level for the first; the need for product (horizontal) specialization for the second; and the desirability of vertical specialization in the form of the production of parts, components, and accessories on an efficient scale for the third. In all these cases, production in protected domestic markets will involve high costs in most developing countries, and the establishment of small-scale and insufficiently specialized firms will make the transition to exportation difficult. This contrasts with the case of nondurable consumer goods and their inputs, where efficient production does not require large plants or horizontal and vertical specialization.

It follows that, rather than enter into second-stage import substitution as a prelude to subsequent exports, it is preferable to undertake the manufacture of intermediate goods and producer and consumer durables for domestic and foreign markets simultaneously. This will permit the exploitation of economies of scale and ensure efficient import substitution in some products, while others continue to be imported. At the same time, it will require the provision of equal incentives to exports and to import substitution instead of import protection that discriminates against exports. . . .

Policy Prescriptions and Prospects for the Future

The experience of developing countries in the postwar period leads to certain policy prescriptions. First, while infant-industry considerations call for the preferential treatment of manufacturing activities, such treatment should be applied on a moderate scale, both to avoid the establishment and maintenance of inefficient industries and to ensure the continued expansion of primary production for domestic and foreign markets.

Second, equal treatment should be given to exports and to import substitution in the manufacturing sector, in order to ensure resource allocation according to comparative advantage and the exploitation of economies of scale. This is of particular importance in the case of intermediate goods and producer and consumer durables, where the advantages of large plant size and horizontal and vertical specialization are considerable and where import substitution in the framework of small domestic markets makes the subsequent development of exports difficult. The provision of equal incentives will contribute to efficient exportation and import substitution through specialization in particular products and in their parts, components, and accessories.

Third, infant-industry considerations apart, variations in incentive rates within the manufacturing sector should be kept to a minimum. This amounts to the application of the "market principle" in allowing firms to decide on the activities to be undertaken. In particular, firms should be free to choose their export composition in response to changing world market conditions.

Fourth, in order to minimize uncertainty for the firm, the system of incentives should be stable and automatic. Uncertainty will also be reduced if the reform of the system of incentives necessary to apply the principles just described is carried out according to a time-table made public in advance.

Selection IV.A.5. Exchange Control, Liberalization, and Economic Development*

Export Promotion Versus Import Substitution

Among the more interesting results that appear to emerge from our preliminary analysis of individual countries' experience is that countries which have had export-oriented development strategies appear, by and large, to have intervened virtually as much and as "chaotically" on the side of promoting new exports as other countries have on the side of import substitution. Yet, the economic cost of incentives distorted toward export promotion appears to have been less than the cost of those distorted toward import substitution, and the growth performance of the countries oriented toward export promotion appears to have been more satisfactory than that of the import-substitution oriented countries. If that conclusion is valid, the lesson is that policy should err on the side of allowing a higher marginal cost for earning than for saving foreign exchange.

There are several theoretical reasons which would explain such an asymmetry in outcomes, and the empirical evidence does point in their direction. In theory, there are four reasons why export promotion may be the superior strategy.

(1) Generally speaking, the costs of excess export promotion are more visible to policymakers than are those of import substitution. If there are departures from unified exchange rates, export-promoting growth can be sustained only by subsidies or other incentives costly to the government budget. Thus, there are built-in forces within the government against excessive export subsidization and promotion. The equivalent costs of import substitution are borne by firms and consumers and, hence, no obvious intragovernmental pressure group emerges as rapidly when incentives are biased toward import substitution.

(2) An export-oriented development strategy generally entails relatively greater use of indirect, rather than direct, interventions. There is considerable evidence from the individual country studies that direct intervention may be considerably more costly than is generally recognized. When policy makers are concerned with export promotion, direct controls cannot be as pervasive as they can be

under import substitution. Price controls, distribution controls, and a host of other detailed interventions make little sense, even to bureaucrats, when firms' outputs are intended largely for overseas markets, but appear attractive when production is oriented toward the home market under import substitution. The fact that, under import substitution, government officials have power to remove or enhance domestic monopoly positions of import-competing firms implies that those firms can be induced to accept otherwise intolerable (and socially unprofitable) interventions with their decisions. By contrast, officials simply do not have the same degree of power over firms engaged primarily in the export market.

(3) Exporting firms, however much they may be sheltered on the domestic market, must face price and quality competition in international markets. Import-substituting producers, with no competition for domestic markets, are a pervasive fact of life in the developing countries where import substitution has been stressed. While there is little hard evidence on the subject, there is considerable reason to believe that sheltered monopoly positions may be important explanations of low productivity growth in the newly established manufacturing industries in developing countries. Insofar as the adverse side effects of inadequate competition are less severe under the export-oriented strategy, it may be that export promotion is superior simply because it reduces the incidence of the problem.

(4) If there are significant indivisibilities or economies of scale, an export-oriented strategy will enable firms of adequate size to realize them. When import-substituting incentives dominate the domestic market, import-substituting firms generally are confronted with powerful incentives for expansion through diversification; each new product line provides one more domestic monopoly position. If indivisibilities and/or economies to scale are important, an export-oriented strategy will provide better incentives for expansion of capacity in existing lines. As such, an export-oriented growth strategy is better suited to achieving whatever economies of scale are present than is an import-substitution strategy where firms are generally limited in their horizons by the size of the domestic market.

These and other arguments supporting the case

*From Jagdish N. Bhagwati and Anne O. Krueger, "Exchange Control, Liberalization, and Economic Development," *American Economic Review* 63 (May 1973): 420–421, 424–427. Reprinted by permission.

for an asymmetrical behavior of the export-promoting versus import-substituting economies appear to be borne out by the contrast in the success of South Korea and the relative failure of India, for example, in the countries studied in the project. Since approximately 1960, the economic policies of South Korea have been heavily oriented toward growth through exporting. The rate of growth of exports has been almost double that of real GNP. Close inspection of South Korean policies indicates that the kinds of detailed and chaotic interventions which we have found in other countries are abundantly present in Korea's case as well: numerous *QR*'s [quantitative restrictions], high tariffs, and physical targeting of exports and imports. The striking difference, however, is in the remarkable degree to which the government has been willing to use exchange-rate changes and to lean in favor of export promotion *via* preferential allocation of import licenses, etc. Thus, aside from other special factors, such as the high inflow of foreign resources (official and private), the one striking aspect of Korean success has clearly been the significantly less discrimination against exports than in other developing countries, and not (it would appear) the presence of a neoclassically efficient allocation mechanism in toto in the system. . . .

Logic of *QR*'s

Once a *QR* regime is established, it seems to have an internal, self-contradictory logic all its own. The tariff equivalent of existing quotas tends to fluctuate widely and the unintended side effects of *QR*'s tend to force other changes. Decision makers do not receive visible feedbacks as to the effects of their actions. Thus, one finds quota categories where the quotas are redundant and there is a zero premium side by side with quota applications exceeding the amount of the quota by exorbitant multiples. Yet these multiples provide little information to those allocating quotas, because the amount of applications is itself influenced by expectations as to the probable disparity between the amount applied for and the amount received.

But that is only a small part of the story. For, once a *QR* regime is established, quotas inevitably become a tool seized upon by governments to accomplish a host of purposes other than the initial one of restraining *ex ante* payments imbalances. Thus, "priorities" are established and preferential treatment is given to applicants willing to further an officially desired goal. For example, efforts are generally made to encourage capital goods imports at the expense of consumer goods imports, in the hope of accelerating the rate of investment. In turn, the newly established manufacturing capacity often has intermediate goods import "requirements" which can be met only at the cost of reducing capital goods imports, thus defeating the initial purpose of the priority. Moreover, in increasing capital goods imports, consumer goods imports are the first to go, and the production structure of the domestic economy becomes increasingly oriented toward consumer goods.

Once that happens, growth in investment becomes increasingly dependent upon expansion of imports, itself a function of export growth. Yet the protection afforded to producers in domestic markets by *QR*'s is so great that profitability lies in expanding domestic sales and disincentives to export increase. By this point, governments are trapped: if they devalue the currency (which could have been done in the first place as an alternative to *QR*'s), they fear that the rate of capital formation will decline as capital goods become more expensive. If they do not devalue the currency, they must resort to ad hoc measures such as export rebates, import entitlement schemes for exporters, and the like in order to stimulate export growth. As these "incentives" grow over time, the regime becomes increasingly piecemeal. In virtually all the countries studied in the project which have had *QR* systems, governments themselves have reacted against these undesired side effects and proliferation of special regulations that seem to result from *QR* systems.

The tendency toward increasingly detailed, often internally inconsistent, controls and the resulting frustration of initial intentions shows up in numerous ways. In India, a major goal was the reduction of concentration in economic power, which presumably meant reducing the share of the large industrial concerns in industrial output. Yet the regulations and procedures surrounding licensing applications (for investment and for imports) became so complex that the large firms had a strong competitive advantage in satisfying license requirements: their share actually increased. In Turkey, import licenses were granted to establish assembly industries in the expectation that those (import-substitution) industries would save foreign exchange and provide incentives for domestic production of parts and components. Instead, people invested in the assembly industries in order to earn import licenses, and the value of licenses for assembly industry requirements of intermediate goods increased, rather than decreased, during the 1960's, while domestic content requirements had to be employed to induce investments in parts-and-components producing activities.

Wide Variations in Economic Costs

When producers know that they will benefit from complete protection from imports once domestic productive capacity is established, there are powerful profitability incentives to establish capacity regardless of the social opportunity costs of so doing. The drive to industrialize has been such an important goal that few of the countries covered in the Project have been able to resist using *QR*'s to provide those incentives. In India and Turkey, goods have simply become ineligible for importation once domestic productive capacity was established. In Egypt and Ghana, the same thing happened de facto. In Brazil, the Law of Similars, combined with domestic content requirements, and a provision that tariff rates be doubled once domestic production started, achieved the same result.

It is easily predictable that under such systems the variation in domestic resource cost among and within industries will be great. One of the purposes of the country studies was to quantify the extent of this variation, and the results show remarkably wide differences. We do *not* find that all import-substitution firms are inefficient. On the contrary, some appear to have very low costs while others require a large multiple of all resources in order to save an equal amount of foreign exchange.

In view of this, a major defect of the *QR* system seems to be its inevitably indiscriminate nature. If, within such a system, low-cost activities could be differentially encouraged, the excess costs of the system should be significantly lower. Yet, the workings of the system seem invariably to result in an inability to reflect differentials in social profitability to individual decision makers.

Actual User Licensing

We have already shown that the allocation of import licenses to firms using imported goods in their production process has different resource-allocational implications from those that arise when premia on licenses accrue to individuals who then resell to actual users. One feature of most *QR* systems is that they have tended to become increasingly actual-user oriented, and the fraction of import licenses allocated directly to user firms has increased over time.

The motive for this method of allocation seems reasonable enough: it is designed to avoid allowing large windfall gains to accrue to persons who apparently do nothing but apply for import licenses and, in addition, it rewards those individuals who have contributed toward the industrialization goal, as well as providing an implicit subsidy for recipient firms.

Difficulty, however, arises from the fact that criteria for allocation of licenses among actual users are needed in the presence of excess demand. Without such criteria, the allocating officials are naturally accused of favoritism. The most frequently adopted criterion has been to allocate licenses to recipients in proportion to different firms' capacities, although almost all countries have made provisions whereby new entrants would be entitled to an initial allocation.

This allocational criterion has had two closely interrelated and deleterious side effects: (1) it has, predictably enough, encouraged the development of excess capacity, and (2) it has resulted in roughly proportionate expansion of all firms in a given industry with little competition between them.

Turning to excess capacity first, in many newly established industries, firms' output levels are determined, within fairly narrow limits, by the volume of imports they obtain. Hence, summing over firms within an industry, the industry's output is closely tied to the imports of intermediate goods allocated to it. The fact that there are excess profits to most firms at that level of output is reflected by the premium on import licenses: any individual firm could increase its total profit if it obtained more imports.

The only way to get more imports, however, is to expand capacity, since one's import rights are a function of his share in total capacity of the industry. Thus, even with existing excess capacity, it may pay to build more, since the return on the investment is the premium to be earned per unit of imports times the expected increment in import licenses.

When policy makers perceive this result, a natural response is to attempt to control the expansion of capacity. Then, investment licensing follows import licensing. Again, criteria are needed and the circle has one more twist: profitability cannot be used as a criterion, since it emanates from import-licensing procedures, and also is regarded with suspicion (the bureaucrats are rewarding the already rich large firms). Thus, the natural temptation is to allow expansion proportionately over all applicants or over all firms. Decisions about the relative rates at which different industries shall be expanded must then be made and private profitability departs further and further from social profitability.

This brings us to the effect of import, and investment, licensing upon competition. For those industries where a firm's imports determine its output, the firm-specific allocation of imports determines market shares. With output fixed in the short run, there is little competition among firms. If there were no investment licensing, it might be that more profitable firms would expand more, with higher equilibrium levels of excess capacity in the long run. In general, however, investment licensing rules out even that form of competition, perhaps diminishing excess capacity, but insuring the growth of efficient and inefficient firms alike. We spoke earlier of the asymmetries of export promotion and import substitution. It may well be that, in dynamic terms, the inability of QR systems to foster relatively more rapid growth of more efficient firms is one of the gravest drawbacks of the QR-import-substitution development pattern.

Selection IV.A.6. Trade Policy Reform*

The number of countries that have experimented seriously with trade reform is limited. This limited progress reflects a number of problems—real or perceived—in the transition from inward to outward orientation. The transition means that some activities become more profitable and others less so. Often it is protected manufacturing activities whose profitability is most threatened. The more inward-oriented the original policies, the greater these shifts—and the costs associated with them—will be. The pattern of transition may need to be designed to suit specific national situations.

- The more rapid and fundamental the policy changes, the greater the immediate benefits to the economy. But there is also a greater likelihood that more people will face transitional costs as workers are displaced from old jobs and firms abandon old activities.
- As some activities or occupations become less remunerative, resistance to policy change will emerge. Those who are threatened will use political means to obstruct reform.
- Trade policy reform is closely related to reform of other economic policies. In particular, the exchange rate and the way domestic inflation affects it in real terms are crucial to competitiveness in import-replacing and export activities. In turn these are influenced by domestic fiscal, monetary, and credit policies and by policies affecting capital flows.

All these problems of transition make the design of policy reform important. How can policies best be selected, phased, and sequenced to gain the benefits of reform as quickly as possible while minimizing transitional costs and political resistance?

The Design of Trade Policy Reform

Reform in the conventional instruments of trade policy can be discussed under three headings: replacing quantitative restrictions with tariffs, reforming tariff protection, and the direct promotion of exports.

Replacing Quantitative Restrictions with Tariffs

It is broadly accepted that moving from nontariff barriers to tariffs is a move toward a more open trade policy. This is so for two reasons. First, tariffs are generally less protective than quantitative restrictions (although it is possible to have tariffs set so high that they prohibit imports). Second, a tariff is a price instrument, not a quantity instrument. As a result, tariffs are more "transparent"—changes in foreign prices feed through more readily to the domestic economy. Quotas, by contrast, uncouple national economies from the world economy. For example, in India cotton is protected by quantitative restrictions, and textile producers are required to use Indian cotton. As a result, movements in the price of this crucial raw material are not always related to those of world cotton prices, which determine the cost of this input to competitors. It is therefore difficult for Indian producers to commit themselves to production for export: the conditions under which they have to compete are unpredictable.

In many cases a shift from quotas to tariffs has been a key element in the early stages of trade policy reform. Sometimes it has been the only element. For example, Israel's first and second phases of reform focused on imports and consisted of the gradual removal of quotas and their replacement with tariffs. Greece's first reforms removed almost all quotas and replaced them with tariffs which were for the most part lower than the tariff equivalent of the quotas.

The evidence of similar episodes strongly suggests that this shift in the form of protection was highly beneficial. Often, not only did the economy's growth speed up following such shifts, but even in the sectors whose protection had been lowered, production increased as firms began to operate in a less restrictive and more transparent regime. This suggests that in an economy in which trade is regulated largely by quantitative restrictions—and this is true for most economies in which trade is severely restricted—a liberalization policy should start with a shift from the use of quotas to the use of tariffs, even if it means very high tariffs. . . .

Reforming Tariffs

The movement toward greater neutrality has two dimensions: the lowering of the average level of protection and the reduction in the average dispersion, or variance, of protection. If the dispersion of tariffs is not reduced as the tariff average is reduced, the tariff structure may not become more neutral. Indeed, a reform that reduces tariffs on in-

*From World Bank, *World Development Report, 1987* (1987), pp. 95, 109–12. Reprinted by permission.

termediate and capital goods but leaves intact those on final outputs could *increase* effective protection—the level of protection afforded to domestic value added—even though it *reduced* the average level of tariffs.

Of course, it is possible to reduce at the same time both the average level of tariffs and their dispersion. Governments have approached the task in several ways: an equiproportional cut in all tariffs, an equiproportional reduction of the excess of each tariff over some target level, higher proportional reductions of higher tariffs, or some combination of these and other methods. As a rule, simple schemes widely applied work better than case-by-case and fine-tuning methods. Some tariff reforms have attempted to target the effective, rather than the nominal, rate of protection (the Philippine reforms of 1981–85 are an example). This is unnecessarily complicated and may misfire anyway because of measurement problems.

Many economists favor the so-called concertina approach to tariff cutting. First, all tariffs above a certain ceiling are lowered to that ceiling; next, all tariffs above a new, lower ceiling are lowered to that ceiling; and so on. This should yield the lowest adjustment costs without leading to inadvertent increases in effective protection. Chile's tariff reductions in the 1970s more or less followed this scheme.

Lessons about the amount of time necessary to eliminate quantitative restrictions and tariffs are difficult to draw. Some reforms have taken a long time—Korea and the countries of southern Europe, for instance, have still not completed their reforms after at least two decades. Fewer have been completed within the medium term—the process lasted five years in Chile, for example. But none have been fully implemented over the short term. There is no obvious relationship between the length of the period of policy reform and its chances of success. But the apparently low adjustment costs in most trade reforms, together with the danger that lengthier reforms will be less credible, are arguments for faster reform. . . .

Direct Promotion of Exports

The logic of trade liberalization is that the tariffs should be as low as possible. As long as the average tariff is not zero, an element of discrimination against exports remains (unless they are equivalently subsidized). Chile's reforms achieved a uniform tariff of 10 percent with no exceptions. Later, this was revised, and Chile ended up with a uniform tariff of 20 percent, which left a mild discrimination against exports, but not enough to pre-

vent export growth. The experience of Brazil and the Philippines shows that export growth can be achieved in the presence of significant import protection, as long as governments can prevent the real exchange rate from appreciating.

Where significant import protection remains, governments might consider offsetting the discrimination against exports with administrative measures to provide imported inputs at world prices or with subsidies. Directly promoting exports in this way may also help to form a constituency for continued protection. But it may come to be seen as a long-term alternative to further import liberalization. This appears to have been the case in Pakistan and, in the 1970s at least, in the Philippines.

Direct export promotion is a difficult alternative to cuts in import protection. It raises administrative problems and often requires significant budgetary resources. Like any other selective intervention, it will also encourage rent seeking. Above all, the risk of GATT disputes and of countervailing duties in importing countries has made direct export promotion increasingly unattractive.

The Lessons of Trade Liberalization

Trade policy reform is complicated. It is closely linked to liberalization in capital, labor, and domestic product markets and to macroeconomic policy. It is partly a political process, in which credibility and expectations play an important role. Feasible policy choices may differ from country to country, and reform may be vulnerable to changes in the international environment. Because of this complexity, there is no single optimal path to reform. But there are, nonetheless, lessons to be drawn from previous attempts.

- Trade liberalization must involve large shifts of resources, but it has not always raised unemployment by as much as is commonly supposed.
- Strong and decisive reforms have carried greater credibility and have been better sustained than more timid reforms.
- Replacing quantitative restrictions with tariffs is a useful first stage of trade liberalization.
- Providing a realistic real exchange rate is vital to the successful introduction of trade reform. Keeping it stable is essential if the reform is to be sustained. All this requires a macroeconomic policy that manages inflation and the nominal exchange rate so as to keep domestic costs in line with world prices.
- The scope for successful trade liberalization depends on complementary reforms in the domestic economy—especially in financial and labor markets.

Comment IV.A.2. Stabilization-cum-Liberalization Programs

Stabilization-cum-liberalization programs involve the liberalization of external trade, decontrol of domestic financial markets, and liberalization of capital flows from abroad. The timing and sequencing of these liberalization measures have differed among countries. But more attention to the sequencing of policies is essential for the success of the program. As Bruno observes,

> Economic theory tells us that a fully liberalized economy is most probably Pareto superior to a heavily controlled economy. It can also tell us something about the advantages of certain departures from full liberalization in some markets. However, theory tells us virtually nothing about optimal transition paths from a distorted system to one that is more liberalized. Unfortunately, this is the most important problem for any successful reform. The study of actual cases may, however, eventually lead to theoretical insights on optimal transition paths or the kind of economic policies that should accompany the process of transition.
>
> Should all markets be liberalized at the same time? If they cannot, can one say anything about the sequencing of market liberalization? . . . A major distinction should be drawn between the real and the financial sides of opening up. No general case can be made against the opening up of the current account. The most successful development histories are those in which a country very early on switched from an import-substitution-led towards an export-led development strategy. There are problems of adjustment speed and of what kind of investment and/or trade policy should be adopted in the transition, but there is little doubt, from a pure efficiency point of view, as to the wisdom of opening up the real side of the economy, as quickly as is consistent with the other major social objectives. Moreover, there seems to be substantial evidence attesting to productivity gains coming from the trade liberalization process.
>
> The liberalization of financial markets has turned out to be much more problematic. There are obvious efficiency gains to be obtained when a country moves from a repressed capital market, with negative real interest rates, to one which is less regulated. In practice, however, various factors caused real interest rates to rise to excessively high levels. This, coupled with the opening up to foreign capital inflows, proved disastrous. The issue of credibility is clearly at the heart of the success or failure of any reform. Even the most drastic reforms take time to be implemented and to work themselves out. The behavior of economic agents is dictated by their perception of the future, which incorporates the government's present and expected behavior as a key input. Thus, the maintenance of high government deficits will be inconsistent with the announced slowing down of the rate of devaluation as an anti-inflationary device (the case of Argentina). Not only will prices be slow in coming down, if at all, thus bringing about a real appreciation, with consequences to the current account, but the expected large devaluation will force capital flight today. Like the building up of real assets, credibility formation is an asymmetric process. Once eroded, credibility is very hard to restore.[1]

Several studies attempt to distill the lessons from the reform undertaken in various countries. From the experiences of Argentina, Chile, and Uruguay, some observers conclude that for countries with annual inflation rates of 25 percent or more, anti-inflation stabilization programs should precede liberalization. This is because inflation reduces substantially the information content of relative prices, and the main aim of liberalization is to adjust relative prices in accordance with economic costs. Stabilization is also necessary because successful liberalization depends on credibility and on a stable and competitive real exchange rate. These objectives cannot be fulfilled when inflation is rapid. See Anne O. Krueger, *Foreign Trade Regimes and Economic Development: Liberalization Attempts and Consequences* (1978); R. Dornbusch, "Stabilization Policies in Developing Countries: What Have We Learned?" *World Development* (September 1982); S. Fischer, "Issues in Medium-term Macroeconomic Adjustment," *World Bank Research Observer* (July 1986); Michael Mussa, "Macroeconomic Policy and Trade Liberalization: Some Guidelines," *World Bank Research Observer* (January 1987); Vittorio Corbo and Jaime de Melo, "Lessons from the Southern Cone Policy Reforms," *World Bank Research Observer* (July 1987); and Dani Rodrik, "The Limits of Trade Policy Reform in Developing Countries," *Journal of Economic Perspectives* (Winter 1992).

A major eight-volume research project has reviewed the experience of 18 countries with respect to policy prescriptions for successful implementation of liberalization policies: Michael

---

[1]Michael Bruno, "The Reforms and Macroeconomic Adjustments," *World Development* (August 1985): 867–69.

Michaely et al., *Liberalizing Foreign Trade,* vol. 7 (1990). It is concluded that the successful programs of trade reform had certain elements in common: momentum, reduced quantitative restrictions, competitive real exchange rates, prudent macroeconomic policies, proper sequencing of reform (trade liberalization should precede capital-market liberalization), and political stability.

Selection IV.A.7. Getting Interventions Right: How South Korea and Taiwan Grew Rich*

The Coordination Failure Interpretation

The Argument

First, by 1960 Taiwan and South Korea shared a set of advantageous initial conditions relating to social infrastructure. In particular, both economics had a skilled labour force, relative to their physical capital stock and income levels. These initial conditions made both countries ready for economic take-off, in the sense that the latent return to capital accumulation was high.

Second, for a number of reasons, the economic take-off could not take place under decentralized market conditions. Chief among these reasons are the imperfect tradability of key inputs (and technologies) associated with modern-sector production, and some increasing returns to scale in these activities. These conditions created a situation of coordination failure. In other words, while the rate of return to coordinated investments was extremely high, the rate of return to individual investments remained low.

Third, governments in both countries undertook a set of measures starting in the late 1950s that not only removed some policy-induced distortions, but also served to coordinate and subsidize private investment. These measures included: credit subsidies, tax incentives, administrative guidance and public investment.

Fourth, this active government role helped remove the coordination failure that had blocked industrial growth. As private entrepreneurs responded to these measures, the resulting investments turned out to be profitable not only in financial terms, but in social terms as well.

Fifth, government intervention could be implemented in an effective manner (without leading to rent-seeking behaviour) because initial conditions, once again, had endowed the government in each country with an extraordinary degree of insulation from pressure groups, and with leadership capability over them. Among these initial conditions, a relatively equal distribution of income and wealth was critical.

Sixth, as investment rose as a share of GDP, so did imports of capital goods, as neither country

had a comparative advantage in such goods. Thanks to appropriate macroeconomic and exchange rate policies, export supply was adequate to meet the increase in import demand, and rose alongside imports.

Seventh, as a consequence, the increase in exports played a critical role in paying for the imports of capital goods. But it is more appropriate to view this increase in exports as a consequence of the increase in investment demand, rather than the other way around.

A Framework of Analysis

There are two critical claims in this story: (1) both countries were ready for economic take-off by the early to mid-1960s, but economic growth was blocked by a coordination failure; (2) governments in both countries were able to undertake the measures needed to override this coordination failure. The evidence on the presence of a coordination failure is necessarily circumstantial. I think the case is reasonably compelling in view of the likelihood that all of the prerequisites for the existence of a coordination failure were met in the two countries. . . . I rely on an intuitive exposition of the economic logic.

Imagine a small open economy, initially specializing in the production of traditional goods. Alongside there exists a relatively capital-intensive modern sector, which yields higher factor returns when it is viable. The modern sector relies on specialized inputs (e.g. particular labour skills, technologies, intermediate inputs or capital goods). These inputs share the following features: (1) they require well-educated workers but at low cost; (2) they exhibit scale economies; and (3) they cannot be perfectly traded in international markets. The viability of the modern sector requires the local presence of these inputs, which in turn depends (in part) on the existence of a sufficiently well-educated workforce.

Such an economy is ready for take-off if there is enough skilled labour that the modern sector would be viable if a large enough share of the economy's resources were devoted to producing the specialized inputs. Yet there is no certainty that labour and capital move from the traditional sector to the modern sector, leading to specialization in the latter and to higher incomes. The reason is that,

*From Dani Rodrik, "Getting Interventions Right: How South Korea and Taiwan Grew Rich," *Economic Policy* 20 (April 1995): 78–84, 88–91. Reprinted by permission.

because of scale economies, only a large-scale movement of resources is guaranteed to be profitable. From the perspective of an individual investor, it will not pay to invest in the modern sector unless others are doing so as well. The profitability of the modern sector depends on the simultaneous presence of the specialized inputs; but the profitability of producing these inputs in turn depends on the presence of demand from a pre-existing modern sector. It is this interdependence of production and investment decisions that creates the coordination problem.

Coordination failure is least likely to happen when the economy is well endowed with both skilled labour and physical capital, for then production in the modern sector is profitable even when entrepreneurs act in an uncoordinated manner. For economies at the other end of the spectrum—lacking both skilled labour and capital—the coordination issue is moot because the modern sector is not viable in the first place. It is in the intermediate economies most reminiscent of Korea and Taiwan in the early 1960s—well endowed with skilled labour but poor in physical capital—that the coordination problem is most severe.

Markets are known to handle resource allocation poorly in the presence of scale economies and non-tradability: market prices reflect the profitability of different activities only as they are currently undertaken; they do not provide any signals about the profitability of activities that would require a large-scale reallocation of resources within the economy (which, after all, is what economic development is all about). These are, of course, old ideas that go back to Scitovsky's (1954) analysis of pecuniary externalities and Rosenstein-Rodan's (1943) advocacy of big-push policies. More recently, the arguments have been formalized in papers by Faini (1984), Pack and Westphal (1986), Murphy et al. (1989), Krugman (1991), Matsuyama (1991), Ciccone and Matsuyama (1993), Rodríguez-Clare (1993) and Rodrik (1993).

One problem with this literature has been that coordination failure is often presented as a generic problem affecting all kinds of economies. The present framework is more specific about the prerequisites. It highlights the following three prerequisites for a coordination failure to become a serious issue: (1) some degree of non-tradability in the technologies and/or goods associated with the modern sector; (2) economies of scale; (3) a reasonably skilled labour force (but a low endowment of physical capital). The last one clearly applies to the case of Korea and Taiwan. Scale economies are also plausible in many of the modern-sector activities. Hence, non-tradability is the feature that requires additional discussion.

Upon a moment's reflection, it should be clear that some degree of non-tradability is necessarily associated with the types of goods produced by rich countries. Otherwise poor countries would not remain poor for long: arbitrage through trade would eliminate the disparities. In practice, the non-tradability of modern-sector inputs is observed in a number of different ways. Labour services are for the most part effectively non-traded, so that skilled and specialized workmanship must be locally available. The fixed costs often required to develop these skills lead to scale economies. Intermediate and capital goods are in principle tradable, but they sometimes require either geographic proximity to the final user (as when they are manufactured to suppliers' specifications) or the use of complementary local inputs before they can be put to use (as when skilled workers are needed to operate sophisticated imported machinery). Often, the requisite technologies also have a non-tradable element, in so far as much of the technological capability is tacit and not explicitly codified in designs and blueprints. As Pack and Westphal (1986) put it:

The tacitness of technology leads to problems in its communication over long distances and across social differences, problems which can be overcome—if at all—only at some cost . . . Moreover, knowledge that exists (somewhere in the world) does not exist everywhere simultaneously because there are costs in advertising its mere existence or in discovering its existence through search. Only knowledge that is "close by" is known to exist . . . Another significant channel for inter-industry externalities is the exchange of technological elements in transactions involving intermediate products and capital goods. Indeed many such exchanges leading to better utilization of local resources and to improvements in the design of capital goods have been observed. A salient aspect of these exchanges is the dependence of their outcome on extensive interaction between suppliers and users in iteratively changing both process and product characteristics.

Some examples drawn from the East Asian experience may help bring these points to life.

Case Studies: Hyundai and Lucky-Goldstar

The importance of specialized labour skills and the complementarities they generate across manufacturing activities is illustrated by the experience of Hyundai, one of Korea's huge conglomerates (*chaebol*). Hyundai first entered manufacturing in 1964 by building a cement plant. According to Amsden (1989):

Hyundai used its cement plant as a laboratory to train its managers with background in construction, before assigning them to other manufacturing affiliates. Trainees gained experience in inventory management, quality and process control, capacity planning, and so on, thus spreading basic production skills throughout the Hyundai organization. After Hyundai Cement, the next manufacturing affiliate in the group was founded in 1967 and named Hyundai Motors. Twenty years later it became the first independent automaker from a late-industrializing country to export globally. The first president of Hyundai Motors was a former president of Hyundai Cement.

Korean government policies were highly partial to conglomerates like Hyundai. By giving them access to subsidized capital, the government allowed them to internalize many of the labour market spillovers in the fashion described in the quote.

Hyundai's experience with shipbuilding provides a concrete instance of the imperfect tradability of technology (and its interaction with scale economies). The company started out by importing its basic design from a Scottish firm, but soon found that this was not working out. The Scottish design relied on building the ship in two halves because the original manufacturer had enough capacity to build only half a ship at a time. When Hyundai followed the same course, it found out that the two halves did not quite fit. Subsequent designs imported from European consulting firms also had problems, in that the firms would not guarantee the rated capacity, leading to costly delays. Engines were available from Japanese suppliers, but apparently only at a price higher than that obtained by Japanese shipyards. Moreover, ship buyers would often require design modifications, which Hyundai would be unable to undertake in the absence of an in-house design capability. Only with large enough capacity would it pay for Hyundai to integrate backwards (into design and engine building). In a highly volatile business, scale in turn depended on having access to a steady and reliable customer (a merchant marine). The Korean government provided Hyundai with substantial assistance, as well as an implicit guarantee of markets. Hyundai eventually integrated both backwards and forwards. The government's guarantee came in handy in 1975 when a shipping slump led to the cancellation of foreign orders. President Park responded by forcing Korean refineries to ship oil in Korean-owned tankers, creating a captive demand for Hyundai (Jones and Sakong, 1980).

The chairman of the Lucky-Goldstar group explains the success of his company in this way:

My father and I started a cosmetic cream factory in the late 1940s. At the time, no company could supply us

with plastic caps of adequate quality for cream jars, so we had to start a plastic business. Plastic caps alone were not sufficient to run the plastic-moulding plant, so we added combs, toothbrushes, and soap boxes. The plastics business also led us to manufacture electrical and electronic products and telecommunication equipment. The plastics business also took us into oil refining which needed a tanker-shipping company. The oil-refining company alone was paying an insurance premium amounting to more than half the total revenue of the then largest insurance company in Korea. Thus, an insurance company was started. This natural step-by-step evolution through related businesses resulted in the Lucky-Goldstar group as we see it today. (cited in Amsden, 1989)

The quotation clearly illustrates the importance of local inputs and customers as well as of scale economies in fuelling the growth of *chaebol*. While the *chaebol* could thus internalize some of the coordination issues, they were greatly assisted in doing so by government policies which will be discussed in the next section.

In both Korea and Taiwan, the rate of return to capital and profitability in key manufacturing activities rose significantly from the late 1950s on. In Korea, Jones and Sakong (1980) report (based on Hong, 1977) steadily rising real rates of return to capital in manufacturing: the range is 9–18% in mid- to late-1950s, 9–26% in 1962–6, 16–38% in 1967–72, and 17–40% after 1972. The rate of profit in manufacturing steadily rose from 9% in 1951–3 to 16% in 1954–6, to 28% in 1957–62, and to 35% in 1963–70 (Hong, 1993, p. 347). Apparently, investment became more profitable as the investment rate rose.[1] In Taiwan, profitability rates rose in most of the private manufacturing industries after the late 1950s, with the notable exception of textiles and wood products, two major exporting industries (Lin, 1973). Interestingly, the greatest increase in profitability in the post-1963 period (outside food, beverages and tobacco) was experienced by public-sector manufacturing. As will be discussed in the next section, it was public enterprises that supplied many of the key intermediate inputs in Taiwan. This is how Lin (1973) explains the increase in their profits:

The domestic consumption of the output of these non-food industries (which produce petroleum products, chemical fertilizers, industrial chemicals, etc.) increased tremendously during the 1960s, due to increased demand

---

[1]Little (1994) calculates that the annualized return to investment in Korea was 31.1% during the period 1963–73. However, his calculations also show a reduction in the rate of return subsequently, to 18.3% during 1974–9. He attributes the decline to the HCI drive.

from chemical-using industries (such as those making polyvinylchloride, monosodium glutamate, and paper and pulp for both the export and domestic market), as well as from the agricultural sector and the transportation industry.

In other words, intermediate industries became profitable thanks to expanding linkages downstream.

We note finally that in both Korea and Taiwan the way policy-makers viewed the economy and their role in it has parallels with the logic of the co-ordination failure. As the discussion in the following section will make clear, the Korean government has always perceived itself as a mediating agent and a facilitator for bringing about industrial change, through arm-twisting, subsidies or public enterprises as the circumstances may demand. In the words of Pack and Westphal (1986):

> In Taiwan, the basic philosophy underlying [the government strategy] is that an economy will undergo certain stages of development, and at each stage there are certain key industries (such as integrated steel mill, large shipyard, and petrochemical plants) which through various linkages will bring about development of the entire economy. This strategy also assumes that government officials know what those key industries are and what policy measures should be adopted to develop these industries. (Hou, 1988, cited in Hong, 1993)

Indeed, Taiwan's Fourth Plan (1965–8) stated:

> For further development, stress must be laid on basic heavy industries (such as chemical wood pulp, petrochemical intermediates, and large-scale integrated steel production) instead of end product manufacturing or processing. Industrial development in the long run must be centred on export products that have high income elasticity and low transportation cost. And around these products there should be development of both forward and backward industries, so that both specialization and complementarity may be achieved in the interest of Taiwan's economy. (quoted in Wade, 1990)

Hence, what these governments thought they were doing has much in common with the ideas discussed here.

Government Policies to Subsidize and Coordinate Private Investment

Under the conditions discussed in the previous section, there exists a large role for government intervention. Such intervention can take many different forms. Most directly, policy-makers can coordinate private-sector production and investment decisions through their control over credit allocation, the tax regime and trade policy, as well as through "administrative guidance." Government policies to subsidize investment in the modern sectors of the economy have a large payoff because they get the private sector to internalize the coordination externalities. The same outcome can also be obtained through investments by public enterprises themselves. The Korean and Taiwanese governments used a combination of these interventions, thereby raising the private return to capital in the modern sectors to the level of the social return. . . .

Direct Co-ordination of Investment Decisions

In addition to providing subsidies, the Korean and Taiwanese governments played a much more direct, hands-on role by organizing private entrepreneurs into investments that they may not otherwise have made. In Taiwan, it was the government that took the initial steps in establishing such industries as plastics, textiles, fibres, steel and electronics. In Korea, in the words of Amsden (1989), "[t]he initiative to enter new manufacturing branches has come primarily from the public sphere. Ignoring the 1950s . . . every major shift in industrial diversification in the decades of the 1960s and 1970s was instigated by the state."

Wade (1990) describes how Taiwan's first plastics plant for PVC was built under government supervision, and handed over to a private entrepreneur upon completion in 1957. In 1966, three more private firms began producing PVC. All four relied on an imported intermediate. Meanwhile, the state-owned Chinese Petroleum Corporation (CPC) produced ethylene, from which an intermediate suitable for processing into PVC could be derived at a cheaper price than the imported intermediate. "So the government forced the four private producers of PVC to merge in a joint venture with the Chinese Petroleum Corporation and another state-owned chemical company, in order to adopt a more efficient ethylene-using production method" (Wade, 1990). (While Wade is not explicit on this, there must have been some scale economies or complementarities that prevented CPC from unilaterally moving into the production of the ethylene-based intermediate, without waiting for a commitment from the downstream producers.) The story illustrates nicely the coordinating role of the government.

A similar account is given regarding fibres:

> The government . . . decided to oversee the creation of a rayon-making plant as part of a plan to diversify the textile industry away from cotton fibre. With much help from US advisors it brought together an American synthetic fibre company with several local textiles from both

public and private firms, and oversaw negotiations on the terms of the joint venture . . . The resulting corporation . . . was the largest "private" firm on the island at the time [1957] . . . In 1962, this same state-sponsored rayon company, together with a state financing agency, created another company to make nylon. It started production in 1964. (Wade, 1990)

Private firms soon followed after this state-led entry into synthetic fibres.

Finally, the role of the Taiwanese state was crucial in the early stages of the electronics industry. In 1974 the publicly owned Electronic Research and Service Organization (ERSO) was formed to bring in foreign technology and disseminate it to local firms. ERSO built the country's first model shop for wafer fabrication and entered a technology transfer agreement with RCA. It trained engineers, who later moved to private firms. The strategy led to many private-sector offshoots that commercialized the technology developed by ERSO (Wade, 1990).

It is interesting to note that the Taiwanese authorities' approach to selecting industries to nurture in this fashion was based on what Wade calls "engineering concepts," such as take-off, linkages, gaps, substitutions and incremental extensions—concepts which have little place in conventional welfare economics. Wade mentions that the justification for building a stainless steel plant in the early 1980s was to "fill a gap in Taiwan's infrastructure." Similarly, "[d]evelopments in electronics are being promoted with the aid of an input-output map which highlights gaps in the production structure within Taiwan." This concern with linkages may sit awkwardly with neoclassical development theory, but it does resonate with our emphasis on coordination failures.

In Korea, as we have seen, the presence of large conglomerates helped internalize some of the industrial complementarities that Taiwanese policymakers had to nurture through more direct interventions. But the Korean government was not hesitant to intervene in order to solve what it perceived to be larger-scale coordination problems:

The state masterminded the early import-substitution projects in cement, fertilizers, oil refining, and synthetic fibres, the last greatly improving the profitability of the overextended textiles industry. The government also kept alive some unprofitable factories inherited from the colonial period, factories that eventually provided key personnel to the modern general machinery and shipbuilding industries, which the state also promoted. The transformation from light to heavy industry came at the state's behest, in the form of an integrated iron and steel mill . . . [The government] was responsible for the Big Push into heavy machinery and chemicals in the late 1970s. (Amsden, 1989)

The case of shipbuilding has already been discussed in some detail. As in Taiwan, the government proceeded on the understanding that some industries and products were more "strategic" than others because they were the source of linkages with the rest of the economy. A recent account about how Daewoo got into the shipbuilding business provides yet another example: "Mr Kim [the founder of Daewoo] found himself in shipbuilding in 1978, when the government twisted his arm to take over a near-bankrupt project to build a giant shipyard at Okpo, on Koje island near the southern port of Pusan. "I did not have a chance to say no," says Mr Kim. Indeed, the government simply announced the move when he was out of the country" (*The Economist,* 26 November 1994, p. 81). The Okpo shipyard is now "at the heart of . . . [Korea's] achievement" in shipbuilding.

Use of Public Investment and Public Enterprise

Public enterprises played a very important role in enhancing the profitability of private investment in both countries (perhaps more so in Taiwan than in Korea). They did so by ensuring that key inputs were available locally for private producers downstream. In Taiwan, as we have seen, it was common for the state to establish new upstream industries and then either hand the factories over to selected private entrepreneurs (as happened in the case of glass, plastics, steel and cement) or run them as public enterprises. In Korea, the government established many new public enterprises in the 1960s and 1970s, particularly in basic industries characterized by a high degree of linkages and scale economies. In both countries, public enterprises were the recipient of favourable credit terms, as well as direct allocations from the government budget.

Not only did public enterprises account for a large share of manufacturing output and investment in each country, their importance actually increased during the critical take-off years of the 1960s. This can be seen clearly in Table 1, where data on three comparator countries are also listed. Public enterprises actually accounted for a larger share of GDP in Taiwan than in such "socialist" developing countries as India and Tanzania.

Jones and Sakong (1980) have analysed in detail the expansion of the public enterprise sector in Korea. They find that the Korean government had a coherent set of preferences with respect to where

Table 1. The Importance of Public Enterprise in GDP and Investment (%)

		Public enterprise share of	
	Year	GDP	Capital formation
South Korea	1963–4	6.7	31.2
	1971–2	9.1	21.7
Taiwan	1954–7	11.7	34.3
	1958–61	13.5	38.1
	1962–5	14.1	27.7
	1966–9	13.6	28.0
	1970–3	13.3	30.5
	1974–7	13.6	35.0
India	1966–9	6.5	29.6
Tanzania	1970–3	12.7	48.2
Argentina	1978–80	4.6	19.6

Sources: Wade (1990, Table 6.2), from original data in Short (1983), except for public enterprise share in GDP for Korea, which is from Jones and Sakong (1980, Table 24).

public enterprises should be set up. They summarize their results thus: "the industries chosen for the public-enterprise sector [were] characterized by high forward linkages, high capital intensity, large size, output-market concentration, and production of non-tradables or import substitutes rather than exports." These are exactly the characteristics associated with a high potential for coordination failure.

The case of POSCO, Korea's state-owned integrated steel mill, is instructive (if not entirely representative). In the early 1970s, the Korean government was turned down by the World Bank when it applied for a loan to construct a steel plant. The World Bank's argument was that Korea did not have a comparative advantage in steel. The government was undeterred and went ahead nonetheless. The government provided POSCO with capital assistance as well as infrastructure subsidies (for the construction of water supply facilities, port facilities, an electricity generating station, roads and a railway line). In addition, the government supported downstream industries to ensure demand for POSCO's production. POSCO eventually became, by the World Bank's reckoning, "arguably the world's most efficient producer of steel" (cited in Wade, 1990), supplying Korean minimills with steel at below world prices. Moreover, the presence of POSCO stimulated in turn a wide range of upstream industries, ranging from capital goods to spare parts. Between 1977 and 1984, the local content of POSCO's output rose from 44 to 75%.

References

Amsden, A. H. (1989). *Asia's Next Giant: South Korea and Late Industrialization,* Oxford University Press, New York.

Ciccone, A. and K. Matsuyama (1993). "Start-up Costs and Pecuniary Externalities as Barriers to Economic Development," NBER Working Paper No. 4363.

Faini, R. (1984). "Increasing Returns, Non-Traded Inputs, and Regional Development," *Economic Journal.*

Hong, W. (1977). "Trade, Distortions and Employment in Korea," Korea Development Institute, Seoul.

——— (1993). "Trade and Development: The Experience of Korea and Taiwan," in G. Hasson (ed.), *International Trade and Development,* Routledge, London.

Hou, C.-M. (1988). "Strategy for Economic Development in Taiwan and Implications for Developing Economies," paper presented at the Conference on Economic Development Experiences of Taiwan, Taipei, 8–10 June.

Jones, Leroy and Il Sakong (1980). *Government, Business, and Entrepreneurship in Economic Development: The Korean Case,* Harvard University Press, Cambridge, MA.

Krugman, P. (1991). "History versus Expectations," *Quarterly Journal of Economics.*

Lin, C.-Y. (1973). *Industrialization in Taiwan, 1946–72: Trade and Import-Substitution Policies for Developing Countries,* Praeger, New York.

Little, I. M. D. (1994). "Trade and Industrialization Revisited," unpublished paper, Nuffield College, Oxford.

Matsuyama, K. (1991). "Increasing Returns, Industrialization and Indeterminacy of Equilibrium," *Quarterly Journal of Economics.*

Murphy, K., A. Shleifer and R. Vishny (1989). "Industrialization and the Big Push," *Journal of Political Economy.*

Pack, H. and L. E. Westphal (1986). "Industrial Strategy and Technological Change: Theory versus Reality," *Journal of Development Economics.*

Rodríguez-Clare, A. (1993). "The Division of Labor and Economic Development," unpublished manuscript, Stanford University, CA.

Rodrik, D. (1993). "Coordination Failures and Government Policy in Intermediate Economies: A Model with Applications to East Asia and Eastern Europe,"

unpublished manuscript, Columbia University, New York.

Rosenstein-Rodan, P. (1943). "Problems of Industrialization of Eastern and South-Eastern Europe," *Economic Journal.*

Scitovsky, T. (1954). "Two Concepts of External Economies," *Journal of Political Economy.*

Short, R. (1983). "The Role of Public Enterprises: An International Statistical Comparison," International Monetary Fund, Washington, DC.

Wade, R. (1990). *Governing the Market: Economic Theory and the Role of Government in East Asian Industrialization,* Princeton University Press, Princeton, NJ.

Note IV.A.2. Tradeability of Intermediate Goods, Linkages, and Bottlenecks

In the preceding selection Rodrik claims that the Taiwanese government intentionally and successfully fostered forward and backward "linkages" among domestic producers of intermediate and final goods. In contrast, Riedel (1976, p. 320) claims that Taiwan is a "prime example" of a country "characterized by a rather 'footloose,' import-dependent industrial structure" and states "it might be argued that Taiwan has been so successful precisely because its industrial structure lacks backward linkages." These differing perceptions of Taiwanese industry and trade reflect a more general difference of opinion regarding the tradeability of intermediate goods and the desirability of domestic linkages versus reliance on imports (or exports, if intermediate goods are produced domestically but then sold to foreign downstream users).

When intermediate goods are used to produce a final product, they must fit together, literally and figuratively. This may require that downstream and upstream producers be in regular consultation in order to make necessary modifications. As Rodrik points out, geographic proximity reduces the cost of such consultation. The relationships between downstream assemblers and upstream suppliers have been especially well studied for the automobile industry. Transnational auto companies from Europe, Japan, or the United States typically rely on their home suppliers when they begin production in LDCs (Dobson and Yue 1997), but often later try to establish supplier networks within the host country (see, e.g., Doner 1997, pp. 220–21), consistent with the need for geographic proximity.

The tolerance for "poor fit" among components may be much greater for labor-intensive industries such as apparel and toys than for capital-intensive industries such as automobiles, and components for the former set of industries may be more standardized. In these industries it may be considerably less difficult for a downstream producer to find the right inputs abroad or for an upstream producer to find a foreign assembler for which his part will work. (We discussed the relative ease of trading standardized versus differentiated products in Note II.1.) It may therefore be much more feasible to have an "unlinked," import-dependent structure for consumer nondurables than for consumer durables and machinery. This could explain why Riedel and Rodrik perceived Taiwan so differently. Riedel was writing in the mid-1970s when Taiwan could still be described as a "labor-abundant LDC" and its manufacturing production was more concentrated in light industry than it was two decades later when Rodrik was writing.

This discussion suggests that the case for a policy of promoting linkages is much weaker when appropriate imported inputs are easily available. Balassa (1980, p. 14) notes that the four Latin American countries engaged in second-stage import substitution that he studied (Argentina, Brazil, Colombia, Mexico) "did not, however, provide exporters with a free choice between domestic and imported inputs. Rather, in order to safeguard existing industries, exporters were required to use domestic inputs produced under protection." Forcing downstream firms to rely on domestic upstream production is risky, because if upstream production develops only slowly (due perhaps to difficulty in mastering the requisite technology), it becomes a bottleneck for expansion of all the downstream producers. One can also argue that diversification for its own sake reduces both static and dynamic economies of scale (the latter generated, for example, by learning-by-doing) achievable by any given industry. Weinhold and Rauch (1999) find that productivity growth in the manufacturing sector in LDCs is higher when production is more specialized.

References

Balassa, Bela. 1980. *The Process of Industrial Development and Alternative Development Strategies.* Princeton University International Finance Section, Essays in International Finance No. 141 (December).

Dobson, Wendy, and Chia Siow, Yue, eds. 1997. *Multinationals and East Asian Integration.* Singapore: IDRC Books and ISEAS.

Doner, Richard F. 1997. "Japan in East Asia: Institutions and Regional Leadership, " in Peter J. Katzenstein and Takashi Shiraishi, eds., *Network Power: Japan and Asia.* Ithaca, N.Y.: Cornell University Press), pp. 197–233.

Riedel, James. 1976. "A Balanced Growth Version of the Linkage Hypothesis: Comment." *Quarterly Journal of Economics* 90 (May): 319–22.

Weinhold, Diana, and James E. Rauch. 1999. "Openness, Specialization, and Productivity Growth in Less Developed Countries." *Canadian Journal of Economics,* 32 (August).

IV.B. FOREIGN CONTACT AND TECHNOLOGY TRANSFER

Note IV.B.1. Learning in International Production Networks

Economists have typically modeled technology transfer as an arm's-length phenomenon. Firms are not *taught* the new technology. Rather they engage in purposive imitative activity on their own (e.g., Grossman and Helpman 1991), employ machinery and equipment that embodies foreign knowledge (e.g., Coe et al. 1997), license the new technology, and so on. However, as Rodrik points out in his selection in the preceding section, it is difficult to learn new technology from a distance. There is a growing body of evidence that for LDC firms in particular a major and perhaps predominant source of technology transfer (and transfer of managerial know-how) is instruction by developed country buyers: producers seeking cheaper suppliers of inputs and distributors seeking cheaper suppliers of final goods. Pack and Page (1994, pp. 220–21) state:

> The motivation of the purchasers is to obtain still lower-cost, better quality products from major suppliers whose products account for a significant percentage of profits. To achieve this they are willing to transmit tacit and occasionally proprietary knowledge from their other OECD suppliers. Such transfers of knowledge are more likely to characterize simpler production sectors such as clothing and footwear or more generally those older technologies that are not hedged by restrictions adopted to increase appropriability, such as patents and trade secrets.

One example of such evidence is a study by Egan and Mody (1992), who surveyed U.S. buyers operating in LDCs, including "manufacturers, retailers, importers, buyers' agents, and joint venture partners" (p. 322). They found (p. 328):

> Buyers also render long-term benefits to suppliers in the form of information on production technology. This occurs principally through various forms of in-plant training. The buyer may send international experts to train local workers and supervisors. . . . Buyers may also arrange short-term worker training in a developed country plant.

Rhee, Ross-Larson, and Pursell (1984) surveyed Korean exporters of manufactures. Their findings (p. 61) were similar to those of Egan and Mody:

> The relations between Korean firms and the foreign buyers went far beyond the negotiation and fulfillment of contracts. Almost half the firms said they had directly benefited from the technical information foreign buyers provided: through visits to their plants by engineers or other technical staff of the foreign buyers, through visits by their engineering staff to the foreign buyers . . .

The Rhee, Ross-Larson, and Pursell survey was conducted in 1975. More recently Korea and the other advanced East Asian countries have played the role for LDCs that foreign buyers used to play for them. The role of Korea in developing garment exports from Bangladesh is an especially interesting case that is studied in Rhee and Belot (1990). This case is part of the broader phenomenon of "triangle manufacturing" (Gereffi 1999) in East Asia: countries such as Korea and Taiwan continue to accept and fulfill the orders of developed country buyers for labor-intensive goods, but have "outsourced" the actual production to countries with lower wages.

This process of learning foreign technology can be thought of as taking place within international production networks or "global commodity chains" (Gereffi 1994, 1999). This theoretical framework predicts that once LDC firms are incorporated into the "bottoms" of the chains, their learning will continue by movement up the chains. There are two types of chains: "producer-driven" and "buyer-driven" (Gereffi 1994). In the former, large manufacturers play the central roles in coordinating the production networks. Producer-driven chains are typical in capital- and technology-intensive industries such as automobiles, aircraft, computers, semiconductors, and heavy machinery. In the latter, large retailers, branded marketers, and branded manufacturers play the coordinating roles. Buyer-driven commodity chains are typical in labor-intensive, consumer goods industries such as garments, footwear, toys, housewares, and consumer electronics. Profitability is highest at the tops of the chains where barriers to entry are greatest: scale and technology in producer-driven chains, design and marketing expertise in buyer-driven chains.

In buyer-driven commodity chains, one mode through which learning is predicted to continue is *organizational succession:* from assembler to original equipment manufacturer (OEM) to original brand-name manufacturer (OBM), which is from more subordinate, competitive, and low-profit positions to more controlling, oligopolistic, high-profit positions. In the apparel industry, Gereffi (1999) finds that LDC firms that have parts provided to them for assembly learn how to find on their own the parts needed to make the product according to the design specified by the buyer (and may then subcontract the assembly); firms that have reached this level learn how to design and sell their own merchandise, becoming branded manufacturers (and may then subcontract the production, becoming branded marketers). Additional study is needed to determine whether this pattern of learning is common in other consumer goods industries, and what kind of learning modes might be present in producer-driven commodity chains. At the same time, work is needed to reconcile the kind of findings discussed in this Note with econometric analyses (surveyed in Rodrik 1999, chap. 2) that conclude that more productive firms export, but exporting does not make firms more productive.

References

Coe, David T., Elhanan Helpman, and Alexander W. Hoffmaister. 1997. "North-South R&D Spillovers." *Economic Journal* 107(440): 134–49.

Egan, Mary Lou, and Ashoka Mody. 1992. "Buyer-Seller Links in Export Development." *World Development* 20(3): 321–34.

Gereffi, Gary. 1994. "The Organization of Buyer-Driven Global Commodity Chains: How U.S. Retailers Shape Overseas Production Networks." In Gary Gereffi and Miguel Korzeniewicz, eds., *Commodity Chains and Global Capitalism* (Westport, Conn. Praeger), pp. 95–122.

Gereffi, Gary. 1999. "International Trade and Industrial Upgrading in the Apparel Commodity Chain." *Journal of International Economics* 48 (June): 37–70.

Grossman, Gene, and Elhanan Helpman. 1991. "Endogenous Product Cycles." *Economic Journal* 101(408): 1214–29.

Pack, Howard, and John M. Page Jr. 1994. "Accumulation, Exports, and Growth in the High-performing Asian Economies." *Carnegie-Rochester Conf. Ser. Pub. Pol.* (June) 40: 199–257.

Rhee, Yung Whee, Bruce Ross-Larson, and Garry Pursell. 1984. *Korea's Competitive Edge: Managing the Entry into World Markets.* Baltimore: Johns Hopkins University Press.

Rhee, Yung Whee, and Therese Belot. 1990. "Export Catalysts in Low-Income Countries: A Review of Eleven Success Stories." World Bank Discussion Paper 72, Washington, D.C.

Rodrik, Dani. 1999. *Making Openness Work: The New Global Economy and the Developing Countries.* Washington, D.C.: Overseas Development Council.

Selection IV.B.1. Technology Gaps Between Industrial and Developing Countries: Are There Dividends for Latecomers?*

Firms have several alternatives for obtaining new technology that, if mastered, yield a higher level of TFP [total factor productivity] for any given capital-labor ratio. These alternatives include: (a) the purchase of new equipment; (b) direct foreign investment; (c) the purchase of technology licenses for domestic production of new products or the use of new processes; (d) the use of nonproprietary technology, including that obtained from purchasers of exports; (e) acquisition of knowledge from returning nationals who have been educated or have worked in industrial countries and from nationals who remain in industrial countries; and (f) domestic research and development and efforts in reverse engineering.

All these possibilities, except for the research and development efforts, represent an attempt to move toward international best practice by transferring technologies available abroad. The research and development alternative may have an element of aiding the identification, modification, and absorption of foreign technology rather than generating a completely indigenous technology.

The Experience of Two Successful Asian Economies

This section describes some of the means by which two of the fastest-growing newly industrializing economies—Korea and Taiwan (China)—were able to shift toward an international production function.[1]

Korea and Taiwan (China)

Until the mid- to late 1970s neither Korea nor Taiwan (China) employed explicit technology policies. The main exceptions were the restrictions placed on direct foreign investment and a fairly perfunctory review of technology licensing agreements in Korea. The ability of the two countries to close the initial productivity gaps was a result of firms' responses to the incentives contained in national economic policies. Among these policies

*From Howard Pack, "Technology Gaps Between Industrial and Developing Countries: Are There Dividends for Latecomers?" *World Bank Economic Review Supplement* (1992): 295–99. Reprinted by permission.

[1]The evidence for the interpretations in this section is set forth in Dahlman and Sananikone (1990), Westphal, Rhee, and Pursell (1981), Pack and Westphal (1986), and Pack (1992).

were: (a) the relative neutrality of the foreign trade regime with respect to profitability between domestic and foreign sales and the relatively low variance in protection across sectors; (b) export targeting in Korea and undervaluation of the real exchange rate in Taiwan (China) to encourage exports to a greater extent than would have been the case given the protection afforded to new industries in the domestic market; (c) a relatively undistorted labor market that, along with some movement toward market rates of interest (particularly in Taiwan, China), kept the wage-rental ratio closer to its scarcity value than in other developing countries.

The responses to these incentives led to a set of favorable but unintended technological consequences. For example, as a result of the rapid rates of export growth that these policies encouraged, there was a substantial inflow of nonproprietary technology, embodied in equipment and in the knowledge provided by customers (Westphal, Rhee, and Pursell 1981). This inflow was greater because exports and production increased most in older labor-intensive sectors in which technology from industrial countries was less protected. Technology and knowledge were relatively easy to acquire and absorb in these sectors even without a large stock of highly educated engineers. Much of the relevant information was based on mechanical knowledge rather than on electronic, biological, or chemical principles that would have required more formal education of employees.

Moreover, the machinery that was employed to manufacture the increased output was quite labor-intensive, in response to the low wage-rental ratio (Ranis 1979; Rhee and Westphal 1977). The simple equipment and the absence of continuous processing were conducive to minor innovations for increasing productivity, which were often suggested by blue-collar workers. Thus, the trade and factor price regimes were complementary and were conducive both to obtaining static gains in output and to fostering the move toward best practice. In this period, until the late 1970s, it is likely that much of the growth in productivity was the unplanned consequence of getting the prices right. Dollar and Sokoloff (1990) find that TFP growth in labor-intensive sectors in Korea exceeded that in the capital-intensive sectors. Technology policy was implicit in the standard economic policies, and technological learning complemented the conventional economic responses, stimulating further growth in production and exports as a consequence of reduced production costs.

In the 1970s a more explicit policy toward technology acquisition appeared. This policy differed in the two economies. In Korea the growth of large local firms was encouraged by the use of selected credit and other instruments. As domestic real wages increased and newer lower-wage competitors entered the international market, large Korean firms were encouraged to acquire the technological capacity to enter sectors that were more capital- and technology-intensive and to achieve best-practice productivity (Pack and Westphal 1986). Information about production technology in these more complex producer goods sectors was likely to be more closely guarded than in the consumer goods industries, and importers in industrial countries were less likely to transfer such technology. The Korean government encouraged firms to obtain technology licenses, acquire advanced equipment, and engage in their own research and development.

In Taiwan (China) the transfer of knowledge in the consumer industries, in which the early export drive was concentrated, was similar to that in Korea (Pack 1992). As Taiwan entered newer areas, however, it did not encourage the growth of large-scale firms capable of substantial research and development. The industrial structure was characterized by many small firms, reflecting the prevalence of high interest rates and the limited use of selected credit directed to larger firms. Therefore Taiwan utilized central institutions such as the Industrial Technology Research Institute, as well as technology diffusion institutions such as the China Productivity Center, to introduce new technologies, develop new products and processes, diffuse knowledge of them, and scan international markets for both products and processes (see Dahlman and Sananikone 1990). Moreover, in the newest sectors the ability to attract back Taiwanese nationals or to utilize the knowledge of those who remain abroad has been critical (Pack 1992).

Efforts to obtain international knowledge will have lower payoffs if they are not accompanied by a growth in the stock of capital per worker. Capital, both physical and human, can be partly supplied by other countries in the form of direct foreign investment. The remarkable development of Singapore, for example, demonstrates the potency of externally provided capital and skills in facilitating a rapid movement to international best practice (Lim and Fong 1991). In the initial period of rapid growth of industrial productivity, Korea and Taiwan (China) benefited from both capital accumulation and the move toward international best practice.

It may be conjectured that the extent of the shift in the production function would have been less if the sectors in which exports grew had been those in which these countries were close to world best practice. In Chile, a more recent example of improved policies, TFP growth has been much slower. Part of the explanation for this may lie in its emphasis on primary exports, minerals, and agricultural products. It is likely that these sectors in Chile were much closer to international best practice than were the industrial growth sectors in Korea and Taiwan (China). Moreover, in some of the expanding export sectors, such as electronics, the best-practice frontier was itself shifting rapidly, and the two Asian economies were able to take advantage of this. If these conjectures are correct, early proponents of import-substituting industrialization such as Singer and Prebisch may have been correct in their intuition of the dynamic (TFP growth) benefits of industrialization. They were mistaken, however, in their emphasis on import substitution rather than export growth as the process for realizing these benefits.

In both economies, people (and the knowledge they embody) who have been educated abroad return because of the high wages made possible by growing exports. Purely domestically oriented firms with smaller sales bases could not have offered sufficiently high wages to attract them. The newly acquired international knowledge was embedded in a framework conducive to efficiency. Competitive pressures led to a search within plants for better productivity performance. As a result, imported practices were improved, and purely domestic efforts were made to increase productivity.

The Interaction of Knowledge Acquisition, Investment, and Human Capital

Both Korea and Taiwan (China) invested extensively in education and in the accumulation of substantial physical capital. The ratio of investment to GDP increased from relatively low levels to more than 30 percent in the 1980s. Figure 1 elucidates the process. Initially the economy is at point A on production function f_0. As physical and human capital accumulation proceed, it moves to point E on production function f_1. The shift to the higher production function is realized because of the growing utilization of international best practice. Note, however, that the benefit from this accumulation of knowledge would have been less—

Figure 1

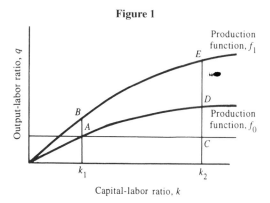

Capital-labor ratio, k

$AB < DE$—if capital per worker had not grown (Nelson 1973). Thus the size of the benefit from the growing import of knowledge and from local efforts to increase productivity depends on the stock of physical investment and skills complementing local unskilled labor.

References

Dahlman, Carl J., and Ousa Sananikone. 1990. "Technology Strategy in the Economy of Taiwan (China): Exploiting Foreign Linkages and Investing in Local Capability." World Bank, Industry and Energy Department, Washington, D.C.

Dollar, David, and Kenneth Sokoloff. 1990. "Patterns of Productivity Growth in South Korean Manufacturing Industries, 1963–1979." *Journal of Development Economics* 33: 309–27.

Lim, Linda Y. C., and Pang Eng Fong. 1991. *Foreign Direct Investment and Industrialization in Malaysia, Singapore, Taiwan, and Thailand.* Development Centre Studies. Paris: Organization for Economic Cooperation and Development.

Nelson, Richard R. 1973. "Recent Exercises in Growth Accounting: New Understanding or Dead End?" *American Economic Review* 73: 162–68.

Pack, Howard. 1992. "New Perspectives on Industrial Growth in Taiwan." In Gustav Ranis, ed., *Taiwan: From Developing to Mature Economy.* Boulder, Colo.: Westview.

Pack, Howard, and Larry E. Westphal. 1986. "Industrial Strategy and Technological Change: Theory versus Reality." *Journal of Development Economics* 22: 87–128.

Ranis, Gustav. 1979. "Industrial Development." In Walter Galenson, ed., *Economic Growth and Structural Change in Taiwan.* Ithaca, N.Y.: Cornell University Press.

Rhee, Yung W., and Larry E. Westphal. 1977. "A Microeconometric Investigation of Choice of Technique." *Journal of Development Economics* 4: 205–38.

Westphal, Larry E., Yung W. Rhee, and Garry G. Pursell. 1981. "Korean Industrial Competence: Where it Came From." World Bank Staff Working Paper no. 469, Washington, D.C.

Selection IV.B.2. The Benefits of FDI*

In 1993, direct foreign investment was the largest single source of external finance for developing countries, accounting for about half of all private resource flows. Following the virtual disappearance of commercial bank lending to these countries in the 1980s, many countries liberalized their restrictions on incoming foreign investment. Some countries even tilted the balance towards foreign firms by offering special incentives: in Czechoslovakia, joint ventures pay lower income taxes than domestic enterprises; foreign firms in much of the Caribbean receive income tax holidays, import duty exemptions and subsidies for infrastructure.

The pro-investment policies of the 1990s are very different from the wave of nationalizations which drove out foreign investment in many regions during the 1960s and 1970s. The new attitude is in part driven by the need for alternative sources of new capital, and in part driven by increasing skepticism about import-substituting trade and investment strategies. India, within one year, liberated both its trade regime and opened up its internal market to foreign investors, leading to what Indian Finance Secretary Montek Ahluwalia dubbed a "quiet economic revolution."[1]

Foreign Investment and Technology Transfer: Morocco and Venezuela

One reason to subsidize incoming foreign investors is the idea that they convey benefits which cannot be completely captured by the firm, such as new technology. Although technology transfer occurs through many different avenues, foreign investment could play an unusual role in several respects. New technology may not be commercially available and innovating firms may refuse to sell their technology via licensing agreements. In this case, alliances with innovating firms or close proximity to these firms may be the best means of learning about new technology. Foreign investment may also provide the competition necessary to stimulate technology diffusion, particularly if local firms are protected from import competition. Finally, foreign investors may provide a form of worker training which cannot be replicated in domestic firms or purchased from abroad, such as managerial skills. Technology diffusion may occur

through labor turnover as domestic employees move from foreign to domestic firms.

The studies on Morocco and Venezuela tested the magnitude of technology transfer from foreign subsidiaries (or joint ventures) to wholly domestically owned firms.[2] This is a working definition for the idea of a technology "spillover." I explored two related questions. First, to what extent do joint ventures or foreign subsidiaries perform better than domestic firms? Second, are there technology spillovers from firms with foreign equity investment to domestically owned firms?

Multinational enterprises (MNEs) are defined as any firm with foreign equity participation in the firm. Firm performance is measured as either labor productivity (output per worker) or a multi-factor productivity measure—which measures the productivity of all the firm's inputs simultaneously. Technological change is defined as an increase in output after taking into account all increases in the various inputs in production. Obviously, this concept of technological change is not an engineering concept. Technological change is synonymous with increases in observed productivity at the enterprise level.

In both Morocco and Venezuela, MNEs—firms with foreign equity participation—exhibit much higher levels of productivity. In Venezuela, increases in foreign equity participation also led to higher productivity growth. There is strong evidence that an infusion of foreign investment does more than simply provide additional capital to enterprises—it is also accompanied by knowledge transfers which lead to better firm performance.

Yet there is no evidence that the benefits accruing to joint ventures or local subsidiaries of multinationals are diffused to domestic firms. In other words, foreign investors provide direct benefits to those firms receiving the investment, but there are no "spillovers" to other plants. In fact, an increased multinational presence in Venezuela hurt the productivity of domestic competitors, in part because the multinationals took market share away from domestic plants.

These research results reinforce earlier case study evidence as well as interviews with plant managers in Morocco and Venezuela. The lack of technology transfer to domestic competitors can be explained by the limited hiring of domestic employees in higher level positions, very little labor mobility between domestic firms and foreign subsidiaries, limited subcontracting to local firms, no

*From Ann Harrison, "The Benefits of FDI," *Columbia Journal of World Business* (Winter 1994): 7–9. Reprinted by permission.

research and development by subsidiaries, and few incentives by multinationals to diffuse their knowledge to local competitors.

Foreign Investment and Breaking into Export Markets: Mexico

Anecdotal evidence, mostly derived from case studies in developing countries, suggests that the process of breaking into foreign markets can be very difficult. In order to export, firms must obtain information about foreign tastes and establish distribution channels in foreign markets. One obvious way for firms to learn about export markets is to observe other exporters who have already acquired experience selling abroad. Those exporters may be other domestic firms, or multinationals.

Case studies suggest that multinationals bring information about export markets to local producers, enabling them to access markets abroad. In Bangladesh, one Korean garment producer started a booming export business, triggering the entry into export markets of hundreds of new Bangladeshi garment producers. If this phenomenon is widespread, then governments may want to encourage foreign investors in sectors with high export potential but little know-how about foreign markets.

In a research project with Brian Aitken at the IMF and Gordon Hanson at the University of Texas, we test for the possibility that other exporters can reduce the cost of foreign market access for a firm contemplating the jump into export markets.[3] In particular, we examine whether locating near multinational exporters helps a firm to gain information about the export process.

Ours is the first study which provides statistical evidence on the role of foreign firms as "catalysts" for other exporters.[4] The basis for our study is 2,113 Mexican manufacturing plants over the period between 1986 and 1990. Following Mexico's trade reform in 1985, many Mexican manufacturers turned away from the previously protected domestic market towards outside markets. These changes during the 1980s allow us to identify the kinds of firms most likely to become exporters.

The analysis shows that multinational firms in Mexico do act as export catalysts. Domestic firms located near multinational exporters are much more likely to export than other firms. This suggests that foreign investors bring valuable information about export possibilities to developing countries—which then "spills over" to domestic rivals. One implication is that firms wishing to break into export markets should locate in areas with a concentration of multinational export activity. Another implication is that governments may wish to encourage exporters or potential exporters to locate near each other.

One policy option for developing countries is to encourage export processing zones (EPZs), special economic zones reserved for exporting firms. These zones often confer special benefits to exporters, such as duty-free imported inputs, tax holidays, or subsidized infrastructure. Our research suggests one unintended benefit of EPZs: by forcing potential exporters to locate near each other, they may help reduce the costs of breaking into foreign markets. However, EPZs need to be carefully designed to avoid isolating exporters from other enterprises. EPZs in countries like Jamaica, for example, are placed in fortress-like enclaves which isolates exporters from other enterprises.

Notes

1. Montek S. Ahluwalia, "India's Quiet Economic Revolution," *Columbia Journal of World Business* 29 (1), (Spring 1994): 6–12.

2. See: Mona Haddad and Ann Harrison, "Are there positive spillovers from direct foreign investment? Evidence from panel data for Morocco," *Journal of Development Economics* 42, (1993); and, Brian Aitken and Ann Harrison, "Do Domestic Firms Benefit from Foreign Direct Investment?" World Bank Policy Research Working Paper 1248, February 1994.

3. See: Brian Aitken, Gordon Hanson, and Ann Harrison, "Spillovers, Foreign Investment, and Export Behavior," World Bank, November 1994.

4. The term, export "catalyst," however, is not our creation. See the paper by Y. Rhee and T. Belot, "Export Catalysts in Low-Income Countries," World Bank, 1989, which presents case study evidence of this phenomena.

Note IV.B.2. Trade as Enemy, Handmaiden, and Engine of Growth

The effect of international trade on the economic growth of less developed countries has long been one of the most passionately debated subjects in the field of development economics. In this concluding Note we describe three views that span the range from negative to positive, all of which can draw some support from this section and the preceding one.

It is easiest to make the case for trade as the enemy of growth by building on the open economy version of the Matsuyama model, already discussed in the Overview for Chapter II and described in more detail and extended in Selection IV.A.1 by Sachs and Warner. Recall that in Matsuyama's model all productivity increase takes place through learning-by-doing in the manufacturing sector. Productivity in agriculture (or, more broadly, in the primary product sector) is constant by assumption. Now consider a country that is well endowed with natural resources compared with labor (and also relative to human and physical capital, if these are assumed to be used more intensively in manufacturing). Comparative advantage will lead this country to export primary products and import manufactures. Exports of primary products draw workers out of manufacturing and thereby reduce productivity growth both in that sector and in the aggregate (since there is no productivity growth in primary products). In this way trade reduces growth in per capita income in countries with abundant natural resources. It is interesting that the sociology literature on "dependency" and "world systems" comes to the same conclusion, that development of "peripheral" countries is hindered by their exports of primary products to "core" industrialized countries. For a summary of these arguments and a review of empirical studies see Crowly, Rauch, Seagrave, and Smith (1999).

We should note that the case for trade as the enemy of growth does not depend on the assumption that productivity in the primary product sector is constant. Obviously, learning-by-doing and other forms of productivity increase occur in this sector in the real world. What is crucial is only that this productivity increase tends to be substantially less rapid or less able to be sustained for a long period than it is in manufacturing.

The phrase "trade as handmaiden of growth" is from the title of an article by Kravis (1970). He states (p. 869),

> The term "engine of growth" is not generally descriptive and involves expectations which cannot be fulfilled by trade alone; the term 'handmaiden of growth' better conveys the notion of the role that trade can play. One of the most important parts of this handmaiden role for today's developing countries may be to serve as a check on the appropriateness of new industries by keeping the price and cost structures in touch with external prices and costs.

This supportive role can be usefully compared with that of financial development. As discussed in Chapter III, a well-developed financial system increases the efficiency of investment by helping to channel savings to the most profitable projects. One way that trade can increase the efficiency of investment is by helping to ensure that the most privately profitable projects are also the most socially profitable ones. Foreign competition discourages investors from attempting to establish monopoly positions in small domestic markets and from producing substandard goods. Other ways in which trade can increase the efficiency of investment are enabling producers to realize economies of scale through exporting, and relieving bottlenecks that might reduce the returns to well-conceived downstream investments or divert resources from them.

The view of trade as the engine of growth takes technological progress rather than investment to be the ultimate source of growth, and sees imported ideas as the main determinant of technological progress in LDCs. In other words, trade with more technologically advanced countries acts as a vehicle for the flow of knowledge from them and thereby drives growth in less advanced countries. Foreign direct investment from more to less developed countries plays the same role. (This contemporary view of trade as the engine of growth must be distinguished from the older view, in which growth is driven by expansion of land devoted to production of technologically stagnant primary products to meet the demand of industrialized countries.) This view is associated with the work of Romer (1993a, 1993b). Some specific mechanisms through which firms in LDCs absorb knowledge through contact with technologically advanced countries were discussed in the preceding Note and selections in this section.

The three views are not necessarily inconsistent with each other. Trade could be an enemy of growth for resource-abundant countries and a handmaiden or engine of growth for other countries. The mechanisms by which trade is said to operate as a handmaiden or engine of growth are not mutually exclusive.

References

Crowly, Angela M., James E. Rauch, Susanne Seagrave, and David A. Smith. 1998. "Quantitative Cross-National Studies of Economic Development: A Comparison of the Economics and Sociology Literatures." *Studies in Comparative International Development* 33 (Summer): 30–57.

Kravis, Irving B. 1970. "Trade as a Handmaiden of Growth: Similarities Between the Nineteenth and Twentieth Centuries." *Economic Journal* 80 (December): 850–72.

Romer, Paul M. 1993a. "Two Strategies for Economic Development: Using Ideas and Producing Ideas." *Proceedings of the World Bank Annual Conference on Development Economics 1992*. Washington, D. C.: World Bank.

Romer, Paul M. 1993b. "Idea Gaps and Object Gaps in Economic Development." *Journal of Monetary Economics* 32 (December): 543–73.

Human Resources

Overview

In Chapter III, on Savings and investment, and in Chapter IV, on international trade and technology transfer, we have seen several ways in which education, or more broadly human capital, can contribute to development. Education is a form of saving, causing accumulation of human capital and growth of aggregate output if human capital is an input in the aggregate production function. Taking a more disaggregated view, greater educational attainment helps a country to "move up the ladder" from production and export of less to more skill- and capital-intensive goods. An educated work force is also better able to absorb foreign technology. We begin section V.A on education with a Note that tries to trace these different views to differences in thinking about how education is used in production processes. A key distinction is whether education should be seen as a direct input to production or as a means of learning the production process and improving it to yield more output for given levels of inputs.

In Selection V.A.1 Jess Benhabib and Mark Spiegel find using cross-country regressions that growth in average years of schooling is not associated with growth in per capita income during the period 1965–85. They take this result as evidence against the view that education is a direct input to production. On the other hand, they find that the *level* of average years of schooling is positively associated with growth during this period, once the initial level of income is taken into account. Benhabib and Spiegel interpret these results as showing that, for a given distance behind the technological leader (a given initial income), countries with higher levels of education learn the leader's technology faster and catch up to the leader's income level faster.

In the next selection George Psacharopoulos summarizes evidence that social returns to investment in education in less developed countries are greatest for primary education and least for university education. The following Comment describes possible upward and downward biases from computing rates of return to educational investments using differences between earnings of more and less educated workers. An additional Comment suggests further readings on the subject of the impact of education on development.

If education is indeed important for development, how should countries go about it? In Selection V.A.3 Eric Hanushek stresses the uncertain effectiveness of putting more resources into education. The studies of education in less developed countries that he surveys are especially negative concerning any benefits from higher teacher-pupil ratios. Jong-Wha Lee and Robert Barro in Selection V.A.4 find, on the other hand, that students in countries with higher teacher-pupil ratios do better on internationally standardized tests. The effects of resources on educational outcomes in both more and less developed countries remain highly controversial, but Hanushek notes that there is broad agreement that schools make a difference: it is what makes a good school that is in doubt. In the last selection of this section, the World Bank shows that the high-performing East Asian countries concentrated their educational expenditure on primary and secondary rather than university education, in effect following the prescription implied by the differences in returns to educational investment reported in the selection by Psacharopoulos. These East Asian countries have thereby achieved universal primary enrollment and higher rates of secondary enrollment than would be predicted given their income levels.

Section V.B, on population, begins with a Note on the effect of population growth on development. The Note draws a distinction between the effects of a large world population and a large average family size, the former the consequence and the latter a major cause of rapid population growth. It is perhaps surprising that a larger world population cannot be shown to have any negative impact on development, and if anything the contrary position is consistent with the evidence. On the other hand, in Selection V.B.1 Nancy Birdsall notes the existence of substantial evidence that children from large families have lower educational attainment, and as we saw in the previous section higher educational attainment is widely believed to make an essential contribution to economic growth, however much the exact mechanism may be in dispute. In the remainder of her selection Birdsall summarizes the findings of studies of the determinants of fertility, the major factor influencing family size. Female education above about four years has one of the strongest and most consistent negative associations with fertility. Family planning programs are also found to have some negative effect on fertility.

The extent of poor health and nutrition in the less developed compared with the more developed world is documented in Exhibit V.C.I. In Selection V.C.1 Jere Behrman and Anil Deolalikar summarize the findings of studies of the determinants of health status and nutrition at the individual and family levels. One of the more robust findings is that a higher level of women's schooling improves the nutrient consumption of their children. The World Bank in its selection and the Exhibit that concludes this section both focus on health policy. It is clear that there is considerable scope for improvements in the efficiency and equity of expenditures on health care by less developed country governments.

Women play an especially important role in determining family size, nutrition, and health. The previous two sections thus lead naturally to the concluding section, V.D., on gender and development.

In view of findings that more educated women have smaller and better nourished families, it is ironic that education of women in poor countries has lagged behind that of men. In Selection V.D.1 M. Anne Hill and Elizabeth King document this "gender gap." It is largest in sub-Saharan Africa, South Asia, and the Middle East and North Africa. In Latin America and East Asia the gender gap in education has largely disappeared. Hill and King also discuss why the gender gap persists. Interactions of traditional practices with incentives provide part of the answer. For example, girls may be more valued in the home because by tradition they do much more housework than boys, and parents therefore have less incentive to send girls to school.

In the next selection the International Labour Office describes the nature of women's work throughout the less developed world. Women's work is typically less productive and less well paid than that of men. Mayra Buvinic and Margaret Lycette describe the disproportionate poverty of female-headed households in Selection V.D.3, and Paul Collier describes the discrimination encountered by women in labor and credit markets in Selection V.D.4. Of course women face less severe versions of these same problems in more developed countries. One problem they do not face in more developed countries, however, is lower survival rates. In Selection V.D.5 Amartya Sen notes that the ratio of women to men in Asia and North Africa is substantially below that in Europe and North America. Comparative neglect of female health and nutrition appears to be the main cause.

Women might be less willing to follow the traditional paths for themselves and their daughters if they have their own assets and independent income. In Bangladesh, the Grameen Bank has primarily targeted women for loans that support agriculture and other small business and house-building. Shahidur Khandker, Baqui Khalily, and Zahed Khan in Selection V.D.6 describe how the Grameen Bank makes loans to groups rather than individuals, thereby enlisting peer pressure as an aid in loan performance. The following Comment lists several studies that confirm that the increased financial independence conferred on women by participation in Grameen Bank credit programs has increased women's decision-making power within the household and improved household outcomes of special concern to women such as schooling of girls. The section concludes with a Comment suggesting additional readings in the area of gender and development.

One theme that runs through most of this diverse chapter is the importance of government as a provider of services, whether they be education, family planning, or health care. Perhaps governments should be more involved in redressing discrimination against women, but to date this task has fallen largely to nongovernmental organizations (NGOs) such as the Grameen Bank.

V.A. EDUCATION

Note V.A.1. Three Views of the Contribution of Education to Economic Growth

It is possible to think of the role of education in a production process in at least three different ways. These correspond to three different views of how education contributes to economic growth.

First, we can think of uneducated and educated workers as perfectly substitutable inputs to production. Two workers who have completed primary school, say, are equivalent to one worker who has completed secondary school. Put differently, labor is homogeneous and can be measured in terms of "efficiency units." Holding constant the number of actual workers, an increase in the average level of education of the labor force increases the size of the labor force measured in efficiency units. This increase in the number of efficiency units per worker generates greater output per worker since labor is an input to production. Growth in the average years of schooling per worker is thus associated with growth in output per worker.

Second, uneducated and educated workers can be seen as imperfectly substitutable inputs to production. In constructing a suspension bridge, say, three (or 30) workers with a primary school education cannot replace one civil engineer. With educated and uneducated labor treated as different inputs, different production processes can be thought of as making more or less intensive use of educated relative to uneducated labor. If the aircraft and the apparel industries face the same costs of hiring educated and uneducated labor, the aircraft industry will employ a higher ratio of educated to uneducated workers because of the nature of its production process compared with that of the apparel industry. As we saw in Selection IV.A.3 by Deardorff and in the following Comment, increasing the number of educated workers helps a country to "move up the ladder" to production of more technologically sophisticated goods. Consider the following newspaper report on Thailand (Stier 1993):

> In the past decade, Thailand's economic growth has been fueled by export-oriented industries dependent on an abundance of low-skilled, low-wage workers. But those industries have lost much of their competitive advantage because Thai wage increases have outpaced labor costs in other developing Asian nations—including China, Indonesia, Vietnam and India—that are now competing in international trade. Thus within a relatively short period of industrialization, Thailand is under pressure to make a transition to more sophisticated, higher-skilled industries. . . . A serious problem for Thailand in taking the economy to a higher level is that the education and skill of the work force has not kept pace. More than 80% of Thai workers in a labor force of 34 million has a primary school education or less. Only about 4% of school-age youth make it through universities. Thailand has a shortage of skilled workers across the board—from doctors to auditors and engineers to middle managers. . . . Analysts say it could be years before Thailand's education system produces enough skilled workers for the next stage of industrialization.

Lack of educated workers is also seen as an obstacle to the continued rapid economic growth of Thailand in Selection V.A.5 by the World Bank.

An industry's production process could make intensive use of educated labor because it requires sophisticated monitoring and quality control, say, or because technology is rapidly changing and highly educated workers are needed to learn it. Generalizing from the latter case, the role of educated labor in any production process can be seen as learning or creating technology that generates more output holding levels of inputs constant, rather than as an input itself. This leads to the third view of the contribution of education to the economic growth of less developed countries: it helps them absorb foreign technology. As they state in selection V.A.1, the cross-country regressions of Benhabib and Spiegel can be interpreted as evidence in favor of this third view. Though their work is a promising start, we judge that the three views of the contribution of education to economic growth described in this Note are as yet insufficiently precisely formulated and inadequately tested to inform educational policy.

Reference

Stier, Ken. 1993. "Thailand Caught Between Economic Levels." *Los Angeles Times* (November 8): D2.

Selection V.A.1. The Role of Human Capital in Economic Development: Evidence from Aggregate Cross-Country Data*

1. Introduction

How does human capital or the educational attainment of the labor force affect the output and the growth of an economy? A standard approach is to treat human capital, or the average years of schooling of the labor force, as an ordinary input in the production function. The recent work of Mankiw, Romer, and Weil (1992) is in this tradition. An alternative approach, associated with endogenous growth theory,[1] is to model technological progress, or the growth of total factor productivity, as a function of the level of education or human capital. The presumption is that an educated labor force is better at creating, implementing, and adopting new technologies, thereby generating growth. In this paper, we attempt to empirically distinguish between these two approaches. At the end we also briefly comment on the impact of some ancillary variables, such as political instability and income inequality, on economic growth and factor accumulation.

Because of data constraints, the literature has often attempted to proxy the variables relevant to growth accounting by those which are directly observable. For example, although physical capital stocks are necessary to estimate the growth accounting equations, the literature has usually used gross investment rates as a proxy for physical capital accumulation (Barro, 1991).[2] In addition, human capital has been proxied in the literature by enrollment ratios or literacy rates. At best, however, enrollment ratios represent investment levels in human capital. Literacy is a stock variable, but there are important empirical problems associated with the use of literacy as a proxy for human capital.[3]

This paper uses estimates of physical and human capital stocks to examine cross-country evidence on the determinants of economic growth. We begin with estimation of a standard Cobb–Douglas production function in which labor and human and physical capital enter as factors of production. Our findings shed some doubt on the traditional role given to human capital in the development process as a separate factor of production. In our first set of results, we find that human capital growth has an insignificant, and usually negative effect in explaining per capita income growth. This result is robust to a number of alternative specifications and data sources, as well as to the possibility of bias which is encountered when regressing per capita income growth on accumulated factors of production.

Nonetheless, human capital accumulation has long been stressed as a prerequisite for economic growth. As pointed out by Nelson and Phelps (1966), by treating human capital simply as another factor in growth accounting we may be misspecifying its role. Below, we introduce an alternative model which allows human capital levels to directly affect aggregate factor productivity through two channels: Following Romer (1990a), we postulate that human capital may directly influence productivity by determining the capacity of nations to innovate new technologies suited to domestic production. Furthermore, we adapt the Nelson and Phelps (1966) model to allow human capital levels to affect the speed of technological catch-up and diffusion. We assume that the ability of a nation to adopt and implement new technology from abroad is a function of its domestic human capital stock. In our model, at every point in time there exists some country which is the world leader in technology. The speed with which nations "catch up" to this leader country is then a function of their human capital stocks.

The combination of these two forces, domestic innovation and catch-up, produces some noteworthy results: First, under certain conditions (in particular when the innovation parameter dominates), growth rates may differ across countries for a long time due to differences in levels of human capital stocks. Second, a country which lies below the "leader nation" in technology, but possesses a higher human capital stock, will catch up and overtake the leader in a finite time period. Third, the country with the highest stock of human capital will always eventually emerge as the technological leader nation in finite time and maintain its leader-

*From Jess Benhabib and Mark M. Spiegel, "The Role of Human Capital in Economic Development: Evidence from Aggregate Cross-Country Data," *Journal of Monetary Economics* 34 (October 1994): 143–151, 158–161. Reprinted by permission.

[1]For example, see Romer (1990a, b).

[2]An exception is the work of Mankiw, Romer, and Weil (1992). In their study, they are able to generate a specification in terms of investment rates by assuming that all countries are in their steady state.

[3]These include quality of measurement differences across countries, biases introduced by the skewness of sampling towards urban areas, and the fact developed countries typically have literacy rates which are close to unity.

ship as long as its human capital advantage is sustained.

We test the specification indicated by this alternative model below. Our findings assign a positive role to the levels of human capital in growth accounting. Our results below generally confirm that per capita income growth indeed depends positively upon average levels of human capital, although not always measurably at a 5% confidence level.
. . .

2. Growth Accounting with Human Capital as a Factor of Production

The standard growth accounting methodology with human capital specifies an aggregate production function in which per capita income, Y_t, is dependent upon three input factors—labor, L_t, physical capital, K_t, and human capital, H_t. Assuming a Cobb–Douglas technology, $Y_t = A_t K_t^\alpha L_t^\beta K_t^\gamma \varepsilon_t$, and taking log differences, the relationship for long-term growth can be expressed as

$$(\log Y_T - \log Y_0) = (\log A_T - \log A_0)$$
$$+ \alpha(\log K_T - \log K_0) + \beta(\log L_T - \log L_0)$$
$$+ \gamma(\log H_T - \log H_0) + (\log \varepsilon_T - \log \varepsilon_0). \quad (1)$$

A difficulty associated with estimating aggregate production functions such as Eq. (1) concerns the possibility that because physical and human capital are accumulated factors, they will be correlated with the error term ε_t. This would imply the possibility of biased estimates. . . . Our results indicate that there is likely to be an upward coefficient bias on the α and γ estimates, and a downward bias on our estimate of β. In particular, this bias may lead us to overestimate the importance of human and physical capital accumulation in the growth equations.

We estimate Eq. (1) in the standard growth accounting framework by regressing log differences in income on log differences of factors. If this specification is correct, this methodology would provide estimates of the magnitudes of α, β, and γ. In addition, we introduce a number of 'ancillary variables' to allow for some productivity differences, such as proxies for political instability and distortionary activity. . . . See Table 1. Regressions were run using ordinary least squares with White's heteroscedasticity-consistent covariance estimation method. The coefficient on the log difference of capital stocks, dK, enters positively and significantly at the 1% confidence level in all the specifications. The capital coefficient estimate for the full sample regression is approximately 0.5.

The coefficient on log differences in 'labor', measured by both reported labor and population stocks, dL, also enters with the expected positive coefficient, although the coefficient estimate appears to be low and the variable rarely enters significantly at a 5% confidence level.[4]

The most surprising result concerns the coefficient on the log difference in human capital, dH. The log difference in human capital always enters insignificantly, and almost always with a negative coefficient. One explanation for the negative coefficient is that a number of countries, most notably many from Africa, began the period with extremely low stocks of human capital. Consequently, those that achieved a modicum of improvement in their educational levels were credited with large improvements in this stock. However, it is well-known that many of these countries did not experience similar improvements in output, implying a small coefficient for γ in the growth accounting regressions. Nevertheless, even when we include African and Latin American country dummies, *AFRICA* and *LAAMER,* to account for the special experiences of these countries (Model 4), the results hold. Therefore, even though the experience of these countries over the period provides evidence against the standard growth accounting framework, these countries alone do not drive the results found in Table 1.[5]

Also, note that these country dummies, as well as the dummy for oil-exporting countries in Model 3, fail to enter significantly once one accounts for disparities in rates of factor accumulation. It seems that proper accounting for capital and labor obviate the necessity for including these dummies. Many previous works which did not include factor accumulation due to lack of capital stock data, such as Barro (1991), found that these dummies entered significantly.

The negative point estimate on human capital accumulation is robust to the inclusion of the log of initial wealth, *LOG* Y_0, and cannot be explained by the negative correlation between human capital accumulation and initial income per worker. Initial income itself robustly enters with a negative and highly significant parameter estimate.

---

[4] When we exclude Botswana, the coefficient on physical labor growth increases to 0.27, while the other results are similar.

[5] Using maximum likelihood techniques, we also ran a C.E.S. specification. The elasticity of substitution was not measurably different from one. The implied factor shares with a unitary elasticity were about 0.5 each for physical capital and labor, while human capital was still insignificant with a point estimate of 0.03.

Table 1. Cross-Country Growth Accounting Results: Standard Specification[a] Dependent Variable: DY 1965–1985

	Model 1	Model 2	Model 3	Model 4	Model 5	Model 6
Const.	0.269[b]	1.947[b]	1.871[b]	1.968[b]	1.127[b]	1.654[b]
	(0.090)	(0.322)	(0.349)	(0.398)	(0.287)	(0.296)
DK	0.457[b]	0.545[b]	0.555[b]	0.530[b]	0.607[b]	0.472[b]
	(0.085)	(0.066)	(0.068)	(0.088)	(0.064)	(0.056)
DL	0.209	0.130	0.164	0.225	0.362[c]	0.219
	(0.207)	(0.163)	(0.164)	(0.192)	(0.156)	(0.138)
DH	0.063	−0.059	−0.043	−0.080	−0.028	−0.031
	(0.079)	(0.058)	(0.066)	(0.064)	(0.065)	(0.059)
LOG Y_0	—	−0.190[b]	−0.185[b]	−0.190[b]	−0.143[b]	−0.152[b]
		(0.036)	(0.038)	(0.041)	(0.038)	(0.030)
OIL	—	—	−0.097	—	—	—
			(0.141)			
AFRICA	—	—	—	−0.024	—	—
				(0.144)		
LAAMER	—	—	—	−0.107	—	—
				(0.065)		
MID	—	—	—	—	0.675	—
					(0.761)	
PIQ	—	—	—	—	—	0.057
						(0.057)
Obs.	78	78	78	78	40	67
F-stat.	26.609	37.693	30.228	25.610	27.740	22.736

[a] dX refers to the log difference in variable X. Standard errors are in parentheses.
[b] 1% confidence level.
[c] 5% confidence level.

We should note that for a specification with an aggregate production function the accumulation of factors are accounted for, and the role of initial income in our regressions is unclear. However, initial income may proxy for initial technological advantage and, as argued in the next section, the negative coefficient may be interpreted as a "catch-up" result.

Models 5 and 6 introduce ancillary variables to incorporate other factors which may play a role in determining per capita growth rates. *MID* represents the relative size of the middle class in a country and is the variable used as a measure of income distribution by Persson and Tabellini (1991). Note that the sample size available with the introduction of this variable is much smaller, as income distribution data is relatively scarce. Once one adjusts for differences in rates of factor accumulation, this ancillary variable fails to significantly affect growth, contrary to Persson and Tabellini (1991). However, the variable does enter with the expected positive sign.

The final model introduces political instability, *PIQ*, measured as average annual levels of the political instability coefficient, obtained from

Gupta (1990).[6] Note that once again the political instability variable fails to enter significantly once one accounts for differences in rates of factor accumulation. . . .

3. Growth Accounting with Human Capital Stocks Entering into Productivity

Table 2 reports the results of ordinary least squares estimation using White's heteroskedasticity correction method. Model 1 simply substitutes the log of average human capital levels for log differences of human capital. Physical capital accumulation and labor force growth enter with their predicted signs, but labor force growth fails to enter significantly. However, the performance of human capital appears disappointing. Both in levels and in growth rates, human capital fails to enter significantly, and the point estimates are of incorrect sign.

Nevertheless, as pointed out above, the human

[6] Gupta (1990) uses discriminant analysis of a variety of political events from the Taylor and Jodice (1983) data set to form his index of political instability.

Table 2. Cross-Country Growth Accounting Results: Human Capital in Log Levels[a] Dependent Variable: DGDP 1965–1985

	Model 1	Model 2	Model 3	Model 4	Model 5	Model 6
Const.	0.416[b]	2.093[b]	2.065[b]	2.044[b]	1.176[b]	1.730[b]
	(0.103)	(0.326)	(0.345)	(0.392)	(0.391)	(0.308)
DK	0.495[b]	0.500[b]	0.505[b]	0.479[b]	0.594[b]	0.440[b]
	(0.100)	(0.075)	(0.079)	(0.094)	(0.077)	(0.063)
DL	0.132	0.253	0.260	0.391[c]	0.385[c]	0.303
	(0.218)	(0.166)	(0.169)	(0.191)	(0.174)	(0.150)
LOGH	−0.079	0.128[c]	0.121[c]	0.167[c]	0.045	0.089
	(0.060)	(0.055)	(0.059)	(0.054)	(0.101)	(0.058)
LOG Y_0	—	−0.233[b]	−0.230[b]	−0.235[b]	−0.161[c]	−0.179[b]
		(0.043)	(0.045)	(0.046)	(0.067)	(0.036)
OIL	—	—	−0.032	—	—	—
			(0.127)			
AFRICA	—	—	—	0.007	—	—
				(0.133)		
LAAMER	—	—	—	−0.135[c]	—	—
				(0.065)		
MID	—	—	—	—	0.746	—
					(0.747)	
PIQ	—	—	—	—	—	−0.045
						(0.053)
Obs.	78	78	78	78	40	67
F-stat.	27.551	41.225	32.583	29.198	27.832	23.830

[a]*dX* refers to the log difference in variable *X*. Standard errors are in parentheses.

[b]1% confidence level.

[c]5% confidence level.

capital rich country need not always be the high growth country because of the catch-up factor. Therefore, Model 1 is likely to be misspecified. To account for differences in initial technology levels across countries, we introduce initial income levels in Model 2, which will capture the role of the catch-up effect.[7]

As soon as initial income levels are introduced, human capital enters significantly in levels with the predicted positive sign. This result suggests that catch-up remains a significant element in growth, and that countries with higher education tend to close the technology gap faster than others. It is not particularly surprising that this transition effect appears in twenty years of growth experiences. The transition towards a common growth

rate set by the leading country may be quite long, and stochastic technological innovations by the leader can set countries on new transition paths. The results suggest that the role of human capital is indeed one of facilitating adoption of technology from abroad and creation of appropriate domestic technologies rather than entering on its own as a factor of production.[8]

In addition, we used likelihood ratio tests to examine whether human capital in levels should be added to a regression which included growth rate of population and physical and human capital as well as initial per capita income. The likelihood tests indicated that human capital in levels should be included in the specification with a 1% level of confidence.

Initial income enters significantly and negatively in all the specifications. This may imply some support for the convergence hypothesis. However,

[7]Strictly speaking, . . . [theory] suggests that the catch-up term should be log($Y_{max} - Y_i$), where Y_{max} is the initial income per worker for the leading country. Since Y_{max} is constant across countries, it enters into the constant term which can no longer be viewed, unlike Model 1, as accounting for exogenous growth. If the catch-up is operative at higher frequencies, such as annually, then the modified specification requires us to include not initial income, but an average of incomes over the years as well as adjusting the constant term for changes in Y_{max}.

[8]One caveat is again the possibility of a bias in these coefficient estimates as discussed in Section 2. . . . However, the coefficient estimates on physical capital are close to its expected factor share and do not indicate a significant upward bias.

given the model above, a negative coefficient estimate on initial income levels may not be a sign of convergence due to diminishing returns, but of catch-up from adoption of technology from abroad. These two forces may be observationally equivalent in simple cross-country growth accounting exercises.

The ancillary variables are introduced in Models 3 through 6. The positive and significant coefficient estimate on levels of human capital is robust to the introduction of these variables, with the exception of the income distribution variable *MID*. However, the sample size is severely curtailed by the introduction of this variable.

With the exception of the Latin American dummy, note that none of the ancillary variables are statistically significant at the 5% confidence level. As above, once one accounts for differences in rates of factor accumulation, the residual role for characteristics such as political stability and skewness of income distribution appears to be limited.

References

Barro, Robert, 1991. Economic growth in a cross section of countries, Quarterly Journal of Economics 106, 407–444.

Gupta, Dipak, 1990. The economics of political violence: The effect of political instability on economic growth (Praeger, New York, NY).

Mankiw, Gregory, David Romer, and David Weil, 1992. A contribution to the empirics of economic growth, Quarterly Journal of Economics 106, 407–437.

Nelson, Richard and Edmund Phelps, 1966, Investment in humans, technological diffusion, and economic growth, American Economic Review: Papers and Proceedings 61, 69–75.

Persson, Torsten and Guido Tabellini, 1991, Is inequality harmful for growth? Discussion paper 581 (C.E.P.R., London).

Romer, Paul, 1990a, Endogenous technological change, Journal of Political Economy 98, S71–S102.

Romer, Paul, 1990b, Human capital and growth: theory and evidence, Carnegie Rochester Conference Series on Public Policy 32, 151–286.

Section V.A.2. Economic Impact of Education*

In this paper I review the evidence on the economic impact of education produced in the past thirty years and compile a number of lessons from the literature that might be useful to policy makers. And since no field is without controversy, I also review the major debates that have surrounded human capital theory and its applications.

The Evidence

The evidence on the economic impact of education can be divided into two distinct types: micro and macro.

Micro

If expenditure on education is a kind of investment leading to the formation of human capital, either for the individual or for society at large, one should be able to estimate the rate of return to this investment. In its most simplified form, the rate of return to investment in education (r) can be estimated by dividing the permanent annual benefits stream due to education ($Y_1 - Y_0$) by the cost of obtaining such education ($Y_0 + C_1$),

$$r = \frac{(Y_1 - Y_0)}{S(Y_0 + C_1)}$$

In this case Y_1 and Y_0 could refer to the mean earnings of workers who are literate and illiterate, respectively, S to the number of years of schooling it takes for someone to become literate, and C_1 to the annual cost of keeping someone in school. Note the appearance of Y_0 in the denominator of the expression, representing the opportunity cost of attending school rather than working in the labor market.

There are several ways to examine rates of return to education: by whether the returns refer to the individual investor or to society at large, namely, the private or social rate of return; by the country's level of economic development; by the type of curriculum—say, general or vocational secondary education; by type of economic sector the worker is in, say, modern wage employment or self-employment; and by gender.

Hundreds of studies have been conducted in the past thirty years on the profitability of investment in education in a large number of countries across the dimensions cited above (for a summary see Psacharopoulos 1985). Figures 1 and 2 offer an impressionistic summary of the results of these studies. The figures are impressionistic in the sense that I want the reader to focus on the structure of the returns to education rather than the exact percentage points represented by the vertical axes. As a point of reference I give an illustrative 10 percent opportunity cost of capital or alternative discount rate. This might be more realistic in a developed country than in a developing country, although the 10 percent rate could be defended in a developing country setting if the country could borrow internationally for investment in education at this interest rate.

The first notable result of the application of rate of return studies to education is that the rates are not far off the yield of more conventional investments. The returns to investment in education in advanced industrial countries are roughly the same as those of investment in physical capital. By contrast, the returns to education in developing countries stand at a much higher level relative to industrial countries. This reflects both the continuing scarcity of human capital in poorer countries and barriers to the allocation of funds to human capital investment, so that the returns to any kind of capital (physical or human) equalize at the margin.

A typical pattern, found since the early days of rate of return estimation in education, is that returns decline by level of schooling. Thus, returns to primary education are higher relative to returns to secondary education, and the latter are higher than returns to university education. This finding, corroborated in study after study, has fundamental policy implications.

Another result worth noting is the difference between social and private rates of return. Because of the public subsidization of education in all parts of the world, private rates are typically several percentage points higher than social rates of return. By definition, the cost in a private rate-of-return estimation refers only to what the individual pays out of his or her pocket, whereas the cost in a social rate of return estimation refers to the full resource cost of someone attending school. The distortion incurred by the public subsidization of education means that, in some instances, individuals will find it profitable to pursue education to a given level whereas, from the point of view of society, this investment is not profitable. The maxi-

*From George Psacharopoulos, *The Economic Impact of Education: Lessons for Policymakers* (San Francisco: ICS Press, 1991), pp. 8–15. Reprinted by permission.

Figure 1. The returns to investment in education by level and country type.

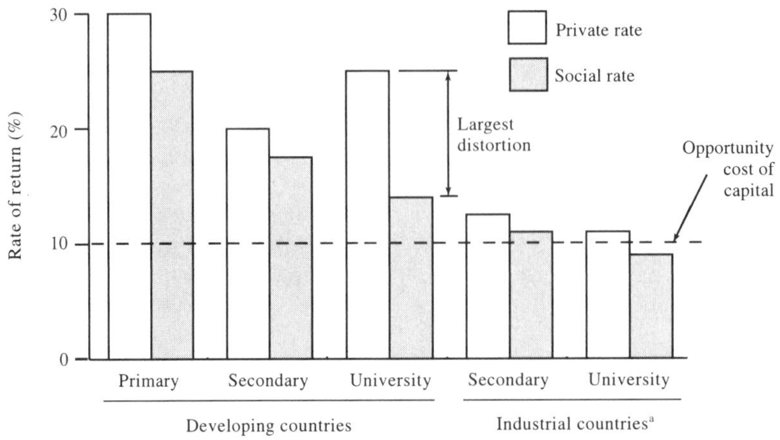

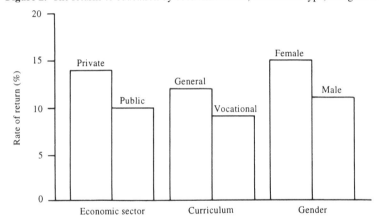

^aThe rate of return for primary education in industrial countries is undefined because of universal enrollment at this level of schooling.
Source: Based on Psacharopoulos 1985.

Figure 2. The returns to education by economic sector, curriculum type, and gender.

Source: Based on Psacharopoulos 1985.

mum distortion between the private and the social rates refers to education at the university level. This level is more heavily subsidized in most countries relative to any other level.

Figure 2 presents three additional rate-of-return patterns that have been found in studies in many countries, irrespective of whether the rate of return is social or private. The first comparison shows that the return to education is typically higher in the private or competitive sector than in the public sector. It is well known that the public pay structure is very compressed, leading to a lower rate of return relative to estimates based on earnings in the private sector, where there is no limit to rewards. To the extent that private sector earnings truly approximate a worker's productivity, rates of

return based on earnings in the competitive sector provide a better fix for the scarcity of human capital than rates of return based on civil service pay scales. The latter, however, are very important for explaining the private behavior of individuals in seeking different levels and types of education. Given the dominance of the public sector in hiring university graduates in any kind of country, a private rate-of-return estimation using civil service data is very appropriate, if not a must, in understanding the demand for university education. However, a private earnings base would be more appropriate for setting priorities for educational investment in a given country.

The second pattern in Figure 2 provides a well documented yet highly counterintuitive finding:

within a given level of education, say, secondary schooling or university education, the more general the curriculum the higher the returns to education. This startling finding is due to two factors. First, the unit cost of vocational education, at any level, is higher than that of general education, because of the more specialized faculty and equipment that vocational education entails. Second, graduates of general programs are more flexible in fitting a wide spectrum of occupations—and perhaps are more easily trained on the job—than graduates of vocational programs that are earmarked to enter a particular occupation (to put it at the extreme, mechanical watch repairers).

The last pattern presented in Figure 2 refers to the worker's gender. Investment in the education of females often yields a higher rate of return than investment in the education of males. This finding could also be considered counter-intuitive, in the sense that males typically earn much more than females. One must remember that the rate of return to investment in education is a *relative* concept, comparing the *difference* between more- and less-educated workers with the cost of their education. A major component of the cost is the forgone earnings of the worker while studying, which can lead to a higher rate of return for females than for males.

Macro

If investment in education yields returns at the individual or social level, this must be reflected at the level of the economy. Growth accounting in the post-World War II period was based on the so-called aggregate production function.

$$\text{Output} = f(\text{Land, Labor, Capital})$$

expressing a country's output (measured by gross domestic product) as a function of the traditional triad of factors of production: land, measured in terms of cultivated area; labor, measured in terms of the number of persons or man-hours worked; and capital, measured in terms of the value of the physical plant in operation. Fitting the above relationship to time-series data for the United States left a huge unexplained residual, named "the coefficient of our ignorance." Output grew much faster than increases in the traditional factors of production could account for. Relabeling the residual "technical change" was simply begging the question "what determines technical change?"

It was then that Schultz (1961) and Denison (1967), using computationally different although conceptually similar approaches, introduced the quality of labor or human capital into the traditional production function. Schultz, for example, plugged in the amount of investment represented by expenditures on education and explained a great part of the previously puzzling residual. The macro approach has been replicated by others over the past thirty years with similar results.[1]

Figure 3 shows that in Africa, investment in education explains nearly twice the proportion of economic growth that it does in more affluent Europe and North America. This macro result essentially replicates the rate-of-return structure by country type presented above, given that human capital is much scarcer in the poorer countries.

Beyond the results cited above, which have been generated by econometricians, economic historians took a stab at the matter by taking a much longer-term view than sophisticated statistical analysis permits. Thus it has been established that bouts of long-term economic growth were preceded by increases in the population's literacy level. The examples of Japan and Korea are the classic cases in which an educated population base has provided the necessary infrastructure for industrial advances to take place at a later date (see Saxonhouse 1977 and Easterlin 1981).

Wider Social Impact

Beyond the above "strict" or monetary impact of education, investment in human beings also has many other social values. Some come under the heading of externalities—namely, values captured by persons other than the individual investor. Others are labeled "nonmarket effects" (for a superb account of this see Haveman and Wolfe 1984). And others are simply means or mechanisms by which the overall impact of education is realized.

When a person becomes literate, this person will enjoy a higher lifetime consumption path, according to statistics for a large number of countries. Others will also benefit if the country has a more literate population—through lower transaction costs than if they were dealing with illiterates, for example.

Many educated females may choose not to participate in the labor force. This does not mean, however, that such females are not more productive (relative to their less educated counterparts) in the variety of goods and services produced within the household that are not readily marketable. For example, they may provide better sanitation conditions for all members of the family and more nutri-

---

[1]For a review see Psacharopoulos (1984).

Figure 3. The contribution of education to economic growth by continent.

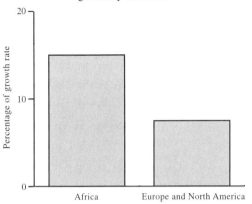

Source: Based on Psacharopoulos 1984.

tional meals. Such effects should be counted as part of the social impact of education.

Education increases the opportunity cost to a woman staying in the household and induces her to participate in the labor market. This contributes to overall efficiency in the economy to the extent that her market wage is higher than her implicit, shadow wage of being engaged in household activities.

Migration is an illustrative example of the means by which the returns to education are realized. To the extent that education makes the worker aware of employment opportunities elsewhere, or simply makes him or her employable in other contexts, it will instigate a more efficient allocation of labor to the most productive uses.

Health status is a very important part of human well-being. Several studies have shown that literacy and other measures of education are more closely correlated with life expectancy than per capita income is. The mechanism of this relationship is that education helps determine both the level of knowledge about how to combat disease and the ease with which it can be transmitted and utilized (Cochrane, O'Hara, and Leslie 1980).

The relationship between education and fertility

is a very complex one, although most observers would agree that the link is negative—that increased literacy and school attendance in general delay marriage and increase the opportunity cost of having children. Consequently, families desire and have fewer children. This has been clearly demonstrated in urban areas on a global scale (see Cochrane 1979).

Last but not least, another often mentioned wider effect of education is that of having a more informed body of consumers and a literate electorate, leading to democratic government.

References

Cochrane, S. H. (1979). *Fertility and Education: What Do We Really Know?* Baltimore: Johns Hopkins University Press.

Cochrane, S. H., D. O'Hara, and J. Leslie (1980). *The Effects of Education on Health.* Staff Working Paper no. 405. Washington, D.C.: World Bank.

Denison, E. F. (1967). *Why Do Growth Rates Differ?* Washington D.C.: Brookings Institution.

Easterlin, R. (1981). "Why Isn't the Whole World Developed?" *Journal of Economic History* 41 (March): 1–19.

Haveman, R. H., and B. Wolfe (1984). "Schooling and Economic Well-being: The Role of Nonmarket Effects." *Journal of Human Resources* 19:377–407.

Psacharopoulos, G. (1984). "The Contribution of Education to Economic Growth: International Comparisons." In J. W. Kendrick, ed., *International Comparisons of Productivity and Causes of the Slowdown.* New York: Ballinger, pp. 335–60.

——— (1985). "Returns to Education: A Further International Update and Implications." *Journal of Human Resources* 20 (Fall): 583–604.

Saxonhouse, G. R. (1977). "Productivity Change and Labor Absorption in Japanese Cotton Spinning, 1881–1935." *Quarterly Journal of Economics* 91: 195–200.

Schultz, T. W. (1961). "Education and Economic Growth." In N. B. Henry, ed., *Social Forces Influencing American Education.* Chicago: University of Chicago Press.

Comment V.A.1. Ability Differences, Spillovers, and the Returns to Education

The returns to investment in education reported by Psacharopoulos in Figure 1 of the preceding selection are computed using the differences in average earnings between workers with and workers without a given level of education. These computations are based on the implicit assumption that the average innate abilities of the more and less educated groups of workers are the same, and therefore have no effect on the average earnings differential. This assumption is accurate if the only cause of differences in educational attainment is differences in the resources to which the workers had access when students: for example, whether or not primary schools were present in their villages. Suppose, to the contrary, that another cause of differences in educational attainment is differences in ability: high-ability students graduate from secondary school, say, while low-ability students drop out. In this case part of the higher earnings of secondary school graduates reflects their higher ability, and the return to secondary education is overestimated.

The ability bias argument suggests that the social returns to investment in education may not be as high relative to those on alternative investments as Figure 1 in Psacharopoulos's selection implies. However, this argument probably does not work against Psacharopoulos's claim that social returns to investment are greatest for primary education and least for university education. If anything, one would guess that ability bias in estimates of the return to education increases with the level of education, since the extent to which school attendance is compulsory decreases.

One can also argue that earnings differentials *under*estimate the social return to investment in education. People learn from those around them, so if I have an education I improve the learning environment for my co-workers. This positive spillover or "human capital externality" is not captured by the computations behind Figure 1 in Psacharopoulos's selection. Evidence for the existence of such spillovers in the United States is given by James E. Rauch, "Productivity Benefits from Geographic Concentration of Human Capital: Evidence from the Cities," *Journal of Urban Economics* (November 1993). He finds that workers earn more, the higher is the average level of education in their city, controlling for their individual characteristics and other important attributes of the city. Again, the implications of this argument for the relative returns to investments in different levels of education are unclear. If this spillover is most important for learning new technology it may have the greatest impact on the social return to university education.

Comment V.A.2. Education and Development

The World Bank's *Education Sector Policy Paper* (1980) concludes that "studies have shown that economic returns on investment in education seem, in most instances, to exceed returns on alternative kinds of investment, and that developing countries obtain higher returns than the developed ones."

For an extensive bibliography on education and development see Mark Blaug, ed., *Economics of Education,* vols. 1 and 2 (1968, 1969). Several writings by Theodore W. Schultz are highly instructive on the role of education in development: "Capital Formation by Education," *Journal of Political Economy* (December 1960); "Education and Economic Growth," in *Social Forces Influencing American Education,* ed. N. B. Henry (1961); and "Investment in Human Capital in Poor Countries," in *Foreign Trade and Human Capital,* ed. P. D. Zook (1962). "Investment in Human Beings," the special supplement of the *Journal of Political Economy* (October 1962), also contains a number of pertinent papers covering particular aspects of the problem.

For a comprehensive survey of the state of knowledge about the effects of education on income, see Timothy King, ed., "Education and Income," *World Bank Staff Working Paper,* no. 402 (July 1980).

A critique of social cost–benefit analysis in educational planning is offered by G. S. Fields, "Assessing Educational Progress and Commitment," *Report for the U.S. Agency for International Development* (October 1978). See also World Bank, *Education* (1980); Ronald Dore, *The Diploma Disease* (1976); Marcelo Selowsky, "On the Measurement of Education's Contribution to Growth," *Quarterly Journal of Economics* (August 1969); and Dean T. Jamison and Lawrence J. Lau, *Farmer Education and Farm Efficiency* (1981).

Also informative are Marcelo Selowsky, "A Note on Preschool-age Investment in Human Capital in Developing Countries," *Economic Development and Cultural Change* (July 1976); M. R. Rosenzweig and R. E. Evenson, "Fertility, Schooling and the Economic Contribution of Children in Rural India," *Econometrica* (July 1977); George Psacharopoulos, "Returns to Education: An Updated International Comparison," *Comparative Education* (1981); Christopher

Colclough, "The Impact of Primary Schooling on Economic Development: A Review of the Evidence," *World Development* (March 1982); World Bank, *Education in Sub-Saharan Africa* (1988); Lawrence H. Summers, *Investing in All the People,* World Bank, Policy Research Working Paper 905 (May 1992); and Elizabeth M. King and M. Anne Hill, *Women's Education in Developing Countries: Barriers, Benefits and Policies* (1993).

Selection V.A.3. Interpreting Recent Research on Schooling in Developing Countries*

Table 1 summarizes the effects of five educational inputs on student performance in developing countries on the basis of ninety-six studies: teacher-pupil ratio; teacher education, experience, and salary; expenditure per pupil. A more recent review (Velez, Schiefelbein, and Valenzuela 1993) contains a larger number of studies, but the general conclusions are the same. Table 1 shows which inputs have a statistically significant correlation (by sign of coefficient or direction of effect) and which are statistically insignificant. (The insignificant findings, unfortunately, cannot be divided by direction of effect.) In all cases, the reported correlations are those that hold after allowing for differences in the family backgrounds of students and in other educational inputs.

The evidence provides no support for policies to reduce class size. Of the thirty studies investigating teacher-pupil ratios, only eight find statistically significant results supporting smaller classes; an equal number are significant but have the opposite sign; and almost half are statistically insignificant. These findings qualitatively duplicate those in the U.S. studies, but are particularly interesting here. Class sizes in the developing-country studies are considerably more varied than those in the U.S. studies and thus pertain to a wider set of environments, providing even stronger evidence that the enthusiasm for policies to reduce class size is misplaced.

The effect of the teachers' experience yields results that are roughly similar to findings for the United States. Although 35 percent of the studies (sixteen out of forty-six) display significant positive benefits from more teaching experience (the analogous figure for the United States is 29 percent), the majority of the studies—twenty-eight out of forty-six—found this input statistically insignificant.

The results for teacher education, on the other hand, diverge in relative terms from those seen in the U.S. studies, with a majority (thirty-five out of sixty-three) supporting the conventional wisdom that more education for teachers improves student performance. (In the U.S. studies, teachers' education was the least important of all inputs.) Although these results are still surrounded by consid-

erable uncertainty (twenty-six estimates are insignificant and two display significantly negative effects), they do suggest a possible differentiation by stage of development and general level of resources available.

The evidence on teacher salaries in developing countries contains no compelling support for the notion that higher wages yield better teachers. Because these results aggregate studies across different countries, school organizations, and labor markets, however, it is difficult to take these results too far. For policy purposes, one would generally want information on what happens if the entire salary schedule is altered (as opposed to simply moving along a given schedule denominated, say, in experience, education, or some other attribute of teachers). But it is not possible with available studies to distinguish between the two effects.

Data on total expenditure per pupil are rarely available in analyses of developing countries, but the twelve studies that include such estimates are evenly split between statistically significant and statistically insignificant. Given questions about the quality of the underlying data, not too much should be inferred from these findings.

One of the clearest divergences between the findings in developing and industrial countries is the effect of facilities, suggesting that differences in the school environment are of some importance in developing countries. Twenty-two of the thirty-four investigations support the provision of quality buildings and libraries. The specific measures of facilities vary widely, however, so the interpretation almost certainly depends on local conditions.

Several other factors have been investigated in the course of the developing-country analyses, including an assortment of curriculum issues, instructional methods, and teacher training programs. Many of these inputs, however, are difficult to assess here because of the multicountry evidence and the probable importance of local institutions. One input—the provision of textbooks—has received widespread endorsement, although this support is as much for conceptual reasons as for solid empirical ones. The relationship of textbooks and writing materials to student performance is found to be important with reasonable consistency in developing countries, but relatively few studies are available (Lockheed and Hanushek 1988; Lockheed and Verspoor 1991). Investigations of technological or organizational differences have

*From Eric A. Hanushek, "Interpreting Recent Research on Schooling in Developing Countries," *World Bank Research Observer* 10 (August 1995): 230–231, 235–239, 243–244. Reprinted by permission.

Table 1. Summary of Ninety-six Studies on the Estimated Effects of Resources on Education in Developing Countries

Input	Number of studies	Statistically significant		Statistically insignificant
		Positive	Negative	
Teacher-pupil ratio	30	8	8	14
Teacher's education	63	35	2	26
Teacher's experience	46	16	2	28
Teacher's salary	13	4	2	7
Expenditure per pupil	12	6	0	6
Facilities	34	22	3	9

Source: Harbison and Hanushek 1992.

shown mixed results. In three extensive investigations in Nicaragua, Kenya, and Thailand, interactive radio teaching, an approach to "distance education," has been found to be effective in teaching children in sparse settlements in rural areas. This result should not be generalized to all new technologies, however. In particular, there is little evidence at this time to support the widespread introduction of computers (Lockheed and Verspoor 1991). . . .

My own interpretation of existing evidence, based on results for both the United States and developing countries, is that schools differ in important ways, but we cannot describe what causes these differences very well. To take one example, Hanushek and Lavy (1994) investigated differences in the quality of schools across a sample of primary schools in Egypt. We defined school quality implicitly. After allowing for individual differences among students in achievement and in parental education, we labeled schools that had large gains in student achievement in a given year as high-quality schools; those with small gains, low quality. A continuous measure of school quality was developed by looking at growth in student achievement (after considering family and other influences on achievement growth). This exercise found enormous differences in the sixty sample schools. Table 2 shows the variation in the quality of schools by looking at achievement relative to a randomly chosen base school. The worst school shows an average achievement gain that is 62 percent below the base school, while the best school is 30 percent above. These results indicate dramatically that schools do differ in quality and that the difference is enough to be relevant to policymaking.

At the same time, measured attributes of teachers and schools explain only a small portion of these differences. From our estimation, only 16

percent of the variance in school quality is related to teacher attributes (such as education and gender) and school attributes (such as class size and facilities). Although we did not look further, I seriously doubt that adding more detailed measures of resources, or of pedagogy, or of curricular differences would have allowed us to explain the differences much more fully.

A similar approach undertaken in rural Brazil (Harbison and Hanushek 1992) pointed to very similar conclusions: schools show very large differences in their ability to improve student achievement, but these differences are not highly correlated with measured characteristics of teachers and schools.

In short, the findings summarized in table 1 do *not* indicate that schools and teachers are all the same. Large differences exist, even though these differences are not captured by the simple measures commonly employed. Neither, it appears, are they captured by more detailed measures of classroom organization or pedagogical approach. This leads me to conclude that the educational process is very complicated and that we do not understand it very well. We cannot describe what makes a good or bad teacher or a good or bad school. Nor are we likely to be able to describe the educational process very well in the near future. My view is that we should learn to live with that fact: living with it implies finding policies that acknowledge and work within this fundamental ignorance.

Quality Versus Access

A third major aspect of current research relates to the importance of school quality and particularly to the perceived policy tradeoff between quality and access. The traditional concern goes something like this: given limited budgets for schools, and the commonly accepted twin objectives of expanding access and improving quality, policymakers face a particularly unpleasant dilemma. They must choose between expanding the availability of education or providing high-quality schools.

A second way of viewing these policy concerns, while apparently different, is actually quite closely related. Analyses of labor market implications and the rate of return to schooling in developing countries suggest strongly that schooling is a very good investment. A year of schooling typically shows a 25–30 percent real rate of return, which appears noticeably better than that of other investment alternatives. At the same time, school completion rates in low-income countries are very low (Lockheed and Verspoor 1991). These two facts are inconsistent. If education yields such a high rate of return, why are people not taking advantage of it?

Emerging analyses of school quality have something to say about both elements of education policy. I believe that the common conception of a simple tradeoff between access and quality is misleading—if not wrong; and I think that low school quality may frequently be an important explanation for the widespread failure to take advantage of the apparently high returns available from education.

The central theme here is that school quality is directly related to students' decisions about attending school and schools' decisions about promoting students. High-quality schools raise student achievement and speed students through primary (and perhaps secondary) school, thus saving costs. Additionally, students respond to higher school quality with lower dropout rates: they tend to stay in good schools and drop out of poor ones.

Both of these mechanisms indicate a direct relationship between the quantity of schooling attained and the quality of that schooling. Thus, studies of the rate of return to schooling that consider only the quantity of schooling produce a misleading estimate of the potential gains. Estimates of the rate of return to schooling that do not account for quality differences will systematically overstate the productivity gains that are associated with additional years of schooling, because the estimates will include quality differences that are correlated with quantity. The evidence shows that those who do not complete a given level tend to have attended poorer schools. If a policy simply pushes students to stay in school but makes no changes in the fundamental quality of the schools, the new school completers will get only the returns associated with years of schooling and not with quality. Thus, their rate of return on their investment in schooling will not be as high as the estimates suggest.

Table 2. Distribution of Estimated School Quality in Egyptian Primary Schools

Distribution	All schools	Rural	Urban
Mean	−.084	−.111	−.057
Minimum	−.62	−.62	−.52
Maximum	.30	.30	.21

Note: Values indicate the average proportional achievement gain of a school in comparison with that of the arbitrarily chosen base school, Taha Hussein School.
Source: Hanushek and Lavy 1994.

Many countries, concerned about very high grade repetition rates, directly intervene to ensure regular promotion through school (Lockheed and Verspoor 1991), but they typically ignore school quality. Neglecting the quality of schools is a serious mistake. In studying primary school students in the rural northeast of Brazil, Ralph Harbison and I discovered a very direct relationship between what a student knows and the student's promotion probabilities. Students who learn more than the curriculum requires (as measured by specifically designed tests) are significantly more likely to be promoted through primary school than those who do not learn what is expected. Schools, not surprisingly, have an important impact on student achievement. These findings suggest that policies that improve the quality of schools—that is, that enhance student achievement—will simultaneously lead to more rapid progress by students through the grades.

The magnitude of the overall effects of improving school quality, when converted to a monetary metric, is remarkable. Hanushek, Gomes-Neto, and Harbison (1994) summarize the expected savings from two simple policies—improving the availability of textbooks and writing materials (software) or improving components of the facilities (hardware). They show that if $1 is invested in useful resources such as textbooks, an immediate savings of more than $12 is obtained from speeding students through school. (These savings are pure efficiency savings from getting through school more quickly and include none of the increased productivity benefits that typically justify schooling investments; increases in future productivity simply reinforce the efficiency gains.) Where facilities are lacking, each $1 improvement has an expected cost saving of more than $3.

These estimates of the savings that can be expected from quality improvements are subject to some uncertainty. Nonetheless, the lowest plausible savings still indicate substantial efficiency gains from improving the quality of schools. The availability of books and writing materials and school facilities is consistently important for student achievement and promotion.

These results highlight the importance of providing minimal resources for schools and are consistent with previous findings about the importance of basic textbooks, materials, and facilities. But these estimates—as startling as they are—may not represent the largest opportunities and are really lower-bound estimates of the potential for change. Specifically, all the research points to the importance of the teacher. Because the variations in teacher quality appear to be much more important than the variations in software or hardware, the savings from ensuring the former would almost certainly exceed those obtained from improvements in the latter. Unfortunately, because we do not know how to hire particularly effective teachers—nor what it would cost—we cannot calculate straightforward benefit-cost ratios.

Grade repetition is not entirely bad, because students do learn more with each time through the same grade, but it is an expensive way to improve student learning (Gomes-Neto and Hanushek 1994). One alternative explanation is that repetition reflects demand-side factors—that is, student choices that lead to low attendance during each school year. Little is actually known about attendance patterns, but anecdotal evidence suggests that normal crop cycles and requirements for children to work in the fields at planting and harvest times may be important in some settings. Such attendance patterns could severely constrain the chances of completing a given grade, at least in the likely absence of well-integrated, self-paced instruction. Dealing with these issues might require different policies aimed at lessening the current consumption constraints of families. In any event, however, the continued production of low-grade schools is no more effective in the face of such demand-side influences than without them.

In work on Egypt, Hanushek and Lavy (1994) pursue a related question: whether school quality affects students' decisions to drop out. In that analysis, the school quality estimates (Table 2) were included as one of the determinants of the decisions of individual students. Additionally, the analysis considered the students' own achievements and abilities as well as their earnings opportunities outside of school. If we hold achievement and opportunities constant, students going to high-quality schools are much more likely to stay in school than those going to low-quality schools. This makes sense. If a student is not going to get anything out of school, why waste the time?

The magnitude of the effect is particularly important. The primary schools sampled had average dropout rates in 1980 of 9.3 percent. If all the schools were at the quality level of the best one, the dropout rate would fall to 3.2 percent or less, a decline that indicates the huge impact of quality on school attainment.

Research in Brazil and Egypt points to similar conclusions. School quality has large and direct effects on school access and school attainment. These effects are complements, not substitutes, as suggested by the simple budgetary analysis that is commonly employed. And the research in both countries indicates that quality adds a dimension that is extremely important in thinking about schooling in developing countries. Finally, efforts to pursue quality improvement must confront the policy challenges described in the earlier sections. Inefficiency and general lack of knowledge about the production function in education imply that dealing with quality will require new and innovative approaches.

These conclusions are supported in Glewwe and Jacoby (1994), whose work on Ghana shows the direct relationship between school quality and school attainment. Improving the schools (in this case, the facilities) tends to hold students in school longer, other things equal. The authors do not obtain estimates of the total effects of school quality (as was done for Egypt), but the indication that measured effects have this influence confirms the quantity-quality correlation. This correlation in turn confirms the bias in rates of return flowing from analyses that ignore variations in school quality. . . .

Conclusions

The research into the educational process, both in the United States and in the developing world, promises some very distinct payoffs. In policy dimensions, we appear to have learned a great deal. At the same time, the results do not always conform to what was expected. Research conclusively demonstrates an inefficiency in the current organization of schools. Resources are being spent in unproductive ways—ways that do not contribute to improving student performance. Correcting these inefficiencies is not simple. There is no blueprint for a model school that can be reproduced and handed out to policymakers, and such a blueprint is unlikely to be developed in the near future. Instead, we must turn to new organizations and new incentives if we are to improve schools.

Research suggests that the most likely path to

improvement involves the introduction of performance incentives. Although several ways to introduce incentives have been suggested, none has been tried extensively. An extensive and systematic program of experimentation and evaluation is thus in order.

Finally, the evidence underscores the importance of establishing good schools. Although translating this goal into policy will be difficult, there are powerful reasons to believe that providing quality schools should be very high on the policy agenda. The continued expansion of low-quality schools—often thought to be a step on the path both to high access and to high-quality schools—may actually be a self-defeating strategy.

References

Glewwe, Paul, and Hanan Jacoby. 1994. "Student Achievement and Schooling Choice in Low Income Countries: Evidence from Ghana." *Journal of Human Resources* 29(3):841–64.

Gomes-Neto, João Batista, and Eric A. Hanushek. 1994. "Causes and Consequences of Grade Repetition: Evidence from Brazil." *Economic Development and Cultural Change* 43(1):117–48.

Hanushek, Eric A., João Batista Gomes-Neto, and Ralph W. Harbison. 1994. "Self-financing Educational Investments: The Quality Imperative in Developing Countries." University of Rochester, Department of Economics, Rochester, N.Y. Processed.

Hanushek, Eric A., and Victor Lavy. 1994. *School Quality, Achievement Bias, and Dropout Behavior in Egypt.* Living Standards Measurement Study Working Paper 107. Washington, D.C.: World Bank.

Harbison, Ralph W., and Eric A. Hanushek. 1992. *Educational Performance of the Poor: Lessons from Rural Northeast Brazil.* New York: Oxford University Press.

Lockheed, Marlaine E., and Eric A. Hanushek. 1988. "Improving Educational Efficiency in Developing Countries: What Do We Know?" *Compare* 18(1):21–38.

Lockheed, Marlaine E., and Adriaan Verspoor. 1991. *Improving Primary Education in Developing Countries.* New York: Oxford University Press.

Velez, Eduardo, Ernesto Schiefelbein, and Jorge Valenzuela. 1993. "Factors Affecting Achievement in Primary Education." HROWP Working Paper 2. World Bank, Department of Human Resources Development and Operations Policy, Washington, D.C.

Selection V.A.4. Schooling Quality in a Cross Section of Countries*

... The education production function that relates test scores to inputs in a broad panel of countries can be specified as follows:

$$Q_{ijt} = \alpha_{ijt} + \beta_1 * F_t + \beta_2 * R_t + \varepsilon_{ijt} \qquad (1)$$

where Q_{ijt} denotes test scores of subject i (mathematics, science, and reading) for students of age group j (10- and 14-year-olds) in year t (1964, 1970–72, 1982–83, 1984, and 1990–91); F_t denotes family factors (income and schooling) in year t; R_t denotes school resources (pupil-teacher ratio, average teacher salary, educational expenditure per pupil, school length) in year t; and ε_{ijt} denotes unmeasured factors influencing school quality. The panel consists of a system of 13 equations. The system is estimated by the seemingly-unrelated-regression (SUR) technique. This procedure allows for different error variances in each equation and for correlation of these errors across the equations. We allow for different constant terms in each equation but assume that the slope coefficients are the same for each input measure. The regressions apply to a total of 214 observations. Each equation has a varying number of observations depending to the availability of test-score data.

Column 1 of Table 1 presents the results of the basic regression. The results show the strong effects of family inputs on student achievement. The positive coefficient on the log of per capita GDP (3.41, t = 3.20) confirms that school children from higher income countries tend to achieve higher test scores, holding fixed other factors that influence student achievement. This result suggests that parents' income has a strong positive effect on children's academic performance. The estimated coefficient implies that a one-standard-deviation increase in the log of per capita GDP (by 0.9 in 1990) raises test scores by 3.1 percentage points.

The average educational level, entered in the form of average years of primary school attainment for adults aged 25 and above, has a significantly positive effect on test scores. The estimated coefficient on the schooling variable (1.35, t = 4.90) indicates that a one-standard-deviation increase in average years of primary schooling (by 1.7 years in 1990) is estimated to raise test scores by 2.3 percentage points. Hence, this result sug-

gests that parents' education has an important positive effect on the children's test scores.[1]

The regression also includes three measures of school resources—pupil-teacher ratio, the log of public educational expenditure per pupil, and the log of the average salary of primary school teachers. The pupil-teacher ratio has a negative relation with test scores, confirming that smaller classes are better for pupil achievement. The estimated coefficient (–0.22, t = 2.54) implies that a one-standard-deviation decrease in the pupil-teacher ratio (by 12.3 in 1990) raises test scores by 2.7 percentage points.

The log of the average salary of primary school teachers has a positive and significant relation with test scores. However, the log of total educational spending per student is insignificant (with a negative sign). Since the three school-resource variables—school spending per pupil, average salary of teachers, and the pupil-teacher ratio—are highly correlated, it is difficult to separate their effects.[2] However, a chi-square test for the three variables together has a p-value of 0.00. Therefore, there is a clear overall indication that more school resources produce better student outcomes.

The regression in column 1 of Table 1 also includes the length of the school term as a measure of the intensity of education. This variable turns out to be insignificant.

Column 2 of Table 1 includes a regional dummy for the East Asian countries.[3] This dummy variable has a large and significant coefficient (3.6, t = 3.6). Therefore, a major component of East Asia's academic performance is left unexplained by the family and school inputs that were included in the re-

---

[1] The average years of schooling variable is interpreted as education of parents, but it can also reflect education of teachers. Thus, the regression result may indicate that education of teachers, as well as parents, is important for children's achievement.

[2] Because the regression includes four school variables—teacher-pupil ratio, teacher salary, education spending, and school length—, the effect of each variable on test scores may reflect shifts of expenditure among categories, rather than the direct effect of more spending in one category. For example, the estimated coefficient on the teacher-pupil ratio indicates the effect on student achievement of smaller class sizes when total educational spending is held fixed. Regressions without the total education spending variable reveal slightly smaller effects of the teacher-pupil ratio and teachers' salary on test scores, but maintain all the same qualitative results.

[3] The East Asian dummy indicates East and Southeast Asia geographical region. The seven countries in our sample include Hong Kong, Indonesia, Singapore, Korea, the Philippines, Taiwan, and Thailand.

---

*From Jong-Wha Lee and Robert J. Barro, "Schooling Quality in a Cross-Section of Countries," National Bureau of Economic Research Working Paper No. 6198 (September 1997), pp. 22–25, 27–29, tables 3 and 6. Reprinted by permission.

Table 1. Regressions for Test Scores

Independent variable	(1)	(2)
log(GDP per capita)	3.41 (3.20)	3.43 (3.43)
Primary Education of Adults	1.35 (4.90)	1.18 (4.56)
Pupil-Teacher Ratio	−0.22 (2.54)	−0.21 (2.53)
log(Average teacher salary)	2.88 (2.09)	2.19 (1.66)
log(Educ. expend. per pupil)	−1.34 (1.13)	−0.30 (0.26)
Length of School Days	0.003 (0.14)	−0.02 (0.93)
Dummy for East Asia		3.61 (3.57)

Exam	R^2 (number of observations)	
Math, 1964, age 14	−0.16 (11)	−0.24 (11)
Math, 1982, age 14	0.10 (15)	0.11 (15)
Math, 1990, age 10	−0.57 (12)	−0.29 (12)
Math, 1990, age 14	0.24 (18)	0.27 (18)
Science, 1970, age 10	0.54 (14)	0.53 (14)
Science, 1970, age 14	0.50 (16)	0.51 (16)
Science, 1984, age 10	0.18 (15)	0.14 (15)
Science, 1984, age 14	0.34 (17)	0.27 (17)
Science, 1990, age 10	−0.19 (12)	0.15 (12)
Science, 1990, age 14	0.11 (17)	0.21 (17)
Reading, 1970, age 10	0.74 (12)	0.73 (12)
Reading, 1990, age 14	0.66 (29)	0.73 (29)
Reading, 1990, age 10	0.47 (26)	0.54 (26)

Notes: The system has 13 equations, where the dependent variables are the scores on internationally comparable tests in mathematics, science, and reading in various years for the students aged 10 or 14. Each equation has a different constant term (not shown). Absolute values of t-statistics are reported in parentheses. The R^2 values and number of observations apply to each equation individually.

Estimation is by the SUR technique. The estimation allows for different error variances in each equation and for correlation of these errors across equations.

gressions. Also, the log of teacher salary is no longer significant in column 2, but the pupil-teacher ratio remains negative and significant.

The significance of the East Asian dummy may reflect the existence of an "Asian value," which is broadly defined by the cultural and religious features unique to the East Asian countries (see Stevenson [1992, 1993] and *Economist* [1996]). In East Asia, parents tend to provide strong support for children's education. Children are often sent to cramming schools in the evening to supplement their regular classes. (In this sense, the reported figures on educational spending and school length are an underestimate of the true values.) Also, in the Confucian tradition, teachers in East Asia receive considerably more respect and prestige than do those in other societies.

The regressions in Table 1 restrict the slope coefficients for each explanatory variable to be the same in each equation. That is, the effect of a variable such as per capita GDP is the same regardless of the subject area and the age group of students who take the test. . . .

Dropout and Repetition Rates

Table 2 shows results for the two other indicators of school outcomes: the repetition and dropout rates.[4] The forms of these regressions parallel those for test scores in Table 1. Columns 1 and 3 of Table 2 show that the repetition and dropout rates are each significantly negatively related to the two family variables, the log of per capita GDP and the primary education of adults.[5] These results parallel those for test scores; that is, richer and better educated adults appear to generate children who perform better on all three measures of school performance.

With respect to school inputs, the pupil-teacher

[4]The regressions are based on the complete data set of primary repetition and dropout rates at five-year intervals from 1970 to 1990. If the number for the five-year value was missing, then we used the observed value for the nearest year; for example, we would use a value for 1980 to represent 1975. For a few countries, we interpolated to fill in missing values.

[5]Secondary schooling variable is insignificant in the regressions when included as an additional explanatory variable.

Table 2. Regressions for School Repetition and Dropout Rates

Independent variable	(1)	(2)	(3)	(4)
log(GDP per capita)	−2.18 (2.52)	−2.17 (2.56)	−4.90 (2.27)	−5.13 (2.28)
Primary Education of Adults	−1.11 (3.63)	−0.96 (3.15)	−2.29 (2.76)	−2.40 (2.89)
Pupil-Teacher Ratio	0.16 (3.58)	0.15 (3.38)	0.34 (2.66)	0.30 (2.30)
log(Average teacher salary)	−0.02 (0.01)	−0.38 (0.37)	−4.29 (1.55)	−3.76 (1.36)
log(Educ. expend. per pupil)	0.15 (0.14)	−0.35 (0.32)	−0.03 (0.01)	−0.54 (0.18)
Length of School Days	−0.08 (3.50)	−0.07 (2.93)	−0.08 (1.13)	−0.06 (0.83)
East Asia		−4.39 (3.21)		−8.07 (1.93)
Year	R^2 (number of observations)			
1970	0.41 (64)	0.48 (64)	0.46 (71)	0.49 (71)
1975	0.32 (68)	0.36 (68)	0.45 (72)	0.44 (72)
1980	0.43 (74)	0.46 (74)	0.48 (73)	0.49 (73)
1985	0.45 (66)	0.49 (66)	0.49 (68)	0.50 (68)
1990	0.53 (65)	0.55 (65)	0.42 (62)	0.43 (62)

Notes: The systems have five equations corresponding to 1970, 1975, 1980, 1985 and 1990. The dependent variable in columns 1 and 2 is the primary school repetition rate. In columns 3 and 4, the dependent variable is the school dropout rate. Each equation has a different constant term (not shown). Absolute values of t-statistics are reported in parentheses. The R^2 values and number of observations apply to each equation individually.

Estimation is by the SUR technique. The estimation allows for different error variances in each equation and for correlation of these errors across equations.

ratio is significantly positive for the repetition and dropout rates in columns 1 and 3 of Table 2. These results again parallel those for test scores; a lower ratio of pupils to teachers is estimated to improve all three indicators of educational outcomes. Two other input measures—the log of average teacher salary and the log of educational spending per pupil—are not significantly related to the repetition and dropout rates. However, the estimated coefficient of the log of average teacher salary is negative and marginally significant for the school dropout rate in column 3 of Table 2. The results for test scores are basically similar, with a weak indication that higher teacher salaries are associated with better performance.

The length of the school year is significantly negative for the repetition rate in column 1 of Table 2 and is negative but not significant for the dropout rate in column 3. However, the overall association between school length and test scores in Table 1 is essentially nil.

Finally, the East Asian dummy variable is significantly negative for the repetition and dropout rates in columns 2 and 4 of Table 2. These findings parallel those for test scores in column 2 of Table

1. That is, the East Asian region does better on all three measures of school performance, even after holding constant the family variables and the measures of school inputs.

Overall, the three indicators of school performance—international test scores, repetition rates, and dropout rates—yield a similar picture in regard to the roles of family factors and school inputs. The general pattern is that family influences (in the sense of richer and better educated parents) and school inputs (especially smaller class sizes but probably also higher teacher salaries and greater school length) enhance educational outcomes.

References

Economist (1996), "Asia's Educational Edge," September 21.

Stevenson, W. Harold (1992), "Learning from Asian Schools," *Scientific American,* 267, December, 70–76.

Stevenson, W. Harold, Chuansheng Chen and Shin-Ying Lee (1993), "Mathematics Achievement of Chinese, Japanese, and American Children: Ten Years Later," *Science,* 259, January, 53–58.

Selection V.A.5. Creating Human Capital*

Figures 1 and 2 present a stylized summary of the results of regressing primary and secondary enrollment rates on per capita national income for more than 90 developing economies for the years 1965 and 1987. Enrollment rates are higher at higher levels of per capita income. But the HPAE's [high-performing Asian economics] enrollment rates have tended to be higher than predicted for their level of income. At the primary level, this was most obvious in 1965, when Hong Kong, Korea, and Singapore had already achieved universal primary education, well ahead of other developing economies, and even Indonesia with its vast population had a primary enrollment rate above 70 percent. By 1987, East Asia's superior education systems were evident at the secondary level. Indonesia had a secondary enrollment rate of 46 percent, well above other economies with roughly the same level of income, and Korea had moved from 35 to 88 percent, maintaining its large lead in relative performance. Only in Thailand was the 28 percent secondary enrollment rate well below the income-predicted 36 percent and the 54 percent mean for middle-income economies. In recent years Thailand's weak educational performance has been felt, as serious shortages of educated workers have begun to threaten continued very rapid growth. . . .

Policies that Promoted Human Capital Formation

Higher shares of national income devoted to education cannot fully explain the larger accumulation of human capital in the HPAEs. In both 1960 and 1989, public expenditure on education as a percentage of GNP was not much higher in East Asia than elsewhere (see table 1). In 1960 the share was 2.2 percent for all developing economies, 2.4 percent for Sub-Saharan Africa, and 2.5 percent for East Asia. During the three decades that followed, the governments of East Asia markedly increased the share of national output they invested in formal education, but so did governments in other developing regions. In 1989 the share in Sub-Saharan Africa, 4.1 percent, was higher than the East Asian share, 3.7 percent,

which barely exceeded the average share for all developing economies, 3.6 percent.

Nor were initial conditions, for example the colonial legacy, decisive. While Korea did have much higher enrollment rates in 1950 than most developing economies, subsequent increases in primary and secondary enrollment rates account for Korea's present wide lead in enrollments over other middle-income economies. A comparison of Indonesia, a success story, and Pakistan, a laggard, is also illustrative. In 1987 Indonesia had achieved universal primary enrollment and a 48 percent secondary enrollment rate. By contrast, Pakistan's enrollment rates were 52 percent at the primary level and 19 percent at the secondary level. What proportion of these gaps is due to initial conditions? At the primary level, Indonesia increased its enrollment rate by nearly 80 percentage points since 1950, while Pakistan managed an increase of only 34 percentage points, implying that most of the current gap is explained by the pace of increase rather than initial conditions. For secondary schooling, Pakistan's enrollment rate in 1950 was actually higher than Indonesia's; all of the current gap is explained by the rates of increase during the past thirty-seven years.

Primary and Secondary Education. The allocation of public expenditure between basic and higher education is the major public policy factor that accounts for East Asia's extraordinary performance with regard to the quantity of basic education provided. The share of public expenditure on education allocated to basic education has been consistently higher in East Asia than elsewhere. Korea and Venezuela provide an extreme example that nicely illustrates the point. Table 2 indicates that in 1985 Venezuela allocated 43 percent of its education budget to higher education; by contrast, in the same year Korea allocated only 10 percent of its budget to higher education. Public expenditure on education as a percentage of GNP was actually higher in Venezuela (4.3) than in Korea (3.0). After subtracting the share going to higher education, however, public expenditure available for basic education as a percentage of GNP was considerably higher in Korea (2.5) than in Venezuela (1.3). Box 1 shows how Indonesia's emphasis on primary education, contrasted with Bolivia's relative neglect of primary schooling, is reflected in rural educational opportunities.

The share of public funds allocated to tertiary

*From World Bank, "Creating Human Capital and Policies that Promoted Human Capital Formation," *The East Asian Miracle: Economic Growth and Public Policy* (Washington, D.C.: The World Bank, 1993), pp. 43–46, 198–201. Reprinted by permission.

Figure 1. Cross-Economy Regression for Primary Enrollment Rates, 1965 and 1987

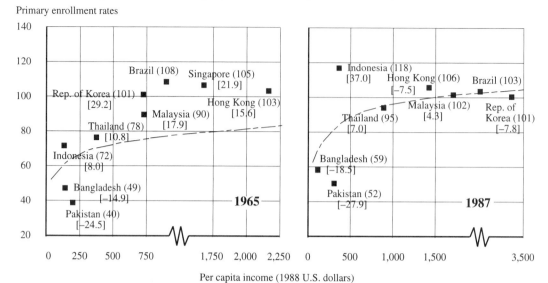

Note: Figures in parentheses are enrollment rates; bracketed numbers show residuals.
Source: Behrman and Schneider (1992).

Figure 2. Cross-Economy Regression for Secondary Enrollment Rates, 1965 and 1987

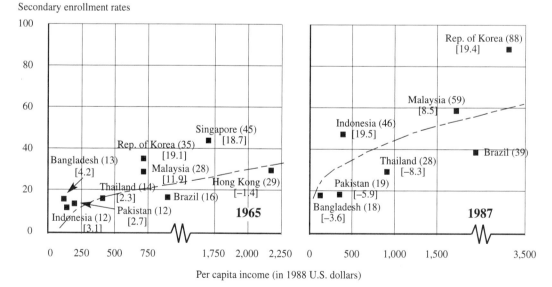

Note: Figures in parentheses are enrollment rates; bracketed numbers show residuals.
Source: Behrman and Schneider (1992).

Table 1. Public Expenditure on Education as a Percentage of GNP

Economy/region	1960	1989
HPAEs		
Hong Kong	—	2.8
Korea, Rep. of	2.0	3.6
Singapore	2.8	3.4
Malaysia	2.9	5.6
Thailand	2.3	3.2
Indonesia[a]	2.5	0.9
Average[b]	2.5	3.7
Other		
Brazil	1.9	3.7
Pakistan	1.1	2.6
Less developed economies[c]	1.3	3.1
Sub-Saharan Africa	2.4	4.1

—Not available

[a]Alternative sources of data indicate that expenditure on public education as a percentage of GDP was 3.0 percent in Indonesia in 1989.

[b]Average does not include Indonesia.

[c]Low- and middle-income economies.

Source: UNDP (1991).

education in East Asia has tended to be low, averaging roughly 15 percent during the past three decades. In Latin America the share has been roughly 24 percent. In South Asia, the share is close to the Latin American level. This had been the case in Sub-Saharan Africa as well, but in recent years the share has declined to East Asian levels.

By giving priority to expanding the primary and secondary bases of the educational pyramid, East Asian governments have stimulated the demand for higher education, while relying to a large extent on the private sector to satisfy that demand. In all developing regions the probability of going to university is markedly higher for secondary school graduates from high- than from low-income families. Typically, in low- and middle-income economies government subsidies of university education are not related to need, implying that they benefit families with relatively high incomes that

Table 2. Allocation of Education Budgets, 1985

Economy	Public expenditure on education as a percentage of GNP	Public expenditure on basic education as a percentage of GNP	Percentage of education budget allocated to higher education	Percentage of education budget allocated to basic education
Hong Kong	2.8	1.9	25.1	69.3
Indonesia[a]	2.3	2.0	9.0	89.0
Korea, Rep. of	3.0	2.5	10.3	83.9
Malaysia	7.9	5.9	14.6	74.9
Singapore	5.0	3.2	30.7	64.6
Thailand	3.2	2.6	12.0	81.3
Venezuela	4.3	1.3	43.4	31.0

[a]Alternative sources of data indicate that in Indonesia public expenditure on education as a percentage of GDP was 3.3 in 1984–85 and 4.3 in 1985–86, and that the percentage of the education budget allocated to basic education was 81 in 1984–85 and 80 in 1985–86.

Row percentages do not add up to 100 since three of the categories into which educational funding is channeled—pre-primary, other types, and not distributed—have not been included in this table.

Source: Column 1, UNDP (1990); columns 2 and 3, UNESCO (1989).

Box 1 Spending on the Kids: Primary Education in Bolivia and Indonesia

The impact of differing spending priorities within education budgets is starkly evident in a comparison of primary schools in Bolivia and Indonesia. Both economies are at roughly similar levels of development, and both have predominantly rural populations, national illiteracy rates of about 20 percent, and social and cultural factors that hinder the education of girls. Moreover, the proportion of national resources devoted to education at all levels is roughly similar. Bolivia has an annual per capita GNP of about $650; Indonesia, $610. Both spend 2.3 percent of their GDP on education. But while Bolivia devotes only 41 percent of its education budget to primary schools, Indonesia spends nearly 90 percent on basic education.

The resulting differences are striking. In Bolivia, the education system officially covers only 60 percent of children. But even that low figure overstates educational attainment. Only 45 percent of rural schools provide education through the fifth grade; the remainder, mostly in remote areas, offer only three years of instruction. Repetition and dropout rates are high, especially for girls, and only one in ten children has a textbook. Partly because of inadequate resources, teacher training is poor, and administrative corruption is widespread.

Indonesia, by contrast, has deliberately focused resources on primary education, to good effect. Beginning in 1974 with a massive school construction drive, and continuing in 1978 with the abolition of primary school fees, the government endeavored to make primary education available to all children. By 1987, 91 percent of children in rural areas were enrolled in primary school, only slightly less than the 92 percent enrolled nationwide. With near universal education, the gender gap in enrollments has disappeared. While dropout and repetition rates are higher in the countryside than in the cities, and large regional gaps in enrollment ratios and illiteracy rates persist, the focus on primary education has been an effective way to make the most of limited education resources.

Like other developing economies, Indonesia must balance the desire to fund more intermediate and advanced education against the reality that stretching education budgets means less for the lower grades. In 1987, the government expanded free education, which had previously covered up to the sixth grade, to include up to the ninth grade. Educational quality declined, however, and the government has since identified improvement of primary schooling as a key educational objective.

Sources: World Bank (1990; internal World Bank reports).

could afford to pay fees closer to the actual cost of schooling.

At the same time, in many economies, Brazil and Kenya being notable examples, low public funding of secondary education results in poorly qualified children from low-income backgrounds being forced into the private sector or entirely out of the education system. Because of the higher concentration on basic education in East Asia, public funds for education are more likely to benefit children of low-income families who might otherwise have difficulty remaining in school.

References

Behrman, Jere R., and Ryan Schneider. 1992. "An International Perspective on Schooling Investment in the Last Quarter Century in Some Fast-Growing Eastern and Southeastern Countries." Background paper for *The East Asian Miracle*. World Bank, Policy Research Department, Washington, D.C.

UNESCO. Various years. *Statistical Yearbook*. Paris.

UNDP (United Nations Development Programme). 1991. *Human Development Report*. New York: Oxford University Press.

World Bank. 1990. *Indonesia: Strategy for a Sustained Reduction in Poverty*. Washington, D.C.

V.B. POPULATION

Note V.B.1. The Size of the World's Population and the Size of the Average Family

Recently a growing "revisionist" literature has contradicted the commonly accepted view that rapid population growth is a hindrance to development. Especially influential was a report by the National Research Council of the National Academy of Sciences (1986), which identifies positive as well as negative impacts of population growth and claims that the net impact cannot be determined given current evidence.

The revisionist view has gained credence in part from the failed predictions of many non-economists (and a few economists) of dire consequences from an expanding world population. These predictions included famines and metal and mineral shortages. In fact, both food and metal and mineral prices fell between 1960 and 1995, and food production per person climbed steadily during the same period (*Economist* 1997). The rise in metal and mineral prices during the 1960s and early 1970s stimulated conservation, invention of substitute materials, and successful new exploration. Continued improvement in agricultural technology, practices, and infrastructure increased the supply of food. There is, however, reason to be less sanguine about the impact of an expanding world population on unpriced resources such as clean air (see Selection X.1).

One of the arguments in favor of a large world population is that it increases the worldwide rate of technological progress. This argument has been formalized in the endogenous growth literature. For example, Kremer (1993, p. 681) "constructs a highly stylized model in which each person's chance of being lucky or smart enough to invent something is independent of population, all else equal, so that the growth rate of technology is proportional to total population." Robinson and Srinivasan (1997, p. 1262) phrase the argument as, "larger populations have more geniuses, and . . . presumably, there are increasing returns to geniuses." The basis of this presumption is that ideas are "nonrival," in contrast to most goods and services: the use of an idea by one person does not make it more difficult for another person to use the idea, but when one person eats a peach another person cannot eat it as well.

The case for efforts to slow population growth through family planning programs, for example, is much stronger when we examine the microeconomic impact of large family size than when we focus on the macroeconomic impact of a large world population. Put simply, it is harder for parents to find the time and resources to educate a large family than a small one. Although the mechanisms through which education contributes to economic development are in dispute, there is little doubt that education is essential to development. Concerning the worldwide rate of technological progress, the World Bank (1984) points out that "ideas may be lost and Einsteins go undiscovered if many children receive little schooling." The selection we have chosen for this section focuses on the effects of family size on educational attainment and health, and on the determinants of fertility (births per woman), the most important factor in family size.

References

The Economist. 1997. "Plenty of Gloom." *The Economist* 345 (December 20): 19–21.

Kremer, Michael. 1993. "Population Growth and Technological Change: One Million B.C. to 1990." *Quarterly Journal of Economics* 108 (August): 681–716.

National Research Council. 1986. *Population Growth and Economic Development: Policy Questions* (Washington, D. C.: National Academy Press).

Robinson, James A., and T. N. Srinivasan. 1997. "Long-Term Consequences of Population Growth: Technological Change, Natural Resources, and the Environment." In Mark R. Rosenzweig and Oded Stark, eds., *Handbook of Population and Family Economics* (Amsterdam: Elsevier).

World Bank. 1984. *World Development Report 1984* (New York: Oxford University Press).

Selection V.B.1. Economic Approaches to Population Growth*

Health and Education

There is substantial evidence that children from large families have lower educational attainment and reduced levels of health, in developed as well as developing countries.[1] Though many studies have inadequate controls for parents' income and education, there is some evidence that the negative association is greater at lower levels of family income, and pertains especially after four children.[2] Since families in poor countries have on average lower income and higher family size than families in rich countries, in poor countries the negative association of large family size and reduced health and education of children, will have greater weight in the population as a whole.

However, the strong cross-section association should not be interpreted necessarily as a causal one—of family size on health and education. It is possible that parents decide jointly and simultaneously on both the number of children to have and the size of their parental investment in child health and education. Low income, low returns to education and health investments, and reasonable concern about their own long-term security could lead parents to choose simultaneously both large numbers of children and low investments per child. Thus, an exogenous shock which reduced the number of children—for example the unexpected death of a child—would not necessarily raise parental investments in the health and education of remaining children, in the absence of other changes in the family's environment.

The question thus arises whether parents consciously trade off more children against higher inputs per child, deciding jointly on the quantity and "quality" of children and viewing these as substitutes, or whether they invest in children taking the number as given. The question is an important one for policy. If there is a quantity–quality tradeoff, and parents are not "altruistic" toward their children, that is they do not incorporate into their own utility that of their children, then the negative rela-

tion of large families with children's health and education may signal a negative intertemporal externality (arising perhaps because parents do not believe they can capture the returns on investing in their children's health and education)—a market failure which could justify public intervention to discourage high fertility. But if parents are altruistic, then efforts to force parents into higher investments in child health and education through certain kinds of interventions, such as quantitative restrictions on numbers of children or imposition of mandatory school attendance, could simply reduce overall family welfare.[3] From a welfare point of view it is reasonable to assume, except in the case of "unwanted" children, that parents have another child only when they feel that the benefits of an additional child to the family as a whole, including to the children already born, exceed the costs.

Governments have generally taken the view that parents are altruistic (or at least that if they are not, they still retain total rights over their own reproductive lives), and that the decision regarding family size should be left to parents. The most widespread form of population policy is public support for family planning programs, justified as a means to assist parents avoid unwanted children for whom the private costs would add to any social costs of additional births. If some children are unwanted, then even altruistic parents must in effect take the number of children as given, and are forced into sequential decision-making and possibly lower investments in child health and education than they would otherwise have made. In a few countries, especially in Asia (where governments view the social costs of high fertility as substantially above the private costs), government spending on family planning is also justified to provide information and "education" to parents about the likely effects of their own high fertility on the health and education of their own children.

The best evidence that unwanted births do reduce parental investments in children is from a study of the effects of twins on children's school enrollment in India. Rosenzweig and Wolpin (1980) posit that the birth of twins is likely in at least some cases to constitute the exogenous imposition of an "unwanted" child; they report that children from families in which the most recent birth

*From Nancy Birdsall, "Economic Approaches to Population Growth," in Hollis Chenery and T. N. Srinivasan, eds., *Handbook of Development Economics, Volume I* (Amsterdam: North-Holland, 1988), 497–499, 514–521. Reprinted by permission.

[1]Work on the consequences of high fertility for child health and development has been largely the domain of psychologists, public health specialists and demographers. See Blake (1983) and Maine and McNamara (1985). For an economic view, see Birdsall and Griffin (1988).

[2]Birdsall (1980). See also studies cited in Birdsall (1977).

[3]A whole range of pricing policies could distort parental demand for the number and "quality" of children.

was of twins were significantly less likely to be in school. Here the causal link—from an exogeneously-imposed extra birth to less child schooling—can easily be inferred. The implication is that the elimination of unwanted births, through for example a reduction in the cost of family planning, would raise average education levels among children. . . .

Female Education, Labor Force Participation, and Wages

There is some evidence that at low levels of education (e.g. between zero and three or four years), education's effect on fertility is positive [Cochrane (1979)]. This may be due to an increase in fecundity (supply of children) as education increases from very low levels in populations in which fertility is initially below desired fertility, as posited in the synthesis model. It may be that more education is associated with higher income (a variable often missing from studies Cochrane cites), and that the higher income is having a positive effect on fertility (by increasing fecundity or increasing the demand for children), without any offsetting change in a woman's shadow price of time (especially in the largely illiterate populations where this positive effect tends to obtain).

Female education above about four years, however, bears one of the strongest and most consistent negative relationships to fertility. Its negative effect is consistent with the price of time effect postulated in the household model, with a "taste" effect of education on a desire for fewer, more educated children postulated in the synthesis model, and with an efficiency effect, operating through a woman's improved efficiency in the use of contraception. Female education is also associated with a higher age at marriage, and may well have some intangible effect on a woman's ability to plan and on her taste for non-familial activities.

Distinguishing empirically among the postulated mechanisms by which education reduces fertility is difficult. For women who work, the wage rate in theory represents the price of time; but labor supply is endogenous to the fertility decision, and high labor supply and low fertility could result from the taste effect as well as the price of time effect of education. Using U.S. data, Rosenzweig and Seiver (1982) and Rosenzweig and Schultz (1985) have shown that at least part of the education effect operates through greater efficiency in contraceptive use. Rosenzweig and Schultz demonstrate that the efficiency effect operates through more effective use by educated women of

relatively ineffective methods (and their greater ability to decipher information about their own fecundity). Since education's effect is partly one of information-processing, schooling and birth control information programs are substitutes as public programs to encourage low fertility (and both are substitutes for birth control services). (No comparable studies using developing country data are known to this author. Insofar as birth control information is less available in developing countries, the efficiency effect of education may well be critical.)

Female education is also associated with entry by women into the formal market, especially into jobs in the modern sector. Participation in the labor market is negatively associated with fertility only for women in relatively high-wage modern sector jobs. Though there may be a causal effect of work in the formal labor market on fertility, virtually no studies in developing countries have allowed for the simultaneity of the fertility and labor supply decisions—for example, the possibility that women who have few children due to low fecundity decide to work more.[4] The identification problem in a simultaneous model is severe, since most factors that influence labor supply would also influence fertility.[5] Jobs outside the modern sector—in agriculture, cottage industry and so on—which do not take women far from the household and allow flexible hours, do not increase the time cost of raising children and are not associated with low fertility.[6]

As female education and female wages rise, the differential between female and child wages widens. This in itself tends to reduce fertility, since it means that the family's loss of the mother's income when children are young is not easily and quickly made up by children's work.

Child Schooling (the "Quality" of Children)

Though the effect of changing prices for child quality on quantity of children is a fundamental idea in the household demand model, only a few

---

[4]But see McCabe and Rosenzweig (1976).

[5]Fertility but not labor supply would be affected by the price of contraceptives. As Rosenzweig and Wolpin (1980) point out, in estimating a labor supply equation, if the only source of variation in fertility not due to preferences is the price of contraceptives, two-stage least squares in a simultaneous equations model is redundant. The contraceptive price variable should simply be included in a reduced-form labor supply equation.

[6]See Standing (1983) for a review of the literature on fertility and female labor force participation.

studies have rigorously explored this cross-price effect, i.e. the hypothesis that a decline in the price of child schooling (or child health) will reduce fertility. . . . Rosenzweig and Wolpin (1982) show that in India, households in villages with a school have, all other things the same, lower fertility than households in villages without a school. (They also confirm the converse cross-price effect.) Their study is a classic in its demonstration of the use of simple reduced-form ordinary least squares regressions to test the effects of various governmental interventions (more schools, more family planning) on various outcomes—direct own-price effects and indirect cross-price effects. In a subsequent study using the same Indian data, Rosenzweig (1982) shows that farm households more intensively exposed to (exogenous) new agricultural technologies have lower fertility and higher child schooling, similarly implying an alteration in the household's allocation of resources between child quantity and quality in the face of exogenous price changes.

Family Income and Income Distribution

In studies controlling for parents' education and taking into account the endogeneity of family income [e.g. Kelley (1980)], income has a positive effect on fertility.[7] This positive effect is consistent with the pure income effect of the household demand model,[8] and with the increased fecundity or supply of births postulated when income rises in low income households in the synthesis model. Within the same socioeconomic group, e.g. among small farmers, higher income parents also tend to have more children,[9] and in industrial countries, income growth in the short run is associated with higher fertility (e.g. in the United States in the 1950s). In the long run, however, income growth tends to be offset by social changes that reduce fertility—such as rising education, so that people with more income want and have fewer children.

As a result, the association of income and fertility tends to vary according to absolute levels of income. Below some minimum income, increases in income are associated with higher fertility. In the poorest countries of Africa and South Asia, many families are below that threshold. Above that

threshold, further increases in income are associated with lower fertility—for a given increase in income, the reduction is greater for low-income groups. Raising the incomes of the rich (be it of rich countries or of rich groups within countries) reduces fertility less than does raising the incomes of the poor. There is, however, no good evidence that the distribution of income has an independent effect on fertility; it is influential only to the extent that poor households usually have higher absolute incomes if their share of the total is higher.

Markets and Old-Age Security

An important feature of development is that markets enlarge and diversify. Contacts and kin begin to matter less as guarantors of jobs and help with the harvest; children begin to matter less as a form of old-age security. Children's greater geographical mobility in an expanding labor market makes them less dependable as a form of old-age support; at the same time, an expanding capital market means other instruments for old-age security, including private savings and social insurance, emerge.

The household and synthesis models of fertility emphasize the importance to fertility decline of increases in the relative costs of children, especially the time costs as women's education and wages increase and as the market for women's labor expands [see also Lindert (1980, 1983)]. Cain (1981, 1983), however, has criticized the failure of empirical studies based on these models to take into account the pension value of children as security in old age in societies where land and capital markets are poor and means of accumulation other than children are limited.[10] He examines, for example, the near-total reliance of women in societies such as Bangladesh on their sons' support should they be widowed, as an explanation of persistent high fertility that pertains irrespective of the rearing costs of children.

Williamson (1985) incorporates the effect of a poor capital market and an expanding labor market in a study of fertility decline in nineteenth-century England. He notes the importance of "default risk," i.e. the probability that adult children will

---

[7]Kelley shows that use of ordinary least squares, rather than two-stage least squares with income endogenous, produces a non-significant coefficient on income in a fertility regression.

[8]For a full discussion see Simon (1977).

[9]World Bank (1984, p. 108).

[10]Rosenzweig and Wolpin (1985) argue that Cain's approach requires an assumption of a poor capital and land market, but that in fact, the apparent absence of such markets (e.g. of land sales) may itself be simply a manifestation of an optimal implicit contract across generations which maximizes the gains from farm-specific knowledge; older people in effect trade information they have on own-farm characteristics, for support from children.

emigrate from rural areas, and thus leave the parents' household just as they become a net economic benefit at the margin, both to the net cost of a child and to a child's pension value.[11] Using data from nineteenth-century England on rural emigration rates, he shows that rising rates throughout the period reduced the present value of rural male children to parents (but not female children) by about 18 percent of farm wages (using a 5 percent discount rate).[12] The emigration rate matters only if remittances from absent children to parents were small; Williamson notes there is little evidence of remittances, and that capital markets that might have eased transfers were poor. His emphasis on the importance of rural emigration in explaining fertility decline thus relies on the combined assumptions of an increasingly integrated labor market and a poor capital market—a combination of assumptions that has not been explored in developing country settings.

Hammer (1986) has proposed that improvements in capital markets should lower fertility (and increase savings; he argues that increased savings per se are not the cause of lower fertility), and Nugent et al. (1983), using household data from India, show in a fully specified structural model that a weak local capital market is positively associated with higher fertility in nuclear households (and not in extended households, which presumably have greater access to capital through family networks).

Infant Mortality and Fertility

The demographic transition idea posits that a decline in infant mortality brings about a compensating decline in fertility. The exact nature of any causal link is not well understood, however. At the aggregate level, declines in fertility have tended to lag behind declines in mortality, producing in the 1950s through the early 1970s rapid rates of population growth. The real issue, however, is the effect of declining mortality at the individual and family level. At this level, several problems complicate empirical analyses of the effect of infant mortality on fertility behavior. First, at the family level, high mortality and high fertility may be jointly determined, so that ordinary least squares estimates will

be biased. Only recently have analysts attempted to isolate the family-specific exogenous component of life expectancy, in order to analyze the effect on fertility of exogenous changes in mortality; these effects appear much smaller than the endogenous mortality component [Olsen and Wolpin (1983)]. The problem of bias due to simultaneity can also occur because high fertility may cause high mortality, rather than vice versa, for example when the birth of a new child leads to rapid weaning (and poor nutritional status, diarrhea and death) of the preceding child.

Second, there is a biological as well as a behavioral effect of mortality on fertility, for example when with the death of a child a woman ceases breastfeeding, and is then more likely to become pregnant. To predict the long-run effects of declines in mortality on fertility, isolation of the behavioral effect is critical.

Schultz (1981, pp. 131–132) notes that knowledge that some fraction of children is likely to die has two offsetting effects on parents: it increases the cost per surviving child, and increases the number of births required to obtain a survivor. The effect on fertility of declines in the probability that children will die depends on the price elasticity of parental demand for surviving children; if demand is elastic, a reduction in the cost or "price" of births with a decline in (exogenous) mortality should increase the demand for children and raise fertility. If demand is inelastic, mortality decline should reduce fertility. The latter is likely if an exogenous reduction in mortality, by lowering the price of child "quality," encourages investment in child quality, i.e. in schooling and health, as allowed for in the quantity–quality model outlined above.

Finally, once a behavioral response to mortality decline is established, an additional question arises: whether the effect represents a reduction in "replacement" behavior (individual couples replacing lost children) or in "insurance" or "hoarding" behavior (couples having more births than they might otherwise have in order to insure against the possibility of loss). Replacement behavior is purported to be more prominent in populations at the highest and lowest levels of development, such as the industrial economies on the one hand, Bangladesh on the other [Preston (1975)]; for a country like Malaysia, replacement effects appear small [Wolpin (1984), Olsen (1983)].

On average, the evidence is that families do not completely replace a lost child, so that in the short run infant mortality reduces overall population growth, all other things the same. However, the in-

---

[11]Caldwell's (1976, 1978) restatement of demographic transition theory emphasizes the shift from child-to-parent "wealth" transfers to parent-to-child transfers in explaining fertility decline, but does not refer explicitly to the "default risk" issue.

[12]The lower the discount rate the greater the relative effect of the default (or emigration rate) on the present value of children. Cain's view that the pension motive affects fertility in effect favors a low discount rate.

direct and long-run effect of reduced mortality is probably to reduce fertility in a more than compensating amount—as, with greater certainty about child survival, parents reduce "insurance" births and shift toward child "quality" investments. The need for hoarding or insurance births would appear limited, given the sequential nature of childbearing (which allows replacement); however, it is likely that in high mortality environments, couples begin childbearing earlier (which increases aggregate population growth), and have children more rapidly. Thus, hoarding effects appear to be greater than replacement effects [e.g. Olsen (1983)]. However, the likely root of the apparent long-run response of lower fertility to declining mortality is in the shift toward an entirely new pattern of child investment, as parents adjust their behavior in response to a new environment of costs and benefits of children, of which reduced mortality may be only one component.

Family Planning Programs and Fertility

Whether organized family planning programs, privately or publicly subsidized, contribute to fertility decline is of obvious policy interest; governments of many developing countries, especially in Asia, have subsidized family planning in an effort to reduce fertility, and donors, especially the United States, have supported such efforts financially.

Measuring the impact of family planning programs on fertility decline requires controlling for other possible causes of fertility decline discussed above—such as increases in education or declines in mortality. It also requires data on some exogenous change in the availability or quality of family planning to a household, community or nation. Any such exogenous change would correspond to a change (increase) in the price of child quantity in the household demand model or change (reduction) in the cost of fertility control in the synthesis model. Information on change in the use of services is generally more widely available than information on availability, but does not suffice, since use is endogenous to people's fertility goals.

Lack of good information on change of the "price" of family planning (i.e. in the availability and quality of information or services) meant that until about a decade ago it was difficult to resolve the debate about the relative importance to fertility decline of the supply of family planning services vs. the "demand" factors—increasing education, falling infant mortality and so on. Early family planning programs in Korea, Hong Kong, and oth-

er areas of East Asia had been established in countries where a marked fall in fertility was already in progress; some of the continued decline might have occurred even without official programs. In other countries (such as India and Pakistan), where programs were also established in the 1950s and 1960s, fertility was changing little during the 1960s.

More recently, however, such information has accumulated, especially at the national level, e.g. the nation-level measures of family planning program effort of Mauldin and Lapham (1985), and at the community level; and though this and other such measures remain controversial due to measurement problems, they have permitted analyses of fertility change taking into account both supply and demand factors.

In general, the evidence from these analyses is that family planning programs do matter, having some negative effect on fertility independent of demand factors. The negative effect is relatively weak where other factors do not encourage low fertility, but powerful where other factors do. Boulier (1985), for example, estimates a variant of the household demand model for a sample of developing countries, using the Mauldin and Lapham 1972 index of family planning as one variable explaining fertility change over the period 1965–75. Other variables include the change during the same period in life expectancy, in adult literacy, in income per capita, in the proportion of the population in cities of 100000 or more, and in fertility change 1960–65. The 1972 index is treated as an endogenous variable, statistically identified using pre-1965 socioeconomic data. (Boulier himself notes that this is rather arbitrary.) Fertility decline in the period 1960–65 turns out to be an important predictor of the 1972 index; it is plausible that fertility decline itself induces government officials to augment resources for encouraging more fertility decline, particularly if it represents real demand for more services. However, even taking into account that a stronger family planning program in 1972 is associated with prior fertility decline (in 1960–65), the effect of the program on fertility decline in the concurrent period (1965–75) is still positive.

In a similar analysis, Wheeler (1985) estimates the effect of change in the Mauldin–Lapham index between 1972 and 1982 on fertility change from 1970 to 1980. He experiments with various functional forms in a simultaneous equations model, and concludes that in explaining fertility change over this period in developing countries, it is the combination of family planning availability with female education which must be stressed, since specifications including the interaction of these two are the most powerful.

Studies within countries tend to complement these nation-level studies. Not surprisingly, cross-section studies of households, summarized by Boulier (1985), find that people are more likely to know about and use contraception the closer they live to a reliable source. Use of contraception does not necessarily reduce aggregate fertility, of course. However, Schultz (1973) in a study of administrative regions of Taiwan, found that fertility over the period 1964–69 declined more rapidly where health and family planning workers were more plentiful. Consistent with Wheeler's findings, the impact of workers was greater where child school enrollment rates were greater and infant mortality had declined more.

In another study, Rosenzweig and Wolpin (1982) examined the determinants of recent fertility among women in India in 1968–71, measuring family planning inputs by the fraction of villages having a family planning clinic in the district in which a woman resides. Holding constant wife's and husband's education, wife's age, farm and non-farm residence, and district level health, schooling, and sanitation characteristics, they reported that doubling the number of villages in a district with a family planning clinic (from 2 to 4 percent) would reduce fertility by 13 percent, as well as reducing child mortality and raising school attendance. In a later study [Rosenzweig and Wolpin (1986)], they examined the possibility that the availability of public services such as family planning and health to households cannot be treated as exogenous, given that governments may locate such services in specific places in an effort to compensate for or to complement "demand" factors. For the particular case they study, of the Philippines, they conclude that family planning services do reduce fertility; they also show that conventional tests could understate the true price effect of public programs in reducing fertility and improving health, since government appears to be following a compensatory strategy, locating services where other factors would mitigate against lower fertility and better health.

Finally, recent experimental studies testing the impact of family planning, summarized in World Bank (1984, pp. 119–121) suggest sustained programs can reduce fertility even in rural relatively uneducated populations; the most widely noted of these is that in Matlab, Bangladesh.

Greater availability or improved quality of family planning services, usually at no charge, re-duces the overall price to potential users most obviously by reducing the cost of information or of travel. The economic models predict such a price reduction will reduce fertility (except where demand for births still falls short of biological supply); the empirical evidence is consistent with the prediction.

References

Birdsall, N. (1977) "Analytical approaches to the relationship of population growth and development," *Population and Development Review,* 3:63–102.

Birdsall, N. (1980) "A cost of siblings: Child schooling in urban Colombia," in: J. Simon and J. DaVanzo, eds., *Research in population economics,* Vol. 2. Greenwich, CT: JAI Press.

Birdsall, N. and Griffin, C. C. (1988) "Fertility and poverty in developing countries," *Journal of Policy Modeling,* forthcoming.

Blake, J. (1983) "Family size and the quality of children," *Demography,* 18:421–442.

Boulier, B. L. (1985) "Family planning programs and contraceptive availability: Their effects on contraceptive use and fertility," in: N. Birdsall, ed., *The effects of family planning programs on fertility in the developing world.* World Bank Staff working paper no. 677, Washington, DC.

Cain, M. T. (1981) "Risk and insurance perspectives on fertility and agrarian change in India and Bangladesh," *Population and Development Review,* 7:435–474.

Cain, M. T. (1983) "Fertility as an adjustment to risk," *Population and Development Review,* 9:688–702.

Caldwell, J. C. (1976) "Toward a restatement of demographic theory," *Population and Development Review,* 2:321–366.

Caldwell, J. C. (1978) "A theory of fertility: From high plateau to destabilization," *Population and Development Review,* 4:553–577.

Cochrane, S. H. (1979) *Fertility and education: What do we really know?* World Bank Staff occasional paper, no. 26. Baltimore, MD: Johns Hopkins University Press.

Hammer, J. (1986) "Population growth and savings in LDCs: A survey article," *World Development,* 14:579–591.

Kelley, A. C. (1980) "Interactions of economic and demographic household behavior," in: R. A. Easterlin, ed., *Population and economic change in developing countries.* Chicago, IL: University of Chicago Press.

Lindert, P. H. (1980) "Child costs and economic development," in: R. A. Easterlin, ed., *Population and economic change in developing countries.* Chicago, IL: University of Chicago Press.

Lindert, P.H. (1983) "The changing economic costs and

benefits of having children," in: R. A. Bulatao and R. D. Lee, eds., *Determinants of fertility in developing countries.* New York: Academic Press.

Maine, D. and McNamara, R. (1985) *Birth spacing and child survival.* New York: Columbia University.

Mauldin, W. P. and Lapham, R. J. (1985) "Measuring family planning effort in LDCs: 1972 and 1982," in: N. Birdsall, ed., *The effects of family planning programs on fertility in the developing world,* World Bank Staff working paper no. 677. Washington, DC: World Bank.

McCabe, J. and Rosenzweig, M. R. (1976) "Female labor force participation, occupational choice and fertility in developing countries," in: R. G. Ridker, ed., *Population and development: The search for selective interventions.* Baltimore, MD: Johns Hopkins University Press.

Nugent, J., Kan, K. and Walther, R. J. (1983) "The effects of old-age pensions on household structure, marriage, fertility and resource allocation in rural areas of developing countries," University of Southern California, mimeo.

Olsen, R. J. (1983) "Mortality rates, mortality events and the number of births," *American Economic Review,* 73:29–32.

Olsen, R. J. and Wolpin, K. I. (1983) "The impact of exogenous child mortality on fertility: A waiting time regression with dynamic regressors," *Econometrica,* 51:731–749.

Preston, H. (1975) "Health programs and population growth," *Population and Development Review,* 1:189–199.

Rosenzweig, M. R. (1982) "Educational subsidy, agricultural development and fertility change," *Quarterly Journal of Economics,* February: 67–88.

Rosenzweig, M. R. and Schultz, T. P. (1985b) "Schooling, information and non-market productivity: Contraceptive use and its effectiveness," Yale University, mimeo.

Rosenzweig, M. R. and Seiver, D. (1982) "Education and contraceptive choice: A conditional demand framework," *International Economic Review,* 23: 171–198.

Rosenzweig, M. R. and Wolpin, K. (1980a) "Testing the quantity-quality fertility model: The use of twins as a natural experiment," *Econometrica,* 48:227–240.

Rosenzweig, M. R. and Wolpin, K. (1982) "Governmental interventions and household behavior in a developing country," *Journal of Development Economics,* 209–225.

Rosenzweig, M. R. and Wolpin, K. (1985) "Specific experience, household structure and intergenerational transfers: Farm family land and labor arrangements in developing countries," *Quarterly Journal of Economics,* C (supplement): 961–988.

Rosenzweig, M. R. and Wolpin, K. (1986) "Evaluating the effects of optimally distributed public programs: Child health and family planning interventions," *American Economic Review,* 76:470–482.

Schultz, T. P. (1973) "Explanation of birth rate changes over time: A study of Taiwan," *Journal of Political Economy,* 31 (supplement): 238–274.

Schultz, T. P. (1981) *Economics of population.* Reading, MA: Addison-Wesley Publishing Company.

Simon, J. L. (1977) *The economics of population growth.* Princeton, NJ: Princeton University Press.

Standing, G. (1983) "Women's work activity and fertility," in: R. A. Bulatao and R. D. Lee, eds., *Determinants of fertility in developing countries,* Vols. 1 and 2. New York: Academic Press.

Wheeler, D. (1985) "Female education, family planning, income and population: A long-run econometric simulation model," in: N. Birdsall, ed., *The effects of family planning programs on fertility in the developing world,* World Bank Staff working paper no. 677. Washington, DC: World Bank.

Williamson, J. G. (1985) "Did rising emigration cause fertility to decline in 19th century rural England? Child costs, old-age pensions and child default," Harvard Institute for Economic Research, Harvard University, Cambridge, MA.

Wolpin, K. (1984) "An estimable dynamic stochastic model of fertility and child mortality," *Journal of Political Economy,* 92:852–874.

World Bank (1984) *World development report 1984.* New York: Oxford University Press. Also available as *Population change and economic development.* New York: Oxford University Press (1985).

V.C. HEALTH AND NUTRITION

Exhibit V.C.1. Health Indicators

| | Percentage of total population with access to | | | | | | Infant mortality rate (per 1,000 live births) | | Prevalence of malnutrition (% under 5) 1989–95 | Contraceptive prevalence rate (%) 1989–95 | Total fertility rate | | Maternal mortality ratio (per 100,000 live births) 1989–95 |
| | Health care | | Safe water | | Sanitation | | | | | | | | |
	1980	1993	1980	1994–95	1980	1994–95	1980	1995			1980	1995	
Low-income economies							98 w	69 w			4.3 w	3.2 w	
Excluding China and india							116 w	89 w			6.3 w	5.0 w	
1 Mozambique	..	..	9	28	10	23	145	113	..	..	6.5	6.2	1,512[a]
2 Ethiopia	..	55	4	27	..	10	155	112	47	4	6.6	7.0	1,528[a]
3 Tanzania	72	93	..	49	..	86	104	82	28	10	6.7	5.8	748[a]
4 Burundi	..	80	..	58	..	48	121	98	..	..	6.8	6.5	1,327[a]
5 Malawi	40	..	..	54	..	63	169	133	27	13	7.6	6.6	620[b]
6 Chad	..	26	..	29	..	32	147	117	..	..	5.9	5.9	1,594[a]
7 Rwanda	..	..	..	..	..	..	128	133	28	21	8.3	6.2	1,512[a]
8 Sierra Leone	26	..	..	..	13	..	190	179	23	..	6.5	6.5	..
9 Nepal	10	..	11	48	0	6	132	91	70	..	6.4	5.3	515[c]
10 Niger	..	30	..	57	..	15	150	119	..	4	7.4	7.4	593[b]
11 Burkina Faso	..	..	35	..	5	14	121	99	..	8	7.5	6.7	939[a]
12 Madagascar	..	74	..	32	..	17	138	89	32	17	6.5	5.8	..
13 Bangladesh	80	..	..	83	..	30	132	79	84	40	6.1	3.5	887[a]
14 Uganda	..	..	..	42	..	60	116	98	23	15	7.2	6.7	506[c]
15 Vietnam	75	..	..	38	..	21	57	41	45	..	5.0	3.1	105[d]
16 Guinea-Bissau	30	..	24	27	..	20	168	136	..	..	6.0	6.0	..
17 Haiti	..	..	..	28	..	24	123	72	27	18	5.9	4.4	600[b]
18 Mali	20	..	..	44	..	44	184	123	..	..	7.1	6.8	1,249[a]
19 Nigeria	40	67	..	43	..	63	99	80	43	6	6.9	5.5	..
20 Yemen, Rep.	16	..	..	52	..	51	141	100	30	..	7.9	7.4	1,471[a]
21 Cambodia	..	..	..	13	..	..	201	108	..	..	4.7	4.7	..
22 Kenya	..	..	..	49	..	43	72	58	23	27	7.8	4.7	..
23 Mongolia	90	..	..	..	..	..	82	55	10	..	5.4	3.4	..
24 Togo	..	..	..	..	..	20	110	88	..	..	6.6	6.4	626[a]
25 Gambia, The	90	..	42	67	..	34	159	126	..	..	6.5	5.3	..
26 Central African Republic	..	..	16	61	..	..	117	98	..	..	5.8	5.1	649

Exhibit V.C.1. Continued

| | Percentage of total population with access to | | | | | | Infant mortality rate (per 1,000 live births) | | Prevalence of malnutrition (% under 5) | Contraceptive prevalence rate (%) | Total fertility rate | | Maternal mortality ratio (per 100,000 live births) |
| | Health care | | Safe water | | Sanitation | | | | | | | | |
	1980	1993	1980	1994–95	1980	1994–95	1980	1995	1989–95	1989–95	1980	1995	1989–95
27 India	50	..	..	63	..	29	116	68	63	43	5.0	3.2	437[d]
28 Lao PDR	..	..	..	41	..	30	127	90	40	..	6.7	6.5	..
29 Benin	..	42	..	70	..	22	122	95	36	..	6.5	6.0	..
30 Nicaragua	..	..	..	57	..	..	90	46	12	44	6.2	4.1	..
31 Ghana	..	25	..	56	..	29	100	73	27	20	6.5	5.1	742[a]
32 Zambia	..	..	..	47	..	42	90	109	27	15	7.0	5.7	..
33 Angola	70	24	..	32	..	16	153	124	20	..	6.9	6.9	..
34 Georgia	..	..	..	..	..	..	25	18	..	..	2.3	2.2	55[d]
35 Pakistan	65	85	38	60	16	30	124	90	40	14	7.0	5.2	..
36 Mauritania	..	..	..	41	..	64	120	96	..	..	6.3	5.2	..
37 Azerbaijan	..	..	..	..	..	..	30	25	16	..	3.2	2.3	29[d]
38 Zimbabwe	55	..	..	74	5	58	82	55	18	..	6.8	3.8	..
39 Guinea	..	45	..	49	12	6	161	128	19	..	6.1	6.5	880[d]
40 Honduras	..	..	..	70	..	68	70	45	..	47	6.5	4.6	..
41 Senegal	..	40	..	..	..	..	91	62	20	7	6.7	5.7	..
42 China	..	..	..	83	..	..	42	34	17	83	2.5	1.9	115[e]
43 Cameroon	20	..	..	41	..	40	94	56	14	16	6.5	5.7	..
44 Côte d'Ivoire	..	..	20	82	17	54	108	86	..	11	7.4	5.3	887[a]
45 Albania	100	..	92	..	..	100	47	30	..	..	3.6	2.6	23[d]
46 Congo	..	..	..	60	..	9	89	90	..	..	6.2	6.0	822[a]
47 Kyrgyz Republic	..	..	..	75	..	53	43	30	..	..	4.1	3.3	80[d]
48 Sri Lanka	90	..	..	57	..	66	34	16	38	..	3.5	2.3	30[d]
49 Armenia	..	..	..	..	..	..	26	16	..	..	2.3	1.8	35[d]
Middle-income economies							65 w	39 w			3.8 w	3.0 w	
Lower-middle-income							68 w	41 w			3.7 w	3.0 w	
50 Lesotho	..	..	18	57	12	35	108	76	21	23	5.6	4.6	598[a]
51 Egypt, Arab Rep.	100	99	90	84	70	..	120	56	9	48	5.1	3.4	..
52 Bolivia	..	..	..	60	..	44	118	69	13	45	5.5	4.5	373[b]
53 Macedonia, FYR	..	..	..	..	..	..	54	23	..	..	2.5	2.2	12[d]
54 Moldova	..	..	..	..	..	50	35	22	..	..	2.4	2.0	34[d]
55 Uzbekistan	..	..	..	..	..	18	47	30	..	..	4.8	3.7	43[d]

		1	2	3	4	5	6	7	8	9	10	11	12	13
56	Indonesia	..	..		63		55	90	51	39	55	4.3	2.7	390
57	Philippines	..	..		84		75	52	39	30	40	4.8	3.7	208[b]
58	Morocco	..	62	32	59	50	63	99	55	9	50	5.4	3.4	372[c]
59	Syrian Arab Republic	..	99	71	87	45	78	56	32	..	..	7.4	4.8	179[d]
60	Papua New Guinea	..	..	..	31	..	26	67	64	..	..	5.7	4.8	
61	Bulgaria	..	..	96	..	..	99	20	15	..	..	2.1	1.2	20[d]
62	Kazakstan	..	..	..	..	..	..	33	27	..	..	2.9	2.3	53[d]
63	Guatemala	..	..	..	64	..	71	75	44	..	32	6.2	4.7	464[a]
64	Ecuador	..	..	..	70	..	64	67	36	45	57	5.0	3.2	..
65	Dominican Republic	..	..	..	79	..	85	76	37	10	56	4.2	2.9	..
66	Romania	..	..	77	..	50	49	29	23	..	57	2.4	1.4	48[d]
67	Jamaica	..	..	..	70	..	74	21	13	10	55	3.7	2.4	..
68	Jordan	..	90	..	89	76	30	41	31	17	..	6.8	4.8	132[a]
69	Algeria	..	77	89	..	..	..	98	34	9	51	6.7	3.5	140[d]
70	El Salvador	..	..	77	62	..	73	81	36	22	53	5.3	3.7	..
71	Ukraine	95	..	..	97	50	49	17	15	..	..	2.0	1.5	33[d]
72	Paraguay	..	90	..	..	..	30	50	41	4	48	4.8	4.0	180[d]
73	Tunisia	..	..	72	86	46	72	71	39	..	..	5.2	2.9	138[a]
74	Lithuania	..	..	..	..	..	..	20	14	..	..	2.0	1.5	16[d]
75	Colombia	88	88	..	96	..	70	45	26	10	72	3.8	2.8	107[a]
76	Namibia	..	..	..	57	..	36	90	62	..	29	5.9	5.0	518
77	Belarus	..	..	..	..	50	100	16	13	..	..	2.0	1.4	25[d]
78	Russian Federation	..	..	..	..	..	..	22	18	..	..	1.9	1.4	52[d]
79	Larvia	100	..	..	..	..	..	20	16	..	..	2.0	1.3	..
80	Peru	..	..	..	60	..	47	81	47	16	55	4.5	3.1	..
81	Costa Rica	..	..	..	100	..	99	20	13	2	..	3.7	2.8	..
82	Lebanon	..	59	92	..	59	..	48	32	..	..	4.0	2.8	..
83	Thailand	30	..	..	81	..	87	49	35	13	..	3.5	1.8	..
84	Panama	..	..	..	82	..	87	32	23	7	..	3.7	2.7	..
85	Turkey	..	..	67	92	..	94	109	48	..	..	4.3	2.7	183[c]
86	Poland	100	..	67	..	50	100	21	14	..	..	2.3	1.6	10[d]
87	Estonia	..	..	..	..	..	..	17	14	..	..	2.0	1.3	41[d]
88	Slovak Republic	..	..	..	..	43	51	21	11	..	..	2.3	1.5	8[d]
89	Botswana	..	..	..	70	..	55	69	56	6	..	6.7	4.4	220[a]
90	Venezuela	..	..	..	88	..	55	36	23	..	..	4.1	3.1	200[d]
	Upper-middle-income						57 w		35 w			3.9 w	2.9 w	
91	South Africa	..	..	..	..	..	46	67	50	..	..	4.9	3.9	404[a]
92	Croatia	..	..	..	96	..	68	21	16	..	..	1.9	1.5	10[d]
93	Mexico	51	..	..	87	..	70	51	33	..	..	4.5	3.0	..
94	Mauritius	100	99	99	100	..	100	32	16	..	75	2.7	2.2	112[d]
95	Gabon	..	..	..	67	..	76	116	89	..	..	4.5	5.2	483[a]
96	Brazil	..	..	..	92	..	73	70	44	18	..	3.9	2.4	200[d]
97	Trinidad and Tobago	..	..	..	82	..	56	35	13	..	..	3.3	2.1	..

Exhibit V.C.1. Continued

| | Percentage of total population with access to | | | | | | Infant mortality rate (per 1,000 live births) | | Prevalence of malnutrition (% under 5) 1989–95 | Contraceptive prevalence rate (%) 1989–95 | Total fertility rate | | Maternal mortality ratio (per 100,000 live births) 1989–95 |
| | Health care | | Safe water | | Sanitation | | | | | | | | |
	1980	1993	1980	1994–95	1980	1994–95	1980	1995			1980	1995	
98 Czech Republic	..	..	..	..	..	..	16	8	..	69	2.1	1.3	12[d]
99 Malaysia	..	88	..	90	75	94	30	12	23	..	4.2	3.4	34[f]
100 Hungary	..	..	..	..	..	94	23	11	..	..	1.9	1.6	10[d]
101 Chile	..	..	..	96	..	71	32	12	1	..	2.8	2.3	..
102 Oman	75	89	15	56	..	72	41	18	..	9	9.9	7.0	..
103 Uruguay	..	..	..	83	..	82	37	18	..	..	2.7	2.2	..
104 Saudi Arabia	85	98	91	93	76	86	65	21	..	..	7.3	6.2	18[d]
105 Argentina	..	..	..	64	..	89	35	22	..	..	3.3	2.7	140[d]
106 Slovenia	..	..	..	..	..	90	15	7	..	..	2.1	1.3	5[d]
107 Greece	..	..	..	..	..	96	18	8	..	..	2.2	1.4	..
Low- and middle-income							87 w	60 w			4.1 w	3.1 w	
Sub-Saharan Africa							114 w	92 w			6.7 w	5.7 w	
East Asia and Pacific							56 w	40 w			3.1 w	2.2 w	
South Asia							120 w	75 w			5.3 w	3.5 w	
Europe and Central Asia							40 w	26 w			2.5 w	2.0 w	
Middle East and N. Africa							97 w	54 w			6.1 w	4.2 w	
Latin America and Carribbean							60 w	37 w			4.1 w	2.8 w	
High-income economies							13 w	7 w			1.9 w	1.7 w	
108 Korea, Rep.	..	100	..	89	..	100	26	10	..	..	2.6	1.8	30[d]
109 Portugal	..	..	57	..	..	100	24	7	..	..	2.2	1.4	21
110 Spain	..	..	98	99	95	97	12	7	..	..	2.2	1.2	..
111 New Zealand	..	100	87	..	..	..	13	7	..	..	2.1	2.1	..
112 Ireland	..	..	..	99	..	100	11	6	..	60	3.2	1.9	..
113 †Israel	..	..	..	99	..	70	15	8	..	..	3.2	2.4	..
114 †Kuwait	100	..	100	..	100	..	27	11	..	..	5.3	3.0	18[d]
115 †United Arab Emirates	96	90	100	98	75	95	55	16	..	..	5.4	3.6	20[a]
116 United Kingdom	..	..	..	100	..	96	12	6	..	..	1.9	1.7	..
117 Australia	99	..	99	95	99	90	11	6	..	..	1.9	1.9	..
118 Italy	..	..	99	..	99	100	15	7	..	..	1.6	1.2	..

119	Canada	:	97	100	60	85	10	6	:	1.7	1.7	:
120	Finland	:	100	100	100	100	8	5	:	1.6	1.8	:
121	†Hong Kong	:	:	:	:	:	11	5	:	2.0	1.2	:
122	Sweden	:	:	:	85	100	7	4	:	1.7	1.7	:
123	Netherlands	:	100	100	100	100	9	6	:	1.6	1.6	:
124	Belgium	:	:	:	99	96	12	8	:	1.7	1.6	:
125	France	:	:	100	85	100	10	6	:	1.9	1.7	:
126	†Singapore	:	100	100	:	100	12	4	14	1.7	1.7	:
127	Austria	:	100	:	85	85	14	6	:	1.6	1.5	:
128	United States	:	:	90	98	100	13	8	:	1.8	2.1	:
129	Germany	:	:	:	:	100	12	6	:	1.6	1.2	:
130	Denmark	:	100	100	100	100	8	6	:	1.5	1.8	:
131	Norway	:	:	100	100	85	8	5	:	1.7	1.9	:
132	Japan	100	:	95	:	100	8	4	3	1.8	1.5	6[d]
133	Switzerland	:	:	100	85	100	9	6	:	1.6	1.5	:
	World	:	:	:	:	:	80 w	55 w	:	3.7 w	2.9 w	:

Note: Figures in italics are for years other than those specified. w = weighted average.

[a] UNICEF/WHO estimate based on statistical modeling.

[b] Indirect estimate based on sample survey.

[c] Based on sample survey.

[d] Official estimate.

[e] Based on a survey covering thirty provinces.

[f] Based on civil registration.

Source: World Bank, World Development Report 1997 (New York: Oxford University Press, 1997), pp. 224–225.

Selection V.C.1. Health and Nutrition*

Although there is substantial variation in the estimates, the extent of malnutrition and poor health in the developing world as measured by conventional standards is considerable. Consideration of the adaptability of the human body to its environment and the extent of inter- and intraperson variations leads to a less pessimistic characterization of the current situation and somewhat different identification of who is at risk. Nevertheless, large numbers of individuals in the developing world have lower nutritional input and health status than many would think desirable. Such inadequacies are likely to be exacerbated at times of unfavorable relative price movements for the poorer members of societies, such as during famines. Such as characterization is appropriate for the late 1980s despite very considerable absolute and relative gains in indicators of average nutrition and health status in developing countries—such as life expectancy—in recent decades. These gains have been larger in fact than the gains indicated by narrowly defined economic indicators. Of course the national averages hide a wide range of variances and, since the situation for the poorer may be particularly critical in determining average health and nutrition, countries that appear similar according to the per capita income averages have had widely different average nutrition and health status. The life expectancy at birth in 1983 of 69 years in Sri Lanka as compared to 38 years in Sierra Leone, though both have per capita income estimates of $330 for that year, provides a vivid example.[1]

Efforts to investigate the micro level determinants of health status or of health-care utilization, whether by estimating health production functions or reduced-form demand equations, have met with some, but fairly limited success. Some micro health production function estimates suggest that direct nutritional supplements improve child, but not adult, health. This contrast between the health production function results for children versus those for adults may not be surprising given the apparent relatively greater importance of nutrients in the child development stage and strong intraperson serial correlation in health status. For adults, nutrient increases seem to result in increased energy expenditures, in some cases associated with increased productivity. Reduced-form micro demand relations for both child and adult health find little evidence of responses to relative market prices, income, or wealth. The micro estimates, however, contrast sharply with the aggregate estimates of fairly strong associations between measures such as life expectancy and per capita real income or product. This contrast raises the question of whether the micro results are misleading because of measurement errors for health and/or income and specification errors regarding lags and time use, or whether in the macro estimates per capita income or product is representing not the purchasing power of individuals so much as the general level of development and associated public health measures that are not well represented in micro estimates. For a number of both the micro and the macro estimates, furthermore, standard estimates often indicate a substantial role for women's schooling, in some cases substituting for other inputs. In the one sample for which adult sibling deviations permit extensive control for the women's unobserved childhood background characteristics, however, the impact of women's schooling on health vanishes with such a control.

Studies of the reduced-form demand relations for nutrient intakes suggest some substantial price responses, not only for foods consumed, but also for agricultural products and inputs in the case of farm households. The substantial price responses mean that many policies and market developments may affect nutrition whether or not that is their intent. Policy-makers need to be sensitive to such possibilities in their policy design and implementation. The food price responses, moreover, are not always negative; in some cases, particularly for farm or rural labor households, the price elasticities for locally produced foods may be positive and considerable in magnitude. For such households, food price floors may improve nutrition more than the price subsidies that often are rationalized on such grounds. Of course, the same result is not likely to be true for the nonrural poor, but many of the poorest and most malnourished are in the rural areas. Another interesting characteristic of the price elasticities is a tendency for them to be larger for poorer households. Differential price elasticities across the income distribution presents some possibilities of price policies that favor the poor for distributional reasons without too great leakages to those who are better off. Allocation of nu-

*From Jere R. Behrman and Anil B. Deolalikar, "Health and Nutrition," in Hollis Chenery and T. N. Srinivasan, eds., *Handbook of Development Economics, Volume I* (Amsterdam: North-Holland, 1988), 698–701. Reprinted by permission.

[1]Bhalla (1984) and Bhalla and Glewwe (1986) discusses in some detail the Sri Lankan experience.

trients within households, finally, seems to favor males and older children in absolute terms, but there is some interesting evidence for rural south India that adjustments to price changes are relatively smaller for girls than for other household members—suggesting that in this sense nutrients for girls are treated less as luxuries than are those for others.

Estimates of nutrient determinants indicate a wide range of income or expenditure elasticities. However, in a number of cases large expenditure elasticities result from aggregate (with respect to foods) estimates based on a priori assumptions that nutrient elasticities are identical to a weighted average of food elasticities at a high level of aggregation. But this assumption may be very misleading if the prices paid for nutrients vary positively with income, as appears to be the case. Comparison of directly estimated nutrient elasticities with food elasticities for rural south India, in fact, suggest that the former are much smaller than the latter. Apparently other food characteristics—taste, appearance, status value, degree of processing—are valued much more than nutrition at the margin even among individuals in this relatively poor population. Cross-country estimates also suggest that in part the low income elasticities of nutrients (as compared with those for food expenditures) reflect an increasing taste for food variety as income increases. If non-nutritive food characteristics are fovored highly at the margin, then income increases and the general development process will not alleviate malnutrition nearly as much as the World Bank (1980), Srinivasan (1985), and others have claimed. On the other hand, the limited importance placed by individuals in such populations on increasing nutrient consumption at the margin (if they are making informed choices) raises doubts about whether they are so malnourished as conventional estimates suggest, and thus provides a different type of evidence consistent with the Sukhatme–Srinivasan–Seckler–Payne hypothesis about individual adaptability to nutrient availabilities and "small but healthy" people. Of course such evidence does not speak to the question, why are many people in some populations so small, nor does it allay the suspicion that the malnutrition experienced by many children in such populations is associated not only with small adults, but also with high infant and child mortality.

Beyond relative prices and perhaps income, some—but far from all—studies point to the possible importance of women's schooling, nutritional knowledge, and public health measures in improving nutrient consumption (particularly for chil-

dren). The impact of women's schooling and nutrient knowledge may reflect that better-educated consumers make more nutritious food choices, ceteris paribus. The impact of women's schooling on nutrient consumption, in contrast to that on health, is robust to control for unobserved background characteristics in the one sample that permits such adult sibling control. Better public health services such as safer water may reflect the greater value of nutrients when such factors are present because of their complementarity with nutrients in the health production function. Of course women's schooling also may be playing such a role in addition to or instead of working only by improving information about nutrient qualities of different foods.

Nutrient intakes and health status both appear to affect positively agricultural productivity and labor market wages and possibly schooling productivity for some poor populations. Nutrient intakes might affect productivity without altering indicators of health status because nutrient changes may be transferred largely to energy expenditure changes, including some that are productivity related. Except in extreme cases, malnourishment does not seem to alter fertility. However, declines in infant mortality do seem broadly to reduce fertility. Therefore health and nutrition are not only important ends in themselves, but also may be important means through which productivity and population goals are affected.

Investigations on the supply side have focused on the impact of subsidy policies for food and, to a lesser extent, other health-related inputs. Such studies suggest that general food subsidies are not very effective in redistributing income to the poor, but that targeted food programs can be used to shift income to some segments of the poor that depend on market purchases for food. However, the small nutrient elasticities with respect to income imply that nutrient intakes do not improve substantially as a result of such subsidies. Recent studies of actual nutrition and other health-related input pricing policies suggest that in fact they often redistribute income *from* the poor and are not justified on the grounds of externalities, though subsidies for preventive measures for contagious diseases may be justifiable on the latter grounds.

Strong claims have been made by UNICEF and others about very negative multiplied effects of macroeconomic adjustment policies on health and nutrition. Careful examination of the relevant studies, however, suggests that the empirical basis for such a claim currently is quite weak. In fact the underlying studies seem to be characterized better as reflecting how well societies and people have adapted to minimize negative health and nutrition effects rather than the more negative interpretation given by UNICEF.

References

Bhalla, S.S. (1984) "Is Sri Lanka an exception? A comparative study of living standards," mimeo.

Bhalla, S.S. and Glewwe, P. (1986) "Growth and equity in developing countries: A reinterpretation of the Sri Lankan experience," *World Bank Economic Review,* 1:35–64.

Srinivasan, T.N. (1985) "Malnutrition in developing countries: The state of knowledge of the extent of its prevalence, its causes and its consequences," mimeo.

World Bank (1980) *World development report, 1980.* Washington: World Bank.

Selection V.C.2. Investing in Health*

Despite remarkable improvements, enormous health problems remain. Absolute levels of mortality in developing countries remain unacceptably high: child mortality rates are about ten times higher than those in the established market economies. If death rates among children in poor countries were reduced to those prevailing in the rich countries, 11 million fewer children would die each year. Almost half of these preventable deaths are a result of diarrheal and respiratory illness, exacerbated by malnutrition. In addition, every year 7 million adults die of conditions that could be inexpensively prevented or cured; tuberculosis alone causes 2 million of these deaths. About 400,000 women die from the direct complications of pregnancy and childbirth. Maternal mortality ratios are, on average, thirty times as high in developing countries as in high-income countries.

Although health has improved even in the poorest countries, the pace of progress has been uneven. In 1960 in Ghana and Indonesia about one child in five died before reaching age 5—a child mortality rate typical of many developing countries. By 1990 Indonesia's rate had dropped to about one-half the 1960 level, but Ghana's had fallen only slightly. Table 1 provides a summary of regional progress in mortality reduction between 1975 and 1990.

In addition to premature mortality, a substantial portion of the burden of disease consists of disability, ranging from polio-related paralysis to blindness to the suffering brought about by severe psychosis. To measure the burden of disease, this Report uses the disability-adjusted life year (DALY), a measure that combines healthy life years lost because of premature mortality with those lost as a result of disability.

There is huge variation in per person loss of DALYs across regions, mainly because of differences in premature mortality; regional differences in loss of DALYs as a result of disability are much smaller. The total loss of DALYs is referred to as the global burden of disease.

The world is facing serious new health challenges. By 2000 the growing toll from acquired immune deficiency syndrome (AIDS) in developing countries could easily rise to more than 1.8 million deaths annually, erasing decades of hard-won reductions in mortality. The malaria parasite's

increased resistance to available drugs could lead to a doubling of malaria deaths, to nearly 2 million a year within a decade. Rapid progress in reducing child mortality and fertility rates will create new demands on health care systems as the aging of populations brings to the fore costly noncommunicable diseases of adults and the elderly. Tobacco-related deaths from heart disease and cancers alone are likely to double by the first decade of the next century, to 2 million a year, and, if present smoking patterns continue, they will grow to more than 12 million a year in developing countries in the second quarter of the next century.

Health Systems and Their Problems

Although health services are only one factor in explaining past successes, the importance of their role in the developing world is not in doubt. Public health measures brought about the eradication of smallpox and have been central to the reduction in deaths caused by vaccine-preventable childhood diseases. Expanded and improved clinical care has saved millions of lives from infectious diseases and injuries. But there are also major problems with health systems that, if not resolved, will hamper progress in reducing the burden of premature mortality and disability and frustrate efforts to respond to new health challenges and emerging disease threats.

- *Misallocation.* Public money is spent on health interventions of low cost-effectiveness, such as surgery for most cancers, at the same time that critical and highly cost-effective interventions, such as treatment of tuberculosis and sexually transmitted diseases (STDs), remain underfunded. In some countries a single teaching hospital can absorb 20 percent or more of the budget of the ministry of health, even though almost all cost-effective interventions are best delivered at lower-level facilities.
- *Inequity.* The poor lack access to basic health services and receive low-quality care. Government spending for health goes disproportionately to the affluent in the form of free or below-cost care in sophisticated public tertiary care hospitals and subsidies to private and public insurance.
- *Inefficiency.* Much of the money spent on health is wasted: brand-name pharmaceuticals are purchased instead of generic drugs, health workers

*From World Bank, *World Development Report 1993* (New York: World Bank by Oxford University Press, 1993), pp. 1–8. Reprinted by permission.

Table 1. Population, Economic Indicators, and Progress in Health by Demographic Region, 1975–90

Region	Population, 1990 (millions)	Deaths, 1990 (millions)	Income per Capita Dollars, 1990	Income per Capita Growth Rate, 1975–90 (percent per year)	Child Mortality 1975	Child Mortality 1990	Life Expectancy at Birth (years) 1975	Life Expectancy at Birth (years) 1990
Sub-Saharan Africa	510	7.9	510	−1.0	212	175	48	52
India	850	9.3	360	2.5	195	127	53	58
China	1,134	8.9	370	7.4	85	43	56	69
Other Asia and islands	683	5.5	1,320	4.6	135	97	56	62
Latin America and the Caribbean	444	3.0	2,190	−0.1	104	60	62	70
Middle Eastern crescent	503	4.4	1,720	−1.3	174	111	52	61
Demographically developing group[a]	4,123	39.1	900	3.0	152	106	56	63
World	5,267	50.0	4,000	1.2	135	96	60	65

Note: Child mortality is the probability of dying between birth and age 5, expressed per 1,000 live births; life expectancy at birth is the average number of years that a person would expect to live at the prevailing age-specific mortality rates

[a]The countries of the demographic regions Sub-Saharan Africa, India, China, Other Asia and islands, Latin America and the Caribbean and Middle Eastern crescent.

Source: For income per capita, World Bank data.

are badly deployed and supervised, and hospital beds are underutilized.

- *Exploding costs.* In some middle-income developing countries health care expenditures are growing much faster than income. Increasing numbers of general physicians and specialists, the availability of new medical technologies, and expanding health insurance linked to fee-for-service payments together generate a rapidly growing demand for costly tests, procedures, and treatments.

World health spending—and thus also the potential for misallocation, waste, and inequitable distribution of resources—is huge. For the world as a whole in 1990, public and private expenditure on health services was about $1,700 billion, or 8 percent of total world product. High-income countries spent almost 90 percent of this amount, for an average of $1,500 per person. The United States alone consumed 41 percent of the global total—more than 12 percent of its gross national product (GNP). Developing countries spent about $170 billion, or 4 percent of their GNP, for an average of $41 per person—less than one-thirtieth the amount spent by rich countries.

In the *low-income countries* government hospitals and clinics, which account for the greatest part of the modern medical care provided, are often inefficient, suffering from highly centralized deci-

sion-making, wide fluctuations in budgetary allocations, and poor motivation of facility managers and health care workers. Private providers—mainly religious nongovernmental organizations (NGOs) in Africa and private doctors and unlicensed practitioners in South Asia—are often more technically efficient than the public sector and offer a service that is perceived to be of higher quality, but they are not supported by government policies. In low-income countries the poor often lose out in health because public spending in the sector is heavily skewed toward high-cost hospital services that disproportionately benefit better-off urban groups. In Indonesia, despite concerted government efforts in the 1980s to improve health services for the poor, government subsidies to health for the richest 10 percent of households in 1990 were still almost three times the subsidies going to the poorest 10 percent of Indonesians.

In *middle-income countries* governments frequently subsidize insurance that protects only the relatively wealthy—a small, affluent minority in the case of private insurance in South Africa and Zimbabwe and, in Latin America, the larger industrial labor force covered by compulsory public insurance (so-called social insurance). The bulk of the population, especially the poor, relies heavily on out-of-pocket payments and on government services that may be largely inaccessible to them. In Peru, for example, more than 60 percent of the poor have to travel for more than an hour to obtain primary health care, as compared with less than 3 percent of the better-off. The quality of care is also low: drugs and equipment are in short supply, patient waiting times are long and medical consultations are short; and misdiagnoses and inappropriate treatment are common. . . .

The Roles of the Government and of the Market in Health

Three rationales for a major government role in the health sector should guide the reform of health systems.

- Many health-related services such as information and control of contagious disease are *public goods.* One person's use of health information does not leave less available for others to consume; one person cannot benefit from control of malaria-carrying mosquitoes while another person in the same area is excluded. Because private markets alone provide too little of the public goods crucial for health, government involvement is necessary to increase the supply of these goods. Other health services have large *externalities:* consumption by one individual affects others. Immunizing a child slows transmission of measles and other diseases, conferring a positive externality. Polluters and drunk drivers create negative health externalities. Governments need to encourage behaviors that carry positive externalities and to discourage those with negative externalities.
- Provision of cost-effective health services to the poor is an effective and socially acceptable approach to *poverty reduction.* Most countries view access to basic health care as a human right. This perspective is embodied in the goal, "Health for All by the Year 2000," of the conference held by the World Health Organization (WHO) and the United Nations Children's Fund (UNICEF) at Alma-Ata in 1978, which launched today's primary health care movement. Private markets will not give the poor adequate access to essential clinical services or the insurance often needed to pay for such services. Public finance of essential clinical care is thus justified to alleviate poverty. Such public funding can take several forms: subsidies to private providers and NGOs that serve the poor; vouchers that the poor can take to a provider of their choice; and free or below-cost delivery of public services to the poor.
- Government action may be needed to compen-

sate for problems generated by *uncertainty* and *insurance market failure.* The great uncertainties surrounding the probability of illness and the efficacy of care give rise both to strong demand for insurance and to shortcomings in the operation of private markets. One reason why markets may work poorly is that variations in health risk create incentives for insurance companies to refuse to insure the very people who most need health insurance—those who are already sick or are likely to become ill. A second has to do with "moral hazard"; insurance reduces the incentives for individuals to avoid risk and expense by prudent behavior and can create both incentives and opportunities for doctors and hospitals to give patients more care than they need. A third has to do with the asymmetry in information between provider and patient concerning the outcomes of intervention; providers advise patients on choice of treatment, and when the providers' income is linked to this advice, excessive treatment can result. As a consequence of these last two considerations, in unregulated private markets costs escalate without appreciable health gains to the patient. Governments have an important role to play in regulating privately provided health insurance, or in mandating alternatives such as social insurance, in order to ensure widespread coverage and hold down costs.

If governments do intervene, they must do so intelligently, or they risk exacerbating the very problems they are trying to solve. When governments become directly involved in the health sector—by providing public health programs or financing essential clinical services for the poor—policymakers face difficult decisions concerning the allocation of public resources. For any given amount of total spending, taxpayers and, in some countries, donors want to see maximum health gain for the money spent. An important source of guidance for achieving value for money in health spending is a measure of the cost-effectiveness of different health interventions and medical procedures—that is, the ratio of costs to health benefits (DALYs gained).

Until recently, little has been done to apply cost-effectiveness analysis to health. This is, in part, because it is difficult. Cost and effectiveness data on health interventions are often weak. Costs vary between countries and can rise or fall sharply as a service is expanded. Some groups of interventions are provided jointly, and their costs are shared. Nonetheless, cost-effectiveness analysis is already demonstrating its usefulness as a tool for choosing among possible health interventions in individual countries and for addressing specific health problems such as the spread of AIDS.

Just because a particular intervention is cost-effective does not mean that public funds should be spent on it. Households can buy health care with their own money and, when well informed, may do this better than governments can do it for them. But households also seek value for money, and governments, by making information about cost-effectiveness available, can often help improve the decisions of private consumers, providers, and insurers.

Government Policies for Achieving Health for All

This Report focuses primarily on the relation between policy choices, both inside and outside the health sector, and health outcomes, especially for the poor.

- Since overall economic growth—particularly poverty-reducing growth—and education are central to good health, governments need to pursue sound macroeconomic policies that emphasize reduction of poverty. They also need to expand basic schooling, especially for girls, because the way in which households, particularly mothers, use information and financial resources to shape their dietary, fertility, health care, and other life-style choices has a powerful influence on the health of household members.
- Governments in developing countries should spend far less—on average, about 50 percent less—than they now do on less cost-effective interventions and instead double or triple spending on basic public health programs such as immunizations and AIDS prevention and on essential clinical services. A minimum package of essential clinical services would include sick-child care, family planning, prenatal and delivery care, and treatment for tuberculosis and STDs. Low-income countries would have to redirect current public spending for health and increase expenditures (by government, donors, and patients) to meet needs for public health and the minimum package of essential clinical services for their populations; less reallocation would be needed in middle-income countries. Tertiary care and less cost-effective services will continue, but public subsidies to them, if they mainly benefit the wealthy, should be phased out during a transitional period.
- Because competition can improve quality and

drive down costs, governments should foster competition and diversity in the supply of health services and inputs, particularly drugs, supplies, and equipment. This could include, where feasible, private supply of health care services paid for by governments or social insurance. There is also considerable scope for improving the quality and efficiency of government health services through a combination of decentralization, performance-based incentives for managers and clinicians, and related training and development of management systems. Exposing the public sector to competition with private suppliers can help to spur such improvements. Strong government regulation is also crucial. . . .

Improving the Economic Environment for Healthy Households

Advances in income and education have allowed households almost everywhere to improve their health. In the 1980s, even in countries in which average incomes fell, death rates of children under age 5 declined by almost 30 percent. But the child mortality rate fell more than twice as much in countries in which average incomes rose by more than 1 percent a year. Economic policies conducive to sustained growth are thus among the most important measures governments can take to improve their citizens' health.

Of these economic policies, increasing the income of those in poverty is the most efficacious for improving health. The reason is that the poor are most likely to spend additional income in ways that enhance their health: improving their diet, obtaining safe water, and upgrading sanitation and housing. And the poor have the greatest remaining health needs. Government policies that promote equity and growth together will therefore be better for health than those that promote growth alone.

In the 1980s many countries undertook macroeconomic stabilization and adjustment programs designed to deal with severe economic imbalances and move the countries onto sustainable growth paths. Such adjustment is clearly needed for long-run health gains. But during the transitional period, and especially in the earliest adjustment programs, recession and cuts in public spending slowed improvements in health. This effect was less than originally feared, however—in part because earlier expenditures for improving health and education had enduring effects. As a result of this experience, most countries' adjustment programs today try to rationalize overall government spending while maintaining cost-effective expenditures in health and education. Despite these improvements, much is still to be learned about more efficient ways of carrying out stabilization and adjustment programs while protecting the poor.

Policies to expand schooling are also crucial for promoting health. People who have had more schooling seek and utilize health information more effectively than those with little or no schooling. This means that rapid expansion of educational opportunities—in part by setting a high minimum standard of schooling (say, six full years) for all— is a cost-effective way of improving health. Education of girls and women is particularly beneficial to household health because it is largely women who buy and prepare food, maintain a clean home, care for children and the elderly, and initiate contacts with the health system. Beyond education, government policies that support the rights and economic opportunities of women also contribute to overall household well-being and better health.

Exhibit V.C.2. Life Expectancies and Health Expenditures in Selected Countries

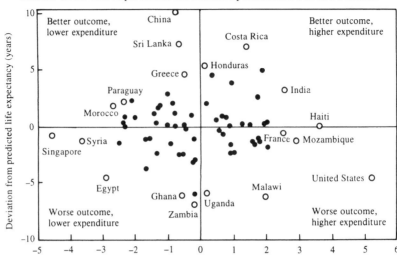

Deviation from predicted percentage of GDP spent on health

Differences in health spending are an obvious starting point in the search for why some countries have better health levels than others. But as this chart shows, health spending alone cannot explain the discrepancies—nor can income and education, or even spending, income, and schooling taken together.

The vertical axis shows how far life expectancy in a country differs from the value predicted on the basis of that country's income and average schooling. France, Haiti, Singapore, and Syria have almost exactly the life expectancy predicted. China, Costa Rica, Honduras, and Sri Lanka all achieve five years or more of life beyond what would be expected. Egypt, Ghana, Malawi, Uganda, the United States, and Zambia all have a life expectancy about five years lower than expected.

The horizontal axis shows how far total health spending differs from the value predicted by income and education. Egypt, Morocco, Paraguay, Singapore, and Syria spend relatively little. France, Haiti, India, Mozambique, and the United States spend more than expected.

At any level of income and education, higher health spending should yield better health, all else being equal. But there is no evidence of such a relation. Countries are scattered in all quadrants. The countries that appear in the upper-left quadrant obtain better health for less money. China, for instance, spends a full percentage point less of its GNP on health than other countries at the same stage of development but obtains nearly ten years of additional life expectancy. The United States is another extreme case, spending 5 percent more of GNP than predicted to achieve several years less of life expectancy than would be typical for its high income and educational level.

So why do some countries have better health levels than others? The missing link looks to be the quality of a government's health policy.

Source: Dean T. Jamison, "Investing in Health," *Finance & Development* (September 1993), p. 4.

V.D. GENDER AND DEVELOPMENT

Selection V.D.1. Women's Education in Developing Countries: An Overview*

Several indicators—including measures of literacy, enrollment, and years in school—reveal important patterns and trends in women's education in developing countries. Each of these indicators leads to the same conclusions: the level of female education is low in the poorest countries, with just a handful of exceptions, and by any measure, the gender gap is largest in these countries.

Literacy Rates

Literacy is one of the principal goals of education around the world. The ability to read and write is considered almost a basic human right. Yet low literacy rates prevail among women in many countries (figure 1). In fourteen of the fifty-one developing countries for which school data or estimates are available for the 1980s, female adult literacy is less than 20 percent; in none is the male literacy rate as low. In Afghanistan, Burkina Faso, Nepal, Somalia, and Sudan, where fewer than 10 percent of adult women are literate, the percentage of men who are literate is three to four times larger. Among those countries with male literacy rates greater than 70 percent, the gender gap is notably large in Libya (30 percentage points), China (28), Zaire (26), Turkey (23), and Botswana (21). In contrast, the literacy rates for men and women are about equal in Colombia, the Dominican Republic, and the Philippines.

Primary School Enrollment

Low adult literacy rates are a result of past underinvestment in the education of women and thus do not necessarily reflect recent progress. We look next, therefore, at how the differences between primary school enrollment rates for boys and girls have changed over time. Figure 2 illustrates the trend since 1960 for countries grouped by gross national product (GNP) per capita; figure 3 shows the trend by geographic region.

Without question, enrollment rates at all school levels have been rising in the developing world for

*From M. Anne Hill and Elizabeth M. King, "Women's Education in Developing Countries: An Overview," in Elizabeth M. King and M. Anne Hill, eds., *Women's Education in Developing Countries: Barriers, Benefits, and Policies* (Baltimore: Johns Hopkins, 1993), pp. 2–9, 21–28. Reprinted by permission.

both sexes. But this expansion has not substantially diminished gender disparities. The enrollment rates of girls remain much lower than those of boys, with the widest gap in the poorest countries. For the group of forty low-income countries, defined as those with a GNP per capita below $500 in 1988, the gap in primary school enrollment between boys and girls averages 20 percentage points. This gap has persisted in large part since 1960.

Both enrollment rates and gender disparities in enrollment differ dramatically by region. Except for South Asia and Sub- Saharan Africa, all regions have achieved nearly universal primary education for boys. Only in East Asia and in Latin America and the Caribbean, however, have enrollment rates for girls approached similar levels; in the other three regions they continue to lag behind. In South Asia the gender gap in primary enrollment has actually widened over the twenty-eight-year period because policies to expand the education system improved access for boys more than for girls. . . . As countries approach universal primary education, the gender gap in enrollment becomes more apparent beyond the primary level. . . .

Table 1 shows that, despite the large increases in enrollment rates in most countries, expected attainment levels in the poorest countries remain low, especially for females. For example, a six-year-old girl entering school in Nepal in 1985 is expected to complete only 3.1 years of schooling by the time she reaches eighteen. For a girl in Burkina Faso, the figure is lower still, 1.5 years. Since 1965 the primary school enrollment rate for girls has increased fivefold in Nepal and almost threefold in Burkina Faso. But of all the girls enrolled in primary school in Nepal in 1985, almost 45 percent were in grade one and only about 10 percent were in grade five (the final year of the primary cycle). In Burkina Faso 26 percent were in grade one and 13 percent in grade five. In both countries the rate at which boys stayed in school, called the retention rate, was higher.

The gender gap in educational attainment, measured by years of schooling, tends to fall as one moves from low-income to middle-income countries. The expected years of schooling in 1985 ranged from averages of 2.7 and 4.8 years for fe-

Figure 1. Women's and Men's Literacy Rates in Developing Countries

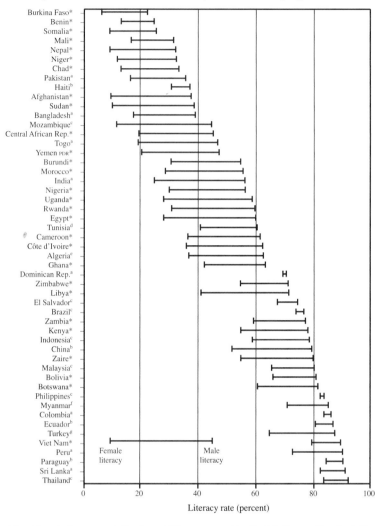

Note: The criteria for determining whether a person is literate can differ among countries; the definition used here is whether a person can with understanding both read and write a short, simple statement on his everyday life. Countries marked by an asterisk (*) do not have census-based literacy data after 1980. Most have data going back to the 1960s. For those countries the data reported are UNESCO estimates for 1985; for all other countries the latest survey-based data are used.

[a]1981. [b]1982. [c]1983. [d]1984. [e]1987. [f]1983. [g]1985.

Source: UNESCO data.

males and males, respectively, in eight low-income countries to averages of 10.2 and 10.5 years, respectively, in eleven upper-middle-income countries. In the low-income group the expected length of schooling for males exceeds that for females. For example, in Nepal and Benin girls average 4.4 and 3.5 fewer years of schooling than boys, respectively. In the middle-income group, besides Bolivia, only countries in the Middle East and North Africa show a significant gender gap: girls can expect to be in school two or three years less than boys. . . .

Costs, Benefits, and Gender Differentials

If women's education is so important, why do women remain under-educated compared with men? Why do gender differentials in education persist? In this section we present a conceptual approach for organizing the factors that can explain the current state of women's education and for understanding the dynamics underlying educational outcomes. We propose, in short, that gender differentials in education endure because those persons who bear the private costs of investing in school-

Figure 2. Gross Enrollment in Primary and Secondary Schools by Income Group, 1960–88

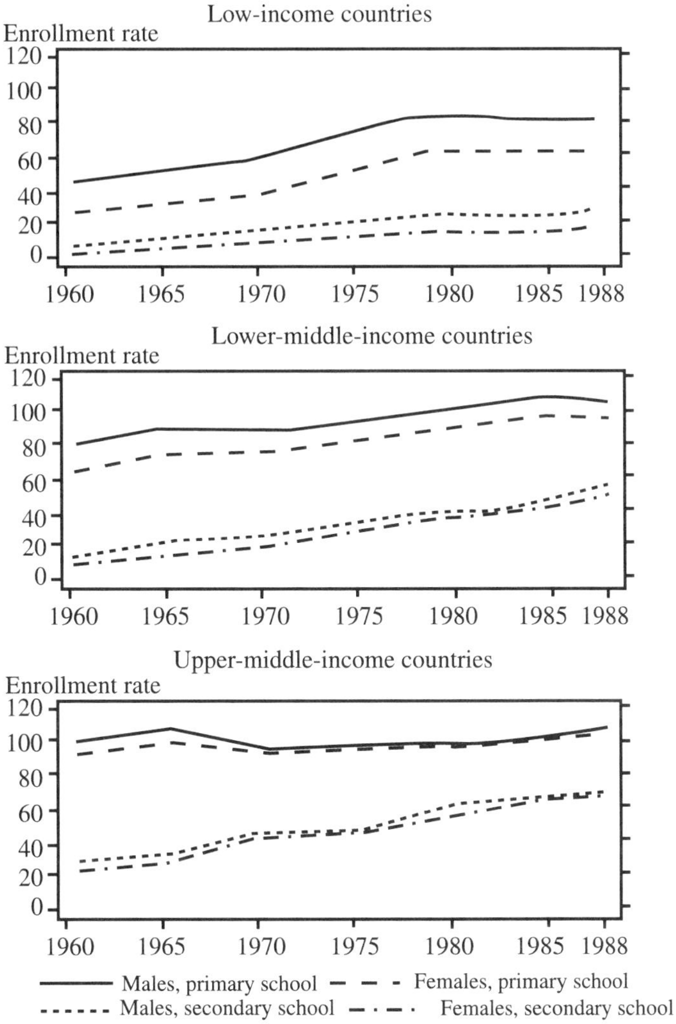

Low-income countries

Lower-middle-income countries

Upper-middle-income countries

——— Males, primary school   – – – Females, primary school
· · · · · · Males, secondary school   — · — · Females, secondary school

Note: The latest year for which data are available after 1985 is shown as 1988; for some countries, however, this date may be any year between 1985 and 1989.

Source: For gross enrollment rates, UNESCO data; for income groups (based on 1988 GNP per capita), World Bank data.

ing for girls and women fail to receive the full benefits of their investment. This is especially true because much of the payoff in educating women is broadly social.

The body of empirical work on the determinants of school enrollment in developing countries is expanding. The contribution of this literature is that it disentangles the many and complex influences on school enrollment. The studies are based, implicitly or explicitly, on a framework that treats education as a family or individual decision influenced by perceptions about current costs and future benefits. The decisionmaker weighs the benefits, net of costs, from spending family resources on educa-

tion against the net benefits of keeping children out of school. The costs include those direct financial costs, indirect or opportunity costs, and nonpecuniary costs that are borne privately by the parents or the student. The benefits include returns both to the family (in higher earnings for the children, some share of which is returned to the parents) and to society (in improved quality of life, as evidenced in our earlier discussion).

Costs are often measured by the availability of, or distance to, school, for lack of better data on the costs that each parent or student faces. A few studies have estimated the effect of the opportunity cost of schooling on enrollment or attainment in

Figure 3. Gross Enrollment Rates in Primary and Secondary Schools by Region, 1960–88

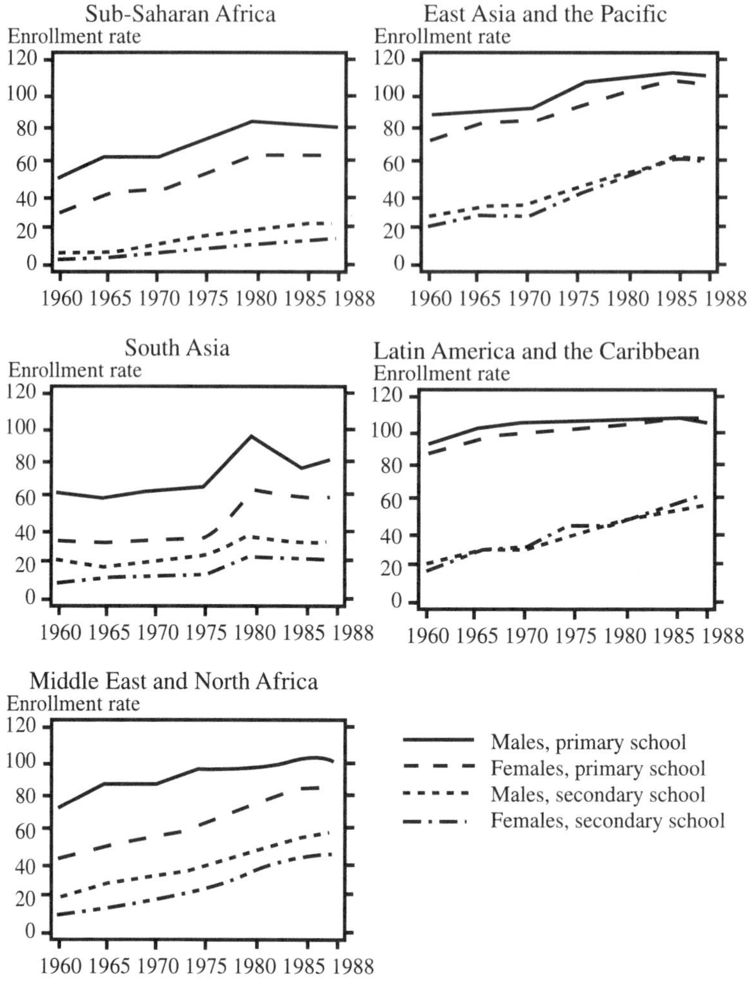

Sub-Saharan Africa
Enrollment rate

East Asia and the Pacific
Enrollment rate

South Asia
Enrollment rate

Latin America and the Caribbean
Enrollment rate

Middle East and North Africa
Enrollment rate

——— Males, primary school
– – – Females, primary school
······ Males, secondary school
–·–· Females, secondary school

Note: The latest year for which data are available after 1985 is shown as 1988; for some countries, however, this date may be any year between 1985 and 1989.
Source: UNESCO data base.

developing countries and have found a negative relationship (for example, Rosenzweig and Evenson 1977). Unlike costs, benefits do not usually find their way into empirical studies of school enrollment, primarily because of measurement difficulties. Improved productivity in the work-place, as measured by expected earnings in the labor market corresponding to given levels of education, is easier to calculate than other returns to schooling, such as increased future productivity in unpaid labor, greater efficiency in taking care of one's children or one's health, or enhanced ability to deal with problems or "disequilibria" in one's daily life (Schultz 1975).

But how do these costs and benefits affect the schooling of men and women differently? Can they account for disparities in the amounts that parents are willing to invest in educating their daughters and their sons?

Although the returns to schooling go primarily to the student, the decision and the resources usually come from the parents, especially in the early school years. Thus the perception of parents may be the key factor. And parents may have different perceptions regarding their sons' and daughters' education. In certain societies they tend to favor sons, not only in education but sometimes also in the allocation of food at mealtime or in the distribution of inheritance (Greenhalgh 1985, Rosenzweig and Schultz 1982). Such behavior on the

Table 1. Average Expected Years of Schooling by Age Eighteen in Selected Countries, 1985

Economy	Females	Males	Difference males—females
Low-income			
Burkina Faso	1.5	2.6	1.1
Nepal	3.1	7.5	4.4
Bangladesh	3.3	5.6	2.3
Burundi	2.8	4.1	1.3
Benin	3.5	7.0	3.5
Somalia	1.2	2.3	1.2
Rwanda	5.0	5.4	0.4
Guinea	1.5	3.5	2.0
Lower-middle-income			
Lesotho	10.3	7.9	−2.4
Philippines	9.0	8.8	−0.2
Morocco	5.0	7.7	2.7
Bolivia	8.0	9.1	1.1
Honduras	8.6	8.1	−0.6
Nicaragua	9.4	7.7	−1.7
El Salvador	7.3	7.0	−0.3
Botswana	9.3	8.5	−0.8
Paraguay	7.8	8.2	0.3
Tunisia	8.5	10.7	2.2
Costa Rica	8.0	8.0	−0.1
Syrian Arab Republic	8.9	11.2	2.3
Upper-middle-income			
Hungary	10.7	10.6	−0.1
Poland	11.2	11.2	−0.1
Portugal	10.5	10.2	−0.2
Panama	10.0	9.9	−0.1
Algeria	8.0	10.3	2.3
Venezuela	9.5	9.0	−0.5
Greece	11.7	11.8	0.1
Ireland	11.2	10.7	−0.6
Trinidad and Tobago	10.6	10.2	−0.4
Hong Kong	11.4	11.0	−0.3
Iraq	8.1	10.7	2.6

Note: Economies were selected on the basis of availability of data on age-specific enrollment in 1985 in the UNESCO data base. They are listed by ascending order of GNP per capita in 1985.

Source: Computed from UNESCO data.

part of parents may not be discriminatory in itself but may be a rational response to constraints imposed by poverty and to expected returns determined by labor market conditions and tradition. This does not make the consequences any less pernicious, however. When the expected returns to sending daughters to school do not exceed the costs of doing so, female education as an investment becomes unattractive to parents. Daughters will then be educated only to the extent that parents are willing to accept low economic returns.
. . .

Financial, Opportunity, and Psychic Costs

Even when education is public and tuition is free, school attendance still entails outlays from family resources. Miscellaneous school charges, learning materials, transportation, and boarding fees are some of the nontuition costs of sending children to school. Parental spending on education can be quite large. In Malawi, for example, a student at the secondary level paid K30 (Malawian kwacha) in tuition and K71 in boarding charges in 1982, or 38 percent of the total cost per student place (World Bank 1986). The families also incurred additional expenses for uniforms and transportation to school. In Korea in the mid-1960s about 70 percent of national educational expenses were paid for by parents and students. These contributions were used for the construction and operation of schools and for books, supplies, room and board, and transportation (McGinn and others 1980).

For a variety of reasons, some of these out-of-pocket expenses may be greater for girls than for boys. For example, parents' greater reluctance to send daughters to school without proper attire raises the cost of their attendance. And in some cultures, parents' concern for the physical and moral safety of their daughters makes them unwilling to let them travel long distances to school each day, necessitating costly boarding and lodging arrangements.

In addition, parents may not be able to afford the opportunity costs of educating their children. These costs vary by sex and from country to country. Although in some countries (for example, Botswana, Côte d'Ivoire, and some areas of the Philippines) boys perform a larger share of family labor, herding livestock or plowing the fields, in most places girls work more in the home and marketplace than boys. They cook, clean house, fetch water, and help their mothers care for younger children, especially those who are ill. In Nepal and Java, for example, most young girls spend at least one-third more hours per day working at home and in the market than boys of the same age; in some age groups this rises to as many as 85 percent more hours (table 2). In Malaysian households, girls between the ages of five and six who do home or market chores work as much as three-fourths more hours per week than boys of the same age. And in Chinese and Indian households in Malaysia, seven-to-nine-year-old girls work as many as

Table 2. Differences in Time Spent on Market and Household Activities by Girls Relative to Boys

Author and location of study	Definition of work	Age group		
Cabañero (1978)		*6–8*	*9–11*	*12–14*
Philippines	Average annual hours in home and market production	0.93	1.49	1.02
de Tray (1983)		*5–6*	*7–9*	*10–14*
Peninsular Malaysia	Annual participation rates in home and market production			
	Malays	1.82	1.17	1.10
	Chinese	2.50	1.78	1.31
	Indians	2.18	1.79	1.35
	Average hours per week if working			
	Malays	1.211	1.74	1.75
	Chinese	1.00	2.19	1.35
	Indians	1.76	2.49	1.80
King (1982)		*7–10*	*11–14*	
Philippines	Labor force participation rates			
	Youths in school	0.60	0.29	
	Youths out of school	—	0.37	
King and Bellew (1989)		*5–7*	*8–10*	*11–13*
Peru	Labor force participation rates			
	Youths in school	0.56	0.89	0.88
	Youths out of school	1.07	1.03	1.14
Mueller (1984)		*7–9*	*10–14*	
Rural Botswana	Proportion of total time in home and market production	0.93	0.92	
Nag and others (1980)		*6–8*	*9–11*	*12–14*
Indonesia	Hours per day in home and market production			
	Javanese village	0.97	1.74	1.85
	Nepalese village	1.32	1.29	1.36
Newman (1988)		*7–14*		
Côte d'Ivoire	Labor force participation rates	0.94		

120–150 percent more hours than boys. Clearly, girls who work more than their brothers will be less likely to attend school or will be more overworked if they do (causing them to perform less well). These examples prove that gender inequality exists even at early ages.

Besides lost work, parents may feel that girls are forgoing important childcare, household, and craft training at home if they go to school. The relative importance of these training opportunities differs from country to country depending on the expected adult occupation. For example, if most women enter the informal labor market by continuing in a crafts tradition or in agriculture, relying on skills imparted by their mothers, then the cost of attending formal schooling must include not only the opportunity cost of current time but also the lost alternative training.

Finally, in addition to the financial costs and the opportunity costs of schooling, educating girls may exact nonpecuniary or "psychic" costs as well. In certain settings, religion as well as sociocultural factors (such as norms delineating the societal, economic, and familial roles of women) strongly influence parents' choices by imposing a heavy cost on nonconformist behavior. These may bear significantly on schooling decisions. In countries in which females are usually secluded, for example, girls may attend only those schools that do not admit boys or employ male teachers. These concerns are usually stronger when girls reach puberty than earlier. Furthermore, parents may consider education itself a negative factor because of prevailing doubts about whether better-educated women make good wives. In many traditional societies, education beyond the acquisition of literacy is contrary to the social pressure for women to become wives and mothers and threatens their possibilities for marriage.

With economic development and expanding work opportunities for women, however, tension builds up between the family's adherence to traditional social norms and its desire to benefit from the changing conditions. The questions then become, when and to what extent will people respond to these shifts, and which families and individuals will respond? Economic theory does not deal formally with the impact of sociocultural forces on individual behavior, but it does predict behavioral adjustments to change in incomes and prices that result from economic growth. For example, it predicts that a rise in women's wages, which in turn increases returns to their education, tends to increase parents' investment in their daughters' education. The magnitude and speed of their response depends on acquisition of new information and on the price and income elasticities of their demand for education. Clearly, parental preferences are both shaped by and shape the economic environment.

Benefits at Work and at Home

Even when the costs of educating girls and boys are identical, parents may still keep girls at home to work and send their sons to school. Although educating a girl benefits not only her parents but also the girl herself and her future family, as well as society at large, it may be parents' expectations of receiving greater returns from educating sons than from educating daughters that determine which of their children they will send to school.

Education enhances women's economic productivity in both the farm and the nonfarm sectors. In a study of the productivity of men and women farmers in Sub-Saharan Africa, the gain in productivity from education was found to be higher for women than for men. Studies on the determinants of wage earnings have found the marginal effect of education to be about as large for women as for men once labor force participation, work experience, and sector of employment have been taken into account. But discriminatory employment practices against women have limited their work opportunities and reduced the earnings they can expect to gain from education. Entry barriers against women, explicit or implicit, in certain occupations serve as deterrents to education; examples include restrictions on hiring married women in wage-paying jobs in the manufacturing or service sectors. Some of the barriers begin even at the primary school level, with teachers and textbooks projecting attitudes that discourage performance by girls, or promoting stereotypes of girls as less capable than boys of learning mathematics or technical subjects. Other barriers arise at the postprimary level with gender-specific admissions policies in certain areas of study.

Unless daughters transfer part of their future income to their parents, parents, who must bear some of the costs of their education, may not have sufficient incentives to do so. For example, the earlier daughters marry and move in with their husbands' families, the less parents enjoy the benefits of their education. In Bangladesh 75 percent of women living in rural areas who have ever been married were married by the age of seventeen. In India 75 percent of this group were married by nineteen. Some evidence suggests that when girls do not marry so early but spend some time working in the labor force, parents are more willing to educate their daughters (see Acharya and Bennett 1981). In Hong Kong, although custom dictates that sons take responsibility for their parents, girls who marry when they are older and help their parents in the interim appear to attain higher levels of schooling than others.

Although women with more education are generally better paid and more likely to find employment in the paid sector than those with less education, married women are more likely to withdraw from the labor market as their schooling increases from the primary to the secondary level. Pregnancy, childbirth, and childcare duties remove women from the paid work force for substantial periods or even permanently. Moreover, this pattern feeds back into employers' decisions about wages, causing them to place a lower value on female than on male workers. But the withdrawal from the labor force by married women is also due partly to the fact that education increases women's productivity in nonmarket activities too, and that unless better-paying jobs outside the home are available to those with secondary education, staying at home is often a superior option.

References

Acharya, Meena, and Lynn Bennett. 1981. *The Rural Women of Nepal: An Aggregate Analysis and Summary of Eight Village Studies.* Tribhuvan University, Centre for Economic Development Administration, Katmandu.

Cabañero, T. A. 1978. "The Shadow Price of Children in Laguna Households." *Philippine Economic Journal* 17(1–2):62–87.

de Tray, Dennis. 1983. "Children's Economic Contributions in Peninsular Malaysia." Rand Note N-1839-AID. Rand Corporation, Santa Monica, Calif.

Greenhalgh, Susan. 1985. "Sexual Stratification: The Other Side of 'Growth with Equity' in East Asia." *Population and Development Review* 2(2):265–314.

King, Elizabeth M. 1982. "Investments in Schooling: An Analysis of Demand in Low-Income Households." Ph.D. diss. Yale University, New Haven, Conn.

King, Elizabeth M., and Rosemary Bellew. 1989. "Gains in the Education of Peruvian Women, 1940 to 1980." Policy Research Working Paper 472. World Bank, Population and Human Resources Department, Education and Employment Division and Women in Development Division, Washington, D.C.

McGinn, Noel F., Donald R. Snodgrass, Yung Boo Kim, Shin Bok Kim, and Quee-Young Kim. 1980. *Education and Development in Korea.* East Asian Monographs. Cambridge, Mass.: Harvard University Press.

Mueller, Eva. 1984. "The Value and Allocation of Time in Rural Botswana." *Journal of Development Economics* 15:329–60.

Nag, Moni, Benjamin N. F. White, and Robert C. Peet. 1980. "An Anthropological Approach to the Study of the Economic Value of Children in Java and Nepal." In Hans Binswanger, R. Evenson, C. Florencio, and B. White, eds., *Rural Household Studies in Asia.* Singapore University Press.

Newman, John L. 1988. *Labor Market Activity in Côte d'Ivoire and Peru.* Living Standards Measurement Study Working Paper 36. Washington, D.C.: World Bank.

Rosenzweig, Mark R., and Robert E. Evenson. 1977. "Fertility, Schooling, and the Economic Contribution of Children in Rural India: An Econometric Analysis." *Econometrica* 45:1065–79.

Rosenzweig, Mark R., and T. Paul Schultz. 1982. "Market Opportunities, Genetic Endowments, and the Intrafamily Distribution of Resources: Child Survival in Rural India." *American Economic Review* 72(4):803–15.

Schultz, Theodore W. 1975. "The Value of the Ability to Deal with Disequilibria." *Journal of Economic Literature* 13:872–76.

World Bank. 1986. *Financing Education in Developing Countries: An Exploration of Policy Options.* Washington D.C.: World Bank.

Selection V.D.2. Women in the Labor Force*

Rural women in the developing world, and particularly those who are poor, invariably work hard at a variety of tasks, with little time for leisure and little control over productive resources or even over their own income or labour. Yet they often must assume a large share of the responsibility for the survival of their families, through direct production for consumption, income earning, providing health care, etc. Women constitute a substantial part—in some countries the majority—of the agricultural labour force, including workers on plantations; they are engaged in home-based production of modern as well as traditional products, sometimes working for a contractor under the putting-out system; and many migrate from impoverished rural areas to work in the urban informal sector as traders, or in export processing zones as industrial workers.

Women in rural areas throughout the Third World are typically farmers. In Sub-Saharan Africa, subsistence farming is essentially a female activity, and women are the primary labourers on small farms, where they contribute two-thirds or more of all hours of work. Food production (as well as processing and often marketing) is essentially a female responsibility—a situation that also prevails in the Caribbean.

A more complex picture emerges in Asia. In India, while overall female labour force participation has been falling in the face of surplus labour, more and more women are becoming agricultural wage labourers because of growing landlessness. Between 30 and 40 percent of the agricultural labour force is composed of women. In Bangladesh, where women are still presumed to be secluded, they are increasingly seen in the fields, and poverty forces them to come forth for other hard work, such as road construction; these activities are in addition to their long-standing essential but largely invisible work behind compound walls in seed selection, processing, winnowing, and threshing. In China, the female labour force in rural areas has greatly increased over the past 25 years, as women's participation in agricultural work and in many non-farm activities has been strongly encouraged, both to increase production and to combat discriminatory practices and prejudices. A new dimension is emerging with the recent shift toward family farming and the promotion of family-based domestic sidelines. In South-east Asian countries, such as Indonesia, women are very active in the rice fields, a crop which usually requires intensive farming.

In Latin America, women work more in agriculture than is commonly thought, even without counting such activities as processing done in the fields and services provided to field workers. Andean agriculture, often considered a male farming system, is in fact better characterised as a family farming system.

There is a large proportion of female labour in the plantation sector as well. Working as tea pluckers, as rubber tappers, or as casual workers on coconut plantations, women in Malaysia and Sri Lanka, for example, constitute more than half of the labour force; but they receive lower pay than men for the same work, face extra burdens because of inadequate child-care facilities and the long distances between home and work, and often see others collecting their pay. Despite a high rate of trade union membership on the part of women plantation workers, their particular needs and interests have seldom been given attention by the union leadership.

In addition to agricultural work, many women are engaged in home-based production, either fulltime or in slack seasons to increase family income. In some cases such production is traditional; in others it is relatively new—particularly where traditional sources of production and income have been lost with modernisation and commercialisation; in still others it is the result of the promotion of "income-generating activities" designed to allow women to increase their cash income without disturbing their domestic responsibilities. Sometimes the result is a good income for women. In many cases, however, the returns to labour are very low. And at its worst, such home-based production definitely involves exploitation. . . . Secluded women in poor households working at home rolling beedies (popular cigarettes) or crocheting lace for contractors under the putting-out system do not receive anywhere near the minimum wage, nor do they control their own labour, let alone the labour process or marketing. They constitute an invisible labour force, dependent on traders and intermediaries who control the work. Wages (or piece rate payments) may be very low, yet they account for a substantial proportion of the income of poor households. Data on such workers

*From International Labour Office, *World Labour Report,* Vol. 2 (Oxford University Press, 1985), pp. 205–10. Reprinted by permission.

are very scanty, but the beedi industry in India alone employs between 2 and 3 million women. And this system has begun to encompass the manufacture of some modern products, such as electronics assembly units.

Access to and Control over Resources

Land is obviously the principal asset in rural areas: access to credit, extension services, technologies, and even cooperative organisations are generally linked to land titles. Yet even where women perform the bulk of agricultural work, as in much of Sub-Saharan Africa, they seldom have full title (but rather, land use rights). Where rights are collectively held, it is almost invariably the male head of household who participates in the peasant association. In family farming systems, women have even less access to basic assets. The provision of land rights and access to related resources (credit, technology, etc.) would alter the production relations, which are now characterised by the unequal bargaining position of the women. In many societies (particularly in Asia and Latin America), the process of agricultural growth and modernisation is leading to pauperisation and increasing landlessness, thus drawing more and more women into agricultural wage labour even where overall employment opportunities for women are shrinking. In North Africa and the Middle East, a little-heralded effect of male migration to the oil-producing countries of the region is the increase of female-headed households and women's participation in agricultural labour. And in Sub-Saharan Africa, while land in itself may be relatively abundant and accessible, women usually neither own nor control improved cultivable land. However, in many parts of the developing world women are beginning to organise themselves and to raise these issues within their communities and nations.

Forests are another resource that is very important to women in rural areas, as a source of fuel, food, fodder, and livelihood. Reduced access to forests, which may occur because of drought, deforestation, or changes in land tenure or forest policy, can have a devastating effect on family welfare. But it is the women who are most dependent on this resource, and whose work and income are at stake. When fuel is not readily available, families either have fewer cooked meals or have to work harder to find fuel or have to earn cash to buy fuel and/or cooked food.

There is increasing evidence that the income of household members is not automatically pooled, and that it does matter to family welfare who earns and, particularly, who controls "household" income. For example, a case-study in India has found that increasing women's wages has a visible effect on child nutrition. Therefore, increasing women's income and entitlement to or control over resources can be an important means of improving the welfare of households in rural areas.

Changing Division of Labour Between Men and Women

While domestic work is almost universally considered to be the domain of women, great variations are found in the division of labour between men and women in non-domestic activities (and even the domestic division may eventually change). Social and economic development affects men and women in specific ways, producing significant changes in the division of labour between men and women. In many developing countries great changes have occurred in agriculture during the past three decades, which have profoundly but differently affected the work of rural men and women in various income groups. The introduction of new technologies, changes in the agrarian structure, the spread of commodity production and growing inequality in rural areas have displaced women from many traditional activities, while at the same time increasing women's workload in certain agricultural tasks.

Labour mobility and the changing patterns of work and employment that accompany economic growth are often detrimental to women workers in rural areas. Modernisation has done away with many traditional income-earning opportunities, and rural development policies and programmes do not generally recognise women as producers. This is happening at a time when the incomes of poor households are dwindling, forcing women in many countries to provide for an increasing share of their family's needs. In the struggle for survival, women face great obstacles, such as their limited mobility due to family responsibilities and social and cultural restrictions. In Africa growing labour displacement towards cash crops is leaving rural women increasingly on their own to produce food with no means of improving productivity. The best arable land is usually allocated to cash crops. Yet concern is growing about falling per capita food production. This should logically lead to support for Africa's food producers—the rural women. ILO research has indicated that women's productivity can be increased by using improved technologies.

In green revolution areas in Asia, agricultural

modernisation has increased the demand for casual labour while marginalising small tenants and dispossessing smallholders of their land. Male tasks have been more commonly mechanised than those of women, thereby decreasing male employment opportunities and income and pushing women into agricultural wage labour. Women are also seeking needed income in the informal sector or as home-based workers, or they may migrate to look for work elsewhere. Landlessness and poverty have dramatically increased the number of women working as casual labourers. Improved transport facilities and the spread of manufactured goods threaten many petty commodity trade activities undertaken by women and men without opening up new employment opportunities for women, as jobs in the modern sector are seldom available to them. Permanent or seasonal male out-migration in Asia, west and southern Africa is affecting farming practices. In Lesotho, for instance, the plight of migrant workers' families is such that the departure of able-bodied men to the mining industry in South Africa calls for additional work by women, and is hardly compensated by insecure and meagre migrant remittances. Strained family bonds and reduced household income are leaving women in a very vulnerable position. In Malawi about a quarter of rural households are headed by women, and this rate is even higher among the lowest income groups. Rural development programmes and extension services have failed to reach these women, who in the absence of male workers are unable to increase agricultural productivity. In some countries, such as Ghana, Malawi, and the Sudan, female-headed households constitute between one-fourth and one-third of all rural households, while in other countries the proportion is estimated at between 5 and 20 percent (about 12 in Indonesia, 17 in Mauritania, and 13 in Panama, for instance).

Increasing rural poverty has also precipitated female out-migration as a means of supplementing family income. Export processing zones in Asia (e.g., in Malaysia, the Philippines, and Singapore) have increasingly attracted a young and docile female labour force for export-oriented industries relying on a cheap but intensive labour process.

Women as Industrial Workers

Rapid industralisation, while expanding employment opportunities, has not fully benefited working women, since they often lose traditional sources of income without getting new jobs. This has happened for example in such newly industrialised countries as Brazil, India, Mexico, and Ni-

geria. Various studies show that women are increasingly confined to home work (as in the textiles, clothing, and tobacco industries) and in marginal service jobs in the urban informal sector where employment is casual and irregular and where incomes are very low. It is also characteristic of most developing countries that mainly young unmarried women (in the 20–25 age group) obtain employment in the formal sector.

Why do certain employers prefer to recruit young unmarried women as employees? Some studies indicate that this preference is based less on the job requirements than on social perceptions. Women are supposed to have dexterity, speed, and endurance in certain assembly-line jobs in old industries such as clothing or new industries such as electronics. They are considered to be more disciplined and docile than male workers, and ready to accept low wages. In some cases young girls have been dismissed when they reached the legal age at which they would be entitled to adult wages.

The fact that women are concentrated in the traditionally "female industries" and in low-skilled jobs keeps their wages low, hinders their upward mobility, and makes them prone to long periods of unemployment in times of economic and technological restructuring. It is well known that in female industries, such as textiles, clothing, electronics, food, and beverages, wages are usually lower than in other industries.

What is the impact of new technologies on women's jobs? While technological progress over the years has widened women's employment opportunities in the modern sector, it has had the effect of frequently displacing them into low-skilled and low-status occupations. This trend is illustrated by the commerce, finance, and services sectors where their employment at first expanded enormously but may now be affected in two ways: those who are already employed may lose the jobs or see the content of their jobs change, while those who are looking for jobs may not find one corresponding to their qualifications. This situation, combined with high rates of unemployment, may cause serious setbacks to the emancipation of women through work. It appears that even in newer industries, such as electronics, the dynamics of technological change require higher levels of technical skills, generally not accessible to women. In plants located in several industrial estates and export processing zones, young, inexperienced rural women are considered to be the best choice, since they are believed to be more patient and diligent and to have keener eyesight and more nimble fingers than men.

In developing countries lack of skills leads women to seek employment as domestic servants, an occupation in which they are often exploited and which offers low wages and uncertain and long hours, with no paid leave or other social benefits. Other occupations in which women find themselves are those of barmaids, hostesses, and receptionists, which are outside the reach of labour regulations. Sometimes young girls under the minimum age of admission to employment work as domestic servants or entertainers under harsh conditions and often without adequate pay, food, or shelter.

The number of women working in offices and commerce varies from country to country. In developing countries secretaries and teachers are still occupational categories filled by both men and women. There is, however, a trend for these occupations to become more feminised. This is true of first-grade teachers in Asia and secondary-level teachers in Africa, where the number of women occupying such posts rose from 22 to 29 percent and from 25 to 33 percent respectively between 1975 and 1980. Community, social, and health services in many countries show a high concentration of women since welfare services are considered to be a female sphere of activity. But even in these occupations women hold jobs in the lower echelons, while the higher echelons are almost exclusively occupied by men. This is particularly true of the health sector where women are usually nurses, etc., but not hospital managers, surgeons, or research technicians.

There are occupations, however, in which there is a neat division of labour between men and women. For example, it is mainly women who are engaged in the retail trade of certain African and Asian countries, while men dominate the wholesale trade and commerce.

In the public service sector women usually have reasonable opportunities to reach responsible positions, owing to the scope of labour legislation and other regulations. Although their numbers are still very small, in some countries they work in ministries of health, education, and social affairs at intermediate levels and in various government departments and agencies.

Selection V.D.3. Women, Poverty, and Development in the Third World*

The relative intensity of women's poverty is apparent from data on: (1) the income of house-holds that are headed by women, and (2) the productivity and earnings of women's work in developing countries. This selection reviews the evidence related to these measures and describes some of the factors that explain why income tends to be lowest in women-headed households and why women's work is less productive than men's work and the lowest paid.

The Poverty of Women-Headed Households

The incidence of households headed by women is increasing rapidly in the Third World. In Africa in the 1980s, the seasonal migration of males seeking work abroad or in domestic urban labor markets has resulted in large numbers of rural households headed by "left behind" women. From one-third to one-half of all rural households are at any one time headed by women in, for example, Botswana, Kenya, and Zambia. In the Arab, Islamic countries of North Africa, the male exodus has created women-headed households on a large scale, even though this household category is scarcely recognized in the applicable family law. In Latin America and in the Caribbean region, steady rural-to-urban migration of young women since the 1960s—combined with marital abandonment and unstable unions—has led to a heavy incidence of households headed by women in the urban areas.

The available data show that in rural Africa, in the Commonwealth Caribbean territories, and in urban Latin America, women-headed house-holds are poorer than those jointly headed or headed by men. In Latin America, comparative analyses of the earnings of household heads show that the type of occupation, rather than age or education, explains most of the differential earnings between male and female heads. Female-headed households also are poorer because they have fewer secondary earners and more dependents to support than male-headed house-holds. The pattern is the same in the English-speaking Caribbean. Similarly, in Africa, comparisons of male and female household heads reveal no significant differences

*From Mayra Buvinic and Margaret A. Lycette, "Women, Poverty and Development in the Third World," in John P. Lewis, ed., *Strengthening the Poor: What Have We Learned?* (Overseas Development Council, 1989), pp. 150–56. 160–61. © 1989. Reprinted by permission from Transaction Publishers.

as to age and education. Instead, women-headed households are poorer because they have fewer resident working members than male-headed house-holds, but more dependents and smaller landholdings. It is also true that these house-holds are much less likely to have access to productive services such as agricultural extension and credit for more explicitly gender reasons. In any event, in Latin America, the Caribbean, and Africa, female-headed households are on average distinctly worse off.

The situation in Asia is more hopeful in that poverty does not seem to be concentrated on women-headed households. Evidence from India, Nepal, Sri Lanka, Taiwan, and peninsular Malaysia indicated that women-headed households are not found disproportionately among the bottom deciles of the household distributions of per capita income and expenditure. This is probably due to the fact that in Asia—in contrast to Africa and Latin America—few women of prime reproductive age have sole responsibility for the care of young children and the extended family household is more common. Even in Asia, however, a substantial number of women, often widows, do head households, especially among the lower castes.

Women's Earnings

Women-headed households are not the only cases of poverty among women—nor should they be the only ones targeted for gender-oriented interventions. Women in male- and jointly-headed households contribute to family income through both unremunerated home labor and production for income, and the low compensation some of them receive keeps their households' incomes in the poverty zone.

To a large extent, the poverty of women (including heads of households) is related to the type of work women do and the meager returns they obtain for it. Their lower earnings are a direct function of their limited access to capital and modern technologies. Women perform low-productivity, labor-intensive work both as homemakers and income earners. The result is overwork and low pay for women and harder times for their families.

Moreover, the poorer the country, the more hours women work. In parts of East Africa, for example, women work sixteen hours a day doing housework, caring for children, preparing food, and raising 60–80 percent of the food for the fami-

Table 1. 1980 Distribution of Economically Active Population by Sector (percentage)

	Agriculture		Industry		Services	
	Males	Females	Males	Females	Males	Females
Latin America and Caribbean	38	15	28	20	34	66
Asia	63	71	17	13	21	16
Africa	64	78	15	6	21	17

Source: International Labour Office, *Economically Active Population, 1950–2025,* Vols. I, II, III, and V (Geneva: ILO, 1986).

ly. In Burkina Faso, women have only a little more than one hour a day in which to perform personal care, undertake community responsibilities, and engage in leisure activities. In fact, in all regions women devote significantly more time than men to a combination of work for income and home maintenance, food preparation, and childcare. As the demand for child-rearing time and for cash income increases over the household life cycle, women's work hours increase and leisure decreases. The burdens of poverty are aggravated when women, out of need, seek work in the marketplace and, because of their lack of assets, undertake low-productivity work in agriculture, in the informal non-agricultural sector, or in the lowest paid sectors of the modern economy.

In agriculture, because of limited access to credit and modern technologies and services, women's work is labor-intensive and yields very low economic returns. This has been documented for countries as disparate as Cameroon, Indonesia, and Peru. Women wage laborers in agriculture are hired for lower-paid agricultural tasks and/or are paid less than men for similar work. In Sri Lanka they receive only 66–75 percent of the male wage, while in Honduras they are paid about 70 percent of the male wage for performing the same tasks in tobacco cultivation.

In industry and services, women tend to be clustered in low-skilled jobs with little potential for training or advancement. While the proportion of women among unskilled industrial workers is less than 30 percent in developed countries, it is higher than 50 percent in some Asian and African countries. In Latin American countries, women workers tend to be concentrated in lower-status occupations in the service sector rather than in industry. In Brazil, Chile, and Peru, for example, over 50 percent of economically active urban women work in services—a low-wage sector in those countries.

Unable to gain better-paid, formal sector employment, increasing numbers of women have turned to self-employment in the informal sector—either as a supplement to formal sector earn-

ings or as their sole source of support. In much of the Third World, the informal sector rivals formal employment as a source of jobs for both men and women. In Bombay and Jakarta, for example, as well as in many African and Latin American cities, 50 to 60 percent of the labor force is employed in the informal sector, which is often the fastest-growing segment of the economy. Informal sector employment tends to be labor-intensive and to have low output per worker. This is reflected in the close association between informal employment and lower average earnings, particularly for women. In Kenya in 1978, for example, 41 percent of informally employed women—compared with 13.8 percent of men—had incomes of less than 199 shillings. In Bolivia, 48 percent of the self-employed in La Paz in 1983 were women, and their average weekly earnings were 70 percent of those of men.

Even if much of women's increased participation in product and labor markets yields low economic returns, it often makes a crucial difference to family well-being.

The Economic Contributions of Poor Women

Three indicators of the importance of women's earnings in low-income developing-country households are their proportional representation in household budgets, their role in promoting child nutritional status, and their importance in periods of economic crisis.

Women's Earnings in Low-Income Households

Studies have repeatedly shown that the earnings of adult women are proportionately more important in poor families than among the better off. In Indonesia, women and girls of poor landless families, unlike those of upper-income families, devote almost as much time to wage labor as do men and boys. In the Peruvian Sierra, women from landless peasant households provide 35 percent of the total number of family labor days devoted to agricultural production, while women from the middle and rich peasantry provide only 21 percent. Moreover, it is mainly the women in poor near-landless and smallholder households who resort to wage labor or artisan activities to supplement family incomes; in so doing, they are adversely affected by the differential returns to male and female labor.

Women's Earnings and Child Nutrition

Joanne Leslie's 1987 critical review of fifty empirical studies on the relationship between women's market work, infant feeding practices, and child nutrition demonstrates that children of higher-income-earning mothers are nutritionally better off than children of lower-income earners. Efforts to raise women's incomes are critical to the provision of high-quality foods for infants and children.

In the case of women heads of household it is possible that the additional meager income from market work may not compensate for the time lost in child (and self) care, especially since these women may have little access to alternative child caretakers. Nevertheless, evidence for rural Africa suggests that children may actually be nutritionally better off in households headed by women. This is largely because women heads of household have more control over income, and resources controlled by women are more likely to be allocated to family food expenditures. In Kenya, for example, female-headed households (controlled for land size and household composition) allocate a greater proportion of income toward supplying high-calorie foods than do male-headed households.

Women's Earnings in Periods of Economic Adversity

As happened during the Great Depression in the United States, adverse economic conditions in developing economies in the early 1980s seem to have increased the participation of poor women in formal and informal labor markets to help compensate for the loss in real family incomes. In rural Africa, poorer women farmers and nearly landless women have responded to economic contraction and food insecurity by increasing the time they devote to farming marginal lands and to low-productivity informal sector activities.

In Latin America, during the economic crises of the early 1980s, women's labor force participation rates generally increased more than those of men, leveling off or declining during periods of relative economic recovery. In Chile, for example, despite a long-term downward trend in women's labor force participation, women's activity rates in the lowest quintile of household incomes increased sharply—from 18 percent to 22.4 percent—during the economic crisis of 1974–75. Over the same period, the participation rates of women in the higher quintiles of the income distribution declined.

From the foregoing, it is clear that attempts to expand women's economic opportunities and increase their earnings should be a preferred anti-poverty strategy. The next sections examine problems such efforts must overcome and make some recommendations for policy reform.

Constraints on Gender-related Reforms

Five major constraints have to be addressed in poverty-alleviation strategies that are intended to focus in whole or in part on the particular economic and social needs of women.

(1) Perhaps the most important of these constraints is the virtually universal responsibility of women for household production chores such as childcare, food preparation, and provision of water and fuel-wood or other sources of cooking fuel. The dual burden of home labor and production for cash income has far-reaching implications for women's ability to invest the time often required to participate in and benefit from development programs.

(2) Women's educational attainment in developing countries is severely limited, both relative to men and in absolute terms, in most world regions. Only in Latin America are there virtually identical enrollment rates for girls and boys through the secondary school level. Even in this region, however, functional literacy and numeracy rates among women—especially in rural areas—are still low. Until the educational imbalance between women and men is reduced, it will be impossible for adequate numbers of women to be trained for skilled occupations or to participate in development programs that depend on participants' ability to read and write.

(3) Cultural dictates regarding the sexual division of labor in agriculture, formal employment, and, perhaps to a somewhat smaller degree, informal employment, can effectively bar women's participation in what often are the more lucrative areas of economic activity. Such dictates are reflected in, and in turn contribute to, biases regarding the extent, quality, and type of education avail-

able to women. Other biases regarding, for example, the types and levels of women's asset ownership and the "protection" of women, must also be dealt with in the design of many development programs, as such cultural factors often determine when and in what circumstances women can attend a training center or meet collateral conditions for loans.

(4) Some of the restrictive cultural norms are enshrined in laws. In many countries, laws prohibit a woman's participation in education or family planning programs without the consent of her husband or father. More important, laws regarding title to land or housing can determine whether or not women—even women who head households—are able to participate in housing or credit programs; and protective labor laws may result in women being denied the chance to work and be paid for overtime or to work at all in certain occupations in which late night shifts are common.

(5) Because of the factors cited, women are over-represented in the most marginally productive occupations and are among the smallest operators and producers. The scale of women's economic activities, in and of itself, increases the difficulty of reaching women through development programs.

These constraints translate into sectoral policy and program concerns and point to the need for alternative approaches in poverty–alleviation programs that hope to incorporate women. For example, women who operate micro-enterprises face particular constraints in access to credit. First, they may lack access to information about credit programs, especially when the latter are sponsored by organizations to which women do not belong. Because women are less educated than men, they are less likely to be able to fill out loan application forms. Collateral requirements, based on land or property ownership, are another serious constraint, since women seldom hold title to such assets. And in loan programs that accept business ownership as collateral, women may miss out because their businesses are too small or are not formally registered.

Women farmers typically face similar problems. Lack of title to land can block their access to agricultural credit, services, and inputs. In addition, women farmers rarely have direct contact with agricultural extension agents; and when they are reached, their limited education may prevent them from using agricultural information effectively. A study of six rural Peruvian communities revealed that 88 percent of women farmers had never been

offered any agricultural extension services or advice, although 67 percent expressed strong interest in agricultural and livestock training.

Women's access to vocational training is also inhibited by many factors. Low-income and rural women especially are often precluded from participation in such programs by educational prerequisites, timing conflicts between instruction hours and inflexible work and family responsibilities, as well as distance and lack of cheap transport.

Moreover, when women do gain access to training, the effectiveness of the programs often is diminished by sex-biased curricula. Women's training typically concentrates in such traditionally female areas as cosmetology, hairdressing, and typing, while men predominate in such higher-paying areas as machine tool operation and motor vehicle mechanics.

Finally, because of their household responsibilities, women choose courses of short duration, which generally do not lead to high-paying jobs. In Argentina, for example, a recent survey found that 95 percent of the students in short-term training programs were women, while 92 percent of those in long-term training were men.

Conclusions and Recommendations

Given the degree of poverty among women in developing countries and the importance of their economic contributions to households, it is clear that anti-poverty strategies must be designed to address the social, legal, and economic constraints that women face.

An effective strategy for accomplishing this goal should include, first, a focus on women themselves rather than on women as members of households or families. Because there are critical differences in the types of work men and women perform, and in the ways in which they utilize income received, development interventions aimed at the household or family are not effective in alleviating women's poverty nor, in most cases, that of the children for whom women are almost universally responsible. Conversely, programs focused on women, when they are effective in raising women's productivity and income, produce benefits for family well-being.

Micro-enterprise interventions have been successful in reaching women largely because they have been designed to improve entrepreneurial, rather than family, income. Agriculture projects, however, must be reoriented to smallholders and should rely on a farming systems approach that takes into account women's roles as farmers and resource managers. Improvements in women's education and training will depend on the introduction of flexible class timing, incentives for parents to release girls from home production, and the removal of traditional biases regarding "appropriate" training for women.

At the policy level, the need to consider gender implications is becoming increasingly clear. Structural adjustment and other policy reform programs worldwide have produced a number of unforeseen problems because the role of women in various economic activities was not taken into account. To be effective, such reforms must be structured to assist women, not only men, to respond to price and other incentives. Similarly, broader changes in legal, financial, and educational systems must be undertaken in order to genuinely enhance women's social and economic contributions to development in the long term. There is a need to examine carefully, for instance, the ways in which legal inheritance patterns or protective labor legislation can reinforce women's disadvantaged economic position. Financial policies that encourage biases against, or reduce the profitability of, the types of borrowing that poor women seek must be revamped in order to maximize the productivity of women's work. And educational policies and funding must be changed to reflect the very high social and economic returns to women's primary education and literacy.

In essence, policymakers and development practitioners must consider gender differences, and the implications of development interventions for women, at each stage of policy and project development and for all social and economic sectors. Failure to do so may mean not only bypassing women in poverty–alleviation efforts, but perhaps even increasing their relative poverty.

Selection V.D.4. Women in Developing Countries*

Most of the literature on discrimination focuses on the labor market. The most commonly deployed technique, the earnings function, is well suited to show one type of discrimination, namely, differentially low pay for the same characteristics. However, this is perhaps the less important aspect of labor market gender discrimination. The more important is differentially poor access. Evidence on this requires logistic techniques and sampling frames based upon households rather than employers. One such study, for rural Tanzania, found extreme discrimination in access to non-farm wage employment, which was the highest return activity. Access was determined largely by education, age, and gender: a 36-year-old man with secondary education had a three-in-four chance of such employment, whereas a woman of the same age and education had half of that chance. With completed primary education she had only a quarter of the chance, and with partial primary or less she had only one-fifth of the chance. This declension suggests that discrimination may apply differentially at different levels of education. Thus general expansion of the education system may reduce the aggregate incidence of discrimination even if the educational expansion is not targetted to women.

Since the rural non-agricultural labor market commonly contains a large public sector, discrimination is the outcome of government recruitment policies. In turn, this may reflect the use of public sector employment as part of a patronage system rather than its being a competitive entry based upon job-related characteristics. Women may because of their low status in society be badly represented in the lobby for patronage.

In urban areas, the labor market is probably the main arena of discrimination. However, in rural areas, non-agricultural wage employment can usually only be available to a minority of women because it is only available to a minority of men. Rather, it is the savings, credit, and financial markets where discrimination is more important because these constrain the earning capacities of women in agricultural self-employment.

Savings and Credit

Women are severely disadvantaged in the credit market: they usually do not own marketable land

*From Paul Collier, *Women in Developing Countries,* World Bank, Policy Research Working Paper 129 (December 1988), pp. 3–11. Reprinted by permission.

rights and hence have no collateral, and if subordinates in the household may have no capacity to establish reputations for credit-worthiness as independent agents. Formal credit programs are usually channeled to household heads, and are commonly based on non-food crops in which men tend to specialise. It is very hard to see how these obstacles in the credit market can be overcome, except in the case of female-headed households. For this group, who have the capacity to build reputations, formal credit programs could be monitored to see whether discrimination is occurring. Where it is, it should be a relatively simple matter for a public credit program to be redirected to them as a target group.

However, where women are in male-headed households, which is the majority, the alternative is probably to rely upon the savings market. The latter suffers none of the problems intrinsic to the credit market: dependents can hold individual rights to financial assets. Once such assets are accumulated they fulfil the same functions as a credit line, namely, liquidity and the capacity to finance lumpy investments. It is notable that whereas men predominate as borrowers in both the formal and informal rural credit market, women predominate in the informal savings market (both as savers and even as lenders in many cases). A particularly interesting manifestation of this is the savings club. In this arrangement a group of women agree to make regular payments into a common fund, the whole sum being distributed on each occasion to the members of the group in turn, the sequence being determined by lot. This offers two advantages over individual savings: first, it enables any scale economies in expenditure to be reaped earlier, and secondly, the social pressure to make contributions enforces savings behaviour against both temporary lapses on the part of the saver and pressure on the woman from other claimants upon assets. The latter may be particularly difficult to resist because of the dependent status of the woman. To bring out the implications, public interventions in rural financial markets have overwhelmingly been on credit rather than the savings side of the market. Yet we have suggested that the former is intrinsically male biased, whereas the latter is far more likely to be gender neutral. Since the savings market can serve as a substitute for credit, it is therefore likely to be female biased. The neglect of the rural savings market by public programs would be less important were the informal savings market in a position to provide an adequate service. However, this is often not the case. First, due to problems of the high co-variance of withdrawals, informal savings institutions rarely develop (hence money lenders are far more common than deposit takers). Secondly, because of foreign exchange and interest rate controls, formal deposit-taking institutions are not in a position to offer a secure and positive real return upon assets to depositors, despite such returns being available on the world financial market. Thirdly, if as we have suggested, contractual savings schemes (which both compel saving and limit the capacity to make withdrawals) would be popular, this requires a degree of contractual enforcement and continuity more suited to formal than informal agencies. The design of rural formal savings schemes attractive to women is a priority because it contributes on several different fronts. Savings can finance long-term investment in the sectors in which women specialise, thereby rectifying a current misallocation of capital and possibly increasing the overall savings rate. They also provide a cushion for temporary negative shocks and a means of profiting in a sustained way from positive ones. Finally, when women command assets their status and bargaining position is improved, and financial assets being new they are not bound by the conventions which often restrict the major real assets, land and livestock, to male ownership.

Role Models

In rural Africa formal wage employment, non-food crops, and improved livestock are generally innovations of this century. The economy is in disequilibrium in the sense that the rates of return to factors differ systematically among activities. Typically, food production is at the bottom of this hierarchy and formal wage employment and new-technique agricultural investments are at the top. Women are a minority towards the top of the hierarchy and a majority at the bottom. Economic change in rural Africa is to a considerable extent a process of taking up these disequilibrium opportunities by switching into the higher return activities.

Women are at a disadvantage in this process: Bevan et al. (1986) establish that controlling for a wide range of other characteristics, female-headed households are radically less likely to adopt tree crops and improved livestock. Although this is partly due to discrimination, it appears also to be because of the enormous power of role models.

Bevan et al. demonstrated that a "copying effect" is decisive in the entry into new, high-return activities. The peasant population has access to a very restricted stream of trustworthy information, chiefly its own social network. This network is defined by family and spatial proximity. If this social network is indeed the chief determinant of economic innovation then the very fact that women are under-represented in high-return activities creates a powerful role model for its perpetuation. The externalities, which the copying effect constitute, provide a case for temporary positive discrimination to establish a countervailing role model.

The copying effect works both on states and on decisions. That is, in deciding to enter a new activity people are influenced both by the number of other people already in the activity and by the number of other people who have recently decided to enter it. Bevan et al. find that the copying effect is much more pronounced for decisions than for states: that is, the decisions currently being made are much more influential than past decisions. Hence, encouraging one woman to enter a high-return activity may have the same inducement to other women to follow as that provided to men by two men who are already in the activity. This is hopeful because it suggests that although role models are important, their inertial properties can be overcome.

Since gender is only one of the dimensions on which actors identify themselves, and hence appropriate role models, the copying effect can be enhanced by concentrating change among similar women (for example, geographically proximate, young, educated women).

Asymmetric Rights and Obligations

To some extent the household can be viewed as a set of implicit contracts which generate reciprocal rights and obligations. Typically, women incur obligations to grow food crops for subsistence, to gather fuel and water, to cook, and to rear children. In return, the man will provide land and will meet the cash needs of the household. This allocation is commonly unequal—women work much harder than men. This is clearly the case in much of rural Africa as measured by hours of work. It may also be inefficient, labor and land being imperfectly allocated between activities. Returns to factors are generally radically higher in non-food activities, consistent with the hypothesis that women work excessively on food crops because they cannot secure the land for, or would forfeit part of the income from non-food activities. Specialisation is not confined to food versus non-food crops. For example, in Kenya tea picking tends to be women's work. The adoption of tea was found to be significantly affected by the gender composition of the household labour endowment: the more female labor the more likely was the household to adopt the crop. Conversely in coffee, which tends to be a man's crop, adoption was encouraged only by additional male labor. A constant set of asymmetric rights and obligations may give rise to variable material circumstances. First, there may be asymmetric vulnerability—at times of crisis women may suffer relative to men. For example, work by Vaughan on famine in Malawi shows that men took the opportunity to out-migrate, leaving women with a collapse in subsistence production and a reduced command over cash to purchase food in the market. Women may be especially vulnerable to unanticipated rapid changes associated with slumps and rapid structural adjustment. If so this is worrying since the burden of adjustment costs should not, on equity grounds, be borne by an initially disadvantaged group. Further, since women spend disproportionately upon children, an adjustment that involves short-term costs and long-term gains (as most do), may inflict upon a cohort of children an inter-temporal redistribution of consumption which is undesirable (because low but temporary levels of consumption in children may give rise to permanent effects). Secondly, changes in circumstances may make a given set of rights and obligations increasingly unequal or increasingly inefficient. For example, the emphasis upon technical progress and extension in non-food activities relative to food increases the returns to male labor relative to female labor, and factor allocations become less appropriate because of the restrictions upon substitution possibilities. As the returns to non-food activities rise, female labor and land constrained to food production represent an increasing misallocation.

However, this very specialisation by function makes it relatively easy to target programs for women (much easier than for poor households). For example, rural water, fuel, and health services are all pro-women. Water fetching is an arduous and time-consuming activity undertaken almost exclusively by women. Piped water is in effect the supply of leisure to women. Wood gathering for fuel is also a time-consuming female activity. The growing scarcity of such wood reflects the absence of private property rights which, if they are to be created, would most sensibly be vested in women. Reforestation programs have generally been targeted at men. The pricing of firewood substitutes such as kerosene is also, therefore, a woman's issue.

Reference

Bevan, D. L., et al. (1986). *Trade Shocks in Controlled Economies* (London: Oxford University Press).

Selection V.D.5. Missing Women*

In Europe and North America women tend to out-number men. For example, in the United King-dom, France, and the United States the ratio of wo-men to men exceeds 1.05. In many Third World countries, however, especially in Asia and north Africa, the female:male ratio may be as low as 0.95 (Egypt), 0.94 (Bangladesh, China, and west Asia), 0.93 (India), or even 0.90 (Pakistan). These differences are relevant to an assessment of female inequality across the world.[1]

Everywhere about 5 percent more boys than girls are born. But women are hardier than men and, given similar care, survive better at all ages—including in utero. There are other causes for this preponderance of women—for example, some re-maining impact of the deaths of men in the last world war and more cigarette smoking and violent deaths among men. But even taking these into ac-count, women would still outnumber men if given similar care.[2]

Social factors must therefore explain the low fe-male:male ratios in Asian and north African coun-tries. These countries would have millions more women if they showed the female:male ratios of Europe and the United States.[3] Calculated on this basis, China is missing more than 50 million wo-men.

Using European or American ratios may not, however, be appropriate. Because of lower female mortality in Europe and America the female:male ratio rises gradually with age. A lower ratio would therefore be expected in Asia and north Africa partly because of a lower life expectancy and high-er fertility rate. There are several ways of adjusting for this. One is to adopt the female:male ratios of Sub-Saharan Africa, where there is little female disadvantage in terms of relative mortality but where life expectancy is no higher and fertility rates no lower than those in Asia and north Africa. Using the Sub-Saharan ratio of 1.022 yields an es-timate of 44 million missing women in China, 37 million in India, and a total of more than 100 mil-lion worldwide.[4]

Using population models based on Western de-mographic experience, it is possible to estimate roughly how many women there would be without any female disadvantage in survival, given the ac-tual life expectancy and the fertility rates in these countries. Coale estimates 29 million missing wo-men in China, 23 million in India, and an overall total of 60 million for selected countries.[5] Though lower, these numbers are still enormous.

Why is overall mortality for females higher than that for males in these countries? Consider India, where age specific mortality for females consis-tently exceeds that for males until the fourth decade. Although the excess mortality at child-bearing age may be partly due to maternal mortali-ty, obviously no such explanation is possible for female disadvantage in survival in infancy and childhood. Despite occasional distressing accounts of female infanticide, this could not explain the ex-tra mortality or its age distribution. The compara-tive neglect of female health and nutrition, espe-cially—but not exclusively—during childhood, would seem the prime suspect. Considerable direct evidence exists of neglect of female children in terms of health care, admission to hospitals, and even feeding.[6]

Even though the position in India has been more extensively studied than that in other coun-tries, similar evidence of relative neglect of the health and nutrition of female children may be found in other countries in Asia and north Africa. In China some evidence suggests that the extent of neglect may have increased sharply in recent

*From Amartya Sen, "Missing Women," *British Medical Journal* 304 (1992): 587–88. Reprinted by permission.

[1]A. K. Sen, *Resources, Values and Development* (1984), pp. 346–85, and "Women's Survival as a Development Problem," *Bulletin of the American Academy of Arts and Sciences* 43 (1989): 14–29; J. Kynch, "How Many Woman Are Enough? Sex Ratios and the Right to Life," in *Third World Affairs 1985*, ed. A. Gauhar (1985), pp. 156–72; B. Harriss and E. Watson, "The Sex Ratio in South Asia," in *Geography of Gender in the Third World*, ed. J. H. Momson and J. Townsend (1987), pp. 85–115; J. Drèze and A. K. Sen, *Hunger and Public Action* (1989), pp. 50–59, 221–25; A. J. Coale, "Excess Female Mortality and the Balance of the Sexes in the Population: An Estimate of the Number of 'Missing Females,' " *Population and Development Review* 17 (1991): 517–23.

[2]I. Waldron, "The Role of Genetic and Biological Factors in Sex Differences in Mortality," in *Sex Differences in Mortality*, ed. A. D. Lopez and L. T. Ruzicka (1983).

[3]Sen, "Women's Survival as a Development Problem."

[4]Drèze and Sen, *Hunger and Public Action*.

[5]Coale, "Excess Female Mortality and the Balance of the Sexes in the Population."

[6]L. Chen, E. Huq, and S. D'Souza, "Sex Bias in the Family Allocation of Food and Health Care in Rural Bangladesh," *Population and Development Review* 7 (1981): 55–70; A. K. Sen, *Commodities and Capabilities* (1985), pp. 81–104.

years, particularly since compulsory restrictions on the size of families were introduced in some parts of the country in the late 1970s. There are also some new, ominous signs in China, such as a substantial increase in the reported ratio of male to female births—quite out of line with the rest of the world. It could quite possibly indicate "hiding" of newborn female children (to avoid the rigours of compulsory restriction on the size of the family), but it could, no less plausibly, reflect a higher female infant mortality—whether or not induced (with new births and new deaths both going unreported).

What causes the relative neglect of females, and how can it be changed? Possible influences include traditional cultures and values. But some economic links have also emerged, and some connections between economic status and social standing have been identified. For example, the ability to earn an outside income through paid employment seems to enhance the social standing of a woman (which is the case in Sub-Saharan Africa). This makes her contribution to the prosperity of the family more visible. Also, being less dependent on others, she has more voice. The higher status of women also affects ideas on the female child's "due." Secondly, education, especially female literacy, may make a substantial difference. Thirdly, women's economic rights (for example, land ownership and in-heritance) may be important.[7] Public policy can influence all of these.

The Indian state of Kerala provides an illuminating exception to the prevailing experience. It has the most developed school education system in India, which dates from the early nineteenth century, with strongly supportive state policies in the "native kingdoms" of Travancore and Cochin.[8] Adult literacy rate is now over 90 percent. Property inheritance passes through the female line for an influential part of the community (the Nairs). Many women participate in "gainful" economic activities. Kerala also has an extensive health care system, which has been built up through public policy. Even though Kerala is one of the poorer Indian states, life expectancy at birth there now exceeds 73 years for women and 67 years for men.

The female:male ratio of the Kerala population is now around 1.04—similar to that in Europe and America (and most unlike that in the rest of India, Bangladesh, Pakistan, China, west Asia, and north Africa). It seems that the "missing women" may be rescuable, after all, by public policy.

[7]E. Boserup, *Women's Role in Economic Development* (1970), pp. 15–154; A. K. Sen, "Gender and Cooperative Conflict," in *Persistent Inequalities,* ed. I. Tinker (1990), pp. 123–49.

[8]Drèze and Sen, *Hunger and Public Action.*

Selection V.D.6. Grameen Bank: Performance and Sustainability*

The Grameen Bank is a rural bank in Bangladesh that provides credit to the rural poor, particularly women, who own less than half an acre of land or whose assets do not exceed the value of one acre of land. Unlike traditional commercial bank loans, Grameen Bank loans need not be secured by collateral. This serves the landless in Bangladesh who are left out of the conventional banking system.

Dr. Muhammad Yunus, an economics professor, started the Grameen Bank in 1976 as a research project. He held that rural people, owning too little land to support themselves as farmers, could nevertheless make productive use of small loans borrowed without collateral, and would repay loans on time. Lack of access to credit was perceived as the biggest constraint for the rural poor. The Grameen Bank believes that with the appropriate support, the poor can be productively employed in income-generating activities, including processing and manufacturing, transportation, storing and marketing agricultural produce and raising livestock.

The Grameen Bank also maintains that if the rural poor are provided credit on reasonable terms, they can judge for themselves how best to increase their incomes and need only those inputs that they can purchase themselves. Based on these notions, the Grameen Bank creates the social and financial conditions enabling poor men and women to receive credit by identifying for themselves a source of self-employment and by agreeing to guarantee and monitor others in their self-selected group.

The Grameen Bank ultimately aims to improve the well-being of the poor. In addition to financial intermediation, it conducts social intermediation to make the poor both socially and individually accountable. Such accountability leads to more effective use of loans and consequently ensures loan recovery. The Grameen Bank, unlike commercial banks or development financial institutions, addresses the survival concerns of both the borrowers and the lender. Although these concerns may seem to conflict,[1] the Grameen Bank has developed a credit delivery model augmented by a social development program to attain these dual objectives.

This chapter discusses the principles underlying the Grameen Bank's role as an institution for financial intermediation and poverty alleviation, and then assesses how well this unique model works.

The Credit Delivery Model

The Grameen Bank has integrated group organization with credit delivery to assist the rural poor. Individuals take the first step in the banking process by organizing themselves into groups of five. Men and women form separate groups in accordance with the sociocultural norms of rural Bangladesh. Membership in a particular group is strictly limited to people who do not own more than half an acre of land, are not members of the same household, have similar economic resources and, therefore, equal bargaining strength, enjoy mutual trust and confidence, and live in the same village. Past experience suggests that the spatial and social cohesiveness developed among individuals of the same gender, residing in the same village, and having similar economic backgrounds were important factors in the smooth functioning of these groups.

Each group elects a chairperson, who is responsible for the discipline of group members, and a secretary. Both hold office for one year. Each group member must have a chance to be elected before office-holders can be reelected. Members have weekly meetings where they practice, learn and discuss the rules of the Grameen Bank and other group activities.

Two to three weeks after the formation of groups, during which all group members make small savings deposits (Tk 1 per week) and are trained by Grameen Bank employees, credit is issued to individual group members if they conform to the discipline of the Grameen Bank. Initially, two members of a group are given credit and observed for one or two months. If they pay their weekly installments and maintain group discipline, new loans are given to the next two members. The group leader is customarily the last to receive credit. Grameen Bank loans are small (about Tk 2,000–5,000 with an upper limit of Tk 10,000) and must be repaid in equal weekly installments over one year. If any member defaults, the whole group becomes ineligible to receive ad-

*From Shahidur R. Khandker, Baqui Khalily, and Zahed Khan, "Grameen Bank: Performance and Sustainability," World Bank Discussion Paper No. 306 (1995): 9–13. Reprinted by permission.

[1]For various reasons, the survival concerns of borrowers may not match those of the lenders. Lenders are concerned with loan repayment and how much can be recovered if the borrowers default. On the other hand, borrowers are concerned with how much they can make beyond the amount of the loan, which does not interest lenders. This misalignment of interests is the moral hazard problem of lending. For more discussion, see Stiglitz and Weiss (1981).

ditional loans from the Grameen Bank. This rule compels group members to pressure one another to keep up with regular payments. Thus, although credit is given to an individual member, the group is ultimately responsible for repaying loans, as well as for maintaining financial and social discipline.

The loans are provided for activities identified and selected by each member, and members are expected to guide one another. Selections are discussed at group meetings and at meetings of centers, typically composed of five to eight groups and led by an elected center chairperson and secretary. Each center is assisted by a Grameen Bank employee, who visits several on a weekly basis. The group chooses meeting discussions and transactions by consensus, and every member is required to attend all group and center meetings. The chairpersons conduct center meetings and enforce members' attendance, weekly payments, and discipline. Each center chief holds office for one year and a new chief is elected every year. If a center chief does not behave properly, he or she can be replaced by a new chief. Center chiefs and group chairpersons jointly monitor loan utilization on a daily basis. These elected officeholders are not given any remuneration for organizing the group and center activities. Loan use is also monitored at the outset by Grameen Bank staff, which has improved borrower performance. Any irregularity is reported at the center meeting, where group performances are discussed with a Grameen Bank employee in attendance.

A unique feature of the Grameen Bank is the transparency of its credit transactions: all are openly conducted at the center meetings. The virtue of these open procedures is that they mitigate problems or "entrenchment of vested interests and constellations of power" as well as deterring individuals from taking anti-group actions (Fuglesang and Chandler 1988). This peer monitoring mechanism works both within the group and at the center, eliminating the danger of group collusion when the groups are self-selected.

The Grameen Bank, unlike many other development financial institutions, considers savings mobilization to be an integral part of lending. Each member is required to save at least 1 taka every week, which is deposited at the weekly meeting. In addition, each borrower is required to contribute 5 percent of their borrowed amount to the "group fund." The group fund is self-managed and can be used for mutually agreed upon purposes. A borrower is also required to contribute 25

percent of the total interest due on the principal to the "emergency fund."[2] The Grameen Bank manages this fund for use as insurance against potential default due to death, disability, or other misfortune. This fund is also used to provide life and accident insurance to all group members, to repay bad debts, and to undertake activities that will improve group members' health, skills, education and investment opportunities (Yunus 1983). In addition to mandatory saving, each member can purchase a Grameen Bank equity share worth Tk 100. Members thus have a stake in Grameen Bank operations, because they own its shares and because they will lose valuable access to a reliable source of credit and lose face among their peers if they default.

Conceived of as a vehicle to bring banking facilities to the people rather than force the people to come to the bank, the Grameen Bank's lending procedures consist sequentially of group formation, training, loan application and approval, disbursement, supervision, and repayment. The system encourages local monitoring and enforcement among members.

The Social Development Program

Early on, the Grameen Bank leadership realized that in addition to high recovery rates and financial viability, borrowers must receive social benefits. To that end, the Grameen Bank developed a comprehensive social development program, outlined by the "sixteen decisions," in order to promote social and financial discipline among the rural poor. These decisions are guidelines for some activities and codes of conduct that members are encouraged to adopt. For example, the members are encouraged to plant trees, grow kitchen gardens, and build houses and sanitary latrines, which are also intended to address environmental concerns.

The Grameen Bank has deliberately targeted women, realizing that their participation in social development is necessary for economic development because of their primary role in providing health, education, and nutrition. Historically, women have been neglected by development projects, removing them from the growth and development process. Because women are poorer than men, the Grameen Bank actively promotes their member-

[2]This requirement has been changed since July 1, 1991. Currently there is no emergency fund contribution for any loan up to Tk 1,000, but for large loan amounts a contribution of Tk 5 per 1,000 is levied.

ship out of concern for equity. Moreover, over time Grameen Bank has observed that women are better credit risks than men and are more eager to properly use bank loans.

The Bank's social development program also includes a comprehensive training program in maternal health, nutrition and child care. As a result of this training, demand for basic services has increased and the nutritional status of participating women and their children has improved (Quanine 1989). The social development program encourages borrowers to establish schools to tutor and prepare their children to enter the mainstream schooling system and to serve as day-care centers when members are engaged in business activities. The social development program also supplies tree seedlings and seeds for kitchen gardens in order to improve both living conditions and the environment.

References

Fuglesang, Andreas and Dale Chandler. 1988. *Participation as Process: What We Can Learn from Grameen Bank, Bangladesh,* Oslo: NORAD.

Quanine, Jannat. 1989. "Women and Nutrition: The Grameen Bank Experience." *Food and Nutrition Bulletin.* 11 (4):64–66.

Stiglitz, Joseph E. and Andrew Weiss. 1981. "Credit Rationing in Markets with Imperfect Information." *American Economic Review* 71(3): 393–410.

Yunus, Muhammad. 1983. "Group-based Savings and Credit for the Rural Poor: The Grameen Bank in Bangladesh." In *Group-based Savings and Credit for the Rural Poor.* Geneva: ILO.

Comment V.D.1. The Grameen Bank and "Empowerment" of Women

According to Khandker, Khalily, and Khan, World Bank Discussion Paper No. 306 (1995), women received 91.1 percent of cumulative loan disbursement by the Grameen Bank in 1994. Moreover, they state (pp. 27–28),

> The Grameen Bank introduced house-building loans in 1984 as part of its social development program without any prior donor commitment. These are longer-term loans that require weekly repayments over ten years and are lent at a lower rate of 8 percent (5 percent until 1991). It was designed to help Grameen Bank members construct good-quality, low-cost housing. The requirement that the borrower hold title to the land has enabled the legal transfer of home-ownership to thousands of poor women.

Mark M. Pitt and Shahidur R. Khandker, "Household and Intrahousehold Impact of the Grameen Bank and Similar Targeted Credit Programs in Bangladesh," World Bank Discussion Paper No. 320 (1996), evaluate three group-based credit programs: the Grameen Bank, the Bangladesh Rural Advancement Committee, and the Bangladesh Rural Development Board's RD-12 program. They find (p. 41) that "either the set of female credit variables, male credit variables or both are statistically significant at the 0.05 level of significance in all 8 key behaviors studied," that is, girls' and boys' schooling, women's and men's labor supply, total household expenditure, contraception, fertility, and the value of women's nonland assets. They also find (pp. 41–42) that "credit provided by the Grameen Bank had the greatest positive impact on variables typically associated with household wealth and women's power and independence than credit from any other program source. Grameen Bank credit to women had the largest impacts on girls' schooling, women's labor supply and total household expenditure." They conclude (p. 42),

> Our results provide evidence that program participation benefits the poor, especially women and children. Furthermore, the magnitude of the benefits accruing to individuals in a participating household depends on whether the participant is a woman or a man. . . . targeted credit programs such as the Grameen Bank can "empower" women by increasing their contribution to household consumption expenditure, their hours devoted to production for the market, and the value of their assets.

Ainon Nahar Mizan, "Women's Decision-making Power in Rural Bangladesh: A Study of Grameen Bank," in Abu N. M. Wahid, ed., *The Grameen Bank: Poverty Relief in Bangladesh* (1993), finds that Grameen Bank participation, length of borrowing, and income from investing Grameen Bank loans all positively and significantly affect women's decision-making power in the family. The latter is measured by a scale in which decided by wife only equals 3, decided by husband and wife together equals 2, and decided by husband only equals 1. The household decisions included items such as expenditure on education and marriage of children and purchase and sale of land. A more personal and detailed view of women's empowerment by the Grameen Bank is given in Helen Todd, *Women at the Center: Grameen Bank Borrowers After One Decade* (1996).

Comment V.D.2. Gender-Aware Analysis

Numerous gender studies indicate that economic analysis that is aware of gendered relationships can provide a better understanding of the development process and a better understanding of policies required to diminish gender inequality. See Diane Elson, "Gender-Aware Analysis and Development Economics," *Journal of International Development* 5 (1993), and Diane Elson, ed., *Male Bias in the Development Process* (1991).

Also of special significance are Janet Momsen and Vivian Kinnaird, *Different Plans, Different Voices* (1993); Caroline O. N. Moser, *Gender Planning and Development* (1993); John Humphrey, *Gender and Work in the Third World* (1987); Esther Boserup, *Women's Role in Economic Development* (1970); K. Young, ed., *Of Marriage and the Market* (1984); N. Long, ed., *Family and Work in Rural Societies* (1984); J. Nash and P. Fernandes-Kelly, *Women, Men and the International Division of Labor* (1983); and S. Joekes, *Women in the World Economy* (1987).

A number of empirical studies focus on gender asymmetry in intrahousehold activities—distribution of food, health, education. See Mark M. Pitt et al., "Productivity, Health, and Inequality in the Intrahousehold Distribution of Food in Low-Income Countries," *American Economic Review* (December 1990); Jere Behrman, "Intrahousehold Allocation of Nutrients in Rural India," *Oxford Economic Papers* (March 1988); Jere Behrman and Barbara Wolfe, "How Does Mothers' Schooling Affect Family Health, Nutrition, Medical Care Usage, and Household Sanitation?" *Journal of Econometrics* 36 (1987); and Duncan Thomas, "Intra-Household Resource Allocation," *Journal of Human Resources* (Fall 1990).

Gender studies are especially prominent in analyzing women's role in agriculture. They examine how the division of labor by task, field, and product, as well as how different people's access to land and to each other's labor, affect choices of crop and technology. See Uma Lele, "Women and Structural Transformation," *Economic Development and Cultural Change* (January 1986); C. D. Deere, "The Division of Labor by Sex in Agriculture," *Economic Development and Cultural Change* (July 1982); Amartya Sen, "Gender and Cooperative Conflicts" in *Persistent Inequalities: Women and World Development,* ed. I. Tinker (1990); and Ann Whitehead, *Female Farmers in Africa* (1990).

CHAPTER VI

Migration and the Urban Informal Sector

Overview: The Evolving View of Urban Underemployment, the Informal Sector, and Their Connection with Rural-Urban Migration

In the Overview to Chapter I, we pointed out that the share of the labor force employed in agriculture is much smaller in rich than in poor countries. Since agriculture is concentrated in rural areas and industry is concentrated in urban areas, we can expect substantial migration from rural to urban areas as a poor country grows richer. If one visits the major cities in many less developed countries, one gets a powerful impression that this urbanization process is not working very smoothly. The city centers are so congested that it seems impossible to get from one place to another, while outside the centers huge neighborhoods have no access to municipal services such as electricity, running water, and sewers. Judging by the abundance of farm animals, many of the residents of these neighborhoods are of rural origin. It is not surprising that many authors have concluded that the pace of urbanization in less developed countries is excessive.

The historical experience of more developed countries provides one yardstick by which one can assess the current urbanization process of less developed countries. In 1875 the urban population share of the now-rich countries was very close to that of less developed countries in 1950. In Selection VI.1, Samuel Preston reports that the increase in this share in less developed countries during the period 1950–1975 was very similar to the increase that occurred in the now more developed countries during the period 1875–1900. What is unprecedented is the rate of growth of urban populations in less developed countries, which is due to the unprecedented overall rate of population growth in these countries rather than to an unprecedented rate of increase in the share of their populations living in urban areas.

In addition to overcrowding, the major cities in many less developed countries give an impression of massive underemployment. This is colorfully described in several of the selections. W. Arthur Lewis speaks of "the young men who rush forward asking to carry your bag as you appear." Michael Todaro quotes another writer's description of "the urban in-migrant who, instead of doing absolutely nothing, joins Bombay's army of underemployed bootblacks or Delhi's throngs of self-appointed (and tippable) parking directors, or who becomes an extra, redundant salesman in the yard goods stall of the cousin." Gary Fields describes as representative "a woman sitting on a market street in Kuala Lumpur, garlics set out on a piece of newspaper in front of her for sale."

Official unemployment statistics are not a reliable way to measure the extent of this kind of underemployment because the underemployed are working. A crude way to measure underemployment is to label all self-employed workers and unpaid family labor as underemployed. (This is sometimes used as a measure of the size of "the informal sector." We will discuss the relationship between the concepts "informal sector" and "underemployment" below.) This is obviously an inaccurate measure since the self-employed may own substantial firms or be highly educated professionals and unpaid family workers may earn their bed and board. Nevertheless, as shown in Exhibit VI.1, this measure of underemployment (as a share of the nonagricultural labor force) does decline sharply across countries as per capita income increases, suggesting that lack of opportunities for wage employment is a major cause of self-employment and unpaid family labor. (The correlation between the share of self-employed workers and unpaid family labor in nonagriculture and per capita GNP in Exhibit VI.1 is –0.61. It should be noted that in nearly all countries the share of self-employed workers and unpaid family labor is higher in agriculture than in nonagriculture, reflecting the influence of the age-old tradition of family farming.)

We would like, of course, not merely to describe and measure urban underemployment but to understand its causes and its links, if any, to rural-urban migration in less developed countries. There are two leading theories of underemployment in less developed countries. The first is described in Selection VI.2 by W. Arthur Lewis. Lewis argues that in less developed countries there is simply not enough demand for wage labor to employ all who want to work at the minimum wage needed for subsistence. The "surplus" labor survives through a combination of employment in family businesses (especially farms) that are willing to pay family members more than their marginal products, and low-productivity self-employment (again supplemented by family charity). For Lewis there is no conceptual difference between the urban and the rural underemployed, so for a given demand for wage labor rural-urban migration serves only to shift the location of the underemployed from rural to urban areas. A strong point of Lewis's theory is that it is consistent with the reduction of self-employment and unpaid family labor as per capita income increases that is shown in Exhibit VI.1. As capital accumulates in industry, demand for wage labor increases and underemployed labor is absorbed into wage employment by nonfamily firms.

In Selection VI.3, Michael Todaro describes the second leading theory of underemployment in LDCs. Todaro starts from the premise that in LDCs wage employment in the urban "modern sector" provides a substantially higher income than rural employment, even adjusting for differences in cost of living, and that the urban underemployed cannot bid down modern sector wages. This wage differential causes migration from the countryside to the city, where the migrants spend some time underemployed in the urban "traditional sector" until they are lucky enough to obtain modern sector jobs. The larger the number of underemployed seeking jobs in the urban modern sector, the longer a migrant can expect to wait before finding such a job, and the less attractive migration becomes. It follows that any attempt to reduce urban underemployment (by creating more modern sector jobs, for example) will be at least partially self-defeating, because it will make rural-urban migration more attractive. As a proportion of the urban labor force, the underemployed will shrink only if the urban-rural income differential narrows.

Todaro's theory of urban underemployment was incorporated into a larger model (and somewhat modified) by Harris and Todaro (1970). Harris and Todaro (p. 126) assume that the source of the urban-rural income differential is "a politically determined minimum urban wage at levels substantially higher than agricultural earnings." One can then see that the key difference between the Lewis and Harris–Todaro models of underemployment is that in the Lewis model the (subsistence) minimum wage holds in both agriculture and industry whereas in the Harris–Todaro model the (politically determined) minimum wage is enforced only in industry. In Note VI.1 we put the Harris–Todaro and Lewis models of underemployment into a common diagrammatic framework. We observe that one consequence of the difference between the Lewis and Todaro (or Harris–Todaro) views of underemployment is sharply different predictions regarding the effects of expansion of urban labor demand on agricultural output: agricultural output must fall in the Harris–Todaro model but need not do so in the Lewis model.

In Selection VI.4, Gene Tidrick examines official unemployment in Jamaica rather than underemployment. Nevertheless, he finds that the Todaro theory has considerable explanatory power. For example, in the period Tidrick examines, the Jamaican urban economy was highly unionized, and wages of unskilled urban workers in occupations such as construction and transportation were much higher than wages of unskilled agricultural workers. The official unemployment rate never fell below 13 percent despite substantial growth in "modern" non-agricultural jobs and an almost stable labor force. Despite high unemployment, there were labor shortages in rural areas. An econometric study of Jamaican migration cited by Tidrick found that migration occurred largely in response to wage differentials and in spite of higher unemployment levels in high-wage areas. In Note VI.2, which follows Tidrick's selection, we discuss more recent econometric approaches to the study of rural-urban migration.

Subsequent to the writings of Lewis and Todaro, the concept of "underemployment" has fallen out of favor and been largely replaced by the concept of "the informal sector." The latter is most commonly defined as firms (including the self-employed) that operate outside the system of government benefits and regulations. This concept is already latent in Harris and Todaro (1970): one could view the "urban traditional sector" of Todaro as the part of the urban economy where the political forces that determine the minimum wage in the Harris–Todaro model do not apply. However, as the International Labour Office (ILO) makes clear in Selection VI.5, "the informal sector" is seen as dominated not by the underemployed but rather by productive if small firms that supply essential goods and services. The ILO views urban economies in less developed countries as "dualistic," with a sharp distinction between informal activities that are small in scale, labor intensive, and unregulated and formal activities that are large in scale, capital intensive, and regulated. The subsequent selection by Ian Livingstone extends this dualism from the supply to the demand side, stating that the informal and formal sectors cater to poor and well-off urban consumers, respectively.

In Selection VI.7, Gary Fields makes a distinction between the "easy-entry" informal sector and the "upper-tier" informal sector. Workers in the easy-entry informal sector resemble the underemployed of Lewis and Todaro and seek better positions in the formal sector. Workers in the upper-tier informal sector, on the other hand, prefer their positions to formal sector jobs and may even have received training in the formal sector before leaving to start informal sector businesses. Fields's characterization of the informal sector leaves open the possibility that the size of the easy-entry informal sector influences rural-urban migration in just the way that Todaro described: a smaller easy-entry informal sector encourages rural-urban migration by decreasing the time migrants expect to wait before landing a formal sector job.

In contrast to Fields, Biswajit Banerjee takes a strong position against the "probabilistic migration model" of Todaro in Selection VI.8. He argues that access to formal sector jobs is determined largely by one's contacts or social network, and that with good contacts one can line up a formal sector job directly from one's village without engaging in an urban-based job search, whereas without good contacts one is unlikely to obtain a formal sector job even after migrating to the city. Knowing this, rural workers do not see the number of formal sector jobs relative to the size of the informal wage sector as an important indicator of their chances of obtaining a formal sector job and do not migrate in response to this indicator. For more discussion of the importance of social structure in LDC labor markets, the reader can begin with Kannappan (1989, especially pp. 60–62) and the references therein.

References

Harris, John R., and Michael P. Todaro. 1970. "Migration, Unemployment and Development: A Two-Sector Analysis." *Amer. in Economic Review* 60 (March): 126–142.

Kannappan, Subbiah. 1989. "Employment Policy and Labour Markets in Developing Nations." In Bernard Salome, ed., *Fighting Urban Unemployment in Developing Countries* (Paris: OECD).

Selection VI.1. Urban Growth in Developing Countries: A Demographic Reappraisal*

. . . In this review, we rely primarily upon material developed in the course of a United Nations study of urban and rural population change. This study assembled estimates of urban and rural population and of the population of cities larger than 100,000 from 1950 to the present. The study does not deal with all aspects of population distribution, but only with those demographic aspects that relate to distinctions between urban and rural areas and between places of differing size. Conclusions of this study are described here, and their bearing on distribution policy is considered.

(1) The rate of change in the proportion urban in developing countries is not exceptionally rapid by historical standards; rather it is the growth rates of urban populations that represent an unprecedented phenomenon.

The most common measure of the rate of urbanization is the annual change in the percentage of the population living in urban areas. According to this measure, urbanization in developing countries did not proceed with unusual speed in the quarter-century from 1950 to 1975. In this period the percentage urban grew from 16.7 to 28.0 in developing countries. While this is a rapid increase, it is very similar to the one that occurred in more developed countries during the last quarter of the nineteenth century. Between 1875 and 1900, the percentage urban of countries now more developed grew from 17.2 to 26.1. The slight difference from the growth in developing countries 75 years later is well within the margin of error of the estimates. The rates of net rural–urban migration required to achieve the observed increase in the urban percentage may even have been greater in more developed countries, in view of the higher rates of rural than of urban natural increase that typically prevailed at the time. That is, to achieve a certain increase in the urban percentage, higher rates of net rural–urban migration were required in developed countries than in developing countries, where rural-urban differences in rates of natural increase are far less significant.

Nor does it appear that rates of urbanization or of net rural–urban migration are accelerating in de-

veloping countries. Between 1950 and 1960 the proportion urban grew by 5.1 percentage points and between 1960 and 1975, a period 50 percent longer, by 6.2 percentage points. (These figures include China's uncertain estimates, which show decelerated urbanization.) The pace of urbanization has been accelerating in Africa but decelerating in Latin America. . . .

While the rate of urbanization (the rate of change in proportion urban) has not been unprecedented in developing countries, the growth rate of the urban population has been. Between 1875 and 1900, urban populations in now-developed countries grew by 100 percent and rural populations by 18 percent. While developing countries were traversing roughly the same range in proportions urban between 1950 and 1975, their urban populations grew by 188 percent and their rural ones by 49 percent. The growth factors of both rural and urban populations were much larger simply because rates of natural increase were much faster. Urban growth is currently exceptionally rapid in developing countries, but the explanation is not to be found in unusually rapid changes in the urban proportion produced by rural–urban migration but in the rapid changes in total population to which those proportions are applied.

(2) Urban growth through most of the developing world results primarily from the natural increase of urban populations.

This point is readily overlooked in the midst of scholarly and political concern with internal migration. It has been made before by Kingsley Davis, Eduardo Arriaga, Salley Findley, and the United Nations Population Division, and new findings on components of urban growth provide strong confirmation. Of the 29 developing countries whose data support a decomposition of the sources of urban growth during the most recent intercensal period, 24 had faster rates of urban natural increase than of net in-migration (the latter also including area reclassification). The mean percentage of urban growth attributable to natural increase for the 29 countries was 60.7 percent. Among the largest developing countries the percentage was 67.7 in India (1961–71), 64.3 in Indonesia (1961–71), and 55.1 in Brazil (1960–70). There is apparently a slight tendency for the percentage of

*From Samuel H. Preston, "Urban Growth in Developing Countries: A Demographic Reappraisal," *Population and Development Review* 5 (June 1979): 196–199. Reprinted by permission.

urban growth attributable to natural increase to grow over time. . . .

It should be noted that the coverage of African populations in the data set is very poor and that results pertain primarily to Latin America and Asia (except China). Judging from the unusually rapid urban growth in Africa, it is likely that rural–urban migration is a more important source of growth there than is implied by the above account.

Exhibit VI.1. Self-employment* and Unpaid Family Workers Circa 1990

	Year	As share of total labor force (%)	As share of nonagricultural labor force (%)**	GNP per capita $ in 1990
Low-income economies				
Malawi	1987	81.2	24.0	200
Nigeria	1986	75.3	58.6	290
Haiti	1990	69.5	38.1	370
Pakistan	1990–1991	61.4	38.0	380
Central African Republic	1988	83.4	38.3	390
Indonesia	1989	71.0	49.5	570
Egypt, Arab Rep.	1990	40.6	18.2	600
Average		68.9	37.8	400
Middle-income economies				
Lower-middle-income				
Bolivia	1991	41.3	41.0	630
Philippines	1990	49.9	28.8	730
Guatemala	1989	50.4	36.0	900
Ecuador	1990	50.1	40.7	980
Syrian Arab Republic	1989	31.2	26.5	1,000
Paraguay	1991	30.5	30.0	1,110
El Salvador	1991	34.6	34.6	1,110
Peru	1991	39.3	39.3	1,160
Colombia	1990	27.2	27.0	1,260
Thailand	1990	69.5	34.3	1,420
Tunisia	1989	28.9	19.3	1,440
Turkey	1990	57.7	28.7	1,630
Romania	1992	15.8	1.5	1,640
Poland	1992	25.9	9.6	1,690
Panama	1991	32.8	20.9	1,830
Costa Rica	1990	29.0	24.0	1,900
Chile	1990	29.5	29.1	1,940
Botswana	1991	23.6	10.0	2,040
Algeria	1987	19.4	12.4	2,060
Mauritius	1990	14.0	12.6	2,250
Malaysia	1990	34.0	20.5	2,320
Iran	1986	40.7	25.1	2,490
Average		35.2	25.1	1,524
Upper-middle-income				
Mexico	1991	43.5	32.1	2,490
Uruguay	1991	24.8	24.2	2,560
Venezuela	1990	30.4	26.8	2,560
Brazil	1990	34.0	25.8	2,680
Hungary	1990	8.6	7.6	2,780
Czech Republic	1991	2.2	2.4	3,140
Trinidad and Tobago	1990	21.1	17.5	3,610
Portugal	1990	27.8	16.9	4,900
Korea, Rep.	1990	38.8	27.2	5,400
Greece	1990	44.4	29.6	5,990
Average		27.6	21.0	3,611
High-income economies				
Ireland	1990	21.2	11.7	9,550
Israel	1990	18.1	16.1	10,920
Spain	1990	22.1	17.3	11,020
Singapore	1989	14.1	13.6	11,160
Hong Kong	1990	6.3	6.1	11,490

Exhibit VI.1. Continued

	Year	As share of total labor force (%)	As share of nonagricultural labor force (%)**	GNP per capita $ in 1990
High-income economies (continued)				
New Zealand	1991	18.4	14.4	12,680
Belgium	1990	16.2	14.5	15,540
Italy	1990	25.3	22.4	16,830
Australia	1990	14.8	12.0	17,000
Netherlands	1990	10.6	8.3	17,320
Austria	1990	14.0	7.9	19,060
Canada	1990	9.2	7.4	20,470
United States	1990	8.5	7.4	21,790
Denmark	1990	10.8	7.9	22,080
Germany	1990	9.8	7.6	22,320
Norway	1990	8.8	5.3	23,120
Sweden	1990	8.8	7.1	23,660
Japan	1990	20.6	15.3	25,430
Finland	1990	14.1	8.7	26,040
Average		14.3	11.1	17,762

*Self-employment = employers and own-account workers as defined in ILO *Yearbook.*

**Nonagriculture excludes agriculture, hunting, forestry, and fishing.

Sources: International Labour Office. *Yearbook of Labour Statistics,* various years (Geneva: International Labour Office). World Bank. *World Development Report 1992* (New York: Oxford University Press).

Selection VI.2. Economic Development with Unlimited Supplies of Labor*

In the first place, an unlimited supply of labour may be said to exist in those countries where population is so large relatively to capital and natural resources, that there are large sectors of the economy where the marginal productivity of labour is negligible, zero, or even negative. Several writers have drawn attention to the existence of such "disguised" unemployment in the agricultural sector, demonstrating in each case that the family holding is so small that if some members of the family obtained other employment the remaining members could cultivate the holding just as well (of course they would have to work harder: the argument includes the proposition that they would be willing to work harder in these circumstances). The phenomenon is not, however, by any means confined to the countryside. Another large sector to which it applies is the whole range of casual jobs—the workers on the docks, the young men who rush forward asking to carry your bag as you appear, the jobbing gardener, and the like. These occupations usually have a multiple of the number they need, each of them earning very small sums from occasional employment; frequently their number could be halved without reducing output in this sector. Petty retail trading is also exactly of this type; it is enormously expanded in overpopulated economies; each trader makes only a few sales; markets are crowded with stalls, and if the number of stalls were greatly reduced the consumers would be no whit worse off—they might even be better off, since retail margins might fall. Twenty years ago one could not write these sentences without having to stop and explain why in these circumstances, the casual labourers do not bid their earnings down to zero, or why the farmers' product is not similarly all eaten up in rent, but these propositions present no terrors to contemporary economists.

A little more explanation has to be given of those cases where the workers are not self-employed, but are working for wages, since it is harder to believe that employers will pay wages exceeding marginal productivity. The most important of these sectors is domestic service, which is usually even more inflated in over-populated countries than is petty trading (in Barbados 16 per cent. of the population is in domestic service). The reason is that in over-populated countries the code of eth-

ical behaviour so shapes itself that it becomes good form for each person to offer as much employment as he can. The line between employees and dependents is very thinly drawn. Social prestige requires people to have servants, and the grand seigneur may have to keep a whole army of retainers who are really little more than a burden upon his purse. This is found not only in domestic service, but in every sector of employment. Most businesses in under-developed countries employ a large number of "messengers," whose contribution is almost negligible; you see them sitting outside office doors, or hanging around in the courtyard. And even in the severest slump the agricultural or commercial employer is expected to keep his labour force somehow or other—it would be immoral to turn them out, for how would they eat, in countries where the only form of unemployment assistance is the charity of relatives? So it comes about that even in the sectors where people are working for wages, and above all the domestic sector, marginal productivity may be negligible or even zero.

Whether marginal productivity is zero or negligible is not, however, of fundamental importance to our analysis. The price of labour, in these economies, is a wage at the subsistence level (we define this later). The supply of labour is therefore "unlimited" so long as the supply of labour at this price exceeds the demand. In this situation, new industries can be created, or old industries expanded without limit at the existing wage; or, to put it more exactly, shortage of labour is no limit to the creation of new sources of employment. If we cease to ask whether the marginal productivity of labour is negligible and ask instead only the question from what sectors would additional labour be available if new industries were created offering employment at subsistence wages, the answer becomes even more comprehensive. For we have then not only the farmers, the casuals, the petty traders and the retainers (domestic and commercial), but we have also three other classes from which to choose.

First of all, there are the wives and daughters of the household. The employment of women outside the household depends upon a great number of factors, religious and conventional, and is certainly not exclusively a matter of employment opportunities. There are, however, a number of countries where the current limit is for practical purposes only employment opportunities. This is true, for

*From W. Arthur Lewis. 1954. "Economic Development with Unlimited Supplies of Labor." *The Manchester School* 22:141–45. Reprinted by permission.

example, even inside the United Kingdom. The proportion of women gainfully employed in the U.K. varies enormously from one region to another according to employment opportunities for women. For example, in 1939 whereas there were 52 women gainfully employed for every 100 men in Lancashire, there were only 15 women gainfully employed for every 100 men in South Wales. Similarly in the Gold Coast, although there is an acute shortage of male labour, any industry which offered good employment to women would be besieged with applications. The transfer of women's work from the household to commercial employment is one of the most notable features of economic development. It is not by any means all gain, but the gain is substantial because most of the things which women otherwise do in the household can in fact be done much better or more cheaply outside, thanks to the large scale economies of specialisation, and also to the use of capital (grinding grain, fetching water from the river, making cloth, making clothes, cooking the midday meal, teaching children, nursing the sick, etc.). One of the surest ways of increasing the national income is therefore to create new sources of employment for women outside the home.

The second source of labour for expanding industries is the increase in the population resulting from the excess of births over deaths. This source is important in any dynamic analysis of how capital accumulation can occur, and employment can increase, without any increase in real wages. It was therefore a cornerstone of Ricardo's system. Strictly speaking, population increase is not relevant either to the classical analysis, or to the analysis which follows in this article, unless it can be shown that the increase of population is caused by economic development and would not otherwise be so large. The proof of this proposition was supplied to the classical economists by the Malthusian law of population. There is already an enormous literature of the genus: "What Malthus *Really* Meant," into which we need not enter. Modern population theory has advanced a little by analysing separately the effects of economic development upon the birth rate, and its effects on the death rate. Of the former, we know little. There is no evidence that the birth rate ever rises with economic development. In Western Europe it has fallen during the last eighty years. We are not quite sure why; we suspect that it was for reasons associated with development, and we hope that the same thing may happen in the rest of the world as development spreads. Of the death rate we are more certain. It comes down with development

from around 40 to around 12 per thousand; in the first stage because better communications and trade eliminate death from local famines; in the second stage because better public health facilities banish the great epidemic diseases of plague, smallpox, cholera, malaria, yellow fever (and eventually tuberculosis); and in the third stage because widespread facilities for treating the sick snatch from the jaws of death many who would otherwise perish in infancy or in their prime. Because the effect of development on the death rate is so swift and certain, while its effect on the birth rate is unsure and retarded, we can say for certain that the immediate effect of economic development is to cause the population to grow; after some decades it begins to grow (we hope) less rapidly. Hence in any society where the death rate is around 40 per thousand, the effect of economic development will be to generate an increase in the supply of labour.

Marx offered a third source of labour to add to the reserve army, namely the unemployment generated by increasing efficiency. Ricardo had admitted that the creation of machinery could reduce employment. Marx seized upon the argument, and in effect generalised it, for into the pit of unemployment he threw not only those displaced by machinery, but also the self-employed and petty capitalists who could not compete with larger capitalists of increasing size, enjoying the benefits of the economies of scale. Nowadays we reject this argument on empirical grounds. It is clear that the effect of capital accumulation in the past has been to reduce the size of the reserve army, and not to increase it, so we have lost interest in arguments about what is "theoretically" possible.

When we take account of all the sources we have now listed—the farmers, the casuals, the petty traders, the retainers (domestic and commercial), women in the household, and population growth—it is clear enough that there can be in an over-populated economy an enormous expansion of new industries or new employment opportunities without any shortage of unskilled labour becoming apparent in the labour market. From the point of view of the effect of economic development on wages, the supply of labour is practically unlimited.

This applies only to unskilled labour. There may at any time be a shortage of skilled workers of any grade—ranging from masons, electricians or welders to engineers, biologists or administrators. Skilled labour may be the bottleneck in expansion, just like capital or land. Skilled labour, however, is only what Marshall might have called a "quasi-bottleneck," if he had not had so nice a sense of elegant language. For it is only a very temporary bottleneck, in the sense that if the capital is available for development, the capitalists or their government will soon provide the facilities for training more skilled people. The real bottlenecks to expansion are therefore capital and natural resources, and we can proceed on the assumption that so long as these are available the necessary skills will be provided as well, though perhaps with some time lag.

Selection VI.3. A Model of Labor Migration and Urban Unemployment in Less Developed Countries*

. . . It is our opinion that a more realistic picture of labor migration in less developed countries would be one that views migration as a two-stage phenomenon. The first stage finds the unskilled rural worker migrating to an urban area and initially spending a certain period of time in the so-called "urban traditional" sector.[1] The second stage is reached with the eventual attainment of a more permanent modern sector job. This two-stage process permits us to ask some fundamentally important questions regarding the decision to migrate, the proportionate size of the urban traditional sector, and the implications of accelerated industrial growth and/or alternative rural-urban real income differentials on labor participation in the modern economy.

Employment Probability and the Decision to Migrate

In our model, the decision to migrate from rural to urban areas will be functionally related to two principal variables: (1) the urban-rural real income differential and (2) the probability of obtaining an urban job. Since it is this latter variable which will play a pivotal role in the analysis, it might be instructive at this point to explain briefly our reasons for incorporating this probability notion into the overall framework.

As pointed out above, an implicit assumption of typical labor transfer models is that any migrant who enters the modern sector is "absorbed" into the gainfully employed at the prevailing urban real wage. However, the important question to ask in this context is "how long" does the average migrant have to wait before actually obtaining a job. Even if the prevailing real wage is significantly higher than expected rural income, the fact that the "probability" of obtaining a modern sector job, say within the next year or two, is very low must certainly influence the prospective migrant's choice as to whether or not he should leave the farm. In effect, he must balance the probabilities and risks of being unemployed or sporadically employed in the city for a certain period of time against the favorable urban wage differential. A 70 per cent urban real wage premium, for example, might be of little consequence to the prospective migrant if his chances of actually securing a job are, say, one in fifty. Nevertheless, even if expected urban real income is less than rural real income for a certain period following migration, it may still be economically rational from a longer-run point of view (e.g., from a discounted present value approach to the rural-urban work choice) for the individual to migrate and swell the ranks of the urban traditional sector. Our underlying behavioral model, therefore, will be formulated more in the spirit of permanent income theories than present wage differential theories.

To underline the fundamental role played by job opportunities and probabilities of employment in the actual migration decision-making process, we might cite two outstanding illustrations, one historical and one contemporary, which demonstrate the relative, and often overriding, importance of this variable. The first case concerns the movements of American unskilled laborers back and forth between agriculture and industry during the 1930 depression decade. In an extremely informative and well-documented study of American agriculture, Theodore Schultz (1945) argues that in 1932 when urban wages were still considerably higher and falling less rapidly than rural wages, there was a definite reversal of the historical flow of workers from the farm to the city. In fact, 1932 witnessed a net urban to rural labor migration (p. 90). Schultz attributes this seemingly paradoxical phenomenon to the severe lack of job opportunities in depressed urban factories and the more likely prospects of finding agricultural employment in rural areas even though there still existed a significant positive urban wage premium (p. 99).

*From Michael P. Todaro, "A Model of Labor Migration and Urban Unemployment in Less Developed Countries," *American Economic Review,* March 1969: 139–147. Reprinted by permission.

[1]For the purposes of this paper, the urban traditional sector will encompass all those workers not regularly employed in the urban modern sector, i.e., the overtly unemployed, the underemployed or sporadically employed, and those who grind out a meagre existence in petty retail trades and services. J. P. Lewis provides an excellent description of this traditional sector which consists largely of "the urban in-migrant who, instead of doing absolutely nothing, joins Bombay's army of underemployed bootblacks or Delhi's throngs of self-appointed (and tippable) parking directors, or who becomes an extra, redundant salesman in the yard goods stall of the cousin, who according to custom, is going to have to provide him with bed and board anyway" (1962, p. 53). This description aptly fits a typical city in Africa and Latin America as well.

The second, more contemporary case concerns an interesting experiment carried out in Kenya in 1964. In a modified version of a tactic suggested by the International Labor Office (1964) which advocated that governments of less developed countries employ and, through taxes and subsidies, induce private enterprise to employ more labor than would be worthwhile on the basis of a comparison between productivity and wages, the government of Kenya instituted a "tripartite agreement" among itself, private employers, and trade unions. The avowed intention was to wipe out the considerable unemployment existing in the greater Nairobi area by having the two hiring participants agree to increase their employment immediately by 15 per cent. For their part the unions had to agree to forego any demands for general wage increases. In his analysis of this "agreement" Professor Harbison has observed that:

The effort was a colossal failure. The private employers did take on additional workers and *this acted like a magnet attracting new workers into the urban labor markets;* in a few months the working forces in most of the private establishments had dropped to their former levels through attrition not offset by new hires. In the end, the volume of unemployment, as a consequence of the expansion of the modern labor force *in response to the prospect of more jobs* was probably increased rather than decreased (1967, p. 183, fn**). (Italics not in original)

Here once again we can recognize the basic influence exerted by the probability of finding a job (whether real or anticipated) on the supply of rural workers into urban labor markets. . . .

Perhaps the most significant policy implication emerging from the model is the great difficulty of substantially reducing the size of the urban traditional sector without a concentrated effort at making rural life more attractive. For example, instead of allocating scarce capital funds to urban low cost housing projects which would effectively raise urban real incomes and might therefore lead to a worsening of the housing problem, governments in less developed countries might do better if they devoted these funds to the improvement of rural amenities. In effect, the net benefit of bringing "city lights" to the countryside might greatly exceed whatever net benefit might be derived from luring more peasants to the city by increasing the attractiveness of urban living conditions. Like Marshall's famous scissors analogy, the equilibrium level of nonparticipation in the urban economy is as much a function of rural "supply push" as it is one of urban "demand pull." Thus, as long as the urban-rural real income differential continues to rise sufficiently fast to offset any sustained increase in the rate of job creation, then even in spite of the long-run stabilizing effect of a lower probability of successfully finding modern sector employment, the lure of relatively higher permanent incomes will continue to attract a steady stream of rural migrants into the ever more congested urban slums. The potential social, political, and economic ramifications of this growing mass of urban unemployed should not be taken lightly.

References

F. Harbison, "The Generation of Employment in Newly Developing Countries," in J. Sheffield (ed.), *Education, Employment and Rural Development,* Nairobi 1967.

International Labor Office, *Employment and Economic Growth.* Geneva 1964.

J. P. Lewis, *Quiet Crisis in India.* Washington 1962.

T. W. Schultz, *Agriculture in an Unstable Economy.* New York 1945.

Note VI.1. The Lewis Versus the Harris–Todaro View of Underemployment in Less Developed Countries

These two enormously influential models make sharply different predictions regarding the effects of expansion of urban labor demand on underemployment and agricultural output. In this Note we will exposit the two views in a common diagrammatic framework in order to bring the sources of these different predictions into clear focus.

To better understand Lewis's model of underemployment and its predictions it is helpful to refer to Figure 1. The horizontal dimension of the figure is determined by the labor endowment $\bar{L}$ of the economy. We will treat total labor supply as fixed, so we will not consider the possibility that, for example, people might work more or less hours in response to higher wages. Agricultural employment L_A is measured to the right starting from O_A and industrial (manufacturing) employment L_M is measured to the left starting from O_M. The left vertical axis measures the marginal value product of labor in agriculture; the right vertical axis measures the marginal value product of labor in industry, which is assumed to be located in urban rather than rural areas. The prices of agricultural and manufacturing output, p_A and p_M, are assumed to be determined in international markets that the economy is too small to influence. This assumption allows us not to consider how the terms of trade between agriculture and industry might change as the relative outputs of the two sectors change. The marginal physical products of labor in agriculture and manufacturing, MPL_A and MPL_M, are determined by the respective technologies (the production functions) and by the ratio of labor to land in agriculture and the ratio of labor to capital equipment in industry. Land and capital stocks are assumed to be fixed, so the ratios of labor to land and labor to capital only change when employment in agriculture and industry changes, respectively. By diminishing returns, the marginal physical products of labor decrease as these ratios increase, hence the marginal value product of labor curve for agriculture AA slopes down to the right as L_A increases and the marginal value product of labor curve for industry MM slopes down to the left as L_M increases. Finally, $\bar{w}$ gives the subsistence wage mentioned by Lewis in his preceding selection, which is assumed to be equal for both agricultural and industrial (rural and urban) workers.

In Figure 1, farmers and manufacturing firms both find it worthwhile to hire labor until its marginal value product equals the subsistence wage, yielding employment $\hat{L}_A$ in agriculture and $\hat{L}_M$ in industry. This leaves a group of workers $U = \bar{L} - \hat{L}_A - \hat{L}_M$ who must eke out a living in some way other than employment by farmers or manufacturing firms. We call this group the underemployed.

Why do the underemployed not bid wages down below the subsistence level? A popular answer to this question is the nutrition-based efficiency wage model, which asserts that it is not profitable for employers to pay workers less than $\bar{w}$ because of adverse effects on employee nutrition and health. The idea is stated well by Swamy (1997, p. 86), who also provides a fine survey of the relevant literature: "employers do not lower the wage because the worker would then consume less, thereby lowering his productivity; paying a lower wage may raise the cost per efficiency unit of labor." (We should note that Swamy argues against the relevance of this model for rural India.)

How do the underemployed survive? The Malthusian answer is that they do not, or more precisely that they do not marry and reproduce. Over time, then, the horizontal dimension of Figure 1 ($\bar{L}$) will shrink until the marginal value product of labor curves in agriculture and industry intersect each other at rather than below $\bar{w}$, at which point the economy is in long-run equilibrium. Lewis had a very different answer: the underemployed would survive through family sharing, where by "family" we mean "extended family," not only one's parents and siblings. Some family members may earn an income above the subsistence level through ownership of assets other than unskilled labor such as land or capital equipment, and by altruism or tradition they may be willing to share some of this "extra" income with less fortunate family members who are underemployed. In terms of Figure 1, the areas $A\bar{w}a$ and

Figure 1. Underemployment in the Lewis model

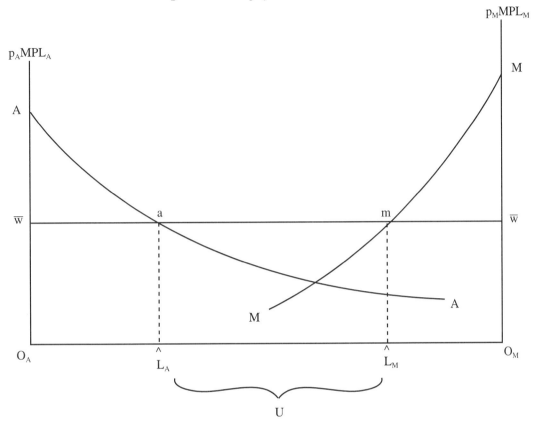

$M\bar{w}m$ are potential sources of income the underemployed can receive through family sharing. There are a number of ways in which this family sharing can take place: the underemployed can be retained as workers on the family farm or in an urban family business and be paid more than their marginal products; or they can be self-employed (Lewis gives the example of petty retail trading) and receive supplemental income from family members (either in cash or in kind).

The model of Figure 1 generates powerful predictions concerning the effects of expansion of the manufacturing sector. Suppose that capital equipment accumulates, causing the marginal value product of labor curve for industry to shift to the left, but not so far as to raise its intersection with the marginal value product of labor curve in agriculture above $\bar{w}$. We first see that underemployment decreases: $\hat{L}_M$ increases while $\hat{L}_A$ remains constant, causing $U = \bar{L} - \hat{L}_A - \hat{L}_M$ to fall. Since $\hat{L}_A$ is constant, the only reduction in agricultural output is due to rural-urban migration of previously underemployed agricultural workers who were sustained by family sharing. Finally, the wages in both agriculture and industry remain constant, rather than increasing in response to the greater demand for labor. This last point was especially emphasized by Lewis, since it meant that earnings of owners of capital equipment (the area $M\bar{w}m$) would not be reduced by rising wages, and he believed that these earnings were the main source of savings that would finance further investment and drive economic growth. Nurkse (1953) argued that the resources used by families to support their underemployed constituted a source of "hidden savings" that were available to finance investment once these underemployed found jobs in the expanded manufacturing sector. Ranis and Fei (1961) noted that the reduction in underemployment could be viewed as a "commercialization" of the economy because the fraction of workers whose income was determined by market forces rather than family sharing increased.

We now turn to Figure 2, which is based on the model of Harris and Todaro (1970). We see that the marginal value product of labor curves from Figure 1 have been retained. The first major change in Figure 2 relative to Figure 1 is that the minimum wage now applies only to industry rather than to both industry and agriculture. It is therefore relabeled $\bar{w}_M$. Harris and Todaro view the minimum wage as determined not by the need for subsistence but rather by institutional forces such as government regulations and union contracts, which in turn are seen as effective in urban but not in rural areas. The notion of a subsistence wage is absent from the Harris–Todaro model entirely, so there is no floor underneath the agricultural wage. This raises the question, why does the agricultural wage not fall to $\underline{w}_A$, at which agricultural employment $L_A = \bar{L} - \hat{L}_M$ and there is no underemployment? To answer we need to describe how the urban labor market functions in the Harris–Todaro model. We will then be able to generate the second major change in Figure 2 relative to Figure 1, the addition of the *ii* curve.

In the Harris–Todaro model the urban labor market can be described as a market for casual labor, in which every day employers hire anew the amount of workers they need that day. (This is more typically observed in construction or dock work than in manufacturing.) All workers picked on a given day receive the wage $\bar{w}_M$, and the remainder are unemployed that day and earn zero. Moreover, each day's drawing is random and independent of the previous day's drawing: being picked today does not make a worker more or less likely to be picked tomorrow. Every urban worker's odds of being picked on any day are thus equal to the ratio of total urban labor demand $\hat{L}_M$ to total urban labor supply L_U. It follows that every urban worker's income averages out to $(\hat{L}_M/L_U)\bar{w}_M$ in the long run. Returning to Figure 2, we see that if

Figure 2. Underemployment in the Harris–Todaro model

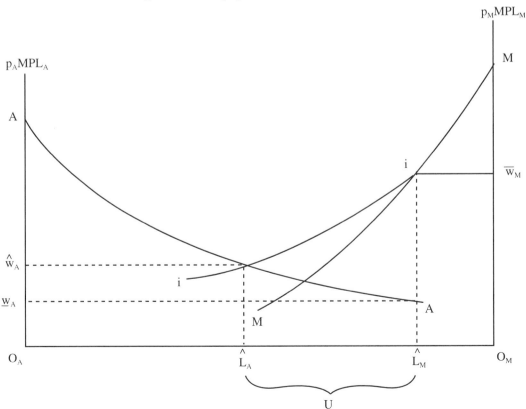

the agricultural wage is $\underline{w}_A$, then the size of the urban labor force exactly equals $\hat{L}_M$, in which case every urban worker earns $\bar{w}_M$ on average. This is obviously preferable to earning $\underline{w}_A$, so it will pay for agricultural workers to migrate to the city even though they will raise L_U above $\hat{L}_M$ and therefore obtain sporadic rather than regular employment. Agricultural employment must therefore fall below $L_A = \bar{L} - \hat{L}_M$ and the agricultural wage must rise above $\underline{w}_A$.

To determine the level of underemployment that makes workers indifferent between remaining in the countryside and earning w_A and migrating to the city and earning $(\hat{L}_M/L_U)\bar{w}_M$ on average, we note that urban workers not picked on a given day are underemployed (actually, unemployed) so we can write $L_U = \hat{L}_M + U$. The condition for indifference is then:

$$w_A = \frac{\hat{L}_M}{\hat{L}_M + U}\, \bar{w}_M \tag{1}$$

Equation (1) is depicted by the *ii* curve in Figure 2. It shows the agricultural wage for which a worker is indifferent between agricultural employment and migration to the city. This wage declines with U, given the levels of $\hat{L}_M$ and $\bar{w}_M$, hence the *ii* curve slopes down to the left starting from $w_A = \bar{w}_M$ at $U = 0$: as U increases, a worker is willing to stay in agriculture for lower and lower wages. At the intersection between the marginal value product of labor curve in agricultural and the *ii* curve, what agricultural employers are willing to pay equals what agricultural workers are willing to accept. (This depiction of labor market equilibrium in the Harris–Todaro model was introduced by Corden and Findlay (1975).)

Note that in the Harris–Todaro model every worker in agriculture is paid his marginal product. Lewis would argue that many of the agricultural workers who live with their families and work on the family farm are underemployed in the sense that their bed and board exceeds their marginal products. If there are well-functioning labor and land markets in rural areas, however, one could argue to the contrary that the families of any underemployed workers would insist that they get jobs on other farms or would rent land from other farms so that these workers could earn their keep. Thus the Harris–Todaro view that there is no underemployment in rural areas need not be inconsistent with the fact that there is a great deal of unpaid family labor in agriculture.

Let us now consider the effects in the model of Figure 2 of an increase in urban labor demand, just as we did for the model of Figure 1. Unfortunately graphical analysis is more complicated than in the earlier case, because the increase in $\hat{L}_M$ resulting from the leftward shift of the marginal value product of labor curve for industry also causes the origin of the *ii* curve to shift left. Let us instead turn to equation (1). We see that if we hold the agricultural wage w_A constant, an increase in urban employment $\hat{L}_M$ actually causes an increase rather than a decrease in urban underemployment U. The actual change in U depends on how fast the agricultural wage rises in response to the out-migration of agricultural workers induced by the increased income they can expect in the city. Could all of the increase in urban employment come from reduced urban underemployment, leaving the agricultural labor force unchanged? Clearly not, since then the ratio $\hat{L}_M/(\hat{L}_M + U)$ must increase, implying an increase in w_A by equation (1), which in turn requires a decrease in L_A. In sum, expansion of urban labor demand in the model of Figure 2 is much less beneficial than in the model of Figure 1: it need not reduce underemployment, whereas it must do so in the model of Figure 1, and it must reduce agricultural output (and raise the agricultural wage), whereas it need not do so in the model of Figure 1.

To conclude this Note, let us consider the effects in the model of Figure 2 of an increase in agricultural labor demand, caused for example by an increase in the quantity of irrigated land. Since the *ii* curve now remains stationary (because $\hat{L}_M$ and $\bar{w}_M$ do not change), when the marginal value product of labor curve for agriculture shifts right it must intersect the *ii* curve at a lower level of U. We have the paradoxical policy implication, emphasized by Todaro at the end of his preceding selection, that the surest way to reduce underemployment in the city is to improve employment opportunities in the countryside.

References

Corden, W. Max, and Ronald Findlay. 1975. "Urban Unemployment, Intersectoral Capital Mobility and Development Policy." *Economica* 42: 59–78.

Harris, John R., and Michael P. Todaro. 1970. "Migration, Unemployment and Development: A Two-Sector Analysis." *American Economic Review* 60 (March): 126–42.

Nurkse, Ragnar. 1953. *Problems of Capital Formation in Underdeveloped Areas* (New York: Oxford University Press).

Ranis, Gustav, and John C. H. Fei. 1961. "A Theory of Economic Development." *American Economic Review* 51 (September): 533–65.

Swamy, Anand V. 1997. "A Simple Test of the Nutrition-Based Efficiency Wage Model." *Journal of Development Economics* 53 (June): 85–98.

Selection VI.4. Wage Spillover and Unemployment in a Wage-Gap Economy: The Jamaican Case*

Jamaican Wage and Employment Patterns

A casual survey of urban unemployment levels in the Caribbean raises an intriguing question: Why does poor and stagnant Haiti seemingly have less open urban unemployment than comparatively rich and rapidly growing Jamaica, Puerto Rico, and Trinidad? There are no unemployment statistics for Haiti, but to all appearances open unemployment is lower than in the more prosperous islands. In Puerto Rico and Jamaica, unemployment has probably not fallen below 10 percent of the labor force since at least 1950, and Trinidad has more recently achieved this dubious distinction.[1] Why should the poorest of these structurally similar economies have the least unemployment problem? . . .

This is not the only perplexing question about Jamaican unemployment. Between 1953 and 1960 total output in real terms increased 76.8 percent while the labor force increased by only 2.5 percent (15,800 workers) due to massive emigration to the United Kingdom. "Modern" nonagricultural jobs[2]

increased by an estimated 50,000 during this same period. Yet unemployment fell only slightly from 98,000 to 88,100. Why did this spectacular output growth in the face of an almost stable labor force fail to cut unemployment more? Why did the relatively large increase in modern sector jobs not create more net employment in the economy as a whole? Why did migration not reduce unemployment, especially since so many of the migrants were unemployed?

Finally, what can we make of Jamaican wage behavior? Real average earnings (money earnings deflated by the cost-of-living index) rose by 2.6 percent per year between 1942 and 1960. In recent years the rate of increase has been more like 4 percent. The Jamaican economy is heavily unionized and output growth has been high, but these trends are still noteworthy for two reasons. First, the rate of open unemployment (where the definition of unemployment embraces all workers wanting work but working less than 1 day in a survey week) has remained extremely high since the 1930s. The lowest rate ever recorded was 13 percent in 1960. More importantly, wages in unorganized sectors of the economy rose by about the same amount as in unionized sectors. For example, real average earnings of female personal service workers (mostly domestic servants) rose 46.6 percent between 1942 and 1960 compared with an increase of 60 percent for all workers. Scattered evidence from the unorganized parts of agriculture suggests a similar pattern. Why were real wages not bid down in unorganized sectors? Moreover, despite rising rural wages and high overall unemployment, genuine labor shortages in rural areas have existed since the mid 1950s. How can we account for these shortages in the midst of high unemployment?

None of these puzzling features of Jamaican wage and employment patterns can be fully understood without reference to the distorted wage structure, that is, a wage structure in which workers of the same skill level receive different wages in different industries. The Jamaican wage structure is clearly distorted by this definition. Disparities among major sectors are dramatic. Unskilled

*From Gene M. Tidrick, "Wage Spillover and Unemployment in a Wage-gap Economy: The Jamaican Case," *Economic Development and Cultural Change*, 1975, 307–323. Reprinted by permission.

[1]On Puerto Rico, see Lloyd G. Reynolds and Peter Gregory, *Wages, Productivity, and Industrialization in Puerto Rico* (Homewood, Ill.: Richard D. Irwin, Inc., 1965); and for Trinidad, see Jack Harewood, *Employment in Trinidad and Tobago 1960* (Mona, Jamaica: Institute of Social and Economic Research, University of the West Indies, n.d.). For more recent figures, see David Turnham, *The Employment Problem in Less Developed Countries* (Paris: Development Centre of the OECD, 1971), p. 46. Employment data for Jamaica in this paper and some wage data are from Jamaica, Department [formerly Central Bureau] of Statistics, *Census of Jamaica and Its Dependencies, 1943; The Census of Jamaica: 7th April, 1960;* and *Report on a Sample Survey of the Population of Jamaica, Oct./Nov. 1953.* Other wage or average earnings data are from Jamaica, Department of Statistics, *Employment and Earnings in Large Establishments* and *Wage Rates,* 1957–1965. Output figures are from Jamaica, Department of Statistics, *National Accounts: Income and Expenditure,* 1950–1961, and *National Income and Product,* 1965–; and from Alfred P. Thorne, "Size, Structure, and Growth of the Economy of Jamaica," *Social and Economic Studies* 4, suppl. (December 1955): 1–156. For a detailed discussion of Jamaican wage, employment, and output data, and of the adjustments made to achieve comparability of data from different sources, see Gene M. Tidrick, "Wages and Unemployment in Jamaica" (Ph.D. diss., Harvard University, 1972), esp. chap. 3.

[2]For statistical purposes, the modern sector is defined to include all mining workers, factory workers in manufacturing, all other workers in secondary industries except own-account workers and employers in construction and distribution, and ser-

vice workers excluding domestic service. Between 1942 and 1960, modern jobs thus defined increased by 94,000 to 194,700, or about one-third of the labor force in 1960. Figures for the subperiod 1953–60 are not available, but output trends suggest that 50,000 plus or minus 10,000 is a reasonable estimate.

bauxite mining workers earn about twice as much per week as unskilled workers in transportation or construction, the two next most highly paid industries. (In fact, unskilled mining workers earn more than skilled construction workers.) Unskilled construction workers, in turn, earn almost two and one-half times as much as agricultural workers. . . .

The Wage-Gap Model

. . . In figure 1, the demand for labor in the sugar sector (*Ds*) is measured from left to right. The demand for labor in the mining sector (*Dm*) is measured from right (at *L′*) to left. The *Dm* is completely inelastic at *L′P*. In a competitive labor market, the allocation of the fixed supply of labor *LL′* between the two sectors and the equilibrium wage rate will be determined by the intersection of the two demand curves. In equilibrium, *LP* workers will be employed in sugar and *L′P* will be employed in mining at a wage in both sectors of *We*. There is full employment and the equilibrium is stable. As long as the labor market is competitive, there is no tendency for the wage level to rise above *We* in either sector.

Assume, however, that in mining the wage is set at *Wm*, perhaps at the initiative of employers seeking better public relations or of government or unions who see an opportunity to raise mining

wages without curtailing mining employment. Under certain assumptions, the effect of setting the mining wage at *Wm* will be to create an incentive for some workers to withdraw from sugar employment to seek a job in the high-wage mining sector. The number who choose to withdraw from the sugar sector is a function of the wage gap between the two sectors. Thus, if the mining-sector wage is *Wm* and the sugar-sector wage is *Ws, QP* workers would choose to withdraw from sugar employment to seek mining employment. If the sugar wage were lower, more workers would withdraw, and if it were higher, fewer workers would withdraw. Only if the sugar-sector wage were also *Wm* would no workers withdraw from sugar employment. We can plot the succession of such points to obtain the supply curve of labor to the sugar sector, given a mining wage equal to *Wm*. The curve is labeled *Ss* in figure 1. If the sugar-sector labor market remains competitive and the mining wage remains fixed at *Wm,* the new "equilibrium" sugar wage will be *Ws*. Then *LQ* workers will be employed in sugar, *L′P* will be employed in mining, and *QP* workers will be unemployed. If the mining wage were raised above *Wm,* the supply curve of labor to sugar would shift upward, thereby raising the equilibrium sugar wage above *Ws* and creating unemployment greater than *QP*.

To see this, assume that the fixed supply of labor

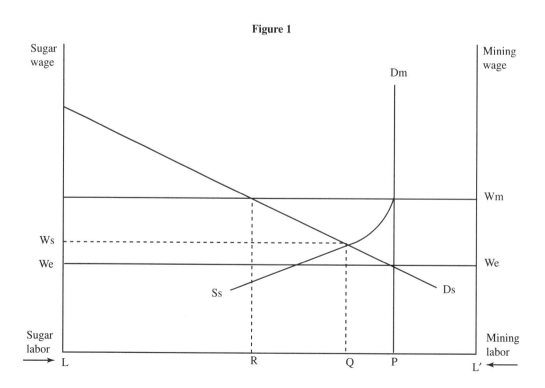

Figure 1

is the result of a balanced flow of new entrants into the labor force and of retirements. At any given time, therefore, there will be new job openings in mining. Assume, further, that the probability of getting a mining job is higher if a worker is not employed in sugar, perhaps because hiring is done at the gate and sugar and mining activities are located in different parts of the country. It will then be rational for a new entrant to remain unemployed rather than take a job in sugar, or for a sugar worker to quit his job in order to seek a job in mining so long as: (1) the present value of his forgone earnings in sugar is less than the expected lifetime earnings in mining and (2) he has some means of subsistence during his period of unemployment. Expected lifetime earnings in mining are simply the probability of having a mining job in each period times the mining wage summed over the worker's remaining work life, or

$$PVm = \sum_{t=0}^{n} \frac{P(t)Wm}{(1+r)^t}, \qquad (1)$$

where PVm is the present value of lifetime earnings in mining and $P(t)$ is the probability of having a mining job at time t. For simplicity assume that $P(t)$ is the ratio of the number of hirings mining in period t, $H(t)$, to the number of unemployed workers, $U(t)$. That is,

$$P(t) = H(t)/U(t) \qquad (2)$$

The present value of lifetime earnings in sugar, PVs, is

$$PVs = \sum_{t=0}^{n} \frac{Ws}{(1+r)^t}, \qquad (3)$$

and the equilibrium labor market condition is

$$PVs = PVm \qquad (4)$$

I defer the question of how the unemployed survive until a later section.

When the mining wage is raised, workers will leave sugar employment (or new entrants will remain unemployed) until the probability of getting a mining job is lowered sufficiently (unemployment raised sufficiently) to reestablish equality between PVs and PVm. In terms of figure 1, a rise in the mining wage to Wm will shift the supply curve of labor to sugar to Ss, cause the sugar wage to rise to Ws, and create unemployment of PQ. This supply-withdrawal unemployment is overt by any conventional measure. Workers could truthfully answer a labor force questionnaire that they wanted but could not obtain more work in either sector at the going wage. They could get a job in sugar at a lower wage rate, but their reserve supply price

has risen and they would not accept it. They would take a lower wage in mining and bid that wage down but are prevented from doing so by market imperfections. They are voluntarily unemployed with respect to sugar but involuntarily unemployed with respect to mining.

Even if an increased mining wage does not reduce employment directly in the mining sector itself, it will reduce employment (and output) indirectly in sugar. Moreover, the mining wage increase spills over into the sugar sector, raising the sugar wage. This effect does not depend on unionization. Wages rise in sugar even though sugar workers remain completely unorganized. . . .

An increase in mining employment will increase the probability of getting a high-wage job and hence the expected lifetime earnings of workers seeking mining employment. In figure 1, if the Dm curve shifts outward (to the left) at a constant wage Wm, the supply curve of labor to sugar will also shift farther upward as the increased probability of securing mining employment induces more workers to leave sugar employment. Thus, if mining employment increased to $L'Q$ in figure 1, unemployment would not be eliminated because the shift in the Dm curve would induce a shift in the supply curve of labor to sugar above Ss. Whether total unemployment would be less or greater than the original PQ after an increase in mining employment of QP depends on many factors, but it is clear that the net employment increase in the economy as a whole is less than the gross employment increase in mining in a wage-gap economy. Continued employment growth in mining at a constant wage Wm would not completely eliminate unemployment until mining employment was $L'R$. Outward shifts in the Ds curve would decrease unemployment by the amount that sugar employment increased, however. Net and gross employment effects are equal. . . .

The Sharing Mechanism

Unemployment is a rational response to a distorted wage structure only if the unemployed have some means of subsistence. The nature of the sharing mechanism will be an important determinant of the level of unemployment which the system can sustain. . . .

High-wage casual employment is a fairly important source of income for the "unemployed" in Jamaica. Counting opportunities in dock working, construction, tourism, and illegal activities, it is not hard to imaging that from a quarter to a half of unemployed males might earn at least as much or more over a year's time as a full-time wage earner in agriculture. The large number of casual jobs available also explains why unemployment is such a different phenomenon in less developed countries. A 10 percent unemployment rate is more likely to mean that 20 percent of the labor force is unemployed half the time.

Sharing mechanisms which allow the unemployed to subsist while looking for high-wage jobs are also undoubtedly important. . . . Assume that $L'P$ mining workers are hired on a full-time basis. Earnings in mining cannot be bid down as in a casual labor system, and it becomes rational for some workers to remain unemployed at a subsistence level while seeking permanent full-time employment in mining. The number who can afford to remain unemployed, and hence the number forced back into sugar, are determined by the sharing mechanism. . . . it is clear that an increase in mining wages or employment would increase the number of unemployed which the system could support, as well as raise expected lifetime earnings of those remaining temporarily unemployed.

Some sharing mechanisms may place a constraint on unemployment no matter how favorable the expected lifetime earnings differential. If the unemployed are supported largely by the low-wage sector, as in parts of Africa, increased wages or employment in the high-wage sector will not increase the capacity of the system to support unemployment as much as a high-wage-sector sharing mechanism. If the high-wage sector has a high propensity to share, however, support capacity will increase pari passu with the increased tendency of the system to generate unemployment. As suggested earlier, this is why Jamaica and Puerto Rico, with large high-wage sectors, can support more unemployment than Haiti.

The sharing mechanism helps determine not only how many but who will be unemployed. Where high-wage workers have a high propensity to share with dependents, for example, many of the unemployed will be new entrants whose reserve price is higher than the sugar wage because they live in a high-income household. This poses an interesting welfare issue. Since unemployment is voluntary with respect to low-wage employment, it appears that those who are worst off are not the unemployed but those forced to accept employment in the low-wage sector—the involuntarily employed as it were. . . .

Empirical Evidence

. . . The limited evidence from Jamaica on how the unemployed live suggests that many of the un-

employed, though by no means all, may be better off than those fully employed in the low-wage sector.

In the first place, there are many casual job opportunities in Jamaica, some at very high wages. The most extreme example is the water transport industry (mostly dock workers). In the 1960 census survey week, less than half of the 5,522 workers (nearly 1 percent of the labor force) in this industry worked 5 or more days and more than one-fourth worked only 1–2 days. Dock workers could earn more in 2 7-hour days in 1965 than the typical agricultural worker earned in a full week. In this extreme case, many workers registered as unemployed in a given week may have been better off over the course of a year than other fully employed workers. Second, in spite of the much larger population of unemployed in the Kingston Metropolitan Area, average household working-class income in the KMA in 1963–64 was about twice that in rural areas, a difference not nearly offset by the cost-of-living differential. More strikingly, only 10 percent of KMA households earned less than the median rural household income.[3]

Finally, 92 percent of the unemployed were dependents in 1960. Or, to put it in a different perspective, 98 percent of heads of households wanting work were employed. Of course, some might not have been heads of households because they were unemployed, rather than the other way around, but the presumption is that most were unemployed because they could afford to be.[4]

A closely related bit of evidence bearing on the presumed voluntary nature of unemployment comes from interviews with unemployed Jamaican workers. Two such surveys largely confirm the expectation that the reserve supply price of the unemployed is higher than the ruling wage in the low-wage sector. An official study of the rural labor shortage by M. G. Smith in 1955 found that over 90 percent of those looking for work in areas of "good" labor supply and over 80 percent in "bad" areas would not accept regular employment at the going agricultural wage rate in their respective areas.[5] A survey by Robert Kerton of unem-

[3]Jamaica, Department of Statistics, *Expenditure Patterns of Working Class Households* (Kingston: Department of Statistics, 1967), p. 10.

[4]Turnham, p. 55, cites similar evidence from Puerto Rico where a 1959 study showed "that family income tended to be higher than average for the families to which unemployed workers belonged and that such families, on average, included more working members."

[5]M. G. Smith, *A Report on the Labour Supply in Rural Jamaica* (Kingston: Government Printer, 1956), pp. 137–56.

ployed men in the Kingston area in 1966–67 found that one-third of those surveyed would not have accepted employment in the medium-wage, un-skilled job of garbage collection and about two-thirds had a reserve supply price higher than the average weekly earnings on large farms.[6] Of course, garbage collection is a low-status and un-pleasant job, but probably no less so in Jamaica than agricultural work, which paid only half as much. Moreover, for some of these men, their choice of residence in an urban area is evidence of their voluntary unemployment as far as agricultur-al work is concerned.

Kerton also found that the reserve supply price of the unemployed fell with age.[7] Again, this is what the wage-gap model predicts. Young workers have a longer lifetime over which to offset low earnings in the initial period of unemployment and a lower discount rate for future earnings because of fewer family responsibilities. Thus, the reserve supply price tends to fall with age, the unemployed tend to be disproportionately young, and workers in the low-wage sector tend to be older than aver-age. All three age-structural characteristics are borne out by Jamaican data.

Finally, the most important evidence supporting the hypothesis that most Jamaican unemployment is generated by the wage gap is the pattern of mi-gration flows within Jamaica. An econometric study by Nassau Adams[8] found that distance and wage differentials among the 14 Jamaican parishes explained almost all the variance ($R^2 = .860$ for Ja-maican males age 15–54) of internal migration flows. Other variables—degree of urbanization, educational levels of sending areas, and unem-ployment levels—added negligibly to the explana-tion of migration flows. The unemployment level in receiving areas was positively (but insignifi-cantly) correlated with migration rates, whereas the unemployment level in sending areas was pos-itively (and significantly) associated with migra-tion. The results confirm a central prediction of the wage-gap model. Migration occurs largely in re-sponse to wage differentials and in spite of higher unemployment levels in high-wage areas.

The size of the wage coefficient in receiving areas indicated that when wages in a high-wage

area rose by 10 percent, the rate of migration rose by nearly 30 percent. Since Adams's study in-volved intercensal migration, this was cumulative migration over a number of years. Nevertheless, it implies a very powerful impetus to supply-with-drawal unemployment due to wage increases in the high-wage sector. Separate regressions for males age 15–29 and those age 30–54 showed a higher wage coefficient for the younger group, in-dicating both that the effect of wage differentials was more pronounced for younger workers and that the effect worked in a relatively short time period. . . .

Conclusion

The wage-gap model provides answers to the questions posed early in this paper and in the pre-vious section.

Why does comparatively prosperous and rapid-ly growing Jamaica seemingly have more unem-ployment than poor and stagnant Haiti? Because the larger the high-wage modern sector, the more unemployed an economy can afford to support. In an economy without a high-wage sector, neither the incentive for nor the means to support unem-ployment may exist.

Why did employment growth in the high-wage sector and heavy migration abroad fail to reduce unemployment by a like amount? Because any re-duction in the number of unemployed or any in-crease in the rate of hiring raises the probability of obtaining a high-wage job and induces further sup-ply withdrawal from the low-wage sector.

Why did wages in unorganized, low-wage sec-tors rise along with wages in the unionized, high-wage sectors? Because the increased wage gap causes the supply curve of labor to the low-wage sector to shift. Why is there a long-standing labor shortage in agriculture when open unemployment levels have remained so high? Because the unem-ployed prefer unemployment and the uncertain prospect of a high-wage job to the certain prospect of low-wage steady employment.

Why do they prefer unemployment? Because their expected lifetime earnings are greater if they remain temporarily unemployed and because they have adequate means of support while searching for a high-wage job.

Why do migrants continue to pour into areas with high levels of unemployment? Because the higher wages the migrant will receive when he fi-nally gets a job will more than compensate him for his forgone earnings in his place of origin.

[6]Robert Kerton, "Labour Theory and Developing Countries: The Individual's Supply of Effort in the Caribbean" (Ph.D. diss., Duke University, 1968), pp. 58–59.

[7]Ibid., p. 65.

[8]Nassau A. Adams, "Internal Migration in Jamaica: An Eco-nomic Analysis," *Social and Economic Studies* 18 (June 1969): 137–51.

Note VI.2. Econometric Studies of Migration

The key question of what determines rural-urban migration can be explored further in studies that set forth probabilistic job-search models and in empirical investigations of migration functions. Field studies and econometric analyses indicate the importance of the economic motive in the decision to migrate. Econometric estimates of migration functions have also demonstrated that the probability of urban employment, independent of the differences in actual rural and urban wages, contributes significantly to the explanation of variance among time periods and subgroups of the rural population in rates of urban migration.

In an excellent survey of numerous studies, however, Yap indicates several problems with the econometric functions that limit their usefulness for prediction.[1]

The basic form of the migration function is as follows:

$$\bar{M}_{ij} = f(Y_i, Y_j; U_i, U_g; Z_i, Z_j; d_{ij}; C_{ij})$$

The specification is usually log linear. Typical independent variables used to explain migration from place i to place j ($\bar{M}_{ij}$) include wage or income levels (Y), unemployment rates (U), the degree of urbanization (Z) for the population in areas i and j, the distance between i and j (d_{ij}), and the friends and relatives of residents of i in the destination j (C_{ij}). Population in areas i and j is sometimes included.

Limitations of these studies are: (1) the level of demographic and geographic aggregation masks different patterns of migration; (2) the migration variable used in some of the studies presents conceptual and econometric difficulties; and (3) the independent variables are often poorly measured, especially the income estimates.

According to Stark and Bloom,

> Recent empirical research on the economics of labor migration has benefited a great deal more from the development of new econometric techniques than from new theoretical ideas. The techniques that have substantially improved our ability to use micro data sets in the estimation of relatively standard models of labor migration include techniques for the analysis of qualitative dependent variables, techniques that correct for sample selection bias, and techniques for the analysis of longitudinal and pseudo-longitudinal data. At the micro level, most empirical studies have attempted to test simple microeconomic models of migration according to which individuals (or families) make locational decisions primarily by comparing their income opportunities at alternative locations. The key feature of recent studies of this type is their focus on the estimation of structural, as opposed to reduced-form, models of the migration decision.[2]

In his *The Migration of Labor* (1991), Stark extends portfolio investment theory to migration and to the remittance of earnings. Under this theory, migration decisions are ordered by family needs for stable income levels, provided by a diversified portfolio of laborers, both male and female, and the need to jointly insure the family's well-being. In brief, group decision making and objectives, rather than the wishes of individual migrants, determine migration patterns and remittance flows. Viewed in light of portfolio investment theory, families allocate their labor assets over geographically dispersed and structurally different markets to reduce risk. Research indicates that after migration, family members pool and share their incomes. This pooling, or co-insurance, covers risks of losing income in individual markets and allows the family to smooth its consumption.

As Yap concludes, additional empirical research on migration would be useful to define the migration rate appropriately, adjust for simultaneous equation biases, and include more policy variables to provide more predictive value.

Notes

1. L. Y. L. Yap, "The Attraction of Cities: A Review of the Migration Literature," *Journal of Development Economics* 4 (1977): 239–64.

2. Oded Stark and David E. Bloom, "The New Economics of Labor Migration," *American Economic Review* (May 1985) 176–77.

Selection VI.5. The Informal Sector*

The popular view of informal-sector activities is that they are primarily those of petty traders, street hawkers, shoeshine boys and other groups "underemployed" on the streets of the big towns. The evidence suggests that the bulk of employment in the informal sector, far from being only marginally productive, is economically efficient and profit-making, though small in scale and limited by simple technologies, little capital and lack of links with the other ("formal") sector. Within the informal sector are employed a variety of carpenters, masons, tailors and other tradesmen, as well as cooks and taxi-drivers, offering virtually the full range of basic skills needed to provide goods and services for a large though often poor section of the population.

Our analysis lays great stress on the pervasive importance of the link between formal and informal activities. We should therefore emphasise that informal activities are not confined to employment on the periphery of the main towns, to particular occupations or even to economic activities. Rather, informal activities are the way of doing things, characterised by—

1. ease of entry;
2. reliance on indigenous resources;
3. family ownership of enterprises;
4. small scale of operation;
5. labour-intensive and adapted technology;
6. skills acquired outside the formal school system; and
7. unregulated and competitive markets.

Informal-sector activities are largely ignored, rarely supported, often regulated and sometimes actively discouraged by the Government.

The characteristics of formal-sector activities are the obverse of these, namely—

1. difficult entry;
2. frequent reliance on overseas resources;
3. corporate ownership;
4. large scale of operation;
5. capital-intensive and often imported technology;
6. formally acquired skills, often expatriate; and
7. protected markets (through tariffs, quotas and trade licenses).

*From ILO Mission, *Employment, Incomes, and Equality: A Strategy for Increasing Productive Employment in Kenya,* Geneva, 1972, pp. 5–8, 503–8. Copyright 1972, International Labour Organisation, Geneva. Reprinted by permission.

Our strategy of a redistribution from growth aims at establishing links that are at present lacking between the formal and the informal sectors. A transfer of incomes from the top income groups to the working poor would result in new types of labour-intensive investments in both urban and rural areas. This should not only generate demand for the products of the informal sector but also encourage innovations in labour-intensive techniques in this sector. The various policies which we recommend in other parts of the report are intended to reduce risk and uncertainty on the part of those employed in the informal sector and to ensure a dynamic growth of this large segment of the Kenyan economy.

There are marked contrasts between the relative security and income levels of those with wage-earning jobs in the bigger firms and those self-employed in the informal sector. These sharp inequalities inevitably create strong ambitions to migrate to the towns, to strive for higher education, to search for a job. As long as extreme imbalances persist, so will unemployment, since large differentials will always attract a margin of job seekers to hover in the towns, near the chances of the good jobs, in the hopes of snapping one up. This explains why the analysis of inequality is fundamental to the explanation of employment problems in Kenya.

But unemployment is not only the result of imbalance in differentials and opportunities. Even with perfect equality, unemployment could arise. Fast rates of population growth, of urbanisation and school expansion inevitably make it more difficult to absorb the growing labour force and reduce the time that might otherwise be available for structural adjustments. Here a second set of imbalances arise—dynamic imbalances relating to the structure of economic growth in the economy and to the constraints upon it. Rapid growth is needed, but rapid growth can itself generate imbalances which will frustrate its continuation—most notably a shortage of foreign exchange, of domestic savings, of skills and entrepreneurship, of demand or of the political support needed to keep the system workable. For this reason our report is not merely concerned with alleviating unemployment, poverty and gross inequality, but with economic growth on a pattern which can be sustained in the future, and which generates wider and more productive employment opportunities in the process. . . .

The Relation Between the Formal and Informal Sectors

The process of economic transformation and growth in Kenya has been marked by growing inequalities in the distribution of wealth and income among Africans. The usual explanation is the traditional–modern division of the economy, in which the westernised modern sector is the source of dynamism and change and the traditional sector slowly withers away. This view does not correspond to the reality of Kenya; we reject it for that reason, and because it ignores the dynamism and progressive elements indigenous to the Kenyan economy. We have considerable evidence to refute a view that attributes the sources of economic and social change almost exclusively to outside forces.

Furthermore, the traditional–modern analysis focuses only on the positive effects of the westernisation of the Kenyan economy and ignores the negative effects. In particular, it ignores inter-sectoral dynamics, which are the key to the employment problem. The accumulation of wealth in a small part of the modern sector is the consequence of the concentration of political power in that sector, and has given rise to the development of an impoverished and economically deprived modern sub-sector. The slums of Nairobi, Mombasa and to a lesser extent other urban areas are completely modern and due to the differences of wealth and income between different sectors of the economy. These differences draw migrants toward the concentrations, and bring about the modernisation of almost the entire economy, but not the spread of wealth. Because of the slow growth of high-wage employment, migration to urban areas by income seekers has led to the growth of a low-income periphery. This low-income sector is peripheral both literally and figuratively. In Nairobi it sprang up, and continues to grow, just outside the borders of the wealthy urban zone, to supply goods and services to the fortunate few inside that zone and to its own population. Figuratively, it is peripheral in that it has only fortuitous and restricted access to the sources of wealth.

Characteristics and Dynamics of the Informal Sector

We describe these two urban sectors as being the "formal" and the "informal" sector. This designation is not intended to contribute to an academic proliferation of labels; we merely seek an analytical terminology to describe a duality that avoids the bias against the low-income sector inherent in the traditional-modern dichotomy. Both sectors are modern; both are the consequence of the urbanisation that has taken place in Kenya over the last 50 years. We might have used the terms "large-scale" and "small-scale," but those terms are purely descriptive and tell us nothing about why one sector is large-scale and the other is small-scale. An explanation of this is central to explaining and solving the employment problem in Kenya. One important characteristic of the formal sector is its relationship to the Government. Economic activities formally and officially recognised and fostered by the Government enjoy considerable advantages. First, they obtain the direct benefits of access to credit, foreign exchange concessions, work permits for foreign technicians, and a formidable list of benefits that reduce the cost of capital in relation to that of labour. Indirectly, establishments in the formal sector benefit immeasurably from the restriction of competition through tariffs, quotas, trade licensing and product and construction standards drawn from the rich countries or based on their criteria. Partly because of its privileged access to resources, the formal sector is characterised by large enterprise, sophisticated technology, high wage rates, high average profits and foreign ownership.

The informal sector, on the other hand, is often ignored and in some respects helped and in some harassed by the authorities. Enterprises and individuals within it operate largely outside the system of government benefits and regulation, and thus have no access to the formal credit institutions and the main sources of transfer of foreign technology. Many of the economic agents in this sector operate illegally, though often pursuing similar economic activities to those in the formal sector—marketing foodstuffs and other consumer goods, carrying out the repair and maintenance of machinery and consumer durables and running transport, for example. Illegality here is generally due not to the nature of the economic activity but to an official limitation of access to legitimate activity. Sometimes the limitations are flouted with virtual abandon, as in the case of unlicensed *matatu* taxis; sometimes the regulations are quite effective. The consequence is always twofold: the risk and uncertainty of earning a livelihood in this low-income sector are magnified, and the regulations ensure a high quality of services and commodities for the wealthy few at the expense of the impoverished many.

The formal-informal analysis applies equally well to the agricultural sector. The parallels are obvious and striking. The division between favoured operators with licences and those without in urban areas is reproduced in agriculture between those who grow tea and coffee with official sanction and those who do so illegally. Similarly, with other agricultural products such as beef, there are those whose wealth enables them to conform to and benefit from standards officially laid down, while others can make a livelihood only by contravening the regulations. In the agricultural sector extension services take the place of the industrial estates and of loans from the Industrial and Commercial Development Corporation in the urban areas: farmers whose wealth and income allow them to conform to bureaucratic criteria benefit. Perhaps the most striking rural-urban parallel is with illegal rural squatters, who move unofficially on to land scheduled for resettlement and face a continual danger of eviction. Their similarity to urban squatters is obvious—both are irresistibly drawn to real or perceived sources of wealth, despite legal restrictions of access.

These characteristics of the informal sector, both agricultural and non-agricultural, result in low incomes for those who work in it. A natural consequence of these low incomes is that monetary exchanges within the informal sector are different in quality from those in the formal sector. A most important consequence of a low income is the primacy of risk and uncertainty. The loss a small farmer or a small entrepreneur can bear is disproportionately smaller than that which can be borne by a wealthy operator, particularly when the former has no access to institutionalised sources of credit. As a consequence, the entrepreneur in the informal sector must act continually to protect himself against risk. Accordingly he establishes semi-permanent relations with suppliers and buyers, frequently at the expense of his profits. For the same reason he may be hesitant to innovate, particularly in agriculture, for he cannot take the chance of failure. These characteristic behavioural responses are not inherent in the informal sector; they are adaptive responses to low income.

Despite the vitality and dynamism we see in the informal sector, we do not delude ourselves that it will develop successfully under present conditions. Although it has the potential for dynamic, evolutionary growth, under the existing nexus of restrictions and disincentives, the seeds of involutionary growth have been sown. Unlike the determinants of growth of the formal sector, the determinants of growth of the informal sector are largely external to it. The relevant question is not whether the informal sector is inherently evolutionary or involutionary, but what policies should be followed to cause evolutionary growth. Irrespective of policy changes, the informal sector will grow in the next 15 years. If policy continues as at present, the growth will be involutionary and the gap between the formal and informal sectors will widen. The employment problem will then be worse.

Selection VI.6. A Reassessment of Kenya's Rural and Urban Informal Sector*

The informal/microenterprise sector turns out to be quite a heterogeneous set of activities, many of them in trade and services, so that it is unwise to make blanket judgments, completely positive or negative, regarding its potential contribution to development: rather, one should assess its various roles and consider in what ways its contribution can be enhanced.

The quantitative importance of the sector within the urban and rural economy shows that it is capable of substituting for large-scale units, both large-scale factories and "modern" small-scale enterprises. This is despite the pursuit of microeconomic and sectoral policies which are generally biased against microenterprises. Even if special small-industry development programs exist, the basic industrial development strategy pursued in Kenya and other African countries has been one of import-substituting industrialization, usually centering on large-scale, capital-intensive industry, often foreign-owned and using imported technologies. Other macroeconomic policies are well-known: duty-free import of capital goods (but taxed imports of microenterprise capital goods, treated as consumer goods) assisting large-scale units but competing with potential small-scale capital goods production; special depreciation provisions, subsidized real interest rates and special access to finance; and overvalued exchange rates, apart from direct support measures. A particular feature of SSI promotional programs and assistance measures, moreover, is usually a complete absence of technology improvement and product development components. With more even-handed macroeconomic and sectoral policies—including positive measures to promote linkages between large- and small-scale industry, and to upgrade microenterprise products and technologies—it should be possible to shift the boundary of production between large-scale and small-scale production.

A principal reason why informal sector producers are able to substitute for larger enterprise is that, in a market dominated quantitatively by low-income consumers, they offer cheap and "appropriate" goods and demand only a very low supply price for their services.

One form of "appropriateness" is to make goods last longer, hence the share of repair services of all

*From Ian Livingstone, "A Reassessment of Kenya's Rural and Urban Informal Sector," *World Development* 19, no.6 (1991): 667–68. Reprinted by permission from Elsevier Science Ltd. Oxford, England.

kinds within the sector. Cheap but risky and uncomfortable transportation is another example.

This aspect has led some economists to suggest that informal sector manufacturing has no long-run development role, inevitably to be replaced by factory production as incomes rise. This neglects the time scale involved: only when development has proceeded far enough to substantially raise the supply price of labor will informal sector production modes become uneconomic. Even Asian countries with significantly higher per capita incomes than most African countries continue to have substantial informal sectors.

The sector expands not through the growth of individual enterprises but through an increase in the number of establishments, each employing only one or two persons. Given the numbers to be absorbed, and the inability of the formal sector to absorb them, labor is sufficiently cheap to make 1–2 person enterprises competitive. Informal sector enterprises represent a means of providing employment rather than potential developing firms (though not exclusively).

A substantial portion of rural Kenyan households are "divided": nonfarm self-employment and farm employment both contribute to rural household viability, even though family members may need to work in urban areas to secure the former. Household-based nonfarm activities also provide supplementary income to maintain viability. The substantial proportion of such "divided households" in rural Kenya implies a relatively favorable return to labor in the informal sector, but may in turn cause labor shortages and lower productivity in agriculture. It would be desirable to raise technology to improve productivity simultaneously in both sectors.

Disdain for the informal sector is produced by frequent reference to marginal activities such as shoe shining, car washing, or selling discarded whisky bottles. Evidence from an actual study of shoe shining in Nairobi (Elkan et al., 1983) puts a different perspective on this. Although House clearly places shoe shiners within his "community of the poor," Elkan found average net earnings in the trade to be around KShs600 a month, noting that this was "a good deal higher than had been expected." The significant finding, however, was that the chief customers were Kenyans, not tourists, and not even well-to-do Kenyans, but an intermediate category of "shop assistants, office clerks, and civil servants of the lower grades, none of whom have servants but all of whom like to look smart." This suggests that, rather than being a marginal occupation and a form of disguised unemployment, shoe shining has a natural place in the market economy of Kenya at its present stage of development. Many other "informal sector activities," of course, will have a much more important place in that economy, and the whole set of activities will basically reflect the level of income in the population. Thus in Asian developing economies, the urban and rural informal sectors may be much richer in content. Conversely, it is evident that in other African countries, where rural incomes and rural purchasing power are much lower than Kenya, the informal sector is thin. This wide variation was observed also within one country, in different districts of Kenya.

Part of the dichotomy, in fact, between the formal and informal sectors arises out of a corresponding income dichotomy between the mass of consumers making use of informal sector goods and services (and, of course, some mass-produced factory goods) and a wealthy class largely patronizing the formal sector. In some cases there may be a clear element of price discrimination involved, reflecting the effect of income levels. Thus a short taxi ride in the "formal" sector across Nairobi for the tourist or middle-class Kenyan will cost the same as an 80-mile ride from Nairobi to Embu in an "informal sector" taxi, even when the city taxi is considerably more ramshackle. Much of the service sector in Kenya and other developing countries (prostitution is an example) is characterized by price discrimination and segmented markets. However, informal manufacturing may be similarly if less obviously based on price discrimination, by supplying rough-and-ready goods such as furniture, household utensils, and garments for the mass market, while leaving the often much *smaller* quality market to the formal sector. Low-income consumers do not simply consume less: they consume goods and services which serve similar purposes but at a much lower price—informal sector taxis, local beer instead of canned beer, charcoal instead of electricity, simple houses instead of expensive houses, and less hygienic eating houses and food kiosks instead of modern hotels. There are, indeed, usually two price levels depending on the income category of the consumer.

The sharper the division between income categories, the clearer will be the gap between formal and informal producing sectors: also because a larger poor sector provides the necessary source of ultra-cheap labor. It is not a coincidence that much of the early literature on the informal sector focused on Kenya, and less so on West African countries such as Nigeria, and that the issue was taken up subsequently by the Latin American countries especially. In many Asian countries there is more of a spectrum than a dichotomy, but there remains a complex set of low-priced activities which reflect the general level of incomes, as these evolve over time, in each country. It is especially this level of income difference which produces differences in the content of the typical African economy and many of the Asian economies at the present time.

Reference

Elkan, W., T. C. I. Ryan, and J. T. Mukui (1983). "The economics of shoe shining in Nairobi." *African Affairs* 18, no. 323.

Selection VI.7. Labour Market Modelling and the Urban Informal Sector: Theory and Evidence*

The existence of earning opportunities in the informal sector gives each member of the labour force yet another search option: he might take up a job in the urban informal sector and search from there in the evenings, on weekends, or during the day when working hours are variable. In the typical developing country, most of the formal sector jobs are located in the cities. Urban informal sector workers would therefore be expected to have a better chance of obtaining an urban formal sector job than would an agricultural worker, if for no other reason than simple proximity to places of hiring. Writing in the early 1970s, based upon observation of the Kenyan situation, I characterized the search process as follows:

New arrivals in the cities ordinarily stay with friends or relatives who help house and feed them while they look for work. A dozen or more people crowded into one room is not uncommon. They need not live in housing which is rented or provided as part of job compensation. Squatter settlements and shanty towns house a substantial portion of urban populations, particularly in Africa.

Open unemployment is not very common. Additional household members are expected to contribute to their support. Frequently, they assist with the household chores by preparing meals, washing clothes, or caring for children. Simultaneously, they search for work (albeit on an irregular basis) and are classified as unemployed.

The most fortunate new migrants obtain a permanent modern-sector job as a clerk, messenger, or whatever. However, these are the best jobs and the typical migrant is forced to find some lesser means of earning a cash income. He may secure one or more typically a succession of wage jobs (e.g., house-servant, cook in a small lunch kiosk, assistant in a family shop) or engage in self-employment (e.g. selling produce, newspapers, curios, or shoe shines on the street corner).

The defining characteristics of the (informal) sector are ease of entry and the lack of a stable employer-employee relationship. The urban areas of less developed countries typically have a wide variety of such open entry, casual employment types of jobs. For instance, a person can get started by buy-

ing some peas in the market, removing the pods at the side of the road, and selling podded peas to passers-by at a higher price. Prostitution is another occupation which has notoriously easy entry.

Workers in the (informal) sector are ordinarily classified as employed although they themselves and the statisticians who measure those things would be inclined to consider them underemployed. [Fields, 1975, pp. 171–172]

I would maintain that this characterization is equally valid today as a characterization of a broad range of economic activity, not only in Kenya but in a wide variety of developing countries.

Others agree. For example, Oberai and Singh (1984) conducted a study in Ludhiana in the Indian Punjab. They found (p. 509) "that more than 90 percent of migrants seeking work found a job within two months of their arrival, which means that migrants are being absorbed fairly quickly into the urban labour market". But much of this is free-entry self-employment. In Oberai and Singh's words (pp. 516–517): ". . . a fair proportion of migrants who take up self-employment on arrival start in the informal sector where they work as street vendors, porters, shoeshine boys and the like. Perhaps some of them also work in small family enterprises. All such employment requires little capital or skill. The proportion of migrants who are engaged in the formal sector as own-account workers or employers rises in most cases with length of stay; the increase is particularly sharp during the first few years." And in a study of Jamaica, Doeringer (1988) has written:

In particular, a distinction is drawn between those jobs (generally in what is often called the informal sector) where easy entry and work sharing are the principal determinants of income-earning opportunities, and those which are protected by formal sector internal labour markets. This distinction is critical for understanding how employment and productivity are affected by economic change, and by institutional forces in the workplace.

Thus, the main features of the urban informal sector, as I characterized it in my 1975 paper and as it remains characterized in many people's minds today are:

- *Free entry,* in the sense that all who wish to enter this sector can find some sort of work which will provide them with cash earnings;
- *Income-sharing,* because of the institutional cir-

*From Gary S. Fields, "Labour Market Modelling and the Urban Informal Sector: Theory and Evidence," in David Turnham, Bernard Salomé, and Antoine Schwartz, eds., *The Informal Sector Revisited* (Paris: OECD, 1990), 55–56, 64–68. Reprinted by permission.

cumstances of that sector's production and sales patterns;

- *Positive on-the-job search opportunities,* in that those who are engaged in the urban informal sector have a non-zero chance of finding a formal sector job;
- *An intermediate search probability,* in that those in the urban informal sector have a better chance of finding a formal sector job than do those in agriculture but a worse chance than those who are openly unemployed and searching full time; and
- *A lower wage in the urban informal sector than in agriculture,* arising endogenously as result of the higher on-the-job search opportunity here.

Free entry is the defining feature of the informal sector, and the other characteristics just listed are attributed of that sector in a typical developing economy. . . .

A Restatement of Results

. . . We may say that for some countries, the evidence shows:

i) Some of the activities which appear to be free-entry are not.

ii) The earnings of workers in small firms are lower on average than the earnings in large firms. However, the earnings in small firms are not uniformly lower. Rather, the two distributions overlap.

iii) The earnings of workers in small urban firms are not lower than the earnings of rural traditional workers.

iv) Those presently working in small firms, in firms not covered by social security, and in self-employment have been in those jobs for long periods of time.

v) Formal sector jobs are mostly filled by rural residents, not by informal sector workers.

vi) Many of those who are in small firms and in self-employment are there by choice.

When the studies are viewed this way—in terms of what the evidence actually shows rather than in terms of the labels and terminology of the authors—the early theoretical models are found for the most part not to be seriously challenged or contradicted by the empirical evidence.

There is one exception, though: contrary to the earlier theoretical models, empirical studies show that workers do indeed move into the informal sector by choice. Because this point leads to a major

conclusion of this paper, I elaborate on it at some length below.

Some Economic Anthropology-Type Findings

To get a better handle on the the workings of the informal sector labour market, I led a research team in conducting a series of interviews with informal sector workers in the two cities: Kuala Lumpur, Malaysia and San José, Costa Rica. Three major findings emerged.

1. Diversity Within the Informal Sector

Informal activities prove to be quite diverse. Some are activities with easy entry and no fixed hours of operation. They may be characterized by self-employment or employment of unpaid family labour or of unskilled labour with non-specific work relations. By contrast, other informal activities exhibit limited entry due to higher set-up costs and/or complicated licensing requirements, irregular hours of operation, and employment of family labour and unskilled labour with semi-specified work relations. These contrast with formal sector enterprises, which are characterized by restricted entry, regular place and hours of operation, and employment of non-family labour with specific work-relations. These belong in the category of formal sector, even if they are very small in scale. One example would be professional services companies which, although small in scale, cannot be viewed in any meaningful way as part of the informal sector.

Some examples may help clarify the distinction between the three types of activities. In transportation, trishaws in Malaysia (pedi-cabs) are examples of easy entry activities. They require very little capital investment. They are usually operated and owned by one person. Their owners operate them at irregular hours and at negotiable prices. No particular skill is required to be a pedi-cab driver. Typical of the upper-tier informal activities are the individually owned and operated taxi-cabs. Taxis are much more expensive to purchase than trishaws and the operating costs of taxis are much higher. Hours of operation can be regular or irregular, and the owner may hire a second driver to operate at different times of day (such as the night shift). Finally, there are the large established taxi companies which own a fleet of vehicles and hire a number of drivers to operate them. The taxi-drivers are expected to report to work at regular, agreed-upon hours. Sometimes they are paid fixed wages, sometimes a percentage of the fares. These taxi companies are examples of formal sector activities.

In commerce, street-vending is an obvious representative of free-entry activities. Street-vending (e.g. a sugar cane juice stand or a fruit stand) requires relatively low set-up costs. There is no skill requirement to this work. Street-vending licenses are easily procured. Location rental fees are nominal. Hours of operation are irregular. Paid employees are rare; even unpaid family workers are not very numerous. For the upper-tier informal sector in the commerce industry, examples are small retail stores such as sundry shops. They face higher set-up costs than do street-vendors because of higher rental fees and also because more licenses are involved. Although these shops are opened and closed at the same hours on most days, they may without notice close up earlier or not open at all at the wish of their owners. These shops are usually family-run with some hired help. The hired workers can be non-relatives, although relatives are sometimes employed with semi-specified responsibilities. Supermarkets owned by a large company exemplify the formal sector in commerce.

In manufacturing, backyard industries belong to the easy entry informal sector. Entry is easy because capital costs are small and rental fees are minimal, since the owners live and work in the same house. These backyard industries use manual labour, sometimes with very few tools. Workers may have to put in long hours to fill an order, or when there is no order, the shop may have to close up. These workers are usually family members or paid relatives and are generally unskilled. The small manufacturing industries in the upper-tier informal sector have higher capital and property costs. Because of the kinds of machinery used and the larger number of workers hired in these activities, licensing requirements may be more complicated and time-consuming. Workers in the upper-tier informal sector are both family members and hired labourers who are either unskilled or semi-skilled. Work relations are semi-formal.

Thus, within the informal sector, we find considerable diversity. The UIS does not consist uniformly of free-entry, low-wage, unorganized enterprises and workers, although, some activities do indeed fit this characterization; I would refer to these as the easy entry informal sector. Others do not. These others have significant barriers to entry, higher capital or skill requirements, and fairly regular labour relations arrangements; yet, they too may also be small, employ family labour, and op-

erate at irregular hours and places. I shall refer to these as the upper-tier informal sector. In Malaysia and Costa Rica, there are really two urban informal sectors.

2. Voluntary Participation in Upper-Tier Informal Activities but Not Easy Entry Ones

Another major conclusion from the interviews is that many people are in informal activities by choice. When asked their reasons for doing what they were doing, many informal workers in Costa Rica gave the following answers most frequently: *i*) They felt they could make more money at the informal sector job they were doing than they could earn in the formal sector, or *ii*) Even though they made a little less money, they enjoyed their work more, because it allowed them to choose their own hours, to work in the open air, to talk to friends, etc.

Here are some examples of such people. One man, 46 years old, sells a peanut-sugar-butter candy called "melcochas" in downtown San José. He has been selling melcochas on the streets for 37 years, and before that his father made and sold them. He was very insistent that he was there voluntarily, doing what he likes to do, and that it pays better than formal sector work. His brother had, at one time, started up a small factory making melcochas, which he then sold to the public. The brother eventually gave up this factory because he realized that he could make more money selling in the streets himself. That is, the informal sector work paid better than formal sector work.

Another interview was with a 50-year-old man selling fruit on a corner. This man had worked in the United States in several paid positions, and could easily have become a formal sector job in Costa Rica. Yet he sold fruits, because he earned more money (US $36 a day) than in any other type of work he could get in San José.

These examples illustrate what I call the constrained voluntary nature of much upper-tier informal activity. That is, given the constrained choices open to them, a great many of informal sector workers are in that sector voluntarily. These people know that job opportunities are available in the urban formal sectors for people like themselves and that they could get such jobs. Yet, they choose not to seek such jobs, the foremost reason being that they prefer the combination of monetary rewards and psychic aspects of their informal sector jobs.

Of course, not all informal sector activities are of such a type. Many people face such severely constrained options that the informal sector involvement can only be seen as their making the best of a bad situation. Representative of this kind of informal sector activity is a woman sitting on a market street in Kuala Lumpur, garlics set out on a piece of newspaper in front of her for sale. She calls out the price of her products to shoppers who pass by. Whenever she sells off her garlics, she is ready to go home. If the market turns out to be slow for the day, she sometimes stays for longer hours; other times, she sells her products at a substantial discount. If it happens to be raining, she takes the day off. This kind of activity is clearly small in scale. It also has free entry; all anyone has to do to enter similar economic activity is buy a supply of garlics from a rack jobber. The owner is self-employed and manages her business in a very casual (though not necessarily inefficient) way. She is very poor.

3. Linkages Between the Formal Sector and Informal Sector Labour Markets

A third important conclusion is that the upper-tier informal sector and the easy-entry informal sector are linked to the formal sector in very different ways. Whereas most participants in the easy-entry sector reported themselves dissatisfied with their positions and sought better jobs in the formal sector, those in the upper-tier informal sector had typically come from the formal sector and were glad to leave the formal sector behind.

There are barriers to entry to many upper-tier informal sector activities. One needs skills and tools to repair shoes or watches. Even to sell fruit, one needs capital for the initial stock, contacts with fruit wholesalers in the market, and money to buy a license for a good street location. However, these barriers can be overcome by working in the formal sector.

The formal sector was found to provide training for workers to move into upper-tier small-scale employment. Examples are food industry workers who leave jobs in the formal sector to set up their own small food processing activities, office-workers who leave to work in small family stores, and repairmen who learn their trades in large work places and then leave to set up their own shops. In Costa Rica, a study by the Ministry of Planning found that more than 70 per cent of those self-employed in the informal sector had previously held wage or salary jobs in the formal sector. This finding was reaffirmed in our interviews of such workers in San José.

The formal sector also provides the opportunity for workers to accumulate savings to start up their own businesses. Examples are repairmen and small manufacturers who save part of their wages to buy their own machinery, tools, and raw materials for use in their own businesses. In Costa Rica, these savings from formal sector jobs are a much more important source of finance for new businesses than are loans from banks or other financial institutions.

At the other end of the spectrum, the formal sector was found to employ preferentially those workers who have acquired training in the easy entry segment of the informal sector. Examples are managers of appliance stores who had previously worked in small family businesses. These people tend to be young and well-educated. The growth of the formal sector enables workers to move out of the easy entry informal sector into newly-created formal sectors jobs. This is especially true in Malaysia, where the economy has been on a sustained positive economic growth path. It is much less the case in Costa Rica, where the severe economic crisis of the early 1980s led to a loss of formal sector employment. Examples in Malaysia are young people who start out in family stores but end up as clerks in fast-food restaurants or as mechanics in car-repair shops—jobs that have opened up due to the growth of the formal sector.

Although on balance the linkages between the informal sector and the formal sector were found to be positive, there is one identifiable group of losers among informal sector firms: those who fail to respond to the dynamic changes in the economy. Yet, a repeated finding from the interviews in Malaysia and Costa Rica, as surprising as it was consistent, is that those who do not respond often have deliberately decided not to. Many do not want to change. For example, proprietors of small family shops (often older people) prefer to go on operating them in much the same way as before despite growing competition from shopping centres. Another reason for losing out due to economic growth, much less common than the first, is technical change. An example is the reluctance of watch repairmen to enter new lines of work despite the fact that demand for their services has plummeted due to the advent of cheap digital watches which cost less to replace than to repair. It was rare for informal sector workers to report that they themselves or others in similar lines of work lost out because they were squeezed by formal sector firms.

References

Doeringer, Peter, "Market Structure, Jobs, and Productivity: Observations from Jamaica," *World Development,* Vol. 16, No. 4, April, 1988.

Fields, G., "Rural-Urban Migration, Urban Unemployment and Underemployment, and Job Search Activity in LDCs," *Journal of Development Economics,* June, 1975.

Oberai, A. S. and H. K. Manmohan Singh, "Migration, Employment and the Urban Labour Market: A Study in the Indian Punjab," *International Labour Review,* July–August, 1984.

Selection VI.8. The Role of the Informal Sector in the Migration Process: A Test of Probabilistic Migration Models and Labour Market Segmentation for India*

Attitude Towards the Informal Sector at Time of Entry

Seventy-one per cent of those who were absorbed in non-wage employment on arrival stated during the survey that they had come to the city with the specific intention of pursuing non-wage activity. The issue about the objectives of those who entered the informal wage sector cannot be resolved as easily, as the survey did not collect information on the type and size of establishments that migrants expected to join. However, some insight can be obtained from estimates of the prevalence of moving to the city with job prospects made certain from the rural area, and of job search after entering the informal wage sector.

Of those who entered the informal wage sector, 12 per cent had prearranged their urban jobs (in the sense that they had received *firm commitment* of employment from the *employer*), and 42 per cent had migrated on the suggestions of urban-based contacts.[1] For all practical purposes informal wage sector entrants who received suggestions from urban contacts have no uncertainty in their minds of getting a job in this sector on arrival at the urban centre. The survey data indicate that because of the responsibilities incurred, urban-based contacts are not likely to make suggestions until they have lined up specific jobs for their candidates or are sure of doing so.[2] Moreover, the ability of contacts to locate jobs for others outside their own sector is likely to be limited. Contacts have most influence with their own employers, and they are most knowledgeable about vacancies in their own occupations and establishments.

It can be argued that the evidence that many migrants expected to enter the informal wage sector and acquired such jobs through contacts does not establish that these migrants did not move to the city to engage in job search there. For it may be that they simply expected to start lower down the job ladder. However, the survey data suggest that this was not so. If informal sector entrants considered their job as a holding operation they would be looking for alternative employment. The continuation of job search after taking up first job was more prevalent among those who entered the informal wage sector, but the majority of migrants entering this sector did not search. Forty-one per cent of those who entered the informal wage sector continued job search, compared to 21 per cent and 20 per cent of those who entered the formal sector and non-wage employment respectively. Thus, it can be claimed with some confidence that a sizeable proportion, possibly one-half or more, of migrants who entered the informal wage sector and the non-wage sector had been attracted to the city by opportunities in these sectors, and did not consider employment there as a means of survival while waiting in the queue for formal sector jobs.

Mobility from the Informal Sector to the Formal Sector

Only 24 per cent of those who entered the informal wage sector on arrival and 6 per cent of the non-wage workers had found their way into the formal sector by the time of the survey. These figures represent the average experience of a large number of cohorts over varying periods of time. Thus they are not adequate measures of the degree of mobility, though the mobility from the non-wage sector is obviously on the low side. To overcome this deficiency, we suggested a comparison of the proportion of direct entrants in the formal sector in any particular year with the proportion of informal sector entrants in the previous year who moved to the formal sector within twelve months of arrival.

The results of such an exercise are presented in Table 1. The table shows that for migrants who entered the informal wage sector, the percentage who moved to the formal sector within twelve months of arrival was between 5 per cent and 15 per cent (col. 3). This was considerably lower than the percentage of all new arrivals and of those with no education who entered the formal sector directly. The percentage who had entered the formal sector directly varied from 38 per cent to 48 per cent for the

*From Biswajit Banerjee, "The Role of the Informal Sector in the Migration Process: A Test of Probabilistic Migration Models and Labour Market Segmentation for India," *Oxford Economic Papers* 35 (1983): 411, 414–420. Reprinted by permission.

[1] These two categories of migrants overlap. In all, 48 per cent of the informal wage sector entrants had pre-arranged job and/or moved on the suggestion of a contact.

[2] This point is discussed in detail in Banerjee (1984).

Table 1. Direct Entry into the Formal Sector and Mobility from the Informal Sector, by Year of Arrival in Delhi

Year of arrival	Percentage of migrants who entered the formal sector directly (1)	Percentage of migrants with no education who entered the formal sector directly (2)	For those who entered the informal wage sector, the percentage who moved to the formal sector within 12 months of arrival (3)	For those who entered the informal wage sector, the percentage who were in the formal sector at the time of the survey (1975–76) (4)
1965	37.8	25.8	5.9	29.4
1966	44.3	32.0	7.1	31.0
1967	46.2	25.8	10.4	33.3
1968	45.4	43.9	4.8	20.6
1969	45.9	45.5	14.6	31.3
1970	43.9	29.5	11.6	30.4
1971	42.9	52.3	8.7	26.1
1972	41.8	37.2	12.5	20.8
1973	49.5	38.5	9.8	22.0
1974	40.5	35.7	14.3	16.7
1975	46.2	37.9	3.9[a]	3.9

[a]This figure is low because many of the new arrivals in 1975 had not completed 12 months of urban residence at the time of the survey.

entire sample (col. 1), and from 26 per cent to 46 per cent for migrants with no education (col. 2).[3] To give a specific example, of those migrants who had entered the informal wage sector in 1966, only 7.1 per cent had moved to the formal sector within twelve months of their arrival. But in 1967, 46.2 per cent of all new arrivals and 25.8 per cent of new arrivals with no education entered the formal sector directly. Thus in 1967 new arrivals were at least four to six times more likely to get formal sector employment than those who entered the informal wage sector in 1966. This suggests, in contrast to the assumption of probabilistic migration models, that the migrant labour market in Delhi is segmented.

It can be argued that in the context of Delhi the above criterion for judging segmentation is too stringent. Limiting the reference period to twelve months would be appropriate if job search was entirely urban based. But the survey data indicate that over one-half of the direct entrants to the formal sector had engaged in rural-based search. Therefore the reference period for measuring mo-

[3]The percentage of direct formal sector entrants in any particular year has been calculated with respect to those who had arrived in the city that year and were living there at the time of the survey. This neglects those who had come in that year and had returned to their origin. To the extent these return migrants had entered the urban informal sector, the figures on direct formal sector entry are overestimates. But then, so also are the figures on mobility from the informal sector to the formal sector.

bility from the informal sector ought to match the average length of rural-based search of formal sector entrants. Unfortunately, we are unable to do this as information on length of rural-based search was not collected in the survey. However, a consideration of mobility measured over a longer period (see col. 4) and the econometric evidence reported below on the influence of length of urban residence suggests that the conclusion of segmentation is still valid.

We now estimate the factors that contributed to mobility from the informal wage sector to the formal sector by estimating a binary logit model. The estimates, obtained by the maximum likelihood method, are presented in Table 2. The results indicate, contrary to the assertion of the segmentation model, that education has an important influence on mobility. In particular, having middle school- or intermediate college-level education increases the likelihood of mobility. However, age on arrival does not have any significant effect. Thus, the advantage that migrants who arrive between the age of 20 and 24 have over other age groups in gaining direct access to the formal sector is lost once they enter the informal wage sector.

As might be expected, the likelihood of mobility increases with duration of urban residence. Ceteris paribus, an additional year spent in the city increases the probability of an informal wage sector employee moving to the formal sector by 0.02, when evaluated at the aggregate predicted proba-

Table 2. Logit Estimates of Mobility Between Sectors (Dependent variable: log of odds of moving to the formal sector from the informal wage sector)

Independent Variable	Coefficient (Asymptotic standard error)
Education dummies[a]	
Below primary	−0.06823 (0.34667)
Primary to below middle	−0.18347 (0.28831)
Middle to below matric	0.56045 (0.29552)†
Matric to below intermediate	0.43083 (0.35694)
Intermediate to below graduate	2.10030 (0.62826)*
Graduate and above	−25.71200 (237.00 × 10³)[b]
Age on arrival dummies[c]	
20 to 24	0.11364 (0.25274)
25 to 29	0.33029 (0.32886)
30 to 39	0.13475 (0.38893)
40 and above	−0.19849 (0.68002)
Years of urban residence	0.14667 (0.03044)*
Unmarried	−0.42204 (0.22976)†
Scheduled caste	0.44327 (0.23079)†
Region of origin dummies[d]	
Haryana	−0.34077 (0.45692)
Punjab	−1.59160 (0.85051)†
Rajasthan	−0.43204 (0.51791)
Eastern Uttar Pradesh	0.09134 (0.33322)
Hill Uttar Pradesh	0.51610 (0.44980)
Central Uttar Pradesh	0.15181 (0.74723)
Western Uttar Pradesh	−1.06220 (0.39815)*
Constant	−2.04740 (0.44978)*
Log likelihood	−323.04
Likelihood ratio test	63.51
Degrees of freedom	20
(N)	(646)
Predicted probability at mean values of independent variables	0.18

[a]The omitted category was those with no education.

[b]There were very few observations in this education category, which has affected the size and reliability of the coefficient.

[c]The omitted category was those less than 19 years of age.

[d]The omitted category was those from "Rest of India."

*Significant at the 1 per cent level, using a two-tailed test.

†Significant at the 10 per cent level.

bility for mean values of the explanatory variables ($p = 0.18$).

The finding on the unmarried worker dummy is similar to that obtained in the model of sector of entry restricted to wage employees. This suggests that formal sector employers perhaps prefer to hire married workers or that informal sector employment is less acceptable to married than to unmarried workers. The evidence suggests that Scheduled caste migrants are more likely to move out of the informal wage sector to the formal sector than those who belong to other castes, reflecting their awareness and exploitation of the advantage they have from the government policy of reserving jobs for Scheduled castes.[4]

As for *potential mobility* from the informal sector to the formal sector, the probability appears to be low. At the time of the survey, only 15 per cent of the informal sector wage employees and 12 per cent of the non-wage workers were actively searching for alternative wage employment.

[4]For a detailed analysis of the influence of caste in the urban labour market see Banerjee and Knight (1982).

The lack of mobility from the non-wage sector and the lack of interest of non-wage workers in wage employment is not surprising given that the average monthly earnings of these workers were 47 per cent higher than those of workers in the formal sector. One reason for the low propensity of workers in the informal wage sector to seek alternative employment may be that the wage differential with the formal sector is not large enough to make it worthwhile to bother looking for formal sector employment. The informal sector migrants may currently be working together with their relatives and co-villagers, and may not like to sacrifice this working environment to seek employment elsewhere for slightly higher pay. Further, the cumulative loss from being in the informal sector rather than in the formal sector is minimal since education and experience are rewarded at similar rates in both sectors.[5] Another, and perhaps more important, reason may be that there are constraints on obtaining specific information and gaining access to formal sector employment. If information on formal sector opportunities is generally transmitted through contacts, informal sector employees will come to know of them only if they are able to widen their contacts after arrival. The widening of contacts is not easy, and is largely a matter of chance. The urban social network is based on kinship, caste membership, area of origin, and place of work. When jobs are scarce, social groups are likely to accommodate their own members first. An alternative way to obtain information would be to search personally at factory gates. But this search would have to be carried out during working hours, and may require giving up the current job. This option is therefore quite risky, and may not be preferred by many individuals. An additional consideration in rejecting this option may be the belief that jobs cannot be obtained without the influence of contacts. This belief may also inhibit individuals from searching for formal sector jobs through newspaper advertisement and employment exchange. Thus, migrants may not search because they do not know of any jobs that are available, or because they know that what is available cannot be obtained. The presence of contacts plays a crucial role in both these considerations. The role of contacts in mobility between sectors in Delhi is highlighted by individual level data: of those migrants in the sample who had moved from the informal wage sector to the formal sector, about 60 per cent came to know about their current employment from relatives and friends.

The above discussion suggests a reason why the proportion of new arrivals entering the formal sector was greater than the proportion of informal wage sector workers moving to the formal sector. Informal sector wage employees were not aware of the formal sector vacancies which the new arrivals filled. Only if there was a perfect market mechanism for transmission of information would all persons have an equal chance to search.

Conclusions

A basic hypothesis of probabilistic migration models is that informal sector employment is a temporary staging post for new migrants on their way to formal sector employment. In this paper we have argued that there are no conclusive tests of probabilistic models in the empirical migration literature, and we then went on to examine evidence from a sample survey which tests the validity of the assumptions that underlie such models. We also tested some of the main hypotheses of the segmented labour market theory, a popular alternative to neo-classical theory for analyzing the structure of urban labour markets in developing countries. The empirical evidence indicates that the migration process postulated in probabilistic models does not seem to be realistic in the case of Delhi, and that the segmentation model is only partially valid.

Slightly more than one-half of the migrants in the sample joined the informal sector on arrival in Delhi, but only a small fraction entered non-wage employment. Not all informal sector entrants saw their job as a means of financing search for formal sector employment. A substantial proportion of informal sector entrants were attracted to Delhi by opportunities in the informal sector. About one-half of the informal wage sector entrants moved to Delhi after prearranging their job or on the suggestion of an urban-based contact, and nearly three-quarters of the non-wage sector entrants expected to set up such activities on arrival in the city. Only two-fifths of the informal wage sector entrants and one-fifth of the non-wage workers continued to search for alternative employment after finding their first job. The survey data also suggest that a majority of formal sector entrants too had engaged in rural-based search and had lined up their jobs from the rural area. These findings do not lend support to the basic assumptions of probabilistic migration models.

---

[5]The superiority of the formal sector must not be gauged in terms of earnings differentials alone. This sector is likely to have greater non-pecuniary benefits and better terms and conditions of work than the informal sector.

Actual mobility and potential mobility from the informal sector was low. Slightly less than one-quarter of informal wage sector entrants were able to move to the formal sector. The proportion who moved from the informal wage sector to the formal sector during any twelve month period was four to six times lower than the proportion of all new arrivals and of those with no education during that period who entered the formal sector directly. Moreover, only a small proportion of informal sector wage employees were seeking alternative jobs at the time of the survey. This was interpreted as evidence of a segmented labour market, and was attributed in part to imperfect information flows, resulting from the importance of contacts in the recruitment process. Individual level data indicate that friends and relatives were heavily relied on to obtain employment by entrants to all sectors and by those who moved from the informal wage sector to the formal sector. Moreover, the dummy variables on region of origin, included as proxies for the influence of contacts, were statistically significant in the econometric analysis of earnings, sector of entry, and mobility between sectors.

An analysis of earnings of wage employees suggest that a meaningful distinction could be made between the formal sector and the informal wage sector. Earnings were lower in the informal wage sector and the process of wage determination in this sector differed from that in the formal sector. But, contrary to the assertion of the segmented labour market model, returns to education and experience were similar to both sectors. The differences observed were in the effect of employment status, nature of work, and caste on earnings. In the formal sector daily-wage workers, manual workers, and individuals belonging to the Scheduled castes had lower earnings, but there was no such discrimination in the informal sector. This suggests that the informal sector was, as might be expected, more competitive.

Informal sector entrants were, on the average, slightly less well educated than those who entered the formal sector, and the likelihood of moving from the informal to the formal sector was greater for those who had above middle school level education. The latter finding goes against the hypothesis of the segmentation model that human capital is not important in explaining mobility between sectors. However, this should not detract attention from the fact that over one-third of those with no

education entered the formal sector directly on arrival in the city, and that the likelihood of uneducated informal sector entrants moving to the formal sector was small. The probability of mobility increased with duration of urban residence but only by small magnitude, and it was higher for married migrants and those who belonged to the Scheduled castes.

The findings of this paper have important implications. The implication of the rejection of probabilistic models for policy decisions is that employment creation in the urban formal sector can play a part in the solution of the urban "employment problem," and that the contribution of migration to urban surplus labour and social costs is much less than is usually visualized. The importance of pre-arranging jobs and moving on the suggestion of contacts suggest that migration in response to job creation in the formal sector is not likely to exceed the number of openings by a large margin. Only those who have contacts in the formal sector and also have the necessary qualifications will receive information about new opportunities and stand some chance of obtaining employment. If jobs are created in establishments and occupations dominated by urban natives, induced migration will be particularly low. The findings also suggest that for migrants attracted to the city by informal sector opportunities, labour market segmentation is not a constraint on the achievement of their objectives formed at the time of migration. There is no reduction in the perceived increase in welfare through migration, arising out of segmentation of the market. Individuals in the informal sector are better off in the city than they were in the rural area, though their position could be even better if there was no segmentation. Further, the importance of education and experience in the determination of earnings of wage employees in the informal sector suggests that low earnings in this sector can be eliminated through human capital formation.

Reference

Banerjee, Biswajit (1984) "Information flow, expectations and job search: rural-to-urban migration process in India," *Journal of Development Economics* 15: 239–57.

Banerjee, Biswajit and Knight, J. B. (1982) "Caste discrimination in the Indian urban labour market," mimeo.

CHAPTER VII

Agriculture

Overview

Agricultural productivity in poor countries is an even smaller fraction of that of rich countries than is industrial productivity, as we saw in the Overview to Chapter I. Raising agricultural productivity is crucial for raising incomes of agricultural workers, who make up a large fraction or even the majority of the labor force in less developed countries. Increased agricultural productivity may yield other benefits for LDC economies such as reduced urban underemployment, as was claimed by Todaro in Selection VI.3. In this chapter W. Arthur Lewis reviews the reasons agriculture has proven to be "the weakest link in the development chain" and the consequences of this relative failure in Selection VII.A.1. The following Note on food, hunger, and famine discusses studies of some of the more extreme consequences of agricultural failure.

What special characteristics of agriculture have made it so difficult to raise productivity? To begin, in a large LDC millions of individuals and households are making production decisions, whereas in other important industries the number of decision-makers might range from a handful to thousands. Next, the seasonality and geographical dispersion of agricultural production create the need for an extensive system of storage and transportation. The weather adds an extra element of uncertainty to the agricultural production process and contributes to exceptional volatility of output prices. All of these special characteristics complicate the task of policymakers and increase the risk that government intervention will fail, yet, as Timmer (1988, p. 301) points out, "Designing new technology and fostering its adoption is primarily a public sector activity because of the relatively small scale of individual farmers." The same could be said of rural infrastructure such as roads and irrigation projects.

Given these special characteristics, how should less developed countries go about "transforming traditional agriculture" (Schultz 1964) or "getting agriculture moving" (Mosher 1966)? In the first selection of section VII.B on designing an agricultural strategy, Joseph Stiglitz lists the justifications for government intervention in agricultural markets and assesses the prospects that policies can succeed given the limited information that governments have available. In the following selection Bruce Johnston advocates a "unimodal" agricultural strategy, in which the government promotes diffusion of technical innovations that can be used efficiently by small-scale farmers, over a "bimodal" strategy that promotes modernization of the small fraction of farms that have enough land to use efficiently the kind of capital equipment employed by farmers in more developed countries. Whether small farmers have benefited from diffusion of "Green Revolution" technology has been a subject of much controversy, and the Comment following Johnston's selection lists some of the key studies and issues. Johnston also discusses the interaction between land reform and a unimodal agricultural strategy. The case for land reform and the relevant literature are the subject of the second Comment following his selection. C. Peter Timmer argues in Selection VII.B.3 that the strategy advocated by Johnston gives too active and direct a role for the government and insufficient attention to the influence of world markets on domestic agriculture. The Note concluding this section describes the theory of Hayami and Ruttan (1985) that the direction of technical and institutional change in agriculture toward saving labor or saving land is "induced" by relative scarcity of labor versus land. Also included in the Note is the less optimistic view, expressed by Braverman and Stiglitz (1986), that beneficial innovations may not be adopted and undesirable innovations may be given the structure of incentives in the landlord-tenant relationship. This need to carefully take into account the nature of agricultural contracts and the incentives they generate leads to section VII.C, on the microeconomics of the rural sector.

In Selection VII.C.1, Joseph Stiglitz discusses the incentive effects of sharecropping arrangements that are widely used in less developed countries. Unlike a wage system, sharecropping provides an incentive for the tenant to work in the absence of monitoring by the landlord, and unlike a rental system, the landlord and tenant face the same risks. Hans Binswanger and Mark Rosenzweig in Selection VII.C.2 note the difficulty for contractual choice models of explaining "tenancy ladders" where workers first become sharecroppers, then fixed-rent tenants, and finally acquire land of their own. In the following selection Pranab Bardhan criticizes the tendency of researchers in this area to "explain" the existence of certain contractual arrangements by showing that they benefit the parties involved. Collective action and bargaining problems may allow inefficient institutions to persist, vitiating the power of such "explanations."

Complementary fixed capital investments are often required to achieve the maximum benefits from adopting technical innovations in agriculture, making effective provision of credit to small farmers a key ingredient in raising agricultural productivity. Avishay Braverman and J. Luis Guasch in Selection VII.C.4 review some of the fundamental problems with rural financial markets in less developed countries. In the following selection Inderjit Singh, Lyn Squire, and John Strauss try to capture in a formal model the complexity of agricultural household behavior. This complexity stems from the fact that the typical agricultural household must make decisions regarding production, family labor supply, and commodity consumption. They show that if the household is a price taker in all markets its production decisions are consistent with profit maximization and independent of the household's utility function. An important consequence is that output supply will increase with price. Empirical studies of the response of agricultural production to prices are listed in the Comment following this selection.

In the final section, VII.D, we turn to the subject of agricultural pricing policy. Timmer (1988, p. 294) states, "Given the large number of farmers within a typical developing country, government extension agents cannot teach each individual farmer new agricultural techniques. Price policy for farm crops and agricultural inputs, on the other hand, is an intervention that reaches most farmers quite directly while being amenable to effective government control." A major World Bank study of agricultural pricing policy is summarized in the Note that begins this section. The study found that the typical LDC government discriminates against the agricultural sector, partly by policies that lower agricultural prices directly but mostly by policies that raise the prices of what farmers buy by protecting the manufacturing sector from import competition. The following selection by Michael Lipton gives a less detached account of policy bias in favor of urban and against rural interests.

Poverty does appear to be greater in rural than in urban areas of LDCs, as shown in Exhibit VII.D.1. One formulation of the urban bias thesis, discussed in the Comment following this Exhibit, is that unfavorable terms of trade for agriculture are used to transfer resources from the agricultural to the industrial sector. The urban bias thesis has also drawn criticism that is briefly summarized in Comment VII.D.2. The question of urban bias leads naturally to discussions of income distribution and political economy, which are the subjects of the next two chapters of this book.

References

Braverman, Avishay, and Joseph Stiglitz. 1986. "Landlords, Tenants and Technological Innovations." *Journal of Development Economics* 23 (October): 313–32.

Hayami, Yujiro, and Vernon W. Ruttan. 1985. *Agricultural Development: An International Perspective,* revised and expanded edition (Baltimore: Johns Hopkins University Press).

Mosher, Arthur T. 1966. *Getting Agriculture Moving: Essentials for Development and Modernization* (New York: Praeger).

Schultz, Theodore W. 1964. *Transforming Traditional Agriculture* (New Haven, Conn.: Yale University Press).

Timmer, C. Peter. 1988. "The Agricultural Transformation." In Hollis Chenery and T. N. Srinivasan, eds., *Handbook of Development Economics, Volume I* (Amsterdam: North-Holland).

VII.A. THE IMPORTANCE OF AGRICULTURE FOR ECONOMIC DEVELOPMENT

Selection VII.A.1. Development Strategy in a Limping World Economy*

Agriculture has been the weakest link in the development chain. Industry in LDCs has grown at around 7 percent per annum, the number of children in school has multiplied by four, the domestic savings ratio has risen by three percentage points—the picture is everywhere bright until one turns to agriculture, where the dominant fact is that, in LDCs as a whole, food production has failed to keep pace with the demand for food, thereby causing or aggravating a whole series of other problems.

The basic reasons for this failure are well known, so I will list but not dwell on them.

The first has been fast population growth. Population has grown at around 2.5 percent per annum, and per capita demand has pushed the growth of total demand well beyond three percent, while output has grown at significantly less than 3 percent, turning what used to be an export surplus into an import surplus of food.

Second, the technological revolution in tropical food production has only just begun, research in the colonial days having been confined almost but not exclusively to commercial crops exportable to the world market. We have made spectacular progress with maize, wheat for subtropical conditions, and rice for areas of controlled irrigation, but have still far to go with other rice, with sorghums, and millets, and with livestock management.

Third, even where there is new technology to impart, the agricultural extension services and the network for supplying modern inputs to the farmer—especially seeds, fertilisers and pesticides, are gravely deficient, and in many areas virtually non-existent.

Fourth, investment in rural infrastructure is inadequate. Road systems have improved immensely, and the penetration of the countryside by buses and trucks is altering the patterns of rural life. But not enough has been invested in irrigation, or in storage facilities.

Fifth, everyone speaks in favour of land reform, but very few governments have done it in any of its various forms, whether distributing land to the landless, or converting from rental to ownership tenures, or fixing rental ceilings. The case for some sort of land reform remains unquestionable from the standpoint of justice; the case from the standpoint of its effects on production is now stated with greater sophistication, recognising the extent to which higher output is tied to improved technology, extension and investment. Indeed several writers now speak not of land reform but of "the land reform package," to distinguish what they see as good land reform from bad land reform.

And finally to complete our list of factors that have inhibited agricultural output we must add poor terms of trade. The prices of agricultural commodities in world trade fell throughout the 1950s and most of the 1960s, while industrial prices rose all the time. This was anomalous, since prosperity usually improves agriculture's terms of trade. The basic factor was the enormous increase in agricultural productivity in the United States, resulting in the build up of stocks of cereals; since agricultural commodities compete with each other either on the demand side or on the supply side, this depressed all other agricultural prices. Add to this that in several LDCs governments wanted to keep farm revenues low, whether by imposing taxes on exportable crops, or by placing price ceilings on food for the domestic market. This is at first sight a curious phenomenon. One would expect that farm populations, being more than half the nation (in most cases), would carry enough political clout to be able to defend themselves against such measures—and would on the contrary be manipulating the terms of trade in their favour, but this is not automatic. European farmers were doing this at the end of the nineteenth century, but the contemporaneous efforts of American farmers—though they were still in the majority—were a failure.

Let me now turn from the causes of the low level of agricultural output in the LDCs to some of its effects. Agricultural failure is not the sole cause of the problems I shall mention, but makes in each case a significant contribution.

Take first the probability that inequality of the income distribution has increased along with recent growth. This is not a novel phenomenon. Increased inequality is inherent in the classical system of economics because population growth keeps labour income down while profits and rents increase. Given the long and strident debate between economic historians as to what happened to

*From Sir W. Arthur Lewis, "Development Strategy in a Limping World Economy," The Elmhurst Lecture, The International Conference of Agricultural Economists, Banff, Canada, September 3–12, 1979 (processed), pp. 2–9. Reprinted by permission.

the European living standards in the first half of the century, no modern economist should have assumed that economic growth would automatically raise the incomes of those at the lower end of the scale. Rapid population growth has also played its negative role in our day, restraining the wage level and farm income per head. Since the majority of the labour force in LDCs consists of farm people, who also have the lowest incomes, the standard of living of the great bulk of the population can be raised only by raising farm income. Discussions of the effects of growth on income distribution or income distribution on growth lead nowhere unless farm income is at the centre of the alleged relationship.

The worst effects of population growth combined with technological standstill are to be seen in the arid zones of the tropical world, where some 500 million people live, especially along the fringes of the African and Asian deserts. There we have the largest concentration of human poverty; the numbers continue to grow rapidly; and we have not yet had the technological breakthrough in dry farming that might promise higher productivity. To raise the living standards of these hundreds of millions is the greatest challenge to those who work for development.

Consider next the huge flow of migrants from the countryside into the towns. Central to this of course is the growth of population. Relatively under-populated countries can cope with population growth by opening up new land, as has been happening over much of Africa, but in less favoured countries population growth means smaller farms, more landless labourers and lower output per head. Unless a green revolution is set in motion, the natural reaction of farmers caught in this situation is to put pressure on the young to migrate to the cities, which they will do if the cities show signs of expanding employment. This is not a complete solution. The towns cannot provide employment for the whole of the natural increase in the countryside, not to speak of women now also leaving the family tasks and seeking wage employment; so unemployment mounts. The government is also trapped. The towns exert great pressure for expansion of the public services—of water, bus transport, schools, hospitals, and so on—eating up more funds than exist, and leaving nothing to spend in the countryside. So the differential in amenities between town and country widens all the more, and the stream of migrants is increased. Unemployment in the towns cannot be ended by spending more in the towns. The basic solution is rather to make the countryside economically viable, with a larger cultivated area, with rising productivity on the farms, more rural industry, and better social amenities.

Note "the larger cultivated area." Development economists have been mesmerized by European experience into assuming that the development process always involves a decline in the number of persons in agriculture. This is true of relative decline, but it extends to an absolute decline only in the later stages of development. For example, around 1850 in Western Europe the agricultural population was only 50 percent of the whole, and the rate of natural increase about one and a quarter percent. So the agricultural population would decline absolutely if the non-agricultural population grew at over 2.5 percent per year. Whereas with 70 percent in agriculture and a rate of natural increase of 2.5 percent, an absolute decline of the agricultural labour force requires non-agricultural employment to expand at 8.3 percent per annum, which it cannot do.

An increase in the absolute numbers engaged in agriculture is therefore an essential item in coping with the current flood of population. The fact that the green revolution in cereals is labour-intensive helps, especially if the natural propensity of the more enterprising farmers to invest in labour saving machinery can be restrained. But there is no escaping the need to bring more land under cultivation, by opening up roads, irrigation, terracing, drainage, and other investment in infrastructure. Some governments are actively engaged in colonisation schemes of this sort, which, if highly planned to meet modern standards, are costly and troublesome. The subject is neglected in our textbooks. It needs more research and experimentation, leading to action.

A third consequence of the weakness of agriculture is that it is one of the reasons why so many LDCs have had balance of payments troubles, have incurred large external debts, or have found themselves defaulting on their obligations. It is not just that a larger output would earn more foreign exchange, or save on food imports. Indirectly it would reduce urbanization, the high cost of which is the prime cause of their needing so much capital and having to borrow so much. Also, in countries suffering from the two-gap disease, it would facilitate the translation of domestic saving into foreign exchange.

A fourth and final consequence of the weakness of agriculture has been to inhibit the growth of manufacturing industry because of the farmers' low purchasing power. The physical output of LDC commercial export crops grew rapidly, aided on the supply side by the expansion of internal transport, and on the demand side by the unusually rapid growth of the developed countries. But the prices at which these commodities sold were poor; exports are a small part of agricultural output, so their prices are linked on the supply side to the price of food, which as we saw earlier, was depressed by American surpluses. The individual LDC can do well out of exporting agricultural raw materials or tropical beverages; but for the group of LDCs as a whole the elasticity of supply of these commodities is so high, at prices yielding roughly the same incomes as domestic food production, that the factoral terms of trade stay much the same despite increases in demand or improvements in technology. The road to riches does not run in these directions.

At the same time farm incomes from domestic production were also low, for reasons which we have already considered. So import substitution of manufactures, which was the starting point of industrialization, was limited by the narrowness of the domestic market. LDCs soon discovered that if

industry is to grow at 7 percent per annum, in the face of a peasantry with only a small marketable surplus, industry must look to foreign markets. By the year 1970 this lesson had been learnt, and nearly every LDC has begun exporting some manufactures to developed countries. Unfortunately this range was very narrow, dominated by textiles and clothing; broadening only as the protests and restrictions of MDCs forced the more advanced LDCs into light metals, electronics and other fields. The LDC effort was clearly successful, since LDC exports of manufactures were growing at 10 percent a year, despite the barriers erected by the MDCs. Whether world trade will revive, and if so whether LDC exports of manufactures will again grow at 10 percent, are crucial questions for LDC development strategy. . . . But no matter how they may be answered, it will be to the advantage of LDCs to raise their agricultural productivity, since this would simultaneously raise the living standards of their farmers, create a domestic market for their manufactures, and improve their terms of trade.

Note VII.A.1. Food, Hunger, Famine

Can developing countries attain levels of food consumption that will ensure adequate nutrition even for the lowest deciles in their income distribution? To guarantee adequate nutrition, agricultural development must be concerned simultaneously with the rate of increase in food production and the means by which production is increased. Unless a country's "pattern" of agricultural development facilitates the absorption of a large segment of the rural labor force into productive employment, even a large increase in food output will leave many households with inadequate access to food supplies.

Rather than being a race between food and population, the food equation is to be viewed as a dynamic balance in individual countries between food supply and food demand that depends on complex relationships among a number of variables. Equilibrium in this vital food equation can range from a low one—a small increase in food supplies and little purchasing power in the hands of the poor—to high levels of each. The level at which the food supply–food demand equation is balanced is largely dependent on the design and implementation of a country's development strategy, especially as it influences the rate of expansion of employment.

These views are presented in detail in John W. Mellor and Bruce F. Johnston, "The World Food Equation: Interrelations Among Development, Employment, and Food Consumption," *Journal of Economic Literature* (June 1984).

There is now deeper understanding of the causes and consequences of hunger and famine. The cause is not so much deficient food output as it is the absence of "entitlements" and the lack of "capability" for poor people without the financial means or political influence. This understanding follows from Sen's analysis in section I.A and is elaborated in Jean Drèze and Amartya Sen, *Hunger and Public Action* (1989).

Drèze and Sen also submit that capability and nutritional requirements encompass more than food intake—health care, basic education, clean drinking water, sewage, and adequate shelter. They point out that most of those who die in famines succumb to disease, not to starvation. Gender bias is also a cause.

Analyzing the Great Bengal Famine of 1943 and more recent famines in Bangladesh and Ethiopia, Sen has shown that it was not the decline in available food that was the major cause of famine. In Bengal, military expenditures in urban areas and the consequent inflation in food prices were responsible. Especially hard hit were landless agricultural laborers and self-employed rural artisans whose incomes lagged behind the inflation. When a threat of famine arises, relief works to provide employment and real purchasing power to the poorest can do much to avert famine. See A. K. Sen, *Poverty and Famines* (1981).

As demonstrated by India, famines can be averted, even in the event of harvest failure, by targeted and timely employment programs, direct relief to the unemployable, and careful use of food reserves. Drèze and Sen note that, in contrast to China, India's democratic political system and free press induced government action to avert famine. They contrast India, which has eliminated famine but retained chronic hunger, with China, which has reduced chronic undernutrition but has suffered famines.

For estimates of hunger and its causes and consequences, see also D. Gale Johnson and G. Edward Schuch, eds., *Role of Markets in the World Food Economy* (1983); Nicole Ball, *World Hunger* (1981); A. Macbean, "Achieving Food Security," in *Current Issues in Development Economics,* ed. U. N. Balasutramanyam and S. Lall (1991), chap. 4; and Paul Streeten, "Hunger," in *Equity and Efficiency in Economic Development,* ed. Donald J. Savoie and Irving Brecher (1992).

VII.B. DESIGNING AN AGRICULTURAL STRATEGY

Selection VII.B.1. Some Theoretical Aspects of Agricultural Policies*

What are the legitimate reasons for government intervention in agricultural markets? In particular, what makes the market's own allocation either inefficient or otherwise "unacceptable"? There is a standard litany of such reasons; five are relevant to agriculture.

(1) *Incomplete markets in insurance futures and credit.* Farmers cannot get complete insurance against the big (output and price) risks they face. Rural credit markets, like agricultural insurance markets, are notoriously imperfect. Farmers' access to credit is limited, if they can obtain it at all. They often have to pay usurious interest rates, though this may have something to do with the likelihood of default.[1]

(2) *Public goods and increasing returns.* These provide the justification for governments to finance water projects. In some cases, the marginal cost of using irrigated water, once the dam has been built, is relatively low, and the cost of monitoring water usage is relatively high. Water projects therefore satisfy both the criteria of pure public goods. The provision of water is almost always a natural monopoly, and a common (though not universal) response to such monopolies is production by government.

(3) *Imperfect information.* Government supply of information can be thought of as a type of public good. (Where the government ascertains what crops grow best in a particular area, the information is best described as a local public good.) However, disseminating information is costly, and the

benefits accrue mainly to those who receive it. So it is probably wrong to think of agricultural extension as a pure public service. It may be justified, however, by the next category of market failure.

(4) *Externalities.* The successful adoption of a new technology by one farmer conveys valuable information to his neighbors and hence gives them a significant externality. The existence of this externality has been used to justify subsidies for farmers to adopt new technologies.

(5) *Income distribution.* Perhaps the most important reason for government intervention in agriculture is concern with the distribution of income generated by free markets. Given the initial holdings of assets, this distribution need not, and often does not, satisfy society's ethical judgments. In particular, it may result in significant numbers of people having unacceptably low incomes or supplies of food. This suggests the government should design programs that increase the incomes of small farmers—and, for urban dwellers, a program of food subsidies.

Though this list provides various rationales for government action, the link between them and actual government policies may be tenuous. Thus, measures aimed at reducing risk (like price stabilization programs) may actually increase the riskiness of farmers' income, and they often entail large subsidies. Though government policies may be defended in terms of helping the small farmer, the main beneficiaries may be large farmers. And though governments may claim that their policies redistribute income, the net impact of the programs may be regressive.

Critics of government programs thus claim that market failures are matched by a corresponding list of government failures. The fact that markets face certain problems does not in itself justify government intervention; it only identifies the potential area for it. This caveat is particularly important in any assessment of public remedies for those market failures affected by imperfect information (for instance, imperfect credit markets), since the government is likely to face similar problems if it intervenes.[2]

To understand the nature of government inter-

*From Joseph E. Stiglitz, "Some Theoretical Aspects of Agricultural Policies," *World Bank Research Observer,* Vol. 2, No. 1 (January 1987), pp. 43–47, 49, 51. Reprinted by permission.

[1] Insurance markets are notoriously bad in many contexts other than agricultural markets. Particular problems in agricultural markets are adverse selection and moral hazard: the farmer is likely to be better informed about the hazards he faces than the insurer (this is referred to as the adverse selection problem); and there are actions the farmer can take that affect output (or, more generally, the insurance companies' expected liability; this is referred to as the moral hazard problem). Thus, though the farmer cannot affect whether there is a hailstorm, he can affect the losses he incurs if one happens, by taking precautionary action. Adverse selection and moral hazard problems need to be taken into account in the design of insurance contracts.

Government policies that ignore adverse selection and moral hazard may exacerbate the problems. Thus, government stabilization programs may induce farmers to increase their production of risky crops, thus imposing a greater cost on government than it would otherwise have to face.

[2] Indeed, the problems associated with distinguishing between good and bad borrowers and of monitoring the actions of borrowers enhance the scope for political abuse within subsidized credit schemes.

ventions in agricultural markets, one must approach the problem from the perspective of the *second best.* Whether government or market failures are of greater importance may differ from country to country, and this will crucially affect the nature of the appropriate government policy. Failure to recognize this fact has given rise to much of the controversy over state intervention. Simplistic views—such as "governments should not intervene in free markets"—or even the more sophisticated view (based on optimal tax theory for developed countries) that "government should not impose trade taxes" become inappropriate once it is recognized that the government has limited instruments for collecting revenue (thus, some distortionary taxation is necessary) and for redistributing income (so that the surest way of improving the lot of the rural poor may be through trade taxes). But the prescription that the government use trade taxes to redistribute income may be inappropriate when the redistributive impact of trade taxes is likely to be regressive.

An analysis of the appropriate policy for a particular country must therefore begin by specifying the reasons for market failure and the instruments the government can use to remedy it. The role of general theories is to identify the circumstances under which one kind of policy is more likely to be appropriate, thereby developing a taxonomy for analyzing policies in different countries. The models for specific countries help to frame the policy discussion. They enable one to establish whether the source of disagreement over policy is differences in objectives (welfare weights associated with different groups or between current generations and future generations); or differences in views about the structure of the economy; or differences in views about the values of key parameters.

The following sections organize the evaluation of alternative policies around several themes: risk, credit, dynamic effects.

Risk

Most economists acknowledge that farmers face significant risks and have only limited opportunity to avoid them through insurance and other markets. However, appropriate remedies are the subject of theoretical and practical disagreement.

What is of crucial importance to farmers is stabilizing their *income,* not stabilizing the prices of their produce. If price and quantity are negatively correlated, stabilizing prices may actually exacerbate the fluctuations in income.

Some economists favor the use of futures mar-

kets. These have the advantage of allowing a farmer to choose how much of his crop to sell forward, to "adapt" the extent of price stabilization to his own circumstances and preferences. But futures markets have two important drawbacks. First, they involve bigger transactions costs than those price stabilization schemes that work through the market. To the extent that such schemes serve to stabilize incomes, they do so without any farmer taking special action for himself. Second, to the extent that crop sizes are uncertain, no farmer can completely hedge his position unless he purchases crop insurance (which in general is unavailable). These disadvantages are not necessarily as bad as those produced by schemes in which the government does not stabilize the market price, but makes separate agreements with different farmers to buy given amounts of a crop at a guaranteed price.

Despite their transactions costs, futures markets dominate most types of price stabilization schemes. The intuitive reason is that futures markets allow the farmer to choose how much he wishes to divest himself of price risk. However, even in developed countries in which futures markets exist, farmers have not (at least until recently) used these markets to any significant extent. Thus, it remains an open question whether futures markets could be an effective way of sparing small farmers from risks.

If governments decide to stabilize prices, they have several ways to do so. They can, for instance, use buffer stocks, which can be operated according to various rules. Perfect price stability is, in essence, impossible. Even simple rules, such as setting a band within which prices can move, are not immune to speculative attack. The only generally feasible rules involve prices being a function of the size of the current stock; as the amount in storage decreases, the government allows the price to rise.

The limited calculations done so far suggest that the welfare gains from well-designed rules may be significantly greater than those from certain simple rules, such as keeping prices within a band (even if that were possible). Indeed, questions may be raised about the significance of the latter gains altogether (Newbery and Stiglitz, 1982). As for buffer stocks, a major criticism is that it is usually more efficient to store general purchasing power than specific commodities—that is, to use savings and reserves—except when transport and transactions costs are large.

Another way for governments to try to affect price variability is to impose trade restrictions. These may have marked transactional advantages over other forms of price stabilization, though they may be less effective in stabilizing incomes. It is now widely recognized that, in the presence of uncertainty (and with limited governmental ability to respond to changing circumstances), quotas and tariffs are not interchangeable. Tariffs do not insulate a country from foreign-induced price fluctuations, but quotas may do so. Quotas are particularly effective when the source of price fluctuations is neither domestic demand nor supply; they can then completely insulate the producers from foreign shocks (at the cost, of course, of preventing a country from taking full advantage of its current comparative advantage). Quotas are also effective in the extreme case in which the only source of variability is domestic output; they then serve to raise prices whenever farmers are suffering from lower volume. Even in these circumstances, however, it is not clear that the gains from reducing risk exceed the costs of failing to take advantage of temporary comparative advantage. The calculations depend partly on supply responses.

With any price stabilization scheme, supply responses are a major uncertainty. How do farmers react to a reduction in risk? And to what extent do a government's price stabilization programs serve simply to replace the stabilizing (arbitrage) activities of the private sector? Little empirical work has been done on either of these issues, though the effects can clearly be large: some countries have had to restrict their farmers' production so as to limit the costs of government programs.

Though there often is a role for government intervention to reduce the risks faced by farmers, many of the programs justified on these grounds serve more to redistribute income than to stabilize it. Indeed, in some instances, they may actually increase the variability of income. The appeal of these programs may lie in the way that they conceal the size and allocation of subsidies. Were the subsidies provided more openly, they might not be politically acceptable.

Credit

It is a common observation that farmers in developing countries are unable to obtain credit, or that they can do so only at usurious interest rates. This is not, in itself, evidence of a market failure. Interest rates will be high if the probability of default is high—which is indeed often the case. At the same time, the fact that there is imperfect information on the credit risks of different individuals (the adverse selection problem) and on the actions of those individuals (the moral hazard problem) means that the market equilibrium is not, in general, (constrained) Pareto efficient.

Nonetheless, government policies to boost credit for farmers need to take account of these adverse selection and moral hazard problems. The government is usually in no better (indeed, often worse) position for gathering information on the varying probabilities of default. Furthermore, a government credit program that involves some discretion in the granting of loans also contains scope for giving subsidies to particular individuals: whenever a "high-risk" farmer is granted a loan for which the interest rate has not been increased accordingly, he is obtaining an implicit subsidy. It is naturally difficult for an outsider to judge whether a subsidy has been granted; precisely for this reason, such programs are open to abuse.

Dynamic Effects

A justification for subsidizing inputs has to do with the adoption of new technologies. If peasants were perfectly rational and risk markets were perfect, then farmers would adopt the new technology if it increased their expected utility. No government subsidy would be needed.

Reality is different: risk markets are imperfect, and peasants are risk averse. Moreover, technologies that are riskier, but offer higher returns, yield more tax revenue for the government. Thus, the government has a real interest in encouraging the adoption of such technologies. If such technologies use a lot of fertilizer, for example, then a fertilizer subsidy may be an effective way of encouraging the adoption of the riskier technologies.

There is an added (and rather distinct) justification for governments to encourage the use of new technologies: when one farmer tries a new technology, he conveys a large amount of information to his neighbors. The presence of these informational externalities implies that farmers will have insufficient incentives for trying new technologies; the solution is to levy corrective (Pigovian) taxes or to provide subsidies.

The conflict between these dynamic efficiency objectives and distributional considerations raises a familiar problem. The farmers that are least risk averse are likely to be the large ones, so they are likely to be willing to try the new technology. Thus, subsidies for those who introduce the new technology are likely to be regressive. (The effect may be exacerbated if the new technologies are also capital intensive, and the larger farmers have easier access to capital markets or can borrow at lower interest rates.)

References

Newbery, David N., and Joseph E. Stiglitz. 1981. *The Theory of Commodity Price Stabilization.* London: Oxford University Press.

Newbery, David N., and Joseph E. Stiglitz. 1982. "Optimal Stockpiling Rules." *Oxford Economic Papers* 34, no. 3 (November): 403–27.

Selection VII.B.2. Criteria for the Design of Agricultural Development Strategies*

The historical experience in a number of countries, and the recent technical breakthroughs of the Green Revolution, justify major emphasis on increases in factor productivity. It is, however, the experience of Japan and Taiwan that is especially useful in demonstrating that an *appropriate* sequence of innovations based on modern scientific knowledge and experimental methods makes possible an expansion path for the agricultural sector that is characterized by large increases in factor productivity *throughout* the agricultural sector. Such a strategy enables a widening fraction of the working population in agriculture to be associated with increasingly productive technologies, based mainly on expanded use of purchased inputs that are divisible and neutral to scale. It is because the new inputs of seed and fertilizer, that are the essence of the Green Revolution, are complementary to the large amounts of labor and land already committed to agriculture that these increases in factor productivity can have such a large impact on total farm output. At the same time, by involving an increasing large fraction of the rural population in the process of technical change, such a strategy means that the fruits of economic progress are widely shared.

The Choice Between Unimodal and Bimodal Agricultural Strategies

The most fundamental issue of agricultural strategy faced by the late developing countries is to choose between a bimodal strategy whereby resources are concentrated within a subsector of large, capital-intensive units or a unimodal strategy which seeks to encourage a more progressive and wider diffusion of technical innovations adapted to the factor proportions of the sector as a whole. The essential distinction between the two approaches is that the unimodal strategy emphasizes sequences of innovations that are highly divisible and largely scale-neutral. These are innovations that can be used efficiently by small-scale farmers and adopted progressively. A unimodal approach does not mean that all farmers or all agricultural regions would adopt innovations and ex-

*From Bruce F. Johnston, "Criteria for the Design of Agricultural Development Strategies," *Food Research Institute Studies in Agricultural Economics, Trade, and Development,* Vol. 11, No. 1, 1972, pp. 35–37, 42–54. Copyright 1972 by the Board of Trustees of Leland Stanford Junior University. Reprinted by permission.

pand output at uniform rates. Rather it means that the type of innovations emphasized are appropriate to a progressive pattern of adoption in the twofold sense that there will be progressive diffusion of innovations within particular areas and extension of the benefits of technical change to new areas as changes in environmental conditions, notably irrigation facilities, or improved market opportunities or changes in the nature of the innovations available enable farmers in new areas to participate in the process of modernization. Although a bimodal strategy entails a much more rapid adoption of a wider range of modern technologies, this is necessarily confined to a small fraction of farm units because of the structure of economies in which commercial demand is small in relation to a farm labor force that still represents some 60 to 80 percent of the working population.

The late developing countries face a wide choice of farm equipment embodying large investments in research and development activity in the economically advanced countries. The performance characteristics of these machines are impressive, and representatives of the major manufacturing firms in the economically advanced countries are experienced and skillful in demonstrating their equipment. And they now have added incentive to promote sales in the developing countries to more fully utilize their plant capacity which is large relative to domestic demand (mainly a replacement demand since the period of rapid expansion of tractors and tractor-drawn equipment in the developed countries has ended). The availability of credit under bilateral and international aid programs temporarily eliminates the foreign exchange constraint to acquiring such equipment; and when such loans are readily available it may even appear to be an attractive means of increasing the availability of resources—in the short run. Within developing countries there is often considerable enthusiasm for the latest in modern technologies. But little attention is given to research and development activity and support services to promote the manufacture and wide use of simple, inexpensive equipment of good design, low import content, and suited to the factor proportions prevailing in countries where labor is relatively abundant and capital scarce. . . .

Under a bimodal strategy frontier firms with their high capital to labor ratio would account for the bulk of commercial production and would have the cash income required to make extensive use of purchased inputs. Inasmuch as the schedule of aggregate commercial demand for agricultural products is inelastic and its rightward shift over time is essentially a function of the rate of structural transformation, to concentrate resources within a subsector of agriculture inevitably implies a reduction in the ability of farm households outside that subsector to adopt new purchased inputs and technologies. In addition, the high foreign exchange content of many of the capital inputs employed in the frontier sector implies a reduction in the amount of foreign exchange available for imported inputs for other farm firms (or for other sectors). It is, of course, because of these purchasing power and foreign exchange constraints that it is impossible for the agricultural sector as a whole to pursue a crash modernization strategy. It might be argued that a proper farm credit program could eliminate the purchasing power constraint, but the availability of credit (assuming that repayment takes place) merely alters the shape of the time horizon over which the constraint operates. And capital and government revenue are such scarce resources in a developing country that government subsidy programs are not feasible means of escaping from this constraint. In brief, bimodal and unimodal strategies are to a considerable extent mutually exclusive.

Under the bimodal approach the divergence between the factor intensities and the technical efficiency of "best" and average firms is likely to become progressively greater as agricultural transformation takes place. Moreover, both the initial and subsequent divergences between the technologies used in the two sectors are likely to be accentuated because the factor prices, including the price of imported capital equipment, faced by the modern sector in contemporary developing countries typically diverge from social opportunity cost. This divergence is obvious when subsidized credit is made available on a rationed basis to large farmers and when equipment can be imported with a zero or low tariff at an official exchange rate that is overvalued. In addition, the large-scale farmers depend on hired labor rather than unpaid family labor. The wages paid hired labor may be determined by minimum wage legislation, and even without a statutory minimum the price of hired labor is characteristically higher than the opportunity cost of labor to small farm units. . . .

Under the unimodal strategy with its emphasis on highly divisible and scale-neutral innovations, the best firms in the agrarian sector display essentially the same factor intensities as average firms. Interfarm differences in performance will be large,

especially during transitional periods as farmers are learning how to use new inputs efficiently, but this will reflect mainly differences in output per unit of input rather than major differences in factor proportions. Inasmuch as the expansion path for the agricultural sector associated with a unimodal strategy implies a level of capital intensity and foreign exchange requirements that are compatible with a late developing country's economic structure, more firms within the agricultural sector are able to expand their use of fertilizer and the other divisible inputs that dominate purchases under this strategy. Thus, the diffusion of innovations and associated inputs will be more broadly based, and the divergence in factor intensities between frontier firms and average firms will be moderate.

Although the foregoing has emphasized the contrast in the pattern of technical change, it is apparent that the two strategies will have significantly different impacts on many dimensions of economic and social change. Most obvious are the differences in the nature of demand for farm inputs, but the structure of rural demand for consumer goods will also be very different under a unimodal as compared to a bimodal strategy.

A major difference in income distribution is to be expected because of the likelihood that under a bimodal strategy the difficult problem of absorbing a rapidly growing labor force into productive employment would be exacerbated whereas under a unimodal strategy there is a good prospect that the rate of increase in demand for labor would be more rapid than the growth of the labor force. Underemployment and unemployment would thus be reduced as a result of wide participation of the rural population in improved income-earning opportunities. This improvement in income opportunities available to members of the rural work force would result in part from increased earnings as hired labor since rising demand for labor would tend to raise wage rates and the number of days of work available during the year for landless laborers and for very small farmers whose incomes derive to a considerable extent from work on farms that are above average size.

Most important, however, would be the increased incomes earned by farm households cultivating their own or rented land. The extent to which tenants would be able to share in the increased productivity resulting from yield-increasing innovations will be determined by forces related to land reform as an aspect of broadly based improvements in the welfare of the rural population. Basically, however, it will depend upon the rate of growth of the rural population of working age seeking a livelihood in farming or in nonfarm activities relative to the rate of expansion of income-earning opportunities. The latter will be influenced strongly by the demand on the part of landowners for labor "hired" indirectly as laborers on owner-operated farms.

The Multiple Objectives of an Agricultural Strategy

In the paragraphs that follow I comment briefly on some of the reasons why the design of an efficient strategy for agriculture should be guided by explicit consideration of four major objectives of an agricultural strategy and the interrelationships among them. . . .

Contributions to Overall Economic Growth and Structural Transformation. It is conventional when considering agriculture's role in economic development to catalog a number of specific "contributions." Several of these contributions imply a net transfer of factors of production out of the agricultural sector as the process of structural transformation takes place. Typically the farm sector provides foreign exchange, public and private investment resources, and labor to the more rapidly expanding sectors of the economy as well as increased supplies of food and raw materials to support a growing urban population and manufacturing sector.

These contributions are, of course, synonymous with the increased sectoral interdependence that characterizes a developing economy. Outward labor migration and increased farm purchasing power are synchronized with the growing importance of commodity flows between agriculture and other sectors: a flow of food and raw materials out of agriculture and a return flow of farm inputs and consumer goods from the manufacturing sector. Tertiary activities of government, transport, marketing and other service industries expand to meet the needs of individual sectors and to facilitate the linkages between them.

Agricultural exports have special significance here for two reasons. First, in countries that have experienced little structural transformation there are usually few alternative means of meeting the growing demands for foreign exchange that characterize a developing economy. Secondly, expanded production for export makes it possible to enlarge farm cash incomes when the domestic market for purchased food is still very small, and at the same time it provides a stimulus and the means to establish some of the physical infrastructure and institutions that are necessary for the creation of a national, market-oriented economy.

The structure of rural demand for farm inputs associated with alternative agricultural strategies exerts an important influence on the growth of local manufacturing as well as on the pattern of productivity advance within agriculture. I emphasize the composition of this demand because the capacity of the agricultural sector to purchase inputs from other sectors is powerfully constrained by the proportion of the population living outside agriculture. Pathological growth of population in urban areas only loosely related to the growth of off-farm employment opportunities is a conspicuous and distressing feature of many of the contemporary less developed countries, but basically this growth of urban population depends on the transformation of a country's occupational structure that is a concomitant of economic growth.

The nature of the linkages between agriculture and the local manufacturing sector and the seriousness of foreign exchange and investment constraints on development will be influenced significantly by the structure of rural demand for both inputs and consumer goods. Because of their differential effects on the sequence of innovations and on rural income distribution, a bimodal and a unimodal strategy will differ greatly in their aggregate capital and foreign exchange requirements.

The more capital-intensive bimodal strategy emphasizes rapid adoption of mechanical innovations such as tractors along with chemical fertilizers and other inputs essential for increasing crop yields. Even if that type of machinery is manufactured locally, the foreign exchange requirements for capital equipment and for components are high, and the production processes require a high level of technical sophistication, large plants, and capital-intensive technologies.

The unimodal strategy with its emphasis on mechanical innovations of lower technical sophistication and foreign exchange content, such as improved bullock implements and low-lift pumps, appears to offer greater promise for the development of local manufacturing which is less demanding in its technical requirements and which is characterized by lower capital-labor ratios and lower foreign exchange content. On the basis of experience in Japan and Taiwan as well as an analysis of the nature of the supply response to the two patterns of demand, it seems clear that a unimodal strategy will have a much more favorable impact on the growth of output and especially on the growth of employment in local manufacturing and supporting service industries. The reasons cannot be pursued here except to note the wider diffusion of opportunities to develop entrepreneurial and technical skills through "learning by doing" that leads to increasing competence in manufacturing. Progress in metalworking and in the domestic manufacture of capital goods are especially significant because they are necessary to the creation of an industrial sector adapted to the factor proportions of a late developing economy.

Increasing Farm Productivity and Output. The differences in farm productivity between modern and traditional agriculture are, of course, to be attributed mainly to their use of widely different technologies. Those differences in turn are based on large differences in their use of fixed and working capital and associated differences in their investments in human resources that affect the level and efficiency of agricultural research and other supporting services as well as the knowledge, skills, and innovativeness of the farm population.

The importance of distinguishing between inputs and innovations that are mainly instrumental in increasing output per acre and those that make it possible for each farm worker to cultivate a larger area has already been noted. Biological and chemical innovations increase agricultural productivity mainly through increasing yields per acre. In general the effect on yield of farm mechanization per se is slight, although certain mechanical innovations, notably tubewells and low-lift pumps may be highly complementary to yield-increasing innovations. Indeed, for some high-yielding varieties, especially rice, an ample and reliable supply of water is a necessary precondition for realizing the genetic potential of the new varieties. This distinction between yield-increasing and labor-saving innovations is significant because the relative emphasis given to these two types of innovations largely determines whether development of agriculture will follow a unimodal or bimodal pattern.

The thrust of a unimodal strategy is to encourage general diffusion of yield-increasing innovations and such mechanical innovations as are complementary with the new seed-fertilizer technology. The bimodal strategy emphasizes simultaneous adoption of innovations that increase substantially the amount of land which individual cultivators can efficiently work in addition to the yield-increasing innovations emphasized in the unimodal approach.

For reasons discussed above, it is not possible for developing countries to pursue the unimodal and bimodal options simultaneously. In placing emphasis on reinforcing success within a subsec-

tor of large and capital-intensive farms, a bimodal strategy may have an advantage in maximizing the rate of increase in the short run because it bypasses the problems and costs associated with involving a large fraction of the farm population in the modernization process. In a longer view, however, a unimodal strategy appears to be more efficient, especially in minimizing requirements for the scarce resources of foreign exchange and loanable funds.

Policies and programs to ensure that the seed-fertilizer revolution is exploited as widely and as fully as possible are clearly of central importance. This emphasizes the importance of adaptive research and of training and extension programs to promote further diffusion of new varieties and to narrow the gap between yields at the farm level and the potential yields obtainable. Investment in infrastructure and in land and water development required to provide environmental conditions favorable to the introduction of more productive technologies are also priority needs. . . .

The distribution of land ownership and, more particularly, the size distribution of operational units are highly important factors influencing the choice of technique and the factor proportions that characterize the expansion path of the agricultural sector. Both are influenced by policies and practices affecting land tenure which are discussed in the following section.

Achieving Broadly Based Improvement in the Welfare of the Rural Population. In a longer term view substantial improvement in the welfare of the rural population depends upon the process of structural change which, inter alia, makes possible a reduction in the absolute size of the rural population, a large increase in commercial demand for farm products, and large increases in the capital-labor ratio in agriculture. There are, however, some more direct relationships between strategies for agriculture and the improvement of rural welfare that need to be considered.

Rural works programs are probably the more frequently discussed measure aimed directly at improving the welfare of the poorest segments of the farm population. There is much to be said for such programs as a means of providing supplemental employment and income to the most disadvantaged members of the rural population and at the same time building infrastructure important to agriculture and other sectors. But because of the organizational problems and particularly the severe fiscal constraints that characterize a developing country, it seems doubtful whether this approach can have a very substantial effect on under-employment and unemployment in rural areas. . . .

Other programs also merit attention because they offer the promise of substantial benefits relative to their cost, and some of them can also make a substantial contribution to the expansion of output by improving the health and productivity of the rural population. Public health programs such as malaria control are notable examples. The success of such programs is, of course, a major factor underlying the population explosion and the urgent need for policies and programs that will have both direct and indirect effects in encouraging the spread of family planning. Nutritional programs also deserve attention. The effects on well-being of increased farm productivity and incomes can be enhanced considerably if diet changes are informed by practical programs of nutrition education. . . .

Although it is foolhardy to attempt to treat the complex and controversial subject of land tenure in a few paragraphs, the positive and negative effects on rural welfare of land reform programs cannot be ignored. In Asia the land tenure situation is dominated by the fact that the area of arable land is small relative to the large and growing farm population entirely or mainly dependent on agriculture for their livelihood. One implication of this, which is distressing but beyond dispute, is that for the agricultural sector as a whole in these countries the average farm size will become even smaller—or at least that the number of agricultural workers per acre of arable land will continue to increase for several decades until a structural transformation turning point is reached.

It is sometimes argued that because of the connection between size of holding and choice of technique, redistributive land reform is a necessary condition for a unimodal strategy. Indeed it is even claimed that the success of unimodal strategies in Japan and Taiwan is attributable to their postwar land reforms, notwithstanding the fact that in both countries the basic pattern of progressive modernization of small-scale, labor-intensive, but technically progressive farm units was established long before World War II.

I am persuaded that an effectively implemented land reform program that brings about a more equal distribution of landed wealth will not only contribute to the goal of equity but will also tend to facilitate low-cost expansion of farm output based primarily on yield-increasing innovations. Although such a program would appear to be desirable, there is reason to believe that for a good many Asian countries it is not a likely outcome. It therefore seems important to emphasize that historical evidence and logic both contradict the view that in the absence of land reform the pattern of agricultural development will inevitably accentuate the problems of rural underemployment and unemployment and the inequality of income distribution.

The critical factor determining the choice of technique and factor proportions in agriculture is the size distribution of operational (management) units rather than ownership units. Past experience, for example in prewar Japan and Taiwan, demonstrates that a highly skewed pattern of land ownership is not incompatible with a unimodal size distribution of operational units. To a considerable extent the widespread condemnation of tenancy, particularly of share tenancy, seems to stem from a tendency to confuse what is really a symptom with the root cause of the miserable existence that is the plight of so many tenant households in underdeveloped countries. The fact that tenants are prepared to accept rental arrangements that leave them such a meager residual income is fundamentally a consequence of the extreme lack of alternative income-earning opportunities. The proposition, briefly stated, is that bargaining between land-owners and tenants will tend to result in equilibrium arrangements with respect to the rental share, the amount of land rented to individual tenants, the cropping pattern and other farm practices, and sharing of expenses of inputs. These arrangements will tend to maximize the landowner's rental income subject to the constraint that a tenant and members of his household must obtain residual income that represents a "wage" approximately equal to his best alternative earnings or they will not enter into the agreement. To the extent that the proposition is valid, it means that improvement in the welfare of tenants must depend primarily on improving the income-earning opportunities available, including the possibility of enlarging their own holdings by redistributive land reform as well as the increase in demand for labor within and outside agriculture.

The advantages of organizing agricultural production primarily on the basis of small-scale units appropriate to the unfavorable man-land ratios that characterize the agricultural sector in late developing countries are enhanced by the new technical possibilities resulting from the seed-fertilizer revolution. Although those advantages are to a considerable extent a function of the size of operational units, there are some specific advantages of owner cultivation related to productivity considerations as well as the more obvious effects on income distribution. Although in principle investments in land improvement that are profitable will be made by the landowner, by the tenant, or under some joint agreement, the division of responsibility in decision-making is likely to delay or prevent investments even though they would be to the advantage of both parties. Owner cultivation also avoids the difficulties that arise when landlords, responding to higher yields, raise the percentage share of output that they demand as rent. But if redistributive land reform is not a realistic possibility, widespread renting of land seems clearly preferable to the further concentration of land in large operational units and the bimodal pattern which is thereby accentuated.

Facilitating the Processes of Social Modernization by Encouraging Widespread Attitudinal and Behavioral Changes. The spread of economic and technical change among the rural population, buttressed by a network of institutions and communication links, undoubtedly has significant effects on the process of social modernization that go beyond their effects on economic growth. It seems likely that the broad impact of a unimodal strategy would have favorable effects in three areas important to this process of social change. First, the wide diffusion of familiarity with the calculation of costs and returns and of opportunities to acquire managerial experience would appear to provide a favorable environment for the training and recruitment of entrepreneurs. The same would apply, of course, to the wider diffusion of learning experiences in manufacturing which is associated with a unimodal strategy.

Secondly, a broadly based approach to agricultural development seems likely to generate strong support for rural education as well as the institutions more directly related to promoting increased agricultural productivity. It is sometimes argued that large-scale, highly commercialized farm enterprises are easier to tax than millions of small units. Because of the power structure maintained or created by a bimodal strategy, however, the greater administrative convenience may in practice mean very little. The fact that public education, and especially rural education, in most of South America seems to lag behind progress in other developing countries where average incomes are considerably lower seems to provide some support for this generalization.

Thirdly, and most important, the reduction in birthrates in the countryside, resulting from spontaneous changes in attitudes and behavior as well as behavioral changes induced by government population programs, are likely to be more widespread and have a greater effect on the national birthrate under a unimodal than a bimodal strategy. For reasons examined earlier, the bulk of the population in the late developing countries is going to be in the agricultural sector for several decades or more. Under those circumstances rapid reduction in a country's birthrate to bring it into tolerable balance with a sharply reduced death rate cannot be achieved unless family planning spreads in the country-side as well as in towns and cities. It seems probable that reasonably rapid changes in this domain of behavior are more likely to take place if the dynamic processes of economic and technical change affect a large fraction of a rural population involved to an increasing extent in formal and informal education and communication networks (including mass media). It also seems likely that the wider spread of improved income and educational opportunities will affect motivations in ways favorable to the practice of family planning. . . .

Comment VII.B.1. The Green Revolution

Studies of the green revolution include T. T. Poleman and D. K. Freebairn, eds., *Food, Population, and Employment: The Impact of the Green Revolution* (1973); Clive Bell, "The Acquisition of Agricultural Technology," *Journal of Development Studies* (October 1972); Bruce F. Johnston and J. Cownie, "The Seed-Fertilizer Revolution and Labor Force Absorption," *America Economic Review* (September 1969); John W. Mellor, *The New Economics of Growth* (1976); C. Wharton, "The Green Revolution: Cornucopia or Pandora's Box?" *Foreign Affairs* (April 1969); W. Ladejinsky, *Agrarian Reform as Unfinished Business* (1978); and Walter P. Falcon, "The Green Revolution: Second-Generation Problems," *American Journal of Agricultural Economics* (December 1978).

Radical political economists have argued that the green revolution's technology tends to be monopolized by large commercial farmers who have better access to new information and better financial capacity. A large profit resulting from the exclusive adoption of modern varieties of technology by large farmers stimulates them to enlarge their operational holdings by consolidating the farms of small nonadopters through purchase or tenant eviction. As a result, polarization of rural communities into large commercial farmers and landless proletariat is promoted. See Harry M. Cleaver, "The Contradictions of the Green Revolution," *American Economic Review* (May 1972); Ali M. S. Fatami, "The Green Revolution: An Appraisal," *Monthly Review* (June 1972); Keith Griffin, *The Political Economy of Agrarian Change* (1974); and Richard Grabowski, "The Implications of an Induced Innovation Model," *Economic Development and Cultural Change* (July 1979), and "Reply," *Economic Development and Cultural Change* (October 1981).

The green revolution is also often compared with the "Japanese model" of increases in agricultural productivity associated with the use of improved seed varieties, fertilizers, implements, and other complementary inputs within the framework of Japan's small-scale farming system. For a comparative study of Japan's experience and what has been brought about by the green revolution, see Kazushi Ohkawa, *Differential Structure and Agriculture—Essays on Dualistic Growth* (1972).

Experience with the green revolution has been mixed, with differential growth rates of agriculture in different countries or in agriculture in different regions within the same country. This has been because of differences in the availability of inputs, extent of information, and attitude toward risks.

For an appraisal of the recent history of high-yielding cereals, see Michael Lipton with Richard Longhhurst, *New Seeds and Poor People* (1989). This study examines the impact of the new varieties on the poor and claims that the increases in food supplies have had little impact on the nutrition of the poor and on their poverty.

Comment VII.B.2. Land Reform

The case for a small-farm or reformed agricultural system claims several advantages— more employment, more equitable distribution of income, and a wider home market for the manufacturing sector. But the case for smallholdings must also address itself to other requirements. It is essential to consider the effects of land reform on agricultural production, both for exports and for increasing food production. Capital formation is also necessary in both agricultural and industrial sectors. And efficiency must be achieved, as well as employment and equity.

The economic gains to be had from a radical modification of land-tenure patterns appear to be greatest during periods when rapid technical changes are opening up new production possibilities that are inhibited by existing tenure relationships. See Yujiro Hayami and Vernon W. Ruttan, *Agricultural Development: An International Perspective* (1971). In view of the technical revolution in grain production and the explosive rate of growth in the agricultural labor force, the authors conclude that the payoff to tenure reforms, involving a shift from share tenure, plantation, and collective tenure systems to smallholder owner-operator systems, may be greatly increased in the future.

On the need for reform in connection with the development of agriculture, see Peter Dorner, *Land Reform and Economic Development* (1972); Louis J. Walinsky, ed., *Agrarian Reform as Unfinished Business* (1977); Albert Berry and William Cline, *Agrarian Structure and Productivity in Developing Countries* (1979); and Alain de Janvry, "The Role of Land Reform in Economic Development," *American Journal of Agricultural Economics* (May 1981).

Selection VII.B.3. The Agricultural Transformation*

Several main lessons have been learned in the last two decades about the functioning of the agricultural sector and its potential role in the development process: the emergence of the agricultural sector into a general equilibrium perspective; the recognition of the importance of macroeconomic policy for agricultural performance; the necessity (and feasibility because of the potential for technical change) of rapid economic growth to deal with the human welfare concerns that stem from poverty and hunger; and the superior performance of trade- and market-oriented systems in achieving this growth. These lessons do not define a single strategic approach to agricultural development, however. In fact, three sharply different paths would seem to be open for appropriate policies toward agriculture that view development of the sector as a means to an end—as part of the effort to speed the overall process of development—rather than as an end in itself.

The Alternatives

The first path has parallels to the philosophy of the 1950s, in which benign neglect of agricultural policy was thought to be sufficient for stimulating the process of economic growth. This perspective grows out of the recognition of the role of well-functioning markets and decision makers operating in a world of "rational expectations." In this view, most policy is irrelevant to farmers in more than a very transitory sense, and this is especially true of price policy. . . .

In this world, agricultural incomes are determined by employment opportunities outside agriculture, the agricultural sector *must* decline in proportional output terms and absolutely in the labor force, and the long-run decline in basic agricultural commodity prices due to technical change simply emphasizes that society is best served by getting resources out of agriculture as rapidly as possible. Although the clearest case for this view of the world is in the OECD countries, a host of middle-income countries, and even some quite poor countries, are also facing the problem of declining real incomes in the agricultural sector under the impact of rapid technical change domestically and lower world

*From C. Peter Timmer, "The Agricultural Transformation," in *Handbook of Development Economics*, Vol. I, H. Chenery and T. N. Srinivasan (eds.), Elsevier Science Publishers, North Holland Publishing Company, Amsterdam, 1988, pp. 321–28. Reprinted by permission.

prices for the resulting output. This perspective is obviously consistent with the view that open economies will show better performance than those with substantial trade barriers.

A sharply different path has been sketched by Mellor and Johnston (1984). Building on their earlier stress on balanced growth (1961), Johnston and Mellor call for an "interrelated strategy" that improves nutrition in one dimension while it fosters the broader growth process in the other. The approach calls for a major role of government in strategic design and program implementation, a role that is in marked contrast with the free-market approach sketched out above.

We have, therefore, emphasized that improvements in nutrition [one of Mellor and Johnston's key objectives for agricultural development] require a *set of interacting forces:* accelerated growth in agriculture; wage goods production; a strategy of development that structures demand towards high employment content goods and services; increased employment; and increased effective demand for food on the part of the poor. Agricultural growth not only satisfies the need for food to meet nutritional requirements (which is the other side of the wage-goods coin), but fosters a favorable employment-oriented demand structure as well. Agriculture's role in generating a structure of demand, favorable to rapid growth in employment, is central. (pp. 567–68, emphasis added)

Mellor and Johnston go on to summarize their earlier argument that agriculture can play this multiplicity of roles only if a unimodel development strategy is followed, that is, one in which a broad base of smallholders are the central focus of agricultural research and extension services and the recipient of the bulk of receipts from agricultural sales. The authors see the dualism inherent in bimodal strategies—those placing modernization efforts primarily on large, "progressive" farms while neglecting the "backward" smallholders—as the major obstacle to putting their set of interacting forces in motion.

The most common barrier to the interrelated strategy indicated is pronounced dualism in capital allocations—too much to industry and the unproductive elements of the private sector rather than to agriculture, and to capital intensive elements within those, as well as to large-scale and therefore capital-intensive allocations within agriculture. The outcome of the strategy will depend upon national-level decisions about macroeconomic policies, exchange rates, interest rates, and investment allocations among sectors and regions, not just within agriculture itself. Indeed, the whole strategy fails if it is viewed simply as the responsibility of agriculture ministries. (Mellor and Johnston, 1984, p. 568)

This interrelated strategy must be directed by government planners; there is relatively little concern or role for the private sector, other than small farmers. The analysis leading to the strategy remains heavily influenced by closed economy considerations, and little attention is given to either domestic marketing activities or their relationship to international markets. Three key elements are suggested as essential to meeting all objectives of agricultural development—massive investment in human capital through nutrition, health, and family planning services in the countryside, creation of the complex, rural organizational structures seen in Japan and Taiwan that provide services to small farmers while also serving as a voice for their interests, and investment in rapid technical change appropriate to these small farmers in order to raise agricultural output and rural incomes simultaneously.

Notably missing in this list of key elements is significant concern for the structure of incentives for agriculture relative to industry or for the country's tradables relative to foreign competitors. Although it is realized that the macroeconomic setting is no doubt important to agriculture, it remains outside the scope of appropriate strategy for agricultural development. Not surprisingly, given the argument in Johnston and Clark (1982), the intellectual foundation for this strategy lies in rural development, not in a vision of agriculture linked to the macro economy and world markets by powerful market mechanisms. It is this latter vision which provides the third potential path for agricultural development strategy for the rest of the 1980s and into the 1990s.

The third approach contrasts with both the "free market" and "interrelated strategy" approaches. It calls for government policy interventions into market outcomes but uses markets and the private marketing sector as the vehicle for those policy interventions. This "market policy" approach recognizes widespread "market failures" in agriculture as well as extensive "government failures" in implementation of economic tasks. The strategic dilemma is how to cope with segmented rural capital and labor markets, poorly functioning land markets, the welfare consequences of sharp instability of prices in commodity markets, the pervasive lack of information about current and future events in most rural economies, and the sheer absence of many important markets, especially for future contingencies involving yield or price risks.

One powerful lesson of the postwar development record is that direct government interventions to correct market failures frequently make matters worse by inhibiting whatever market responses were possible in the initial circumstances, without providing greater output or more efficient utilization of resources. The agricultural sector in particular is vulnerable to well-intended but poorly conceived and managed state organizations that attempt a wide array of direct economic activities, including monopoly control of input supplies, capital-intensive state farms, and mandated control over crop marketing and processing. As Bates (1981) has demonstrated, these direct controls and agencies have a strong political economy rationale for a government that tries to reward its supporters and centralize power and resources in the hands of the state (see also Lipton, 1977).

The answer to the dilemma over making matters worse, in this approach, is to gain a much clearer understanding of the necessary interaction between the public and private sectors. . . . Political objectives for the performance of agriculture—its capacity to feed the population regularly and cheaply, or its ability to provide fair incomes to farmers caught in the pressures of successful structural transformation—are inevitable and, in some long-run sense, highly desirable.

The "market policy" path argues that these objectives are best served by making carefully considered interventions into the prices determined in markets, not by leaving markets alone or by striving to reach the objectives through direct activities by the government. If the "free market" approach incurs heavy political costs as markets relentlessly redistribute incomes to the winners in the course of economic development, and the "interrelated strategy" incurs heavy managerial and administrative costs as the government plays an active and direct economic role, the "market policy" approach incurs heavy analytical costs.

These analytical costs come from the need to understand each country's path of structural change, the workings of factor and commodity markets, and the potential impact of macro and commodity price interventions on these markets and ultimately on the structural path itself. It requires that government intervention be based on an empirical understanding of economic responses to a change in policy and the political repercussions from them. There is an important role for models in illuminating where to look for these responses, but the models themselves cannot provide the answers. This is especially true as attempts are made to build into the models the response of policy itself to changes in the economic environment. Such endogenous policy models may reveal some of the historical factors that accounted for policy shifts, but they seldom provide a sense of when the degrees of freedom for policy initiative are about to expand. Frequently, this is in times of crisis. Policy makers often embark on bold experiments in such times, and the payoff would be very high if sufficient analytical understanding already existed in order to anticipate the response to a policy change.

Agricultural Policy and Structural Change

Hayami and Ruttan (1985) have asked why agricultural growth has not been faster and more evenly spread around the world:

We indicated that the basic factor underlying poor performance was neither the meager endowment of natural resources nor the lack of technological potential to increase output from the available resources at a sufficiently rapid pace to meet the growth of demand. The major constraint limiting agricultural development was identified as the policies that impeded rather than induced appropriate technical and institutional innovations. As a result, the gap widened between the potential and the actual productive capacities of LDC agriculture. (p. 416)

This perspective, with its emphasis on the relationship between policy and agriculture's role in structural change, has provided the organizing theme for this selection. The progression of topics has followed from understanding why the agricultural sector is different from the industrial and ser-

vice sectors and how the differences condition the nature of effective policy interventions. The factors needed for inducing the agricultural transformation, to "get agriculture moving," involves a complex mix of appropriate new technology, flexible rural institutions, and a market orientation that offers farmers material rewards for the physical effort they expend in their fields and households and for the risks they face from both nature and markets.

References

Bates, Robert H. 1981. *Markets and States in Tropical Africa: The Political Basis of Agricultural Policies.* Berkeley: University of California Press.

Hayami, Yujiro, and Vernon Ruttan. 1985. *Agricultural Development: An International Perspective* (revised and expanded edition). Baltimore and London: Johns Hopkins University Press.

Johnston, Bruce F., and William C. Clark. 1982. *Redesigning Rural Development: A Strategic Perspective.* Baltimore and London: Johns Hopkins University Press.

Johnston, Bruce F., and John W. Mellor. 1961. "The Role of Agriculture in Economic Development," *American Economic Review* 51, no. 4: 566–93.

Lipton, Michael. 1977. *Why Poor People Stay Poor: Urban Bias in World Development.* Cambridge, Mass.: Harvard University Press.

Mellor, John W., and Bruce F. Johnston. 1984. "The World Food Equation: Inter-relations Among Development, Employment, and Food Consumption." *Journal of Economic Literature* 22: 531–74.

Note VII.B.1. Induced Technical and Institutional Change

Hayami and Ruttan have presented an "induced innovation" model to explain growth in agricultural productivity:

> The model attempts to make more explicit the process by which technical and institutional changes are induced through the responses of farmers, agribusiness entrepreneurs, scientists, and public administrators to resource endowments and to changes in the supply and demand of factors and products.
>
> The state of relative endowments and accumulation of the two primary resources, land and labor, is a critical element in determining a viable pattern of technical change in agriculture. Agriculture is characterized by much stronger constraints of land on production than most other sectors of the economy. Agricultural growth may be viewed as a process of easing the constraints on production imposed by inelastic supplies of land and labor. Depending on the relative scarcity of land and labor, technical change embodied in new and more productive inputs may be induced primarily either (a) to save labor or (b) to save land.
>
> The nonagricultural sector plays an important role in this process. It absorbs labor from agriculture. And it supplies to agriculture the modern technical inputs that can be substituted for land and labor in agricultural production.
>
> The critical element in this process is an effective system of market and non-market information linkages among farmers, public research institutions, private agricultural supply firms, and political and bureaucratic entrepreneurs. It is hypothesized that the proper functioning of such interactions is a key to success in the generation of the unique pattern of technical change necessary for agricultural development in any developing economy.[1]

According to the theory of induced technical innovation, progress in agricultural technology is largely an endogenous phenomenon. As formulated by Hayami and Ruttan, the theory states that the high price associated with a scarce factor of production (e.g., land) induces farmers to choose technologies that conserve the scarce factor. A rise in the price of land relative to the price of labor induces the substitution of labor for land. Or mechanization relaxes labor constraints. Or new high-yield seeds and fertilizer relax land constraints. But the advance in technology is itself a function of institutional innovation. Therefore, farmers exert political pressure to induce institutional innovations that will advance technological change (e.g., by public research institutions or institutions of land reform). Shifts in the demand for institutional change are thus induced by changes in relative factor supply and technical change.

Evidence in support of the Hayami-Ruttan theory, however, has been questioned: see Michael Lipton with Richard Longhurst, *New Seeds and Poor People* (1989). Lipton and Longhurst also place more emphasis on the need for a global research and planning apparatus that will give more attention to the effects of modern agricultural technologies on the poor. In particular, they argue that research must focus not only on increasing output, but also on generating employment, on provision of cheap calories, and on the "full social systemic influences" of any new seed or technology.

Recognizing some special characteristics of the institutional structure of an agrarian economy, Braverman and Stiglitz have presented another interpretation of technological innovation in agriculture. They investigate two common beliefs: that landlords have used their control over the means of production to direct the development and adoption of technologies that have increased their own welfare at the expense of workers; and that interlinkage between credit and tenancy markets provides an impetus to the resistance of innovations: innovations that make tenants better off reduce their demand for loans, and thereby make landlords—as creditors—worse off.

Those who apply purely competitive models dismiss these beliefs, arguing that if an economy is competitive these results would not occur.

Braverman and Stiglitz, however, point out that, contrary to the competitive model in many

LDCs, sharecropping contracts are widely employed, widespread unemployment prevails, and there is not the full set of risk and capital markets required by the competitive paradigm.

Under these different institutional conditions Braverman and Stiglitz conclude that

(i) landlords may wish to—and can—resist innovations which unambiguously increase production whenever sharecropping contracts are employed.

(ii) conversely, landlords may adopt innovations which not only lower the welfare of workers, but even lower net national product.

(iii) the presence of interlinkage may, indeed, affect the adoption of a new technology; however, the reason for this is only partly related to the effect of innovations on tenants' borrowing. Indeed, innovations may increase as well as decrease the tenants' demand for borrowing.[2]

Notes

1. Yujiro Hayami and Vernon W. Ruttan, *Agricultural Development: An International Perspective,* rev. ed. (1985), pp. 4–5; for a detailed exposition, see also Vernon W. Ruttan, "Innovation and Agricultural Development," *World Development* (September 1989).

2. Avishay Braverman and Joseph Stiglitz, "Landlords, Tenants and Technological Innovations," *Journal of Development Economics* (October 1986): 313–32; see also Selection VII.B.1.

Selection VII.C.1. The New Development Economics*

There are a wide variety of institutional arrangements observed in different LDCs. One set that has been of long-standing interest to economists is sharecropping. Earlier views of sharecropping held that it was an inefficient form of economic organization: the worker received less than the value of his marginal product, and thus he had insufficient incentives to exert effort. The question was, how could such a seemingly inefficient form of economic organization have survived for so long (and why should it be such a prevalent form of economic organization at so many different places at different times?). For those who believe in even a modicum of economic rationality, some explanation had to be found.

One explanation that comes to mind is that peasants are more risk averse than landlords; if workers rented the land from the landlords, they would have to bear all of the risk. Though workers' risk aversion is undoubtedly of importance, it cannot be the entire explanation: there are alternative (and perhaps more effective) risk-sharing arrangements. In particular, in the wage system, the landlord bears all of the risk, the worker none. Any degree of risk sharing between the landlord and the worker can be attained by the worker dividing his time between working as a wage-laborer and working on his own or rented land.

The other central part of the explanation of sharecropping is that it provides an effective incentive system in the presence of costly supervision. Since in a wage system, the worker's compensation is not directly related to his output, the landlord must spend resources to ensure that the worker actual works. In a sharecropping system, since the worker's pay depends directly on his output, he has some incentives to work. The incentives may not be as strong as they would if he owned the land (since he receives, say, only half the product); but that is not the relevant alternative. Sharecropping thus represents a compromise between the rental system, in which incentives are "correct" but all the risk is borne by the worker, and the wage system, in which the landlord who is in a better position to bear risk, bears all the risk but in which effort can only be sustained through expenditures on supervision. This new view (Stiglitz, 1974) turns the tradi-

tional criticism of sharecropping on its head: it is precisely because of its incentive properties, relative to the relevant alternative, the wage system, that the sharecropping system is employed.

The contention that the rental system provides correct incentives is, however, not quite correct. The rental system provides correct incentives for effort decisions. But tenants make many decisions other than those involving effort; they make decisions concerning the choice of technique, the use of fertilizer, the timing of harvest, etc. These decisions affect the riskiness of the outcomes. For instance, many of the high-yielding seed varieties have a higher mean output, but a greater sensitivity to rainfall. Whenever there is a finite probability of default (that is, the tenant not paying the promised rent), then tenants may not have, with the rental system, the correct incentives with respect to these decisions. Of course, with unlimited liability, the worker could be made to bear all of the costs. But since the tenant might be unable to pay his rent even if he had undertaken all of the "right" decisions, and since it is often difficult to ascertain whether the individual took "unnecessary" risks, most societies are reluctant to grant unlimited liability, or to use extreme measures like debtor prisons, to ensure that individuals do not take unnecessary risks. Hence, in effect, part of the costs of risk taking by the tenant is borne by the landlord. With sharecropping, both the landlord and the tenant face the same risks.

Thus, sharecropping can be viewed as an institution which has developed in response to (a) risk aversion on the part of workers; (b) the limited ability (or desire) to force the tenant to pay back rents when he is clearly unable to do so; and (c) the limited ability to monitor the actions of the tenant (or the high costs of doing so).

The general theory has been extended in a number of directions, only three of which I can discuss here: cost sharing, interlinkage, and technical change.

In many situations, there are other important inputs besides labor and land, such as bullocks or fertilizer. How should these inputs be paid for? Clearly, if the worker pays all of the costs, but receives only a fraction of the benefits, he will have an insufficient incentive to supply these other inputs. Cost sharing is a proposed remedy. If the worker receives 50 percent of the output, and pays

*From Joseph E. Stiglitz, "The New Development Economics," *World Development* 14, no. 2 (1986): 258–61. Reprinted by permission from Elsevier Science Ltd., Oxford, England.

50 percent of the cost, it would appear that he has the correct incentives: both benefits and costs have been cut in half.

But in fact, though cost shares equal to output shares are common, they are far from universal. How do we explain these deviations from what seems both a simple, reasonable rule, and a rule which ensures economic efficiency? To find the answer, we again return to our general theoretical framework, which focuses on the role of imperfect information. First, it is clear that the landlord may want the tenant to supply more fertilizer than he would with a 50-50 rule, if increasing the fertilizer increases the marginal product of labor, and thus induces the worker to work harder. Remember, the central problem of the landlord is that he cannot directly control the actions of his worker; he must induce them to work hard. The reason that share-cropping was employed was to provide these additional incentives.

But if a cost-sharing arrangement can be implemented, it means that the expenditures can be monitored; and if the expenditures can be monitored, there is no necessity for engaging in cost sharing; rather the terms of the contract could simply specify the levels of various inputs. But workers typically have more information about current circumstances than the landlord (in the fashionable technical jargon, we say there is an asymmetry of information). A contract which specifies the level of inputs cannot adapt to the changing circumstances. Cost-sharing contracts provide the ability and incentives for these adaptations, and thus are more efficient contracts than contracts which simply specified the level of inputs.

Another aspect of economic organization in many LDCs is the interlinkage of markets: the landlord may also supply credit (and he may also supply food and inputs as well). How can we explain this interlinkage? Some have claimed that it is simply another way that landlords exploit their workers. We shall comment later on these alternative explanations. For now, we simply note that our general theory can explain the prevalence of interlinkage (both under competitive and noncompetitive circumstances). We have repeatedly noted the problem of the landlord in inducing the worker both to work hard and to make the "correct" decisions from his point of view (with respect to choice of technique, etc.). Exactly analogous problems arise with respect to lenders. Their concern is that the borrower will default on the loan. The probability of a default depends in part on the actions taken by the borrower. The actions of the tenant-borrower thus affect both the lender and the

landlord. Note too that the terms of the contract with the landlord will affect the lender, and vice versa: if the landlord can, for instance, reduce the probability of default by supplying more fertilizer, the lender is better off. The actions of the borrower (both with respect to the effort and the choice of technique) may be affected by the individual's indebtedness, so that the landlord's (expected) income may be affected by the amount (and terms) of indebtedness. There appear to be clear and possibly significant externalities between the actions of the landlord and the actions of the lender. Whenever there are such externalities, a natural market solution is to internalize the externality, and that is precisely what the interlinkage of markets does.

Thus, interlinkage is motivated by the desire for economic efficiency, not necessarily by the desire for further exploitation of the worker.

Interlinkage has, in turn, been linked to the incentives landlords have for resisting profitable innovations. Bhaduri (1973) has argued, for instance, that landlords-cum-creditors may resist innovations, because innovations reduce the demand for credit, and thus the income which they receive in their capacity as creditors. Braverman and Stiglitz (1982) have shown that there is no presumption that innovations result in a reduction in the demand for credit. Credit is used to smooth income across periods, and under quite plausible conditions, innovations may either increase or decrease the aggregate demand for credit. But they argue further that what happens to the demand for credit is beside the point.

The central question is simply whether the innovation moves the economically relevant utilities possibilities schedule outward or inward. The utilities possibilities schedule gives the maximum level of (expected) utility to one group (the landlord) given the level of (expected) utility of the other (the workers). The economically relevant utilities possibilities curve takes into account the information problems which have been the center of our discussion thus far, for instance, the fact that with sharecropping, individuals' incentives are different from what they would be with costless monitoring. The utilities possibilities schedule with costless monitoring might move one way, the economically relevant utilities possibilities schedule the other. Thus, for instance, there are innovations which, at each level of input, increase the output, but which, at the same time, exacerbate the incentives-monitoring problem. Such innovations would not be socially desirable. Landlords would resist such innovations, as well they should, though from an "engineering" point of view, such innovations might look desirable.

The consequences of interlinkage for the adoption of innovations, within this perspective, are ambiguous. There are innovations which would be adopted with interlinkage, but would not without it, and conversely; but the effect of the innovation on the demand for credit does not seem to play a central role.

Though the landlord correctly worries about the incentive–monitoring consequences of an innovation, one should not jump to the conclusions either that the landlords collectively make decisions which maximize their own welfare, or that the landlord always makes the socially efficient decision. The landlord, within a competitive environment, will adopt an innovation if at current prices (terms of contracts, etc.) it is profitable for him to do so. Of course, when all the landlords adopt the innovation, prices (terms of contracts) will change, and they may change in such a way that landlords are adversely affected. In a competitive environment landlords cannot resist innovations simply because it is disadvantageous to them to do so. (By contrast, if they are in a "monopoly" position, they will not wish to resist such innovations, since presumably they will be able to capture all the surplus associated with the innovation.)

But just as the market allocation is not constrained Pareto efficient (even assuming a perfectly competitive economy) whenever there are problems of moral hazard, so too the market decisions concerning innovation are not constrained Pareto efficient. (We use the term *constrained Pareto efficient* to remind us that we are accounting for the limitations on information; we have not assumed the government has any information other than that possessed by private individuals.) Though in principle there exist government interventions which (accounting for the costs of information) could make everyone better off, whether such Pareto-improving interventions are likely to emerge from the political process remains a moot question.

Alternative Theories

In this section, I wish to present in summary form what I view to be the major competing approaches to understanding the organization of economic activity in the rural sector.

In many respects, I see my view as lying between other more extreme views. In one, the peasant is viewed as rational, working in an environment with reasonably complete information and complete and competitive markets. In this view,

then, the differences between LDCs and more developed countries lies not so much in the difference between sophisticated, maximizing farmers and uneducated rule-bound peasants, as it does in differences in the economic environments, the goods produced by these economies, their endowments, and how their endowments are used to produce goods. In this view, sharecropping is a rational response to the problems of risk sharing; but there is less concern about the incentive problems than I have expressed; with perfect information and perfect enforceability of contracts, the sharecropping contract can enforce the desired level of labor supply and the choice of technique which is efficient. These theories have had little to say about some of the other phenomena which I have discussed: interlinkage, technical change, cost sharing. Interlinkage might be explained in terms of the advantages in transactions costs, but if transactions costs were central, one should only have observed simple cost-sharing rules (with cost share equalling output share).

By contrast, there are those who view the peasant as irrational, with his behavior dictated by customs and institutions which may have served a useful function at some previous time but no longer do so. This approach (which I shall refer to, somewhat loosely, as the institutional–historical approach) may attempt to describe the kinds of LDCs in which there is sharecropping, interlinkage, or cost sharing. It may attempt to relate current practices to earlier practices. In particular, the institutional–historical approach may identify particular historical events which lead to the establishment of the sharecropping system, or to the development of the credit system. But this leaves largely unanswered the question of why so many LDCs developed similar institutional structures, or why in some countries cost shares equal output shares, while in others the two differ. More fundamentally, a theory must explain how earlier practices developed; and to provide an explanation of these, one has to have recourse to one of the other theories. Thus, by itself, the institutional–historical approach is incomplete.

Still a third view emphasizes the departures from competitiveness in the rural sector, and the consequent ability of the landlords to exploit the workers. In some cases, workers are tied to their land; legal constraints may put the landlord in a position to exploit the worker. But in the absence of these legal constraints, one has to explain how the landlords exercise their allegedly coercive powers. In many LDCs there is a well-developed labor market. Many landlords need laborers at harvest time and at planting time. The worker chooses for whom he will work. It is important to recognize that the exploitation hypothesis fails to explain the mechanisms by which, in situations where there are many landlords, they exercise their exploitative power. More generally, it fails to explain variations in the degree of exploitation over time and across countries. The fact that wages are low is not necessarily evidence of exploitation: the competitive market will yield low wages when the value of the marginal product of labor is low.

The exploitation hypothesis also fails to explain the detailed structure of rural organization: why cost shares are the way they are, or why (or how) landlords who can exploit their workers use the credit market to gain further exploitative capacity.

There may be some grain of truth in all these approaches. Important instances of currently dysfunctional institutions and customs can clearly be identified. Institutional structures clearly to not adapt instantaneously to changed circumstances. Yet, as social scientists, our objective is to identify the systematical components, the regularities of social behavior, to look for general principles underlying a variety of phenomena. It is useful to describe the institutions found in the rural sector of LDCs, but description is not enough.

Therefore, I view the rationality hypothesis as a convenient starting point, a simple and general principle with which to understand economic behavior. Important instances of departures from rationality may well be observed. As social scientists, our objective is to look for *systematic* departures. Some systematic departures have been noted, for instance in the work of Tversky, in individuals' judgments of probabilities, particularly of small probability events; but as Binswanger's 1978 study has noted, departures from the theory appear less important in "important" decisions than in less important decisions. Many of the seeming departures from "rationality" that have been noted can be interpreted as "rational" decision-making in the presence of imperfect information.

I also view the competitiveness hypothesis as a convenient starting point. Many of the central phenomena of interest can be explained without recourse to the exploitation hypothesis. Some degree of imperfect competition is not inconsistent with the imperfect information paradigm: the imperfect information paradigm provides part of the explanation for the absence of perfect competition; it can help identify situations where the landlords may be in a better position to exploit the workers. Moreover, to the extent that imperfect information limits the extent to which even a monopoly landlord can extract surplus from his workers, the imperfect information paradigm can provide insights into how he can increase his monopoly profits. The theory of interlinkage we have developed can thus be applied to the behavior of a monopolist landlord.

There is one other approach that has received some attention that is, in fact, closely related to the one I have advocated: the transactions cost approach, which attempts to explicate economic relations by focusing on transactions costs. Information costs are an important part of transactions costs (though information problems arise in other contexts as well). My reservations concerning the transactions cost approach lie in its lack of specificity: while the information paradigm provides a well-defined structure which allows one to derive clear propositions concerning, for instance, the design of contracts, the transactions cost paradigm does not. Thus, the transactions cost approach might provide some insight into why cost sharing is employed, but not into the terms of the cost-sharing agreement. The transactions cost paradigm might say that economies of scope provide an explanation for why the landlord also supplies credit, but it does not provide insights into when the landlord-cum-creditor would subsidize credit, or when he would "tax" it. Moreover, while the information paradigm identifies parameters which affect the magnitude of the externalities between landlords and creditors, and thus enables, in principle, the identification of circumstances under which interlinkage is more likely to be observed, the transactions cost paradigm can do little more than to say that there are circumstances in which the diseconomies of scope exceed the economies, and in these circumstances there will not be interlinkage.

References

Bhadari, A. (1973). "Agricultural Backwardness Under Semi-Feudalism." *Economic Journal* (March): 120–37.

Binswanger, H. P. (1978). "Attitudes Towards Risk: Implications and Psychological Theories of an Experiment in Rural India." Yale University Economic Growth Center DP 286.

Braverman, A., and J. E. Stiglitz (1982). "Sharecropping and the Interlinking of Agrarian Markets." *American Economic Review* (September): 695–715.

Stiglitz, J. E. (1974). "Alternative Theories of Wage Determination and Unemployment in LDCs: The Labor Turnover Model. *Quarterly Journal of Economics* 87 (May): 194–227.

Tversky, A. (1969). "Intransitivity of Preferences." *Psychological Review* 76: 31–48.

Selection VII.C.2. Contractual Arrangements, Employment, and Wages in Rural Labor Markets: A Critical Review*

In a world of perfect markets for all factors of production (including credit and insurance), a person's annual income would simply represent the employment of his or her factor endowments valued at the market rate per unit. In such a world, the initial distribution of endowments among people—for given tastes and aggregate quantities of each factor—would uniquely determine the distribution of income among people. Moreover, production—total output—would be not only maximal but unrelated to the distribution of factor ownership. Production techniques would be identical on all farms facing the same market environment and operating the same quality of land; for example, because output and employment per acre would be unrelated to farm size, barring scale economies, productive efficiency could not be improved by a rearrangement of factor uses or distributions. To explain labor earnings in a world of perfect markets with a given distribution of endowments requires that one explain the returns to each factor (wage rates, rent), a task for which the competitive supply-demand model has proved a powerful tool. The failure of one or more markets, however, would have important implications for the distribution of earnings and productive efficiency and would probably mean that more complex models would be required to understand earnings determination. An important, unresolved question is whether such models can outpredict the simpler, competitive models when only some markets are imperfect or absent.

Attention to market failure, however, is important not only for understanding the determination of earnings and the achievement of productive efficiency. It may also help us to understand the existence of and changes in the labor market's many and diverse institutional arrangements—different types of contracts and labor recruitment strategies and the interlinking of labor and one or more factors of production within one transaction. Indeed, because of the general nonindependence, or interrelatedness, of all factor markets, market failures anywhere in the rural sector may have a significant effect on labor market earnings or arrangements even if the market for labor operates perfectly. In

these circumstances, explaining earnings requires information beyond the determination of wages and labor supply.

In the rural economy, it is a fact that some labor is combined with land, not by the temporary sale of labor services but by the temporary acquisition of land. It is clear that the terms and arrangements associated with the market for land have a significant effect on the earnings of rural households and the production of aggregate output. . . . [This raises] two primary issues: First, what are the efficiency characteristics of a contract that provides laborers with a share of total agricultural output, an important contractual arrangement in the rural economy? Second, how do the welfare levels or earnings of such sharecroppers compare with those of laborers who work only for wages—that is, what determines the contractual terms?

Recent Tenancy Models

If the sales market for land is absent or involves very high transaction costs, landowners can hire all cooperating factors of production, including bullocks and management, in quantities that are optimal for their own land. Landowners can then rent out any nonland factors owned that are in excess of these optimal quantities. Productive efficiency—that is, equal factor ratios on all farms with land of equal quality—can still be achieved. Thus the absence of a sales market for land is not sufficient to force the use of tenancy. However, the institution of tenancy and the market for tenancies do substitute for the sales market. When there are no scale economies, at least one other factor market must be absent before the temporary rental of land becomes a necessary tool to achieve the most efficient factor ratios for all factors of production and all agents. The absent or incomplete markets (which involve high risks or high transaction costs) may be those for insurance, family labor, bullocks, or managerial skills. . . .

Cheung's (1968, 1969) work set the stage for the recent sharecropping literature in terms of the major reasons for share tenancy and the major issues to be addressed. His work both attacked the negative efficiency (incentive) implication of sharecropping and broadened the scope of inquiry of the sharecropping literature to include discussion of the manner in which size of tenancy and share of crop are determined. All writers from

*From Hans P. Binswanger and Mark R. Rosenzweig, *Contractual Arrangements, Employment and Wages in Rural Labor Markets: A Critical Review,* Agricultural Development Council, 1981, pp. 3–4, 21–27. Reprinted by permission.

Cheung onward have regarded both tenancy size and share level as endogenous to a particular model, while they have taken the wage rate as exogenously given. Contractual terms, but not the wage rate, are thus determined by economic forces, and the equilibrium solution to the contract choice problem involves maximization by both landlord and worker. The worker's equilibrium requires that "of the set of contracts available in the economy, there [exist] none which the individual worker prefers to the one which he has" (Stiglitz, 1974, p. 222). And landlord equilibrium implies that "there exists no subset [of the available contracts] which the landlord prefers to the subset which he employs" (ibid.).

Cheung also assigned *risk* and *risk aversion* a much larger role in determining share tenancy than others have accorded them. He did not include them, however, in his formal model. Clearly, under a wage labor system all the risks of cultivation are borne by the owner-cultivator; owner-cultivator income is the residual after payment of production costs at fixed wages. Under a fixed-rate tenancy, tenants bear all the risk since their income is the residual after payment of a fixed rent. Under share tenancy, however, the risk is divided between tenant and owner in proportion to the crop share of each.

As Jaynes (1979) has shown, however, Cheung's model achieves its efficiency outcome because it simply assumes away two problems—the negative incentives of sharing and the difficulty of monitoring effort. If these problems did not exist, we would not observe share tenancy. Thus Cheung must indeed introduce risk, risk aversion, and transaction costs in order to explain the existence of the contracts his formal model explores under conditions in which such sources of market imperfections do not exist.

With respect to risk aversion motivation for sharecropping, Newbery (1975) and Reid (1976) have shown that, with constant returns to scale, sharecropping provides no risk-sharing benefits that landlord and worker could not achieve by dividing a plot of land "into two subplots, one of which is rented out at a fixed rental R and the other is operated by the landlord who hires labor at a wage W" (Newbery and Stiglitz, 1979, p. 314). Thus a model in the Cheungian tradition—that is, one without problems of worker incentives—does not explain the existence of share tenancy, even in the presence of production risk and risk aversion. Sharecropping can, however, be a means of risk avoidance under more complex characterizations of risk. Newbery and Stiglitz (1979) have demon-

strated that with a second independent source of risk, such as wage rate risk in the labor market, share contracts are superior to a mixture of wage and fixed-rent contracts. If there are no incentive (monitoring) problems or economies of scale but there are multiple sources of risk, the sharecropping contract acts as the necessary instrument to achieve productive efficiency; that is, it prevents rather than creates an inefficient allocation of resources.

Another class of tenancy models focuses on the costliness of labor supervision as a cause of sharecropping—the *Marshallian inefficiency.* One of Stiglitz's (1974) models assumes costly supervision: the landlord sets the size of the tenancy just like the share, taking into account the impact of tenancy size on the tenant's input decision. The landlord can prevent the tenant from renting any other land or from working for wages, or he can include these restrictions in the contract and monitor and enforce them. The landlord thus has an extra control instrument and can, by means of maximization, control the contractual terms in such a way as to limit the tenant to his or her reservation utility—that is, the wage rate. Of course, given the effort monitoring problem, productive efficiency cannot be achieved in this model.

Braverman and Srinivasan (1979) have extended the Stiglitz model of costly supervision so as to allow tenant and landlord to engage in a simultaneous share-cum-credit contract, the credit being used for the tenant's consumption. Such a tied contract becomes superior to an untied contract if the landlord has access to credit from third parties at lower rates of interest than the tenant can obtain. The landlord sets four contractual terms: crop share, tenancy size, rate of interest to be charged the tenant, and proportion of credit requirements that the tenant borrows from the landlord. Given that the landlord has two extra instruments available, the landlord can almost always hold the tenant to the utility level the latter would obtain as a wage laborer. As a result, policies like tenancy reform or provision of credit to tenants at lower than market rates cannot improve the tenant's utility level. Nothing less than land redistribution, intervention in several markets, or rising alternative wage levels can improve tenants' welfare.

In the models discussed, costly supervision arises because of imperfect information. Information is asymmetrically distributed between landlord and tenant because only the tenant can know how much effort he or she will provide; the landlord cannot know this at sufficiently low cost. And a central planner, who shares the landlord's lack of information, cannot improve on the existing allocation. Such improvement can be achieved only if the central planner has cheaper means of monitoring effort than the landlord, which, in agriculture, is not likely. Alternatively, the central planner will have to redistribute land to tenants in order to overcome their inability to buy land in the land market, which inability has led to their status as tenants. Such a policy, however, will also improve efficiency in a decentralized economy. As long as the underlying constraints on information or land transfer remain in place, the share tenancy equilibrium achieved is optimal with respect to these constraints; that is, it is a second best optimum, relative to the set of informational constraints assumed in the model. This point is an important recurrent theme in the literature.

A problem that the models we have discussed so far fail to address explicitly is the coexistence in the same region of all forms of contracts: owner cultivation, share contracts, and fixed rent contracts. Moreover, *tenancy ladders* appear to be important in both developed and developing countries: workers first become sharecroppers, then fixed-rent tenants, and finally acquire land of their own.

There are three explanations for the coexistence of tenurial contractural arrangements: (1) differences in risk aversion, (2) screening of workers of different quality, and (3) market imperfections for inputs other than labor. But differential risk aversion cannot account for the tenancy ladder, since there is little reason to expect the same person to become completely risk neutral as he or she becomes older, even if the person accumulates assets. It must be recognized, therefore, that workers differ in other respects, such as ability, management skills, and capital endowments.

If productivity per hour of work differs among otherwise homogeneous workers but the productivity differences are known only to the workers and cannot be observed by the landlord without cost, landowners or workers face a screening cost. In this case, Hallagan (1978) and, independently, Newbery and Stiglitz (1979) have shown that the choice of contract conveys information about workers' perception of their abilities. "Individuals who believe they are most productive [as workers] will choose the rental contract; individuals who believe they are very unproductive will choose the wage contract and those in between will choose the share contract" (Newbery and Stiglitz, 1979, p.

323). Each class of workers prefers its respective contract. Utility levels for the more able workers are higher than the levels they could achieve in a labor market without screening. Again, since information is asymmetrically distributed between landlord and workers, productive efficiency cannot be achieved. The implicit screening by means of contract choice again represents a second best improvement in efficiency over the situation without tenancy contracts. This model leads to coexistence of contracts but not to a tenancy ladder unless workers move to higher efficiency classes as they grow older.

The clearest route to the tenancy ladder, the social differentiation of laborers, and different types of tenants is through absent markets or imperfect markets for inputs other than labor.

References

Braverman, Avishay, and T. N. Srinivasan. Conference Paper, "Agrarian Reforms in Developing Rural Economies Characterized by Interlinked Credit and Tenancy Markets," 1979.

Cheung, S. N. S. "Private Property Rights and Sharecropping," *Journal of Political Economy*, Vol. 76, 1968, pp. 1117–1122.

Cheung, S. N. S. *The Theory of Share Tenancy* (Chicago: University of Chicago Press, 1969).

Hallagan, W. "Self-selection by Contractual Choice and the Theory of Sharecropping," *Bell Journal of Economics*, Vol. 9, 1978, pp. 344–54.

Jaynes, Gerald D. Conference Paper, "Economic Theory and Land Tenure," 1979.

Newbery, D. M. G. "The Choice of Rental Contracts in Peasant Agriculture" in Lloyd G. Reynolds (ed.), *Agriculture in Development Theory* (New Haven: Yale University Press, 1975).

Newbery, D. M. G., and J. E. Stiglitz. "Sharecropping, Risk Sharing and the Importance of Imperfect Information" in James A. Roumasset, Jean Marc Boussard, and Inderjit Singh (eds.), *Risk, Uncertainty, and Agricultural Development* (College, Laguna, Philippines and New York: Southeast Asian Regional Center for Graduate Study and Research in Agriculture and Agricultural Development Council, 1979).

Reid, Joseph D., Jr. "Sharecropping and Agricultural Uncertainty," *Economic Development and Cultural Change*, Vol. 24, 1976, pp. 549–76.

Stiglitz, Joseph E. "Incentives and Risk Sharing in Agriculture," *Review of Economic Studies*, Vol. 41, 1974, 209–56.

Selection VII.C.3. The New Institutional Economics and Development Theory*

In recent years two strands of non-Walrasian economic literature have developed well-articulated endogenous theories of institutions, and they are both getting to be prominent in the new microeconomics of development. One is the transaction cost school, flowing out of the famous paper by Coase (1960), . . . The other school is associated with the theory of imperfect information. . . . Although there is some family resemblance between the two strands, there are important differences in their points of emphasis. But they both deny the validity of some of the principal results of mainstream economics. For example, one of the main pillars of Walrasian neoclassical economies—the separability of equity and efficiency—breaks down when transaction costs and imperfect information are important; the terms and conditions of contracts in various transactions, which directly affect the efficiency of resource allocation, now crucially depend on ownership structures and property relations. Development economics, which deals with cases where market failure and incomplete markets (often the result of the substantive presence of transaction costs and information problems) are predominant, clearly provides hospitable territory for such institutional analysis.

According to the transaction cost school, institutions that evolve to lower these costs are the key to the performance of economies. These costs include those of information, negotiation, monitoring, coordination, and enforcement of contracts. When transaction costs are absent, the initial assignment of property rights does not matter from the point of view of efficiency, because rights can be voluntarily adjusted and exchanged to promote increased production. But when transaction costs are substantial, as is usually the case, the allocation of property rights is critical. In the historical growth process there is a trade-off between economies of scale and specialization on the one hand and transaction costs on the other. In a small, closed, face-to-face peasant community, for example, transaction costs are low, but the production costs are high, because specialization and division of labor are severely limited by the extent of market defined by the personalized exchange process of the small community. In a large-scale complex economy, as the network of interdependence widens the impersonal exchange process gives considerable scope for all kinds of opportunistic behavior (cheating, shirking, moral hazard) and the costs of transacting can be high. In Western societies over time, complex institutional structures have been devised (elaborately defined and effectively enforced property rights, formal contracts and guarantees, corporate hierarchy, vertical integration, limited liability, bankruptcy laws, and so on) to constrain the participants, to reduce the uncertainty of social interaction, in general to prevent the transactions from being too costly and thus to allow the productivity gains of larger scale and improved technology to be realized.

The imperfect–information theory of institutions is closely related to that of transaction costs, since information costs constitute an important part of transaction costs. But the former theory is usually cast in a more rigorous framework clearly spelling out assumptions and equilibrium solution concepts, drawing out more fully the implications of strategic behavior under asymmetric information, and sharply differentiating the impact of different types of information problems. Imperfect–information theory yields somewhat more concrete and specific predictions about the design of contracts, with more attention to the details of terms and conditions of varying contractual arrangements under varying circumstances, than the usual presentations of transaction cost theory.

The imperfect–information theory has been fruitfully used in modeling many key agrarian institutions which are seen to emerge as substitutes for missing credit, insurance, and futures markets in an environment of pervasive risks, information asymmetry, and moral hazard. It started with the literature on sharecropping, then on interlocking of transactions in labor, credit and land lease, on labor tying, on credit rationing, and so on. Radical economists have often cited some of these production relations as institutional obstacles to development in a poor agrarian economy, overlooking the microeconomic rationale of the formation of these institutions. Under a set of informational constraints and missing markets, a given agrarian institution (say, sharecropping or interlocking of contracts) may be serving a real economic function. Its simple abolition, as is often demanded on a radical platform, without taking care of the factors that gave rise to the institution in the first place, may not necessarily improve the conditions of the intended beneficiaries of the abolition pro-

*From Pranab Bardhan, "The New Institutional Economics and Development Theory," *World Development* 17, no. 9 (1989): 1390–94. Reprinted by permission from Elsevier Science Ltd. Oxford, England.

gram. There may be some important political lessons here from what can be called the economics of second-best reformism.

The transaction–cost and imperfect–information theories are equally murky on the mechanism through which new institutions and property rights emerge. One gets the impression that more efficient institutions and governance structures evolve as the parties involved come to appreciate the new benefit-cost possibilities. The literature is marked by a certain ahistorical functionalism and even vulgar Darwinism on this point. An institution's mere function of serving the interests of potential beneficiaries is clearly inadequate in *explaining* it, just as it is an incompetent detective who tries to explain a murder mystery only by looking for the beneficiary and, on that basis alone, proceeds to arrest the heir of the murdered rich man. One cannot get away from the enormity of the collective action problem that limits the ability of potential gainers to get their act together in bringing about institutional changes. There are two kinds of collective action problems involved here: one is the well known free-rider problem about sharing the costs of bringing about change, the other is a bargaining problem where disputes about sharing the potential benefits from the change may lead to a breakdown of the necessary coordination.

A related question is that of the presumed optimality of persistent institutions. The transaction–cost (as well as the imperfect–information) school often unthinkingly implies the application of the market analogy of competitive equilibrium to the social choice of institutions or the biological analogy of natural selection in the survival of the fittest institution. In fact transaction costs themselves, by raising barriers to entry and exit, reduce pressures from any social selection process; sunk costs and asset-specificity insulate internal governance structures from market forces. As Greenwald and Stiglitz (1986) have shown, the market equilibrium under imperfect information and incomplete markets is, in general, constrained Pareto inefficient; and, as Farrell (1987) has shown, with imperfect information even bilateral relationships may not be efficient on account of complexity of private bargaining.

In the recent development literature the institution of interlocking of transactions (in labor, credit, and land relations) has been rationalized as a device to save transaction costs and to substitute for incomplete or nonexistent credit and insurance markets. But one should not overlook that such interlocking itself may act as a barrier to entry for third parties and be a source of additional monopoly power for the dominant partner (usually the employer-creditor-landlord) in such transactions. Personalized interlocking of labor commitments and credit transactions (involving selective exclusion of others) also divides the workers and emasculates their collective bargaining strength vis-à-vis employers, who use this as an instrument of control over the labor process.

As we all know from experience, dysfunctional institutions often persist for a very long period. Akerlof (1984) has built models to show how economically unprofitable or socially unpleasant customs may persist as a result of a mutually sustaining network of social sanctions when each individual conforms out of fear of loss of reputation from disobedience. In such a system, potential members of a breakaway coalition fear that it is doomed to failure and thus failure to challenge the system becomes a self-fulfilling prophecy. . . .

The biological analogy of survival of the fittest is particularly inappropriate as path dependence is assigned an important role in biological processes. To quote Gould (1980, p. 16): "Organisms are not billiard balls propelled by simple and measurable external forces to predictable new positions on life's pool table. . . . Organisms have a history that constrains their future in myriad, subtle ways. . . . Their complexity of form entails a host of functions incidental to whatever pressures of natural selection superintended the initial construction." The arguments against the operation of natural selection in social institutions are obviously much stronger. . . .

References

Akerlof, G. (1984). *An Economic Theorist's Book of Tales.* Cambridge: Cambridge University Press.

Coase, R. (1960). "The problem of social cost." *Journal of Law and Economics* 3 (October): 144.

Farrell, J. (1987). "Information and the Coase theorem." *Journal of Economic Perspectives* 1 (Fall): 113–129.

Gould, S. J. (1980). *The Panda's Thumb.* New York: Norton.

Greenwald B., and J. E. Stiglitz (1986). "Externalities in economies with imperfect information and incomplete markets." *Quarterly Journal of Economics* 101 (May): 229–64.

Selection VII.C.4. Rural Credit Markets and Institutions in Developing Countries: Lessons for Policy Analysis from Practice and Modern Theory*

Until recently conventional wisdom held that imposing low ceilings on interest rates and allocating massive amounts of credit to rural financial markets would speed rural development and improve income distribution. But by and large policies directed along these lines have failed. Indeed, most often they have made matters worse. Low interest rate ceilings provide income transfers to loan recipients, distorting the real price ratio of investment opportunities by undervaluing the real cost of capital in different sectors. To the standard cost of distorted resource allocation, add the specific costs and consequences of implementing credit programs in rural financial markets for the full measure of impact. The record overwhelmingly shows credit programs' objectives have not been met.

These credit policy failures can be attributed to basic flaws intrinsic to formal rural credit markets out of which arise persistent problems as described in Table 1.

Informal lending was once the only form credit took in rural settings. Evidence suggests that as farm size increases, private credit sources, village moneylenders and pawnbrokers, chit funds with an array of implicit interest rates, and friends or relatives grow less important than banks. With the implementation of development plans, official lending complements but clearly does not supersede informal sources.

Sample surveys supply the information on the extent of informal lending practices. They indicate that its volume is far greater than that of organized institutions. It is characterized by a much shorter processing time, better screening techniques or enforcement devices (noted in the lower default rate), and higher interest rates, with a median around 50 percent and a variance much higher than institutionalized credit rate.

The lower delinquency rates reported in informal credit sources are to a large extent due to better assessment of creditworthiness, ability to exert social pressure for repayment, and the frequent practice of tying (interlinking) credit contracts with other input or output contracts. Documentation of the use and characteristics of the latter practice is quite extensive. Sharecropping contracts are quite often interlinked with credit contracts. . . . Credit contracts between landlords and tenants are often in the form of production loans and tied to the purchase of fertilizer, seeds, and other forms of capital with different tenants paying different interest rates on their loans. These interlinkage practices have been viewed as a way to address the adverse selection problem and the moral hazard problem indigenous to these markets.

Two approaches have been put forward in the past to explain why landlords (employers) transact with their tenants (workers) in credit. They are: (1) reduction of transaction costs and (2) exploitation of weaker agents by more powerful ones. Though both have merits under certain circumstances, they fail to explain such interlinkages under a wider range of circumstances. In particular, they do not pay attention to the particular information structure. Even though information costs are part of the transaction cost, it is essential to specify them in order to explain the details of the contractual equilibrium, for example, why some landlords may subsidize tenants' credit while others charge their tenants higher interest rates. The exploitation theory fails to explain why monopolist landlords choosing tenants (workers) from a pool of the "reserve army of the unemployed" need any extra instrument (credit) for exploitation beyond the rental (tenant) or wage (worker) contract.

The modern theory of contractual equilibrium under imperfect information focuses on the moral hazard and adverse selection features commonly found in rural developing economies. The "moral hazard" features as pertaining to the interlinking credit with labor and land contracts are:

(a) Individuals are not paid on the basis of their input (effort) in general since this is not observable and they often do not rent land for a fixed sum since that imposes too much risk on them. Hence the contractual arrangements involve at least some form of sharecropping; as a result, tenants do not obtain the full marginal product of their efforts.

(b) The landlord cannot completely specify the actions to be taken by the tenant: the tenant has considerable discretion both with respect to the allocation and level of effort, and the choice of production technique. Some of these decisions may be easily monitored by the landlord, but there are oth-

*From A. Braverman and J. L. Guasch, "Rural Credit Markets and Institutions in Developing Countries: Lessons for Policy Analysis from Practice and Modern Theory," *World Development*, Vol. 14, Nos. 10/11 (October/November 1986), pp. 1253–55, 1257, 1260–62. Reprinted by permission from Elsevier Science Ltd., Oxford, England.

Table 1. Characteristics of Rural Financial Markets

Basic Flaws

Weakness of competitive forces.

Weak legal enforcement of contracts.

Corruption and lack of accountability in institutions, patronage and income transfer practices, which are partly due to poorly designed or non-existent incentive mechanisms to induce accountability on both sides of the market.

Significant information problems and uncertainty regarding the ability of borrowers to meet future loan obligations.

Inability to monitor the use of funds.

Lack of collateral often due to land tenure arrangements or ill-defined property rights (e.g. parts of Africa).

Lack of coherent financial savings mobilization program.

Higher opportunity cost of capital in other sectors because of interest rate ceilings.

Persistent Problems

Credit loans to wealthy farmers, small farmers rationed out of the credit market.

Loans for agricultural programs diverted to non-agricultural uses.

Credit policies that encourage consumption and discourage savings.

The term structure of agricultural loans contracts or fails to expand.

Low adoption rates of cost-savings technologies in agriculture and in financial services.

Low recovery rate.

Significant distortions in the optimal allocation of resources across markets.

Extensive use of interlinking credit contracts with labor and land contracts.

---

ers, perhaps equally important, for which the cost of monitoring would be very high.

The tenant's considerable discretion over his own actions combined with their significant impact on the landlord's expected profits have some further implications. In particular, the landlord has an incentive to *induce* tenants to behave as he wishes. This is attempted through influencing the amount and terms of credit the tenant borrows and by the goods he can purchase and the prices he pays.

The behavior affected includes the effort supplied by the tenant and the choice of technique (risk distribution) applied by him. For instance, if the landlord makes credit less expensive, under reasonable conditions the tenant will be induced to borrow more. If there are severe penalties associated with default (e.g., bonded labor), the tenant will then need to work harder to avoid this contingency.

Similarly the landlord may observe that his tenants are employing techniques of production which are too safe; the landlord's income might be increased if his tenants were willing to employ techniques with higher means and higher variances. He may note that his tenants are acting in a particularly risk-averse manner because of the consequences of defaulting on outstanding loans. To change their behavior, the landlord may require that his tenants only borrow from him. He may charge them interest above the market rate in order to induce them to limit their borrowing, and at the same time he may offer a tenancy contract which

is much more attractive in some other dimensions. Such a phenomenon prevails both in competitive and non-competitive environments and shifts the utilities possibilities frontier. Since interlinking is really the internalization of the externality from the credit to the labor/land markets in the absence of a complete set of markets, the utilities possibilities frontier moves outward while the distribution effects of interlinkage are ambiguous. The rationale for interlinkage becomes even stronger where law or custom restricts certain contractual arrangements, for example usury laws or floors on tenants' crop shares.

Another rationale for interlinking is the "adverse selection" effect, where interlinking credit and tenancy contracts may screen the high-ability from the low-ability types. . . .

Braverman and Stiglitz have shown that there is no presumption that innovation results either in a reduction or in an increase in tenants' demand for credit. Whether the demand for credit itself is increased or decreased depends critically on both how the technical change affects the probability distribution of yields and on tenants' utility functions. The presence of interlinkage between credit and land markets does not preclude either resistance to or encouragement of the adoption of technological innovations. Either is possible. In some cases, it might actually encourage the adoption of some technologies which otherwise would not be adopted, even though the innovation itself reduces tenants' demand for credit.

As explained before, the amount borrowed affects the landlord's return (through its effect both on the tenants' effort and on his decisions concerning choices of technique), and conversely, the terms of the landlord's contract affect returns to the lender (through its effect on the likelihood of default). Interlinkage was a method by which these "externalities" could be internalized. What then concerns the landlord-cum-lender is the total impact of the innovation on his income; the decomposition of his income into a return as a lender, or return as a landlord, has no particular significance. So it becomes clear that the impact of an innovation on a landlord-cum-lender may be quite different from the impact of the same innovation on a landlord who does not control the borrowing activities of his tenants. . . .

Selection VII.C.5. A Survey of Agricultural Household Models: Recent Findings and Policy Implications*

Efforts to predict the consequences of agricultural policies are often confounded by the complex behavioral interactions characteristic of semicommercialized, rural economies. Most households in agricultural areas produce partly for sale and partly for own-consumption. They also purchase some of their inputs—such as fertilizer and labor—and provide some inputs—such as family labor—from their own resources. Any change in the policies governing agricultural activities will therefore affect not only production but also consumption and labor supply.

Agricultural household models are designed to capture these interactions in a theoretically consistent fashion and in a manner that allows empirical applications so that the consequences of policy interventions can be illuminated. The existence of such models would enable the analyst to examine the consequences of policy in three dimensions.

First, one could examine the effects of alternative policies on the well-being of representative agricultural households. Well-being may be interpreted here to mean household income or some other measure such as nutritional status. For example, in examining the effect of a policy designed to provide cheap food for urban consumers, an agricultural household model would allow the analyst to assess the costs to farmers of depressed producer prices. The nutritional benefits for the urban population may be more than offset by the reduced nutritional status of the rural population that results from lower farm incomes.

Second, an understanding of the behavior of agricultural households would shed light on the spillover effects of government policies on other segments of the rural population. For example, since most investment strategies are designed to increase production, their primary impact is on the incomes of agricultural households. As a result, rural investment strategies may not reach landless households or households engaged in nonagricultural activities. A model that incorporates total labor demand and family labor supply, however, would allow the analyst to explore the effects of investment policy on the demand for hired labor and hence on the rural labor market and the in-

comes of landless households. Similarly, a model that incorporates consumer behavior would allow the analyst to explore the consequences of increased profits for agricultural households on the demand for products and services provided by nonagricultural, rural households. Since the demand for nonagricultural commodities is often thought to be much more responsive to an increase in income than the demand for agricultural staples, this spillover effect may well be important.

Third, governments are interested in the performance of the agricultural sector from a more macroeconomic perspective. For example, agriculture is often an important source of revenue for the public budget and a major earner of foreign exchange. In assessing the effects of pricing policy on the budget or the balance of payments, the government is obliged to consider how agricultural households will alter their production and consumption in response to changes in prices. A reduction in export taxes, for example, may increase earnings of foreign exchange and budget revenues if households market enough additional production. Since agricultural household models capture both consumption and production behavior, they are an appropriate vehicle for examining the effect of pricing policy on marketed surplus and hence on foreign exchange earnings and budget revenues.

The importance of agricultural households in the total population and the significance of sector policies combine to make the behavior of agricultural households an area warranting thorough theoretical and empirical investigation.

Modeling the Agricultural Household

In general, any analysis of the consumption or labor supply of agricultural households has to account for the interdependence of household production and consumption. Agricultural households combine the household and the firm, two fundamental units of microeconomic analysis. When the household is a price taker in all markets, for all commodities which it both consumes and produces, optimal household production can be determined independent of leisure and consumption choices. Then, given the maximum income level derived from profit-maximizing production, family labor supply and commodity consumption decisions can be made.

*From Inderjit Singh, Lyn Squire, and John Strauss, "A Survey of Agricultural Household Models: Recent Findings and Policy Implications," *World Bank Economic Review*, Vol. 1, No. 1, September 1986, pp. 149–50, 152–54. Reprinted by permission.

Given this sequential decisionmaking, the appropriate analytical framework is a recursive model with profit- and utility-maximizing components. Empirical analysis of both household consumption and production becomes considerably more tractable in a recursive model, which as a result has been used by most (but not all) empirical analyses.

In this section, a prototype static model is developed. (A more detailed treatment with derivations is found in Strauss, 1986.) For any production cycle, the household is assumed to maximize a utility function:

$$U = U(X_a, X_m, X_l) \qquad (1)$$

where the commodities are an agricultural staple (X_a), a market-purchased good (X_m), and leisure (X_l). Utility is maximized subject to a cash income constraint:

$$p_m X_m = p_a(Q_a - X_a) - p_l(L - F) - p_v V + E$$

where p_m and p_a are the prices of the market-purchased commodity and the staple, respectively; Q_a is the household's production of the staple (so that $Q_a - X_a$ is its marketed surplus); p_l is the market wage; L is total labor input; F is family labor input (so that $L - F$, if positive, is hired labor and, if negative, is off-farm labor); V is a variable input (for example, fertilizer); p_v is the variable input's market price; and E is any nonlabor, nonfarm income.

The household also faces a time constraint; it cannot allocate more time to leisure, on-farm production, or off-farm employment than the total time available to the household:

$$X_l + F = T$$

where T is the total stock of household time. It also faces a production constraint or production technology that depicts the relationship between inputs and farm output:

$$Q_a = Q(L, V, A, K)$$

where A is the household's fixed quantity of land and K is its fixed stock of capital.

In this presentation, various complexities are omitted. For example, the possibility of more than one crop is ignored. In addition, it is assumed that family labor and hired labor are perfect substitutes and can be added directly. Production is also assumed to be riskless. Finally, and perhaps most importantly, it is assumed that the four prices in the model—p_a, p_m, p_v, and p_l—are not affected by actions of the household. That is, the household is assumed to be a price taker in the four markets; as seen below, this will result in a recursive model.

The three constraints on household behavior can be collapsed into a single constraint. Substituting the production constraint into the cash income constraint for Q_a and substituting the time constraint into the cash income constraint for F yields a single constraint:

$$p_m X_m + p_a X_a + p_l X_l = p_l T + \pi + E \qquad (2)$$

where $\pi = p_a Q_a (L, VA, K) - p_l L - p_v V$ and is a measure of farm profits. In this equation, the left-hand side shows total household "expenditure" on three items: the market-purchased commodity, the household's "purchase" of its own output, and the household's "purchase" of its own time in the form of leisure. The right-hand side is a development of Becker's concept of full income, in which the value of the stock of time ($p_l T$) owned by the household is explicitly recorded, as is any labor income. The extension for agricultural households is the inclusion of a measure of farm profits, $p_a Q_a - p_l L - p_v V$, with all labor valued at the market wage, this being a consequence of the assumption of price-taking behavior in the labor market. Equations 1 and 2 are the core of all the studies of agricultural households reported in this article.

Equations 1 and 2 reveal that the household can choose the levels of consumption for the three commodities, the total labor input, and the fertilizer input into agricultural production. Maximization of household utility subject to the single constraint yields the following first-order conditions:

$$p_a \frac{\partial Q_a}{\partial L} = p_l \qquad (3a)$$

$$p_a \frac{\partial Q_a}{\partial V} = p_v \qquad (3b)$$

$$\frac{\partial U/\partial X_a}{\partial U/\partial X_m} = \frac{p_a}{p_m} \qquad (4a)$$

$$\frac{\partial U/\partial X_l}{\partial U_l/\partial X_m} = \frac{p_l}{p_m} \qquad (4b)$$

plus the constraint. Equations 3a and 3b show that the household will equate the marginal revenue products for labor and fertilizer to their respective market prices. An important attribute of these two equations is that they contain only two endogenous variables, L and V. The other endogenous variables, X_m, X_a, and X_l, do not appear and do not, therefore, influence the household's choice of L or V (provided second-order conditions are met). Accordingly, farm labor and fertilizer demand can be determined as a function of prices (p_a, p_l and p_v), the technological parameters of the production function, and the fixed area of land and quantity of capital. Since equations 3a and 3b depict the standard conditions for profit maximization, it can be concluded that the household's production decisions are consistent with profit maximization and independent of the household's utility function.

The maximized value of profits can be substituted into equation 2 to yield:

$$p_m X_m + p_a X_a + p_l X_l = Y^* \qquad (5)$$

where Y^* is the value of full income associated with profit-maximizing behavior. Equations 4a, 4b, and 5 can be thought of as the first-order conditions of a second maximization. That is, having first maximized profits (see equations 3a and 3b), the household then maximizes utility subject to its (maximized) value of full income. Equations 4a, 4b, and 5 can then be solved to obtain the demand equations for X_m, X_a, and X_l as functions of prices (p_m, p_a, p_l) and full income (Y^*). This demonstrates, given the assumptions made about markets, that even though the household's production and consumption decisions may be simultaneous in time, they can be modeled recursively (Nakajima, 1969; Jorgenson and Lau, 1969).

The presence of farm profits in equation 5 demonstrates the principal message of the farm household literature—that farm technology, quantities of fixed inputs, and prices of variable inputs and outputs affect consumption decisions. The reverse, however, is not true provided the model is recursive. Preferences, prices of consumption commodities, and income do not affect production decisions; therefore, output supply responds positively to own price at all times because of the quasi-convexity assumption on the production function. However, for consumption commodities (X_a) which are also produced by the household (Q_a), own-price effects are

$$\frac{dX_a}{dp_a} = \left. \frac{\partial X_a}{\partial p_a} \right|_{Y^*} + \frac{\partial X_a}{\partial Y^*}\frac{\partial Y^*}{\partial p_a} \qquad (6)$$

The first term on the right-hand side of this expression is the standard result of consumer demand theory and, for a normal good, is negative. The second term captures the "profit effect," which occurs when a rise in the price of the staple increases farm profits and hence full income. Applying the envelope theorem to equation 6,

$$\frac{\partial Y^*}{\partial p_a}dp_a = \frac{\partial \pi}{\partial p_a}dp_a = Q_a dp_a \qquad (7)$$

that is, the profit effect equals output times the price increase and therefore is unambiguously positive. The positive effect of an increase in profits (and hence farm income), an effect totally ignored in traditional models of demand, will definitely dampen and may outweigh the negative effect of both income and substitution in standard consumer demand theory. The presence of the profit effect is a direct consequence of the joint treatment of production and consumption decisions.

References

Jorgenson, Dale, and Lawrence Lau. 1969. "An Economic Theory of Agricultural House-hold Behavior." Paper presented at Fourth Far Eastern Meeting of Econometric Society.

Nakajima, Chihiro. 1969. "Subsistence and Commercial Family Farms: Some Theoretical Models of Subjecture Equilibrium." In C. F. Wharton, Jr., ed., *Subsistence Agriculture and Economic Development.* Chicago: Aldine.

Strauss, John. 1986. "The Theory and Comparative Statics of Agricultural Household Models: A General Approach." In I. J. Singh, L. Squire, and J. Strauss, eds., *Agricultural Household Models: Extensions, Applications, and Policy.* Baltimore, Md.: Johns Hopkins University Press.

Comment VII.C.1. Supply Functions and Price Responsiveness

A number of empirical studies offer evidence on the positive supply elasticity of agricultural production in response to price incentives. An excellent summary of empirical estimates of supply elasticities is presented by Hossein Askari and John T. Cummings, *Agricultural Supply Response: A Survey of the Econometric Evidence* (1976). See also Raj Krishna, "Agricultural Price Policy and Economic Development," in *Agricultural Development and Economic Growth,* ed. Herman M. Southworth and Bruce F. Johnston (1967); Theodore W. Schultz, ed., *Distortions of Agricultural Incentives* (1978); Walter Falcon, "Farmer Response to Price in a Subsistence Economy," *American Economic Review, Papers and Proceedings* (May 1964); and K. Bardhan, "Price and Output Response of Marketed Surplus of Foodgrains," *American Journal of Agricultural Economics* (February 1970).

Considering the efficiency of farmer decision making, several studies have examined the allocational behavior of peasant producers from the viewpoint of efficiency across farm size groups, risk, pricing policy, credit, and marketing. See Theodore W. Schultz, *Transforming Traditional Agriculture* (1964); Amartya K. Sen, "Peasants and Dualism With or Without Surplus Labor," *Journal of Political Economy* (October 1966); D. W. Hopper, "Allocational Efficiency in Traditional Indian Agriculture," *Journal of Farm Economics* (August 1965); Michael Lipton, "The Theory of the Optimizing Peasant," *Journal of Development Studies* (August 1968); and M. Schluter and T. Mount, "Some Management Objectives of the Peasant Farmer," *Journal of Development Studies* (August 1977).

In an important study, *Palanpur: The Economy of an Indian Village* (1982), C. J. Bliss and N. H. Stern examine whether farmers' decisions about inputs and outputs can be explained by an optimizing model (whether farmers are rational profit- or utility-maximizing agents) and whether sharecropping tenancy is inefficient.

VII.D. AGRICULTURAL PRICING POLICY AND URBAN BIAS

Note VII.D.1. Agricultural Pricing Policy

A five-volume research project, *The Political Economy of Agricultural Pricing Policy* (1991–92), sponsored by the World Bank, presents some significant findings on the experience of 18 developing countries.

The project provides systematic estimates of the degree of price discrimination against agriculture within individual countries and explains how it changed over time; determines how this intervention affected such key variables as foreign exchange earnings, agricultural output, and income distribution; and offers further insight into the political economy of agricultural pricing policy through a study of the motivations of policy makers, the economic and political factors determining the degree of agricultural intervention, and the attempts to reform unsuccessful policies.

The main findings of the comparative study of agricultural price interventions are

- The indirect tax on agriculture from industrial protection and macroeconomic policies was about 22 percent on average for the eighteen countries over 1960–85—nearly three times the direct tax from agricultural pricing policies (about 8 percent). The total tax (direct plus indirect) was thus 30 percent.
- Industrial protection policies taxed agriculture more than did real overvaluation of the exchange rate.
- High taxation of agriculture was associated with low growth in agriculture—and low growth in the economy.
- The transfers out of agriculture have been enormous. The net effect of total (direct plus indirect) interventions averaged 46 percent of agricultural gross domestic product (GDP) from 1960 to 1984. These transfers ranged from 2 percent for the protectors (Korea and Portugal) to 140 percent of actual agricultural GDP in Sub-Saharan African countries. Such enormous transfers must have severely depressed private investment and growth in agriculture.
- Surprisingly, most countries protected importables. On average, the direct protection of importables was about 18 percent and the direct taxation of exportables about 16 percent, for an average impact on the relative price of importables to exportables of about 40 percent. These distortions within agriculture increased between the early 1960s and mid-1980s.
- Direct price policies stabilized domestic agricultural prices relative to world prices, with an average reduction in variability of 25 percent and even more when world prices were highly volatile. Indirect policies contributed little, if anything, to price stability.
- Public investment in agriculture did not compensate for adverse price policies.
- The effect of removing agricultural price interventions is not regressive. In most countries, removing direct (or total) interventions changed the real incomes of the poorer urban and rural groups by less than 5 percent (up or down). More often than not, the rural poor gained from the removal of the interventions.
- The contribution of agriculture to fiscal revenues has fallen over time and is on average small.[1]

It is concluded:

Discrimination against agriculture in developing countries has generally been pronounced. It has been more extreme the more ideologically committed those influencing policy have been to the notions of modernization through industrialization and import substitution; it has been more extreme where agricultural production consists predominantly of traditional exportable commodities; and it has been more extreme when agricultural interests have not been part of the governing coalition.

Indirect discrimination against agriculture through trade regime and exchange rate policies is generally of greater importance than direct discrimination. Interestingly, however, most major reforms of direct agricultural pricing policies have been carried out in conjunction with major reforms of the overall trade and payments regimes.[2]

Notes

1. World Bank, The Political Economy of Agricultural Pricing Policy (1992), vol. 4, pp. 199–200.
2. Ibid., vol. 5, p. 139.

Selection VII.D.1. Urban Bias*

The most important class conflict in the poor countries of the world today is not between labour and capital. Nor is it between foreign and national interests. It is between the rural classes and the urban classes. The rural sector contains most of the poverty, and most of the low-cost sources of potential advance; but the urban sector contains most of the articulateness, organisation and power. So the urban classes have been able to "win" most of the rounds of the struggle with the countryside; but in so doing they have made the development process needlessly slow and unfair. Scarce land, which might grow millets and beansprouts for hungry villagers, instead produces a trickle of costly calories from meat and milk, which few except the urban rich (who have ample protein anyway) can afford. Scarce investment, instead of going into water-pumps to grow rice, is wasted on urban motorways. Scarce human skills design and administer, not clean village wells and agricultural extension services, but world boxing championships in showpiece stadia. Resource allocations, within the city and the village as well as between them, reflect urban priorities rather than equity or efficiency. The damage has been increased by misguided ideological imports, liberal and Marxian, and by the town's success in buying off part of the rural elite, thus transferring most of the costs of the process to the rural poor.

The disparity between urban and rural welfare is much greater in poor countries now than it was in rich countries during their early development. . . . This huge welfare gap is demonstrably inefficient, as well as inequitable. . . . It persists mainly because less than 20 percent of investment for development has gone to the agricultural sector . . . although over 65 percent of the people of less-developed countries (LDCs), and over 80 percent of the really poor who live on $1 a week each or less, depend for a living on agriculture. The proportion of skilled people who support development—doctors, bankers, engineers—going to rural areas has been lower still; and the rural-urban imbalances have in general been even greater than those between agriculture and industry. Moreover, in most LDCs, governments have taken numerous measures with the unhappy side-effect of accentuating rural-urban disparities: their own allocation of public expenditure and taxation; measures raising

the price of industrial production relative to farm production, thus encouraging private rural saving to flow into industrial investment because the value of industrial output has been artificially boosted; and educational facilities encouraging bright villagers to train in cities for urban jobs.

Such processes have been extremely inefficient. For instance, the impact on output of $1 of carefully selected investment is in most countries two to three times as high in agriculture as elsewhere yet public policy and private market power have combined to push domestic savings and foreign aid into non-agricultural uses. The process has also been inequitable. Agriculture starts with about one-third the income per head of the rest of the economy, so that the people who depend on it should in equity receive special attention not special mulcting. Finally, the misallocation between sectors has created a needless and acute conflict between efficiency and equity. In agriculture the poor farmer with little land is usually efficient in his use of both land and capital, whereas power, construction and industry often do best in big, capital-intensive units; and rural income and power, while far from equal, are less unequal then in the cities. So concentration on urban development and neglect of agriculture have pushed resources away from activities where they can help growth *and* benefit the poor, and towards activities where they do either of these, if at all, at the expense of the other.

Urban bias also increases inefficiency and inequity *within* the sectors. Poor farmers have little land and much underused family labour. Hence they tend to complement any extra developmental resources received—pumpsets, fertilisers, virgin land—with much more extra labour than do large farmers. Poor farmers thus tend to get most output from such extra resources (as well as needing the extra income most). But rich farmers (because they sell their extra output to the cities instead of eating it themselves, and because they are likely to use much of their extra income to support urban investment) are naturally favoured by urban-biased policies; it is they, not the efficient small farmers, who get the cheap loans and the fertiliser subsidies. The patterns of allocation and distribution within the cities are damaged too. Farm inputs are produced inefficiently, instead of imported, and the farmer has to pay, even if the price is nominally "subsidised." . . . The processing of farm outputs, notably grain milling, is shifted into big ur-

*From Michael Lipton, *Why Poor People Stay Poor,* 1977, Gower Publishing Limited. Reprinted by permission.

ban units and the profits are no longer reinvested in agriculture. And equalisation between classes inside the cities becomes more risky, because the investment-starved farm sector might prove unable to deliver the food that a better-off urban mass would seek to buy.

Moreover, income in poor countries is usually more equally distributed within the rural sector than within the urban sector. Since income creates the power to distribute extra income, therefore, a policy that concentrates on raising income in the urban sector will worsen inequalities in two ways: by transferring not only from poor to rich, but also from more equal to less equal. Concentration on urban enrichment is triply inequitable: because countryfolk start poorer; because such concentration allots rural resources largely to the rural rich (who sell food to the cities); and because the great inequality of power *within* the towns renders urban resources especially likely to go to the resident elites.

However, urban bias does not rest on a conspiracy, but on convergent interests. Industrialists, urban workers, even big farmers *all* benefit if agriculture gets squeezed, provided its few resources are steered, heavily subsidised, to the big farmer, to produce cheap food and raw materials for the cities. Nobody conspires; all the powerful are satisfied; the labour-intensive small farmer stays efficient, poor and powerless, and had better shut up. Meanwhile, the economist, often in the blinkers of industrial determinism, congratulates all concerned on resolutely extracting an agricultural surplus to finance industrialisation. Conspiracy? Who needs conspiracy?

Thirdly, how far does the urban bias thesis go towards an agricultural or rural emphasis? It was noted that there is a rather low limit to the shifts than *can* swiftly be made in allocations of key resources like doctors or savings between huge, structured areas of economic life like agriculture and industry. In the longer run, if the arguments of this section are right, how high do they push the allocations that should go to agriculture in poor countries: from the typical 20 percent of various sorts of scarce resource (for the poorest two-thirds of the people, who are also those normally using scarce resources more efficiently, as will be shown) up to 50 percent, or 70 percent, or (absurdly) 100 percent? Clearly the answer will differ according to the resource being reallocated, the length of time for the reallocation, and the national situation under review. The optimal extra proportion of doctors for rural India, of investment for rural Peru, and of increase in farm prices for rural

Nigeria will naturally differ. However, it remains true that pressures exist to set all these levels far below their optima. To acquire the right to advise against letting children go naked in winter, do I need to prescribe the ideal designs of babies' bonnets?

Linked to the question "Is there a limit to the share of resources agriculture ought to get?" is a more fundamental question. Does the need for a high share of rural resources last for ever? Does not development imply a move out of agriculture and away from villages? Since all developed countries have a very high proportion of resources outside agriculture, can it make sense for underdeveloped countries to push more resources *into* agriculture? And—a related question—as a poor country develops, does it not approach the British or U.S. style of farming, where it is workers rather than machines or land that are scarce, so that the concentration of farm resources upon big labour-saving farms begins to make more sense?

The best way to look at this question is to posit four stages in the analysis of policy in a developing country towards agriculture. Stage I is to advocate leaving farming alone, allowing it few resources, taxing it heavily if possible, and getting its outputs cheaply to finance industrial development, which has top priority. This belief often rests on such comfortable assumptions as that agricultural growth is ensured by rapid technical change; does not require or cannot absorb investment; and can be directed to the poor while the rich farmers alone are squeezed to provide the surpluses. Such a squeeze on agriculture was overtly Stalin's policy, and in effect (though much more humanely) the policy of the Second Indian Plan (1956–61) as articulated by Mahalanobis, its chief architect. The bridge between the two was the economic analysis of Preobrazhensky and Feldman. The underlying argument, that it is better to make machines than to make consumer goods, especially if one can make machines to make machines, ignores both the possible case for international specialisation, and the decided inefficiency of using scarce resources to do the right thing at the wrong time.

The second stage in policy for rural development usually arises out of the failures of Stage I. In Stage II, policy-makers argue that agriculture cannot be safely neglected if it is adequately to provide workers, materials, markets and saving to industry. Hence a lot of resources need to be put into those parts of agriculture (mainly big farms, though this is seldom stated openly) that supply industry with raw materials, and industrial workers with food. That is the stage that many poor countries have reached in their official pronounce-ments, and some in their actual decisions. Stage II is still permeated by urban bias, because the farm sector is allocated resources not mainly to raise economic welfare, but because, and insofar as, it uses the resources to feed urban-industrial growth. Development of the rural sector is advocated, but not for the people who live and work there.

In Stage III, the argument shifts. It is realised that, so long as resources are concentrated on big farmers to provide urban inputs, those resources will neither relieve need nor—because big farmers use little labour per acre—be used very produc-tively. So the sequence is taken one step further back. It is recognised, not only (as in Stage II) that efficient industrialisation is unlikely without major growth in rural inputs, but also (and this is the dis-tinctive contribution of Stage III) that such growth cannot be achieved efficiently or equitably—or maybe at all—on the basis of immediately "ex-tracting surplus." Stage III therefore involves ac-cepting the need for a transformation of the *mass* rural sector, through major resource inputs, *prior* to substantial industrialisation, except insofar as such industrialisation is a more efficient way than (say) imports of providing the mass rural sector with farm requirements or processing facilities. For development to "march on two legs," the best foot must be put forward first.

It is at Stage III that I stop. I do not believe that poor countries should "stay agricultural" in order to develop, let alone instead of developing. The ar-gument that neither the carrying capacity of the land, nor the market for farm products, is such as to permit the masses in poor countries to reach high levels of living without a major shift to non-farm activities seems conclusive. The existence of

a Stage IV must be recognised, however. Stage IV is the belief that industrialism degrades; that one should keep rural for ever. This is attractive to some people in poor countries because it marks a total rejection of imitativeness. Neither Western nor Soviet industrialism, but a "national path," is advocated. Other people, notably in rich countries, argue that environmental factors preclude an in-dustrialised world where all consume at U.S. lev-els; that there would be too little of one or more key minerals, or that the use of so much energy would disastrously damage the world's air, water, climate or other aspects of the ecosystem. . . .

The learning process, needed for modern indus-trialisation, is sometimes long; but it is fallacious for a nation, comprising above all a promising but overwhelmingly underdeveloped agriculture, to conclude that, in order to begin the process of learning, a general attack on numerous branches of industrial activity should be initiated. A far better strategy is to concentrate first upon high-yielding mass rural development, supported (partly for learning's sake) by such selective ancillary indus-try as rural development makes viable. Rapid in-dustrialisation on a broad front, doomed to self-strangulation for want of the wage goods and savings capacity that only a developed agricultural sector can provide, is likely to discredit industrial-isation itself.

The arguments for rapid general industrialisa-tion, prior to or alongside agricultural develop-ment, assume against most of the evidence that such a sequence is likely to succeed. But no na-tional self-esteem, no learning-by-doing, no jam tomorrow, can come from a mass of false starts. If you wish for industrialisation, prepare to develop agriculture.

Exhibit VII.D.1. Rural and Urban Poverty in the 1980s

Region and Country	Rural Population as Percentage of Total	Rural Poor as Percentage of Total	Infant Mortality (per thousand live births)		Access to Safe Water (percentage of population)	
			Rural	Urban	Rural	Urban
Sub-Saharan Africa						
Côte d'Ivoire	57	86	121	70	10	30
Ghana	65	80	87	67	39	93
Kenya	80	96	59	57	21	61
Asia						
India	77	79	105	57	50	76
Indonesia	73	91	74	57	36	43
Malaysia	62	80	—	—	76	96
Philippines	60	67	55	42	54	49
Thailand	70	80	43	28	66	56
Latin America						
Guatemala	59	66	85	65	26	89
Mexico	31	37	79	29	51	79
Panama	50	59	28	22	63	100
Peru	44	52	101	54	17	73
Venezuela	15	20	—	—	80	80

Source: World Bank, *World Development Report 1990* (1990), p. 31.

Comment VII.D.1. Rural–Urban Terms of Trade

For a discussion of methods chosen to test the urban-bias thesis and a critical examination of the evidence, see Michael Lipton, "Urban Bias Revisited," *Journal of Development Studies* (April 1984).

Highly relevant to urban bias are the rural–urban terms of trade as determined by government policies that influence the output and input prices for agriculture and the output and input prices for the urban industrial sector. The terms of trade for the rural sector are an indication of the profitability of agriculture and the purchasing power of agricultural income. To the extent that the types of government interventions reflect urban bias, the terms-of-trade level for the rural sector will be more unfavorable than a market-determined level in the absence of government intervention.

The following are instructive on the terms of trade manipulation and resource transfer from agriculture: G. T. Brown, "Agricultural Pricing Policies in Developing Countries," in *Distortion of Agricultural Incentives,* ed. Theodore W. Schultz (1978); A. K. Dixit, "Marketable Surplus and Dualistic Development," *Journal of Economic Theory* (August 1969); and R. K. Sah and J. E. Stiglitz, "The Economics of Price Scissors," *American Economic Review* (March 1984), and "Price Scissors and the Structure of the Economy," *Quarterly Journal of Economics* (February 1987).

Comment VII.D.2. The Rural–Urban Divide

Critics of the formulation of "urban bias" contend that the pattern of rural–urban relations is not the prime cause of slow economic growth or of continuing mass poverty. They further argue that the rural–urban dichotomy has been asked to bear too heavy a burden, that there is considerable overlap between and differentiation within the two sectors, and that the complexities of actual patterns of political action beyond an urban-biased coalition are ignored. See John Harris and Mick Moore, eds., "Development and the Rural–Urban Divide" [special issue], *Journal of Development Studies* (April 1984). In this same issue, Michael Lipton defends his formulation of urban bias against the major criticisms.

Also relevant is Robert Bates's theory of urban bias for tropical Africa: *Markets and States in Tropical Africa* (1981). Compare also the symposium "Robert Bates, Rational Choice and the Political Economy of Development in Africa," *World Development* (June 1993).

Income Distribution

Overview

This chapter begins with a Note that describes some of the problems involved in estimating the income distribution for a country and discusses the measures of inequality for a given distribution of income that are used in the subsequent selections. The first section concerns the impact of economic development on income distribution and in particular on measures of income inequality. It is theoretically possible, of course, that development has no impact on income distribution. For example, suppose it were the case that the distribution of income is determined entirely by the distribution of innate ability in the population. It is plausible that development will not change the distribution of innate ability, and therefore will not change the distribution of income. Against the hypothesis that development does not affect income distribution and therefore leaves income inequality unchanged, the alternative that has received by far the most attention is the hypothesis that income inequality first rises and then falls with development. A plot of inequality against a measure of development such as per capita income would then look like an inverted U. This hypothesis has therefore become known as the inverted-U hypothesis.

The inverted-U hypothesis originated with Simon Kuznets in the work featured in the first selection. Kuznets observed falling inequality in Germany and especially in the United Kingdom and the United States, beginning from roughly the last quarter of the nineteenth century for the United Kingdom and the First World War for Germany and the United States. He conjectured that inequality was falling after having risen during an earlier period, perhaps 1780 to 1850 in the United Kingdom and 1840 to 1890 in Germany and the United States. The reasoning behind his conjecture was that he believed that in these countries the distribution of income in agriculture was more equal than the distribution of income in urban areas, so that as development and urbanization proceeded, measured inequality overall should have risen. The subsequent fall in inequality that he actually observed was then due, he argued, to a decline in inequality within urban areas caused by better adaptation of the children of rural–urban migrants to city economic life and growing political power of urban lower-income groups to enact legislation favoring their interests.

Kuznets published his conjecture in 1955. Because the long swings in income inequality he described occurred (at least in his examples) over periods of a century or more, existing data are inadequate to test the inverted-U hypothesis as he formulated it even now, more than 40 years later. Two approaches have therefore been taken by researchers who nevertheless want to test the inverted-U hypothesis. The more popular of the two approaches is to make the heroic assumption that different countries observed at different levels of development at a given point in time trace out the path that a typical country would take over a very long period of time. One then looks at whether the cross-country data yield an inverted-U plot of inequality against level of development, the latter typically measured by per capita income. The less popular of the two approaches is to look at changes in inequality within countries over the short time periods for which data are available, and see whether inequality has tended to increase in relatively less developed countries and decrease in relatively more developed countries.

The first approach is taken in Selection VIII.A.2 by Montek Ahluwalia. Using a sample of 60 countries, he finds that income shares of all percentile groups except the top 20 percent first decline and then rise as per capita GNP increases, whereas the income share of the top 20 percent follows the opposite pattern. Findings of later studies using the cross-sectional approach have been similarly supportive of the inverted-U hypothesis (e.g., Papanek and Kyn 1986). The second approach is taken in Selection VIII.A.3 by Gary Fields. He examines the change in income inequality during 43 spells in 19 countries during which per capita income increased. None of the spells is longer than a decade. He finds no tendency for spells in poorer countries to yield increased rather than decreased inequality or for spells in richer countries to yield decreased rather than increased inequality.

While this mixed evidence regarding the validity of the inverted-U hypothesis has been accumulating, other researchers have sought to clarify the argument underlying Kuznets's original conjecture. Selection VIII.A.4 by Sherman Robinson considers a two-sector economy for which average income is higher in one sector. He shows that overall income inequality as measured by the variance in the logarithm of income follows an inverted U as the population is reallocated from one sector to another, provided that within-sector inequalities and the average sector log incomes are held constant. We can think of the two sectors as the rural and urban sectors, with average income and inequality both higher in the urban sector, but the point of Robinson's selection is that this interpretation is irrelevant: the inverted-U result holds regardless of which sector has higher average income or higher inequality. If the Gini coefficient rather than the log variance is used to measure income inequality, the inverted-U result can again be demonstrated in the special case where within-sector inequalities are zero, so that all inequality is attributable to the difference in incomes between the two sectors (see Knight 1976 and Fields 1979). Focusing on between-sector inequality yields a simple intuition for Robinson's result. When all of the population is in sector 1, between-sector inequality is zero. When some of the population has migrated to sector 2, between-sector inequality is positive. When all of the population has migrated to sector 2, between-sector inequality is again zero.

Robinson's result makes it appear that an inverted-U path of income inequality, should we observe it, is a rather uninteresting artifact of the way in which we measure inequality. This position is challenged in Selection VIII.A.5 by James Rauch and in the following Comment on the grounds that all individuals in Robinson's economy would prefer to be in the sector with higher average income, and that once the need for migration equilibrium is taken into account the cause of the inverted-U path of income inequality completely changes. Specifically, Rauch supposes that individuals are indifferent in equilibrium between earning the agricultural income with certainty or taking their chances in the urban sector, where they earn a high income if they are lucky and find a formal-sector job and a low income if they are unlucky and get stuck in informal-sector underemployment (which we can think of as the easy-entry informal sector described in Selection VI.7 by Fields). The main source of inequality in the Rauch model is not inequality between the rural and urban sectors but rather inequality within the urban sector between informally and formally employed workers. As urbanization increases the urban sector gains greater weight in the determination of overall inequality, causing it to rise, but at the same time the share of the underemployed in the urban population falls, eventually causing inequality within the urban sector and overall inequality to fall. The inverted U in income inequality is thus closely related to the growth and decline of the proportion of the population that falls into the poorest class, the underemployed. Rauch's result for overall income inequality is similar to Kuznets's original hypothesis that inequality should first increase with urbanization because population was being shifted from a sector with low inequality (agriculture) to a sector with high inequality and later decrease with urbanization because inequality within the urban sector would be reduced.

The second section of this chapter reverses the arrow of causality in the first section and addresses the impact of income distribution on economic development. For many years the dominant view was that income inequality promoted savings and therefore promoted development. This opinion was closely linked to the view that savings is the engine of growth (see the Overview for Chapter III), and like that view it was succinctly expounded by W. Arthur Lewis (1954, pp. 156–57):

> We are interested not in the people in general, but only say in the 10 percent of them with the largest incomes. . . . The remaining 90 percent of the people never manage to save a significant fraction of their incomes. . . . saving increases relatively to the national income because the incomes of the savers increase relatively to the national income. The central fact of economic development is that the distribution of income is altered in favour of the saving class.

The view that inequality helps to generate rapid economic growth was called into question by the combination in the "high-performing East Asian economies" (see the *East Asian Miracle,* Selection I.B.1) of relatively equal distributions of income with rates of growth in per capita income (and with savings rates) that were among the world's highest. Selection VIII.B.1 by Alberto Alesina and Dani Rodrik shows that both income inequality and inequality of land ownership are negatively associated with per capita income growth during the periods 1960–85 and 1970–85 for the countries with available data. As a result of such findings it is now more commonly believed that the impact of inequality on development is negative rather than positive. One must then ask, what is the mechanism by which inequality harms development? Alberto Alesina and Roberto Perotti in Selection VIII.B.2 describe one possible mechanism and find evidence to support it using cross-country data, and indeed this is the only one of the various proposed mechanisms to receive substantial empirical support to date. The key intervening variable in this mechanism is political instability: income inequality is hypothesized to cause political instability, which in turn is hypothesized to reduce investment. If investment is inhibited by political instability, it will be difficult to sustain development. In their sample of 71 countries during the period 1960–85, Alesina and Perotti find that the share of income received by the "middle class" (the two quintiles just below the top) is negatively associated with their index of sociopolitical instability and that this index in turn is negatively associated with the share of investment in GDP.

In the final section we return to the impact of economic development on income distribution, but consider case studies rather than cross-country statistical analysis or theory. The two countries and time periods covered are Taiwan from 1953 to 1964, in the selection by John Fei, Gustav Ranis, and Shirley Kuo, and Brazil from 1960 to 1970, in the selection by Albert Fishlow. In both cases the crucial factor causing income distribution to change was redistribution of assets by government policy, a factor considered in none of the previous selections. In the study of Taiwan the key asset is land, whereas in the study of Brazil the key asset is human capital (education). Taiwan instituted a major land reform between 1949 and 1953, and Fei, Ranis, and Kuo argue that it continued to have its impact on income distribution well into the 1950s, in part due to complementary farm programs and dispersed rural industry that allowed new owner-cultivators to take full advantage of the land reform. Income inequality fell to levels among the lowest in the world by 1964. Fishlow notes that the variance of educational attainment in the Brazilian labor force increased 48 percent between 1960 and 1970 due to policies that emphasized secondary school and university enrollment rather than extension of primary education. He attributes to this increased variance in educational attainment about half the increase in Brazilian income inequality during this period, from an already high level to one of the world's highest.

References

Fields, Gary S. 1979. "A Welfare Economic Approach to Growth and Distribution in the Dual Economy." *Quarterly Journal of Economics* 93 (August): 325–53.

Knight, John B. 1976. "Explaining Income Distribution in Less Developed Countries: A Framework and an Agenda." *Oxford Bulletin of Economics and Statistics* 38 (August): 161–77.

Lewis, W. Arthur. 1954. "Economic Development with Unlimited Supplies of Labour." *The Manchester School* 22: 139–91.

Papanek, Gustav F., and Oldrich Kyn. 1986. "The Effect on Income Distribution of Development, the Growth Rate and Economic Strategy." *Journal of Development Economics* 23 (September): 55–65.

Note VIII.1. Measurement of Income Inequality

For a given distribution of income there are many ways to measure inequality. In this Note we will discuss only the measures that are used in the selections included in this chapter.

Estimation of the distribution of income presents many difficulties. Ideally we would like to use estimates of the incomes of all households in a country. By contrast, to estimate income or GNP per capita we only need estimates of two quantities: total income and total population. Because the data collection requirements are so great, countries rarely report estimates of their income distributions more frequently than every 10 years, and for many countries there exist no reliable estimates of income distribution at all. The estimates we do have are invariably based on the incomes of households in a given year rather than averaged over many years. (They are also almost always based on before-tax rather than after-tax incomes and are sometimes based on incomes received by individuals rather than households.) To see the problem this presents for measurement of inequality, consider a hypothetical country inhabited entirely by farmers, some of whom grow crops that benefit from above average rainfall and the rest of whom grow crops that benefit from below average rainfall. Suppose that all farmers within each group are identical, and that on average (that is, for average rainfall) these two groups of farmers earn the same household incomes. We would then want to say that there is no inequality in the distribution of income for this country. However, in any given year rainfall will differ from the average, and unequal incomes will be observed. Simon Kuznets lists the specifications for an ideal estimate of income distribution at the beginning of Selection VIII.A.1.

Ignoring these difficulties, we can measure inequality using the estimated income distributions that we have. A popular measure is the ratio of the share of income received by the fifth *quintile* (richest 20 percent) of households to the share of income received by the first quintile (poorest 20 percent) or first two quintiles (poorest 40 percent) of households. The shares of income received by various quintiles are the variables used in the empirical analyses of the selections in this chapter by Montek Ahluwalia (VIII.A.2) and by Alberto Alesina and Roberto Perotti (VIII.B.2).

A more rigorous way to measure income inequality is to use *Lorenz curves*. A Lorenz curve plots the percentage of a country's income received by the poorest x percent of households against x. Thus in Figure 1, OX percent of households (the poorest group) receives a percent of income, and so on, giving the Lorenz curve L. Complete equality would occur only if a percent of households received a percent of income, yielding the curve of complete equality E. The curve of perfect inequality is OGH, with a right angle at G. This curve represents the case where one household has 100 percent of the country's income. In practice the Lorenz curve is typically fitted to data giving income shares by decile, that is, the points on the Lorenz curve that are actually observed are the percentage of income received by the poorest 10 percent of households, the percentage of income received by the poorest 20 percent of households, and so on. If the Lorenz curve for one income distribution α lies above that of another income distribution β for at least one point and never lies below it, that is, if distribution α *Lorenz dominates* distribution β, we say that distribution α is more equal than distribution β. It can be shown (see, e.g., Fields and Fei 1978) that if distribution α Lorenz dominates distribution β for the same level of income, α can be obtained from β by transferring positive amounts of income from the relatively rich to the relatively poor. If an additional dollar of income is worth less to the relatively rich than to the relatively poor (i.e., if there is diminishing marginal utility of income), we can judge that this transfer increases social welfare. In short, for a given level of income, Lorenz dominance gives us a measure of income inequality that we can link to social welfare, with lower inequality implying higher welfare.

This feature makes measurement of income inequality using Lorenz curves very attractive. Unfortunately, it does not allow us to compare inequality of income distributions whose

Figure 1. The Lorenz Curve

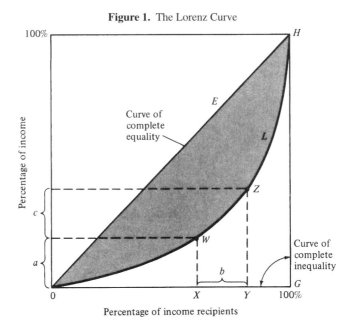

Percentage of income recipients

Lorenz curves cross. One way to deal with this problem is to measure inequality using the *Gini coefficient,* computation of which is illustrated in Figure 1. The shaded area in the figure, enclosed by the theoretical line of equality *E* and the observed Lorenz curve *L,* is known as the concentration area or area of inequality. The Gini coefficient is the ratio of this area to the total area under the line of equality. One way to compute the Gini coefficient is to take the sum of the areas of all "trapezoids" such as *WXYZ* and subtract it from the area under *E* to obtain the concentration area. The required ratio then follows. As a measure of income inequality, the Gini coefficient ranges from 0 to 1—the larger the coefficient, the greater the inequality. Thus 0 represents perfect equality, and 1 represents perfect inequality. It is clear that if one income distribution Lorenz dominates another, its Gini coefficient will be smaller, but the Gini coefficient also allows us to rank inequality for income distributions whose Lorenz curves cross. The Gini coefficient is the measure of income inequality used in the selections here by Gary Fields (VIII.A.3); by Alberto Alesina and Dani Rodrik (VIII.B.1); by John Fei, Gustav Ranis, and Shirley Kuo (VIII.C.1); and by Albert Fishlow (VIII.C.2).

A disadvantage of the Gini coefficient is that it cannot be decomposed into inequality within and inequality between groups, that is, the sum of inequality within and inequality between groups will not add up exactly to the overall Gini coefficient. This disadvantage is especially important when one wants to analyze a change in inequality that occurs over time, since one can often obtain a great deal of insight by analyzing how much of the change can be attributed to a change in within-group inequality and how much can be attributed to a change in between-group inequality. Many groupings are interesting, for example, by levels of education of the heads of households, but in the selections in this chapter attention is focused primarily on the division between rural and urban or agricultural and nonagricultural households. The decomposable measure of income inequality that is used to analyze changes in inequality in the selections by Sherman Robinson (VIII.A.4) and by James Rauch (VIII.A.5) is the variance in the logarithm of income. One reason the log variance is used rather than the variance is that it does not change when the units of measurement for income change, for example, it is the same whether incomes are measured in dollars or cents. For a more thorough discussion of the advantages and disadvantages of various measures of inequality, see Foster (1985).

References

Fields, Gary S., and John C. H. Fei. 1978. "On Inequality Comparisons." *Econometrica* 46 (March): 303–16.

Foster, James. 1985. "Inequality Measurement." In Peyton Young, ed., *Fair Allocation* (Providence, R.I.: American Mathematical Society).

VIII.A. THE IMPACT OF DEVELOPMENT ON INCOME DISTRIBUTION

Selection VIII.A.1. Economic Growth and Income Inequality*

The central theme of this paper is the character and causes of long-term changes in the personal distribution of income. Does inequality in the distribution of income increase or decrease in the course of a country's economic growth? What factors determine the secular level and trends of income inequalities?

These are broad questions in a field of study that has been plagued by looseness in definitions, unusual scarcity of data, and pressures of strongly held opinions. While we cannot completely avoid the resulting difficulties, it may help to specify the characteristics of the size-of-income distributions that we want to examine and the movements of which we want to explain.

Five specifications may be listed. First, the units for which incomes are recorded and grouped should be family-expenditure units, properly adjusted for the number of persons in each—rather than income recipients for whom the relations between receipt and use of income can be widely diverse. Second, the distribution should be complete, i.e., should cover all units in a country rather than a segment either at the upper or lower tail. Third, if possible we should segregate the units whose main income earners are either still in the learning or already in the retired stages of their life cycle—to avoid complicating the picture by including incomes *not* associated with full-time, full-fledged participation in economic activity. Fourth, income should be defined as it is now for national income in this country, i.e., received by individuals, including income in kind, before and after direct taxes, excluding capital gains. Fifth, the units should be grouped by *secular* levels of income, free of cyclical and other transient disturbances.

For such a distribution of mature expenditure units by secular levels of income per capita, we should measure shares of some fixed ordinal groups—percentiles, deciles, quintiles, etc. In the underlying array the units should be classified by average income levels for a sufficiently long span so that they form income-status groups—say a generation or about 25 years. Within such a period, even when classified by secular income levels, units may shift from one ordinal group to another. It would, therefore, be necessary and useful to study separately the relative share of units that, throughout the generation period of reference, were continuously within a specific ordinal group, and the share of the units that moved into that specific group; and this should be done for the shares of "residents" and "migrants" within all ordinal groups. Without such a long period of reference and the resulting separation between "resident" and "migrant" units at different relative income levels, the very distinction between "low" and "high" income classes loses its meaning, particularly in a study of long-term changes in shares and in inequalities in the distribution. To say, for example, that the "lower" income classes gained or lost during the last twenty years in that their share of total income increased or decreased has meaning only if the units have been classified as members of the "lower" classes throughout those 20 years—and for those who have moved into or out of those classes recently such a statement has no significance. . . .

I. Trends in Income Inequality

Forewarned of the difficulties, we turn now to the available data. These data, even when relating to complete populations, invariably classify units by income for a given year. From our standpoint, this is their major limitation. Because the data often do not permit many size-groupings, and because the difference between annual income incidence and longer-term income status has less effect if the number of classes is small and the limits of each class are wide, we use a few wide classes. This does not resolve the difficulty; and there are others due to the scantiness of data for long periods, inadequacy of the unit used—which is, at best, a family and very often a reporting unit—errors in the data, and so on through a long list. Consequently, the trends in the income structure can be discerned but dimly, and the results considered as preliminary informed guesses.

The data are for the United States, England, and Germany—a scant sample, but at least a starting point for some inferences concerning long-term changes in the presently developed countries. The general conclusion suggested is that the relative distribution of income, as measured by annual income incidence in rather broad classes, has been moving toward equality—with these trends partic-

*From Simon Kuznets, "Economic Growth and Income Inequality," *American Economic Review* 45 (March 1955): 1–8, 16–19. Reprinted by permission.

ularly noticeable since the 1920's but beginning perhaps in the period before the first world war.

Let me cite some figures, all for income before direct taxes, in support of this impression. In the United States, in the distribution of income among families (excluding single individuals), the shares of the two lowest quintiles rise from 13 1/2 per cent in 1929 to 18 per cent in the years after the second world war (average of 1944, 1946, 1947, and 1950); whereas the share of the top quintile declines from 55 to 44 per cent, and that of the top 5 per cent from 31 to 20 per cent. In the United Kingdom, the share of the top 5 per cent of units declines from 46 per cent in 1880 to 43 per cent in 1910 or 1913, to 33 per cent in 1929, to 31 per cent in 1938, and to 24 per cent in 1947; the share of the lower 85 per cent remains fairly constant between 1880 and 1913, between 41 and 43 per cent, but then rises to 46 per cent in 1929 and 55 per cent in 1947. In Prussia income inequality increases slightly between 1875 and 1913—the shares of the top quintile rising from 48 to 50 per cent, of the top 5 per cent from 26 to 30 per cent; the share of the lower 60 per cent, however, remains about the same. In Saxony, the change between 1880 and 1913 is minor: the share of the two lowest quintiles declines from 15 to 14 1/2 per cent; that of the third quintile rises from 12 to 13 per cent, of the fourth quintile from 16 1/2 to about 18 per cent; that of the top quintile declines from 56 1/2 to 54 1/2 per cent, and of the top 5 per cent from 34 to 33 per cent. In Germany as a whole, relative income inequality drops fairly sharply from 1913 to the 1920's, apparently due to decimation of large fortunes and property incomes during the war and inflation; but then begins to return to prewar levels during the depression of the 1930's.[1]

Even for what they are assumed to represent, let alone as approximations to shares in distributions by secular income levels, the data are such that differences of two or three percentage points cannot be assigned significance. One must judge by the general weight and consensus of the evidence— which unfortunately is limited to a few countries. It justifies a tentative impression of constancy in the relative distribution of income before taxes, followed by some narrowing of relative income inequality after the first world war—or earlier.

Three aspects of this finding should be stressed. First, the data are for income before direct taxes and exclude contributions by government (e.g., relief and free assistance). It is fair to argue that both the proportion and progressivity of direct taxes and the proportion of total income of individuals accounted for by government assistance to the less privileged economic groups have grown during recent decades. This is certainly true of the United States and the United Kingdom, but in the case of Germany is subject to further examination. It follows that the distribution of income after direct taxes and including free contributions by government would show an even greater narrowing of inequality in developed countries with size distributions of pretax, ex-government-benefits income similar to those for the United States and the United Kingdom.

Second, such stability or reduction in the inequality of the percentage shares was accompanied by significant rises in real income per capita. The countries now classified as developed have enjoyed rising per capita incomes except during catastrophic periods such as years of active world conflict. Hence, if the shares of groups classified by their annual income position can be viewed as approximations to shares of groups classified by their secular income levels, a constant percentage share of a given group means that its per capita real income is rising at the same rate as the average for all units in the country; and a reduction in inequality of the shares means that the per capita income of the lower-income groups is rising at a more rapid rate than the per capita income of the upper-income groups.

The third point can be put in the form of a question. Do the distributions by annual incomes properly reflect trends in distribution by secular incomes? As technology and economic performance

[1]The following sources were used in calculating the figures cited:

United States. For recent years we used *Income Distribution by Size, 1944–1950* (Washington, 1953) and Selma Goldsmith and others, "Size Distribution of Income Since the Mid-Thirties," *Rev. Econ. Stat.*, Feb. 1954, XXXVI, 1–32; for 1929, the Brookings Institution data as adjusted in Simon Kuznets, *Shares of Upper Groups in Income and Savings* (New York, 1953), p. 220.

United Kingdom. For 1938 and 1947, Dudley Seers, The *Levelling of Income Since 1938* (Oxford, 1951) p. 39; for 1929, Colin Clark, *National Income and Outlay* (London, 1937) Table 47, p. 109; for 1880, 1910, and 1913, A. Bowley, *The Change in the Distribution of the National Income, 1880–1913* (Oxford, 1920).

Germany. For the constituent areas (Prussia, Saxony and others) for years before the first world war, based on S. Prokopovich, *National Income of Western European Countries*

(published in Moscow in the 1920's). Some summary results are given in Prokopovich, "The Distribution of National Income," *Econ. Jour.*, March 1926, XXXVI, 69–82. See also, "Das Deutsche Volkseinkommen vor und nach dem Kriege," *Einzelschrift zur Stat. des Deutschen Reichs*, no. 24 (Berlin, 1932), and W. S. and E. S. Woytinsky, *World Population and Production* (New York, 1953) Table 192, p. 709.

rise to higher levels, incomes are less subject to transient disturbances, not necessarily of the cyclical order that can be recognized and allowed for by reference to business cycle chronology, but of a more irregular type. If in the earlier years the economic fortunes of units were subject to greater vicissitudes—poor crops for some farmers, natural calamity losses for some nonfarm business units—if the over-all proportion of individual entrepreneurs whose incomes were subject to such calamities, more yesterday but some even today, was larger in earlier decades, these earlier distributions of income would be more affected by transient disturbances. In these earlier distributions the temporarily unfortunate might crowd the lower quintiles and depress their shares unduly, and the temporarily fortunate might dominate the top quintile and raise its share unduly—proportionately more than in the distributions for later years. If so, distributions by longer-term average incomes might show less reduction in inequality than do the distributions by annual incomes; they might even show an opposite trend.

One may doubt whether this qualification would upset a narrowing of inequality as marked as that for the United States, and in as short a period as twenty-five years. Nor is it likely to affect the persistent downward drift in the spread of the distributions in the United Kingdom. But I must admit a strong element of judgment in deciding how far this qualification modifies the finding of long-term stability followed by reduction in income inequality in the few developed countries for which it is observed or is likely to be revealed by existing data. The important point is that the qualification is relevant; it suggests need for further study if we are to learn much from the available data concerning the secular income structure; and such study is likely to yield results of interest in themselves in their bearing upon the problem of trends in temporal instability of income flows to individual units or to economically significant groups of units in different sectors of the national economy. . . .

II. An Attempt at Explanation

. . . An invariable accompaniment of growth in developed countries is the shift away from agriculture, a process usually referred to as industrialization and urbanization. The income distribution of the total population, in the simplest model, may therefore be viewed as a combination of the income distributions of the rural and of the urban populations. What little we know of the structures of these two component income distributions reveals that: (a) the average per capita income of the rural population is usually lower than that of the urban; (b) inequality in the percentage shares within the distribution for the rural population is somewhat narrower than in that for the urban population—even when based on annual income; and this difference would probably be wider for distributions by secular income levels. Operating with this simple model, what conclusions do we reach? First, all other conditions being equal, the increasing weight of urban population means an increasing share for the more unequal of the two component distributions. Second, the relative difference in per capita income between the rural and urban populations does not necessarily drift downward in the process of economic growth: indeed, there is some evidence to suggest that it is stable at best, and tends to widen because per capita productivity in urban pursuits increases more rapidly than in agriculture. If this is so, inequality in the total income distribution should increase. . . .

We deal with two sectors: agriculture (A) and all others (B). . . . It seems most plausible to assume that in earlier periods of industrialization, even when the nonagricultural population was still relatively small in the total, its income distribution was more unequal than that of the agricultural population. This would be particularly so during the periods when industrialization and urbanization were proceeding apace and the urban population was being swelled, and fairly rapidly, by immigrants—either from the country's agricultural areas or from abroad. Under these conditions, the urban population would run the full gamut from low-income positions of recent entrants to the economic peaks of the established top-income groups. The urban income inequalities might be assumed to be far wider than those for the agricultural population which was organized in relatively small individual enterprises (large-scale units were rarer then than now).

If we grant the assumption of wider inequality of distribution in sector B, the shares of the lower-income brackets should have shown a downward trend. Yet the earlier summary of empirical evidence indicates that during the last 50 to 75 years there has been no widening in income inequality in the developed countries but, on the contrary, some narrowing within the last two to four decades. It follows that the intrasector distribution—either for sector A or for sector B—must have shown sufficient narrowing of inequality to offset the increase called for by the factors discussed.

This narrowing in inequality, the offsetting rise

in the shares of the lower brackets, most likely occurred in the income distribution for the urban groups, in sector B. While it may also have been present in sector A, it would have had a more limited effect on the inequality in the countrywide income distribution because of the rapidly diminishing weight of sector A in the total. Nor was such a narrowing of income inequality in agriculture likely: with industrialization, a higher level of technology permitted larger-scale units and, in the United States for example, sharpened the contrast between the large and successful business farmers and the subsistence sharecroppers of the South. Furthermore, since we accept the assumption of *initially* narrower inequality in the internal distribution of income in sector A than in sector B, any significant reduction in inequality in the former is less likely than in the latter.

Hence we may conclude that the major offset to the widening of income inequality associated with the shift from agriculture and the countryside to industry and the city must have been a rise in the income share of the lower groups within the nonagricultural sector of the population. This provides a lead for exploration in what seems to me a most promising direction: consideration of the pace and character of the economic growth of the urban population, with particular reference to the relative position of lower-income groups. Much is to be said for the notion that once the early turbulent phases of industrialization and urbanization had passed, a variety of forces converged to bolster the economic position of the lower-income groups within the urban population. The very fact that after a while, an increasing proportion of the urban population was "native," i.e., born in cities rather than in the rural areas, and hence more able to take advantage of the possibilities of city life in preparation for the economic struggle, meant a better chance for organization and adaptation, a better basis for securing greater income shares than was possible for the newly "immigrant" population coming from the countryside or from abroad. The increasing efficiency of the older, established urban population should also be taken into account. Furthermore, in democratic societies the growing political power of the urban lower-income groups led to a variety of protective and supporting legislation, much of it aimed to counteract the worst effects of rapid industrialization and urbanization and to support the claims of the broad masses for more adequate shares of the growing income of the country. Space does not permit the discussion of demographic, political, and social considerations that could be brought to

bear to explain the offsets to any declines in the shares of the lower groups, declines otherwise deducible from the trends suggested in the numerical illustration.

III. Other Trends Related to Those in Income Inequality

One aspect of the conjectural conclusion just reached deserves emphasis because of its possible interrelation with other important elements in the process and theory of economic growth. The scanty empirical evidence suggests that the narrowing of income inequality in the developed countries is relatively recent and probably did not characterize the earlier stages of their growth. Likewise, the various factors that have been suggested above would explain stability and narrowing in income inequality in the later rather than in the earlier phases of industrialization and urbanization. Indeed, they would suggest widening inequality in these early phases of economic growth, especially in the older countries where the emergence of the new industrial system had shattering effects on long-established pre-industrial economic and social institutions. This timing characteristic is particularly applicable to factors bearing upon the lower-income groups: the dislocating effects of the agricultural and industrial revolutions, combined with the "swarming" of population incident upon a rapid decline in death rates and the maintenance or even rise of birth rates, would be unfavorable to the relative economic position of lower-income groups. Furthermore, there may also have been a preponderance in the earlier periods of factors favoring maintenance or increase in the shares of top-income groups: in so far as their position was bolstered by gains arising out of new industries, by an unusually rapid rate of creation of new fortunes, we would expect these forces to be relatively stronger in the early phases of industrialization than in the later when the pace of industrial growth slackens.

One might thus assume a long swing in the inequality characterizing the secular income structure: widening in the early phases of economic growth when the transition from the pre-industrial to the industrial civilization was most rapid; becoming stabilized for a while; and then narrowing in the later phases. This long secular swing would be most pronounced for older countries where the dislocation effects of the earlier phases of modern economic growth were most conspicuous; but it might be found also in the "younger" countries like the United States, if the period preceding marked industrialization could be compared with the early phases of industrialization, and if the latter could be compared with the subsequent phases of greater maturity.

If there is some evidence for assuming this long swing in relative inequality in the distribution of income before direct taxes and excluding free benefits from government, there is surely a stronger case for assuming a long swing in inequality of income net of direct taxes and including government benefits. Progressivity of income taxes and, indeed, their very importance characterize only the more recent phases of development of the presently developed countries; in narrowing income inequality they must have accentuated the downward phase of the long swing, contributing to the reversal of trend in the secular widening and narrowing of income inequality.

No adequate empirical evidence is available for checking this conjecture of a long secular swing in income inequality;[2] nor can the phases be dated precisely. However, to make it more specific, I would place the early phase in which income inequality might have been widening, from about 1780 to 1850 in England; from about 1840 to 1890, and particularly from 1870 on in the United States; and, from the 1840's to the 1890's in Germany. I would put the phase of narrowing income inequality somewhat later in the United States and Germany than in England—perhaps beginning with the first world war in the former and in the last quarter of the 19th century in the latter.

---

[2]Prokopovich's data on Prussia, from the source cited in footnote 1, indicate a substantial widening in income inequality in the early period. The share of the lower 90 per cent of the population declines from 73 per cent in 1854 to 65 per cent in 1875; the share of the top 5 per cent rises from 21 to 25 per cent. But I do not know enough about the data for the early years to evaluate the reliability of the finding.

Selection VIII.A.2. Inequality, Poverty, and Development*

1. Introduction

The relationship between the distribution of income and the process of development is one of the oldest subjects of economic enquiry. Classical economic theory accorded it a central position in analysing the dynamics of economic systems, and while this pre-eminence was somewhat obscured in the heyday of neoclassical theory, in recent years it has again come to occupy the center stage of development economics. The purpose of this paper is to explore the nature of this relationship on the basis of cross country data on income inequality. The use of cross country data for the analysis of what are essentially dynamic processes raises a number of familiar problems. Ideally, such processes should be examined in an explicitly historical context for particular countries. Unfortunately, time series data on the distribution of income, over any substantial period, are simply not available for most developing countries. For the present, therefore, empirical investigation in this field must perforce draw heavily on cross country experience.

The results presented in this paper are based on a sample of 60 countries including 40 developing countries, 14 developed countries and 6 socialist countries. In the established tradition of cross country analysis, the approach adopted is essentially exploratory. We have used multivariate regression analysis to estimate cross country relationships between the income shares of different percentile groups and selected variables reflecting aspects of the development process which are likely to influence income inequality.[1] The estimated equations are then used as a basis for broad generalisations about the relationship between income distribution and development. The difficulties inherent in this methodology are well known, although all too often ignored. It is self-evident that the relationships thus identified are primarily associational. They do not necessarily establish the nature of the underlying causal mechanism at work

for the simple reason that quite different causal mechanisms might generate the same observed relationship between selected variables. Such alternative mechanisms (or hypotheses) are observationally equivalent in the sense that our estimated equations do not always permit us to choose between them.

The cross country relationships presented in this paper must be viewed in this perspective. We should treat them as "stylised facts" which can be observed, but which still need to be explained, by an appropriate theory. The documentation of such "stylised facts" is obviously not the same thing as the development of a tried and tested theory, but it may contribute to the development of such a theory in two ways. Firstly, the observed relationships may suggest hypotheses about the nature of the underlying causal mechanisms at work, which then need to be further tested and fashioned into a broader theory. Secondly, they provide yardsticks for verifying theories of distribution and development by defining the observed "behaviour" that such theories must explain.

What, then, do we know of the "stylised facts" about income distribution and development? A logical point of departure for our investigation is the hypothesis, originally advanced by Kuznets (1955, 1963), that the secular behavior of inequality follows an inverted "U-shaped" pattern with inequality first increasing and then decreasing with development. . . .

2. Kuznets' Hypothesis: The "U-shaped Curve"

We begin by documenting the evidence for Kuznets' hypothesis that inequality tends to widen in the early stages of development, with a reversal of this tendency in the later stages. Following convention, we have tested this hypothesis by taking the per capita GNP of each country (in US$ at 1965–1971 prices) as a summary measure of its level of development and including it as an explanatory variable in regression equations in which the income share of different percentile groups is taken as the dependent variable.

The cross country regressions provide a substantial measure of support for the hypothesis that there is a U-shaped pattern in the secular behaviour of inequality. Table 1 reports the estimated equations describing the relationship between income shares of five different percentile groups (the

*From Montek S. Ahluwalia, "Inequality, Poverty, and Development," *Journal of Development Economics* 3 (December 1976): 307–312. Reprinted by permission.

[1]We have used income shares as the dependent variables instead of summary indices of inequality such as the Gini coefficient because this permits us to focus on the impact of the development process over different ranges of the income distribution. The Gini coefficient is also a relatively insensitive measure and its limited variation across countries makes it difficult to identify statistically significant relationships. See, for example, Papanek (1976).

Table 1. The Kuznets Curve

Dependent variable Income shares of:	Estimated coefficients on explanatory variables[a]				$\bar{R}^2$	F	D.W.[b]	Turning point per capita GNP US$ (1965–71)
	Constant	Log per capita GNP	[Log per capita GNP]^2	Socialist Dummy				
(A) Full sample								
(1) Top 20 percent	−57.58 (2.11)	89.95 (4.48)	−17.56 (4.88)	−20.15 (6.83)	0.58	27.9	2.05	364
(2) Middle 40 percent	87.03 (4.81)	−45.59 (3.43)	9.25 (3.88)	8.21 (4.20)	0.47	18.6	2.08	291
(3) Lowest 60 percent	119.4 (5.85)	−73.52 (4.90)	14.06 (5.23)	17.52 (7.95)	0.61	31.4	1.97	412
(4) Lowest 40 percent	70.57 (5.38)	−44.38 (4.61)	8.31 (4.82)	11.95 (8.45)	0.59	29.8	2.04	468
(5) Lowest 20 percent	27.31 (4.93)	−16.97 (3.71)	3.06 (3.74)	5.54 (8.28)	0.54	24.3	1.93	593
(B) Developing countries only								
(1) Top 20 percent	−99.74 (1.56)	123.80 (2.35)	−24.18 (2.26)		0.12	3.6	2.24	363
(2) Middle 40 percent	92.93 (2.12)	−49.13 (1.36)	9.65 (1.32)		0.01	1.4	2.19	351
(3) Lowest 60 percent	171.50 (3.79)	−116.40 (3.12)	22.72 (2.99)		0.22	6.5	2.20	364
(4) Lowest 40 percent	106.80 (3.83)	−74.69 (3.25)	14.53 (3.10)		0.24	7.2	2.20	371
(5) Lowest 20 percent	44.15 (3.43)	−31.33 (2.96)	6.07 (2.81)		0.22	6.3	1.98	381

[a] t-statistics in parentheses.

[b] In estimating these equations the observations were entered in ascending order of per capita GNP. The Durbin-Watson statistic therefore gives some idea of the pattern of residuals with this ordering. The lack of serial correlation of residuals in the above equations provides some reassurance that the quadratic formulation captures the underlying nonlinearity reasonably well.

top 20 percent, the next or "middle" 40 percent, the lowest 60 percent, the lowest 40 percent and the lowest 20 percent) and the logarithm of per capita GNP.[2] Two equations are reported for each income share, one estimated from the full sample of 60 countries and the other estimated from the restricted sample of 40 developing countries only. For the full sample, we have included a dummy variable for the socialist countries in order to take account of the much higher degree of equality observed in these countries. The results obtained can be summarised as follows:

(*i*) Taking the results from the full sample to begin with, there is clear evidence of a nonmonotonic relationship between inequality and the level of development. The estimated equations test for a quadratic relationship with the logarithm of per capita GNP. We find that in all cases, both terms of the quadratic are significant[3] and the coefficients have the appropriate opposite signs to generate the U-shaped pattern hypothesised by Kuznets. Income shares of all percentile groups except the top 20 percent first decline and then increase as per capita GNP rises. Income shares of the top 20 percent display a corresponding opposite pattern.

(*ii*) The turning point for income shares implied by the estimated equations are also reported in table 1. It is interesting to note that this turning point occurs at different levels of per capita GNP for different income groups. In the case of the full sample, the turning point for the income share of the top 20 percent occurs at per capita GNP levels of US\$ 364 (for the economy as a whole) after which the income share of this group begins to decline. However, the income shares of the middle 40 percent appear to improve after a per capita GNP level of US\$ 291 is reached. As shown in table 1, the turning point of income shares shifts systematically further out as we go down the percentile groups, with the lowest 20 percent having to wait until per capita GNP levels of about \$600 are reached. Taking these estimates at face value (i.e. ignoring the question whether these estimated differences are significant), the cross section evidence suggests that the reversal of the "deteriorat-

ing phase" of relative inequality begins fairly early, first for the middle income group and much later for the lower income groups. It appears that if there is a "trickle down" process, then it takes substantially longer to reach the bottom!

(*iii*) The basic pattern described in (*i*) and (*ii*) above can also be discerned in the equations estimated from the restricted sample of 40 developing countries, with slight differences. Except for the equation explaining income shares of the middle 40 percent, the coefficients on both terms in the quadratic are again significant and have the same sign patterns as in the full sample, indicating a U-shaped pattern in the income shares of the lower income groups offset by an opposite pattern in the income shares of the top 20 percent. The absolute magnitudes of the estimated coefficients in these equations are, however, somewhat different, implying that there are differences in the shape of the Kuznets' curve obtained in the two cases. The exclusion of the developed countries and socialist countries from the sample has the effect of (a) shifting the turning point of the Kuznets' curve slightly inwards and (b) increasing the steepness of the observed U-shape in both phases. The extent of the shift can be seen in fig. 1, which compares the curve of estimated income shares for the lowest 40 percent at different levels of per capita GNP from eq. (A.4), with the curve of estimated shares from eq. (B.4), which includes developing countries only. We note that the improvement in relative income shares in the later phases of development appears markedly more modest if we look at the full sample than at the reduced sample of developing countries only. This is because the quadratic formulation forces a symmetry of shape with respect to the logarithm of per capita GNP and this allows the equations for the restricted sample to fit a steeper U curve in conformity with the steepness observed over the \$75–500 range, which is where most of the developing countries are concentrated. By contrast, the equation for the full sample is forced to fit a somewhat less steep curve to reflect the relatively modest improvement in equality observed between the middle income countries at the bottom of the U and the developed countries of today.

(*iv*) A major problem in interpreting the U shape revealed in cross country data is the possibility that it may be generated solely by the fact that the middle income range is dominated by countries with particular characteristics which generate high inequality. If so, the U shape has little relevance to the long-term prospect facing the low income countries of today, unless these countries share the same characteristics. Thus it is sometimes argued that the

---

[2] The logarithmic transformation gives equal weight to equal proportional differences in GNP in measuring "levels of development." This has an intuitive appeal since growth occurs at a compound rate over time.

[3] Throughout this paper the term significant will be used to indicate that the estimated coefficients are significantly different from zero with the sign indicated at least at the 10 percent level for a two-tailed test. The critical value of *t* for this level of significance is 1.68 for our sample size.

Figure 1

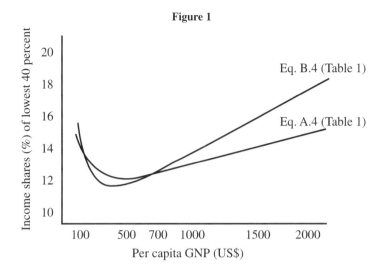

U shape simply reflects the concentration in the middle income range of Latin American countries, which display greater inequality because of particular historical and structural characteristics not applicable to others. We have tested for this 'Latin America effect' by including a dummy variable for the Latin American countries in each of the equations (A.1)–(A.4). We find that the coefficient on this dummy variable is insignificant in all cases and its inclusion leaves both the sign pattern and the significance of the coefficients on the income quadratic largely unaffected.

References

Kuznets, S., 1955, Economic growth and income inequality, American Economic Review, March.

Kuznets, S., 1963, Quantitative aspects of the economic growth of nations: VIII distribution of income by size, Economic Development and Cultural Change, January.

Papanek, G.F., 1976, Economic growth, income distribution, and the political process in less developed countries, Paper presented at a Symposium on Income Distribution and Economic Inequality, June, Bad Homburg, West Germany.

Selection VIII.A.3. Growth and Income Distribution*

Hypothesis: Growth tends to raise inequality in the low income countries and to reduce inequality in the high income countries.

Discussion and Evidence: The pathbreaking work relating inequality and economic growth to a country's level of economic development is, of course, by Simon Kuznets. In Kuznets (1955), he measured inequality in five countries and found greater inequality in the developed countries than in the less developed countries. This result was sustained in subsequent work on ever-larger samples of countries, first by Kravis (1960) and then by Kuznets (1963). Both Kuznets and Oshima (1962) reasoned that the less developed countries had greater equality in their earlier stages of development, because everyone was thought to be more or less equally poor. From this emerged the hypothesis of the so-called "Kuznets curve"—the idea that income inequality increases in the early stages of economic development and decreases in the later stages, thus tracing out an inverted-U curve.

The Kuznets curve has received support in cross-sectional studies by Paukert (1973), Cline (1975), Chenery and Syrquin (1975), Ahluwalia (1976), and Papanek and Kyn (1987), among others. However, in a careful econometric study allowing for various functional forms, Anand and Kanbur (1986) found that the cross-sectional data were best fit by a *U-shaped* curve, not an inverted-U. In any event, regardless of which cross-sectional pattern is in fact correct, the hypothesis that growth raises inequality in low income countries

and lowers it in higher income countries is a statement about change over time and is properly tested using intertemporal data.

Data on changes in inequality over time in various countries' development experiences have not, until now, been plentiful enough to permit Hypothesis 6 to be tested intertemporally. Now, however, we have enough data to be able to divide the developing countries into higher and lower income groups and compare changes in the two groups' inequality over time.

To determine the effect of growth on inequality in the high income and low income groups, a spell is included here if it is a growth spell (i.e., spells of economic decline are omitted). The division between high income and low income was set at U.S. $728 in 1980 prices; this is the level of GNP in 1980 prices at which income inequality was found in the cross-sectional study by Paukert (1973) to have peaked.[1]

Table 1 reports the findings. In the low-income countries, ten out of twenty-one growth spells (48%) were marked by an increase in inequality. In the high-income countries, it was nine out of twenty-two (42%). These two percentages are very close and not significantly different from one another. Thus:

Finding: inequality increases with growth as frequently in the low-income countries as in the high-income countries. There is *no* tendency for inequality to increase more in the early stages of economic development than in the later stages.

*From Gary S. Fields, "Growth and Income Distribution." [From George Psacharopoulos, ed., *Essays on Poverty, Equity, and Growth* (Oxford: Pergamon, 1991), 41–45.] Reprinted by permission.

[1]Paukert's turning point was U.S.$300 in 1965 prices. Prices were inflated using the U.S. inflation rate reported in *World Tables 1987.*

Table 1. Change in Gini Coefficient in High Income and Low Income Countries, Growth Spell Analysis

Part A   Low-Income Countries

Growth Spells in Which Gini Coefficient Increased (n = 10):

Bangladesh, 1973/74–1976/77
Indonesia, 1970–1976
Indonesia, 1976–1978
Pakistan, 1971/72–1979
Pakistan, 1979–1984
Sri Lanka, 1973–1978/79
Sri Lanka, 1978/79–1981/82
Thailand, 1962/63–1968/69
Thailand, 1968/69–1975/76
Thailand, 1975/76–1981

Growth Spells in Which Gini Coefficient Decreased (n = 11):

Bangladesh, 1976/77–1981/82
Egypt, 1964/65–1974/75
Indonesia, 1967–1970
Indonesia, 1978–1980
Pakistan, 1963/64–1966/67
Pakistan, 1966/67–1968/69
Pakistan, 1968/69–1969/70
Pakistan, 1969/70–1970/71
Philippines, 1965–1971
Philippines, 1971–1975
Sri Lanka, 1963–1973

Part B   High-Income Countries

Growth Spells in Which Gini Coefficient Increased (n = 9):

Bahamas, 1977–1979
Brazil, 1970–1972
Costa Rica, 1971–1977
Hong Kong, 1976–1981
Jamaica, 1968–1973
Korea, 1970–1976
Malaysia, 1970–1976
Mexico, 1958–1963
Mexico, 1963–1969

Growth Spells in Which Gini Coefficient Decreased (n = 10):

Bahamas, 1975/1977
Brazil, 1976–1978
Costa Rica, 1977–1979
Hong Kong, 1966–1971
Korea, 1976–1982
Malaysia, 1976–1979
Mexico, 1969–1977
Singapore, 1972/73–1977/78
Trinidad and Tobago, 1971/72–1975/76
Turkey, 1968–1973

Growth Spells in Which Gini Coefficient Was Unchanged (n = 3):

Brazil, 1978–80
Chile, 1968–1971
Hong Kong, 1971–1976

Note: The dividing line between high income and low income is U.S.$728; see text for explanation.

For determining whether a country is high income or low income-GNP per capita taken from *IMF Financial Statistics Supplement No. 8.*

References

Ahluwalia, Montek, "Inequality, Poverty and Development," *Journal of Development Economics,* 1976.

Anand, Sudhir, and Ravi Kanbur, "Inequality and Development: A Critique," Paper prepared for the Yale University Economic Growth Center 25th Anniversary Symposium on The State of Development Economics: Progress and Perspectives, 1986.

Chenery, Hollis and M. Syrquin, *Patterns of Development, 1950–1970.* (New York: Oxford University Press, 1975).

Cline, William, "Distribution and Development: A Survey of the Literature," *Journal of Development Economics,* 1975.

IMF, *International Financial Statistics Supplement No. 8.*

Kravis, Irving, "International Differences in the Distribution of Income," *Review of Economics and Statistics,* November, 1960.

Kuznets, Simon, "Economic Growth and Income inequality," *American Economic Review,* March, 1955.

Kuznets, Simon, "Quantitative Aspects of the Economic Growth of Nations: VIII, Distribution of Income by Size," *Economic Development and Cultural Change,* January, 1963, Part 2.

Oshima, Harry, "The International Comparison of Size Distribution of Family Incomes with Special Reference to Asia," *Review of Economics and Statistics,* November, 1962.

Papanek, Gustav F. and Oldrich Kyn, "Flattening the Kuznets Curve: The Consequences for Income Distribution of Development Strategy, Government Intervention, Income and the Rate of Growth," *The Pakistan Development Review,* Spring, 1987.

Paukert, Felix, "Income Distribution at Different Levels of Development: A Survey of Evidence," *International Labour Review,* August-September, 1973.

Selection VIII.A.4. A Note on the U Hypothesis Relating Income Inequality and Economic Development*

The purpose of this note is to demonstrate that the U hypothesis can be derived from a very simple model with a minimum of economic assumptions. One need only assume that the economy can be divided into two sectors with different sectoral income distributions and that there is a monotonic increase in the relative population of one of the sectors over time. . . .

Assume that the economy is divided into two sectors with different income distributions. The *log* mean and *log* variance of income in the two sectors are given by Y_1 and Y_2 and σ_1^2 and σ_2^2, respectively. Define the population shares of the two sectors as W_1 and W_2 with:

$$W_1 + W_2 = 1 \tag{1}$$

The overall *log* mean income is given by:

$$Y = W_1 Y_1 + W_2 Y_2 \tag{2}$$

and the overall *log* variance is given by:

$$\sigma^2 = W_1 \sigma_1^2 + W_2 \sigma_2^2 + W_1 (Y_1 - Y)^2 + W_2 (Y_2 - Y)^2 \tag{3}$$

The *log* variance is itself an increasing measure of income inequality. One need not use *log* means and *log* variances, but they are convenient since the *log* variance is a commonly used inequality measure. The arithmetic mean and variance would also do—the algebra is exactly the same.

Assuming that the within-sector distributions remain unchanged over time (σ_1^2, σ_2^2, Y_1, and Y_2 are constant), then from equation (3) inequality is a function only of sectoral population shares and overall *log* mean income. By equation (2), the overall *log* mean is itself a function of sectoral population shares.

Assume that sector 1 is the sector whose relative

*From Sherman Robinson, "A Note on the U Hypothesis Relating Income Inequality and Economic Development," *American Economic Review* 66 (June 1976): 437–438. Reprinted by permission.

population share is increasing. Then, substituting (1) and (2) into (3) and doing a bit of algebra, one finally gets:

$$\sigma^2 = AW_1^2 + BW_1 + C \tag{4}$$

where
$$A = -(Y_1 - Y_2)^2$$
$$B = (\sigma_1^2 - \sigma_2^2) + (Y_1 - Y_2)^2$$
$$C = \sigma_2^2$$

If one assumes that the *log* mean incomes are different in the two sectors, then inequality is a quadratic function of W_1. Since $A < 0$, the parabola has a maximum. As W_1 increases, inequality first increases, reaches a maximum, then decreases—precisely the U hypothesis.

There is one possible problem. Since by assumption $0 \le W_1 \le 1$, it is possible that the maximum value of σ^2 occurs for a value of W_1 outside the zero to one range. Setting the first derivative of (4) equal to zero, the maximum value of σ^2 occurs when W_1 is equal to $\hat{W}_1$:

$$\hat{W}_1 = \frac{\sigma_1^2 - \sigma_2^2}{2 \cdot (Y_1 - Y_2)^2} + 1/2 \tag{5}$$

Thus, the more equal are the *log* variances, and the more different are the *log* mean incomes, the closer is $\hat{W}_1$ to 1/2. . . .

Some properties of these equations are interesting. The U hypothesis in no way depends on which sector has the higher income. If total income is to rise then Y_1 must be greater than Y_2, but the U hypothesis depends only on their being different. It also does not matter which sector has the more unequal distribution of within sector income. The difference between σ_1^2 and σ_2^2 affects $\hat{W}_1$, but not the existence of the U. If $\sigma_1^2 < \sigma_2^2$, then it will take longer for the distribution to start becoming more equal (for a given rate of change of sector population shares), but the turning point exists. It is interesting that even if people are moved from a sector with relatively more equality to one with less, the overall distribution will still become more equal.

Selection VIII.A.5. Economic Development, Urban Underemployment, and Income Inequality*

1. Introduction

Economic development invariably involves a transfer of labour from the agricultural to the non-agricultural sector, a process that for the purposes of this paper will be identified with urbanization. This transfer appears to take place monotonically over time. A check of the share of economically active population engaged in agriculture as reported in the Food and Agriculture Organization *Production Yearbook* showed a decline in every year for which data were available for all except one (Ireland) of 121 countries checked.[1] Kuznets (1955) saw this labour transfer as having important consequences for the size distribution of income over time. He hypothesized that income inequality will increase during the early stages of development as population shifts from the agricultural sector, where he believed incomes are more equally distributed, to the urban sector, where he believed incomes are less equally distributed. During the later stages of development this force for inequality is more than offset, he supposed, by growing equality of income distribution *within* the urban sector, owing to better adaptation of the children of rural-urban migrants to city economic life and growing political power of urban lower-income groups to effect "protective and supportive legislation" (17). A graph of income inequality against the urbanization rate or per capita income would therefore have the shape of an inverted υ.

An important innovation in the formulation of Kuznets's hypothesis was made by Robinson (1976), who showed that, under the assumption of a constant difference between mean incomes in the rural and urban sectors, the inverted-υ result required neither that urban income be more unequally distributed than rural income nor that urban income inequality decline as the urban share of the population increased. Specifically he showed that, if the within sector income distributions remain constant, then overall inequality as measured by

the variance of the logarithms of income is a quadratic function of the share of the population in the urban sector, and it achieves its maximum (under reasonable empirical assumptions) for a share between zero and one. The same result was established by Knight (1976) and independently by Fields (1979) for the Gini coefficient for the case where the difference in incomes between the two sectors is the *only* source of inequality.[2]

Their results led both Knight and Fields to question the importance of the inverted-υ path of income inequality. Knight asks, "Should we be concerned about an increase in measured inequality [during the upswing of the inverted υ] if it simply reflects a relative transfer of people from low- to high-income groups or sectors? No-one is made worse off—total income is allowed to increase—and some of the poor are made better off" (172–3). Before we accept the process described in the quotation as pertaining to real-world economic development, however, we must look more deeply into the situation described by Robinson, Knight, and Fields (hereafter called RKF).

The RKF assumptions are based on the numerous studies of LCDs (see, e.g., Tidrick 1975) that have shown that wages for comparably skilled labour tend to be higher in "formal" urban jobs than in rural jobs by a margin that is too large to be attributed to measurement error (such as failure to correct for lower cost of living in rural areas). These studies formed the basis for new models of LDC labour markets, beginning with Todaro (1969) and Harris and Todaro (1970), that themselves are absent from the RKF framework. Like the RKF economy, the Harris–Todaro economy consists of two sectors, which they label agriculture and urban manufacturing. Harris and Todaro argued that the wage in the urban manufacturing sector is set above the competitive equilibrium wage by institutional forces, which may in practice include trade unions, governments (e.g., through

*From James E. Rauch, "Economic Development, Urban Underemployment, and Income Inequality," *Canadian Journal of Economics* 26 (November 1993): 901–904, 912–915. Reprinted by permission.

[1] I am referring to data for the years 1960, 1970, and 1975–84. In 1985 the FAO appears to have revised its definitions, since many countries show a dramatic increase in the agricultural share of the economically active population. The 121 countries are the market economies covered in the study of Summers and Heston (1988).

[2] Since reliable time series on income inequality spanning several decades exist for extremely few countries, the Kuznets hypothesis has been empirically tested using cross-country data on the assumption that cross-country and intertemporal "Kuznets curves" are identical. In the most recent study of which I am aware, Papanek and Kyn (1986) find a statistically significant quadratic relationship between the Gini coefficient measure of income inequality and the log of per capita GNP using 145 observations for eighty-three countries. Inclusion of other economic, social, and regional explanatory variables did not weaken this relationship.

minimum wage legislation enforced only in urban areas), or both acting together. The key insight of Todaro (1969), used again in a different form in Harris and Todaro (1970), is that unlike the situation in the RKF economy, the equilibrium involving the minimum urban wage is *not* one where there is full employment, with all urban manufacturing jobs filled, and the remainder of the labour force employed in agriculture at a wage lower than the original competitive equilibrium wage. Instead, this equilibrium involves an excess supply of workers in the urban sector, with the resulting unemployment or underemployment acting to equate *expected utility* between the rural and urban sectors. It is this equation that allows labour market equilibrium to exist in the presence of rural-urban wage differentials.

Surprisingly, the way this equation is formulated in Harris and Todaro (1970) and in most of the subsequent theoretical work based on their paper implies that, in effect, there is *no* wage inequality within the urban sector or between the urban and rural sectors. It is assumed that in equilibrium the rural wage is equated to the expected urban wage, where the latter equals the urban minimum wage times the ratio of urban employment to the total urban labour force. This assumption can be justified by the following characterization of the urban labour market. Suppose we interpret the static Harris–Todaro equilibrium as a steady state persisting indefinitely in time. Suppose further that the labour market reopens in every period, at the beginning of which workers are drawn at random from the total urban labour pool for the given number of urban manufacturing jobs. Workers not drawn are unemployed during that period. If the draws are independent, then by the Law of Large Numbers, workers are certain to earn on average the expected wage described above, which should therefore be equal to the certain rural wage in equilibrium. Obviously there is no inequality in *lifetime* wage income in this model.

More recent research into the nature of LDC labour markets has shown that upon arriving in the city some rural migrants immediately obtain jobs in the protected labour market, while others wind up in what has become known as the "informal sector," meaning small businesses and self-employment that escape government and union intervention. The latter group earns less than comparably skilled workers in the former group (Banerjee 1983). While there is some mobility over time from the informal to the formal (protected) sector, most informal sector workers view their situations as permanent (Sethuraman 1981). This more re-cent research suggests that it is the risk of long-term underemployment in the informal sector that equates expected utility between the urban and rural sectors and thus allows for labour market equilibrium. The risk is substantial, since according to the studies surveyed by Sethuraman (appendix table 4, 213), the share of the urban labour force in LDC cities engaged in the informal sector ranges from 19 to 69 per cent, with a mean of roughly 41 per cent. If we modify the Harris–Todaro model in this way, we wind up with three classes of wage earners: rural (agricultural) workers, urban formal-sector workers, and urban informal-sector workers. I will thus address the evolution of income inequality by examining how the relative sizes and incomes of these three groups change during the course of economic development.

It turns out that the log variance measure of inequality in this economy tends to follow an inverted υ. It rises when urbanization is low and consequent pressure on the land keeps rural incomes low, making agents willing to incur high risks of underemployment in the urban informal sector. It eventually falls after urbanization, and consequently rural incomes, has increased sufficiently to allow agents to make better than even bets in the industrial sector. This inverted υ in inequality is associated with another inverted υ in the share of the informal sector in the total labour force, the upswing of which is driven by the "Todaro paradox" that an increase in the number of urban manufacturing jobs may *increase* rather than decrease underemployment. . . .

2. Empirical Investigation of the Model: A Beginning

Is there evidence for my view of the causes of inverted-υ behaviour of income inequality? We need incomes data reported by agricultural, urban formal, and urban informal sectors for a number of countries and years. Unfortunately, incomes data disaggregated by formal versus informal sector have typically been collected as part of one-time surveys of particular urban areas rather than as part of ongoing nationwide censuses. Moreover, the definitions of the informal sector tend to vary from survey to survey. While it therefore appears that the accuracy of our model's description of inequality behaviour cannot be assessed empirically at the present time, the model makes other predictions that are necessary though not sufficient for this description to be accurate. If they are supported by the stylized facts, I can at least claim that further investigation of my inequality results as better data become available is a promising direction for future research.

Underlying my inequality results are results on labour market behaviour. In particular, two predictions concerning the behaviour of the informal sector that can be checked against data emerge from the analysis. First, the informal sector share of the urban labour force $(1 - N_a - N_m)/(1 - N_a)$ should decrease with the level of urbanization. . . . Second, the informal sector share of the total labour force or underemployment rate $1 - N_a - N_m$ should follow an inverted U with urbanization. To facilitate the following empirical discussion of these predictions, I denote by URB and UNDER the variables used to measure $1 - N_a$ and $1 - N_a - N_m$, respectively. The ratio $(1 - N_a - N_m)/(1 - N_a)$ is measured by UNDER/URB, which is given the mnemonic SHARE.

Unlike the incomes data we would like, there do exist data on UNDER and URB (and therefore SHARE) that were collected for many countries on a nationwide basis using standardized definitions. This apparently unique data set was collected by PREALC (1982) under the direction of Victor E. Tokman, a leading scholar of the informal sector. It is based on the decennial censuses taken by almost every Latin American country. The variables of interest to us are defined as follows. URB is the non-primary share of the economically active population. It is further disaggregated into the classifications formal, informal, and wage-earning domestic service. Workers are classified as informal if they are either self-employed or unpaid family help, excluding professionals and technicians. This definition of UNDER is more restrictive than we would like, since it excludes the many wage earners in firms small enough to be bypassed by unions and government regulation.[3] We simply have to assume that the ratio of those omitted from UNDER to those included does not vary in any systematic way with URB.

The PREALC data cover seventeen Latin American countries[4] for the years 1950, 1960, 1970, and 1980. Perhaps more troubling than the obvious limitation resulting from inclusion in our sample of only one region of the globe is the fact that all the countries covered are classified by the World Bank as either "lower-middle income" or "upper-

Table 1

Variable	Mean	Std Dev.	Minimum	Maximum
URB	50.9	16.6	18.9	84.4
UNDER	11.3	3.4	4.5	20.4
SHARE	23.8	8.4	10.9	44.0

Note: All variables are expressed as percentages.

middle income": no countries classified as low income or high income are included. Presumably this truncation of the sample at the low and high ends decreases the likelihood of finding an inverted U in UNDER. Nevertheless, table 1 shows that there is substantial variation in the data. The reader may also note from table 1 that the mean of SHARE is substantially below the figure of roughly 41 per cent (cited in the introduction to this paper) computed from the surveys of LDC cities listed by Sethuraman (1981). This result can be partly explained by the undercounting of the informal sector mentioned above, since the survey definitions, though not standardized, were typically more inclusive than the PREALC definition. Moreover, if my hypothesis concerning the decline of SHARE with URB is correct, the difference may also be explained by the inclusion of observations for several low-income countries (accounting for seven out of thirty-two observations, with a mean SHARE of 48 per cent) in the Sethuraman sample.

As in all studies that have checked for the existence of an inverted U in income distribution data (see the extensive references in Papanek and Kyn 1986), I shall seek to establish the stylized facts by applying ordinary least squares regressions to pooled data, a procedure that may be less troubling when one is working with a relatively homogeneous sample of countries such as Latin America. Table 2 shows that both predictions of my model concerning labour market behaviour are strongly supported by the PREALC data. Particularly impressive is the performance of the quadratic specification of the dependence of the underemployment rate on urbanization compared with the naïve linear specification that assumes that the urban informal sector expands pari passu with the rest of the urban sector.[5] The quadratic results imply that the peak of the inverted U in the underemployment rate occurs when 61.0 per cent of the labour force has left the primary sector. If these results are representative of labour market behaviour in the world

[3]Two studies of Latin American cities cited in Portes et al. (1989, 17, 97) expand the definition of the urban informal sector to include wage workers without social security protection. This change causes a shift from the formal to the informal sector of 3.1 per cent of the urban labour force in Montevideo in 1983 and 11.8 per cent in Bogotá in 1984.

[4]The countries included are Argentina, Bolivia, Brazil, Chile, Colombia, Costa Rica, Dominican Republic, Ecuador, El Salvador, Guatemala, Honduras, Mexico, Nicaragua, Panama, Peru, Uruguay, and Venezuela.

[5]Including $(URB)^2$ in the SHARE equation leads to statistically insignificant coefficients on both explanatory variables and a lower adjusted R^2.

Table 2

Variable	Dependent variable: SHARE	Dependent variable: UNDER	
	Coefficient (*t*-value)	Coefficient (*t*-value)	Coefficient (*t*-value)
CONSTANT	38.9	8.2	−3.0
	(14.5)	(6.3)	(0.8)
URB	−0.30	0.061	0.52
	(5.93)	(2.52)	(3.51)
(URB)^2			−0.0043
			(3.13)
R^2	0.35	0.09	0.21
$\hat{\sigma}$	6.8	3.3	3.1

Note: Number of observations = 68.

as a whole, they hold out considerable promise for future empirical support of my model's predictions concerning the source of inverted-u behaviour of income inequality.

3. Conclusions: Interpreting Inverted-u Behaviour of Income Inequality

For reasons noted in the introduction to this paper, Fields (1987) proposes that for the purpose of measuring change in income inequality during the course of economic development we discard the traditional indices in favour of ones that do not have the inverted-u property under the hypothetical conditions of pure "modern-sector enlargement" (expansion of the urban sector in the presence of a fixed rural-urban income differential). Moore (1990) argues against Fields's proposal. The present paper suggests that both sides of this debate may be misguided because they are using an incomplete economic model where there is no equilibrium condition that determines the intersectoral allocation of the labour force. In the complete model, the rise and fall of income inequality as measured by the log variance are closely related to the rise and fall of the proportion of the labour force that falls into the poorest class, the underemployed. Far from being an unimportant artifact of traditional inequality indices, then, the inverted u reflects the rise and fall of urban slums and of the share of the population with disappointed expectations, which are phenomena of political as well as economic significance.

Perhaps surprisingly, the model can be seen as a complement to the human-capital-based explanation of income inequality associated with the Uni-

versity of Chicago. According to this school of thought, exemplified by the work of Becker and Tomes (1979), inequality among identically endowed individuals is generated over time by differences in "market luck," which parents can pass on to their children by investing in the children's human capital. Market luck is exactly the source of inequality in the model: the lucky wind up in the formal sector, while the unlucky wind up in the informal sector. Over time, market luck first becomes more important, as the movement from an agrarian to an industrial society opens up more opportunities for both success and failure, and later becomes less important, simply because rising incomes in the agricultural sector provide a "safety net" that allows everyone to make much safer bets in the industrial sector. From this point of view, then, market luck is the driving force behind the inverted u, and the advantage of the model over the human capital model of income inequality is its ability to endogenize market luck. Its disadvantage is its inability to incorporate "inheritance" of market luck through parental investment in children. Overcoming this disadvantage should be a subject for future research.

References

Banerjee, Biswajit (1983) "The role of the informal sector in the migration process: a test of probabilistic migration models and labour market segmentation for India." *Oxford Economic Papers* 35, 399–422

Becker, Gary S., and Nigel Tomes (1979) "An equilibrium theory of the distribution of income and intergenerational mobility." *Journal of Political Economy* 87, 1153–89

Fields, Gary S. (1979) "A welfare economic approach to growth and distribution in the dual economy." *Quarterly Journal of Economics* 93, 325–53

—— (1987) "Measuring inequality change in an economy with income growth." *Journal of Development Economics* 26, 357–74

Harris, John R., and Michael P. Todaro (1970) "Migration, unemployment, and development: a two-sector analysis." *American Economic Review* 60, 126–42

Knight, John B. (1976) "Explaining income distribution in less developed countries: a framework and an agenda." *Oxford Bulletin of Economics and Statistics* 38, 161–77

Kuznets, Simon (1955) "Economic growth and income inequality." *American Economic Review* 45, 1–28

Moore, Robert E. (1990) "Measuring inequality change in an economy with income growth: reassessment." *Journal of Development Economics* 32, 205–10

Papanek, Gustav F., and Oldrich Kyn (1986) "The effect on income distribution of development, the growth rate and economic strategy." *Journal of Development Economics* 23, 55–65

Portes, Alejandro, Manuel Castells, and Lauren A. Benton, eds. (1989) *The Informal Economy: Studies in Advanced and Less Developed Countries* (Baltimore: Johns Hopkins University Press)

PREALC (Programa Regional del Empleo para Amèrica Latina y el Caribe) (1982) *Mercado de Trabajo en Cifras, 1950–1980* (Santiago: Oficina International del Trabajo)

Robinson, Sherman (1976) "A note on the U hypothesis relating income inequality and economic development." *American Economic Review* 66, 437–40

Sethuraman, S.V., ed. (1981) *The Urban Informed Sector in Developing Countries* (Geneva: International Labour Office)

Summers, Robert, and Alan Heston (1988) "A new set of international comparisons of real product and price levels estimates for 130 countries, 1950–1985." *Review of Income and Wealth* 34, 1–25

Tidrick, Gene M. (1975) "Wage spillover and unemployment in a wage-gap economy: the Jamaican case." *Economic Development and Cultural Change* 23, 306–24

Todaro, Michael P. (1969) "A model of labor migration and urban unemployment in less developed countries." *American Economic Review* 59, 138–48

Comment VIII.A.1. The Informal Sector, Intraurban Inequality, and the Inverted U

As urbanization (*URB*) increases in the Rauch model, the informal sector share of the urban labor force (*SHARE*) falls, the informal sector share of the total labor force (*UNDER*) follows an inverted U, and inequality measured by the log variance also follows an inverted U. This Comment is intended to give the interested reader a better understanding of the sources of these results and the connections among them.

The labor market equilibrium condition in the Rauch model is that the expected utility from working in the agricultural sector is equal to the expected utility from working in the urban sector. This is analogous to the labor market equilibrium condition that holds in the Todaro and Harris–Todaro models of Chapter VI. Under the assumption of intertemporally log-linear utility (the same utility function used in Note III.1), this equilibrium condition boils down to an equality between the agricultural log wage and a weighted average of the log wages in urban informal and urban formal employment, where the weights are *SHARE* and 1 – *SHARE*, respectively. (This equality is consistent with a higher average wage in the urban sector measured in natural units.) It follows immediately that, since the population average log wage is equal across sectors, there is no contribution to the log variance measure of inequality from inequality between the agricultural and urban sectors. If the log variance measure of inequality follows an inverted U as the population is reallocated from one sector to the other, it cannot be because of changes in between-sector inequality as it was in Selection VIII.A.4 by Robinson.

As *URB* increases in the Rauch model the land-labor ratio in agriculture rises, increasing the marginal product of labor in agriculture and the agricultural wage. This is consistent with labor market equilibrium only if the weighted average log wage in the urban sector increases. This can only happen if *SHARE* (the weight on the smaller urban log wage) falls, because both the minimum wage enforced in urban formal employment and the self-employment wage of informal workers remain constant by assumption. The change in *UNDER* is then seen to be the result of two conflicting trends. On the one hand, holding *SHARE* constant the increase in *URB* must increase *UNDER*. On the other hand, *SHARE* falls as *URB* increases, tending to decrease *UNDER*. The first effect dominates when *URB* is low and the second effect dominates when *URB* is high, yielding an inverted U in *UNDER*. Intuitively, it is clear that the second effect must dominate when *URB* is sufficiently high because the agricultural wage must catch up to the urban formal wage, yielding *SHARE* equal to zero by the labor market equilibrium condition.

The same logic that leads to an inverted U in *UNDER* leads to an inverted U in the log variance measure of inequality in the Rauch model. Since between-sector inequality is zero, overall inequality is just a weighted average of inequalities within the rural and urban sectors, where the weights are the rural and urban population shares 1 – *URB* and *URB*, respectively.

Inequality within agriculture is zero but inequality within the urban sector is positive because of the difference in earnings between informally and formally employed workers. The change in overall inequality is then the result of the same two conflicting trends that determined the change in *UNDER*. Holding inequality within the urban sector constant, as *URB* increases overall inequality must increase because urban inequality is greater than rural inequality. Once *SHARE* shrinks below one-half, however, the further decline in *SHARE* as *URB* increases reduces inequality within the urban sector, tending to decrease overall inequality. This second effect eventually dominates the first effect, just as it did for *UNDER*. It can be shown, with an additional assumption on the agricultural production function, that the log variance measure of inequality cannot decline in the Rauch model until after *UNDER* declines.

VIII.B. THE IMPACT OF INCOME DISTRIBUTION ON DEVELOPMENT

Selection VIII.B.1. Distributive Politics and Economic Growth*

We attempt to determine whether initial inequality is a statistically significant predictor of long-term growth across countries.

Comparable data on wealth distribution for a large enough sample of countries do not exist. What we do have are distributional indicators on *income* and on *land*. With respect to income there exist several compilations of Gini coefficients and other indices drawn from national surveys [Jain 1975; Lecallion et al. 1984; Fields 1989]. Some countries have distributional indicators available for different time periods, but the intertemporal and cross-country comparability of these data is quite weak. Fields [1989] has recently reviewed the sources of income distribution estimates for 70 *developing* countries and has found that only 35 of them have data that satisfy minimum criteria of quality and comparability.[1] The problem of data quality is less acute for developed countries. Therefore, we define and use a "high quality sample" that includes all the OECD countries for which we have data (from Jain [1975]) and the developing countries chosen by Fields [1989].[2] In addition, we present results for a larger sample, which includes *all* countries for which we have distributional data. . . .

With respect to land distribution we are aware of only one compendium [Taylor and Hudson 1972], and this source provides the Gini coefficient of land distribution for 54 countries around 1960.[3] Land is only one component of wealth, and thus the Gini coefficient of land ownership is only a very imperfect proxy of a true measure of wealth distribution. . . . Since only Gini coefficients are available for land, we restrict the presentation of results to Gini coefficients for income as well. (However, we have also done work with quantile measures of income distribution and have reached very similar results; these additional results are available upon request.) The correlation coefficient between the land and income Gini's is 0.35 in the sample of 41 countries for which both indicators are available.

To avoid reverse causation from growth to distribution, we tried to limit the sample to countries for which we had Gini coefficients measured not too far beyond the beginning of the time horizon for growth. In the case of Gini coefficients for land, this did not prove to be a problem because the most recent data point comes from 1964 and the majority of Gini's date from before 1960. However, many of the earliest income Gini coefficients are measured in the 1960s, and some in the 1970s. . . . Throwing out all of these cases would have reduced our sample size significantly. We have dealt with the simultaneity problem in two ways: first, by running two-stage least squares regressions and instrumenting for the Gini coefficients,[4] and second, by running regressions for the 1970–1985 period as well as for the 1960–1985 period.

In addition to the Gini coefficients, we have included in our regressions two additional explanatory variables emphasized in the recent growth literature [Barro 1991]: (i) the initial level of per capita income and (ii) the primary school enrollment ratio. The first variable is entered to account for the possibility of convergence, and the second is a measure of the initial level of human capital. . . . Except for the Gini coefficients, all data are from Heston and Summers [1988] and Barro and Wolf [1989].

Table 1 shows our results for the 1960–1985 period. Columns (1) and (2) restrict the sample to countries for which income distribution data are more reliable: this is the high-quality sample described above. Columns (3) and (4) are the regressions for the larger sample of countries, where the previous sample is augmented by 24 additional developing countries. Columns (5)–(8) are the regressions that include the Gini coefficient for land,

*From Alberto Alesina and Dani Rodrik, "Distributive Politics and Economic Growth," *Quarterly Journal of Economics* 109 (May 1994): 479–484. Reprinted by permission.

[1]His four criteria are (i) the estimates must be based on an actual household survey or census; (ii) the survey or census must be national in coverage; (iii) the data must be tabulated in enough categories that a meaningful index can be calculated if one is not already published; and (iv) for more than one year to be included, the surveys must have been comparable. See Fields and Jakubson [1993, pp. 3–4].

[2]Of the 35 countries in the Fields sample, we could use only 29 because 4 of them were not in the Barro-Wolf [1989] data set (Bahamas, Puerto Rico, Reunion, and Seychelles) and 2 had data only for the 1980s (Cote d'Ivoire and Peru). The high-quality sample is made up of these 29 plus 17 developed countries from Jain [1975]. Turkey, an OECD member, is included in the Fields sample of developing countries.

[3]In our regressions, we actually use only 49 of these countries as the rest (Puerto Rico, Libya, Vietnam, Poland, and Yugoslavia) are not included in the Barro-Wolf [1989] 118-country data set from which our other data are drawn.

[4]The instruments we use are listed in the notes to Table 1. We have experimented with alternative sets of instruments, and found that the results are generally robust.

Table 1. Growth Regressions for 1960–1985

	High-quality sample (N = 46)		Largest possible sample (N = 70)		Largest possible sample			
					(N = 49)		(N = 41)	
	OLS (1)	TSLS (2)	OLS (3)	TSLS (4)	OLS (5)	OLS (6)	OLS (7)	OLS (8)
Const.	3.60	8.66	1.76	6.48	3.71	6.22	6.24	6.21
	(2.66)	(3.33)	(1.50)	(2.93)	(3.86)	(4.69)	(4.63)	(4.61)
GDP60	−0.44	−0.52	−0.48	−0.58	−0.38	−0.38	−0.39	−0.38
	(−3.28)	(−3.17)	(−3.37)	(−3.47)	(−3.61)	(−3.25)	(−3.06)	(−2.95)
PRIM60	3.26	2.85	3.98	3.70	3.85	2.66	2.62	2.65
	(3.38)	(2.43)	(4.66)	(3.72)	(4.88)	(2.66)	(2.53)	(2.56)
GINI60	−5.70	−15.98	−3.58	−12.93		−3.47	−3.45	−3.47
	(−2.46)	(−3.21)	(−1.81)	(−3.12)		(−1.82)	(−1.79)	(−1.80)
GINILND					−5.50	−5.23	−5.24	−5.21
					(−5.24)	(−4.38)	(−4.32)	(−4.19)
DEMOC*							0.12	
GINILND							(0.12)	
DEMOC								0.02
								(0.05)
$\bar{R}^2$	0.28	0.27	0.25	0.26	0.53	0.53	0.51	0.51

The dependent variable is average per capita growth rate over 1960–1985, *t*-statistics are in parentheses. Independent variables are defined as follows:

GDP60:   Per capita GDP level in 1960

PRIM60:   Primary school enrollment ratio in 1960

GINI60:   Gini coefficient of income inequality, measured close to 1960

GINILND: Gini coefficient of land distribution inequality, measured close to 1960

DEMOC: Democracy dummy.

Two-stage least squares regressions use GDP60, PRIM60, literacy rate in 1960, infant mortality in 1965, secondary enrollment in 1960, fertility in 1965, and an Africa dummy as instruments.

either alone or jointly with the income Gini (columns (6)–(8)).

The results indicate that income inequality is negatively correlated with subsequent growth. When either one of the two Gini's is entered on its own, the relevant coefficient is almost uniformly statistically significant at the 5 percent level or better and has the expected (negative) sign. The only exception is the OLS regression for the large sample (column (3)), where the income Gini is statistically significant only at the 10 percent level. We also note that the *t*-statistics for the land Gini are remarkably high (above 4), as are the R^2's for the regressions that include the land Gini's. When the land and income Gini's are entered together, the former remains significant at the 1 percent level, while the latter is significant only at the 10 percent level (the sample size shrinks to 41 countries in this case, since many countries have only one of the two indicators). The estimated coefficients imply that an increase in, say, the land Gini coefficient by one standard deviation (an increase of 0.16 in the Gini index) would lead to a reduction in growth of 0.8 percentage points per year.

Column (7) reports the results obtained including a dummy variable for democracies interacted with the land Gini. The coefficient is not statistically significant, rejecting the hypothesis that the relationship between inequality and growth is different in democracies and nondemocracies. We have included this interactive democracy dummy in all other versions of our regressions; the results were uniformly insignificant. . . .

. . . Finally, column (8) indicates that democracies do not grow faster than or more slowly than dictatorships. . . .

Table 2 repeats these regressions for the 1970–1985 period (except for the two-stage least squares regressions). As mentioned above, this may be a more relevant time period to try our story out as many of our income Gini's are measured during the 1960s (and some in the 1970s). The results are indeed even stronger: the coefficient on the Gini is consistently significant at the 5 percent level or better. Moreover, both the land and income Gini's remain statistically significant (at the 1 percent and 5 percent levels, respectively) when they are entered jointly. The magnitude of the coefficients is commensurate with those in Table 1.

Our results imply that countries that experi-

Table 2. Growth Regressions for 1970–1985

	High-quality sample (N = 46)	Largest possible sample (N = 70)	Largest possible sample			
			(N = 49)		(N = 41)	
	OLS (9)	OLS (10)	OLS (11)	OLS (12)	OLS (13)	OLS (14)
Const.	4.56	2.80	4.88	7.22	7.18	7.22
	(2.67)	(2.00)	(3.16)	(3.79)	(3.69)	(3.74)
GDP70	−0.29	−0.27	−0.21	−0.28	−0.28	−0.27
	(−2.60)	(−2.33)	(−2.09)	(−2.58)	(−2.23)	(−2.15)
PRIM70	3.28	3.79	3.45	2.77	2.81	2.81
	(2.46)	(3.52)	(2.65)	(1.83)	(1.79)	(1.80)
GINI70	−9.71	−7.95		−5.71	−5.74	−5.73
	(−3.62)	(−3.49)		(−2.33)	(−2.30)	(−2.30)
GINILND			−8.14	−6.41	−6.39	−6.46
			(−5.49)	(−3.79)	(−3.69)	(−3.71)
DEMOC*					−0.11	
GINILND					(−0.13)	
DEMOC						−0.09
						(−0.15)
$\bar{R}^2$	0.28	0.23	0.43	0.46	0.45	0.45

The dependent variable is average per capita growth rate over 1970–1985, t-statistics are in parentheses. Independent variables are defined as follows:

GDP70:   Per capita GDP level in 1970
PRIM70:   Primary school enrollment ratio in 1970
GINI70:   Gini coefficient of income inequality, measured close to 1970
GINILND: Gini coefficient of land distribution inequality, measured close to 1960
DEMOC: Democracy dummy.

enced a land reform in the aftermath of World War II and hence reduced the inequality in land ownership should have had higher growth than countries with no land reform. This argument is often mentioned in the literature on economic development as one explanation for the successful experience of several Asian countries, such as Japan, South Korea, or Taiwan, compared with the less stellar performance of most Latin American countries (see, for example, Ranis [1990] and Wade [1990, Chapter 8]). Asian countries had land reforms; Latin American countries did not.

References

Barro, Robert, "Economic Growth in a Cross Section of Countries," *Quarterly Journal of Economics,* CVI (May 1991), 407–44.

Barro, Robert, and Holger Wolf, "Data Appendix for Economic Growth in a Cross-Section of Countries," unpublished manuscript, 1989.

Fields, Gary, "A Compendium of Data on Inequality and Poverty for the Developing World," Cornell University, unpublished manuscript, 1989.

Fields, Gary, and George Jakubson, "New Evidence on the Kuznets Curve," Cornell University, unpublished manuscript, 1993.

Heston, Alan, and Robert Summers, "A New Set of International Comparisons of Real Product and Price Levels: Estimates for 130 Countries," *The Review of Income and Wealth,* XXXIV (1988), 1–25.

Jain, S., "Size Distribution of Income: A Comparison of Data," The World Bank, unpublished manuscript, 1975.

Lecallion, Jack, Felix Paukert, Christian Morrison, and Dimitri Gemiolis, "Income Distribution and Economic Development: Analytical Survey" (Geneva: International Labor Office, 1984).

Ranis, Gustav, "Contrasts in the Political Economy of Development Policy Change," in Gary Gereffi and Donald L. Wyman, eds., *Manufacturing Miracles: Paths of Industrialization in Latin America and East Asia* (Princeton, NJ: Princeton University Press, 1990).

Taylor, C. L., and M. C. Hudson, *World Handbook of Political and Social Indicators,* 2nd. ed. (New Haven, CT: Yale University Press, 1972).

Wade, Robert, *Governing the Market: Economic Theory and the Role of Government in East Asian Industrialization* (Princeton, NJ: Princeton University Press, 1990).

Selection VIII.B.2. Income Distribution, Political Instability, and Investment*

1. Introduction

This paper studies the effects of income distribution on investment, by focusing on political instability as the channel which links these two variables. Income inequality increases social discontent and fuels social unrest. The latter, by increasing the probability of coups, revolutions, mass violence or, more generally, by increasing policy uncertainty and threatening property rights, has a negative effect on investment and, as a consequence, reduces growth.

Several authors have recently argued that income inequality is harmful for growth: in more unequal societies, the demand for fiscal redistribution financed by distortionary taxation is higher, causing a lower rate of growth.[1] Alesina and Rodrik (1993), Alesina and Rodrik (1994) and Persson and Tabellini (1994) present reduced form regressions supportive of this hypothesis.

An important question, still unresolved empirically, is what exactly is the channel through which inequality harms investment and growth. Perotti (1996) explicitly investigates the fiscal channel described above, with, however, rather inconclusive results.

In this paper we emphasize and test a different link from income inequality to capital accumulation: political instability. Therefore, our paper is related to the research on the effects of political instability on growth. For instance, Barro (1991), Alesina et al. (1996), and Mauro (1993) find an inverse relationship between political instability and growth or investment, using different techniques, approaches and data.[2] Venieris and Gupta (1986) identify an inverse relationship between political instability and the savings rate.

We estimate on a cross-section of 71 countries for the period 1960–85 a two-equation system in which the endogenous variables are investment in physical capital and a measure of political instability.[3] In our model, economic and political variables are jointly endogenous, an issue that has been generally ignored in the recent literature on the political economy of growth.[4] We are specifically interested in two questions:

1. Does income inequality increase political instability?
2. Does political instability reduce investment?

According to our findings, the answer to both questions is "yes." First, more unequal societies are more politically unstable: in particular, our results suggest that political stability is enhanced by the presence of a wealthy middle class. Second, political instability has an adverse effect on investment and, therefore, on growth. Furthermore, these two effects (from inequality to instability, and from instability to investment) are not only statistically significant, but also economically significant. . . .

2. Definition and Measure of Political Instability

. . . Socio-political instability is measured by constructing an index which summarizes various variables capturing phenomena of social unrest. . . . The index is constructed by applying the method of principal component to the following variables: *ASSASS,* the number of politically motivated assassinations; *DEATH,* the number of people killed in conjunction with phenomena of domestic mass violence, as a fraction of the total population; SCOUP, the number of successful coups; *UCOUP,* the number of attempted but unsuccessful coups; *DEM,* a dummy variable that takes the value of 1 in democracies, 0.5 in "semi-democracies" and 0 in dictatorships. A "democracy" is defined as a country with free competitive elections; a semi-democracy is a country with some form of elections but with severe restrictions on political rights (for instance, Mexico); a dictatorship is a country without competitive elections. All the variables are expressed as the average of annual values over the sample period, 1960–85. A

*From Alberto Alesina and Roberto Perotti, "Income Distribution, Political Instability, and Investment," *European Economic Review* 40 (June 1996): 1203–1219. Reprinted by permission.

[1]A non-exhaustive list of papers in this area includes Alesina and Rodrik (1993), Alesina and Rodrik (1994), Persson and Tabellini (1994), Bertola (1993) and Perotti (1993).

[2]Londegran and Poole (1990), and Londegran and Poole (1991) in related work do not seem to find such evidence. For a discussion of their results and comparisons with other literature see Alesina et al. (1996).

[3]The number of countries used in different specifications and different tests may vary slightly because of data availability. We have always chosen the largest sample of countries for which data were available.

[4]Some exceptions are Londegran and Poole (1990), Londegran and Poole (1991), and Alesina et al. (1996).

more detailed definition of the variables used in this paper, including sources, is in Table 1. . . .

Applying the method of principal components to the five variables listed above leads to the following index of socio-political instability:

$$SPI = 1.39\ ASSASS + 1.21\ DEATH$$
$$+ 7.58\ SCOUP + 7.23\ UCOUP$$
$$- 5.45\ DEM \qquad (1)$$

3. Data and Sample Period

We perform cross-sectional regressions using a sample of 71 countries for the period 1960–1985. The binding constraint on the number of countries is the data availability. We have income distribution data for 74 countries, but for only 71 of these we have data on political instability and the other variables we use in our regressions, like investment shares in 1960–85 and GDP per capita in 1960.

We use the same dataset on income distribution assembled by Perotti (1996). The income distribution data consist of the income shares of the five quintiles of the population, measured as close as possible to the beginning of each sample period, 1960. In our framework, income distribution is predetermined; therefore, it is appropriate to mea-

sure this variable at the beginning of the sample period. In fact, in the long run income distribution is likely to be endogenous, as it is arguably affected by such factors as land reforms, the savings behavior of the population etc. These problems of endogeneity are clearly hard to overcome: however, measuring income distribution at the beginning of the sample period is a way of minimizing them.

. . .

The binding constraint on the initial date of the sample period is the availability of economic data. Our main sources for this variable is the Barro–Wolf and the Barro–Lee datasets, with the exceptions noted in Table 1. The end of our sample period (1985) is imposed by the availability of economic and socio-political variables. The list of these variables with their sources is included in Table 1, as well.

Table 2 reports the average of our SPI index for the sample 1960–85, ordered from the poorest to the richest country, in terms of their per capita income in 1960. This ordering immediately highlights a positive correlation between poverty and socio-political instability. Furthermore, a few countries suggest interesting observations. Japan has a much lower index of instability than countries at comparable level of development in 1960. Thirty years later this country is one of the richest in the world. The opposite observation holds for

Table 1. Definition of Variables and Data Sources

GDP:	GDP in 1960 in hundreds of 1980 dollars;
PRIM:	Primary school enrollment rate in 1960, from Barro and Lee (1993);
SEC:	Secondary school enrollment rate in 1960, from Barro and Lee (1993);
MIDCLASS:	Share of the third and fourth quintiles of the population in or around 1960;
INV:	Ratio of real domestic investment (private plus public) to real GDP (average from 1960 to 1985);
PPPI:	PPP value of the investment deflator (U.S. = 1.0), 1960;
PPPIDE:	Magnitude of the deviation of the PPP value for the investment deflator from the sample mean, 1960;
SPI:	Index of socio-political instability, constructed using averages over 1960–85 of the variables that appear in the formula of Eq. 1;
SPIG:	Index of socio-political instability, constructed using annual data from the formula in Gupta (1990), average over 1960–85;
HOMOG:	Percentage of the population belonging to the main ethnic or linguistic group, 1960, from Canning and Fay (1993);
URB:	Urban population as percentage of total population in 1960. Source: World Bank Tables;
GOV:	Government consumption as share of GDP, average 1970–85;
DEATH:	Average number of deaths in domestic disturbances, per millions population, 1960–85, from Jodice and Taylor (1988);
ASSASS:	Average number of assassinations, 1960–85, from Jodice and Taylor (1988);
UCOUP:	Average number of unsuccessful coups, 1960–85, from Jodice and Taylor (1988);
SCOUP:	Average number of successful coups, 1960–85, from Jodice and Taylor (1988);
DEM:	Dummy variable taking the value 1 for democracies, 0.5 for semi-democracies, and 0 for dictatorships, average 1960–85, from Jodice and Taylor (1988).

This table describes the data used in the regressions. All the data are from the Barro and Wolf (1989) data set, except for the income distribution data which are mainly from Jain (1975) (see Perotti (1996) for a more detailed list of the original sources) or unless otherwise indicated

Table 2. SPI Index (sample 1960–85)

Country	SPI	Country	SPI
Tanzania	−0.73	Panama	5.42
Malawi	−2.66	Brazil	−0.19
Sierra Leone	9.11	Colombia	−4.69
Niger	3.42	Jamaica	−11.60
Burma	1.58	Greece	2.41
Togo	6.80	Costa Rica	−11.76
Bangladesh	8.39	Cyprus	−5.55
Kenya	−0.72	Peru	7.46
Botswana	−9.68	Barbados	−11.76
Egypt	1.83	Iran	−1.13
Chad	7.61	Mexico	−4.15
India	−8.92	Japan	−11.68
Morocco	2.41	Spain	−2.77
Nigeria	12.69	Iraq	30.64
Pakistan	9.11	Ireland	−11.37
Congo	21.66	South Africa	−7.08
Benin	30.34	Israel	−11.67
Zimbabwe	−1.76	Chile	0.50
Madagascar	2.42	Argentina	30.54
Sudan	15.09	Italy	−8.10
Thailand	9.31	Uruguay	4.80
Zambia	−3.46	Austria	−11.68
Ivory Coast	−2.74	Finland	−11.76
Honduras	5.00	France	−9.44
Senegal	−0.98	Holland	−11.68
Gabon	4.05	U.K.	−7.63
Tunisia	−2.57	Norway	−11.76
Philippines	−4.14	Sweden	−11.68
Bolivia	44.19	Australia	−11.68
Dom. Republic	8.22	Germany	−11.45
Sri Lanka	−9.91	Venezuela	4.03
El Salvador	7.94	Denmark	−11.76
Malaysia	−11.21	New Zealand	−11.76
Ecuador	19.91	Canada	−11.68
Turkey	2.88	Switzerland	−11.76
		U.S.A.	−11.06

Argentina: it has the second highest *SPI* index and from 1960 to 1985 it has dropped several steps in the income ladder. Not surprisingly, the most stable countries are OECD democracies, even though several LDCs, such as Botswana, are also relatively stable. The case of Venezuela is also interesting: in 1960 it had the fifth highest per capita income in the sample, but a much higher *SPI* index than the countries in the same group. . . .

4. Model Specification

Our hypothesis is that income inequality increases socio-political instability and the latter reduces the propensity to invest. A large group of im-

poverished citizens, facing a small and very rich group of well-off individuals is likely to become dissatisfied with the existing socio-economic status quo and demand radical changes, so that mass violence and illegal seizure of power are more likely than when income distribution is more equitable. Several arguments justify the second link, from political instability to investment. Broadly speaking, political instability affects investment through three main channels. First, because it increases the expected *level* of taxation of factors that can be accumulated,. . . . Second, because phenomena of social unrest can cause disruption of productive activities, and therefore a fall in the productivity of labor and capital. Third, because socio-political instability increases *uncertainty,* thereby inducing investors to postpone projects, invest abroad (capital flights) or simply consume more. In turn, a high value of the *SPI* index implies high uncertainty for two reasons. First, when social unrest is widespread, the probability of the government being overthrown is higher, making the course of future economic policy and even protection of property rights more uncertain. Second, the occurrence of attempted or successful coups indicates a propensity to abandon the rule of law and therefore, in principle, a threat to established property rights.

We capture these two links in a simple bivariate simultaneous equation model with *SPI* and investment as endogenous variables. The most basic specification of this model is as follows:

$$INV = \alpha_0 + \alpha_1 SPI + \alpha_2 GDP + \alpha_3 PPPIDE$$
$$+ \alpha_4 PPPI + \varepsilon_1, \tag{2}$$

$$SPI = \beta_0 + \beta_1 PRIM + \beta_2 INV$$
$$+ \beta_3 MIDCLASS + \varepsilon_2. \tag{3}$$

. . . As discussed above, we expect α_1 in the investment equation to be negative. In the same equation, we control for the initial level of GDP per capita, as it is common in the literature. Note that the sign of the coefficient of *GDP*, α_2, is a priori ambiguous: according to the exogenous growth theory, long-run convergence would imply a negative sign. However, as Levine and Renelt (1992) have shown, empirically *GDP* enters with a consistently positive sign in cross-country investment regressions, suggesting that the convergence in GDP per capita occurs through channels different from increases in physical investment. The two variables *PPPI* (the PPP value of the investment deflator in 1960 relative to that of the U.S.) and

PPPIDE (the magnitude of the deviation of PPPI from the sample mean) capture the effects of domestic distortions which obviously would affect investment directly.

Turning to the *SPI* equation, we included the variable *PRIM* (the enrollment ratio in primary school in 1960) as a proxy for human capital, on the ground that a higher level of education may reduce political violence and channel political action within institutional rules (see Huntington (1968) or Hibbs (1973)).[5] Therefore, we expect β_1 to be negative. Investment is also included to test whether rapidly growing economies tend to be more stable: on the one hand, more growth means more prosperity, less dissatisfaction and possibly more stability, implying a negative sign for β_2. On the other hand, periods of very high growth may temporarily lead to social disruptions and economic transformation which may actually *increase* political instability. Finally, as discussed at length above, we expect a positive relation between inequality and instability: accordingly, under the null hypothesis the sign of β_3 should be negative when an index of equality is used. . . .

5. Estimation of the Basic Specification

We start by estimating the basic specification of Eqs. (2) and (3) in columns (1a) and (1b) of Table 3. The two key coefficients are those that capture the effects of *SPI* on *INV* and of *MIDCLASS* on *SPI*. Both coefficients have the expected signs and are significant at the 5% level: socio-political instability depresses investment and a rich middle class reduces socio-political instability. A "healthy" middle class is conducive to capital accumulation because it creates conditions of social stability. . . . the share of income of the middle class has a correlation of almost −1 with the share of the richest quintile; thus, a wealthier middle class implies more equality in the distribution of income.

An increase by one standard deviation of the share of the middle class is associated with a decrease in the index of political instability by about 5.7, which corresponds to about 48% of its stan-

dard deviation. This in turn is associated with an increase in the share of investment in GDP of about 2.85 percentage points. The effect of income distribution on investment implied by these estimates is definitely not negligible, since the difference between the highest and lowest value of *MIDCLASS* in the sample is about 4 standard deviations. In addition, an exogenous increase in the *SPI* index by one standard deviation causes a decrease in the share of investment in GDP of about 6 percentage points.

The coefficient on *PPPI* in the investment equation has the expected negative sign and is significant at high levels of confidence: market distortions do have negative effects on investment. The second proxy for market distortions, *PPPIDE,* is insignificant. Consistently with the results of the existing literature, initial GDP per capita has a positive, although insignificant, coefficient.[6]

The estimation results for the *SPI* equation are also very sensible. *PRIM* has a negative and significant coefficient: as expected, countries with higher levels of education tend to be more stable.

In columns (2a) and (2b) we add three regional dummies, *ASIA* (for the East Asian countries), *LAAM* (for Latin American countries) and *AFRICA* (for Sub-Saharan countries), in the *SPI* equation. There are at least two reasons for this: first, cultural and / or historical reasons may influence the amount of socio-political unrest in different regions of the world. Second, in certain regions, particularly Africa, under-reporting of socio-political events can be particularly acute. Of the three regional dummies, only *LAAM* is significant: as expected, on average Latin American countries tend to be much more unstable than the other countries in the sample. The coefficient of *SPI* in the investment equation is very similar to that of column (1a), while the coefficient of *MID-CLASS* in the *SPI* equation drops (in absolute value) by about 30% to −0.68, although it remains strongly significant. This is hardly surprising, since the Latin America countries in the sample are more unstable than the average and, especially, have a particularly unequal distribution of income. Since regional dummies do appear to be important in our regressions, from now on we include them in all our reported estimates; it might be worthwhile nothing that, if we did not include them, in general our results on the income distribution variable would be *stronger* than the ones we report.

---

[5]In addition to providing new measures of primary enrollment, Barro and Lee (1993) have recently estimated several stock measures of human capital, and they kindly made all their data available to us. We prefer to use their primary enrollment ratio which is not an estimate but a direct observation. When we use their estimated human capital stock our regressions are less successful, possibly because of measurement errors in the constructed stock variables.

[6]Note that our results in the investment equation are consistent with the reduced-form results in Barro (1991).

Table 3. Investment and SPI Equations, 1960–85[a]

	INV (1a)	SPI (1b)	INV (2a)	SPI (2b)
Constant	27.36 (9.34)	37.43 (4.54)	27.85 (9.49)	32.44 (3.02)
GDP	0.07 (1.09)		0.06 (0.91)	
SPI	−0.50 (−2.39)		−0.57 (−3.14)	
PPPI	−0.14 (−2.39)		−0.15 (−3.14)	
PPPIDE	0.04 (0.62)		0.05 (0.79)	
PRIM		−0.23 (−2.45)		−0.32 (−2.82)
MIDCLASS		−1.01 (−3.42)		−0.68 (−2.34)
INV		0.72 (1.30)		0.66 (1.38)
LAAM				9.89 (2.39)
ASIA				2.59 (0.38)
AFRICA				−3.17 (−0.76)
NOBS	71	71	71	71
s.e.e.	6.71	11.62	7.09	10.90

[a]2SLS. *t*-statistics in parentheses. Estimates using 3SLS are very similar.

References

Alesina, Alberto and Dani Rodrik, 1993, Income distribution and economic growth: A simple theory and some empirical evidence, In: Alex Cukierman, Zvi Hercovitz and Leonardo Leiderman, eds., The political economy of business cycles and growth (MIT Press, Cambridge, MA).

Alesina, Alberto and Dani Rodrik, 1994, Distributive politics and economic growth, Quarterly Journal of Economics, 109, 465–490.

Alesina, Alberto, Sule Ozler, Nouriel Roubini and Philip Swagel, 1996, Political instability and economic growth, Journal of Economic Growth, forthcoming.

Barro, Robert J., 1991, Economic growth in a cross-section of countries, Quarterly Journal of Economics 106, 407–444.

Barro, Robert J. and Jong-Waa Lee, 1993, International comparisons of educational attainments, Unpublished (Harvard University, Cambridge, MA).

Barro, Robert J. and Holger Wolf, 1989, Data appendix for economic growth in a cross section of countries, unpublished (National Bureau of Economic Research, Cambridge, MA).

Bertola, Giuseppe, 1993, Market structure and income distribution in endogenous growth models, American Economic Review 83, 1184–1199.

Canning, David and Marianne Fay, 1993, Growth and infrastructure, Unpublished (Columbia University, New York).

Gupta, Dipak K., 1990, The economics of political violence (Praeger, New York).

Hibbs, Douglas, 1973, Mass political violence: A cross-sectional analysis (Wiley and Sons, New York).

Huntington, Samuel, 1968, Political order in changing societies (Yale University Press, New Haven, CT).

Jain, Shail, 1975, Size distribution of income: A compilation of data (World Bank, Washington, DC).

Jodice, D. and D. L. Taylor, 1988, World handbook of social and political indicators (Yale University Press, New Haven, CT).

Levine, Ross and David Renelt, 1992, A sensitivity analysis of cross-country growth regressions, American Economic Review 82, 942–963.

Londegran, John and Keith Poole, 1990, Poverty, the coup trap and the seizure of executive power, World Politics 92, 1–24.

Londegran, John and Keith Poole, 1991, Leadership turnover and unconstitutional rule, Unpublished.

Mauro, Paolo, 1993, Political instability, growth and investment, Unpublished (Harvard University, Cambridge, MA).

Ozler, Sule and Guido Tabellini, 1991, External debt and political instability, Mimeo.

Perotti, Roberto, 1993, Political equilibrium, income distribution, and growth, Review of Economic Studies, Sep.

Perotti, Roberto, 1996, Income distribution, democracy and growth: What the data say, Journal of Economic Growth, forthcoming.

Persson, Torsten and Guido Tabellini, 1994, Is inequality harmful for growth? Theory and Evidence, American Economic Review 84, 600–621.

Venieris, Yannis and Dipak Gupta, 1986, Income distribution and socio-political instability as determinants of savings: A cross-sectional model, Journal of Political Economy 96, 873–883.

Selection VIII.C.1. Economic Growth and Income Distribution in Taiwan, 1953–64*

Despite considerable wartime destruction, the physical and institutional infrastructure established under colonial rule in Taiwan was instrumental in the rapid growth of agriculture during the 1950s. The irrigation system, which extended over more than half of Taiwan's cultivated area, proved valuable in ensuring the equitable distribution of benefits of green-revolution technology. Linkages between agriculture and the rural-based food-processing industry led to a marked spatial dispersion of economic growth. This pattern later enabled the provision of substantial nonagricultural employment to farmers. Progress in public health and education during the colonial period provided the basis for a highly productive labor force in both agriculture and industry. In addition, the overwhelmingly Japanese ownership of manufacturing enterprises contributed to a more equal distribution of income in two ways: it reduced the concentration of industrial assets in private Taiwanese hands in the period immediately after independence; and it provided a source of industrial assets that could be distributed as compensation to landowners under the program of land reform. The preconditions for rapid economic growth and an improved distribution of income thus were considerably more favorable in Taiwan than in the typical developing country. . . .

Land Reform

The land reform that government instituted between 1949 and 1953 probably was the most important factor in improving the distribution of income before the beginning of the subphase of export substitution in the early 1960s.[1] Although much of the reform took place before 1952, the year for which sample data on the distribution of income first exist, it continued to have its impact well into the 1950s. The reform thus remained an important factor in explaining improvements in

FID [family distribution of income] during that decade.

Land reform was initiated for several reasons. Although the Japanese had developed a substantial agricultural infrastructure in Taiwan, they paid relatively little attention to the distribution of land. . . . Given the large class of tenants, competition for the scarce land was so fierce that the average lease was less than one year. As a result, rents often were equal to 50 percent of the anticipated harvest, especially in the more fertile regions. Contracts frequently were oral; rent payments had to be made in advance; no adjustments were made for crop failures. These conditions and practices left the typical tenant helpless in any dispute with his landlord. The record of landlord abuse and the need to meet the food demands of postwar Taiwan—which, in addition to its own increased population, included hundreds of thousands of mainland Chinese—laid the groundwork for reform.[2] In addition, the principle of land ownership by the tiller, although never receiving much attention, had always been part of the ideology of the Chinese Nationalists. The loss of the mainland and the social unrest threatening in Taiwan made the redistribution of wealth a particularly important issue for government. Land reform was also considered to be an essential ingredient of agricultural growth and economic recovery. Moreover, it could be imposed by a government free of obligations and ties to the landowning class.

Government's conception of land reform was broad. Strengthening farmers' associations and other elements of organizational and financial infrastructure in rural areas was considered to be important. Moreover the repair of physical infrastructure, started as soon as Taiwan was retroceded to China and almost completed by 1952, increased the effect of land reform on both growth and equity. But the main component of the successful reorganization of the agricultural sector clearly was the three-pronged package of land reform: the program to reduce farm rents, the sale of public lands, and the land-to-the-tiller program.

The first step taken to promote agricultural incentives and output was to reduce farm rents and

*From John C. H. Fei, Gustav Ranis, and Shirley W. Y. Kuo, "Economic Growth and Income Distribution, 1953–64," *Growth with Equity: The Taiwan Case* (New York: Oxford University, 1979), pp. 37–43, 45–52, 65–66. Reprinted by permission.

[1]Discussion of land reform draws heavily on Samuel P. S. Ho, *Economic Development in Taiwan: 1860–1970* (New Haven: Yale University Press, 1978) and Chao-Chen Chen, "Land Reform and Agricultural Development in Taiwan" (paper read at Conference on Economic Development of Taiwan, June 19–28, 1967, Taipei; processed).

[2]In 1945 and 1946, 640,000 mainlanders moved to Taiwan. Kuang Lu, "Population and Employment," in *Economic Development of Taiwan,* ed. Kowie Chang (Taipei: Cheng Chung Books, 1968), p. 532.

thereby to increase the share of tenant farmers in crop yields. Promulgated in 1949, this program had five basic provisions: first, farm rents could be fixed at no more than 37.5 percent of the anticipated annual yield of the main crops; second, if crops failed because of natural forces, tenant farmers could apply to local farm-tenancy committees for a further reduction; third, tenant farmers no longer had to pay their rent in advance; fourth, written contracts and fixed leases of three to six years had to be registered; fifth, tenants had the first option to purchase land from its owners. The reform affected about 43 percent of the 660,000 farm families, 75 percent of the 410,000 part owners and tenants, and 40 percent of the 650,000 hectares of private farmland. Prices of farmland immediately dropped: paddy field prices by 20 percent; dry field prices by more than 40 percent by December 1949 and a further 66 percent by 1952.[3] Equally important, the requirement for written contracts and the fixing of standard reduced rents enabled tenants to benefit from their own increased efforts for the first time. This incentive was a primary ingredient of the sustained increase in Taiwan's agricultural productivity during the early 1950s. With higher yields and lower rents, the average income of tenant farmers rose by 81 percent between 1949 and 1952.[4] These rising incomes enabled tenants to purchase land put up for sale by their landlords; about 6 percent of private farmland changed hands.

Given the success of the program to reduce farm rents, government decided to accelerate the program initiated in 1948 to sell public land to tenant farmers. Formerly owned by the Japanese, about 170,000 hectares of public land, or about 25 percent of Taiwan's arable land, were suitable for cultivation. Taiwan Sugar Corporation owned most of this land and leased part of it to tenant farmers. The program gave priority in land purchases to cultivators of public land and landless tenants. The size of parcels was limited according to predetermined fertility grades, and the average size was 1 chia. Selling prices were 2.5 times the value of the annual yield of the main crops; payments in kind were set to coincide with the harvest season over a ten-year period. In all, 35 percent of Taiwan's arable public land was sold during 1948–53; 43 percent during 1953–58.

With government setting the example of returning land to the tiller, the stage was set for the most dramatic component of the three-pronged pack-

age: the compulsory sale of land by landlords. This program stipulated that privately owned land in excess of specified amounts per landowner had to be sold to government, which would resell that land to tenants.[5] The purchase price was set at 2.5 times the annual yield of the main crops. Landlords were paid 70 percent of the purchase price in land bonds denominated in kind and 30 percent in industrial stock of four public enterprises previously owned by the Japanese. The selling prices and conditions of repayment were the same as those provided in the sale of public lands. This third program had a dual objective. The new owner-cultivators were encouraged to work harder because they would benefit from any increases in agricultural output. The landlords, deprived of the privilege of living comfortably off the land, were encouraged to participate in the industrial development of Taiwan through ownership of four large-scale industrial enterprises. Between May and December of 1953, tenant households acquired 244,000 hectares of farmland, or 16.4 percent of the total area cultivated in Taiwan during 1951–55.

Effects of Land Reform on the Distribution of Assets

Tables 1, 2, and 3 summarize the extent of land reform and its importance for the redistribution of wealth in Taiwan. Because of the reform, the distribution of land holdings dramatically changed between 1952 and 1960. The rising share of families owning medium-sized plots of land ranging from 0.5 to 3 chia reflects this change: their share increased from 46 percent in 1952 to 76 percent in 1960. The largest rise was in the share of families owning between 0.5 and 1 chia. What is even more dramatic, the average size of holdings in all categories of less than 5 chia increased. The combined share in total land of families owning less than 3 chia increased from 58 percent in 1952 to 85 percent in 1960. The proportion of land cultivated by tenants fell from 44 percent in 1948 to 17 percent in 1959. The proportion of tenant farmers in farm families fell from 38 percent in 1950 to 15 percent in 1960.

Although government compensated landlords for the land they were forced to give up, this compensation was only 2.5 times the standard annual yield; market values of land ranged between 5 and 8 times the annual yield. The exercise thus repre-

---

[3]Chen Cheng, *Land Reform in Taiwan* (Taipei: China Publishing, 1961), p. 310.

[4]Cheng, *Land Reform in Taiwan*, p. 309.

[5]Individual landowners were allowed to retain three chia of medium-grade land. Anthony Y. C. Koo, *The Role of Land Reform in Economic Development—A Case Study of Taiwan* (New York: Frederick A. Praeger, 1968), p. 38.

Table 1. Area and Households Affected by Land Reform, by Type of Reform

Item	Reduction of farm rents	Sale of public land	Land-to-the-tiller program	Total redistribution[a]
		Type of Reform		
Area affected (thousands of chia)	256.9	71.7	193.6	215.2
Farm households affected (thousands)	302.3	139.7	194.9	334.3
Ratio of cultivated area affected to total area[b] (percent)	29.2	8.1	16.4	24.6
Ratio of farm households affected to total farm households (percent)	43.3	20.0	27.9	47.9

Note: Figures may not reconcile because of rounding.

[a]Comprises land distributed under the sale of public land and the land-to-the-tiller program.

[b]Total area is the total area cultivated in 1951–55.

Source: Samuel P. S. Ho, *Economic Development in Taiwan: 1860–1970* (New Haven: Yale University Press, 1978), p. 163.

Table 2. Distribution of Land and Owner-Cultivator Households, by Size of Holding, 1952 and 1960

Size of holding (chia)[a]	Distribution of owner-cultivator households (percent)		Distribution of land (percent)		Average size of holding (chia)	
	1952	1960[b]	1952	1960[b]	1952	1960[b]
0–0.5	47.3	20.7	9.9	5.2	0.23	0.30
0.5–1	23.3	45.9	15.1	30.5	0.72	0.81
1–2	16.9	15.3	21.1	19.3	1.39	4.58
2–3	5.7	14.8	12.3	30.3	2.42	2.50
3–5	3.9	2.7	13.2	10.2	3.79	4.58
Over 5	3.4	0.6	28.4	4.6	10.14	9.10
Total (chia)	611,193	776,002	681,154	948,738	—	—

—Not applicable.

[a]One chia is equal to 0.97 hectare or 2.47 acres.

[b]Includes only individual farm households; excludes public and private commercial farms, which all are larger than 10 chia and account for about 6 percent of total land and less than 0.1 percent of the number of holdings.

Source: Ho, *Economic Development in Taiwan.*

sented a substantial redistribution of wealth. The total value of wealth redistributed as a result of this price difference was equivalent to about 13 percent of Taiwan's gross domestic product (GDP) in 1952.[6] Furthermore bonds used to reimburse landowners paid an interest rate of only 4 percent, substantially less than the prevailing market rates. Because of the landlords' lack of experience in nonagricultural matters, most landlords did not place much value on the 30 percent of their compensation received as industrial stocks. They promptly sold the stocks at prices far below value. Most of their proceeds went to consumption; some went to investments in small businesses. The majority of land-

lords thus ended up being not much better off than the new owner-cultivators.[7]...

Reorganization of Institutional Infrastructure

The institutional infrastructure of Taiwan's agriculture was extensively reorganized and improved during the 1950s. The farmers' associations and credit cooperatives, set up by the Japanese to facilitate agricultural extension programs and rice procurement, were top-down institutions dominated by landlords and nonfarmers. As a result, most farmers did not directly benefit from them. In 1952 government consolidated those institutions in mul-

[6]Ho, *Economic Development in Taiwan*, p. 166.

[7]T. Martin Yang, *Socio-Economic Results of Land Reform in Taiwan* (Honolulu: East-West Center, 1970).

Table 3. Distribution of Farm Families and Agricultural Land, by Type of Cultivator, 1948–60

Item and type of cultivator	1948	1950	1953	1955–56	1959–60
Total farm families	n.a.	638,062	n.a.	732,555	785,592
Distribution of families (percent)					
Owner	n.a.	36.0	n.a.	59.0	64.0
Part-owner	n.a.	26.0	n.a.	24.0	21.0
Tenant	n.a.	38.0	n.a.	17.0	15.0
Distribution of land (percent)					
Owner	55.9	n.a.	82.9	84.9	85.6
Tenant	44.1	n.a.	17.1	15.1	14.4

n.a. Not available.

Sources: Family distribution from Ho, *Economic Development in Taiwan;* land distribution from Chen Cheng, *Land Reform in Taiwan* (Taipei: China Publishing, 1961).

tipurpose farmers' associations restricted to farmers and serving their interests. In addition to the original function of agricultural extension, the activities of farmers' associations expanded to include a credit department, which accepted deposits from farmers and made loans to them, and to provide facilities for purchasing, marketing, warehousing, and processing.[8] The associations thus became clearing-houses for farmers, who controlled and maintained them and viewed them as their own creatures.

The other major institutional reform affecting agriculture during the 1950s was the establishment of the Joint Commission on Rural Reconstruction (JCRR) by the U.S. Congress in 1948. Its main functions were to allocate U.S. aid, provide technical assistance, and help the Taiwanese government plan and coordinate programs for agricultural extension, research, and experimentation. Thus, while the farmers' associations provided the much-needed organizational structure at local levels and facilitated the efficient flow of agricultural surpluses to the industrial sector, the JCRR was a major catalyst. It funded and initiated many innovations in

[8]Deposits of the credit divisions of farmers' associations increased from about NT$100 million to NT$2,700 million by the end of 1965. Loans increased commensurately. (At the time of writing, the new Taiwan dollar was equal to about US$0.025.) Wen-Fu Hsu, "The Role of Agricultural Organizations in Agricultural Development" (paper read at Conference on Economic Development of Taiwan, June 19–28, 1967, Taipei; processed). Also during this period, credit became available to farmers from the JCRR, government-owned banks, and government agencies and monopolies. Between 1949 and 1960 the proportion of farm loans provided through the organized money market rose from 17 percent to 57 percent. Ho, *Economic Development in Taiwan,* pp. 179–80.

farming techniques, and it introduced new crops and new markets. For example, the JCRR was behind the introduction of asparagus and mushroom cultivation, which led to the highly successful production and export performance of those commodities in the 1960s.

Agricultural Development During the 1950s

Land reform alone could not solve the primary constraint facing Taiwan's agriculture: the shortage of land for a rapidly growing agricultural population. Although an ever-increasing number of farmers left agriculture to live and work in Taiwan's expanding urban areas, the population pressure on farmland was severe, especially during the early 1950s. The agricultural population rose from 4.3 million in 1952 to 5.8 million in 1964, an increase of 33 percent. During the same period the total area of cultivated land remained nearly fixed, culminating in a decline of the average size of holding from 1.29 hectares per family to 1.06 hectares (table 4). Taiwan overcame these pressures in three ways: by the achievement of substantial increases in agricultural productivity at the intensive margin; by the diversification of agricultural production into more profitable crops; and by the part-time reallocation of labor to nonagricultural activities, including off-farm employment for many members of agricultural families.

The growth of the agricultural sector during the 1950s was impressive. The real net domestic product (NDP) by agricultural origin increased by about 80 percent during the 1952–64 period, or at an average rate of 5 percent a year, even though agriculture's share in NDP declined, from 36 percent to

Table 4. Parameters and Indexes of Agricultural Employment, Production, and Development, 1952–64

Item	1952	1956	1960	1964
Agricultural population (thousands)	4,257	4,699	5,373	5,649
Agricultural employment (thousands)	1,792	1,806	1,877	2,010
Cultivated land (thousands of hectares)	876	876	869	882
Cropped land (thousands of hectares)	1,506	1,537	1,595	1,658
Percentage of agricultural population in total population	52.4	50.0	49.8	46.1
Hectares of cultivated land				
Per farm family	1.29	1.17	1.11	1.06
Per capita on farm	0.21	0.19	0.16	0.16
Per agricultural employee	0.49	0.48	0.46	0.44
Indexes				
Agricultural population	100.0	110.4	126.2	132.7
Agricultural employment	100.0	100.1	104.7	112.2
Total agricultural production	100.0	121.0	142.8	178.7
Agricultural crop production[a]	100.0	116.8	132.1	159.7
Output of crops and livestock	100.0	121.4	139.1	168.5
Agricultural crop production per worker	100.0	115.4	126.1	142.4
Man-days of labor	100.0	104.1	111.5	116.9
Agricultural crop production to man-days of labor	100.0	112.2	118.8	136.6
Man-days of labor to employment	100.0	104.0	106.5	104.2
Fixed capital	100.0	107.5	116.6	133.6
Working capital	100.0	151.5	169.7	240.2
Multiple cropping	171.9	175.5	183.6	188.0
Diversification[b]	3.54	4.07	4.01	5.75

[a]Excludes forestry, fishing, and livestock.

[b]The diversification index is calculated for 181 different crops by the formula: $1/\Sigma$ (value of each product/value of total products)^2.

Sources: Parameters of land and population and indexes of production from Economic Planning Council, *Taiwan Statistical Data Book, 1975*, pp. 47–51; indexes of labor man-days, output of crops and livestock, working capital, and fixed capital from Ho, *Economic Development in Taiwan*, p. 245; index of diversification from Shirley W. Y. Kuo, "Effects of Land Reform, Agricultural Pricing Policy, and Economic Growth on Multiple Crop Diversification in Taiwan," in *Economic Essays*, vol. 4 (Taipei: National Taiwan University, Graduate Institute of Economics, November 1973); other indexes from calculations by the authors.

28 percent. Because the agricultural population increased by only a third, an agricultural surplus was assured. Although this 5 percent annual increase in net output during the subphase of import substitution is considerably smaller than that of the industrial sector, it still is an impressive figure by any international standard of comparison. It is even more impressive when two additional factors are considered: the natural fertility of the soil is low; the land frontier on the mountainous island already had essentially been reached. The growth in agricultural output could only be called dramatic. Between 1952 and 1964 total agricultural production, including forestry, fishing, and livestock, rose by 78 percent, with the production of crops alone rising by 59.7 percent (see table 4). These production increases were primarily the result of increased yields in traditional crops, but they were also the result of the introduction of new crops. While the yields of such traditional crops as rice increased 50 percent, the yields of relatively new specialty crops, such as cotton and fruits, increased more than 100 percent.[9]

Fixed capital in agriculture expanded by about 34 percent between 1952 and 1964 (see table 4). Much of this expansion was in irrigation and flood control facilities, which deteriorated during the war and were rebuilt and expanded during the 1950s. Farm buildings and other structures were added to and improved. The water buffalo was gradually replaced by small tillers and other small mechanical devices. Working capital increased even more dramatically than fixed capital, growing

[9]Economic Planning Council, *Taiwan Statistical Data Book, 1975* (Taipei, 1975), pp. 48, 53–55.

by 140 percent between 1952 and 1964 (see table 4). The continuous introduction of new seed varieties, responsive to intensive fertilizer applications, and the gradual reduction in fertilizer prices and government restrictions enabled Taiwan's total fertilizer use to grow by 91 percent over the same period.[10] As livestock production grew by nearly 120 percent, more and more commercial feeds were imported. Further increases in working capital included widespread use of pesticides, a major postwar innovation which helped to reduce high losses caused by disease and insects.

Technology change, introduced mainly by such government-supported research agencies as the JCRR, clearly was a significant factor in generating the increased agricultural output.[11] In 1960 Taiwan had 79 agricultural research workers for every 100,000 persons active in agriculture, compared with 60 in Japan, 4.7 in Thailand, 1.6 in the Philippines, and 1.2 in India.[12] The research agencies successfully introduced new strains of rice and sugar and such new crops as asparagus and mushrooms, as well as pesticides, insecticides, and new agricultural tools and machinery. In the Hayami-Ruttan terminology, most of the technology change was of the chemical variety, not the mechanical.[13]

Taiwan's impressive success in agriculture can thus be attributed to many factors. Although the purpose of this volume is not to analyze these factors in detail, their relation to the distribution of income nevertheless is relevant to the argument here. Given the physical and organizational improvement of the environmental infrastructure and the pervasive package of land reform, farmers had the incentives and the tools to improve their situation during the subphase of primary import substitution, which usually discriminates against agriculture. Moreover the technology change seemed to be of a type that generally used labor and saved land and capital. Although the number of persons employed in agriculture increased by 12 percent between 1952 and 1964, the number of man-days increased by 17 percent (see table 4). Consequently the number of working days per worker steadily increased. In 1965 the average worker had 156

days of farm employment, compared with 90 days in 1946 and 134 days in 1952.[14] As a result, the number of working days per hectare of land increased from approximately 170 in 1948–50 to about 260 in 1963–65.[15]

Larger labor inputs to the cultivation of traditional crops and the diversification into new crops resulted in more intensive cultivation of land. Between 1952 and 1964 the multiple-cropping index increased from 171.9 to 188; the diversification index increased from 3.54 to 5.75 (see table 4). The shift toward such labor-intensive crops as vegetables and away from the complete dominance of the traditional crops of rice and sugar was continuous. As an indication of the labor intensity of vegetable cultivation, the cultivation of one hectare of asparagus requires 2,900 times the labor input of the cultivation of one hectare of rice.

Despite the substantial increase in the absorption of labor in agriculture between 1952 and 1964, rural underemployment continued during the 1950s and has been estimated at about 40 percent.[16] The smaller, poorer farms were especially unable to generate sufficient income or to keep the entire family fully employed. This pattern led to a small amount of net physical migration out of the agricultural sector, estimated at less than one percent annually during the 1950s. Mostly, however, farmers increasingly sought off-farm employment in the rapidly growing rural industrial sector. Consequently underemployment did not develop into as serious a problem as in most other LDCs.[17] The pattern of agricultural growth and the participation in that growth by rich and poor farmers were the basic ingredients of the dramatic improvement in the distribution of income in Taiwan during the 1950s.

The Distribution of Assets and Industrial Growth

What can be said about the distribution of assets outside agriculture during this period? Obviously

---

[10]*Taiwan Statistical Data Book, 1975*, p. 58.

[11]Ho estimated that 44.9 percent of the growth of agricultural output during 1951–60 can be attributed to changes in total factor productivity, 10.3 percent to increases in crop area, and 34.7 percent to increases in working capital. Ho, *Economic Development in Taiwan*, pp. 147–85.

[12]Ho, *Economic Development in Taiwan*, p. 178.

[13]Yujiro Hayami and Vernon W. Ruttan, *Agricultural Development in International Perspective* (Baltimore: Johns Hopkins University Press, 1971), passim.

[14]You-tsao Wang, "Agricultural Development," in *Economic Development of Taiwan*, ed. Kowie Chang, p. 176.

[15]W. H. Lai, "Trend of Agricultural Employment in Post-war Taiwan" (paper read at Conference on Manpower in Taiwan, 1972, Taipei; processed).

[16]The estimation difficulties here are well known, and the authors do not place much confidence in these numbers.

[17]Ho, *Economic Development in Taiwan*, p. 158. Ho derived his figures from S. F. Liu, "Disguised Unemployment in Taiwan Agriculture" (Ph.D. dissertation, University of Illinois, 1966) and Paul K. C. Liu, "Economic Development and Population in Taiwan since 1895: An Overview," in *Essays on the Population of Taiwan* (Taipei: Academia Sinica, Institute of Economics, 1973).

Table 5. Distribution of Industrial Production, by Public and Private Ownership, 1952–64 (percent)

Year	Total Public	Total Private	Manufacturing Public	Manufacturing Private	Mining Public	Mining Private	Electricity, gas, and water Public
1952	56.6	43.4	56.2	43.8	28.3	71.7	100.0
1953	55.9	44.1	55.9	44.1	24.4	75.6	100.0
1954	52.7	47.3	49.7	50.3	32.5	67.5	100.0
1955	51.1	48.9	48.7	51.3	28.5	71.5	100.0
1956	51.0	49.0	48.3	51.7	26.5	73.5	100.0
1957	51.3	48.7	48.7	51.3	26.3	73.7	100.0
1958	50.0	50.0	47.2	52.8	24.2	75.8	100.0
1959	48.7	51.3	45.2	54.8	22.6	77.4	100.0
1960	47.9	52.1	43.8	56.2	24.2	75.8	100.0
1961	48.2	51.8	45.3	54.7	18.8	81.2	99.9
1962	46.2	53.8	42.3	57.7	19.6	80.4	98.6
1963	44.8	55.2	40.6	59.4	19.1	80.4	99.7
1964	43.7	56.3	38.9	61.1	20.5	79.5	98.8

Source: Economic Planning Council, *Taiwan Statistical Data Book, 1975,* p. 75.

much less, but broad patterns nevertheless are indicative. The 56.6 percent share of the public sector in industrial output in 1952 characterized the Taiwanese economy in the early 1950s (table 5). This pattern was mainly a consequence of the Chinese takeover of Japanese assets at the end of the Second World War. In addition, before the evacuation from the mainland, the Nationalist government dismantled and shipped industrial equipment, such as textile spindles, and in some cases entire enterprises to Taiwan. Firms under public ownership were initially plagued with typical problems: inefficiency, over-staffing, rigid pay structures, and bureaucratic interference. Meanwhile small firms and simple equipment characterized the private sector. As late as 1961, 31 percent of all manufacturing establishments employed fewer than ten workers.[18] All industry was hampered by the shortage of foreign exchange.[19]

This situation undoubtedly was favorable to the equity of the initial distribution of industrial assets. Because private ownership of capital was not on a large scale; entrepreneurs generally were not in a position to gain monopolistic control of industries or to accumulate great wealth from property income. In the private sector the small size and labor intensity of firms was favorable to the share of workers. Profits of the larger, more capital-inten-

sive firms went to government, not to private entrepreneurs.

During the early 1950s government began transferring the four public enterprises under its control to private ownership: Taiwan Cement Corporation, Taiwan Pulp and Paper Corporation, Taiwan Industrial and Mining Corporation, and Taiwan Agriculture and Forestry Development Corporation. This transfer was not easily accomplished. Government had difficulty finding buyers because of the lack of accumulated private wealth and entrepreneurial expertise and because of the poor track records of these enterprises. In 1953 a large portion of government assets was nevertheless transferred as partial payment to landlords under the land-to-the-tiller program. As a result of this transfer and such other factors as the increasingly rapid growth of private industry, the government-owned share of total industrial production fell to 43.7 percent in 1964 (see table 5). Industries remaining in the public sector included utilities, railroads, shipbuilding, and iron and steel. Thus, despite the substantial drop in government ownership, the public control of assets continued to be important, particularly in the most capital-intensive industries, in which growth is least favorable to the distribution of income. . . .

Overall FID

The pattern of overall FID for 1953, 1959, and 1964 shows a striking improvement by almost

[18]Ho, *Economic Development in Taiwan,* p. 597.

[19]Council on U.S. Aid, *Industry of Free China,* vol. 1, no. 4 (1954).

Table 6. Measures of the Equity of the Family Distribution of Income, 1953, 1959, and 1964

Item	1953[a]	1959[b]	1964[c]
Distribution of income by percentile of households (percent)			
0–20	3.0	5.7	7.7
21–40	8.3	9.7	12.6
41–60	9.1	13.9	16.6
61–80	18.2	19.7	22.1
81–95	28.8	26.3	24.8
96–100	32.6	24.7	16.2
Mean income per household (N.T. dollars in 1972 prices)	22,681	31,814	32,452
Per capita GNP in market prices (N.T. dollars in 1972 prices)	6,994	8,629	10,875
Ratio of income share of top 10 percent to that of bottom 10 percent	30.40	13.72	8.63
Gini coefficient	0.5580	0.4400	0.3280

[a]Data are based on a sample of 301 families, or a sample fraction of 2/1,000.

[b]Data are based on a sample of 812 families, or a sample fraction of 4/1,000.

[c]Data are based on a sample size of 3,000 families, or a sample fraction of 14.6/1,000.

Sources: 1953 from Kowie Chang, "An Estimate of Taiwan Personal Income Distribution in 1953—Pareto's Formula Discussed and Applied," *Journal of Social Science,* vol. 7 (August 1956), p. 260; 1959 from National Taiwan University, College of Law, "Report on Pilot Study of Personal Income and Consumption in Taiwan" (prepared under the sponsorship of a working group of National Income Statistics, DGBAS; processed in Chinese), table A, p. 23; 1964 from DGBAS, *Report on the Survey of Family Income Expenditure, 1964* (Taipei: DGBAS, 1966); Shirley W. Y. Kuo, "Income Distribution by Size in Taiwan Area—Changes and Causes," in *Income Distribution, Employment, and Economic Development in Southeast and East Asia,* 2 vols. (Tokyo: Japan Economic Research Center, 1975), vol. 1, pp. 80–146.

every measure (table 6). In 1953 the Gini coefficient was 0.56, which is comparable to patterns of income distribution now prevailing in Brazil and Mexico. By 1964 the Gini coefficient dropped to 0.33, a level comparable to that of the best performers anywhere.[20] This substantial decline in overall FID during the 1950s can be traced primarily to the rapidly improving rural FID, as noted earlier, and secondarily to the distribution of nonagricultural income, which probably did not worsen and may even have slightly improved.

[20]The quality of the data, particularly for the 1950s, is suspect. Calculation of total personal income in 1953, by aggregating the product of average family income and the number of households in each income group, gives a figure 20 percent lower than that of the national accounts data. A similar calculation found that the 1953 data underestimated the total family income given in the national accounts data by 16.7 percent, but that the 1959 data overestimated total family income by 15.3 percent. The 1964 DGBAS data were found to underestimate total family income by only about 5 percent.

Although more than half of Taiwan's population in 1953 was in agriculture, 84 percent of the 1953 sample group came from the more urbanized and industrialized areas; 58 percent of that group lived in Taiwan's four largest cities. If rural income was better distributed than urban income, as was seen earlier, any overweighting of urban income may have resulted in a low estimate of total personal income and a high estimate of the Gini coefficient. In turn, although DGBAS data for 1964 did not include an appropriate number of families with income exceeding NT$200,000, the downward bias in the Gini probably is too small to be of much importance. Nevertheless the survey results for the 1950s must be accepted with caution.

With respect to the underestimation of FID inequality—the 1964 Gini coefficient based on decile groups is 0.328—households with income exceeding NT$200,000 accounted for only 0.1 percent of the population and 1.15 percent of total income. Even if the income share of these households is increased by 1 percentage point, which almost doubles their income share, and if the 1 percent loss is equally assigned to the first nine decile groups, the Gini coefficient increases by only 3.1 percent to 0.3307. The increase really is not that large. To give an idea of the effect of the underestimation of the Gini coefficient, again for the 1964 data, suppose the income share of the top decile group to be increased by 2, 3, and 4 percentage points. Then the Gini coefficients respectively rise by 6.2 percent, 9.3 percent, and 12.4 percent to 0.3406, 0.3505, and 0.3604. Thus the smaller the population, income share, underestimation of the wealthiest households, or any combination of these elements, the smaller the downward bias of the Gini coefficient.

Selection VIII.C.2. Brazilian Size Distribution of Income*

The four distributions of income set out in Table 1 derive from a stratified sample of approximately eleven thousand families drawn from the 1960 Brazilian census returns and accurately reproducing the population as a whole. The distributions labeled as "original" include monetary remuneration only, as requested by the census. To these, four adjustments are then made, leading to the corrected distributions. The adjustments are of two basic types, one set to incorporate nonmonetary income excluded from the census inquiry, the other to reallocate income to family workers reported as economically active but without monetary remuneration. After allowance for income in kind for imputed rent, imputed rural home consumption, and imputed room and board for domestic servants, and distribution of some fraction of household chief's income to family workers, income per worker is increased almost 20 percent and concentration significantly reduced. Family income is affected in the same direction but to a lesser degree.

The resultant concentration of income reported in Table 1, as measured by the Gini coefficient, is similar to that of most of the Latin American countries. Such an index also bespeaks considerably more inequality than currently prevails for the United States, Canada, Japan, and Western Europe. (See Irving B. Kravis 1962 and Econ. Comm. for Latin America 1967.) . . .

Since 1967 Brazil has grown at real rates of 9 percent and greater, and the immediate prospects seem equally auspicious. This economic "miracle" has already begun to rival the earlier German example. The common ingredient of greater scope to market forces and freer rein to the private sector has not gone unnoticed; there is already talk of the applicability of the Brazilian model to other parts of the developing world.

Yet the recent publication of the preliminary results of the 1970 census give much less cause for satisfaction on the income distribution front (Brasil 1971). In Table 2 I have presented estimates of the income distribution for the total economically active population and its agricultural and nonagricultural components. The coverage of the censuses of 1960 and 1970 are quite comparable, and the treatment of the open-ended class is identical for the two dates. The conclusion that inequality has increased over the course of the decade accordingly seems correct, if lamentable. The upper 3.2 percent of the labor force commands 33.1 percent of the income in 1970, compared to about 27 percent in 1960. Although the concentration of income is less in agriculture than nonagriculture, thereby reversing their 1960 ordering, this accomplishment is not indicative of greater welfare in rural areas. Rather, the sectoral differential in reported census incomes has widened, a phenomenon corroborated by the independent quarterly surveys of households conducted since 1968 (Brasil 1968).

It is legitimate to object that the 1970 data are not a fair test of what rapid growth in a capitalistic mold implies. Little more than half the decade is spanned by the continuity of military government since 1964, and only the last segment of that is characterized by substantial material progress. In fact, it is reasonable to presume that stabilization was more responsible than growth for the widening inequality portrayed in Table 2 (Fishlow). Between 1964 and 1967, as the consequence of policies both severely restraining nominal wages and inducing "corrective inflation"—adjustment of governmentally administered prices—real minimum wages declined 20 percent. They subsequently barely held their own. Average real salaries in industry fared somewhat better, declining by less and increasing more rapidly from their nadir. The 1970 level stands about 10 percent above 1964 receipts. Since per capita income rose considerably more rapidly over the same interval, 22 percent, someone gained relatively. As we have seen, it likely was not the rural sector, but rather urban, above-average income recipients in finance, commerce, etc. Such an interpretation is consistent with the aggregate income distribution for 1970.

The concentration of income, resultant from stabilization was not wholly intentional. It occurred because actual inflation exceeded programmed price rises, and the latter were applied to the official wage formula. The increased inequality thus measures the failure of the conventional monetary and fiscal instruments applied during the Castello Branco administration. In a larger sense, however, the result was accurately indicative of priorities: destruction of the urban proletariat as a political threat, and reestablishment of an economic order geared to private capital accumulation.

Because such goals persist, it is not easy to be sanguine about the distributional implications of

*From Albert Fishlow, "Brazilian Size Distribution of Income," *American Economic Review* 62 (May 1972): 391–392, 399–402. Reprinted by permission.

Table 1. Brazilian[a] Size Distributions of Income, 1960

Monthly Income in 1960, NCr$	Economically Active Population[b]				Families			
	Original		Corrected		Original		Corrected	
	Percentage of Population	Percentage of Income	Percentage of Population	Percentage of Income	Percentage of Population	Percentage of Income	Percentage of Population	Percentage of Income
None	14.7	0.0	.5	0.0	2.7	0.0	1.7	0.0
0–2.1	22.3	5.2	26.1	5.2	14.8	2.1	5.4	.7
2.1–3.3	14.4	7.0	16.2	6.4	15.0	4.3	12.5	2.9
3.3–4.5	10.5	7.4	11.8	7.1	12.9	5.5	12.1	4.4
4.5–6.0	13.1	12.3	14.0	11.3	13.1	7.4	14.6	7.1
6.0–10.0	13.8	20.0	17.3	21.0	16.7	14.3	22.3	16.0
10.0–20.0	8.2	22.2	10.5	23.6	15.5	24.2	20.4	26.7
20.0–50.0	2.6	16.4	3.1	16.8	7.5	25.0	8.9	25.3
Over 50.0	.5	9.4	.5	8.6	1.8	17.2	2.1	16.8
Mean	5.52		6.51		9.24		10.95	
Mean (US$/year)[c]	513		606		860		939	
Gini Coefficient	.59		.52		.55		.50	

[a]Excludes Center-West and North, which accounted for 7.7 percent of the population in 1960.

[b]The distribution of the economically active population plus individuals receiving income is not significantly different: the top 3.2 percent receive 26.8 percent of the income (uncorrected). Since most of the analysis applied subsequently is more appropriate to the economically active population, we shall use it as our basic distribution of individuals.

[c]Converted at an exchange rate of .129 NCr$ per dollar, the purchasing power equivalent rates in June 1960 as reported in *Econ. Bull. for Latin America*, Oct. 1963, 203.

Source: See text.

more rapid growth over an extended period. The very strength of the recent expansion, after all, partially derives from the prior concentration of income. The leading sectors in the industrial revival have been consumer durables, automobiles especially, rather than foodstuffs or textiles. The differential is more than one would expect on the basis of income elasticities of demand, or perhaps even the greater facilities for credit, and is presumably not unassociated with some reallocation of income shares.

Governmental policy instruments as presently applied, moreover, hardly favor equity. One of the distinguishing characteristics of fiscal policy is its liberal concession of tax incentives for investment in the securities market, application in certain regions and specified sectors, etc. By its very nature this is a boon to those with tax liabilities and of no corresponding advantage to the poor. Despite progressivity of the tax structure, increased withholding, and attempts to eliminate evasion, the proportion of revenues originating in direct taxes has declined since the early 1960's. On the financial side, positive real rates of interest for savers, and

an ebullient stock exchange, may satisfy the requirements of an efficient capital market but will also benefit relatively those with above-average incomes. Such apparent distributional counterweights as the Programa de Integracao Social and the Programa de Integracao Nacional (*PIN*) hardly rectify the balance. The former, financed by a tax levied upon employers, creates a fund to which workers have limited access. Its benefits are scaled to earnings, rather than the inverse relationship that is implied by distributional objectives. Depending upon the ultimate incidence of the tax, there will likely be modest redistribution from capital to labor at best. In the meantime, the fund runs a surplus and these forced savings ultimately finance the acquisition of private assets that will set up skewed distributions of income in the future. The *PIN* is based upon the questionable premise that colonization is to be a major component of the solution of rural poverty. A proposal of doubtful direct economic profitability, it has the further cost of detracting energies from more effective alternatives designed to increase agricultural productivity directly.

Table 2. Size Distribution of Income, 1970 (in Percent)

NCr$ per Month	Total Economically Active Population		Agriculture		Nonagriculture	
	Population	Income	Population	Income	Population	Income
None	11.7	0.0	20.1	0.0	5.1	0.0
0–100	31.7	8.0	46.8	28.4	19.7	3.4
101–150	12.8	6.2	15.3	17.8	10.7	3.6
151–200	15.6	10.6	10.0	16.3	20.0	9.3
201–250	4.5	3.9	1.7	3.7	6.6	3.9
251–500	14.6	21.2	4.6	16.0	22.7	22.6
501–1000	5.9	17.1	1.0	7.2	9.7	19.3
1001–2000	2.2	13.0	.3	4.3	3.8	14.9
2001+	1.0	20.1	.1	6.4	1.7	23.0
Mean NCr$	258.1		107.3		377.1	
Mean U.S. 1960 $ per year[a]	679		282		992	
Gini coefficient	.63		.53		.58	

[a]Converted at the 1960 parity rate multiplied by the Brazilian implicit *GDP* price deflator: NCr$ 4.56.
Source: See text.

It is important, however, not to place undue emphasis upon the possibilities of conventional policies in influencing the distribution of income. Even highly progressive tax systems have limited leverage. In the instances of the United States, Sweden, and the United Kingdom, the shares of income of the upper 5 percent of the population are diminished only by between 10 and 20 percent after taxes. (Simon Kuznets 1966, pp. 208–11). In the case of Brazil this would at best mean an after-tax distribution in which the wealthiest 5 percent would have claim on something more than a third of the income. This is a considerable improvement, to be sure, well beyond what Brazilian fiscal policy is likely to achieve, and still leaves matters in an unsatisfactory state by comparative international standards.

In light of such constraints, it is especially disturbing to discover that such structural factors as the distribution of educational opportunities and the sectoral allocation of the labor force are not tending in favor of equality, but instead the opposite. Between 1960 and 1970 the average number of years of schooling of labor force participants increased from 2.24 to 2.95 years. Yet because the increase resulted from the disproportionate gain in persons with training beyond the primary level, the variance increased by an even greater 48 percent. The consequence, to the extent that education is causal, is that the more skewed distribution of educational attainment itself accounts for about half

the observed increase in total inequality over the decade.

The causal factor making for inequality is the variance rather than the level of education. While in principle the greater educational attainment could tend to increase the concentration of income, in fact its quantitative contribution appears to be negligible. Thus there are some degrees of freedom for governmental policy. Some increase in variance and inequality may virtually be inevitable owing to the age structure of the labor force and the prior lack of education, but there is clearly scope for a policy that emphasizes to a greater extent extension of educational opportunities to the underprivileged—and various calculations of the rate of return to elementary schooling suggest it is a highly profitable strategy as well (Lerner 1970, Levy 1970). Thus an educational policy that succeeded in elimination of illiteracy among the young between 1960 and 1970 could have simultaneously increased the average level of educational attainment more, while increasing the variance less, than the pattern actually occurring. Current plans, however, seem to favor continuing emphasis upon secondary and university enrollment, without sensibility to the distributional implications of such a structure.

Similarly, while the reallocation of labor from agriculture to the nonagricultural sector has positive, albeit limited, possibilities for greater equality, the widened divergence in average incomes has produced the opposite result. Despite absorption of labor in the secondary sector in the 1960's at a much more rapid rate than in the 1950's, in large measure owing to opportunities in construction activity, the sectoral contribution to overall inequality actually increased.

In sum, in the absence of effective and far-reaching alteration in governmental attitudes, there is likely to be little progress and, quite possibly, retrogression in the distribution of income. It is mistaken to view such a result as an unfortunate but inevitable consequence of rapid growth. There is no necessary inconsistency between greater equity and expanding output. Brazilian poverty is directly linked to low levels of productivity, particularly rural, that are subject to attack. Policies can be developed. But first there must be recognition of an accounting system that reckons and applauds not only increases in aggregate output, but also tabulates the differential gains in welfare that are reflected in the distribution of income.

References

A. Fishlow, "Some Reflections on Post-1964 Brazilian Economic Policy," unpublished paper, forthcoming in volume on recent developments in Brazil, Alfred Stepan, ed.

I. B. Kravis, *The Structure of Income,* Philadelphia 1962.

S. Kuznets, *Modern Economic Growth: Rate, Structure and Spread,* New Haven 1966.

M. O. Lerner, "Determinants of Educational Attainment in Brazil, 1960," unpublished Ph.D. dissertation, University of California, Berkeley 1970.

S. Levy, "An Economic Analysis of Investment in Education in the State of Sao Paulo," unpublished paper, Instituto de Pesquisas Economicas, Sao Paulo 1970.

Brasil, Instituto Brasileiro de Estatistica, *Pesquisa Nacional por Amostra de Domicilios,* quarterly, 1968.

Brasil, Servico Nacional de Recenseamento, *Censo Demografico,* 1970, *Tabulacocs Avancadas,* Rio de Janeiro 1971.

Economic Commission for Latin America, *Economic Bulletin for Latin America,* Oct. 1967, 12, 38–60.

Political Economy

Overview

Since the origin of modern development economics in the 1950s, thinking about the state and economic development has gone through three phases. The first, most optimistic phase viewed the state as an essentially benevolent leader of the development process, an "omniscient social-welfare maximizer" in the words of Dani Rodrik in Selection IX.C.3 below. The second, most pessimistic phase views the state as a major obstacle to development, acting on behalf of narrow interest groups or on behalf of politicians and bureaucrats (i.e., on its own behalf) rather than for the greater good. Both the theoretical reasoning and the empirical findings constituting this second, ongoing phase are represented in section IX.B. The third phase identifies wide variations in state performance and seeks to explain them, focusing in particular on institutional determinants of "state capacity," meaning the ability of the state to formulate policy independent of corrupting influences and to implement policy effectively. The last section in this chapter is devoted to this newest phase.

While today few specialists in development believe in a benevolent and omniscient state, no one doubts the value of knowing what the state should do if its goal is to maximize social welfare. This is the subject of section IX.A. Under the implicit assumption that "government is well intentioned, well informed, and competent," Nicholas Stern in Selection IX.A.1 identifies five groups of arguments for state intervention: market failure, income distribution, rights to certain facilities or goods such as education, paternalism (relating to drugs, for example), and the rights of future generations. These arguments "point fairly directly to particular areas of government expenditure, notably education, health, social support, and the environment." In Exhibit IX.A.1 Stern summarizes both reasons for market failure and problems with state intervention.

As noted in the first Comment following Stern's selection, comprehensive development planning has clearly fallen out of favor. Yet some argue for a more limited form of government guidance of the economy, often under the heading of "industrial policy." One of the most prominent advocates of this position is Robert Wade, whose views on "governing the market" are summarized in the Comment that concludes section IX.A. Disagreement regarding the desirability of industrial policy is the chief remaining controversy in what Fischer and Thomas (1990) describe as "the new consensus on development policy":

> The new consensus on development policy places greater stress than before on the central role of markets, and on the private sector (in some countries, the informal private sector) as the engine of growth. The role of the public sector is seen as the creation of a favorable enabling environment for economic activity. The enabling environment consists of the legal, institutional, and policy framework within which economic agents operate.
>
> A government that creates a favorable enabling environment has a large role to play, for instance in ensuring the provision of infrastructure, including social services, such as poverty alleviation, basic education, and access to health care; public security; a stable macroeconomic framework; and an efficient fiscal and regulatory system.
>
> The most difficult question about the role of the government is whether it should take an active part in promoting particular industries, that is, whether it should pursue an industrial policy. Some successful elements of an active policy are clear: export development and assistance in marketing, information, technology, and know-how. Expanding manufactured exports requires sustained efforts on both macroeconomic and microeconomic levels. Japan, Korea, and Taiwan have paid attention to the many nonprice requirements of export development. For a period of time, they also pursued export development while maintaining a certain degree of import protection.

We should note that priorities are not part of this new consensus. Given its limited resources, should the government build roads or schools first? Should the most attention of policymakers and the best and brightest civil servants be devoted to tax collection or macroeconomic management? How should these priorities differ depending on the level of development and other country characteristics? To date economists have had very little to say on this subject.

As evidence for failure of government leadership of the development process mounted, particularly in sub-Saharan Africa (see section I.B), the view of the state as a major obstacle to development gained momentum. Advocates of this view were hampered, however, by conventional welfare economics analysis that predicts that the "deadweight losses" generated by government interventions in the economy will be small relative to national income. In the first selection of the second section, Anne Krueger points out that when government interventions take the form of restrictions on economic activity that create rents, resources may be wasted in competing for these rents, causing these interventions to be much more costly than conventional analysis predicts. Under certain assumptions it can be shown that the value of the resources wasted by competitive rent seeking will equal the value of the rents; Krueger estimates the value of rents to have been 7.3 percent of Indian GNP in 1964 and roughly 15 percent of Turkish GNP in 1968. Krueger's selection is preceded by a Note explaining exactly what "rents" are and showing that rents and thus the cost of rent seeking can be large relative to deadweight losses. The first Comment following Krueger's selection shows how the Harris–Todaro model presented in Note VI.1 above can be seen as an example of the complete rent dissipation predicted by Krueger. The second Comment clarifies the relationship between rent seeking and corruption.

In Krueger's analysis, rent seeking is an unintended side effect of well-intentioned (if sometimes misguided) state interventions in the economy. Other writers in the "neoclassical political economy" tradition have argued that these interventions are the result of lobbying by interest groups. For example, import quotas may be designed to protect politically powerful industries. Government failure is thus generated by interest groups that use their influence on the state to cause it to enact inefficient policies that redistribute income in their favor, and such failure is amplified by the rent-seeking activities to which these policies give rise. The neoclassical political economy literature is surveyed in Selection IX.B.2 by T. N. Srinivasan.

The next two selections take us from the theory of government failure to cases. Pranab Bardhan describes the failure of Indian government policies intended to alleviate rural poverty. Many of these policies, such as land reform, were similar to those that successfully stimulated agricultural production by small farmers and reduced income inequality in Taiwan, as described in Selection VIII.C.1 by Fei, Ranis, and Kuo. According to Bardhan, these policies failed in India because they were not effectively implemented or enforced. Lack of enforcement in turn can be explained by the dominance of the Indian political system by "a complex constellation of forces representing rich farmers, big business, and the so-called petite bourgeoisie, including the unionized workers of the organized sector. In such a context," Bardhan asserts, "it is touchingly naive not to anticipate the failures of asset distribution policies or the appropriation by the rich of a disproportionate share of the benefits of public investment."

Bardhan is not writing about unnecessary state interventions in the economy but rather about desirable interventions that were not enforced. Moreover, his analysis of government failure in this instance is closer to a Marxist tradition than to neoclassical political economy. The following selection by Robert Bates, IX.B.4, is different from Bardhan's in both these respects. Bates notes that sub-Saharan African governments that seek increased farm production tend to employ project-based rather than price-based policies. He explains this tendency by the fact that price-based policies affect rural supporters and opponents of the government alike, whereas projects can be targeted to supporters. Unfortunately, targeted projects have proven to be a much less efficient way to increase farm production than high output prices, and agricultural performance in sub-Saharan Africa has been extremely poor. Similarly, the tendency for sub-Saharan African governments to regulate markets heavily for agricultural outputs and inputs is explained by Bates as a way to give governments the ability to reward supporters by granting exceptions to the rules and to punish opponents by threatening to enforce them.

Sub-Saharan African countries are among the world's most ethnically fractionalized, and in the last selection of this section, William Easterly and Ross Levine argue that ethnically divided societies are more prone to government failure. On the one hand, valuable infrastructure investments may not be made because groups cannot agree on large expenditures, perhaps because of different preferences or because of suspicions that one's own ethnic group will benefit least. On the other hand, if different ethnic groups control different branches of the government there may be an especially strong tendency to enact rent-generating legislation, with each group believing its members can capture the rents while the costs fall on other groups. (One could also argue, following the reasoning of Bates, that ethnically divided societies are more likely to adopt project-based policies that can be targeted to co-ethnics.) Either of these arguments can be reversed—each group may agree to support infrastructure investments that benefit other groups in return for support of its favorite projects ("log-rolling"), and each group may veto the rent-generating legislation of the other groups—so ultimately the effects of ethnic diversity on infrastructure expenditure and rent-generating legislation are empirical questions. Using data for roughly 100 countries, Easterly and Levine find that ethnic diversity is associated with lower school attainment, fewer telephones per worker, and a higher black-market exchange rate premium (a good source of rents). Through its impact on these and other policy indicators, ethnic diversity tends to reduce economic growth, and thus accounts for much of the poor growth performance of sub-Saharan Africa.

The theoretical and empirical grounds for viewing the state as an obstacle to economic development appear very strong. Yet readers of this book will be able to recall a number of examples of beneficial state action, particularly in East Asia. In the first selection of the final section, Stephen Knack and Philip Keefer present more systematic evidence that state performance, rather than being uniformly bad, varies widely, and that this variation has substantial consequences for economic growth. As explanatory variables in cross-country growth regressions they use indices based on ratings compiled by two private international investment risk services of aspects of state performance such as rule of law, infrastructure quality, and bureaucratic delays. An increase of one standard deviation in either index is associated with an increase in average annual per capita GDP growth of more than 1.2 percentage points.

Writers seeking to explain government success as well as government failure in less developed countries reject the model of the state as a tool of narrow interest groups, but must then confront the issue of why "autonomous" states do not simply maximize the income of politicians and bureaucrats. Indeed, Peter Evans finds in Selection IX.C.2 that some LDC states, notably the government of Zaire, do use their autonomy for this purpose. The Korean and Taiwanese states, on the other hand, have worked hand in glove with the private sector to promote investment and enhance the capacity of private firms to enter international markets, earning these governments the moniker "developmental states." Evans argues that a necessary (but not sufficient) condition for a state to be "developmental" is professionalization of the state bureaucracy. Meritocratically recruited officials, partially insulated from society by civil service procedures, identify with the corporate goals of the state and seek to advance their self-interests not through corruption but rather by impressing their colleagues with superior performance and thereby moving up the bureaucratic hierarchy.

In Evans's view, bureaucratic professionalism may be adequate for the state to create the "favorable enabling environment" for private sector economic activity called for in the new consensus on development policy described above, but it is not sufficient for the state to pursue successfully the more controversial task of industrial policy. For this the state needs good communications networks with key private sector decision-makers, that is, it needs to be "embedded" in society yet maintain its autonomy—a difficult feat.

In Selection IX.C.3, Dani Rodrik focuses the discussion of state capacity around the ability of the government to successfully implement export subsidies. While he agrees with Evans regarding the importance of autonomy for the ability of the state to implement policy without being manipulated by interest groups, he is much less confident about what state characteristics cause this autonomy to be put to good use. Rather than citing "embeddedness" of bureaucrats as a complement to autonomy, Rodrik emphasizes the need for "coherence" of policy priorities set by the politicians at the top of the decision-making hierarchy.

In the final selection, James Rauch and Peter Evans seek to test Evans's hypothesis that bureaucratic professionalism improves state performance by examining the effects of measures of meritocratic recruitment, internal promotion and career stability, and competitive official salaries on ratings of corruption, bureaucratic quality, and bureaucratic delays collected by Knack and Keefer. To construct their measures Rauch and Evans surveyed three experts per country for 35 LDCs regarding personnel practices in those countries' core economic agencies. Controlling for country per capita income, level of education, and ethnic diversity, they find that their measure of meritocratic recruitment is positively associated with all three ratings of bureaucratic performance collected by Knack and Keefer, and that their measure of salary competitiveness is positively associated with one of these three ratings.

Looking back from the last to the first section, it appears that development specialists are much closer to a consensus on what the government should do than they are on how to get the government to do what it should effectively.

Reference

Fischer, Stanley, and Vinod Thomas. 1990. "Policies for Economic Development." *American Journal of Agricultural Economics* 72 (August): 809–14.

IX.A. THE (PROPER) ROLE OF THE STATE IN LESS DEVELOPED COUNTRIES

Selection IX.A.1. Public Policy and the Economics of Development*

The Role of the State

Early writers on development, governments of recently independent developing countries, and many Western countries facing reconstruction after World War II saw a major role for the state in the production process. Behind these judgements were a pessimism about the market's ability to deliver economic change in key dimensions with the speed deemed necessary. . . . More recently the pendulum has swung the other way with a sizeable fraction of the herd of both politicians and economists charging in the direction of minimalist government, privatisation, and so on. I shall argue, on the basis of theory, of rights, and of experience, that the state's role should not be minimal. The state's emphasis, however, should not be on production. It should rather be on health, education, protection of the poor, infrastructure, and providing the right environment for entrepreneurial activity to flourish. When we add to the list basic administration, law and order, and defence, we see that a substantial fraction of GDP will be involved. It should be emphasised that the organisation and finance of this expenditure can take many forms, particularly concerning the tier of government and the relationship between government and community, but the discussion of these important issues would take us too far afield.

I begin with a brief review of what standard microeconomic theory has to say about market and government failures. First note that it would be a mistake to see the issue of the role of the state in terms of finding an appropriate balance along a single dimension such as the fraction of productive capacity owned by the state. Many activities and institutions have public and private aspects to them and many of the crucial policy issues involve finding an effective integration of the market and the government.

Five groups of arguments for state intervention in the economy may be distinguished:

(i) market failure, which may arise from many possible sources including externalities, missing markets, increasing returns, public goods, and imperfect information;

*From Nicholas Stern, "Public Policy and the Economics of Development," *European Economic Review* 35 (1991): 250–57. Reprinted by permission.

(ii) a concern to prevent or reduce poverty and/or to improve income distribution;

(iii) the assertion of rights to certain facilities or goods such as education, health, and housing;

(iv) paternalism (relating, for example, to education, pensions, and drugs); and

(v) the rights of future generations (including some concerns relevant to the environment).

The first two groups of arguments arise from standard welfare economics but the others arise rather differently. Strands from all five provide grounds for government action for both developed and developing countries although they are perhaps stronger for the latter. Together they point fairly directly to particular areas of government expenditure, notably education, health, social support, and the environment.

There is a further substantial role for government in improving market functioning and private sector activity through such measures as building infrastructure, providing a regulatory and legislative framework which allows competition to work effectively, and intervening selectively in industry and agriculture. The market failure arguments are especially persuasive concerning infrastructure, where increasing returns, public goods, and externalities can all be of considerable importance. The arguments therefore help identify important areas for state activity, but, as we have remarked, the case for direct state activity in the production of ordinary producer and consumer goods such as steel, cars, shoes, or ice cream does not appear to be strong, at least from the perspectives included here.

Until now, we have assumed implicitly that the government is well intentioned, well informed, and competent. Governments, however, may be craven or manipulated, they may be very badly informed, and they may be incompetent. In recent years much of the profession seems to have swung towards an emphasis on government failures in contrast to market failures (see, for example, the symposium in the June 1990 issue of the *Journal of Economic Perspectives,* in particular, Krueger 1990), and this shift in the climate of opinion has gone hand-in-hand with the reduction of government activities in a number of countries, although it is not clear that it is economic analysis that has led the way. There is no doubt, however, that failures of government are indeed important and are particularly severe for developing nations.

In the recent past there has been substantial attention in development economics given to the generation by government action (including quotas, prohibitions, restrictions, and the like) of rent-seeking and unproductive activities. It has been argued that this type of economic loss associated with government activity can be very large, relative to traditional calculations of deadweight losses (usually associated with government action in the form of taxes) of the "triangle" variety (or suitable general equilibrium generalisations) which have often been viewed as quite small (1% or so of GNP is a common figure for these losses).

Rent-seeking is no doubt important, but in my judgement the empirical evidence on its magnitude has been weak. Attempts, however insecure, to measure the size of rents are generally far more secure than estimates of the resources used in the pursuit of those rents. Those resources are usually estimated simply by the magnitude of the rents themselves. This rests on the rather dubious assumption that the competition for rents take place in a manner which is perfect in an important sense. Indeed, one of the complaints about the generation of rents is precisely that they are allocated in ways which favour certain groups (such as close relations of the President) and the market for them is not competitive. While this causes aggravation, it may imply that efficiency losses are much smaller than the rents themselves. The effects, however, of the creation of special privileges for certain groups by government may be rather more pernicious and long-term than is portrayed in the simple static descriptions embodied in the arguments just described. Rent-seeking is not limited to developing countries, of course. The New Yorkers see Washington as the rent-seeking capital of the world and the Milanese have a similar view of Rome.

Let us now turn to an examination of empirical evidence. Consideration of the expenditure figures shown in Table 1 indicates that health and social security receive relatively less attention in developing than in industrial nations while defence and general public services show a greater share. It is reasonable to ask why it is that industrial countries attach greater (proportional) weight to social security expending when problems of poverty are clearly far greater in developing nations. One can also argue the share of expenditure on infrastructure proxied by Transport and Communications in Table 1) is too low given its backward state in many LDCs and its central role in generating growth and aiding market functioning. There appears to be considerable scope for alteration of the composition of expenditures in order to improve living standards and market functioning in developing countries. In support of this view evidence is provided on the impact of various type interventions drawn from a wide range of countries.

Health and Nutrition

The performance of China and Sri Lanka in reducing mortality rates and increasing life expectancy has been outstanding in relation to their incomes. This high performance appears largely to have been the result of public action. I shall describe some central elements briefly. China's life expectancy of 70 and infant mortality rate of 31 per thousand may be compared with India's of 58 and 97, respectively. It seems reasonable to relate this to the extensive social support system in China. Through in large part, a strong focus on the food supply and distribution system China has attained a high level of food consumption per capita (2,630 daily calories per person in 1986) as compared with India at 2,238 (World Bank 1990, table 28). In 1984 there were 1,000 people per physician China as compared with 2,520 in India and much greater attention was paid to maternal and child health care and support of the elderly.

Aggregate income would not appear to be the main issue here. Brazil with an income per capita of $2,160 (conventionally measured), as compared with $330 for China, has only managed a life expectancy of 65 and an infant mortality rate of 61, and the gains in life expectancy and infant mortality rate in China were achieved prior to the very rapid growth since the reforms began in 1979. The crude comparisons of aggregates understates the achievements of China's support system. Whereas China provides a fairly universal system of support, reaching all parts of the country, coverage in India and Brazil is haphazard. For example, the poorest part of Brazil, the north-east which contains most of the country's poor (but only a quarter of the population) receives few social services. Indeed, Brazil's population per physician (1,080) and food consumption per capita (2,656 calories) are similar to China's but the distribution is much worse. The distribution of services probably plays a major part in explaining the higher life expectancy and lower infant mortality rate—the weak and the old in China receive much better support than in most developing countries. Further, China has placed a great emphasis on preventive measures including education, the provision of pure water supply, and adequate sanitation.

The explanation behind Sri Lanka's outstanding performance is similar to that of China although

Table 1. Central Government Expenditures by Type (percent total expenditure, 1986–87)

Area	General Public Services	Defense	Education	Health	Social Security	Transport and Communication	Other Economic Services	Other	Central Expenditures (% GDP)
Industrial	8.05	7.34	8.45	9.61	37.71	5.12	7.15	16.57	31.46
Developing	16.94	11.97	14.11	6.21	12.60	7.19	16.04	14.94	25.40
Africa	18.54	8.85	15.97	5.51	8.25	7.12	17.49	18.27	25.63
Asia	17.87	12.99	14.39	5.18	7.14	11.23	19.41	11.79	19.89
Europe	16.88	13.63	7.26	6.26	23.07	6.53	21.18	5.19	29.15
Middle East	13.29	26.69	12.54	4.85	13.22	3.71	11.06	14.64	33.12
Western Hemisphere	16.09	7.53	13.98	8.32	18.77	6.80	11.88	16.63	25.04

Source: International Monetary Fund, *Government Finance Statistics Yearbook* (1989).

Sri Lanka's advance came rather earlier (primarily prior to 1960). The subsidised rice system was introduced in 1942 and the promotion of primary education goes back to the early part of this century (see Drèze and Sen 1990, chap. 12). Like China, Sri Lanka has long had an emphasis on public health—a particularly important example being the eradication of malaria. Chile reduced its infant mortality from 103 per thousand in 1965 to 20 per thousand in 1988 in large part as a result of reforms begun in the early 1970s, including an expansion of primary health care with an emphasis on vulnerable groups (World Bank 1990, chap. 5).

Improved health and nutrition are important in their own right. They may also improve economic performance and there are a number of cases from, for example, Indonesia, Kenya, and India (see Berg 1987, chap. 6) where it has been claimed that improved nutrition in manual workers led to higher productivity.

Protection of Living Standards

To a major extent the reduction of age-specific mortality rates and the lengthening of life expectancy are achieved by protecting the poor from death and illness by, for example, providing clean water, adequate sanitation, and ensuring that they can obtain food. The protection of health and nutrition constitutes a central aspect of social support in developing countries. Over the last ten years or so we have come to understand much more about how protection can be provided (see, for example, Sen 1981, Drèze and Sen 1990, and Ahmad, Drèze, Hills, and Sen 1991). These authors have argued persuasively for careful integration of public action with the market. An important example is the employment-based famine prevention and poverty reduction schemes which have been effective where applied in India throughout this century—see Drèze (1988). The Employment Guarantee Scheme in Maharastra, as well as providing longer-term support, was also effective in meeting the threat of famine in the early 1970s. The cash-for-work element in these schemes embodies both the self-selection device of presentation for work and the provision of purchasing power to buy food. Markets seem effective in ensuring that the supply becomes available to meet the demand. Cash allows that demand to manifest itself.

Education

We have already discussed the Barro (1989a, b) results relating growth rates to human capital mea-

sured in terms of education. The *World Development Report 1990* (chap. 5) reports similar statistical relationships (although between the level of the real GDP and average years of education—Box 5.2) plus estimates of social returns to primary education in Sub-Saharan Africa (16%), Asia (27%), and Latin America (26%) based on Psacharopoulos (1985).

Infrastructure

Looking back over the World Bank's successes and failures (as seen through the eyes of its Operation Evaluation Department) in different areas of activity, Pohl and Mihaljek (1989) found investments in roads and irrigation to have been particularly productive. The *World Development Report 1990* (p. 85) indicates an economic rate of return, on average, for agricultural infrastructural projects of 17 percent. The *World Development Report 1987* noted a study of the Indian economy that put the costs of power cuts in the mid-1970s at 2 percent of GDP. In Bangladesh a study of sixteen villages found that those which had benefitted from public programmes for infrastructure (roads, power, and so on) displayed an increase in average household income approaching one-third (World Bank 1990, p. 60). . . .

The Environment for Economic Activity

Health, education, and infrastructure all play a critical role in the economic environment. So too does competition. Indeed one of the critical lessons of the British privatisation experience has been that competition seems to be of greater importance than whether an industry is publicly or privately owned (see Vickers and Yarrow 1988). A number of discussions of agriculture and the environment in Africa (for example, Platteau 1990) point to the importance of the establishment of clear property rights if investment and land development are to be encouraged. A similar interpretation may be attached to the substantial negative effect of political instability on growth in the Barro analysis. Reynolds (1983), in a study of comparative growth from a perspective of 100 years or so, suggests that the single most important explanatory variable is "political organisation and the administrative competence of government" (p. 978).

The role of government in encouraging private industry can involve much more than defining property rights and promoting a competitive environment. . . . To take some examples from developing countries which have exhibited rapid growth, the government has been very actively involved in channeling credit to selected industries in South Korea, Singapore, and Taiwan. It is interesting that in most of the countries just cited the strategies have involved neither the command economy nor the free market. In some cases international trade has been substantially less than free. One should not view the apparent collapse of the Eastern European economies and the success of Hong Kong together with the (strong) evidence on the beneficial effects of trade-oriented strategies (see, for example, Papageorgiou et al. 1990) as establishing an overwhelming case for minimalist government and a free trade policy. Looking to agriculture we see that governments, such as those of Mexico, India, and Indonesia, have been very influential in developing and disseminating the new technologies that created what is sometimes called "the green revolution." Economic coordination and the encouragement of new ideas and adoption do seem to be areas where the state can play a productive role in assisting the market.

References

Ahmad, E., J. P. Drèze, J. Hills, and A. K. Sen, eds. (1991). *Social Security in Developing Countries.* Oxford: Oxford University Press.

Barro, R. J. (1989a). "Economic Growth in a Cross Section of Countries." National Bureau of Economic Research, Working Paper no. 3120, September.

Barro, R. J. (1989b). "Economic Growth in a Cross Section of Countries." University of Rochester, Working Paper no. 201, September.

Berg, A. (1987). *Malnutrition: What Can Be Done? Lessons from World Bank Experience.* Baltimore: Johns Hopkins University Press.

Drèze, J. P. (1988). "Famine Prevention in India." Development Economics Research Programme Discussion Paper no. 3 (London School of Economics) February.

Drèze, J. P., and A. K. Sen. (1990). *Hunger and Public Action.* Oxford: Oxford University Press.

International Monetary Fund. (1989). *Government Finance Statistics Yearbook,* vol. 13 (Washington, D.C.: International Monetary Fund).

Krueger, A. O. (1990). "Government Failures in Development." *Journal of Economic Perspectives* 4:9–24.

Papageorgiou, D., M. Michaely, and A. M. Choksi (1990). *Liberalizing Foreign Trade.* Oxford: Basil Blackwell for the World Bank.

Platteau, J. Ph. (1990). *Land Reform and Structural Adjustment in Sub-Saharan Africa: Controversies and Guidelines.* Report prepared for the Food and Agricultural Organisation, August.

Pohl, G., and D. Mihaljek. (1989). *Project Evaluation in Practice: Uncertainty at the World Bank.* Economic Advisory Staff, The World Bank.

Reynolds, J. (1983). "The Spread of Economic Growth to the Third World, 1850–1980. *Journal of Economic Literature* 21: 941–80.

Sen, A. K. (1981). *Poverty and Famines.* Oxford: Oxford University Press.

Vickers, J., and G. Yarrow. (1988). *Privatisation: An Economic Analysis.* Cambridge, Mass.: MIT Press.

World Bank. (1987, 1990). *World Development Report.* Oxford: Oxford University Press/World Bank.

EXHIBIT IX.A.1. Market Failure and State Intervention

Reasons for Market Failure

   (i) Markets may be monopolised or oligopolistic.

  (ii) There may be externalities.

 (iii) There may be increasing returns to scale.

 (iv) Some markets, particularly insurance and futures markets, cannot be perfect and, indeed, may not exist.

  (v) Markets may adjust slowly or imprecisely because information may move slowly or marketing institutions may be inflexible.

 (vi) Individuals or enterprises may adjust slowly.

(vii) Individuals or enterprises may be badly informed about products, prices, their production possibilities, and so on.

(viii) Individuals may not act so as to maximise anything, either implicitly or explicitly.

 (ix) Government taxation is unavoidable and will not, or cannot, take a form which allows efficiency.

Some Problems of State Intervention

   (i) Individuals may know more about their own preferences and circumstances than the government.

  (ii) Government planning may increase risk by pointing everyone in the same direction—governments may make bigger mistakes than markets.

 (iii) Government planning may be more rigid and inflexible than private decision-making since complex decision-making machinery may be involved in government.

 (iv) Governments may be incapable of administering detailed plans.

  (v) Government controls may prevent private sector individual initiative if there are many bureaucratic obstacles.

 (vi) Organisations and individuals require incentives to work, innovate, control costs, and allocate efficiently and the discipline and rewards of the market cannot easily be replicated within public enterprises and organisations.

(vii) Different levels and parts of government may be poorly coordinated in the absence of the equilibrating signals provided by the market, particularly where groups or regions with different interests are involved.

(viii) Markets place constraints on what can be achieved by government, for example, resale of commodities on black markets and activities in the informal sector can disrupt rationing or other non-linear pricing or taxation schemes. This is the general problem of "incentive compatibility."

 (ix) Controls create resource-using activities to influence those controls through lobbying and corruption—often called rent-seeking or directly unproductive activities in the literature.

  (x) Planning may be manipulated by privileged and powerful groups which act in their own interests and further, planning creates groups with a vested interest in planning, for example, bureaucrats or industrialists who obtain protected positions.

 (xi) Governments may be dominated by narrow interest groups interested in their own welfare and sometimes actively hostile to large sections of the population. Planning may intensify their power.

Source: Nicholas Stern, "The Economics of Development," *Economic Journal* (September 1989), p. 616. Reprinted by permission.

Comment IX.A.1.   *Development Planning*

Beginning in the early 1950s with India's first Five-Year Plan, many countries attempted to formulate a central plan for their economy's development. General introductions to development planning were provided by Maurice Dobb, *An Essay on Economic Growth and Planning* (1960); W. Arthur Lewis, *Development Planning* (1966); Jan Tinbergen, *Development Planning* (1967); K. Griffin and J. Enos, *Planning Development* (1971); and Michael P. Todaro, *Development Planning* (1971).

In the 1970s and 1980s, however, the failures of central planning were more widely recognized. Deficiencies in the formulation and especially the implementation of development plans became acute. One critic of the practice of development planning lists the following causes of poor plan performance:

1. Deficiencies in the plans: they tend to be over-ambitious; to be based upon inappropriately specified macro-models; to be insufficiently specific about policies and projects; to overlook important non-economic considerations; to fail to incorporate adequate administrative provision for their own implementation.

2. Inadequate resources: incomplete and unreliable data; too few economists and other planning personnel.

3. Unanticipated dislocations to domestic economic activity: adverse movements in the terms of trade; irregular flows of development aid; unplanned changes in the private sector.

4. Institutional weaknesses: failures to locate the planning agency appropriately in the machinery of government; failures of communication between planners, administrators, and their political masters; the importation of institutional arrangements unsuited to local circumstances.

5. Failings on the part of the administrative civil service: cumbersome bureaucratic procedures; excessive caution and resistance to innovations; personal and departmental rivalries; lack of concern with economic considerations. (Finance Ministries are a particularly frequent target, often said to undermine the planning agency by resisting the co-ordination of plans and budgets).[1]

See also S. Chakravarty, "Development Planning: A Reappraisal," *Cambridge Journal of Economics* (March 1991).

Among the numerous country studies of development planning, of particular interest are those related to India: S. Chakravarty, *Development Planning: The Indian Experience* (1987); B. S. Minhas, "Objectives and Policy Frame of the Fourth Indian Plan," in *The Crisis in Planning,* vol. 2, ed. Mike Faber and Dudley Seers (1972); J. Bhagwati and P. Desai, *India—Planning for Industrialization* (1970); and P. Bardhan, *The Political Economy of Development in India* (1984).

[1]Tony Killick, "The Possibilities of Development Planning," *Oxford Economic Papers* (July 1976): 164.

Comment IX.A.2. Governing the Market

Although many developing countries have abandoned central planning of a comprehensive character, an active public sector still exercises substantial influence in most countries. Of special interest—and subject to varying interpretations—is the role of government in the high-performing economies of Asia. Some neoclassical economists read the success of these economies as having been the result of the "invisible hand"—little government intervention and neutral incentives across activities that promote allocative efficiency. A revisionist view, however, sees the visible hand of government in "picking winners," protecting infant industries, and promoting exports.

The latter view is presented by Robert Wade, *Governing the Market: Economic Theory and the Role of Government in East Asian Industrialization* (1990). He rejects the claims of those who interpret the East Asian story as a vindication of either free-market principles or the confinement of government intervention only to promoting exports and correcting market failures. Equally, he disputes those who maintain that it all resulted from government intervention. Instead of "market supremacy," Wade's interpretation emphasizes "government leadership"—that is,

a synergistic connection between a public system and mostly private market system, outputs of each becoming inputs for the other, with the government setting rules and influencing decision-making in the private sector in line with its view of an appropriate industrial and trade profile for the economy. Through this mechanism, the advantages of markets (decentralization, rivalry, diversity and multiple experiments) have been combined with the advantages of partially insulating producers from the instabilities of free markets and of stimulating investment in certain industries selected by government as important for the economy's future growth. This combination has improved upon the results of free markets.[1]

Wade concludes that

[1]Robert Wade, *Governing the Market: Economic Theory and the Role of Government in East Asian Industrialization* (1990), p. 5.

a necessary but not sufficient condition for more rapid industrialization is state deployment of a range of industrial promotion policies, including ones to intensify the growth of selected industries within the national territory. This is not to say that effectiveness increases with the sheer amount of intervention, nor that it increases the more the state imposes its will on society, ignoring other groups. State effectiveness is a function of the range of options, given by the number and force of policy instruments, and the flexibility with which those policy instruments are used. Flexibility means that the capacity to intervene, as given by the number and force of policy instruments, is used to varying degrees, more in some industries than in others at any one time, and more in one industry at some times than at others, always with an eye on the costs of interventions in political as well as economic terms.[2]

What distinguishes the use of state power in the high-performing economies is that government intervened in accordance with market opportunities, national economic management was independent of interest groups, government was capable of undertaking an entire set of appropriate policies (especially monetary and fiscal as well as industrial), government and business had close consultations, and policy instruments were used promotionally rather than restrictively.

From the experience of the high-performing economies, we can conclude that the most important questions about the role of the state are not how large should be the public sector or how much government intervention there should be, but rather what kind of intervention. What can government do best? And in what types of policy instruments does government have a comparative advantage? Answers do not point to a minimalist state, but rather to a shift from policies of planning and control to policies that work through markets. See Tony Killick, *A Reaction Too Far* (1990), pp. 27–32.

A similar interpretation of market friendly interventionism is given by Christopher Colclough and James Manor. The problem is not "too much government" but too much of government doing the wrong things. "The task is to dismantle the disabling state . . . [and] . . . establish the enabling state."[3]

Being realistic, we should endorse the conclusion of Dwight Perkins:

Making markets work is a much more complex process than slogans such as "getting the prices right," "privatization," or "getting rid of controls" would imply. Making markets work involves fundamental changes in enterprise behavior in most cases and substantial changes in the way government itself carries out its functions. Finally, most developing nations are never going to be willing to turn as much over to the market as, say, Hong Kong. Nonmarket controls or hierarchical commands will continue to play a major role in many sectors of most economies. Reform, therefore, is not just a matter of getting rid of such commands. A high growth economy must learn to make both the market and the bureaucracy perform efficiently.[4]

---

[2]Ibid., pp. 370–71.

[3]Christopher Colclough and James Manor, eds., *States or Markets?* (1991), pp. 276–77.

[4]Dwight H. Perkins, *Reforming Economic Systems in Developing Countries* (1991), p. 45.

IX.B. RENT SEEKING AND GOVERNMENT FAILURE

Note IX.B.1. What Are Rents?

Economists use the term *rent* in two very different ways. Sometimes it has the same meaning as in everyday life: the payment one makes to use a piece of equipment or a structure one does not own. Other times it means *the return to an asset in excess of its best alternative earning.* This latter concept is often called "economic rent" to distinguish it from rent as conventionally defined. In the literature on the political economy of development, "rent" is always short for "economic rent." In fact, one can go further and state that in this literature "rent" is short for "economic rent created by government action."

To further clarify the concept of rent it helps to consider some examples of rents *not* created by government action. A classic example is the return earned by the holder of a piece of rich mineral-bearing land, the best alternative use of which is farmland. The difference between what the owner can earn by extracting the minerals and what he can earn by using the land to grow crops is the economic rent on the land. Another example is the earnings of an employee who has become extremely valuable to a particular firm by virtue of having learned all the ins and outs of its production process, but whose knowledge is of no special value to any other firm. The difference between his earnings at his current firm and what he would earn at another firm is the rent to his firm-specific knowledge. (If the employee is not actually paid more than his best alternative earning, this rent accrues to his employer rather than to him.)

From this second example it is easy to see one way in which the government can create rents. Suppose the government chooses to pay its employees more than they would earn in positions of comparable responsibility and skill in the private sector. The difference between the earnings in the government jobs and the earnings in comparable private sector employment are the rents received by holders of government jobs. It is also easy to see how this government action could give rise to rent-seeking behavior. We can expect that government jobs would be in excess demand, and that the government will need some way to choose among qualified applicants. One way might be to hire only applicants with college degrees, even though skills learned in college are not needed to perform the jobs. People might then attend college not in order to learn but rather as a means of obtaining access to rents on government jobs.

The most important way in which governments create rents is by issuing licenses or permits to engage in various forms of economic activity. Examples are a license to import some units of a particular good and a permit to make an investment by building a factory. Such licenses and permits have no alternative uses, hence insofar as they have any value to their holders we can consider this value to be rent. Rents will be generated only insofar as the licenses or permits effectively restrict the level of economic activity to below what it would be in their absence. For this reason it is often assumed that the existence of positive rents to holders of licenses or permits indicates that government policies are reducing economic efficiency. This need not be true. Consider a license, such as a patent, that gives the holder exclusive rights to produce and market a new product for a number of years. Without the rents generated by this license, there might be no incentive to expend the resources necessary to invent the new product in the first place. Similarly, rent seeking is often assumed to be a socially wasteful activity, as it was in the example at the end of the previous paragraph. Yet inventive activity pursued with the intent of securing a patent can also be labeled rent seeking.

The selection that follows by Anne Krueger concentrates on rents and rent seeking generated by import licenses. Figure 1 shows how the welfare effects of an import quota and the total rents obtained by holders of import licenses can be quantified. The figure shows the domestic market for an internationally tradeable commodity. Domestic supply is given by the upward-sloping schedule S and domestic demand is given by the downward-sloping schedule

Figure 1. Welfare Loss From a Tariff or Equivalent Quota

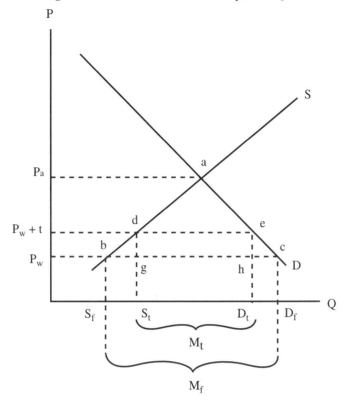

D. In the absence of international trade the domestic market clears at point *a* (for *autarky*). With free international trade the country can import the commodity at the world price P_w. We assume that the country is too small to affect the world price, so that P_w prevails regardless of how much the country imports. Under this assumption the country's consumers purchase D_f units of the commodity and its producers supply S_f units, leaving $M_f = D_f - S_f$ units of demand to be satisfied by imports.

We see that, compared with autarky, free trade increases consumer surplus (the area to the left of the demand curve) and decreases producer surplus (the area to the left of the supply curve). According to standard welfare analysis, national gains from international trade can be approximated by the sum of the changes in consumer and producer surplus. This sum is given by the trapezoid acP_wP_a less the trapezoid abP_wP_a, which equals the triangle *abc*. Now suppose the government imposes a tariff *t* per unit of imports. Under the assumption of perfect competition in import supply, the domestic price of the importable commodity will rise by exactly the amount of the tariff to $P_w + t$. Units purchased will fall to D_t, units supplied will rise to S_t, and imports will fall to $M_t = D_t - S_t$ units. Gains from trade shrink from *abc* to *ade*. However, the country also collects tariff revenue $t \times M_t$, equal to the rectangle *dehg*. The net loss in national welfare from the tariff policy (sometimes called the "deadweight loss") is therefore given by the sum of the triangles *bdg* and *ceh*.

Finally, suppose that instead of imposing a tariff the government imposes a quota that limits imports to M_t units. This creates an excess demand at the price P_w, causing the domestic price to be bid up to $P_w + t$, at which point demand for imports $D_t - S_t$ equals supply M_t. Holders of import licenses can purchase imports at the price P_w and resell them in the domestic market at the price $P_w + t$, earning a rent of *t* per unit. The total amount of quota rents equals *t* $\times M_t$, exactly equal to the tariff revenue collected by the government under the tariff policy.

Note that if the quota had been set at M_f units (or higher), no excess demand at the price P_w would have been created and the domestic price would not have risen above the world price. The quota licenses would then have been worthless: they would simply have conveyed the right to purchase imports at the price P_w and resell them at the same price. We see that licenses create rents only by restricting the level of economic activity (in this case, importing) to below what it would be in their absence.

Because the net loss in national welfare is the same whether the government imposes a tariff t or a quota M_t, these are sometimes called "equivalent" policies. One of the main points of Krueger's selection is that if resources are devoted to rent seeking (i.e., if resources are devoted to competing for quota licenses), the policies are not equivalent: the welfare loss from the quota policy will exceed the welfare loss from the tariff policy. Krueger argues that the value of the resources wasted in rent seeking will be roughly equal to the value of the rents themselves. A comparison of the rectangle *dehg* in Figure 1 with the triangles *bdg* and *ceh* suggests that if Krueger is right the welfare cost of a quota could far exceed that of the "equivalent" tariff. In lieu of her model, in the Comment following her selection we demonstrate the result that the value of rents is completely dissipated for the Harris–Todaro model.

Selection IX.B.1. Political Economy of the Rent-Seeking Society*

In many market-oriented economies, government restrictions upon economic activity are pervasive facts of life. These restrictions give rise to rents of a variety of forms, and people often compete for the rents. Sometimes, such competition is perfectly legal. In other instances, rent seeking takes other forms, such as bribery, corruption, smuggling, and black markets.

It is the purpose of this paper to show some of the ways in which rent seeking is competitive, and to develop a simple model of competitive rent seeking for the important case when rents originate from quantitative restrictions upon international trade. In such a case 1) competitive rent seeking leads to the operation of the economy inside its transformation curve; 2) the welfare loss associated with quantitative restrictions is unequivocally greater than the loss from the tariff equivalent of those quantitative restrictions; and 3) competitive rent seeking results in a divergence between the private and social costs of certain activities. Although the analysis is general, the model has particular applicability for developing countries, where government interventions are frequently all-embracing. . . .

Competitive Rent Seeking

A. Means of Competition

When quantitative restrictions are imposed upon and effectively constrain imports, an import license is a valuable commodity. It is well known that under some circumstances, one can estimate the tariff equivalents of a set of quantitative restrictions and analyze the effects of those restrictions in the same manner as one would the tariff equivalents. In other circumstances, the resource-allocational effects of import licensing will vary, depending upon who receives the license.[1]

It has always been recognized that there are *some* costs associated with licensing: paperwork, the time spent by entrepreneurs in obtaining their licenses, the cost of the administrative apparatus necessary to issue licenses, and so on. Here, the argument is carried one step further: in many cir-cumstances resources are devoted to competing for those licenses.

The consequences of that rent seeking are examined below. First, however, it will be argued that rent-seeking activities are often competitive and resources are devoted to competing for rents. It is difficult, if not impossible, to find empirically observable measures of the degree to which rent seeking is competitive. Instead, some mechanisms under which rent seeking is almost certain to be competitive are examined. Then other cases are considered in which it is less obvious, but perhaps equally plausible, that competition results.

Consider first the results of an import-licensing mechanism when licenses for imports of intermediate goods are allocated in proportion to firms' capacities. That system is frequently used, and has been analyzed for the Indian case by Jagdish Bhagwati and Padma Desai. When licenses are allocated in proportion to firms' capacities, investment in additional physical plant confers upon the investor a higher expected receipt of import licenses. Even with initial excess capacity (due to quantitative restrictions upon imports of intermediate goods), a rational entrepreneur may still expand his plant if the expected gains from the additional import licenses he will receive, divided by the cost of the investment, equal the returns on investment in other activities.[2] This behavior could be perfectly rational even if, for all entrepreneurs, the total number of import licenses will remain fixed. In fact, if imports are held constant as domestic income grows, one would expect the domestic value of a constant quantity of imports to increase over time, and hence installed capacity would increase while output remained constant. By investing in additional capacity, entrepreneurs devote resources to compete for import licenses.

A second sort of licensing mechanism frequently found in developing countries is used for imports of consumer goods. There, licenses are allocated pro rata in proportion to the applications for those licenses from importers-wholesalers. Entry is generally free into importing-whole-saling, and firms usually have U-shaped cost curves. The result is a larger-than-optimal number of firms, operating on the downward sloping portion of their

*From Anne Krueger, "The Political Economy of the Rent-Seeking Society." From *American Economic Review* 64 (June 1974): 291–294, 301–302. Reprinted by permission.

[1]This phenomenon is explored in detail in Bhagwati and Krueger.

[2]Note that: 1) one would expect to find greater excess capacity in those industries where rents are higher; and 2) within an industry, more efficient firms will have greater excess capacity than less efficient firms, since the return on a given amount of investment will be higher with greater efficiency.

cost curves, yet earning a "normal" rate of return. Each importer-wholesaler receives fewer imports than he would buy at existing prices in the absence of licensing, but realizes a sufficient return on those licenses he does receive to make it profitable to stay in business. In this case, competition for rents occurs through entry into the industry with smaller-than-optimally sized firms, and resources are used in that the same volume of imports could be efficiently distributed with fewer inputs if firms were of optimal size.

A third sort of licensing mechanism is less systematic in that government officials decide on license allocations. Competition occurs to some extent through both mechanisms already mentioned as businessmen base their decisions on expected values. But, in addition, competition can also occur through allocating resources to influencing the probability, or expected size, of license allocations. Some means of influencing the expected allocation—trips to the capital city, locating the firm in the capital, and so on—are straightforward. Others, including bribery, hiring relatives of officials or employing the officials themselves upon retirement, are less so. In the former case, competition occurs through choice of location, expenditure of resources upon travel, and so on. In the latter case, government officials themselves receive part of the rents.

Bribery has often been treated as a transfer payment. However, there is competition for government jobs and it is reasonable to believe that expected total remuneration is the relevant decision variable for persons deciding upon careers. Generally, entry into government service requires above-average educational attainments. The human capital literature provides evidence that choices as to how much to invest in human capital are strongly influenced by rates of return upon the investment. For a given level of educational attainment, one would expect the rate of return to be approximately equated among various lines of endeavor. Thus, if there appear to be high official-plus-unofficial incomes accruing to government officials and higher education is a prerequisite for seeking a government job, more individuals will invest in higher education. It is not necessary that government officials earn the same total income as other college graduates. All that is necessary is that there is an excess supply of persons seeking government employment, or that highly educated persons make sustained efforts to enter government services. Competition takes place through attaining the appropriate credentials for entry into government service and through accepting unem-

ployment while making efforts to obtain appointments. Efforts to influence those in charge of making appointments, of course, just carry the argument one step further back.

To argue that competition for entry into government service is, in part, a competition for rents does not imply that all government servants accept bribes nor that they would leave government service in their absence. Successful competitors for government jobs might experience large windfall gains even at their official salaries. However, if the possibility of those gains induces others to expend time, energy, and resources in seeking entry into government services, the activity is competitive for present purposes.

In all these license-allocation cases, there are means, legal and illegal, for competing for rents. If individuals choose their activities on the basis of expected returns, rates of return on alternative activities will be equated and, in that sense, markets will be competitive.[3] In most cases, people do not perceive themselves to be rent seekers and, generally speaking, individuals and firms do not specialize in rent seeking. Rather, rent seeking is one part of an economic activity, such as distribution or production, and part of the firm's resources are devoted to the activity (including, of course, the hiring of expediters) . . .

B. Are Rents Quantitatively Important?

Granted that rent seeking may be highly competitive, the question remains whether rents are important. Data from two countries, India and Turkey, suggest that they are. Gunnar Myrdal believes India may ". . . on the balance, be judged to have somewhat less corruption than any other country in South Asia" (p. 943). Nonetheless, it is generally believed that "corruption" has been increasing, and that much of the blame lies with the proliferation of economic controls following independence.[4]

Table 1 presents crude estimates, based on fairly conservative assumptions of the value of rents of all sorts in 1964. One important source of rents—investment licensing—is not included for lack of

---

[3]It may be objected that illegal means of competition may be sufficiently distasteful that perfect competition will not result. Three comments are called for. First, it requires only that enough people at the margin do not incur disutility from engaging in these activities. Second, most lines of economic activity in many countries cannot be entered without some rent-seeking activity. Third, risks of detection (especially when bribery is expected) and the value judgments associated with illegal activities differ from society to society. See Ronald Wraith and Edgar Simpkins.

[4]Santhanam Committee, pp. 7–8.

Table 1. Estimates of Value of Rents: India, 1964

Source of Rent	Amount of Rent (Rs. million)
Public investment	365
Imports	10,271
Controlled commodities	3,000
Credit rationing	407
Railways	602
Total	14,645

Sources:

1) Public investment: The Santhanam Committee, pp. 11–12, placed the loss in public investment at *at least* 5 percent of investment. That figure was multiplied by the average annual public investment in the *Third Five Year Plan.*

2) Imports: The Santhanam Committee, p. 18, stated that import licenses were worth 100 to 500 percent of their face value. Seventy-five percent of the value of 1964 imports was used here as a conservative estimate.

3) Controlled commodities: These commodities include steel, cement, coal, passenger cars, scooters, food, and other price- and/or distribution-controlled commodities, as well as foreign exchange used for illegal imports and other unrecorded transactions. The figure is the lower bound estimate given by John Monteiro, p. 60. Monteiro puts the upper bound estimate at Rs. 30,000 billion, although he rejects the figure on the (dubious) ground that notes in circulation are less than that sum.

4) Credit rationing: The bank rate in 1964 was 6 percent; Rs. 20.3 billion of loans were outstanding. It is assumed that *at least* an 8 percent interest rate would have been required to clear the market, and that 3 percent of bank loans outstanding would be equivalent to the present value of new loans at 5 percent. Data source: Reserve Bank of India, Tables 534 and 554.

5) Railways: Monteiro, p. 45, cites commissions of 20 percent on railway purchases, and extra-official fees of Rs. 0.15 per wagon and Rs. 1.4 per 100 maunds loaded. These figures were multiplied by the 1964 traffic volume; 203 million tons of revenue-paying traffic originated in that year. Third plan expenditure on railroads was Rs. 13,260 million. There were 350,000 railroad goods wagons in 1964–65. If a wagon was loaded once a week, there were 17,500,000 wagons of freight. At Rs. 0.15 per load, this would be Rs. 2.6 million; 100 maunds equal 8,228 pounds so at 1.4 Rs. per 100 maunds, Rs. 69 million changed hands; if one-fifth of railroad expenditures were made in 1964–65, Rs. 2652 million was spent in 1964; at 20 percent, this would be Rs. 530 million, for a total of Rs. 602 million.

any valid basis on which to estimate its value. Many smaller controls are also excluded. Nonetheless, it is apparent from Table 1 that import licenses provided the largest source of rents. The total value of rents of Rs. 14.6 billion contrasts with Indian national income of Rs. 201 billion in 1964. At 7.3 percent of national income, rents must be judged large relative to India's problems in attempting to raise her savings rate.

For Turkey, excellent detailed estimates of the value of import licenses in 1968 are available. Data on the c.i.f. prices of individual imports, their landed cost (c.i.f. price plus all duties, taxes, and landing charges), and wholesale prices were collected for a sizeable sample of commodities representing about 10 percent of total imports in 1968. The c.i.f. value of imports in the sample was TL

547 million and the landed cost of the imports was TL 1,443 million. The value at the wholesale level of these same imports was TL 3,568 million. Of course, wholesalers incur some handling, storage, and transport costs. The question, therefore, is the amount that can be attributed to normal wholesaling costs. If one assumes that a 50 percent markup would be adequate, then the value of import licenses was TL 1,404 million, or almost three times the c.i.f. value of imports. Imports in 1968 were recorded (c.i.f.) as 6 percent of national income. On the basis of Aker's data, this would imply that rents from import licenses in Turkey in 1968 were about 15 percent of *GNP*. . . .

Conclusions and Implications

While import licenses constitute a large and visible rent resulting from government intervention, the phenomenon of rent seeking is far more general. Fair trade laws result in firms of less-than-optimal size. Minimum wage legislation generates equilibrium levels of unemployment above the optimum with associated deadweight losses, as shown by John Harris and Michael Todaro, and Todaro. Ceilings on interest rates and consequent credit rationing lead to competition for loans and deposits and/or high-cost banking operations. Regulating taxi fares affects the average waiting time for a taxi and the percent of time taxis are idle, but probably not their owners' incomes, unless taxis are also licensed. Capital gains tax treatment results in overbuilding of apartments and uneconomic oil exploration. And so on.

Each of these and other interventions lead people to compete for the rents although the competitors often do not perceive themselves as such. In each case there is a deadweight loss associated with that competition over and above the traditional triangle. In general, prevention of that loss can be achieved only by restricting entry into the activity for which a rent has been created.

That, in turn, has political implications. First, even if they *can* limit competition for the rents, governments which consider they must impose restrictions are caught on the horns of a dilemma: if they do restrict entry, they are clearly "showing favoritism" to one group in society and are choosing an unequal distribution of income. If, instead, competition for the rents is allowed (or cannot be prevented), income distribution may be less unequal and certainly there will be less appearance of favoring special groups, although the economic costs associated with quantitative restrictions will be higher.

References

J. Bhagwati and P. Desai, *Planning for Industrialization: A Study of India's Trade and Industrial Policies Since 1950,* Cambridge 1970.

——— and A. Krueger, *Foreign Trade Regimes and Economic Development: Experience and Analysis,* New York forthcoming.

J. R. Harris and M. P. Todaro, "Migration, Unemployment, and Development: A Two-Sector Analysis," *Amer. Econ. Rev.,* Mar. 1970, *60,* 126–42.

J. B. Monteiro, *Corruption,* Bombay 1966.

G. Myrdal, *Asian Drama,* Vol. III, New York 1968.

M. P. Todaro, "A Model of Labor Migration and Urban Unemployment in Less Developed Countries," *Amer. Econ. Rev.,* Mar. 1969, *59,* 138–48.

R. Wraith and E. Simpkins, *Corruption in Developing Countries,* London 1963.

Santhanam Committee, *Report on the Committee on Prevention of Corruption,* Government of India, Ministry of Home Affairs, New Delhi 1964.

Comment IX.B.1. Complete Rent Dissipation Through Competitive Rent Seeking in the Harris–Todaro Model

At the end of her selection Krueger mentions the work of John Harris and Michael Todaro, "Migration, Unemployment and Development: A Two-Sector Analysis" *American Economic Review* (March 1970), as an example of a model in which rent seeking leads to welfare losses. Since we have already presented their model in Note VI.1, we can build on that presentation here to demonstrate Krueger's result that when rent seeking is competitive the value of the resources wasted in rent seeking equals the value of the rents.

One interpretation of the Harris–Todaro model is that the government enforces a minimum wage $\bar{w}_M$ in urban areas that exceeds the market-clearing wage. Workers who obtain employment at this minimum wage can then be said to earn rents equal to the difference between $\bar{w}_M$ and their best alternative, the agricultural wage w_A. Migration into urban areas to obtain high-wage jobs constitutes the competitive rent-seeking behavior in the Harris–Todaro model. The unemployment of urban workers not chosen for the available high-wage jobs gives the quantity of resources wasted in rent seeking. To show the equality between the value of resources wasted in rent seeking and the value of the rents, we use the condition that determines the level of unemployment for which workers are indifferent between remaining in the countryside and migrating to the city, $w_A = [\hat{L}_M/(\hat{L}_M + U)]\bar{w}_M$, where $\hat{L}_M$ is urban employment at wage $\bar{w}_M$ and U is unemployment. This condition can be rearranged as $w_A U = (\bar{w}_M - w_A)\hat{L}_M$. The right-hand side of this equation gives the value of the rents earned by workers who obtain high-wage employment, while the left-hand side gives the value of the resources wasted when workers withdraw from agriculture to engage in rent seeking.

Comment IX.B.2. The Relationship Between Rent Seeking and Corruption

In her selection Krueger mentions "corruption" as a means of seeking rents. Later writers have often used the concepts of corruption and rent seeking interchangeably. Here we wish to clarify the relationship between the two concepts, partly by amplifying points already made in both the Krueger selection and the selection by Stern in the first section of this chapter.

Let us define corruption as the use of public office for private gain. This is typically illegal. Yet Krueger is quite clear that many forms of rent seeking are perfectly legal, so that rent seeking should not be seen as only a form of corruption. It is also easy to find examples in which corruption, rather than being a form of rent seeking, actually eliminates rent seeking. Consider again the case of import quota licenses. Suppose that the government official in charge of allocating import licenses gives them away to members of his extended family. No resources have been expended in competing for the quota rents, yet the official's action fits the definition of corruption. (It is possible that resources will be expended in competition for entrance to the official's extended family, however.)

As Krueger points out, insofar as corruption creates rents by raising the incomes of government officials above what they would earn in positions of comparable responsibility and skill in the private sector, it may give rise to rent seeking. Here it is more accurate to say that corruption causes rent seeking than to say that corruption and rent seeking are identical, and in this case the two are actually separate activities carried out by different groups of people.

Perhaps the most complex relationship between corruption and rent seeking occurs when officials enact restrictions on economic activity for the main purpose of creating rents which they can capture through rent-seeking bribery (or allocate to family, friends, and political supporters). This "large-scale" corruption may be the type most damaging to economic development. Many examples are to be found in sub-Saharan agricultural policy, as described in Selection IX.B.4 by Robert Bates.

Selection IX.B.2. Neoclassical Political Economy, the State, and Economic Development*

A curious facet of neoclassical [competitive equilibrium] is that it is "institution free" in that it does not explicitly refer to any state. However, a complete set of smoothly functioning commodity, factor, insurance and capital markets is presumed. Above all, it is presumed that producer and consumer decisions, particularly those involving trades across time, space or conditions of nature, are taken with full confidence that the parties to a trade will fulfill their obligations. Thus, contracts will be observed or at the very least a mechanism for enforcing contracts is implicit. Some view this feature as a strength rather than a weakness, in the sense that the informationally efficient decentralization of decisions brought about by price-guided allocations can, in principle, be exploited by a capitalist or a socialist state. Others argue that the state itself is an actor in the scene rather than an impartial enforcer of contracts.

In the dominant stream of development literature, the assigned role for the state extends beyond maintaining law and order and enforcing contracts. The argument is familiar. Because of pervasive externalities and increasing returns, some markets fail and others such as insurance and capital markets either do not exist or do not function well because of, among others, moral hazards and adverse selections. The very existence of markets and other vital institutions can be viewed as the availability of a public good, in the sense that their "use" by one agent does not reduce their potential use by other agents. And for well-known reasons, including the "free-rider" problem, most public goods will be underprovided if left to private decisions. However, it was believed that a well-informed government motivated solely by social welfare can correct all these market failures through appropriate intervention and also provide public goods. Further, such government intervention will also promote distributional justice. And the literature is full of sophisticated analyses and recommendations in regard to optimal taxation of income and wealth, import tariffs, and taxes or subsidies on commodity inputs, outputs and primary factors. It is hard to say whether governments of developing countries were influenced by this advice. But it is a fact that they intervened massively. More often than not, these interventions either proved to be ineffective or worse than the disease of market failure that they were meant to cure.

From a somewhat different perspective, some students of the economies of developed countries began focusing attention on the interaction between public policies and private lobbies and interest groups. An important element of this analytical effort is an attempt to understand why some economies grow faster than others.[1] This is of particular interest from the viewpoint of economic development of developing countries. Equally relevant is the contribution of some economic historians to this research on the theory of three important institutions, viz., *property rights* that describe and circumscribe individual and group incentives, the *state* that formulates and enforces these rights, and *ideology* that relates to different perceptions of and reactions to the same change in objective situations by individuals. Independently of this, students of international trade interested in the continuing strength of protectionism in developed countries and the cost of inward-oriented import-substituting industrialization policies in developing countries also began analyzing the impact of lobbies on the creation and sustenance of protection and on the competition for the "rents" so created.

Neoclassical Political Economy

Colander christened this area of research Neoclassical Political Economy. He distinguished it from neoclassical economics by its assumption that the state, far from being "an exogenous force, trying to do good . . . is at least partially endogenous and the policies it institutes will reflect vested interests in society."[2] Such a view of the state is not particularly new and goes back to Marx, if not earlier. What is new and interesting in the analysis of neoclassical political economists is their application of the standard tools of individual optimization to lobbies and interest groups. It turns out that the benign Smithian metaphor of the "invisible hand" guiding self-interested individuals to achieve social good has to be replaced by Magee's colorful metaphor of

*From T. N. Srinivasan, "Neoclassical Political Economy, the State, and Economic Development," *Asian Development Review,* Vol. 3, No. 2 (1985), pp. 40–45. Reprinted by permission.

[1]D. C. Mueller, *The Political Economy of Growth* (New Haven: Yale University Press, 1983); and M. Olson, *The Rise and Decline of Nations* (New Haven: Yale University Press, 1982).

[2]D. Colander, ed., *Neo-Classical Political Economy* (Cambridge: Ballinger Publishing Co., 1984), p. 2.

the "invisible foot" symbolizing the welfare-reducing effects of competitive self-interested behavior in the political arena over redistribution.[3]

The three major strands of this literature are: (i) the collective choice analysis of Olson and his associates; (ii) the public choice school of Buchanan, Tullock and their followers; and (iii) the international trade and development school of Bhagwati and Srinivasan, Brock and Magee, Findlay and Wellisz, Krueger, Mayer and Wilson. The contributions of economic historians led by North, while not belonging to this genre, address some of the same set of issues. Also noteworthy is the work of Assar Lindbeck on "endogenous politicians."

Olson observes that even though a group of individuals or firms had some interest in common and can be expected to organize and lobby for that interest, in the absence of special arrangements or circumstances, rational individuals will not act in their group interest.[4] The reason is that the services of such a lobby, like those of a state, are "public goods" such that their provision to *anyone* in the group means provision to *everyone.* This results in each rational individual trying to be a "free-rider" by contributing nothing to the group while enjoying the fruits of the contributions of others. Of course, it follows that "if there is only voluntary and rational individual behavior, then for the most part neither governments nor lobbies and cartels will exist, unless individuals support them for some reason *other* than the collective goods they provide."[5] However, since governments and lobbies obviously exist, the reason for their existence has to be sought elsewhere. Governments have monopoly over coercion and force and to levy taxes. The existence of large private organizations depends on whether they can institute a set of *selective incentives,* that is, an incentive that applies selectively to individuals depending on whether they contribute to the provision of the collective good. Small groups *can* engage in collective action without selective incentives. The reason is that in small groups bargaining is feasible and not unduly costly. Therefore, bargaining among members can lead to a group-optimal outcome, even though to begin with, benefits of an individual contribution are shared by the entire group.

Olson draws several implications from his analysis, of which those relating to "distributional coalitions" are of particular interest. These coalitions are "overwhelmingly oriented to struggles over the distribution of income and wealth rather than to the production of additional output."[6] The "free-rider" argument extended to organizations suggests that a typical lobby in a society is more likely to be a narrow special interest group or distributional coalition since the benefits of any resources spent by the group to *expand* the society's output have to be shared with the rest of society, while the benefits of the same resources spent on redistributing society's output in its favor accrue entirely to the group. Stable societies with unchanged boundaries are likely to accumulate more such coalitions over time; these coalitions make decisions more slowly than their members, slow down a society's capacity to introduce technical change and adapt quickly to changing conditions, and lower the rate of economic growth.[7] And the accumulation of such coalitions inevitably increases the role of government and the complexity of regulations.

An implication of Olson's analysis is that since distributional coalitions such as cartels can operate through markets, and not only by influencing government policy, laissez-faire per se would not be sufficient to counter them, at least in a closed economy, although a free trade policy in an open economy is an effective cartel buster. However, distributional coalitions that congeal into social classes and castes are not easily countered this way. The distributional coalitions operating at all levels will slow down growth and redistribute national product, not necessarily to the poor.

Neoclassical economic theory presumes that the only social loss associated with a distortion introduced by a policy is the deadweight loss associated with it. For instance, the loss due to an import tariff imposed by a country which cannot influence its terms of trade is equated to the value of the resources that could be saved by abolishing the tariff while assuring the consumers their post-tariff level of welfare. On the other hand, as Buchanan of the public choice school put it, the loss is not confined only to the deadweight loss. For it to be so, the

---

[3]S. Magee, "The Theory of Endogenous Tariffs," in D. Colander, ed., *Neo-Classical Political Economy* (Cambridge: Ballinger Publishing Co., 1984), chap. 3.

[4]M. Olson, *The Logic of Collective Action* (Cambridge, Mass.: Harvard University Press, 1965); and M. Olson, *The Rise and Decline of Nations.*

[5]M. Olson, *The Rise and Decline of Nations,* pp. 19–20.

[6]Ibid., p. 44.

[7]One has to be careful about drawing conclusions in regard to growth. A resource diversion to non-productive lobbying per se need not slow down growth. That is, a society can be operating inside its production possibility frontier at each time-point because of the diversion, yet it can grow as fast as another in which there is no such diversion. Olson's argument depends on the effect of the activities of distributional conditions on the *growth process.*

only response of producers and consumers to the tariff must be to shift their production and consumption patterns.[8] But in fact a person or group that is differentially affected, favorably or unfavorably, by a government may: (i) engage in *lobbying efforts* to institute or repeal it; (ii) engage *directly in politics* to secure access to decision-making power; and (iii) *shift resources* into or out of the affected activity. Resources may be employed at all three levels simultaneously while the traditional deadweight loss calculation is confined only to the last level. The analysis of all such activities falls under the rubric of public choice theory that is concerned with non-market decision-making. It "shifts attention to interactions and to institutions outside of and beyond the confined competitive market process, while applying essentially the same tools as those applied to interactions within the process."[9] Activities, legal and illegal, such as tax avoidance, tax evasion, and smuggling, are also covered by the analysis.

The essential feature of all these activities is that while they are rational and not wasteful from a private viewpoint they are often socially wasteful. The important policy implication drawn by Buchanan is that "so long as governmental action is restricted largely, if not entirely, to protecting individual rights, persons and property, and enforcing voluntarily negotiated private contracts, the market process dominates economic behavior and ensures that any economic rents that appear will be dissipated by the force of competitive entry. Furthermore, the prospects for economic rents enhance the dynamic process of development, growth and orderly change. If, however, governmental action moves significantly beyond the limits defined by the minimal or protective state, if government commences, as it has done on a sweeping scale, to interfere in the market adjustment process, the tendency toward the erosion or dissipation of rents is countered and may be shortly blocked."[10] If political allocation is to be undertaken without giving rise to rent seeking, then such allocation has to be done without creating differential advantages to some groups and, more important, a credible precommitment not to depart in future from such an allocation procedure needs to be given. This suggests that such a scheme will be more difficult to implement the larger is the size

of government and the extent and scope of its intervention.

The approach of North and his fellow economic historians to the evolution of the state is also based on the importance of the structure of property rights which in their view "causes growth or stagnation or economic decline" depending on its efficiency.[11] In a "neutral" state, property rights that would emerge from competition would be efficient relative to the existing constraints of technology, information costs and uncertainty, efficiency presumably being identified with the minimization of transaction costs. In postulating a "neutral" state thereby allowing it a role and level of activity, this school differs from the extreme that is sometimes attributed to the public choice and rent-seeking schools, namely, the belief that the state is nothing more than a gigantic redistributive machine! But in the real world, the state is not "neutral" and the emerging property rights would reflect the tension "between the desires of rulers of the state, on the one hand and efforts of the parties to exchange to reduce transaction costs on the other."[12] The state emerges as a monopolistic provider of protection and justice because these activities are subject to indivisibility and increasing returns to scale. It attempts to maximize revenue acting as a discriminating monopolist in setting property rights, subject only to the constraint that it does not force its constituents to other available means of assuring themselves the same services. Since the revenue potential will in general increase with the production potential of the economy, the state will also attempt to devise a structure of property rights that will reduce transaction costs and hence raise output. Yet the structure that maximizes state revenue need not coincide with the one that maximizes output and growth. Lal, for instance, argues that successive empires in North India were essentially predatory revenue-maximizing states and each fell when it attempted to extract more than the maximum natural "rent" that the system could provide.[13]

In modeling the politico-economic institution of the state and the structure of property rights as a result of a trade-off between revenue maximization and minimization of transaction costs, North's theory differs from an interest-group modeling of the political system *à la* Buchanan et al. and the

[8]J. M. Buchanan, "Rent Seeking and Profit Seeking," in J. M. Buchanan, R. D. Tollison, and G. Tullock, eds., *Toward a Theory of Rent-Seeking Society* (College Station: Texan A&M University Press, 1980).

[9]Ibid., p. 14.

[10]Ibid., p. 9.

[11]D. C. North, *Structure and Change in Economic History* (New York: Norton & Co., 1981), p. 17.

[12]Ibid., p. 18.

[13]D. Lal, *The Political Economy of the Predatory State,* Discussion Paper DRD 105, Development Research Department (Washington, D.C.: World Bank, 1984).

collective choice approach of Olson. Also, North differs from others in assigning, along with Marx, an important role for ideology. In his scheme, ideology combats the "free-rider" problem. The individual incentive to ride free is tempered if he or she considers the institution (of which he or she is a member) to be legitimate. And legitimacy is an ideological evaluation. It leads individuals to obey rules and law, even if such obedience is not in their narrow private interest, because of an ideological conviction as to the legitimacy of the institution imposing the rules and laws. Thus, an ideology is successful only to the extent it mitigates, if not eliminates, the "free-rider" problem by acting as "an economizing device by which individuals come to terms with their environment" and come to acquire "a 'world view' so that decision making is simplified."[14] The degree of success of a particular ideology in deterring an individual from riding free will depend on the extent to which his or her perception about the "fairness" of the world (an important aspect of which is the perceived fairness of the income distribution) is consistent with the moral and ethical judgments that the ideology inculcates. In particular, an individual will change his currently held ideological perspective if his ex-

perience consistently runs counter to it. An implication of this is that when there is a dominant ideology and its tenets are consistent with behavior that promotes rapid economic development, such development will occur. A pluralistic society, such as India, with many competing ideologies is placed at a disadvantage in this respect compared with, for example, the Republic of China or the Republic of Korea.

Let me briefly sum up the discussion. The dominant view of the early development literature that a benevolent state, acting solely in the societal interest, and equipped with needed information, knowledge and policy instruments, can intervene in an optimal way to correct any market failure and launch a society along the road to self-sustained and rapid development turned out to be much too optimistic, if not completely out of touch with the realities. Instead, the state is seen to be pushed and pulled by lobbies and interest groups that are mostly interested in redistribution rather than growth and development. State interventions *intended* at best to improve the efficiency of resource allocation and channel it in socially desired directions and *at worst* by creating fairly small deadweight losses due to distortions may instead end up diverting resources to a significant extent from production to "rent seeking."

[14]North, p. 49.

Selection IX.B.3. India*

Removal of social and economic injustices and assurance of minimum levels of living have been among the most important Directive Principles laid down in the Indian Constitution. Right from the inception of planning these have been among the most prominent explicitly stated objectives of government economic policy. In the last two decades or more, a whole host of policy measures (at least ostensibly resembling many of the suggestions made in different parts of this volume) had been taken towards achieving these objectives. Yet, by most accounts, about half of the total population continue to live in abject poverty and the distribution of income, wealth, and economic power continues to be extremely unequal. The Indian experience, therefore, is highly instructive in understanding the nature of various types of constraints on the effective implementation of good-intentioned redistributive policies in the framework of a so-called mixed economy.

Asset Redistribution Policies

Let us first take the set of policies aimed at direct redistribution of existing assets. The most important asset in India is land. On paper, the volume of land reform legislation in India is very impressive. Laws setting ceilings (often fixed at reasonably low levels) on the private ownership of land with provision for the redistribution of surplus land adorn the statute books of all states in India. Yet by the end of 1970, for the country as a whole, the "declared surplus" has been only 2.4 million acres and the "area distributed" just half of that, or 0.3 percent of the total cultivated land. (Even then this distributed land includes, to a large extent, very poor quality land, wasteland, and the like.) Laws were frequently enacted with deliberate loopholes and telltale exemptions designed to induce fictitious transfers of land to close and distant relatives and to keep the size of permissible retentions high. These laws were executed by a local bureaucracy largely indifferent, occasionally corrupt, and biased in favor of the rural oligarchy; they were enforced by an enormously costly and excruciatingly slow judicial process. For roughly similar reasons, equally miserable has been the fate, except in a couple of states, of tenancy legis-

lation designed to bestow occupancy rights or security of tenure on the tenant cultivators. Implementation has been particularly hampered by a lack of systematic land records (with most of the tenancy existing on the basis of informal and oral lease) and weak revenue administration in many states. Quite frequently, protective tenancy legislation (actual or anticipated) may have worsened the condition of tenants; it has led to resumption of land by the landlords and eviction of tenants under the guise of "voluntary surrender" of land.

As for nonland assets, the major attempts at redistribution have been indirect through the substantial extension of public ownership over the last two decades. The public sector now owns more than 25 percent of the total reproducible tangible wealth in the country, which is a large increase over its share twenty-five years ago. But it is doubtful if this has had any significant impact on personal income inequalities. Much of the "nationalization" has been on payment of heavy compensation and the poor utilization of capacity and low rate of profits in many public enterprises (several exceptions notwithstanding) have led to a lower surplus available for either growth or distribution. The general tendency of many public enterprises to underprice their products and to yield relatively easily to union pressures on wage and salary settlements and provision of relatively liberal housing and other amenities to workers does not necessarily mean that the benefits of the public sector flow to the really poor people, most of whom do not belong to the organized sector and do not in general consume products which are highly intensive—directly or indirectly—in what the public sector produces.

Public Investment

From the point of view of poverty, a more important class of policies is related to public investment in the provision of various types of facilities and to infrastructure aimed at helping to raise productivity and asset formation on the part of the poor themselves. In the 1950s, major attempts in this direction were made through state-sponsored or state-patronized institutions like village cooperatives (to provide subsidized credit) and Community Development Programmes (to provide extension services and to create various infrastructural facilities). But by the end of the 1950s it was admitted on all hands (including reports of the Programme Evaluation Organization of the Planning Commission) that

*From Pranab K. Bardhan, "India," in Hollis Chenery et al., eds., *Redistribution with Growth* (London: Oxford, 1974), pp. 255–262. Reprinted by permission.

most of these benefits in the rural areas were being appropriated by rich farmers by virtue of their social and economic dominance in the countryside and their political and administrative control over these new institutions. The cooperatives became essentially sources of subsidized credit for the big farmers and village moneylenders; the Community Development Programmes provided some of the infrastructure (like roads, land improvement, and so on) to be utilized mostly by the big farmers and traders. Similar has been the case with the large amount of public investment in major irrigation programs, partly because the powerful and "well-connected" people in the villages have direct influence on the distribution of canal water and partly because the small farmers do not have the finances to invest in tubewells, pumps, and other mechanical devices for supplementary water supplies. In the industrial sector also, the overwhelming share of benefits of public investment in the creation and operation of public financial institutions for long-term lending has gone to the rich.

Credit and Services for the Rural Poor

In very recent years some special agencies like the Small Farmers Development Agency (SFDA) and Agency for Marginal Farmers and Agricultural Labour (MFAL) have been created to aid improvements in the productive capacity of the rural poor. It is as yet too early to attempt an evaluation of the performance of these agencies. But one may point to some inherent problems in their effectiveness. The task of the special agencies is to identify and promote viable activities for the poor and to activate and subsidize existing institutions (like cooperatives, commercial banks, extension agencies, and the like) to provide inputs, services, and credit to the small and marginal farmers. But there are problems of identifying economically viable activities for the individual small farmer because of deficiencies of *farm level* infrastructure (for example, the frequent recommendation of dairy farming as a way of making the small man viable often ignores the limitations imposed by a small or no-land base); on the other hand, attempts to compensate for these deficiencies are made by strengthening the *area-level* infrastructure (like development of general facilities of marketing, processing, storage, transport, and so forth), but these additional facilities, being in their very nature area-specific rather than individual farm-specific, largely flow to those who are better off and more well equipped to utilize them. Second, as the mode of operation of the special agencies essentially involves subsi-

dizing and underwriting the loans of existing institutions like cooperatives, the implicit assumption is that these institutions have not been effective in helping the poor so far, primarily due to lack of adequate resources and, particularly, of risk funds (some studies have, however, shown that the extent of default on repayment of cooperative credit has *not* been larger in the case of smaller farmers). If big farmers, moneylenders, and traders continue to control the operation of cooperatives and other existing institutions, it may not be difficult for them to influence the priorities and flow of benefits from the special agencies. There are already several reports that big farmers—who, in view of the land ceilings legislation, have fictitiously parceled their land among several relatives—are now taking advantage of the subsidies of the SFDA program on account of their "small farms."

The main problem with the credit policies of cooperatives, land mortgage banks, or branches of nationalized banks is that credit continues to be given on the basis of land ownership as the primary collateral. Even when these credit institutions have very liberal lending policies, they usually insist that cultivators must be in a position to mortgage at least four to seven acres of land in order to obtain a large enough long-term or medium-term credit for the purchase of a tubewell or a pumpset. The majority of small farmers are left out. If as a result the small farmer does not have assured water supply, this in turn means that he cannot utilize short-term production credit for buying fertilizers, and so on, a phenomenon often interpreted by the cooperative bank officials as "lack of demand." Even when the farmer owns the requisite amount of land, as long as it is "encumbered" (i.e., mortgaged to some other credit institution or private moneylender), he cannot use it as collateral for any other loan negotiation. All these problems are, of course, much more acute for the large numbers of tenants and sharecroppers who do not own but only cultivate land and have, therefore, little creditworthiness. Since most of the small tenants are on oral lease, they do not in general have access even to short-term cooperative or bank credit for current production purposes, and have to fall back on the village moneylender's tender mercy. Attempts at introducing the crop loan system where credit is production oriented rather than security-oriented have been fragmentary and limited.

Education

Public investment in human capital formation, particularly through education, is often regarded as an important way of affecting the long-run distribution of income. Evidence on the distribution of benefits from such investment in India is scanty, but most studies of enrollment, wastage, and drop-out rates in school, as well as participation in higher education, suggest that the benefits of educational subsidies accrue disproportionately less to the lower income groups at each level of education. Even when one has access to education, the poor man with less "contacts" and mobility has a smaller opportunity to get jobs commensurate with his education (the government's policy of ensuring job quotas for some backward castes and groups is clearly inadequate and is sometimes misused).

Rural Investment and Employment Creation

The other area of redistributive public investment advocated in the Indian Plans, particularly since the late 1950s, is investment in rural works programs creating alternative employment for rural unskilled and underemployed labor and at the same time producing durable assets (in the form of roads, soil conservation, minor irrigation, afforestation, and so on) without involving much use of scarce inputs like steel or cement. But the actual expenditure incurred on this account has been extremely small, the programs have been badly administered and, whenever resource constraints have necessitated curtailing of plans midway, the axe has usually fallen first on programs like these. Very recently the government has adopted, somewhat more earnestly, a Crash Scheme for Rural Employment (CSRE) designed to provide in every district in the country employment for 1,000 persons for a period of ten months a year on public works at off-season market wage rates. This is only an experimental scheme and is not aimed at more than touching the bare fringe of the massive problem of unemployment and underemployment in rural India. Yet it is worth pointing to some of the major problems in the actual operation of CSRE. One such problem is that of organization. The rigidities of government departmental organization are well known. The district administrative machinery is often woefully inadequate in preparing technically sound projects suited to the specific problems of timing, location, skills, and other constraints of the local underemployed. Frequently, the task of organizing the works is entrusted to labor contractors. This immediately leads to a big cut in the wage share of the workers. Then, the contractor usually hires people from around the village of his own residence, and that may not be among the pockets of acute unemployment in the

district. Since the contractor is usually paid according to the amount of work done, he is sometimes in a hurry to get the job done in bouts of intensive activity for a few weeks. Over this period, the official requirement of the Scheme to provide employment to those who belong to families where no adult member is employed is quite often ignored. For the same reason the Scheme, in spite of its intentions, does not provide continuity of employment. Second, in a private-ownership economy the benefits of public works (like construction of roads or land improvement) accrue differentially to different groups and this is limited with problems of mobilizing responsible local participation in terms of financial and organizational efforts involved in such programs, problems which the Chinese have successfully tackled through the institution of the commune. Third, because of the very nature of public works, there is relatively low participation by female members of poor households and by laborers attached to big farms who may not have much freedom in working outside even in off seasons. Finally, because of political pressures and regional pulls, programs like CSRE tend to be thinly spread over the country as a whole rather than concentrated in areas of severe incidence of poverty and underemployment.

Price, Incomes, and Tax-Subsidy Policy

Let us now turn to the more conventional arena of price, incomes, and tax-subsidy policies to help the poor. In agricultural prices, the government policy in the last decade or so has been to provide relatively high support prices for foodgrains and to try to distribute the procured grains at fair price shops with a large subsidy. Since the major part of marketable surplus of grains is controlled by big farmers, the high support prices mostly help them rather than small farmers (although the latter may have benefited to some extent from the reduction in interseason price fluctuations that high support prices may have brought about). The system of public distribution of grains is, however, very weak except in about four states. The poor, including the small farmers, are largely dependent on the open market for their grains consumption and have been directly hit by the steep price rises of recent years. The statutory stipulation of minimum wages in industry or agriculture has been virtually inoperative in the vast unorganized nonunionized sectors where the overwhelming majority of the poor work; nothing more could be expected in a situation of acute underemployment. Similarly inoperative has been the rent control legislation in protective tenancy reforms in agriculture, as can be expected in a situation of inexorable pressure on land.

In the Indian context there are only limited possibilities of substantial expansion of employment in the organized sector through price-induced changes in product pattern or techniques of production. The major use of price policy for increasing employment has therefore been to encourage and protect, at the expense of large subsidies and grants, traditional village industries, particularly hand-spinning and hand-weaving of cloth which involve nearly four million poor households. The Indian planning discussion has held long and unending debates on the wisdom of protecting what is quite often an admittedly inferior technology from the competition of a superior technology of mill production for the sake of helping—or at least not uprooting—large numbers of poor households. Other kinds of price policy which may have affected choice of technology relate to underpricing of capital and foreign exchange—in agriculture this has encouraged labor-displacing mechanization, particularly of harvesting and threshing operations in some regions; in the industrial sector this has reinforced or at least failed to counter the tendency of wholesale transfer of labor-saving technical progress of industrially advanced countries.

As for direct provision of public consumption and welfare measures for the poor in the form of health and sanitation, nutrition, drinking water, housing, education, transport, and communication and electricity, there has been some progress over the last two decades, but facilities in proportion to minimum needs remain apparently meagre. Apart from the problem of developing an adequate administrative delivery infrastructure, finance has been a major constraint: whenever the overall financial situation gets worse, these social welfare programs have been the first to be shelved in order to save the so-called core sectors in the Plan. There is also some evidence that the upper-income groups have been able to appropriate for themselves a disproportionate share of some of the expanding social services (particularly education, transport and communication facilities, and low-cost housing).

Conclusions

In sum, the problems of poverty in India remain intractable, not because redistributive objectives were inadequately considered in the planning models, nor because general policies of the kind prescribed in this volume were not attempted. Of course, on the micro level there were specific programs that were ill-conceived and uncoordinated and there were familiar problems of administrative rigidities on the part of an ex-colonial bureaucracy largely oriented to maintaining law and order and collecting revenue. But the major constraint is rooted in the power realities of a political system dominated by a complex constellation of forces representing rich farmers, big business, and the so-called petite bourgeoisie, including the unionized workers of the organized sector. In such a context it is touchingly naïve not to anticipate the failures of asset distribution policies or the appropriation by the rich of a disproportionate share of the benefits of public investment.

Two other kinds of constraints follow from the same primary political constraint. One has to do with the generation and mobilization of the surplus necessary to finance redistributive programs. With a vast network of deliberately designed exemptions and loopholes in the tax laws, all catering to the various pressure groups in the top deciles of the population, the system of income and wealth taxation is largely incapacitated to yield much extra surplus; already nearly three-fourths of total tax revenue come from indirect taxes which, apart from frequently stoking the fires of inflation, are not progressive in their overall incidence in spite of some stiff taxes on selected luxury items. With low rates of profits in public enterprises and huge subsidies in supporting prices paid to big farmers and wages and salary increases paid to white-collar workers, there is little surplus left to help the poor. Faced with a financial squeeze, the government immediately prunes social welfare programs for the poor, or resorts to deficit financing, or both; the inflationary consequences hit the poor hardest. It is paucity of surplus and the consequent fall in the rate of public investment which largely explain why in recent years India has had a miserable performance in overall growth as well as in mitigation of poverty.

The second set of constraints that follows from the ultimate political constraint mentioned above relates to the nature of the local bureaucracy which administers the poverty programs. More often than not the local administrative machinery is manned by people belonging to the families of the rural oligarchy and the urban elite. One does not have to believe in conspiracy theories to note the good-intentioned redistributive programs are sometimes negated by the local vested interests with at least tacit administrative connivance. To quote a Bengali rural proverb, "if there are ghosts inside your mustard seeds, how would you use them to exorcise the ghosts?"

Selection IX.B.4. Governments and Agricultural Markets in Africa*

Governments in Africa intervene in agricultural markets in characteristic ways. They tend to lower the prices offered for agricultural commodities. They tend to increase the prices which farmers must pay for the goods they buy for consumption purposes. And although African governments subsidize the prices that farmers pay for the goods they use in farming, the benefits of these subsidies are appropriated by the rich few—the small minority of large-scale farmers.

There are other characteristics of patterns of government market intervention. Insofar as African governments seek increased farm production, their policies are project-based rather than price-based. Insofar as they employ prices to strengthen production incentives, they tend to encourage production by lowering the prices of inputs (i.e., by lowering costs) rather than by increasing the prices of products (i.e., by increasing revenues). A last characteristic is that governments intervene in ways that promote inefficiency; they create major price distortions, reduce competition in markets, and invest in poorly conceived agricultural projects. In all of these behaviors, it should be stressed, the conduct of African governments resembles the conduct of governments in other parts of the world.

The Regulation of Commodity Markets

It is useful to distinguish between two kinds of agricultural commodities: food crops, many of which could be directly consumed on the farm, and cash crops, few of which are directly consumable and which are instead marketed as a source of cash income. Many cash crops are in fact exported; they provide not only a source of cash incomes for farm families but also a source of foreign exchange for the national economies of Africa.

Export Crops

An important feature of the African economies is the nature of the marketing systems employed for the purchase and exportation of cash crops. The crops are grown by private farm families, but they are then sold through official, state-controlled mar-

*Reprinted by permission from "Governments and Agricultural Markets in Africa" by Robert H. Bates. *The Role of Markets in the World Food Economy,* edited by D. Gale Johnson and G. Edward Schuh. Westview Press, Boulder, Colorado, 1983.

keting channels. At the local level, these channels may take the form of licensed agents or registered private buyers; they may also take the form of cooperative societies or farmers' associations. But the regulated nature of the marketing system is clearly revealed in the fact that these primary purchasing agencies can in most cases sell to but one purchaser: a state-owned body, commonly known as a marketing board. . . .

Upon independence, many African governments found themselves the inheritors of bureaucracies that held a legal monopoly over the purchase and export of commodities in the most valuable sector of their domestic economies. These new states possessed extremely powerful instruments of market intervention. They could purchase export crops at an administratively set, low domestic price; they could then market these crops at the prevailing world price; and they could accumulate the revenues generated by the difference between the domestic and world prices for these commodities.

Government Taxation. Initially, the revenues accumulated by the marketing boards were to be kept in the form of price assistance funds and used for the benefit of the farmers. At times of low international prices, they were to be employed to support domestic prices and so shelter the farmers from the vagaries of the world market. In the case of the Western Nigerian marketing board, for example, 70 percent of the board's revenues were to be retained for such purposes. But commitments to employ the funds for the benefit of the farmers proved short-lived. They were overborn by ambitions to implement development programs and by political pressures brought to bear upon governments from nonagricultural sectors of the economy. . . .

The movement from an instrument of price stabilization, largely for the benefit of farmers, to an instrument of taxation, with the diversion of revenues to nonfarm sectors, can be seen as well in changes in the pricing formulas employed by the marketing boards. Insofar as the boards were employed to stabilize producer prices, the domestic prices—i.e., the price offered the farmers—should have moved independently of the world prices; moreover, a policy of price stabilization implies that domestic prices should have at times exceeded world prices, as the marketing board attempted to protect farmers from falls in the world price. But investigations clearly suggest that what was being stabilized was not the domestic price but rather the difference between the domestic and world price, i.e. the tax on the farmers' income.

Food Crops

African governments also intervene in the market for food crops. And, once again, they tend to do so in ways that lower the price of agricultural commodities.

Price Controls. One way in which African governments attempt to secure low-priced food is by instructing bureaucracies to purchase food crops at government-mandated prices. A recent study by the U.S. Department of Agriculture examined the marketing systems for food crops in Africa and discovered a high incidence of government market intervention. In the case of three of the food crops studied, in over 50 percent of the countries in which the crop was grown, the government had imposed a system of producer price controls; in over 20 percent the government maintained an official monopsony for the purchase of that food crop.

Projects. In order to keep food prices low, governments take additional measures. In particular, they attempt to increase food supplies, either by importing food or by investing in food production projects.

Foreign exchange is scarce. Especially since the rise of petroleum prices, the cost of imports is high. To conserve foreign exchange, African governments therefore attempt to become self-sufficient in food. But they seek to do so within the context of a low-price policy; and therefore invest in projects that will yield increased food production.

In some cases, governments turn public institutions into food production units: youth league and prison farms provide illustrative cases. In other instances, they invest in large-scale efforts to furnish scarce factors of production. In Africa, water is commonly scarce and governments invest heavily in river basin development schemes and irrigation projects. Capital equipment is also scarce; by purchasing and operating farm machinery, governments attempt to promote farm production. Some governments invest in projects to provide particular crops; rice production in the case of Kenya, for example, or wheat production in the case of Tanzania. In other instances, governments divert large portions of their capital budgets to the financing of food production schemes.

Nonbureaucratic Forms of Intervention

Thus far I have emphasized direct forms of government intervention. But there is an equally important, less direct form of intervention: the overvaluation of the domestic currency.

Most governments in Africa maintain an overvalued currency. One result is to lower the prices received by the exporters of cash crops. For a given dollar earned abroad, the exporters of cash crops receive fewer units of the domestic currency. In part, overvaluation also inflicts losses on governments; deriving a portion of their revenues from taxes levied by the marketing boards, the governments command less domestic purchasing power as a result of overvaluation. But because their instruments of taxation are monopolistic agencies, African governments are able to transfer much of the burden of overvaluation: they pass it on to farmers in the form of lower prices.

In addition to lowering the earnings of export agriculture, overvaluation lowers the prices paid for foreign imports. This is, of course, part of the rationale for a policy of overvaluation: it cheapens the costs of importing plant, machinery and other capital equipment needed to build the base for a nascent industrial sector. But things other than plant and equipment can be imported, and among these other commodities is food. As a consequence of overvaluation, African food producers face higher levels of competition from foreign food stuffs. In search of low-priced food, African governments do little to protect their domestic food markets from foreign products—whose prices have artificially been lowered as a consequence of public policies.

Industrial Goods

In the markets for the crops they produce, African farmers therefore face a variety of government policies that serve to lower farm prices. In the markets for the goods they consume, however, they face a highly contrasting situation: they confront consumer prices that are supported by government policy.

In promoting industrial development, African governments adopt commercial policies that shelter local industries from foreign competition. To some degree, they impose tariff barriers between the local and international markets. To an even greater extent, they employ quantitative restrictions. Quotas, import licenses, and permits to acquire and use foreign exchange: all are employed to conserve foreign exchange on the one hand, while on the other hand they protect the domestic market for local industries. In connection with the maintenance of overvalued currencies, these trade barriers create incentives for investors to import capital equipment and to manufacture goods domestically that formerly had been imported from abroad.

Not only do government policies shelter industries from low-cost foreign competition; they shelter them from domestic competition as well. In part, protection from domestic competition is a by-product of protection from foreign competition. The policy of allocating licenses to import in conformity with historic market shares provides an example. The limitation of competition results from other policies as well. In exchange for commitments to invest, governments guarantee periods of freedom from competition. Moreover, governments tend to favor larger projects; seeking infusions of scarce capital, they tend to back those proposals that promise the largest capital investments. Given the small markets typical of most African nations, the result is that investors create plants whose output represents a very large fraction of the domestic market; a small number of firms thus come to dominate the industry. Lastly, particularly where state enterprises are concerned, governments sometimes confer virtual monopoly rights upon particular enterprises. The consequence of all these measures is to shelter industries from domestic competition.

Discussion

Governments intervene in the market for products in an effort to lower prices. They adopt policies that tend to raise the price of the goods farmers buy. And while they attempt to lower the costs of farm inputs, the benefits of this policy are experienced by a small minority of the richer farmers. Agricultural policies in Africa thus tend to be adverse to the interests of most producers.

We may accept for the moment the premise that states act as agencies for maximizing the social welfare. Nonetheless, we are left with the fact that this premise is not very useful, particularly when applied to food policy, for it yields little by way of predictive power. To secure social objectives, governments can choose among a wide variety of policy instruments; and knowledge of the public objectives of a program often does not allow us to predict or to explain the particular policy instrument chosen to implement it.

For example, an important objective of African governments is to increase food supplies. To se-

cure greater supplies, governments could offer higher prices for food or invest the same amount of resources in food production projects. There is every reason to believe that the former is a more efficient way of securing the objective. But governments in Africa systematically prefer project-based policies to price-based policies.

To strengthen the incentives for food production, African governments can increase the price of farm products or subsidize the costs of farm implements. Either would result in higher profits for producers. But governments prefer the latter policy.

To increase output, African governments finance food production programs. But given the level of resources devoted to these programs, they often create too many projects; the programs then fail because resources have been spread too thin. Such behavior is nonsensical, given the social objectives of the program.

To take a last example: In the face of shortages, governments can either allow prices to rise or they can maintain lower prices while imposing quotas. In a variety of markets of significance to agricultural producers African governments choose to ration. They exhibit a systematic preference for the use of this technique—a preference that cannot readily be accounted for in terms of their development objectives.

A major problem with an approach that tries to explain agricultural policies in terms of the social objectives of governments, then, is that the social objectives underlying a policy program rarely determine the particular form the policies assume. The approach thus yields little predictive power. There is a second major difficulty. Insofar as this approach does make predictions, they are often wrong.

This problem is disclosed by the self-defeating nature of many government policies. To secure cheaper food, for example, governments lower prices to producers; but this only creates shortages which lead to *higher* food prices. To increase resources with which to finance programs of development, governments increase agricultural taxes; but this leads to declines in production and to shortfalls in public finances and foreign exchange. And to secure rapid development, governments seek to transfer resources from agriculture to industry; but this set of policies has instead led to reduced rates of growth and to economic stagnation.

The policy instruments chosen to secure social objectives are thus often inconsistent with the attainment of these objectives. The approach thus makes false predictions and it should therefore be rejected. And yet the choices of governments are clearly stable; despite undermining their own goals, governments continue to employ these policy instruments. Some kind of explanation is required, and other kinds of theories must therefore be explored.

There are other grounds for rejecting the development economics approach to the explanation of governmental behavior. One is that the approach assumes autonomy on the part of governments: they are viewed as having the capability of making meaningful choices. It could be that domestic forces impose binding constraints on governments in the developing areas; alternatively, their position in the international political economy may offer them a highly impoverished menu of alternatives. In either case, it would make little sense to view governments as possessing the capacity for making choices. Another basis for rejecting this approach is that it posits benign motives for governments. In contrast to welfare economists, political scientists like myself view governments as possessing their own private agendas, and regard it as the duty of all who bear a commitment to the public interest to make it in the private interest of governments to do the same. Quite apart from philosophic predisposition, however, recent experiences in Africa and elsewhere make it clear that the preference of governments often bears little correspondence to any idealization of the public interest. Rather, governments engage in bureaucratic accumulation and act so as to enhance the wealth and power of those who derive their incomes from the public sector; they also act on behalf of private factions, be they social classes, military cliques, or ethnic groups. They engage in economic redistribution, often from the poor to the rich and at the expense of economic growth. These are central themes in policy formation in Africa and their prominence serves to discredit any approach based on a conviction that governments are agencies of the public interest.

Pluralist Theory

The pluralist approach views public policy as the outcome of political pressures exerted by members of the domestic economy, i.e., by local groups seeking the satisfaction of their private interests from political action.

Particularly in the area of food price policy, this approach has much to recommend it. Put bluntly, food policy in Africa appears to represent a form of political settlement designed to bring peaceful relations between African governments and their urban constituents. It is a settlement whose costs tend to be borne by the farmers.

Urban consumers in Africa constitute a vigilant and potent pressure group demanding low-priced food. Because they are poor, they spend much of their income on food; most studies suggest that urban consumers in Africa spend between 50 and 60 percent of their incomes on food. Changes in the price of food therefore have a major impact on the economic well-being of urban dwellers in Africa, and this group pays close attention to the issue of food prices.

Urban consumers are potent because they are geographically concentrated and strategically located. Because of their geographic concentration, they can quickly be organized; because they control such basic services as transport, communications, and public services, they can impose deprivations on others. They are therefore influential. Urban unrest forms a significant prelude to changes of governments in Africa, and the cost and availability of food supplies is a significant factor promoting urban unrest.

It is not only the worker who cares about food prices. Employers care about food prices because food is a wages good; with higher food prices, wages rise and, all else being equal, profits fall. Governments care about food prices not only because they are employers in their own right but also because as owners of industries and promoters of industrial development programs they seek to protect industrial profits. Indicative of the significance of these interests is that the unit that sets agricultural prices often resides not in the Ministry of Agriculture but in the Ministry of Commerce or Finance.

When urban unrest begins among food consumers, political discontent often rapidly spreads to upper echelons of the polity: to those whose incomes come from profits, not wages, and to those in charge of major bureaucracies. Political regimes that are unable to supply low-cost food are seen as dangerously incompetent and as failing to protect the interests of key elements of the social order. In alliance with the urban masses, influential elites are likely to shift their political loyalties and to replace those in power. Thus it was that protests over food shortages and rising prices in Ghana in 1972 formed a critical prelude to the coup that unseated Busia and led to the period of political maneuvers and flux that threatened to overthrow the government of Arap Moi in Kenya in 1980.

It is ironic but true that among those governments most committed to low-cost food are the "radical" governments in Africa. Despite their stress on economic equality, they impose lower prices on the commodity from which the poorest of the poor—the peasant farmers—derive their incomes. A major reason for their behavior is that they are deeply committed to rapid industrialization: moreover, they are deeply committed to higher real wages for urban workers and have deep institutional ties to organized labor.

We can thus understand the demand for low-cost food. Its origins lie in the urban areas. It is supported by governments, both out of political necessity and, on the part of more radical ones, out of ideological preference. It arises because food is a major staple and higher prices for such staples threaten the real value of wages *and* profits. . . .

Governments as Agencies That Seek to Retain Power

Nonetheless, the pluralist explanation is also incomplete. Its primary virtue is that it helps to account for the essentially draconian pricing policies adopted by African governments. Its primary limitation is that it fails to explain how governments get away with these policies. How, in nations where the majority of the population are farmers and the majority of the resources are held in agriculture, are governments able to succeed in implementing policies that violate the interests of most farmers? In search of answers to this question, another approach is needed: one that looks at agriculture programs as part of a repertoire of devices employed by African governments in their efforts to secure political control over their rural populations and thus to remain in power.

Organizing a Rural Constituency

We have already seen that adopting policies in support of higher prices for agricultural commodities would be politically costly to African governments. It is important to note that this stance would generate few political benefits as well. From a political point of view, conferring higher prices offers few attractions for politicians, for the benefits would be enjoyed by rural opponents and supporters alike. The benefits could not be restricted exclusively to the faithful and withheld from the politically disloyal. Pricing policies therefore cannot be employed by politicians to organize political followings in the countryside.

Project-based policies, however, suffer less from this liability. Officials can exercise discretion in locating projects; they can also exercise discretion in staffing them. This allows them to bestow benefits selectively upon those whose political support they desire. Politicians are therefore more likely to be attracted to project-based policies as a measure of rural development.

Disorganizing the Rural Opposition

We have seen that government policies are often aimed at establishing low prices for agricultural products. Particularly in the market for cash crops, governments maintain monopsonistic agencies and use their market power to lower product prices, thereby imposing deprivations on all producers. What is interesting, however, is that they return a portion of the resources they exact to selected members of the farm community. Some of the earnings taxed from farmers are returned to a privileged few in the form of subsidies for farm inputs. While imposing collective deprivations, governments thus confer selective benefits. The benefits serve as "side payments": they compensate selected members of the rural sector for the losses they sustain as a consequence of the governments' programs. They thereby make it in the private interests of particular members of the rural sector to abide by policies that are harmful to rural dwellers as a whole. By so doing, they secure the defection of favored farmers from a potential rural opposition and insure their adherence to a governing coalition that implements agricultural programs harmful to farming as a whole.

We have already noted that agricultural producers are both subsidized and taxed. What is of concern at this point is the use of subsidy programs for political purposes. In northern Ghana in the late 1970s, for example, subsidized credit was given to large-scale, mechanized producers who were close allies of the ruling military government.

In conferring selective benefits in the markets for farm inputs while imposing collective deprivations in the markets for products, governments secure the deference of a privileged few to programs that are harmful to the interests of most farmers. By politicizing their farm programs and making access to their benefits contingent upon political loyalty, governments secure acquiescence to those in power and compliance with their policies. The political efficacy of these measures is underscored by targeting the large producers who have the most to gain from a change in pricing policy, and who might otherwise provide the "natural leadership" for efforts on the part of farmers to alter the agricultural policies of their governments.

Markets as Instruments of Political Organization

As part of their development programs, African governments intervene in markets to alter prices. At least in the short run, market intervention establishes disequilibrium prices, i.e., prices at which demand exceeds supply. Such prices artificially induce scarcities, and the allocation of these scarce resources through regulated market channels becomes a significant source of political power. Regulated markets can be used to organize political support and to perpetuate governments in power.

As we have seen, in the markets for agricultural products public monopsonies depress the price of commodities below the market price. Those in charge of the market can then bestow the right of entry; persons given access to the market can reap excess profits and owe their special fortunes to the favor of those in charge. Members of the Cocoa Marketing Board in Ghana, for example, frequently allowed private trading on the part of persons whose political backing they wished to secure.

Disequilibrium product prices also facilitate political control by yielding the capacity to *dis*-organize those most hurt by the measure: the farmers themselves. For a portion of the gains, the bureaucrat in charge of the market can turn a blind eye while farmers make sales at market-clearing prices. The structure of regulation vests legal powers in the bureaucrats; the farmers have no right to make such sales. Only by securing an individual exception to the general rule can the farmer gain access to the market-clearing price. Within the framework established by marketing policy, the farmers thus do best by securing individual exceptions. The capacity for discretion therefore allows the bureaucrat to separate the individual interests of particular producers from the interests of their class, and collective organization on the part of rural producers becomes more difficult. In addition, the structure of regulations creates for the government essential elements of political power. By allowing exceptions to the rules, the bureaucracy grants favors; by threatening to enforce the rules, it threatens sanctions. Market regulations thus become a source of political control, and this, in a sense, is most true when they are regularly breached.

Governments establish disequilibrium prices in the markets for inputs as well; the result, once again, is the enhancement of their capacity for political control. When they lower the price of inputs, private sources furnish lesser quantities, users demand greater quantities, and the result is excess demand. One consequence is that the inputs acquire new value; the administratively created shortage creates an economic premium for those who acquire them. Another is that, at the mandated price, the market cannot allocate the inputs; they are in short supply. Rather than being allocated through a pricing system, they must be rationed. Those in charge of the regulated market thereby acquire the capacity to exercise discretion and to confer special benefits upon those whose favor they desire.

Selection IX.B.5. Africa's Growth Tragedy: Policies and Ethnic Divisions*

I. Introduction

Africa's economic history since 1960 fits the classical definition of tragedy: potential unfulfilled, with disastrous consequences. In the 1960s a leading development textbook ranked Africa's growth potential ahead of East Asia's, and the World Bank's chief economist listed seven African countries that "clearly have the potential to reach or surpass" a 7 percent growth rate. Yet, these hopes went awry. On average, real per capita GDP did not grow in Africa over the 1965–1990 period, while, in East Asia and the Pacific, per capita GDP growth was over 5 percent and Latin America grew at almost 2 percent per year. Much of Africa has even suffered negative per capita growth since 1960, and the seven promising countries identified by the World Bank's chief economist were among those with negative growth (Figure 1). Sub-Saharan Africa's growth tragedy is reflected in painful human scars. The typical African mother has only a 30 percent chance of having all of her children survive to age five. Average life expectancy for a person born in 1980 in Sub-Saharan Africa is only 48 years compared with 65 in Latin America, and daily calorie intake is only 70 percent of Latin America's and East Asia's.

Although an enormous literature points to a diverse set of potential causes of Sub-Saharan Africa's ills, ranging from bad policies, to poor education, to political instability, to inadequate infrastructure,[1] existing work does not explain why

some countries choose growth-enhancing policies and others adopt growth-retarding ones. Why did so many public policies all go so badly wrong in Africa? This paper examines a simple hypothesis: cross-country differences in ethnic diversity explain a substantial part of the cross-country differences in public policies, political instability, and other economic factors associated with long-run growth. This paper seeks a better understanding of cross-country growth differences by examining the direct effect of ethnic diversity on economic growth and by evaluating the indirect effect of ethnic diversity on public policy choices that in turn influence long-run growth rates. Though motivated by Africa's growth tragedy and its considerable ethnic diversity, none of the results is particular to Africa since we conduct the analysis on a broad cross section of countries. Thus, this paper examines the general proposition that ethnic diversity influences economic performance, and most of this effect works indirectly through public policies, political stability, and other economic factors. We illustrate the economic importance of ethnic diversity by demonstrating that it helps account for Africa's growth tragedy.

The paper first quantifies the empirical relationship between economic growth and a wide array of factors using data over the last 30 years. We include standard variables such as initial income to capture convergence effects, schooling, political stability, and indicators of fiscal, trade, exchange rate, financial sector policies, and infrastructure. We find that low school attainment, political instability, poorly developed financial systems, large black market exchange rate premiums, large government deficits, and inadequate infrastructure are significantly correlated with economic growth and enter the growth regressions with economically large coefficients. These variables account for about two-fifths of the growth differential between the countries of Sub-Saharan Africa and fast growing East Asia.

Next, the paper turns to its main focus: do higher levels of ethnic diversity encourage poor policies, poor education, political instability, inadequate infrastructure, and other factors associated with slow growth? While debate persists, an assortment of political economy models suggest that polarized societies will be both prone to competitive rent-seeking by the different groups and have difficulty agreeing on public goods like infrastruc-

*From William Easterly and Ross Levine, "Africa's Growth Tragedy: Policies and Ethnic Divisions," *Quarterly Journal of Economics* 112 (November 1997): 1203–1219, 1223–1227, 1230–1236, 1241. Reprinted by permission.

[1]See Bevan, Collier, and Gunning [1993], Collier and Gunning [1992], Soludo [1993], Husain and Faruquee [1994], Pack [1993], Lewis [1986], Wheeler [1984], Ndulu [1991], Elbadawi [1992], Elbadawi and Ndulu [1994], Helleiner [1986], Fosu [1992a, 1992b], Gyimah-Brempong [1991], Killick [1991], Berg [1993], Pickett [1990], Hadjimichael et al. [1994], and Rimmer [1991]. Chhibber and Fischer [1992] edited a book on economic reform in Sub-Saharan Africa that discusses changes in exchange rate, fiscal, financial sector, trade, educational, and regional integration policies that could potentially stimulate sustained growth in Africa. Other books include Blomstrom and Lundahl [1993], Borgin and Corbett [1982], Glickman [1988], Ravenhill [1986], Sadiq Ali and Gupta [1987], and Turok [1987]. From the World Bank, see World Bank [1981, 1989, 1994a]. A recent and thorough World Bank study on Sub-Saharan Africa is *Adjustment in Africa: Reforms, Results, and the Road Ahead* [World Bank 1994], with an update in Bouton, Jones, and Kiguel [1994]

Figure 1. Regional Distribution of Negative Growth

Countries that had negative per capita growth 1960–1988 are shaded gray.

ture, education, and good policies [Alesina and Tabellini 1989; Alesina and Drazen 1991; Shleifer and Vishny 1993; Alesina and Rodrik 1994; Alesina and Spolaore 1997]. Alesina [1994, p. 38] recently argued that "society's polarization and degree of social conflict" are key factors underlying policy decisions. Ethnic diversity may increase polarization and thereby impede agreement about the provision of public goods and create positive incentives for growth-reducing policies, such as financial repression and over-valued exchange rates, that create rents for the groups in power at the expense of society at large.

To assess the hypothesis that ethnic divisions influence economic growth and public policies, we assemble a diverse set of measures of ethnic diversity. We focus most of our attention on a measure of ethnolinguistic diversity, ETHNIC, that measures the probability that two randomly selected individuals in a country belong to different ethnolinguistic groups. ETHNIC is derived from Soviet data collected in the early 1960s. . . .

The data indicate that high levels of ethnic diversity are strongly linked to high black market

premiums, poor financial development, low provision of infrastructure, and low levels of education. Although ethnic diversity is not significantly correlated with every economic indicator, the evidence is consistent with the hypothesis that ethnic diversity adversely affects many public policies associated with economic growth. The evidence regarding the direct link between ethnic diversity and growth is more ambiguous. While some indicators of ethnic diversity remain significantly negatively correlated with growth after controlling for a diverse set of factors, other ethnic diversity measures are so strongly correlated with the other factors included in the regression that they lose their significance when entered jointly in cross-country growth regressions. The indirect link between ethnic diversity and public policies, however, is robust to alternative measures of ethnolinguistic diversity. While not fully accounting for Africa's growth performance, the extraordinarily high levels of ethnic diversity in Africa importantly contribute to our understanding of Africa's growth tragedy. Indeed, after accounting for the effects of ethnic diversity on education, political stability, fi-

nancial depth, black market premiums, fiscal policy, and infrastructure development, ethnic diversity alone accounts for about 28 percent of the
growth differential between the countries of Africa
and East Asia. . . .

II. Using Cross-Country Regressions to Explain Growth

We begin by quantifying the empirical association between long-run economic growth and a
wide variety of indicators. The goal here is not to
establish that any particular economic or political
indicator has an empirical relationship with long-
run growth that is independent of other indicators.
That is, the goal is not to establish "robustness" as
defined by Levine and Renelt [1992]. Instead, this
section shows that many indicators have a close
association with growth and these indicators account for a substantial amount of the cross-country
variation in growth rates over the last 30 years.
This section sets the stage for the remainder of the
paper, where we ask: why do countries select
growth-retarding policy-packages?

A. Regression Framework

Since we are focusing on long-run growth, we
attempt to abstract from business cycle fluctuations by studying economic performance over
decades. Specifically, the explanatory variable in
our regressions is the average annual growth rate
of GDP per capita in the 1960s, 1970s, and 1980s
for all countries with data (excluding Gulf Oil
States). Thus, each country has three observations,
data permitting. The equations are estimated using
the technique of seemingly unrelated regressions,
where each decade forms one-third of the system.
This procedure allows for country random effects
that are correlated across decades. It should be noted that the AR(1) coefficient across decades is typically smaller than 0.25, and the simple ordinary
least squares results are virtually identical to those
reported below.

To account for cross-country growth differences, we use an array of right-hand-side variables. Besides different intercept terms for each
decade, we include dummy variables for Sub-Saharan Africa and Latin America and the Caribbean
called AFRICA and LATINCA that Barro [1991]
and many others have found to be significant and
negative.

We include two variables to control for initial
income (at the start of each decade) and thereby
capture the convergence effect highlighted by Barro and Sala-i-Martin [1992]. This convergence result, however, is nonlinear, first rising and then
falling with per capita income [Baumol, Blackman, and Wolff 1992; Easterly 1994]. Consequently, we include two terms: the logarithm of GDP per
capita at the start of the decade and the square of
the logarithm of initial income at the start of each
decade.

The cross-country growth regressions also include the logarithm of the average educational attainment variable constructed by Barro and Lee
[1993], which is measured at the beginning of each
decade. Also, we control for political instability by
including a measure of political assassinations,
which Barro [1991] found to be negatively associated with growth. We used other indicators of political instability, such as measures of civil liber-
ties, the number of revolutions and coups, and the
number of casualties from war, but these did not
alter the results.

We include three economic indicators that have
been linked to economic growth in past studies.
First, we include a measure of the black market exchange rate premium, averaged over each decade.
The black market exchange rate premium is frequently used as a general indicator of trade, exchange rate, and price distortions.[2] Second, we
measure the fiscal stance of the country by including the central government surplus to GDP ratio,
averaged over each decade.[3] Finally, we include a
measure of financial depth that equals liquid liabilities of the financial system divided by GDP, averaged over each decade.[4] Unlike the black market
premium and the fiscal surplus, financial depth is
not directly linked to a policy lever. Collier and
Mayer [1989] and Levine [1997], however, show
that financial depth is closely linked with measures
of financial sector policies and measures of the legal treatment of outside creditors developed by La
Porta, López-de-Silanes; Shleifer, and Vishny
[1996]. With the caveat that financial depth is not a

[2] See Easterly [1994], Fischer [1993], and Levine and Zervos
[1993].

[3] Fischer [1993] and Easterly and Rebelo [1993] find a negative relationship between government deficits and economic
growth.

[4] King and Levine [1993a, 1993b] show that financial depth
is closely associated with long-run growth. Furthermore, alternative measures of financial development, such as (1) the fraction of credit banks allocate to enterprises relative to the fraction
of credit provided to central, state, and local governments and
(2) the fraction of credit intermediated by commercial banks relative to credit intermediated by the central bank, produced similar results.

Table 1. Growth Regressions: Pooled Decades (1960s, 1970s, 1980s) (dependent variable: real per capita GDP growth)

Variable	(1)	(2)	(3)	(4)
Dummy for the 1960s	−0.142 (−1.66)	−0.169 (−1.96)	−0.246 (−2.60)	−0.267 (−2.82)
Dummy for the 1970s	−0.145 (−1.70)	−0.171 (−1.99)	−0.243 (−2.56)	−0.261 (−2.76)
Dummy for the 1980s	−0.165 (−1.93)	−0.191 (−2.22)	−0.259 (−2.74)	−0.277 (−2.93)
Dummy variable for Sub-Saharan Africa	−0.014 (−3.24)	−0.015 (−3.45)	−0.016 (−3.39)	−0.018 (−3.58)
Dummy variable for Latin America and the Caribbean	−0.021 (−5.58)	−0.019 (−5.21)	−0.015 (−4.22)	−0.016 (−4.56)
Log of initial income	0.047 (2.11)	0.055 (2.43)	0.079 (3.22)	0.090 (3.74)
(Log of initial income) squared	−0.003 (−2.26)	−0.004 (−2.60)	−0.006 (−3.59)	−0.007 (−4.58)
Log of schooling	0.012 (2.93)	0.013 (3.04)	0.011 (2.53)	0.009 (1.89)
Assassinations		−23.783 (−2.26)	−17.868 (−1.82)	−22.923 (−2.52)
Financial depth			0.018 (3.08)	0.013 (2.19)
Black market premium			−0.020 (−4.48)	−0.018 (−4.09)
Fiscal surplus/GDP			0.093 (3.00)	0.177 (4.93)
Log of telephones per worker				0.007 (2.71)
No. of observations	83; 89; 96	78; 88; 95	45; 72; 76	41; 70; 67
R^2	0.21, 0.18, 0.32	0.20, 0.18, 0.34	0.42, 0.43, 0.49	0.42, 0.49, 0.59

t-statistics are in parentheses.

Estimated using Seemingly Unrelated Regressions: a separate regression for each period.

policy lever, we sometimes refer to these three variables as policy indicators.[5]

B. Growth Regression Results

Regressions (1)–(3) in Table 1 present the results using these traditional measures of initial income, schooling, political stability, and policies. All of the variables are significant at the 0.05 significance level and of the anticipated sign. Countries with greater financial depth, larger fiscal surpluses, and lower black market exchange rate premiums grew significantly faster than countries with more shallow financial systems, large fiscal deficits, and sizable black market premiums. The regression also indicates that political assassinations are negatively correlated with long-run growth, while educational attainment is positively linked to growth.

The dummy variables for both Sub-Saharan African countries and Latin America and Caribbean countries are significant and negative. While the

regressors are able to account for some of the poor growth performance of Africa, the regression does not explain all of it. Africa (and Latin America) grow more slowly than predicted by the cross-country growth regressions. A Chow test does not reject the hypothesis that the reported coefficients are the same for only the sample of Sub-Saharan African countries. Although the power of the Chow test is probably low, the data do not make us believe that the tragedy of Africa lies in different sensitivities to various economic indicators.

The coefficients on the catch-up variables, 0.079 on the logarithm of initial income and −0.006 on the logarithm of initial income squared in regression (3), imply that the catch-up effect is a concave function of initial income. For the given parameter values, the catch-up effect is strongest for countries with incomes of $1020.[6] Africa's initial per capita income (averaging over 1960, 1970, and 1980) is $883. Thus, the regression indicates that Africa should enjoy a catch-up effect, even though this effect will, on average, be slightly less pronounced for Africa than for countries right

[5]We experimented with including measures of inflation and other variables frequently included in cross-country regressions, but these other variables did not enter significantly, nor did they alter this paper's conclusions. Trade or export shares are not significant as explanatory variables in cross-country growth studies. Helleiner [1986] has previously pointed out the lack of explanatory power of export shares for Africa specifically.

[6]To compute this, set the derivative of growth in the core regression with respect to INCOME equal to zero: 0 = 0.078936 − (0.005697)(2)(log of initial real per capita GDP). Thus, initial real per capita GDP with the maximum catch-up effect is exp{0.078936/(2*0.005697)} = $1020.

around the "convergence maximum" of about $1000.

Many studies of Africa cite the poor state of infrastructure. Low-quality infrastructure can hinder growth by depressing the marginal product of private investment. An influential study by Aschauer [1989] claimed that infrastructure had large effects on U.S. productivity growth; Canning and Fay [1993] and Easterly and Rebelo [1993] have similar findings for a cross-country sample, emphasizing transport and communication infrastructure.[7]

As an indicator of the state of a country's infrastructure, we use Canning and Fay's [1993] measure of telephones per worker. We find a strong, positive link between growth and telephones per worker as shown in regression (4) of Table 1. . . .

The Table 1 results suggest that a variety of economic indicators are closely associated with economic growth in a cross section of economies. These indicators account for between 42 percent and 59 percent of the cross-country variance of growth rates depending on the decade.

To illustrate the importance of these public policy indicators in accounting for growth differences, we compare the most slowly growing region, Africa, with the most rapidly growing region, East Asia. Table 2 gives average values of the explanatory variables of regression (4) of Table 1 for East Asia and Africa. East Asia's country characteristics were uniformly more favorable for growth than those of Africa. East Asia's average years of school attainment at the beginning of each decade was 72 percent higher than Africa's. The number of assassinations in East Asia was one-third of those in Africa. East Asia had twice the financial depth and its black market premium was practically one-tenth that of Africa's. East Asia's government deficits were half the size of those in Africa. East Asia had three times as many telephones per worker as Africa. (Hong Kong had more telephones in 1960 than Nigeria, even though Nigeria's population was seventeen times larger. By 1980 Hong Kong had more telephones than all of Sub-Saharan Africa.) Thus, East Asia enjoyed substantially better country characteristics—from policies, to infrastructure, to political stability—than Africa. These country characteristics—budget deficits, black market premiums, financial depth, political instability, infrastructure, and human capital—account for a substantial amount of the cross-country variation in growth rates. Specifically, as

we document below, these public policy indicators account for about 44 percent of the growth differential between Africa and East Asia. The importance of public policies in accounting for growth differences, however, leaves open an important question: why did so many factors all go wrong in Africa? . . .

III. Ethnicity: Growth and Policy Choices

A. *Ethnic Diversity: Concepts and Country Examples*

The borders of African nations were determined through a tragicomic series of negotiations between European powers in the nineteenth century that split up ethnic groups and exacerbated preexisting high levels of ethnic and linguistic diversity.[8] A vast political science literature argues that these high levels of ethnic diversity have encouraged growth-impeding policies. For example, a leading Nigerian social scientist, Claude Ake, argues that a "conflict among nationalities, ethnic groups, and communal and interest groups" broke out after the independence of African nations. The resulting "struggle for power was so absorbing that everything else, including development, was marginalized" [Ake 1996, pp. 5, 7].[9]

Besides the analyses of political scientists, economic theories suggest that ethnically polarized societies are more likely to select socially suboptimal policies under many circumstances. Alesina and Drazen [1991] describe how a war of attrition between interest groups can postpone macroeconomic stabilization. In this model, the first group to concede and accept stabilization bears a disproportionate share of the cost. The groups differ in the welfare loss they suffer from postponing stabilization, but their type is not known to the other group. The stabilization is delayed as the groups

---

[7]Easterly and Rebelo [1993] used consolidated public sector investment in transport and communications; these data are available for too few African countries to be of use here.

[8]Negotiations about African nation borders paid far more attention to where explorers of each European nationality had happened to wander than to existing ethnic borders, so that many ethnic groups were split between neighboring countries. For a popular historical treatment see Pakenham [1991].

[9]Scarritt [1993] concurs that in Africa, "The prevalent form of conflict . . . is competition over political and economic distribution in the context of unstable multiethnic coalitions" [p. 252]. The historian Davidson [1992] states flatly that African economic decline was due to the destruction caused by "rival kinship networks, whether of 'ethnic' clientelism or its camouflage in no less clientelist 'multiparty systems'" [p. 291]. Chazan [1988] says these ethnic groupings in Africa "have been proven to be effective channels for the extraction of state resources" [p. 134]. All of this contrasts, according to Gurr [1993], with Western democracies, which "have devised strategies that have contributed to a substantial decline in most kinds of ethnic conflict" [p. 290].

Table 2. Economic Indicators: Africa Versus East Asia

Variable	Africa mean	East Asia mean
Log of schooling	1.031	1.574
Assassinations	1.13E-05	3.73E-06
Financial depth	0.240	0.474
Black market premium	0.450	0.054
Log of telephones per worker	2.436	3.538
Fiscal Surplus/GDP	–0.051	–0.025

accumulate information on the other group's like-lihood of conceding. Although they focus on infla-tion, the logic applies equally to any distortion such as a black market premium or financial re-pression. We see ethnic diversity entering their model by making it more likely that there will be polarized groups engaged in a war of attrition.

For another example, corruption may be partic-ularly damaging when there is more than one bribe-taker [Shleifer and Vishny 1993]. If each in-dependent bribe-taker does not internalize the ef-fect of his bribes on the other bribe-taker's rev-enues, then the result is more bribes per unit of output and less output. Ethnically diverse societies may be more likely to yield independent bribe-tak-ers since each ethnic group may be allocated a re-gion or ministry in the power structure. Mauro [1995] has already demonstrated the empirical as-sociation between ethnic fragmentation and high corruption.

Moreover, ethnically diverse societies may pro-duce situations formally analogous to Shleifer and Vishny's [1993] uncoordinated bribe-takers, be-yond straight bribe collection. Specifically, unco-ordinated ministries may each pursue a rent-seek-ing strategy without taking into account the effect of their actions on the other groups' rents. For ex-ample, one group may impose an overvalued ex-change rate and strict exchange controls for the purpose of generating rents from reselling foreign exchange on the black market. Another group may impose very low interest rates (e.g., negative in real terms) on savers for the purpose of generating rents in the form of low-interest loans to their eth-nic supporters. Different groups do not internalize the effects of their actions on other groups or soci-ety at large. For example, an overvalued official exchange rate creates incentives to smuggle local currency savings out of the country because of fear of devaluation, lowering the amount of financial savings that the other group can appropriate as low-interest loans. Likewise, highly negative do-mestic real interest rates create incentives to invest

in foreign assets, giving exporters an additional in-centive to underinvoice and keep foreign exchange outside of the country, lowering the amount of for-eign exchange the group setting the official ex-change rate can implicitly tax. As in Shleifer and Vishny, the results from uncoordinated rent-seek-ing are lower output and higher "bribes"—in this case higher black market premiums and more fi-nancial repression—than would occur in a mono-lithic government.

More generally, separation of powers between distinct groups can lead to "common pool" prob-lems, where each group seizes its share of the "pool" of rents until the pool is exhausted [Pers-son, Roland, and Tabellini 1997]. The common pool problem is alleviated only if checks and bal-ances exist that give each group a veto over the other groups' rent appropriation. As we will see below, ethnically diverse societies not only by def-inition have distinct groups but are also empirical-ly less likely to have the kind of political institu-tions that create effective checks and balances, i.e., democratic institutions and rule of law. To mix metaphors, the "common pool" story could help explain the otherwise inexplicable phenomenon of "killing the goose that lays the golden egg." It is not uncommon to observe in Africa some activity nearly taxed out of existence, that is, taxed far be-yond the revenue-maximizing tax rate.

Other models tell us that polarized preferences lead to a low provision of public goods. In Alesina and Spolaore [1997] a public good like a school brings less satisfaction to everyone in an ethnically diverse situation because of the different prefer-ences for language of instruction, curriculum, loca-tion, etc. So less of the public good is chosen by so-ciety, lowering the level of output or growth. Although this lower provision may be socially opti-mal, given the constraint that the school must rec-oncile very different preferences by ethnic groups, the existence of this constraint is costly for output and growth compared with a homogeneous society.

Some work on data from U.S. localities finds

evidence for ethnic diversity affecting public goods choice. Poterba [1996] finds that a larger fraction of elderly in a jurisdiction leads to lower public spending on education and that "this reduction is particularly large when the elderly residents and the school age population are from different racial groups." Alesina, Baqir, and Easterly [1997] find that a variety of public goods—roads, schools, trash pickup, libraries—worsen or receive less funding with higher ethnic diversity in a sample of U.S. cities.[10]

A few country anecdotes help give a flavor of how ethnic divisions can foster growth-retarding policies. Kenya has more than 40 ethnic groups, including Kikuyu (21 percent of population), Luhya (13), Luo (13), Kalenjin (11), Kamba (11), Masai (2), and Somali (2). A large Indian business community and some remaining white Kenyans add to the complicated mix. The Kikuyu led the fight for independence and dominated politics under President Kenyatta until 1978, at first in alliance with the Luo and then with the Kamba. Since 1978 the Kalenjin group of President Moi has been prominent in government, in alliance with Kamba, Luhya, and smaller groups [Cohen 1995; Throup 1987]. In the 1992 presidential elections, the Luo candidate won 75 percent of the vote in the Luo region, the two Kikuyu candidates together received 96 percent of the vote in the Kikuyu region, and the Kalenjin candidate—President Moi—received 71 percent of the vote in the Kalenjin region.[11]

Barkan and Chege [1989] analyze the allocation of road-building investments in Kenya between

what they consider to be the home regions of the Kenyatta and the Moi ethnic coalitions during their respective governments. Each regional grouping contains a third of Kenya's population. They report that after Moi took over in 1978, the road-building investment share of the Kenyatta coalition home regions fell from 44 percent in 1979–1980 to 16 percent in 1987–1988. The share of the Moi coalition home regions rose from 32 percent to 57 percent. The share of health expenditures in 1987–1988 going to the regions of the Kenyatta ethnic coalition was 18 percent, while the regions of the Moi coalition received 49 percent.[12]

The history of Ghana provides an illustrative example of how ethnic conflict over economic rents adversely affects policy choices. Ghana's main export crop is cocoa, production of which is concentrated in the region of the Ashanti group who make up 13 percent of the population. The Ashanti Empire was dominant in precolonial times, to the resentment of other groups such as the coastal Akan groups (30 percent of population). Beginning with the runup to independence in the 1950s, cocoa replaced historical resentments as a bone of interethnic contention [Mikell 1989].

In the early 1950s Kwame Nkrumah, himself from one of the coastal Akan groups, split off from the traditional Ashanti-based independence party. He pushed a bill through the colonial legislature in 1954 to freeze the producer price of cocoa. An Ashanti-based opposition party to Nkrumah ran against him in the 1956 elections with the slogan, "Vote Cocoa," while also pushing for secession. With most of the other groups favoring Nkrumah, these efforts failed. Nkrumah continued to tax cocoa heavily—through the Cocoa Marketing Board and through the growing overvaluation of the official exchange rate.

In 1969–1971 Kofi Busia led the only Ashanti-based government in modern Ghanaian history, having co-opted some of the coastal Akan groups as allies. One of Busia's first acts was to raise the producer price of cocoa. Later in his term, in 1971, he instituted a large devaluation that raised the domestic currency price of cocoa at a time when the world cocoa price was falling. The military over-

---

[10]Other models in which it is more difficult to achieve a consensus for good policies in a polarized environment include Persson and Tabellini [1994], Alesina and Tabellini [1989], Lane and Tornell [1995], and Alesina and Rodrik [1994]. We should note that it is theoretically conceivable that the effect of diversity on public goods could go the other way. If each public good is purely "local" to each ethnic group, then the "common pool" type model could imply more public goods from ethnic fragmentation. Under other models, like those that feature "logrolling," each ethnic representative gets his favorite local public projects funded while agreeing in return to support the other representatives' projects and so the result is *excessive* spending on public goods. Whether these considerations are relevant is an empirical issue our results will address.

[11]Miller and Yeager [1994, p. 116]. Moi was elected with a plurality (36 percent) of the votes due to the splitting of opposition votes. Of course, ethnic bloc voting is hardly unique to Kenya, or to Africa. In Fiji's 1977 elections, 82 percent of people of Fijian origin voted for one party, while 86 percent of people of Indian origin voted for the other party [Milne 1981]. In Washington, DC's mayoral election in 1994, the white candidate got over 90 percent of the vote in the mostly white Ward 3, while the black candidate got over 90 percent of the vote in the mostly black Ward 8 (*Washington Post*).

[12]Background studies of parliamentarians find that "the one characteristic they share with their constituents is ethnicity," since communities "want to be sure that a candidate will represent their interests" [Miller and Yeager 1994, p. 77]. Cohen [1995] says the group in power has systematically manipulated the multiple exchange rate system to extract rents for its particular ethnic group, which illustrates "how brazen ethnic-based rent-seeking coalitions can become." See also Nyangira [1987], Throup [1987], Haugerud [1995], and Bates [1989] for other examples of ethnic distributional conflicts in Kenya.

threw him three days later and partially reversed the devaluation.

Though ethnic coalitions rotated with dizzying speed through the 1970s and early 1980s in Ghana, they all seemed to concur on punitive taxation of cocoa exports through the ludicrously overvalued official exchange rate (reflected in a high black market premium). Granting of permission to import goods at the official exchange rate was one way to dissipate these rents to political and ethnic supporters. The black market premium reached its historical peak in 1982, with the black market exchange rate at 22 times the official exchange rate [Wetzel 1995, p. 197]. The cocoa producers had received 89 percent of the world price of cocoa in 1949 [Bates 1981]. By 1983 they received 6 percent of the world price. Cocoa exports were 19 percent of GDP in 1955; by 1983 they were only 3 percent of GDP. Ghanaian cocoa is one of the classic examples of "killing the goose that laid the golden egg." Reforms finally began in the mid-1980s. The case of Ghana suggests that the interethnic struggle over rents from a commodity like cocoa has something to do with the choice of growth-retarding policies—like an overvalued exchange rate resulting in a high black market premium.

Finally, in contrast to Ghana and Kenya, Botswana is an African success story with growth comparable to South Korea's. In terms of this paper's focus, it is noteworthy that Botswana has one of the most ethnically homogeneous populations in Africa and has adopted some of the best policies in Sub-Saharan Africa. . . .

B. Measuring Ethnic Diversity

Table 3 shows the most and the least ethnically diverse societies in the world according to the Soviets' measure of ETHNIC. Fourteen out of the fifteen most ethnically heterogeneous societies in the world are in Africa; eight countries classified as high-income countries by the World Bank's Development Report are among the most ethnically homogeneous, and no such rich countries are among the top-fifteen most ethnically diverse countries. Two of the East Asian fast growers (Japan and Hong Kong) are among the most ethnically homogeneous. . . .

C. Growth Regressions

The simple regression of growth on ETHNIC (with decade dummies) is highly significant, with a t-statistic of -4.4. The magnitude of the coefficient ($-.023$) indicates that going from complete homogeneity to complete heterogeneity is associated with a fall in growth of 2.3 percentage

Table 3. Ethnolinguistic Fractionalization Index (ETHNIC) (66 Countries, 1960)

Country	ETHNIC	Country	ETHNIC
15 Most fractionalized:		15 Least fractionalized:	
Tanzania	93	Haiti	1
Uganda	90	Japan	1
Zaire	90	Portugal	1
Cameroon	89	Hong Kong	2
India	89	Yemen	2
South Africa	88	Germany	3
Nigeria	87	Burundi	4
Ivory Coast	86	Dominican Republic	4
CAR	83	Egypt	4
Kenya	83	Ireland	4
Liberia	83	Italy	4
Zambia	82	Norway	4
Angola	78	Iceland	5
Mali	78	Jamaica	5
Sierra Leone	77	Jordan	5

ETHNIC measures the probability that two randomly selected persons from a given country will not belong to the same ethnolinguistic group. The more groups there are, the higher ETHNIC. The more equally distributed the groups, the higher the ETHNIC.

Source: Taylor and Hudson [1972].

points.[13] A one-standard-deviation increase in ETHNIC is associated with a decrease in per capita growth of about 30 percent of a standard deviation in growth across countries. ETHNIC is not simply proxying for the Africa dummy here, because it also remains significant in the non-Africa sample (coefficient of −.016 and t-statistic of −2.3). This simple, reduced-form regression is an important result because we will argue that many of the standard explanatory variables in growth regressions are themselves endogenous to ETHNIC.[14]

Table 4 presents evidence on the empirical association between ETHNIC and economic growth, controlling for other factors. Regression (1) shows that ETHNIC is significantly correlated with growth after controlling for initial income and including dummy variables for countries in Sub-Saharan Africa and Latin America. In regression (2) we introduce measures of educational attainment and political stability. Ethnic diversity remains significant with little change in the coefficient. Moreover, ethnic diversity remains significantly negatively correlated with growth after controlling for financial depth, the fiscal surplus, and the black market exchange rate premium as shown in regression (3).[15] The economic magnitude of the coefficient on ETHNIC is substantial. Taken literally, the coefficient in regression (3) implies that if

[13]We estimate this and the following regressions with the method of seemingly unrelated regressions with one equation for each decade. We believe the pooled decade average, cross section sample is useful despite the lack of intertemporal variability of ETHNIC so that we can—as we will see—capture the intertemporal variation in the other variables. If we run the simple correlation between growth and ETHNIC as a cross section by averaging the decade growth rates, the association remains highly significant.

[14]Many readers have wondered whether the relationship between growth and ETHNIC was nonlinear; for example, maybe having two equal groups is just as damaging to political economy as four equal groups; alternatively, maybe ethnic diversity only matters when there are many small ethnic groups (the upper range of ETHNIC). Unfortunately, our efforts to estimate a spline regression were unavailing; we found no evidence of a change in slope at ETHNIC = .5 and at ETHNIC = .75, which may simply reflect our small sample.

[15]We have already noted that war is associated with ethnic fragmentation. Over the past three decades, many military conflicts have occurred in Africa. To gauge whether our results merely reflect the economic disruptions caused by war, we examine the relationships between wars and growth and between wars and policy choices. We use a dummy variable, WAR, that takes on the value 1 when Sivard [1993] reports a war taking place on the territory of a given country in a given decade. When we include WAR in the pooled cross-country, decade growth regressions of Table 1 that include policy indicators (regressions (3)–(4)), WAR enters with a P-value of greater than 0.10 and the results on the other variables remain unaffected.

Nigeria had the sample mean value of ETHNIC (0.42) instead of its actual value of 0.87, its per capita growth rate over the 1960–1989 period would have been almost double its actual value of 0.7 percent per annum. In regression (4) we also include the logarithm of the number of telephones per worker as an indicator of national infrastructure. The significance of ethnic diversity weakens, and the coefficient diminishes when we also include the infrastructure measure. Apparently, ETHNIC is sufficiently correlated with public policy indicators such that it loses its independent association with long-run growth in regression (4) of Table 4. We get similar results when the analysis is restricted to the non-African countries. Thus, as suggested by theory and country studies, ETHNIC may primarily affect growth indirectly by influencing public policy decisions. . . .

D. Ethnic Diversity, Political Instability, and Policy Choices

Ethnically fragmented economies may find it difficult to agree on public goods and good policies. They also may be politically unstable. Table 5 presents evidence on the effects of ethnic diversity on political instability and policy choices. The simple relationship between ethnic diversity and assassinations is insignificant. There is no evidence that ethnic diversity affects this manifestation of political instability. This lack of correlation is not unique to this indicator—out of a set of nine indicators of political instability, we found only one (constitutional changes) to be correlated with ethnic diversity. A related observation is that Africa does *not* have significantly above average political instability by these measures, despite its well-documented ethnic conflicts.[16] These results suggest that, for some countries, high levels of ethnic conflict coexist with governments that for long periods successfully suppress overt political opposition.

Although ethnic diversity is not significantly correlated with fiscal surpluses, ethnic diversity is significantly negatively correlated with school attainment, financial depth, and the number of tele-

[16]The nine measures of political instability were antigovernment demonstrations, assassinations, cabinet changes, constitutional changes, coups, government crises, purges, revolutions, and riots. The source, as in some of the measures used by Barro [1991] and Alesina, Ozler, Roubini, and Swagel [1996], was Banks [1994]. . . . Africa was below average for the whole sample on six of these measures, and above average for three of them; constitutional changes was the only indicator significantly above average for Africa.

Table 4. Ethnic Diversity and Long-Run Growth (Dependent Variable is Growth of per Capita real GDP)

Variable	(1)	(2)	(3)	(4)	(5)
Dummy for the 1960s	−0.072	−0.096	−0.186	−0.254	−0.224
	(−0.88)	(−1.15)	(−1.94)	(−2.66)	(−2.37)
Dummy for the 1970s	−0.074	−0.098	−0.182	−0.248	−0.217
	(−0.90)	(−1.17)	(−1.90)	(−2.59)	(−2.30)
Dummy for the 1980s	−0.094	−0.117	−0.198	−0.263	−0.232
	(−1.14)	(−1.40)	(−2.07)	(−2.76)	(−2.46)
Dummy variable for Sub-Saharan Africa	−0.013	−0.014	−0.012	−0.013	−0.013
	(−2.82)	(−2.98)	(−2.46)	(−2.53)	(−2.49)
Dummy variable for Latin America and the Caribbean	−0.022	−0.021	−0.017	−0.018	−0.019
	(−6.52)	(−5.88)	(−4.74)	(−4.90)	(−5.22)
Log of initial income	0.033	0.039	0.066	0.086	0.081
	(1.56)	(1.82)	(2.69)	(3.58)	(3.41)
(Log of initial income) squared	−0.003	−0.003	−0.005	−0.007	−0.006
	(−1.83)	(−2.09)	(−3.10)	(−4.25)	(−4.23)
Log of schooling	0.011	0.011	0.009	0.009	0.010
	(2.85)	(2.83)	(2.28)	(1.98)	(2.22)
Assassinations		−20.730	−14.874	−21.480	−21.862
		(−2.04)	(−1.56)	(−2.45)	(−2.45)
Financial depth			0.015	0.012	0.011
			(2.54)	(2.10)	(1.90)
Black market premium			−0.020	−0.019	−0.019
			(−4.63)	(−4.46)	(−4.52)
Fiscal surplus/GDP			0.088	0.171	0.158
			(2.88)	(4.82)	(4.40)
Log of telephones per worker				0.005	0.005
				(1.74)	(1.86)
ETHNIC	−0.020	−0.017	−0.016	−0.011	
	(−3.19)	(−2.74)	(−2.54)	(−1.53)	
AVG-ETHNIC					−0.020
					(−2.73)
No. of observations	78; 84; 90	75; 83; 89	44; 69; 72	40; 68; 64	41; 70; 67
R^2	0.31, 0.24, 0.35	0.27, 0.23, 0.36	0.43, 0.44, 0.51	0.43, 0.49, 0.61	0.45, 0.52, 0.60

t-statistics are in parentheses.
Estimated using Seemingly Unrelated Regressions: a separate regression for each period.
AVG-ETHNIC is the average value of ETHNIC and the Muller [1964], Roberts [1962], and two Gunnemark [1991] measures of ethnolinguistic diversity.

phones per worker, and ethnic diversity is significantly positively correlated with the black market premium.[17] (Ethnic diversity was also positively correlated with the other infrastructure measures mentioned earlier: electrical system losses and the percentage of roads that are unpaved.) Although the results do not hold for every policy indicator, the data are consistent with the view that ethnic diversity tends to slow growth by making it more difficult to agree on the provision of public goods

[17]The associations between ETHNIC and telephones, black market premium, financial depth, and school attainment are also highly significant in a pure cross section.

and policies that foster economic growth. Since Africa is much more ethnically diverse than other regions, this feature of African economies helps explain their tendency to choose growth-retarding policies. . . .

Econometrically, the correlation between ETHNIC and the public policy indicators helps clarify why the partial correlation between long-run growth and some measures of ethnolinguistic diversity are not robust to the inclusion of the wide array of public policy indicators used in regression (4) of Table 4: ethnic diversity affects many of the explanatory variables used in standard growth regressions. Our interpretation of those results is *not* so much that one should throw one more variable—ETHNIC—into growth regressions.[18] Our interpretation is that ETHNIC helps explain some of the explanatory variables used in growth regressions and, through these policy indicators, growth itself.

E. Assessing Africa's Performance: The East Asia Comparison

We now put our results in context by comparing East Asia's growth miracle with Africa's growth tragedy. We start by ignoring the role of ethnicity and simply showing how much of the East Asia–Africa growth differential is accounted for by the public policy indicators used in regression (4) of Table 4. By subtracting Africa's value for each explanatory variable from East Asia's country value and multiplying this difference by the regression coefficient (from regression (4) in Table 4), we compute that part of the difference in growth rates between East Asian and African countries associated with each explanatory variable.[19] Table 2 gives the values for the public policy variables. Taken together, Africa's high budget deficits, financial shallowness, substantial black market exchange rate premiums, high political instability, weak infrastructure, and low human capital account for 2.6 percentage points of the 3.4 percentage point differential between East Asia and Africa (Table 6).[20] Although these factors appear to explain most of the East Asia–Africa growth difference, they are offset by one factor that was in Africa's favor. Africa's income at the beginning of each decade was much lower than East Asia's. This convergence effect predicts that Africa should have grown 1.1 percentage points faster than East Asia, so that on net, the non-ETHNIC explanatory variables in regression 4 of Table IV account for 1.5 percentage points (2.6 – 1.1) of the 3.4 percentage point growth differential. The non-ETHNIC variables account for about two-fifths of the growth difference.

Now consider the direct effect of ETHNIC on

growth. As discussed above, this direct effect is relatively modest. The direct effect explains an additional 0.2 percentage points of the growth differential. Thus, all explanatory variables in regression (4) of Table 4 account for about half (1.7 percentage points) of the difference between East Asian and African growth rates. Of the unexplained differential, most is due to the Africa dummy, and the remainder to the positive East Asia residual.[21]

Next, consider the indirect effect of ETHNIC on growth: ETHNIC helps account for long-run growth differences by explaining public policy decisions. ETHNIC is 0.74 in the 27 observations for the Africa group included in this sample and 0.53 in the 19 observations for the East Asia group. (This sample excludes Korea and Hong Kong, as discussed earlier, so likely understates the difference in ethnic diversity between the two regions.) We use the policy regressions in Table 5 to explain how much of the East Asia–Africa policy differences are attributable to ETHNIC. Although these types of calculations may be sensitive to the simple linear functional form that we have used throughout this paper, we present these calculations to illustrate the potential importance of ethnic diversity on economic growth. We find that ETHNIC indirectly accounts for about 28 percent of the 2.6 percentage point growth difference attributable to political/policy indicators. When we include the direct effects of ETHNIC, ETHNIC alone explains about one percentage point of the 3.4 percentage point East Asia–Africa growth differential. . . .

IV. Conclusions

Understanding Africa's growth tragedy requires not only an accounting of the relationship between slow growth and unfavorable country characteristics, but also an understanding of why country characteristics were so unfavorable. Africa's poor growth—and resulting low income—is associated with low schooling, political instability, underdeveloped financial systems, distorted foreign exchange markets, high government deficits, and insufficient infrastructure. High ethnic diversity is

---

[18]Here we are careful to hedge by using the phrase ". . . not so much . . ." because some measures of ethnolinguistic diversity maintain a robust independent partial correlation with growth after controlling for a wide array of public policy indicators.

[19]Recall that we demonstrated earlier that the coefficients on the explanatory variables are not significantly different for Africa from the rest of the sample.

[20]These decomposition results are virtually indential to those obtained from regression (4) of Table 1, which does not include ETHNIC. We use the regression results from Table 4 to facilitate comparisons across the different scenarios presented in Table 6.

[21]The positive East Asia residual reminds us that not all of the Africa dummy is necessarily due to "Africa." The Africa and Latin America dummies reflect how these two underachieving regions compare with the rest of the sample, which includes at least one overachieving region—East Asia. If we put for symmetry a dummy to measure how much of *East Asia's* performance is not fully captured by the regressions, then the Africa dummy is reduced in magnitude and significance compared with regressions (4) and (5) of Table 4. With the Soviet ETHNIC, AFRICA is just barely significant and with AVG-ETHNIC, the AFRICA dummy is no longer significant.

Table 5. Determinants of Economic Indicators

Dependent variable	C	ETHNIC	R^2	Number of observations
Log of schooling	1.508 (17.12)	−0.991 (−6.21)	0.08, 0.09, 0.10	83; 85; 91
Assassinations	1.24E-05 (1.52)	1.03E-06 (0.07)	−0.01, −0.06, −0.02	98; 105; 105
Financial depth	0.417 (11.44)	−0.266 (−3.67)	0.09, 0.06, −0.02	94; 100; 103
Black market premium	0.070 (1.82)	0.252 (3.39)	0.05, 0.08; −0.04	97; 107; 106
Fiscal surplus/GDP	−0.026 (−5.48)	−0.013 (−1.37)	−0.14, −0.02, −0.13	55; 87; 82
Log of telephones per worker	4.331 (18.95)	−3.067 (−7.17)	0.21, 0.23, 0.04	95; 103; 92

t-statistics are in parentheses.

Equations estimated using Seemingly Unrelated Regression procedures.

Table 6. Decomposition of Growth Differential Between Africa and East Asia (based on regression (4), Table 4 with Soviet ETHNIC measure)

	Africa–East Asia growth differential accounted for this variable	% of difference in each variable explained by ETHNIC	Growth differential implicitly explained by ETHNIC through this variable
Political/policy indicator RHS variables:			
Log schooling	0.5%	43%	0.2%
Assassinations	0.0%	3%	0.0%
Financial depth	0.3%	21%	0.1%
Black market premium	0.8%	13%	0.1%
Fiscal surplus/GDP	0.5%	11%	0.1%
Log telephones per worker	0.5%	60%	0.3%
(1) Total effect through political/policy indicator RHS variables on growth	2.6%	28%	0.7%
ETHNIC—Soviet (the partial effect of ETHNIC in regression (4), Table 4)	0.2%		0.2%
(2) Joint effect of all policy indicator and ETHNIC RHS variables	2.8%	34%	1.0%
Convergence effect (growth effect includes both linear and quadratic terms on initial income)	−1.1%		
(3) Joint growth effect of all RHS variables	1.7%	56%	1.0%
Residual	1.7%		
unexplained difference of which: Africa dummy	*1.3%*		
(4) Actual per capita growth differential, East Asia–Africa	3.4%	28%	1.0%
Ethnic diversity:			
Africa: 0.744			
East Asia: 0.527			

closely associated with low schooling, underdeveloped financial systems, distorted foreign exchange markets, and insufficient infrastructure. While motivated by Africa, these results are not particular to Africa. In evaluating the extent to which cross-country differences in ethnic diversity explain cross-country differences in public policies and political stability, we conduct the analysis on a broad cross section of countries. The results lend support to theories that interest group polarization leads to rent-seeking behavior and reduces the consensus for public goods, creating long-run growth tragedies.

References

Ake, Claude, *Democracy and Development in Africa* (Washington, DC: The Brookings Institution, 1996).

Alesina, Alberto, "Political Models of Macroeconomic Policy and Fiscal Reforms," in Stephen Haggard and Steven Webb, eds. *Voting for Reform: Democracy, Political Liberalization, and Economic Adjustment* (New York, NY: Oxford University Press, 1994).

Alesina, Alberto, Reza Baqir, and William Easterly, "Public Goods and Ethnic Divisions," Harvard University and World Bank mimeo, March 1997.

Alesina, Alberto, and Allen Drazen, "Why Are Stabilizations Delayed?" *American Economic Review,* LXXXI (1991), 1170–1188.

Alesina, Alberto, Sule Ozler, Nouriel Roubini, and Phillip Swagel, "Political Instability and Economic Growth," *Journal of Economic Growth,* I (1996), 189–211.

Alesina, Alberto, and Dani Rodrik, "Distributive Politics and Economic Growth," *Quarterly Journal of Economics,* CIX (1994), 465–490.

Alesina, Alberto, and Enrico Spolaore, "On the Number and Size of Nations," *Quarterly Journal of Economics,* CII (1997), 1027–1056.

Alesina, Alberto, and Guido Tabellini, "External Debt, Capital Flight and Political Risk," *Journal of International Economics,* XXVII (1989), 199–220.

Aschauer, David A., "Is Public Expenditure Productive?" *Journal of Monetary Economics,* XXIII (1989), 177–200.

Banks, Arthur S., "Cross-National Time Series Data Archive," Center for Social Analysis, State University of New York at Binghamton, 1994.

Barkan, Joel, with Michael Chege, "Decentralising the State: District Focus and the Politics of Reallocation in Kenya," *Journal of Modern African Studies,* XXVII (1989), 431–453.

Barro, Robert, "Economic Growth in a Cross Section of Countries," *Quarterly Journal of Economics,* CVI (1991), 407–443.

Barro, Robert, and Jong-Wha Lee, "International Comparisons of Educational Attainment," *Journal of Monetary Economics,* XXXII (1993), 363–394.

Barro, Robert, and Xavier Sala-i-Martin, "Convergence," *Journal of Political Economy,* C (1992), 223–251.

Bates, Robert H., *Markets and States in Tropical Africa: the Political Basis of Agricultural Policies* (Berkeley, CA: University of California Press, 1981).

———, *Beyond the Miracle of the Market: The Political Economy of Agrarian Development in Kenya* (Cambridge and New York: Cambridge University Press, 1989).

Baumol, William J., Sue Anne Batey Blackman, and Edward N. Wolff, *Productivity and American Leadership: The Long View* (Cambridge, MA: MIT Press, 1992).

Berg, Elliot, "L'Integration Economique en Afrique de l'Ouest: Problemes et Strategies," *Revue d'Economie du Developpement,* XCIII (1993), 51–82.

Bevan, David, Paul Collier, and Jan Willem Gunning, "Trade Shocks in Developing Countries: Consequences and Policy Responses," *European Economic Review,* XXXVII (1993), 557–565.

Blomstrom, Magnus, and Mats Lundahl, eds., *Economic Crisis in Africa: Perspectives on Policy Responses* (New York, NY: Routledge, 1993).

Borgin, Karl, and Kathleen Corbett, *The Destruction of a Continent: Africa and International Aid* (San Diego, CA: Harcourt Brace Jovanovich, 1982).

Bouton, Lawrence, Christine Jones, and Miguel Kiguel, "Macroeconomic Reforms and Growth in Africa: *Adjustment in Africa* Revisited," Working Paper Series No. 1394, Washington, DC, World Bank, 1994.

Canning, David, and Marianne Fay, "The Effect of Transportation Networks on Economic Growth," Discussion Paper Series, Columbia University, Department of Economics, 1993.

Chazan, Naomi, *The Precarious Balance: State and Society in Africa,* Naomi Chazan and Donald Rothchild, eds. (Boulder, CO: Westview Press, 1988).

Chhibber, Ajay, and Stanley Fischer, eds., *Economic Reform in Sub-Saharan Africa* (Washington, DC: World Bank, 1992).

Cohen, John M., "Ethnicity, Foreign Aid, and Economic Growth: The Case of Kenya," HIID Development Discussion Paper No. 520, 1995.

Collier, Paul, and J.W. Gunning, "Aid and Exchange Rate Adjustment in African Trade Liberalization," *Economic Journal,* CII (1992), 925–939.

Collier, Paul, and Colin Mayer, "Financial Liberalization, Financial Systems, and Economic Growth: The Assessment," *Oxford Review of Economic Policy,* V (1989), 1–12.

Davidson, Basil, *Black Man's Burden: Africa and the Curse of the Nation-State* (New York, NY: Times Books, 1992).

Easterly, William, "Economic Stagnation, Fixed Factors, and Policy Thresholds," *Journal of Monetary Economics,* XXXIII (1994), 525–557.

Easterly, William, and Sergio Rebelo, "Fiscal Policy and Economic Growth: An Empirical Investigation," *Journal of Monetary Economics,* XXXII (1993), 417–457.

Elbadawi, Ibrahim, "World Bank Adjustment Lending and Economic Performance in Sub-Saharan Africa in the 1980s: A Comparison of Early Adjusters, Late

Adjusters, and Nonadjusters," Working Paper Series No. 1001, Washington, DC, World Bank, 1992.

Elbadawi, Ibrahim, and Benno Ndulu, "Long-Term Development and Sustainable Growth in Sub-Saharan Africa," AERC, mimeo, 1994.

Fischer, Stanley, "The Role of Macroeconomic Factors in Growth," *Journal of Monetary Economics,* XXXII (1993), 485–511.

Fosu, Augustin K., "Effect of Export Instability on Economic Growth in Africa," *Journal of Development Areas,* XXVI (1992a), 323–332.

———, "Political Instability and Economic Growth: Evidence from Sub-Saharan Africa," *Economic Development and Cultural Change,* XL (1992b), 829–841.

Glickman, Harvey, *The Crisis and Challenge of African Development* (New York, NY: Greenwood Press, 1988).

Gunnemark, Erik V., *Countries, Peoples and Their Languages: The Linguistic Handbook* (Gothenburg, Sweden: Lanstryckeriet, 1991).

Gurr, Ted Robert, *Minorities at Risk: A Global View of Ethnopolitical Conflicts* (Washington, DC: United States Institute of Peace Press, 1993).

Gyimah-Brempong, Kwabena, "Export Instability and Economic Growth in Sub-Saharan Africa," *Economic Development and Cultural Change,* XXXIX (1991), 815–28.

Hadjimichael, Michael T., Dhaneshwar Ghura, Martin Muhleisen, Roger Nord, and E.Murat Ucer, "Effects of Macroeconomic Stability on Growth, Savings, and Investment in Sub-Saharan Africa: An Empirical Investigation," IMF Working Paper 94/98, 1994.

Haugerud, Angelique, *The Culture of Politics in Modern Kenya* (Cambridge, MA: Cambridge University Press, 1995).

Helleiner, Gerald K, *Theory and Reality in Development: Essays in Honor of Paul Streeten,* Saniaya Lall, and Stewart Frances, eds. (New York, NY: St. Martin's Press, 1986).

Husain, Ishrat, and Rashid Faruqee, eds. *Adjustment in Africa: Lessons from Case Studies* (Washington, DC: World Bank, 1994).

Killick, Tony, "The Developmental Effectiveness of Aid to Africa," Working Paper Series No. 646, Washington, DC, World Bank, 1991.

King, Robert G., and Ross Levine, "Finance and Growth: Schumpeter Might Be Right," *Quarterly Journal of Economics,* CVIII (1993a), 717–738.

King, Robert G., and Ross Levine, "Finance, Entrepreneurship, and Growth: Theory and Evidence," *Journal of Monetary Economics,* XXXII (1993b), 513–542.

Lane, Philip, and Aaron Tornell, "Power Concentration and Growth," Harvard Institute of Economic Research, Discussion Paper No. 1720, Harvard University, 1995.

La Porta, Rafael, Florencio López-de-Silanes, Andrei Shleifer, and Robert W. Vishny, "Law and Finance," NBER Working Paper No. 5661, July 1996.

Levine, Ross. "Law, Finance, and Economic Growth," University of Virginia, mimeo, 1997.

Levine, Ross, and David Renelt, "Sensitivity Analysis of Cross-Country Growth Regressions," *American Economic Review,* LXXXII (1992), 942–963.

Levine, Ross, and Sara J. Zervos, "What We Have Learned about Policy and Growth from Cross-Country Regressions," *American Economic Review, Papers and Proceedings,* LXXXIII (1993), 426–30.

Lewis, John Prior, *Development Strategies Reconsidered* (New Brunswick, NJ: Transaction Books, 1986).

Mauro, Paolo, "Corruption and Growth," *Quarterly Journal of Economics,* CX (1995), 681–712.

Mikell, Gwendolyn, *Cocoa and Chaos in Ghana* (New York, NY: Paragon House, 1989).

Miller, Norman, and Rodger Yeager, *Kenya: The Quest for Prosperity* (Boulder, CO: Westview Press, 1994).

Milne, R. S. *Politics in Ethnically Bipolar States: Guyana, Malaysia, Fiji* University of British Columbia Press (Vancouver: 1981).

Muller, Siegfried H., *The World's Living Languages: Basic Facts of Their Structure, Kinship, Location, and Number of Speakers* (New York, NY: Ungar, 1964).

Ndulu, Benno J., *Economic Reform in Sub-Saharan Africa,* Ajay Chhibber and Stanley Fischer, eds. (Washington, DC: World Bank, 1991).

Nyangira, Nicholas, *The Political Economy of Kenya,* Michael G. Schatzberg, ed. (New York, NY: Praeger, 1987).

Pack, Howard, "Productivity and Industrial Development in Sub-Saharan Africa," *World Development,* XXI (1993), 1–16.

Pakenham, Thomas, *The Scramble for Africa* (New York, NY: Random House, 1991).

Persson, Torsten, Gérard Roland, and Guido Tabellini, "Separation of Powers and Accountability," *Quarterly Journal of Economics,* CXII (1997), 1163–1202.

Persson, Torsten, and G. Tabellini, "Is Inequality Harmful for Growth?" *American Economic Review,* LXXXIV (1994), 600–621.

Pickett, James, "Low-Income Economies of Sub-Saharan Africa: Problems and Prospects," *African Development Bank, Economic Research Papers,* XII (1990), 1–48.

Poterba, James, M. "Demographic Structure and the Political Economy of Public Education," NBER Working Paper No. 5677, July 1996.

Ravenhill, John, ed., *Africa in Economic Crisis* (Basingstoke, NH: Macmillan, 1986).

Rimmer, Douglas, ed., *Africa 30 Years On* (London: Villiers Publications Ltd., 1991).

Roberts, Janet, "Sociocultural Change and Communication Problems," in *Study of the Role of Second Languages in Asia, Africa, and Latin America,* Frank A.

Rice, ed. (Washington DC: Center for Applied Linguistics of the Modern Language Association of America, 1962), pp. 105–123.

Sadiq Ali, Shanti, and Anirudha Gupta, eds., *Africa: Dimensions of the Economic Crisis; An Analysis of the Problems and Constraints of Development* (New Delhi: Sterling Publishers, 1987).

Scarritt, James R., *Minorities at Risk: A Global View of Ethnopolitical Conflicts,* Ted Robert Gurr, ed. (Washington, DC: United States Institute of Peace Press, 1993).

Shleifer, Andrei, and Robert Vishny, "Corruption," *Quarterly Journal of Economics,* CVIII (1993), 599–617.

Sivard, Ruth L., *World Military and Social Expenditures: 1993,* 15th ed. (Washington, DC: World Priorities, 1993).

Soludo, Charles C., "Growth Performance in Africa: Further Evidence on the External Shocks versus Domestic Policy Debate," UNECA Development Research Paper Series No. 6 (November), United Nations, 1993.

Taylor, Charles Lewis, and Michael C. Hudson, *World Handbook of Political and Social Indicators,* 2nd ed. (New Haven, CT: Yale University Press, 1972).

Throup, David W., *The Political Economy of Kenya* Michael G. Schatzberg, ed. (New York, NY: Praeger, 1987).

Turok, Ben, *Africa: What Can Be Done?* (London: Zed Books, 1987).

Wetzel, Deborah L., *The Macroeconomics of Fiscal Deficits in Ghana: 1960–94,* Ph.D. thesis, Oxford University, 1995.

Wheeler, David, "Sources of Stagnation in Sub-Saharan Africa," *World Development,* XII (1984), 1–23.

World Bank, *Accelerated Development in Sub-Saharan Africa: An Agenda for Action* (Washington, DC: World Bank, 1981).

———, *Sub-Saharan Africa: from Crisis to Sustainable Growth—a Long-Term Perspective Study* (Washington DC: World Bank, 1989).

———, *Adjustment in Africa: Reforms, Results, and the Road Ahead* (New York, NY: Oxford University Press, 1994).

IX.C. STATE CAPACITY

Selection IX.C.1. Institutions and Economic Performance: Cross-Country Tests Using Alternative Institutional Measures*

The Institutional Data

The focus of this paper is on institutional indicators compiled by two private international investment risk services: International Country Risk Guide (ICRG) and Business Environmental Risk Intelligence (BERI). We use the first observations that these services have for any country; for BERI, the vast majority of observations are from 1972 and for ICRG, nearly all observations are from 1982. . . .

ICRG variables *Expropriation Risk,* measuring the risk of expropriation, and *Rule of Law,* measuring whether there are established peaceful mechanisms for adjudicating disputes, are interpreted here as proxies for the security of property and contract rights. If countries score low on these dimensions, they are likely to suffer a reduction in the quantity and efficiency of physical and perhaps even human capital investment. As the probability increases that investors will lose the proceeds from the investment, or the investment itself, investors reduce their investment and channel their resources to activities that are more secure from the threat of expropriation (trading rather than manufacturing, for example), although they may be less profitable.

Repudiation of Contracts by Government is another indicator of contract enforcement. It is likely that if private actors cannot count on the government to respect the contracts it has with them, they will also not be able to count on the government enforcing contracts between two private parties. In the absence of impartial state enforcement, the only impersonal exchanges taking place between private economic actors will be those that are "self-enforcing"—those in which the benefits of compliance exceed the gains from cheating or reneging. This restriction on economic activity severely limits the universe of possible Pareto-improving exchanges that would otherwise be undertaken.

Repudiation is also an indicator of government credibility. Regimes in which officials have the power unilaterally to modify or to repudiate contractual agreements will likely be unconstrained in numerous other areas that impinge on economic activity. In particular, entrepreneurs are likely to be suspicious about the institutional or other barriers on state officials that keep them from pursuing policies of confiscatory taxation (directly, or through inflation), or outright expropriation.[1]

The remaining two ICRG variables used in this paper are *Corruption in Government* and *Quality of Bureaucracy.* They are taken as proxies for the general efficiency with which government services are provided, and for the extent and damage of rent-seeking behavior. When countries score poorly (low) on these dimensions, it is a strong indication that a bureaucracy lacks procedural clarity or technical competence and is likely to introduce criteria other than efficiency into the determination of government policies or the allocation of public goods. In particular, the bureaucracy is likely to award contracts, business and trade licenses, police protection and so forth on the basis of criteria other than those of allocative and technical efficiency. In addition, bureaucracies where corruption is higher or competence is low are less likely to provide a strong bulwark against infringements on property rights. The resulting distortions in investment and trade may reduce the quantity and efficiency of capital investment and foreign technology introduced into the country.

Theoretically, the use of corrupt allocation schemes in the political marketplace need not produce less efficient results than other forms of political allocation. However, in those countries where ICRG records high levels of corruption, entrepreneurs are also beset by greater uncertainty regarding the credibility of government commitments. That is, the same institutions that allow public officials to demand large and arbitrary bribes, such as failed law enforcement systems, also inhibit those officials from credibly pledging not to renege on their future commitments. This discourages investment and encourages forms of economic activity that are less vulnerable to expropriation.[2]

[1]See Weingast (1993) and Keefer (1993) for a discussion of the effects of government credibility on investment and growth.

[2]The predominance of trading as the object of most new entrepreneurial effort in Russia during the transition is likely due not only to the high returns to trading, but also to the low returns to other forms of economic activity that are driven down by riskiness of investments and the difficulties of making credible deals with corrupt government officials.

*From Stephen Knack and Philip Keefer, "Institutions and Economic Performance: Cross-Country Tests Using Alternative Institutional Measures," *Economics and Politics* 7 (November 1995): 210–212, 214–222. Reprinted by permission.

The measures from BERI that are used for this paper are *Contract Enforceability* and *Infrastructure Quality,* which do not have close analogues in the ICRG data set, and *Nationalization Potential* and *Bureaucratic Delays,* which parallel the ICRG variables *Expropriation Risk* and *Quality of Bureaucracy.* The relevance of all the BERI variables is indicated by the foregoing discussion, with the exception of *Infrastructure Quality.* This variable allows some approximation to be made to the efficiency with which governments allocate public goods.

Because of strong correlations among these separate indicators, with the consequent risk of multicollinearity, and in order to avoid omitting any of them from the equation, the five ICRG variables and the four BERI variables have been aggregated to form an ICRG index (*ICRG82*) and a BERI index (*BERI72*) of the security of contractual and property rights. Although the aggregation is accomplished through simple addition, the results reported below do not change significantly when individual components of these indices are used, or when the indices are compiled with different weights. Higher values of the ICRG and BERI indices indicate better conditions for investment. . . .

The Growth Equation

. . . Barro (1991) is the specification that is relied upon below to compare the effects of political violence and institutional indicators on growth:

$$GR6085 = \alpha + \beta_1 GDP60 + \beta_2 SEC60$$
$$+ \beta_3 PRIM60 + \beta_4 GOVCONS$$
$$+ \beta_5 REVCOUP + \beta_6 ASSASS$$
$$+ \beta_7 PPI60DEV + \varepsilon_i \qquad (1)$$

Here, growth is a function of initial income,[3] secondary and primary school enrollment in 1960, the percent of government consumption in GDP, frequencies of revolutions and assassinations, and the magnitude of the deviation of the Summers and Heston investment deflator (U.S. = 100) from the sample mean. . . .[4]

Unlike Barro (1991), this paper focuses on

growth over the period 1974–1989 to mitigate the effects of possible measurement error in the ICRG and BERI indices that might have been introduced by evaluator bias. The evaluators of the investor services might be influenced by the level of income of the countries that they evaluate. Current levels of GDP are a product of past growth, naturally. To the extent that evaluators are influenced by the current level of GDP, estimates of the effect of property rights on growth might be biased upwards. This is a problem that afflicts all such measures, including the Gastil measures. Our choice of period reduces problems of simultaneity that might cloud inferences about the effect of property rights. . . .

Empirical Results—Growth

Equations (1) of Tables 1 and 2 are benchmark regressions for the ICRG and BERI samples, respectively, and include no institutional variables. Equations (2) add the political violence indicators, but not the ICRG and BERI indices. . . .

In equations (3) of Tables 1 and 2 the ICRG and BERI indices, respectively, replace the political violence indicators. Both are more significant than the political violence indicators. . . .

In the final equations of these two tables, the political violence indicators enter with either *ICRG82* or *BERI72.* In the regression with the ICRG index, the magnitude and statistical significance of the violence indicators drop substantially and *ICRG82* remains significant. *BERI72* performs less well, but still exhibits at least as much economic and statistical significance as the political violence indicators.[5]

Comparing these variables in terms of their economic impact also reveals the greater explanatory power of the ICRG/BERI indices relative to the political violence indicators. Since the units of the variables are not comparable, standardized estimates of their regression coefficients were calculated. These denote the change in the dependent variable, in standard deviation units, for a one unit change in the standard deviation of the independent variable. For the ICRG case in Table 1, the sum of the standardized estimates of *REVC7499* and *ASSN7489* in Equation (2) is –0.36. The standardized estimate of ICRG82 when it replaces these

---

[3]Other research has employed the log of initial GDP. The regressions reported below, employing initial GDP, were also run with the log of this variable. In nearly all cases the qualitative findings, that the institutional variables add significant additional information that explains growth, remain unchanged.

[4]Barro (1991) uses economic growth and investment data from Summers and Heston. For this paper, data on these variables come from the World Bank and are taken from Levine and Renelt (1992).

[5]Using log of initial income and the BERI sample of countries, and including the two political violence indicators along with *BERI72*, all three variables are statistically insignificant, although *BERI72* is more significant than *ASSN7489*, and the standardized estimate of *BERI72* is equal to the sum of the standardized estimates of the two political violence indicators.

Table 1. Growth, Institutions and Political Violence: ICRG

	(1)	(2)	(3)	(4)
Intercept	1.980	3.028	0.254	1.345
	1.980	*2.851*	*0.237*	*1.091*
ICRG82			0.092	0.072
			3.420	*2.499*
REVC7489		−1.630		−1.115
		−1.904		*−1.302*
ASSN7489		−3.486		−2.278
		−1.695		*−1.108*
GDP70	−0.401	−0.482	−0.692	−0.683
	−2.564	*−3.141*	*−4.055*	*−4.030*
SEC70	6.083	6.284	5.051	5.411
	3.819	*4.083*	*3.286*	*3.524*
PRIM70	−0.690	−0.959	−0.532	−0.752
	−0.758	*−1.072*	*−0.617*	*−0.862*
GCON7489	−5.222	−6.388	−4.289	−5.286
	−1.213	*−1.527*	*−1.051*	*−1.293*
PPI74DEV	−0.920	−0.985	−0.892	−0.941
	−2.243	*−2.482*	*−2.3*	*−2.439*
R-Square	0.198	0.270	0.291	0.318
N	97	97	97	97

Dependent variable: Average annual per capita GDP growth, 1974–1989.

Numbers in italics are t-statistics.

Table 2. Growth, Institutions and Political Violence: BERI

	(1)	(2)	(3)	(4)
Intercept	1.022	0.356	−0.977	−0.627
	0.644	*0.205*	*−0.545*	*−0.336*
BERI72			0.376	0.263
			2.111	*1.357*
REVC7489		−1.653		−1.630
		−1.304		*−1.300*
ASSN7489		−23.015		−14.695
		−1.710		*−1.003*
GDP70	−0.501	−0.594	−0.694	−0.721
	−2.751	*−3.277*	*−3.520*	*−3.566*
SEC70	5.376	4.624	4.047	4.026
	2.805	*2.411*	*2.083*	*2.067*
PRIM70	0.653	2.793	0.580	2.018
	0.377	*1.389*	*0.349*	*0.976*
GCON7489	−1.145	−1.508	−2.968	−3.052
	−0.183	*−0.249*	*−0.489*	*−0.500*
PPI74DEV	−0.929	−0.894	−0.711	−0.748
	−1.921	*−1.938*	*−1.495*	*−1.595*
R-Square	0.276	0.375	0.350	0.405
N	46	46	46	46

Dependent variable: Average annual per capita GDP growth, 1974–1989.

Numbers in italics are t-statistics.

two variables in Equation (3) of Table 1, however, is 0.504: an increase of one standard deviation in *ICRG82* leads to an increase in growth equal to 0.504 of its standard deviation. The standard deviation of the growth variable *GR7489* is 2.465, indicating that an increase of one standard deviation in *ICRG82* [equal to approximately 12 points on the 40 point scale, or the difference between the *ICRG82* scores of Honduras (15) and Costa Rica (27), or of Argentina (25) and Italy (30)] increases growth by more than 1.2 percentage points. The importance of the effect of *ICRG82* can be seen by comparing its standardized coefficient to the standardized coefficient on secondary education enrollment (*SEC70*), which is not much higher at 0.57. When *ICRG82* and the political violence variables are all included in the same regression, the standardized estimate of *ICRG82* is 0.393 and the sum of the standardized estimates of the violence indicators is −0.235. In all cases, the economic impact of *ICRG82* is significant and greater than that of the political violence indicators.

A similar story can be told with regard to *BERI72*. Alone, the two political violence indicators have a combined standardized estimate of −0.47. When it replaces these variables, however, the BERI index has a standardized estimate of 0.54. When the three variables enter into the same regression, the combined political violence standardized estimate is −0.37 and the standardized estimate of *BERI72* is 0.38.

These results were robust to a number of alternative specifications. The institutional variables were statistically and economically significant in growth regressions that included rates of factor accumulation (investment and labor force growth); that deleted OPEC members from the 1974–1989 period regressions; that substituted *REVC6088* and *ASSN6088* for their 1974–1988 counterparts in growth regressions; and that employed the log of initial income.

The coefficients on the institutional variables were somewhat lower when investment was included. This is to be expected; one way that insecure property rights hinder growth is by deterring investment, an effect that is captured by investment itself when it enters the regression. However, it is noteworthy that the institutional variables were still significant, even in the presence of an investment term. This suggests that institutions measured by the BERI and ICRG indices matter not only because secure property rights encourage fixed investments, but also because they encourage the efficient allocation of factor inputs. In response to expropriatory threats of one kind or another, en-

Table 3. Investment, Institutions and Political Violence

Institutional Variable:	ICRG82			BERI72		
	(1)	(2)	(3)	(4)	(5)	(6)
Intercept	0.160	0.112	0.125	0.159	0.124	0.123
	5.188	3.443	3.404	2.678	2.487	2.174
Institut'l var.		0.002	0.001		0.014	0.014
		2.151	1.741		3.087	2.554
REVC7489	−0.017		−0.014	−0.011		−0.008
	−0.578		−0.480	−0.216		−0.174
ASSN7489	−0.083		−0.042	−0.560		−0.118
	−1.201		0.072	−1.346		−0.281
GDP70	−0.0002	−0.004	−0.004	−0.002	−0.009	−0.009
	−0.050	−1.000	−0.942	−0.461	−1.754	−1.643
SEC70	0.019	−0.002	−0.00007	0.033	0.007	0.005
	0.447	−0.044	−0.002	0.528	0.131	0.085
PRIM70	0.065	0.071	0.067	0.090	0.026	0.037
	2.529	3.011	2.662	1.323	0.519	0.564
GCON7489	0.005	0.043	0.048	−0.103	−0.215	−0.204
	0.043	0.345	0.381	−0.527	−1.221	−1.105
PPI74	−0.022	−0.019	−0.014	−0.014	−0.011	−0.011
	−2.549	−2.325	−2.375	−1.329	−1.136	−1.099
R-Square	0.312	0.338	0.345	0.215	0.356	0.359
N	69	69	69	38	38	38

Dependent variable: Average private investment/GDP, 1974–1989. Numbers in italics are t-statistics.

trepreneurs not only reduce investment, they also invest in less specialized capital (human and physical), which can be moved more easily from one activity to another. This has static efficiency effects, but also discourages dynamic gains from innovation, since innovation is most likely to thrive when specialization is encouraged. . . .

Empirical Results—Investment

Another basis for comparing the different institutional variables is in their ability to explain investment. Barro excludes investment from his growth estimations at least implicitly because many of the variables in the growth equation, including institutional variables, operate, at least in part, through factor accumulation. The importance of institutions, then, can also be examined through empirical estimates of the determinants of investment. Barro (1991) estimates variants of the following equation for private investment, for which cross country data is available beginning in the 1970s:

$$PINV7085 = \alpha + \beta_1 GDP60 + \beta_2 SEC60$$
$$+ \beta_3 PRIM60 + \beta_4 GOVCONS$$
$$+ \beta_5 REVCOUP + \beta_6 ASSASS$$
$$+ \beta_7 PPI60DEV + \beta_8 PPI60 + \varepsilon_i \quad (2)$$

where *PINV7085* is the average ratio of real private investment to real GDP over the period, equal to the ratio of real total investment over real GDP less the same ratio for real public investment. The 1960 purchasing power parity investment deflator (from Summers and Heston) is also employed.[6] Initial income, *GDP60,* enters as a proxy for initial capital stock. The higher the initial capital stock, the greater the effect of diminishing returns on investment, and the less investment that would be expected.

As before, the ICRG and BERI indices perform substantially better than the political violence variables: their statistical and economic significance is greater and the explanatory power of models that contain only the ICRG and BERI indices is greater than those that contain the political violence measures.

Table 3 summarizes the investment results comparing the political violence, ICRG and BERI indicators. Contrary to the Barro (1991) results for the time period 1960–1985, Table 3 indicates that for

---

[6]Barro runs this model with and without dummy variables for Africa and Latin America. These dummies remain significant even in the presence of the ICRG and BERI indices. They disappear in the work on political instability by Alesina, et al. (1992), who attempt to take into account simultaneity that might exist between political instability and growth.

the time period 1974–1989 revolutions and assassinations are statistically insignificant, alone or in combination with *ICRG82* and *BERI72,* while the institutional indicators are statistically significant wherever they appear.[7] Economically, as well, the institutional indicators offer a more powerful explanation of growth. The sum of the standardized coefficients for *REVC7489* and *ASSN7489* in regression (4) of Table 3 is –0.31. When the BERI variable enters alone, in regression (5), its standardized coefficient is 0.815. When the three variables enter together, the difference remains equally dramatic, –0.08 versus 0.77. The ICRG results are qualitatively the same, although the magnitude of the differences in absolute value is smaller: –0.20 versus 0.37 when they enter in separate equations, and –0.12 versus 0.33 when they enter in the same equation.

References

Alesina, A., O. Sule, R. Nouriel, and P. Swagel, 1992, Political Instability and Growth. NBER Working Paper No. 173.

Barro, R., 1991, Economic Growth in a Cross Section of Countries. *Quarterly Journal of Economics* 106, 407–444.

Keefer, P., 1993, Institutions, Credibility and the Costs of Rent-seeking. Manuscript, The IRIS Center, University of Maryland.

Levine, R. and D. Renelt, 1992, A Sensitivity Analysis of Cross-Country Growth Regressions. *American Economic Review* 82, 942–963.

Weingast, B., 1993, The Political Foundations of Democracy and the Rule of Law. IRIS Working Paper No. 54.

---

[7]The ICRG/BERI variables are much weaker at predicting total investment. This is consistent with the theory, however. We would not expect public investment to be sensitive to risks of expropriation.

Selection IX.C.2. The State as Problem and Solution: Predation, Embedded Autonomy, and Structural Change*

Perspectives on the State

Even theories of development that privilege the market as an institution have always recognized that "the existence of the state is essential for economic growth,"[1] but the essential state was a minimal one, "restricted largely, if not entirely, to protecting individual rights, persons and property, and enforcing voluntarily negotiated private contracts."[2] In its minimal neoclassical form, the state was treated as an exogenous black box whose internal functionings were not a proper or worthy subject for economic analysis. Neoutilitarian political economists, however, became convinced that the negative economic consequences of state action were too important to leave the black box closed. To unravel its workings, they applied the "standard tools of individual optimization" to the analysis of the state itself.[3]

The exchange relation between incumbents and supporters is the essence of state action. Incumbents require political supporters to survive and the supporters, in turn, must be provided with incentives sufficient to prevent their shifting support to other potential officeholders. Incumbents may either distribute resources directly to supporters,

*From Peter B. Evans, "The State as Problem and Solution: Predation, Embedded Autonomy, and Structural Change," in Stephan Haggard and Robert R. Kaufman, eds., *The Politics of Economic Adjustment* (Princeton, NJ: Princeton, 1992), pp. 143–179. Reprinted by permission.

[1] Douglas North, *Structure and Change in Economic History* (New York: Norton, 1981), p. 20.

[2] James M. Buchanan, Robert D. Tollison, and Gordon Tullock, eds., *Toward a Theory of the Rent-Seeking Society* (College Station, Tex.: Texas A&M University Press, 1980), p. 9.

[3] T. N. Srinivasan, "Neoclassical Political Economy, the State and Economic Development," *Asian Development Review* 3, no. 2 (1985): 38–58, 41. Among public choice theorists Nobel Laureate James Buchanan and his collaborators Tollison and Tullock are best known (see Buchanan, Tollison and Tullock, *The Rent-Seeking Society*). Others would include William A. Niskanen, *Bureaucracy and Representative Government* (Chicago: Aldine-Atherton, 1971); Richard D. Auster and Morris Silver, *The State as Firm: Economic Forces in Political Development* (The Hague: Martinus Nijhoff, 1979). The recent re-emergence of neoclassical political economy represents a similar, though usually less extreme, perspective. See David C. Colander, ed., *Neoclassical Political Economy: An Analysis of Rent-seeking and DUP Activities* (Cambridge, Mass.: Ballinger, 1984). Elements of the neoutilitarian view are also present in collective action perspectives, e.g., Mancur Olson, *The Rise and Decline of Nations* (New Haven, Conn.: Yale University Press, 1982), and the new institutional economics, which emphasizes property rights, e.g., Douglas North, *Structure and Change in Economic History*.

through subsidies, loans, jobs, contracts, or the provision of services, or use their rule-making authority to create rents for favored groups by restricting the ability of market forces to operate. Rationing foreign exchange, restricting entry through licensing producers, and imposing tariffs or quantitative restrictions on imports are all ways of creating rents. Incumbents may also exact a share of the rent for themselves. Indeed, it is hypothesized that "competition for entry into government service is, in part, a competition for rents."[4] In the economy as a whole, high returns from "directly unproductive profit-seeking" make investment in productive activities less attractive. Efficiency and dynamism decline.

In order to escape the deleterious effects of state action, the state's sphere should be reduced to the minimum, and bureaucratic control should be replaced by market mechanisms wherever possible. The range of state functions considered susceptible to marketization varies but some authors even speculate on the possibility of using "prizes" and other incentives to induce "privateers" and other private citizens to provide at least partially for the national defense.[5]

It would be foolish to deny that the neoutilitarian vision captures a significant aspect of the functioning of most states, perhaps the dominant aspect of the functioning of some states. Rent seeking, conceptualized more primitively as corruption, has always been a well-known facet of the operation of Third World states. Some states' apparatuses consume the surplus they extract, encourage private actors to shift from productive activities to unproductive rent seeking, and fail to provide collective goods. They have no more regard for their societies than a predator does for its prey and are legitimately called "predatory."[6]

[4] Anne O. Krueger, "The Political Economy of the Rent-Seeking Society," *American Economic Review* 64, no. 3 (June 1974): 291–303, 293.

[5] Auster and Silver, *The State as Firm*, p. 102.

[6] It is important to note that this vernacular way of conceptualizing the predatory state is quite different from the way the term is used by it advocates. Deepak Lal, *The Hindu Equilibrium: Cultural Stability and Economic Stagnation, India c. 1500BC–AD1980,* vol. 1 (Oxford: Clarendon Press, 1988), and Margaret Levi, *Of Rule and Revenue* (Berkeley: University of California Press, 1988) both equate predatory behavior with revenue maximizing behavior. In Levi's use states may maximize revenue in ways that promote development or in ways that impede it. Thus, the term *predatory* in her usage has no necessary developmental implications. States that others call developmen-

476

Because it reintroduces politics, the neoutilitarian view should even be considered an improvement on the traditional neoclassical vision of the state as neutral arbiter. Indeed, the assumption that state policies "reflect vested interests in society" partially recaptures some of Marx's original insights into the biases that characterize state policy.[7] As an explanation of one pattern of the incumbent behavior which may or may not dominate in a particular state apparatus, neoutilitarian thinking is a useful contribution. As a monocausal master theory applicable to states generically, which the neoutilitarian view tends to become in the hands of its more dedicated adherents, the neoutilitarian model is problematic.

To begin with, it is hard to explain why, if officeholders are primarily interested in individual rents, they do not all "freelance." Neoutilitarian logic provides little insight into what constrains individual incumbents to work together as a collectivity at all. If we postulate that somehow the state solves its own collective action problem, there is no reason, within the logic of neoutilitarian arguments, for those who have a monopoly on violence to rest content being nightwatchmen and every reason for them to try to expand rental havens. In short, strict adherence to a neoutilitarian logic makes the existence of the state difficult to explain and the nightwatchman state almost a theoretical impossibility.[8]

At the same time, the neoutilitarian assumption that exchange relations are natural, that is epistomologically prior to other kinds of social relationships, is not well supported by empirical evidence. Detailed studies of real processes of exchange (as opposed to analytical summaries of their results) find that markets operate well only when they are supported by other kinds of social networks.[9] An efficient system of property relations is not enough. The smooth operation of exchange requires the dense, deeply developed medium of trust and culturally shared understandings, summarized by Durkheim under the deceptively simple heading of the "noncontractual elements of contract."

For better or worse, markets are always inextricably embedded in a matrix that includes both cultural understandings and social networks composed of polyvalent individual ties. In some cases support for exchange relations may be generated by informal interaction. In other cases, formal hierarchical organizations may "internalize" exchange relations.[10] If markets must be surrounded by other kinds of social structures in order to operate, then neoutilitarian attempts to free the market from the state may end up destroying the institutional underpinnings that allow exchange to operate. This is, of course, the position of the classic tradition of comparative institutionalist scholarship which emphasized the essential complementarity of state structures and market exchange, particularly in the promotion of industrial transformation.

This tradition has always been critical of the proposition that exchange was a natural activity that required only the most minimal institutional underpinnings. Forty years ago Polanyi argued, "The road to the free market was opened and kept open by an enormous increase in continuous, centrally organized and controlled interventionism."[11] From the beginning, according to Polanyi, the life of the market has been intertwined not just with other kinds of social ties, but with the forms and policies of the state.

Looking at established market societies, Weber carried this line of reasoning further, arguing that the operation of large scale capitalist enterprise depended on the availability of the kind of order that only a modern bureaucratic state could provide. As he put it: "Capitalism and bureaucracy have found each other and belong intimately together."[12] Weber's assumption of the intimate relation was, of course, based on a conception of the bureaucratic state apparatus that was the mirror image of the neoutilitarian view. Weber's bureaucrats were concerned only with carrying out their assignments and contributing to the fulfillment of the goals of the apparatus as a whole. Use of the prerogatives of office for maximizing private interests was, for Weber, a feature of earlier prebureaucratic forms.

---

tal could easily be labeled predatory under Levi's definition. Lal is more convinced of the negative relation between revenue maximization and development. For him, as for the neoutilitarians, the alternative to the predatory state is the minimal nightwatchman state and there is no analytical space for a developmental state.

[7]Colander, *Neoclassical Political Economy*, p. 2.

[8]It is important to note that this critique is intended to highlight some of the problems inherent in the thinking that supported the radical second wave approach to the state, not as a review of the wide variety of literature on the state that has emerged under the general rubric of rational choice. For one such review see Levi, *Of Rule and Revenue*, appendix.

[9]See Mark Granovetter, "Economic Action and Social Structure: The Problem of Embeddedness," *American Journal of Sociology* 91, no. 3 (November 1985): 481–510.

[10]Cf. Oliver E. Williamson, *Markets and Hierarchies: Analysis and Antitrust Implications* (New York: Free Press, 1975).

[11]Karl Polanyi, *The Great Transformation* (Boston: Beacon Press, 1957), p. 140.

[12]Max Weber, *Economy and Society*, ed. Guenter Roth and Claus Wittich (New York: Bedminster Press, 1968), p. 1395, n. 14.

For Weber, the state was useful to those operating in markets precisely because the actions of its incumbents obeyed a logic quite different from that of utilitarian exchange. The state's ability to support markets and capitalist accumulation depended on the bureaucracy being a corporately coherent entity in which individuals see furtherance of corporate goals as the best means of maximizing their individual self-interest. Corporate coherence requires that individual incumbents be to some degree insulated from the demands of the surrounding society. Insulation, in turn, is enhanced by conferring a distinctive and rewarding status on bureaucrats. The concentration of expertise in the bureaucracy through meritocratic recruitment and the provision of opportunities for long-term career rewards was also central to the bureaucracy's effectiveness. In short, Weber saw construction of a solid, authoritative framework as a necessary prerequisite to the operation of markets.

Later observers extended Weber's vision of the state's role. The ability to implement rules predictably, however necessary, is not sufficient. Gerschenkron's work on late developers complements Weber by focusing on the specific contributions of the state apparatus to overcoming problems created by a disjunction between the scale of economic activity required for development and the effective scope of existing social networks.[13] Late industrializers confronting production technologies with capital requirements in excess of what private markets were capable of amassing were forced to rely on the power of the state to mobilize the necessary resources. Instead of simply providing a suitable environment, as it did in Weber's model, the state was now actively organizing a crucial aspect of the market. Gerschenkron's argument also raises a new issue—the problem of risk taking. The crux of the problem faced by late developers is that institutions that allow large risks to be spread across a wide network of capital holders do not exist, and individual capitalists are neither able nor interested in taking them on. Under these circumstances the state must serve as surrogate entrepreneur.

Hirschman takes up this emphasis on entrepreneurship as the missing ingredient for development in much more detail. Based on his observations of the "late late" developers of the twentieth-century Third World, Hirschman argues that capital, in the sense of a potentially investable surplus, is not the principal ingredient that is lacking in developing countries. What is lacking is entrepreneurship in the sense of willingness to risk the available surplus by investing it in productive activities, or in Hirschman's own words, "the perception of investment opportunities and transformation into actual investments." If "maximizing induced decision-making" is the key as Hirschman argues it is, then the state's role involves a high level of responsiveness to private capital.[14] It must provide disequilibrating incentives to induce private capitalists to invest and at the same time be ready to alleviate bottlenecks that are creating disincentives to investment. . . .

The Gershenkronian/Hirschmanian vision makes the relationship between state capacity and insulation (or "autonomy") more ambiguous than a strictly Weberian perspective or, for that matter, a neo-Marxist one.[15] For the insulated state to be effective, the nature of a project of accumulation and the means of implementing it must be readily apparent. In a Gerschenkronian or Hirschmanian scenario of transformation, the shape of a project of accumulation must be discovered, almost invented, and its implementation demands close connections to private capital. A Prussian-style bureaucracy might well be effective at the prevention of force and fraud, but the kind of surrogate entrepreneurship that Gerschenkron talks about or the kind of subtle triggering of private initiative that Hirschman emphasizes would demand more than an insulated, corporately coherent administrative apparatus. It demands accurate intelligence, inventiveness, active agency and sophisticated responseness to a changing economic reality. Such arguments demand a state that is more embedded in society than insulated.[16]

Whatever the structural features that underlie state capacity, arguments for the central role of the state apply most strongly to situations in which structural transformation is the order of the day. Industrialization, which is the focus of the case studies that follow, is the classic example of this kind of transformation, but structural adjustment also

---

[13]Alexander Gerschenkron, *Economic Backwardness in Historical Perspective* (Cambridge, Mass.: Belknap, 1962).

[14]Albert Hirschman, *The Strategy of Economic Development* (New Haven, Conn.: Yale University Press, 1958), pp. 35, 44.

[15]Neo-Marxist arguments for the necessity of relative autonomy from the particularistic demands of individual capitalists reinforce the idea of a positive relation between capacity and autonomy. Cf. Dietrich Rueschemeyer and Peter Evans, "The State and Economic Transformation: Toward an Analysis of the Conditions Underlying Effective State Intervention," in Peter Evans, Dietrich Rueschemeyer, and Theda Skocpol, eds., *Bringing the State Back In* (New York: Cambridge University Press, 1985), pp. 44–77.

[16]Cf. Granovetter, "Economic Action and Social Structure," for a discussion of embeddedness.

requires more than incremental movement. It is also when transformation is on the agenda that the contrast between predatory and developmental states comes into sharpest relief. As Callaghy points out, the potential existence of a positive state role creates no logical necessity of the potential being realized. Societies and economies that "need" developmental states don't necessarily get them, as the case of Zaire amply demonstrates.

Zaire: An Exemplary Case of Predation

Since Joseph Mobutu Sese Seko gained control over Zaire in 1965, he and his coterie within the Zairian state apparatus have extracted vast personal fortunes from revenues generated by exporting the country's impressive mineral wealth. Over the next 25 years Zaire's GNP per capita *declined* at an annual rate of 2 percent a year, gradually moving the country toward the very bottom of the world hierarchy of nations and leaving the country's population in misery as bad or worse than that which they suffered under the Belgian colonial regime.[17] Zaire is, in short, a textbook case of a predatory state in which the preoccupation of the political class with rent-seeking has turned society into its prey.

Following Weber, Callaghy emphasizes the patrimonial qualities of the Zairian state; the mixture of traditionalism and arbitrariness that Weber argued retarded capitalist development.[18] True to the patrimonial model, control of the state apparatus is vested in a small group of personally connected individuals. At the pinnacle of power is the "presidential clique," which consists of "50-odd of the president's most trusted kinsmen, occupying the most sensitive and lucrative positions such as head of the Judiciary Council, secret police, Interior Ministry, President's office and so on."[19] Next is the "presidential brotherhood" who are not kin, but whose positions still depend on their personal ties with the president, his clique, and each other.

One of the most striking, and ironic, aspects of the Zairian state is the extent to which market relations dominate administrative behavior, again almost as a caricature of the neoutilitarian image of how rent-creating state apparatuses are likely to work. A Zairian archbishop described it as follows:

Why in our courts do people only obtain their rights by paying the judge liberally? Why do the prisoners live forgotten in prisons? They do not have anyone who can pay the judge who has their dossiers at hand. Why in our office of administration, like public services, are people required to return day after day to obtain their due? If they do not pay the clerk, they will not be served.[20]

President Mobutu himself characterized the system in much the same way saying: "Everything is for sale, everything is bought in our country. And in this traffic, holding any slice of public power constitutes a veritable exchange instrument, convertible into illicit acquisition of money or other goods."[21]

The prevalence of such a thoroughgoing market ethic might at first seem inconsistent with what Callaghy characterizes as an "early modern absolutist state,"[22] but it is in fact quite consistent. Personalism and plundering at the top destroy any possibility of rule-governed behavior in the lower levels of the bureaucracy. Moreover, the marketization of the state apparatus makes the development of a bourgeoisie oriented toward long-term productive investment almost an impossibility by undermining the predictability of state action.

The persistence of the regime itself might be taken as evidence that Mobutu has managed to at least construct a repressive apparatus with the minimal amount of corporate coherence necessary to fend off potential competitors. It is not clear that even this is the case. As Gould puts it bluntly: "The bureaucratic bourgeoisie owes its existence to past and continued foreign support."[23] Aid from the World Bank as well as individual Western nations has played an important role, but French and Belgian troops at critical moments (e.g., in Shaba in 1978) have been the sine qua non of Mobutu's remaining in power.[24] Thus, Mobutu provides only a weak test of the limits to which rent seeking can be allowed to prevail without undermining even the repressive apparatus necessary for regime survival.[25]

[17]World Bank, *World Development Report, 1991* (New York: Oxford University Press, 1991), p. 204.

[18]Thomas Callaghy, *The State-Society Struggle: Zaire in Comparative Perspective* (New York: Columbia University Press, 1984), pp. 32–79.

[19]David Gould, "The Administration of Underdevelopment," in Guy Gran, ed., *Zaire: The Political Economy of Underdevelopment* (New York: Praeger, 1979), p. 93.

[20]Cited in Callaghy, *The State-Society Struggle*, p. 420.

[21]Crawford Young, "Zaire: The Unending Crisis," *Foreign Affairs* 57, no. 1 (Fall 1978): 172.

[22]Callaghy, *The State-Society Struggle*.

[23]Gould, "The Administration of Underdevelopment," p. 93.

[24]Galen Hull, "Zaire in the World System: In Search of Sovereignty," in Gran, *The Political Economy of Underdevelopment*, pp. 263–83.

[25]Obviously, a full analysis of both the original character of the regime and its persistence would require more careful attention to the nature of Zaire's social structure. For a general approach to the question of the state and development which begins with an analysis of social structure see Joel Migdal, *Strong*

Zaire confirms clearly that it is not the bureaucracy that impedes development so much as the *absence* of a coherent bureaucratic apparatus. The "kleptopatrimonial" Zairian state is an amalgam of personalism and a thoroughly marketized administrative apparatus.[26] It is precisely the kind of exchange-dominated state that the neoutilitarians postulate and fear, but it is not only rampant rent seeking and distorted incentives that are produced. Weakness at the center of the political-economic system undermines the predictability of policy required for private investment. The state fails to provide even the most basic prerequisites for the functioning of a modern economy: predictable enforcement of contract, provision and maintenance of infrastructure, and public investment in health and education.

Zaire also poses some problems for conventional views of the importance of state autonomy in formulating coherent adjustment and growth strategies. On the one hand, since the state as a corporate entity is incapable of formulating coherent goals and implementing them, and since policy decisions are up for sale to private elites, the state might be seen as completely lacking in autonomy. This lack of autonomy is what permits pervasive rent seeking to prevail. At the same time, however, the Zairian state is strikingly unconstrained by society. It is autonomous in the sense of not deriving its goals from the aggregation of societal interests. This autonomy does not enhance the state's capacity to pursue goals of its own, but rather removes critical social checks on arbitrary rule. The Zairian case suggests that the relationship between capacity and autonomy needs rethinking. This becomes even more evident in looking at the developmental states of East Asia.

Developmental States

While states like Mobutu's were providing practical demonstrations of the perversions predicted by neoutilitarian visions of the state, a different set of nations halfway around the world were writing historical records that confirmed institutionalist expectations. By the end of the 1970s, the economic success of the major East Asian newly industrialized countries (NICs), Korea and Taiwan, was increasingly interpreted as depending on the active involvement of the state,[27] even by observers with a neoclassical bent.[28] . . .

The Japanese Model

Looking for institutional bases on which to build rapid industrialization, the East Asian NICs drew on the regional model of the active state—Japan. Analyses of the Japanese case provide a nice starting point for understanding of the developmental state. Chalmers Johnson's account of the golden years of the Ministry of International Trade and Industry (MITI) provides one of the best pictures of the developmental state in action.[29] His description is particularly fascinating because it corresponds so neatly to what a sophisticated implementation of ideas from Gerschenkron and Hirschman might look like in practice.

In the capital-scarce years following World War II, the Japanese state acted as a surrogate for weakly developed capital markets, while inducing transformative investment decisions. State institutions from the postal saving system to the Japan Development Bank were crucial in getting the needed investment capital to industry. The state's centrality to the provision of new capital, in turn, allowed MITI to aquire a central industrial policy role. Given its role in the approval of investment loans from the Japan Development Bank, its authority over foreign currency allocations for industrial purposes and licenses to import foreign technology, its ability to provide tax breaks, and its capacity to articulate "administrative guidance cartels" that would regulate competition in an industry, MITI was in a perfect position to "maximize induced decision-making."[30]

Some might consider Johnson's characterization of MITI as "without doubt the greatest concentration of brainpower in Japan" an exaggera-

---

Societies and Weak States: State-Society Relations and State Capabilities in the Third World* (Princeton, N.J.: Princeton University Press, 1988).

[26]The conjunction of leviathan and the invisible hand is not as contradictory as it might seem but is, in fact, quite common. It does take different forms in different states. For example, in the less traditionally corrupt military regimes of Argentina and Chile, brutal, leviathan-like control over political dissension was combined with fierce imposition of market logic on the surrounding society.

[27]Alice Amsden, "Taiwan's Economic History: A Case of Etatisme and a Challenge to Dependency Theory," *Modern China 5,* no. 3 (1979): 341–80.

[28]For example, Leroy Jones and Sakong II, *Government, Business and Entrepreneurship in Economic Development: The Korean Case. Studies in Modernization of the Korean Republic, 1945–1975* (Cambridge, Mass.: Harvard University Press, 1980).

[29]Chalmers Johnson, *MITI and the Japanese Miracle: The Growth of Industrial Policy, 1925–1975* (Stanford, Calif.: Stanford University Press, 1982).

[30]See, for example, Johnson's description of MITI's nurturing of the petrochemical industry in the 1950s and 1960s, *MITI and the Japanese Miracle,* p. 236.

tion, but few would deny the fact that until recently, "official agencies attract the most talented graduates of the best universities in the country and positions of higher level official in these ministries have been and still are the most prestigious in the country."[31]

There is thus clearly a Weberian aspect to the Japanese developmental state. Officials have the special status that Weber felt was essential to a true bureaucracy. They follow long-term career paths within the bureaucracy and operate generally in accordance with rules and established norms. These characteristics vary somewhat across the Japanese bureaucracy, but the less bureaucratic, more clientelistic agencies like the Ministry of Agriculture are generally viewed as "pockets of conspicuous inefficiency."[32] If Japan confirms Weberian pronouncements regarding the necessity of a coherent, meritocratic bureaucracy, it also indicates the necessity of going beyond such prescriptions. All descriptions of the Japanese state emphasize the indispensability of informal networks, both internal and external, to the state's functioning. Internal networks, particularly the *gakubatsu,* or ties among classmates at the elite universities from which officials are recruited, are crucial to the bureaucracy's coherence.[33] These informal networks give the bureaucracy an internal coherence and corporate identity that meritocracy alone could not provide. The fact that formal competence, rather than clientelistic ties or traditional loyalties, is the prime requirement for entry into the network, makes it much more likely that effective performance will be a valued attribute among loyal members of the various *batsu.* The overall result is a kind of "reinforced Weberianism," in which the "nonbureaucratic elements of bureaucracy" reinforce the formal organizational structure in the same way that Durkheim's "noncontractual elements of contract" reinforce the market.[34]

External networks connecting the state and private powerholders are even more important. As Chie Nakane puts it, "the administrative web is woven more thoroughly into Japanese society than

perhaps any other in the world."[35] Japanese industrial policy depends fundamentally on the ties that connect MITI and major industrialists.[36] Ties between the bureaucracy and private powerholders are reinforced by the pervasive role of MITI alumni, who through *amakudari* (the "descent from heaven" of early retirement), end up in key positions not only in individual corporations but also in the industry associations and quasi-governmental organizations that comprise "the maze of intermediate organizations and informal policy networks, where much of the time-consuming work of consensus formation takes place."[37]

The centrality of external ties has led some to argue that the state's effectiveness emerges "not from its own inherent capacity but from the complexity and stability of its interaction with market players."[38] This perspective is a necessary complement to descriptions like Johnson's, but it runs the danger of setting external networks and internal corporate coherence as opposing alternative explanations. Instead internal bureaucratic coherence should be seen as an essential precondition for the state's effective participation in external networks. If MITI were not an exceptionally competent, cohesive organization, it could not participate in external networks in the way that it does. If MITI were not autonomous in the sense of being capable of independently formulating its own goals and able to count on those who work within it to see implementing these goals as important to their individuals careers, then it would have little to offer the private sector. MITI's relative autonomy is what allows it to address the collective action problems of private capital, helping capital as a whole to reach solutions that would be hard to attain otherwise, even within the highly organized Japanese industrial system.

This embedded autonomy is the mirror image of the incoherent absolutist domination of the predatory state and constitutes the organizational key to the effectiveness of the developmental state. Embedded autonomy depends on an apparently contradictory combination of Weberian bureaucratic insulation with intense immersion in the surrounding social structure. How this contradictory combination is achieved depends, of course, on both the

---

[31]Johnson, *MITI and the Japanese Miracle,* pp. 26, 20. Johnson reports that in 1977 only thirteen hundred out of fifty-three thousand passed the higher-level Public Officials Examination and cites an overall failure rate of 90 percent for the years 1928–43 (p. 57).

[32]Daniel I. Okimoto, *Between MITI and the Market: Japanese Industrial Policy for High Technology* (Stanford, Calif.: Stanford University Press, 1989), p. 4.

[33]In 1965 an astounding 73 percent of higher bureaucrats were graduates of Tokyo University Law School.

[34]Cf. Rueschemeyer and Evans, "The State and Economic Transformation."

[35]Cited in Okimoto, *Between MITI and the Market,* p. 170.

[36]Okimoto, *Between MITI and the Market,* p. 157, estimates that the deputy director of a MITI sectoral bureau may spend the majority of his time with key corporate personnel.

[37]Okimoto, *Between MITI and the Market,* p. 155.

[38]Richard J. Samuels, *The Business of the Japanese State: Energy Markets in Comparative and Historical Perspective* (Ithaca, N.Y.: Cornell University Press, 1987), p. 262.

historically determined character of the state apparatus and the nature of the social structure in which it is embedded, as a comparison of Japan with the East Asian NICs illustrates.

Korea and Taiwan

Korea and Taiwan have different state structures linked to different social bases of support, different patterns of industrial organization, and different policy strategies.[39] Nonetheless, they share crucial features. In both, the policy initiatives that facilitated industrial transformation was rooted in coherent, competent bureaucratic organization. Though both of the East Asian NICs look more autonomous than the Japanese state, both reveal elements of the embedded autonomy that was crucial to Japan's success.

In comparing the Korean bureaucracy to Mexico's, Kim Byung Kook points out that while Mexico has yet to institutionalize exam-based civil service recruitment, meritocratic civil service examinations have been used for recruiting incumbents into the Korean state since A.D. 788, more than a thousand years.[40] Despite Korea's chaotic twentieth-century political history, the bureaucracy has been able to pick its staff from among the most talented members of the most prestigious universities. Data on the selectivity of the Higher Civil Service Examinations are almost identical to the data offered by Johnson for Japan. Despite a sevenfold increase in the annual number of recruits to the higher civil service between 1949 and 1980, only about 2 percent of those who take the exam are accepted.[41]

Along with similar recruitment patterns comes the inculcation of a particular corporate culture. Choi's discussion of the Economic Planning Board, for example, notes the same kind of confidence and esprit de corps that characterize MITI in Johnson's description.[42] Finally, as in Japan, meritocratic recruitment via elite universities and the existence of a strong organizational ethos creates the potential for constructing *batsu*-like solidary interpersonal networks within the bureaucracy. Looking at those who passed the civil service examination in 1972, Kim found 55 percent were graduates of Seoul National University and of these, 40 percent were graduates of two prestigious Seoul high schools.[43]

While the Korean bureaucracy seems an archetype, Korea's experience also shows the insufficiency of a bureaucratic tradition. In the 1950s under Rhee Syngman, the civil service exam was largely bypassed, with only about 4 percent of those filling higher entry level positions entering via the civil service exam. Nor were those who entered the higher civil service able to count on making their way up through the ranks via a standard process of internal promotion. Instead higher ranks were filled primarily on the basis of politically-driven "special appointments."[44]

The character of bureaucratic appointment and promotion under Rhee is, of course, quite consistent with the character of his regime. While Rhee presided over a certain amount of import-substituting industrialization, his regime was more predatory than developmental. Massive U.S. aid, in effect, financed substantial government corruption. Rhee's dependence on private sector donations to finance his political dominance made him dependent on clientelistic ties with individual businessmen and, not surprisingly, "rent-seeking activities were rampant and systematic."[45]

Without a deep, thoroughly elaborated, bureaucratic tradition, neither the Park regime's reconstruction of bureaucratic career paths nor its reorganization of the economic policy making apparatus would have been possible. Without some powerful additional basis for cohesion in the upper ranks of the state, the bureaucratic tradition would have remained ineffectual. Without both in combination it would have been impossible to transform the state's relationship to private capital.

Only with the ascension to power of a group with strong ideological convictions and close personal and organizational ties was the state able to "regain its autonomy."[46] The junior officers involved in the coup led by Park Chung Hee were united by both reformist convictions and close interpersonal ties both on service experience and close *batsu*-like network ties originating in the

[39]Cf. Tun-jen Cheng, "The Politics of Industrial Transformation: The Case of the East Asia NICs" (Ph.D. diss., Department of Political Science, University of California, 1987).

[40]Kim Byung Kook, "Bringing and Managing Socioeconomic Change: The State in Korea and Mexico" (Ph.D. diss., Department of Government, Harvard University, 1987), pp. 101–2.

[41]Kim, "Bringing and Managing Socioeconomic Change," p. 101.

[42]Choi Byung Sun, "Institutionalizing a Liberal Economic Order in Korea: The Strategic Management of Economic Change" (Ph.D. diss., Kennedy School, Harvard University, 1987).

[43]Kim, "Bringing and Managing Socioeconomic Change," p. 101.

[44]Ibid., pp. 101–2.

[45]Cheng, "The Politics of Industrial Transformation," p. 200.

[46]Ibid., p. 203.

military academy.[47] The super-imposition of this new brand of organizational solidary sometimes undercut the civilian state bureaucracy as military men were put in top posts but, in general, the military used the leverage provided by their own corporate solidarity to both strengthen and discipline the bureaucracy. Under Park the proportion of higher entry-level positions filled with Higher Civil Service examinees quintupled and internal promotion became the principal means of filling all ranks above them, with the exception of the highest political appointments.[48]

One of the features of the revitalized state bureaucracy was the relatively privileged position held by a single pilot agency, the Economic Planning Board (EPB). Headed by a deputy prime minister, the EPB was chosen by Park to be a "superagency" in the economic area.[49] Its power to coordinate economic policy through control of the budgetary process is enhanced by mechanisms like the Economic Ministers Consultation Committee and by the fact that its managers are often promoted into leadership positions in other ministries.[50] As in the Japanese case the existence of a pilot agency does not mean that policies are uncontested within the bureaucracy. The EPB and the Ministry of Trade and Industry (MTI) are often at loggerheads over industrial policy.[51] Nonetheless, the existence of a given agency with generally acknowledged leadership in the economic area allows for the concentration of talent and expertise and gives economic policy a coherence that it lacks in a less clearly organized state apparatus.

When the Park regime took power its goal seemed to be not just insulation from private capital but complete dominance over it. Criminal trials and confiscation were threatened and the leaders of industry were marched through the street in ignominy as corrupt parasites. This soon changed as Park realized that he needed to harness private entrepreneurship and managerial expertise to achieve

his economic goals.[52] Over time, and particularly in the 1970s, the ties between the regime and the largest *chaebol* (conglomerates) became so tight that visiting economists concluded that "Korea, Inc." was "undoubtedly a more apt description of the situation in Korea than is 'Japan, Inc.'"[53]

As in the case of Japan, the symbiotic relationship between the state and the *chaebol* was founded on the fact that the state had access to capital in a capital scarce environment.[54] Through its ability to allocate capital the state promoted the concentration of economic power in the hands of the *chaebol,* and "aggressively orchestrated" their activities.[55] At the same time, the Park regime was dependent on the *chaebol* to implement the industrial transformation that constituted its primary project and the basis for its legitimacy.

The embeddedness of the Korean state under Park was a much more top-down affair than the Japanese prototype, lacking the well-developed intermediary associations and focused on a much smaller number of firms. The size and diversification of the largest *chaebol* did give them interests that were relatively "encompassing" in sectoral terms so that the small number of actors did not limit the sectoral scope of the shared project of accumulation.[56] Still, the Korean state could not claim the same generalized institutional relation with the private sector that the MITI system provided and never fully escaped the danger that the

---

[47]See for example Kang's (1988) description of the Hanahoe club, founded by members of the eleventh military academy class.

[48]Kim, "Bringing and Managing Socioeconomic Change," pp. 101–8.

[49]Ibid., p. 115.

[50]For example, according to Choi, "Institutionalizing a Liberal Economic Order," p. 50, "four out of five Ministers of the Ministry of Trade and Industry between December 1973 and May, 1982 were former Vice-Ministers of the EPB."

[51]Cheng, "The Politics of Industrial Transformation," p. 231–32, claims that the MTI rather than the EPB dominated industrial policy making in the early 1970s, but clearly by the late 1970s the EPB was again dominant.

[52]See Kim Eun Mee, "From Dominance to Symbiosis: State and *Chaebol* in the Korean Economy, 1960–1985" (Ph.D. diss., Department of Sociology, Brown University, 1987); Kim Myoung Soo, "The Making of the Korean Society: The Role of the State in the Republic of Korea (1948–1979)" (Ph.D. diss., Department of Sociology, Brown University, 1987).

[53]Mason et al., *The Economic and Social Modernization of the Republic of Korea* (Cambridge: Harvard University Press, 1980), cited in Bruce Cumings, "The Origins and Development of the Northeast Asian Political Economy: Industrial Sectors, Product Cycles and Political Consequences," in F. Deyo, ed., *The Political Economy of the New Asian Industrialism* (Ithaca, N.Y.: Cornell University Press, 1987), p. 73.

[54]The importance first of foreign aid and then of foreign loans, both of which were channeled through the state and allocated by it was a cornerstone of the state's control over capital. See Kim, "From Dominance to Symbiosis"; Woo Jung-en, *Race to the Swift: State and Finance in Korean Industrialization* (New York: Columbia University Press, 1991); and Barbara Stallings, "The Role of Foreign Capital in Economic Development," in Gary Gereffi and Donald L. Wyman, eds. *Manufacturing Miracles: Paths of Industrialization in Latin America and East Asia* (Princeton: Princeton University Press, 1990), pp. 55–89.

[55]Robert Wade, *Governing the Market: Economic Theory and the Role of Government in East Asian Industrialization* (Princeton: Princeton University Press, 1990), p. 320.

[56]Cf. Mancur Olson, *The Rise and Decline of Nations.*

particularistic interests of individual firms might lead back in the direction of unproductive rent seeking. This, at least, was the perception of the Young Turk technocrats in the EPB at the beginning of the 1980s who felt that it was past time that the state begin to distance itself from resource claims of the largest *chaebol*.[57]

Korea is pushing at the limit to which embeddedness can be concentrated in a few ties without degenerating into particularistic predation. The opposite risk, of weak links to private capital threatening the state's ability to secure full information and count on the private sector for effective implementation, is represented by the region's second prominent pupil of the Japanese model, Taiwan.

In Taiwan, as in Korea, the state has been central to the process of industrial accumulation, channeling capital into risky investments, enhancing the capacity of private firms to confront international markets, and taking on entrepreneurial functions directly through state-owned enterprises. In Taiwan, as in Korea, the ability of the state to play this role depended on a classic, meritocratically-recruited, Weberian bureaucracy, crucially reinforced by extra-bureaucratic organizational forms. As in the case of the Korean state, the Kuomintang (KMT) regime is built on a combination of longstanding tradition and dramatic transformation, but differences in the historical experience of the two states led to very different patterns of relations with the private sector and, in consequence, very different patterns of state entrepreneurship. The transformation of the Kuomintang state following its arrival on Taiwan is as striking as the changes in Korea between the Rhee and Park governments. On the mainland the KMT regime had been largely predatory, riddled with rent seeking and unable to prevent the particular interests of private speculators from undermining its economic projects. On the island, the party remade itself. Freed of its old landlord base, and aided by the fact that the "most egregiously corrupt and harmful" members of the capitalist elite did not follow Chiang Kai Shek to the island,[58] the KMT was able to completely rework its ties with private capital. A corrupt and faction-ridden party organization came to approximate the Leninist party-state that it had aspired to be from the beginning,[59] thus providing the state bureaucracy with a reinforcing source of organizational cohesion and coherence more powerful and stable than could have been provided by military organization alone.

Within the reinforced governmental apparatus, the KMT put together a small set of elite economic policy organizations similar in scope and expertise to Japan's MITI or Korea's EPB.[60] The Council on Economic Planning and Development (CEPD) is the current incarnation of the planning side of the economic general staff. It is not an executive agency but "in Japanese terms lies somewhere between MITI and the Economic Planning Agency."[61] The Industrial Development Bureau (IDB) of the Ministry of Economic Affairs is staffed primarily by engineers and takes a more direct role in sectoral policies. Both of these agencies, like their counterparts in Korea and Japan, have traditionally been successful in attracting the best and the brightest. Staff members tend to be both KMT members and graduates of the country's elite Taiwan National University.[62]

Without negating the fundamental transformation in the character of the Kuomintang apparatus, it is also noteworthy that as in the case of Korea, the existence of a long bureaucratic tradition gave the regime a foundation on which to build. Not only was there a party organization that provided political cohesion at the top, but there was also an economic bureaucracy with considerable managerial experience. For example, the National Resources Commission (NRC), founded in 1932, had a staff of twelve thousand by 1944 and managed over one hundred public enterprises whose combined capital accounted for half of the paid-up capital of all Chinese enterprises. It was an island of relatively meritocratic recruitment within the mainland regime and its alumni eventually came to play a major role in managing industrial policy on Taiwan.[63]

The punishing experience of being undercut by the particularistic interests of private speculators on the mainland led the political leadership of the KMT as well as the alumni of the NRC to harbor a fundamental distrust of private capital and to take seriously the anticapitalist elements of Sun Yat Sen's ideological pronouncements. These predilections were reinforced by the pragmatic fact that strengthening private capitalists on Taiwan in-

---

[57]See Stephan Haggard and Chung-in Moon, "Institutions and Economic Policy: Theory and a Korean Case Study," *World Politics* 42, no. 2 (January 1990): 210–37.

[58]Tom Gold, *State and Society in the Taiwan Miracle* (New York: M.E. Sharpe, 1986), p. 59.

[59]Cheng, "The Politics of Industrial Transformation," p. 97.

[60]The discussion that follows draws primarily on Wade, *Governing the Market*.

[61]Wade, *Governing the Market*, p. 198.

[62]Ibid., p. 217.

[63]According to Wade, *Governing the Market*, pp. 272–73, the pool of NRC technocrats provided among other leading economic bureaucrats eight out of fourteen Ministers of Economic affairs.

volved increasing the power of an ethnically distinct, politically hostile private elite. It is therefore hardly surprising that instead of turning Japanese properties over to the private sector as its American advisors recommended, the KMT retained control, generating one of the largest state-owned sectors in the non-Communist world.[64] What is surprising is that Taiwan's state-owned enterprises (SOEs), in contrast to the pattern of inefficiency and deficit financing that is often considered intrinsic to the operation of such firms, were for the most part both profitable and efficient.[65]

On Taiwan, SOEs have been key instruments of industrial development. In addition to the banking sector, which was state-owned as in post-Rhee Korea, state-owned enterprises accounted for the majority of industrial production in the 1950s[66] and, after falling off a bit in the 1960s, their share expanded again in the 1970s.[67] SOEs are particularly important in basic and intermediary industries. China Steel, for example, has enabled Taiwan to successfully outcompete all Organization for Economic Cooperation and Development (OECD) steel exporters in the Japanese market.[68] The state enterprise sector not only makes a direct entrepreneurial contribution, but is also a training ground for economic leadership in the central state bureaucracy.[69] Thus, economic policy formation in Taiwan grows out of "a little understood but apparently vigorous policy network which links the central economic bureaus with public enterprises [and] public banks."[70]

What is striking in comparing Taiwan with Korea and Japan is the extent to which the Taiwanese private sector has been absent from economic policy networks. Even though the current trend is to "expand and institutionalize decision-making inputs from industrialists, financiers and others,"[71] historical relations between the KMT state and private (mainly Taiwanese) capital have been suffi-

ciently distant to raise the question of whether embeddedness is really a necessary component of the developmental state.

The Taiwanese state unquestionably operates effectively with a less dense set of public-private network ties than the Korean or Japanese versions of the developmental state. Nonetheless, its lack of embeddedness should not be exaggerated. It is hardly isolated from the private sector. Gold has shown the close relations that existed between the government and the nascent textile sector in the 1950s, as well as the key intermediary role the government played in the development of the semiconductor industry in the 1970s. Wade notes that IDB officials spend a substantial portion of their time visiting firms and are engaged in something very much like MITI's "administrative guidance."[72] He provides a revealing example of the state's close interaction with private capital in his discussion of negotiations between raw materials producers and textile companies in the synthetic fiber industry. While the formal negotiations involved the downstream industry association (Man-made Fibers Association) and the upstream domestic monopolist (a state-MNC joint venture), state managers were continuously involved.[73] By engaging in this kind of negotiation state managers ensure that neither the Country's efforts at backward integration into intermediary products nor the export competitiveness of its textile producers is threatened by unresolved private conflicts. Informal public-private networks may be less dense than in the other two cases, but they are clearly essential to Taiwan's industrial policy.

In addition to defining the limits to which embeddedness can be reduced, the Taiwanese case highlights the symbiotic relationship between state autonomy and the preservation of market competition. The role of state autonomy in preserving market relationships is also crucial in Korea and Japan, but it is most apparent in the case of Taiwan.[74]

The evolution of the textile industry offers the best illustration.[75] In the early 1950s, K. Y. Yin, ignoring the American-trained economists advis-

[64]See Cheng, "The Politics of Industrial Transformation," p. 107; Wade, *Governing the Market,* p. 302.

[65]Cf. Waterbury, chapter 4.

[66]Wade, *Governing the Market,* p. 78. Even in the 1980s, the state accounted for almost half of Taiwan's gross domestic capital formation and state enterprises accounted for two-thirds of the state's share (Cheng, "The Politics of Industrial Transformation," p. 166).

[67]Wade, *Governing the Market,* p. 97.

[68]P. Bruce, "World Steel Industry: The Rise and Rise of the Third World," *Financial Times* (London, 22 November 1983), cited in Wade, *Governing the Market,* p. 99.

[69]According to Wade, *Governing the Market,* p. 275, "most Ministers of Economic Affairs have had management positions in public enterprises."

[70]Wade, *Governing the Market,* p. 295.

[71]Ibid., p. 293.

[72]Ibid., p. 284.

[73]Ibid., p. 281.

[74]Cf. Stephan Haggard, *Pathways from the Periphery: The Politics of Growth in the Newly Industrializing Countries* (Ithaca, N.Y.: Cornell University Press, 1990), pp. 44–45.

[75]Cf. Peter Evans and Chien-kuo Pang, "State Structure and State Policy: Implications of the Taiwanese Case for Newly Industrializing Countries" (Paper presented at the International Conference on Taiwan: A Newly Industrialized Country, National Taiwan University, 3–5 September 1987).

ing his government, decided that Taiwan should develop a textile industry. The result was the textile entrustment scheme that, by providing an assured market and raw materials, minimized the entrepreneurial risk involved in entering the industry and successfully induced the entry of private capital. In this initial phase, the state was supportive in a classic Hirschmanian way, inducing investment decisions and stimulating the supply of entrepreneurship.[76]

The entrustment scheme in itself is unusual only in the lengths to which the state was willing to go in order to ensure that entrepreneurship was forthcoming; otherwise it was very similar to the policies of most Latin American countries in the initial phases of industrialization. What is unusual is that the entrustment scheme did not become the instrument of the entrepreneurs it had created. Instead, the KMT regime progressively exposed its "greenhouse capitalists" to the rigors of the market, making export quotas dependent on the quality and price of goods, gradually shifting incentives toward exports, and finally diminishing protection over time.[77] Thus, the state was able to enforce the emergence of a free market rather than allowing the creation of rental havens. Without the autonomy made possible by a powerful bureaucratic apparatus, it would have been impossible to impose the unpleasantness of free competition on such a comfortable set of entrepreneurs.

The example reinforces the point made earlier in relation to embeddedness and autonomy in Japan. Private capital, especially private capital organized into tight oligopolistic networks, is unlikely to be a political force for competitive markets. Nor can a state that is a passive register of these oligopolistic interests give them what they are unwilling to provide for themselves. Only a state that is capable of acting autonomously can provide this essential collective good. Embeddedness is necessary for information and implementation, but without autonomy embeddedness will degenerate into a supercartel, aimed, like all cartels, at protecting its members from changes in the status quo.

A final, equally important characteristic of the developmental state is also well illustrated by the Taiwanese case. While the government has been deeply involved in a range of sectors, the Taiwanese state is extremely selective in its interventions. The bureaucracy operates in Wade's words as a "filtering mechanism," focusing the attention of policy makers and the private sector on products and processes crucial to future industrial growth.[78] Like most of the KMT's Taiwan strategy, selectivity was in part a response to previous experience on the mainland; having experienced the disasters of an overextended state apparatus, the KMT was determined to husband its bureaucratic capacity in its new environment.[79] Selectivity would, however, seem to be a general feature of the developmental state. Johnson describes how the Japanese state, having experimented with direct and detailed intervention in the pre-World War II period, limited itself to strategically selected economic involvement after the war,[80] and Okimoto goes so far as to note that in terms of its overall size, the Japanese state could be considered "minimalist."[81]

The Dynamics of Developmental States

The salient structural features of the development state should now be clear. Corporate coherence gives them the ability to resist incursions by the invisible hand of individual maximization by bureaucrats; internally, Weberian characteristics predominate. Highly selective, meritocratic recruitment and longterm career rewards create commitment and a sense of corporate coherence. Developmental states have benefited from extraordinary administrative capacities, but they also restrict their interventions to the strategic necessities of a transformative project, using their power to selectively impose market forces. The sharp contrast between the prebureaucratic, patrimonial character of the predatory state and the more closely Weberian character of developmental states should give pause to those who attribute the ineffectiveness of Third World states to their bureaucratic nature. Lack of bureaucracy may come closer to the correct diagnosis.

At the same time, the analysis of the East Asian cases has underlined the fact that the nonbureau-

[76]See Gold, *State and Society in the Taiwan Miracle,* p. 70; Pang Chien Kuo, "The State and Economic Transformation: The Taiwan Case" (Ph.D. diss., Department of Sociology, Brown University, 1987), pp. 167–69.

[77]The same strategy continues to be used. Wade, *Governing the Market,* pp. 207–8, recounts the IDB's efforts to induce local VCR production at the beginning of the 1980s. Two local companies were at first given a monopoly, but when, after a year and a half, they were still not producing internationally competitive products, Japanese firms were allowed to enter the market (with local joint venture partners) despite the protests of the original entrants.

[78]Wade, *Governing the Market,* p. 226.

[79]Johnson notes in his discussion of the Japanese case how the state apparatus, having attempted with very mixed success detailed and direct intervention in the pre-War period, limited itself to strategically chosen interventions after the war.

[80]Johnson, *MITI and the Japanese Miracle.*

[81]Okimoto, *Between MITI and the Market,* p. 2.

cratic elements of bureaucracy may be just as important as the non-contractual elements of contract.[82] Historically deep, informal networks, or tightknit party or military organization have enhanced the coherence of the East Asian bureaucracies. Whether these ties are based on commitment to a parallel corporate institution or performance in the educational system, they reinforce the binding character of participation in the formal organization structure rather than undercutting in the way that informal networks based on kinship or parochial geographic loyalties do in the predatory pattern.

Having successfully bound the behavior of incumbents to its pursuit of collective ends, the state can act with some independence in relation to particularistic societal pressures. The autonomy of the developmental state is, however, of a completely different character from the aimless, absolutist domination of the predatory state. It is not just relative autonomy in the structural Marxist sense of being constrained by the generic requirements of capital accumulation. It is an autonomy embedded in a concrete set of social ties which bind the state to society and provide institutionalized channels for the continual negotiation and renegotiation of goals and policies.

In order to understand how this felicitous combination of autonomy and embeddedness emerged, it is necessary to set the developmental state in the context of a conjuncture of domestic and international factors. East Asian developmental states began the post-World War II period with legacies of long bureaucratic traditions and considerable prewar experience in direct economic intervention, in Korea and Taiwan under Japanese colonialism. World War II and its aftermath provided all these states with unusual societal environments. Traditional agrarian elites were decimated, industrial groups were disorganized and undercapitalized, and external resources were channeled through the state apparatus. The outcome of the war, including, ironically, American occupation in Japan and Korea, qualitatively enhanced the autonomy of these states vis-à-vis private domestic elites.[83] The combination of historically accumulated bureaucratic capacity and conjuncturally generated autonomy, placed them in an exceptional historical position.

At the same time, the state's autonomy was constrained by the international context, both geopolitical and economic. These states were certainly not free to make history as they chose. The international context excluded military expansion, but generated clear external threats. Economic expansion was not only the basis for shoring up legitimacy, but for maintaining defensive capabilities in the face of these threats. American hegemony on the one side and expansionary Asian communism on the other left them little choice but to rely primarily on private capital as the instrument of industrialization. The environment conspired to create the conviction that rapid, market-based industrialization was necessary to regime survival. Their small size and lack of resources made the place of export competitiveness in successful industrialization obvious.

Commitment to industrialization motivated these states to promote the growth of local industrial capital. Their exceptional autonomy allowed them to dominate (at least initially) the formation of the ties that bound capital and the state together. Out of this conjuncture the kind of embedded autonomy that characterized these states during the most impressive periods of their industrial growth emerged: a project shared by a highly developed bureaucratic apparatus and a relatively organized set of private actors who could provide useful intelligence and decentralized implementation.

. . . Recent developments suggest that embedded autonomy is not a static characteristic of the developmental state. In contrast to the absolutist domination of the predatory state, which seems self-reinforcing, embedded autonomy has been, to a surprising extent, its own gravedigger. The very success of the developmental state in structuring the accumulation of industrial capital has changed the nature of relations between capital and the state. As private capital has become less dependent on the resources provided by the state, the state's relative dominance has diminished. MITI influence in the 1980s cannot be compared to the golden era of the 1950s and early 1960s. Korean *chaebol* can now tap international capital markets directly[84] and the state's ability to veto their projects has correspondingly eroded.[85]

The capacity of state apparatuses to command the loyalties of the most talented graduates of the best universities has also begun to erode as private careers become more rewarding. For example, Wade notes that the proportion of Masters and Ph.D.s entering government service in Taiwan has dropped substantially while the share entering the

---

[82]Cf. Rueschemeyer and Evans, "The State and Economic Transformation."

[83]See Johnson, *MITI and the Japanese Miracle;* Pang, "The State and Economic Transformation."

[84]See Woo, *Race to the Swift.*

[85]See, for example, Kim, "From Dominance to Symbiosis," on the interaction of the state and the *chaebol* in the auto industry in the early 1980s.

private sector has risen,[86] which is not surprising given the increasing salary differentials between the public and private sector. Whether the bureaucracy's traditional esprit de corps and corporate coherence can be preserved in the face of these trends remains to be seen. Even more fundamentally, the achievement of higher standards of living has made it more difficult to legitimize a national project justified solely on grounds of its contribution to the growth of GNP. Resurgent distributional demands, both political and economic, do not fit comfortably with the elite networks and bureaucratic structures which fostered the original project of industrial accumulation.[87]

There is no reason to presume that the developmental state will persist in the form that has been described here. Nor can we presume that if these state apparatuses persisted in their present form they would promote the satisfaction of future societal goals. They proved themselves formidable instruments for instigating the accumulation of industrial capital but, in all likelihood, they will have to be transformed in order to deal with the problems and opportunities created by the success of their initial project.

Brazil and India: "Intermediate" Cases

Having developed the contrast between the embedded autonomy of the East Asian developmental state and the incoherent absolutism of the predatory Zairian regime, it is time to look at how elements from these two ideal types can be combined in different ways to produce results that are neither purely predatory nor consistently developmental. Brazil and India provide ample illustration of how elements from the developmental ideal type may be combined with characteristics that negate Weberian insulation and undercut embeddedness. . . .

Brazil

A plethora of historical and contemporary research make the differences between Brazil and the ideal typical developmental state clear.[88] The

differences begin with the simple question of how people get government jobs. Barbara Geddes chronicles the unusually extensive powers of political appointment and the corresponding difficulty Brazil has experienced in instituting meritocratic recruitment procedures.[89] Ben Schneider points out that while Japanese prime ministers appoint only dozens of officials and American presidents appoint hundreds, Brazilian presidents appoint thousands.[90] It is little wonder that the Brazilian state is known as a massive *cabide de emprego* (source of jobs), populated on the basis of connection rather than competence.

The negative consequences of patronage are exacerbated by the character of the career patterns that such a system encourages. Instead of being tuned to the longterm gains via promotions based on organizationally relevant performance, Brazilian bureaucrats face staccato careers, punctuated by the rhythms of changing political leadership and periodic spawning of new organizations. A 1987 survey by Schneider of 281 Brazilian bureaucrats found that they shifted agencies very four or five years. Since the top four or five layers of most organizations are appointed from outside the agency itself, long-term commitment to the agency has only a limited return and construction of an ethos and of agency- and policy-relevant expertise

---

[86]Wade, *Governing the Market,* table 7.1, p. 218.

[87]As Rueschemeyer and Evans, "The State and Economic Transformation," p. 53, argue, the state capacity required to implement distributional policies is likely to be significantly higher than that required to implement policies aimed at accumulation, further complicating prospects for success.

[88]Among historical studies those by Jose de Carvalho Murilo, "Elite and State-building in Brazil" (Ph.D. diss., Department of Political Science, Stanford University, 1974); and Fernando Uricoechea, *The Patrimonial Foundations of the Brazilian Bureaucratic State* (Berkeley: University of California Press,

1980) are particularly relevant to this discussion. Important recent contemporary studies include Sergio Abranches, "The Divided Leviathan: The State and Economic Policy Making in Authoritarian Brazil" (Ph.D. diss., Department of Political Science, Cornell University, 1978); Michael Barzelay, *The Politicized Market Economy: Alcohol in Brazil's Energy Strategy* (Berkeley: University of California Press, 1986); Frances Hagopian, "The Politics of Oligarchy: The Persistence of Traditional Elites in Contemporary Brazil" (Ph.D. diss., Department of Political Science, MIT, 1987); Barbara Geddes, *Economic Development as a Collective Action Problem: Individual Interests and Innovation in Brazil* (Ann Arbor, Mich.: University of Michigan Microfilms, 1986); Silvia Raw, "The Political Economy of Brazilian State-Owned Enterprises" (Ph.D. diss., Department of Economics, University of Massachusetts, 1986); Ben R. Schneider, "Politics within the State: Elite Bureaucrats and Industrial Policy in Authoritarian Brazil" (Ph.D. diss., Department of Political Science, University of California, 1987); Ben R. Schneider, "Framing the State: Economic Policy and Political Representation in Post Authoritarian Brazil," in John D. Wirth, Edson de Oliveira Nunes, and Thomas E. Bogenschild, eds., *State and Society in Brazil: Continuity and Change* (Boulder, Colo.: Westview Press, 1987); Helen Shapiro, "State Intervention and Industrialization: The Origins of the Brazilian Automotive Industry" (Ph.D. diss., Department of Economics, Yale University, 1988); and Eliza J. Willis, "The State as Banker: The Expansion of the Public Sector in Brazil" (Ph.D. diss., University of Texas at Austin, 1986). The discussion that follows draws especially on Schneider.

[89]Geddes, *Economic Development as a Collective Action Problem.*

[90]Schneider, "Politics Within the State," pp. 5, 212, 644.

is difficult. There is thus little to restrain strategies oriented toward individual and political gain.[91]

Unable to transform the bureaucracy as a whole, Brazilian leaders have tried to create pockets of efficiency (*bolsoes de eficiencia*) within the bureaucracy,[92] modernizing the state apparatus incrementally rather than through a broader transformation.[93] The National Development Bank (BNDE), favored especially by Kubitschek as an instrument of his developmentalism in the 1950s, was, until recently, a good example of a pocket of efficiency.[94] Unlike most of Brazil's bureaucracy, the BNDE offered "a clear career path, developmental duties and an ethic of public service."[95] Early in its institutional life (1956) the BNDE started a system of public examinations for recruitment. Norms grew up against arbitrary reversal of the judgments of the bank's technical personnel (*opiniao do tecnico*) by higher-ups. A solid majority of the directors was recruited internally, and a clear esprit de corps developed within the bank.[96]

Agencies like the BNDE are, not surprisingly, more developmentally effective than the traditional parts of the Brazilian bureaucracy.[97] According to Geddes those projects in Kubitschek's Target Plan that were both under the jurisdiction of executive groups or work groups and under the financial wing of the BNDE fulfilled 102 percent of their targets whereas those projects that were the responsibility of the traditional bureaucracy achieved only 32 percent.[98] Because the BNDE was a major source

of long term investment loans, its professionalism was a stimulus to improving performance in other sectors.[99] Tendler notes, for example, that the necessity of competing for loan funds was an important stimulus to the improvement of proposals by Brazil's electrical power-generating companies.[100]

Unfortunately, the pockets of efficiency strategy has a number of disadvantages. As long as pockets of efficiency are surrounded by a sea of traditional clientelistic norms, they are dependent on the personal protection of individual presidents. Geddes, for example, chronicles the decline in the effectiveness of the Departmento Administrativo de Servico Publico (DASP) established by Vargas in 1938 as part of the Estado Novo once Vargas' protection was no longer available.[101] Willis emphasizes the dependence of the BNDE on presidential support, both in terms of the definition of its mission and in terms of its ability to maintain its institutional integrity.[102]

Incrementalism, or reform by addition, is likely to result in uncoordinated expansion and make strategic selectivity much more difficult to achieve. Having entered power with the intention of shrinking the state by as much as two hundred thousand positions, the Brazilian military ended up creating "hundreds of new, often redundant, agencies and enterprises" and expanding the federal bureaucracy from seven hundred thousand to 1.6 million.[103] Trying to modernize by piecemeal addition also undercuts the organizational coherence of the state apparatus as a whole. As new pieces are added, a larger and ever more baroque structure emerges. The resulting apparatus has been characterized as "segmented,"[104] "divided,"[105] or "fragmented."[106] It is a structure that not only makes policy coordination difficult, but encourages resort to personalistic solutions.

Just as the internal structure of the Brazilian state apparatus limits its capacity to replicate the

[91]Ibid., p. 106. As Schneider points out, there are positive as well as negative features to this pattern. It discourages organizationally parochial perspectives and generates a web of inter-organizational ties among individuals. The main problem with these career patterns is that they provide insufficient counterweight either to the idiosyncratic decision-making from the top political leadership or to the tendencies toward individualized rent seeking.

[92]Geddes, *Economic Development as a Collective Action Problem,* p. 105.

[93]See Philippe Schmitter, *Interest Conflict and Political Change in Brazil* (Stanford, Calif.: Stanford University Press, 1971); Schneider, "Politics Within the State," p. 45.

[94]The BNDE later became the BNDES (National Bank for Economic and Social Development). Its history is discussed by both Geddes and Schneider, but the fullest discussions are Luciano Martins, *Estado Capitalista e Burocracia no Brasil Pos64* (Rio de Janeiro: Paz e Terra, 1985), and Willis, "The State as Banker."

[95]Schneider, "Politics Within the State," p. 633.

[96]Willis, "The State as Banker," pp. 96–126.

[97]Among the agencies highlighted by Geddes, *Economic Development as a Collective Action Problem,* p. 117, are the BNDES, CACEX, SUMOC, DASP, Itamaraty, Kubitscheks Executive Groups and Work Groups and the foreign exchange department of the Bank of Brazil.

[98]Geddes, *Economic Development as a Collective Action Problem,* p. 116.

[99]According to Willis, "The State as Banker," p. 4, the bank has "virtually monopolized the provision of long term credit in Brazil, often accounting for as much as 10 percent of gross domestic capital formation."

[100]Judith Tendler, *Electric Power in Brazil: Entrepreneurship in the Public Sector* (Cambridge, Mass.: Harvard University Press, 1968). See also Schneider, "Politics Within the State," p. 143.

[101]Geddes, *Economic Development as a Collective Action Problem,* p. 97.

[102]Willis, "The State as Banker."

[103]Schneider, "Politics Within the State," pp. 109, 575, 44. This was the goal of Roberto Campos (p. 575).

[104]Barzelay, *The Politicized Market Economy.*

[105]Abranches, "The Divided Leviathan."

[106]Schneider, "Politics Within the State."

performance of the East Asian developmental states, the character of its embeddedness makes it harder to construct a project of industrial transformation jointly with industrial elites. While the Brazilian state has been an uninterruptedly powerful presence in the country's social and economic development since colonial times, it is important to keep in mind that, as Fernando Urichochea, Jose Murilo de Carvalho and others have emphasized, "the efficiency of government . . . was dependent . . . on the cooperation of the landed oligarchy."[107] Despite the increasing weight of industrial capital in the economy, the persistent legacy of rural power continues to shape the character of the state. Hagopian argues that contemporary rural elites have turned increasingly to trying to use the state as an instrument for reinforcing their traditional clientelistic networks.[108] Thus, rather than being able to focus on its relationship with industrial capital, the state has always had to simultaneously contend with traditional elites threatened by the conflictful transformation of rural class relations.

At the same time, relations with industrial capital have been complicated by the early and massive presence of transnational manufacturing capital in the domestic market.[109] The threat of domination by transnational corporations (TNCs) created an atmosphere of defensive nationalism and made it more difficult to discipline domestic capital. It is much harder to force industrial capital to confront the market, as K. Y. Yin did with the Taiwanese textile industry, when transnational capital is the probable beneficiary of any gale of creative destruction.

Problems created by divisions in dominant economic elites were reinforced by the nature of state structures. The lack of a stable bureaucratic structure also made it harder to establish regularized ties with the private sector of the administrative guidance sort and pushed public-private interaction into individualized channels. Even the military regime, which had the greatest structural potential for insulation from clientelistic pressures, proved unable to construct an administrative guidance relationship with the local industrial elite.[110] The regime was "highly legitimate in the eyes of the local bourgeoisie, yet unconnected to it by any well-institutionalized system of linkages."[111] Instead of becoming institutionalized, relationships became individualized, taking the form of what Cardoso called "bureaucratic rings": small sets of individual industrialists connected to an equally small sets of individual bureaucrats, usually through some pivotal office holder.[112] As Schneider points out, the ad hoc, personalized character of these linkages makes them both undependable from the point of view of industrialists and arbitrary in terms of their outcomes.[113] They are, in short, quite the opposite of the sort of state-society ties that are described by Samuels and others in their discussions of the developmental state.

Overall, this reading of the internal structure and external ties of the Brazilian state is consistent with Schneider's lament that "the structure and operation of the Brazilian state should prevent it from fulfilling even minimal government functions."[114] But it is important to underline that despite its problems the Brazilian state has been entrepreneurially effective in a variety of industrial areas, and that these areas have undoubtedly contributed to its long-term growth and industrialization. These successes are, as we would expect, found in areas where the relevant state organizations had exceptional coherence and capacity. These coherent state organizations, in turn, also rested on a more institutionally effective set of linkages with the private sector, the precise pattern visible in the developmental states of East Asia.

Shapiro's discussion of the role of the Grupo Executivo para Industria Automobilistica (GEIA) in the implantation of Brazil's auto industry during the late 1950s and early 1960s is a good example. She concludes that overall "the Brazilian strategy was a success" and that the planning capacity and subsidies provided by the state through the GEIA

[107]Uricoechea, *The Patrimonial Foundations*, p. 52.

[108]Hagopian, "The Politics of Oligarchy."

[109]See Peter Evans, *Dependent Development: The Alliance of Multinational, State and Local Capital in Brazil* (Princeton: Princeton University Press, 1979); for a discussion of the consequences of foreign capital in Brazil, "Reinventing the Bourgeoisie: State Entrepreneurship and Class Formation in Dependent Capitalist Development," *The American Journal of Sociology* 88 (Supplement 1982): S210–47. For a more general contrast between Latin America and East Asia see Peter Evans, "Class, State and Dependence in East Asia: Some Lessons for Latin Americanists," in F. Deyo, ed., *The Political Economy of the New Asian Industrialism* (Ithaca, N.Y.: Cornell University Press, 1987); Stallings, "The Role of Foreign Capital in Economic Development."

[110]As a very cohesive corporate group whose lack of combat opportunities brought technocratic (i.e., educational) criteria for internal mobility to the fore, the Brazilian military approximated a KMT-style institutional reinforcement to the state's bureaucracy. See Alfred Stepan, *The Military in Politics: Changing Patterns in Brazil* (Princeton: Princeton University Press, 1971), and especially Geddes, *Economic Development as a Collective Action Problem*, chap. 7.

[111]Evans, "Reinventing the Bourgeoisie," p. S221.

[112]Fernando Henrique Cardoso, *Autoritarismo e Democratizacao* (Rio de Janeiro: Paz e Terra, 1975).

[113]Schneider, "Framing the State," pp. 230–31.

[114]Schneider, "Politics Within the State," p. 4.

were crucial to inducing the required investments.[115] The GEIA served as a sectorally specific minipilot agency. Because it combined representation from all the different agencies that needed to pass on plans, it "could implement its program independently of the fragmented policy-making authority" that plagued the government as a whole.[116] Its ability to provide predictable timely decisions was critical to risk reduction as far as the TNCs that were being asked to invest were concerned. In addition, again much like MITI or the IDB, the GEIA "played a critical coordinating role between the assemblers and the parts producers."[117]

The later development of the petrochemical industry exhibited an even more potent variant of embedded autonomy.[118] Trebat concludes that state-led investment in the petrochemical industry saved foreign exchange[119] and was economically reasonable given the prevailing opportunity costs of capital.[120] At the heart of the initiative was Petrobras, the most autonomous and corporately coherent organization within the state enterprise system. Equally crucial to the explosive growth of Brazil's petrochemical capacity in the 1970s, however, was the dense network of ties that were constructed to link the Petrobras system to private capital, both domestic and transnational.

Out of these sectoral examples a clear overall difference between the Brazilian state and the archetypal developmental state emerges. Embedded autonomy is a partial rather than a global attribute, limited to certain pockets of efficiency. The persistence of clientelistic and patrimonial characteristics has prevented the construction of Weberian corporate coherence. Brazil's complex and contentious elite structure makes embeddedness much more problematic. It is hardly surprising that embedded autonomy remains partial.

India

The Indian state is even more ambiguously situated in the space between predatory and developmental than the Brazilian one. Its internal structure, at least at the apex, resembles the Weberian norm, but its relation to the country's convoluted social structure more thoroughly undercuts its capacity to act. Its harsher critics see it as clearly predatory and view its expansion as perhaps the single most important cause of India's stagnation.[121] Others, like Pranab Bardhan, take almost the reverse point of view, arguing that state investment was essential to India's industrial growth in the 1950s and early 1960s and that the state's retreat from a more aggressively developmental posture has been an important factor in India's relatively slow growth in the 1960s and 1970s.[122]

At the time of independence the Indian Civil Service (ICS) was the apex of a venerable bureaucracy. It was the culmination of a tradition that stretched back at least to the Mughal empire.[123] Its eleven hundred members formed a prestigious elite, providing "the steel frame of empire" for two hundred years.[124] Its successor, the Indian Administrative Service (IAS) has carried on the tradition. Entry is primarily via a nationwide examination which, historically at least, has been as highly competitive as its East Asian counterparts.[125] While educational training is not concentrated in a single national university in the way that it is in East Asia, solidary networks are enhanced by the fact that each class of recruits spends a year together at the National Academy of Administration.[126]

Despite an historically deep tradition of solid state bureaucracy, the colonial traditions that the IAS inherited were by no means an unambiguous asset from the perspective of development. Assimilation of imperial culture and a humanistic training was an important criteria of acceptance into the ICS. Even after the English had departed, IAS exams still had three parts, English, English essay,

---

[115]Shapiro, "State Intervention and Industrialization," p. 57.

[116]Ibid., p. 111.

[117]Ibid., p. 58.

[118]See Evans, *Dependent Development; "Reinventing the Bourgeoisie"; "Class, State and Dependence in East Asia"; and "Collectivized Capitalism: Integrated Petrochemical Complexes and Capital Accumulation in Brazil," in Thomas C. and Philippe Faucher Bruneau, eds., *Authoritarian Brazil* (Boulder, Colo.: Westview, 1981).

[119]Thomas Trebat, *Brazil's State-Owned Enterprises: A Case Study of the State as Entrepreneur* (Cambridge, England: Cambridge University Press, 1983).

[120]See Evans, "Collectivized Capitalism."

[121]E.g., Lal, *The Hindu Equilibrium.*

[122]Pranab Bardhan, *The Political Economy of Development in India* (Oxford: Basil Blackwell, 1984).

[123]See Lloyd I. Rudolf and Susanne Hoeber Rudolf, *In Pursuit of Lakshmi: The Political Economy of the Indian State* (Chicago, Ill.: University of Chicago Press, 1987).

[124]Richard P. Taub, *Bureaucrats Under Stress: Administrators and Administration in an Indian State* (Berkeley: University of California Press, 1969), p. 3.

[125]Taub, *Bureaucrats Under Stress,* p. 29, reports that in 1960 eleven thousand college graduates competed for one hundred places.

[126]An example of the solidary created is the statement by one of Taub's (*Bureaucrats Under Stress,* p. 33) informants that he could "go anywhere in India and put up with a batch mate [member of his IAS class]," a possibility that the informant considered unheard of in terms of normal relations with nonkin.

and general knowledge.[127] An intelligent generalist might, of course, perform well, if career patterns provided the opportunity for the gradual acquisition of relevant technical knowledge and skills. Unfortunately, career patterns do not generally afford this kind of opportunity. Careers are characterized by the same kind of rapid rotation of people in jobs that characterize the Brazilian bureaucracy. Rudolf and Rudolf report, for example, that chief executives in the petrochemical industry have an average tenure in office of about fifteen months.[128] In addition to the problems of the IAS tradition itself, the extent to which the "steel frame" has remained uncorroded is questionable. The Rudolfs argue that there has been an "erosion of state institutions" at least since the death of Nehru.[129] Contemporary fieldstudies have found corruption not just endemic but overwhelming.[130] Erosion may be due in part to problems internal to the bureaucracy, but the difficulties of building connections to the surrounding social structure seem the more serious source of difficulty. In a "subcontinental, multinational state" like India state-society relations are qualitatively more complex than in the East Asian cases.[131] Given the diseconomies of scale inherent in administrative organizations, it would take a bureaucratic apparatus of truly extraordinary capacity to produce results comparable to what can be achieved on an island of twenty million people or a peninsula of forty million. Class, ethnic, religious, and regional divisions compound administrative difficulties.

From the time of independence, the political survival of Indian regimes has required simultaneously pleasing a persistently powerful rural landowning class and a highly concentrated set of industrial capitalists. The shared interests of larger landowners and the millions of "bullock capitalists" in the countryside give this group daunting political weight.[132] At the same time, the large business houses like the Tatas and Birlas must be kept on board.[133] Since business houses and landowners share no encompassing developmental project, the divided elite confronts the state in search of particularistic advantage. They comprise in Bardhan's terms, "a flabby and heterogeneous dominant coalition preoccupied in a spree of anarchical grabbing at public resources."[134]

The micropolitics of state-private interactions further diminish the possibility of the state leading a coherent developmental project. Historically, the stereotypical IAS veteran was an anglophile Brahman of Fabian socialist ideological leanings. The private capitalists with whom he was dealing were likely to be of lower caste, different cultural tastes, and opposing ideology. While these stereotypes have gradually changed over time, shared discourse and common vision, on the basis of which a common project might be constructed, are often still lacking, leaving the exchange of material favors as the only alternative to hostile stalemate. Policy networks that allow industry experts from within the state apparatus to collect and disseminate information, build consensus, tutor, and cajole are missing. Nor do we find sectorally specific networks comparable to the one that binds together the state and private capital in the Brazilian petrochemical industry. Unlike the developmental states, the Indian state cannot count on the private sector either as a source of information about what kind of industrial policy will fly or as an effective instrument for the implementation of industrial policy.

It would be unfair and incorrect to say that the Indian state has made no developmental contribution. State investment in basic infrastructure and intermediate goods was a central element in maintaining a respectable rate of industrial growth in the 1950s and early 1960s. Even Deepak Lal admits that infrastructural investments and the increase in the domestic savings rate, both of which depended largely on the behavior of the state, were "the two major achievements of post-Independence India."[135] State investment in basic agricultural inputs, primarily irrigation and fertilizers, played an important role in increasing agricultural

[127]Take, for example, the question cited by Taub (*Bureaucrats Under Stress,* p. 30): "Identify the following: Venus de Milo, Mona Lisa, the Thinker, William Faulkner, Corbusier, Karen Hantze Susman, Major Gherman Titov, Ravi Shankar, Disneyland."

[128]Rudolf and Rudolf, *In Pursuit of Lakshmi,* p. 34.

[129]Ibid., chap. 2.

[130]E.g., Robert Wade, "The Market for Public Office: Why the Indian State Is Not Better at Development," *World Development* 13, no. 4 (1985): 467–97.

[131]Rudolf and Rudolf, *In Pursuit of Lakshmi.*

[132]Ibid.

[133]Dennis Encarnation, *Dislodging the Multinationals: India's Strategy in Comparative Perspective* (Ithaca, N.Y.: Cornell University Press, 1990), p. 286.

[134]Bardhan, *The Political Economy of Development in India,* p. 70. It is interesting to contrast this vision with a quite different social structural dilemma, equally difficult for a would-be developmental state. In Maurice Zeitlin and Richard E. Ratcliff's *Landlords and Capitalists: The Dominant Class of Chile* (Princeton: Princeton University Press, 1988), analysis of Chile they found not a split elite but one which united agrarian and industrial interests, thus ensuring that the elite as a whole would resist transformation of the agrarian sector and the kind of single-minded focus on industrialization that characterized East Asian cases.

[135]Lal, *The Hindu Equilibrium,* p. 237.

output. The state has invested effectively, if not always efficiently,[136] in basic and intermediate industries like steel and petrochemicals and even in more technologically adventurous industries like electrical equipment manufacture.[137]

Unfortunately, these are largely accomplishments of the past, of the 1950s and early 1960s. Increasingly, lack of selectiveness in state intervention has burdened the bureaucracy and helped propel the erosion of state institutions. The "license, permit, quota raj" has attempted to enforce detailed control over the physical output of a broad range of manufactured goods.[138] At the same time, the state is directly involved in production of a variety of goods greater than even relatively expansive states like Brazil have attempted. Indian SOEs produce not only computers but also televisions, not only steel but also automobiles.[139] The state-owned share of corporate assets moved from one-sixth to a half between 1962 and 1972,[140] as the number of state enterprises grew from five in 1951 to 214 in 1984.[141] Given the overwhelming demands created by the sheer task of supplying even minimalist governance, unselective state involvement is simply unsustainable.

Relative to Brazil, it might be argued that India suffers from excessive autonomy and inadequate embeddedness and consequently has more difficulty in executing the kind of sectoral projects that are the focus here. At the same time, the degree to which the "steel frame" still retains some residual coherence may help account for India's ability to avoid the disastrous excesses that Brazil has fallen prey to.

Given their continental scale, Brazil and India may appear as sui generis, and of limited comparative relevance. Yet their states share many of the same problems, both with one another and with many of the middle-income developing countries as well. Their bureaucracies, which are not patrimonial caricatures of Weberian structures as in the predatory case, still lack the corporate coherence of the developmental ideal type. Consistent career ladders that bind the individual to corporate goals while simultaneously allowing him to acquire the expertise necessary to perform effectively are not well institutionalized. India has a more thoroughly Weberian organizational structure, but lacks the ties that might enable it to mount a shared project with social groups interested in transformation.

With less well-developed bureaucratic capacity, these intermediate apparatuses must nevertheless confront more complex and divided social structures. Their ability to construct a project of industrialization is specifically complicated by the continuing social power of agrarian elites. In the Brazilian case the problem is complicated even further by the historical importance of foreign firms at the core of the industrial establishment. In the Indian case it is exacerbated by the cultural divergence between state managers and private capitalists. In both countries the state has tried to do too many things; it has been unable to strategically select a set of activities commensurate with its capacity. Lesser capacity and a more demanding array of tasks combine to make embedded autonomy impossible. . . .

State Structures and Adjustment

. . . The comparative evidence argues strongly in favor of focusing more on state capacity as an important factor in policy choice and outcomes and helps clarify the structures and processes that underlie capacity. Most specifically, this analysis challenges the tendency to equate capacity with insulation. It suggests instead that transformative capacity requires a combination of internal coherence and external connectedness that can be called embedded autonomy.

The first and most obvious lessons to be extracted from these cases is that bureaucracy is in *under,* not over-, supply. This is not only a problem in the post-colonial societies of the sub-Sahara. Even in countries like Brazil that enjoy relatively abundant supplies of trained manpower and a long tradition of state involvement in the economy, predictable, coherent, Weberian bureaucracies are hard to find. The standard perception to the contrary flows from the common tendency for patrimonial organizations to masquerade as Weberian bureaucracies. There is an abundance of rule-mak-

---

[136]For a good discussion of problems in the inefficiency of state investments in terms of extraordinarily high capital output ratios etc., see Isher Judge Aluwalia, *Industrial Growth in India: Stagnation since the Mid-Sixties* (Delhi: Oxford University Press, 1985).

[137]Ravi Ramamurti, *State-owned Enterprises in High Technology Industries: Studies in India and Brazil* (New York: Praeger, 1987).

[138]See Encarnation, *Dislodging the Multinationals.*

[139]This lack of selectivity is not always evident in aggregate comparisons. For example, the distribution of public enterprises in Korea and India looked quite similar when Leroy Jones and Edward S. Mason, "Role of Economic Factors in Determining the Size and Structure of the Public-Enterprise Sector in Less-developed Countries with Mixed Economies," in Jones, ed., *Public Enterprise in Less-developed Countries* (New York: Cambridge University Press, 1982), p. 22, considered manufacturing a single sector rather than disaggregating it.

[140]Encarnation, *Dislodging the Multinationals,* p. 283.

[141]Lal, *The Hindu Equilibrium,* p. 257.

ing or administrative organizations, but most have neither the capability of pursuing collective goals in a predictable, coherent way nor an interest in doing so. Weber misled his successors by insisting that bureaucracy would naturally sweep all other forms before it. Just as markets are less natural than Smith would have had us believe, so bureaucracies need more nurturing than Weber led us to expect.

The second lesson is an extension of the first. The state's ability to perform administrative and other functions must be treated as a scarce good. Early visions of the developmental state seemed to assume that the resources necessary to undertake new tasks would be automatically generated by the performance of the tasks themselves, just as expanding firm sales generate resources for new production. The analogy is false. Unjudicious expansion of the menu of tasks leads too easily to a vicious cycle. State capacity grows more slowly than tasks expand. Administrative and organizational diseconomies of scale and scope lead to declining performance. Inadequate performance undercuts legitimacy and makes it hard to claim the resources necessary to increase capacity. The gap between capacity required and capacity available yawns wider until even the effective execution of nightwatchman duties is threatened.

Almost all Third World states try to do more than they are capable of doing. The contrasting balance of capacity and tasks that separates India and Brazil from the East Asian developmental states illustrates the point. The developmental states not only had higher levels of capacity but exercised greater selectivity in the tasks they undertook. They focused on industrial transformation and their strategies of promoting industry were designed to conserve administrative resources. . . .

Autonomy and corporate coherence, like insulation, are well within the Weberian tradition. Emphasis on embeddedness as the necessary complement to autonomy not only contradicts the notion that insulation is the most important feature of capacity, it also departs from a Weberian perspective. Embeddedness represents a different solution to the shortage of capacity. Embeddedness is necessary because policies must respond to the perceived problems of private actors and rely in the end on private actors for implementation. A concrete network of external ties allows the state to assess, monitor, and shape private responses to policy initiatives, prospectively and after the fact. It extends the state's intelligence and enlarges the prospect that policies will be implemented. Admitting the importance of embeddedness turns arguments for insulation on their head. Connections to civil society become part of the solution rather than part of the problem.

The obvious question is: Why doesn't embeddedness devolve into clientelism, corruption and undermining the effectiveness of the state? Most of the answer lies in the fact that embeddedness is assumed to have value only in the context of autonomy. In the absence of a coherent, self-orienting, Weberian sort of administrative structure, embeddedness will almost certainly have deleterious effects. . . . It is the *combination* of embeddedness and autonomy that works, not either on its own.

Selection IX.C.3. Taking Trade Policy Seriously: Export Subsidization as a Case Study in Policy Effectiveness*

Preliminary Considerations

There are three sets of economic models that I think are invaluable in thinking about policy formulation and implementation: (i) models of dynamic inconsistency of policy; (ii) models with irreversibilities and hysteresis; and (iii) models of rent seeking. Each of these has a distinct lesson for what makes policy effective.

The basic model of dynamic inconsistency points to the costs of discretionary behavior by government officials and brings out the advantage of rule-based policy regimes which entail high degrees of precommitment. Two significant applications of these ideas in the area of trade policy can be found in Staiger and Tabellini 1987 and Matsuyama 1990. The first of these papers shows the bias towards excessive protection on the part of governments that care about income distribution, while the second demonstrates the difficulties of disciplining firms by threatening to remove protection, a threat that is hardly credible *ex post*. In each case, a clear implication is that designing schemes that would enhance the commitment of policymakers to ex-ante rules would be desirable.

Models with irreversibilities demonstrate the importance of policy stability, or more accurately, predictability in coaxing the desired response from the private sector. When supply decisions are subject to sunk costs, unpredictability about future policy can seriously dampen the supply response to any policy change (Dixit 1989; Pindyck and Solimano 1993), and potentially render a prima-facie desirable policy change harmful (Rodrik 1991). Combined with Calvo's 1989 demonstration that a lack of credibility in trade policy amounts to an intertemporal distortion, this literature underscores the importance of building predictability into the policy making process.

Finally, the rent-seeking approach to trade policy, originating from Krueger's 1974 venerable article, reminds us that policies that create rents will also create rent seekers. This in turn generates incentives for bureaucrats to create rents in the first place (Shleifer and Vishny 1991). These ideas lie at the core of the neoclassical political-economy literature on trade policy, where rent-seeking interest groups and rent-providing policy makers interact to produce inefficient policy configurations (Grossman and Helpman 1992 provide a recent example[1]). The implications are bleak for policy making: policy interventions should be avoided as a rule, but if they cannot, they should be undertaken in manner that keeps private groups at arms length.

Taken together, these theoretical ideas yield quite a coherent story about what constitutes a good policy regime. Successful government programs are likely to contain the following characteristics:

- they apply simple and uniform rules, rather than selective and differentiated ones;
- they endow bureaucrats with few discretionary powers;
- they contain safeguards against frequent, unpredictable alteration of the rules;
- they keep firms and other organized interests at arms length from the policy formulation and implementation process.

These conclusions seem broadly reasonable, and lists like the above are often drawn in policy discussions.

When I first decided to take on export subsidies as a case study, I was expecting that the evidence on what makes some programs successful and others failures would validate these conclusions. I was wrong. While the models mentioned above *are* useful in understanding what happens, the broad generalizations that one is tempted to draw from them are much less so. In fact, as a first cut, these broad conclusions have more explanatory power when they are turned upside down! The two most successful programs of export subsidization I found, those in South Korea and Brazil, were highly complex and selective, differentiated by firm, subject to frequent changes, gave bureaucrats enormous discretionary powers, and entailed close interaction between bureaucrats and firms. On the other hand, the least successful programs in my sample, those in Kenya and Bolivia, consisted of simple, across-the-board, and non-selective subsidies.

What is going on here? I think the answer is that there is a lot that we do not know or under-

*From Dani Rodrik, "Taking Trade Policy Seriously: Export Subsidization as a Case Study in Policy Effectiveness," in Alan V. Deardorff et al., eds., *New Directions in Trade Theory* (Ann Arbor: University of Michigan, 1995), pp. 350–378. Reprinted by permission.

[1]However, they also allow the government to place an exogenous weight on aggregate efficiency.

stand about state capabilities and policy effectiveness. . . . With regard to export subsidies, there are two concepts that I have found useful in characterizing the differences in outcomes across countries. The first, and more fundamental, one is the notion of *state autonomy*. This refers to the degree to which the state and administrative apparatus of a society is insulated from organized private interests and, consequently, can exercise discipline over them.[2] The second useful notion is that of *policy coherence,* meaning a clearly articulated, stable, and non-conflicting set of policy priorities. I will be using these terms in a descriptive, rather than explanatory, fashion, as it remains unclear whether they can be operationalized in a meaningful manner.

The evidence from the case studies points to some simple conclusions. Policies work best when autonomy and coherence are both present; they fail when neither is. However, policy coherence on its own is worth something: coherent programs can be successfully formulated and implemented even when autonomy is lacking, but at the cost of some abuse. An important implication for economic analysis is the following one: while the state may not be an omniscient social-welfare maximizer, neither is it a tool of lobbying groups as in much of the recent political-economy literature. To understand where each case fits, we have to dig deeper than we are prone to do.

As mentioned above, the concept of state autonomy is borrowed from the political science literature. However, it has an important antecedent in Gunnar Myrdal's magisterial work on Asian development, *Asian Drama* 1968. In his study of Asian societies, Myrdal was struck by how little states asked of their citizens, and how incapable they were of eliciting compliance when they tried. The result was a pattern of economic policy making that was all carrots and no stick. Myrdal christened such states as "soft states," and contrasted them with their opposite, "strong states." This distinction, under different names, has survived. For example, Jones and Sakong's 1980 excellent study of policy making in South Korea harks back to this distinction, and the authors locate the key to that country's stellar performance in the presence of a "hard" state (more on this below).

State autonomy, as the term is usually used, is effectively a measure of how "strong" or "hard" a state is. Migdal 1988 is a good source on how po-

litical scientists have approached the issue of state strength and societal control, as well as on attempts to quantify these concepts. I find it helpful to think of autonomy as the extent to which the state can act as a Stackelberg leader over private groups, rather than as a Stackelberg follower; states that fall in the first category are strong, while states in the second category are weak.[3] The existing literature is not very helpful on where autonomy comes from and how it is acquired. Most studies point to distinctive historical experience: Migdal 1988, for example, emphasizes massive social dislocations, such as war, revolution, or mass migration, as a precondition to the existence of strong states.[4]

Going back to our list of what constitutes a good policy regime, then, these conclusions turn out to be too pessimistic about state capabilities in societies governed by strong states. On the other hand, they are too optimistic about the capabilities of weak states—and that is really bad news! In either case, they provide a bad fit.

I will expand on these points in the following sections. Export subsidization is a good area to try some of these ideas out for a number of reasons. For one thing, it is the policy on which the strategic trade policy literature has focussed. Second, it is very common: most countries have tried it at some time or another, and this provides a large sample. Third, the administration of export subsidies tends to be "organizationally demanding" (Levy 1993 p. 257), opening a window into contrasts in state capabilities. Finally, the received wisdom on export subsidies is that they have not been effective (Nogués 1990 and Thomas and Nash 1991).

Two Successful Cases: Korea and Brazil

Korea

Korea's phenomenal export boom starting in the early 1960s is well known. Less well known is the significant role played by the Korean government's micro-management of export incentives in produc-

---

[2]Occasionally the literature draws a distinction between the two parts of this definition, referring to the first as "autonomy" and the second as "capacity." See Barkey and Parikh 1991 pp. 525–26.

[3]See Rodrik 1992 for a first attempt to formalize this. Using a highly stylized model of interaction between the government and the private sector, I show that, compared to a strong state (the Stackelberg leader), a weak state (a Stackelberg follower) systematically underprovides economically desirable interventions, and systematically overprovides politically motivated (and economically harmful) interventions.

[4]As Migdal 1988 p. 269 puts it, "[a]ll these cases [Israel, Cuba, China, Japan, Vietnam, Taiwan, North Korea, and South Korea] of relatively strong states have occurred in societies in which major social disturbances rocked existing structures within the last half-century."

ing the boom. It is not a great exaggeration to say that the manner in which the Korean bureaucracy administered and coordinated the export push of the 1960s and 1970s is reminiscent of the way that the military command of a nation would run a war.

Under the Rhee government of the 1950s, Korean policy was preoccupied by largely political considerations, and the government attached no particular importance to either economic growth or exports (Jones and Sakong 1980 pp. 272–273). While there were some export subsidies, they were implemented haphazardly and often not budgeted at all (Frank et al. 1975 pp. 38–39). This changed dramatically after Park took over in a military coup on May 16, 1961. Park made exports his top priority, and aside from devaluing the won, greatly expanded the scope of export subsidization. Table 1 shows estimates of the combined ad-valorem equivalents of export subsidies during 1958–70. Two significant jumps in the subsidies are evident from the data, one in 1961–62 and another one in 1966–67.

Exporters had access to a bewildering array of subsidies in this period. Direct cash grants were important very early on, but they were phased out by 1965 and replaced by tax and import duty exemptions. In that year, the priority given to exporters in acquiring import licenses was formalized and expanded: exporters were allowed duty-free imports of raw materials and intermediate inputs up to a limit. This limit was determined administratively, on the basis of firm and industry input-output coefficients plus a margin of "wastage allowance." Since the imports acquired under the wastage allowance could be sold in the domestic market, this was a significant subsidy and was consciously used as such. Frank et al. 1975, p. 66 estimate that the wastage allowance alone provided an export subsidy of 4.6 percent in 1968 on average, and up to 17–21 percent in certain fabrics and footwear. Bureaucrats had virtually unrestricted discretion in setting wastage allowances, and their generosity varied from time to time (Frank et al. p. 50). Businesses and trade associations regularly lobbied for increased allowances.

Subsidized credit to exporters was another significant incentive. As Table 1 shows, it became particularly important after 1966. Frank et al. 1975 table 5-5 list twelve different types of preferential loans to exporters that were operative in the 1967–1970 period.

A noteworthy feature of the Korean export subsidies is that they applied not only to the final exporters, but to the indirect exporters as well (i.e., the firms that supplied the intermediate inputs used

in exportables). The available econometric evidence indicates that exports were highly sensitive to subsidies: Jung and Lee 1986 estimate that a 1 percent increase in export subsidies eventually led to more than a 2 percent increase in export supply. Intriguingly, they also find that the elasticity of export supply with respect to the real exchange rate was smaller than this.

These subsidies were disbursed against a background of highly unusual government-business relationship. One of the first acts of the Park regime was to arrest most of the country's leading businessmen and to threaten the confiscation of their assets under a recently passed Law for Dealing with Illicit Wealth Accumulation (Jones and Sakong 1980 p. 69).[5] A compromise was then arranged by which these businessmen would build factories and turn their shares over to the government in exchange for their release. The matter was eventually closed in December 1964 with most businessmen paying their fines in cash (with fines amounting to a total sum of $16 million). The planned transfer of ownership never took place. "Nonetheless," as Jones and Sakong remark (1980, p. 70), "the basic pattern was set, with businessmen in a decidedly subordinate role" to the state.

The ability of the government to elicit the desired response from firms by a combination of cajoling, arm-twisting, and threats was characteristic of the manner in which the export subsidies were administered. Westphal's description of the situation is worth quoting at length:

[T]he [Korean] government has not relied solely on market forces acting in response to incentives. It has also used publicly announced, quarterly export targets for individual commodities, markets, and firms. Contact between government and business in the day-to-day implementation of these targets has been close. Next to the responsible minister's office, an "export situation room" was established, laid out so that potential export shortfalls could be identified at a glance. A large staff has maintained almost daily contact with major exporters, and it has not been uncommon for the minister to intervene in difficult situations; for example, to obtain immediate customs clearance for inputs being delayed on some pretext. Progress towards targets and the current trade situation have been regularly reviewed at a Monthly Trade Promotion Conference, chaired by the president and attended by ministers, bankers, and the more successful exporters, large and small.

The highest export achievements have brought national awards as well as material benefits bestowed through

---

[5]This law was actually passed by the short-lived Chang Myon regime intervening between the Rhee and Park years, but its implementation took place under Park's government.

Table 1. Export Subsidies in Korea, 1958–70 (%)

	Direct Subsidies	Tax Exemptions	Duty Exemptions	Credit Subsidies	Total
1958	0.00	0.00	0.00	2.30	2.30
1959	0.00	0.00	0.00	2.53	2.53
1960	0.00	0.00	0.00	1.85	1.85
1961	5.89	0.00	0.00	0.75	6.64
1962	7.94	4.35	3.58	0.66	16.54
1963	3.14	4.67	5.06	2.20	15.07
1964	1.36	3.86	4.66	2.80	12.68
1965	0.00	6.11	5.79	2.86	14.76
1966	0.00	7.54	7.85	3.79	19.18
1967	0.00	8.52	9.07	5.45	23.04
1968	0.00	8.27	14.32	5.50	28.10
1969	0.00	9.07	11.89	5.11	26.06
1970	0.00	9.61	12.66	5.57	27.84

Source: Calculated from Frank et al. 1975, Tables 5–8.

discretionary means . . . [including] additional preferences in the general allocation of credit under a system of government directed bank lending and relaxed tax surveillance under a revenue system that gives government officials considerable latitude in determining tax liabilities. . . . Conversely, indolence has been deterred by the perception that discretion could be—indeed, sometimes was—exercised in ways that impose material costs or deny potential benefits in other areas of a firm's activity. (Westphal 1990 pp. 45–46)

There was a clear understanding on the part of firms that good export performance would be rewarded by various kinds of government benefits, while poor performance would bring forth penalties. Most notable among the penalties were tax inspection and collection applied more rigorously than usual (Rhee et al. 1984 p. 92).

As the passage quoted above makes clear, the government issued specific export targets for firms (as well as commodities and export markets). When the government first began to issue such targets, the heads of firms are reported to have willingly complied, "with the[ir] memory still fresh of their being jailed by the new regime for the illicit accumulation of wealth" (Rhee et al. 1984 p. 21). Eventually, firms began to set their own targets, but remained constrained by past performance as well as the vigilance of bureaucrats in extracting maximum export performance.[6,7]

The extent to which the government's priorities

and resources were organized around export performance is striking. As mentioned in the passage by Westphal above, the monthly trade promotion conferences were chaired by President Park himself, and he often took decisions on the spot. Exports were monitored literally on a daily basis:

The head of the export promotion office in the Ministry of Commerce and Industry has at his side a computer printout of progress against targets by industry and by firms. The data is for the preceding day, which is all the more remarkable when it is considered that most developing countries do not have aggregate information on exports for many months. The printout is also broken down by geographic region. If sales in a region are not up to target, the Korean ambassadors there are recalled to find out what the problems are and what can be done to spur Korean sales. And in the foyer of the head office of the Korean Traders' Association is a big board tracking the progress of each industry towards its target. The export associations of each industry, the nodes for all information flows on exports, have their own boards tracking progress. So do firms on the shop floors, where workers—dressed in uniforms that give all of industry a paramilitary air—keep track of their firm's progress toward targets and of that by competitors down the street. (Rhee et al. 1984 p. 22.)

The extreme discretion that trade officials had allowed them to be flexible and respond quickly to changes in circumstances. For example, export targets for automotive products were scaled down more than once during the 1970s (Westphal 1990

---

[6]Around half or more of the firms surveyed by Rhee et al. 1984 reported that the export targets had negative effects on the firm in terms of profitability or sales diversion. Enterprise-level export targets have also been used, apparently quite successfully, in China (see Panagariya 1993).

[7]As it turned out, most firms regularly exceeded their targets. Balassa 1978 reads this as evidence that targets did not play an

important role. However, that fact itself says nothing about how binding these requirements were ex ante: for one thing, Korean exports grew at a stupendous rate that would have been impossible to predict beforehand; secondly, there was a general expectation that failure to meet targets would attract penalties, creating strong incentives for fulfillment; and third, over-fulfillment brought rewards from the administration.

p. 54), and a survey by Rhee et al. 1984 found that nearly a third of the respondents had their targets revised during 1973–75.[8] But when asked whether a firm had any say in setting the export target for itself, 47 of the 97 firms replied negatively.

Without these two institutional innovations—the practice of setting and monitoring export targets and the holding of monthly trade promotion conferences—the export incentives themselves would arguably not have been as effective (Rhee et al. 1984). These were instrumental in communicating the top leadership's priorities to lower level bureaucrats and to firms alike, in resolving administrative problems quickly, and as a combined carrot-and-stick strategy more broadly. To the question of why firms did not systematically manipulate the incentives or set low targets (as in socialist economies), the simple answer is that state officials were on top of things. In turn, low-level corruption on the part of bureaucrats themselves was ruled out by the high priority given to the export drive by the top leadership.

The Korean state's strength (or autonomy) is usually ascribed to a number of distinctive circumstances. According to Amsden 1989 p. 54, "[t]he Korean state was able to consolidate its power in the 1960s because of the weakness of the social classes. Workers were a small percentage of the population, capitalists were dependent on state largesse, the aristocracy was dissolved by land reform, and the peasantry was atomized into smallholders." Others like Evans 1992 also stress the importance of a tradition of meritocratic bureaucracy. Such historical considerations, however, do not explain how the Korean state under Park was able to metamorphose itself from its poor cousin under Rhee.[9] We also need to take into account the *coherence* of export policies under Park—the consistent priority given to them at the expense of other objectives—and the lack thereof under Rhee.

Brazil

Brazil's economy has been so mismanaged since the early 1980s that it is hard to imagine the presence there of an effective program of export subsidies. Yet starting in the second half of the 1960s an extensive set of export incentives was successfully implemented and led—alongside a crawling exchange rate policy—to an impressive increase in manufactured exports. It was this export performance that prompted many observers to talk about a "Brazilian miracle," until the debt crisis of 1982 and macroeconomic mismanagement turned the economy into a big mess.

Prior to the military coup of 1964, government policy in Brazil did not attach particular attention to exports, in keeping with the bias towards import substitution. The incoming government, like Park's regime, developed a clear commitment to exports. There was some liberalization of import restrictions, a move (in 1968) to a crawling peg regime to maintain competitiveness, and the development of an extensive and generous system of export subsidies for manufactures. These subsidies included duty and tax rebates, income tax exemption, credit subsidies, and many others (see table 2). By the latter half of the 1970s, the combined value of these subsidies stood close to 50 percent of exports. As in Korea, these subsidy programs were implemented in a highly selective and discriminatory manner.[10] Export subsidization varied greatly from industry to industry, as well as from firm to firm. Almost without exception, the larger firms obtained a disproportionate share of the subsidies (Fasano-Filho et al. 1987 p. 66).

The effectiveness of these subsidies appears beyond question. In a survey of export subsidies in Latin America, Nogués 1990 lists only the Brazilian case as a success. Fasano-Filho et al. 1987 provide econometric evidence of their importance in export supply decisions. A World Bank study (1983 p. 121) credits the BEFIEX program (discussed below) for stimulating a significant amount of new investments oriented towards world markets. Perhaps most telling of all is that Brazilian manufactured exports expanded at an annual average rate of 38 percent during the 1970s.

Among the subsidies listed in table 2, one stands out in terms of effectiveness and distinctiveness. This is the BEFIEX program, introduced in 1972. (BEFIEX is the Brazilian acronym for Fiscal Benefits for Special Export Programmes.) According to

---

[8]Here is how Jones and Sakong 1980 p. 61 describe the down side of the discretionary environment: "Businessmen often complain about the sudden shifts in policy direction, and (at a decidedly lower level of importance) academics are regularly frustrated when their critiques of policy become outdated before reaching print." But according to Rhee et al. 1984 p. 36: "Firms . . . saw the flexibility and frequent adjustments in the incentive system not as characteristics that would create uncertainty about the automaticity and stability of that system. They saw them as part of the government's long-term commitment to keep exports profitable. . . . "

[9]Survey results reported in Jones and Sakong 1980 Table 22 show a striking difference in firms' perceptions with regard to the effectiveness and hardness of economic policies under the two regimes.

[10]Evans 1979 pp. 93–94 characterizes post-1964 Brazil as "a case of espousing liberal free enterprise while acting to increase vastly the economic role of the state, both regulatory and entrepreneurial."

Table 2. Export Subsidies in Brazil, 1969–1985 (%)

	Duty Drawback	BEFIEX	Tax Credit Premium	Credit Subsidies	Income Tax Exempt.	Total
1969	4.0	—	6.7	4.1	0.0	14.8
1970	4.0	—	13.5	7.5	0.0	25.0
1971	4.0	—	13.2	7.8	1.3	26.3
1972	4.9	n.a.	16.3	8.2	1.3	30.7
1973	7.2	n.a.	16.2	6.5	1.3	31.2
1974	12.6	n.a.	12.0	6.1	1.8	32.5
1975	8.3	n.a.	12.1	11.5	1.7	33.6
1976	11.8	3.6	11.7	15.9	1.3	44.3
1977	12.6	4.6	12.4	19.6	1.5	50.7
1978	9.1	5.0	12.8	17.0	1.8	45.7
1979	10.5	5.4	12.8	13.9	2.1	44.7
1980	9.0	8.1	0.0	2.0	1.9	21.0
1981	9.4	10.2	6.5	18.7	1.8	46.6
1982	10.3	7.7	9.1	21.7	1.6	50.4
1983	8.6	4.9	7.8	9.3	1.6	32.2
1984	9.1	4.3	7.8	2.7	1.6	25.5
1985	9.1	5.9	1.4	3.6	1.6	21.6

Source: Clements 1988 pp. 15–17, and GATT 1992 Table IV, pp. 14–15.

Fritsch and Franco 1992 p. 9, this was the most important of the export subsidies. The scheme was unusual in that it entailed the signing of long-term contracts (for usually 10 years) by participating firms detailing their export commitments. Aside from these export commitments, firms also had to satisfy minimum local-content requirements in order to qualify for BEFIEX incentives. The contracts were negotiated with the BEFIEX administration on the basis of detailed information on firms' activities and strategic plans. The incentives, in turn, typically included "90% reduction of import duties and the Industrialized Products Tax (IPI) on imported machinery and equipment; 50% reduction on import duties and IPI tax on imported raw materials, parts and components, and other intermediate products; exemption from the 'similarity' test; and income tax exemption on profits attributable to exports of manufactured products" (GATT 1992 p. 104).[11]

Between 1972–1985, 316 contracts were signed, mainly with multinational enterprises in the transport equipment and textile and clothing industries. In the automotive sector, GM, Ford, and VW each committed to $1 billion of exports over ten years, Fiat to $550 million, and Mercedes Benz to $500 million (Shapiro 1993 p. 213; World Bank 1983 p. 257). The effect of the program in this sector was nothing short of dramatic. As shown in figure 1, au-

tomotive exports rose from virtually nothing in 1972 to more than $1 billion in 1980. Total exports under BEFIEX contracts increased to $8.2 billion by 1990, at which time the program was phased out as part of an overall trade liberalization. According to a GATT study (1992, p. 104), BEFIEX-linked exports eventually covered about *half* of all manufactured exports.

To an economist, perhaps the most striking thing about BEFIEX is the apparent absence of gaming between firms and the government and of renegotiation of initial contract terms. Participation in BEFIEX meant that firms were under legal obligation to live up to their export commitments, irrespective of economic circumstances such as foreign demand conditions or exchange-rate fluctuations. These were tough terms, and firms apparently lived by them. In her study of the Brazilian automotive industry, Shapiro 1993 mentions instances in which multinationals had to make adjustments to their global strategies—by cutting back exports from third countries, for example—so as not to run afoul of BEFIEX export commitments.[12] This must be confounding to economists who generally believe

[11]The "similarity test" in the quote refers to the infamous law that prohibited the importation of foreign products when similar products were available domestically.

[12]In the late 1980s, GM headquarters allowed the Brazilian subsidiary to export engines to GM-Opel (Germany) for the first time, even though the firm's global strategy had assigned the European market to its Australian subsidiary. "GM was forced to grant Brazil access to the European market . . . [because otherwise] GMB [GM-Brazil] would not have been able to meet its export commitments. . . ." (Shapiro 1993 p. 222). Fiat began to export the Uno from Brazil, even though it would not have done so without BEFIEX (ibid. p. 223).

Figure 1. Brazilian Automotive Exports

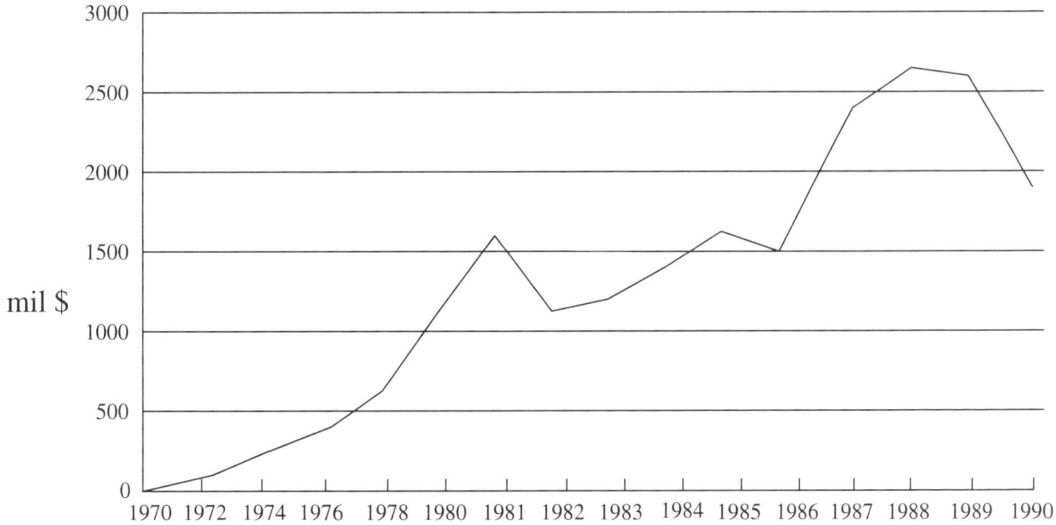

Source: Shapiro (1993, Table 5-4).

that long-term contracts are not enforceable, especially when the government is on one side, and must come under severe renegotiation pressure in response to unforeseen circumstances. In this instance the Brazilian state had the capacity to discipline firms and was perceived as such. It is difficult to envisage this kind of discipline being exerted in the countries that we will turn to next.[13]

Just as in the Korean case, the reasons for the Brazilian state's strength and autonomy in the area of export policy remain murky. Leff argues in his study of economic policy making during the earlier 1947–64 period that the Brazilian government could always act autonomously from special interest groups, and impose policy rather freely (Leff 1968). His description of Brazil is reminiscent of Jones and Sakong's 1980 analysis of Korea. On pre-1964 export policy, he writes: "policy here was made in direct opposition to the interests of major private groups, the exporters and the landed elites producing primary products, in deference instead to doctrines which commanded widespread influence among the government administrators and in elite opinion" (Leff 1968 p. 77).[14] He lists several reasons for the state's autonomy,

and notes in particular the emergence of a strong government *prior* to the development of manufacturing interests.

Evans 1992 presents a rather different picture of the Brazilian state, much less autonomous, and having to contend with important social groups. Evans notes that clientelism was rampant, that the bureaucracy had (compared to Korea, for example) much less of a tradition of meritocracy, and that there was no policy coordination within the state. "Even the military regime, which had the greatest structural potential for insulation from clientelistic pressures, proved unable to construct an administrative guidance relationship with the local industrial elite" (Evans 1992 p. 170). However, he notes the presence of "important pockets of state efficiency," mentioning in particular the state's relationship with the auto sector. The co-existence of pockets of autonomy with general state weakness rings true in light of the macroeconomic crisis in which the Brazilian state—virtually alone in Latin America—still remains deeply mired. It suggests the possibility that state strength may vary not only across time but also across sectors and issues.

---

[13]Indeed, in Turkey's case export commitments were formally demanded, but remained on paper.

[14]Hence, Leff leaves no doubt that autonomy did not come with the military coup—it existed prior to 1964. This is important because it suggests that authoritarianism need not be a pre-

condition for autonomy. Jones and Sakong also express doubt about the relationship between authoritarianism and autonomy in the case of Korea: "Until the early 1970s, the Park regime was both hard and reasonably democratic" (1980 p. 140).

Two Failures: Kenya and Bolivia

Kenya

Kenya's export subsidization policy is undistinguished in many respects, including effectiveness. The only thing that recommends it to our attention is the presence of a good study by Patrick Low 1982, who observed it at close distance.

Compared to the Korean and Brazilian programs we have just discussed, the Kenyan scheme was on paper an economist's dream: it could not have been simpler, less discretionary, or more uniform. The Local Manufactures (Export Compensation) Act of 1974 applied a straightforward 10 percent export subsidy to most manufactures. (The rate was increased to 20 percent in 1980.) The only restriction was that the value of imported goods could not amount to more than 70 percent of the value of the export. The subsidy was to be paid through commercial banks, after export proceeds were received and after government officials processed the subsidy claims.

The effects of the program were imperceptible. Low 1982 interviewed 55 firms and found that only 16 (29 percent) of them had responded by increasing exported output. The plurality of firms (17, or 31 percent) treated the subsidy simply as a windfall, while 7 firms (13 percent) did not even bother to claim the subsidy. Even more telling is Low's calculation that at the aggregate level less than 30 percent of eligible exports actually received the subsidy. A very large number of exporters either did not claim the subsidy or did not get it.

What seems to have happened is a bit of both. Government officials processing the subsidy claims exercised such zeal that many applications were rejected on trivial grounds. Low spent a day with these officials and observed two claims being rejected, "one because a date had been inadvertently omitted on a form and the other because the quadruplicate instead of the sextuplicate copy of the Export Entry form had been submitted with the claim" (1982 p. 297). The officials also took their time. More than a quarter of the firms interviewed by Low expected to wait more than six months after claims had been filed. And since the claims could not be filed before export proceeds were actually received, the total waiting time was even longer than this. The delay and unpredictability explain why many firms did not bother to claim, and why those that treated the subsidy as a lump-sum payment, did not allow it to influence their export decisions.

At a deeper level, the failure of this program must be attributed to the fact that the Kenyan government never clearly sorted out and prioritized its objectives as they impinged on the export subsidy policy. While encouraging exports (or more correctly reducing the anti-export bias due to import restrictions) was obviously an objective, it did not rank very high in the overall scheme of things. Neither was the apparent conflict with the negative fiscal implications of the program ever resolved. Note that the program was administered by the Customs and Excise Department, a revenue-raising body. Since providing the subsidy was expensive, the program as it stood was subject to a clear time inconsistency: the dynamically consistent policy was to promise to pay the subsidy but not to do so (since payment was to occur *after* exports had gone out). There was no commitment to exports on the part of the top leadership (as in Korea or Brazil) that would help resolve this dilemma on the side of exports.

In partial recognition of these problems, the government reformed the program in 1980. The subsidy was raised to 20 percent, coverage of the scheme was expanded to almost all non-traditional exports, and an attempt was made to streamline administrative procedures. Two features of the reform deserve special mention. First, the increase in the subsidy was accompanied by an equivalent 10 percent surcharge on imports. This was intended to de-emphasize fiscal considerations in the implementation of the subsidy, but is also indicative of the incoherence of policy: by the Lerner symmetry theorem, the import surcharge served to cancel the effect of the increase in the export subsidy.[15] Second, administrative responsibility for the subsidy scheme was moved from the Customs and Excise Department to the Central Bank, an institution with less stake in revenue and greater reputation for bureaucratic efficiency.

Low's study does not extend to the period after 1980, so we do not have a good account of how these reforms fared. There is reason to be skeptical however. A recent account in *The Economist* (August 14, 1993, pp. 37–38) relates the scandalous story of a Kenyan firm called Goldenberg. This firm, the sole recipient of a license to export gold and jewelry, apparently received $54 million in export subsidies from the Central Bank (amounting to 5 percent of Kenya's total exports!). Not only was the firm paid a subsidy of 35 percent (rather than 20 percent, as the law requires), but the for-

---

[15]Almost. The equivalence was not exact, of course, because there were prevailing tariffs that were generally higher than the pre-existing 10 percent export subsidy.

eign firms to which Goldenberg claimed to have shipped its exports were either fictituous or had never heard of Goldenberg. Kenya's export policy has apparently moved from the Scylla of incentive-blunting diligence to the Charybdis of corrupt generosity.

Bolivia

Between 1987 and 1991, Bolivia had an export subsidy program similar to the Kenyan scheme, which also failed for virtually identical reasons. As the authorities never resolved the conflicting objectives of safeguarding revenue versus stimulating exports, the exporters reacted by alternatively ignoring the scheme and badly abusing it.

The export subsidy introduced in July 1987 was in principle aimed at reimbursing exports for duties paid in imported inputs (hence the acronym CRA, standing for the initials for Tariff Refund Certificate in Spanish). However, rather than create an explicit drawback scheme which can be an administrative nightmare, the government sensibly set the subsidy at a uniform 10 percent for non-traditional exports and 5 percent for traditional exports. (The top rate was subsequently lowered to 6 percent in August 1990, following a tariff reduction.)

Bolivia had recently come out of a hyperinflation, with inflation running at more than 40,000 percent per annum and a budget deficit of more than 20 percent of GDP prior to the stabilization of August 1985. The authorities were naturally more than slightly nervous about the budgetary implications of the subsidy. Partly for that reason, the entry into force of the CRA was delayed. No CRA certificates were issued before April 1988, and a new regulation in September 1988 retroactively limited the benefits accruing to some of the exporters having earned CRA rights between July 1987 and April 1988. Apparently, no CRA payments were made until 1989 (see GATT 1993 table IV.8). And once payments began to be made, enterprising individuals and firms freely abused the system: there was a famous case of so-called tourist cows (*vacas turistas*) in which cow herds were led across the Bolivian borders several times, collecting CRA benefits at each crossing (GATT 1993 p. 93). The system was finally scrapped in April 1991, and replaced by a narrower scheme with lower financial benefits.

Hence we have once more a clear example of a uniform, transparent scheme which fails because: (i) delays in payments blunt incentive effects early on; and (ii) when payments are made, fraudulent practices take over and cannot be reined in. The government is then forced to narrow the scope of a scheme which has a large fiscal impact but little incentive effect.[16]

Two Intermediate Cases: Turkey and India

Turkey

Turkish economic policy experienced a radical shift to export orientation as a result of a dramatic package of measures undertaken in January 1980 by Turgut Özal (then a top technocrat, and subsequently prime minister and president). Undertaken in the midst of a macroeconomic crisis, the package included a devaluation, fiscal actions, and a series of measures designed to enhance export incentives. Alongside a flexible exchange-rate policy, the generous package of export subsidies did much to contribute to the export boom that ensued (see Arslan and van Wijnbergen 1990 and Uygur 1993 for econometric evidence linking subsidies to export supply). However, it also led to much abuse and a phenomenon that came to be called "fictitious exports"—various forms of fraud designed to take advantage of the financial incentives.

These subsidies were of many types. They comprised export tax rebates (supposedly to compensate for indirect taxes, but going well beyond them), sub-market export credits, foreign exchange allocations which conferred the right to duty-free imports, corporate tax reductions (after 1981), and additional tax rebates for enterprises exporting above a threshold (Milanović 1986, Krueger and Aktan 1992, Togan 1993). The combined ad-valorem equivalent of these subsidies rose to 34 percent in 1983, coming down thereafter to around 26 percent (see table 3). Exports were a top priority for Özal, to the point where "the success of the export drive became almost synonymous with the success of the stabilization program" (Milanović 1986 p. 73). He took pains to ensure that no obstacle stood between an exporter and his claim to a subsidy. One of his key institutional innovations was the centralization of export incentives, which had been previously dispersed among numerous government agencies, into a specific agency, the Directorate of Incentives and Implementation (TUD) within the State Planning Organization. Exporters now had to apply to the TUD

---

[16]This combination of delays with fraudulent response is apparently quite general. Additional cases appeared in Senegal and Côte d'Ivoire during the second half of the 1980s, when the governments in both cases decided to undertake a simulated devaluation by increasing import tariffs and export subsidies simultaneously.

Table 3. Export Subsidies on Manufactures in Turkey, 1980–86 (%)

	Tax Rebates	Export Credits	Foreign Exchange Retention & Allocation	VAT Exemption	Others	Total
1980	5.9	5.5	5.8	—	0.0	17.2
1981	3.6	6.4	4.9	—	4.0	15.3
1982	9.5	7.2	6.7	—	6.0	24.0
1983	11.8	7.9	13.0	—	1.5	34.2
1984	11.3	6.0	4.0	—	2.0	23.3
1985	3.1	3.2	3.9	10.0	5.8	26.0
1986	1.9	3.6	6.5	10.2	4.6	26.8

Source: Krueger and Aktan 1992 Table 14.

to obtain an "export investment certificate," which served as the basis for receiving all the subsidies discussed above. This stood in stark contrast with previous practice whereby an exporter would have to establish his standing with each agency separately. The new system was simple and rapid, and exporters could get their certificates within weeks or days (Krueger and Aktan 1992 p. 76).[17]

Obtaining the export certificate entailed the undertaking of a quantitative export commitment on whose realization the granting of incentives in principle depended (Milanović 1986 p. 6). In practice, this was a commitment that the government easily waived. According to Krueger and Aktan 1992 p. 247 fn. 5: "If, for some reason, the export was not realized, [the firms] simply notified TUD/TUB that they would not be exporting that amount, and there was no penalty." Firms believed that the authorities would impose penalties only in cases where the certificate had been obtained with no intent to export at all (ibid.).

As mentioned above, these subsidies led to widespread abuse. Documented cases included instances in which: (i) low-value items such as scrap metal or stones were exported under the guise of industrial products with high tax-rebate rates; (ii) low- or medium-grade items (such as common rugs) were over-invoiced as high-grade (silk rugs); (iii) the quantity shipped was overstated, as in the case of leather wallets whose number was blown up by a factor of 100[18]; and (iv) the most egregious of all, entire export operations took place on paper

only, with no physical transaction ever taking place (these and other cases are detailed in a popular book by Çetin 1988).

An attempt to quantify the extent of over-invoicing and other mischief that took place is shown in figure 2. These estimates are based on comparisons of Turkish export statistics with OECD statistics for imports from Turkey. The presence of over-invoicing is unmistakable. Until 1981, the calculations reveal a small *under*-invoicing, which is not surprising in view of the black-market premium for foreign currency that existed prior to the 1980 stabilization. But over the course of the first half of the 1980s, over-invoicing increased steadily, reaching more than 25 percent of export value by 1984. It thereafter decreased sharply, partly because of the decline in subsidies and partly because "fictitious exports" became a hot political issue and became risky for all but the most adventurous of firms. It should be mentioned, however, that the Turkish export boom of the 1980s looks only slightly less impressive when over-invoicing is taken into account. In other words, the boom was not a statistical illusion by any stretch of the imagination.

Özal, who was a brilliant technocrat, was fully aware of the abuses that the subsidies were giving rise to. State officials had large numbers of files on suspected abuses. But Özal firmly resisted the Turkish bureaucracy's inclination to tighten the regulations and prosecute the fraudulent cases (Çetin 1988). He feared that unleashing the bureaucracy on exporters would do more harm than good and discourage the legitimate exporter alongside the fictitious one. Put differently, unlike in the Korean and Brazilian cases, the Turkish bureaucracy could not be trusted to find the right balance between providing incentives and discouraging potential abusers. He thus understood very well

---

[17]There were occasional glitches though. In 1983 and 1984 shortage of government funds led to important arrears in both tax refunds due to exporters and interest rate rebates for export credits due to commercial banks (Milanovic 1986 p. 48).

[18]This case came to light because the exporting firm had neglected to raise the weight of the shipment by the same factor, leading to ridiculously low unit weights (Çetin 1988 p. 34).

Figure 2. Over-invoicing in Turkish Exports to the OECD

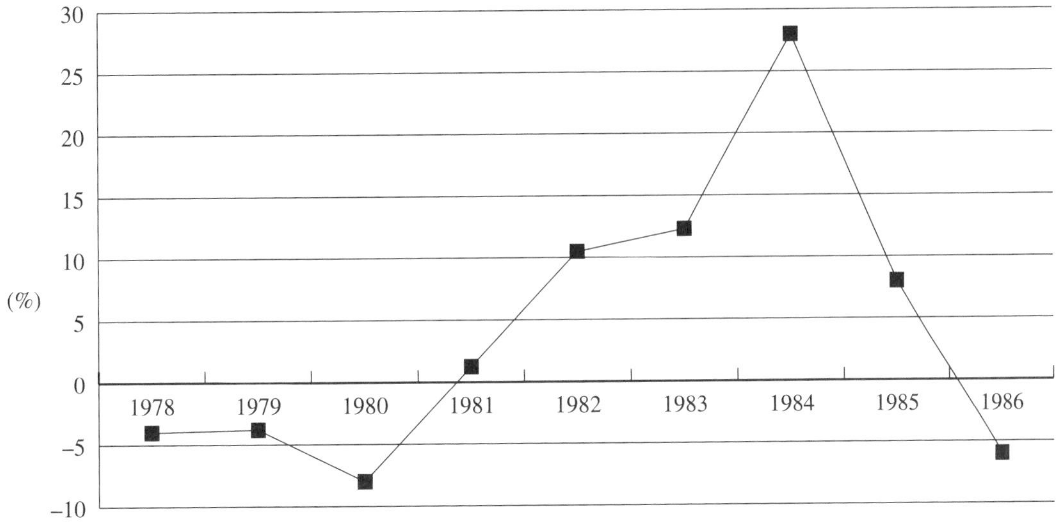

Source: Rodrik (1988)

the dilemma of a weak state: the carrot and the stick may not be available simultaneously, so one has to go with one or the other. A corollary is what we may call the second-best law for weak states: a weak state may become less effective in trying to act strong.

India

Until very recently, India was hardly known for its pro-export policies. Export subsidies of one kind or another have always been part of the Indian policy landscape, but these were greatly overshadowed by a highly restrictive import regime. Here I will focus on the period before the devaluation of 1966, on which we have the excellent and enormously detailed study by Bhagwati and Desai 1970. This is a case of mixed success, somewhat like Turkey's except less stark. The subsidies in place appear to have played a role in stimulating exports, but they also led to fraud.

Indian exporters had already access to a variety of fiscal subsidies during the late 1950s, but these were considerably strengthened in the course of the early 1960s. The most significant subsidy, on which I will concentrate, was an import entitlement scheme under which exporters were awarded import licenses in proportion to the value of their exports. According to Bhagwati and Desai 1970 p. 406, the average premiums for import licenses were of the order of 70–80 percent, so the incentive effect of this policy can be easily imagined.

Bhagwati and Desai characterize Indian state

administration in the trade policy area as "*ad hocism* at the top and corruption at the bottom" (1970 p. 134). Yet the import entitlement scheme started out as a relatively non-discretionary program with well-defined rules. Two principles were laid down at the outset to govern the scheme's administration: (i) import entitlements would not exceed 75 percent of the f.o.b. value of exports; and (ii) subject to the previous constraint, the entitlement would equal only twice the value of an exporting firm's import content (ibid. p. 409). As it turned out, these rules were frequently flouted by the authorities who were anxious to demonstrate success on the export front. Note that since subsidies consisted of import licenses, they had no immediate fiscal impact (unlike in Bolivia and Kenya), and there was consequently little inherent resistance to awarding them. In turn, the officials were aided in this by exporters themselves who naturally lobbied for the most generous terms possible. As Bhagwati and Desai put it, the increasing subsidy "reflected the growing pressure to make exports more profitable, on the part of the exporters, combined with an accommodating Ministry whose objective was to maximize export earnings" (ibid. p. 426).

Given these pressures, the Indian export subsidy scheme eventually took on a perverse quality with subsidies awarded in inverse relationship to an exporter's competitiveness. That is, exporters could get a subsidy large enough to make their exports profitable by manipulating the government: "it became generally possible to ask the Ministry of International Trade for *ad hoc* entitlements, for chemical and engineering exports, to make up for any ostensible difference between the domestic sale price of a product and its supposed f.o.b. export price plus the subsidy normally available" (ibid. pp. 465–66). Bhagwati and Desai also note that the scheme resulted in significant over-invoicing, as in Turkey.[19]

For all its problems, Bhagwati and Desai credit the export subsidies of the period as being "undoubtedly instrumental in sustaining the spurt in the Indian export performance during the Third Plan [April 1961–March 1966]" (ibid. p. 429).

Concluding Remarks

These stories reveal a wide variety of experience with export subsidies. Policies that look identical on the books often produce different results, and policies that appear ex ante well designed frequently result in failure. Perhaps the greatest surprise is that the most successful programs in our sample were the ones in which state officials exercised the greatest discretion, applied the least uniformity (at least ex ante), and interacted the most intensively with firms. The other cases, however, make clear that these successful experiences cannot easily be replicated in settings characterized by weak states.[20]

The message that comes out of the cases is both pessimistic and optimistic as regards state capabilities. On the one hand, the importance of state autonomy, which seems to be determined largely by historical and structural factors, underscores the

point that the range of options open to most governments may be fairly limited. On the other hand, policy coherence alone counts for something: weak states can achieve some of their objectives if their priorities are sufficiently crystallized and if they are creative in designing appropriate institutional frameworks. Centralizing subsidy functions in a high-visibility agency (as in Turkey) or processing claims through the trade ministry rather than the finance ministry (as in India) are examples of institutional considerations that may make a large difference in practice. Priorities are most clearly articulated and communicated when there exists political commitment on the part of the top leadership: in Korea, Brazil, Turkey, success derived in part from the clear, unmitigated commitment to exports by new regimes. The case of export subsidies shows that normally incoherent states can produce coherent policies when they attach a sufficiently high priority to them. On the other hand, nothing is more distinctive about weak states than a multiplicity of conflicting government objectives.

---

[19]They point out that partner-country trade statistics were not helpful to get a sense of the magnitude of over-invoicing in this case because the over-invoicing occurred with free ports like Aden, Hong Kong, and Panama.

[20]It is useful to interject here Hernando de Soto's poignant complaints about the unpredictability of policy-making in Peru: "It is simply untrue that, in Peru, we are all equal before the law, because no two people pay the same tax, no two imports are taxed in the same way, no two exports are subsidized in the same way, and no two individuals have the same right to credit. . . . Uncertainty is constant in the redistributive state, for the Peruvians are aware that the executive branch, which issues some 110 regulations and decisions each working day, can change the rules of the game at any moment without prior consultation or debate" (1989 pp. 195–199). These complaints ring true to anyone who has observed policy making in developing countries. The trouble is that, absent the reference to the redistributive state, this statement is equally valid for Korean policy making. Jones and Sakong resolve the paradox in the following manner: "the lesson of the Korean case is that in a hard state with leadership commitment to growth, the Myrdalian objections to discretionary controls on economic grounds may be obviated. Just as compulsion is necessary, so also is discretion. Both mechanisms are potentially subject to great abuse, and their use constitutes a high-risk/high-gain strategy which is feasible only in a Myrdalian hard state" (1980 p. 139).

References

Amsden, Alice H. 1989. *Asia's Next Giant: South Korea and Late Industrialization.* New York: Oxford University Press.

Arslan, İsmail, and Sweder van Wijnbergen. 1990. "Turkey: Export Miracle or Accounting Trick?" Washington, DC: World Bank Discussion Paper WPS 370.

Balassa, Bela. 1978. "Export Incentives and Export Performance in Developing Countries: A Comparative Analysis," *Weltwirtschaftliches Archiv* 114: 24–61.

Barkey, Karen, and Sunita Parikh. 1991. "Comparative Perspectives on the State," *Annual Review of Sociology* 17: 523–49.

Bhagwati, Jagdish N., and Padma Desai. 1970. *India: Planning for Industrialization.* London: Oxford University Press.

Calvo, Guillermo. 1989. "Incredible Reforms," in G. Calvo et al. (eds.), *Debt, Stabilization, and Development: Essays in Honor of Carlos Diaz-Alejandro.* New York: Basil Blackwell.

Clements, Benedict J. 1988. *Foreign Trade Strategies, Employment, and Income Distribution in Brazil.* New York: Praeger.

Çetin, Bilal. 1988. *Soygun: Hayali İhracatın Boyutları* [Hold-Up: Dimensions of Fictitious Exporting]. Ankara: Bilgi Yayınları.

De Soto, Hernando. 1989. *The Other Path: The Invisible Revolution in the Third World.* New York: Harper & Row.

Dixit, Avinash. 1989. "Trade and Insurance with Adverse Selection," *Review of Economic Studies* 56: 235–47.

Evans, Peter. 1979. *Dependent Development: The Alliance of Multinationals, State, and Local Capital in Brazil.* Princeton, NJ: Princeton University Press.

Evans, Peter. 1992. "The State as Problem and Solution: Predation, Embedded Autonomy, and Structural Change," in S. Haggard and R. Kaufman (eds.), *The Politics of Adjustment.* Princeton, NJ: Princeton University Press.

Fasano-Filho, Ugo, Bernard Fischer, and Peter Nunnenkamp. 1987. *On the Determinants of Brazil's Manufactured Exports: An Empirical Analysis.* Tubingen: J.C.B. Mohr (Paul Siebeck).

Frank, Charles R., Jr., Kwang Suk Kim, and Larry E. Westphal. 1975. *Foreign Trade Regimes and Economic Development: South Korea.* New York and London: Columbia University Press.

Fritsch, Winston, and Gustavo H.B. Franco. 1992. "Brazil as an Exporter of Manufacturers," unpublished manuscript.

GATT. 1992. *Trade Policy Review Mechanism: Brazil.* Geneva: GATT.

GATT. 1993. *Trade Policy Review Mechanism: Bolivia.* Geneva: GATT.

Grossman, Gene, and Elhanan Helpman. 1992. "Protection for Sale," unpublished manuscript, Princeton University.

Jones, Leroy P., and Il Sakong. 1980. *Government, Business, and Entrepreneurship in Economic Development: The Korean Case.* Cambridge, MA: Harvard University Press.

Jung, Woo S., and Gyu Lee. 1986. "The Effectiveness of Export Promotion Policies: The Case of Korea," *Weltwirtschaftliches Archiv* 122: 340–357.

Krueger, Anne O. 1974. "The Political Economy of the Rent-Seeking Society," *American Economic Review* 64: 291–303.

Krueger, Anne O., and Okan H. Aktan. 1992. *Swimming Against the Tide: Turkish Trade Reform in the 1980s.* San Francisco: ICS Press.

Leff, Nathaniel H. 1968. *Economic Policy-Making and Development in Brazil 1947–1964.* New York: John Wiley & Sons.

Levy, Brian. 1993. "An Institutional Analysis of the Design and Sequencing of Trade and Investment Policy Reform," *The World Bank Economic Review* 7: 247–262.

Low, Patrick. 1982. "Export Subsidies and Trade Policy: The Experience of Kenya," *World Development* 10: 293–304.

Matsuyama, Kiminori. 1990. "Perfect Equilibria in a Trade Liberalization Game," *American Economic Review* 80: 480–92.

Migdal, Joel. 1988. *Strong Societies and Weak States.* Princeton, NJ: Princeton University Press.

Milanović, Branko. 1986. *Export Incentives and Turkish Manufactured Exports, 1980–1984,* The World Bank, Staff Working Papers No. 768, Washington, DC.

Myrdal, Gunnar. 1968. *Asian Drama: An Inquiry into the Poverty of Nations.* New York: Pantheon.

Nogués, Julio. 1990. "The Experience of Latin America with Export Subsidies," *Weltwirtschaftliches Archiv* 126: 97–115.

Panagariya, Arvind. 1993. "Unravelling the Mysteries of China's Foreign Trade Regime," *The World Economy* 16: 51–68.

Pindyck, Robert S., and Andrés Solimano. 1993. "Economic Instability and Aggregate Investment," NBER Working Paper No. 4380.

Rhee, Yung Whee, Bruce Ross-Larson, and Garry Pursell. 1984. *Korea's Competitive Edge: Managing the Entry into World Markets.* Baltimore and London: The Johns Hopkins University Press.

Rodrik, Dani. 1991. "Policy Uncertainty and Private Investment in Developing Countries," *Journal of Development Economics* 36: 229–242.

Rodrik, Dani. 1992. "Political Economy and Development Policy," *European Economic Review* 36: 329–336.

Shapiro, Helen. 1993. "Automobiles: From Import Substitution to Export Promotion in Brazil and Mexico," in D. Yoffie (ed.), *Beyond Free Trade: Firms, Governments, and Global Competition.* Boston, MA: Harvard Business School Press.

Shleifer, Andrei, and Robert Vishny. 1991. "Pervasive Shortages under Socialism," NBER Working Paper No. 3791.

Staiger, Robert W., and Guido Tabellini. 1987. "Discretionary Trade Policy and Excessive Protection," *American Economic Review* 77:823–837.

Thomas, Vinod, and John Nash. 1991. "Reform of Trade Policy: Recent Evidence from Theory and Practice," *The World Bank Research Observer* 6: 219–240.

Togan, Sübidey. 1993. "How to Assess the Significance of Export Incentives: An Application to Turkey," Bilkent University (forthcoming, *Weltwirtschaftliches Archiv*).

Uygur, Ercan. 1993. "Trade Policies and Economic Performance in Turkey in the 1980s," unpublished paper, Faculty of Political Science, Ankara University.

Westphal, Larry E. 1990. "Industrial Policy in an Export-Propelled Economy: Lessons from South Korea's Exprience," *Journal of Economic Perspectives* 4: 41–59.

World Bank. 1983. *Brazil: Industrial Policies and Manufactured Exports.* Washington, DC.

Selection IX.C.4. Bureaucratic Structure and Bureaucratic Performance in Less Developed Countries*

I. Introduction

. . . In this paper we will be especially concerned with ratings of the performance of the central government bureaucracy. Knack and Keefer (1995) use ratings by the International Country Risk Guide (ICRG) of "corruption in government" and "bureaucratic quality" in one of their indices of institutional quality and use a rating by Business and Environmental Risk Intelligence (BERI) of "bureaucratic delays" in the other, and Mauro (1995) uses ratings by Business International (BI) of "bureaucracy and red tape" and "corruption" in his index of bureaucratic efficiency. Knack and Keefer find positive and significant effects of both of their institutional quality indices on growth in per capita GDP, and Mauro finds the same for his index of bureaucratic efficiency.

While the cross-country statistical evidence reinforces the idea that differential governmental performance may have an impact on economic growth, it tells us little about what kind of institutional characteristics are associated with lower levels of corruption or red tape. If the findings just listed are meaningful, it is worth identifying which characteristics of government bureaucracies lead to good ratings from the ICRG, BERI, and BI on the variables cited above. This is our aim in the present paper. . . .

Our data collection and analysis will be guided by what we call the "Weberian state hypothesis." Drawing on the original insight of Weber (1968 [1904–1911]), Evans (1992, 1995) argues that replacement of a patronage system for state officials by a professional state bureaucracy is a necessary (though not sufficient) condition for a state to be "developmental." The key institutional characteristics of what he calls "Weberian" bureaucracy include meritocratic recruitment through competitive examinations, civil service procedures for hiring and firing rather than political appointments and dismissals, and filling higher levels of the hierarchy through internal promotion.

To test the Weberian state hypothesis (actually several related hypotheses), we collected original data on various elements of bureaucratic structure for 35 countries. The next section of this paper describes our hypotheses more fully and contrasts them with other views of the determinants of bureaucratic performance. . . .

II. Theoretical Approach

In the economics literature, bureaucratic performance is typically addressed using a principal-agent model. The case studies described by Klitgaard (1988) leave little doubt that a powerful and determined outside monitor (principal) can reduce corruption and improve delivery of services by his bureaucratic agents. Milgrom and Roberts (1992) give a comprehensive theoretical treatment of the strategies a principal can use to elicit better performance from his agents, such as performance-based pay and (implicit) tournaments among employees for higher-level positions.[1] These strategies have been incorporated into "the new public management" (Aucoin 1990, Caiden 1988), which to date has been applied most extensively in New Zealand (Boston et al. 1991).

A drawback of the principal-agent approach is that to some extent it assumes away the problem, especially in an LDC context, because the political will to engage in vigorous monitoring and implement appropriate strategies is lacking, or worse yet the principal is himself corrupt. Rose-Ackerman (1997, p. 48) notes that "behind all proposals for civil service reform is an effective set of internal controls or of antibribery laws with vigorous enforcement," leaving one to wonder what can be done if vigorous enforcement is not available. It follows that reforms that make weaker demands on outside monitors or the political system for their implementation and enforcement are of considerable interest.

We believe that the reforms that constitute the Weberian state have this property. Enforcement of meritocratic recruitment requires verification of whether entry into government service has been conditioned on passage of a civil service exam or attainment of a university degree. Implementation of internal promotion requires that higher-level agency positions be filled by current agency employees or at least current members of the civil service. Maintenance of competitive salaries requires

---

*From James E. Rauch and Peter B. Evans, "Bureaucratic Structure and Bureaucratic Performance in Less Developed Countries," *Journal of Public Economics* 75 (January 2000): 49–62.

[1]Another strand of the literature addresses the effects of interagency competition on corruption (Rose-Ackerman 1978, Shleifer and Vishny 1993). In this paper we examine only intraagency bureaucratic structure.

a simple comparison with private sector numbers. It is precisely the relative ease with which one can observe whether and to what extent these rules are being followed that makes possible our empirical analysis below. In contrast, consider the effort that must be made to evaluate "performance" in pay-for-performance schemes (Milgrom and Roberts 1992, pp. 464–469), or the initiative that must be taken to implement "strong financial management systems that audit government accounts and make financial information about the government public" (Rose-Ackerman 1997, pp. 49–50).

How do the ingredients of the Weberian state combine to produce good bureaucratic performance? We first present an argument based on Evans (1992, 1995). Making entry to the bureaucracy conditional on passing a civil service exam or attaining a university degree, and paying salaries comparable to those for private positions requiring similar skills and responsibility, should produce a capable pool of officials. The stability provided by internal promotion allows formation of stronger ties among them. This improves communication, and therefore effectiveness. It also increases each official's concern with what his colleagues think of him, leading to greater adherence to norms of behavior. Since the officials entered the bureaucracy on the basis of merit, effective performance is likely to be a valued attribute among them rather than, say, how much one can accomplish on behalf of one's clan. The long-term career rewards generated by a system of internal promotion should reinforce adherence to codified rules of behavior. Ideally, a sense of commitment to corporate goals and "esprit de corps" develop.

The work of Rauch (1995) attempts to marry the Weberian state hypothesis to a principal-agent framework. Internal promotion is defined as recruiting the principal from the ranks of the agents. Only the principal exercises power in the sense of deciding (or at least influencing) the mix of services the bureaucracy will supply. Individuals are assumed to differ in their desire to impose their preferences over collective goods on the public. Imposing preferences requires that the bureaucracy as a whole be effective in fulfilling its mission. A principal who values exercise of power highly will spend more time supervising her agents to ensure that they are carrying out their tasks (and thereby implementing her preferences), and less time looking for ways to line her own pockets. With internal promotion, agents who hope to exercise power themselves will be more responsive to any effective supervision in order to increase their chances of becoming principal. Since agents who care about

power are more likely to become principal, principals are more likely to care about power and therefore supervise their agents more closely. It follows that given any positive initial level of supervision, internal promotion generates a virtuous circle that increases (in expectation) the value the principal places on exercise of power, tending to increase the extent to which the bureaucracy as a whole carries out its assigned tasks of public goods provision and decrease the extent to which it implicitly taxes the private sector through large-scale corruption. Competitive salaries and meritocratic recruitment are of only secondary importance for bureaucratic performance in this model.

The arguments of both Evans (1992, 1995) and Rauch (1995) for the virtues of the Weberian state are based largely on the effects of selection and the development of norms. A more standard incentive-based analysis may reach different conclusions. Regarding meritocratic recruitment, a civil service system typically entails not only examinations but also civil service protection, and it could be argued that bureaucrats with civil service protection are less motivated to perform since it is more difficult to fire them. In other words, a civil service system entails worse monitoring conditions for the bureaucracy. . . . Exams and other credentials may not select for relevant skills but instead may function mainly as barriers to entry that shield incumbent officials from competition from qualified outsiders. Similarly, internal promotion may simply prevent the best candidates from being appointed to higher positions when they are open.[2] Only regarding the benefits of competitive salaries will the standard analysis agree, pointing in particular to the reduction in the incentives to take bribes given the presumed reduction in the marginal utility of income and increase in the disutility of being fired if one is caught in corrupt activity.

In the long run, however, we feel that there is no contradiction between the Weberian approach to bureaucratic reform and "the new public management." Instead, the former can be seen as part of the preconditions for implementing the latter, as suggested by the following quotation from a World Bank debate (Bale and Dale 1998, Schick 1998) over the applicability of New Zealand's reforms to LDCs (p. 116):

The following precedents formed the basis for the reforms adopted in New Zealand: a tradition of a political-

---

[2] Overall, the Weberian state hypothesis is similar to a "Williamsonian" (1985) argument that governance structures that limit the extent of competition may sometimes have more than compensating benefits.

ly neutral, relatively competent civil service; little concern about corruption or nepotism; a consistent and well-enforced legal code, including contract law; a well-functioning political market; and a competent, but suppressed, private sector. The right reform mix for any developing country must reflect any major differences in these preconditions; New Zealand's reforms cannot simply be transplanted.

III. Collection of Original Data

Our collection of data on bureaucratic structure proceeded in three steps. First, we developed and pretested a survey to be filled out by country experts. Second, we identified a sample of countries for which we thought it was feasible to collect accurate data on the core economic agencies. Third, we sent out the final version of our survey with the goal of obtaining responses from at least three experts per country for purposes of cross-validation. We met this goal in all but three cases (see Table 1). . . .

Feasibility and maintenance of data quality required us to sample less than the entire universe of countries. The same concerns led us to restrict our coverage of agencies within a country. We chose to focus on the core economic agencies.[3] . . . Using our data on the bureaucratic structure of core economic agencies to explain the privately produced measures of bureaucratic performance cited in the Introduction creates a problem if these agencies are, for example, "pockets of efficiency" with bureaucratic structures that are more "Weberian" than is typical of the rest of the state bureaucracy. Since these measures of bureaucratic performance are intended to serve the needs of transnational investors, this problem may be somewhat mitigated if these investors mainly deal with officials who are employed by (or heavily influenced by) the core economic agencies. . . .

The [survey] questions that we deemed relevant for this study, and their codings, are reproduced in Table 2. We used the average of the coded expert responses for each country.[4] These questions were

[3]The respondents were asked to choose "the four most important agencies in the central state bureaucracy in order of their power to shape overall economic policy." The Ministry of Finance was the most commonly listed agency, followed at a distance by the Planning Ministry/Board and Ministry of Trade/Commerce/Industry. Other agencies represented include the President's/Prime Minister's office (or Royal Palace), Central Bank, and Ministry of Defense.

[4]For all questions used in the analysis below, the between-country variance far outweighed the variance among experts assessing the same country.

Table 1. Sample of 35 Countries World Bank Country ID and Number of Expert Survey Respondents Per Country

Country	ID	Number
Argentina	ARG	3
Brazil	BRA	4
Chile	CHL	4
Cote D'Ivoire	CIV	3
Colombia	COL	4
Costa Rica	CRI	3
Dominican Republic	DOM	5
Ecuador	ECU	3
Egypt	EGY	3
Greece	GRC	5
Guatemala	GTM	4
Haiti	HTI	4
Hong Kong	HKG	3
India	IND	3
Israel	ISR	3
Kenya	KEN	3
(S.) Korea	KOR	3
Malaysia	MYS	3
Mexico	MEX	4
Morocco	MAR	2
Nigeria	NGA	3
Pakistan	PAK	3
Peru	PER	5
Philippines	PHL	4
Portugal	PRT	4
Singapore	SGP	4
Spain	ESP	5
Sri Lanka	LKA	5
Syria	SYR	4
Taiwan	OAN	4
Thailand	THA	2
Tunisia	TUN	5
Turkey	TUR	4
Uruguay	URY	2
Zaire	ZAR	3

almost always answered in terms of an assessment of the period 1970–1990 as a whole. The questions virtually always require quantitative rather than qualitative answers in order to minimize the possibility that the expert responses would be influenced by their perceptions of bureaucratic performance, thereby introducing spurious correlation between our measures of bureaucratic structure and the ratings of bureaucratic performance we seek to explain.

Questions 4–5 in Table 2 address the extent to which recruitment is meritocratic at the entry level. *MERIT* is an equal-weight index of the two questions, where each question and the index itself have

Table 2. Construction of Bureaucratic Structure Indices from Survey Responses

[We are interested primarily in what these bureaucracies looked like in the recent past, roughly 1970–1990. In answering the following questions, assume that "higher officials" refers to those who hold roughly the top 500 positions in the core economic agencies you have discussed above.]

Q4. Approximately what proportion of the higher officials in these agencies enter the civil service via a formal examination system?
   Codes: 1 = less than 30%, 2 = 30%–60%, 3 = 60%–90%, 4 = more than 90%

Q5. Of those that do *not* enter via examinations, what proportion have university or post-graduate degrees?
   Codes: 1= less than 30%, 2 = 30%–60%, 3 = 60%–90%, 4 = more than 90%

$$MERIT \text{ index} = [(Q4 - 1)/3 + (Q5 - 1)/3]/2$$

Q6. Roughly how many of the top levels in these agencies are political appointees (e.g., appointed by the President or Chief Executive)?
   Codes: 1 = none, 2 = just agency chiefs, 3 = agency chiefs and vice-chiefs, 4 = all of top 2 or 3 levels.

Q7. Of political appointees to these positions, what proportion are likely to already be members of the higher civil service?
   Codes: 1 = less than 30%, 2 = 30%–70%, 3 = more than 70%

Q8. Of those promoted to the top 2 or 3 levels in these agencies (whether or not they are political appointees), what proportion come from within the agency itself or (its associated ministry(ies) if the agency is not itself a ministry)?
   Codes: 1 = less than 50%, 2 = 50%–70%, 3 = 70%–90%, 4 = over 90%

Q10. What is roughly the modal number of years spent by a typical higher-level official in one of these agencies during his career?
   Codes: 1 = 1–5 years, 2 = 5–10 years, 3 = 10–20 years, 4 = entire career

Q11. What prospects for promotion can someone who enters one of these agencies through a higher civil service examination early in his/her career reasonably expect? Assuming that there are at least a half dozen steps or levels between an entry-level position and the head of the agency, how would you characterize the possibilities for moving up in the agency?
   Codes: 2, if respondent circled "if performance is superior, moving up several levels to the level just below political appointees is not an unreasonable expectation" or "in at least a few cases, could expect to move up several levels within the civil service and then move up to the very top of the agency on the basis of political appointments" and *not* "in most cases, will move up one or two levels but no more" or "in most cases, will move up three or four levels, but unlikely to reach the level just below political appointees"; 1 otherwise.

$$CAREER \text{ index} = [(4 - Q6)/3 + (Q7 - 1)/2 + (Q8 - 1)/3 + (Q10 - 1)/3 + (Q11 - 1)]/5$$

Q14. How would you estimate the salaries (and perquisites, not including bribes or other extralegal sources of income) of higher officials in these agencies relative to those of private sector managers with roughly comparable training and responsibilities?
   Codes: 1 = less than 50%, 2 = 50%–80%, 3 = 80%–90%, 4 = comparable, 5 = higher

Q16. Over the period in question (roughly 1970–1990) what was the movement of legal income in these agencies relative to salaries in the private sector?
   Codes: 1 = declined dramatically, 2 = declined slightly, 3 = maintained the same position, 4 = improved their position

$$SALARY \text{ index} = [(Q14 - 1)/4 + (Q16 - 1)/3]/2$$

---

been normalized to lie in the range 0–1. Question 8, and to a lesser extent questions 6, 7, and 11, pertain to the extent of internal promotion, whereas question 10 addresses career stability. *CAREER* is an equal-weight index of questions 6–8 and 10–11. Question 14 concerns the level and question 16 concerns the change of bureaucratic compensation relative to the private sector. *SALARY* is an equal-weight index of these two questions. . . .

IV. Testing the Weberian State Hypotheses

We will seek to explain the cross-country variation in the five measures of bureaucratic performance, cited in the Introduction, that are available to us from private ratings services. These are described in Table 3, listed in the order in which we will use them as dependent variables in the data analysis. Two of these measures require additional

Table 3. Available Measures of Bureaucratic Performance

Variable	Country Coverage	Time Coverage	Definition
CORRUPT1 Source: ICRG Scored 0–6	complete	1982–1990	Low scores indicate "high government officials are likely to demand special payments" and "illegal payments are generally expected throughout lower levels of government" in the form of "bribes connected with import and export licenses, exchange controls, tax assessment, police protection, or loans" (quoted from Knack and Keefer 1995)
BURQUAL Source: ICRG Scored 0–6	complete	1982–1990	High scores indicate "autonomy from political pressure" and "strength and expertise to govern without drastic changes in policy or interruptions in government services"; also existence of an "established mechanism for recruiting and training" (quoted from Knack and Keefer 1995).
BURDELAY Source: BERI Scored 1–4	missing Costa Rica, Dominican Republic, Guatemala, Haiti, Hong Kong, Sri Lanka, Syria, Tunisia, and Uruguay	1972–1990	High scores indicate greater "speed and efficiency of the civil service including processing customs clearances, foreign exchange remittances and similar applications" (quoted from Knack and Keefer 1995).
REDTAPE Source: BI Scored 0–10	missing Costa Rica, Guatemala, Syria, and Tunisia	1981–1989; only certain years in this period for a few countries	Measures "the regulatory environment foreign firms must face when seeking approvals and permits; the degree to which government represents an obstacle to business" (quoted from Mauro 1995); lower scores indicate greater levels of regulation and/or government obstruction.
CORRUPT2 Source: BI Scored 0–10	missing Costa Rica, Guatemala, Syria, and Tunisia	1981–1989; only certain years in this period for a few countries	Measures "the degree to which business transactions involve corruption or questionable payments" (quoted from Mauro 1995); lower scores indicate greater levels of corruption.

comment. First, the definition of BURQUAL indicates that it measures not only an aspect of bureaucratic performance but also some of the same elements of bureaucratic structure that are addressed by our survey. It follows that while a positive and significant effect of our indices on this variable provides some information, in the absence of similar effects on other measures of bureaucratic performance such a finding could not be considered important evidence in favor of our hypotheses. Second, it should be noted that unlike COR-RUPT1, CORRUPT2 is not necessarily an indicator of bureaucratic performance: it is not clear whether the "corruption or questionable payments" in the definition are made to government officials or to private sector managers such as purchasing agents. . . .

In attempting to explain these measures of bureaucratic performance, the question arises as to

what control variables to include along with our measures of bureaucratic structure. Rauch and Evans (1999, Figure 1a) show a strong tendency for high income countries to have high bureaucratic performance ratings, and Weberian state characteristics are also likely to be positively correlated with country income, so it seems clear that we should control for level of development. Our measure of level of development, RGDP, will be GDP per capita at the beginning of the time period for which the dependent variable is available, corrected for differences in purchasing power across countries (Summers and Heston 1991). It also seems prudent to control for country level of education. Countries with higher levels of education may be more likely to adopt meritocratic recruitment procedures, and at the same time education could affect bureaucratic performance by enabling the population to better monitor the state bureaucracy, and may also help on

Table 4. Testing the Weberian State Hypotheses

Dependent Variable	CORRUPT1	CORRUPT1	BURQUAL	BURQUAL	BURDELAY	BURDELAY	REDTAPE	REDTAPE	CORRUPT2	CORRUPT2
Intercept	0.762	0.751	1.344	1.391	0.724	0.783	1.986	3.621	2.588	2.487
	(0.542)	(0.344)	(0.526)	(0.354)	(0.248)	(0.176)	(1.024)	(0.513)	(1.190)	(0.756)
MERIT	2.175[c]	1.671[a]	2.287[b]	2.032[a]	0.067	0.589[b]	1.832		2.544	
	(1.108)	(0.542)	(1.074)	(0.558)	(0.521)	(0.267)	(2.138)		(2.485)	
CAREER	-0.876		-0.468		0.580		-0.514		-1.407	
	(1.391)		(1.349)		(0.592)		(2.513)		(2.921)	
SALARY	0.451		0.810		1.161[a]	1.220[a]	1.998		-1.368	
	(0.849)		(0.823)		(0.348)	(0.307)	(1.548)		(1.800)	
RGDP	0.000332[a]	0.000373[a]	0.000119	0.000136[b]	0.000010	0.000084[b]	0.000276	0.000509[a]	0.000370[c]	0.000382[b]
	(0.000097)	(0.000063)	(0.000094)	(0.000064)	(0.000058)	(0.000036)	(0.000178)	(0.000121)	(0.000207)	(0.000167)
HUMCAP	0.036		-0.009		0.099[c]		0.239		0.333	0.418[b]
	(0.101)		(0.098)		(0.052)		(0.189)		(0.220)	(0.198)
ETHFRAC	-0.0015		-0.0014		-0.000326		-0.0018		-0.0052	
	(0.0059)		(0.0058)		(0.0024)		(0.0112)		(0.0130)	
n	32	35	32	35	23	26	28	31	28	28
R^2	0.672	0.666	0.505	0.442	0.698	0.636	0.558	0.378	0.545	0.507
Root MSE	0.825	0.754	0.799	0.776	0.289	0.281	1.432	1.534	1.664	1.587

1970 value of *HUMCAP* and *RGDP* for *BURDELAY*; 1980 value of *HUMCAP* and *RGDP* for all other dependent variables. Standard errors in parentheses.

[a]Significant at the one percent level.
[b]Significant at the five percent level.
[c]Significant at the ten percent level.

the supply side by improving the pool of applicants for the officialdom. Our education measure, *HUM-CAP,* is the average years of schooling in the population over age 25, as compiled by Barro and Lee (1993). This variable is available only at five-year intervals, is missing for three countries in our sample (Cote d'Ivoire, Morocco, and Nigeria), and is available only in 1975 for Egypt. Except for Egypt, we use the 1980 value to explain all dependent variables except *BURDELAY,* for which we use the 1970 value. (For consistency we also use the 1980 or 1970 values of *RGDP.*) Finally, we control for the ethnic diversity of a country. Easterly and Levine (1997) present both arguments and country anecdotes supporting the view that ethnic diversity generates more competition for government-created rents, leading to greater corruption and poorer bureaucratic performance generally. At the same time, if government patronage is organized along ethnic lines, ethnic diversity may make it more difficult to replace a clientelistic bureaucratic structure with a more rule-based one. We use the same measure of ethnolinguistic fractionalization used by Mauro (1995) and Easterly and Levine (1997), pertaining to the year 1960 and originally collected by the Department of Geodesy and Cartography of the State Geological Committee of the Soviet Union. The variable, *ETHFRAC,* measures the probability that two randomly selected individuals in a country will belong to different ethnolinguistic groups.

In Table 4 we report two ordinary least-squares regressions for each measure of bureaucratic performance, where the dependent variables are the time averages of the variables in Table 3. The first regression for each dependent variable contains all the bureaucratic structure indices and control variables, while the second regression is a more parsimonious specification that results from retaining all explanatory variables that are statistically significant in the first regression, plus any that is significant when added back individually to a regression containing only the significant variables. . . .

Table 4 shows that bureaucratic structure indices are statistically significant determinants of the bureaucratic performance measures produced by the ICRG and by BERI but not of the bureaucratic performance measures produced by BI. *MERIT* is retained in the more parsimonious specifications for the ICRG and BERI measure of bureaucratic performance while *SALARY* is retained in the more parsimonious specification for the BERI measure of bureaucratic performance only. Among the control variables, *RGDP* is retained in the more parsimonious specifications for all five

measures of bureaucratic performance and *HUM-CAP* is retained in the more parsimonious specification for *CORRUPT2* only, though . . . it could have been retained instead of *RGDP* in the *BUR-DELAY* equation. *ETHFRAC* is not a statistically significant determinant of any measure of bureaucratic performance. . . .

These results indicate that meritocratic recruitment is the element of Weberian bureaucracy that is most important for improving bureaucratic performance. Internal promotion and career stability are at best of secondary importance, given that *CAREER* is a statistically significant determinant of bureaucratic performance only when *MERIT* is omitted. Whether or not competitive salaries have any effect on bureaucratic performance is unclear.

References

Aucoin, P., 1990. Administrative reform in public management: paradigms, principles, paradoxes, and pendulums. *Governance* 3(1), 115–137.

Bale, M., Dale, T., 1998. Public sector reform in New Zealand and its relevance to developing countries. *World Bank Research Observer* 13(1), 103–121.

Barro, R. J., Lee, J., 1993. International comparisons of educational attainment. *Journal of Monetary Economics* 32(3), 363–394.

Boston, J., Martin, J., Pallot, J., Walsh, P. (Eds), 1991. *Reshaping the State: New Zealand's Bureaucratic Revolution.* Oxford University Press, Auckland.

Caiden, G., 1988. The vitality of administrative reform. *International Review of Administrative Sciences* 54(3), 331–358.

Easterly, W., Levine, R., 1997. Africa's growth tragedy: policies and ethnic divisions. *Quarterly Journal of Economics* 112(4), 1203–1250.

Evans, P. B., 1992. The state as problem and solution: predation, embedded autonomy, and structural change. In: Haggard, S., Kaufman, R. R. (Eds), *The Politics of Economic Adjustment.* Princeton University Press, Princeton, NJ, pp. 139–191.

Evans, P. B., 1995. *Embedded Autonomy: States and Industrial Transformation.* Princeton University Press, Princeton, NJ.

Knack, S., Keefer, P., 1995. Institutions and economic performance: cross-country tests using alternative institutional measures. *Economics and Politics* 7(3), 207–227.

Klitgaard, R., 1988. *Controlling Corruption.* University of California Press, Berkeley, CA.

Mauro, P., 1995. Corruption and growth. *Quarterly Journal of Economics* 110(3), 681–712.

Milgrom, P., Roberts, J., 1992. *Economics, Organization, and Management.* Prentice-Hall, Englewood Cliffs, NJ.

Rauch, J. E., 1995. Choosing a dictator: bureaucracy and welfare in less developed polities. National Bureau of Economic Research Working Paper No. 5196.

Rauch, J. E., Evans, P. B., 1999. Bureaucratic structure and bureaucratic performance in less developed countries. UCSD Discussion Paper No. 99–06.

Rose-Ackerman, S., 1978. *Corruption: A Study in Political Economy.* Academic Press, New York.

Rose-Ackerman, S., 1997. The political economy of corruption. In: Elliott, K. A. (Ed), *Corruption and the Global Economy.* Institute for International Economics, Washington, D.C., pp. 31–60.

Schick, A., 1998. Why most developing countries should not try New Zealand's reforms. *World Bank Research Observer* 13(1), 123–131.

Shleifer, A., Vishny, R. W., 1993. Corruption. *Quarterly Journal of Economics* 108(3), 599–617.

Summers, R., Heston, A., 1991. The Penn World Table (Mark 5): an expanded set of international comparisons, 1950–1988. *Quarterly Journal of Economics* 106(2), 327–368.

Weber, M., 1968 [1904–1911]. *Economy and Society.* Roth, G., Wittich, C. (Eds), Bedminster Press, New York.

Williamson, O. E., 1985. *The Economic Institutions of Capitalism: Firms, Markets, Relational Contracting.* Free Press, New York.

World Bank, 1993. *The East Asian Miracle: Economic Growth and Public Policy.* Oxford University Press, New York.

CHAPTER X

Development and the Environment

Overview: Environmental Problems in Less Versus More Developed Countries

Concern with environmental degradation that began in the industrialized countries in the 1960s and 1970s extended to the less developed countries by the 1980s. The most pressing issues in the latter countries are not necessarily the same as in the former countries, however. A particularly dramatic example is "indoor air pollution," of which the World Bank states in the first selection of this chapter:

> For hundreds of millions of the world's poorer citizens, smoke and fumes from indoor use of biomass fuel (such as wood, straw, and dung) pose much greater health risks than any outdoor pollution. Women and children suffer most from this form of pollution, and its effects are often equivalent to those of smoking several packs of cigarettes a day.

The reason environmental problems differ so substantially between less and more developed countries is that few if any forms of environmental degradation tend to remain constant with economic growth. Figure 3 of the first selection shows that some environmental problems such as inadequate urban sanitation tend to improve as income increases, others such as urban air pollution initially worsen but then improve as incomes rise, and still others such as carbon dioxide emissions tend to worsen steadily with increasing income. The tendency of many forms of environmental degradation to follow an "inverted U" when plotted against income has been christened the "environmental Kuznets curve." The Comment that follows the first selection goes into the possible causes of the environmental Kuznets curve in more detail and suggests some additional readings on this subject.

The environmental problems of less and more developed countries are of course not completely independent of each other. If, as seems probable, the carbon dioxide emissions that come primarily from rich countries are causing greenhouse warming, less developed countries are affected. Loss of biodiversity due to destruction of tropical rainforests in less developed countries is a problem for more developed countries as well. Environmental problems and policies of less and more developed countries may also interact indirectly through international trade. If, for example, "dirty" industries locate in less developed countries and export to more developed countries, environmental degradation is worsened in the former and improved in the latter. By one view, such a pattern of trade is desirable because the demand for environmental quality or the (implicit) economic valuation of life is lower in LDCs. An opposing view holds that this pattern of trade is undesirable because weaker government regulation leads to a greater divergence between the private and social costs of environmental degradation in less than in more developed countries. Selection X.2 by Graciela Chichilnisky identifies a particularly clear theoretical case where international trade between poor and rich countries promotes socially inefficient environmental degradation. This case arises when property rights to a natural resource are better enforced in rich countries, leading to overexploitation of the natural resource in poor countries that is exacerbated by international trade. The Comment that follows Chichilnisky's selection reviews some of the empirical evidence regarding the impact of international trade on the environment in less developed countries.

Tropical deforestation is the chief example given by Chichilnisky of environmental degradation that is exacerbated by international trade in the presence of weak property rights in less developed countries. The link between property rights and deforestation (setting aside any effect of international trade) is given a systematic empirical investigation in Selection X.3 by Robert Deacon. We should note that Chichilnisky considers property rights within a harvest period whereas Deacon considers property rights across harvest periods, yielding different though complementary arguments why better property rights will reduce deforestation. Chichilnisky's argument is essentially that if a forest is the private property of the harvester, he will take full account of the fact that each tree he harvests raises his cost of harvesting an additional tree (by forcing him deeper into the forest, say). This will lead to a lower overall level of harvesting than if the forest is unregulated common property harvested by many small producers, each of whom does not take into account the impact of his actions on the costs of the others. Deacon argues that preservation or restoration of forests is an act of investment and is therefore encouraged if those making the initial sacrifice feel confident that they will receive the future benefits. A harvester has a greater incentive to replant if he expects to have the rights to harvest the new trees. Deacon uses indicators of political instability and nonrepresentative government as proxies for the strength of property rights. These indicators should affect the security of any investment, not just investment in preservation or restoration of forests. Across countries they generally have the expected associations with deforestation, but it is not clear that these associations hold when population growth is controlled for. The weakness of Deacon's results may be due to lack of direct measures of forest property rights or of policies that specifically regulate use of forests.

As the first selection of this chapter points out, clarification and enforcement of property rights is a practical means of reducing some but not all types of environmental degradation. Other types of government policies are needed, such as pollution taxes or requirements to use emission control equipment. These kinds of regulation are quite weak in most less developed countries, which might lead one to expect production of uniformly high pollution intensity. In Selection X.4, Hemamala Hettige, Mainul Huq, Sheoli Pargal, and David Wheeler find to the contrary that there is wide variation in the pollution intensity of manufacturing production in the countries of South and Southeast Asia, with some plants even satisfying more developed country regulatory standards. They identify a number of different sources of this variation, such as whether a plant is state owned. A particularly interesting result is that higher per capita income in the community surrounding the plant is associated with greater installation of pollution control technologies or lower measured pollution intensity. This and related findings suggest that informal regulation in the form of community pressure can play a significant role in protecting the environment in less developed countries.

The policies suggested by the World Bank in the first selection of this chapter are intended to adjust the private costs of environmentally degrading activities to equal their social costs, following the principles of neoclassical welfare economics. In the last selection, David Pearce, Edward Barbier, and Anil Markandya propose an additional objective for policy of maintaining a nondecreasing "natural capital stock" as a way of achieving "sustainable development." The concluding Comment suggests some readings in which this objective is weakened to allow for increases in the man-made physical capital stock or human capital stock to make up for decreases in the natural capital stock.

Selection X.1. Development and the Environment*

. . . Recent years have witnessed rising concern about whether environmental constraints will limit development and whether development will cause serious environmental damage—in turn impairing the quality of life of this and future generations. This concern is overdue. A number of environmental problems are already very serious and require urgent attention. Humanity's stake in environmental protection is enormous, and environmental values have been neglected too often in the past.

This Report explores the two-way relationship between development and the environment. It describes how environmental problems can and do undermine the goals of development. There are two ways in which this can happen. First, environmental quality—water that is safe and plentiful and air that is healthy—is itself part of the improvement in welfare that development attempts to bring. If the benefits from rising incomes are offset by the costs imposed on health and the quality of life by pollution, this cannot be called development. Second, environmental damage can undermine future productivity. Soils that, are degraded, aquifers that are depleted, and ecosystems that are destroyed in the name of raising incomes today can jeopardize the prospects for earning income tomorrow.

The Report also explores the impact—for good and bad—of economic growth on the environment. It identifies the conditions under which policies for efficient income growth can complement those for environmental protection and identifies tradeoffs. Its message is positive. There are strong "win-win" opportunities that remain unexploited. The most important of these relates to poverty reduction: not only is attacking poverty a moral imperative, but it is also essential for environmental stewardship. Moreover, policies that are justified on economic grounds alone can deliver substantial environmental benefits. Eliminating subsidies for the use of fossil fuels and water, giving poor farmers property rights on the land they farm, making heavily polluting state-owned companies more competitive, and eliminating rules that reward with property rights those who clear forests are examples of policies that improve both economic efficiency and the environment. Similarly, investing in better sanitation and water and in improved research and extension services can both improve the environment *and* raise incomes.

But these policies are not enough to ensure environmental quality; strong public institutions and policies for environmental protection are also essential. The world has learned over the past two decades to rely more on markets and less on governments to promote development. But environmental protection is one area in which government must maintain a central role. Private markets provide little or no incentive for curbing pollution. Whether it be air pollution in urban centers, the dumping of unsanitary wastes in public waters, or the overuse of land whose ownership is unclear, there is a compelling case for public action. Here there may be tradeoffs between income growth and environmental protection, requiring a careful assessment of the benefits and costs of alternative policies as they affect both today's population and future generations. The evidence indicates that the gains from protecting the environment are often high and that the costs in forgone income are modest if appropriate policies are adopted. Experience suggests that policies are most effective when they aim at underlying causes rather than symptoms, concentrate on addressing those problems for which the benefits of reform are greatest, use incentives rather than regulations where possible, and recognize administrative constraints.

Strong environmental policies complement and reinforce development. It is often the poorest who suffer most from the consequences of pollution and environmental degradation. Unlike the rich, the poor cannot afford to protect themselves from contaminated water; in cities they are more likely to spend much of their time on the streets, breathing polluted air; in rural areas they are more likely to cook on open fires of wood or dung, inhaling dangerous fumes; their lands are most likely to suffer from soil erosion. The poor may also draw a large part of their livelihood from unmarketed environmental resources: common grazing lands, for example, or forests where food, fuel, and building materials have traditionally been gathered. The loss of such resources may particularly harm the poorest. Sound environmental policies are thus likely to be powerfully redistributive.

Making decisions about some environmental problems is complicated by uncertainties about physical and ecological processes, by the long-term nature of their effects, and by the possibility of thresholds beyond which unexpected or irre-

*From World Bank, "Overview: Development and the Environment," *World Development Report* 1992 (New York: Oxford University Press, 1992), pp. 1–15. Reprinted by permission.

versible change may occur. New evidence that the impact of chlorofluorocarbons (CFCs) on stratospheric ozone depletion is greater than earlier thought is a timely reminder of how little we know. Such uncertainties call for much greater attention to research and to designing flexible precautionary policies.

Because this Report is about development and the environment, it focuses primarily on the welfare of developing countries. The most immediate environmental problems facing these countries—unsafe water, inadequate sanitation, soil depletion, indoor smoke from cooking fires and outdoor smoke from coal burning—are different from and more immediately life-threatening than those associated with the affluence of rich countries, such as carbon dioxide emissions, depletion of stratospheric ozone, photochemical smogs, acid rain, and hazardous wastes. Industrial countries need to solve their own problems, but they also have a crucial role to play in helping to improve the environments of developing countries.

- First, developing countries need to have access to less-polluting technologies and to learn from the successes and failures of industrial countries' environmental policies.
- Second, some of the benefits from environmental policies in developing countries—the protection of tropical forests and of biodiversity, for example—accrue to rich countries, which ought therefore to bear an equivalent part of the costs.
- Third, some of the potential problems facing developing countries—global warming and ozone depletion, in particular—stem from high consumption levels in rich countries; thus, the burden of finding and implementing solutions should be on the rich countries.
- Fourth, the strong and growing evidence of the links between poverty reduction and environmental goals makes a compelling case for greater support for programs to reduce poverty and population growth.
- Fifth, the capacity of developing countries to enjoy sustained income growth will depend on industrial countries' economic policies; improved access to trade and capital markets, policies to increase savings and lower world interest rates, and policies that promote robust, environmentally responsible growth in industrial countries, will all help. . . .

Table 1 outlines the potential consequences for health and productivity of different forms of environmental mismanagement. Since environmental problems vary across countries and with the stage of industrialization, each country needs to assess its own priorities carefully.

Clean Water and Sanitation

For the 1 billion people in developing countries who do not have access to clean water and the 1.7 billion who lack access to sanitation, these are the most important environmental problems of all. Their effects on health are shocking: they are major contributors to the 900 million cases of diarrheal diseases every year, which cause the deaths of more than 3 million children; 2 million of these deaths could be prevented if adequate sanitation and clean water were available. At any time 200 million are suffering from schistosomiasis or bilharzia and 900 million from hookworm. Cholera, typhoid, and paratyphoid also continue to wreak havoc with human welfare. Providing access to sanitation and clean water would not eradicate all these diseases, but it would be the single most effective means of alleviating human distress.

The economic costs of inadequate provision are also high. Many women in Africa spend more than two hours a day fetching water. In Jakarta an amount equivalent to 1 percent of the city's gross domestic product (GDP) is spent each year on boiling water, and in Bangkok, Mexico City, and Jakarta excessive pumping of groundwater has led to subsidence, structural damage, and flooding.

Clean Air

Emissions from industry and transport and from domestic energy consumption impose serious costs for health and productivity. Three specific problems stand out for their effect on human suffering.

Suspended Particulate Matter. In the second half of the 1980s about 1.3 billion people worldwide lived in urban areas that did not meet the standards for particulate matter (airborne dust and smoke) set by the World Health Organization (WHO). They thus faced the threat of serious respiratory disorders and cancers (see Figure 1). If emissions could be reduced so that the WHO standards were met everywhere, an estimated 300,000 to 700,000 lives could be saved each year, and many more people would be spared the suffering caused by chronic respiratory difficulties.

Lead. High levels of lead, primarily from vehicle emissions, have been identified as the greatest environmental danger in a number of large cities in

Table 1. Principal Health and Productivity Consequences of Environmental Mismanagement

Environmental problem	Effect on health	Effect on productivity
Water pollution and water scarcity	More than 2 million deaths and billions of illnesses a year attributable to pollution; poor household hygiene and added health risks caused by water scarcity	Declining fisheries; rural household time and municipal costs of providing safe water; aquifer depletion leading to irreversible compaction; constraint on economic activity because of water shortages
Air pollution	Many acute and chronic health impacts: excessive urban particulate matter levels are responsible for 300,000–700,000 premature deaths annually and for half of childhood chronic coughing; 400 million–700 million people, mainly women and children in poor rural areas, affected by smoky indoor air	Restrictions on vehicle and industrial activity during critical episodes; effect of acid rain on forests and water bodies
Solid and hazardous wastes	Diseases spread by rotting garbage and blocked drains. Risks from hazardous wastes typically local but often acute	Pollution of groundwater resources
Soil degradation	Reduced nutrition for poor farmers on depleted soils; greater susceptibility to drought	Field productivity losses in range of 0.5–1.5 percent of gross national product (GNP) common on tropical soils; offsite siltation of reservoirs, river-transport channels, and other hydrologic investments
Deforestation	Localized flooding, leading to death and disease	Loss of sustainable logging potential and of erosion prevention, watershed stability, and carbon sequestration provided by forests
Loss of biodiversity	Potential loss of new drugs	Reduction of ecosystem adaptability and loss of genetic resources
Atmospheric changes	Possible shifts in vector-borne diseases; risks from climatic natural disasters; diseases attributable to ozone depletion (perhaps 300,000 additional cases of skin cancer a year worldwide; 1.7 million cases of cataracts)	Sea-rise damage to coastal investments; regional changes in agricultural productivity; disruption of marine food chain

the developing world. Estimates for Bangkok suggest that the average child has lost four or more IQ points by the age of seven because of elevated exposure to lead, with enduring implications for adult productivity. In adults the consequences include risks of higher blood pressure and higher risks of heart attacks, strokes, and death. In Mexico City lead exposure may contribute to as much as 20 percent of the incidence of hypertension.

Indoor Air Pollution. For hundreds of millions of the world's poorer citizens, smoke and fumes from indoor use of biomass fuel (such as wood, straw, and dung) pose much greater health risks than any outdoor pollution. Women and children suffer most from this form of pollution, and its effects on health are often equivalent to those of smoking several packs of cigarettes a day.

Other Forms of Pollution. An estimated 1 billion people live in cities that exceed WHO standards for sulfur dioxide. Nitrogen oxides and volatile organic compounds are a problem in a smaller but growing number of rapidly industrializing and heavily motorized cities.

Soil, Water, and Agricultural Productivity

The loss of productive potential in rural areas is a more widespread and important problem, although less dramatic, than that evoked by images of advancing deserts. Soil degradation, in particular, is the cause of stagnating or declining yields in parts of many countries, especially on fragile lands from which the poorest farmers attempt to wrest a living. Erosion is the most visible symptom of this degradation. Data on soil conditions are of low

Figure 1. Urban air pollution: Average concentrations of suspended particulate matter, by country income group

Micrograms per cubic meter of air

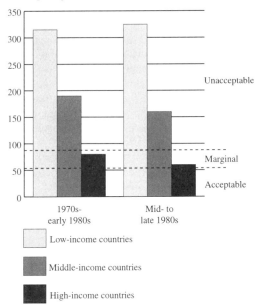

Note: Periods of time series differ by site. World Health Organization guidelines for air quality are used as the criteria for acceptability.

Source: Environmental data appendix table A.5.

quality, but crude estimates suggest that in some countries the losses in productive potential attributable to soil depletion may amount to 0.5–1.5 percent of GDP annually. Erosion can also damage economic infrastructure, such as dams, downstream. Even when erosion is insignificant, soils may suffer from nutrient, physical, and biological depletion.

Waterlogging and salinization are serious problems in some irrigated areas and are often the result of policies and infrastructure that inadequately recognize the growing scarcity of water. The increasing conflicts over the use of water mean that in the future, additional growth in agricultural productivity will have to make do with more efficient irrigation and, in some regions, less water overall.

Agricultural intensification will continue as it becomes harder to expand the area of cultivation. High levels of inputs and changes in land use will cause problems for farm communities and other parts of the economy. These problems, once confined mainly to the highly intensive agricultural systems of Europe and North America, are now increasing in such areas as the Punjab, Java, and parts of China.

Natural Habitats and Loss of Biodiversity

Forests (especially moist tropical forests), coastal and inland wetlands, coral reefs, and other ecosystems are being converted or degraded at rates that are high by historical standards. Tropical forests have declined by one-fifth in this century, and the rate has accelerated. As Figure 2 shows, in the 1980s tropical deforestation occurred at a rate of 0.9 percent a year, with Asia's rate slightly higher (1.2 percent) and Sub-Saharan Africa's lower (0.8 percent). The loss of forests has severe ecological and economic costs—lost watershed protection, local climate change, lost coastal protection and fishing grounds—and affects people's lives. African women have to walk farther for fuelwood, indigenous forest dwellers in the Amazon have succumbed to settlers' diseases, and 5,000 villagers in the Philippines were recently killed by flooding caused in part by the deforestation of hillsides.

Extinction of species is occurring at rates that are high by historical standards, and many more species are threatened because their habitats are being lost. Models that link species extinction to habitat loss suggest that rapid rises in the rate of extinction to levels approaching those of prehis-

Figure 2. Loss of tropical forests in developing regions, 1980–90

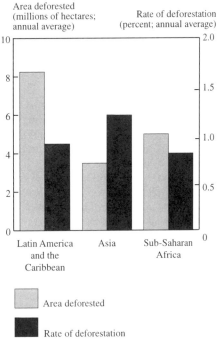

Source: FAO data.

toric mass extinctions may be difficult to avoid in the next century unless current rates of deforestation and other habitat loss are sharply reduced.

Greenhouse Warming

The buildup of carbon dioxide and other greenhouse gases will raise average temperatures on earth. The size of the effect remains unclear, but the best estimate of the International Panel on Climate Change (IPCC) is that average world temperatures may rise by 3° Celsius by the end of the next century under their "business as usual" scenario, with a range of uncertainty of from less than 2° Celsius to more than 5° Celsius. There is even more uncertainty about the consequences than about the extent of global warming. Although recent research has reduced fears that icecaps might melt or that the sea level might rise precipitously, there are still grounds for concern. Low-lying nations are at risk, and forests and ecosystems may not adapt easily to shifts in climatic zones. The consequences will depend both on whether policies are adopted to reduce emissions and on how effective economies are in adapting to rising temperatures. . . .

Economic Growth and the Environment

What pressures will economic growth place on the natural environment in the coming years? To assess this question, the Report explores a long-term projection of economic output. Under present productivity trends, and given projected population increases, developing country output would rise by 4–5 percent a year between 1990 and 2030 and by the end of the period would be about five times what it is today. Industrial country output would rise more slowly but would still triple over the period. World output by 2030 would be 3.5 times what it is today, or roughly $69 trillion (in 1990 prices).

If environmental pollution and degradation were to rise in step with such a rise in output, the result would be appalling environmental pollution and damage. Tens of millions more people would become sick or die each year from environmental causes. Water shortages would be intolerable, and tropical forests and other natural habitats would decline to a fraction of their current size. Fortunately, such an outcome need not occur, nor will it if sound policies and strong institutional arrangements are put in place.

The earth's "sources" are limited, and so is the absorptive capacity of its "sinks." Whether these limitations will place bounds on the growth of human activity will depend on the scope for substitution, technical progress, and structural change. Forcing decisionmakers to respect the scarcity and limits of natural resources has a powerful effect on their actions. For example, whereas fears that the world would run out of metals and other minerals were fashionable even fifteen years ago, the potential supply of these resources is now outstripping demand. Prices of minerals have shown a fairly consistent downward trend over the past hundred years. They fell sharply in the 1980s, leading to gluts that threatened to impoverish countries dependent on commodity exports.

With some other natural resources, by contrast, demand often exceeds supply. This is true of the demand for water, not only in the arid areas of the Middle East but also in northern China, east Java, and parts of India. Aquifers are being depleted, sometimes irreversibly, and the extraction from rivers is often so great that their ecological functions are impaired and further expansion of irrigation is becoming severely limited.

The reason some resources—water, forests, and clean air—are under siege while others—metals, minerals, and energy—are not is that the scarcity of the latter is reflected in market prices and so the forces of substitution, technical progress, and structural change are strong. The first group is characterized by open access, meaning that there are no incentives to use them sparingly. Policies and institutions are therefore necessary to force decisionmakers—corporations, farmers, households, and governments—to take account of the social value of these resources in their actions. This is not easy. The evidence suggests, however, that when environmental policies are publicly supported and firmly enforced, the positive forces of substitution, technical progress, and structural change can be just as powerful as for marketed inputs such as metals and minerals. This explains why the environmental debate has rightly shifted away from concern about *physical limits* to growth toward concern about incentives for *human behavior* and policies that can overcome *market and policy failures.*

Figure 3 illustrates how rising economic activity can cause environmental problems but can also, with the right policies and institutions, help address them. Three patterns emerge:

- Some problems decline as income increases. This is because increasing income provides the resources for public services such as sanitation and rural electricity. When individuals no longer

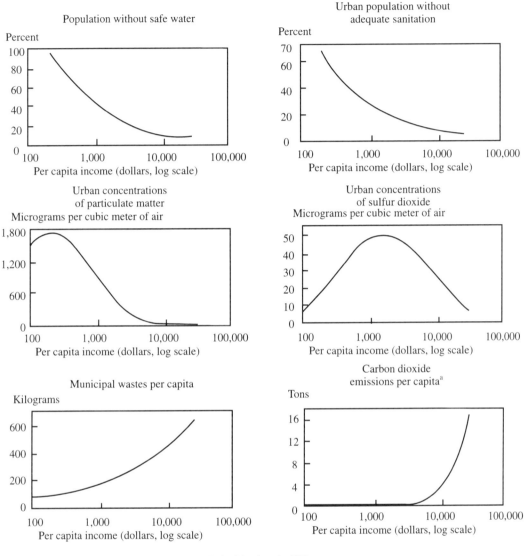

Figure 3 Environmental indicators at different country income levels

Note: Estimates are based on cross-country regression analysis of data from the 1980s.

a. Emissions are from fossil fuels.

Sources: Shafik and Bandyopadhyay, background paper; World Bank data.

have to worry about day-to-day survival, they can devote resources to profitable investments in conservation. These positive synergies between economic growth and environmental quality must not be underestimated.

- Some problems initially worsen but then improve as incomes rise. Most forms of air and water pollution fit into this category, as do some types of deforestation and encroachment on natural habitats. There is nothing automatic about this improvement; it occurs only when countries

deliberately introduce policies to ensure that additional resources are devoted to dealing with environmental problems.

- Some indicators of environmental stress worsen as incomes increase. Emissions of carbon and of nitrogen oxides and municipal wastes are current examples. In these cases abatement is relatively expensive and the costs associated with the emissions and wastes are not yet perceived as high—often because they are borne by someone else. The key is, once again, policy. In most countries individuals and firms have few incentives to cut back on wastes and emissions, and until such incentives are put into place—through regulation, charges, or other means—damage will continue to increase. The experience with the turnarounds achieved in other forms of pollution, however, shows what may be possible once a policy commitment is made.

Figure 3 does not imply an inevitable relationship between income levels and particular environmental problems; countries can choose policies that result in much better (or worse) environmental conditions than those in other countries at similar income levels. Nor does it imply a static picture; as a result of technological progress, some of these curves have shifted downward over recent decades, providing an opportunity for countries to develop in a less damaging manner than was possible earlier.

Policies for Development and the Environment

Two broad sets of policies are needed to attack the underlying causes of environmental damage. Both are necessary. Neither will be sufficient on its own.

- Policies that seek to harness the positive links between development and the environment by correcting or preventing policy failures, improving access to resources and technology, and promoting equitable income growth
- Policies targeted at specific environmental problems: regulations and incentives that are required to force the recognition of environmental values in decisionmaking.

Building on the Positive Links

Fortunately, many policies that are good for efficiency are also good for the environment. Policies that encourage efficiency lead to less waste, less consumption of raw materials, and more technological innovation. . . .

Removing Distortions. Some government policies are downright harmful to the environment. Notable here are distorted prices in general and subsidized input prices in particular. Subsidies for energy, for example, cost developing country governments more than $230 billion a year—more than four times the total world volume of official development assistance. The former U.S.S.R. and Eastern Europe account for the bulk of this amount ($180 billion); estimates suggest that more than half of their air pollution is attributable to these distortions. The removal of all energy subsidies—including those on coal in industrial countries—would not only produce large gains in efficiency and in fiscal balances but would sharply reduce local pollution and cut worldwide carbon emissions from energy use by 10 percent. Other distortionary incentives have also had serious environmental consequences. Logging fees in a sample of five African countries ranged from 1 to 33 percent of the costs of replanting. Irrigation charges in most Asian countries covered less than 20 percent of the costs of supplying the water. And pesticide subsidies in a sample of seven countries in Latin America, Africa, and Asia ranged from 19 to 83 percent of costs.

Distorted incentives are often particularly evident in the behavior of state-owned enterprises. This is important because many sectors in which state enterprises are prominent—power generation, cement, steel, and mining—are heavy polluters; the "commanding heights" are also the "polluting heights." Thus, the environment can benefit if the managers of state enterprises are made more accountable and are exposed to the same competition as is the private sector.

Clarifying Property Rights. When people have open access to forests, pastureland, or fishing grounds, they tend to overuse them. Providing land titles to farmers in Thailand has helped to reduce damage to forests. The assignment of property titles to slum dwellers in Bandung, Indonesia, has tripled household investment in sanitation facilities. Providing security of tenure to hill farmers in Kenya has reduced soil erosion. Formalizing community rights to land in Burkina Faso is sharply improving land management. And allocating transferable rights to fishery resources has checked the tendency to overfish in New Zealand.

The most serious mistake that governments make in seeking to eliminate open access is to nationalize resources in the name of conservation. Nationalization has often reflected the failure of policymakers and aid agencies to distinguish between traditional common-property systems, which promote sound management of natural resources, and open-access systems that result in excessive exploitation. When land and water have been nationalized and traditional management arrangements abandoned, the environmental consequences have often been severe, as they were in the forests of Nepal.

Targeted Policies to Change Behavior

The policies described above are important, but they are not enough. Eliminating fuel subsidies will not be sufficient to end air pollution in Beijing or Mexico City. And it simply is not practical to find property-rights solutions for most of those environmental problems that adversely affect a large number of people "offsite"—air and water pollution, watershed destruction, loss of biodiversity, and the like. For these situations specific policies are required to induce or require resource users to take account of the spillover effects that their actions have on the rest of society.

Policies designed to change behavior are of two broad types: those based on incentives ("market-based" policies), which tax or charge polluters according to the amount of damage they do, and those based on quantitative restrictions ("command-and-control" policies), which provide no such flexibility.

Market-based instruments are best in principle and often in practice. They encourage those polluters with the lowest costs of control to take the most remedial action, and they thus impose less of a burden on the economy. A survey of six studies of air pollution control in the United States found that least-cost policies could reduce the costs of control by 45–95 percent in comparison with the actual policies implemented. Economic incentives have been used for years in indirect, or blunt, forms such as fuel and vehicle taxes (most OECD countries), congestion charges (Singapore), and surcharges on potentially damaging inputs such as pesticides and plastics (Denmark and Sweden). More specific charges, such as the newly introduced carbon taxes in some European countries, tradable permits for air pollution (in the United States), deposit-refund schemes for bottles and batteries (in several European countries), hazardous waste charges and performance bonds, which are under consideration in Bangkok, and surcharges on stumpage fees to pay for replanting, as in Indonesia, are growing in importance. Industrial countries have been slow to adopt market-based strategies, in part because environmentalists contended that degrading the environment was unacceptable at any price, but more importantly because corporations feared that they would have to adopt emissions standards *and also* pay charges on the remaining emissions. Most now agree that market-based instruments have been underutilized. They are particularly promising for developing countries, which cannot afford to incur the unnecessary extra costs of less-flexible instruments that have been borne by OECD countries.

Quantitative command-and-control instruments, such as specific regulations on what abatement technologies must be used in specific industries, have acquired a bad name in recent years for their high costs and for stifling innovation. But in some situations they may be the best instruments available. Where there are a few large polluters, as was the case in the industrial city of Cubatão in Brazil, direct regulation may be the quickest and most effective instrument. Management of land use in frontier areas is another example of situations that may require direct controls.

The appropriate choice among instruments will depend on circumstances. Conserving scarce administrative capacity is an important consideration. For many developing countries blunt instruments that avoid the need for detailed monitoring will be attractive. These may involve taxes or charges on polluting inputs rather than on the pollution itself. Also attractive will be policies that provide self-enforcing incentives, such as deposit-refund and performance-bond schemes.

Several lessons can be drawn from recent experience:

- *Standards should be realistic and enforceable.* Many developing countries have set unrealistically tight standards—often those of OECD countries—and have enforced them only selectively. This has wasted resources, facilitated corruption, and undermined the credibility of all environmental policies. Laws on the books and zoning charts on the walls of government offices are often a genuine indication of concern, but unless policies are implemented, they can give a false sense that serious problems are under control. Better to have fewer and more realistic standards that are truly implemented.
- *Controls must be consistent with the overall policy framework.* Many well-intentioned policies have been thwarted by other policies that pull in the opposite direction. Both China and Poland have had pollution taxes for years, but to no effect; state-owned enterprises were not interested in profitability. Land-use planning in Sub-Saharan Africa has usually failed in the face of policies that did not encourage intensification and off-farm employment. Brazil's concern about overfishing off the Bahia coast was undermined in the early 1980s by government subsidies for new nylon nets.
- *A combination of policies will often be required.* Because environmental damage is frequently caused by different actors and for different reasons, a single policy change may not be enough.

Reducing air pollution from vehicles in Mexico City, for example, will require mandated emissions and engine standards, fuel improvements, and gasoline taxes.

Reviewing Public Expenditures

Public expenditures can have a remarkable effect on the environment—for bad or for good. It is now clear that numerous public investments—often supported by development agencies, including the World Bank—have caused damage by failing to take environments considerations into account or to judge the magnitude of the impacts. Indonesia's transmigration program, Sri Lanka's Mahaweli scheme, and Brazil's Polonoreste projects are examples of large programs that caused unanticipated damage in earlier years. But equally important are design issues relating to individual project components—road alignments, the design of water systems, and the provision of access to forests and wetlands.

Beginning with analysis in the 1950s and 1960s of hydroelectric projects in the United States, considerable progress has been made in applying cost-benefit techniques to environmental concerns. Such analyses have tripled estimated returns for some forestry programs and halved returns on some hydroelectric and road projects, making the latter unattractive.

Most countries and aid agencies have recently introduced environmental assessment procedures. These are still early days for such arrangements; technical skills need to be developed, and lessons are being learned about the difficulties of incorporating assessment results, which are often non-quantitative, into decisionmaking. Making the process transparent has been found to be an important way of improving its quality and impact. Listening to local views has also proved essential; some lessons from the World Bank experience are that information must be shared with local people early in the life of the project and that comments from affected communities must be incorporated into project design.

Removing Impediments to Action

Even when straightforward ways of tackling environmental problems exist, governments have often found it difficult to translate them into effective policy. The reason for the gap between intentions and performance include political pressures, an absence of data and knowledge, weak institutions, and inadequate participation of local people in finding solutions.

Counteracting Political Pressures

Stopping environmental damage often involves taking rights away from people who may be politically powerful. Industrialists, farmers, loggers, and fishermen fiercely defend their rights to pollute or to exploit sources. Examples of the results include modification of proposed carbon taxes in Europe to assist energy-intensive industries, delay in the introduction of transferable fishing rights in Chile because of pressure from powerful fishing interests, and lack of progress almost everywhere in introducing irrigation charges. Those who are hurt when the environment is degraded, and who stand to gain most from sound policies, are often the poor and the weak. They may be less potent politically than the polluters whom governments must challenge.

A second reason for disappointing performance has to do with the inability of governments to regulate themselves. The problem arises partly because state bodies have conflicting social and economic objectives, which allow them to use resources less efficiently, and partly because of the inherent contradictions of being both gamekeeper and poacher. In the United States, for example, publicly owned municipal wastewater treatment plants are the most persistent violators of effluent discharge standards.

While private and public polluters may obstruct policy, other influences may persuade governments to set the wrong priorities. International pressures may favor issues of interest to donors rather than to developing countries. And there is always a tendency to focus on dramatic problems rather than chronic ones; few pressure groups, for example, lobby for improved sanitation or for reduced indoor air pollution. Moreover, governments may be pressed to address problems such as air pollution that affect everybody, including the rich, rather than problems such as fecal coliforms in rivers from which the rich can insulate themselves.

Improving Information

Ignorance is a serious impediment to finding solutions. Governments often make decisions in the absence of even rudimentary information. International initiatives are urgently needed to overcome a grave lack of knowledge in some areas, including soil depletion (especially in Africa), land productivity in and around tropical forests, and global atmospheric issues. Countries can reap large returns from investments in basic environmental data on exposure to emissions and unsanitary conditions, soil and water depletion, land capability, and loss of forests and natural habitat.

Understanding the causes and effects of environmental damage and the costs and benefits of action is the next stage. Following a careful analysis, authorities in Bangkok found that attacking lead and particulate emissions deserved the highest priority. The U.S. Environmental Protection Agency estimated that, as a measure for avoiding deaths, placing controls on unvented indoor heaters was 1,000 times more cost-effective than further tightening certain hazardous wastes standards. A study in southern Poland discovered that the benefits from reducing emissions of particulates would greatly exceed costs but that this would not be true of controls on sulfur dioxide.

Independent commissions have proved a useful way for governments to draw on technical expertise; a growing number of developing countries, including Hungary, Nigeria, and Thailand, are finding that ad hoc commissions can bring professional objectivity to highly charged issues. In Africa, national environmental action plans, which have already been completed for Lesotho, Madagascar, and Mauritius and are under preparation for seventeen other countries, are bringing technical experts and citizens' groups into the process of setting priorities and policies. . . .

Involving Local People

Making choices between economic and social benefits and environmental costs often requires subjective judgments and detailed local knowl-edge. Neither governments nor aid agencies are equipped to make judgments about how local people value their environment. A participatory process is essential. Local participation also yields high economic and environmental returns in implementing programs of afforestation, soil management, park protection, water management, and sanitation, drainage, and flood control.

Development projects that have not built on the strengths of existing practices have often failed. Haiti's top-down reforestation program was unsuccessful until small farmers and community groups were allowed to choose what kinds of trees should be planted, and where. Then, instead of the target of 3 million trees on 6,000 family farms, 20 million trees were planted on 75,000 farms. A large irrigation project in Bali, Indonesia, that failed to recognize the advantages of traditional approaches to pest management had disastrous results. A follow-up project that built on indigenous strengths succeeded.

Involving people can be expensive and in some instances can paralyze decisionmaking, hold public investments hostage to unproductive NIMBY ("not-in-my-backyard") activism, and reinforce local power structures. Experience suggests that success is greatest when tasks are devolved selectively and on the basis of actual performance. Increasing responsibilities for local governments is an important part of this process. Public agencies need training in participatory approaches and a clear indication from senior management of the importance of participation.

Comment X.1. The "Environmental Kuznets Curve"

The middle row of Figure 3 of the preceding selection shows two types of air pollution that first increase and then decrease with per capita income. Because this is reminiscent of Kuznets's conjecture for income inequality (see section VIII.A in this book), this inverted-U relationship has become known as the "environmental Kuznets curve." (As the selection points out, the environmental Kuznets curve is not limited to air pollution, but at the same time there are some forms of environmental degradation to which it clearly does not apply.) The cause of the upswing of the inverted U is simply that greater output per head generates more emissions, all else equal. The cause of the downswing is more controversial. The conventional explanation is that richer consumers demand higher environmental quality, richer governments are better able to enforce regulations that yield the higher environmental quality their constituents demand, and more technologically advanced producers are better able to control their emissions. A more pessimistic explanation focuses on the composition of output. Richer countries produce more services relative to manufactures, and within manufacturing they tend to specialize in "cleaner" industries. Demand for the output of "dirty" industries is met by imports from poorer countries. If this latter explanation is correct, then at the global level economic growth of countries with per capita incomes above the "turning point" of the inverted U for a certain form of environmental degradation does not improve environmental quality but instead redistributes degradation to poorer countries. This point is made in more detail by Gilles Saint-Paul, "Discussion," in Ian Goldin and L. Alan Winters, eds., *The Economics of Sustainable Development* (1995).

Some evidence in favor of the conventional explanation of the downswing of the environmental Kuznets curve is contained in an article by Richard T. Carson, Yongil Jeon, and Donald R. McCubbin, "The Relationship Between Air Pollution Emissions and Income: U.S. Data," *Environment and Development Economics* (1997). They reason that since even the poorest U.S. state has a per capita income above most estimated "turning points" of the inverted U, per capita air pollutant emissions should decline monotonically with state per capita income. The data confirm their expectation. It is possible that this result obtains because dirty industries have moved from richer states to poorer states, or because richer states import the products of dirty industries from abroad to a greater extent. However, Carson et al. find that their result holds even when they include controls for industry mix in their cross-state regressions.

The paper by Carson, Jeon, and McCubbin appeared in an environmental Kuznets curve special issue of *Environment and Development Economics*. This special issue is an excellent source of additional information on the subject.

Selection X.2. North–South Trade and the Global Environment*

Why do developing countries tend to specialize in the production and the export of goods which deplete environmental resources such as rain forests (see Chichilnisky and Geoffrey Heal, 1991)? Do they have a comparative advantage in "dirty industries," and if so, does efficiency dictate that this advantage should be exploited? Is it possible to protect resources without interfering with free markets? Are trade policies based on traditional comparative advantages compatible with environmental preservation?

This paper proposes answers to these questions. It does so by studying patterns of North-South trade in a world economy where the North has better-defined property rights for environmental resources than the South. . . . It considers a trade model with two countries (North and South), two goods, and two factors. . . . The environment, which is one of the factors of production, is owned as unregulated common property in the South, and as private property in the North. . . .

The paper considers a general completely symmetric case: a world economy consisting of two identical countries, both with the same inputs and outputs, and with the same endowments, technologies, and preferences. The two countries engage in free trade in unregulated and competitive markets. The countries differ only in the pattern of ownership of an environmental resource used as an input to production. I consider this case to demonstrate that lack of property rights alone can create trade, and that trade itself can exacerbate the common-property problem. No trade is necessary for efficiency when the two countries are identical, yet trade occurs when they have different property-rights regimes. In this context I establish two general propositions. First, the country with ill-defined property rights overuses the environment as an input to production, and these ill-defined property rights by themselves create a motive for trade between two otherwise identical countries. Second, for the country with poorly defined property rights, trade with a country with well-defined property rights increases the overuse of resources and makes the misallocation worse, transmitting it to the entire world economy. Trade equalizes the prices of traded goods and of factors worldwide, but this does not improve resource allocation. In the resulting world economy, resources are under-

priced; there is overproduction by one country and over-consumption by the other. . . .

These results offer a new perspective on a current debate, initiated in 1992 by Lawrence Summers, a World Bank economist, about whether developing countries have a comparative advantage in "dirty industries" (see e.g., *The Economist,* 8 February 1992, Vol. 322, p. 66). If so, the argument goes, is it not efficient that they specialize in "dirty industries" and environmentally intensive production?

One response to this is that the apparent comparative advantages may not be actual comparative advantages, an issue which this paper addresses rigorously. They may derive neither from a relative abundance of resources nor from differences in productivity or preferences, not even from lower factor prices, but rather from historical and institutional factors: the lack of property rights for a common-property resource. In this context the South produces and exports environmentally intensive goods to a greater degree than is efficient, and at prices that are below social costs. This happens even if all factor prices are equal across the world, all markets are competitive, and the two regions have identical factor endowments, preferences and technologies. Under those conditions the trade patterns which emerge are inefficient for the world economy as a whole, and for the developing countries themselves. Developing countries are not made better off by specializing in "dirty industries," nor is the world better off if they do. . . .

The problems described in this paper appear when societies that are still in transition between agricultural and industrialized economies trade with societies already industrialized. Many traditional societies had well developed systems for inducing cooperative outcomes in the use of shared resources. Laws to protect the citizens' property rights in running water were in operation in the United Kingdom in the Middle Ages. Japan had well developed systems for the management of traditional communal lands (*Iriaichi*). Other examples are the communal-field agriculture in the Andes and in medieval England, and the successful sea-tenure systems in Bahia, Brazil, before the arrival of outsiders (see Daniel Bromley, 1992). These traditional systems, however, appear to lapse in the period of transition between agricultural and industrial economies.

Today many environmental resources are unregulated common property in developing countries.

*From Graciela Chichilnisky, "North-South Trade and the Global Environment," *American Economic Review* 84 (September 1994): 851–853, 864. Reprinted by permission.

Examples are rain forests, which are used for timber or destroyed to give way to the production and export of cash crops such as coffee, sugar, and palm oil. Other examples include grazing land, fisheries, and aquifers, which by the nature of things must usually be shared property even when the land covering the aquifer is privately owned (see Partha Dasgupta, 1992). These are common-property resources whose ownership is shared with future generations. They are typically used as inputs to the production of goods that are traded internationally.

Recent studies show that 90 percent of all tropical deforestation is for the agricultural use of forests, particularly for the international market (C. S. Binley and Jeffrey R. Vincent, 1990; Torsten Amelung, 1991; Edward Barbier et al., 1991; W. F. Hyde and D. H. Newman, 1991). The Korup National Park between Cameroon and Nigeria, at 60 million years old, one of the oldest rain forests in the world and one of the richest in biodiversity, is exploited as an unregulated common-property resource for the production of palm oil, trapping, and other forest products sold in the international market (H. J. Ruitenbeck, 1990). So is the Amazon basin, which is cleared and used as a source of land for the production of cash crops, such as soy beans and coffee, for the international market.

In the now industrialized countries communal land was frequently observed prior to industrialization. Industrialization in England was preceded by the "enclosure" (privatization) of common lands (Cohen and Weitzman, 1975). Now, however, industrial countries have much better defined property rights for their resources than do developing countries. The United States has property-rights regimes for petroleum. These include laws to prevent the overexploitation of common-property resources such as the Conally "Hot Oil Act" of 1936 and "unitization" laws (Steven McDonald, 1971). Water, however, is still treated as common property in parts of Texas and California, leading to misallocation. Japan is well known for its protection of property rights in environmental resources, including even sunlight. Germany recently initiated a parallel system of national accounts which records the depreciation of environmental assets, effectively treating the accounting of national property on the same basis as that of private property. . . .

A main argument in favor of property-rights policies is that once these have been implemented, no market intervention is needed. Consider, for example, any policy which improves the property of Amazonian small farmers, such as rubber-tappers. This will change the supply function of Amazon-

ian resources, reducing output at each price. In turn this will change the computation of comparative advantages and of gains from trade from agricultural exports based on deforestation of the Amazon. Production patterns shift, and export patterns will reflect more fully the social cost of deforesting the Amazon.

Examples of such property-rights approaches are provided by recent agreements involving debt-for-nature swaps (Ruitenbeck, 1990). Another example is provided by recent agreements between the United States pharmaceutical industry and Costa Rica. The spearhead of this project is a pair of ingenious efforts to exploit the forests to obtain medicinal products. A Costa Rican research institute (INBIO) is prospecting for promising plants, microorganisms, and insects to be screened for medical uses by Merck and Company, the world's largest drug company. Merck, in turn, is supporting the prospecting effort financially and will share any resulting profits with Costa Rica. Thus Costa Rica has acquired property rights over the "intellectual property" embodied in the genetic information within its forests. A similar initiative was taken by a small Californian company, Shaman Pharmaceuticals, which is tapping the expertise of traditional healers, "Shamans" or medicine people, in various parts of the tropics (see Chichilnisky, 1993). The company intends to promote the conservation of the forests by channeling some of its profits back to the localities whose medicine people provided the key plants. The theory behind both ventures is that everybody wins: the world gets new drugs, the pharmaceutical companies earn profits, and people in the localities are justly compensated for their "intellectual property" and their conservation and collection efforts.[1]

Similar examples hold for land resources. Recently the government of Ecuador allocated a piece of the Amazon the size of the state of Connecticut to its Indian population, a clear property-rights policy.[2] Under the conditions examined here, this policy should lead to a better use of the forest's resources and to a more balanced pattern of trade between Ecuador and the United States.

---

[1]Examples of successful medical discoveries from rain forests and other natural sources include widely used medicines such as aspirin, morphine, quinine, curare, the rosy periwinkle used to treat childhood leukemia and Hodgkin's disease, and (more recently) taxol.

[2]Indian groups will gain title to land in Pastaza Province, a traditional homelands area covering 4,305 square miles in eastern Ecuador. Ecuador's move is part of a wider trend in the Amazon basin. Achuar, Shiwiar, and Quiche Indians will soon administer an area where population density averages five people per square mile.

References

Amelung, Torsten. "Tropical Deforestation as an International Economic Problem." Unpublished manuscript presented at the Egon-Sohmen Foundation Conference on Economic Evolution and Environmental Concerns, Linz, Austria, 30–31 August 1991.

Barbier, Edward B.; Burgess, J. C. and Markandya, Anil. "The Economics of Tropical Deforestation." *AMBIO*, April 1991, *20*(2), pp. 55–58.

Binkley, C. S. and Vincent, Jeffrey R. "Forest Based Industrialization: A Dynamic Perspective." World Bank (Washington, DC) Forest Policy Issues Paper, 1990.

Bromley, Daniel W., ed. *Making the commons work.* San Francisco: ICS Press, 1992.

Chichilnisky, Graciela. "Biodiversity and Property Rights in the Pharmaceutical Industry." Case study, Columbia University School of Business, 1993.

Chichilnisky, Graciela and Heal, Geoffrey M. *The evolv-ing international economy.* Cambridge: Cambridge University Press, 1987.

Cohen, Jon S. and Weitzman, Martin L. "A Marxian Model of Enclosures." *Journal of Development Economics,* February 1975, *1*(4), pp. 287–336.

Dasgupta, Partha. *The control of resources.* Cambridge, MA: Harvard University Press, 1992.

Hyde, W. F. and Newman, D. H. "Forest Economics in Brief—With Summary Observations for Policy Analysis." Unpublished manuscript (draft report), Agricultural and Rural Development, World Bank, Washington, DC, 1991.

McDonald, Steven, L. *Petroleum conservation in the United States: An economic analysis.* Baltimore, MD: Johns Hopkins University Press, 1971.

Ruitenbeck, H. J. "The Rainforest Supply Price: A Step Towards Estimating a Cost Curve for Rainforest Conservation." Development Research Programme Working Paper No. 29, London School of Economics, 1990.

Comment X.2.   Empirical Studies of the Impact of International Trade on the Environment in Less Developed Countries

Empirical studies of the impact of international trade on environmental quality in LDCs have mostly been inconclusive or suggested small effects. There appears to be a consensus that pollution-intensive industries expanded faster in lower-income countries during the 1970s and 1980s, but the contribution of international trade to this trend is not clear. Patrick Low and Alexander Yeats find that the share of the output of dirty industries in the exports of many LDCs increased between 1965 and 1988. On the other hand, Nancy Birdsall and David Wheeler find that within Latin America dirtier industries tend to be located in the economies that are less open to international trade. These studies are included in a book edited by Patrick Low, *International Trade and the Environment* (1992). Gunnar S. Eskeland and Ann Harrison, "Moving to Greener Pastures? Multinationals and the Pollution-Haven Hypothesis," World Bank Policy Research Working Paper No. 1744 (March 1997), examine the pattern of foreign investment in Côte d'Ivoire, Mexico, Morocco, and Venezuela and find almost no evidence that foreign investment is concentrated in dirty industries. They also find no evidence that foreign investment in these countries is related to pollution abatement costs in more developed countries. Werner Antweiler, Brian R. Copeland, and M. Scott Taylor, "Is Free Trade Good For the Environment?," National Bureau of Economic Research Working Paper No. 6707 (August 1998), argue on theoretical grounds that we might not expect increased openness to trade to have a large effect on the pollution intensity of output in low-income countries. Even if dirty industries are attracted to LDCs by lax environmental regulation, this could be offset by a comparative advantage effect, whereby output becomes more concentrated in labor-intensive industries that tend to be cleaner than capital-intensive industries.

There is perhaps more evidence to support a connection between international trade and deforestation than there is for links between international trade and any other form of environmental degradation in less developed countries. A particularly ambitious attempt to establish such a link is Ramón López, "Environmental Externalities in Traditional Agriculture and the Impact of Trade Liberalization: The Case of Ghana," *Journal of Development Economics* 3 (June 1997). For villages in western Ghana during the period 1988–1989 López finds an overexploitation of biomass through a more than optimal level of land cultivated: fallow periods appear to be too short and the level of deforestation too high. A simulation of his model predicts that trade liberalization will exacerbate this problem, just as the selection by Chichilnisky would lead one to expect, but López has no direct estimate of the impact of trade liberalization on deforestation in Ghana.

Selection X.3. Deforestation and the Rule of Law in a Cross Section of Countries*

I. Introduction

The use of forests and other natural resources in developing countries has received growing attention from environmentalists, the media, and government decision makers. Concern for forests, particularly tropical forests, stems both from the recent recognition that they provide critical services to host nations and worldwide, and from reports that global forest cover is shrinking. Many observers have attributed this shrinkage to population growth, the process of economic development, and misguided government policies. Much of the economic literature on deforestation stresses different factors—the importance of property rights and the role of ownership security in promoting conservation of forests and other natural assets. This paper examines these hypotheses empirically by testing for relationships between deforestation and three possible causes: population pressure, growth in income, and insecure property rights as reflected in measurable legal and political attributes of countries. . . .

The causes of deforestation are not well understood. Popular discussions often mistake associated effects and proximate causes for underlying forces (Panayotou 1990). Deforestation in developing countries is sometimes attributed to slash and burn agriculture, logging, and demands for fuel wood, fodder, and forest products. Yet temperate forests in many developed countries also face growing demand for forest products, logging activity, and agricultural competition for land, but generally are not experiencing the rapid forest depletion and land degradation found in the developing world. . . .

Southgate, Sierra, and Brown (1991) have examined the effect of ownership security and found that security of tenure, as measured by the prevalence of adjudicated land claims, is negatively related to deforestation rates. In addition, there is ample case study evidence that enforcement of property rights is lacking in countries experiencing rapid deforestation. Leases to harvest from government forests in developing countries often are of very short duration so the harvester's self-interest does not provide sufficient incentive to conserve the economic value of the forest. Governments could of course encourage conservation on forests they own by closely controlling the harvest and regeneration practices of concessionaires. However, the associated costs and benefits are such that they seldom choose to do so (Repetto et al. 1989, 23; Boado 1988, 176, 186–87). . . .

The present paper examines this property rights hypothesis indirectly, by testing for associations between deforestation and measures of political turmoil and repression. The potential role of these political factors in deforestation is summarized here and a more detailed discussion is presented in Section V. Conserving a forest to yield a stream of output in future years rather than consuming it immediately is an act of investment. Intuitively, investors will not forego current consumption for a future return without some assurance that the future benefit will be received by the party who makes the initial sacrifice. Such assurances normally result from legal contracts and the force of reputation. When legal and political institutions are volatile or predatory, the degree of assurance is lowered and the incentive to invest is diminished. The empirical analysis that follows tests for relationships between changes in forest cover and relevant political factors using data from a cross section of 120 countries.

As used here, deforestation is simply defined as a reduction in the land area covered by forests, using Food and Agriculture Organization (FAO) definitions of forested land (FAO 1988). . . .

II. Empirical Approach and Data Used

. . . The primary source of forest cover data is *An Interim Report on the State of Forest Resources in the Developing Countries* (FAO 1988). This source provides data on "total forest" cover for 129 countries in 1980 and 84 countries in 1985. Total forest includes land area covered by both closed and open forests.[1] A secondary source, FAO's *Production Yearbook*, reports "forest and woodland area," defined as land area under natural or planted stands of trees plus logged-over area that will be reforested in the near future. This source is available annually for most countries.

---

[1] A closed forest includes broad-leaved, coniferous, and bamboo forests, with tree crown cover exceeding 20 percent of the land. An open forest consists of mixed forest/grasslands with at least 10 percent tree cover. See World Resources Institute (1992, 292) for further details on these definitions.

*From Robert T. Deacon, "Deforestation and the Rule of Law in a Cross-Section of Countries," *Land Economics* 70 (November 1994): 414–425, 427–429. Reprinted by permission.

The *Interim Report* is considered the more reliable of the two and hence is used as the primary source of data on forest cover. The fact that this series is unavailable for many countries in 1985 is a drawback, however. In order to extend it, a statistical relationship between *total forest* and *forest and woodland area* was estimated using data on 84 countries for which both series are available. The estimated equation was then used to predict total forest cover in 1985 for the missing observations. The form of the equation used to predict total forest is motivated by postulating a general functional relationship between total forest, T, and forest and woodland area, w. This relationship, denoted $T(w)$, is then expressed as a second-order Taylor series expansion of T around 1980 values

$$T_1 = T_0 + T'(w_1 - w_0) + (T''/2)(w_1 - w_0)^2$$

where 0 and 1 represent values in 1980 and 1985. Ordinary least squares regression yielded the following estimates, with standard errors in parentheses,

$$T_1 = .9995T_0 + 1.2451(w_1 - w_0)$$
$$\quad (.0056) \qquad (.1510)$$

$$\qquad + 10.2301(w_1 - w_0)^2$$
$$\qquad (1.9863)$$

$$R^2 = .998$$

$$N = 84$$

where T and w are measured as fractions of the land area of countries. The high R^2 is of course due to the close correlation between T_0 and T_1. As the other coefficient estimates clearly indicate, however, changes in total forest are strongly related to changes in forest and woodland area.

In addition, measures of population, national income, and country specific indicators of the rule of law—variables that indicate the degree of political stability and popular representation—are needed. Data on population were taken from Banks (1990) and data on income, actually gross domestic product, were taken from Summers and Heston (1991). Political/legal indicators were obtained from Banks (1990). Indicators of political and legal stability include frequencies of political assassinations, riots, major constitutional changes, guerrilla warfare, attempts at revolution, riots, and government regime changes. As explained later, measures of political representation were also examined, including type of government executive (military, elected, monarch), frequency of political purges, and existence of an elected legislature.

These variables are defined more precisely in Section IV.

Table 1 lists the 120 countries examined, 20 of which are defined as "high income" by the World Bank. It also partitions the overall sample into two deforestation groups, depending on whether countries lost more or less than 10 percent of their 1980 forest cover during 1980–85. This sample excludes countries with less than 500,000 population or having less than 1 percent of land area covered by forests in 1980. It may seem surprising to see Brazil, Indonesia, and the Philippines included among low deforestation countries, as they often appear prominently in discussions of worldwide forest conversion. While these three countries account for large absolute areas of forest loss per year, this is partly due to the fact that the total forest areas in these countries are large. Their percentage deforestation rates ranged from 0.5–0.9 percent per year during 1980–85. By comparison, average annual deforestation rates in Afghanistan, Cote d'Ivoire, and Haiti were 3.7–5.0 percent during the same time span.

In what follows, each of the three hypotheses of interest is examined in isolation, by testing for associations between deforestation rates and, alternatively, population growth, income growth, and political attributes. These simple tests are useful for determining the sensitivity of results to the choice of sample, the exact definition and lag structure of determining variables, and so forth. These results are then used to formulate a more general model that allows for the presence of all three influences at once.

III. Deforestation and Population Growth

Many cite population growth as the single most important cause of deforestation (Allen and Barnes 1985, 175; World Bank 1992, 26–29; World Rainforest Movement 1990, 78). Population growth often leads to migration to the forests by peasants seeking land to clear for subsistence farming. Population growth also increases fuel wood collection, which removes nutrients from the forest. If nutrient loss is sufficiently intense, the result is slowed regeneration and eventual degradation of forest cover.

Table 2 provides a simple test of this hypothesis, where the dependent variable is the proportionate rate of deforestation during 1980–85. Positive population growth is associated with deforestation but the effect is not immediate. Rather, the strongest association is with the rate of population increase five years earlier. In this simple model, a 1

Table 1. Countries in Sample

High Deforestation	Low Deforestation		
Low and Middle Income Countries			
Afghanistan	Albania	German D. R.	Papua New Guinea
Costa Rica	Angola	Ghana	Paraguay
Cote d'Ivoire	Argentina	Greece	Peru
Ecuador	Bangladesh	Guatemala	Philippines
El Salvador	Benin	Guinea	Poland
Gambia	Bhutan	Guyana	Portugal
Guinea-Bissau	Bolivia	Hungary	Romania
Haiti	Botswana	India	Rwanda
Honduras	Brazil	Indonesia	Senegal
Iraq	Bulgaria	Iran	Sierra Leone
Jamaica	Burkina Faso	Kenya	Somalia
Lebanon	Burundi	Korea, North	Sudan
Liberia	Cambodia	Korea, South	Swaziland
Malawi	Cameroon	Lao P. D. R.	Tanzania
Nepal	Cent. African Rep.	Madagascar	Togo
Nicaragua	Chad	Malaysia	Trinidad and Tobago
Niger	Chile	Mali	Tunisia
Nigeria	China	Mauritius	Turkey
South Africa	Colombia	Mexico	Uganda
Sri Lanka	Congo	Mongolia	Uruguay
Syria	Cuba	Morocco	Venezuela
Thailand	Czechoslovakia	Mozambique	Vietnam
	Dominican Rep.	Myanmar	Yugoslavia
	Ethiopia	Namibia	Zaire
	Fiji	Pakistan	Zambia
	Gabon	Panama	Zimbabwe
High Income Countries			
Israel	Australia	F. R. Germany	Spain
	Austria	Ireland	Sweden
	Canada	Italy	Switzerland
	Cyprus	Japan	United Kingdom
	Denmark	Netherlands	United States
	Finland	New Zealand	
	France	Norway	

Note: Excludes countries with fewer than 500,000 population. See text for definitions.

percent increase in population during 1975–80 is associated with a proportionate forest cover reduction of 0.24–0.28 percent during 1980–85.

The simple correlation between cross country population growth rates in 1975–80 and 1980–85 is fairly high, 0.86 in this sample. For this reason the model was reestimated with the 1980–85 population growth rate excluded. As the figures in the third and fourth columns indicate, this increases the significance of the lagged growth rate but has no appreciable effect on the coefficient estimates. The second and fourth columns of coefficients indicate that these results are largely unchanged when countries with relatively light forest cover

are dropped from the sample.[2] The general tenor of these results—that deforestation is associated with lagged population growth—does not change appreciably when countries are separated by income levels. Reestimating these models with high income countries excluded yielded coefficients that are slightly smaller in algebraic value than those in Table 2, but the change is not significant. Surprisingly, perhaps, the population growth coefficients are all larger in algebraic value when estimated for

[2]The countries excluded are Afghanistan, Burundi, Haiti, Iran, Iraq, Israel, Kenya, Lebanon, Niger, Pakistan, South Africa, Syria, Tunisia, and Uruguay.

Table 2. Deforestation and Population Growth (ordinary least squares estimates)

Countries in Sample	All	Forest > 5%	All	Forest > 5%
Log change in population, 1980–85	−.0304 (−0.17)	.0009 (0.01)	—	—
Log change in population, 1975–80	.2593 (1.52)	.2815 (2.01)	.2357 (2.55)	.2814 (3.34)
Log change in population, 1970–75	.0575 (0.69)	−.0221 (−0.20)	.0544 (0.67)	−.0218 (−0.22)
Constant	.0274 (2.27)	.0188 (1.08)	.0270 (2.30)	.0188 (1.82)
R^2	.08	.14	.08	.14
N	112	98	112	98

Notes: t-statistics in parentheses. The dependent variable is the 1980–1985 change in the logarithm of land area classified as forest. The heading "Forest > 5%" indicates that forest cover in 1980 exceeds 5 percent of the country's land area.

Table 3. Deforestation and Income Growth (correlation coefficients)

	All Countries	Forest > 5%	Low and Middle Income
Log change in per-capita GDP, 1980–85	−.1776	−.1061	−.1423
Log change in per-capita GDP, 1975–80	−.0642	−.0890	−.0110
Log change in total GDP, 1980–85	−.0917	−.0044	−.1066
Log change in total GDP, 1975–80	.0380	.0227	.0349
N	105	92	85

Notes: Low and middle income countries are identified in Table 1. See note to Table 1 for other definitions.

high income countries. That is, a given rate of population growth is associated with a higher deforestation rate if it occurs in a high income country than in a low income country. Again, the most significant association is with population growth lagged five years.

IV. Deforestation and Income Growth

Growth in measured national income is often identified as an important correlate, and sometimes as a cause, of deforestation. This is implicit in discussions that attribute deforestation to economic development strategies that promote conversion of forests to plantation agriculture and the production of cash crops for export (World Rainforest Movement 1990, 41, ff.). It also appears at the heart of proposals to revise national income to appropriately incorporate the consumption of natural assets. Those who advocate such revisions point out that an important share of measured GNP, particularly in developing countries, is actually consumption

of natural capital such as forests (see Repetto et al. 1989, 4–9; Solorzano et al. 1991).

Table 3 presents evidence relevant to this hypothesis. These simple correlation coefficients indicate that, if anything, the association between deforestation and growth in measured income is negative—rapid deforestation accompanies slow, or negative, measured economic growth. Experimentation with different samples indicates that this lack of association is robust. Although not shown in the table, a negative relationship between income growth and deforestation exists for high income countries as well.

Of course this does not invalidate the proposition that some growth in measured income actually is consumption of forest capital. It may indicate, however, that any such relationship based on capital consumption is outweighed by the increase in demand for forest preservation that comes with increases in income. Alternatively, it may indicate the presence of a third factor that is positively related to both income growth and the maintenance of forest cover. A possible set of such factors is examined next.

V. Deforestation, Ownership Security, and the Nature of Political Systems

Forest cover is a form of capital that is productive in several land uses. Land continuously covered by forest can yield a sustained flow of minor forest products such as fruit, latex, rattan, oils, or grazing (Peters, Gentry, and Mendelsohn 1989). Alternatively, forested land can be harvested intermittently to obtain timber, in which case the standing biomass at any time is capital that enables future timber growth. If a forest is used for sustainable shifting cultivation, with relatively long fallow periods during which forest cover is allowed to increase, then the growing stock is a store of nutrients that can be harvested periodically. The latter two land uses are very similar. Both involve an investment period during which forest capital accumulates followed by harvest, either of timber or of nutrients for agriculture, and both allow the possibility for this cycle to be repeated indefinitely.

A Simple Model of Default Risk and Land Use

Poorly enforced ownership exposes standing forests and other kinds of capital to a form of confiscation or default risk and thereby discriminates against capital intensive land uses. Long fallow periods between harvests of nutrients are attractive only if the individual, family, or tribe has some assurance that a parcel of land and its forest cover will not be invaded by squatters, harvested by a timber company, or confiscated by a government official. The same point applies to land used to grow timber. Likewise, land that would be used to grow minor forest products if ownership were enforced might be deforested instead if ownership becomes insecure, in order to obtain timber or simply to make the land available for less capital intensive uses. In general, poorly defined ownership favors either the conversion of forested land to noncapital intensive permanent agriculture or its degeneration to wasteland. . . .

The Role of Political Factors in Ownership Security

Insecure property rights, either to assets or income streams, might arise from two sorts of political circumstances. First, government may lack the power, stability, and popular support to enforce laws of property. Absent reliable third party enforcement and predictable legal interpretations of property claims, the individual's incentive to invest is weak. While this argument seems straightforward when applied to privately held property, a similar argument can be made for assets nominally owned by government. When government lacks the ability to enforce controls on how government forests are used they tend to be treated as free access resources. This is manifest in Latin America and elsewhere by the colonization of national parks and government forest reserves by squatters. Further, if the institutions of government are weak or short-lived, proposals for long-term investment in government-owned assets will lack credibility since the segments of society making the initial sacrifice will have no guarantee of receiving the ultimate reward. Measures of general lawlessness, guerrilla warfare, armed revolt, and rapid changes in laws or constitutions are used as empirical indicators of such instability.

Second, it is hypothesized that the average individual's ownership security tends to be weak in countries that are governed by the rule of individuals and dominant elites rather than the rule of law and anonymous institutions. In such circumstances, one's property claim may depend heavily on the favor of a specific individual or clique rather than the persistence of a set of political and legal institutions. If the clique is deposed, its allies may lose their property. For those who are not in favor with the ruling elite, property claims are even more problematic since those who control government may choose to enforce laws selectively and redistribute property toward themselves or their allies. Such redistribution need not be direct, it may take the form of opportunistic taxation or regulation. Accumulating capital in such circumstances may simply invite confiscation. Empirically assessing the degree to which a country is ruled by individuals as opposed to laws is approached by determining whether its governmental system exhibits attributes of popular representation, for example, whether its leaders are elected, whether a legislature exists, whether political opposition is tolerated, and so forth.

Empirical Results

This general set of hypotheses initially was tested in a very simple way. Data on the attributes of political and governmental systems were obtained in each country, and country averages were formed over 1980–85. These average political attributes were then compared for countries experiencing high versus low deforestation during 1980–85, using the sample of countries shown in Table 1. The ten variables selected to measure general lawlessness and governmental/legal instability are shown in Table 4. The mean number of political assassinations per million population is a measure of general lawlessness, and may also indicate government instability. Other variables are primarily indicators of instability in a given regime's grip on power or, as in the case of major constitutional changes, a measure of the frequency of changes in the basic legal structure regardless of regime.

All variables in Table 4 are defined in such a way that figures in the first column will exceed those in the second if the hypothesis is correct. This expectation is confirmed for nine of the ten measures. The differences are significant at 10 percent using a one-tailed test for frequencies of revolutions, guerrilla warfare, and major constitutional changes. Contrary to expectations, coups de'état are slightly more frequent in low deforestation countries, but the difference is small and insignificant. All high income countries were excluded in

these comparisons. When high income countries are included the differences become much sharper: t-statistics rise for all comparisons except coups d'état, which falls to near zero, and six of the ten differences become significant at 10 percent.

The second set of tests concerns the effect of popular representation on deforestation. The variables used to measure representation in each country are defined in Table 5. The first three of these are self-explanatory. Regarding the fourth, the chief executive of government is a premier only if chosen by elected representatives. This indicates, jointly, that the selection process is democratic and that the legislative branch exercises substantial power, hence the degree of representation is high. Representation is thus weaker if the executive is not a premier. Frequent political purges indicate that opposition, and hence competition for political power, is not tolerated. Consequently, the first five measures are *larger* in less representative systems and are expected to be greater in high deforestation countries. The sixth, "Legislature is elected," is expected to be *smaller* in less representative governments, and hence smaller in high deforestation countries. Regarding the last measure, fre-

Table 4. Deforestation and Measures of Lawlessness and Governmental/Legal Instability (mean political attributes by deforestation rate, 1980–1985)

	High Deforestation Countries, μ_H	Low Deforestation Countries, μ_L	t-statistic* H_0: $\mu_L < \mu_H$	$Pr > t$
Political assassinations**	.0822	.0264	0.94 (24)	.18
General strikes**	.0245	.0142	0.88 (34)	.19
Riots**	.0468	.0284	1.04 (28)	.15
Anti-gov't. demonstrations**	.0645	.0482	0.82 (49)	.21
Guerrilla warfare	.3333	.2051	1.31 (31)	.10
Revolutions	.3258	.1859	1.63 (29)	.06
Major government crises	.1439	.0684	1.08 (25)	.14
Coups d'état	.0303	.0384	0.39 (31)	.36
Major constitutional changes	.1136	.0705	1.41 (31)	.08
Government regime changes	.0727	.0436	1.08 (30)	.14
Number of countries	22	78	—	—

*t-statistic is for the one-tailed test H_0: $\mu_H \leq \mu_L$ versus H_a: $\mu_H > \mu_L$. Degrees of freedom are in parentheses.

**Per million population.

Notes: Excludes 20 countries classified as "high income" by the World Bank. A *high deforestation* country is one that lost at least 10 percent of the forest cover existing in 1980 during 1980–85. A *political assassination* is any politically motivated murder or attempted murder of a high government official or politician. A *general strike* is a strike of 1,000 or more workers aimed at national government policies or authority. A *riot* is any violent demonstration of more than 100 citizens involving the use of physical force. *Anti-government demonstrations* are peaceful gatherings of at least 100 people for the primary purpose of displaying opposition to government policies or authority. *Guerrilla warfare* is the presence of any armed activity, sabotage, or bombings carried on by independent bands of citizens or irregular forces and aimed at the overthrow of the present regime. A *revolution* is an attempted illegal or forced change in top government elite, or armed rebellion intended to gain independence from the central government. A *major government crisis* is a rapidly developing situation that threatens to bring the downfall of the present regime—excluding revolt aimed at such overthrow. A *coup d'état* is a successful extraconstitutional or forced change in the top government elite and/or its effective control of the nation's power structure—including successful revolutions. *Major constitutional changes* reports the number of basic alterations in a state's constitutional structure, e.g., adoption of a new constitution that alters roles of different branches of government (minor constitutional amendments are excluded). A *government regime change* is any change in the type of regime, e.g., civilian, military, protectorate, in charge of government.

Source: A. S. Banks, *Cross-National Time-Series Data Archive,* SUNY Binghamton, 1990.

Table 5. Deforestation and Indicators of Nonrepresentative Government (mean indicators by deforestation rate, 1980–1985)

	High Deforestation Countries, μ_H	Low Deforestation Countries, μ_L	t-statistic* H_0: $\mu_L < \mu_H$	$Pr > t$
Government executive is military	.2424	.0940	1.80 (27)	.04
Nonelected executive	.4394	.3184	1.11 (33)	.14
No legislature exists	.1742	.1410	0.49 (36)	.31
Executive is not a premier	.6136	.4124	1.79 (36)	.04
Political purges	.0909	.0620	0.74 (30)	.23
Legislature is elected*	.7879	.8419	0.72 (35)	.24
Changes in executive*	.1136	.1624	1.16 (50)	.13
Number of countries	22	78	—	—

*t-statistic is for the one-tailed test H_0: $\mu_H \leq \mu_L$ versus H_a: $\mu_H > \mu_L$, except in tests involving *Legislature is elected* and *Changes in executive* where the inequalities are reversed.

Notes: Excludes 20 countries classified as "high income" by the World Bank. A *high deforestation* country is one experiencing a loss of forest cover during 1980–85 exceeding 10 percent of the amount existing in 1980. *Government executive is military* indicates that the individual who exercises primary influence in shaping the country's major internal and external decisions is in the armed services. *Executive is not a premier* indicates that the executive is not drawn from the legislature of a parliamentary democracy. A *purge* is the systematic elimination by jailing or execution of political opposition within the ranks of the regime or the opposition. *Legislature is elected* indicates that a legislature exists and that legislators are chosen either by direct or indirect election. *Changes in executive* are the number of times in a year that control of the executive changes to a new individual independent of the predecessor. Other measures are self-explanatory.

Source: A. S. Banks, *Cross-National Time-Series Data Archive*, SUNY Binghamton, 1990.

quent changes in executive might plausibly indicate competition in the executive branch. If so, such changes should be more common in low deforestation countries. Alternatively, more frequent executive change might signal greater instability in government policy and hence greater deforestation. The comparison in Table 5 supports the former hypothesis, although the difference is not highly significant.

To summarize the results obtained, all seven comparisons are as expected. Only two of the differences are significant at 10 percent, however, those for "military executive" and for "executive is not a premier." Again, the results become much sharper when high income countries are included. In this case four of the seven are significant at 10 percent.

The 17 political measures in Tables 4 and 5 clearly are not independent. To test their joint association with deforestation, a logit regression equation was estimated using the political measures as regressors and testing their joint ability to predict a categorical variable denoting high versus low deforestation countries. When all 17 measures are included and the sample includes all 120 countries, the chi square statistic indicates the regression is significant at a probability level of 0.02. All but four of the coefficients have signs that accord with the differences in means reported earlier, and none of the four with perverse signs approach significance. When high income countries are excluded,

the probability of no relationship rises to 0.15. If variables with z statistics below 0.5 are excluded, however, the probability level falls to 0.02 and the number of perverse signs falls to one. Overall, then, the null hypothesis that these measures of political instability and nonrepresentation are not related to deforestation is rejected. . . .

VI. A Preliminary Synthesis

The preceding results are broadly consistent with the hypotheses that deforestation results both from population growth—and the increased competition for land and natural resources that accompany it—and from political environments that are not conducive to investment. . . . The political factors identified as correlates of deforestation were combined with population growth rates in a single regression equation for deforestation. In addition, . . . a variable was formed as the residual from a regression equation of the investment rate on political variables found important in explaining deforestation. This residual is intended to capture aspects of the investment climate not reflected in available political attributes.

Regression results are reported in Table 6. The sign patterns exhibited earlier are largely unchanged. The elasticity of deforestation with respect to lagged population change is reduced noticeably from the level shown in Table 2 (.23–.28), however, and its significance is reduced. As before,

Table 6. Deforestation, Population Growth, and Political Attributes (OLS regression coefficients)

Sample	All Countries		Low and Middle Income	
Population growth, 1975–80	.1744	.1860	.0704	.1247
	(1.84)	(2.21)	(0.60)	(1.27)
Guerrilla warfare, 1980–85	.0539	.0462	.0451	.0392
	(1.75)	(1.66)	(1.34)	(1.32)
Guerrilla warfare, 1975–79	−.0297	−.0156	−.0141	−.0024
	(1.00)	(0.63)	(0.43)	(0.08)
Revolutions, 1980–85	.0313	.0606	.0415	.0662
	(0.95)	(2.10)	(1.16)	(2.19)
Revolutions, 1975–79	−.0536	−.0597	−.0579	−.0636
	(−2.00)	(−2.38)	(1.92)	(2.34)
Constitutional changes, 1980–85	.0200	—	.0122	—
	(0.32)		(0.18)	
Constitutional changes, 1975–79	−.0339	—	−.0357	—
	(0.81)		(0.79)	
Military executive, 1980–85	.0220	—	.0192	—
	(0.66)		(0.55)	
Military executive, 1975–79	.0017	—	.0029	—
	(0.06)		(0.10)	
Executive is not a premier, 1980–85	.0177	.0168	.0227	.0207
	(1.25)	(1.29)	(1.42)	(1.43)
Investment residual	.0154	—	.0200	—
	(0.21)		(0.25)	
N	106	118	86	98
R^2	.21	.20	.19	.19

Note: Absolute values of *t*-statistics in parentheses.

the association between deforestation and population growth is stronger in the full sample than in the sample that omits high income countries. Guerrilla warfare and revolutionary activity are correlated with one another, so including both in the same equation causes the coefficients of both to decline somewhat.[3] For each measure, the coefficients for 1980–85 and 1975–80 are of opposite sign and similar magnitude, which suggests that deforestation is responsive to changes in these variables. With other variables in the model the frequency of constitutional changes and the presence of a military head of government becomes insignificant, though their signs are as expected. Again, the variable "executive is a premier" was included for 1980–85 only since its values in different time periods are highly correlated. The investment residual, included to capture unmeasured effects on investment incentives, is (perversely) positive but insignificant. It is unavailable for 12 countries so its inclusion alters the sample substantially. Figures in the second and fourth columns present estimates obtained by ex-

cluding political and other measures that lacked significance in the original regressions.

VII. Conclusions

The intent of this paper was to present descriptive statistical results and simple hypothesis tests on alternative causes of deforestation, particularly insecure ownership. Consistent associations were found between deforestation and political variables reflecting insecure ownership, and this is encouraging. The explanatory power of the model is fairly low, however, so firm conclusions would be premature. One likely reason for low explanatory power is the exclusion of relevant variables that presently are unavailable, hence an obvious task for continuing research is to obtain and examine additional data.

References

Allen, Julia C., and Douglas F. Barnes. 1985. "The Causes of Deforestation in Developing Countries." *Annals of the Association of American Geographers* 75 (2):163–84.

[3] Simple correlation coefficients range from .47 to .72.

Banks, A. S. 1990. "Cross-National Time-Series Data Archive." Center for Social Analysis, State University of New York, Binghamton, September 1979 (updated to 1990).

Boado, Eufresina L. 1988. "Incentive Policies and Forest Use in the Philippines." In *Public Policies and the Misuse of Forest Resources,* ed. R. Repetto and M. Gillis. Cambridge: Cambridge University Press.

Food and Agriculture Organization (FAO). 1988. *An Interim Report on the State of the Forest Resources in the Developing Countries.* Rome: United Nations.

Panayotou, Theodore. 1990. "The Economics of Environmental Degradation: Problems, Causes, and Responses." Harvard Institute for International Development. Mimeo.

Panayotou, Theodore, and Somthawin Sungsuwan. 1989. "An Econometric Study of the Causes of Tropical Deforestation: The Case of Northeast Thailand." Discussion Paper No. 284, Harvard Institute for International Development.

Peters, Charles M., Alwyn J. Gentry, and Robert O. Mendelsohn. 1989. "Valuation of an Amazonian Rainforest." *Nature* 399 (June 29):655–56.

Repetto, Robert, William Magrath, Michael Wells, Christine Beer, and Fabrizio Rossini. 1989. *Wasting Assets: Natural Resources in the National Income Accounts.* Washington, DC: World Resources Institute.

Solorzano, Raul, Ronnie de Camino, Richard Woodward, Joseph Tosi, Vincente Watson, Alexis Vasquez, Carlos Villalobos, Jorge Jimenez, Robert Repetto, and Wilfredo Cruz. 1991. *Accounts Overdue: Natural Resource Depreciation in Costa Rica.* Washington, DC: World Resources Institute.

Southgate, Douglas, Rodrigo Sierra, and Lawrence Brown. 1991. "The Causes of Tropical Deforestation in Ecuador: A Statistical Analysis." *World Development* 19 (9):1145–51.

Summers, Robert, and Alan Heston. 1991. "The Penn World Table Mark V." *Quarterly Journal of Economics* 61 (May):225–39.

World Resources Institute. 1992. *World Resources, 1992–93.* New York: Oxford University Press.

World Bank. 1992. *World Development Report 1992: Development and the Environment.* Oxford: Oxford University Press.

World Rainforest Movement. 1990. *Rainforest Destruction: Causes, Effects, and False Solutions.* Penang, Malaysia: World Rainforest Movement.

Selection X.4. Determinants of Pollution Abatement in Developing Countries: Evidence from South and Southeast Asia*

1. Introduction

Developing countries, particularly those in Asia, are fast adopting industrial pollution control standards similar to those in developed countries. Some end-of-pipe water pollution control is already evident in many South and Southeast Asian economies. Formal regulation has been greatly hampered, however, by the absence of clear and legally binding regulations; limited institutional capacity; lack of appropriate equipment and trained personnel; and inadequate information on emissions. At present, the government-imposed "price of pollution" is nearly zero for many manufacturing facilities in these economies.

One would predict highly pollution-intensive production under such conditions. Our research, however, has uncovered strongly contradictory evidence. Despite weak or nonexistent formal regulation and enforcement, there are many clean plants in the developing countries of South and Southeast Asia. Of course, there are also many plants which are among the world's most serious polluters. What explains such extreme interplant variation? This paper reviews evidence drawn from three empirical studies which we conducted during 1992–94:

A case study of plants in two sectors in one country: fertilizer and pulping in Bangladesh;
A survey and econometric evaluation of abatement efforts by plants in one sector in four countries: 26 pulp and paper plants in Bangladesh, India, Indonesia and Thailand;
An econometric analysis of many plants across many sectors in one country: Indonesia.

We are particularly interested in policy-relevant variables which are not conventionally associated with environmental regulation. Formal regulation will undoubtedly remain weak for some time, but other determinants of plant-level abatement may provide useful tools for directly or indirectly inducing pollution control. Our analysis incorporates three sets of factors which are relevant for decisions affecting the pollution intensity of an industrial process: plant characteristics, economic considerations, and external pressure.

*From Hemamala Hettige, Mainul Huq, Sheoli Pargal, and David Wheeler, "Determinants of Pollution Abatement in Developing Countries: Evidence from South and Southeast Asia," *World Development* 24 (December 1996): 1891–1902. Reprinted by permission.

Relevant plant characteristics may include production scale, choice of technology, vintage, ownership, management quality, available human resources and technical expertise. Plants' responsiveness to pressure for abatement may also vary significantly with economic considerations: input prices, profitability, market characteristics, availability of information on abatement technology, and sources of financing. Finally, plants may adapt to external pressure from government regulators, buyers, investors, and neighboring communities which suffer damage from pollution. In our empirical studies, we have assessed the significance and relative importance of these factors in determining plants' environmental performance.

The rest of section 1 reviews the current extent of regulation in the study countries and presents some evidence on variations in plant-level abatement. Section 2 develops a conceptual framework for analyzing interplant variation. Our evidence to date is summarized in section 3, while section 4 discusses the implications.

(a) The Current State of Regulation

During the past two decades, many developing countries have instituted pollution-control systems which are similar, at least on paper, to those in developed countries. Quantity-based regulation has been nearly universal, with considerable cross-country variation in reliance on instruments such as effluent concentration standards, volume standards, and mandated installation of pollution control equipment. There has also been great variation in the strictness of monitoring and enforcement of regulations. Our study countries illustrate the existing range of regulatory experience in developing countries.

(i) Bangladesh. The environmental absorptive capacity of this densely populated, riverain country is very low; current environmental concerns focus on the impact of water pollution. Industrial facilities in pollution-intensive sectors such as food, wood pulping, chemicals, and fertilizer nearly always discharge their wastes into rivers which serve large downstream populations.

National regulation of industrial effluents has been weak, with severe shortages of supporting funds and trained personnel. Formal regulatory standards exist only for waste water. It therefore seems clear that formal monitoring and enforcement procedures have had little impact on plants' environmental performance in Bangladesh. In many cases, however, local communities have been able to identify and bring pressure to bear on plants whose discharges have caused fish kills, illness, and damage to irrigated paddy crops.

(ii) India. The formal regulatory structure in India presents a strong contrast to that of Bangladesh. National and state environmental management systems have been highly organized for over a decade. Air and water effluent concentration standards have been legislated for a large number of pollutants. The central government sets reference standards, but lacks legislative and enforcement authority over the individual states. Differences in local political, economic and environmental conditions have led to different degrees of enforcement of the reference standards. There is extensive emissions reporting by plants in some states, with a growing trend toward verification of reports by state-approved research laboratories and consulting firms. Formal sanctions such as fines and threatened shutdowns seem to have generated some abatement efforts at the plant level.

(iii) Indonesia. Indonesian waste-water regulation has only been in place since 1992, so implementation does not meet developed-country standards. Environmental management authority is decentralized, with different effective standards across provinces and uniform standards within provinces. The government's major water pollution control initiative to date is the PROKASIH (Clean Rivers) program. Although it is voluntary, it has produced a response which suggests that current and prospective environmental regulations are taken seriously by plant managers. Since 1990, PROKASIH has elicited substantial pollution reduction from plants in 11 provinces and 23 river basins. It has also apparently been taken by non-PROKASIH plants as a credible signal that the government is serious about combating industrial pollution.

(iv) Thailand. Thailand has had environmental guidelines and pollution standards for several industrial sectors since the early 1980s. The regulatory program has lacked credibility because industrial plants are simply asked to comply with standards without any serious pressure or legal enforcement.

Figure 1. Percentage of plants in the Pasig River Basin (Philippines) by BOD removal rates.

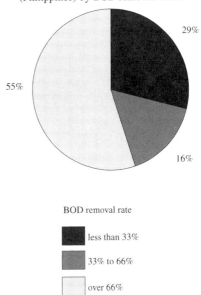

BOD removal rate

■ less than 33%

■ 33% to 66%

□ over 66%

(b) Existing Variations in Abatement

Given the weakness of formal regulation in our sample countries, a conventional economic analysis would predict high emissions discharges in pollution-intensive sectors. If cost-minimizing polluters do not expect to pay for emissions, they should regard the environment as a free input and exploit it accordingly. Evidence gathered by World Bank field surveys and national regulators suggests, however, that such an analysis is far too simplistic.

Figure 1 shows the distribution of treatment rates of organic water pollution (BOD) by approximately 100 factories in the Pasig River Basin, Philippines.[1] These plants are all in the same region of the same developing country, operating under the supervision of the same national regulatory agency (DENR). Nevertheless, some are operating at or near high international standards while others are hardly cleaning their waste water at all.

[1]Biological Oxygen Demand (BOD) is one of the most commonly regulated water pollutants. Organic water pollutants are oxidized by naturally occurring microorganisms. These remove dissolved oxygen from the water and can seriously damage some fish species which have adapted to the previous dissolved oxygen level. Low levels of dissolved oxygen may also enable disease-causing pathogens to survive longer in water. The most common measure for BOD is the amount of oxygen used by microorganisms to oxidize the organic waste in a standard sample of pollutant during a five-day period.

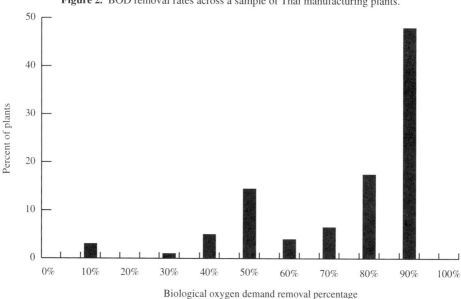

Figure 2. BOD removal rates across a sample of Thai manufacturing plants.

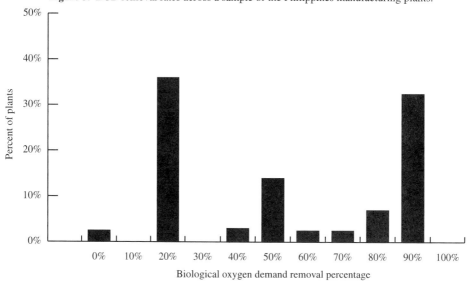

Figure 3. BOD removal rates across a sample of the Philippines manufacturing plants.

Figures 2 and 3 compare samples of approximately 100 plants in the Metro Manila area (the Philippines) and the Bangkok region (Thailand: Suskawat and Ransig). The bar charts in the two figures depict the relative frequency of BOD removal rates in the two sets of plants, which were surveyed by the World Bank in the course of projects in these areas.

In the Philippines, DENR has overall regulatory authority. By contrast, Thailand's extremely "lais-

sez-faire" approach to pollution control would seem to make it a likely candidate for "pollution haven" status. The average BOD reduction rate in Thailand is considerably higher than in the Philippines, however, and many Thai plants are running near OECD emissions standards. Approximately 50% of the plants are removing 90% of the BOD from the waste water stream, and 70–80% are removing over 70%. In the Philippines the distribution is less skewed, with about a third of the sample in each of the high, medium and low removal categories.

In Indonesia, the available plant-level data reveal the same pattern. Figures 4 and 5 show the distribution of effluent concentrations relative to US and Indonesian standards for large samples of Indonesian pulp and paper plants and textile mills.

While the US Environmental Protection Agency (EPA) is well staffed and has operated for over 20 years, the Indonesian national pollution control agency (BAPEDAL) is quite new, operates with a small staff and has little power to punish plants which are not in compliance with existing standards. Nevertheless, the actual distribution of In-

Figure 4. Distribution of BOD load intensity, Indonesian paper plants.

Plants complying with US Std. = ~3.8kg/ton

Plants in violation of Indonesian Std. = 10kg/ton

Kg of BOD/ton of paper

Paper plants

Figure 5. Distribution of BOD load intensity, Indonesian textile plants.

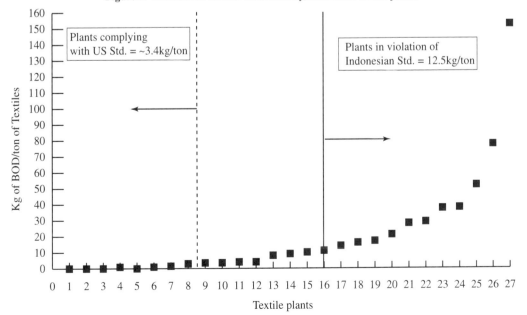

Plants complying with US Std. = ~3.4kg/ton

Plants in violation of Indonesian Std. = 12.5kg/ton

Kg of BOD/ton of Textiles

Textile plants

donesian plants is extremely broad, overlapping both US and Indonesian standards. Approximately two-thirds of the plants are in compliance with Indonesian standards, and one-third would be in compliance with US standards.

To summarize, the existing evidence does not conform to the predictions of conventional environmental economics. Pollution is undeniably an externality, and regulation in all our sample countries is quite weak by OECD standards. Cost-minimizing plants should all favor pollution-intensive production under these circumstances. Analysis of plant-level emissions reveals, however, a distribution of emissions reduction rates which overlaps typical OECD distributions. Average pollution reduction is clearly lower in the Asian developing economies, but more than a few plants are operating at or near world-class environmental performance standards.

2. The Economics of Industrial Pollution in Developing Countries: Some Hypotheses

The variation in pollution intensity of plants in developing countries, even in the absence of formal regulation, has led us to consider community pressure and environmental reputation as two potentially important factors influencing plants' environmental performance.

(a) Community Pressure

The recent literature includes many accounts of plants' response to community pressure in Asia. Cribb (1990) details several agreements reached by plants and communities in Indonesia. Khator (1991) uses several case studies to illustrate ways in which plants have responded to community pressure in India. In some instances, plants reduce their emissions by installing new treatment facilities. In other instances, they compensate the community indirectly by providing drinking water, blankets, or new facilities such as temples and community halls. Some plants, however, successfully refuse to address the pollution problem.

Khator notes that directly affected communities are usually the first to react to industrial pollution problems. Most activism begins with incidents such as fish kills, crop damage or the spread of disease, which can easily be associated with pollution from neighboring plants. Villagers' ability to organize and modify polluters' behavior is often limited, however, by a high illiteracy rate, lack of resources, or lack of influence over government officials. In addition, their capacity to pressure of-fending plants is sometimes compromised by their dependence on those same plants for employment.

(b) Reputation

The ability and willingness of plants to respond to community pressure may also depend on reputation-related factors. Evidence from the United States suggests that large polluters have strong incentives to improve their environmental reputations through participation in voluntary cleanup programs. Arora and Cason (1995) find that large plants with high toxic releases have been more likely to participate in the US EPA's voluntary, highly publicized 33/50 program. Their results also suggest that the probability of joining such programs is enhanced by a plant's profitability and the competitiveness of the markets in which it operates. Arora and Cason argue that higher profits in imperfect capital markets enable some plants to finance voluntary cleanup, and that competitive markets prompt them to differentiate their products on environmental quality. Their results also suggest that such effects are more pronounced in consumer goods industries. . . .

3. Evidence from South and Southeast Asia

(a) A Case Study of Publicly Owned Plants in Bangladesh

This study by Huq and Wheeler (1993) draws on a 1992 survey of seven manufacturing plants in two sectors: fertilizer and wood pulp. The survey included four of the five urea fertilizer plants in Bangladesh, a superphosphate fertilizer plant and two large pulping facilities. All were public enterprises managed by the Bangladesh Chemical Industries Corporation (BCIC). They were of widely varying ages, and evenly distributed between urban and rural locations scattered throughout Bangladesh. The survey investigated process technologies, end-of-pipe treatment efforts, and the efficiency of general waste management. Results are summarized in Table 1, which categorizes plants by pollution intensity, abatement effort, relevant characteristics, location, and the nature of the surrounding community.

Weak vintage effects are suggested by Table 1, but the power of "clean technology bundling" is apparent: each of the four fertilizer plants was built with foreign aid, which was tied to technical assistance and equipment acquisition from the donor country. Each plant's environmental performance therefore reflects donor-country standards at the

Table 1. Plant and Community Characteristics Data from a Plant-Level Survey in Bangladesh

| | Technology Choice | | | Community | | | |
Plant	Donor Country	Year of Installation (Vintage)	Process Pollution Intensity	Cleanup Effort	Local Pressure	Identifiable	Job Options
Urea Fertilizer Factory (UFF—Ghorasal, Narsingdi)	Japan	1968	Medium	High	High	Y	Medium
Polash Urea Fertilizer Factory (PUFF—Polash, Narsingdi)	China	1985	Medium	Medium	High	Y	Medium
Chittagong Urea Factory Ltd (CUF—Rangudia, Chittagong)	Japan	1989	Low	None	Zero	Y	High
Natural Gas Fertilizer Factory (NGFF—Fenchuganj, Sylhet)	Japan	1961	High	Medium	Low	Y	Low
Triple Superphosphate Complex (TSPC—North Patenga, Chittagong)	N.A.	1970	High	None	High	Y	High
Khulna Newsprint Mill (KNM—Khalishpur, Khulna)	Canada	1959	Medium	None	Zero	N	High
Sylhet Pulp and Paper Mill (SPPM—Chatak, Sylhet)	FRG	1975	High	High	Zero	Y	Low

Source: Huq and Wheeler (1993).

time of installation. The three Japanese plants constructed in 1961 (NGFF), 1968 (UFF) and 1989 (CUF) have been successively cleaner. The newest plant (CUF) has internalized environmental concerns to such an extent that there is little need for end-of-pipe (EOP) treatment. In contrast, the PUFF plant installed by China in 1985 has process technology and environmental performance similar to those of UFF, which was constructed by Japan in 1968.

In the absence of formal regulation, community pressure has apparently been quite effective in many instances. Negotiated settlements have included monetary compensation for damage to fisheries and paddy fields, and installation of EOP treatment equipment. Of the three plants which experienced pressure from adjacent communities, two undertook to clean up. The outlier in this context is TSPC, a highly polluting plant which has been identified as a major problem by the Bangladesh government. Its failure to respond to external pressure seems to reflect intractable management problems. Of the four plants where little local pressure was evident (CUF, NGFF, KNM,

and SPPM), only one (SPPM) undertook a substantial cleanup effort.

In all three instances where community pressure was evident (UFF, PUFF and TSPC), the plants were clearly identifiable polluters and other employment opportunities were plentiful. CUF was also clearly identifiable and operating in an area where employment opportunities were abundant. It did not face any local pressure, however, because it was already a very clean plant. The lack of community pressure on SPPM and NGFF, clearly identifiable as the only polluting facilities in a rural setting, may have been due to the scarcity of employment in their areas. In contrast, the location of the KNM plant among several other polluting facilities may have made it more difficult for the community to single out.

(b) A Crosscountry Survey of Paper and Pulp Plants

This section reviews the evidence from a survey of 26 pulp and paper plants in four countries (Bangladesh, India, Indonesia and Thailand) analyzed by Hartman, Huq and Wheeler (1995). The survey was sponsored by the World Bank and conducted by one of the authors (Huq) during a period of three months in 1992. The pulp and paper sector was chosen because it has both high pollution potential and alternative process technologies with highly varied pollution intensities. The sample was chosen to maximize variation in location- and ownership-related variables within the four countries. In Indonesia and Thailand the survey was conducted in Java and the Bangkok region, respectively; in India it spanned four states: Maharashtra, Kerala, Karnataka and West Bengal. The Bangladesh survey was a countrywide exercise.

The study focused on the degree to which plants had installed pollution-control technologies which were directly observable. This was the only feasible approach for a rapid survey, and it had the additional advantage of circumventing uncertainties about the quality of reported emissions data. As previously noted, emissions monitoring and reporting in the sample economies have been very weak in most cases. . . . Table 2 presents final regression results for the abatement effort equations, after nonsignificant variables have been dropped. Although degrees of freedom are modest, the results are quite strong.

(i) Formal and Informal Regulations. The results suggest that both formal and informal regulatory pressure have been significant determinants of abatement effort. As the formal regulation index increases, it is associated with a strong increase in

the abatement effort index (ABI: scaled 0–36). Plants which experienced significant local pressure to abate score approximately 10 points higher on the ABI in Model I. Model II replaces the Pressure dummy with two hypothesized determinants of effective pressure: per capita income and the visibility of the plant (with relative invisibility proxied by location in a large city). Although the overall regression fit is not as good, it seems clear that these variables are robust instruments. Abatement effort rises strongly with national income per capita. In addition, plants operating "invisibly" in large urban/industrial clusters score nearly 12 points lower on the ABI.

(ii) Scale. Scale effects are tested with a quadratic specification in plant employment. The results suggest powerful scale economies for abatement, which apparently decline at the margin. They may also have significance for the analysis of community pressure. In local economies, large plants should be more visible and therefore more susceptible to pressure for cleanup. On the other hand, larger employers might expect more leniency from communities which value the jobs they provide. These results suggest that the combined effects of scale economies and visibility strongly outweigh any leniency effect.

(iii) Vintage, Process Technology. Age of plant has no measurable impact, probably because the survey's focus is on abatement at the end-of-pipe. Age of plant, however, may not be a good proxy

Table 2. Regression Results (dependent variable: Abatement Effort Index)

Variable	Model I (Adj. R^2 = 0.871)		Model II (Adj. R^2 = 0.752)	
	Coefficient estimate	t stat.	Coefficient estimate	t stat.
Intercept			−47.210	−2.69**
Community variables				
Degree of formal regulation	3.366	3.530**	2.991	1.926*
D [pressure]	9.676	2.341**		
Log [per capita income]			6.763	2.482**
D [big city location]			−11.946	−4.366**
Firm variables				
Employment	0.007	2.498**	0.004	1.956*
(Employment)^2	−1.04e^{-06}	−2.517**	−5.69e^{-07}	−1.834*
Competitive	3.487	1.723*	5.712	3.649**
D [state ownership]	−12.794	−2.798**		
D [clean technology]	−6.899	−1.912*		
No. of observations	22		20	

*Significant at 10% confidence level.
**Significant at 1% confidence level.
Source: Hartman, Huq and Wheeler (1995).

for equipment vintage in this survey, because many plants have replaced or improved their process technologies over time. The results do suggest that EOP abatement was not significantly more costly in older pulp and paper plants. As expected, they also show substantially less abatement effort—seven fewer ABI points—in plants whose cleaner process technologies already gave them a lower pollution intensity.

(iv) Competitiveness, Profitability. The results suggest an increase in the ABI of 4–5 points for each unit increase in management's assessment of plant competitiveness and profitability. This may reflect both greater availability of resources for financing cleanup and the superior implementation ability of well-managed plants.

(v) Ownership, Financing, Market Orientation. The results suggest that publicly owned facilities undertake far less abatement, even after controlling for vintage, efficiency and scale. Other things equal, SOE's score nearly 13 points lower on the ABI. Clearly, the bureaucratic shielding effect outweighed any soft budget constraint effect in the sample.

Multinational branch plants do not have higher ABI scores than their domestic private counterparts, ceteris paribus. In addition, the study finds no effect for export orientation or foreign financing of construction. These results certainly run counter to the conventional wisdom, but the latter seems to have been based on only a few anecdotes in any case.

(c) A Cross-sectoral Econometric Analysis of Indonesian Plants

This section draws on an econometric analysis by Pargal and Wheeler (1995) of organic water pollution (BOD) in Indonesian factories. The data are for 1989–90, when there was no effective national regulation of water pollution. This exercise therefore provided the opportunity to test a "pure" model of informal regulation, or community pressure, for a relatively large sample of manufacturing facilities located throughout the country.

As before, the analysis incorporated both economic factors and plant/firm-specific variables. It was possible to construct a relatively comprehensive data-base because the data collection system in Indonesia is one of the most efficient and comprehensive in the developing world. . . .

Regression results from the study of 243 Indonesian factories are presented in Table 3. The dependent variable is the log of annual BOD emissions. Since the log of output is incorporated on the right-hand side, the regressions can be interpreted as explaining variations in pollution intensity (or pollution per unit of output). The results are generally consistent with the findings of the four-country survey.

(i) Economic Variables. Although it is plausible to assume significant relations of complementarity or substitution for pollution with labor and energy, the results provide no supporting evidence. Complementarity with materials is consistent with the result for the Java dummy, which proxies higher transport costs for materials imported from the other Indonesian islands. This, however, is clearly a very crude index.

(ii) Plant/Firm Characteristics. These results are all consistent with the prior results, with the exception of plant vintage. They suggest higher pollution intensity for older plants, although the result does not have high significance. This may be because of the weak proxy used for plant vintage. As before, the results suggest very significant scale economies in abatement. Ceteris paribus, pollution intensity declines 0.35% for each 1% increase in output. Economic efficiency decreases pollution intensity; state ownership increases it; foreign ownership has no effect; and more visible plants are under significantly greater pressure to abate. The visibility effect is measured by two variables: the plant's share of total local manufacturing employment, and local degree of urbanization (measured by population density). Plants which are larger relative to the local economy pollute less, ceteris paribus; plants in more urbanized areas surrounded by other plants are able to pollute more. Because of the visibility effect it is harder to identify the plants which contribute to severe pollution exposure problems in cities.

(iii) Community Characteristics. As before, community per capita income has a very powerful effect on pollution intensity. Local education, although highly correlated with income, is still estimated to have an independent effect on pollution intensity. There is no independent estimate of community pressure in this case, but the mechanism is presumed to be the same as that discussed in the previous sections. . . .

4. Conclusions

(b) Policy Implications

The message of our results to date is an extremely hopeful one for sustainable development,

Table 3. Regression Results (dependent variable: Log BOD Load)

N = 243	Model [Adj R^2 = 0.3146]	
Variable	Coefficient*†	t stat.
Intercept	31.580 (6.76)	4.67**
Economic variables		
Log [OUTPUT]	0.647 (0.19)	3.34**
Log [WAGE]	−0.740 (0.62)	−1.2
Log [FUEL PRICE]	−2.257 (2.42)	−0.93
D [JAVA]	−1.231 (0.55)	−2.23*
Plant/firm variables		
Log [VA/WORKER]	−0.325 (0.18)	−1.81*
LOG [AGE]	0.273 (0.17)	1.64
FOREIGN OWNERSHIP	−0.002 (0.01)	−0.27
STATE OWNERSHIP	0.017 (0.01)	2.64**
Community Variables		
Log [LOCAL EMPLOYMENT]	−0.352 (0.18)	−1.94*
Log [INCOME PER CAPITA]	−4.021 (0.91)	−4.41**
Log [% GT PRIMARY]	−1.072 (0.57)	−1.87*
Log [POP. DENSITY]	0.344 (0.17)	2.04*

*$H_0 \cdot b = 0$ rejected with 90% confidence (two-tail).

**$H_0 \cdot b = 0$ rejected with 99% confidence (two-tail).

†White heteroscedasticity-consistent standard errors in parentheses.

Source: Pargal and Wheeler (1995).

because several major policy trends appear favorable for environmental performance. The current wave of privatization implies declining significance for pollution-intensive public enterprises. Deregulation during the 1980s has presumably increased plant-level efficiency in the private sector, with significant reductions in pollution intensity. Rapidly spreading multinational facilities are relatively clean, and their performance is matched by otherwise comparable domestic plants. The equipment vintage effect may also have some importance. New facilities contribute a major share of output in rapidly industrializing economies, and our results provide some support for the proposition that many of these plants will be cleaner because they employ newer technology.

Our results on informal regulation also suggest that improvements in the quality of life will have an important impact. Post-primary education and per capita income are now advancing steadily in many Asian and Latin American countries, and this should lead to stronger local pressure on many polluting facilities.

The important role for informal regulation has several implications for environmental policy in developing countries. First, it is consistent with a model of local equilibrium pollution which reflects community differences, the market value of environmental reputation, and a number of insights from conventional environmental economics. Widespread informal regulation in a developing country represents a promising foundation for decentralized regulatory policy. Our results suggest that new formal regulatory systems may be able to build on local arrangements rather than replacing them at unnecessarily high cost.

Second, the economics of informal regulation have implications for formal regulation as well. Application of similar principles to national and state-level regulation would encourage the use of market-based instruments with regionally variable "pollution prices" associated with emissions charges or tradable emissions permits.

Third, and probably most important, our results suggest that community income and education are very important determinants of informal regulatory outcomes. Does this mean that "environmental injustice" is an important policy issue in developing countries? Income-based differences in pollution prices certainly reflect inequity in the distribution of income. As such, they may reflect a general problem of social justice. They do not necessarily imply additional "environmental injustice," however, because poor communities with limited resources may trade environmental quality against other social goods.

The effect of education on the price of pollution may, however, provide a stronger case. Poor communities with low levels of education and information may permit inappropriately high pollution, either because they are not aware of it, they cannot evaluate its consequences, or they are unable to organize to combat it. To compensate, formal regulation could be targeted particularly on the pollution control problems of poor communities. Alternatively, governments could try to raise environmental awareness while developing programs to empower poor communities.

References

Arora, Seema and Timothy Cason, "An experiment in voluntary environment regulation: Participation in EPA's 33/50 program," *Journal of Environmental Economics and Management,* Vol. 28 (1995), pp. 271–286.

Cribb, R., "Politics of pollution control in Indonesia," *Asian Survey,* Vol. 30 (December 1990), pp. 1123–1135.

Hartman, Raymond, Mainul Huq and David Wheeler, "Why paper mills clean up: Results from a four-country survey in Asia," Policy Research Department Working Paper (Washington, DC: The World Bank, 1995).

Huq, Mainul and David Wheeler, "Pollution reduction without formal regulation: Evidence from Bangladesh," Environment Department Working Paper, No. 1993–39 (Washington, DC: The World Bank, 1993).

Khator, Renu, *Environment, Development and Politics in India* (Lanham, MD: University Press of America, 1991).

Pargal, Sheoli and David Wheeler, "Informal regulation of industrial pollution in developing countries: Evidence from Indonesia," Policy Research Department Working Paper, No. 1416 (Washington, DC: The World Bank, 1995).

Selection X.5. Sustainable Development: Ecology and Economic Progress*

Introduction

While "sustainable development" is the acknowledged subject of much recent development thinking (see e.g. World Commission on Environment and Development, 1987; Repetto, 1986; Redclift, 1987; Turner, 1988; Stockholm Group, 1988), little headway appears to have been made in terms of a rigorous definition of the concept. Therefore, not surprisingly, efforts to "operationalize" sustainable development and to show how it can be integrated into practical decision-making have been few and generally unpersuasive. The use of the term "development," rather than "economic growth," implies acceptance of the limitations of the use of measures such as gross national product (GNP) to measure the well-being of nations. Instead development embraces wider concerns of the quality of life—educational attainment, nutritional status, access to basic freedoms and spiritual welfare. The emphasis on sustainability suggests that what is needed is a policy effort aimed at making these developmental achievements last well into the future. By implication, some at least of past development efforts have achieved only short-lived gains.

In this chapter we suggest a simple *definition* of sustainable development, and elaborate a set of *minimum* conditions for development to be sustainable, the conditions being based on the requirement that the *natural capital stock* should not decrease over time. Natural capital stock, in this context, is the stock of all environmental and natural resource assets, from oil in the ground to the quality of soil and groundwater, from the stock of fish in the oceans to the capacity of the globe to recycle and absorb carbon. We keep the definition of natural capital stock deliberately vague in order to capture the more general picture, and in the belief that a more detailed investigation will not raise insuperable problems. The meaning of a *constant* natural capital stock is more problematic, however, and we therefore devote a little time to alternative meanings.

The idea that the natural capital stock should be held constant or improved, broadly reduces to an embodiment of the idea that resource and environ-

mental degradation has gone "too far." This basic feeling is what we detect as the undertone to much recent environmental campaigning and discussion. In the language of economics, as degradation increases so the economic value of the next unit of environment at risk from destruction, whether tropical forest or wetland or whatever, is seen to be higher than the unit that has just disappeared or been degraded. Of itself, this idea of a rising "marginal" economic value of natural environments the less there is of them will not justify maintaining what there is at any given moment of time. As we shall see, economists would typically argue that environmental degradation *should* take place so long as the gains from the activities causing the degradation (e.g. agricultural clearance of forests, development of wetlands) are greater than the benefits of preserving the areas in their original form. The idea that there is some "optimum" stock of natural assets based on this comparison of costs and benefits needs to be addressed directly in order to see why the conservation of the existing stock should be elevated to be a goal of sustainable development. The rest of this chapter investigates this question.

Defining Sustainable Development

Since "development" is a value word, implying change that is *desirable,* there is no consensus as to its meaning. What constitutes development depends on what social goals are being advocated by the development agency, government, analyst or adviser. We take development to be a *vector* of desirable social objectives; that is, it is a list of attributes which society seeks to achieve or maximize. The elements of this vector might include:

- increases in real income per capita;
- improvements in health and nutritional status;
- educational achievement;
- access to resources;
- a "fairer" distribution of income;
- increases in basic freedoms.

Correlation between these elements, or an agreed system of weights to be applied to them, might permit development to be represented by a single "proxy" indicator, but this is not an issue pursued here.

Sustainable development is then a situation in which the development vector D does not decrease over time. However, such a simple definition is not

*From David Pearce, Edward Barbier, and Anil Markandya, "Sustainable Development: Ecology and Economic Progress," *Sustainable Development: Economics and Environment in the Third World* (London: Earthscan Publications Ltd, 1990), pp. 1–11. Reprinted by permission.

problem-free. For example, use of the term implies the adoption of an infinite time horizon—i.e. that the aim is to achieve everlasting development—whereas practical decision-making requires adoption of some finite horizon. Nor does it tell us if the rate of change of D with respect to time t must be positive for each and every time period (which we might term *strong sustainability*), or whether only the trend of dD/dt must be positive (*weak sustainability*). One variant of the weak sustainability measure is that the *present value* of development benefits should be positive. A present value is a way of expressing a stream of benefits (or costs) that occur over time as a value perceived from the standpoint of the present. To do this future benefits and costs are *discounted*—i.e. given a lower weight relative to a similar benefit or cost in the present. Chapter 2 investigates the discounting issue in detail. For the moment, however, it is sufficient to note that present value maximization is consistent with the extinction of resources. How far those extinctions result in the development objectives themselves becoming unsustainable is open to question. But they lend some support to the idea that present value maximization is not a sufficient criterion for sustainable development. Sustainable development is better interpreted in its weak form—i.e. as saying that the rate of change of development over time is *generally* positive over some selected time horizon.

Subject to the above caveats, we suggest that sustainability be defined as the general requirement that a vector of development characteristics be non-decreasing over time, where the elements to be included in the vector are open to ethical debate and where the relevant time horizon for *practical* decision-making is similarly indeterminate outside of agreement on intergenerational objectives. This level of generality may seem unsatisfactory, but the essential point is that *what* constitutes development, and the *time horizon* to be adopted, are both ethically and practically determined. Such an ethical debate can be illuminated by discussion of the alternative views on both issues, but it cannot be resolved other than by ethical consensus.

The Conditions for Sustainable Development: Constant Capital Stock

Much of the sustainable development literature has confused *definitions* of sustainable development with the *conditions* for achieving sustainability. The preceding discussion suggests that the definition, the meaning, of sustainable development,

is evident from the phrase itself. We now consider a key necessary condition for achieving sustainable development. These conditions, elaborated below, are not sufficient, however. A sufficient set of conditions is likely to include, for example, institutional requirements for implementing sustainable development policy, and it may even require systematic changes in social values.

We summarize the key necessary condition as "constancy of the natural capital stock." More strictly, the requirement is for non-negative change in the stock of natural resources and environmental quality. In basic terms, the environment should not be degraded further but improvements would be welcome.

The presumption that sustainability has something to do with non-depreciation of the natural capital stock is explicit in the Brundtland Report. Thus, "If needs are to be met on a sustainable basis the Earth's natural resource base must be conserved and enhanced" (World Commission on Environment and Development, 1987, p. 57). It is somewhat more vaguely embraced in the World Conservation Strategy in terms of maintaining "essential ecological processes and life support systems," "preserving genetic diversity" and ensuring "sustainable utilization of species and ecosystems" (IUCN, 1980, I). Both sources offer rationales for conserving natural capital in terms of moral obligation and the alleged mutual interdependency of development and natural capital conservation. A similar definition is advanced by economist Robert Repetto:

sustainable development [is] a development strategy that manages all assets, natural resources, and human resources, as well as financial and physical assets, for increasing long-term wealth and well-being. Sustainable development, as a goal *rejects policies and practices that support current living standards by depleting the productive base, including natural resources,* and that leaves future generations with poorer prospects and greater risks than our own. (Repetto, 1986, p. 15)

Existing and Optimal Capital Stock

Conserving the natural capital stock is consistent with several situations. The stock in question might be that which exists at the point of time that decisions are being taken—the *existing* stock—or it might be the stock that *should exist.* The latter is clearly correct in terms of the application of neoclassical economic principles to resource issues. Economics would argue that there are costs and benefits of changing the natural capital stock. If it is reduced, it will be for some purpose; for example, much tropical forest clearance takes place for agricultural purposes. Similarly, wetlands are drained to gain the fertile soil for crop growing; natural habitats are reduced for housing development, and so on. Thus each destructive act has benefits in terms of the gains from the use to which the land is put. In the same way, using the atmosphere or the oceans as "waste sinks" has benefits, in that alternative means of disposal are often more expensive. Thus the environment as a waste sink reduces production and consumption costs compared to what they would have been. Environmental destruction also has costs since a great many people use natural environments (for wildlife observation, recreation, scientific study, hunting, etc.). These "use benefits" are lost (i.e. there are costs of destruction) if the land is converted for some other purpose. Similarly, one of the benefits of keeping the atmosphere unpolluted is that we avoid the damage that is done by pollution—e.g. better health and, globally, the avoidance of impacts such as global warming through trace gas emissions. Natural environments do not just have "use values." Many people like to think of environments being preserved for their own sake, an "existence value." These "non-use" values need to be added to the use values to get the *total economic value* of the conserved resource or environment.

Figure 1 depicts the cost-benefit comparison. The stock of natural assets is shown on the horizontal axis and costs and benefits are shown on the vertical axis. The cost curve shows that as the stock of natural capital (K_N) increases, there are increasing costs in the form of forgone benefits from *not* conserving the environment. The benefit curve captures the benefits to users and non-users of natural environments. Economic analysis would identify K_N* as the optimal stock of the environment. If the existing stock is to the right of K_N*, then it will be beneficial in net terms to reduce the stock—i.e. to engage in environmental degradation and destruction. If the existing stock is to the left of K_N*, then improvements in environmental quality are called for.

If our overview of the meaning of sustainable development is correct, it appears to be inconsistent with the idea of maintaining optimal stocks of natural assets or, at least, it will only be consistent if we are to the left of the optimum depicted in Figure 1 (since sustainability is consistent with increasing environmental assets) or coincident with it. We therefore need to investigate further the rationale for maintaining and improving existing levels of environmental assets.

Several observations are in order. First, existing stocks would generally be regarded as being below optimal stocks in many developing countries. For some Sahelian countries they are significantly below the optimum, in that desertification and deforestation actually threaten livelihoods (Falloux and Mukendi, 1988). Nor is there evidence that the further reduction of soil quality, tree cover or water

Figure 1. The costs and benefits of environmental change.

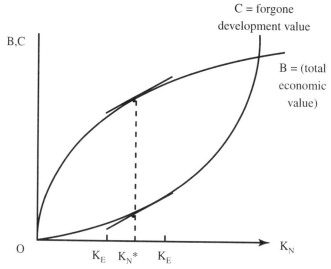

K_N is the natural capital stock; B shows the benefits from increasing it, benefits that accrue as use and non-use values; and C is the cost of increasing the natural capital stock, and these costs are the forgone benefits from using the natural assets for some other purpose. K_N* is the optimal stock.

supplies will result in some form of surplus which can be reinvested in other man-made capital assets. Therefore, to some extent, deliberations about what precisely constitutes an optimum are redundant in the contexts of these countries.

The second observation relates to the identification of the "optimum" in Figure 1. To say that capital stocks "should" be optimal is tautologous. The interesting feature of optimality is how the benefits of augmenting natural capital are calculated. The critical factor here is that the *multifunctionality* of natural resources needs to be recognized, including their role as integrated life support systems. Thus a cost-benefit analysis that compares the "value" of, say, afforestation with the opportunity cost of land in terms of forgone development values needs more careful execution than might otherwise appear to be the case. How far life support functions, such as contributions to geochemical cycles, can be captured by cost-benefit is open to question. In the face of uncertainty and irreversibility, conserving what there is could be a sound risk-averse strategy. Put another way, even in countries where it might appear that we can *afford* to reduce natural capital stocks further, there are risks from so doing because of (a) our imperfect understanding of the life support functions of natural environments, (b) our lack of capability to substitute for those functions, even if their loss is reversible in theory, and (c) the fact that losses are often irreversible. There is therefore a rationale in terms of *uncertainty* and *irreversibility* for conserving the existing stock, at least until we have a clearer understanding of what the optimal stock is and how it might be identified. . . .

A fourth reason for supposing that existing stocks are important arises from recent research on the use of willingness-to-pay and willingness-to-accept measures of benefit. A simple conceptual basis for estimating a benefit is to find out what people are willing to pay to secure it. Thus, if we have an environmental asset and there is the possibility of increasing its size, a measure of the economic value of the increase in size will be the sums that people are willing to pay to ensure that the necessary land or other asset is obtained. Whether there is an actual market in the asset or not is not of great relevance. We can still find out what people would pay if only there were a market. In the same way, if there is to be reduction in the size of the asset, we can ask what people are willing to accept to give it up. Economic theory predicts that the difference between the willingness to pay and willingness to accept measures (the "equivalent and compensating variation"

measures of welfare gain) will not differ significantly. That is, a measure of willingness to pay for a small gain will be approximately equal to the requirement for compensation to give up a small amount of an asset. Empirical work suggests otherwise, with very large discrepancies between willingness to pay and willingness to accept being recorded. Prospect theory offers a rationale for compensation requirements being very much larger. Essentially, what exists is seen as a reference point and attitudes to surrendering some of what is already owned or experienced are quite different to those that come into play when there is the prospect of a gain. Put another way, the valuation function B in Figure 1 is "kinked" at the existing stock of assets. The result of modifying Figure 1 is shown in Figure 2. The existence of the kink means that the optimal level of K_N is likely to be at the point of the kink: existing and optimal natural capital stocks coincide. In terms of the "constant capital" idea in sustainable development, it implies that a high valuation should be placed on reductions in the existing capital stock, thus supporting the view that conservation of existing stocks itself has a high priority.

Overall, while there is a powerful case in analytical economics for thinking in terms of maintaining optimal rather than existing natural capital stocks as the basic condition for sustainability, there are also sound reasons for conserving at least the existing capital stock. For poor countries dependent upon the natural resource base, optimal stocks will in any event be above the existing stock. In other cases, there is a rationale in terms of incomplete information about the benefits of conservation (the failure to appreciate and measure multifunctionality), uncertainty and irreversibility for conserving the existing stock. Additionally, resource conservation serves non-efficiency objectives, whereas optimality tends to be defined only in terms of efficiency. Finally, even in terms of efficiency, the existence of a valuation function which is kinked at the existing endowment of natural resources adds emphasis to the conservation of existing stocks.

The Meaning of Constant Capital Stock

Constancy of the natural capital stock can take on several different meanings. A common interpretation is in terms of constant *physical* capital stock. This is appealing for renewable resources, but, clearly, has little relevance to exhaustible resources since any positive rate of use reduces the stock. An alternative interpretation is in terms of a

Figure 2. Costs and benefits of conservation when the valuation function is kinked.

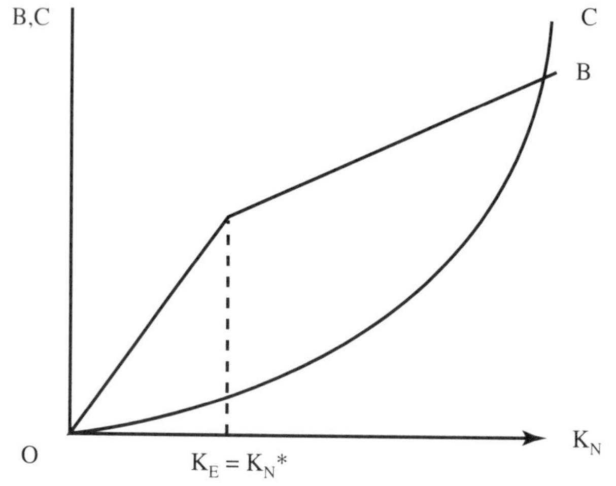

The benefit function of Figure 1 is now kinked at the existing stock of natural capital, making the existing and optimal stocks probably coincident.

constant *economic value* of the stock. This allows for a declining physical stock with a rising real price over time, maintaining a constant economic value. The problem here is that the "price" variable needs to be interpreted with considerable care to reflect all the economic values deriving from multifunctional resources. Valuation problems, especially with functions such as contributions to reducing future catastrophes, are formidable. An additional complication lies with the presence of discontinuities in the valuation function—i.e. threshold effects such that stocks below a minimum critical level result in major costs.

A variant of the constant economic value concept is the view that a constant capital stock can be interpreted as one where the *price* of the stock remains constant over time. The motivation behind this idea is that scarcity can often be effectively measured in terms of the price of a natural resource, higher prices reflecting scarcity and lower prices reflecting abundance. This has some appeal in terms of exhaustible resources with uncertain reserves, where scarcity results in increased exploration effort or technological substitution. But for renewable resources, current prices are less likely to reflect future scarcity. As an example, fuelwood prices may remain constant in real terms, despite stock reductions, because the *flow* of harvest is not significantly affected. Price may then rise only as the last units of the resource are extracted.

A broader version of the constant value rule would require that the total value of *all* capital stocks be held constant, man-made and natural.

Here the basic idea is that future generations would inherit a combined capital stock no smaller than the one in the previous generation. In this way, a depleted resource, say oil, would be compensated for by other investments generating the same income. This argument is considered in more detail shortly; but if it is to be advanced, it is clearly important that natural capital stocks be correctly valued, and that threshold effects be allowed for.

In general, there is no easy interpretation to the idea of a constant capital stock. Some combination of an equal value rule with indicators of physical stocks to allow for critical minimum stocks (which, in turn, might qualify as 'sustainability indicators") appears appropriate, but the issues have yet to be resolved.

References

Falloux, F. and Mukendi, A. (eds) (1988), *Desertification Control and Renewable Resource Management in the Sahelian and Sudanian Zones of West Africa,* World Bank Technical Paper No. 70, World Bank, Washington DC.

International Union for the Conservation of Nature (IUCN) (1980), *World Conservation Strategy,* Gland, Switzerland: IUCN.

Redclift, M. (1987), *Sustainable Development: Exploring the Contradictions,* London: Methuen.

Repetto, R. (1986), *World Enough and Time,* New Haven, Conn.: Yale University Press.

Stockholm Group for Studies on Natural Resource Management (1988), *Perspectives of Sustainable Development,* Stockholm Group, Stockholm.

Turner, R. K. (ed.) (1988), *Sustainable Environmental Management,* London: Belhaven Press, and Boulder, Col: Westview Press.

World Commission on Environment and Development (1987), *Our Common Future* (The "Brundtland Report"), Oxford University Press.

Comment X.3.   Weak Sustainability, Genuine Savings, and Green National Accounting

In other work David Pearce has developed different concepts of "weak sustainability" and "strong sustainability" than those in the preceding selection. By these definitions strong sustainability requires that the natural capital stock not decrease (exactly the condition for sustainable development given in the preceding selection), while weak sustainability requires only that the total value of the man-made physical capital stock, human capital stock, and natural capital stock not decrease. The idea of weak sustainability is that increases in other capital stocks can substitute for decreases in the natural capital stock. See for example, David Pearce and Giles Atkinson, "Measuring Sustainable Development," in Daniel W. Bromley, ed., *The Handbook of Environmental Economics* (1995).

This definition of weak sustainability leads directly to the concept of "genuine savings." These are savings adjusted not only for depreciation of the man-made capital stock but also for depletion of natural resources and degradation of the environment. We can see that there is a rough equivalence between nonnegative genuine savings and weak sustainability, and indeed Pearce and Atkinson use the existence of nonnegative genuine savings as a test for whether a country's development is weakly sustainable, finding that many countries fail this test even though their net savings as conventionally defined are positive. The concept of genuine savings is developed further in Kirk Hamilton and Michael Clemens, "Genuine Savings Rates in Developing Countries," World Bank Environment Department (August 1998).

Just as savings rates can be adjusted for resource depletion and environmental degradation, so can the entire system of national accounts. This adjustment has become known as "green national accounting." Approaches to green national accounting are discussed extensively in Yusuf J. Ahmad, Salah El Serafy, and Ernst Lutz, eds., *Environmental Accounting for Sustainable Development* (1989), and many examples of the practice of green national accounting are given in Ernst Lutz, ed., *Toward Improved Accounting for the Environment* (1993).

APPENDIX: HOW TO READ A REGRESSION TABLE

National accounts, social indicators, and other data have been accumulating for most less developed countries for more than 30 years. Writers on development frequently apply the technique of *multiple regression* to these data to estimate what they believe are underlying behavioral relationships among various economic, political, and social variables. They report their results in *regression tables.*

A number of selections in this book contain regression tables. Fortunately, lack of training in econometrics or statistics need not prevent the reader from understanding the important *economic* (as opposed to statistical) information contained in a regression table. The purpose of this Appendix is to show the untrained reader how to extract this information, using as an illustration a table adapted from the widely cited paper by Robert J. Barro, "Economic Growth in a Cross Section of Countries," *Quarterly Journal of Economics* 106 (May 1991): 407–43. The presentation applies to multiple regressions performed using a method called *ordinary least squares,* but the most important aspects of the discussion carry through even if other methods were used.

A regression table is read one column at a time. Each column reports an estimated relationship between the values of a *dependent variable,* y_i, and the values of a set of *explanatory variables,* $x_{1i}, x_{2i}, \ldots, x_{Ki}$, where i indexes *observations* and K is the number of explanatory variables. This estimated relationship takes the form

$$y_i = b_0 + b_1 x_{1i} + b_2 x_{2i} + \ldots + b_K x_{Ki} + e_i \tag{A1}$$

where the number b_0 is the *constant* or *intercept,* the numbers $b_1, b_2, \ldots, b_K$ are the *estimated coefficients,* and e_i is the *residual.* The quantity $b_0 + b_1 x_{1i} + b_2 x_{2i} + \ldots + b_K x_{Ki}$ is the *predicted value* of the dependent variable for observation $i,$ so called because it gives the value of the dependent variable we would predict for observation i given knowledge of the values of the explanatory variables for observation i. It follows that the residual is simply the difference between the actual value of the dependent variable and its predicted value for each observation. By construction, the average or *mean* of the predicted values taken over all observations equals the mean of the actual values; equivalently, the mean of the residual is zero. As a consequence, if we know the estimated coefficients and the means of the dependent variable and the explanatory variables, we can compute the constant:

$$b_0 = \bar{y} - b_1 \bar{x}_1 - b_2 \bar{x}_2 - \ldots - b_K \bar{x}_K \tag{A2}$$

where the bar over a variable denotes its mean.

The estimated coefficients are the same for all observations because they are supposed to be estimates of underlying behavioral relationships between the dependent variable and the explanatory variables. The estimated coefficient b_1, for example, tells us that a one-unit increase in the value of the explanatory variable x_1 should cause the value of the dependent variable to increase by b_1 units, holding the values of all other explanatory variables constant. These estimated behavioral relationships are the most important economic information contained in a regression table.

With these preliminaries out of the way, we now turn to Table 1. In all regressions reported, an observation consists of the values of the dependent variable and the explanatory variables for one country for one time period. The number of observations used to estimate the coeffi-

Table 1. Regressions for per Capita Growth

	(1)	(2)	(3)	(4)
Dep. var.	GR6085	GR7085	GR6085	GR6085
No. obs.	98	98	98	98
Const.	0.0302	0.0287	0.0288	0.0345
	(0.0066)	(0.0080)	(0.0065)	(0.0067)
GDP60	−0.0075	−0.0089	−0.0073	−0.0068
	(0.0012)	(0.0016)	(0.0011)	(0.0009)
SEC60	0.0305	0.0331	0.0254	0.0133
	(0.0079)	(0.0137)	(0.0110)	(0.0070)
PRIM60	0.0250	0.0276	0.0324	0.0263
	(0.0056)	(0.0070)	(0.0077)	(0.0060)
SEC50	—	—	0.0183	—
			(0.0121)	
PRIM50	—	—	−0.0085	—
			(0.0064)	
g^c/y	−0.119	−0.142	−0.121	−0.094
	(0.028)	(0.034)	(0.027)	(0.026)
REV	−0.0195	−0.0236	−0.0189	−0.0167
	(0.0063)	(0.0071)	(0.0060)	(0.0062)
ASSASS	−0.0333	−0.0485	−0.0298	−0.0201
	(0.0155)	(0.0185)	(0.0130)	(0.0131)
PPI60DEV	−0.0143	−0.0171	−0.0141	−0.0140
	(0.0053)	(0.0078)	(0.0052)	(0.0046)
AFRICA	—	—	—	−0.0114
				(0.0039)
LAT.AMER.	—	—	—	−0.0129
				(0.0030)
R^2	0.56	0.49	0.56	0.62
$\hat{\sigma}$	0.0128	0.0168	0.0129	0.0119

Source: Barro (1991), pp. 410–413.

cients in each regression therefore equals the number of countries included in the analysis. (Barro included all countries for which data were available. They are listed in Appendix 3 of his paper.) In some regression tables in this book more than one time period per country is used in the estimation, so that the number of observations equals the number of countries multiplied by the number of time periods. In general, however, the units of analysis need not be countries. For example, in the regression tables included in Selection X.4 by Hettige et al., the units of analysis are manufacturing plants, and each observation consists of the values of the dependent and explanatory variables for one plant.

Let us focus on column (1). The dependent variable (dep. var.) is GR6085. (If the dependent variable were the same for all regressions it would be described completely in the title of the table rather than listed column by column.) We see from Table 2 that GR6085 is defined as the growth rate of real per capita GDP from 1960 to 1985. From Table 3 we see that the mean of GR6085 is 0.022: on average, per capita GDP grew by 2.2 percent per year from 1960 to 1985 in the sample of countries used in the estimation. Moving down column (1), we see that the number of observations (No. obs.) is 98: 98 countries are included in the sample. Next we see that the value of the constant (Const.) is 0.0302. Underneath this value is another number in parentheses. We will ignore all numbers in parentheses for now. After the constant begins the list of explanatory variables, all of which are defined in Table 2 and have sample means and standard deviations reported in Table 3. For example, GDP60 is defined as the 1960 value of real per capita GDP, and its mean is $1,920. The estimated coefficient for GDP60 is −0.0075. Moving down column (1), we can fill in all the explanatory vari-

Table 2. Definitions of Variables in Tables 1

GR6085 (GR7085): Growth rate of real per capita GDP
   from 1960 to 1985 (1970 to 1985).
GDP60 (GDP70, GDP85): 1960 (1970, 1985) value of
   real per capita GDP (1980 base year).
g^c/y: Average from 1970 to 1985 of the ratio of real
   government consumption (exclusive of defense and
   education) to real GDP.
SEC50 (SEC60): 1950 (1960) secondary-school
   enrollment rate.
PRIM50 (PRIM60): 1950 (1960) primary-school
   enrollment rate.
REV: Number of revolutions and coups per year
   (1960–1985 or subsample).
ASSASS: Number of assassinations per million
   population per year (1960–1985 or subsample).
PPI60DEV: Magnitude of the deviation of 1960 PPP
   value for the investment deflator (U.S. = 1.0) from
   the sample mean.
AFRICA: Dummy variable for sub-Saharan Africa.
LAT. AMER.: Dummy variable for Latin America.

Source: Barro (1991), p. 439.

ables and their estimated coefficients plus the dependent variable in equation (A1) above, obtaining

$$\text{GDP6085}_i = 0.0302 - 0.0075(\text{GDP60}_i) + 0.0305(\text{SEC60}_i) + 0.0250(\text{PRIM60}_i)$$
$$- 0.119(g^c/y)_i - 0.0195(\text{REV}_i) - 0.0333(\text{ASSASS}_i)$$
$$- 0.0143(\text{PPI60DEV}_i) + e_i \tag{A1$'$}$$

As an exercise, the reader may also want to use the means reported in Table 3 to verify that equation (A2) above holds given the numbers reported in column (1). Note that no coefficients are reported in column (1) for SEC50, PRIM50, AFRICA, and LAT. AMER. These explanatory variables were not included in the regression of column (1) but are included in subsequent regressions.

As we stated above, the coefficients in equation (A1$'$) are supposed to be estimates of underlying behavioral relationships. Thus the coefficient on SEC60 indicates that an increase in a country's 1960 secondary-school enrollment rate of 10 percentage points (0.1) would raise its per capita GDP growth by roughly 0.3 percentage points ($0.0305 \times 0.10 = 0.00305$), all else equal. One common way to estimate the strength of a behavioral relationship is to ask how much effect an increase of one standard deviation in the explanatory variable has on the dependent variable. From Table 3 we see that the standard deviation of GDP60 is 1.81 ($1,810). Thus an increase of one standard deviation in GDP60 would reduce a country's per capita GDP growth by roughly 1.4 percentage points ($-0.0075 \times 1.81 = -0.0136$).

Continuing down column (1), we next see a value reported for R^2. R is the correlation coefficient between the actual and predicted values of the dependent variable. R^2 can be shown to equal the share of the variation of the dependent variable about its mean that is accounted for by the explanatory variables rather than by the residual. All else equal, the higher is R^2 the better. The number 0.56 in column (1) indicates that 56 percent of the variation in GR6085 can be "explained" by GDP60, SEC60, PRIM60, g^c/y, REV, ASSASS, and PPI60DEV.

$\hat{\sigma}$, sometimes labeled the standard error of estimate (s.e.e.), is the standard deviation of the actual value of the dependent variable from its predicted value, adjusted for the number of explanatory variables included in the regression. One can think of $\hat{\sigma}$ as the typical prediction er-

Table 3. Means and Standard Deviations of Variables

Variable	Mean	σ
GR6085	0.022	0.019
GR7085	0.016	0.023
GDP60 ($1,000)	1.92	1.81
g^c/y	0.107	0.053
SEC50[a]	0.10	0.14
SEC60	0.23	0.21
PRIM50[b]	0.65	0.39
PRIM60	0.78	0.31
REV	0.18	0.23
ASSASS	0.031	0.086
PPI60DEV	0.23	0.25
AFRICA (dummy)	0.276	0.449
LAT. AMER. (dummy)	0.235	0.426

[a]Sample of 95 countries.
[b]Sample of 97 countries.
Source: Barro (1991), p. 438.

ror. All else equal, the lower is $\hat{\sigma}$ the better. The number 0.0128 in column (1) indicates that the typical prediction error for GR6085 is roughly 1.3 percentage points, or slightly more than half its mean value.

In column (2) of Table 1 the dependent variable is changed from GR6085 to GR7085 but all the explanatory variables are kept the same. Comparing the estimated coefficients between columns (1) and (2), we can see that the relationships found for GR6085 are robust to a change in the time period over which growth is computed from 1960–1985 to 1970–1985. In column (3) the dependent variable is again GR6085, but two explanatory variables, SEC50 and PRIM50, have been added to the set used in column (1). We will discuss the regression results reported in column (3) later. In column (4) two *dummy variables,* AFRICA and LAT. AMER., have been added to the set of explanatory variables used in column (1). A dummy variable is a variable that takes the value 1 if a certain relationship is true (e.g., a country is located in Latin America) and 0 if that relationship is false. The estimated coefficients on dummy variables are especially easy to interpret: the numbers reported in column (4) indicate that, all else equal, a country's per capita GDP growth is 1.1 percentage points lower if it is located in sub-Saharan Africa and 1.3 percentage points lower if it is located in Latin America. Note that inclusion of these two dummy variables reduces the coefficients on most of the other explanatory variables (in absolute value) compared with column (1), indicating that some of their effects were actually attributable to special characteristics of Africa and Latin America.

We now turn to an explanation of the numbers in parentheses reported in each column underneath the constant and estimated coefficients. These are called the *standard errors* of the constant and estimated coefficients. We will denote by s_j the standard error of the estimated coefficient b_j. To understand the economic information conveyed by these standard errors we first need to introduce the idea that the regression (A1) can be thought of as an estimate of an unobserved "true" model (A3):

$$y_i = \beta_0 + \beta_1 x_{1i} + \beta_2 x_{2i} + \ldots + \beta_K x_{Ki} + \varepsilon_i \qquad (A3)$$

where the numbers $\beta_0, \beta_1, \beta_2, \ldots, \beta_K$ are the *parameters* of the model (the "true" constant and "true" coefficients) and ε_i is the *error term* that accounts for random variation in the dependent variable that is not captured by the explanatory variables. We can then ask, what do the estimated constant and coefficients tell us about the values of the model parameters?

The answer is that, under certain assumptions, we can be roughly 95 percent confident that the true parameters are within 2 standard errors of their estimates. We can thus think of $2s_j$ as the "margin of error" for the estimate b_j. More precisely, we can state with a 95 percent degree of confidence that the value of β_j lies within $b_j - 1.96s_j$ and $b_j + 1.96s_j$:

$$b_j - 1.96s_j \leq \beta_j \leq b_j + 1.96s_j \tag{A4}$$

(A4) gives us the 95 percent *confidence interval* for the parameter β_j. The smaller is the standard error s_j, the narrower is the confidence interval, and the more information we can be said to have about the value of β_j. Ninety-five percent is the most common conventional level of confidence; the other conventional levels are 90 percent and 99 percent. To construct a 90 or 99 percent confidence interval we replace the number 1.96 in (A4) with 1.645 or 2.576, respectively. Note that greater confidence is associated with wider intervals, as we would expect.

For the interested reader we will indicate here how the confidence interval (A4) can be derived formally; other readers can skip this paragraph without loss of continuity. We begin by making the assumptions that ε_i is uncorrelated with the explanatory variables, is uncorrelated with itself across observations, and is *normally distributed* with mean zero and constant variance (i.e., the sampling distribution for ε_i follows the same bell-shaped curve centered around zero for all i). Under this assumption it can be shown that $(b_j - \beta_j)/s_j$, the ratio of the difference between an estimated coefficient and the corresponding parameter to the standard error of the coefficient, follows a t *distribution* with n-K-1 degrees of freedom, where n is the number of observations used in the regression. For most regressions reported in the selections in this book the number of observations relative to the number of explanatory variables is sufficiently large that the t distribution with infinite degrees of freedom (i.e., the normal distribution with mean 0 and variance 1) is an excellent approximation to the true t distribution. Ninety-five percent of the mass of this distribution falls within -1.96 and $+1.96$, so the probability that $(b_j - \beta_j)/s_j$ falls within -1.96 and $+1.96$ equals 0.95. Put differently, we can state with a 95 percent degree of confidence that

$$-1.96 \leq \frac{(b_j - \beta_j)}{s_j} \leq +1.96$$

Multiplying this inequality by s_j throughout, we get

$$-1.96s_j \leq (b_j - \beta_j) \leq +1.96s_j.$$

Subtracting b_j from all sides, multiplying throughout by -1, and switching the sides around yields (A4) above.

We now return to column (1) of Table 1 and reconsider our estimate of the effect of an increase in SEC60 of 10 percentage points on GR6085. Using (A4), we can find the 95 percent confidence interval for the "true" coefficient on SEC60:

$$0.0305 - 1.96(0.0079) \leq \beta_{\text{SEC60}} \leq 0.0305 + 1.96(0.0079),$$

$$\text{or} \quad 0.0150 \leq \beta_{\text{SEC60}} \leq 0.0460 \tag{A4$'$}$$

Using (A4$'$) we can compute that the "true" model yields an effect of a 10-percentage point increase in SEC60 on GR6085 that lies within 0.15 and 0.46 percentage points. Our earlier estimate of 0.305 percentage points is, of course, the midpoint of this interval.

From (A4) we can see that, if b_j is positive, then if $b_j > 1.96s_j$ or $b_j/s_j > 1.96$ we can be (at least) 95 percent confident that β_j is positive. Similarly, if b_j is negative, then if $|b_j| > 1.96s_j$ or $|b_j|/s_j > 1.96$ we can be (at least) 95 percent confident that β_j is negative. Put differently, if the absolute value of the ratio b_j/s_j exceeds 1.96, we can be 95 percent confident that explanatory variable j has *some* impact on the dependent variable in the direction indicated by the estimated coefficient. If we cannot be at least 95 percent confident (or, sometimes, at least 90 percent confident), it is conventionally argued that explanatory variable j should not be considered to be part of the "true" model (A3). For this reason the ratio b_j/s_j, known as the *t statistic* for the coefficient b_j, is often reported in regression tables in parentheses underneath the coefficient instead of s_j. Note that if *t* statistics are reported instead of standard errors, the standard errors can be recovered by dividing the estimated coefficients by their *t* statistics. (It is customary to state that, if the absolute value of the *t* statistic for b_j exceeds 1.96, we can *reject the hypothesis that* $\beta_j = 0$. Equivalently, it is stated that b_j is *significantly different from zero at the 95 percent level,* or simply that b_j is *statistically significant.* We prefer not to develop the concept of hypothesis testing here.)

We now return for the final time to Table 1. We can easily compute that all estimated coefficients in columns (1) and (2) have *t* statistics larger than 1.96 in absolute value. This remains true in column (3) except for the coefficients on SEC50 and PRIM50, which have *t* statistics of 1.51 and 1.33 in absolute value, respectively. We can conclude that SEC50 and PRIM50 are superfluous explanatory variables, which is not surprising given the inclusion of SEC60 and PRIM60. In column (4) all estimated coefficients have *t* statistics that exceed 1.96 in absolute value except for the coefficients on SEC60 and ASSASS. The *t* statistic of 1.90 for the coefficient on SEC60 indicates that we can be 90 percent (but not 95 percent) confident that SEC60 has some positive impact on GR6085, while the *t* statistic of 1.53 (in absolute value) for the coefficient on ASSASS indicates that we cannot be even 90 percent confident that ASSASS has some negative impact on GR6085. We noted earlier that the addition of the dummy variables AFRICA and LAT. AMER. reduced the coefficients on most of the other explanatory variables (in absolute value). For SEC60 and ASSASS the changes were substantial enough so that by conventional standards inclusion of the former in the "true" model is now marginal and inclusion of the latter is no longer justified.

The reader who wishes to deepen his understanding of multiple regression can consult any econometrics text. Two popular texts are Damodar N. Gujarati, *Basic Econometrics,* 3rd ed. (New York: McGraw-Hill, 1995) and Ramu Ramanathan, *Introductory Econometrics with Applications* 4th ed. (Fort Worth: Dryden, 1998).

INDEX OF SELECTION AUTHORS

INDEX